The Principles of Finance:

THE COMPETITIVE ECONOMIC ENVIRONMENT

Principle of Self-Interested Behavior:
People act in their own financial self-interest

Principle of Two-Sided Transactions:
Each financial transaction has at least two sides

Signaling Principle:
Actions convey information

Behavioral Principle:
When all else fails, look at what others are doing for guidance

VALUE AND ECONOMIC EFFICIENCY

Principle of Valuable Ideas:
Extraordinary returns are achievable with new ideas

Principle of Comparative Advantage:
Expertise can create value

Options Principle:
Options are valuable

Principle of Incremental Benefits:
Financial decisions are based on incremental benefits

FINANCIAL TRANSACTIONS

Principle of Risk-Return Trade-Off:
There is a trade-off between risk and return

Principle of Diversification:
Diversification is beneficial

Principle of Capital Market Efficiency:
The capital markets reflect all information quickly

Time-Value-of-Money Principle:
Money has a time value

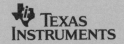

TEXAS INSTRUMENTS

BAII PLUS Rebate Terms and Conditions

This offer is valid only for BAII PLUS purchases between December 1, 1996 and October 31, 1998. All claims must be postmarked by November 15, 1998. Allow 8 to 10 weeks for processing. All purchases must be made in the U.S. or Canada. Rebates will be sent only to addresses in the U.S. and Canada and paid in U.S. dollars. Not redeemable at any store. Send this completed form along with the cash register receipt (original or copy) and the UPC bar code to the address indicated. This original mail-in certificate must accompany your request and may not be duplicated or reproduced. Offer valid only as stated on this form. Offer void where prohibited, taxed, licensed, or restricted. Limit one rebate per household or address. Texas Instruments reserves the right to discontinue this program at any time and without notice.

Yes! I Want $5 Back On My Purchase of the BAII PLUS.

CORPORATE
FINANCIAL
MANAGEMENT

DOUGLAS R̲... ...NERTY

The Koffman
and
Professor of
Binghamton
(SU...

...key
...akin

...inance
...versity

PRENTICE HALL, Upper Saddle River, NJ 07458

Acquisitions Editor: Paul Donnelly
Development Editor: David Cohen
Assistant Editor: Gladys Soto
Editorial Assistant: MaryBeth Sanok
Editor-in-Chief: James Boyd
Director of Development: Steve Deitmer
Marketing Manager: Sandra Steiner
Production Editor: David Salierno
Production Coordinator: Renee Pelletier
Managing Editor: Carol Burgett
Manufacturing Supervisor: Arnold Vila
Manufacturing Manager: Vincent Scelta
Senior Designer: Ann France
Design Director: Patricia Wosczyk
Interior Design: Rosemarie Votta
Cover Design: Maureen Eide
Illustrator (Interior):   ElectraGraphics, Inc.
Composition/Project Management: Maryland Composition Company, Inc.
Cover Image: Hiroshi Inoue/Photonica

Copyright © 1997 by Prentice-Hall, Inc.
A Simon & Shuster Company
Upper Saddle River, New Jersey 07458

Library of Congress Cataloging-in-Publication Data
Emery, Douglas R.
    Corporate financial management/Douglas R. Emery, John D.
Finnerty.
        p.   cm.
    Includes bibliographical references and index.
    ISBN 0–13–433533–3 (hardcover)
    1. Corporations—Finance.   I. Finnerty, John D.   II. Title.
HC4026.E468   1997
658. 15—dc20   96–36716
                                                         CIP

Prentice-Hall International (UK) Limited, London
Prentice-Hall of Australia Pty. Limited, Sydney
Prentice-Hall Canada, Inc., Toronto
Prentice-Hall Hispanoamericana, S.A., Mexico
Prentice-Hall of India Private Limited, New Delhi
Prentice-Hall of Japan, Inc., Tokyo
Simon & Schuster Asia Pte. Ltd., Singapore
Editora Prentice-Hall do Brasil, Ltda., Rio de Janeiro

Printed in the United States of America

10   9   8   7   6   5   4   3   2   1

To our families with love and appreciation

Cindy, Ryan, Lacey, and Logan   *Louise and William*

The authors are long-time friends and collaborators. Currently, they are the editors of *Financial Management*. The journal is one of the oldest finance journals, and has the second largest circulation after the *Financial Analysts Journal*. A major goal of the journal is to bridge the gap between theory and practice. Their first book together, *Principles of Finance with Corporate Applications,* was published in 1991. More recently, some of their joint research was published in the *Journal of Applied Corporate Finance*.

Douglas R. Emery is The Koffman Fellow and Professor of Finance in the School of Management at Binghamton University (SUNY). Doug has also taught at Purdue University, Washington University in St. Louis, the University of Missouri—Columbia, Nanjing University in China, the University of Calgary in Canada, and Kansas University. He currently serves as an Associate Editor of *Decision Sciences* and has been a Director of the Financial Management Association. His research has been published in a wide variety of journals including the *Journal of Finance, Journal of Financial and Quantitative Analysis, Financial Management, Journal of Accounting Research, Journal of Banking and Finance, Decision Sciences, Psychometrika*, and the *Journal of Marketing Research*.

John D. Finnerty is Director of Houlihan Lokey Howard & Zukin and Professor of Finance in the Graduate School of Business Administration at Fordham University. He has previously worked for Morgan Stanley & Co., Lazard Frères & Co., and was the Chief Financial Officer of the College Savings Bank. He currently serves on the advisory boards of the *Journal of Portfolio Management* and *The Financier*, and is an associate editor of the *Journal of Financial Engineering*. He has served as President of the Fixed Income Analysts Society and has been a Director of the Financial Management Association. He has authored, co-authored, or co-edited six other books, including *Corporate Financial Analysis: A Comprehensive Guide to Real-World Approaches for Financial Managers*. His research has been published in a wide variety of journals including the *Journal of Money, Credit and Banking, Journal of Financial and Quantitative Analysis, Financial Management, Journal of Portfolio Management*, and *Management Science*. He co-holds four patents on financial products.

Brief Contents

The teaching of finance has evolved over the past 40 years from simple descriptions of observed practice into a sound body of theory that represents our collective understanding of finance. In this book, we have summarized that collective understanding by detailing, for the first time, the principles of finance. Our principles of finance are a set of fundamental tenets designed to help you develop intuition about financial decision making.

Today, finance continues to evolve at a dizzying pace. Changes in the economic environment and innovations in the practice of finance seem to occur almost daily. How can you prepare for such a fast-paced changing field as finance? The answer lies in the very evolution of finance. You must look past simple descriptions and seek a conceptual understanding of a situation. Then, when the inevitable changes occur, you can use that understanding to make good decisions in the new situation by simply taking into account the changes that have occurred.

To the Student: Our Teaching Philosophy

We believe that if you understand the "first principles," every problem and issue can be addressed and solved with these principles; essentially, if you understand the general concept, you can use them to solve specific problems. This is why we have created the principles of finance, and designed this book around them. Our principles of finance provide an integrated view of the theory of finance so that financial decision making can be treated as an application of our collective understanding. By understanding the principles of finance, rather than simply memorizing a collection of seemingly disparate decision rules, you will be better able to cope with the unforeseen and inevitable changes and problems you will encounter in the future. Our principles of finance provide "ready intuition" for solving problems you have never seen before.

We will show you how to apply this intuition to the world of corporate financial management. Many of our applications come from the "real world," where John Finnerty has spent his entire career of more than 20 years. Most of the applications involve well-known corporations. In other applications, we have changed the name "to protect the innocent." All of the applications are designed to illustrate how financial principles are useful and immediately applicable to the real world.

Of course, like every field, there is always more to learn. We are honest about the limits of our understanding. We indicate what is known, what is believed, and what is still being debated. The evolution of our understanding represents the very important process of research. Some professors spend part of their time doing research, and have contributed to the development and testing of financial theory. It's not possible to cite all of them, but many are included in the end-of-chapter bibliographies.

A Few Words from a Practitioner about the Importance of Theory

This book focuses on the practice of corporate financial management. It's an applied book. So why should I be wasting your time with talk about theory? Quite simply, because it's important. After all, what is it that *applied* refers to? Theory. Yet some people view theory as an irritation. Almost as though theory gets in the way of good practice.

To be able to apply theory successfully, you must understand it. A "mindless cookbook" approach is fine for routine problems. But what do you do when a problem doesn't fit one of the rules? Understanding the underlying principles—the theoretical concepts—allows you to go beyond simple rules. If you understand the financial theory, you can identify the point of departure for evaluating a newly encountered problem. Then you can ask the questions necessary to get the information you need, process this information, and solve the problem.

Our principles of finance provide the framework for financial theory. The first principle, the Principle of Self-Interested Behavior, is the most basic. Without this principle, we cannot explain financial behavior. However, it also deserves special comment. Regrettably, some people misapply this principle.

I have had the unfortunate experience of encountering individuals who "crossed the line" by pursuing self-interested behavior without regard to the law. They paid a heavy price: in three cases, the price included time in jail and lifelong restriction from the securities industry. In a fourth, the price was still high, even without jail time.

In your career, you are likely to face illegal "opportunities" to make literally millions of dollars by, for example, insider trading. Our Principle of Self-Interested Behavior explicitly excludes such behavior; individuals should obey the rules and regulations to ensure legal—and ethically sound—behavior. There is nothing wrong with pursuing self-interested behavior—provided you play by the rules.

We all marvel at certain people who have had self-interested success in finance without formal training. Some very successful traders and sales people I've known didn't even have college degrees. What they had developed was an understanding of the principles of finance—and a well-honed ability to apply them. They probably couldn't articulate them, but they surely understood how to apply them in their own self-interest. Whether it's a corporate treasurer deciding what type of security to issue, an investment banker determining the structure of a new security, a bond trader deciding which bonds to buy, or a stock portfolio manager deciding which stocks to sell, in my experience, it is their grasp of financial theory and their ability to apply it in *any* situation that distinguishes the successful people.

So my advice is to take time to understand the basics—the theory—because it's in your own self-interest.

John D. Finnerty

To the Instructor: Our Goals for this Book

Following the Markowitz-Modigliani-Miller-Fama finance revolution, Akerlof (1970), Black and Scholes (1973), and Jensen and Meckling (1976) engendered a follow-on revolution involving asymmetric information, contingent claims, and agency theory. These articles in turn spawned hundreds, perhaps even thousands, of subsequent papers exploring their implications. Our goal in writing this book is to enrich the teaching of finance by *weaving* these important research advances into the very fabric of the traditional corporate finance course.

When these research advances are presented, students are fascinated. They are impressed by their immediate application and obvious relevance to the real world. The underlying intuitions are as appealing as a downward-sloping demand curve.

However, over the years, the textbook treatment of this new material has been almost ornamental. The material's importance may be discussed in the first chapter, and after that, perhaps mentioned in one or two chapter introductions. Yet the chapters really only contain the traditional material.

This book brings the excitement of this profoundly important material directly to the student. These are concepts that students *can*—and should—understand, within the context of finance. This new material is integrated throughout, so you can include it without having to "reinvent the wheel."

Many of us have participated in research involving agency theory, contingent claims, or asymmetric information, but have kept it essentially separate from our teaching. Like existing textbooks, we might mention the concepts briefly but, essentially, we only cover the standard material. It's no wonder. The alternative of developing your own unique course material is unreasonably costly, not to mention inefficient.

This book provides the necessary background directly to the students to enrich your topical coverage. Students can read and actually understand much, if not all, of the background material on their own. For example, it takes only a few hours to read our chapter on financial contracting. And our early explanation of contingent claims is given in very intuitive terms, without the usual overwhelming technicalities associated with options. In this way, we have minimized the disruption to the normal in-class topical treatment. In short, the marginal cost can be very low. You don't have to spend a lot of valuable class time on this material. In fact, some of our colleagues assign Chapters 8 and 9 only as outside reading.

We have one other comment on course coverage. Some of our colleagues prefer to cover capital market efficiency earlier in the course. Chapter 14 does not require background beyond the material in Chapter 3. Therefore, it can be covered wherever you believe it best fits. Also, like Chapters 8 and 9, Chapter 14 is very student friendly and can, should you so choose, be assigned as outside reading.

The Curriculum Revolution   This book's design lends itself very comfortably to the new environment in which many of us find ourselves. Schools of business/management programs all over North America are going through, or have already made, dramatic curricular changes. These changes frequently involve integration of material across areas and perhaps team teaching. This new environment is forcing us to rethink, and change, how we teach finance. With change comes opportunity. We believe this new environment provides an excellent opportunity for the finance discipline to provide a leadership role.

The other business/management disciplines have enthusiastically embraced the idea of a corporation as a set of stakeholders. Beyond accounting, areas such as organizational behavior, strategic management, business law, marketing, and production are currently working to incorporate the implications of agency theory, contingent claims, and asymmetric information into their views of the organizational world. This makes the principal-agent framework of financial contracting a natural framework for integrating the areas. Therefore, this book offers the chance for the core finance class to play a central role in the new curricular environment.

Innovations of Special Note

Principles of Finance   In Chapter 3, we describe our dozen principles of finance, which provide the foundation for learning finance. These principles provide a framework for integrating and learning corporate financial management.

Financial Contracting   In addition to providing the first formal enumeration of the principles of finance, we further modernize the teaching of finance by including a separate chapter on principal-agent problems in financial contracting. Throughout the book, we recognize the existence of information asymmetries and point out the agency problems it creates. After introducing the problems of financial contracting, we explicitly show how the important insights from this material can be used to solve many practical problems throughout the rest of the book.

Options   We use the term *option* in its broadest sense: any right without an obligation attached to it. This definition allows us to apply the important insights of option theory to a wide variety of topics. For example, we use option concepts in financial contracting, capital budgeting, and capital structure, among many others.

A Practitioner's Perspective   John Finnerty's more than 20 years of experience in the everyday world of finance brings a unique perspective to this book. Based on his first-hand experience, John brings the real world into the classroom.

Internationalization   A great deal is heard today about the importance of internationalizing the curriculum. We

believe that our country's continued economic well-being demands that we be international in our thinking. It is imperative that today's firms incorporate into their decision-making the specific constraints and additional market imperfections introduced by operating in an international economy. Of course, the principles of finance don't stop at the border. Therefore, the concepts and principles developed in this book are readily applicable to international transactions. With this in mind, we treat the international aspects of finance throughout the book as both a point of view and a particular market environment in which to operate.

Learning Aids

Chapter Objectives   The introduction to each chapter includes a set of learning objectives, which highlight the things students should be able to do after mastering the material in the chapter.

Principles of Finance Boxes   In Chapters 5 through 29, there are "principles boxes" in the introductions. These boxes highlight how particular finance principles apply to the chapter material. This sets the stage for the material to follow. It also helps students develop and apply financial intuition. In addition, the boxes tie the chapters together and reduce the chance of becoming bogged down in mechanical computations.

Practice Problems   The end-of-chapter problems are numerous, with an average of more than 35 per chapter. They were written by the authors specifically for this book. The problems are differentiated according to the type of instructional purpose: Problems in problem set A are very straightforward. They review the chapter material and can be answered by direct reference to the text material. Problems in problem set B also relate fairly closely to the material in the chapter but are somewhat more complex. Problems in problem set C are extensions of material presented in the chapter. The C-type problems are designed to challenge the students with complex situations, puzzles, or the examination of more subtle implications of the material in the chapter. Occasionally, problems are drawn from material in earlier chapters to reinforce the retention of important concepts.

Real-World Applications   Following the practice problems, there is a real-world application, which asks students to apply some of the concepts covered in the chapter. Every one of these applications comes from a real-world situation.

Decision Summary Boxes   At the end of each chapter, in the Summary section, we provide a *Decision Summary Box*, which summarizes the important dimensions of each type of decision situation covered in the chapter—a sort of "what really matters" for each type of decision. They provide a set of policy guidelines that are consistent with financial theory, yet take into account those areas where "gaps" in the theory make it difficult, if not impossible, to make unambiguous financial policy choices (for example, choosing a dividend policy).

New Terms and Jargon   Terms are defined and redefined in early usage to minimize effort wasted on looking up definitions. Examples given early in the book are deliberately drawn from everyday experience to minimize feelings of being overwhelmed by new jargon. Key terms appear in boldfaced type in their first usage, and are listed in the back of the chapter in the key terms list. The definitions are collected in the glossary, which appears at the end of the book.

Glossary   The glossary is extensive and is designed to serve as a convenient reference source, both for usage in later chapters and after graduation.

Humor   We interrupt the dry dullness from time to time to bring you occasional messages with humor and levity. Our tone is purposefully somewhat informal, so as not to let the words get in the way of the message.

Targeted Audience

This book was written for use in masters-level core finance classes, and for advanced courses in undergraduate programs. There is an abundance of applications material, so the book can also be used subsequently in other advanced-level courses such as case classes at both the graduate and undergraduate levels.

We assume throughout the book a familiarity with the standard prerequisites in business/management programs: college-level algebra, financial accounting, microeconomics, and probability and statistics. Although we explicitly assume that students have this background, we provide reminders of basic definitions and concepts that will have been covered in prerequisite courses. Also, while an understanding of mathematics is necessary, we facilitate the learning process by providing simple examples and analogies. By providing both verbal/logical *and* rigorous mathematical descriptions, we hope to enlist each student's "learning strength," as well as have the descriptions reinforce one another.

Finally, this book has been written with the intent that it will become a useful future reference tool for students as they move through their business careers. For example, the abundance of applications material will provide a reference source for material not covered in class; the extensive glossary facilitates later reference use; and the decision summary boxes provide an easily accessed summary of the important dimensions and concepts connected with particular topics.

Supplementary Materials

Instructor's Manual   The instructor's manual provides suggestions on how to use the book as a teaching tool. The first part focuses on using the book in a masters-level core finance class. The second part focuses on using the book in an advanced undergraduate class. Each part provides chapter-by-chapter teaching notes that contain a real-world situation to introduce and motivate the material, an outline and summary, including key concepts and definitions, demonstration problems with transparency masters for class usage, and class syllabi with suggested problem assignments for alternative course lengths and coverage. A guide for cross-referencing to other texts is also given.

PowerPoint Notes   The PowerPoint notes provide a complete set of color slide presentations for lecturing on the material.

Test Bank   The test bank provides a wide variety of problems like those at the back of the chapters as well as multiple choice and true–false questions, designed to test student comprehension. It is provided on computer disk with solutions.

Solutions Manual   The solutions manual contains solutions to all of the end-of-chapter problems and is available separately for students.

Software   The computer software in the form of spreadsheets covers specific decision/valuation models such as capital budgeting project analysis, lease-versus-buy analysis, and the Black–Scholes option pricing model, among others. Each topic includes a master model that can be used for calculation, problems that ask the student to complete the logic of partially created models, and problems that ask the student to use the model for computational purposes.

Acknowledgments

As with any book, this book is not simply the work of its authors. Many people have contributed to its creation and development from initial concept to finished product. We are very grateful to our friend and collaborator John D. Stowe for help with this project, especially with respect to the material pertaining to short-term finance.

We also deeply appreciate the invaluable comments and suggestions we have received from the following people who read all or part of various drafts of the manuscript:

Sankar Acharya, *New York University*
James S. Ang, *Florida State University*
Robert J. Angell, *North Carolina A&T State University*
Robert Boldin, *Indiana University of Pennsylvania*
Ronald C. Braswell, *Florida State University*
Greggory A. Brauer, *Texas Christian University*
Ivan E. Brick, *Rutgers University*
Douglas Carman, *Southwest Texas State University*
Richard P. Castanias, *University of California—Davis*
Mary C. Chaffin, *University of Texas—Dallas*
Susan Chaplinsky, *University of Virginia*
K.C. Chen, *California State University—Fresno*
Su-Jane Chen, *University of Wisconsin—Eau Claire*
James J. Cordeiro, *SUNY—Brockport*
Larry Y. Dann, *University of Oregon*
Anand S. Desai, *Kansas State University*
Diane K. Denis, *Purdue University*
Upinder S. Dhillon, *Binghamton University*
John R. Ezzell, *Pennsylvania State University*
Richard Fendler, *Georgia State University*
M. Andrew Fields, *University of Delaware*
Robert L. Finley, *Queens College*
Mona J. Gardner, *Illinois State University*
Chinmoy Gosh, *University of Connecticut*
Atul Gupta, *Bentley College*
Delvin D. Hawley, *University of Mississippi*
Puneet Handa, *University of Iowa*
James D. Harriss, *University of North Carolina at Wilmington*
Kathleen L. Henebry, *University of Nebraska at Omaha*
J. Lawrence Hexter, *Kent State University*
Shalom J. Hochman, *University of Houston*
Keith M. Howe, *DePaul University*
Mai E. Iskandar, *University of Massachusetts*
David N. Ketcher, *Drake University*
Ronald J. Kudla, *University of Wisconsin—Eau Claire*
Bruce R. Kuhlman, *University of Toledo*
Raman Kumar, *Virginia Polytechnic Institute and State University*
Edward C. Lawrence, *University of Missouri—St. Louis*
Ilene F. Levin, *University of Minnesota—Duluth*
Richard D. MacMinn, *University of Texas—Austin*
Judy E. Maese, *New Mexico State University*
Gershon N. Mandelker, *University of Pittsburgh*
Terry Maness, *Baylor University*
Surendra K. Mansinghka, *San Francisco State University*
David C. Mauer, *University of Miami*
Ronald W. Melicher, *University of Colorado*
Edward M. Miller, *University of New Orleans*
Mark J. Moran, *Case Western Reserve University*
Ken Motamed, *Columbia College*

Dina Naples, *Baruch College—CUNY*
William Nelson, *Indiana University Northwest*
Dennis T. Officer, *University of Kentucky*
Robert M. Pavlik, *California State University—Fullerton*
Annette Poulsen, *University of Georgia*
Gabriel G. Ramírez, *Binghamton University*
Debra K. Reed, *Texas A&M University*
Jong-Chul Rhim, *University of Southern Indiana*
Ralph W. Sanders, Jr., *University of South Florida*
Barry Schachter, *Comptroller of the Currency*
Lemma W. Senbet, *University of Maryland*
Dennis P. Sheehan, *Pennsylvania State University*
David C. Shimko, *University of Southern California*
D. Katherine Spiess, *University of Notre Dame*
Suresh C. Srivastava, *University of Alaska—Anchorage*
Robert J. Sweeney, *Marquette University*
John Thatcher, *Marquette University*
Berry D. Thomas, *DePaul University*
M. Mark Walker, *University of Mississippi*
Ray E. Whitmire, *Texas A&M University*
Daniel T. Winkler, *University of North Carolina—Greensboro*
Emilo Zaruk, *Florida Atlantic University*

We also thank Robert J. Kueppers of Deloitte & Touche LLP, who reviewed portions of the manuscript dealing with accounting issues, and Stephen B. Land, Esq., of Howard, Darby & Levin and Jeffrey D. Summa of Deloitte & Touche LLP, both of whom reviewed portions of the manuscript dealing with tax issues. As we remind you repeatedly in the book, taxes play an important role in financial decision making, and tax laws change frequently. It is therefore important to check on the current tax provisions that may affect a financial decision when you undertake a financial analysis.

We are grateful to too many other people for their help and encouragement to mention them all individually. We appreciate the supportive helpful discussions we have had with our many colleagues and friends over the years. We are particularly grateful to several individuals who have helped shape our thinking. These include, but are certainly not limited to, discussions with Victor Marek Borun, Sris Chatterjee, Kevin P. Collins, Cynthia L. Cordes, Uphinder S. Dhillon, Karen K. Dixon, Louis H. Ederington, Adam K. Gehr, Jr., Paul C. Grier, Keith M. Howe, Dennis J. Lasser, Dean Leistikow, Wilbur G. Lewellen, David C. Mauer, Roni Michaely, Philip C. Parr, David A. Preisser, Gabriel G. Ramírez, Jong-Chul Rhim, Anthony Saunders, Donald V. Smith, Charles W. Smithson, John D. Stowe, F. Katherine Warne, Frank M. Werner, and Richard Wohl.

We thank John Finnerty's colleagues at Houlihan Lokey Howard & Zukin, who have provided a stimulating environment within which to apply the principles of finance and a laboratory for testing new analytical techniques based on these principles.

We thank all of the people who helped with the project, including Jim Boyd, Teresa Cohan, Dave Cohen, Leah Jewell, Bill Oldsey, Helen Powers, Dave Salierno, MaryBeth Sanok, Gladys Soto, and especially our editor, Paul Donnelly. The insights, thoughtfulness, and hard work of our development editors, Jerry Ralya and Mike Buckman, deserve special thanks.

Lifelong appreciation goes to our fathers, E. Ward Emery and John P. Finnerty, to Doug Emery's undergraduate professor, mentor, and friend, William Graziano of Baker University, and to John Finnerty's great uncle, O. K. Taylor, who started his career at what is now Exxon Corporation as an office boy and retired many years later as deputy treasurer. After years of trying they finally got it across to us: "When in doubt, always go back to first principles."

In this book we say a great deal about the 12 principles of finance that are explained in Chapter 3. In writing this book we regularly encountered a 13th principle—the unlucky one that is the bane of all authors. We call it the Underestimation Principle. Its circularity highlights its inevitability: Writing a book always takes longer than you think—even when you take into account the Underestimation Principle! So we sincerely thank our spouses and families for their tremendous forbearance during the long and arduous process that culminated in this book. Yes, it did take considerably longer than we originally estimated, and it even took longer than every subsequent estimation. But we never lied; it's just that the basic principles always assert themselves.

Douglas R. Emery   John D. Finnerty
Binghamton, NY   *New York, NY*

Contents

PART IV CAPITAL STRUCTURE AND DIVIDEND POLICY 433

Chapter 14
Capital Market Efficiency: Explanation and Implications 434

Chapter 15
Why Capital Structure Matters 463

Chapter 16
Managing Capital Structure 495

Part I

FOUNDATIONS

OVERVIEW OF CORPORATE FINANCIAL MANAGEMENT

O B J E C T I V E S

After studying this chapter, you should be able to

1. Define the field of finance and its three main areas: corporate financial management, investments, and financial markets and institutions.

2. Describe the three major types of corporate financial management decisions: investment, financing, and managerial decisions.

3. Explain the advantages and disadvantages that the corporate form of organization has over sole proprietorships and partnerships.

4. Identify the rights of corporate shareholders.

5. Compare and contrast the investment-vehicle, accounting, and set-of-contracts models of the firm.

6. Explain the basis for the firm's goal of maximizing shareholder wealth, and explain why, as a firm becomes large, conflicts of interest can arise that can interfere with this goal.

Most people are interested in money in one way or another. Money, and therefore finance, is an integral part of life. Understanding finance can empower you, can help you use your money efficiently, and, yes, can even help you make *more* money.

Suppose you have a great new idea for meeting an important need that isn't already being met (for example, an idea like overnight delivery of packages, which was the basis for creating the phenomenally successful Federal Express Corporation). If you want to make money on your great new idea, how will you go about it? If you don't have a lot of money already, you'll need financing—and critical business know-how. Among other things, you'll need to understand finance. But even if you're not destined to be a business tycoon such as Bill Gates, founder of Microsoft Corporation (another incredible success story), you can benefit from finance.

Finance is not as specialized or complex as you might think. In fact, it is a daily concern of people and of organizations such as businesses and governments. The study of finance can benefit anyone. It can help with your career and your personal financial transactions, such as taking out a loan. It can also help when you are trying to understand world economic events or thinking about investing some money. Learning the ins and outs of finance will enlarge your perspective on important aspects of your present and future life.

In this chapter, we'll introduce you to finance and to the main area of finance on which this book focuses, corporate financial management.

1.1 WHAT IS FINANCE?

First and foremost, **finance** is concerned with determining value. The question "What is something worth?" is asked again and again. Finance is also concerned with how to make the best decisions. For example, should you make an investment? The decision rule in finance says you should buy an asset if it's worth more than it costs. Though seemingly obvious, this principle can easily be overlooked in a complex situation, as in the heat of a corporate takeover battle, such as when Viacom took over Paramount.

Finance has three main areas: corporate financial management, investments, and financial markets and intermediaries. These areas often involve the same financial transactions, but each area deals with them from a different viewpoint.

Corporate financial management is the major focus of this book. However, you can apply the principles and theories of finance to your personal financial transactions as well. For example, we'll show you how to calculate which is more valuable when you are buying a car, special financing such as a 1.9% APR loan or a special price such as $1500 cash back.

Corporate Financial Management

Corporate financial management focuses on how a corporation can create and maintain value. The amounts of money at stake can be huge. For example, Microsoft invested more than $1 billion developing and marketing Windows 95. More generally, *financial management* involves the efficient use of resources to further the goals of any organization, including not-for-profit organizations such as hospitals and government agencies. Financial management decisions are based on fundamental concepts and on the principles of finance, which we will describe in this book.

Netscape's Decision to Go Public

EXAMPLE

In 1994 Jim Clark founded Netscape. Clark put up $4 million. In return he got 9.4 million shares of the firm's stock, which represented 30% of its ownership. The firm was to produce server software to help other firms set up electronic addresses on the Internet. Netscape also created a software package called Navigator. Navigator helps people browse around ("surf") the Internet. In an effort to build a dominant 75% market share for its server software, Netscape gave away copies of Navigator. It hoped such dominance would help it make money by selling its server software, along with the associated service contracts.

In 1995 Netscape's growth strategy was working. However, such rapid growth meant that Netscape risked having trouble keeping up with demand. If it was to meet that continually accelerating demand, it would require substantially more money to finance the firm's phenomenal growth. As a result, Netscape considered *going public*. That is, it considered selling shares of its common stock to the general public for the first time. But Netscape was a very new firm still developing its business. In fact, investment analysts had estimated that Netscape might not become profitable for at least two years. Who would want to invest in a firm that was still unprofitable? As it turned out, it seemed like just about everybody.

Netscape went to *underwriters* for advice. Underwriters specialize in selling new shares of stock. The underwriters saw the potential in the new idea. They estimated that Netscape could expect to sell 3.5 million shares for between $12 and $14 per share. That would provide about $40 to $50 million in additional financing. The owners of Netscape found this attractive. They decided to go for it.

The underwriters soon discovered the extent of Wall Street's fascination with the Internet. Anticipated demand for the shares was building far beyond their initial expectations. As the day the new shares were to be issued approached, the underwriters substantially raised their estimates. They advised Netscape that it could sell 5 million new shares at $21 to $24 per share. At $22.50, Netscape would be worth $859 million. Not bad for a firm whose gross sales in the first half of 1995 were only $16.6 million! But it didn't stop there.

Demand for the shares continued to build. On August 9, 1995, Netscape went public. It sold the 5 million shares at $28 per share. But when the stock started public trading, it was at a price of $72 per share. It traded as high as 74\frac{3}{4}$ the first day, before closing at 58\frac{1}{4}$. The first day's volume was nearly 14 million shares—almost 3 times the number of shares available for trading! You might think of this as a sharks' feeding frenzy. Traders described the market for Netscape shares as "frothing."

On the basis of the first day's closing stock price, Netscape was worth nearly $2 billion. That made Clark's stake worth over $540 million—more than 135 times his initial investment just 17 months before. Clark's new idea, server software for the Internet and a free "surfboard" for browsing around the Internet, proved valuable indeed! ■

Corporate financial management decisions fall into three major categories. The first two reflect the two sides of a *balance sheet*. **Investment decisions** are primarily concerned with the asset (left-hand) side. They determine what assets a firm invests in and address questions such as whether to build a new manufacturing plant.

Financing decisions are primarily concerned with the liabilities and stockholders' equity (right-hand) side. They determine how the firm will obtain the money to make its investments. For example, Netscape obtained additional money for investing by selling new shares of its common stock.

Managerial decisions are the third major type of corporate financial management decisions. Such decisions include the firm's numerous day-to-day operating and financing decisions. How large should the firm be, and how fast should it grow? Should the firm grant credit to a customer? Should the firm change its advertising program? How should the firm compensate its managers and other employees?

CAREERS IN CORPORATE FINANCIAL MANAGEMENT

Among the three areas of finance, corporate financial management offers the greatest number of job opportunities. Financial management is important in business organizations, such as manufacturing firms and financial institutions. It is also important in not-for-profit organizations and government agencies.

ENTRY-LEVEL POSITIONS

Financial Analyst
Financial analysts assist in the firm's decision-making process. They gather and process financial information, and they prepare financial analyses that decision makers can rely on. This work includes capital budgeting studies, analysis of long-term financing alternatives, capital structure policy studies, dividend policy studies, and merger analysis, among others. Indeed, a competent corporate financial analyst should be able to perform a study involving any of the corporate finance issues discussed in this book.

Credit Analyst

In addition to generalists, there are a variety of more specialized financial analysts. One type is the credit analyst. Credit analysts assess the credit strength of the firm's customers who apply for credit. This analysis is useful to the firm when it decides whether to grant credit. (Just think, a former classmate of yours might be the one who processes your next credit card application.)

Cash Manager

Cash managers manage the firm's short-term investments of cash. This involves comparing the returns on short-term securities, purchasing short-term securities, and monitoring the short-term investments to make sure the firm remains fully invested at all times in securities that satisfy its investment objectives.

MORE SENIOR POSITIONS

Assistant Treasurer

A large firm usually has more than one assistant treasurer. They typically divide the responsibility of assisting the treasurer. For example, one may handle international treasury operations, another corporate financial policy, and another working capital management.

Manager of Corporate Financial Analysis

Ensuring high-quality financial analysis is so important that many firms put one individual in overall charge of it. (Titles are flexible, so an assistant treasurer may be given this role.)

Corporate Risk Manager

More and more firms are assigning managers responsibility for managing the interest rate risk, foreign exchange risk, and commodity risk that the firm faces. Risk managers are responsible for quantifying these risks and for designing and implementing strategies for managing them.

Pension Fund Manager

This individual either manages the firm's pension fund investments or selects, and monitors the performance of, outside investment managers.

Director of Financial Reporting

Publicly traded firms must meet the financial reporting requirements imposed by the securities laws. The director of financial reporting ensures compliance with these standards.

VERY SENIOR POSITIONS

Chief Financial Officer

The chief financial officer (CFO) is ultimately responsible for all financial aspects of the firm's operations, including both day-to-day and long-term decisions. One of the most senior executives in the firm, the CFO often moves on to become the chief executive officer (CEO) of the entire firm.

Treasurer

The treasurer is usually responsible for the day-to-day financial management of the firm's operations. The treasurer is concerned with any flow of funds into or out of the firm. The treasurer works very closely with, and reports to, the CFO.

Controller

The controller is usually responsible for the auditing, management accounting, and financial reporting functions. In most firms, the treasury and controllership functions complement one another. Like the treasurer, the controller works very closely with, and reports to, the CFO.

Vice President of Corporate Development

This position doesn't have a consistent title. Some firms call it vice president of corporate planning. It involves long-range financial planning, corporate strategy, and mergers and acquisitions.

Investments

The area of **investments** examines financial transactions from the viewpoint of investors outside the firm. Investors provide funds when they *invest in* (buy) financial securities, such as stocks and bonds. For example, we can view our Netscape example from the "other side" of the transaction: Should you have bought some of the Netscape stock being offered?

CAREERS IN INVESTMENTS

ENTRY-LEVEL POSITIONS

Securities Analyst

Brokerage houses, banks, mutual funds, insurance companies, and other financial institutions employ analysts to evaluate securities as potential investments for the money they manage. College endowments and foundations that manage their own investments also employ securities analysts.

Personal Financial Planner

Personal financial planners help families make financial decisions, which often includes advising them in managing their investments. This often involves helping them save to meet specific needs, such as their retirement or paying for their children's college education.

MORE SENIOR POSITIONS

Pension Fund Manager

Pension fund managers manage money on behalf of pension funds. The proportion of financial assets held in public and private pension funds has increased dramatically over the past 25 years. As the assets under management increase, so do the number of job opportunities in this area.

Portfolio Manager

Commercial banks, brokerage houses, money management firms, and other financial institutions that manage funds employ investment portfolio managers. Like pension fund managers, they try to achieve the maximum possible returns consistent with the financial institution's stated investment policies.

VERY SENIOR POSITIONS

Financial institutions involved in the investments area have senior executives who are responsible for the overall day-to-day operations, as well as the long-term strategies, of these firms. These very senior positions are similar to those described in the "Careers in Corporate Financial Management" box.

Financial Markets and Intermediaries

When we consider financial markets and intermediaries, we are exploring the firm's financing decisions from yet another viewpoint—that of a third party. Rather than viewing the transaction as either a corporation or an investor, financial markets and intermediaries act as go-betweens who facilitate transactions between investors and corporations.

Financial markets are markets where financial securities, such as stocks and bonds, are bought and sold. Some financial market participants, such as brokers and dealers, facilitate the purchases and sales of securities by other parties. They charge fees or commissions for their services. For example, they helped bring Netscape's stock offering to market. In contrast, **financial intermediaries** purchase financial securities, such as stocks and bonds of other firms, but rather than reselling them, intermediaries hold them as investments. Financial intermediaries finance these investments by issuing claims against themselves (for example, shares of stock in themselves).

CAREERS IN FINANCIAL MARKETS AND INTERMEDIARIES

ENTRY-LEVEL POSITIONS

Corporate Finance Associate

Corporate finance associates are also known as entry-level *investment bankers.* Investment bankers assist firms in issuing securities, merging with other firms, managing outstanding liabilities, disposing of unwanted assets, and the like. Commercial banks and consulting firms have expanded into the investment banking business, so these positions are available at a range of financial institutions. These positions require expertise in all aspects of corporate finance.[1]

Lending Officer

Lending officers work for banks and other financial institutions that lend money. They help design and negotiate the loan arrangements and monitor the borrower's performance while the loan is outstanding.

---

[1] If you are interested in being an investment banker, be sure to add the C-type problems to your list of things to do in this course.

Debt Rating Analyst

The debt rating agencies employ a flock of credit analysts who participate in the debt rating process. Usually such analysts specialize in an industry or particular type of security, so these positions offer a good opportunity to learn about particular industries as well as to sharpen your credit skills.

Securities Trader

Brokerage houses, banks, money management firms, and many other types of financial institutions employ individuals who actively trade securities. They play an important role in helping the securities markets function.

Stockbroker

Stockbrokers help investors make investments. They usually make investment recommendations as well as place orders to buy or sell securities on behalf of their clients.

Life Insurance Salesperson

Life insurance salespersons help their clients determine how much life insurance is appropriate and which life insurance products are most suitable for them.

Mortgage Broker

These individuals help people and firms arrange mortgage financing for real estate assets they want to buy.

MORE SENIOR POSITIONS

Branch Manager

The branch manager is responsible for the day-to-day operation of a brokerage house branch office or insurance sales office. Branch managers have usually excelled at their entry-level position and thus earned greater management responsibility.

VERY SENIOR POSITIONS

Financial institutions involved in the financial intermediation area have senior executives who are responsible for the overall day-to-day operations, as well as the long-term strategies, of these firms. These very senior positions are similar to those described in the "Careers in Corporate Financial Management" box.

The Science of Finance

Finance is a science. Like other sciences, it has fundamental concepts, principles, and theories. In Chapter 3 we describe the principles of finance, which we will apply throughout the book. A downward-sloping demand curve is an example of an economics principle you already know: If you lower a product's price, you will sell more of it.

An important tool of science is called modeling. Modeling is a method of describing reality. There are different types of models. Many of our finance models are mathematical models; the downward-sloping demand curve is an example. The primary benefit of using a mathematical model is its precision in specifying relationships. To the extent that we can control the inputs, we can use such a model to predict outcomes.

The relationships in a model are established by a variety of methods. One method is empirical estimation. For example, a firm often estimates future sales of a new product by using past sales observed during marketing research. Other relationships are contractually specified, such as the repayment of borrowed money according to a loan agreement. Finally, many come from logical, conceptual, or theoretical ideas, as in the case of expecting a downward-sloping demand curve.

But models have limitations. One famous marketing case offers an example of an *upward-sloping* demand curve. That is, a firm sold more after raising its price. The product was the beach sandal known as flip-flops.[1] Very few flip-flops sold at first. Apparently, people thought the sandals couldn't be worth much if they didn't cost very much. When marketers figured out the problem, they raised the price. Sales then increased as people tried the new product. Of course, after flip-flops caught on, competition drove the price back down. And today, flip-flops have a downward-sloping demand curve, just as we would expect.[2]

Does this temporary upward-sloping demand curve invalidate the principle of a downward-sloping demand curve? Of course not. The complication in this case was the initial impression that a low price signaled a poorly made product. Once this impression was corrected, flip-flops became extraordinarily popular—and cheap. But people know they are cheap because they are inexpensive to make rather than because they are poorly made.

Despite its limitations, even an imperfect model can provide useful insights and may be the best starting point for solving new and challenging problems.

Finance and Accounting

Finance frequently employs accounting information, as we will in the next section when we use an accounting balance sheet to describe a firm. Consequently people often ask how finance is different from accounting.

The fundamental difference between finance and accounting is the viewpoint. Accounting generally has an historical outlook. Its major purpose is to account for past activities. In marked contrast, finance emphasizes determining value and making decisions; it focuses solidly on the future. Picking up where accounting leaves off, finance concentrates on the implications for the future. Finance asks such questions as "What do we do now?" and "Where do we go from here?"

Self-Check Questions

1. What are the major concerns of the field of finance?

2. What are the three main areas of finance?

3. Describe the three major types of corporate financial management questions.

4. What role do financial intermediaries play in the financial markets?

1.2 OWNERSHIP, CONTROL, AND RISK

Corporations are often very large and complex organizations. However, we can gain insight into them by tracing the development of a firm from one person's idea into a major corporation. Consider the following fictionalized account of Henry Ford's automobile manufacturing firm. Note how each decision in the firm's evolution can affect the value and related decisions of the firm. Each step adds another interested party, called a stakeholder. A **stakeholder** is a constituent who has a legitimate claim of any sort on the firm.

---

[1] A friend of ours, Phil Parr, calls them "go-aheads." He says, "Did you ever try going backward in them?"

[2] You might say the demand curve for flip-flops flip-flopped.

Cash C	
Raw materials . . . . R	
Tools . . . . T	
Garage . . . . G	Henry's equity . . . . HE
Total Assets . . . . TA	Liabilities + Stockholders' Equity . . . . TA

Start-up

Henry started with the idea of making a car affordable for a large number of people. Using his own money, he bought raw materials, built one car by himself, and sold it to a satisfied customer, earning a profit. He reinvested the money from the sale, bought more raw materials, and made more cars. Figure 1-1 shows Henry's first *balance sheet.*

Note that the basic **balance sheet identity,**

$$\text{Total Assets} = \text{Liabilities} + \text{Stockholders' Equity}$$

must always hold. Note also that the financing decision is represented by the right-hand side of the balance sheet. Henry provided the entire financing himself. (Hence liabilities and stockholders' equity are made up solely of Henry's equity, HE.) Henry is also the manager of the firm. In fact, at this point, besides suppliers and customers, Henry is the only person directly involved in the firm.

Henry's primary motivation was to earn money. But what happens if the firm is unsuccessful? That is, what happens if Henry can't sell his cars for a profit? Eventually Henry would run out of money. Under some circumstances, then, Henry can lose the money he invested, but no one else stands to lose anything.

At this initial point, we want to note three things: First, Henry has exclusive *ownership* of the firm and its assets. Second, Henry has complete *control* of the firm and its assets (within legal limits). Third, Henry is bearing all the *risk* associated with the firm's investment.

Debt

Building one car at a time was OK, but it occurred to Henry that if he could buy more materials with each order, he could save money on shipping charges. Henry (and therefore the firm) did not have enough money to place such large orders, so Henry went to a bank and borrowed some money. He promised to repay the money out of revenues from future car sales. Figure 1-2 shows the revised balance sheet for Henry's firm.

Note that the firm's financing—its *capital structure*—is now made up of two parts. (We use TA′ to represent the liabilities plus stockholders' equity to emphasize that the accounting identity must always hold.) The two parts of the firm's new financing are debt and equity. **Equity** represents ownership, whereas **debt** is a legal obligation for borrowed money. As the only **shareholder** (or **stockholder** or **equityholder**[3]), Henry still has exclusive ownership of the firm and its assets. Henry also retains direct control over the firm and its assets, because he is the manager of the firm. However, Henry is now constrained by bank-loan obligations. His firm is required to pay interest on the loan and to repay the money it borrowed. The bank has become a stakeholder in Henry's firm.

As with Henry, the bank's primary motivation for making this loan was to earn money. Because of this, Henry agreed to pay interest in addition to repaying the loan. But now what happens if the firm is unsuccessful? That is, what if Henry can't sell his cars for a profit? Un-

---

[3] We follow financial industry practice and use the terms *shareholder, stockholder,* and *equityholder* interchangeably.

Cash .... C′		
Raw materials .... R′		
Tools .... T′	Bank loan .... B′	
Garage .... G′	Henry's equity .... HE′	
Total Assets .... TA′	Liabilities + Stockholders' Equity .... TA′	

FIGURE 1-2

Balance sheet for Henry's firm after the bank loan.

der some circumstances, the firm might not have sufficient cash to repay the bank fully. Because of this possibility, the bank is bearing some risk. But how much risk?

On the downside, if it is not fully paid, the bank may still get something, whereas Henry will have lost all the money he invested. On the upside, if the firm does well, the bank will receive only the loan repayment plus the promised interest, whereas Henry will get all of the "excess net revenue"—everything above the amount promised to the bank. In short, Henry stands to fare worse than the bank on the downside and better than the bank on the upside. Thus Henry is bearing more of the risk than the bank. Of course, the bank must trust Henry to act responsibly and not run off to South America without repaying.

You can see that this situation is more complex than in the start-up, where Henry provided all the financing. Determining the values of the claims on the firm is more difficult. The firm's decisions are more complex because they affect more stakeholders. Let's review the current situation: First, Henry retains exclusive ownership of the firm. Second, Henry still controls the firm's assets but is constrained by bank-loan obligations. Third, the bank now bears some of the risk. Fourth, Henry bears all the *residual* (remaining) risk, which is the majority of the firm's risk.

Employees

After a while, Henry has an even larger number of orders—so large in fact that it would take him longer than the rest of his life to build those cars—and more are coming in every day. To fill these orders, Henry hires some employees. Although the balance sheet doesn't change, Henry's firm now has some implicit obligations to its employees. For example, its employees would be upset if the firm delayed wage payments. And the employees have some implicit obligations to the firm. For example, an employee shouldn't use an expense account for personal benefit. Therefore, although neither the balance sheet nor the ownership of the firm has changed, Henry's control over the firm's assets is further constrained.

Multiple Equityholders

Demand for Henry's cars continues to grow. Now, although Henry has employees to build the cars on backorder, he is again short of money to buy raw materials. He goes to the bank, but the bank refuses to lend him more money. In short, the bank says it won't take the risk of a bigger loan. The bank will agree to lend more money only if Henry puts up more money. But Henry doesn't have any more money; all of his money is already invested in the firm. The bank suggests that Henry get other equity financing, and Henry does. Just like Netscape, he sells shares in his firm to new equityholders. He also creates a board of directors. Figure 1-3 illustrates the firm's new balance sheet.

Where do Henry and his firm stand now? First, the firm is no longer exclusively Henry's. The firm has other equityholders who are part owners. Second, although Henry is still the manager and still has control over the firm's assets, he is now even more constrained. In addition to the bank-loan and employee obligations, Henry now has an obligation to act in the best interests of the other equityholders. Third, the bank continues to bear some of the risk of

FIGURE 1-3
Balance sheet for Henry's firm after it goes public.

Cash .... C″	
Raw materials .... R″	Bank loan .... B″
Tools .... T″	New stockholders' equity .... O″
Garage .... G″	Henry's equity .... HE″
Total Assets .... TA″	Liabilities + Stockholders' Equity .... TA″

the firm. Fourth, Henry no longer bears all of the firm's residual risk. He and the new equity-holders now share the residual risk of the firm in direct proportion to the number of shares each person owns.

Let's also take a moment to point out the new equityholders' motivation for making this investment. As with Henry and the bank, their motivation is to make money. And the more money the firm makes, the more money each equityholder makes (in proportion to the number of shares each person owns). Because all the equityholders, including Henry, have the same motivation, it might appear that all their interests are identical. However, Henry is the only equityholder who has *direct* control over the firm's assets. Therefore, the other equity-holders have to trust Henry to act in their best interests and not, for example, pay himself a huge, inappropriate salary.

Separation of Ownership from Control

More time has passed, and Henry's firm is operating more successfully than ever before. But Henry is now tired of his years of working and has decided to retire and live off investment returns. Accordingly, Henry hires special employees, *managers,* to run the firm. As with other employees, hiring the managers doesn't change the balance sheet. Nevertheless, this change is a *very important* one: Henry no longer has direct control over the firm and its assets. The managers now control the firm's assets, and Henry has become like the other equityholders. In particular, he must trust the managers to run the firm for his benefit, just as the other equityhold-ers trusted him.

At this point Henry's firm has become a very large and complex corporation. At the start, the right-hand side of the balance sheet was very simple; its total was made up solely of Henry's equity. Now it has become complex, involving explicit as well as implicit contracts among its many stakeholders. Each change added to the potential for conflicts of interest among the various stakeholders.

For example, consider an equityholder who does not have direct control over the firm's assets. This equityholder may be willing to place the firm at great risk to have a chance of earning a high return, because he has other assets and can "afford" to take the risk. Contrast this equityholder with the firm's manager. The manager has direct control over the assets but is affected differently by the firm's risk. If the firm goes bankrupt, the manager can lose her job. Because of this, the manager may limit the firm's risk, even passing up investments that offer great potential returns.

Self-Check Questions

1. Describe some of the conflicts of interest between Henry and the bank.

2. Describe some of the conflicts of interest between Henry and the other shareholders.

3. Describe some of the conflicts of interest between the managers and the other shareholders of Henry's firm.

1.3 THREE DIFFERENT VIEWS OF A FIRM

Earlier we talked about modeling. The evolution of Henry's firm highlights three different models of the firm: the *investment-vehicle, accounting,* and *set-of-contracts models.* All three models are important, and each offers insights into particular problems.

The Investment-Vehicle Model

The most basic view of the firm is the investment-vehicle model. It provides the framework for the firm. The investment-vehicle model is shown in Figure 1-4. Figure 1-4 also shows the three main areas of finance. Investors provide funds (financing) in exchange for financial securities. Formally, **financial securities** are contracts that provide for the exchange of money at various points in time. For example, a bond provides for a specified set of cash payments to its owner (who has previously paid money to purchase the bond).

We have already identified the two basic types of financial securities: equity and debt. Recall that equity is the ownership of the firm. Equity is typically represented by shares of **common stock.** A person who owns all the shares of common stock owns the firm, as Henry did when he started his firm. If more than one person owns shares in the firm, each person's ownership portion is simply the number of shares that person owns divided by the total number of existing shares. For example, if a shareholder owns 350 of a firm's total 1000 shares, then that person owns 35% of the firm.

Recall that debt is a legal obligation to make contractually agreed upon future payments, which consist of interest and repayment of the principal (original debt amount). Debtholders have lent the firm money. They have no claim of ownership as long as the firm meets its payment obligations. The firm controls the use of the funds.

In the investment-vehicle model, the firm's managers are neutral intermediaries who act only in the best interest of the shareholders, the owners of the firm. Sometimes, especially in the case of small firms, the owner is the manager. When this happens, there is obviously no conflict between the owner and the manager because they are one and the same.

The investment-vehicle model of the firm is embodied in an often-stated goal: that managers should *maximize shareholder wealth.* In a "perfect" world (one without owner-manager conflicts), maximizing shareholder wealth is the theoretically correct managerial goal. Because it is correct in a "perfect" world, the investment-vehicle model is the best starting point for analyzing financial decisions. We discuss this further in the following section.

FIGURE 1-4
The investment-vehicle model of the firm, and the three main areas of finance.

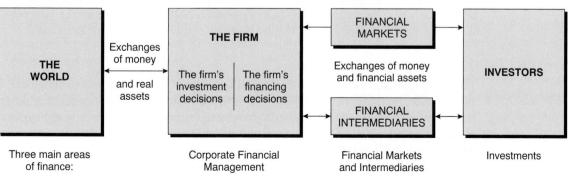

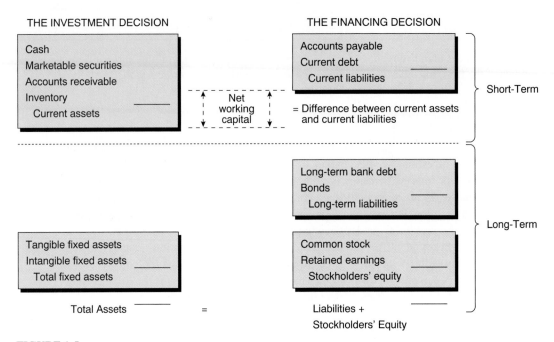

FIGURE 1-5
The accounting model of the firm.

The Accounting Model

The accounting model of the firm is, in a sense, a subset of the investment-vehicle model. In the United States, it is a way to operationalize and approximate the investment-vehicle model. It is embodied in the balance sheet view of the firm, an abbreviated version of which is shown in Figure 1-5. As we have said, the firm's investment decisions concern the asset side, and the firm's financing decisions concern the liabilities and stockholders' equity side. Many day-to-day operating and financial policies (managerial decisions) can also be seen on the balance sheet, as well as on the *income statement* and *statement of cash flows*.

One advantage of the accounting model is that it is highly integrated, showing how the firm's pieces fit together. Another advantage is that accounting is widely familiar, so the accounting model makes communication easier.

There are disadvantages to the accounting model, however. A major one is accounting's primarily historical viewpoint, which we noted earlier. A lot of the information firms use to make decisions is simply not in the accounting system. Although the accounting perspective is important and often helpful, it is frequently inadequate by itself for many decisions.

The Set-of-Contracts Model

The set-of-contracts model of the firm is a refinement of the investment-vehicle model. It starts with the investment-vehicle model but recognizes imperfections that can arise in the relationships within the model. It views relationships as contracts between the firm and its stakeholders. Figure 1-6 shows many of the firm's major stakeholders, those who have contracts with the firm. Major stakeholders include stockholders, bondholders, short-term creditors, employees, customers, managers, communities, and governments.

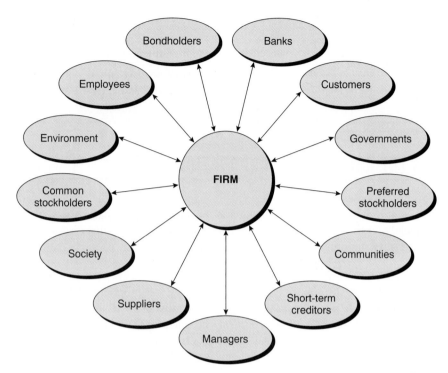

FIGURE 1-6
The set-of-contracts model of the firm.

The set-of-contracts model includes *explicit* as well as *implicit* contracts. Firms have explicit contracts with investors, such as bondholders and short-term creditors, wherein the firm promises to pay them specific amounts of money on specific future dates. Other explicit contracts include such things as outstanding guarantees on previously sold products, severance pay for terminated employees, and pension obligations.

Firms have implicit contracts to be honest and to disclose relevant information. Employees have implicit contracts with firms, wherein the employees agree to be honest and give their best effort. Managers have implicit contracts with the shareholders, wherein the managers agree to act in the shareholders' best interests.

Regulatory and legally mandated contracts, such as workplace safety standards and product liability, include both explicit and implicit aspects. A court of law may be necessary to determine specific obligations in applying the implicit aspects of contracts.

Many contracts depend on the occurrence of particular future outcomes, such as a bonus that employees receive if the firm's profits reach a certain level. The bonus is *contingent* on reaching this profit amount. There are many such contingent contracts. Your 2-week vacation may be contingent on your having worked for the firm for the previous 52 weeks. Your participation in the retirement plan may be contingent on your having worked for the firm for some minimum number of years. This type of contract is called a **contingent claim**. The contract's outcome is contingent on the value of some other asset or on a particular occurrence.

Corporations have many outstanding contingent claims. A loan can be a contingent claim; the lender's claim to the firm's assets is contingent on the firm's actions. If a firm doesn't repay, the lender can take the collateral. Therefore, if a firm fails to meet its obligation, the lender will have some control over the firm's actions. However, that ability to exert control is contingent on the firm's contractual failure. Without such a failure, the lender has no control over the firm's actions.

Self-Check Questions

1. What is the goal of the firm according to the investment-vehicle model of the firm?

2. In what sense is the accounting model a subset of the investment-vehicle model?

3. How does the set-of-contracts model of the firm build on the investment-vehicle model?

4. What types of contracts does the set-of-contracts model recognize?

1.4 THE ROLE OF THE CORPORATION

This book focuses on corporate financial management because the corporate form is the predominant form of business organization in the United States. Corporations issue a variety of financial securities, many of which are publicly traded. This section discusses the advantages of the corporate form over the primary alternative forms.

The Corporate Form and Its Benefits

There are three basic forms of business organization: sole proprietorship, partnership, and corporation. In a **sole proprietorship,** a single individual owns all the firm's assets directly and is directly responsible for all its liabilities. The sole proprietor has *unlimited liability*. That is, the sole proprietor's entire personal wealth is at risk. But a sole proprietorship is not a taxable entity. Instead, the proprietorship's income is added to the owner's other income to determine income taxes due. Most small businesses are set up as proprietorships because they are easy to organize.

A **partnership** is similar to a sole proprietorship except that there are two or more owners. In a *general partnership* all partners have unlimited liability, including unlimited liability for actions taken entirely by other general partners. The partners share in profits and losses, often in proportion to their respective capital contributions to the partnership. As with a proprietorship, the income from the business is taxed directly to the general partners; a partnership does not pay income taxes. Oil and gas ventures and real estate ventures are often organized as partnerships because of tax laws.

The partnership form has another disadvantage besides unlimited liability. If a general partner leaves the partnership or dies, the partnership must be dissolved. This is very inconvenient if there are many partners. Many states permit *limited partnerships,* in which there are one or more limited partners in addition to the general partners. The general partners run the partnership with unlimited liability. The limited partners contribute capital and share in the partnership's profits or losses. But a limited partner's liability is limited to the capital that partner has invested. In addition, limited partners are typically allowed to withdraw by selling their partnerships, which avoids the need to dissolve the partnership when someone dies or wishes to withdraw.

A **corporation** is legally a "person" that is separate and distinct from its owners, who are its shareholders. A corporation is allowed to own assets, incur liabilities, and sell securities to raise capital, among other things. The corporation's officers are agents, who are authorized to act for the corporation.

Table 1-1 compares the corporate form of organization to three other forms of organization. We include the *limited liability company* form because it has recently emerged as a viable alternative to the corporate form. It offers limited liability, like a corporation, but is taxed like a partnership.

TABLE 1-1
Comparison of alternative forms of organization.

	SOLE PROPRIETORSHIP	CORPORATION	PARTNERSHIP	LIMITED LIABILITY COMPANY
Management	The sole proprietor owns and operates the business.	The corporation owns and operates the business. Employees of the corporation manage the business. The shareholders are represented by the corporation's board of directors.	The partnership owns and operates the business. One of the general partners is usually designated the manager of partnership operations. The partnership agreement specifies who exercises operating and management authority.	The company owns and operates the business. Employees of the company manage the business.
Liability for Financial Obligations				
Nature of liability	Sole proprietor bears full liability.	The shareholders have no direct liability for financial obligations of the corporation.	General partners are jointly and severally liable for all obligations of the partnership, as well as for certain liabilities incurred by any general partner. Limited partners have no liability for partnership obligations except obligations they specifically undertake.	The shareholders have no direct liability for financial obligations of the company.

(continued)

The corporate form of organization has four major advantages over sole proprietorships and partnerships:

- **Limited liability.** Shareholders' liability for corporate obligations is limited to the loss of their shares. If a corporation goes bankrupt or loses a large product-liability suit, the most its shareholders can lose is their respective investments. In a sole proprietorship or a general partnership, the owners can lose considerably more—in the extreme case, virtually everything they own.

- **Permanency.** A corporation's legal existence is not affected when some of its shareholders die or sell their shares. Thus its longevity is better assured than that of a proprietorship or a partnership.

- **Transferability of ownership.** Selling shares in a corporation is normally easier than selling a proprietorship or a general-partnership interest.

- **Better access to external sources of capital**. Because of its permanency and its ability to borrow money or sell additional shares, a corporation has greater financing flexibility.

TABLE 1-1
(continued)

	SOLE PROPRIETORSHIP	CORPORATION	PARTNERSHIP	LIMITED LIABILITY COMPANY
Dollar amount of exposure	Liability is unlimited.	Liability is limited to the equity invested.	Liability is unlimited for general partners. Liability is limited to equity invested for limited partners.	Liability is limited to equity invested.
Income Tax Treatment				
Taxable entity	Sole proprietor.	Corporation.	Partners.	Shareholders in the company, which is treated as a partnership for federal income tax purposes.
Deductibility, depreciation, and interest expense	All tax consequences of business flow through directly to the sole proprietor. Sole proprietorship is not a taxable entity.	The tax benefits of ownership are claimed by the corporation.	Tax benefits of ownership usually flow through to partners in the same proportion as ownership percentages.	Tax benefits of ownership usually flow through to shareholders in the same proportion as ownership percentages.
Limitation on tax deductions	No limitations.	Deductions may not be taken directly by the shareholders.	Deductions are usually limited to the tax basis of each partner's investment.	Deductions are usually limited to the tax basis of each shareholder's investment.
Income taxation	Income is taxed at the sole proprietor level only.	Income is taxed at the corporate level. Dividends are taxable to the shareholders as ordinary income.	Income is taxed at the partner level only.	Income is taxed at the shareholder level only.

The corporate form does have a significant drawback, however. A corporation must pay taxes on its income. Operating income paid to shareholders through cash dividends is taxed twice: first to the corporation and then to the shareholder.

Of course, there are many organizations that have still other forms. These include master limited partnerships, mutual organizations, religious organizations, fraternal organizations, not-for-profit corporations, and many kinds of government organizations. Although we will focus largely on profit-making corporations, the principles of finance apply equally well to these other types of organizations.

The Rights of Ownership

A corporation's shareholders are the corporation's owners. As the owners, they have the following rights:

- **Dividend rights.** Shareholders get an identical per-share amount of any dividends.[4] However, the decision to pay dividends is made by the firm's board of directors and is subject to legal and other restrictions, which are discussed in Chapters 17 and 18.

- **Voting rights.** Shareholders have the right to vote on certain matters, such as the annual election of directors. In most cases, each share of common stock entitles its holder to one vote. A corporation's *articles of incorporation* typically specify either majority voting or cumulative voting. Under *majority voting,* shareholders vote for each director separately, casting one vote per share for each director they support. The candidates who receive the largest numbers of votes are elected to the board. Alternatively, under *cumulative voting,* the directors are voted on jointly, and a shareholder can cast all his votes in favor of a single candidate. Cumulative voting makes it easier for a minority-shareholder group to elect a particular representative to the board.

- **Liquidation rights.** Shareholders have the right to a proportional share of the firm's residual value in the event of liquidation. The residual value is what remains after all the corporation's other obligations have been settled.

- **Preemptive rights.** In some corporations, shareholders have the right to subscribe proportionally to any new issue of the corporation's shares. Such offerings, called *rights offerings,* are described in Chapter 23.

When a firm has two or more classes of common stock with differences in dividend, voting, liquidation, or preemptive rights, the different classes of stock usually trade at different prices that reflect these differential rights.

The Goal of the Firm

Many people say the firm's goal is profit. More carefully stated, according to the investment-vehicle model, the firm's goal is to *maximize shareholder wealth.* Shareholder wealth maximization is a more specific form of profit maximization.

WHY NOT PROFIT MAXIMIZATION?   There are at least three important reasons why profit maximization is not an operational goal. First, profit maximization is vague. *Profit* has many different definitions. Do we mean accounting profits (based on book values) or economic profits (based on market values, and beyond a fair return)? Are we measuring private profits or social profits, which include any impacts on all parts of society, not just owners? Are we maximizing short-run profits or long-run profits?

Second, profit maximization ignores differences in when we get the money. These differences are important because of the *time value of money.* Profit maximization does not clearly distinguish between getting a dollar today and getting a dollar in the future, such as a year from today. When costs and benefits extend over time, such as a few years, profit measures fail to adjust properly for the effect that timing differences have on value.

Third, profit maximization ignores risk differences between alternatives. When given a choice between two alternatives that have the same return but different risk, most people choose the less risky one. This makes the less risky alternative more valuable. Profit maximization ignores such differences in value.

SHAREHOLDER WEALTH MAXIMIZATION   **Shareholder wealth maximization** focuses the profit motive squarely on the firm's owners. By maximizing shareholder wealth, we

---

[4] Some corporations have more than one class of common stock, and the classes may have different dividend rights. But within each class, the stockholders share equally on a per-share basis in any dividends.

are directly addressing the problems of profit maximization. First, shareholder wealth is unambiguous. It is based on the future cash flows that are expected to come to the shareholders, rather than on an ambiguous notion of profit or other revenues. Second, shareholder wealth depends explicitly on the timing of future cash flows. Finally, our process for measuring shareholder wealth accounts for risk differences.

For a corporation with publicly traded stock, the value of the firm to its owners is the market value of the shares owned. Managers should therefore make decisions that increase— or at least maintain—the value of these shares. Firms that do not have publicly traded shares can also use the principles of finance and related decision-making techniques to increase the value of the firm. The financial principles and techniques apply for these firms as well.

Self-Check Questions

1. What are the major advantages and disadvantages of the corporate form of organization as compared to sole proprietorships and partnerships?
2. Explain how limited partnerships differ from general partnerships.
3. Describe the four types of rights that corporate stockholders have.
4. What is the goal of the firm? How is it different from the goal of profit maximization?

1.5 THE EVOLUTION OF FINANCE

Finance has flourished only in the broader context of society. It has evolved by addressing the important business, economic, and social problems of its time, thereby contributing to society. For example, finance has long been concerned with the role the firm plays in allocating society's resources. Recently, some have begun to question whether the modern corporate form, as we know it, will be eclipsed by a more efficient organizational form. Another form may be better able to function in a global environment and thus better serve the needs of all its stakeholders.

Contemporary Trends

Three important contemporary trends in finance are globalization, computerization, and corporate reorganization. These trends are rapidly changing the business world.

GLOBALIZATION   Lower trade barriers, cheaper and more reliable transportation, and instantaneous electronic communication have transformed business into a global marketplace. Large securities firms, such as Salomon Brothers, trade U.S. Treasury securities "around the clock." They transfer the "trading book" from New York to Tokyo to London and back to New York in order to maintain continuous markets. Don't think of globalization as merely the importing and exporting of such things as cars and wheat. Globalization is much more.

Almost every product and service has some international content. Financial services are now an important part of the global marketplace. Even corporations themselves are more international. Ownership transcends national boundaries, as do the markets for bonds and for short-term credit. And your own working environment is likely to be multinational and diverse in many ways. We'll point out important aspects of this phenomenon throughout this book.

COMPUTERIZATION AND TELECOMMUNICATIONS   Powerful, low-cost computing has become a fact of life. In addition, there has been a simultaneous development of telecommunications networks that share databases, information, images, and even conferencing almost anywhere in the world. Individual firms have thrived, or have disappeared, because of their ability, or their inability, to use technology effectively. Likewise, individual managers have thrived, or have lost their jobs, on the basis of whether they are willing and able to use computing and telecommunications technology. If you take a job as a financial analyst after graduating, you will have access to vastly more information at the push of a button than ever before possible. Today, many financial analysts have a powerful work station on their desk that is capable of doing what required a large mainframe computer not so many years ago!

CORPORATE REORGANIZATION AND RESTRUCTURING   We have seen a procession of corporate reorganizations, bankruptcies, mergers, acquisitions, and spinoffs. Within large and small firms, the managerial and professional staffs have sometimes been in turmoil. During a recent period, the Fortune 500 corporations (the 500 largest industrial corporations in the United States) laid off over 5 million employees. People can no longer expect their first job to be high-paying, and secure, in a major corporation. And they are not so likely today to spend an entire career with a single firm. This harsh reality should add to your motivation for studying finance.

In the past, many professionals had one or possibly two distinct careers during their working lives, and only a couple of different employers. Today's generation of managers may have very different career paths. You may have three, four, or even more distinct careers, and you may work in shorter stretches for more employers before you retire.

Today, a corporation may be less willing to hire, train, and work to retain employees who are not well trained and highly motivated. We sincerely believe that sound training in corporate financial management is critical to your career. Such training provides valuable skills and insights that will enhance your understanding of the nature of business, the marketplace, and your role in it.

Self-Check Questions

1. How have the trends in globalization, computerization and telecommunications, and corporate reorganization affected the business world?

2. Is a recent graduate more or less likely than in the past to spend her entire career with a single firm?

3. How can sound training in corporate financial management affect your career?

1.6 A FEW WORDS OF ADVICE

There are some things we encourage you to keep in mind as you study. These are things we have found to be helpful to our students.

Financial Principles

This book was written with an overriding belief that if you understand the "first principles," you can address every problem and issue effectively by using them. Essentially, we believe that if you understand the general, you can always apply that understanding to a specific situation. And once you understand the principles and structure of the financial world, using those principles can be interesting and even fun.

Financial Jargon

When you first encounter a subject, you must learn new terms. Finance is no exception. It has its own language, or jargon. And when you learn a new language, it is better to add vocabulary gradually, rather than trying to learn all of it at once. A rich language has many terms for essentially the same thing, but each term has subtle shades of meaning that make it the "best" term to use in a particular situation. This richness provides more precise communication and is welcome in technical situations. However, it can be overwhelming at first.

Toward this end, we will help you avoid getting bogged down in terminology. For now, we'll keep it simple, concentrating on helping you understand the basic concepts rather than forcing you to memorize new terms. Although the new terminology is essential, we will endeavor to familiarize you with the terminology of finance in a way that promotes your understanding of the basics. In the longer term, however, it is very important that you learn the language of finance. Unless you understand it, you will find it very difficult to comprehend fully the more subtle concepts of finance.

Financial Calculators

We recommend that you purchase a good financial calculator. You may have a calculator that will add, subtract, multiply, and divide or a "scientific" calculator with complex math functions. These calculators are good for balancing your checkbook or for courses in statistics, engineering, and chemistry. However, this is a course in finance, and we have written this book with a financial calculator in mind.

Financial calculators are part of the necessary equipment for participating in the business world. When we say simply "calculator" for convenience, we mean a financial calculator. Beyond this class, such a calculator will serve you well in other classes, in your professional life, and in your personal investing and borrowing.

Finance Isn't Just for Finance Majors

Regardless of your major, we believe this will be an important and worthwhile course for you. The principles can be applied immediately in your personal financial transactions, such as borrowing money or using a credit card. If you are a finance major, this course will also provide important preparation for additional study in your major. If you are majoring in another subject, this course will enable you to apply financial principles in that field. If you are undecided about your major, this course may help you select it. We are admittedly biased, but we encourage you to consider finance.

We appreciate the opportunity to teach you about finance. We believe finance can enhance your professional and personal lives in many ways. And we hope your finance studies pay you generous dividends.

SUMMARY

In this chapter, we introduced you to finance and to the main area of finance on which this book focuses. We described three different models of the firm and explained how these models are interrelated. We detailed the evolution of a fictionalized firm from start-up to a large complex corporation, showing how the set-of-contracts model builds on and enriches the investment-vehicle model. We discussed the role and advantages of the corporation, and we set out the objective of corporate financial management: to maximize shareholder wealth.

DECISION SUMMARY

- Finance is concerned with determining value and making decisions.

- The three main areas of finance are corporate financial management, investments, and financial markets and intermediaries.

- The benefits of the corporate form of organization include limited liability, permanency, transferability of ownership, and ready access to capital markets. A significant disadvantage is the double taxation of operating income paid to the shareholders through cash dividends.

- The shareholders are the owners of the firm. They bear the residual risk—they can lose all the money they have invested. On this basis, therefore, the firm's goal is to maximize shareholder wealth. However, as a firm becomes large and complex, and ownership and control become separated, potential conflicts of interest can arise that challenge the implementation of this basic goal.

- Important shareholder rights include dividend rights, voting rights, liquidation rights, and (in some cases) preemptive rights.

- Three important contemporary trends in finance are globalization, computerization and telecommunications, and corporate reorganization.

- The fundamental decisions in corporate financial management involve *investing* (What assets should the firm acquire?), *financing* (How should the firm be financed?) and *managing* (What operating and financial decisions are consistent with the firm's goal of maximizing shareholder wealth?)

- Three models of the firm are (1) the investment-vehicle model, which views the firm from the perspective of shareholders, (2) the accounting model, which views the firm in terms of its financial statements, and (3) the set-of-contracts model, which views the firm as a set of contracts between the firm and its various stakeholders.

KEY TERMS

finance…3	financial intermediaries...7	financial securities...13
corporate financial management...3	stakeholder...9	common stock...13
investment decisions...4	balance sheet identity...10	contingent claim...15
financing decisions...4	equity...10	sole proprietorship…16
managerial decisions...4	debt...10	partnership…16
investments...6	shareholder...10	corporation…16
financial markets...7	stockholder equityholder...10	shareholder wealth maximization...19

BIBLIOGRAPHY

Balachandran, Bala V., Nandu J. Nagarajan, and Alfred Rappaport. "Threshold Margins for Creating Economic Value," *Financial Management,* 1986, 15(1):68–77.

Bessembinder, Hendrik, Kalok Chan, and Paul J. Seguin. "An Empirical Examination of Information, Differences of Opinion, and Trading Activity," *Journal of Financial Economics,* 1996, 40(1):105–134.

Brennan, Michael J. "Corporate Finance Over the Past 25 Years," *Financial Management,* 1995, 24(2):9–22.

Choi, Frederick D. S. "International Data Sources for Empirical Research in Financial Management," *Financial Management,* 1988, 17(2):80–98.

Cooper, Dan, and Glenn Petry. "Corporate Performance and Adherence to Shareholder Wealth-Maximizing Principles," *Financial Management,* 1994, 23(1):71–78.

Cornell, Bradford, and Alan C. Shapiro. "Corporate Stakeholders and Corporate Finance," *Financial Management,* 1987, 16(1):5–14.

Donaldson, Gordon. *Managing Corporate Wealth: The Operations of a Comprehensive Financial Goals System.* New York: Praeger, 1984.

Fama, Eugene F., and Kenneth R. French. "The Cross-Section of Expected Stock Returns," *Journal of Finance,* 1992, 47(2):427–466.

Froot, Kenneth A., David S. Scharfstein, and Jeremy C. Stein. "Herd on the Street: Informational Inefficiencies in a Market with Short-Term Speculation," *Journal of Finance,* 1992, 47(4):1461–1484.

Glosten, Lawrence R. "Is the Electronic Open Limit Order Book Inevitable?" *Journal of Finance,* 1994, 49(4):1127–1161.

Gordon, Lilli A., and John Pound. "Information, Ownership Structure, and Shareholder Voting: Evidence from Shareholder-Sponsored Corporate Governance Proposals," *Journal of Finance,* 1993, 48(2):697–718.

Gordon, M. J. "Corporate Finance Under the MM Theorems," *Financial Management,* 1989, 18(2):19–28.

Jensen, Michael C. "Presidential Address: The Modern Industrial Revolution, Exit, and the Failure of Internal Control Systems," *Journal of Finance,* 1993, 48(3):831–880.

Jensen, Michael C., and William H. Meckling. "Theory of the Firm: Managerial Behavior, Agency Costs and Ownership Structure," *Journal of Financial Economics,* 1976, 3(4):305–360.

Moyer, R. Charles, Ramesh Rao, and Phillip M. Sisneros. "Substitutes for Voting Rights: Evidence from Dual Class Recapitalizations," *Financial Management,* 1992, 21(3):35–48.

Ramirez, Gabriel G., David A. Waldman, and Dennis J. Lasser. "Research Needs in Corporate Finance: Perspectives from Financial Managers," *Financial Management,* 1991, 20(2):17–29.

Roll, Richard. "What Every CO Should Know About Scientific Progress in Financial Economics: What Is Known and What Remains to Be Resolved," *Financial Management,* 1994, 23(2):69–75.

Scholes, Myron S. "Presidential Address: Stock and Compensation," *Journal of Finance,* 1991, 46(3):803–824.

Seitz, Neil. "Shareholder Goals, Firm Goals and Firm Financing Decisions," *Financial Management,* 1982, 11(3):20–26.

Seward, James K. "Corporate Financial Policy and the Theory of Financial Intermediation," *Journal of Finance,* 1990, 45(2):351–378.

Shefrin, Hersh, and Meir Statman. "Behavioral Aspects of the Design of Financial Products," *Financial Management,* 1993, 22(2):123–134.

Thakor, Anjan V. "Corporate Investments and Finance," *Financial Management,* 1993, 22(2):135–144.

Treynor, Jack L. "The Financial Objective in the Widely Held Corporation," *Financial Analysts Journal,* 1981, 37(2):68–71.

Weston, J. Fred. "What MM Have Wrought," *Financial Management,* 1989, 18(2):29–38.

ACCOUNTING, CASH FLOWS, AND TAXES

In Chapter 1 we hinted at the complex relationships among the various stakeholders in the corporation: its stockholders, bondholders, creditors, employees, customers, and suppliers, among others. Beyond complexity, the sheer size of many corporations makes it difficult to comprehend all their activities. The accounting system is a framework for keeping track of it all. It has evolved to serve two basic purposes: reporting the financial activities of the firm to outside stakeholders and providing information to assist decision makers within the firm.

In this chapter we outline the basics of the firm's accounting statements, without going into the details of how they are prepared. We describe important differences between accounting and economic information. We also take a look at how to analyze financial statements. Financial statement analysis rearranges accounting information into ratios that can provide insight into a firm's financial condition and performance.

Finally, we review the federal income tax system. In finance, we make decisions on an *after-tax* basis, so understanding tax effects is very important. Because taxes affect value, they affect many of a firm's corporate financial management decisions. Even at the most basic level, taxes are a significant cost of doing business. Throughout the book we will point out situations where taxes might make a difference. We aren't going to make you a tax expert. Rather, we feel it is important that you realize how tax factors can affect decisions. Thus, when you encounter them in practice, you will know when to seek expert tax advice.

OBJECTIVES

After studying this chapter, you should be able to

1. Explain the structure of a firm's balance sheet, income statement, and statement of cash flows.

2. Explain the inherent limitations of historical accounting information.

3. Describe the differences between net income and cash flow.

4. Understand the differences between book values and market values.

5. Explain the key features of corporate and personal income taxation that have significant implications for corporate financial management.

2.1 UNDERSTANDING ACCOUNTING STATEMENTS

There are several very good reasons why financial managers need to understand accounting statements. Accounting statements are used to communicate with stakeholders outside the firm, such as stockholders, bondholders, and other creditors. They are used within the firm to help plan and organize its activities. Accounting statements are used to monitor employees in connection with such things as performance or even theft. And they are used by the Internal Revenue Service to determine the firm's taxes.

In the United States, accounting statements are prepared according to what are called **generally accepted accounting principles (GAAP)**. GAAP include the conventions, rules, and procedures that define how firms should maintain records and prepare financial reports.[1] In the United States, these rules and procedures are based on guidelines issued by the *Financial Accounting Standards Board (FASB)*. The FASB is the U.S. accounting profession's rule-making organization.

The set of generally accepted accounting principles varies from one country to another. In some cases U.S. GAAP are different from another country's GAAP. British GAAP, for example, differ substantially from U.S. GAAP. As a result, a firm's financial statements can look quite different depending on which country's GAAP are used to prepare them. In any case, you cannot compare the information contained in the financial statements of two firms when the statements were prepared under different systems of GAAP until you first adjust for the differences.

Even under U.S. GAAP, it is possible for accounting numbers to distort economic reality. One of the tasks facing a good manager is to use accounting information effectively. Managers must know what accounting information can—and cannot—be used for. This is a balancing act. They have to combine their knowledge of accounting with other sources of information to make sound business decisions.

The accounting material covered in this chapter is a review of material covered in basic accounting courses. Our focus in corporate financial management is on how to use and interpret this information, rather than on operating an accounting system and generating reports.

The Firm's Financial Statements

A firm's published **annual report** includes, at a minimum, an income statement, a balance sheet, a statement of cash flows, and accompanying notes.[2] We review these statements below, using a basic set of statements for the Ohio Greeting Company as an example.[3] They

---

[1] According to the American Institute of Certified Public Accountants (AICPA), the "phrase 'generally accepted accounting principles' is a technical accounting term that encompasses the conventions, rules, and procedures necessary to define accepted accounting practice at a particular time. It includes not only broad guidelines of general application, but also detailed practices and procedures . . . . Those conventions, rules, and procedures provide a standard by which to measure financial presentations."

[2] A firm's annual report includes income statements and statements of cash flows for the latest three years and balance sheets for the latest two years. It also includes a separate statement of stockholders' equity. This shows how the firm's total stockholders' equity changed from one balance sheet to the next during the past three years.

[3] Publicly traded firms also publish quarterly reports and make public announcements of important information. And they file, with the Securities and Exchange Commission (SEC), disclosures that investors use. Such disclosures include 10-K annual reports (the information in the annual report plus more disclosures), 10-Q reports (the information in quarterly reports plus more), 8-K statements (describing significant events of interest to investors as the events occur), and registration statements (large documents containing financial and business information that must be filed before new securities can be publicly issued).

are the "raw material" for a variety of techniques and procedures that managers and analysts use in financial statement analysis. But first, let's introduce some basic terms we will need.

The **maturity** of an asset is the end of its life. When a financial asset is issued (created), the length of its life is called its **original maturity**. The amount of time remaining until maturity is called the **remaining maturity**.

The **liquidity** of an asset expresses how quickly and easily it can be sold without loss of value. Cash is the most liquid asset.

Market value is the price for which something could be bought or sold in a "reasonable" length of time. A reasonable length of time is defined in terms of the asset's liquidity. It might be several months or even a year for building and land, but only a few days for publicly traded stocks and bonds. **Book value** (net book value) is a net amount shown in the accounting statements.

Balance Sheet

The **balance sheet** reports the financial position of a firm at a particular point in time. The balance sheet shows the **assets** of the firm, which are the productive resources used in its operations. The balance sheet also shows the **liabilities** and **stockholders' equity** of the firm, which are the total claims of creditors and owners against the assets.

A typical balance sheet, that of Ohio Greeting Company, is shown in Table 2-1. Note that the *basic balance sheet identity* is satisfied:

$$\text{Assets} = \text{Liabilities} + \text{Stockholders' equity} \tag{2.1}$$

Assets and liabilities are both broken down into short-term and long-term parts. **Current (or short-term) assets** are expected to become cash within one year. **Current (or short-term) liabilities** mature or are expected to be paid off with cash within one year. A **long-term asset** and a **long-term liability** have remaining maturities of more than one year. Current assets and liabilities are usually arranged in approximate order of remaining maturity, from

ASSETS	1996	1995	TOTAL LIABILITIES & STOCKHOLDERS' EQUITY	1996	1995
Current Assets			**Current Liabilities**		
Cash and equivalents	$ 9.5	$ 12.0	Accounts payable	$ 18.8	$ 14.7
Accounts receivable	233.2	203.3	Notes payable	66.2	33.2
Inventories	133.9	118.8	Accrued expenses	77.7	62.0
Other	0.0	0.0	Total current liabilities	162.7	109.9
Total current assets	376.6	334.1	**Long-Term Liabilities**		
Fixed Assets			Long-term bonds	74.4	70.2
Property, plant, and equip.	450.0	400.0	Other, incl. deferred taxes	19.6	17.7
Less accumulated depr.	(246.2)	(233.0)	Total liabilities	256.7	197.8
Net prop., plant, and equip.	203.8	167.0	**Stockholders' Equity**		
Intangible assets and other	0.0	0.0	Preferred stock	10.0	10.0
Total assets	$ 580.4	$ 501.1	Common stock ($2 par value)	66.4	66.4
			Retained earnings	268.3	247.9
			Less treasury stock	(21.0)	(21.0)
			Total stockholders' equity	323.7	303.3
			Total liabilities and stockholders' equity	$ 580.4	$ 501.1

TABLE 2-1
Ohio Greeting Company, Inc. annual balance sheet (millions of dollars), December 31.

shortest to longest. This arrangement reflects the fact that, generally, the book values of the short-remaining-maturity assets and liabilities tend to be closer to their current market values than those that have long maturities. For example, the book value of receivables may be fairly close to its market value. In contrast, the current market value of net fixed assets can be very different from its book value.

The difference between current assets and current liabilities is the firm's net working capital, often simply called **working capital**:

$$\text{Working capital} = \text{Current assets} - \text{Current liabilities} \qquad (2.2)$$

Working capital provides a measure of the firm's liquidity and of its ability to meet its short-term obligations as they come due. An alternative measure is the **current ratio**:

$$\text{Current ratio} = \frac{\text{Current assets}}{\text{Current liabilities}} \qquad (2.3)$$

The appendix to this chapter describes this and a variety of other ratios and discusses their usefulness in financial statement analysis.

The liabilities and stockholders' equity (right-hand) side of the balance sheet shows the firm's choice of its **capital structure**: the proportions of debt versus equity financing and the mixture of debt maturities, short-term versus long-term.

Income Statement

The **income statement** reports the income, expenses, and profit (or loss) for a firm over a specific interval of time, typically a year or a quarter of a year. Net income, sometimes referred to as profit, is the difference between total revenue and total cost for the period. Table 2-2 shows the income statement for the Ohio Greeting Company. In this income statement, the gross profit is the net sales minus the cost of goods sold. The cost of goods sold is the direct cost for the materials, labor, and other expenses directly associated with the production of the goods or services sold by the firm.

TABLE 2-2
Ohio Greeting Company, Inc. annual income statement (millions of dollars, except per-share data), years ended December 31.

	1996	1995
Net sales	$546.9	$485.8
Cost of goods sold	286.3	247.3
Gross profit	260.6	238.5
Selling, general, & administrative expense	188.5	184.2
Depreciation & amortization	22.7	20.1
Operating profit	49.4	34.2
Nonoperating income	2.3	3.7
Earnings before interest and taxes (EBIT)	51.7	37.9
Interest expense	7.7	8.0
Pretax income	44.0	29.9
Total income tax	18.1	11.9
Net income	25.9	18.0
Preferred dividends	1.0	1.0
Net income available for common	24.9	17.0
Dividends on common stock	4.5	3.6
Addition to retained earnings	$ 20.4	$ 13.4
Per-Share Data:		
Earnings per share	$2.77	$1.89
Dividends per share	0.50	0.40
Shares outstanding (millions)	9.000	9.000

To compute the operating profit, subtract from gross profit (1) the indirect costs associated with selling, general, and administrative expenses and (2) depreciation and amortization (which are noncash items). **Earnings before interest and taxes (EBIT)** equals operating profit plus nonoperating profit (such as investment income). Subtracting interest expense from EBIT gives pretax income of $44.0 million in 1996. Finally, subtracting income taxes yields net income: $25.9 million in 1996, up from $18.0 million in 1995.

If the corporation has preferred stock outstanding, preferred dividends paid are subtracted from net income to get net income available for common stock. After subtracting whatever common stock dividends the firm paid, the remaining earnings are the current period's addition to retained earnings on the balance sheet.

Earnings per share (EPS) and dividends per share are given in the bottom part of the income statement. The firm's common stockholders have a residual claim to the firm's assets after all debts and preferred stock have been paid. The stockholders' welfare, then, depends on the current and future profitability and dividends of the firm. The per-share figures indicate how large the net income is relative to the number of common shares.[4] With nine million shares outstanding, Ohio Greeting shows $2.77 in EPS in 1996.

Corporations occasionally declare an extraordinary gain or loss in addition to income or loss from their normal operations. The Ohio Greeting Company did not report any extraordinary income. If a corporation had an extraordinary gain or loss, the income statement would show net income before and after (that is, without and with) the extraordinary gain or loss. In addition, EPS would be reported before and after the extraordinary income. For valuation purposes, EPS before extraordinary items (without taking them into account) is a more meaningful measure of the firm's sustainable profit.

Finally, dividends per share divided by EPS gives the firm's **payout ratio**. The payout ratio is the proportion of earnings that the firm paid out to common shareholders as cash dividends. Ohio Greeting's 1996 payout ratio is about 18% (= 0.50/2.77).

Statement of Cash Flows

The **statement of cash flows** indicates how the cash position of the firm has changed during the period covered by the income statement. Thus, it complements the income statement and the balance sheet. Changes in a firm's cash position can be the result of any of the firm's many transactions.

The statement of cash flows breaks down the sources and uses of cash into three components. These are cash flows from (1) operating, (2) investing, and (3) financing activities. The flows of funds between a firm and its investors, creditors, workers, customers, and other stakeholders serve as a fundamental starting point for the analysis of the firm, its capital investment projects, and of corporate acquisitions, as well as the analysis underlying many other decisions.

Table 2-3 shows a typical statement of cash flows, that of the Ohio Greeting Company. The sources and amounts of cash flows from operating activities, investing activities, and financing activities are itemized.[5]

---

[4] The earnings-per-share calculation can be fairly complicated. Simple earnings per share is net income divided by the weighted average number of common shares outstanding during the period. Other definitions, such as primary earnings per share and fully diluted earnings per share, take into account what are called the *dilutive effects* of option-like instruments (warrants, convertibles, executive stock options). The rules for computing earnings per share are given in Accounting Principles Board, "Earnings Per Share," APB Opinion No. 15 (New York: AICPA, 1969).

[5] The format of the statement of cash flows shown in Table 2-3 is a presentation called the *indirect* method. Another method, called the *direct method*, sums the cash inflows and outflows associated with operating the firm. The first part of the statement of cash flows (cash flows from operating activities) looks different depending on whether the direct or the indirect method is used; the other two parts are the same. Although their formats differ, the methods give the same numerical result. We use the indirect method here because it is used most widely in published financial statements.

TABLE 2-3
Ohio Greeting Company, Inc. statement of cash flows (millions of dollars), year ended December 31.

	1996
Cash Flows From Operating Activities	
Net income	$ 25.9
Depreciation and amortization	22.7
Accounts receivable decrease (increase)	(29.9)
Inventories decrease (increase)	(15.1)
Accounts payable increase (decrease)	4.1
Accrued expenses increase (decrease)	15.7
Net cash provided by (used in) operating activities	23.4
Cash Flows From Investing Activities	
Purchase of plant and equipment	(59.5)
Net cash provided by (used in) investing activities	(59.5)
Cash Flows From Financing Activities	
Notes payable increase (decrease)	33.0
Issuance of long-term debt, net	4.2
Increase in other long-term liabilities	1.9
Cash dividends (preferred and common)	(5.5)
Net cash provided by (used in) financing activities	33.6
Net increase (decrease) in cash and equivalents	(2.5)
Cash and equivalents, beginning of year	12.0
Cash and equivalents, end of year	$ 9.5

Let's look more closely at the cash flow from operating activities. The net income is taken from Ohio Greeting's income statement (Table 2-2). To arrive at net income, various items are deducted from sales, including some that are noncash expenses. Depreciation is usually the largest of these items. Because these items are not cash flows, they must be added back to determine cash flow. Dividends are *not* subtracted from operating activities. Instead, they are a discretionary part of financing activities. The other items represent changes in several working capital accounts, which are part of operating activities. Decreases (increases) in asset (liability) accounts are positive cash flows (*inflows*). The opposites are negative cash flows (*outflows*). One short-term liability, notes payable, is considered a financing activity and is not included in operating activities.

Investing activities cash flows include those connected with buying or selling long-term assets, acquiring other firms, and selling subsidiaries. Ohio Greeting used $59.5 million to purchase plant and equipment, which is an outflow (negative cash flow).

Financing activities cash flows include those connected with selling or repurchasing common and preferred stock, issuing or retiring long-term debt, issuing and repaying short-term notes, and paying dividends on common stock or preferred stock. For example, Ohio Greeting borrowed $33.0 million in notes payable, which was an inflow.

Net increase (decrease) in cash and equivalents is the sum of the cash flows from the three sections: $23.4 - 59.5 + 33.6 = \$(2.5)$ million. This change is then added to the beginning cash balance of $12.0 million, leaving the ending cash balance of $9.5 million.

In many financial decisions, such as long-term investments, we separate the investing, financing, and operating cash flows. It is important to understand that such separations in the statement of cash flows are somewhat arbitrary, particularly in the case of the first part of the statement, which shows the cash flows from operating activities. For example, dividends are included with financing cash flows, whereas interest expense is treated as an operating cash flow.

- More detailed breakdowns of other income, interest and other financial charges, and provision for income taxes
- A description of the earnings-per-share calculation
- Details concerning extraordinary items, if any, and foreign exchange gains or losses
- Breakdown of inventories, investments (including nonconsolidated subsidiaries), property, plant, and equipment, and other assets
- Costs and amounts of short-term borrowings
- Schedules of long-term debt, preferred stock, and capitalized and operating lease obligations
- Schedule of capital stock issued or reserved for issuance and statement of changes in shareholders' equity (which is often included as a separate financial statement)
- Details concerning significant acquisitions or disposals of assets
- Information concerning employee pension and stock option plans
- Commitments and contingent liabilities
- Events subsequent to the balance sheet date, but prior to the release of the financial statements to the public, that might significantly affect their interpretation
- Quarterly operating results
- Business segment information (by line of business and by geographical region)
- A five-year summary comparison of financial performance and financial position

TABLE 2-4

Items typically covered in the notes to the financial statements in annual reports.

Notes to the Financial Statements

The **notes to the financial statements** are an integral part of the statements. The notes disclose the significant accounting policies used to prepare the financial statements. They also provide additional detail concerning several of the items in the accounting statements. Table 2-4 lists the items usually included in such notes.

Published annual reports also include **management's discussion** of recent operating results. Management's discussion is included along with the financial statements. Usually there is also a letter to the stockholders, which appears at the front of the annual report. This letter and the management's discussion can help you interpret the accounting statements. They can also provide insights into management's philosophy and strategy that simply don't appear in the numerical sections of the annual report.

The notes to the financial statements and management's discussion contain a wealth of useful information. You cannot fully appreciate the information contained in a firm's accounting statements unless you read the notes to the financial statements and the management's discussion.[6]

Self-Check Questions

1. What is the basic balance sheet identity?

2. What is the main purpose of each of the firm's three basic financial statements?

3. How is the firm's statement of cash flows related to its balance sheet?

4. What is the purpose of the notes to the financial statements?

2.2 ACCOUNTING STATEMENTS ARE HISTORICAL

Accounting statements are invaluable aids to analysts and managers. But the statements do not provide certain critical information, and as a result they have inherent limitations. Accounting statements are historical. They do not provide any information about cash flows that might be

---

[6] This is why accounting and securities regulations require firms to furnish this information!

expected in the future. They also do not provide critically important information about the *current* market values of assets and liabilities. Thus accounting statements not only fail to look ahead, they do not even report the current situation. Such missing information limits the usefulness of accounting information.

There are several reasons why accounting statements are historical, but we will not contribute here to the debate over how accounting statements might better be prepared. We will simply review the information accounting statements provide, based on today's practice, and note important implications of the procedures.

Market versus Book Value of Assets

Because the current market value of an asset can be *very* different from its book value, an asset probably can't be sold for its book value. And if an asset can't be sold for its book value, it can't be bought for that value, either. Thus the cost to replace an asset that breaks down is probably different from its current book value as well. At the same time, four factors make a disparity between market and book values more or less likely: the time since the asset was acquired, inflation, the asset's liquidity, and whether the asset is tangible or intangible.

TIME SINCE ACQUISITION   As a rule, the more time that has passed since an asset was acquired, the greater the chance that the asset's current market value will differ from its book value. When an asset is acquired, it is recorded in the accounting statements at its cost. And that cost is a market value, at least in some sense. Therefore, the initial book value is quite likely to be similar to the market value of the asset *at the time it is acquired*. Over time, however, the market value can diverge significantly from the book value. This is because changes in the book value (depreciation each period) are specified by GAAP rather than by economic considerations.

EXAMPLE

Differences in Car Usage

Suppose two firms buy identical cars. In one case, a sales representative is going to drive the car about 10,000 miles per month. In the second case, a manager is going to drive the car about 1000 miles per month. GAAP specifies identical depreciation rules for these cars. The rule is based on the type of asset (an automobile), not on how it will be used. Thus after any significant time, say a year, the book values of the cars will be identical, but the more heavily used car will have a much lower market value. The more time that passes, the larger the difference is likely to be. ■

EXAMPLE

The Sampson Company Waterfront Warehouse

The Sampson Company purchased a warehouse 15 years ago. Since then, the area surrounding the building has changed dramatically from an industrial area of factories and shipping warehouses into an exclusive high-rise condominium area overlooking the waterfront. Sampson's building and land currently have a combined book value of $231,000 (after accounting for depreciation on the building; depreciation cannot be claimed on land). Today the building could be sold for $15 million. Such a difference fundamentally changes the value of the firm. It also has profound implications for the best use of the firm's assets at this point in time. Sampson should consider moving its operations elsewhere and selling the current location. Of course, in other cases the market value may be well *below* the book value, which could have very different policy implications! ■

INFLATION   Inflation during the time since the asset was acquired is a second important factor that can cause a significant difference between market value and book value. When prices change because of inflation, the market values of existing assets also change to reflect the difference in purchasing power. Such changes can be dramatic. For example, from 1970 until 1995, inflation caused the purchasing power of a dollar to change by a factor of 5. This means that what could be purchased for $1.00 in 1970 cost about $5.00 in 1995.

In the early part of this century, when the Coca-Cola Company first issued shares of its common stock to the public, some of the shares went to a predecessor of SunTrust Banks in Atlanta. At the time, the value of the stock was recorded at its current market value of $100,000. Until very recently, the stock was shown on SunTrust's balance sheet as an asset with a book value of $100,000. However, the stock had since gone up in value. Currently, those shares are worth about $1.5 billion, an increase of about 15,000 times over their original value. We know that the stock value has increased well in excess of inflation over the intervening 80 or so years. However, inflation during the same time period was substantial, perhaps changing purchasing power by a factor of 50 or more. Therefore, even if the value of the shares had increased only in step with inflation, the shares would be worth in excess of $5 million. In that case, then, only the remaining 300-times increase ($= 15,000/50$) is due to the success of the Coca-Cola Company! ■

SunTrust's Shares of Coca-Cola Stock

EXAMPLE

LIQUIDITY   An asset's liquidity is a third factor that affects the likelihood that the asset's current market value will differ from its book value. Less liquid assets have higher transaction costs when they are sold, so there's greater uncertainty about the *net* proceeds from a sale. As a consequence, if all else is equal, the current market values of less liquid assets can differ more from their book values.

For example, compare a 2-year-old pickup truck to a unique patented process for producing plastic bags. The pickup truck is a more liquid asset, because it is commonly available and there are many alternatives to that particular truck. In fact, there are established used-truck markets for selling such assets with low transaction costs. Contrast this with the plastic-bag-production process. Such a production process may be worth much more than its book value if it is the leading production technology. Or it may be essentially worthless if another technology has made it obsolete. But in either case, it could be very costly and time-consuming to find the buyer who will pay the most for the process, because there isn't an established market for used plastic-bag-production processes.

TANGIBLE VERSUS INTANGIBLE   A fourth factor that affects the likelihood of there being a significant difference between market and book values is whether the asset is tangible or intangible. The values of intangible assets are much more variable. As with our example of the plastic-bag-production process, intangible assets can be extremely valuable or essentially worthless. Valuation differences can also be caused by extreme differences in liquidity. Even long-term assets such as plant and equipment are more likely to have established markets (real estate and used equipment) than are intangible assets such as patents or the design for a new product. Intangible assets tend to be unique. There aren't active markets for selling them. Consequently, intangible assets tend to be extremely illiquid. Therefore, the current market value of an intangible asset is especially likely to differ from its book value.

Developing a New Product at Murray Corporation

Suppose the Murray Corporation has spent $14 million developing a new product. Now, it can more accurately estimate that the product will provide only about $5 million in profit to offset the development cost. At this point, Murray would like to sell the rights to its product to another firm and let that firm manufacture and market the new product. Would you pay $14 million for something that is worth only $5 million? Despite the $14 million historical cost on Murray's balance sheet, a potential buyer will assess the value of the new product on the basis of its *future* potential.[7] ■

We noted earlier that placement on the balance sheet reflects the general remaining maturity of the assets. We should now point out that balance sheet placement also reflects the general likelihood that there will be a difference between the asset's book value and its market value. As you move down the list of assets, they are less liquid and have generally been held longer. Intangible assets are shown last.

Consider two types of assets that represent opposite extremes in liquidity: cash and a manufacturing plant. Cash is extremely liquid (actually, it is the very *definition* of liquidity), whereas it would probably require considerable effort to find a buyer for the plant.[8] However, despite the fact that the market values of other current assets are generally less likely to differ from their book values, care is always in order when valuing a firm. Accounts receivable can include bad debts. Inventory can be obsolete or can be shown at very low values because of a "last-in–first-out" policy of accounting for inventory. Thus even the book values of current assets other than cash and equivalents can be poor approximations of market value. Therefore, it is wise to look especially carefully at assets other than cash and equivalents when trying to value them.

Market versus Book Value of Liabilities

As with assets, the current market value of a liability can differ from its book value. Generally, however, the potential divergence is smaller, and the relationship between the market and book values is less complex.

REMAINING MATURITY   The time until a liability must be paid off—its remaining maturity—is the main factor that affects the difference between the market and book values of a healthy firm's liabilities. Liabilities have explicit contractual amounts that must be paid at specific points in time. Failure to meet these contractual obligations creates the possibility of bankruptcy. Therefore, when a liability becomes due, the market value of the liability is essentially equal to its book value. In contrast, the market value of liabilities that do not have to be repaid for a long time reflects current economic conditions, as well as expectations about the future.

Consider a loan for $10 million that is due to be paid off in four months. Because the remaining maturity is short, the cost of interest is relatively insignificant compared to the amount borrowed. Now consider a long-term loan for $10 million at 6% interest per year that doesn't have to be repaid for another 25 years, except for yearly interest. If the borrowing rate today is 10%, the market value of this liability is smaller than its book value because its remaining maturity of 25 years provides the firm with 25 more years over which to enjoy the low 6% interest cost on the existing loan.

---

[7] This problem is a major reason why GAAP call for expensing (depreciating) research and development costs over a relatively short time period. Of course, the other side to this is that when a firm does make a great and valuable discovery, its book value grossly *under*states its market value.

[8] Of course, if the firm really wanted to sell the plant quickly, it could probably find a buyer almost instantly for a low enough price, say $2.39. (But even this price might be too high if the plant sat on top of a chemical waste dump that would cost the new owner $100 million to clean up.)

FINANCIAL DISTRESS   In our discussion of the impact of remaining maturity, we referred to a *healthy* firm's liabilities. A second factor that affects the difference between the market and book values of liabilities is the firm's financial health. The market values of a financially distressed firm's liabilities are likely to be below their book values. This state of affairs reflects the fact that the distressed firm may not be able to meet its obligations. Recall that corporate stockholders have limited liability. This increases the likelihood that the liability holders will not get paid. A distressed firm's long-term liabilities are especially likely to have a market value that is below book value because of the uncertainty about the firm's long-term viability. Thus financial distress can intensify the effect of remaining maturity on the market value of a firm's liabilities.

Total Value of a Firm

The total value of a firm is simply the sum of the market values of all its assets. Because the market values of the individual assets can be very different from their book values, the balance sheet amount *Total Assets* should *never* be taken as a reliable estimate of the current value of the firm.

Equity Value

The current book value of the firm's equity is probably the least informative item on a balance sheet. Every factor that affects the difference between the market and book values of each individual item on the balance sheet affects the difference between the market and book values of the firm's equity. This is because the difference between the market and book values of equity is the sum of the differences between the market and book values of all the other items on the balance sheet.

Look back at Equation (2.1), the basic balance sheet identity. We can rewrite that equation as

$$\text{Stockholders' equity} = \text{Assets} - \text{Liabilities}$$

In this form, it is easy to see the residual nature of the equity value, which we discussed in Chapter 1. We have just said that the Assets amount is not the market value of the firm's assets and that the Liabilities amount is not the market value of the firm's liabilities. Therefore, it should be clear that the difference between the two isn't miraculously going to become an accurate measure of market value, either!

If, instead of being book (historical) values, the Assets and Liabilities amounts were current market values, this equation would provide the true residual value of the stockholders' equity. In a GAAP balance sheet, however, the value of Stockholders' Equity is simply the result of applying the required rules to the historical cost of the assets and liabilities—in essence, an amount that forces the balance sheet identity to hold. In a sense, then, the book value of stockholders' equity is a "plug" figure that enforces the basic balance sheet identity.

As we will explain in detail later, stock prices observed in public market trading are a much more accurate basis for estimating the current market value of a firm.

Self-Check Questions

1. Why might the market value of an asset differ from its book value?
2. Why is the difference between market value and book value likely to be greater for intangible assets than for tangible assets?
3. How does the maturity of a liability affect the difference between its book and market values?
4. Your friend believes that the book value of Microsoft Corporation's stockholders' equity is a good measure of what Microsoft's equity is really worth. Do you agree? Explain.

2.3 NET INCOME IS NOT CASH FLOW

Because the income statement contains noncash expenses and accruals, net income is not an accurate measure of cash inflow. This is part of the reason for requiring a statement of cash flows.

Noncash Items

Certain items in the income statement are called noncash items. These are items for which the cash flow connected with the expense occurs at a time outside the reporting period. GAAP require the allocation of all or part of the expense to a time period other than the one in which the cash flow occurs. Depreciation is the most significant such item. When a firm purchases certain assets, such as plant and equipment, the use of the asset is over a prolonged period that spans many income statement periods. On this basis, GAAP require that the total expense for the asset be spread over some extended number of income periods, such as 5, 10, or even 30 years.

It is very important to understand that the only thing at issue here is *timing*. The claim of expense for accounting purposes is separated in time from when the cash flow actually occurs. The cash flow for the item occurs at the time of purchase. The expense charged against income occurs in stages over several income statement periods. Therefore, noncash items make the firm's net income figure very different from its cash inflow. Deferred and accrued taxes are two other examples of noncash items.

Accruals

The revenues and expenses on the income statement include items for which no cash has yet been received. For example, a sale of merchandise that has been agreed to and perhaps even been delivered, but that the customer has not yet paid for, can be included. Also, a sale for which some cash has already been received may not be included, because it has not met certain GAAP requirements. Despite this, the revenues shown over a long time represent a good estimate of the actual revenue that will *ultimately* be collected. However, within a limited time period of, say, one or two years, because of accruals the revenue shown on the income statement can be significantly different from the cash revenue that actually came into the firm.

Estimating Cash Flow

We often estimate cash flow by adding back noncash items to the net income, as in the first two lines of the operating activities part of the statement of cash flows (Table 2-3). This is because the distortion from accruals is typically relatively small. We will use such an estimate in connection with long-term investment decisions, called *capital budgeting decisions*, which are covered in Part III of this book.

Income Statement versus Economic Income

True economic income is the total return on an investment, made up of the cash inflow plus the change in the market value of the assets and liabilities. As we have just discussed, however, net income is not cash flow, and GAAP changes in the firm's assets and liabilities do not reflect changes in market values. Thus the Net Income figure shown on the income statement can be quite different from the firm's actual economic income. As with the balance sheet, however, some items on the income statement are more or less likely than others to be good estimates of economic reality.

OPERATING INCOME   A firm's operating income can be a good estimate of the true economic operating income, provided that (1) the firm has made no changes in its accounting procedures, such as switching inventory accounting from a "last-in–first-out" (LIFO) to a "first-in–first-out" (FIFO) basis, and (2) the accounting period is sufficiently long. With respect to changes in accounting procedures, certain changes make the amounts reported in that period larger or smaller and can therefore distort the amounts reported. With respect to the length of the accounting period, several years is preferable. Good or poor performance may not be revealed in income statements of one or two years. However, over time, significant changes in performance are likely to be revealed in any extended series of income statements.

EXTRAORDINARY INCOME   To interpret accurately the economic meaning of extraordinary income, we need to understand its nature and origin. Without such an understanding, it can be impossible to determine the implications of extraordinary income for the firm's future.

For example, consider an extraordinary item that is the sale of some land that was worth much more than its current book value. Suppose this difference between book and market values was widely known. In such a case, the extraordinary income that is recognized by the land sale is probably only a matter of bookkeeping. Managers and stockholders will have already taken the higher value into account.

In general, extraordinary items occur only once. They do not reflect the firm's *sustainable net income.* We therefore recommend that you use *net income before extraordinary items* when doing calculations that involve net income.

Self-Check Questions

1. What are the main differences between net income and cash flow?

2. Why might the economic income of the firm differ significantly from its net income?

3. Why should you use *net income before extraordinary items* when doing calculations that involve net income?

2.4 CALCULATING TAXES

Taxes make the federal government (and any state and local government that levies income taxes) a partner with every firm. With so much money at stake, taxes can have a significant impact on financial decisions. Both corporate and personal taxes are relevant to corporate financial management. We focus here on income taxes for illustrative purposes and because they are currently the most significant form of taxes.

Corporate Income Taxes

The corporate income tax system is complicated. As shown in Table 2-5, the federal tax rate generally increases with the level of income. The tax rate applied to the last dollar of income is called the **marginal tax rate**. The **average tax rate** is the total taxes paid divided by taxable income. A **progressive tax system** has an average tax rate that increases for some increases in the level of income but never decreases with such increases. The marginal tax rate is greater than the average tax rate in a progressive tax system.

TABLE 2-5
Corporate income tax rates.

CORPORATE TAXABLE INCOME ($)	PAY THIS AMOUNT ON THE BASE OF THE RANGE ($)	PLUS THIS RATE TIMES THE EXCESS OVER THE BASE (%)
0–50,000	0	15
50,000–75,000	7,500	25
75,000–100,000	13,750	34
100,000–335,000	22,250	39
335,000–10,000,000	113,900	34
10,000,000–15,000,000	3,400,000	35
15,000,000–18,333,333	5,150,000	38
over 18,333,333	6,416,667	35

EXAMPLE

Corporate Income Taxes for Sidewell, Inc.

Suppose Sidewell, Inc. has taxable corporate income of $200,000. What will be the corporation's federal corporate income tax liability on this amount?

From the tax rates in Table 2-5, the tax liability will be

$$\text{Tax} = 22{,}250 + 0.39(200{,}000 - 100{,}000) = 22{,}250 + 39{,}000 = \$61{,}250$$

The marginal tax rate is 39%, but the average tax rate on this level of income is

$$\text{Average tax rate} = 61{,}250/200{,}000 = 30.625\%$$

At this income level, the marginal tax rate exceeds the average tax rate. ■

In a progressive tax system, as income is taxed at the higher marginal tax rate, the average tax rate continues to increase toward the marginal tax rate. Figure 2-1 shows the relationship between the marginal and average tax rates at various levels of taxable corporate income for the tax structure shown in Table 2-5. In the first range, indicated by an A (where taxable income is between zero and $50,000), the average and marginal rates are both 15%. In range B, the marginal tax rate is 25%, and the average tax rate increases over the range to 18.3%. In range C, the marginal rate is 34%, and the average rate increases over the range to 22.3%. Because of the lower rate on the "earlier" income, the average tax rate will never become equal to the marginal rate.

To equalize the two rates, Congress set the marginal rate at 39% on income over $100,000 until the average rate increases to 34%. At a taxable income of $335,000, the average and marginal rates are both equal to 34%. For taxable incomes between $350,000 and $10 million, the marginal rate is set back to 34%. For taxable incomes between $10 and $15 million, the marginal tax rate is increased again, to 35%. Once again to raise the average tax rate to this higher marginal rate, the marginal rate is 38% for taxable incomes between $15 and $18.33 million. Above $18.33 million, all incomes are taxed at both a marginal and an average rate of 35%.

There are two more important complications. First, tax structures are often modified. Thus the average and marginal tax rates that apply to a corporation can and do change from time to time, sometimes dramatically. Second, state and local governments often impose additional income (and other) taxes on corporations, so the total tax is the sum of the federal, state, and local tax levies. The result is that no single tax rate will endure through time, and no single tax rate will apply across all geographical locations.

Throughout this book, we will simply specify an income tax rate, such as 40%. We intend whatever rate we specify to reflect all taxes from all levels. The single rate is a simplified

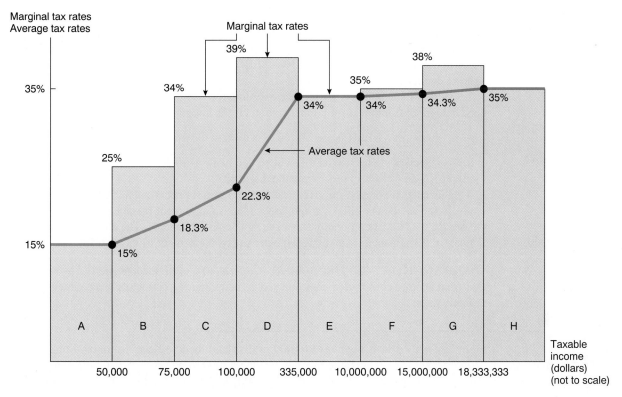

FIGURE 2-1
Marginal and average corporate income tax rates.

approximation of taxes. We use different tax rates to emphasize that actual tax rates vary over time and from one location to another.

CORPORATE CAPITAL GAINS   A long-term capital gain or loss, referred to simply as a **capital gain,** occurs *for tax purposes* when an asset that has been owned for a sufficiently long time (currently, at least one year) is sold for more or less than its tax basis (that is, its net book value for tax purposes). Although an actual gain or loss occurs every time the market value of the asset changes, the gain or loss is not recognized for tax purposes until the asset is sold. This means that the tax on the gain is postponed—indefinitely—until the asset is sold. Of course, this also means no tax-reducing losses can be claimed until the asset is sold. This is an important complicating feature of the tax system. It creates what is called a **tax-timing option**. We will describe and discuss tax-timing options in more detail later.

Currently, corporate capital gains are taxed at the same rates as regular income. Before 1987 corporate capital gains were taxed at a lower rate. A lower tax rate on capital gains provides extra incentive to invest in capital assets. Short-term capital gains (losses) that result from holding assets for less than the required year are taxed as regular income.

TAX TREATMENT OF INTEREST EXPENSE AND DIVIDENDS PAID   Interest paid on debt obligations is a tax-deductible expense. Dividends paid to common and preferred stockholders are not. If a firm is to pay $100 of interest, the firm needs $100 of earnings before interest and taxes (EBIT). However, if a firm is to pay $100 of dividends, it will need more than $100 of EBIT, because taxes will be deducted from EBIT.

In the first case the $100 of interest is a tax-deductible expense, so no taxes will be due on the $100 of EBIT. However, in the second case, the $100 of dividends is not a deductible expense, so taxes are due on the $100 before dividends are paid. Suppose the tax rate is 40%. Taxes of $40 will be paid out of the $100 of EBIT. This will leave only $60 to pay the planned $100 of dividends.

To find the amount of EBIT necessary to cover the dividends, simply divide the dividend amount by 1 minus the marginal tax rate. If the marginal tax rate is 40%,

$$\text{EBIT needed} = 100/(1 - 0.40) = 100/0.6 = \$166.67$$

If EBIT is $166.67, taxes due on this will be $66.67 ($= 0.40 \times 166.67$). This will leave $100 ($= 166.67 - 66.67$) after taxes to pay the dividend.

This unequal, or **asymmetric**, treatment of interest expense and dividend payments effectively lowers the tax bills of corporations that use more debt financing. Conversely, it increases the tax bills of corporations that use more equity financing. The effects of this tax bias in favor of debt financing are discussed extensively in Chapters 14 through 18.

DIVIDENDS-RECEIVED DEDUCTION   At least 70% of dividends *received* by a corporation from another corporation are not taxed.[9] The remaining dividends received are taxed at ordinary rates.

EXAMPLE

The Dividends-Received Deduction at Epic Records

Suppose Epic Records receives $10,000 of dividend income from Columbia Music. It can deduct $7000 from its taxable income, leaving $3000 to be taxed.[10] If Epic's marginal tax rate is 35%, it will owe $1050 ($= 0.35 \times 3000$) in taxes on the $10,000 of dividends. This means that the *effective* tax rate on an intercorporate dividend payment is 30% of the marginal tax rate. In this example, it is 10.5% ($= 1050/10,000 = 0.30 \times 35\%$) for Epic Records. ■

The reason for a dividends-received deduction involves the concept of multiple taxation. In the U.S. tax system, income is taxed once at the corporate level when the firm earns the income, and it is taxed a second time at the personal level when dividends are paid to individual shareholders. This results in what is called double taxation. If intercorporate dividends were fully taxed, this would amount to triple taxation. To reduce the impact of this, a substantial part of intercorporate dividends, currently 70%, are effectively excluded from taxation.

Incidentally, *interest received* by one corporation from another is fully taxable. There are situations wherein a corporation might prefer to purchase preferred stock (over a debt instrument) because the dividends-received deduction results in lower taxes and a higher *after-tax* rate of return on the investment.

IMPROPER ACCUMULATIONS OF INCOME TO AVOID PAYMENT OF TAXES   If a corporation does not pay a dividend, its shareholders do not receive the dividend income and do not incur a personal tax liability. The U.S. tax code imposes a substantial penalty on a corporation if it accumulates earnings for the purpose of enabling its shareholders to avoid the payment of personal income taxes. A corporation is allowed to accumulate $250,000 of re-

---

[9] The proportion not taxed ranges from 70% to 100%, depending on the percentage of ownership.
[10] The effect of the dividends-received deduction is to exclude the amount from income. It is as though the deducted amount is simply not counted as part of Epic's income.

tained earnings without being subject to this tax. Accumulations above $250,000 are subject to the penalty tax if they are considered unnecessary for the reasonable needs of the business. However, if these funds are reinvested in the firm to buy more assets, to pay off debt obligations, or to provide a reasonable amount of liquidity, the improper-accumulations tax is not imposed. Although this penalty tax is very rarely imposed, the threat of the penalty is real. It encourages corporations either to use the funds in the firm or to distribute them as dividends.

TAX LOSS CARRYBACKS AND CARRYFORWARDS   If a corporation shows a loss (has a negative net income), this loss can be "carried back" as much as three years or "carried forward" for as much as 15 years to offset taxable income in those years. For example, suppose a corporation has negative net income this year but had positive net income and paid taxes within the last three years. This year's loss can be used to offset previous profits (carried back), and the government will refund some previously paid taxes. If the corporation's current loss exceeds its previous income, the firm can use the loss to offset future profits (carry the loss forward) and reduce its future taxes.

S CORPORATIONS   The so-called Subchapter S regulation permits small businesses that meet certain requirements to choose to be taxed as partnerships or proprietorships instead of as corporations. This allows the corporation to receive some of the benefits of the corporate form of organization and yet avoid the double taxation of income. Subchapter S corporate income is reported as personal income by its owners. The individual owners then pay personal income taxes on the part of the income that is allocated to each of them.

Personal Income Taxes

Personal income taxes are the federal government's largest source of income. They made up 36% of its total income in fiscal year 1993. Here we'll look at some of the features of the personal income tax system that have implications for corporate financial management.

PERSONAL INCOME TAX RATES   Like corporate income tax rates, personal income tax rates increase with income, going from zero to a maximum of 39.6%. The marginal tax rates for the two most common filing status categories ("single" and "married, filing jointly") are shown in Table 2-6. There are other schedules for people classified as "married, filing separately" or as "head of household." Personal tax rates are further complicated by the elimination of certain exemptions and deductions for higher incomes. The elimination of an exemption or deduction raises the effective tax rate. In addition, individuals pay social security and Medicare taxes and income taxes to state and local governments, so the effective tax rates for individuals can be much higher than the rates in Table 2-6.

EXEMPTIONS AND DEDUCTIONS   Taxable income is equal to gross income minus allowable exemptions and deductions. For each dependent there is an exemption, which was $2450 in 1994 and increases each year with inflation. In addition, you can choose either to itemize your deductions or to take a standard deduction that is based on your filing status. Itemized deductions include such things as home mortgage interest, gifts to charity, state and local income taxes paid, real estate taxes paid, and some medical and job-related expenses. As mentioned above, some exemptions and deductions are eliminated for incomes above certain levels.

DIVIDEND AND INTEREST INCOME   Dividend income received from common stock and preferred stock is fully taxable. Income from interest paid by corporations, financial institutions, and individuals is also fully taxable. For constitutional reasons, interest on most state and local government bonds is not taxable by the federal government. Consequently, these

TABLE 2-6
Personal income tax
rates.

PERSONAL TAXABLE INCOME ($)	PAY THIS AMOUNT ON THE BASE OF THE RANGE ($)	PLUS THIS RATE TIMES THE EXCESS OVER THE BASE (%)
Single Taxpayer		
0–22,750	0	15
22,750–55,100	3,412.50	28
55,100–115,000	12,470.50	31
115,000–250,000	31,039.50	36
over 250,000	79,639.50	39.6
Married Taxpayers Filing Jointly		
0–38,000	0	15
38,000–91,850	5,700	28
91,850–140,000	20,778	31
115,000–250,000	31,039.50	36
over 250,000	79,639.50	39.6

bonds, which are called municipals (*muni's*; pronounced "mu-nees"), can be attractive investments.

PERSONAL CAPITAL GAINS   Like corporate income, the personal income tax system has special provisions for long-term capital gains that result from owning assets for more than one year. And they also lead to tax-timing options.

EXAMPLE

A Capital Gain Tax-Timing Option on Goodyear Stock

Suppose you bought 100 shares of Goodyear for $3000 a little more than a year ago and the shares are worth $4500 today. If you sell the shares for $4500, you will be taxed on a $1500 capital gain. But for as long as you continue to own the shares, you will not have to pay a capital gains tax. Now suppose instead that your shares have gone down in value to $2200. If you sell the shares for $2200, you will be able to claim a capital loss of $800, which could reduce your taxes this year. ■

As with corporate income, short-term capital gains (losses) that result from holding assets for less than the required one year are taxed as regular income. However, personal (long-term) capital gains may be taxed at a lower rate because the maximum capital gains rate is currently 28%. Thus if your marginal ordinary rate is above 28% (such as 31%, 36%, or 39.6%), your capital gains are taxed at the lower rate of 28%. The lower capital gains tax rate provides extra incentive to invest in assets such as stocks, real estate, and, more generally, business.

Self-Check Questions

1. What is a progressive tax system? How do the marginal and average tax rates usually compare in such a system?
2. Explain how interest expense and dividends are treated differently under the tax code.
3. How does the dividends-received deduction work?
4. What is a tax-timing option?
5. Explain how capital gains are taxed differently from ordinary income.

SUMMARY

In this chapter we reviewed the major accounting statements. These include the balance sheet, income statement, and statement of cash flows. We pointed out that the footnotes and the management's discussion that accompany the financial statements also contain useful financial information. However, we also noted that accounting information has certain inherent limitations. The information is historical, and book values can be very different from current market values. Also, remember that a firm's net income is different from its cash flow.

It is worth noting that it would be virtually impossible to set up a "perfect" system of accounting. For example, no set of rules for determining depreciation would ever correspond exactly to the pattern of changes in the market values of the assets. Thus the rules are not necessarily silly or unreasonable, but it is important to understand their impact.

Finally, keep in mind that we have provided only a very basic review. We focused on accounting's connection with finance. You need not become an expert in accounting to become a competent manager (financial or otherwise). But you must develop a complete understanding of the basics and the ability to use and correctly interpret accounting information.

DECISION SUMMARY

- The major accounting statements are the firm's balance sheet, income statement, and statement of cash flows. Footnotes and the management's discussion accompany these statements in the firm's annual report.

- The balance sheet shows the firm's financial position at a point in time. It reports the firm's assets, liabilities, and stockholders' equity.

- The income statement shows the firm's profitability. It reports the firm's revenues, costs, and net income for a period of time, such as one year or one quarter.

- The statement of cash flows shows how the cash position of the firm has changed during the period covered by the income statement. The sources and uses of cash are broken down into three parts: cash flows from operating activities, investing activities, and financing activities.

- Accounting information is historical. The amounts provided are called book values. The current market values of assets, liabilities, and stockholders' equity can be very different from their book values.

- Net income does not equal the firm's cash flow. The most significant difference is caused by depreciation.

- Net income can be quite different from the firm's actual economic income. Over time, however, significant changes in performance are likely to be revealed by an extended series of income statements, especially with respect to operating income.

- In finance, we make decisions on an after-tax basis. Therefore, the features of corporate and personal taxes affect a firm's decisions.

- Corporate and personal income taxes are levied by the federal government as well as by most states and many local governments.

- Personal tax rates and corporate tax rates are progressive; low-income individuals and corporations have lower marginal and average tax rates.

- Currently, capital gains tax rates are similar to ordinary income rates. Lower capital gains tax rates can provide extra incentive to invest in capital assets.

- For corporations, interest paid is a tax-deductible expense, but dividends paid are not tax-deductible. This encourages the use of debt financing.

- Double taxation occurs when some income is taxed twice. Operating profit is taxed once at the corporate level and a second time when dividends are paid to stockholders. To avoid triple taxation, at least 70% of intercorporate dividends are excluded from taxable income. S Corporations avoid double taxation (for those entities that qualify). They allocate their income to their owners, who pay personal taxes on the corporation's income.

- Interest income on municipal bonds is not taxable by the federal government.

EQUATION SUMMARY

(2.1) $$\text{Assets} = \text{Liabilities} + \text{Stockholders' equity}$$

(2.2) $$\text{Working capital} = \text{Current assets} - \text{Current liabilities}$$

(2.3) $$\text{Current ratio} = \frac{\text{Current assets}}{\text{Current liabilities}}$$

KEY TERMS

generally accepted accounting principles (GAAP)...26
annual report...26
maturity...27
original maturity...27
remaining maturity...27
liquidity...27
market value...27
book value...27
balance sheet...27
assets...27
liabilities...27
stockholders' equity...27

current assets...27
current liabilities...27
long-term asset...27
short-term asset...27
long-term liability...27
short-term liability...27
working capital...28
current ratio...28
capital structure...28
income statement...28
earnings before interest and taxes (EBIT)...29
payout ratio...29

statement of cash flows...29
notes to the financial statements...31
management's discussion...31
marginal tax rate...37
average tax rate...37
progressive tax system...37
capital gain...39
tax-timing option...39
asymmetric...40

EXERCISES

PROBLEM SET A

A1. Describe the purpose of each of the following financial statements: a. Income statement, b. Balance sheet, c. Statement of cash flows.

A2. Explain why the notes to a firm's financial statements are an integral part of the financial statements.

A3. What is the basic balance sheet identity?

A4. What primarily distinguishes:

a. Current assets from the other classes of assets on the balance sheet?

b. Current liabilities from the other classes of liabilities on the balance sheet?

A5. Define the term *cash flow*. Explain the difference between cash flow and earnings.

A6. Define the term *working capital*. How is working capital calculated? What does working capital measure?

A7. Cite and briefly discuss four factors that affect the likelihood that the market and book values of an asset will differ.

A8. Cite and briefly discuss two factors that affect the likelihood that the market and book values of a liability will differ.

A9. Briefly describe the difference between economic income and that shown on an income statement.

PROBLEM SET B

B1. Rimbey Sporting Goods has a weird accountant who reported the balance sheet and income statement items in alphabetical order. Please put these items in the correct format for a balance sheet and income statement for Rimbey Sporting Goods for the year ended January 31. All data are in thousands of dollars.

Accounts payable	500
Accounts receivable	600
Addition to retained earnings	250
Cash and equivalents	200
Common stock	100
Cost of goods sold	3700
Depreciation	300
Dividends on common shares	150
Earnings before interest and taxes	800
Earnings before taxes	700
Gross profit	2300
Interest expense	100
Inventories	700
Long-term debt	1100
Net income	400
Net plant and equipment	2500
Notes payable	300
Other current liabilities	500
Retained earnings	1500
Sales	6000
Selling, general, and administrative expenses	1200
Taxes	300
Total assets	4000
Total current assets	1500
Total liabilities and equity	4000
Total current liabilities	1300
Total liabilities	2400

B2. Rimbey's accountant also presented all of the items in the statement of cash flows in alphabetical order. Please put these items in the correct format for a statement of cash flows for Rimbey Sporting Goods for the year ended January 31. All data are in thousands of dollars.

Accounts payable increase	50
Accounts receivable increase	(100)
Cash dividends (common stock)	(100)
Cash and equivalents at beginning of year	100
Cash and equivalents at end of year	200
Depreciation and amortization	300
Increase (decrease) in other long-term liabilities	(50)
Inventories increase	(150)
Issuance of long-term debt, net	200
Net cash provided by (used in) financing activities	100
Net cash provided by (used in) investing activities	(500)
Net cash provided by (used in) operating activities	500
Net income	400
Net increase in cash and equivalents	100
Notes payable increase	50
Purchase of plant and equipment	(500)

B3. Suppose Fisher Electronics reported 1996 net income of $120 million, which included a $15 million extraordinary gain on the sale of a subsidiary and a $25 million extraordinary loss from discontinued operations. Fisher reported interest expense of $20 million. Calculate Fisher's 1996 EBIT.

B4. For the year ended December 31, 1996, Dominion Resources, Inc. recorded the following items:

Cost of goods sold	$485
Interest expense	20
Preferred dividends paid	5
Common dividends paid	10
Selling expenses	30
Administrative expenses	125
Depreciation expense	100
Sales revenues	700
Taxes = 40% of taxable income	

Prepare an income statement for the year ended December 31, 1996, for Dominion Resources, Inc.

B5. A past annual report of Exxon Corporation reported the following items (in millions of dollars):

Sales and other operating revenue (net of excise taxes)	$86,656
Crude oil and product purchases	39,268
Operating expenses	10,535
Selling, general, and administrative expenses	6,398
Depreciation and depletion	5,002
Exploration expenses	872
Other taxes and duties (treat as part of operating expenses)	16,617
Other income	1,112
Minority interest	263
Interest expense	1,265
Income taxes	2,028
Valdez provision (treat as extraordinary cost)	2,545
Effect of accounting change (treat as extraordinary)	+535
Net income	3,510

Calculate Exxon's gross profit, operating income, and net income before extraordinary items for the year.

B6. Bill's Lanes, a Louisiana corporation that owns several bowling alleys, has the following balance sheet:

BILL'S LANES CORPORATION
BALANCE SHEET, DECEMBER 31, 1996
(THOUSANDS OF DOLLARS)

Assets		Liabilities and stockholders' equity	
Current assets	$1200	Current liabilities	$ 800
Net fixed assets	3000	Long-term debt	1000
		Stockholders' equity	2400
Total	$4200	Total	$4200

Assume that the market value of the current assets is equal to the book value and that the market value of the net fixed assets is three times the book value. The market value of current liabilities is equal to the book value, and the market value of long-term debt is 90% of its book value.

a. What is the market value of Bill's Lanes's assets?

b. What is the market value of Bill's Lanes's liabilities?

c. If the market value of equity is equal to the market value of assets minus the market value of liabilities, what is the market value of the equity in Bill's Lanes?

B7. Using the information in Problem B6, determine

a. Bill's Lanes's working capital

b. Bill's Lanes's current ratio

B8. Santiago's Chile Company has sales of $15,000,000, cost of goods sold of $6,000,000, selling and administrative costs of $2,500,000, and depreciation expense of $500,000. Santiago's also paid $200,000 of interest expense and received $150,000 of dividends from other corporations. Santiago's Chile had a long-term capital gain of $400,000 and paid dividends of $250,000 to shareholders. Use the federal income tax rates for 1994, which are given in Table 2-5.

   a. What is the federal income tax liability for Santiago's Chile Company?

   b. What are the marginal and average tax rates for Santiago's?

B9. Assume that you are a single taxpayer and have one personal exemption for $2450 and itemized deductions of $7550. Calculate your federal income tax liability for the three cases given below. What is your marginal income tax rate and your average income tax rate for each case?

   a. Your taxable income is $25,000.

   b. Your taxable income is $75,000.

   c. Your taxable income is $125,000.

B10. The Boston Publishing Company has taxable income of $250,000.

   a. What is its federal corporate tax liability?

   b. What are its average and marginal tax rates?

   c. If Boston had an additional $10,000 from interest income, what additional taxes would it owe?

   d. If Boston had an additional $10,000 of dividend income (from other corporations), what additional taxes would it owe?

B11.

   a. For 1994, Bob and Carol each had a total income of $20,000. They got married in December 1994 and had a tax status of "married filing jointly." They get two personal exemptions at $2450 each and take the standard deduction of $6350. What is their federal income tax liability? Use the personal tax rate schedule shown in Table 2-5.

   b. For 1994, Ted and Alice each had a total income of $20,000. They did not get married in 1994, and each files a return as a "single" taxpayer. They get personal exemptions of $2450 and itemized deductions of $3800. How much federal income tax does Ted owe? Alice? Ted and Alice combined?

   c. Suppose that Bob and Carol receive an additional $500 of interest on a municipal bond. What is the impact of this on their federal income tax obligation?

   d. Suppose that Bob and Carol receive an additional $1000 of long-term capital gains. What is the impact of the capital gain on their federal income tax obligation?

B12. Linn Oil Field Service Company has sales of $5,000,000, cost of goods sold of $2,000,000, selling and administrative costs of $500,000, and depreciation expense of $500,000. Linn also paid $25,000 of interest expense and received $400,000 of dividends from other corporations. Linn had a long-term capital loss of $200,000 and paid dividends of $250,000 to shareholders. What is Linn Oil Field Service Company's federal tax liability? What are the marginal and average tax rates for Linn?

B13. How is working capital related to the current ratio?

PROBLEM SET C

C1. During 1996, McGowan Construction earned net income of $250,000. The firm neither bought nor sold any capital assets. The book value of its assets declined by the year's depreciation charge, which was $200,000. The firm's operating cash flow for the year was $450,000. The market value of its assets increased by $300,000. What was McGowan Construction's economic income for the year? Why is this figure different from its accounting net income?

Real-World Application:
The Value of SunTrust's Coca-Cola Stock

SunTrust Banks, Inc. is one of the premier banks in the southeastern United States. It has grown rapidly by acquiring other banks. Some years ago it acquired Trust Company of Georgia, which owned approximately 24 million shares of common stock of The Coca-Cola Company. Trust Company of Georgia bought its Coca-Cola stock when that firm first issued shares to the public in the early 1900s. (We discuss *initial public offerings* in Chapter 23.)

Trust Company of Georgia paid just pennies per share for the stock. The total purchase price was a mere $110,000. Coca-Cola has since split its stock several times, and the shares have increased tremendously in value. (When a firm splits its stock, it subdivides its shares. For example, a 2-for-1 stock split doubles the number of outstanding shares. We'll tell you why firms split their shares in Chapter 18.)

Here is a summary of SunTrust's balance sheet as of December 31, 1992:

Balance Sheet at December 31, 1992
(Dollar Amounts in Thousands)

ASSETS		LIABILITIES AND STOCKHOLDERS' EQUITY	
Cash and due from banks	$2,298,270	Deposits	$28,843,294
Coca-Cola common stock	110	Other liabilities	5,101,753
Other investment securities	8,384,145	Total liabilities	33,945,047
Net loans	22,340,931	Stockholders' equity	2,703,525
Other assets	3,625,116		
		Total Liabilities and	
Total Assets	$36,648,572	Stockholders' Equity	$36,648,572

1. The price of Coca-Cola's common stock was $41\frac{7}{8}$ on December 31, 1992. Calculate the market value of SunTrust's Coca-Cola stock. By how much did the market value exceed the book value?

2. Suppose the book value of SunTrust's other assets approximates their market value. Calculate their total market value?

3. The price of SunTrust's common stock was $43\frac{3}{4}$ on December 31, 1992. It had 128 million shares outstanding. Calculate the total market value of its stockholders' equity.

4. What's the difference between the total market value and the book value of SunTrust's stockholders' equity? How much of this difference is due to the difference between the market value and book value of its Coca-Cola stock?

5. Calculate SunTrust's market-to-book ratio.

6. Use the summary balance sheet to calculate the debt ratio, the debt/equity ratio, and the equity multiplier for SunTrust. (These ratios are defined on page 53.)

7. Let's redo SunTrust's balance sheet on a market-value basis. List the Coca-Cola stock and SunTrust's stockholders' equity at their market values. Does the balance sheet balance? Can you explain why not?

8. Adjust the value of "other assets" until the basic balance sheet identity holds. Use the adjusted balance sheet to calculate the debt ratio, the debt/equity ratio, and the equity multiplier.

9. Compare the ratios you calculated in item 8 to those in item 6. Which set do you think better reflects SunTrust's true mix of debt and equity?

10. Beginning in 1993, SunTrust was able to adopt a new accounting rule (Financial Accounting Statement No. 115) and carry its Coca-Cola common stock on its balance sheet at its market value. Explain why users of financial statements will find adoptions of this rule like SunTrust's beneficial.

APPENDIX: ANALYZING FINANCIAL STATEMENTS

Despite the built-in limitations of accounting information, published accounting statements can reveal a great deal about a firm. Financial analysts and managers find it helpful to calculate **financial ratios** when interpreting a firm's accounting statements. A financial ratio is simply one quantity divided by another. Financial statement analysis can be useful in at least two ways. First, it can help structure your thinking about business decisions. Second, it can provide some information that is helpful in making those decisions.

The number of financial ratios that could be created is virtually limitless, but certain basic ratios are used frequently. These ratios fall into six classes: *liquidity ratios*, *asset activity ratios*, *leverage ratios*, *coverage ratios*, *profitability ratios*, and *market value ratios*. The calculation and interpretation of these six classes of ratios are discussed below. Our sample calculations are made on the balance sheet and income statement of Anheuser-Busch, which are shown in Tables 2A-1 and 2A-2. Calculations are for 1992, if not otherwise noted.

Liquidity Ratios

Liquidity ratios measure a firm's liquidity. The purpose is to assess the firm's ability to meet its financial obligations on time. Four widely used liquidity ratios are the current ratio, the quick ratio, the working capital ratio, and the cash ratio. The most commonly used measure of overall liquidity is the **current ratio** given by Equation (2.3).

$$\text{Current ratio} = \frac{\text{Current assets}}{\text{Current liabilities}} = \frac{1816}{1460} = 1.24x$$

	1993	1992
Assets		
Cash and equivalents	$ 127	$ 215
Accounts receivable	751	650
Inventories	627	661
Other current assets	290	290
Total current assets	1,795	1,816
Gross plant, property, & equipment	11,727	11,385
Accumulated depreciation	(4,230)	(3,861)
Property & equipment, net	7,497	7,524
Other assets	1,588	1,198
Total assets	$10,880	$10,538
Liabilities & Stockholders' Equity		
Accounts payable	$ 813	$ 737
Taxes payable	91	39
Accrued expenses	610	427
Other current liabilities	302	257
Total current liabilities	1,816	1,460
Long-term debt	3,032	2,643
Deferred taxes	1,170	1,277
Other liabilities	607	538
Total liabilities	6,625	5,918
Preferred stock	0	0
Common stock	343	341
Capital surplus	402	329
Retained earnings	5,990	5,793
Less: treasury stock	(2,480)	(1,843)
Total common equity	4,255	4,620
Total liabilities & equity	$10,880	$10,538

TABLE 2A-1
Anheuser-Busch Companies, Inc. annual balance sheet (millions of dollars, rounded), December 31.

Source: Anheuser-Busch Companies, Inc., *Annual Report 1993,* pp. 42–43.

TABLE 2A-2
Anheuser-Busch Companies, Inc. annual income statement (millions of dollars, except per-share amounts), year ended December 31.

	1993	1992	1991
Sales	$ 11,505	$ 11,394	$ 10,996
Cost of goods sold	6,811	6,742	6,614
Gross profit	4,694	4,652	4,382
Selling, general, & administrative expenses	2,309	2,309	2,126
Depreciation, depletion, & amortization	608	567	534
Operating profit	1,777	1,776	1,722
Interest expense	(208)	(200)	(239)
Capitalized interest	37	48	47
Nonoperating profit (loss)	(556)	(9)	(9)
Earnings before tax	1,050	1,615	1,521
Total income tax	456	621	581
Net income	594	994	940
Preferred dividends	0	0	0
Available for common	$ 594	$ 994	$ 940
Earnings per share	$2.17	$3.48	$3.26
Dividends per share	$1.36	$1.20	$1.06
Shares outstanding (000)	273,963	285,690	288,282

The current ratio measures the number of times the firm's current assets "cover" its current liabilities. Presumably, the higher the current ratio, the greater the firm's ability to meet its short-term obligations as they come due. A widely held but rough rule of thumb is that a current ratio of 2.0 is an appropriate target for most firms.

Inventories are considered current assets, so they are included in the current ratio calculation. Inventories, however, are less liquid than marketable securities and accounts receivables. This is because it is normally more difficult to turn inventory into cash on short notice. Thus analysts often exclude inventories from the numerator in the current ratio and calculate the **quick ratio** (also called the **acid test ratio**).

$$\text{Quick ratio} = \frac{\text{Current assets} - \text{Inventories}}{\text{Current liabilities}} = \frac{1816 - 661}{1460} = 0.79x$$

Another widely held but rough rule of thumb says a quick ratio of 1.0 or more is healthy.

Net working capital (or simply working capital) is the difference between current assets and current liabilities. The **working capital ratio** is simply net working capital expressed as a proportion of sales.

$$\text{Working capital ratio} = \frac{\text{Current asssets} - \text{Current liabilities}}{\text{Sales}} = \frac{1816 - 1460}{11,394} = 3.1\%$$

Net working capital is often considered a measure of liquidity by itself. This ratio shows the amount of liquidity relative to sales.

The **cash ratio** is calculated by dividing cash and equivalents by total assets.

$$\text{Cash ratio} = \frac{\text{Cash and equivalents}}{\text{Total assets}} = \frac{215}{10,538} = 2.0\%$$

Cash and equivalents (such as marketable securities) are the most liquid assets. The cash ratio shows the proportion of assets held in the most liquid possible form.

Ratios for other firms in the same industry and time period are often compared to judge a firm's relative strengths and weaknesses. For example, we can compare Anheuser-Busch's ratios to average ratios for the other large firms in the alcoholic beverages industry.[11]

	ANHEUSER-BUSCH	OTHER ALCOHOLIC BEVERAGE FIRMS
Current ratio	1.24x	2.12x
Quick ratio	0.79x	0.93x
Working capital ratio	3.1%	24.0%
Cash ratio	2.0%	3.0%

Anheuser-Busch has lower liquidity ratios than the other alcoholic beverage firms. Nevertheless, Anheuser-Busch is a healthy firm; nobody expects it to have trouble meeting its obligations as they come due. Its health allows it to carry much greater current liabilities, and it simply doesn't need as much liquidity as the rules of thumb prescribe, a current ratio of 2.0 and a quick ratio of 1.0. Note that the other alcoholic beverage firms have current and quick ratios that are very close to 2.0 and 1.0, respectively.

Asset Activity Ratios

Asset activity ratios are designed to measure how effectively a firm manages its assets. There are several ratios focusing on the management of specific assets as well as total assets.

The **receivables turnover ratio** is

$$\text{Receivables turnover} = \frac{\text{Annual credit sales}}{\text{Accounts receivable}} = \frac{11{,}394}{650} = 17.53x$$

It measures the number of times the accounts receivable balance "turns over" during the year. Note that annual credit sales, which give rise to receivables, are used in the numerator. If a figure for annual credit sales is not available, the firm's net sales figure is used instead. Making that substitution is like assuming that all sales were credit sales.

A closely related figure is the **days' sales outstanding** (DSO). It is the number of days in a year divided by the receivables turnover ratio.[12]

$$\text{Days' sales outstanding} = \frac{365}{\text{Receivables turnover}} = \frac{365}{17.53} = 20.8 \text{ days}$$

The days' sales outstanding shows approximately how long it takes, on average, to collect a receivable. The days' sales outstanding is also called the **average collection period**.

A more detailed picture of the firm's accounts receivable can be obtained by preparing an **aging schedule**. An aging schedule shows the amounts of receivables that have been outstanding for different periods, such as 0 to 30 days, 30 to 60 days, 60 to 90 days, and more than 90 days. An example of an accounts receivable aging schedule is given in Table 2A-3. An external analyst typically lacks the detailed information in an aging schedule unless the firm has chosen to provide it. Of course, managers within the firm want this information to help monitor their accounts receivable.

A measure of the effectiveness of inventory management is the **inventory turnover ratio**, which is calculated as follows:

$$\text{Inventory turnover} = \frac{\text{Cost of goods sold}}{\text{Inventory}} = \frac{6742}{661} = 10.20x$$

---

[11] Brown-Forman Corporation, Canandaigua Wine Co., Adolph Coors Company, The Molson Companies Ltd., and Seagram Co. are the others followed by *The Value Line Investment Survey*. The enormous difference between the working capital ratios for Anheuser-Busch and the other alcoholic beverage firms may look odd. You will find in a moment that Anheuser-Busch also has relatively high receivables and inventory turnover ratios.

[12] Before calculators and computers were widely used, analysts often used a 360-day year for simplicity. Although much of the financial press has continued this practice so far, it is becoming less popular. We will always use a 365-day year.

TABLE 2A-3
Accounts receivable aging schedule.

AGE (DAYS)	ACCOUNTS RECEIVABLE	PERCENTAGE OF TOTAL
0–30	$1500	50.0%
30–60	900	30.0
60–90	450	15.0
over 90	150	5.0
Total	$3000	100.0%

The inventory turnover is a good estimate of how many times per year the inventory is physically turning over. In the past, some analysts calculated the inventory turnover by dividing net sales by inventory. However, this calculation overstates the turnover rate of physical inventory.[13]

Another way to measure inventory turnover is the **days' sales in inventory ratio**. This is the time for "one turnover." For example, if inventory turnover were 12.0x, one turnover would be $\frac{1}{12}$ of a year, which in days is 30.42 (= 365/12). For Anheuser-Busch, it is

$$\text{Days' sales in inventory} = \frac{365}{\text{Inventory turnover}} = \frac{365}{10.20} = 35.8 \text{ days}$$

The day's sales in inventory ratio estimates the average time, in days, that inventory stays with the firm before it is sold.

Finally, two other ratios show how productively the firm is using its assets. These are the **fixed asset turnover ratio** and the **total asset turnover ratio**.

$$\text{Fixed asset turnover} = \frac{\text{Sales}}{\text{Net fixed assets}} = \frac{11,394}{7524} = 1.51x$$

$$\text{Total asset turnover} = \frac{\text{Sales}}{\text{Total assets}} = \frac{11,394}{10,538} = 1.08x$$

These ratios show the sales generated per book-value dollar of fixed assets and total assets, respectively.

We can again compare Anheuser-Busch's ratios to those of the other alcoholic beverage firms.

	ANHEUSER-BUSCH	OTHER ALCOHOLIC BEVERAGE FIRMS
Receivables turnover	17.53x	8.11x
Days' sales outstanding	20.8 days	50.9 days
Inventory turnover	10.20x	2.89x
Days' sales in inventory	35.8 days	189.2 days
Fixed asset turnover	1.51x	3.84x
Total asset turnover	1.08x	1.01x

Anheuser-Busch turns over its receivables and inventory more rapidly than the other firms.[14] Anheuser-Busch's fixed assets turn over more slowly. This implies that Anheuser-Busch requires a larger investment in fixed assets (relative to sales) than these other firms.

---

[13] An example illustrates the problem: 60 units of the firm's product were sold last year; sales were $600; cost of goods sold on these units was $360; and inventory was $120 with 20 units in it. Dividing *sales* by inventory, 600/120 = 5.0x. Dividing *cost of goods sold* by inventory, 360/120 = 3.0x. From knowing the number of units, we can see that the physical turnover rate is in fact 60/20 = 3.0x. The turnover rate of 5.0x is larger than the physical turnover rate, because sales is on a different basis; sales includes profit. Cost of goods sold does not include profit. Cost of goods sold is on the same cost basis as inventory.

[14] We suggest you draw your own conclusions concerning the reasons for this rapid turnover in inventory.

Leverage Ratios

Financial leverage is the extent to which a firm is financed with debt. The amount of debt a firm uses has both positive and negative effects. The more debt, the more likely it is that the firm will have trouble meeting its obligations. Thus the more debt, the higher the probability of financial distress and even bankruptcy. Furthermore, the chance of financial distress, and debt obligations generally, may create conflicts of interest among the stakeholders.

Despite this, debt is a major source of financing. It provides a significant tax advantage, because interest is tax-deductible, as we noted in this chapter. Debt also has lower transaction costs and is generally easier to obtain. Finally, debt affects how the firm's stakeholders bear the risk of the firm. One particular effect is that debt makes the stock riskier because of the increased chance of financial distress. These factors are discussed at length later in the book. At this point, suffice it to say that leverage is very important, and **leverage ratios** measure the amount of (financial) leverage.

Three common leverage ratios are the debt ratio, the debt/equity ratio, and the equity multiplier. The **debt ratio** is the proportion of debt financing.

$$\text{Debt ratio} = \frac{\text{Total debt}}{\text{Total assets}} = \frac{10{,}538 - 4620}{10{,}538} = \frac{5918}{10{,}538} = 0.56x$$

The **debt/equity ratio** is a simple rearrangement of the debt ratio and expresses the same information on a different scale. Whereas the debt ratio can be as small as zero but, assuming positive equity, is always less than 1.0, the debt/equity ratio ranges from zero to infinity. The debt/equity ratio is

$$\text{Debt/equity ratio} = \frac{\text{Total debt}}{\text{Stockholders' equity}} = \frac{5918}{4620} = 1.28x$$

The **equity multiplier** is yet another representation of the same information. It shows how much total assets the firm has for each dollar of equity.

$$\text{Equity multiplier} = \frac{\text{Total assets}}{\text{Stockholders' equity}} = \frac{10{,}538}{4620} = 2.28x$$

All three of these leverage ratios are widely used. As we have said, they are simply different representations of the same information. If you know any one of them, you can derive the other two. For example, suppose a firm has a debt ratio of $0.40x$ and so is 40% debt-financed. From this we know that the firm is 60% equity-financed. Therefore, the firm's debt/equity ratio is $40/60 = 0.67x$. Because total assets is equal to 100% of the financing (the balance sheet equation, A = L + OE), the equity multiplier is $100/60 = 1.67$. Generalizing, we have

$$\text{Equity multiplier} = \text{debt/equity ratio} + 1.0$$

$$\text{Debt/equity ratio} = \frac{\text{Debt ratio}}{1.0 - \text{Debt ratio}}$$

Because it doesn't make any difference which of the three measures is used, we use the debt ratio throughout this book for simplicity and consistency.

Here again we compare Anheuser-Busch to the other alcoholic beverage firms.

	ANHEUSER-BUSCH	OTHER ALCOHOLIC BEVERAGE FIRMS
Debt ratio	$0.56x$	$0.24x$
Debt/equity ratio	$1.28x$	$0.51x$
Equity multiplier	$2.28x$	$1.51x$

The debt ratio shows that Anheuser-Busch is 56% debt-financed. The debt/equity ratio shows that the firm has $1.28 in debt for each $1.00 of equity. The equity multiplier shows that the firm has about $2.28 in total assets for each $1.00 of equity. The comparison shows that Anheuser-Busch has more leverage than the other firms.

Coverage Ratios

Coverage ratios show the number of times a firm can "cover" or meet a particular financial obligation. The **interest coverage ratio**, which is also called the **times-interest-earned ratio**, measures the coverage of the firm's interest expense. It is earnings before interest and income taxes (EBIT) divided by the firm's interest expense. For Anheuser-Busch, EBIT equals operating profit (1776) plus nonoperating profit (-9):

$$\text{EBIT} = 1776 - 9 = 1767$$

The interest coverage ratio is

$$\text{Interest coverage ratio} = \frac{\text{EBIT}}{\text{Interest expense}} = \frac{1767}{200} = 8.84x$$

Many firms lease or rent assets that require contractual payments. Long-term leases are reported on the balance sheet, and the periodic lease payments are included in the firm's interest expense. Rental agreements are different. They are not on the balance sheet. Renting an asset is an alternative to owning it. (Rental payments are therefore an alternative to the interest payments the firm would make if it borrowed the money to buy the same assets). Rental expense is reported in the notes to the financial statements. For these firms, the **fixed-charge coverage ratio** is useful, where fixed charges consist of interest expense plus rental payments:[15]

$$\frac{\text{Fixed-charge}}{\text{coverage ratio}} = \frac{\text{EBIT} + \text{Rental payments}}{\text{Interest expense} + \text{Rental payments}} = \frac{1767 + 5}{200 + 5} = 8.64x$$

The **cash flow coverage ratio** is the firm's operating cash flows divided by its payment obligations for interest, principal, preferred stock dividends, and rent.[16]

$$\frac{\text{Cash flow}}{\text{coverage ratio}} = \frac{\text{EBIT} + \text{Rental payments} + \text{Depreciation}}{\text{Rental payments} + \text{Interest expense} + \dfrac{\text{Preferred stock dividends}}{1-T} + \dfrac{\text{Debt repayment}}{1-T}}$$

$$\frac{\text{Cash flow}}{\text{coverage ratio}} = \frac{1767 + 5 + 567}{200 + 5 + \dfrac{0}{(1-0.4)} + \dfrac{344}{(1-0.4)}} = 3.01x$$

Note that two of the financial obligations in the denominator of the cash flow coverage ratio are divided by $(1 - T)$, where T is the marginal income tax rate. Rental payments and interest charges are tax-deductible expenses. Only one dollar of before-tax cash flow is required to meet one dollar of these obligations. In contrast, preferred stock dividends and principal repayments must be made out of after-tax cash flows. They are divided by $(1 - T)$ to get the equivalent before-tax operating cash flow necessary to meet them. This is similar to the difference in tax treatment between interest expense and dividends that we noted in the chapter.

We can compare Anheuser-Busch's coverage ratios with those of the other alcoholic beverage firms.

	ANHEUSER-BUSCH	OTHER ALCOHOLIC BEVERAGE FIRMS
Interest coverage ratio	8.84x	6.28x
Fixed-charge coverage ratio	8.64x	6.17x
Cash flow coverage ratio	3.01x	8.26x

[15]Rental expense in 1992 is $5 million.
[16]Debt repayment in 1992 is $344 million.

Anheuser-Busch has comparatively better coverage of its interest and fixed-charged obligations. Its cash flow coverage ratio is lower because it had greater long-term debt repayment obligations.

Profitability Ratios

Profitability ratios focus on the profit-generating performance of the firm. These ratios measure how effectively the firm is able to generate profits. They reflect the operating performance, its riskiness, and the effect of leverage. We'll look at two kinds of profitability ratios. These are *profit margins*, which measure performance in relation to sales, and *rate of return ratios*, which measure performance relative to some measure of the size of the investment.

Gross profit is the difference between sales and the cost of goods sold. Gross profit is critical to the firm because it represents the amount of money remaining to pay operating costs, financing costs, and taxes and to provide for profit. The **gross profit margin** is the amount of each sales dollar left after paying the cost of goods sold.

$$\text{Gross profit margin} = \frac{\text{Gross profit}}{\text{Sales}} = \frac{\text{Sales} - \text{Cost of goods sold}}{\text{Sales}} = \frac{4652}{11,394} = 40.8\%$$

The **net profit margin** measures the profit that is available from each dollar of sales after *all* expenses have been paid, including cost of goods sold; selling, general, and administrative expenses; depreciation; interest; and taxes.

$$\text{Net profit margin} = \frac{\text{Net income before extraordinary items}}{\text{Sales}} = \frac{994}{11,394} = 8.7\%$$

Here's how Anheuser-Busch stacks up against the other alcoholic beverage firms:

	ANHEUSER-BUSCH	OTHER ALCOHOLIC BEVERAGE FIRMS
Gross profit margin	40.8%	40.5%
Net profit margin	8.7%	7.2%

Anheuser-Busch has done well. Its gross profit margin is about the same, but its net profit margin is higher.

Unlike profit margins, *rate of return ratios* express profitability in relation to various measures of investment in the firm. Their potential usefulness is inherently limited, however, because they are based on book values. Three ratios are commonly used: return on assets, earning power, and return on equity.

Return on assets (ROA) corresponds to the net profit margin, except that net income is expressed as a proportion of total assets.

$$\text{Return on assets} = \frac{\text{Net income}}{\text{Total assets}} = \frac{994}{10,538} = 9.4\%$$

Earning power is the firm's EBIT divided by total assets.

$$\text{Earning power} = \frac{\text{EBIT}}{\text{Total assets}} = \frac{1767}{10,538} = 16.8\%$$

The difference between ROA and earning power is due to debt financing. Net income is EBIT minus interest and taxes, so ROA will always be less than earning power. Earning power represents the "raw" operating results, whereas ROA represents the combined results of operating and financing.

Return on equity (ROE) is the rate of return on the common stockholders' equity:

$$\text{Return on equity} = \frac{\text{Earnings available for common stock before extraordinary items}}{\text{Common stockholders' equity}} = \frac{994}{4620} = 21.5\%$$

where common stockholders' equity includes common stock (at par value), capital surplus, and retained earnings. ROE shows the residual profits of the firm as a proportion of the book value of common stockholders' equity. The amount of leverage affects both the numerator and the denominator of ROE. Typically, ROE is greater than ROA for healthy firms. In bad years, however, ROE can fall below ROA. This is because financial leverage increases the risk of the stock, as we noted earlier.

Comparing Anheuser-Busch to the other alcoholic beverage firms, we have

	ANHEUSER-BUSCH	OTHER ALCOHOLIC BEVERAGE FIRMS
Return on assets (ROA)	9.4%	5.8%
Earning power	16.8%	10.6%
Return on equity (ROE)	21.5%	11.4%

Anheuser-Busch has higher profitability than the other firms. Note once again, however, that these ratios collectively reflect not only the operating performance and its riskiness but also the effect of the firm's leverage.

Market Value Ratios

Analysts use several **market value ratios** that relate the market value of the firm's common stock to earnings per share (EPS), dividends per share (DPS), and book value per share, which is total common equity divided by the number of common shares outstanding. Book value per share is $16.17(= 4620/285.69). At the time the statements were prepared, the market price of Anheuser-Busch common stock was $58.50 per share.

The **price/earnings ratio (P/E)** is the market price per share of common stock divided by the earnings per share (EPS).

$$\text{P/E} = \text{Price/earnings ratio} = \frac{\text{Market price per share}}{\text{Earnings per share}} = \frac{58.50}{3.48} = 16.8x$$

When earnings are negative, EPS is of course negative, which makes the P/E negative as well. Also, when EPS gets close to zero, the P/E becomes extremely large, because of dividing by the EPS. The P/E is not generally reported when EPS is negative or excessively small, because it is not considered to be economically meaningful under those conditions.

Another form of the same information is **earnings yield**, which is the reciprocal of the P/E.

$$\text{Earnings yield} = \frac{\text{Earnings per share}}{\text{Market price per share}} = \frac{3.48}{58.50} = 5.95\%$$

Unlike the P/E, earnings yield does not "break down" when EPS is excessively small or negative. EPS is on top in the earnings yield and so avoids the division-by-zero problem. A negative EPS is a loss per share. Earnings yield simply represents the loss as a rate of return, a rate of losing value.

The **dividend yield** is the ratio of the dividends per share to the market price per share.

$$\text{Dividend yield} = \frac{\text{Dividend per share}}{\text{Market price per share}} = \frac{1.20}{58.50} = 2.05\%$$

Many firms do not pay a cash dividend. Such firms simply have a dividend yield of zero. The decision to pay cash dividends is essentially a choice between paying out earnings to the owners or reinvesting the money in the firm. We will have more to say about dividends later on.

Finally, the **market-to-book ratio** is the market price per share divided by the book value per share.

$$\text{Market-to-book ratio} = \frac{\text{Market price per share}}{\text{Book value per share}} = \frac{58.50}{16.17} = 3.62x$$

The market-to-book ratio is a very rough index of a firm's historical performance. The higher the ratio, the greater is market value relative to book value. A high ratio says the firm has created more in market value than the GAAP rules have recorded in book value. The implied message is that the firm has done well. Of course, as we noted earlier, there are many possible explanations for a difference between market and book values. Although the implied message of a high market-to-book ratio is likely to be correct in most cases, additional information is generally needed to reach a confident conclusion.

Comparing Anheuser-Busch with other alcoholic beverage firms, we have

	ANHEUSER-BUSCH	OTHER ALCOHOLIC BEVERAGE FIRMS
Price/earnings ratio	16.8x	15.4x
Earnings yield	5.95%	6.40%
Dividend yield	2.05%	2.00%
Market-to-book ratio	3.62x	1.93x

Past increases in the market value of Anheuser-Busch's common stock have significantly exceeded increases in the book value per share. This makes Anheuser-Busch's P/E and market-to-book ratios larger than those of the other firms. Its earnings yield and dividend yield are about the same.

Table 2A-4 presents all of the ratios discussed in this section.

Common-Statement Analysis

Another technique used in financial statement analysis is called common-statement analysis. Common-statement analysis makes some comparisons more meaningful because it puts the things being compared on a common basis. There are two widely used methods of common-statement analysis. **Common-size analysis** shows items as percentages rather than as amounts of money. Balance sheet items are expressed as percentages of total assets, and income statement items are expressed as percentages of sales. Common-size analysis makes possible a more meaningful comparison of firms that are of significantly different sizes and enables us to track a single firm through time.

Common-base-year analysis shows each item as a percentage of its amount in an initial year, such as five years ago. Common-base-year analysis makes it easy to see which items are growing relatively faster or slower, because items more (less) than 100% have increased (declined).

Summary

Despite the inherent limitations of accounting information, financial statement analysis can provide additional insights into the firm. Financial statement analysis can help you structure your thinking about business decisions and can reveal information that is helpful in making such decisions. Numerous widely used financial ratios are given in Table 2A-4.

TABLE 2A-4
Summary of financial ratios.

LIQUIDITY RATIOS

$$\text{Current ratio} = \frac{\text{Current assets}}{\text{Current liabilities}}$$

$$\text{Quick ratio} = \frac{\text{Current assets} - \text{Inventories}}{\text{Current liabilities}}$$

$$\text{Working capital ratio} = \frac{\text{Current assets} - \text{Current liabilities}}{\text{Sales}}$$

$$\text{Cash ratio} = \frac{\text{Cash and equivalents}}{\text{Total assets}}$$

ASSET ACTIVITY RATIOS

$$\text{Receivables turnover} = \frac{\text{Annual credit sales}}{\text{Accounts receivable}}$$

$$\text{Days' sales outstanding} = \frac{365}{\text{Receivables turnover}}$$

$$\text{Inventory turnover} = \frac{\text{Cost of goods sold}}{\text{Inventory}}$$

$$\text{Days' sales in inventory} = \frac{365}{\text{Inventory turnover}}$$

$$\text{Fixed asset turnover} = \frac{\text{Sales}}{\text{Net fixed assets}}$$

$$\text{Total asset turnover} = \frac{\text{Sales}}{\text{Total assets}}$$

LEVERAGE RATIOS

$$\text{Debt ratio} = \frac{\text{Total debt}}{\text{Total assets}}$$

$$\text{Debt/equity ratio} = \frac{\text{Total debt}}{\text{Stockholders' equity}} = \frac{\text{Debt ratio}}{1.0 - \text{Debt ratio}}$$

$$\text{Equity multiplier} = \frac{\text{Total assets}}{\text{Stockholders' equity}} = \text{Debt/equity ratio} + 1.0$$

COVERAGE RATIOS

$$\text{Interest coverage ratio} = \frac{\text{EBIT}}{\text{Interest expense}}$$

$$\text{Fixed-charge coverage ratio} = \frac{\text{EBIT} + \text{Rental payments}}{\text{Interest expense} + \text{Rental payments}}$$

$$\text{Cash flow coverage ratio} = \frac{\text{EBIT} + \text{Rental payments} + \text{Depreciation}}{\text{Rental payments} + \text{Interest expense} + \dfrac{\text{Preferred stock dividends}}{1 - T} + \dfrac{\text{Debt repayment}}{1 - T}}$$

(continued)

PROFITABILITY RATIOS

$$\text{Gross profit margin} = \frac{\text{Gross profit}}{\text{Sales}} = \frac{\text{Sales} - \text{Cost of goods sold}}{\text{Sales}}$$

$$\text{Net profit margin} = \frac{\text{Net income before extraordinary items}}{\text{Sales}}$$

$$\text{Return on assets} = \frac{\text{Net income}}{\text{Total assets}}$$

$$\text{Earning power} = \frac{\text{EBIT}}{\text{Total assets}}$$

$$\text{Return on equity} = \frac{\text{Earnings available for common stock}}{\text{Common stockholders' equity}}$$

MARKET VALUE RATIOS

$$\text{P/E} = \text{Price/earnings ratio} = \frac{\text{Market price per share}}{\text{Earnings per share}}$$

$$\text{Earnings yield} = \frac{\text{Earnings per share}}{\text{Market price per share}}$$

$$\text{Dividend yield} = \frac{\text{Dividend per share}}{\text{Market price per share}}$$

$$\text{Market-to-book ratio} = \frac{\text{Market price per share}}{\text{Book value per share}}$$

APPENDIX KEY TERMS

financial ratios...49	days' sales in inventory ratio...52	profitability ratios...55
liquidity ratios...49	fixed asset turnover ratio...52	gross profit margin...55
current ratio 49	total asset turnover ratio...52	net profit margin...55
quick ratio...50	financial leverage...53	return on assets (ROA)...55
acid test ratio...50	leverage ratios...53	earning power...55
working capital ratio...50	debt ratio...53	return on equity (ROE)...56
cash ratio...50	debt/equity ratio...53	market value ratios...56
asset activity ratios...51	equity multiplier...53	price/earnings ratio (P/E)...56
receivables turnover ratio...51	coverage ratios...54	earnings yield...56
days' sales outstanding...51	interest coverage ratio...54	dividend yield...56
average collection period...51	times-interest-earned ratio...54	market-to-book ratio...57
aging schedule...51	fixed-charge coverage ratio...54	common-size analysis...57
inventory turnover ratio...51	cash flow coverage ratio...54	common-base-year analysis...57

APPENDIX EXERCISE

Compute each of the ratios in Table 2A-4 for Ohio Greeting Company, using the information provided in Tables 2-1, 2-2, and 2-3, and assuming the common stock has a current market value of $47.25. To calculate the book value per share, subtract the preferred stock from total stockholders' equity to get common stockholders' equity.

BIBLIOGRAPHY

AICPA. "The Meaning of Presenting Fairly in Conformity with Generally Accepted Accounting Principles in the Independent Auditor's Report," *Statement on Auditing Standards.* New York: AICPA, 1992.

Amihud, Yakov, and Haim Mendelson. "Liquidity and Asset Prices: Financial Management Implications," *Financial Management*, 1988, 17(1):5–15.

Badrinath, S. G., and Wilbur G. Lewellen. "Evidence on Tax-Motivated Securities Trading Behavior," *Journal of Finance*, 1991, 46(1):369–382.

Ben-Horim, Moshe, Shalom Hochman, and Oded Palmon. "The Impact of the 1986 Tax Reform Act on Corporate Financial Policy," *Financial Management*, 1987, 16(3):29–35.

Brick, Ivan E., and William K. H. Fung. "The Effect of Taxes on the Trade Credit Decision," *Financial Management*, 1984, 13(2):24–30.

Brick, Ivan E., William Fung, and Marti Subrahmanyam. "Leasing and Financial Intermediation: Comparative Tax Advantages," *Financial Management*, 1987, 16(1):55–59.

Dammon, Robert M., and Lemma W. Senbet. "The Effect of Taxes and Depreciation on Corporate Investment and Financial Leverage," *Journal of Finance*, 1988, 43(2):357–373.

Davis, Alfred H. R. "Effective Tax Rates as Determinants of Canadian Capital Structure," *Financial Management*, 1987, 16(3):22–28.

Ferri, Michael G., Steven J. Goldstein, and It-Keong Chew. "Interest Rates and the Announcement of Inflation," *Financial Management*, 1983, 12(3):52–61.

Gombola, Michael J., Mark E. Haskins, J. Edward Ketz, and David D. Williams. "Cash Flow in Bankruptcy Prediction," *Financial Management*, 1987, 16(4):55–65.

Gombola, Michael J., and J. Edward Ketz. "Financial Ratio Patterns in Retail and Manufacturing Organizations," *Financial Management*, 1983, 12(2):45–56.

Gordon, Roger H. "Can Capital Income Taxes Survive in Open Economies?," *Journal of Finance*, 1992, 47(3):1159–1180.

Green, Richard C., and Eli Talmor. "The Structure and Incentive Effects of Corporate Tax Liabilities," *Journal of Finance*, 1985, 40(4):1095–1114.

Griffiths, Mark D., and Robert W. White. "Tax-Induced Trading and the Turn-of-the-Year Anomaly: An Intraday Study," *Journal of Finance*, 1993, 48(2):575–598.

Haugen, Robert A., and Lemma W. Senbet. "Corporate Finance and Taxes: A Review," *Financial Management*, 1986, 15(3):5–21.

Hochman, Shalom J., Oded Palmon, and Alex P. Tang. "Tax-Induced Intra-Year Patterns in Bonds Yields," *Journal of Finance*, 1993, 48(1):331–344.

Jaffe, Jeffrey F. "Taxes and the Capital Structure of Partnerships, REIT's, and Related Entities," *Journal of Finance*, 1991, 46(1):401–408.

John, Teresa A. "Accounting Measures of Corporate Liquidity, Leverage, and Costs of Financial Distress," *Financial Management*, 1993, 22(3):91–100.

Kroll, Yoram. "On the Differences Between Accrual Accounting Figures and Cash Flows: The Case of Working Capital," *Financial Management*, 1985, 14(1):75–82.

Lewis, Craig M. "A Multiperiod Theory of Corporate Financial Policy Under Taxation," *Journal of Financial and Quantitative Analysis*, 1990, 25(1):25–44.

MacKie-Mason, Jeffrey K. "Do Taxes Affect Corporate Financing Decisions?" *Journal of Finance*, 1990, 45(5):1471–1494.

Maloney, Kevin J., and Thomas I. Selling. "Simplifying Tax Simplification: An Analysis of Its Impact on the Profitability of Capital Investment," *Financial Management*, 1985, 14(2):33–42.

Manzon, Gil B., Jr., David J. Sharp, and Nickolaos G. Travlos. "An Empirical Study of the Consequences of U.S. Tax Rules for International Acquisitions by U.S. Firms," *Journal of Finance*, 1994, 49(5):1893–1904.

Mauer, David C., and Wilbur G. Lewellen. "Securityholder Taxes and Corporate Restructurings," *Journal of Financial and Quantitative Analysis*, 1990, 25(3):341–360.

Newbould, Gerald D., Robert E. Chatfield, and Ronald F. Anderson. "Leveraged Buyouts and Tax Incentives," *Financial Management*, 1992, 21(1):50–57.

Papaioannou, George J., and Craig M. Savarese. "Corporate Dividend Policy Response to the Tax Reform Act of 1986," *Financial Management*, 1994, 23(1):56–63.

Pilotte, Eugene. "The Economic Recovery Tax Act of 1981 and Corporate Capital Structure," *Financial Management*, 1990, 19(4):98–107.

Robin, Ashok J. "The Impact of the 1986 Tax Reform Act on Ex-Dividend Day Returns," *Financial Management*, 1991, 20(1):60–70.

Servaes, Henri, and Marc Zenner. "Taxes and the Returns to Foreign Acquisitions in the United States," *Financial Management*, 1994, 23(4):42–56.

Talmor, Eli, and Sheridan Titman. "Taxes and Dividend Policy," *Financial Management*, 1990, 19(2):32–35.

THE FINANCIAL ENVIRONMENT, PRINCIPLES, AND FUNDAMENTAL CONCEPTS

Every field of endeavor has fundamental laws, principles, or tenets that help guide you in understanding that field. Finance is no exception. There are important, basic principles that can help you understand mundane practices in finance as well as new and complex situations.

Suppose you wanted to sell your car. Would you want to get the highest possible price? Sure. Do you think a person who wanted to buy it would want to pay the lowest possible price? Undoubtedly. Suppose you wanted to invest some money. Would you like to triple your money in the next year? That would be nice. But do you want to risk losing all your money? Not really. Do you think you might have to take some risk to get a superior return? Probably. If someone guaranteed to double your money in six months with absolutely no risk, would you doubt them? We hope so. If we owed you $100, would you rather have it today or in three years? Today, of course.

In such straightforward situations, the answers to these questions are obvious. They come from intuition you have developed, based on an understanding of the world. In more complex situations, answers are not always so easy. So you need principles to help you.

In this chapter we describe the principles of finance. They are the foundations on which corporate financial management is built. We will help you understand their application to the practice of finance.

We also take a quick look at what are known as the capital markets, such as the stock market. Capital market transactions (buying and selling) are important, both as a part of corporate financial management and as a place to observe and apply the principles of finance.

3.1 THE COMPETITIVE ECONOMIC ENVIRONMENT

In this section and the two that follow, we describe the "first principles" of finance. These principles provide the basis for understanding financial transactions and making financial decisions. They consist of a set of fundamental tenets that form the basis for financial theory and for decision making in finance. The principles are based on logical deduction and on empirical observation. Even if every principle is not absolutely correct in every case, most practitioners accept the principles as a valid way to describe their world.

Before going any further, we need to remind you of an important definition. A financial security, which we'll call simply a **security**, is a claim issued by a firm to finance itself. Bonds and shares of stock are examples of securities. In essence, securities are simply claims on future cash flows, such as interest and dividends.

Our first group of principles deals with competition in an economic environment.

The Principle of Self-Interested Behavior: People Act in Their Own Financial Self-Interest

Good business decisions require reasonably accurate assumptions about human behavior. Although there may be individual exceptions, we assume that people act in an economically rational way. That is, people act in their own financial self-interest.

The Principle of Self-Interested Behavior may be a little difficult to swallow at first. One reason is that most of us realize money isn't everything. The Principle of Self-Interested Behavior does not deny the truth of this counsel. Nor does it deny the importance of "human" considerations. The principle also does not mean to suggest that money is *the most important thing* in everyone's, or even anyone's, life.

It does mean that when all else is equal, all parties to a financial transaction will choose the course of action most financially advantageous to themselves. This principle has been found to explain actual behavior very well, because most business interactions are "arm's-length" transactions. In these impersonal transactions, getting the most good out of available resources is the primary consideration.

You also might think that giving money to a charity, having children, and being honest when filing your tax return are violations of the Principle of Self-Interested Behavior. These decisions include considerations other than just money. Most people don't give money to charity or have children in order to receive a direct financial benefit. But even if certain actions do violate the Principle of Self-Interested Behavior, the principle is still useful for our purposes. This is because it is right on average. So it's a very good approximation of human behavior.

There is an important corollary to the Principle of Self-Interested Behavior. Frequently, competing desirable actions can be taken. When someone takes an action, that action eliminates other possible actions. The difference between the value of one action and the value of the best alternative is called an **opportunity cost**.

An opportunity cost provides an indication of the relative importance of a decision. When the opportunity cost is small, the cost of an incorrect choice is small. Similarly, when the opportunity cost is large, the cost of not making the best choice is large.

Suppose you sell a car for $3200 without much forethought. You find out the next day that the car could have been sold for $3300. You have incurred an opportunity cost of at least $100. You might not consider that very significant. But suppose you discovered the next day that the car could have been sold for $4500. You probably would consider the opportunity cost of $1300 on an asset worth $4500 significant. ∎

The Opportunity Cost of Selling a Used Car

EXAMPLE

Please don't let the simplicity of our used-car example lull you into thinking such costs are obvious and easy to calculate. In some cases, opportunity costs are very subtle and difficult even to define, let alone calculate. However, the importance of opportunity costs cannot be overstated.

An important application of the Principle of Self-Interested Behavior is called **agency theory**. Agency theory analyzes conflicts of interest and behavior in a principal-agent relationship. A principal-agent relationship is a relationship in which one person, an **agent**, makes decisions that affect another person, a **principal**.

Recall the set-of-contracts model we discussed in Chapter 1. Many of the contracts that make up a firm can be viewed as principal-agent relationships. Examples of principal-agent relationships include those between the firm (as the principal) and employees (agents), such as its managers, salespeople, and others. The firm also has a principal-agent relationship with pension fund managers, with lawyers, and with real estate, travel, and insurance agents. There is also an important principal-agent relationship between the firm's stockholders and bondholders.

The long-time chairman of Occidental Petroleum Corporation, Armand Hammer, died in December 1990. Hammer's name had come to be synonymous with Occidental. He had built it into a major corporation. Now he was gone. And what happened to Occidental's stock price when his death was announced? It jumped up 9%. Trading volume exceeded 8 million shares, many times the stock's average trading volume, making it the most active stock on the New York Stock Exchange that day. Why?

Many oil industry analysts felt that Hammer had begun to operate the firm as his personal fiefdom. They accused him of using the firm's resources to support his own pet projects (such as an art museum to house his collection), even when investing in them was not in the best interests of stockholders. Stockholders believed his successor, Ray Irani, would make better business decisions. And indeed, most would agree that the firm fared much better under Irani. ∎

The Death of Occidental Petroleum Corporation's Long-Time Chairman

EXAMPLE

A critical consideration in principal-agent relationships is the problem of **moral hazard**. Moral hazard refers to situations wherein the agent can take unseen actions for personal benefit even though such actions are costly to the principal. By carefully analyzing individual behavior, agency theory helps us develop more effective provisions for contracts between a principal and an agent. A typical goal of such contract provisions is to reduce conflicts of interest, thereby reducing moral hazard problems.

The Principle of Two-Sided Transactions: Each Financial Transaction Has at Least Two Sides

The Principle of Two-Sided Transactions may seem very straightforward, yet it is sometimes forgotten when things become complex. Understanding financial transactions requires that we not become self-centered. Do not forget that while we are following self-interested behavior and making decisions in *our* financial self-interest, others are also acting in *their own* financial self-interest. That includes those with whom we are transacting business. Consider the sale of an asset—or should we say the purchase? And that is just the point. For every sale, there is a purchase. For each buyer, there is a seller. When we analyze our side of a transaction, we must keep in mind that there is someone else analyzing the other side.

EXAMPLE

Media Doubletalk

An example of the confusion regarding the Principle of Two-Sided Transactions involves reporting stock market transactions. Media commentators sometimes refer to "profit takers *selling off* their holdings" and causing a decline in the price of a particular common stock. The implication is that there was more selling than buying. You may even read in the newspaper that changes in market prices are the result of an "imbalance" between the amount of buying and the amount of selling that is taking place. This, of course, is not true.

When securities, such as stocks, are bought and sold, there is a buyer and a seller for each share that changes hands. And if you will recall the Principle of Self-Interested Behavior, it does not make sense to say that those on the buying side deliberately bought a stock that was going to decline in value. They thought the stock would maintain or increase its value. It just happened that the buyers turned out to be wrong! Quite simply, it is these differences in expectations that give rise to much of the buying and selling of financial securities in the first place. ■

We can describe this sort of situation as one where more people believe the stock is overvalued than believe the stock is undervalued. This difference in beliefs may lead to more *sell orders* than *buy orders*. However, in spite of the disequilibrium in orders (those *willing* to buy or sell), there is *exactly* one share purchased for each share sold. In such situations, people buy or sell until the market price reaches what they think is the correct value of each share.

Most financial transactions are **zero-sum games**. A zero-sum game is a situation in which one player can gain *only* at the expense of another player. In these situations, my gain is your loss, and vice versa. This is exactly the kind of situation we have with most buyer-seller relations. A higher price costs the buyer and benefits the seller. A lower price costs the seller and benefits the buyer. Nevertheless, some transactions may not appear to be zero-sum games. Consider the case of municipal bonds.

EXAMPLE

Tax-Free Municipal Bonds

Municipal bonds (muni's) are issued by state and local governments. In chapter 2, we noted that the interest payments on such bonds are exempt from federal taxes. This allows state and local governments to issue muni's at a lower interest rate than they would have to pay if the interest were taxable. Purchasers of muni's will get a higher after-tax return than they would if they had bought otherwise similar but fully taxable bonds. It appears, then, that this is not a zero-sum game. Both sides are better off. However, this is not so clear when you consider some other parties to the transaction. How about other taxpayers? Reducing one group of taxpayers' tax payments may cause others to bear a larger portion of the cost of running the government. ■

Most financial transactions that are not zero-sum games result from provisions in the tax code. As the municipal bond example illustrates, it is possible under certain conditions for two entities (for example, a securities issuer and an investor) to make an agreement in which both come out ahead by structuring the transaction such that the government collects less total tax from the two than if the transaction had not taken place. Although it is clear that the two entities are indeed better off, whether *everyone* is better off depends on the government's ability to create tax provisions that reduce taxes for people who act in ways that help society as a whole. Because this is a finance textbook, we won't dwell on the debate over the government's ability to write such tax provisions. Suffice it to say that with few exceptions, people and firms seek out ways to pay less in taxes. And this is consistent with the Principle of Self-Interested Behavior. People will seek out tax-created exceptions to the usual zero-sum-game condition and exploit them whenever possible.

Egotistical people often overlook the Principle of Two-Sided Transactions. Some people suffer from *hubris*, an arrogance due to excessive pride and an insolence toward others. They believe, mistakenly, that they are superior to those with whom they are doing business. Such hubris has led to many unfortunate decisions. Common examples involve corporate takeovers. The managers of an acquiring firm often pay an excessive amount for the target firm they are acquiring. They justify this high price by saying that the current market price is too low or claim that they can manage the targeted firm much more profitably than its current management and thereby increase its value. These managers are implicitly saying that the marketplace is stupidly setting too low a value on the stock or that the target's management is incompetent. Unfortunately, in most cases, an accurate assessment is possible only after the fact. Empirical evidence shows that, on average, managers do not increase the value of their own firm while acquiring another firm—despite their claims.

The management of Sun Microsystems Inc. had met with executives of Apple Computer Inc. to discuss a possible business combination. In mid-January 1996, the *Wall Street Journal* reported that Sun might bid $25 per share for Apple. What do you think happened to Sun's stock price? It fell that day from $48.56 per share to $44.13. Investors apparently felt that Sun would be making a bad investment and paying too much for Apple. They registered their opinion "loudly" by reducing the price they were willing to pay for Sun stock. ■

Sun's Offer to Buy Apple Computer

EXAMPLE

There are at least two sides to every transaction, and the parties on the other side can be just as bright, hard-working, and creative as you are. Underestimating your competitors can lead to disaster.

The Signaling Principle: Actions Convey Information

The Signaling Principle is an extension of the Principle of Self-Interested Behavior. Because of self-interested behavior, a decision to buy or sell an asset can imply information about the condition of the asset or about a decision maker's expectations or plans for the future. Likewise, a firm's decision to enter a new line of business may reflect management's belief in the firm's strength and in a favorable outlook for the venture. Similarly, when a firm announces a dividend, a stock split, or a new securities issue, people frequently interpret these actions in terms of the firm's future earnings. In fact, when actions are at odds with the firm's announcements, the actions usually speak louder than the words.

EXAMPLE

*Actions
Versus
Words*

Janus Chemtech's chief executive officer announces at a securities analysts' meeting that he is very encouraged by his firm's prospects for future earnings growth. At the same time, he reports to the Securities and Exchange Commission that the firm's executives—including the chief executive officer—are selling large numbers of their own shares of the firm's stock. The analyst community is understandably suspicious. ▪

In other cases, of course, decisions may be misinterpreted and presumed to provide information they do not actually convey. For example, recall the temporarily upward-sloping demand curve for flip-flops, discussed in Chapter 1. In that case, many consumers incorrectly thought the incredibly low price for a pair of flip-flops signaled that the product was worthless.

The flip-flop example is a variation of a problem known as **adverse selection**. Loosely speaking, adverse selection is operating when offering something for sale is apparently a negative signal. Adverse selection discourages the inclusion of good-quality products in the market. The problem of adverse selection also occurs in used-equipment markets, where potential buyers question whether the equipment offered for sale is broken or even worthless as opposed to no longer needed. In Chapter 14, we discuss the concept of signaling in more detail.

The Behavioral Principle: When All Else Fails, Look at What Others Are Doing for Guidance

The Behavioral Principle is a direct application of the Signaling Principle. The Signaling Principle says that actions convey information. The Behavioral Principle says, in essence, "Let's try to use such information."

To help you understand the Behavioral Principle, we want you to imagine that you have earned your MBA and have been working for a medium-size corporation for about a year and a half in three different positions. Recently, your hard work and the long hours you have been putting in have been noticed by your boss, Mr. Womack, the financial vice president. In recognition of your accomplishments, Mr. Womack has invited you and your spouse to his home for dinner, along with several other members of the department and their spouses.

You and your spouse are just congratulating each other for having successfully navigated the very formal cocktail hour when you arrive at the dining room. It is larger than your whole apartment. As you seat yourselves in your assigned seats, you and your spouse simultaneously nudge each other, motioning toward the silverware. There is more silverware at your place setting alone than you have in your entire kitchen. And you have not a clue about which piece should be used for which food. What do you do?

There is only one reasonable way to proceed. Unobtrusively, look down the table as each course is served and use the same piece of silverware that Mr. Womack is using. But suppose this isn't possible—you can't see Mr. Womack very well from where you sit. What should you do? You can simply "check out" the people immediately around you. Most of us will go with the majority if there isn't someone we especially trust.

Now change the scenario from dinner to finance. Suppose you are a financial manager. You're facing a major decision that seems to have no single, clearly correct course of action. For example, suppose the board of directors has asked you to assess how the firm is currently being financed and perhaps recommend changes. As it turns out, there is no prescribed single optimal capital structure for a firm; managers must make an informed judgment. What should you do?

One reasonable approach is to look for guidance in what other firms similar to your firm are currently doing and have done in the recent past. Either you can imitate the firms that you feel are most likely to be the best guides, or you can imitate the majority. In particular, the policy choices made by other firms in the same industry can provide useful guidance. This form of behavior is sometimes referred to as the "industry effect." This is what we mean by the Behavioral Principle of Finance: When all else fails, look at what others are doing for guidance.

In practice, the Behavioral Principle is typically applied in two types of situations. In some cases, such as the choice of a capital structure, theory does not provide a clear solution to the problem. In other cases, theory provides a clear solution, but the cost of gathering the necessary information outweighs the potential benefit. Valuing certain assets is an example of the latter case. The value of some assets, such as stock or a piece of real estate, can often be estimated at relatively low cost from the observed recent purchase prices of similar assets. In cases such as these, firms use the Behavioral Principle to arrive at an inexpensive approximation of the correct answer.

We have just cited two appropriate applications of the Behavioral Principle: (1) the case where there is a limit to our understanding and (2) the case where its use is more cost-effective than the most accurate method. One application that sometimes occurs in practice is *not* appropriate: "blind imitation" to minimize personal cost and risk. We want to leave you with an important warning to avoid this misapplication.

The Behavioral Principle can be tricky to apply. You have to decide when there is no single, clearly correct, best course of action. Further, once having decided there is no best course of action, you must decide whether there is a "best" other or group of others to look to for guidance. Finally, you must determine from their actions what your best course of action would be. The Behavioral Principle is, admittedly, a second-best principle. It leads to approximate solutions in the best of situations and, in the worst, to imitating the errors of others. Still, it is useful in certain situations, despite its potential shortcomings.

As with several other principles, there is an important corollary to the Behavioral Principle. Application of the Behavioral Principle in many competitive situations gives rise to what is called the **free-rider** problem. In such situations, a "leader" expends resources to determine a best course of action, and a "follower" receives the benefit of the expenditure by simply imitating. Thus the leader is subsidizing the follower. For example, McDonald's does extensive research and analysis concerning the placement of its restaurants. Other fast-food chains have at times chosen their new restaurant locations by simply building near a McDonald's restaurant. Patent and copyright laws are designed to protect innovators, at least to some extent, from the free-rider problem and to reward the introduction of valuable new ideas that improve society.

Self-Check Questions

1. Explain in your own words the Principle of Self-Interested Behavior.
2. What is a principal-agent relationship? Give some examples.
3. Explain in your own words the Signaling Principle.
4. Explain why the Behavioral Principle does *not* suggest blind imitation.

3.2 VALUE AND ECONOMIC EFFICIENCY

Our second group of principles deals with ways of creating value and economic efficiency.

The Principle of Valuable Ideas: Extraordinary Returns Are Achievable with New Ideas

The Principle of Valuable Ideas says you might find a way to get rich! New products or services can create value, so if you have a new idea, you might then transform it into *extraordinary positive value* for yourself.

Most valuable new ideas occur in the physical-asset markets. Physical assets are more likely than financial assets to be unique. For example, the founders of Apple Computer became wealthy by inventing and successfully introducing the personal computer.

Physical assets can be unique in a number of ways. Consider patents. Thomas Edison became a very wealthy man from having invented a large number of unique products, such as the light bulb, the phonograph, the motion picture, and many others. If patent protection had not been available, it is unlikely that he would have become so wealthy. The ability to hold the exclusive rights to produce a unique product enhances the value of a physical asset. Even without patent protection, some firms have been successful at building brand loyalty. They convince consumers that they are the only firms that can produce particular types of products, and this conviction generates more repeat purchases and purchases of related products.

New ideas may also take the form of improved business practices or marketing. For example, a man named Ray Kroc bought a small chain of hamburger stands. By applying his ideas about how to operate the business, he made himself and a large number of other people very wealthy. You might have heard of Ray's little chain—it is called McDonald's. The list of such products and services is almost endless, and the potential for new products and services *is* endless.

The Principle of Comparative Advantage: Expertise Can Create Value

You may find the Principle of Comparative Advantage familiar. In a broad sense, it is the very idea underlying our economic system. If everyone does what she or he does best, we will have the most qualified people doing each type of work. This creates economic efficiency: We pay others to do what they can do better than we can, and they pay us to do what we can do better than they can.

The Principle of Comparative Advantage is the basis for foreign trade. Each country produces the goods and services that it can make most efficiently. Then, when countries trade, each can be better off.

EXAMPLE **Michael Jordan Plays Better Basketball**	Michael Jordan is arguably the best basketball player of all time, but for personal reasons, he left basketball and tried out for a baseball team. Michael Jordan then played only one season of minor league baseball before "throwing in the towel." He left baseball to others who did that better than he did, and he went back to playing basketball, which he does better than anyone else. ■

The Options Principle: Options Are Valuable

An **option** is a right, without an obligation, to do something. In other words, the owner (the buyer of the option) can require the writer (the seller of the option) to make the transaction specified in the option contract (for example, sell a parcel of land), but the writer cannot require the owner to do anything. Often, in finance, an explicit option contract refers to the right to buy or sell an asset for a prespecified price.

The right to buy is a **call option**, and the right to sell is a **put option**. Call options are frequently used by real estate developers. A call option allows the developer to gain the consent of all necessary parties *before* investing a large amount of money—money that could be lost if any of the parties later refused to sell their land.

Insurance is a kind of put option. Suppose you have insurance on your car, and the car is destroyed by a cement truck while it is parked. The insurance settlement can be viewed as selling the destroyed car to the insurance company. Now you may or may not decide to buy another car, but that's your choice.

A corollary to the Options Principle may help you understand its underlying logic: An option cannot have a negative value to the owner because the owner can always decide to do nothing. If the option transaction will never have positive value, the option may be worthless—but the option can never have a negative value. Of course, even the smallest chance that the option's payoff will have a positive value at *any* time in the future gives the option some positive value, however tiny that value might be.

When people hear the word *options*, they may think of explicit financial contracts such as call options and put options. However, we use the term in its broadest sense: a right with no obligation attached. With such a broad definition, you can see that options are widespread. In fact, they exist in many situations without being noticed. The importance of options extends well beyond their easily identified existence, because many assets contain "hidden" options.

An example of a hidden option involving bankruptcy occurs because of *limited liability*. Limited liability is a legal concept stating that the financial liability of an asset owner is limited in some manner. For example, the stockholders of a corporation have limited liability. If the corporation declares bankruptcy, they do not risk losing any more than what they have already invested in the stock. Bankruptcy provides legal protection from creditors, so the law provides the option to default. That is, the law provides the *option* not to fully repay debts. Of course, this isn't an option you think of right away as being valuable, but it is nevertheless a valuable option. ∎

The Hidden Option to Default

EXAMPLE

Hidden options dramatically complicate the process of measuring value. In some cases, such options actually provide an alternative method of valuing an asset, as we will see when we consider valuing shares of common stock. We will discuss options in greater detail at several points in this text. For now, we hope you can see that an asset plus an option is more valuable than the asset alone.

The Principle of Incremental Benefits: Financial Decisions Are Based on Incremental Benefits

The Principle of Incremental Benefits states that the value derived from choosing a particular alternative is determined by the net extra—that is, incremental—benefit the decision provides compared to its alternative. The term *incremental* is very important. The **incremental costs and benefits** are those that would occur *with* a particular course of action but would not occur *without* taking that course of action. For example, if General Motors spends nothing this year on advertising its products, some people will nevertheless buy GM products. Thus the value to GM of advertising its products is based on the difference between whatever future sales they would make *with* the advertising expenditure and whatever future sales they would make *without* the advertising expenditure. And GM's decision, whether and how much to advertise, is based on the profit from the incremental sales that result from the advertising compared to the cost of the advertising. In other words, the advertising decision is based on the *net* (incremental) change in profit.

In many decisions, the incremental benefits are cash flows. The incremental cash flow is the cash flow that would occur as a result of the decision minus the cash flow that would occur without the decision.

Like many of the other principles described in this chapter, the Principle of Incremental Benefits can get lost when things become complex. But this principle is easily overlooked even in some relatively simple situations. There is one situation in which it may be difficult to accept and apply this principle. It involves the concept of a **sunk cost**. A sunk cost is a cost that has already been incurred; subsequent decisions cannot change it.

EXAMPLE

Lockheed Tri-Star

During the development of Lockheed Corporation's L-1011 tri-star jet, critical decisions were made about whether to continue the project. When the wide-body jet was first proposed, there was enthusiasm in the corporation about its potential. But after considerable work on the project, it became clear that the tri-star project would not be nearly as valuable as expected. Some decision makers at Lockheed proposed abandoning the tri-star. Others argued against such a strategy, because so much had already been spent on its development. The decision to continue with the project proved to be a disaster for Lockheed. Bankruptcy was only narrowly avoided, and the tri-star project was eventually scrapped.[1]

If Lockheed decision makers had applied the Principle of Incremental Benefits, they might have saved a lot of money. At some point, the potential benefits from finishing the project were insufficient to justify the remaining development costs. Concentrating on previous expenditures can obscure the fact that in such cases, the firm should proceed with a project only if the necessary *remaining* costs are less than the projected final benefits from the project. Whatever expenditures have already been incurred—sunk costs—are not relevant to the decision to continue the project, because they cannot be changed. ■

In spite of the Principle of Incremental Benefits, some individuals seem to have an emotional attachment to sunk costs. These people continue to own an asset even though they know they could sell the asset and reinvest their money more profitably elsewhere. Clearly, these individuals are not applying the Principle of Incremental Benefits. They are continuing to incur an opportunity cost. Identifying such situations can be difficult.

Suppose that sometime in the future, the asset is sold for more than its historical cost. The decision maker can point to that fact and claim a "profit," even if greater profit could have been realized if the asset had been sold earlier and the money reinvested elsewhere. That is, the "accounting profit" might hide the fact that an opportunity cost was incurred. Some people vigorously resist selling an asset at a "loss," when its current price is below what they paid for it. Try to remember that an asset isn't like a family member. Most of us are emotional about people, but we recommend you not be emotional about your investments.

---

[1] Someone other than us said, "Sunk costs nearly sunk Lockheed."

Self-Check Questions

1. How does the Apple personal computer illustrate the Principle of Valuable Ideas?
2. Explain in your own words the Principle of Comparative Advantage.
3. What is the main difference between a call option and a put option?
4. Which principle does the following situation illustrate? A firm has developed a computer chip that is half the size, but performs at quadruple the speed, of the best computer chip currently on the market.
5. Which principle does the following situation violate? A firm has invested $50 million in a new computer chip. Its chief scientist wants to abandon the effort, but the vice president for research and development tells securities analysts that the firm "can't afford to abandon the project now."

3.3 FINANCIAL TRANSACTIONS

Our third and last group of principles emerges from observing financial transactions.

The Principle of Risk-Return Trade-Off: There Is a Trade-Off Between Risk and Return

The Principle of Risk-Return Trade-Off is another way of saying that if you want to have a chance at some really great outcomes, you have to take a chance on having a really bad outcome. Even without providing a formal definition of *risk*, we can agree on some of the effects of risk. One important dimension of risk is that higher risk brings with it a greater chance of either a bad outcome or worse possible outcomes. You simply cannot expect to get high returns without simultaneously exposing yourself to the chance of low returns.

When we discussed the Principle of Self-Interested Behavior, we did not talk about how we would operationalize it. We'll do that now. In a financial transaction, we assume that *when all else is equal, people prefer higher return and lower risk*. To appreciate the justification for this assumption, simply ask yourself this question: If you are faced with two alternative choices that are identical (including their riskiness) except that alternative A provides a higher return than B, which alternative will you choose? We predict you will choose A.

Similarly, if you are offered two alternatives that are identical (including their return) except that A is riskier than B, which alternative will you choose? If you are like most people, you will choose B. This behavior is called **risk aversion**: avoiding risk when all else is equal. In other words, investors are not indifferent to risk but require compensation for bearing it.

People generally behave as though they are averse to risk. Almost any decision or choice you make involves risk. For example, decisions to make an investment, take a job, or lend money involve varying degrees of risk. Personal decisions also involve risk, and your personal choices will generally reflect your attitude toward risk.

If people prefer higher return and lower risk and they act in their own financial self-interest, competition then creates the Principle of Risk-Return Trade-Off. Competition forces people to make a trade-off between the return and the risk of their investment. You just can't get high returns and low risk simultaneously because that's what *everyone* wants. Therefore, to get a higher expected return, you'll have to take more risk.

A corollary to the Principle of Risk-Return Trade-Off is that most people are willing to take less return in exchange for less risk. When an asset is bought or sold, its return can be adjusted by altering its sale price. A lower (higher) purchase price increases (decreases) the return. Capital markets, such as the stock market, offer such opportunities, and each participant makes his risk-return trade-off.

The Principle of Diversification: Diversification Is Beneficial

The Principle of Diversification is really quite straightforward. It therefore requires little explanation. A prudent investor will not invest her entire wealth in a single firm. That would expose her entire wealth to the risk that the firm might fail. But if the investment is divided among many firms, the entire investment will not be lost unless all of those firms fail. This is much less likely than that one of them will fail. This practice of spreading investments around instead of concentrating them is called **diversification**. We will explain in Chapter 6 how investors can lower their risk by investing in a group of securities, called a **portfolio**, rather than by investing exclusively in one security.

EXAMPLE

Some Ways to Diversify

Mutual funds, commercial banks, and other financial intermediaries all have very diversified portfolios. No single investment makes up a very large part of their overall portfolios. Individual investors are advised to diversify their portfolios broadly. Operating businesses diversify themselves in many ways. They operate in different business segments. They try to diversify their customer base; that is, they try not to depend too heavily on only a few customers. They diversify their sources of supply. Your college curriculum is diversified, because you cannot concentrate too heavily in one area of study to the exclusion of others. Even a healthy diet should be diversified.

Why is diversification so widespread? Quite simply, because it reduces risk. ■

The Principle of Capital Market Efficiency: The Capital Markets Reflect All Information Quickly

The term **capital market** refers to a market in which securities, such as stocks and bonds, are bought and sold. This buying and selling activity is referred to as **trading**. Probably the best-known capital markets are in New York, London, and Tokyo. The New York and American Stock Exchanges and, especially because of recent television advertising, the NASDAQ (National Association of Securities Dealers Automated Quotation) stock markets are the most widely known in the United States. Together with other stock exchanges around the world and smaller ones around the country, they are collectively referred to as the **stock market**. There are many other capital markets as well, which we discuss later in the chapter.

The Principle of Capital Market Efficiency is formally stated as follows: *Market prices of financial assets that are traded regularly in the capital markets reflect all available information and adjust fully and quickly to "new" information.* How do share prices react to new information? We will use the stock market for illustrative purposes at this point, because it is probably familiar to you.

EXAMPLE

Capital Markets React to New Information

Suppose an oil company were to announce the discovery in the United States of a massive new oil field comparable to the North Slope of Alaska. What stock market trading prices would change? Clearly, the share price of the discovering firm would rise. But what about other oil company stocks? Because of the increase in the supply of oil, the price of oil would decline, bringing down the value of the oil reserves owned by other firms. Therefore, we would expect that the share prices of the other oil companies would tend to fall (unless they were participating in the new discovery). Other share prices might change as well.

For example, cheaper oil should lead to cheaper plastic and increased business for a plastics manufacturer. That would suggest higher share prices for plastics manufacturers. However, the share prices of banks that have loaned Mexico a lot of money might decrease. The lower price of oil would reduce Mexico's oil revenue and increase the likelihood that those banks would not be fully repaid.

Alert traders who recognize these effects would act upon the information. Among other things, they might (1) buy the shares of the oil company that made the discovery, (2) sell the shares of oil companies not involved in the discovery, (3) buy the shares of firms such as plastics manufacturers that would benefit from the lower price of oil, and (4) sell the shares of lenders to Mexico that would be hurt by a lower price of oil.

This active trading is the mechanism by which new information becomes reflected in share prices. As you may have gathered by now, an event like a major oil discovery would provide opportunities to make a great deal of money quickly in many different capital markets. This opportunity to profit from new information provides the incentive to act (recall the Principle of Self-Interested Behavior) that causes share prices to respond to new information. ■

The efficiency of the capital markets depends on how quickly new information is reflected in share prices. For a machine, perfect efficiency means there is no wasted energy—no loss to friction. This is certainly one aspect of capital market efficiency. The capital markets are well organized. The cost of making a transaction (buying or selling) is very low, especially when compared to transaction costs in the real-asset markets (such as machines, real estate, and raw materials). It is generally much easier, cheaper, and faster to buy and sell financial assets than to buy and sell real assets.

For example, a full-service brokerage house such as Merrill Lynch would charge a sales commission of about 1% of the sales value to execute an order to buy or sell 1000 shares of stock selling for $60 per share, a $60,000 transaction. Somewhat lower (higher) commission rates would be charged to handle larger (smaller) transactions. In contrast, a real estate brokerage firm such as Century 21 would charge about 6% of the sale value to sell a $60,000 house. We will have more to say about why this difference exists, but for now let's just note the difference.

In addition to offering convenience, low cost, and high speed, the capital markets are unimaginably large. The New York Stock Exchange alone averages more than $10 billion worth of stock traded each day. There are numerous participants, and competition is intense. When anything happens that might alter the value of a financial asset, there are plenty of people paying close attention because there is a lot of money at stake. And those people can buy or sell their financial assets in minutes or even seconds. This explains why transaction costs and operational efficiencies play an important role in determining the degree of **informational efficiency**: the speed and accuracy with which prices fully reflect new information. The lower the transaction costs and the smaller the other impediments to trading activity, the more quickly and easily market participants can act on new information, and the more quickly share prices adjust to reflect the new information.

In an efficient market that had no impediments to trading, the price of each asset would be the same everywhere in the market, except for temporary differences during periods of disequilibrium. In such a market environment, if price differentials existed, traders would take immediate actions to benefit from those differences through **arbitrage**. Arbitrage is the act of buying and selling an asset simultaneously, where the sale price is greater than the purchase price, so that the difference provides a riskless profit. As long as selling prices exceed buying prices, traders can earn a riskless arbitrage profit. And they can continue to do so until the price differential no longer exists.

We can see, then, that arbitrage opportunities enforce the economic principle called the *law of one price*. This law states that equivalent securities must trade at the same price. The law of one price may not hold strictly when there are transaction costs or other impediments to trading, but it is a good approximation of reality. Arbitrage activity ensures that whatever price differentials exist are smaller than the cost of arbitraging them away. For example, you might see small differences in price between the New York and London prices of gold, despite intense competition. This is due to the cost of shipping gold from one place to another. In the capital markets, with the same kind of intense competition but with essentially zero "shipping costs,"[2] differences in the prices of any particular security tend to be virtually zero.

The Principle of Capital Market Efficiency is probably the easiest to accept. Yet it is also the hardest to "internalize" of all of the Principles of Finance. We all know there are people who win the lottery and people who occasionally amass vast fortunes trading in the stock market. How can we become a winner? How can we start with a small sum and amass a great fortune trading in stocks? (The answer to both questions is the same: only with luck or illegal activity!) If there were a reliable way to amass such a fortune, of course, everyone would do it, and then, instead of one great fortune, there would be a multitude of smaller "fortunes." Yet hope springs eternal!

<table>
<tr><td rowspan="2">**EXAMPLE**</td><td>*Hot Tips and Easy Money*</td><td>The logic of the Principle of Capital Market Efficiency is impeccable, and a lot of empirical research supports it. Nevertheless, investors gobble up hot tips and continue to search for "bargains" in the stock market. Just about every major brokerage house regularly publishes a list of "undervalued stocks." If a stock appears on such a list, investors will evaluate the security and bid up the stock's price if they agree with the brokerage analysts' conclusion. In an efficient market, a stock does not remain undervalued for very long. So how can brokerage houses regularly identify and publish extensive lists of them? What special powers do their analysts possess that enable them to identify such undervalued firms?</td></tr>
<tr><td></td><td>If you are skeptical of the value of such lists, you are not alone. Empirical research has not shown them to provide extra value. People who seem to have the gift of "second sight" are more likely to trade for their own account (take the profits for themselves) than to publish a list so that other people can help themselves to the money. Why? You guessed it—the Principle of Self-Interested Behavior. ■</td></tr>
</table>

In Chapter 14, we will explore how competition, size, and the similarity of assets combine to make the capital markets extremely efficient. Frequently, we assume that the capital markets are *perfect* (100% efficient—no losses due to friction) in order to build a decision model. In fact, a perfect market is the best approximation we have of the capital markets. The assumption of perfect capital markets is like the assumption of risk aversion. Though not always correct, it is widely accepted and useful.

RECONCILING CAPITAL MARKET EFFICIENCY WITH VALUABLE NEW IDEAS

You may find it difficult to reconcile the Principle of Valuable Ideas with the Principle of Capital Market Efficiency. Together, they state that the capital markets are efficient, but that even in the capital markets, with all the competition that exists, a *new* market, product, or service can be created that provides an extraordinary return.

---

[2] The cost to "ship" a security is essentially zero because there is nothing physical to move. It is only information exchanged electronically. Thus although there were *fixed costs* to set up the system, the incremental cost (what economists call the *variable cost*) is simply the electricity cost, which is so small as to be virtually zero for any one transaction.

Here is the critical difference between the two principles. The Principle of Valuable Ideas applies to the return associated with being part of the creation of the opportunity. The Principle of Capital Market Efficiency involves the return associated with simply purchasing part of an opportunity that has become known to everyone. The founders of Apple Computer earned a tremendous rate of return on their investment as a result of their innovations. But what happened as other people became aware of the unique advantages that Apple's computer offered? Those advantages became fully reflected in Apple Computer's share price. Thus once the stock became actively traded, a purchaser of Apple Computer common stock could expect, because of capital market efficiency, to earn only a rate of return commensurate with the risk of the investment. Of course, because of the very nature of risk, the outcome could be quite different from what was expected.

The Time-Value-of-Money Principle: Money Has a Time Value

If you own some money, you can "rent" it to someone else. The borrower must pay you interest for the use of your money (or you won't make the loan). Simply stated, the time value of money is how much it costs to "rent" money.

You can think of the time value of money as the opportunity to earn interest on a bank savings account. A sizable amount of money kept in cash at home creates an opportunity cost, the opportunity to earn interest on the money. For this reason, we think of the interest rate as a measure of the opportunity cost. In fact, because of capital market efficiency, we can use our capital market alternatives as benchmarks against which to measure other investment opportunities: Don't make the investment unless it is at least as good as comparable capital market investments.

Suppose you deposit $1000 today in a bank savings account that is paying 7% per year. One year from today, the account will have $1070. Let's call the starting amount PV (for present value) and next year's account balance FV (for future value). Let r be the interest rate. The interest earned over a time period is the interest rate times the amount deposited initially, $r(\text{PV})$. Then FV is the sum of the starting amount, PV, plus the interest, or

$$FV = PV + r(PV) = PV(1 + r) \tag{3.1}$$

For PV = $1000 and r = 0.07, in one year FV is $1070 (= 1000 × 1.07). In words, Equation (3.1) says the future value equals the present value times 1 plus the interest rate.

Equation (3.1) is based on *per-year* interest. But suppose you save the money for two years? At the end of the first year, the account contains $1070. By reapplying Equation (3.1), at the end of 2 years, you will have

$$FV = \$1070(1.07) = \$1144.90$$

Note that the account will earn $70 interest the first year and an additional $74.90 interest the second year. This is because the interest paid at the end of the first year itself earns interest the second year, amounting to $4.90 (7% of $70). Paying interest on interest already earned is called paying **compound interest**. The process of compounding interest can be handled by extending Equation (3.1). Let n be the number of time periods the money remains in the account. Thus

$$FV = PV(1 + r)^n \tag{3.2}$$

Now let's reverse the logic of Equation (3.2). This time, let's rewrite the equation so that we can solve for PV (instead of FV).

$$PV = \frac{FV}{(1+r)^n} \tag{3.3}$$

This is the form in which the equation is most often used. In words, Equation (3.3) says a dollar today is worth more than a dollar in the future. This is because today's dollar can be invested to earn interest until tomorrow. To determine the present value of an amount of money that will be received in the future, divide the future value by the quantity $(1 + r)^n$. This adjustment reflects the cost to rent money at an interest rate of r per period for n periods. That is, it represents the cost from now until you expect to receive the payment.

To compute a present value, you must estimate the amounts to be received in the future. The future amounts are referred to as *expected future cash flows*. Next, you must estimate the appropriate "rental" rate for each of the expected future cash flows from now until you expect to receive each of them. This rental rate has many different names, but the generic term for it is the **discount rate**.

Equation (3.3) is often referred to as the basic **discounted cash flow (DCF) framework** for valuation. It is simple in the form given, but it can become complex as we combine multiple expected future cash flows and allow the discount rate to change over time. Equation (3.3) can be used to value any asset, provided we can estimate the expected future cash flows and determine an appropriate discount rate for each cash flow. The discount rate must accurately reflect each cash flow's riskiness. Selecting the appropriate discount rate often represents a difficult challenge, even for an expert in finance. Estimating expected future cash flows also requires skill.

The Time-Value-of-Money Principle is probably the most useful concept you can learn in this class. The importance of this principle (and for that matter, of all the principles) rests on its ability to keep our thinking clear and logical. Chapter 4 is devoted to the time value of money, and applications of the principle appear throughout the book. You will encounter the time value of money repeatedly for the rest of your life.

Self-Check Questions

1. What does it mean to say that an investor is risk-averse?
2. What does it mean to say that an investor diversifies her portfolio?
3. Explain in your own words the Principle of Capital Market Efficiency.
4. Why is a dollar today worth more than a dollar to be received a year from today?
5. What is the present value of $100 due at the end of one year when the discount rate is 8%?

3.4 THE CAPITAL MARKETS

Having explained the Time-Value-of-Money Principle, we must now tell you that it comes in many different flavors, shapes, sizes, and colors. That's partly because many different types of securities are traded in the capital markets. As you would expect on the basis of the principles of finance, this trading is watched very carefully by many people for several reasons. One reason is simply that firms make numerous transactions in the capital markets, such as issuing, redeeming, or repurchasing their own securities and investing in other securities. A second reason is that many of the concepts and principles that apply to capital markets are the same concepts and principles that managers use in handling their own firm's real assets. Finally, we know from the Signaling Principle that capital markets provide information and signals that help managers make decisions.

Recall that securities are simply claims on future cash flows. Examples include money market securities, bonds, shares of common stock, and derivatives. We will use the term *capital markets* to refer to the markets, collectively, in which these securities are traded.

This section describes many of these types of securities and the capital markets in which they are traded. The section also describes the roles of the professionals in the capital markets. These include a true smorgasbord of investment bankers, brokers, dealers, banks, mutual funds, and other financial intermediaries.

Money Market Securities

Money market securities are short-term claims with an original maturity that is generally one year or less. The largest markets for money market securities are for Treasury bills, commercial paper, certificates of deposit, and bankers' acceptances. Money market securities tend to be high-grade securities with little risk of default. Because of the short maturities involved, the amount of interest earned simply does not allow much margin for default or for expensive credit investigations. Similarly, the securities rarely offer **collateral**, assets that can be repossessed if the borrower defaults. The risk and amount of interest income are too small to justify the added expense involved with collateral.

TREASURY BILLS   A **Treasury bill (T-bill)** is a short-term security issued by the U.S. government. The government regularly issues T-bills with original maturities of 13 weeks, 26 weeks, and 52 weeks. Most T-bills are sold in $10,000 denominations. T-bills do not have explicitly stated interest. Instead, they are sold on what is called a **discount basis**.

Suppose a 52-week T-bill will pay $10,000 at maturity. You buy this T-bill for $9320. What interest rate would you earn by holding it until maturity?

Recall from Equation (3.1) that the difference between PV (the purchase price) and FV (the maturity value) is the amount of interest, r(PV). So the total amount of interest, r(9320), is $680 (= 10,000 − 9320). To solve for the interest rate, we rearrange Equation (3.1).

$$r = r(\text{PV})/\text{PV} = 680/9320 = 0.073 = 7.3\%$$

Thus the implicit interest rate on this investment is 7.3%. In this example we have the simplicity of a time period that is exactly one year. We will show you in Chapter 4 how to compute interest for time periods other than one year. ■

Computing Implicit Interest

EXAMPLE

COMMERCIAL PAPER   **Commercial paper** is a promissory note sold by very large, creditworthy corporations. The minimum size is typically $100,000. Maturities range from 1 day to 270 days. Longer maturities require registration with the Securities and Exchange Commission, which is a fairly expensive process, so corporations simply don't issue maturities longer than 270 days. Firms that issue commercial paper typically have a standby line of credit from a major bank. That way, if the firm finds itself short of the cash it needs to redeem the commercial paper, it can quickly and easily borrow the necessary funds to fulfill its obligation.

CERTIFICATES OF DEPOSIT   **Certificates of deposit (CDs)** are promises to pay, written by a commercial bank, with maturities typically ranging between six months and five years. CDs are sold at face value and pay a fixed interest rate. The principal and the last period's interest are paid to the lender at maturity. Negotiable CDs have denominations of $100,000 or more and can be traded in the capital markets.

BANKERS' ACCEPTANCES **Bankers' acceptances** are short-term loans made to importers and exporters. They help facilitate international trade. The acceptance occurs when the bank "accepts" a customer's promise to pay. The bankers' acceptance is a guarantee that promises to pay the face amount of the security to whoever presents it for payment. The bank customer uses the bankers' acceptance to finance a transaction by giving the security to a supplier in exchange for goods or services. The supplier can either hold the acceptance until maturity and collect from the bank or sell it at a discount. Bankers' acceptances usually have short maturities (180 days or less). The security is a two-party obligation, a direct customer liability and a contingent liability for the bank. Therefore, the risk of default is very low.

Stocks and Bonds

Stocks and **bonds** are long-term securities issued by corporations or governments.

BONDS Bonds are long-term debt securities. Recall that debt is a legal obligation for borrowed money. A debt security is a promise to pay interest, and to repay the borrowed money, the *principal*, on prespecified terms. Failure to make the promised payments is default. It can lead to bankruptcy. *Bonds* have maturities of ten or more years. *Notes* have maturities between one and ten years. Bonds and notes are often referred to as fixed-income securities, because they promise to pay specific (fixed) amounts to their owners. We provide more information about bonds, including how to value them, in Chapter 5.

STOCKS A share of stock is equity in a corporation. Recall that equity represents ownership. *Common stock* is the residual interest in the firm. It is residual because it is a claim on the earnings and assets of the firm *after* all of the firm's other, more senior obligations have been met. The common shareholders have the dividend rights, voting rights, liquidation rights, and preemptive rights we described in Chapter 1. Common stock does not have a maturity.

Preferred stock also represents an equity claim. There are some important differences between common stock and preferred stock. Preferred stockholders are promised a specific periodic dividend, whereas common stockholders receive whatever dividends are decided on (perhaps none) by the board of directors of the corporation each quarter. Preferred stockholders have a higher priority with respect to the payment of dividends and the distribution of liquidation proceeds. This means that preferred stockholders must be paid their dividends before common stockholders can be paid any dividends. However, if the firm is unable to pay its preferred dividends, it cannot be forced into bankruptcy. Preferred stockholders usually do not have a residual claim on the assets of the firm, as do the common shareholders. Nor do preferred stockholders normally have a right to vote on general corporate matters.

Derivatives

Derivatives are securities that derive their value from the value of another security. Options, forward contracts, and futures are among the most common derivatives.

OPTIONS Recall that an **option** is a right without an obligation. Options to buy and sell securities are available for a price. For instance, suppose a stock is currently worth $15. You can purchase an option to buy the stock at a set price of $20 any time during the next three months. You might pay $1 for this option. The value of the option will depend on the value of the stock. If the stock's value goes up to $35, you can use the option to buy the stock for $20 and come out $14 ahead. (You paid $1 for the option and $20 for the stock, and the stock is now worth $35; 14 = 35 − 20 − 1.) On the other hand, if the stock's value remains at $15, you won't use your option to buy the stock for $20. That would be needlessly spending an extra $5, because you could buy the stock in the market for only $15. At the end of the three months, if the stock is not worth more than $20, the option will be worthless. You will have lost the $1 you paid for the option.

There are many securities with option-like features. A warrant is a long-term option issued by a firm giving its holder the right to buy the stock at a fixed price directly from the firm. A convertible security gives holders the right to exchange the security for common shares.

FUTURES A **future** is a standardized **forward contract** that is traded in a **futures market**. A forward contract is an agreement to buy or sell something for a particular price at a future point in time. Note that a forward contract is not an option—the owner has the obligation to make the transaction. Futures are traded on commodities such as corn, oil, and gold. Futures are also traded on financial assets such as bonds, stocks, and foreign currencies. It may seem odd at first to contract to buy something in the future. Why not simply buy it now or wait and buy it when you need it?

The answer lies in the need to plan. Suppose you don't have a way to store what you are going to need. Or suppose what you are going to need hasn't been produced yet, as in the case of next fall's crop of corn. Market prices change according to supply and demand, so future prices may be different from what we expect. By making the contract now, we can lock in our future needs at an agreed-upon price.

For example, a food packer such as Kraft Foods can plan for its needs for corn meal, and farmers can sell their corn before it is harvested. This enables both parties to benefit from the Principle of Comparative Advantage. By arranging the sale-purchase ahead of time, each side of the transaction can concentrate its efforts on what it does best. It need not worry constantly about what it will pay or earn for corn.

Forward contracts are also traded in private transactions. Though useful and common, such nonstandard contracts do not have the liquidity that the futures market provides.

A **spot market** is a market to buy or sell something for immediate delivery. Some of the same assets are also traded in the futures market.

Primary and Secondary Markets

A **primary market** transaction involves the sale by a firm of newly created securities to get additional financing. The issuing firm receives the proceeds from the sale of the securities. A **secondary market** is a market where previously issued securities are bought and sold. The vast majority of trading in the capital markets is secondary. This is because a primary transaction takes place only once, when issued. However, those securities can be traded later many times.

Brokers, Dealers, and Investment Bankers

Brokers, dealers, and investment bankers facilitate securities trading. Brokers and dealers are middlemen who assist investors in trading securities in the secondary market. A **broker** *helps* investors sell or buy securities, charging a sales commission but without taking ownership of the shares. In contrast, a **dealer** actually takes ownership. She buys securities for, and sells them from, her own account. Suppose you buy 100 shares of Sears stock through a broker. The broker arranges the purchase from someone else, typically through a stock exchange. If instead you buy the shares from a dealer, you are buying the shares from that person.

Although some firms get additional financing by selling securities directly to investors, many others raise capital with the assistance of investment bankers. **Investment bankers** specialize in marketing new securities in the primary market. The people who buy the securities can be individuals or financial institutions, such as pension funds, mutual funds, and insurance companies. In some cases, the investment banker acts as a broker, without taking ownership of the securities. In other cases, the investment banker acts as an **underwriter**, who guarantees a minimum price, thereby acting, in effect, as a dealer. The first time a firm issues shares to the public, it is called an **initial public offering (IPO)**. If the firm later issues additional shares to the public, such offerings are called **seasoned offerings**.

Financial Intermediaries

Financial intermediaries are *institutions* that assist in the financing of firms. Financial intermediaries include commercial banks and pension funds. They invest in securities but are themselves financed by other financial claims.

Commercial banks invest primarily in business and personal loans and in marketable securities. They finance their assets by selling various kinds of deposits, such as checking accounts, money market accounts, savings accounts, and certificates of deposit. Pension funds invest primarily in stocks, bonds, and mortgages. They finance their portfolios with the cash contributions made on behalf of pension beneficiaries and keep the funds invested until it is time to pay them out as benefits. With financial intermediaries, savers are investing in securities but are doing so indirectly. Their savings are used to buy securities. Table 3-1 lists examples of the assets and obligations of various financial intermediaries.

Self-Check Questions

1. What are Treasury bills? How are they different from commercial paper?
2. How is preferred stock different from common stock?
3. What are derivatives?
4. What is the difference between a primary market and a secondary market?
5. What role do intermediaries play in the operation of the financial markets?

TABLE 3-1
Financial intermediaries.

TYPE OF FINANCIAL INTERMEDIARY	PRIMARY KINDS OF INVESTMENTS	TYPES OF OBLIGATIONS
Commercial banks	Short-term loans and securities	Deposit liabilities
Pension funds	Stocks, bonds, mortgages	Obligations to pension beneficiaries
Savings and loans	Mortgages	Share deposits
Mutual savings banks	Mortgages	Share deposits
Credit unions	Personal loans, car loans	Share deposits
Mutual funds	Stocks, bonds, or money market securities	Mutual fund shares
Insurance companies	Bonds, mortgages, stocks	Policy obligations

3.5 THE TERM STRUCTURE OF INTEREST RATES

One way to describe the great variety of debt securities is to graph the relationship between interest rate and maturity for a particular class of debt securities, such as U.S. Treasury securities. This shows how the interest rate depends on maturity. This relationship is called a *yield curve*. One form of yield curve has a special name. The yield curve for zero-coupon U.S. Treasury securities is called the **term structure of interest rates**. (Zero coupon means there are no payments until maturity, so that such securities always trade on a discount basis.) Informally, the phrase *term structure* is sometimes used to refer to the relationship between debt maturity and interest rates, generally. We will use this phrase as well.

Available maturities vary widely. At one extreme, investors borrow for less than a day. For example, banks borrow overnight in the federal funds market. At the other extreme, governments and firms regularly issue bonds with maturities of up to 30 years, and sometimes even as long as 100 years. A virtual continuum of maturities exists between these extremes.

More often than not, interest rates increase with maturity. Figure 3-1 shows a typical upward-sloping term structure of interest rates. There also are much less frequent periods when the reverse is true; the term structure is downward-sloping. Figure 3-2 illustrates this unusual structure. Note that in both cases the curve flattens out as maturity increases, because differences in interest rates typically become less and less significant with longer maturity.

Interest rates are affected by the risk of default and the taxability of the returns. Investors require higher rates to offset tax liabilities and the possibility of default. For this reason, the securities used to compile a yield curve must all have the same default risk and tax status, such as the zero-coupon U.S. Treasury securities used to create the term structure of interest rates. In addition to tax considerations, several other factors affect the term structure of interest rates.

At the most basic level, investors sometimes have a particular desired maturity because they plan to use the money for specific needs, such as retirement or a down payment on a house. Thus investors may seek to invest in maturities that match their needs. Beyond specific needs, shorter maturities provide more liquidity and greater financial flexibility, a form of option that the Options Principle tells us is valuable.

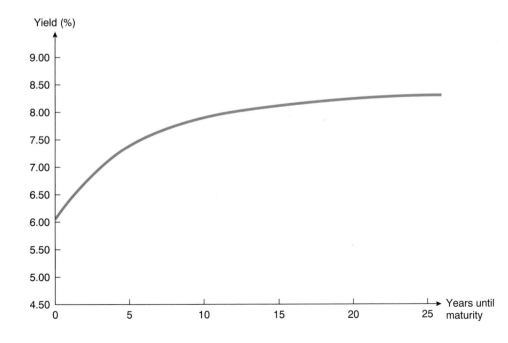

FIGURE 3-1
A typical upward-sloping term structure of interest rates.

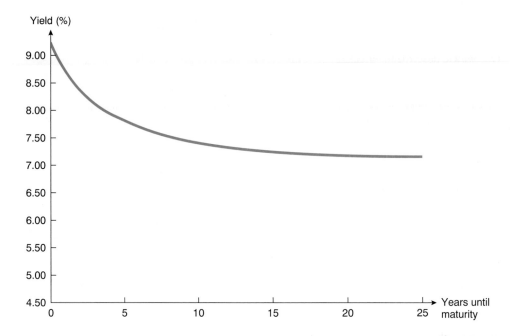

FIGURE 3-2
An example of the unusual downward-sloping term structure of interest rates.

As we will explain in Chapter 5, if all else is equal, longer maturity securities are riskier. Much of this risk depends on inflation expectations, which are an important determinant of interest rates. Therefore, if all else is equal, the Principle of Risk-Return Trade-Off implies that investors will require a higher interest rate (return) to bear the extra risk. This is the basis for the idea that the term structure *should* usually be upward-sloping.

Finally, investors also take into consideration what they expect interest rates to be in the future. That is, if investors believe that long-term interest rates are going to be higher next year, they will want to wait to make a long-term investment. Of course, investors don't hold the cash in a cookie jar while they wait. They put the money in short-term investments, such as money market securities. This kind of "waiting" increases the supply of short-term funds and at the same time decreases the supply of long-term funds. The shift in these supplies lowers the short-term rate and increases the long-term rate, which increases the upward slope of the curve. The reverse happens when investors believe interest rates are going to decrease. This can bring about a downward-sloping term structure. Unusual expectations can even lead to oddly shaped curves that are not consistently upward- or downward-sloping.

The Principle of Capital Market Efficiency tells us that the term structure reflects all the available information about the collective impact of all these factors at any point in time.

Self-Check Questions
1. What is a yield curve?
2. What securities are used to compile the term structure of interest rates?
3. Why is the term structure usually upward-sloping?

3.6 BUSINESS ETHICS

Ethics consists of standards of conduct or moral judgment. Business ethics is a topic of great concern because of the complexity of business relationships. Recall the set-of-contracts model of the firm. The firm is at the center of relationships with many stakeholders, such as customers, employees, managers, shareholders, creditors, suppliers, the community, and governmental units. High standards of ethical conduct require that each stakeholder be dealt with in an honest and fair manner.

There are different levels of ethical behavior. At the most basic level, ethical behavior requires that you comply fully with all of the rules and regulations that apply to your behavior. Failure to do so can result in substantial penalties that include time in jail and fines assessed by regulatory agencies and by courts. The financial consequences often go far beyond these penalties. Many individuals have lost their careers, and businesses have gone bankrupt, because of unethical behavior. The gains from unethical behavior sometimes have been small compared to the ultimate losses due to the loss of trust and reputation.

But behaving ethically means much more than simply following rules and regulations—it requires making personal judgments about right and wrong. Some people believe business is inherently corrupt, immoral, and unethical. However, many others assert that high ethical standards are essential to the profitability and survival of the firm and that ethics in business may be higher than in other segments of society. Why do so many feel that ethical behavior is essential to profitability? There are some clear answers.

1. Ethical behavior avoids fines and legal expenses.

2. It builds customer loyalty and sales.

3. It helps attract and keep high-quality employees and managers.

4. It builds public confidence and adds to the economic development of the communities in which the firm operates.

5. A good reputation enhances relations with the firm's investors.

Ethical behavior can be a necessity for firms to operate profitably and to survive.

Many firms have formal codes of ethics that are a prominent part of their corporate cultures. Managers are often very careful to explore the ethical dimensions of their decisions. Furthermore, if you join a profession—such as accounting, financial analysis, personnel management, or real estate brokerage—there will be professional societies with codes of ethics you must know and follow. In addition, professionals in many fields are regulated by government agencies and are thus subject to special licensing procedures and rules of conduct.

Self-Check Questions

1. Why should a financial manager be concerned with business ethics?

2. Why is ethical behavior essential to profitability?

3. Ethical behavior simply means complying with all explicitly stated rules and regulations. Do you agree or disagree?

SUMMARY

In this chapter we presented the principles of finance and described the financial environment. The principles of finance are simply careful statements about known relationships in the real world.

When combined and built upon, the principles of finance produce useful and sometimes surprising insights. Yet once these insights are understood, they become common sense—as with the principle "What goes up must come down." Taking the analogy one step further, we now know that this principle is not literally correct: The space probe Voyager II will never return to earth. It went up, but it will never come down. In spite of this violation, the principle has provided immeasurable benefits and serves as a foundation for modern technology. So, too, the principles of finance provide a foundation for decision making in the financial world.

As a "first" application of these principles, consider the goal of a firm. What is the appropriate goal? In Chapter 1, we noted that the investment-vehicle model of the firm embodies the often-stated goal of *maximizing shareholder wealth*. You can now see that this goal is a direct application of the Principle of Self-Interested Behavior. The shareholders are the owners of the firm. The owners are entitled to a return (rent) from the use of their money, so how do they want the firm to act? The answer, of course, is that they want the firm to act in their best interests—to maximize their wealth.

The capital markets are well-organized markets in which securities are traded. They process a tremendous volume of transactions. Three broad types of securities are available to investors in the capital markets: money market securities, stocks and bonds, and derivatives.

Primary markets are markets where firms sell new securities to obtain additional financing. The vast majority of trading is in secondary markets, where existing securities trade.

Investment bankers, brokers, and dealers facilitate securities trading. Financial intermediaries are institutions that invest in securities but are themselves financed by issuing other financial claims.

The term structure represents the relationship between interest rates and maturity. Generally, this relationship is upward-sloping. Longer maturities require higher interest rates, but differences become less significant the longer the maturity. The main factors that affect the term structure are taxes, default risk, maturity, and expected future changes in interest rates.

Business ethics, standards of conduct, and moral judgment are central to a firm's operations and profitability. At the most basic level, ethical behavior requires full compliance with all relevant rules and regulations.

DECISION SUMMARY

- People act in their own financial self-interest.
- There are at least two sides to every transaction.
- Actions convey information.
- You can learn from what others are doing.
- New ideas may create extraordinary value.
- Expertise can be a source of value.
- Options are valuable.

- Value is measured incrementally.
- Investors require compensation for taking risk.
- Diversification can reduce risk.
- The capital markets are efficient.
- Money has a time value.
- Money markets offer short-term investments such as Treasury bills, commercial paper, certificates of deposit, and bankers' acceptances.
- Stocks and bonds are long-term investments.
- Derivative markets offer securities, such as options and futures, whose values depend on the value of some other asset, such as a stock, commodity, or foreign currency.
- Investors require higher returns to offset tax liabilities and the possibility of default.
- Shorter maturities provide more liquidity and greater financial flexibility.
- Investors sometimes prefer maturities that exactly match their needs.
- Longer maturity securities are riskier, if all else is equal.
- Anticipated changes in interest rates make some maturities more advantageous.

EQUATION SUMMARY

(3.1) $$FV = PV + r(PV) = PV(1 + r)$$

(3.2) $$FV = PV(1 + r)^n$$

(3.3) $$PV = \frac{FV}{(1 + r)^n}$$

KEY TERMS

EXERCISES

PROBLEM SET A

A1. Define the term *opportunity cost*.

A2. What is a principal-agent relationship?

A3. Cite an example in which the problem of moral hazard can arise in a principal-agent relationship.

A4. Define the term *portfolio*.

A5. What is a zero-sum game?

A6. Define the term *sunk cost*.

A7. Describe a situation that involves information signaling.

A8. Cite a situation in which the problem of adverse selection can arise.

A9. Define the term *arbitrage*.

A10. Distinguish between each of the following pairs of terms:

   a. Spot market and futures market

   b. Call option and put option

   c. Option contract and future contract

   d. Broker and dealer

   e. Investment banker and financial intermediary

   f. Primary market and secondary market

   g. Initial public offering (IPO) and seasoned offering

   h. Forward contract and future contract

   i. Stock and bond

A11. Define the terms *option*, *call option*, and *put option*.

A12. An investor deposits $1000 into a bank account that pays interest at the rate of 10% per year. She leaves the money and all accrued interest in the account for 5 years.

   a. How much money does she have after 1 year?

   b. How much money does she have at the end of the fifth year?

A13. How would your answers to Problem A12 change if interest was paid quarterly—that is, at the end of each quarter in an amount equal to 2.5% of the account balance?

A14. What is the present value of $10,000 to be received seven years from today when the annual discount rate is 12%?

A15. Describe the term structure (of interest rates) and cite the factors that cause it to exist.

PROBLEM SET B

B1. Explain how the Signaling Principle derives from the Principle of Self-Interested Behavior.

B2. Describe in your own words what is meant by the term *efficient capital market*.

B3. Define the term *limited liability*. How does limited liability create an option for a borrower?

B4. *USA Today* once reported that executives of Teradyne had told Wall Street analysts that "business was jumping," but the next day the firm's chairman sold 24,800 shares of his stock in the firm for $32 each, or $793,600. The chairman's secretary said the shares belonged to his daughter. Interpret these events in light of the Signaling Principle.

B5. Explain how the Behavioral Principle derives from the Signaling Principle.

B6. Cite two appropriate and two inappropriate applications of the Behavioral Principle.

B7. Describe a situation wherein you might want to guard against the free-rider problem.

B8. Explain in your own words the idea of compounding interest.

B9. What is the present value of $5000 to be received in two equal installments ($2500 each), four years and five years from today, when the annual discount rate is 10%?

B10. Suppose buy orders are placed for twice as many shares of a stock as the number of shares offered for sale in a 1-hour period. What would be the relationship (higher, lower, or the same) between the reported trading price just before and just after that 1-hour period, assuming no other events occurred?

B11. Explain why the Principle of Two-Sided Transactions is important to financial decision making.

B12. Describe in your own words why financial decisions are based on incremental benefits. How does a sunk cost affect the incremental benefit from a decision?

B13. What is the major distinction between debt and equity? Why is it so important?

PROBLEM SET C

C1. When IBM introduced a new line of personal computers, the *Wall Street Journal* reported that this event would trigger "a new phase of competition in the computer industry." How would you expect the prices of other personal computer manufacturers' common stocks to react to this announcement?

C2. How are the Principles of Self-Interested Behavior and Two-Sided Transactions related to the Principle of Capital Market Efficiency?

C3. Cite an example in which it is not possible to measure *exactly* the opportunity cost of an alternative. Is it possible to measure exactly the opportunity cost of an alternative in most situations?

C4. Suppose you are a manager in a manufacturing business. How are the capital markets relevant to the effective performance of your job?

C5. In our discussion of the Principle of Capital Market Efficiency, we introduced the concept of arbitrage. We also said we would later on assume that the capital markets are perfect. How can the concept of arbitrage be used as the basis for a definition of a perfect capital market?

Real-World Application:
Dividend Policy at Delmarva Power & Light

Suppose you have just graduated and gone to work as a financial analyst in the Treasury Department at Delmarva Power & Light Company. Delmarva supplies electricity to Delaware and parts of Maryland and Virginia, and also gas to the Wilmington, Delaware, area.

Your first task is to help prepare a dividend study to present to Delmarva's Board of Directors. (We discuss *dividend policy* in Chapters 17 and 18. It involves deciding what portion of a firm's profit and cash flow to distribute in cash to its shareholders.)

You gather the following information concerning Delmarva's recent dividend actions:

YEAR	DIVIDEND PER SHARE	EARNINGS PER SHARE	CASH FLOW PER SHARE	YEAR	DIVIDEND PER SHARE	EARNINGS PER SHARE	CASH FLOW PER SHARE
1995	$1.54	$1.79	$3.80	1990	$1.54	$1.49	$3.20
1994	1.54	1.67	3.50	1989	1.51	1.80	3.42
1993	1.54	1.76	3.43	1988	1.47	1.70	3.37
1992	1.54	1.48	3.21	1987	1.43	1.60	3.08
1991	1.54	1.44	3.06	1986	1.36	1.94	3.13

1. What pattern is evident in Delmarva's dividend per share?

2. A firm's *payout ratio* is the ratio of the dividend per share to earnings per share. Calculate Delmarva's payout ratio for each year. Do you see any pattern?

3. What percentage of its cash flow per share did Delmarva pay as a dividend each year? Do you see any pattern?

You also gather the following information concerning dividend actions by the ten electric utility firms that Delmarva considers most similar to itself. Delmarva looks at the dividend policies of these firms for guidance in setting its own dividend policy.

FIRM	PAYOUT RATIO (%)					DIVIDEND/CASH FLOW PER SHARE (%)				
	1995	1994	1993	1992	1991	1995	1994	1993	1992	1991
Allegheny Power	80.5	85.9	86.7	88.0	87.8	39.8	43.6	45.0	45.7	44.9
Atlantic Energy	99.4	109.2	85.6	100.0	85.7	48.1	55.8	50.5	54.3	50.3
Baltimore G&E	76.7	78.2	79.5	87.7	92.1	36.5	37.6	41.2	45.5	44.0
Duquesne Light	55.0	56.8	59.7	57.9	58.1	27.5	27.9	27.9	25.7	24.9
Dominion Res.	96.3	90.7	79.5	90.2	78.6	41.0	40.3	37.5	39.7	36.2
Gen. Pub. Util.	64.6	72.1	63.4	70.5	60.7	30.7	33.3	29.5	30.0	28.1
Peco Energy Co.	65.2	88.1	58.4	61.3	57.2	37.1	41.3	32.8	29.5	28.0
PP&L Resources	81.5	100.0	79.7	78.7	77.1	41.2	47.7	41.9	38.6	36.6
Potomac Elec. Pwr.	97.6	92.7	84.1	96.4	85.0	48.1	50.3	49.7	54.4	52.2
P.S. Enterprise Gp.	79.7	77.7	79.7	109.6	87.7	39.6	40.4	42.0	46.2	41.8

4. Which principle of finance is Delmarva putting into practice when it sets its dividend policy?

5. Calculate the range and average payout ratio for the other ten firms for each year.

6. Calculate the range and average percentage of cash flow paid out for the other ten firms for each year.

7. How does Delmarva's payout ratio and percentage of cash flow paid out compare to the respective averages and ranges?

8. Suppose Delmarva expects to earn $1.90 per share and have $3.90 cash flow per share in 1996. Calculate its payout ratio and percentage of cash flow paid out assuming it doesn't change its dividend per share. Are these ratios in line with the historical averages for the other firms?

9. Suppose Delmarva expects to earn $2.50 per share and have $5.25 cash flow per share. Would its payout ratio and percentage of cash flow paid out be out of line with the averages if it continued the $1.54 dividend?

10. Would these ratios be out of line if Delmarva raised the dividend to $2.00 per share?

BIBLIOGRAPHY

Ackert, Lucy F., and Brian F. Smith. "Stock Price Volatility, Ordinary Dividends, and Other Cash Flows to Shareholders," *Journal of Finance*, 1993, 48(4):1147–1160.

Akerlof, George A. "The Market for 'Lemons': Quality Uncertainty and the Market Mechanism," *Quarterly Journal of Economics*, 1970, 84(August):488–500.

Ambrose, Brent W., and Drew B. Winters. "Does an Industry Effect Exist for Leveraged Buyouts?" *Financial Management*, 1992, 21(1):89–101.

Asquith, Paul, and David W. Mullins, Jr. "Signalling with Dividends, Stock Repurchases, and Equity Issues," *Financial Management*, 1986, 15(3):27–44.

Baker, George P., Michael C. Jensen, and Kevin J. Murphy. "Compensation and Incentives: Practice vs. Theory," *Journal of Finance*, 1988, 43(3):593–616.

Balvers, Ronald J., Thomas F. Cosimano, and Bill McDonald. "Predicting Stock Returns in an Efficient Market," *Journal of Finance*, 1990, 45(4):1109–1128.

Berry, Thomas D., and Keith M. Howe. "Public Information Arrival," *Journal of Finance*, 1994, 49(4):1331–1346.

Black, Fischer, and Myron Scholes. "The Pricing of Options and Corporate Liabilities," *Journal of Political Economy*, 1973, 81(May/June):637–654.

Brous, Peter Alan. "Common Stock Offerings and Earnings Expectations: A Test of the Release of Unfavorable Information," *Journal of Finance*, 1992, 47(4):1517–1536.

Christie, William G., Jeffrey H. Harris, and Paul H. Schultz. "Why Did NASDAQ Market Makers Stop Avoiding Odd-Eighth Quotes?" *Journal of Finance*, 1994, 49(5):1841–1860.

Christie, William G., and Paul H. Schultz. "Why Do NASDAQ Market Makers Avoid Odd-Eighth Quotes?" *Journal of Finance*, 1994, 49(5):1813–1840.

Conrad, Jennifer, and Gautam Kaul. "Long-Term Market Overreaction or Biases in Computed Returns?" *Journal of Finance*, 1993, 48(1):39–64.

Crutchley, Claire E., and Robert S. Hansen. "A Test of the Agency Theory of Managerial Ownership, Corporate Leverage, and Corporate Dividends," *Financial Management*, 1989, 18(4):36–46.

Ederington, Louis H., and Jae Ha Lee. "How Markets Process Information: News Releases and Volatility," *Journal of Finance*, 1993, 48(4):1161–1192.

Fama, Eugene. "Efficient Capital Markets: A Review of Theory and Empirical Work," *Journal of Finance*, 1970, 25(2):383–417.

Fama, Eugene F. "Efficient Capital Markets: II," *Journal of Finance*, 1991, 46(5):1575–1618.

Fisher, Irving. *The Theory of Interest*. New York: Augustus M. Kelley, 1965 (reprinted from the original edition published in 1930).

Froot, Kenneth A., David S. Scharfstein, and Jeremy C. Stein. "Herd on the Street: Informational Inefficiencies in a Market with Short-Term Speculation," *Journal of Finance*, 1992, 47(4):1461–1484.

Hasbrouck, Joel, and George Sofianos. "The Trades of Market Makers: An Empirical Analysis of NYSE Specialists," *Journal of Finance*, 1993, 48(5):1565–1593.

Hirshleifer, David, Avanidhar Subrahmanyam, and Sheridan Titman. "Security Analysis and Trading Patterns When Some Investors Receive Information Before Others," *Journal of Finance*, 1994, 49(5):1665–1698.

Jegadeesh, Narasimhan, and Sheridan Titman. "Returns to Buying Winners and Selling Losers: Implications for Stock Market Efficiency," *Journal of Finance*, 1993, 48(1):65–92.

Jensen, Michael C., and William H. Meckling. "Theory of the Firm: Managerial Behavior, Agency Costs and Ownership Structure," *Journal of Financial Economics*, 1976, 3(4):305–360.

Jordan, James V. "Tax Effects in Term Structure Estimation," *Journal of Finance*, 1984, 39(2):393–406.

Jose, Manuel L., Len M. Nichols, and Jerry L. Stevens. "Contributions of Diversification, Promotion, and R&D to the Value of Multiproduct Firms: A Tobin's q Approach," *Financial Management*, 1986, 15(4):33–42.

Krueger, Thomas M., and William F. Kennedy. "An Examination of the Super Bowl Stock Market Predictor," *Journal of Finance*, 1990, 45(2):691–698.

Lee, Winson B., and Elizabeth S. Cooperman. "Conglomerates in the 1980s: A Performance Appraisal," *Financial Management*, 1989, 18(1):45–54.

Leland, Hayne E., and David H. Pyle. "Informational Asymmetries, Financial Structure, and Financial Intermediation," *Journal of Finance*, 1977, 32(2):371–387.

Liu, Pu, Stanley D. Smith, and Azmat A. Syed. "Stock Price Reactions to the *Wall Street Journal*'s Securities Recommendations," *Journal of Financial and Quantitative Analysis*, 1990, 25(3):399–410.

Longstaff, Francis A., and Eduardo S. Schwartz. "Interest Rate Volatility and the Term Structure: A Two-Factor General Equilibrium Model," *Journal of Finance*, 1992, 47(4):1259–1282.

Markowitz, Harry M. "Portfolio Selection," *Journal of Finance*, 1952, 7(1):77–91.

McCulloch, J. Huston. "A Reexamination of Traditional Hypotheses About the Term Structure: A Comment," *Journal of Finance*, 1993, 48(2):779–789.

McInish, Thomas H., and Robert A. Wood. "An Analysis of Intraday Patterns in Bid/Ask for NYSE Stocks," *Journal of Finance*, 1992, 47(2):753–764.

Merton, Robert C. "A Functional Perspective of Financial Intermediation," *Financial Management*, 1995, 24(2):23–41.

Michel, Allen, and Israel Shaked. "Does Business Diversification Affect Performance?" *Financial Management*, 1984, 13(4):18–25.

Miller, Merton H., and Franco Modigliani. "Dividend Policy, Growth, and the Valuation of Shares," *Journal of Business*, 1961, 34(October):411–433.

Mitchell, Mark L., and J. Harold Mulherin. "The Impact of Public Information on the Stock Market," *Journal of Finance*, 1994, 49(3):923–950.

Modigliani, Franco, and Merton H. Miller. "The Cost of Capital, Corporation Finance, and the Theory of Investment," *American Economic Review*, 1958, 48(June):261–297.

Myers, Stewart C., and Nicholas S. Majluf. "Corporate Financing and Investment Decisions When Firms Have Information That Investors Do Not Have," *Journal of Financial Economics*, 1984, 13(2):187–221.

Netter, Jeffry, and Annette Poulsen. "State Corporation Laws and Shareholders: The Recent Experience," *Financial Management*, 1989, 18(3):29–40.

Pearson, Neil D., and Tong-Sheng Sun. "Exploiting the Conditional Density in Estimating the Term Structure: An Application of the Cox, Ingersoll, and Ross Model," *Journal of Finance*, 1994, 49(4):1279–1304.

Ravid, S. Abraham, and Oded H. Sarig. "Financial Signalling by Committing to Cash Outflows," *Journal of Financial and Quantitative Analysis*, 1991, 26(2):165–180.

Roll, Richard. "What Every CO Should Know About Scientific Progress in Financial Economics: What Is Known and What Remains to Be Resolved," *Financial Management*, 1994, 23(2):69–75.

Sharpe, William F. "Capital Asset Prices: A Theory of Market Equilibrium Under Conditions of Risk," *Journal of Finance*, 1964, 19(3):425–442.

Shefrin, Hersh, and Meir Statman. "Behavioral Aspects of the Design of Financial Products," *Financial Management*, 1993, 22(2):123–134.

Singh, Ajai K., Mir A. Zaman, and Chandrasekhar Krishna-murti. "Liquidity Changes Associated with Open Market Repurchases," *Financial Management*, 1994, 23(1):47–55.

Slovin, Myron B., and Marie E. Sushka. "Ownership Concentration, Corporate Control Activity, and Firm Value: Evidence from the Death of Inside Blockholders," *Journal of Finance*, 1993, 48(4):1293–1321.

Spence, Michael. "Competitive and Optimal Responses to Signals: Analysis of Efficiency and Distribution," *Journal of Economic Theory*, 1974, 7:296–332.

Tobin, J. "Liquidity Preference as Behavior Towards Risk," *Review of Economic Studies*, 1958, 26(February):65–86.

Winton, Andrew. "Limitation of Liability and the Ownership Structure of the Firm," *Journal of Finance*, 1993, 48(2): 487–512.

Part II

VALUATION

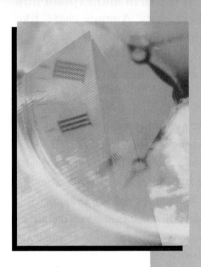

Part II builds on the foundation we established in Part I and constructs the valuation framework we will use in the rest of the book. Valuation is important in just about everything in finance. Part II gives you the valuation basics. Beginning in Part III, we'll show you how to apply these basic techniques to specific problems that firms must solve to manage their assets and liabilities effectively.

Chapter 4 is devoted to the Time-Value-of-Money Principle. In it we will develop the tools for measuring the time value of money. We will demonstrate how to calculate *present value* and how to determine the value, at *any* point in time, of cash flows that actually occur at other points in time. We'll use the time-value-of-money tools in Chapter 5 to value *bonds* and *stocks,* which are the most common and basic types of financial securities.

The value of a security is the present value of its expected future cash flows. The present value reflects both the time value and the risk of the expected cash flows. Chapter 6 explains how to measure risk. We will show you that an asset's risk, and therefore its *required return*, depends on how the asset's expected future cash flows *covary* with all other assets. In Chapter 7, we'll use what we learned about risk in Chapter 6 to develop a very useful model, the *capital-asset-pricing model,* for calculating an asset's required return.

Chapters 8 and 9 explain two special sets of factors that can have an important effect on value: *options* and *agency costs*. They occur frequently but are often difficult to spot. We cover them early in the book to alert you to them. This early coverage also allows us to integrate their significant effects on valuation into our analysis and decision making.

In Chapter 8, we will teach you about the factors that determine an option's value and explore how changes in

4.1 NET PRESENT VALUE AND RATES OF RETURN

Determining the present value of an asset's expected future cash flows—Equation (3.3)—is one way to value the asset. Another way is to find out what it would cost to *buy* such an asset. The difference between what an asset is worth (the present value of its expected future cash flows) and its cost is the asset's **net present value (NPV)**.

$$\text{NPV} = \text{Present value of expected future cash flows} - \text{Cost}$$

A positive NPV increases wealth because the asset is worth more than it costs. A negative NPV decreases wealth, because the asset costs more than it is worth.

It is almost impossible to overstate the importance of the net-present-value concept. NPV appears in connection with virtually every topic in this book, and most financial decisions can be viewed in terms of net present value. NPV measures the value created or lost by a financial decision. However, NPV is measured from a benchmark of the "normal" market return. Therefore, a zero-NPV decision earns the appropriate return, and is "fair." A decision that earns less than the appropriate return is undesirable and has a negative NPV. Positive-NPV decisions earn more than the appropriate return. Firms that pursue the goal of maximizing shareholder wealth seek to make positive-NPV decisions.

The Principle of Capital Market Efficiency says that current market prices of financial securities reflect all available information. That is, financial securities are priced fairly. A **fair price** is a price that does not favor either the buyer's or seller's side of the transaction. Another way to say this is that a fair price makes the NPV from investing equal zero. Sometimes, people ask, "If the NPV is zero, why would anyone purchase a financial security?" The answer is to earn a profit. Remember, a zero NPV implies that the investor will earn an appropriate return for the investment risk, *not* a zero return.

The Principle of Risk-Return Trade-Off implies that investors who take more risk will earn a larger profit, on average. The decision to invest in (purchase) a financial security with NPV = 0 often involves risk. But in exchange for that risk, you get a chance at a higher return.[1]

In the appendix to this chapter, we show how the NPV rule derives from the capital markets' ability to allocate resources efficiently throughout society. Using the NPV rule, in turn, contributes to the efficient allocation of resources. The NPV rule is intuitive and can be readily applied in practice. The appendix provides the theoretical basis for this very practical rule.

Required, Expected, and Realized Rates of Return

An important aspect of any present-value calculation is the *discount rate*, the price for "renting" the money. We describe and discuss here three different rates of return. Distinguishing among these three concepts is critical.

REQUIRED RATE OF RETURN   The **required rate of return** is the return that exactly reflects the riskiness of the expected future cash flows. We can also describe it as the minimum return a person must earn to be willing to make an investment (purchase an asset).[2] An important way to approximate this return is based on the concept of an opportunity cost: The re-

---

[1] Of course, with risky investments, the outcome may be extremely good, extremely bad, or anywhere in between. However, before you make the investment, your expectation must be favorable, despite the risk. Otherwise, you won't make the investment.

[2] At the risk of confusing you, we want to make a very important point that we will explain in detail in Chapter 14. The required return is based on market conditions, *not* on an individual person's situation. This is because in a competitive market, people sell to the highest bidder. As a result, prices reflect only the highest bidder's situation. Regardless of their own circumstances, others must pay this highest-bid market price if they want to participate.

quired return is the return on alternative investments of equal risk. An example of such an alternative might be a financial security with the same risk.

EXPECTED RATE OF RETURN   The **expected rate of return** is what you expect to earn if you make an investment. Another way to say the same thing is to say that the expected return is the return that would make the NPV zero. When the NPV is zero, the investment is expected to earn the rate of return that is appropriate (required) for its level of risk. Therefore, when the NPV is zero, the expected return equals the required return.

REALIZED RATE OF RETURN   The **realized rate of return** is the return that was actually earned during a given time period. It is critical to understand that this is an outcome, the result of having made the decision to invest. You cannot go back and change the realized rate of return. You can only make new decisions in reaction to it.

Confusion between the expected and required returns arises because they are always equal in a perfect capital market environment, where all investment NPVs are zero and all prices are fair prices. In such an environment, everyone can expect to earn the required return for the risk they bear.

Confusion between the expected and realized returns is created by risk. Because of risk, the outcome rarely equals the expected amount. In fact, one way to think about risk is to consider how different the outcome can be from the expected amount. The risk is high when the difference can be great. The risk is low when there cannot be much difference.

Let's review and summarize the relationships among these concepts by using an investment you might make. First, on the basis of other possible investments of the same risk, you determine a minimum return you would have to earn to be willing to invest. (Otherwise, you would simply invest your money in one of these alternatives.) This is the *required* return. Next, you estimate the return if you were to make the investment. This is the *expected* return. Then you decide whether to make the investment. If the expected return is more than the required return, the investment is worth more than its cost, and the NPV is positive. A positive NPV creates value, whereas a negative NPV loses value. Let's say the NPV is positive, and you make the investment.

Finally, later on, the investment pays off. The payoff is the *realized* return. If the realized return is bad (low, negative, or perhaps even zero—you get nothing back), you are not happy, but that is the fundamental nature of risk! After the return is realized, you can't turn back the clock and decide not to make the investment after all. Of course, if the realized return is good (equal to or greater than the expected return), you're glad you made the investment. Therefore, the realized return is disconnected—by risk—from the required and expected returns, despite its vital importance and our desire for it to be large.

Definitions, Assumptions, and Some Advice

We need to give you several additional definitions and underlying assumptions. Please read through the complete list of notations and assumptions now, even though we won't explain some of the terms until later.

CASH FLOWS OCCUR AT THE END OF THE TIME PERIOD   Unless otherwise stated, cash flows occur at the end of the time period.

CASH OUTFLOWS ARE NEGATIVE VALUES   Positive cash flows are inflows, and negative cash flows are outflows from the decision maker's viewpoint. The decision maker can be a firm or an individual. In other words, the algebraic sign indicates whether the amount is an inflow (+) or an outflow (−) to the decision maker.

THE DECISION POINT IS $t = 0$ Unless otherwise stated, "now" is the instant before $t = 0$. That is, $t = 0$ cash flows (in or out) are just about to occur. In other words, you can still make a decision that affects them.

COMPOUNDING FREQUENCY IS THE SAME AS PAYMENT FREQUENCY   Unless otherwise stated, financial transactions assume that the compounding frequency is identical to the payment frequency. For example, if there are monthly payments, the interest compounding is also monthly.

NOTATION

t	A time period. For example, $t = 3$ is time period 3.
CF_t	The net cash flow at time t. For example, CF_3 is the net cash flow at the end of time period 3.
CF	The net cash flow each period for an annuity.
r	The discount rate per period. For example, $r = 0.02$ is 2% per time period.
m	The number of compounding periods per year.
APR	The annual percentage rate (nominal annual rate). The APR equals r times m.
APY	The annual percentage yield (effective annual rate). The APY is the amount you would actually earn if you invested for exactly one year and if the investment paid interest at r per period for m periods.
n	A number of time periods. For example, n might be 36 months.
FV_t	A future value at time t. For example, FV_5 is a future value at the end of time period 5.
FVA_n	The future value of an n-period annuity (at $t = n$).
PV	A present-value amount.
PVA_n	The present value of an n-period annuity (at $t = n$).
NPV	The net present value.

Equations (3.2) and (3.3) were derived in our discussion of the Time-Value-of-Money Principle in Chapter 3. Equation (3.3) is the **present-value formula**, which we restate here for convenience.

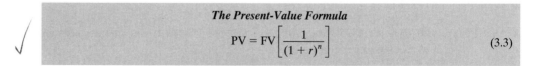

The Present-Value Formula

$$PV = FV \left[\frac{1}{(1 + r)^n} \right] \tag{3.3}$$

The amount $1/(1 + r)^n$ is called the **present-value factor.** Figure 4-1 is a graph of the present-value factor as a function of time and various discount rates. As you can see there, present value is inversely related to both time and the discount rate. That is, the larger the discount

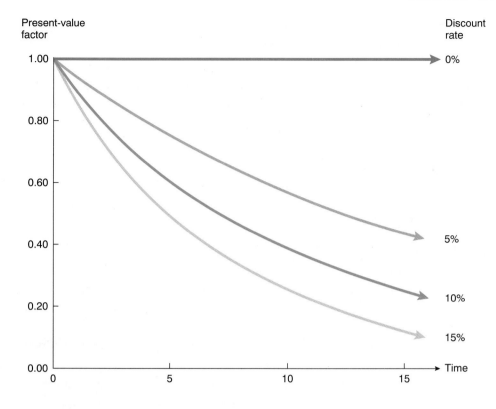

FIGURE 4-1
The present-value factor as a function of time and various discount rates.

rate, the smaller the present value. For positive discount rates, the more time until you get the cash flow, the smaller the present value will be.

Equation (3.2) is the **future-value formula**. We restate this for convenience, too.

> *The Future-Value Formula*
> $$FV = PV(1 + r)^n \qquad (3.2)$$

The amount $(1 + r)^n$ is called the **future-value factor**. Figure 4-2 is a graph of the future-value factor as a function of time and various discount rates. As you can see there, future value is directly related to both time and the discount rate. The larger the discount rate, the larger the future value. For positive discount rates, the more time, the larger the future value.

CALCULATORS   There are five basic input variables to a (financial) calculator:

PV   Present value

FV   Future value

n   The number of time periods.

i, k, or *r*   The discount rate per period. We use *r* throughout this book.

Pmt or CF   A cash flow. Pmt always indicates an annuity. CF can be a single cash flow or the cash flow for an annuity.

The basic calculator formula encompasses each of the four basic time-value-of-money formulas that we will explain in this chapter. For this reason, at the start, you may need to put in a zero for some variables we have not yet explained. Even though you may not understand the basic calculator formula yet, we will state it now. That way, you can refer to it, and see how

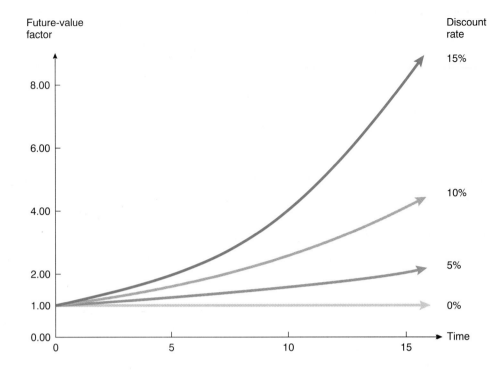

Future-value
factor

Discount
rate

FIGURE 4-2
The future-value factor as a function of time and various discount rates.

each of the basic time-value-of-money formulas is part of it, as we explain that formula.

The Basic Calculator Formula

$$PV = CF \left[\frac{(1 + r)^{n} - 1}{r(1 + r)^{n}} \right] + FV \left[\frac{1}{(1 + r)^{n}} \right]$$

The calculator solves this equation for each time-value-of-money calculation. It computes the variable you want on the basis of the values you put in for all the other variables. Amounts can be positive or negative.[3]

Calculators sometimes retain values from previous calculations. Therefore, if you don't put in a value for a variable, it may use a value from a previous calculation and give you an incorrect answer. You can avoid this problem in two ways. One way is to push the "clear-all" button to zero out all entries. (Be sure to use the "clear-all" rather than the "clear-the-latest-entry" button. The calculator's "how-to" book will describe both procedures.) Another way to avoid the problem is to enter a zero for any variables not otherwise used.

---

[3] Some calculators use a slightly modified version of the basic calculator formula: They put all the cash flows on one side and require the amount to sum to zero. You can think of this in terms of the decision maker's cash flows we described earlier: You are paying out (−) one amount to get in (+) another. For example, let's say you borrow $10,000 (PV), and the money comes to you, which is a positive. But then you pay back $248.85 per month for 48 months, and those payments go from you, which are negatives. For this modified basic calculator formula, then, after you enter the PV as a positive amount, the calculator will display the computed payment as a negative amount. Appendix A at the end of this book shows the key strokes for standard calculations on a calculator of this type.

Whichever type of calculator you have, if you put in a negative value that should be entered as a positive, the calculator will simply give you an error message and not compute an answer. You can adapt quickly to either type. In our calculator procedures, which appear in brackets after various calculations, we will use positive amounts for convenience.

ADVICE   Always use a time line. Valuation problems are easier to understand and the error rate is lower with the visual aid of a time line. Also, you should make the calculations in the chapter yourself, because doing so will help develop your abilities. Similarly, you should follow through the derivations yourself, because this will help you understand the concepts.

Self-Check Questions

1. Why would anyone ever make a *zero*-NPV investment?
2. What is a discount rate?
3. What is the required (rate of) return?
4. Explain the differences among the required return, the expected return, and the realized return.
5. Explain why present value and the discount rate are inversely related.

4.2 MULTIPLE EXPECTED FUTURE CASH FLOWS

In this section, we demonstrate with an example the use and versatility of the present-value and future-value formulas. The example has four expected future cash flows of various sizes that occur at different times. We will calculate the value of the entire set of expected future cash flows at three different points in time.

A Simple Time-Value-of-Money Example

Suppose you expect to receive the cash flows given in Table 4-1 in the time periods indicated, and the required return is 10%.

Time	0	1	2	3
Cash flow	$3000	$2000	$8000	$5000

TABLE 4-1
A simple time-value-of-money example.

QUESTION 1   What is the present value of the set of expected future cash flows given in Table 4-1? Figure 4-3 shows the time line for this problem.

We can compute the present value of the set of cash flows by applying the present-value formula to each cash flow, with $r = 10\%$ and $n =$ the time period when the cash flow is expected to occur.

$$PV = \frac{3000}{(1.1)^0} + \frac{2000}{(1.1)^1} + \frac{8000}{(1.1)^2} + \frac{5000}{(1.1)^3}$$

$$= 3000 + 1818.18 + 6611.57 + 3756.57$$

$$= \$15,186.32$$

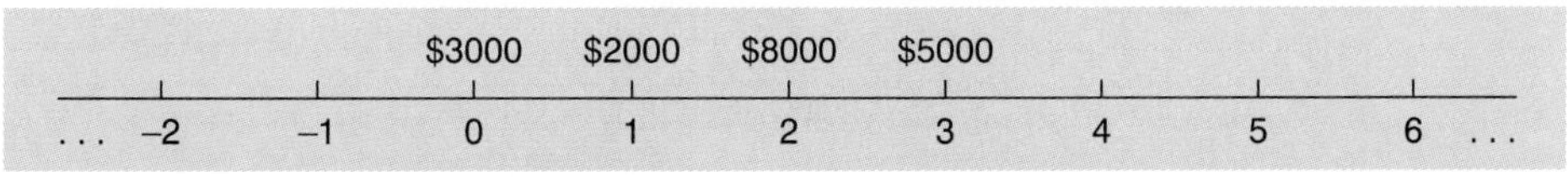

FIGURE 4-3
A time line for the cash flows in Table 4-1.

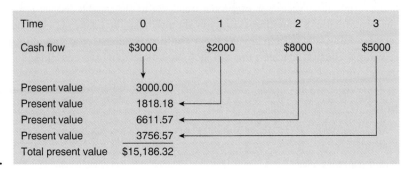

FIGURE 4-4

Present-value calculation for the cash flows in Table 4-1.

Figure 4-4 illustrates this calculation. You can see how each cash flow's present value is calculated using the present-value formula. After you enter the single expected future cash flow, the time it will occur, and the discount rate per period, your calculator can compute each of the present values separately. For example, put in FV = 8000, $n = 2$, $r = 10\%$, and CF = 0. Then compute PV = 6611.57 for the third payment. The total present value is simply the sum of the individual present values.

QUESTION 2   What is the future value at time period 4 ($t = 4$) of the set of expected future cash flows given in Table 4-1? Figure 4-3 again provides a visual aid to the problem.

To compute the future value at $t = 4$, use the future-value formula to value each cash flow with $r = 10\%$ and $n =$ the difference between 4 and the time period when the cash flow is expected to occur.

$$FV_4 = 3000(1.1)^4 + 2000(1.1)^3 + 8000(1.1)^2 + 5000(1.1)^1$$

$$= 4392.30 + 2662.00 + 9680.00 + 5500.00$$

$$= \$22,234.30$$

Figure 4-5 illustrates this calculation. Again, you can see how the future-value formula is applied to each of the cash flows. For example, put in PV = 2000, $n = 3$, $r = 10\%$, and CF = 0. Then compute FV = 2662.00 for the second cash flow. And again, the total future value is the sum of the individual future values.

A SHORT CUT   Once the present value of a set of cash flows is computed, there is a short cut for computing the combined value of the set at any other point in time. The future value at

FIGURE 4-5

Future-value calculation for the cash flows in Table 4-1.

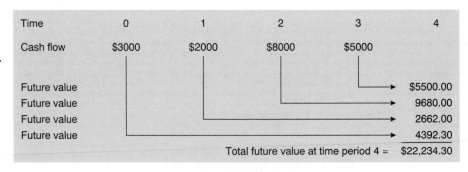

$t = 4$ can be computed by simply applying the future-value formula directly to the total present value, just as though it were a single amount, with $r = 10\%$ and $n = 4$.

$$FV_4 = PV(1 + r)^4 = 15{,}186.32(1.1)^4 = \$22{,}234.29$$

(It's off by one cent due to rounding error.) Once you know the total value at *any* point in time, it is easy to compute the total value at any *other* point in time. [Put in PV = 15,186.32, $n = 4$, $r = 10\%$, and CF = 0. Then compute FV = 22,234.29.]

QUESTION 3   What is the total (future) value at $t = 2$ of the set of expected cash flows given in Table 4-1?

With both the present value and FV_4 already computed, there are three methods for calculating FV_2. (1) Use the future- or present-value formula to value each of the individual cash flows at $t = 2$, and then sum. (2) Use the future-value formula with PV = 15,186.32, $r = 10\%$, $n = 2$, and CF = 0. (3) Use the present-value formula with $FV_4 = 22{,}234.30$, $r = 10\%$, $n = 2$, and CF = 0. Calculations for all three methods produce the one correct answer.

$$FV_2 = 3000(1.1)^2 + 2000(1.1)^1 + 8000 + \frac{5000}{(1.1)^1}$$

$$= 3630.00 + 2200.00 + 8000 + 4545.45$$

$$= \$18{,}375.45$$

$$FV_2 = 15{,}186.32(1.1)^2 = \$18{,}375.45$$

$$FV_2 = \frac{22{,}234.30}{(1.1)^2} = \$18{,}375.45$$

Self-Check Questions

1. Explain why the two methods used to answer Question 2 must give the same answer (except for rounding error).
2. Explain why the three methods used to answer Question 3 must give the same answer.

4.3 ANNUITIES

Any question concerning a time-value-of-money calculation can be answered by using the present-value and/or the future-value formula. However, in complex situations, the calculations can be very tedious. Fortunately, there are extensions of the present-value and future-value formulas that help in some more complex, yet fairly routine, situations. These are formulas for valuing annuities. An **annuity** is a series of identical cash flows that are expected to occur each period for a specified number of periods. Annuities occur in many different financial transactions. One example of an annuity is an installment-debt contract, such as a bank loan for buying a car or house. A bank lends you the money, and in exchange you agree to repay the bank a fixed amount every month for a specified number of months. The series of payments is an annuity.

Valuing an annuity is relatively easy because the payments occur in a regular manner (for example, $200 per month for 48 months), and the combined amount can be calculated by a single formula.

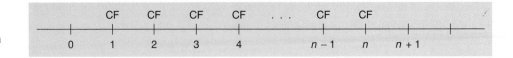

The Future Value of an Annuity

We started our discussion of the time value of money in Chapter 3 with an example of depositing money in a savings account. Now consider a savings plan for depositing the same amount every period for n periods. How much will you have at the end of the n periods?

To analyze this case, let CF be the amount deposited each time period (that is, $CF_1 = CF_2 = \cdots = CF_n = CF$). Recall that the cash flows are made at the end of the time period. Figure 4-6 illustrates an n-period annuity.

The future value of an annuity can be computed by using the future-value formula to value each payment and then adding up the individual values to get the total. Start with the last payment and add backwards to the first payment at time $t = 1$. The future value of the annuity at n, FVA_n, is

$$FVA_n = CF(1 + r)^0 + CF(1 + r)^1 + \cdots + CF(1 + r)^{n-1}$$

Figure 4-7 illustrates this calculation. Note that the first payment (at $t = 1$) earns interest for $(n-1)$ periods, not n periods. Note too that the last payment occurs exactly at the end of the annuity, so it does not earn any interest—$(1 + r)^0 = 1$.

The equation for FVA_n has a CF in every term on the right-hand side. If the CF is factored out, the equation can be rewritten as

$$FVA_n = CF[(1 + r)^0 + (1 + r)^1 + \cdots + (1 + r)^{n-1}]$$

$$= CF\sum_{t=0}^{n-1}(1 + r)^t$$

where Σ is a summation. The summation, which is called a *finite geometric series*, collapses to a formula. The future value of an annuity can then be expressed as

$$FVA_n = CF\left[\frac{(1 + r)^n - 1}{r}\right] \tag{4.1}$$

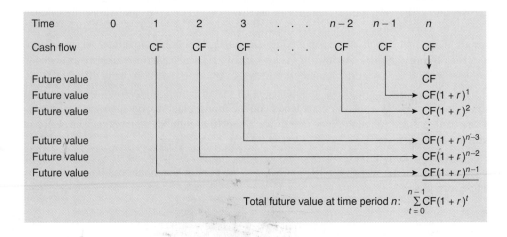

The quantity in brackets on the right-hand side of Equation (4.1) is called the **future-value annuity factor**. The particular values for CF, n, and r, along with Equation (4.1), are all that is needed to determine the future value of the annuity, no matter how many payments the annuity has.

Saving For Retirement at Citibank

Suppose you save $2000 per year for 30 years at Citibank, and the money earns 5% interest per year. How much will you have at the end of the 30 years?

The cash flows are like those in Figure 4-7 with $n = 30$. Because the stream of cash flows is an annuity, its future value can be computed by using Equation (4.1).

$$\mathrm{FVA}_n = \mathrm{CF}\left[\frac{(1 + r)^n - 1}{r}\right] = 2000\left[\frac{(1.05)^{30} - 1}{0.05}\right]$$

$$\mathrm{FVA}_{30} = 2000(66.43885)$$

$$= \$132,877.70$$

[Put in CF = 2000, r = 5%, n = 30, and PV = 0. Then compute FV = 132,877.70.] ■

The Present Value of an Annuity

To compute the present value of an annuity, we will build on what we have already learned. The future value of an annuity is given by Equation (4.1). The present value of the annuity can then be easily found by computing the present value of that amount.

$$\mathrm{PVA}_n = \mathrm{FVA}_n\left[\frac{1}{(1 + r)^n}\right]$$

$$= \mathrm{CF}\left[\frac{(1 + r)^n - 1}{r}\right]\left[\frac{1}{(1 + r)^n}\right]$$

$$\mathrm{PVA}_n = \mathrm{CF}\left[\frac{(1 + r)^n - 1}{r(1 + r)^n}\right] \tag{4.2}$$

The quantity in brackets on the right-hand side of Equation (4.2) is called the **present-value annuity factor**. The particular values for CF, n, and r are all that is needed to determine the present value of the annuity.

Computing the Present Value of a Car Loan from GMAC

GMAC expects to receive future car-loan payments of $200 per month for the next 36 months from one of its customers. The first payment is due 1 month from today. The interest rate on the loan is 1% per month. How much money is being borrowed? In other words, what is the present value of the loan?

The present-value annuity formula, Equation (4.2), can be used to compute the answer to the question with CF = $200, $n = 36$, and $r = 1\%$.

$$\mathrm{PVA}_n = \mathrm{CF}\left[\frac{(1 + r)^n - 1}{r(1 + r)^n}\right] = 200\left[\frac{(1.01)^{36} - 1}{0.01(1.01)^{36}}\right]$$

$$\mathrm{PVA}_{36} = 200(30.1075)$$

$$= \$6021.50$$

[Put in CF = 200, r = 1%, n = 36, and FV = 0. Then compute PV = 6021.50.] ■

The Payments of an Annuity

We have shown you how to compute the present value and the future value of an annuity, given a set of payments and an interest rate. When a person borrows money, however, it is often helpful to be able to verify the required payments. Just as we rearranged the future-value formula to derive the present-value formula, the annuity formulas can be rearranged to solve for the payment amount:

$$CF = PVA_n \left[\frac{r(1 + r)^n}{(1 + r)^n - 1} \right] \qquad (4.3)$$

and

$$CF = FVA_n \left[\frac{r}{(1 + r)^n - 1} \right] \qquad (4.4)$$

The bracketed amounts on the right-hand side of Equations (4.3) and (4.4) are simply the inverse ($= 1/x$) of the present-value and future-value factors, respectively.

EXAMPLE

Computing Annual Loan Payments

Consider a $1000 loan that requires equal payments at the end of each of the next 3 years. If the interest rate is 10% per year, what are the payments?

Using Equation (4.3) yields

$$CF = PVA_n \left[\frac{r(1 + r)^n}{(1 + r)^n - 1} \right] = 1000 \left[\frac{0.1(1.1)^3}{(1.1)^3 - 1} \right]$$

$$= 1000(0.40211)$$

$$= \$402.11$$

[Put in PV = 1000, r = 10%, n = 3, and FV = 0. Then compute CF = 402.11.] ■

EXAMPLE

Saving at the IBM Credit Union to Buy a House

A person is saving money at the IBM Credit Union for a down payment on a house. How much must be saved at the end of every month to accumulate a total of $12,000 at the end of 5 years, if the money is invested at a rate of 0.5% per month?

Equation (4.4) yields

$$CF = FVA_n \left[\frac{r}{(1 + r)^n - 1} \right] = 12,000 \left[\frac{0.005}{(1.005)^{60} - 1} \right]$$

$$= 12,000(0.0143328)$$

$$= \$171.99$$

[Put in FV = 12,000, r = 0.5%, n = 60, and PV = 0. Then compute CF = 171.99.] ■

Amortizing a Loan

A **loan amortization schedule** shows how the loan is paid off over time. That is, it shows how the principal (the original amount borrowed) and interest will be paid. Because an installment loan has the structure of an annuity, an amortization schedule for such a loan shows the relationships among the payments, principal, and interest rate.

To create an amortization schedule, start with the amount borrowed. To this amount add the first period's interest, and then subtract the first period's payment. The result is the starting amount for the second period. Repeat this procedure until the remainder becomes zero at the end of the last period.

Consider again the 3-year 10% $1000 loan. We computed the loan payments to be $402.11. What does the amortization schedule look like for this loan?

The amortization schedule for this loan is given in Table 4-2.

Loan Amortization

EXAMPLE

TABLE 4-2
A loan amortization schedule.

	PERIOD		
	1	**2**	**3**
a. Principal at start of period	$1000.00	$697.89	$365.57
b. Interest for the period (10% of starting principal)	100.00	69.79	36.56
c. Balance (a + b)	1100.00	767.68	402.13
d. Payment	402.11	402.11	402.11
e. Principal at start of next period (c − d)	697.89	365.57	.02*

* Not zero because of rounding error.

Valuing Annuities Not Starting Today

Sometimes, annuities start at a time other than $t = 0$ (where the first payment is at $t = 1$). The present value of such an annuity can be computed from the difference between the present values of two other annuities. The first annuity goes from now until the end of the one in question. The second annuity goes from now until the start of the one in question. The difference between the two values is the value of the annuity in question.

What is the present value of $5000 to be received at the end of each of the years 4 through 7? Figure 4-8 illustrates the timing of the cash flows.

This kind of "postponed" annuity, one not starting until sometime in the future, is equivalent to the difference between two other annuities. In this case, the *difference* between the annuity in Figure 4-9 and the one in Figure 4-10 equals the one in Figure 4-8. That is, the net cash flow in each period in Figure 4-8 equals the cash flow for that period in Figure 4-9 minus the cash flow for that period in Figure 4-10. (The cash flows cancel each other out in the first three periods.) Therefore, the present value of the annuity in Figure 4-8 equals the present

Computing the Present Value of an Annuity Starting in the Future

EXAMPLE

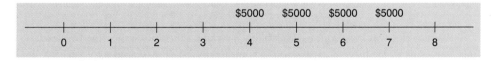

FIGURE 4-8
Equal cash flows occurring $t = 4$ through $t = 7$.

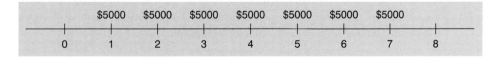

FIGURE 4-9
Cash flows for a 7-year annuity.

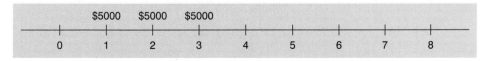

FIGURE 4-10
Cash flows for a 3-year annuity.

value of a 7-year annuity [put in CF = 5000, r = 12%, n = 7, and FV = 0, and then compute PV = 22,818.78] minus the present value of a 3-year annuity [put in CF = 5000, r = 12%, n = 3, and FV = 0, and then compute PV = 12,009.16].

$$PV = 5000\left[\frac{(1.12)^7 - 1}{0.12(1.12)^7}\right] - 5000\left[\frac{(1.12)^3 - 1}{0.12(1.12)^3}\right]$$

$$= 22,818.78 - 12,009.16$$

$$= \$10,809.62$$

Perpetuities

An annuity that goes on forever is called a **perpetuity**. Although perpetuities actually exist in some situations, the most important reason for studying them is that they can be used as a simple and fairly accurate approximation of a long-term annuity.

As we showed in Figure 4-1, the present-value factor becomes smaller as n becomes larger. Therefore, later payments in a long annuity add little to the present value of the annuity. For example, at a required return of 10% per year, the present value of getting $100 in 30 years is only $5.73. It is a mere 85 cents if payment is going to take 50 years. As it turns out, the present value of an annuity has a maximum value, no matter how many payments are expected. That maximum value is the value of a perpetuity.

To examine the present value of a perpetuity, we can start with the present value of an annuity and see what happens when n becomes very large. In mathematical terms, we are taking the limit of the function as n approaches infinity. Let's start by rewriting Equation (4.2), the present-value annuity formula:

$$PVA_n = CF\left[\frac{(1 + r)^n - 1}{r(1 + r)^n}\right]$$

$$= CF\left[\frac{(1 + r)^n}{r(1 + r)^n}\right] - CF\left[\frac{1}{r(1 + r)^n}\right]$$

$$= \left[\frac{CF}{r}\right] - \left[\frac{CF}{r(1 + r)^n}\right]$$

Written this way, you can see what happens when n becomes large. The first term on the right-hand side of the bottom expression is not affected. But the second term gets smaller because $(1 + r)^n$ gets larger when n increases. As n gets really big, the second term goes to zero.

To see this by example, try CF = $100 and r = 10%. Then with n = 25, the second term is $92.30; with n = 50, the second term is $8.52; with n = 75, it is $0.79; with n = 100, it is $0.073, and so on. Therefore, the present value of a perpetuity is

$$PVA_{perpetuity} = \frac{CF}{r} \tag{4.5}$$

What is the present value of $1000 per year, forever, if the required return is 8% per year? The answer can be computed by using Equation (4.5).

$$PVA_{\text{perpetuity}} = \frac{CF}{r} = \frac{1000}{0.08} = \$12{,}500.00$$

Present Value of a Perpetuity

EXAMPLE

Now let's suppose that the $1000 per year lasted for only 50 years. What would be the present value, and how well does the present value of the perpetuity approximate this present value? Using Equation (4.2), we find that the actual present value for the 50-year annuity is

$$PVA_n = CF\left[\frac{(1 + r)^n - 1}{r(1 + r)^n}\right] = 1000\left[\frac{(1.08)^{50} - 1}{0.08(1.08)^{50}}\right]$$

$$PVA_{50} = 1000(12.23348)$$
$$= \$12{,}233.48$$

[Put in CF = 1000, r = 8%, n = 50, and FV = 0. Then compute PV = 12,233.48.] In this case, the perpetuity answer is about 2% above the correct answer. ■

Self-Check Questions

1. What is an annuity?
2. Explain why the present value of the amount FVA_n discounted back over n periods at the rate r must equal PVA_n as expressed by Equation (4.2).
3. What is the purpose of a loan amortization schedule?
4. What is the future value of an annuity?

4.4 SOLVING FOR A DISCOUNT RATE

When you know the expected future cash flows and the discount rate (the generic term for a rate of return), you can compute the present value. Sometimes, however, you already know the present value from a market price, but you don't know the discount rate. For example, suppose you wanted to know how much you could expect to earn on an investment: the investment's expected return. All of the time-value-of-money formulas can be rearranged and solved for the expected return, the rate that would make the NPV equal zero.

Suppose Bank One offers a certificate of deposit (CD) that pays $10,000 in 3 years in exchange for $7938.32 today. What interest rate is Bank One offering? In other words, what is the expected return from investing in this CD? We can rearrange either the future-value or the present-value formula to get

$$r = \left[\frac{FV}{PV}\right]^{1/n} - 1$$

so that

$$r = \left[\frac{10{,}000}{7938.32}\right]^{0.3333} - 1 = 1.08 - 1 = 8.00\%$$

[Put in FV = 10,000, PV = 7938.32, n = 3, and CF = 0. Then compute r = 8.00%.] ■

Computing the Expected Return from a Certificate of Deposit at Bank One

EXAMPLE

Computing the Interest Rate on a Mortgage from Chase Home Mortgage

Assume that Chase Home Mortgage offers a mortgage loan of $97,218.33 to buy a house. It requires payments of $1000 a month for 30 years (360 payments). What interest rate is Chase charging?

Using Equation (4.2) yields

$$97{,}218.33 = 1000\left[\frac{(1 + r)^{360} - 1}{r(1 + r)^{360}}\right]$$

Although this equation has only one unknown, r, we have to solve for r by using trial and error, because it is not possible to solve for r directly. In such cases, a calculator is especially convenient, because finding r without one can be quite tedious. Even though the calculator also uses a trial-and-error program to solve for r, it does so automatically and very quickly. [Put in PV = 97,218.33, CF = 1000, n = 360, and FV = 0. Then compute r = 1.00%.]

Chase is charging 1% per month. ■

Self-Check Questions

1. What does $r = 8.00\%$ in the Bank One example represent?
2. What does $r = 1.00\%$ in the Chase example represent? What is the frequency of compounding?

4.5 COMPOUNDING FREQUENCY

Thus far, we have been careful to use a discount rate that is consistent with the frequency of the cash flows—for example, 1% per *month* with *monthly* payments. In practice, interest rates are typically stated in one of two ways, as an annual percentage rate (APR) or as an annual percentage yield (APY), even though interest is calculated and paid more often than annually.

Annual Percentage Rate (APR)

The **annual percentage rate (APR)** is the periodic rate times the number of periods in a year. This means that the APR is a nominal rate, a rate "in name only." That is, the true (effective) annual rate may be different because of the compounding frequency.

The **compounding frequency** is how often interest is compounded in a year. For example, the compounding frequency might be monthly (12 times per year), quarterly (4 times), or annually (once).

With m compounding periods per year,

$$\text{APR} = (m)(r) \tag{4.6}$$

Suppose Bankers Trust offers a loan, charging 1% per month. What is the APR? From Equation (4.6), the APR is 12%.

$$APR = 12(0.01) = 0.12 = 12.00\%$$

Recall: The compounding frequency is the same as the payment frequency, unless it is otherwise specified.

The periodic rate is an effective rate, but two periods of interest are more than twice one period's interest. This is because the second period's interest includes interest earned on the first period's interest.

Annual Percentage Yield (APY)

The **annual percentage yield** (**APY**) is the effective (true) annual return. It is the rate you actually earn or pay in one year, taking into account the effect of compounding. The APY is computed by compounding the periodic rate for the compounding frequency.

$$APY = \left[1 + \frac{APR}{m}\right]^m - 1 \tag{4.7}$$

What is the APY on Bankers Trust's 12% APR loan, with monthly compounding? From Equation (4.7), the APY is 12.68%.

$$APY = (1.01)^{12} - 1 = 0.1268 = 12.68\%$$

[Put in PV = 1.00, r = 1%, n = 12, and CF = 0, and then compute FV = 1.1268. The APY = FV − 1 = 12.68%.]

The Effect of Compounding Frequency on Future Value

How does compounding frequency affect future value? To answer this question, let's compare yearly, semiannually, quarterly, monthly, and weekly compounding for saving $10,000 for a year at 12% APR.

Yearly compounding.   From Equation (4.6), with m = 1, r is 12% per year. Then, using the future-value formula, we find that the future value at the end of one year, FV_1, is

$$FV_1 = PV(1 + r)^n = 10,000(1.12)^1 = \$11,200.00$$

Semiannual compounding.   From Equation (4.6), r is 6% per half-year. Thus the future value at the end of one year (two half-years), FV_2, is

$$FV_2 = 10,000(1.06)^2 = \$11,236.00$$

Quarterly compounding.   With quarterly compounding, r is 3% per quarter, and the future value at the end of four quarters, FV_4, is

$$FV_4 = 10,000(1.03)^4 = \$11,255.09$$

TABLE 4-3
**Future values and
APYs for various
compounding
frequencies.**

COMPOUNDING FREQUENCY	PV	FV_{year}	ANNUAL INTEREST	APY
Yearly	$10,000	$11,200.00	$1200.00	12.0000%
Semiannually	10,000	11,236.00	1236.00	12.3600
Quarterly	10,000	11,255.09	1255.09	12.5509
Monthly	10,000	11,268.25	1268.25	12.6825
Weekly	10,000	11,273.59	1273.59	12.7359

Monthly compounding.   With monthly compounding, r is 1% per month, and the future value at the end of 12 months, FV_{12}, is

$$FV_{12} = 10,000(1.01)^{12} = \$11,268.25$$

Weekly compounding.   For weekly compounding, r is 0.2308% (= 12/52) per week, and the future value at the end of 52 weeks, FV_{52}, is

$$FV_{52} = 10,000(1.002308)^{52} = \$11,273.59$$

The future values and corresponding APYs for these various compounding periods are given in Table 4-3. From this, you can see that the future value and APY increase as the compounding frequency increases.

Another way to understand an APY is to say that it is the total interest earned in a year (annual interest) divided by the principal. That is,

$$APY = \frac{Annual\ interest}{Principal}$$

For example, the annual interest for monthly compounding is $1268.25, which, divided by $10,000, gives the same 12.68% we found using Equation (4.7).

Continuous Compounding

If more frequent compounding increases the future value, what if we compound daily, hourly, or even every minute? These are all examples of *discrete compounding*, where interest is computed at the end of each compounding period. At the most, we can compound continuously.

Building on our compounding-frequency example further, Table 4-4 shows future values and APYs for several more compounding frequencies (values of m). Note that the change in the future value for each doubling of m is smaller than the previous change.

When m becomes large enough, compounding becomes essentially continuous. Recall that we derived the perpetuity formula by seeing what happens when n gets really large for an

TABLE 4-4
**APY as a function of
compounding
frequency.**

m	FV_{year}	APY
104	$11,274.19	12.7419%
208	11,274.58	12.7458
416	11,274.77	12.7477
832	11,274.87	12.7487
1664	11,274.92	12.7492
3328	11,274.944	12.74944
6656	11,274.957	12.74957

annuity. Similarly, we can look at what happens to APY when *m* gets really large. We will not give the proof, but it turns out that

$$APY = e^{APR} - 1 \tag{4.8}$$

where *e* is approximately 2.718.[4] The function e^x is called the exponential function. It is usually found on a calculator with either e^x or exp on the key.

What is the APY for a 12% APR with continuous compounding?
    Using Equation (4.8) yields

$$APY = e^{APR} - 1 = e^{0.12} - 1 = 0.1274969 = 12.74969\%$$

Note that the APY with continuous compounding is only slightly larger than it is with *m* = 6656 (12.74957% versus 12.74969%), which compounds the interest approximately 18 times per day. For that matter, all of the APYs in Table 4-4 are nearly identical. Thus you can see that a large value for *m* in Equation (4.7) is a good approximation for the APY with continuous compounding. ◼

A Graphical Look at Compounding Frequency

Figure 4-11 shows how compounding frequency affects future value by illustrating future value as a function of annual, semiannual, and continuous compounding. Note how the "stair

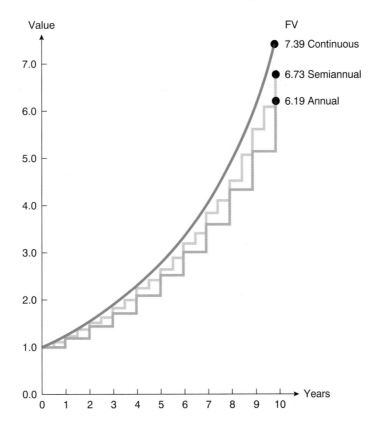

FIGURE 4-11

Future value as a function of annual, semiannual, and continuous compounding for 20% APR.

---

[4] This number occurs frequently in the mathematical and natural sciences. It is the base for what are called *natural logarithms*, usually denoted ln; ln is the inverse function of *e*. That is, $\ln(e^x) = x$.

steps" are smaller and more frequent for semiannual than for annual compounding and how they become a smooth curve with continuous compounding. Note also that the amount increases faster with more frequent compounding.

Time-Value-of-Money Formulas with Continuous Compounding

We can also specify the time-value factors for continuous compounding. For n years, the future-value factor with continuous compounding is $e^{n(\text{APR})}$. Because the present-value factor is the inverse of the future-value factor, the present-value factor with continuous compounding is $e^{-n(\text{APR})}$. (A function with a negative exponent equals 1 over the same function with the same positive exponent. For example, 2^{-2} equals 1 over 2^2, or $\frac{1}{4}$.)

The formulas for the present value and future value of an annuity with continuous compounding can be obtained by modifying the formulas for discrete compounding periods by substituting APR for r and $e^{n(\text{APR})}$ for $(1 + r)^n$ in each formula. There is, however, one additional complication with these annuity formulas.

The cash flows in these annuity formulas are assumed to occur continuously. That is, CF is the total amount of cash flow that will occur in one period, but it is spread out so that it occurs evenly over the period. Table 4-5 provides the time-value-of-money formulas with continuous compounding and continuous annuity cash flows.

EXAMPLE		
Present Value of a Single Cash Flow with Continuous Compounding	What is the present value of $1000 that is expected to be received 3 years from today if the required return is 10% APR compounded continuously? From the present-value formula in Table 4–5,	

$$PV = 1000e^{-3(0.1)} = 1000(0.740818) = \$740.82$$

TABLE 4-5

Time-value-of-money formulas with continuous compounding and continuous annuity cash flows.

Present-value formula	$PV = FV_n[e^{-n(\text{APR})}]$
Future-value formula	$FV_n = PV[e^{n(\text{APR})}]$
Present-value annuity formula	$PVA_n = CF\left[\dfrac{e^{n(\text{APR})} - 1}{(\text{APR})e^{n(\text{APR})}}\right]$
Future-value annuity formula	$FVA_n = CF\left[\dfrac{e^{n(\text{APR})} - 1}{\text{APR}}\right]$

What is the present value of $2000 per year received continuously for 5 years if the required return is 10% APR compounded continuously?

From the present-value annuity formula in Table 4–5,

$$\text{PVA}_5 = \frac{2000(e^{5(0.1)} - 1)}{0.1e^{5(0.1)}} = \frac{2000(1.64872 - 1)}{0.1(1.64872)} = \$7869.38$$

The answer to this question can also be approximated by using a very small compounding period and cash flow. If compounding occurs 4000 times per year, then each compounding period has a cash flow of $0.50 (= 2000/4000). The approximate rate is 0.0025% per period (= 10%/4000). Now put in CF = 0.50, $r = 0.0025\%$, $n = 20{,}000$ (5 years at 4000 per year), and FV = 0, and then compute PV = $7869.31. So this approximation has an error of only 7 cents on an amount of almost $8000. ■

Present Value of a Continuous Cash Flow Annuity with Continuous Compounding

When compounding is continuous but cash flows are discrete, a two-step process is needed. The next example illustrates such a case.

What is the future value of $1000 received at the end of each year for 5 years if the expected return is 6% APR compounded continuously?

First, we must determine the APY to apply to the cash flows, because the cash flows will occur discretely at the end of each year rather than coming in continuously throughout the year. Using Equation (4.8) yields

$$\text{APY} = e^{0.06} - 1 = 0.061837 = 6.1837\%$$

The future value can then be computed using the future-value annuity formula for yearly compounding with $r = 6.1837\%$ and $n = 5$.

$$\text{FVA}_5 = 1000\left[\frac{(1.061837)^5 - 1}{0.061837}\right] = \$5657.80$$

[Put in CF = 1000, $r = 6.1837\%$, $n = 5$, and PV = 0. Then compute FV = 5657.80.] ■

Future Value of a Discrete Cash Flow Annuity with Continuous Compounding

Self-Check Questions

1. What is the annual percentage rate (APR)? Does it reflect the frequency of compounding?
2. What is the annual percentage yield (APY)? How does it take into account the effect of compounding?
3. Explain in your own words the meaning of the term *continuous compounding*.
4. Suppose a bank offers you a 10% APR certificate of deposit. You can specify annual, semiannual, quarterly, monthly, or daily compounding. Which would you choose?
5. Suppose you are going to borrow from a bank at 10% APR. You can specify annual, semiannual, quarterly, monthly, or daily compounding. Which would you choose?

4.6 FRACTIONAL TIME PERIODS

Earlier we used a fractional exponent (0.333) to solve for the 8% expected return from a CD. Using the time-value-of-money formulas with fractional time periods requires care and an understanding of the assumptions underlying the formulas. More than ever, a time line is critical to solving problems that involve fractional time periods.

Single Cash Flows

Computing the present and/or future value of a single cash flow when there is a fractional time period is straightforward, because a fractional exponent can be used directly in the formula.

EXAMPLE

Computing the Present Value of a Single Future Cash Flow

What is the present value of $1000 to be received 46 months from today if the required return is 12% APY?

Use the present-value formula with $n = 3.8333 (= 46/12)$. The present value is

$$PV = 1000\left[\frac{1}{(1.12)^{3.8333}}\right] = \$647.64$$

[Put in FV = 1000, r = 12%, n = 3.8333, and CF = 0. Then compute PV = 647.64.] ∎

Annuities with Fractional Time Periods

Unfortunately, calculator treatment of fractional annuities is not consistent. Some "round down," and treat the fractional time period and payment as though it weren't there. Others "round up," and treat the fractional time period and payment as though it were a full period and payment. Still others account for the fractional time period but assume no payment. Our advice is either to carefully study how your calculator works and use it successfully or to "take matters into your own hands" and account for fractional annuities in other ways. Here are two examples of how to take matters into your own hands and compute a future value by using a two-step process, without relying on whatever assumption is programmed into your calculator.

EXAMPLE

Computing the Future Value of an Annuity After it has Ended

What is the value 3.75 years from now of a 3-year annuity, with the first $1000 payment being made 1 year from today, if the expected return is 10% APY?

The value in 3 years can be computed by using Equation (4.1) as $3310. [Put in CF = 1000, r = 10%, n = 3, and PV = 0. Then compute FV = 3310.] The future value in 3.75 years can then be computed by simply treating the $3310 as though it were a single payment at t = 3 and compounding that amount for 0.75 time periods, to get $3555.27 (= 3310 × 1.1^{0.75}). [Put in PV = 3310, r = 10%, n = 0.75, and CF = 0. Then compute FV = 3555.27.] Figure 4-12 shows the solution using a time line. ∎

FIGURE 4-12
Solution using a time line.

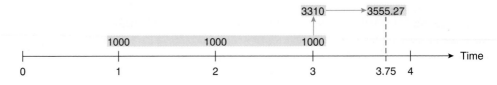

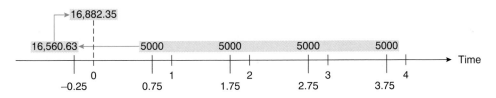

FIGURE 4-13
Solution using a time line.

Computing the Present Value of an Annuity with Early Cash Flows

What is the present value of a 4-year annuity, with the first $5000 payment being made 9 months from today, if the required return is 8% APY?

Three months ago, this annuity would be a "normal" 4-year annuity, so its value as of 3 months ago (at $t = -0.25$) is $16,560.63, from Equation (4.2). [Put in CF = 5000, r = 8%, n = 4, and FV = 0. Then compute PV = 16,560.63.] The present value can then be computed by simply treating that amount as though it were a single payment, and compounding it forward to the present for 0.25 time periods, to get $16,882.35 (= 16,560.63 × $1.08^{.25}$). [Put in PV = 16,560.63, r = 8%, n = 0.25, and CF = 0. Then compute FV = 16,882.35.] Figure 4-13 shows the solution using a time line. ■

Self-Check Questions

1. What is the simplest way to compute the present or future value of a single cash flow when there is a fractional time period involved?
2. Why must you be especially careful when using a calculator to compute the present or future value of an annuity when there is a fractional time period involved?

4.7 VALUING "SPECIAL-FINANCING" OFFERS

Reduced financing costs are often used as part of a sales promotion for consumer goods, such as cars, furniture, and even condominiums. In short, "special financing" has become part of the package in many types of consumer purchases. But how can you tell whether the financing is really special in anything but name only? In this section, we provide an example and some guidelines for dealing with special financing.

Often the interest rate creates the most confusion with special financing. This is because the special rate offered, such as 3.9% APR, is not the opportunity cost for borrowing money. You can't really borrow money at that rate. The special financing is simply a promotional gimmick. In essence, the firm is lowering the effective price to encourage sales. It's just that the lower price is expressed in the form of special financing. The key question, then, is how much does the interest savings lower the price?

To evaluate a special financing deal, you need the interest rate at which you can borrow money for *any* comparable use. That is, you need the market interest rate for such loans. The market interest rate provides a way to measure the opportunity cost of the special financing. You use the market rate to compute the "real" price for the product. The real price is the present value of the payments you would have to make using the special-financing offer. If the present value is smaller than the cash price, the special financing is a better deal; the real price with special financing is lower than the cash price.

Cash Back or 3.9% APR from Ford

Let's say Ford is offering a choice of either "special financing" or "cash back" to buy a car you have already decided to buy. Which offer is better?

The stated price is $20,000. Either you can have $1500 cash back, for a cash price of $18,500, or you can borrow the "$20,000" at 3.9% APR. Monthly payments would be $589.59 for the next 36 months. [Put in PV = 20,000, r = 0.325% (= 3.9/12), n = 36, and FV = 0. Then compute CF = 589.59.] Suppose you could also borrow $18,500 from Citibank (or any of several other banks) at 8% APR and pay cash for the car. Should you take the special-financing offer or take the cash-back offer and borrow from a bank?

The best choice has the lowest present-value cost. The difference between the two costs is the NPV of the choice. On the basis of 8% APR (0.6667% per month), the present value of the special-financing loan payments is $18,814.77. [Put in CF = 589.59, r = 0.6667%, n = 36, and FV = 0. Then compute PV = 18,814.77.] This is more than the $18,500 cash-back-offer price, so taking the cash-back offer and borrowing from the bank is the better deal. The NPV is $314.77 (= $18,814.77 − $18,500.00).

There is another way to see the difference between the two alternatives: Compute what the payments would be on the Citibank loan if Citibank required the same 36 monthly payments.[5] The payments for such a Citibank loan would be $579.73. [Put in PV = 18,500, r = 0.6667%, n = 36, and FV = 0. Then compute CF = 579.73.] Thus the bank loan would be about $10 a month cheaper. The monthly savings have a present value of $314.77, the NPV for the bank loan. [CF = 9.86 (= 589.59 − 579.73), r = 0.6667%, n = 36, and FV = 0. Then compute PV = 314.65, which is 12 cents off due to rounding error.] ∎

In the above example, we assumed you had already decided to purchase that particular car. But what if you are still shopping? In the next example, we will show you how to evaluate competing product offers.

Computing the Value of a Special-Financing Offer from Buick

Suppose that just before you "sign on the dotted line" for that car you were going to buy from Ford, you hear about another offer from Buick. It's a nicer model that you actually like better—except for its higher price of $25,000. Now Buick is offering 1% APR for 48 months on this "$25,000" model. Therefore, you could buy the nicer model for $531.53 per month for the next 48 months. [Put in PV = 25,000, r = 0.0833% (= ¹⁄₁₂), n = 48, and FV = 0. Then compute CF = 531.53.] However, because the loan on the more expensive model is over a different period, the lower monthly payment is not necessarily the best deal.[6]

Is Buick's price on the better model less than the $18,500 cash price on Ford's more basic model? It is a lower monthly payment at a "lower" interest rate, but it is for 12 more months. What is the real price for the Buick? There is no cash-back offer on this nicer model to give a guideline for the price discount.

Again, the real price with the special financing is the present value of the loan payments at the opportunity cost (market) interest rate. On the basis of the bank's 8% APR interest rate, the real price is $21,772.32. [Put in CF = 531.53, r = 0.6667%, n = 48, and FV = 0. Then compute PV = 21,772.32.] Therefore, even with the 1% APR special-financing offer, Buick's nicer model still costs $3272.32 more (= 21,772.32 − 18,500) than the best deal (cash back) on Ford's more basic model. ∎

---

[5] To make a "fair" comparison possible, the repayment process for the bank loan *must* be identical to that for the special-financing offer: 36 equal monthly payments. If the size of the period is different (say weekly), if the length of the loan is different (say 48 months), or if the payments are not identical each period, a comparison of payments can lead to the wrong choice.

[6] We also want to caution that you must *never* multiply the payment amount times the number of payments. Remember, even identical cash flows, if they occur at different times, do not have the same value—because of the time value of money.

Self-Check Questions

1. Why is Ford's "special financing" just like a reduction in the real price of the car?

2. Explain why it is important to calculate the value of special-financing offers correctly when deciding which car to buy.

4.8 PROBLEM SOLVING: A REVIEW

Solving problems reinforces our understanding of important relationships among variables, such as the inverse relationship between a present value and the discount rate: All else equal, a higher discount rate lowers the present value. Although we can memorize particular relationships, solving the end-of-chapter problems can reinforce and improve your understanding of these relationships. Problem solving comes easier to some people than to others, but it is a skill that can be learned. In this section, we provide a reminder about algebra and outline a helpful approach to problem solving.

To solve any problem, you have to have enough information. In mathematical terms, information comes in two forms: (1) as a given value, such as "the discount rate is 10%," or (2) as a relationship, such as the present-value formula. Recall from algebra that you must have at least as many equations as you have unknowns to compute a unique solution to a problem.

For example, the present-value formula cannot be used to determine a present value without knowing the expected future cash flows and the required return. This may seem obvious, but it can be easily forgotten in a complex problem. This provides a starting point for systematically solving problems. Consider the example wherein we compared cash back to 3.9% special financing. Four general steps are necessary to set up the problem for solution:

1. *What must be determined?* The question can be answered by comparing the present value of one alternative with the present value of the other alternative. Thus you need to determine two present values.

2. *What inputs are needed?* The payment schedule and the discount rate are necessary to compute a present value.

3. *What is already known?* The cash-back-offer price is $18,500. Thus the present-value cost for the cash-back offer is known without further calculation. The payments for the special financing are $589.59. [Put in PV = 20,000, r = 0.325%, n = 36, and FV = 0. Then compute CF = 589.59.] The opportunity cost for borrowing money—the market rate—is 8% APR, or r = 0.6667% per month.

4. *What relationships exist?* We know the time-value-of-money formulas and can use them, with what we already know, to compute the other needed inputs. So far, we have one part of the answer: The present value of the cash-back offer is $18,500. We also have the inputs necessary to compute the present value of the special-financing offer, so we can compute the present value using Equation (4.2). It is $18,814.77. [Put in CF = 589.59, r = 0.6667% (8% APR), n = 36, and FV = 0. Then compute PV = 18,814.77.] Finally, we need only compare the two present values and choose the lower-price offer.

Table 4-6 lists the variables, and a source of information for each, for this example. The subscripts c and s denote cash-back offer and special-financing offer, respectively.

The last step is to solve the problem. It involves using known relationships in conjunction with known values. In virtually every case, this last step also involves algebraic manipulation of some sort. We assume you have some knowledge of algebra. Like many skills, how-

TABLE 4-6
Sources of information for the example involving cash back versus 3.9% special financing.

VARIABLE	SOURCE OF INFORMATION
Stated price	Given
Cash back	Given
PV_c	Stated price minus Cash back
PV_s	Present-value formula using CF_s, r, and n
CF_s	Annuity formula using Stated price, Special APR, and n
r	Bank's interest rate, given
Special APR	Given
n	Given

ever, our algebraic skill deteriorates if it is not used regularly. Therefore, you may find it helpful to review some of the basics of algebra.

Remember that whatever you do to one side of the equation you must also do to the other side. This rule is somewhat like the balance scale used by the blindfolded figure of Justice. Thus if you add something, such as 12, or n, or PV, to one side of an equation, then you must add an equivalent amount to the other side to maintain the balance. Likewise, to multiply the equation by some value, you must multiply both sides of the equation by the same value. Using steps such as multiplying or dividing through an equation, and adding or subtracting equal amounts on both sides of an equation, to solve for a particular variable is a matter of practice.

As you work through the end-of-chapter problems, keep the following in mind: Where the example in the chapter may give you A and B and ask you to find C, often the practice problem is simply a "rearrangement" of an example in the chapter, where you are given B and C and asked to find A.

Self-Check Questions
1. What are the four general steps necessary to set up a problem before you can solve it?
2. How are the time-value-of-money formulas useful in financial problem solving?

SUMMARY

This chapter described and discussed uses of the Time-Value-of-Money Principle. We showed how the present-value and future-value formulas can be used to compute the value of cash flows at times other than when they will be paid or received. Annuity formulas enable us to solve more complex problems in a routine manner. Time-value-of-money formulas can also be used to find the payments or true interest cost—the APY—for a loan. The APY depends on the compounding frequency and can differ from the APR, which is a nominal rate. Finally, we showed how to value "special-financing" offers.

DECISION SUMMARY

- The NPV is the difference between present value and cost. The NPV measures the value created by a financial decision. A positive NPV creates value.

- The required return is the minimum return a person must have in order to be willing to invest. The required return *exactly* reflects the risk of the investment.

- The expected return is what you expect to earn if you make the investment.
- The realized return is what was actually earned during a given amount of time.
- The expected return equals the required return in a perfect capital market environment, which makes the NPV equal zero.
- The realized return is disconnected from the expected return because of risk. The realized return is an outcome that cannot be changed after the fact.
- Present value and the discount rate are inversely related: Present value goes down when r goes up, and vice versa.
- Never multiply the annuity payment amount times the number of payments. Because of the time value of money, identical cash flows do not have the same value if they occur at different times.

EQUATION SUMMARY

(4.1)
$$FVA_n = CF\left[\frac{(1+r)^n - 1}{r}\right]$$

(4.2)
$$PVA_n = CF\left[\frac{(1+r)^n - 1}{r(1+r)^n}\right]$$

(4.3)
$$CF = PVA_n\left[\frac{r(1+r)^n}{(1+r)^n - 1}\right]$$

(4.4)
$$CF = FVA_n\left[\frac{r}{(1+r)^n - 1}\right]$$

(4.5)
$$PVA_{perpetuity} = \frac{CF}{r}$$

(4.6)
$$APR = (m)(r)$$

(4.7)
$$APY = \left[1 + \frac{APR}{m}\right]^m - 1$$

(4.8)
$$APY = e^{APR} - 1$$

KEY TERMS

net present value (NPV)...94	present-value factor...96	loan amortization schedule...104
fair price...94	future-value formula...97	perpetuity...106
required rate of return...94	future-value factor...97	annual percentage rate (APR)...108
expected rate of return...95	annuity...101	compounding frequency...108
realized rate of return...95	future-value annuity factor...103	annual percentage yield (APY)...109
present-value formula...96	present-value annuity factor...103	

EXERCISES

PROBLEM SET A

A1. You expect to receive the following future cash flows at the end of the years indicated: $500 in year 2, $1200 in year 4, $800 in year 5, and $1500 in year 6. The discount rate is 7% per year.

   a. What is the present value of all four expected future cash flows?

b. What is the value of the four flows at year 5?

c. What is the value of the four flows at year 10?

A2. The following future cash flows will be received at the end of the years indicated: $1000 in year 1, $1400 in year 2, $900 in year 4, and $600 in year 5. The discount rate is 8% per year.

a. What is the present value of all four expected future cash flows?

b. What is the value of the four flows at year 5?

c. What is the value of the four flows at year 3?

A3. What is the present value of $500 per year for 8 years if the required return is 8.5% per year?

A4. What is the future value, at the end of year 6, of a 6-year annuity of $1000 per year if the expected return is 10%?

A5. What is the future value, at the end of year 5, of $1200 per year for each of the next 5 years if the expected return is 7% per year?

A6. What is the future value, 10 years from now, of an annuity of $350 per year for each of the next 7 years if the expected return is 10% per year?

A7. What is the present value of a 6-year annuity of $1000 per year if the required return is 10% per year?

A8. What are the monthly payments on a 3-year $5000 loan if the interest rate is 1% per month?

A9. What are the annual payments for a 4-year $4000 loan if the interest rate is 9% per year? Make up a loan amortization schedule for this loan.

A10. Create a loan amortization schedule for borrowing $7500 at an interest rate of 20% per year, to be paid off in four equal annual payments.

A11. What is the present value of a perpetuity of $800 per year if the required return is 11% per year?

A12. What are the monthly payments on a 4-year $15,000 loan if the required return is 9% APR?

A13. What is the present value of $100 per week for 5 years if the required return is 10% APR?

A14. What is the future value after 10 years of $200 per month if the expected return is 6% APR?

A15. What are the monthly payments on a 25-year $150,000 mortgage if the required return is 7.5% APR?

A16. What is the present value of $10,000 to be received 7.8 years from today, if the required return is 8.2% APY?

PROBLEM SET B

B1. What is the present value of a stream of $1500 payments received at the end of each of years 3 through 9 if the required return is 10% per year?

B2. If the required return is 8% per year, what is the present value of $1000 per year (a) for 10 years? (b) for 20 years? (c) for 50 years? (d) for 100 years? (e) forever?

B3. Suppose a bank offers to lend you $18,000 if you will pay back $439.43 per month for 48 months.

a. What monthly interest rate is the bank charging?

b. What APR is the bank charging on this loan?

c. What APY is the bank charging on this loan?

B4. What is the APY for a 15% APR with monthly compounding?

B5. What is the APY for a 15% APR with continuous compounding?

B6. Suppose a bank offers a 20-year $130,000 mortgage if you will pay back $1007.89 per month.

a. What monthly interest rate is the bank charging?

b. What APR is the bank charging on this mortgage?

c. What APY is the bank charging on this loan?

B7. What is the present value of $3400 to be received 3 years from today if the required return is 11% APR compounded continuously?

B8. What is the present value of $15,000 per year received continuously for 5 years if the required return is 12% APR compounded continuously?

B9. What is the present value of $4500 to be received 31 months from today if the required return is 10% APY?

B10. What is the future value of $20,000 per year received in lump sums at the end of each year for 5 years if the expected return is 10% per year compounded continuously?

B11. What is the present value of a 5-year annuity, with the first $3000 payment being made 3 months from today, if the required return is 7% APY?

B12. What is the value 4.35 years from now of a 4-year annuity, with the first $1200 payment being made 1 year from today, if the expected return is APY = 10%?

B13. What is the present value of a 6-year annuity, with the first $2500 payment being made 7 months from today if the required return is APY = 12%?

B14. You expect to receive $2000 3 years from today. If the present value of this amount is $1423.56, what is the APY?

B15. You expect to receive $1000 sometime in the future. If the present value of this amount is $592.03 and the discount rate is 10% APY, when is the cash flow expected to occur?

B16. How long does it take a present-value amount to double if the expected return is (a) 4%? (b) 9%? (c) 15%?

B17. If an annuity of $5000 per year for 8 years has a present value of $27,469.57, what is the expected APY?

B18. What is the present value of a 15-year annuity with payments of $1800 per year, where the first payment is expected to occur 4 years from today and the required return is 7.3% APY?

B19. Suppose you expect to receive $1000 per year for each of the next 15 years, except that you will not receive any payments in years 3 and 5. What is the present value of this amount if the required return is 12% APR?

B20. Bob's Bank has offered you a $40,000 mortgage on a house. Payments are to be $374.90 per month for 30 years.

  a. What monthly interest rate is Bob's charging?

  b. What is the APR on this loan?

  c. What is the APY on this loan?

B21. Let's say Chrysler is offering a choice of either "42-month 2.2% APR" financing or "$2000 cash back" on a car you have decided to buy. The stated price for the car is $23,000.

  a. What are the monthly payments required for Chrysler's special-financing deal?

  b. If you can borrow the cash to buy the car from several different banks at 8.3% APR, would you be better off taking the cash-back offer?

B22. Performance Auto is offering you a choice of either special financing or a price discount on their new sports car, the QT-123. The stated price for the car is $31,000, but you can pay $25,500 cash and "drive it home today." Alternatively, you can borrow the $31,000 from Performance Auto and make monthly payments for 3 years with a 1% APR. Suppose the best financing currently available is to borrow money from Bob's Bank for 3 years at 12% APR with monthly installment payments, and you have decided to buy a QT-123 from Performance Auto. Should you take the special financing or borrow the money from Bob's Bank and pay the cash price?

B23. Suppose your parents have decided that after you graduate at the end of this year, they will start saving money to help pay for your younger sister to attend college. They plan to save money for 5 years before she starts college. The instant after they make the last payment, they will withdraw the first payment for her. The payments to her will be $8000 per year at the start of each of her 4 years in college. They will save an equal amount at the end of every month for 5 years. The monthly interest rate they will earn on their savings is 0.45%. How much must they save each month in order to be able to make the four payments with no money left over?

B24. What are the monthly payments on a 3-year $10,000 loan (36 equal payments) if the interest rate is 10% APY?

B25. Suppose you would like to be paid $20,000 per year during your retirement, which starts in 20 years. Assume that the $20,000 is an annual perpetuity with the first payment being made exactly 21 years from today. The expected return is 4% APY. How much should you save per year for the next 20 years so that you can achieve your retirement goal?

B26. Let's say Toyota is offering either "36-month 1.9% APR" financing or "$1400 cash back" on a car you have decided to buy. The stated price for the car is $18,000. You can borrow the cash to buy the car from several different banks at 8.1% APR. Which alternative has the lower "real" price, the special-financing deal or the cash-back offer?

Problem Set C

C1. Annuities have payments that occur at the end of every period. An *annuity due* is an annuity whose payments occur at the start of every period. Make a time line for this problem, and you will be able to see that one way to value an annuity due is to view it as an annuity with "$n - 1$" payments *plus* a payment at $t = 0$.

   a. What is the present value of an 8-year *annuity due* of $750 per year if the required return is 8.2% APY?

   b. What is the future value at the end of 6 years of a 6-year *annuity due* of $400 per year if the expected return is 10.4% APY?

C2. Harry's Home Finance is offering to lend you $10,000 for a home improvement. The loan is to be repaid in monthly installments over 9 years.

   a. If the interest rate on this loan is 15% APR, compounded continuously, what will your monthly payments be if you accept Harry's offer?

   b. If the rate on this loan is 15% APR, compounded weekly, what will your monthly payments be if you accept Harry's offer? (Note that there are more than 4 weeks in a month!)

C3. Billy Bob won a lottery that will pay him $10,000 per year for 10 years. He got the first payment 9 months ago, so the second payment will occur 3 months from today. Billy Bob has decided to sell the rest of the payments. He is offering them to you for $61,825.00. The appropriate required return on this stream of expected future cash flows is 10% APY.

   a. What is the present value of this set of cash flows?

   b. What is the net present value of buying this set of expected future cash flows from Billy Bob for $61,825.00?

C4. What is the future value, 1.75 years from now, if the present value is $900 and the expected return is 12% APR compounded semiannually?

C5.

   a. What is the present value of $5000 per year received at the end of each year for 20 years if the required return is 8% APR compounded continuously?

   b. Under the same conditions except that the money is received continuously during each year, what is the present value?

C6.

   a. What is the present value of $10,000 per year received at the end of each year in perpetuity with a required return of 7.4% APR compounded continuously?

   b. Under the same conditions except that the money is received continuously during each year, what is the present value?

C7. Suppose your parents have decided that after you graduate at the end of this year, they will start saving money to help pay for your younger brother to attend college. They plan to save money for 5 years before he starts college and to continue to save during his college years. They plan to contribute $8000 per year at the start of each of his 4 years in college. Your parents will thus make monthly payments for 8 years (5 before and 3 during your brother's college education). The monthly interest rate earned on their savings is 0.45%. How much must the monthly savings be under these conditions?

C8. What is the present value of $1000 every 2 years forever, with the first payment 2 years from today, if the required return is 12% APY?

C9. What is the present value of $500 every 4 years forever, with the first payment 2 years from today, if the required return is 12% APY?

C10. A firm advertising early-retirement programs promises to repay you forever whatever amount you pay them per year for 12 years. What interest rate are they promising?

C11. Suppose you would like to be paid $30,000 per year during your retirement, which starts in 25 years. Assume the $30,000 is an annual perpetuity and that the expected return is 6% APY. What should you save *per month* for the next 25 years so that you can achieve your retirement goal?

C12. Suppose you are paying $31.73 per week for 10 years to repay a $10,000 loan.

   a. What is the weekly interest rate on this loan?

   b. What is the APR?

   c. What is the APY?

C13. What are the monthly payments on a $50,000 25-year loan if the interest rate is 13% APR with continuous compounding?

Real-World Application:
The Swiss Surprise: $125 Billion Is A Lot of Money

Imagine getting a bill for $125 billion you didn't know you owed. That actually happened to the residents, called "burghers," of the town of Ticino, Switzerland. A court in Brooklyn, New York, ordered Ticino to pay a group of American investors. The investors had sued in the Brooklyn court over a loss they claimed in connection with the 1967 failure of Inter Change Bank, a tiny bank in Ticino. The burghers had known about the suit, but thought the matter was trivial, and were naturally stunned by the bill. Their lead lawyer quipped that if the judgment was upheld by the higher courts, all of Ticino's citizens would have to spend the rest of their lives flipping real burgers (the kind you eat) at McDonald's and Burger King to pay off the debt.[7]

   The root of Ticino's problem was a deposit made in 1966. The estate of one Sterling Granville Higgins deposited $600 million of options on Venezuelan oil and mineral deposits in the Inter Change Bank. The deposit agreement required the bank to pay an interest rate of 1% per week. (No wonder the bank failed the next year!) In

October 1994, the New York State Supreme Court in Brooklyn ruled that Ticino had to pay 1% interest per week compounded weekly for the 7 years between the date of deposit and the date Ticino had the bank liquidated and interest at the rate of 8.54% APY for the remaining 21 years since the bank's liquidation.

1. At an interest rate of 1% per week, how long does it take for $600 million to grow to $1 billion? To $10 billion?

2. At an interest rate of 1% per week, what is the future value of $600 million after 1 year? After 28 years?

3. At an interest rate of 1% per week, what is the future value of $600 million after 7 years?

4. The $125 billion reported in the press was rounded. How much was the bill to the nearest dollar? That is, what is the future value at 8.54% APY after an additional 21 years of the amount you calculated in question 3?

5. What is the APY over the entire 28 years as the $600 million grows to the exact amount you calculated in question 4?

[7] "Poor Swiss Get U.S. Bill: $125 Billion and Change," *The New York Times*, February 28, 1996, p. A4.

6. Suppose Ticino could pay $5 billion per year. How long would it take to pay off the debt, assuming interest continued to be charged at 8.54% APY?

7. Suppose Ticino could pay $12 billion per year. How long would it take to pay off the debt, assuming interest continued to be charged at 8.54% APY?

Postscript: To the burghers' relief, the judgment was thrown out on appeal. This no doubt restored the confidence of the good burghers of Ticino in the American system of justice!

APPENDIX: THE THEORETICAL BASIS FOR THE NPV RULE

The NPV rule is based on how capital markets help allocate resources efficiently. The crucial variable is the "interest rate," which is often referred to as the opportunity cost of capital. The *opportunity cost of capital* is the price to "rent" money. It is the return the users of funds (for example, borrowers) must pay suppliers of funds (for example, lenders) for the use of their capital. The opportunity cost of capital is important, because it determines who will lend, who will borrow, and the amount of total capital supplied and used.

In Chapter 14, we will formally describe an environment called a *perfect capital market environment*. For now, think of a perfect capital market as a streamlined capital market that glosses over the complexities of real capital markets. In a perfect capital market environment, all prices are fair, so all financial assets have a zero NPV. The expected return of every financial asset equals its required return. Our analysis assumes that there is a single capital market where all users and suppliers of capital can make transactions.

We develop the concepts here as though there is a single opportunity cost of capital we call *the* interest rate. This unique rate is determined through competition among suppliers (lenders) and users (borrowers) of funds. It is the key to how the capital market allocates resources efficiently.

In practice, it seems as though there are many different rates. This is because each market return depends on the risk associated with it and on how long the money will be used. From the Principle of Risk-Return Trade-Off, we know that the higher the risk, the higher the required return. But such differences in risk and return do not affect value. That is the nature of the trade-off. Otherwise, if there were differences in value, there wouldn't be a trade-off—everyone would take the choice with the highest value and not the others. To avoid the complication created by risk-return trade-offs, our analysis assumes that all assets are riskless.

Concerning how long the money will be used, recall from our discussion of the term structure of interest rates in Chapter 3 that generally the longer the commitment, the higher the required return. Like differences in risk, differences in *maturity* lead to alternatives (trade-offs) that are equal in value. Therefore, our final simplifying assumption is that all assets last one year.

The Price of Impatience and the Value of Waiting

If the interest rate is 10% per year and you lend $10,000 today, you'll get $11,000 (your principal plus $1000 interest) one year from today. But if you lend the $10,000 today, you can't spend it today. You give up that opportunity. In return for waiting a year, however, you'll be able to spend $11,000, thereby getting an extra $1000 to spend. In this sense, the 10% interest rate measures the *opportunity cost*. It is the price of impatience and the value of waiting.

Figure 4-A1 shows how the capital market allows people to trade off spending (consumption) now against spending (consumption) in the future. Suppose you have income of C today and C a year from today. Without a capital market, you could spend no more than C today, and no more than C a year from today, assuming there was no way to store any unused

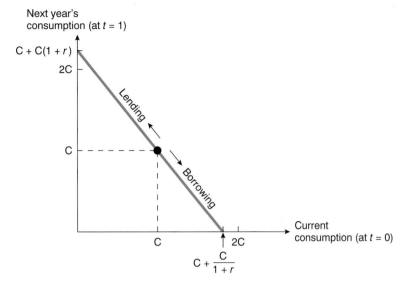

FIGURE 4-A1
All possible consumption (spending) combinations now and next year.

cash. Being so limited could be very inconvenient, especially if you didn't have a regular cash flow each year.

The capital market expands your choices between spending today and spending in the future. The line in Figure 4-A1 shows all the possible combinations of spending today (measured along the horizontal axis) and spending a year from today (measured along the vertical axis). The slope of the line is the rate at which you can trade off current consumption for future consumption, and vice versa. Mathematically, the slope equals $-(1 + r)$, where r is the interest rate. Given your income, you could spend C today and C next year (at $t = 1$). Alternatively, you could lend your entire current income C, spend nothing today, and spend C + C(1 + r) next year. At the opposite extreme, you could borrow the present value of your future income, C/(1 + r), spend C + C/(1 + r) today, and spend nothing next year. Of course, combinations along the line between these two extremes are also possible.

Here is an example to help you see the point. Suppose C = \$10,000 and r = 10%. You can spend \$10,000 today and \$10,000 next year if you don't borrow or lend. Alternatively, you can lend all of this year's income and get to spend \$21,000 (10,000 + 11,000) next year. At the other extreme, you can borrow \$9090.91 (= 10,000/1.1), spend \$19,090.91 now, and have nothing to spend next year. By borrowing or lending, you can take any position along the line in Figure 4-A1.[8]

Smoothing Consumption Patterns

People don't all have the same spending needs and preferences. The capital markets allow people to spend in whatever way they choose, within the limits of their income. In terms of Figure 4-A1, you can be anywhere along the line, but not above it, because you have only \$10,000 per year of income.[9]

Consider two people with the same income C today and C next year (at $t = 1$). Call them Miser and Spendthrift. Miser would like to spend 0.5C today and C + 0.5C(1 + r) next year.

---

[8] Note that the slope of the line is $-(1 + r) = -1.1$, which equals $-21,000/19,090.91$.
[9] If you've had some economic theory, you may recognize the line in Figure 4-A1 as an individual's *consumption-possibilities curve*. We could superimpose an *indifference curve* to find the consumption point where the individual would be best off. This point is where the consumption-possibilities curve is tangent to the indifference curve. This is where the marginal rate of time preference (trading off spending now for spending in the future) equals the interest rate.

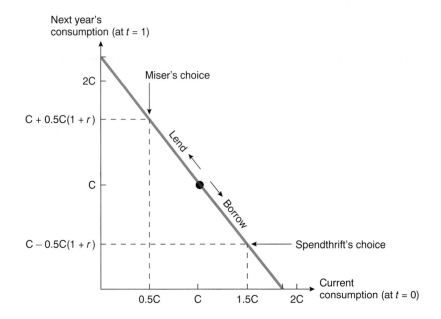

FIGURE 4-A2
Miser's and Spendthrift's consumption (spending) choices.

How can she do this? She lends 0.5C and gets back 0.5C(1 + r) next year. Spendthrift, on the other hand, would like to spend 1.5C today and C − 0.5C(1 + r) next year. Thus he borrows 0.5C today but must pay back 0.5C(1 + r) next year. Figure 4-A2 illustrates Miser's and Spendthrift's consumption (spending) choices.

The capital market lets all individuals have their own preferred spending pattern, within the limit of their total wealth.

All Possible Investment Opportunities

Another way of viewing spending choices is to express them as capital market investment opportunities. By default, this year's spending is, in essence, an investment decision. The less you spend now, the more you invest, and the more you will have next year.

Figure 4-A3 shows the current decision as an investment decision. The line proceeding up and to the right from the origin is a line of all possible investment amounts. If you invest all your current income, C, then next year you will have the investment's future value, C(1 + r). Likewise, an investment of 0.5C will return 0.5C(1 + r), and so on. Thus this capital market investment-opportunities line has a slope of (1 + r).

In addition to capital market investment opportunities, market participants can invest in real assets. Figure 4-A4 presents a real asset investment-opportunities curve, with the opportunities ranked by their expected return from largest to smallest. It shows the combinations of investment today and return next year to be had from investing in real assets.[10] Note that the real asset investment-opportunities curve in Figure 4-A4 is not a straight line. This is because of diminishing returns from investing in real assets. Recall the Principle of Valuable Ideas. Quite simply, some ideas create more value than others. In the extreme, some ideas are actually costly; they will not return enough to be worthwhile.

The opportunity to invest in real assets greatly expands the set of investment possibilities beyond those shown in Figure 4-A3. More significantly, comparing capital market and

---

[10] It might occur to you that the smoothness of the real asset investment-opportunities curve assumes that investment opportunities can be broken into "very small" pieces. That is, the curve isn't "lumpy" the way it would be if opportunities were large and indivisible, as they typically are.

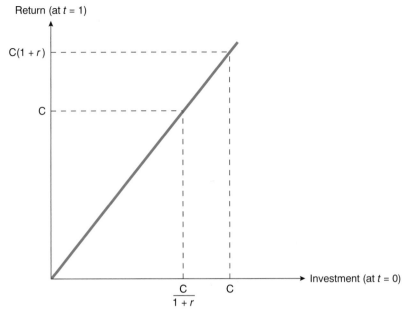

FIGURE 4-A3
The capital market investment-opportunities line.

real asset investment opportunities simultaneously leads us to a very important result: a rule for choosing investments in real assets.

Because of self-interested behavior, people will invest in the most profitable real asset investment opportunity first, in the next most profitable opportunity second, and so on. In Figure 4-A4, the scale is represented in millions of dollars, so the first $1 million of investment produces a return of $2.5 million. Investing the second $1 million produces a return of $2.25 million. Investing additional $1 million amounts would produce successively smaller returns. But how much should the *total* amount of investment be?

If you can earn r per period by investing in the capital market, why would you ever invest in a real asset investment opportunity of identical risk that returned less than r? The an-

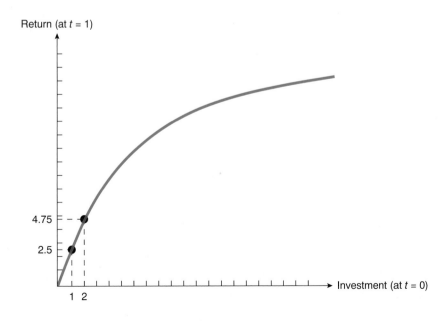

FIGURE 4-A4
The real asset investment-opportunities curve (in millions of dollars).

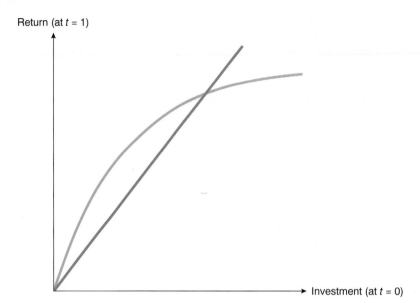

FIGURE 4-A5
Capital market investment-opportunities line superimposed on the real asset investment-opportunities curve.

swer is that you wouldn't. And this is exactly where the net present value (NPV) rule originates. *Don't buy an asset that isn't worth what you have to pay for it*. In other words, don't buy a negative-NPV asset.

Figure 4-A5 superimposes the real asset investment-opportunities curve on the capital market investment-opportunities line. If people use the NPV rule just stated, they will not invest in negative-NPV real assets—those that do not return at least r. These opportunities are where the slope is less than $(1 + r)$. But they should invest in all the opportunities up to that point—those that return at least $(1 + r)$. Therefore, the optimal total investment is found by putting a line parallel to the capital market investment-opportunities line, tangent to the real asset investment-opportunities curve. Figure 4-A6 illustrates this concept by adding this parallel line.

FIGURE 4-A6
The optimal total investment, I*, and the corresponding increase in present value, NPV*.

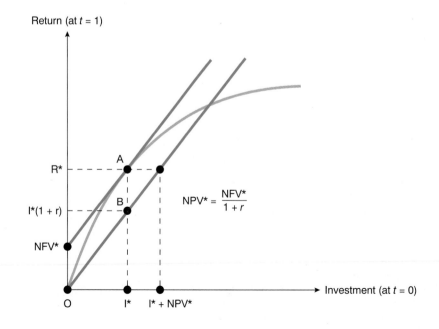

In Figure 4-A6, the optimal total investment is I*, and the total return at $t = 1$ is R*. A fair total return (expected equals required) would be I*$(1 + r)$ = R* − NFV* (because the triangles AR* NFV* and BOI* are congruent). Consequently, the total excess return at $t = 1$ (the net future value) will be NFV*. NFV* has a present value of NPV* $(= $ NFV*$/[1 + r])$.

Our description works if you have *enough* money to invest in a positive-NPV real asset. But suppose you have some money to invest, but not that much? Does this mean you have to give up all real asset investment opportunities? No! The capital market allows both positive and negative investment—that is, lending *and* borrowing. Therefore, when you have found a positive-NPV real asset but lack the cash to make the investment, you can borrow the money in the capital market.[11]

Returning to Miser and Spendthrift, we can see how investing in real assets makes them *both* better off. The value added by investment I* is NPV* in terms of $t = 0$ dollars and is NFV* in terms of $t = 1$ dollars. We can express an individual's value from investing in real assets as IPV at $t = 0$ and as IFV at $t = 1$. This extra value adds to each individual's income. Figure 4-A7 is adapted from Figure 4-A2 by including the value added from investments in real assets. In Figure 4-A7, we can see how investing in real assets can make both Miser and Spendthrift better off. By investing in positive-NPV real assets, they will be able to spend more—both now *and* next year.

It is vital to understand that Spendthrift will borrow (get some type of financing for) the extra money he needs to invest—on top of the amount he was going to borrow anyway to spend (consume) now. But despite this, Spendthrift will be better off because he will get the NPV from those investments (IPV in Figure 4-A7). Miser is also better off, because some of

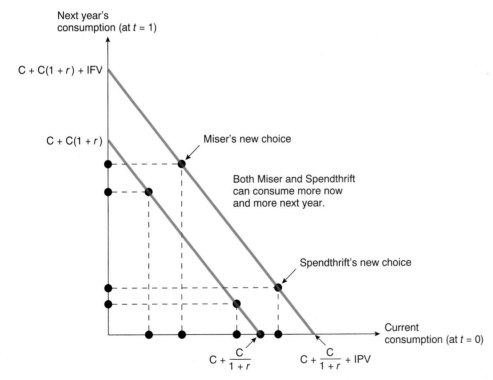

Next year's consumption (at $t = 1$)

$C + C(1 + r) +$ IFV

$C + C(1 + r)$

Miser's new choice

Both Miser and Spendthrift can consume more now and more next year.

Spendthrift's new choice

Current consumption (at $t = 0$)

$C + \dfrac{C}{1 + r}$ $C + \dfrac{C}{1 + r} +$ IPV

FIGURE 4-A7
The individual's gain from investing in real assets.

---

[11] We are using the term *borrowing* to mean any use of capital with any type of financing. The risk-return trade-off makes the various types equivalent in value.

the money she was going to save (lend) will be invested in positive-NPV real assets. Therefore, a key point of the analysis is that the NPV rule applies to all individuals, regardless of their personal spending choices.

The capital markets bring together the combined choices for investing in real and financial assets and borrowing for either spending (consumption) or investment purposes. Thus the capital markets play a crucial role, because they determine the trade-offs among all these choices. These trade-offs are embodied in, or represented by, the rate of interest. The rate of interest, then, is a measure of the opportunity cost of choosing one alternative over another. The rate of interest is the opportunity cost of capital.

Fisher Separation

The NPV rule, which was derived by the American economist Irving Fisher two-thirds of a century ago, means the optimal amount of investment in real assets does not have anything to do with individual spending preferences. As long as people have free access to the capital markets (that is, that they can supply or use capital freely at the market interest rate), each person can choose his or her own spending (consumption) pattern.

This means that a firm's investment decisions are *separate* from individual owners' spending preferences. This result, that investment choices are separate from individual spending preferences, is called **Fisher's separation theorem**.

Fisher's separation theorem has an important implication for firms, some of which have literally hundreds of thousands of shareholders. Such firms are managed by professional managers. The ownership and control of these firms are separated, as we discussed in our set-of-contracts model. Fisher's separation theorem provides a unifying goal for the firm, a goal that the firm's shareholders can all agree on. All the owners, regardless of their spending preferences, will be best off if the firm invests in positive-NPV assets, because all will get their share of the NPV, so each will ultimately be able to spend more. Therefore, *a firm should maximize the NPV of its investments*. This, then, is the basis for the NPV rule.

Fisher's separation theorem—and therefore the NPV rule—rests on the assumption of a perfect capital market environment. To the extent that real capital markets deviate from this, Fisher's separation theorem may only be a first approximation. In Chapter 14, we discuss the existence of capital market imperfections and their implications for the firm.

BIBLIOGRAPHY

Black, Fischer. "A Simple Discounting Rule," *Financial Management*, 1988, 17(2):7–11.

Fisher, Irving. *The Theory of Interest*. New York: Augustus M. Kelley, 1965 (reprinted from the original edition published in 1930).

Hirshleifer, J. *Investment, Interest and Capital.* Englewood Cliffs, N.J.: Prentice-Hall, 1970.

Ross, Stephen A. "Uses, Abuses, and Alternatives to the Net-Present-Value Rule," *Financial Management*, 1995, 24(3):96–102.

VALUING FINANCIAL SECURITIES

Stocks and bonds are the most common and basic types of financial securities. Financial securities provide much of the financing (right-hand side of the balance sheet) for firms. When a firm decides to expand, and lacks the necessary cash, it can raise the money it needs by selling new financial securities.

Stocks and bonds are different. Recall that stock is equity, a form of ownership. A bond is a type of loan.

We know from the previous chapter that the value of something can be expressed as the present value of its expected future cash flows. This is especially convenient for assets that are financial securities, because they're often described mainly by their cash flows. Thus we can make immediate use of the time-value-of-money tools from Chapter 4 to value bonds and stocks.

For a bond, the periodic expected future cash flows are the contractually promised interest and principal payments. For stock, the periodic expected future cash flows are cash dividends. Both have one additional expected future cash flow: the future sale price. Here is the method we will use to value them:

1. Estimate the expected future cash flows.
2. Determine the required return, which depends on the riskiness of the expected future cash flows.
3. Compute the present value, which is what the asset is worth.

Before we go on, let's review some especially relevant terms and concepts. Recall that we defined three different rates of return: required, expected, and realized. Frequently in this chapter, we assume that the required and expected returns are equal. Recall from Chapter 4 that this is like assuming all transactions take place in a perfect capital market, a market in which all securities always have fair prices.

OBJECTIVES

After studying this chapter, you should be able to

1. Describe the typical features of bonds and stocks.

2. Be able to locate and interpret information about bonds and stocks in the financial press.

3. Calculate fair prices for bonds and stocks.

4. Compute expected returns for bonds and stocks, which are called the yield to maturity for a bond and the capitalization rate for a stock.

5. Articulate the relationships among value, required return, and expected future cash flows for bonds and stocks.

6. Identify the main factors that affect the cash flows to bonds and stocks, and understand how changes in them affect bond and stock value.

VALUING SECURITIES AND THE PRINCIPLES OF FINANCE

♦ *Incremental Benefits*: Measure the incremental benefits from owning a financial security, which are its expected future cash flows.

♦ *Time-Value-of-Money*: Determine the value of a financial security by computing the present value of its expected future cash flows.

♦ *Two-Sided Transactions*: Use the fair price of a financial security to compute its expected return, because the fair price does not favor either side of the transaction.

♦ *Efficient Capital Markets*: Estimate the required return for a financial security with its expected return.

♦ *Risk–Return Trade-Off*: Recognize that a financial security's value and required return reflect its risk.

5.1 BONDS

A **bond** is a long-term obligation for borrowed money. It is a promise to pay interest and repay the borrowed money on terms specified in a contract called a **bond indenture**. In addition to U.S. firms, many other entities sell bonds to borrow money. The U.S. government, federal agencies, state governments, municipalities, foreign firms, foreign governments, and international agencies account for most other bond issues. We use U.S. corporate bonds for illustrative purposes, but you can apply the bond valuation techniques we describe here to virtually any bond.

Let's start with an example of a bond contract that governs a six-year $100 million loan. The contract specifies an interest rate of 7% per year payable semiannually (7% APR[1]). It also requires repayment of principal in equal installments three, four, five, and six years from the date the bond was issued. The borrower would then be obligated to pay the lender 3.5% (one-half of 7%) of the unpaid bond loan balance at semiannual intervals. Table 5-1 specifies the bond's future cash flows promised by the borrower.

There are many different types of bonds, but all of them can be described by their pattern of promised future payments. A typical bond indenture includes at a minimum the following provisions:

1. The **par value**, which is also called the **face value**. This is the amount of money the issuer must repay by the end of the bond's life. Most corporate bonds issued in the United States have a par value of $1000. Unless otherwise stated, we assume a $1000 par value.

2. A promise to make **coupon payments** periodically over the life of the bond. Coupon payments are the finance term for what are called interest payments in everyday language. The large majority of corporate bonds make coupon payments semiannually—that is, every six months. Coupon payments are determined by the **coupon rate**. In the example given above, the coupon rate is 7%. Assuming the typical $1000 par value and semiannual interest payments, coupon payments will be $35 (one-half the coupon rate times the par value) every six months.

3. A promise to repay the **principal amount** of the bond issue in one or more installments over the life of the bond issue. The principal is the total amount of money being borrowed. Typically, it is simply the total of the par values of all the bonds that make up the bond issue. For example, a bond issue

---

[1] Recall that the APR, annual percentage rate, is the rate per compounding period times the number of compounding periods in a year.

PERIOD	INITIAL LOAN BALANCE	INTEREST PAYMENT	PRINCIPAL REPAYMENT	ENDING LOAN BALANCE	TOTAL DEBT SERVICE PAYMENT
0.5	$100,000,000	$3,500,000	—	$100,000,000	$3,500,000
1.0	100,000,000	3,500,000	—	100,000,000	3,500,000
1.5	100,000,000	3,500,000	—	100,000,000	3,500,000
2.0	100,000,000	3,500,000	—	100,000,000	3,500,000
2.5	100,000,000	3,500,000	—	100,000,000	3,500,000
3.0	100,000,000	3,500,000	$25,000,000	75,000,000	28,500,000
3.5	75,000,000	2,625,000	—	75,000,000	2,625,000
4.0	75,000,000	2,625,000	25,000,000	50,000,000	27,625,000
4.5	50,000,000	1,750,000	—	50,000,000	1,750,000
5.0	50,000,000	1,750,000	25,000,000	25,000,000	26,750,000
5.5	25,000,000	875,000	—	25,000,000	875,000
6.0	25,000,000	875,000	25,000,000	—	25,875,000

TABLE 5-1
Schedule of semiannual bond payments.

with a $100 million principal would typically have 100,000 (= 100 million/1000) bonds, each with a $1000 par value.

4. The **maturity** of a bond is the end of its life. It occurs at the **maturity date**. When a bond is issued (created), the length of its life is its **original maturity**. The amount of time remaining until maturity is called the **remaining maturity**. Virtually any original maturity is possible, but most U.S. corporate bonds issued in recent years have had original maturities between 5 and 30 years.

5. A **call provision** gives the issuer (the firm) the right (option) to pay off the bonds prior to their maturity by paying a **call price**. When you first think about it, it may seem odd for the issuer to need the right to pay back the money it owes. But as we will explain, bond values change when interest rates change. Therefore, like other options, this one is valuable. Let's step to the other side of the transaction to see how.

If you bought a bond that pays 8% interest and then market interest rates went down, you would be pretty happy to continue to earn 8%. That would be more than you could get in other comparable market investments. But the firm would want to repay you and reborrow the money from others at the new lower interest rate. Because of this difference in view from the two sides of the transaction, the contract must carefully specify the rights of each side. Call provisions typically have a "grace period" of several years after issuance during which the firm cannot repay the bonds. A bond's call price usually starts at a premium above the bond's par value and then declines over time, reaching par value at or near maturity.

A bond issue that requires the repayment of the entire principal amount at maturity is said to have a **bullet maturity**. When a bond issue is repaid in multiple installments, the method of repayment is called a **sinking fund**. Typically, bond issues that have a sinking fund require annual payments that begin after some specified "grace period." Sinking fund payments are a fixed obligation from the firm's viewpoint, but not from the bondholder's. The bonds to be repaid in a given year are chosen by lottery, so any particular bondholder does not know that her bond will be repaid until just before it happens.[2] Sometimes firms repurchase the bonds in the capital markets from owners who want to sell them, rather than by lottery selection. This is especially likely when a bond is selling for less than its par value.[3]

The final repayment of principal is typically larger than the others. When it is, it is called the **balloon payment** (or balloon, for short).

---

[2] This is frequently the opposite of the typical lottery: In this case, you win by *not* being picked!

[3] A sinking fund effectively changes the maturity of the total bond issue. This is because some of the bonds are repaid before the stated maturity date. A calculation that takes this difference into account is called *duration*. Duration, which we describe in Chapter 24, provides a measure of the "effective" length of a bond issue's life.

Valuing a Bond

After they are issued, bonds are traded in the secondary market—and rarely at par value. To understand why, indulge in the following reverie. Imagine that you opened the mail one morning and found a gift from your Uncle Warbucks in the form of a 6% bond with a face value of $1000 and two years remaining until maturity. You realize that this is the perfect time to take that vacation you so richly deserve, so you call your broker to arrange the sale of the bond. While you are on hold, you write a thank-you note to your dear uncle. Imagine your disappointment when you learn that the current interest rate for this bond is 12%. Your broker explains that no one would buy your 6% bond for its face value when he could get an identical bond paying 12% for that price. At that moment you receive a fax from your Aunt Matilda saying your birthday check is in the mail. So you agree to sell your new bond at a lower price and begin to pack. At what price would your bond sell?

The fair price of a bond is the present value of its promised future coupon and principal payments. When a bond is issued, its terms are set by the issuing firm to achieve a particular fair price for the bond. Most often, firms set the terms so that the fair price will be very close to the bond's par value. However, after the bonds have been issued, their fair price will reflect current market conditions for similar bonds. In other words, bond values change over time, just like your bond from Uncle Warbucks. This is because the contract terms, especially the schedule of payments, are usually fixed. As a result, when the interest rate (required return) changes, the bond price (the present value of its future payments) also changes.

WHEN THE REQUIRED RETURN EQUALS THE COUPON RATE   Let's consider what the fair price of the bond you got from Uncle Warbucks would have been if the current interest rate had been the same as the bond's 6% coupon rate. Your bond would be expected to pay $30 every six months for the next two years, plus a $1000 principal repayment at the time of the last coupon payment. The fair price of your bond, denoted B_0, would be the present value of all the payments, which is

$$B_0 = \text{PV(coupon payments)} + \text{PV(par value)}$$

$$= \frac{30}{(1.03)} + \frac{30}{(1.03)^2} + \frac{30}{(1.03)^3} + \frac{30}{(1.03)^4} + \frac{1000}{(1.03)^4} = \$1000.00$$

Figure 5-1 illustrates this computation. The following relationship holds for all bonds of this type: *When the required return equals the coupon rate, the fair price equals the par value.*

Another way to make this same computation is to view the expected future cash flows as having two parts: (1) a 4-period annuity of $30 every six months plus (2) a single $1000 payment two years from today. The present value is

$$B_0 = \text{PV(coupon payments)} + \text{PV(par value)}$$

$$= (30) \left[\frac{(1.03)^4 - 1}{(.03)(1.03)^4} \right] + \frac{1000}{(1.03)^4} = 111.51 + 888.49 = \$1000.00$$

[Put in CF = 30.00, $n = 4$, $r = 3\%$, and FV = 1000. Then compute PV = 1000.][4]

WHEN THE REQUIRED RETURN DIFFERS FROM THE COUPON RATE   Now let's consider the value of your bond when you got it and compute the price you would get from selling it. The only difference in our computation is that the bond's current required return

---

[4] Some calculators require that this calculation be done in parts: 1) Put in CF = 30.00, $n = 4$, $r = 3\%$, and FV = 0, and then compute PV = 111.51. 2) Put in FV = 1000, $n = 4$, $r = 3\%$, and CF = 0, and then compute PV = 888.49. Finally, add the two parts to get 111.51 + 888.49 = $1000.

	Now	6 months	1 year	18 months	2 years
Time	0	1	2	3	4
Cash flow		30.00	30.00	30.00	1030.00
Present value	29.13 ◄				
Present value	28.28 ◄				
Present value	27.45 ◄				
Present value	915.14 ◄				
Total present value:	$1000.00				
Required return:	6% APR				

FIGURE 5-1
The present value of a bond's expected future cash flows when the required return equals the bond's coupon rate.

is 12% APR, which is 6% every six months. Once again, the value is the present value, and your bond is worth

$$B_0 = \text{PV(coupon payments)} + \text{PV(par value)}$$

$$= (30)\left[\frac{(1.06)^4 - 1}{(.06)(1.06)^4}\right] + \frac{1000}{(1.06)^4} = \$896.05$$

Let's hope your birthday check from Aunt Matilda is big enough so that the lower bond value won't cramp your style too much!

GENERALIZING BOND VALUATION   Our valuation method can be generalized to value any bond of this type. The fair price is

$$B_0 = \text{PV(coupon payments)} + \text{PV(par value)}$$

$$= \sum_{t=1}^{2N} \frac{CPN/2}{(1 + r/2)^t} + \frac{1000}{(1 + r/2)^{2N}}$$

$$= \left[\frac{CPN}{2}\right]\left[\frac{(1 + r/2)^{2N} - 1}{(r/2)(1 + r/2)^{2N}}\right] + \frac{1000}{(1 + r/2)^{2N}} \tag{5.1}$$

where

CPN = coupon rate times the par value
N = number of years remaining until maturity
r = current required return for the bond

Suppose a Ford bond has a coupon rate of 8.5%, a remaining maturity of 12 years, and the standard par value of $1000. If the required return on this bond is 10% APR, what is the current fair price for this bond?

The semiannual coupon payments in this case will be $42.50 (= one-half of 8.5% of $1000 = $85/2). The semiannual required return is 5%. Thus using Equation (5.1), we find that the fair price of the bond—the present value of its expected future cash flows—is

$$B_0 = \text{PV(coupon payments)} + \text{PV(par value)}$$

$$= \sum_{t=1}^{24} \frac{42.50}{(1.05)^t} + \frac{1000}{(1.05)^{24}}$$

$$= [42.50]\left[\frac{(1.05)^{24} - 1}{(0.05)(1.05)^{24}}\right] + \frac{1000}{(1.05)^{24}}$$

$$= 586.44 + 310.07 = \$896.51$$

Computing the Fair Price of a Ford Bond

EXAMPLE

[Put in CF = 42.50, n = 24, r = 5%, and FV = 1000. Then compute PV = 896.51.]

Now suppose you're an investor. If you can buy this bond for less than $896.51, it's a positive-NPV investment for you—it is worth more than you have to pay for it. If you have to pay more than $896.51, it's a negative-NPV investment. Of course, at a price of exactly $896.51, it is a fair investment—the NPV is zero. ■

INFERRING THE REQUIRED RETURN   You can infer the required return by observing bond prices and applying the bond price formula to solve for the expected return. The required return equals the expected return in an efficient capital market. This is a consequence of the Principle of Capital Market Efficiency, which says that the market price of a bond will be its fair price. Thus if a bond is actively traded, you can get a very accurate estimate of its fair price by obtaining the most recent sale price. In fact, obtaining a quote from a broker would save the trouble of computation, so why bother with the formula? In fact, you need not bother with the formula unless you have more than just publicly available information. If you want to estimate a fair price for a bond that is actively traded, find the most recent price paid for it.[5]

However, consider another question: How was it decided that the required return for this bond is now 10% APR? Market prices for many bonds are published daily or are available by phone through investment services. But required returns are not as easily obtained. The answer to the second question also relies on the Principle of Capital Market Efficiency. If the market price equals the fair price and the expected cash flows are the same from either viewpoint, the *required* return for computing the fair price *must equal* the *expected* return implied by the market price. Thus, to estimate the required return, compute the expected return for the bond. To compute the expected return, set the bond's market price equal to the present value of its future cash flows (that is, set NPV = 0) and solve for the return.

The benefit of knowing a required return for a market-traded security might not be obvious. After all, you can observe the current market price. In an efficient capital market, that is the fair price. However, there are several potential uses for the required return. The most important is in valuing comparable assets that are *not* currently traded in a public market. For learning purposes, however, we will focus on publicly traded bonds.

Obtaining Bond Information

Suppose you wanted to get information about a particular Coca-Cola bond that is publicly traded. You could look in a newspaper, such as the *Wall Street Journal*, for bond quotes similar to those shown in Figure 5-2.

From the highlighted Coca-Cola bond quote, you know

1. *Coupon rate.* Coca-Cola pays a coupon rate of 6% on these bonds, or $30.00 (one-half of 6.00% of $1000) every six months.

2. *Maturity year.* Assuming that the bonds do not have a sinking fund, Coca-Cola will pay owners $1000 per bond at the bond's maturity in 2003 (indicated by the 03).

3. *Current yield.* The bond's current yield is 7.7%. As discussed below, this is a measure of return based on the current price.

4. *Trading volume.* Yesterday, 49 of these bonds were traded.

5. *Closing price.* Yesterday's **closing price** for this bond was $78\frac{1}{4}$. The closing price is simply the price of a financial security in the last trade before the market closed. Bond prices are quoted as a percentage of the par value. The Coca-Cola bond was selling for $78\frac{1}{4}$% of its face value. The quote in-

---

[5] Of course, for bonds that are not traded regularly, Equation (5.1) is very useful.

Bonds	Cur Yld	Vol	Close	Net Chg.
Caterpinc $9^3/8$ 01	8.3	30	$112^1/2$	$-1^1/2$
Chryslr 10.95s17	9.8	37	$111^1/2$	...
Citicp $6^1/2$ 04	6.5	2	$99^1/2$	$+^1/8$
ClevEl $8^3/4$ 05	8.7	10	$101^1/8$	$-^5/8$
Coca-Cola 6 03	7.7	49	$78^1/4$	$+^1/2$
CrayRs $6^1/8$ 11	cv	31	$79^1/2$	$-^3/4$

FIGURE 5-2
Hypothetical bond quotes with a Coca-Cola bond highlighted.

dicates a dollar price of $782.50 (78.25% of $1000).

6.   *Net change in price.* The closing price is $5 higher than the previous day's closing price ($\frac{1}{2}$% of $1000).

A variety of additional symbols and notation can provide further information in the quote. For example, the Cray Bond has cv for its current yield. This means that this bond is a convertible bond, which can be exchanged at the bondholder's option for some number of shares of Cray common stock. By looking in a publication called a **bond guide**, such as those published by *Moody's* or *Standard & Poor's*, you can find out more about this and other bonds. For example, you can determine the exact date the bond pays interest, its maturity date, and its sinking fund provisions (that is, how the principal is to be repaid). Figure 5-3 illustrates hypothetical information from a bond guide. Check the highlighted bond.

From this quote, you know that

1.   Coca-Cola pays interest on January 15 and July 15 of each year.

2.   Coca-Cola's 6 03 bonds mature on July 15, 2003.

3.   Coca-Cola has $150 million worth of these bonds outstanding.

4.   This bond issue does not include a sinking-fund provision.

Self-Check Questions

1.   What is the par value of most U.S. corporate bonds?

2.   How often do U.S. corporate bonds usually pay interest?

3.   Explain why a bond with a bullet maturity can be viewed as an annuity plus a balloon payment.

4.   A corporate bond is quoted at a price of 95 in a newspaper. What is its dollar price?

Current Yield

The **current yield** equals the annual coupon payment divided by the closing dollar price. It is a measure of the rate of income from the coupon payments. However, it ignores the gain or loss that will result from the difference between the purchase price and the principal repayment. The yield to maturity, which is discussed below, is a better measure of the return, because it measures the *total* return from owning a bond, including capital appreciation. Given that current computer and information technology could easily provide the yield to maturity, there is little need for the bond quote to include the current yield. It appears that the current yield is still in the bond quote simply because of tradition. Traditions are often hard to break!

FIGURE 5-3

Hypothetical excerpt from a bond guide with a Coca-Cola bond highlighted.

CUSIP	ISSUE	RATING	AMT. OUTST. MIL. $	INTEREST DATES	CURRENT PRICE		YIELD TO MAT.	1995 HIGH	1995 LOW	CURRENT CALL PRICE	CALL DATE	SINK FUND PROV.	ISSUED	PRICE	YLD.
126117AC	CNA Financial Corp, nts 6.25 2003	A3	250	M&N 15	$99\frac{1}{8}$	bid	6.38	$99\frac{1}{8}$	$83\frac{3}{4}$	N.C.	–		11-9-93	99.82	6.28
126117AE	deb. 7.25 2023	A3	250	M&N 15	$99\frac{3}{8}$	bid	7.31	$99\frac{1}{8}$	$78\frac{7}{8}$	N.C.	–	Yes	11-9-93	99.68	7.28
12613BAA	CNC Holding Corp. sr.sub.nts. 13.00 1997	B3 r	188.6	M&S 1	–		–	–	–	104.87 to	9-1-97		N.A.	0.00	13.00
190348AC	Coast Fed. Bank FSB cap.nts. 13.00 2002	Ba2	50.0	MJS&D31	$113\frac{3}{4}$	bid	10.20	$113\frac{3}{4}$	$108\frac{1}{2}$	105.57 fr	12-31-97		12-18-92	100.00	13.00
19039MAA	Coast Savings Fin., Inc. sr.nts. 10.00 2000	Ba2	58.0	M&S 1	–		–	–	–		–		4-1-93	100.00	10.00
19041PAA	Coastal Bancorp, Inc. TX sr.nts. 10.00 2002	B1 r	50.0	MJS&D30	–		–	–	–	100.00 fr	6-30-00	No	6-23-95	100.00	10.00
190441AN	Coastal Corp. sr.nts. 8.75 1999	Baa3r	150	M&N 15	104	bid	7.38	104	$101\frac{1}{8}$	N.C.	–	No	5-13-92	100.00	8.75
190441AJ	• sr.nts. 10.375 2000	Baa3	250	A&O 1	$112\frac{5}{8}$	bid	7.18	$111\frac{1}{2}$	$109\frac{1}{4}$	N.C.	–	No	9-25-90	99.88	10.40
190441AL	sr.nts. 10.00 2001	Baa3	300	F&A 1	$111\frac{3}{4}$	bid	7.20	$113\frac{1}{4}$	$111\frac{1}{4}$	N.C.	–	No	1-29-91	99.50	10.08
190441AQ	• sr.nts. 8.125 2002	Baa3	250	M&S 15	109	bid	6.45	$108\frac{1}{2}$	$95\frac{3}{4}$	N.C.	–	No	9-11-92	99.62	8.18
190441AM	• deb. 9.75 2003	Baa3r	300	F&A 1	$113\frac{1}{8}$	bid	7.45	$112\frac{7}{8}$	$103\frac{3}{8}$	N.C.	–	No	7-30-91	99.44	9.83
190441AH	sr.deb. 10.25 2004	Baa3r	200	A&O 15	$118\frac{1}{8}$	bid	7.40	$117\frac{1}{2}$	108	N.C.	–	No	10-3-89	99.85	10.27
190441AF	• sr.deb. 11.75 2006	Baa3r	400	J&D 15	$105\frac{3}{4}$	sale	10.81	$109\frac{1}{8}$	$104\frac{1}{8}$	103.92 fr	6-15-96	Yes	6-24-86	100.00	11.75
190441AK	sr.deb. 10.75 201	Baa3	150	A&O 1	$118\frac{1}{8}$	bid	8.56	120	107	N.C.	–	No	9-25-90	99.59	10.80
190441AP	sr.deb. 9.625 2012	Baa3r	150	M&N 15	108	bid	8.69	$108\frac{7}{8}$	106	N.C.	–	No	5-13-92	99.34	9.70
190441AR	• deb. 7.75 2035	Baa3	150	A&O 15	$106\frac{3}{8}$	bid	7.25	–	–	N.C.	–	No	10-16-95	99.96	7.75
191098AB	Coca-Cola Bottling Consol nts. 6.85 2007	Baa3r	100	M&N 1	$103\frac{1}{2}$	bid	6.42	$103\frac{1}{2}$	$99\frac{1}{8}$	N.C.	–	No	11-1-95	100.00	6.85
191175AB	Coca-Cola Bottling Group sr.sub.nts.9.00 2003	B2 r	140	M&N 15	$100\frac{3}{8}$	bid	8.86	$100\frac{3}{4}$	$87\frac{1}{2}$	104.50 fr	11-15-98		11-8-93	100.00	9.00
191216AB	Coca-Cola Co. nts. 7.75 1996	Aa3r	250	F&A 15	$100\frac{1}{4}$	bid	5.50	$101\frac{1}{8}$	$100\frac{3}{8}$	N.C.	–	No	2-12-91	100.00	7.75
191216AC	nts. 7.875 1998	Aa3r	250	M&S 15	$105\frac{7}{8}$	bid	5.45	$105\frac{7}{8}$	$98\frac{7}{8}$	N.C.	–	No	9-9-91	99.69	7.93
191216AD	nts. 6.625 2002	Aa3	150	A&O 1	$104\frac{1}{4}$	bid	5.84	$104\frac{1}{4}$	$90\frac{7}{8}$	N.C.	–	No	9-30-92	99.32	6.71
191216AE	nts. 6.00 2003	Aa3r	150	J&J 15	$100\frac{3}{8}$	bid	5.93	$100\frac{3}{8}$	$86\frac{3}{8}$	N.C.	–	No	7-15-93	99.81	6.03
191216AF	deb. 7.375 2093	Aa3	117	J&J 29	$110\frac{5}{8}$	bid	6.66	$110\frac{5}{8}$	$86\frac{3}{8}$	N.C.	–	No	7-22-93	98.93	7.46
191219AR	Coca-Cola Enterprises nts. 6.50 1997	A3 r	300	M&N 15	$101\frac{7}{8}$	bid	5.42	$101\frac{7}{8}$	$95\frac{1}{2}$	N.C.	–		11-12-92	99.63	
191219AT	nts. 7.00 1999	A3 r	200	M&N 15	$104\frac{1}{2}$	bid	5.68	$104\frac{1}{2}$	$94\frac{7}{8}$	N.C.	–		11-12-92	99.31	
191219AM	nts. 7.875 2002	A3	500	F&A 1	$109\frac{3}{4}$	bid	5.92	$109\frac{3}{4}$	$97\frac{1}{8}$	N.C.	–	No	1-29-92	100.00	7.87
191219AN	nts. 8.50 2012	A3	250	F&A 1	$118\frac{1}{4}$	bid	6.63	$118\frac{1}{4}$	$99\frac{5}{8}$	N.C.	–	No	1-29-92	100.00	8.50
191219AB	deb 5.75 2005	A3 r	153.3	F&A 2	$100\frac{3}{4}$	bid	5.89	103	$98\frac{5}{8}$	$104.89 to	3-31-96	Yes	1-29-76	98.83	7.98
191219AV	zero cpn.nts. 2020	A3		N.P.	–		–	–	–	N.C.	–		5-9-95	12.93	
191219AP	deb. 8.50 2022	A3	750	F&A 1	$122\frac{1}{8}$	bid	6.69	$122\frac{1}{8}$	$98\frac{1}{2}$	N.C.	–	Yes	Ref. fr. 4-1-97 @ 104.08		

Computing the Expected Return: The Yield to Maturity

In practice, a bond's expected return is estimated by its **yield to maturity (YTM)**. The yield to maturity is simply the APR that equates the bond's market price to the present value of its promised future cash flows.[6] Because most U.S. corporate bonds pay interest semiannually, the yield to maturity equals 2 times the 6-month return implied by the bond's market price.

Once again, Equation (5.1) provides the appropriate relationship. This time, instead of putting in the required return and solving for B_0, we put in the current market price and solve for the required return.

Computing the Yield to Maturity on a Coca-Cola Bond

EXAMPLE

Find the yield to maturity (YTM) of the Coca-Cola bond we described in the previous section, assuming that today is July 15, 1997. In other words, what would be your expected return if you bought this bond today for $782.50?

The inputs are $B_0 = 782.50$, CPN/2 = 30.00 (one-half of 6.00% of $1000), and $2N = 12$. Putting these into Equation (5.1) yields

$$\$782.50 = \text{PV(coupon payments)} + \text{PV(par value)}$$

$$= \sum_{t=1}^{12} \frac{30.00}{(1+r/2)^t} + \frac{1000}{(1+r/2)^{12}}$$

$$= [30.00]\left[\frac{(1+r/2)^{12}-1}{(r/2)(1+r/2)^{12}}\right] + \frac{1000}{(1+r/2)^{12}}$$

Then, from trial and error or a financial calculator, we find that the expected semiannual rate, YTM/2, that solves the equation is 5.528%. [Put in PV = 782.50, CF = 30.00, $n = 12$, and FV = 1000. Then compute $r = 5.528\%$.] Therefore, this bond's YTM equals 2 times 5.528%, or 11.056%. In practice, investors would say the bond has about an 11.1% YTM.[7] ■

Bond Values and Changing Economic Conditions: Interest Rate Risk

The market price of the bond in the example just given is not equal to its par value, even though that was its original selling price. Whenever the required return for a bond changes, the fair price for the bond also changes. A bond selling below its par value is called a **discount bond**. A bond selling above its par value is called a **premium bond**.

A bond's price changes because its present value depends on the required return. With contractually fixed cash flows (interest and principal payments), a drop in the required return raises the present value, and vice versa. Figure 5-4 illustrates how the value of a bond that has a fixed-coupon rate varies with its required return.

In Chapter 3, we described the *term structure of interest rates*. The term structure shows how interest rates depend on maturity. We described several factors that affect the term structure. A very important factor is the risk of interest rate changes. As we said, changes in required returns most often result from changes in the expected rate of inflation.

---

[6] It is important to note that the YTM is only an estimate of the expected return. This is because it ignores the possibility the firm might make late payments, or even go into default. The YTM is a good estimate because this possibility is so small with most high-grade corporate bonds. An important possible exception are the so-called "junk" bonds, named for precisely their greater chance of default.

[7] The YTM is quoted as an APR. However, note that the APY (annual percentage yield) for this bond is larger than the YTM because of semiannual (rather than annual) compounding. The bond's APY equals $[(1 + 0.05528)^2 - 1]$, which is 0.1136, or 11.36%.

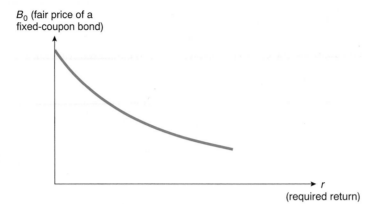

FIGURE 5-4
Relationship between a bond's fair price and its required return.

Because a change in the required return causes a change in a bond's fair price, owning a bond is risky. That is, the fact that a bond's value changes over time creates risk—even if the firm is healthy and will make all the required payments. This risk is called **interest rate risk**. Because of interest rate risk, even bonds that are guaranteed against default have some risk. A bond can be riskless (or as close as possible to being riskless) *only* in the sense that the future cash flows will occur as promised. If you sell the bond before its maturity, you will probably sell it for a price that differs from your purchase price. In fact, a decline in market value can easily exceed the income received from the interest payments while you own the bond!

How much interest rate risk is there? It depends primarily on the bond's remaining maturity. When all else is equal, interest rate risk is greater with a longer remaining maturity.

REMAINING MATURITY AND INTEREST RATE RISK   The present value of a payment due in the distant future changes more with a change in the required return than does a payment due in the near future. To see this, compare a one-year bond and a ten-year bond, both with an 8% coupon rate. Table 5-2 compares the values of these bonds at the required returns of 4% and 15%. At 4% per year, the one-year bond is worth $1038.83 and the ten-year bond is worth $1327.03. At 15% per year, the one-year bond is worth $937.16 and the ten-year bond is worth $643.19. Therefore, an increase in the required return on these bonds from 4% to 15% causes less than a 10% drop in the value of the one-year bond. In contrast, that same rate change causes more than a 50% drop in the value of the ten-year bond.

Figure 5-5 graphs the values of these same bonds as a function of the required return. The slope of the curve for the value of the ten-year bond is much steeper. As a result, any change in the required return will cause a larger change in its value than in the value of the one-year bond.

TABLE 5-2
A comparison of bond value sensitivity to changes in the required return.

REQUIRED RETURN	FAIR PRICE FOR AN 8% COUPON BOND WITH A ONE-YEAR REMAINING MATURITY	FAIR PRICE FOR AN 8% COUPON BOND WITH A TEN-YEAR REMAINING MATURITY
4%	$1038.83	$1327.03
15%	937.16	643.19
Difference in value	101.67	683.84
Drop in value	−9.79%	−51.53%

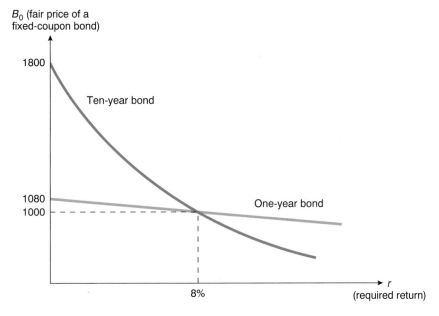

FIGURE 5-5
A comparison of bond value sensitivity to changes in the required return.

BOND VALUES, MATURITY, AND DEFAULT   Although a bond's value may vary over time, it is constrained by its **terminal value**. In most cases, the terminal value of a bond is simply the par value that will be paid at maturity. As a result, the bond's price will tend to converge to its par value as the maturity date approaches. This means that although the value of the bond may have a fluctuating component (due to changes in interest rates), the typical path of a bond's value is somewhat constrained, ending at its par value. This concept is illustrated in Figure 5-6 by hypothetical price paths for both a discount bond (selling below par) and a premium bond (selling above par).

The price paths shown in Figure 5-6 ignore two alternative outcomes: default and early repayment. We will consider the possibility of default now and will discuss the issue of early repayment in the next section.

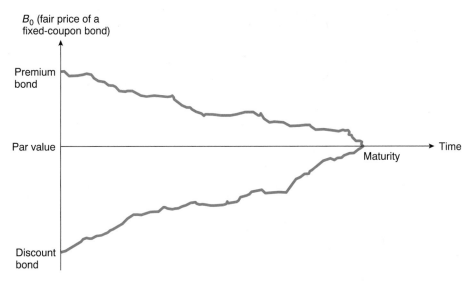

FIGURE 5-6
Hypothetical price paths for a discount bond and a premium bond.

Suppose there is a significant chance that the firm will not be able to pay off its bonds at maturity. If you were going to purchase one of these bonds, you would want to take this potential problem into account. How would you do this? You would offer a lower price. If the firm did pay off the bonds on time, you would earn a higher return (having paid less for the bond). But this possibility is your reward for taking the higher risk that you may not get the full promised payments on time. This is another illustration of the Principle of Risk-Return Trade-Off. Because others will have the same reaction, the bond will be worth less than it would be if full repayment were not in doubt. If repayment continues to be in doubt, as the bond approaches maturity, the bond's price will converge to a lower value. The bond's price at maturity will be the discounted value of the payment the bondholders expect to receive eventually (when the firm makes a settlement after defaulting).

Bond Values and Call Provisions

The call provision (the firm's option to pay off the bonds early) can also change the bond's terminal value and its maturity, because the firm can repay the bonds early by paying the call price to the bondholders. If you know this, you will not pay too much more than the call price for the bond, because the firm could call the bonds right after you buy one.

For example, suppose you could buy a bond for $1230, but the firm could call it for $1080 anytime after you bought it. If you paid $1230 for the bond today, tomorrow you could be forced to sell it back to the firm for only $1080. You would realize a one-day loss of $150, or -12.2%. Thus it is clear that you should not pay much more than the call price for a bond.

But what if the bond cannot be called now but could be called three years from today? In such cases, practitioners compute the **yield to call (YTC)** on bonds selling above their call price. The YTC is a bond's expected return, assuming that the firm will pay off the bonds (pay the bondholders the call price) on a specified call date.

EXAMPLE	**Computing the Yield to Call (YTC) on an IBM Bond**

Suppose IBM has a bond that cannot be called today but can be called in 3 years at a call price of $1090. The bond has a remaining maturity of 18 years and a coupon rate of 12%. It is currently selling for $1175.97. What is the bond's YTC? In other words, what is the expected return from buying this bond today for $1175.97 if the firm redeems the bond in 3 years by paying $1090?

Once again we apply Equation (5.1), but with the call price in place of the par value. The inputs are $B_0 = 1175.97$, CPN/2 is 60.00 (one-half of 12% of $1000), future value is $1090, and $2N$ is 6 because there are 3 years until the firm can call the bond. Putting these into Equation (5.1) yields

$$\$1175.97 = \text{PV(coupon payments)} + \text{PV(call price)}$$

$$= \sum_{t=1}^{6} \frac{60.00}{(1+r/2)^t} + \frac{1090.00}{(1+r/2)^6}$$

$$= [60.00]\left[\frac{(1+r/2)^6 - 1}{(r/2)(1+r/2)^6}\right] + \frac{1090.00}{(1+r/2)^6}$$

Then, from trial and error or a financial calculator, we find that the expected semiannual rate, $r/2$, that solves the equation is 4.0%. [Put in PV = 1175.97, CF = 60.00, n = 6, and FV = 1090. Then compute r = 4.0%.] Therefore, the bond's YTC equals 2 times this value, or 8.0%.

If the firm doesn't call the bond 3 years from now, but instead continues to make all the required payments throughout the life of the bond, the return you will earn could be higher than the yield to call. Of course, this is a "big if" that you might not want to count on! Using Equation (5.1) one more time, you can verify that the bond's YTM is currently 9.89%. Thus if you buy the bond today, and if the firm leaves the bond outstanding until its maturity date and makes all the promised payments, you will earn 9.89% APR. ■

The key point in the IBM bond example is that if the firm calls the bond at its earliest chance, you will earn only an 8% yield, not the 9.89% YTM. This is an important risk to take into account. This risk of calling is why the YTC is, and the YTM is not, the appropriate measure of return when a bond is selling above the call price.

The YTC computation alerts the potential bond buyer to the possibility that the firm will repay the bonds at the first opportunity the contract allows. Of course, we cannot know for certain what will happen. As with every option, the outcome is contingent on the decision of the optionholder—in this case, the firm. And that decision in turn depends on other contingencies—in this case, future market interest rates.

Zero-Coupon Bonds

A **zero-coupon bond** (also called a **pure-discount bond**) is a bond that pays only a terminal value. Its terminal value is the combined repayment of principal and all of the interest over the bond's life. Despite the seeming difference, Equation (5.1) can be used to value a zero-coupon bond, or to determine its YTM.

Suppose J.C. Penney has a zero-coupon bond that will pay $1000 at maturity on April 18, 2017, and today it is April 18, 1997. The bond is selling for $178.43. What is its YTM?

Using Equation (5.1) with semiannual compounding[8] and CPN/2 = 0, the YTM is 8.8%:

$$\$178.43 = PV(\text{coupon payments}) + PV(\text{par value})$$

$$= \sum_{t=1}^{40} \frac{0}{(1+r/2)^t} + \frac{1000}{(1+r/2)^{40}}$$

$$= \frac{1000}{(1+r/2)^{40}}$$

[Put in PV = 178.43, FV = 1000, n = 40, and CF = 0. Then compute YTM/2 = 4.403%.] ■

Calculating the YTM on a J.C. Penney Zero-Coupon Bond

EXAMPLE

Self-Check Questions

1. What is the current yield of a bond?
2. What is a discount bond? What is a premium bond?
3. Explain how a bond's maturity affects its interest rate risk.
4. What is the yield to call? How is it different from the yield to maturity?
5. What is a zero-coupon bond?

---

[8] We chose semiannual compounding for comparability with other bonds. You could use annual compounding, in which case the calculation would provide the APY for the bond.

5.2 STOCKS

Stocks are of two basic types, common stock and preferred stock. **Common stock** represents the residual ownership interest in a firm. Collectively, the common stockholders are the owners of the firm. They elect the firm's directors. In the event the firm is liquidated, they share proportionately in what is left after the bondholders and other higher-legal-priority claimants are legally satisfied (for example, the government gets any taxes owed).

The common stockholders receive dividends, which the firm pays out of cash, presumably out of profits it earns. Profits are calculated after making interest payments. But dividends are not a contractual obligation of the firm. If the firm does not earn any profit, it may even be legally barred from paying dividends in certain cases. As a result, the common stockholders bear more risk than the bondholders. There is greater uncertainty about the payments they will receive. In fact, common stock has no explicitly promised future payments. Of course, we expect the firm to pay cash dividends to its common stockholders, at least at some point in the future.

Preferred stock has a claim higher in priority than the firm's common stock but lower in priority than the firm's debt. There is a stated cash dividend rate, which is like the stated interest rate on debt. But if the firm fails to pay the dividends, the preferred stockholders cannot force the firm into bankruptcy. Compared to common stockholders, preferred stockholders typically have only very limited rights to vote on corporate matters.

Preferred stock is therefore a hybrid; it falls between bonds and common stock in the legal-priority hierarchy of financial securities. The risk of preferred stock also falls between that of the firm's common stock and that of its bonds. Of course, a firm that has preferred stock and wants to keep a good financial reputation will make every effort to pay its preferred stock obligations. Therefore, preferred stock payment obligations are typically viewed like debt obligations. And that stream of payment obligations looks like a debt payment obligation stream. As a result, the bond valuation model can also be used to value preferred stock—under the assumption that the firm will meet its preferred stock payment obligations. However, an adjustment is required. Preferred stock pays dividends quarterly, whereas bonds pay interest semiannually.

EXAMPLE

Valuing Ohio Edison Preferred Stock

Let's say Ohio Edison has preferred stock outstanding that pays a $2.00 quarterly dividend, or $8.00 per year. Ohio Edison must repay the $100 par value 20 years from today. The market price of the stock is $97.50. What is the stock's YTM?

First, adjust Equation (5.1) for quarterly dividends.

$$\text{Preferred stock value} = \text{PV(coupon payments)} + \text{PV(par value)}$$
$$= \left[\frac{\text{annual dividend}}{4}\right]\left[\frac{(1+r/4)^{4N}-1}{(r/4)(1+r/4)^{4N}}\right] + \frac{\text{PAR}}{(1+r/4)^{4N}}$$

where PAR is the stock's par value. Using this equation, in this case we have

$$\$97.50 = [2.00]\left[\frac{(1+r/4)^{4N}-1}{(r/4)(1+r/4)^{4N}}\right] + \frac{100}{(1+r/4)^{4N}}$$

Then, from trial and error or a financial calculator, the expected quarterly rate, YTM/4, that solves the equation is 2.064%. [Put in PV = 97.50, CF = 2.00, n = 80, and FV = 100. Then compute r = 2.064%.] Therefore, Ohio Edison's preferred stock's YTM equals 4 times this, or 8.256%. ∎

Some preferred stocks never mature. Such a *perpetual preferred stock* therefore has no final principal payment and is expected to pay dividends every period into the future. In such situations, the valuation formula collapses to the simpler perpetuity formula (Equation 4.5), and stock value = dividend/required return.

Let's say American Airlines has perpetual preferred stock outstanding that pays a $0.40 quarterly dividend. It has a required return of 12% APR (3% per quarter). What is the stock worth?

Using Equation (4.5), with CF = 0.40 and r = 0.03, we estimate that the stock's value is $13.33.

$$\text{Stock value} = \frac{\text{dividend}}{r} = \frac{0.40}{0.03} = \$13.33$$

Valuing American Airlines Perpetual Preferred Stock

EXAMPLE

Valuing Common Stock

There are two important differences between the factors for valuing common stock and those for valuing bonds. First, the horizon, or life of the investment, is *infinite* rather than finite. For a bond the horizon is called the maturity. Because firms have potentially infinite life, common stocks also have infinite lives; firms never have to redeem them. When an investor sells a stock, its value depends on future expected cash flows, which theoretically continue forever.

Second, as previously mentioned, the future cash flows are not explicitly promised. Future cash flows must be estimated on the basis of expectations about the firm's future earnings and dividend policy.

From a financial point of view, the value of a share of common stock depends *entirely* on the cash flows that the firm will distribute to its owners and on the required return on such cash flows. This is a strong statement. But imagine owning a share of common stock that absolutely could *never* provide any cash to its owner. No one would be willing to pay anything for it. It would be like owning shares in a not-for-profit corporation such as the Red Cross.[9]

The Fair Price of a Share of Common Stock

When you own a stock, you know that its future sale price can largely determine your profit or loss. You may be surprised, then, that the fair price of a stock turns out to depend *only* on its expected future cash dividends. Of course, the future cash flows of a share of common stock are its future cash dividends and its future sale price. But the future sale price depends on the same subsequent variables. As we replace the future sale price with subsequent future discounted cash flows, the future sale price vanishes. The Principle of Two-Sided Transactions is at work. The marketplace expects each subsequent buyer to apply the same valuation formula. Let's see how this works.

The value of a share of common stock today is denoted P_0. The expected future cash dividends are $D_1, D_2, \ldots, D_n$, for time periods 1, 2, ..., n. The cash dividend just paid by the firm is D_0. P_0 can be expressed as the present value of the expected future cash dividends plus the

---

[9] Perhaps this would be a good idea for a fund-raising campaign. "Invest in humanity. Buy shares in the Red Cross." People could be given a "stock certificate," but the dividends would all be personal satisfaction. Of course, we doubt that people would give much to General Motors or IBM if they tried this approach.

present value of the expected future cash sale price of the share of stock at time n, denoted P_n. That is,

$$P_0 = \frac{D_1}{(1+r)} + \frac{D_2}{(1+r)^2} + \cdots + \frac{D_n}{(1+r)^n} + \frac{P_n}{(1+r)^n} \tag{5.2}$$

where r is the required return for this stock.[10]

If Equation (5.2) looks suspiciously like the bond valuation model, that is because it involves the same valuation concept: The price of a financial security equals the present value of the expected future cash flows. For a share of common stock, these are its periodic dividends plus a terminal amount. However, valuing a share of common stock is more difficult than valuing a bond. Specifying the parameter values for a share of common stock is difficult, because the expected cash flows are so uncertain.

As we examine stock valuation further, you should note that each valuation formula represents a special case or rearrangement of Equation (5.2). The cases differ because of the assumptions made to characterize the specific situation. But they all follow the same general rule: *The fair price equals the present value of the expected future cash flows.*

A stock's value has two components. The first is dividends, which are typically referred to as the income component. Note that the cash dividends received periodically during the ownership of the stock are similar to income from any other source. The second component of value consists of the increase (or decrease) in value. It is typically referred to as the capital-gain component. Note that it represents the gain, or growth, in the value of the stock from the time of purchase until the time of sale.

Equation (5.2) assumes the sale of the stock at the end of time period n. But at what price will it be sold? Its value to a second owner who buys it at time n and owns it for the next m periods after time period n can be determined in a similar manner. The second owner expects to sell the stock at time $n + m$. Therefore, we can apply the concept embodied in Equation (5.2) a second time to value the stock for the second owner. P_n, the stock's value at time n, can be expressed as

$$P_n = \frac{D_{n+1}}{(1+r)} + \frac{D_{n+2}}{(1+r)^2} + \cdots + \frac{D_{n+m}}{(1+r)^m} + \frac{P_{n+m}}{(1+r)^m}$$

Putting this expression for P_n into Equation (5.2), P_0 can be rewritten as

$$P_0 = \frac{D_1}{(1+r)} + \frac{D_2}{(1+r)^2} + \cdots + \frac{D_{n+m}}{(1+r)^{n+m}} + \frac{P_{n+m}}{(1+r)^{n+m}}$$

This, of course, is simply a longer horizon until the terminal sale than we had in the first case—an $n + m$ horizon compared to an n horizon. We can apply this same concept again and again for all future owners. The result is that the fair price for the stock can be expressed as the present value of an *infinite* stream of expected future cash dividend payments, or

$$P_0 = \frac{D_1}{(1+r)} + \frac{D_2}{(1+r)^2} + \cdots = \sum_{t=1}^{\infty} \frac{D_t}{(1+r)^t} \tag{5.3}$$

Equation (5.3) is a very general expression for the value of a share of stock. It is expressed in terms of the stock's expected stream of future cash dividends. The formula does not assume any specific pattern of future cash dividends. It also does not make any specific as-

---

[10] For now, we are ignoring tax considerations and treating cash dividends as though payments occur annually rather than quarterly, as they typically do. These simplifications might significantly affect valuation in practice, but they are useful in allowing us to concentrate on the important concepts.

sumption about when the share of stock will be sold; the share might be sold in the future any number of times.

But What Determines Future Dividends?

If the value of a share of common stock is based on expected future cash dividends, it is logical to ask what determines future dividends. Two factors determine cash dividends: (1) the firm's earnings and (2) its dividend policy. A firm's earnings are important, because a firm cannot distribute cash (pay a dividend) to its owners if there is not enough cash available. There are only three ways a firm can obtain cash: (1) sell some of its products, assets, or services; (2) borrow additional money; or (3) sell additional shares of stock. Any of these methods can be used to obtain the cash necessary to pay a dividend.

In the short term, the firm can borrow and/or sell assets to help manage its cash position. But in the long run, a firm cannot sell off its fixed assets, or it soon will have no plant and equipment. Also, it cannot go to the capital markets for additional financing in order to pay cash dividends without convincing lenders and stock buyers of future earning potential. In the long run, then, the cash necessary to pay dividends must come from the firm's earnings.

What should a firm do with its earnings? It must choose either reinvesting its earnings or distributing the earnings to shareholders in the form of dividends. A **dividend policy** is established to guide the firm in determining how much money it will pay out as cash dividends. A simple but very convenient way to characterize a dividend policy is to compute what is called a payout ratio. A **payout ratio** expresses the firm's cash dividend as a proportion of the firm's earnings:

$$\text{Payout ratio} = \frac{\text{dividends}}{\text{earnings}}$$

In any particular year, a firm may deviate, even substantially, from a "target" payout ratio. However, most firms follow a long-term pattern of dividend payments reflecting an average payout ratio. Although a payout ratio is an oversimplification of a firm's dividend policy, we can use this measure to analyze stock valuation. We discuss dividend policy in depth in Chapters 17 and 18.

Self-Check Questions

1. Why is preferred stock a "hybrid" security?
2. When is it appropriate to use the bond valuation model (modified for quarterly payments) to value preferred stock?
3. What are the two components of a stock's value?
4. Explain why a share of common stock can be valued by computing the present value of its expected future dividend stream.
5. What does a firm's payout ratio signify?

5.3 THE DIVIDEND GROWTH MODEL

Now we will show you a method for valuing common stock. Because investors look at a firm (and its stock) as a source of growing wealth, we are interested in the underlying rate of growth of a firm and the implications of that growth rate on the price of the stock. We assume that cash dividend payments will change at some average rate *g* from one period to the next, forever into the future. This characterization of cash dividends is very useful. It is general enough to apply to many situations (for example, the rate of change can be positive or negative). It is also a good *approximation* of actual patterns of dividends.

Although the infinite-horizon assumption may seem at first to be inaccurate (after all, corporations don't really live forever, or at least none has yet), most of a stock's price is determined by the value of its nearest dividends, anyway. As with any cash flow, the further in the future a dividend will occur, the smaller is its present value. As Figure 5-7 shows, very distant future dividends contribute little to the present value of the stock. For example, the present value at 10% of a $2 dividend that is expected to be paid 60 years from now is less than a penny (= $2.00/1.10^{60}$ = 0.007).

Deriving the Dividend Growth Model

Assume cash dividend payments change at the rate of g from one period to the next forever into the future. Then the dividend payment for period t, D_t, can be expressed as the previous dividend, D_{t-1}, times $(1 + g)$. D_{t-1} is a function of D_{t-2}, and so on. Thus D_t can be expressed as a function of any dividend between now and time t, or

$$D_t = (1 + g)D_{t-1} = (1 + g)^2 D_{t-2} = \cdots = (1 + g)^{t-1}D_1$$
$$= (1 + g)^t D_0$$

This relationship is assumed to hold for all future dividend payments. Therefore, every future dividend payment can be expressed as a function of D_1, the next dividend payment. That is,

$$D_t = D_1(1 + g)^{t-1}$$

If each of the future dividend payments in Equation (5.3) is represented in this way, P_0, the current price, can be rewritten as the sum of the growing dividends, discounted by the required return, r:

$$P_0 = \frac{D_1}{1 + r} + \frac{D_1(1 + g)}{(1 + r)^2} + \frac{D_1(1 + g)^2}{(1 + r)^3} + \cdots$$

$$= D_1 \sum_{t=0}^{\infty} \frac{(1 + g)^t}{(1 + r)^{t+1}}$$

FIGURE 5-7
Relative contribution to stock price of near and distant future dividends.

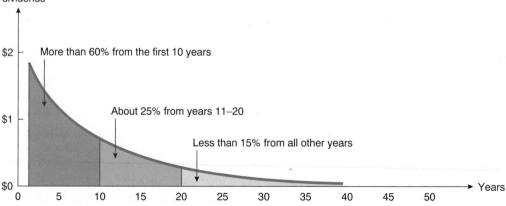

Present value of the expected future dividends

More than 60% from the first 10 years

About 25% from years 11–20

Less than 15% from all other years

Recall that the present value of a perpetuity is CF/r (Equation 4.5). In this situation, D_1 is a *growing* perpetuity. The formula for the present value of a growing perpetuity is very similar to that for a perpetuity. The denominator is reduced by the growth rate, g, so that

$$P_0 = \frac{D_1}{r - g}$$

With positive growth ($g > 0$), the denominator is less than r, which makes the present value, P_0, larger than it would be if the perpetual cash flow were not growing. The positive growth increases the value of the stock. Logically, the more growth, the higher the stock's value. A side benefit from this relationship is that it shows us that the present-value annuity factor for a growing perpetuity is $1/(r - g)$.

We used the notion of hypothetical subsequent owners to derive Equation (5.3). There we showed that the fair price for a share of stock can be expressed as an infinite stream of future cash dividends and a required return. We can use this same notion of a future owner to determine a stock's fair price at any point in time. That price, P_t, can be expressed in terms of the dividend in the next period (D_{t+1}), g, and r, whenever dividends from D_{t+1} on are expected to grow by g every period into the future. Thus whenever g is expected to be constant from time $t + 1$ on, P_t can be written as

$$P_t = \frac{D_{t+1}}{r - g} \qquad\qquad (5.4)$$

Equation (5.4) is the most general version of this concept. Thus, for example, as we just showed, when $t = 0$

$$P_0 = \frac{D_1}{r - g}$$

Recall that dividends grow by g each period in this model, so $D_{t+1} = (1 + g)D_t$. Therefore, we can replace D_{t+1} with $(1 + g)D_t$ in Equation (5.4). This gives us

$$P_t = \frac{(1 + g)D_t}{r - g} = (1 + g)\left[\frac{D_t}{r - g}\right]$$

The amount in brackets on the far right is P_{t-1}, the price at time $t - 1$. (This is because its next dividend, D_t, will grow at g forever.) Substituting P_{t-1} for the bracketed amount gives

$$P_t = (1 + g)P_{t-1}$$

From this relationship, we can see that when dividends grow at g from time $t + 1$ on, the stock's *price* will grow at the rate of g from time t on.

Suppose Procter & Gamble is expected to pay a dividend of $3.00 next year on its common stock, the required return is 12%, and dividend payments are expected to grow at a rate of 4% per year forever. What is the fair price for a share of Procter & Gamble common stock?

Using Equation (5.4) with $D_1 = \$3.00$, $r = 0.12$, and $g = 0.04$, we have

$$P_0 = \frac{3.00}{0.12 - 0.04} = \$37.50$$

Valuing a Constant-Growth Stock: Procter & Gamble

EXAMPLE

EXAMPLE	*Valuing a Zero-Growth Stock: Sargasso*	Suppose Sargasso is expected to pay a dividend of \$3.00 per year on its common stock forever into the future. It has no growth prospects whatsoever. If the required return on Sargasso's common stock is 12%, what is a share worth?

In this case, we simply put in a growth rate of zero. Using Equation (5.4) with $D_1 = \$3.00$, $r = 0.12$, and $g = 0$, we have

$$P_0 = \frac{3.00}{0.12 - 0} = \$25.00$$

An Important Comment on the Relationship Between g and r

One of the first questions students ask when they see Equation (5.4) is what happens if g equals r, or if g is greater than r. The question arises because if we blindly apply Equation (5.4), it implies that the stock's value is infinite if g equals r and that it is negative if g is greater than r. Neither situation makes economic sense. A faster-growing firm is riskier and will have a higher required return, so the larger g is, the larger r will be.

Very simply, g can never be greater than or equal to r. Although we will not prove this statement, briefly consider the following argument: g is the rate at which the cash dividend is expected to grow *every period, forever.* As we noted earlier, in the long run, dividends are paid from a firm's earnings. For cash dividends to grow at the rate of g, the earnings of the firm must grow at a rate that equals or exceeds g (at least, on average over a long time) in order for the firm to have the income to pay the dividends.

It is easy to imagine cases of very high growth in earnings. However, any situation you can imagine will involve a *limited* time period. No firm can grow forever at a rate faster than the rate of growth of economic activity. If a firm grew fast enough for long enough, the total revenue of the firm would equal the total output of the economy. In the limit, the firm would account for 100% of economic activity!

One other comment concerning g might be helpful. Even though g acts like a discount rate in that it compounds amounts, it is a *growth* rate. Be careful to distinguish between the two; it is easy to mix up the rates when you are working problems.

Forming Expectations and Measuring Stock Value

In the Procter & Gamble constant-growth example given above, dividends were expected to grow at a constant rate forever into the future from *now* on. In most situations, we can make better estimates of the near future than of the more distant future. In the same way, it is often possible to describe expected cash dividend payments for the near future more accurately than as simply an "average rate of change" every period. As we estimate further into the future, the extra effort becomes less worthwhile because of the lower present value of the payments. Beyond some point, an average rate of change forever into the future is the most *efficient* estimate we can make, even if it is not the most accurate. A more accurate estimate is not worth the additional resources necessary to produce it.

VALUING A SUPER-NORMAL GROWTH STOCK   Consider a firm that is currently experiencing high dividend growth that is expected to continue for some finite time. After this period of "super-normal" growth, dividend growth will be at a "normal" rate forever into the future. We can compute the value of this firm's stock by using Equation (5.2) and breaking the dividend pattern into two parts: a normal-growth part, which goes on forever into the future, and a super-normal growth part, which is finite. The normal-growth part makes up the sale price, P_n, which can be computed using Equation (5.4). The super-normal growth part is

D_1 through D_{n-1}. Using Equation (5.2), then, P_0 equals the sum of the present values of the two parts.

Let's say Netscape is operating in a new industry that has recently caught on with the public. Sales are growing at the rate of 80% per year. This high growth rate in sales is expected to translate into a 25% growth rate in cash dividends for each of the next 4 years. Thereafter, the growth rate in dividends is expected to be 5% per year forever. The latest annual dividend, paid yesterday, is $0.75. The required return for the stock is 22%. What is a share of Netscape common stock worth?

Valuing a Super-Normal Growth Stock: Netscape

EXAMPLE

First, compute the set of expected future cash dividends, which is

TIME	DIVIDEND	GROWTH
0	0.75	
		25%
1	0.938	
		25%
2	1.172	
		25%
3	1.465	
		25%
4	1.831	
		5%
5	1.923	
		5%
6	2.019	
		5%
.	.	.
.	.	.
.	.	.

Second, compute a fair price for the stock at a future point in time using Equation (5.4). To be able to use this equation, you must pick a point in time after the growth rate in dividends has become constant forever. Let's use Equation (5.4) and time 5 as our future sale point. The hypothetical sale value of the stock, P_5, depends on the next period's dividend, D_6. It equals

$$P_5 = \frac{D_6}{r-g} = \frac{2.019}{0.22 - 0.05} = \$11.876$$

Finally, compute the present value of the expected future sale price, and add that to the present value of all the expected cash dividends between now and then. Applying Equation (5.2), with $n = 5$, we have

$$P_0 = \frac{0.938}{(1.22)} + \frac{1.172}{(1.22)^2} + \frac{1.465}{(1.22)^3} + \frac{1.831}{(1.22)^4} + \frac{1.923}{(1.22)^5} + \frac{11.876}{(1.22)^5}$$

$$= 0.768 + 0.787 + 0.807 + 0.827 + 0.711 + 4.394$$

$$= \$8.295$$

The choice of time period 5 for the hypothetical sale is somewhat arbitrary. We could have used period 6 or 7. In fact, any fair price from period 3 onward can be used. (Period 3 is not a misprint; dividends will grow at the 5% rate from period 4 on. Therefore D_4 can be used to compute P_3, which is $10.77. Again, the present value of the dividends and the sale price equals $8.295. Try it!) ■

VALUING AN ERRATIC-GROWTH STOCK   Now consider a firm that is expected to have erratic dividend growth for some finite time, followed by a "normal" growth rate forever into the future. We can again break the dividend stream into two parts and use Equation (5.2). In fact, we can generalize our procedure further. Suppose the dividend growth rate varies for n periods and then the dividend grows at a constant rate g forever thereafter. The dividend is $(1 + g)D_n$ at time n. Putting this into Equation (5.4), we find that the value of a share of the stock at time n is

$$P_n = \frac{(1 + g)D_n}{r - g}$$

We can now use this expression in place of P_n in Equation (5.2), which gives

$$P_0 = \frac{D_1}{(1 + r)} + \frac{D_2}{(1 + r)^2} + \mathsf{L} + \frac{D_n}{(1 + r)^n} + \frac{(1 + g)D_n}{(1 + r)^n(r - g)} \tag{5.5}$$

Equation (5.5) is a general formula for valuing common stocks with *any* variable dividend growth rates over a finite time period that is followed by a constant growth rate forever. It simply combines Equations (5.4) and (5.2) into a single formula.

EXAMPLE

Valuing an Erratic-Growth Stock: Novell

Let's say Novell is currently in a building stage. It is not expected to change its annual cash dividend while new projects are being developed over the next 3 years. The dividend was $1 last year, and it is to be $1 for each of the next 3 years. After the projects have been developed, earnings are expected to grow at a high rate for 2 years as the sales resulting from the new projects are realized. The higher earnings are expected to result in a 40% increase in dividends for 2 years. After these two extraordinary increases in dividends, the dividend growth rate is expected to be 3% per year forever. If the required return for Novell common stock is 12%, what is a share worth today?

As with our Netscape example, the first step is to compute the set of expected future dividends.

TIME	DIVIDEND	GROWTH
0	1.00	
		0%
1	1.00	
		0%
2	1.00	
		0%
3	1.00	
		40%
4	1.40	
		40%
5	1.96	
		3%
6	2.019	
		3%
7	2.079	
.	.	3%
.	.	.
.	.	.
.	.	.

Second, we see that D_5 is where the growth rate in the dividends is expected to become constant forever. This is the earliest point that satisfies the constant-growth assumption. Using Equation (5.5) with $D_5 = \$1.96$, $g = 3\%$, and $r = 12\%$, we have

$$P_0 = \frac{1.00}{(1.12)} + \frac{1.00}{(1.12)^2} + \frac{1.00}{(1.12)^3} + \frac{1.40}{(1.12)^4} + \frac{1.96}{(1.12)^5} + \frac{(1 + 0.03)1.96}{(1.12)^5(0.12 - 0.03)} = \$17.13$$ ■

Growth versus Income

Recall that the value of a share of stock can be broken into two parts: income and capital gain. Let's say that you have a choice between buying stock in a firm that emphasizes income by paying out all or most of its earnings in cash dividends or buying stock in a firm that emphasizes capital gain by retaining and reinvesting all or most of its earnings. Which stock is the better investment?

As with many situations, the answer is "It depends." In this situation, it depends on the firm's investment opportunities: When all else is equal, a firm should invest its earnings in positive-NPV projects and pay out its residual earnings in dividends when it has only negative-NPV projects to invest in.

DIVIDEND GROWTH, RETAINED EARNINGS, AND THE PAYOUT RATIO   Retaining and reinvesting earnings correspond to pursuing growth and providing a larger capital gain to shareholders. In contrast, paying out earnings as cash dividends corresponds to providing current income to shareholders. Thus one way to think of the question of growth versus income is to pose it as a question of dividend policy: retaining earnings versus paying cash dividends. We said that for now we would characterize a firm's dividend policy by the average payout ratio, the ratio of its cash dividends to its earnings. A lower payout ratio increases retained earnings and provides lower dividends, whereas a higher payout ratio provides higher dividends but slows the growth of retained earnings (and the growth of the firm). Therefore, in addition to being a simple but convenient way to describe a firm's dividend policy, the payout ratio is also a relative measure of the firm's pursuit of growth (retained earnings) versus income. A high payout ratio emphasizes income at the expense of growth. A low payout ratio emphasizes growth at the expense of income.

Typically, firms vary their payout ratios over time. Many firms in new and fast-growing industries such as biotechnology and software production, pay no dividends for a number of years. This is because such firms have many opportunities for investing retained earnings. As a firm grows and becomes well-established, and as new opportunities become more rare in its industry, the firm begins to pay dividends. Thereafter, its payout ratio tends to increase. U.S. firms in well-established industries have average payout ratios of roughly 50% of their earnings.

Self-Check Questions
1. If a stock's dividend is expected to grow at a constant rate g forever, at what rate would you expect the stock's price to grow?
2. Explain why g can never exceed r in the stock valuation model (Equation 5.4).
3. How does the payout ratio serve as a relative measure of the firm's pursuit of growth versus income?
4. Why might a firm wish to retain all its earnings?

5.4 OBTAINING INFORMATION ON COMMON STOCKS

Suppose you wanted to get information about a particular common stock, say PepsiCo, makers of Pepsi-Cola. You could look in a newspaper, such as the *Wall Street Journal* or *The New York Times*, and find a list of New York Stock Exchange quotes like the hypothetical one shown in Figure 5-8.

This quote includes the following information:

1. *Latest 12 months' price range.* The highest and lowest prices paid in the last 52 weeks for a share of PepsiCo common stock were $52.75 and $31.875, respectively.

2. *Exchange symbol.* PepsiCo's stock symbol on the NYSE is PEP.

3. *Estimated dividend.* PepsiCo's estimated current annual dividend rate (based on the latest quarter's dividend) is $0.80.

4. *Dividend yield.* PepsiCo's dividend yield is 1.6%; it is the dividend rate divided by the closing price (= 0.80/48.875).

5. *Price-earnings ratio.* PepsiCo's P/E ratio is 24; it is the closing price divided by the latest 12 months' earnings per share.

6. *Trading volume.* 1,454,600 shares (= 14,546 × 100) changed ownership yesterday.

7. *Latest day's high, low, and closing prices.* Yesterday's high, low, and closing prices for Pepsico common stock were $49.125, $48.625, and $48.875, respectively.

8. *Change in closing price.* Yesterday's closing price was $0.25 (= $\frac{1}{4}$ × $1) higher than the previous day's closing price.

A variety of additional symbols and notation can provide further information in the quote. For example, the second PhilLongD stock has a pf after it and no symbol. This indicates that the stock is a preferred rather than a common stock. Other notations indicate such things as a new 52-week high or low price, or that a dividend has been declared. You can find out more about these and other items by looking in a stock guide, such as *Standard & Poor's Stock Guide*. Additional information published in a stock guide includes the number of shares outstanding and the stated dividend rate for preferred stock. Figure 5-9 illustrates hypothetical information from a stock guide.

From this stock guide quote, we know that

1. PepsiCo has 79,731,500 shares of common stock outstanding and no publicly traded preferred stock.

2. PepsiCo has paid $0.58 per share in dividends this year so far.

3. PepsiCo has $7.675 billion in long-term debt.

4. PepsiCo had $1.405 billion in cash and equivalents on September 4 of the year.

FIGURE 5-8
Hypothetical stock quote with PepsiCo highlighted.

52 Weeks		Stock	Sym	Div	Yld %	P/E	Sales 100s	High	Low	Last	Chg
HI	LO										
$9^1/_8$	$4^3/_4$	PaylessC	PCS		...	8	486	$5^1/_4$	$5^1/_8$	$5^1/_8$	...
$50^1/_4$	$35^3/_8$	Pennzoil	PZL	1.00	2.4	11	1348	$40^1/_2$	$39^7/_8$	$40^1/_8$	$-^1/_8$
$52^3/_4$	$31^7/_8$	PepsiCo	PEP	.80	1.6	24	14546	$49^1/_8$	$48^5/_8$	$48^7/_8$	$+^1/_4$
$38^5/_8$	$26^1/_4$	PerkElmer	PKN	.68	1.8	28	1890	38	$37^1/_8$	$37^3/_4$	+1
$66^7/_8$	$36^1/_8$	Pfizer	PFE	1.04	1.6	26	13254	$64^1/_8$	$62^1/_4$	$62^3/_8$	$-1^1/_4$
$69^1/_2$	$51^5/_8$	PhilLongD	PHI	1.80	2.8	7	412	$64^5/_8$	$61^1/_8$	$63^3/_8$	$+2^1/_4$
$62^5/_8$	47	PhilLongD pf		4.12	7.9	...	260	$52^3/_8$	$51^1/_2$	$52^3/_8$	$+^3/_8$
18	$9^1/_8$	PhillpsVanH	PVH	.15	1.6	41	2511	$9^5/_8$	$9^1/_4$	$9^1/_2$	$-^1/_8$

FIGURE 5-9
Hypothetical excerpt from a stock guide.

S&P 500 #MidCap -Options Index	Ticker Symbol	NAME OF ISSUE (Call Price of pfd. Stocks)	Market	PRINCIPAL BUSINESS	Com. Rank. & Pfd. Rating	Par Val.	Inst Hold Cos.	Inst Hold Shs. (000)	Lg. Trm. Debt Mil-$	Pfd. Shs 000	Com. Shs 000	Cash & Equiv.	Curr. Assets	Curr. Liab.	Balance Sheet Date	Latest Payment Period $	Latest Payment Date	Ex Div.	So Far 1993	Ind. Rate	Paid 1992
1	PTEL	√Peoples Telephone Co	NMS	Oper private pay tel system	NR	1¢	70	7483	40.2	...	14374	3.84	23.1	20.0	9-30-93	None Since Public			...	Nil	...
2	PSFT	√PeopleSoft Inc	NMS	Mfr human resource mgmt softwr	NR	1¢	90	6645	0.97	...	11610	56.3	87.1	27.0	9-30-93	None Since Public			...	Nil	...
◆ 3.¹	PBY	√Pep Boys-Man,Mo,Ja	NY,B,Ch,P,Ph	Retail chain: auto parts, etc.	A+	1	273	39582	265	...	60986	12.8	355	200	10-31-93	Q0.038	1-24-94	1-4	0.14¾	0.15	0.135
◆ 4.²	PEP	√PepsiCo Inc	NY,B,C,Ch,P,Ph	Soft drink: snack fd/ food svc	A+	1¢	1022	463605	7675	...	797315	1405	4759	5141	9-04-93	Q0.16	1-1-94	12-6	0.58	0.64	0.5
5	PRCP	√Perceptron Inc	NMS	Laser-based sensor/ image sys	NR	1¢	11	300	0.08	...	3580	0.91	9.01	1.85	9-30-93	None Since Public			...	Nil	...
6	PFGC	√Performance Food Group	NMS	Market, dstr food products	NR	1¢	24	1021	6.01	...	6032	4.47	52.8	33.9	10-02-93	None Since Public			...	Nil	...
7	PCR	√Perini Corp	AS,B,Ch	Construction: R.E. develop	C	1	27	1363	85.8	100	4331	30.4	266	238	9-30-93	1-0-00	12-18-90	11-20	...	Nil	...
8	Pr	$2.12551Dep Cv52Ex Pfd(5326.275). AS	AS		NR	No	6	198	...	1000	...	Cv into 0.662 com, $37.75				Q0.53⅛	12-15-93	11-18	2.12½	2.125	2.12½
◆ 9.³	PFR	√Perkin-Elmer	NY,B,Ch,P,Ph	Analytical instruments, optics	B−	1	263	34497	6.97	...	43944	29.0	496	400	9-30-93	Q0.17	1-3-94	11-24	0.68	0.68	0.68
10	PKN	√Perkins Family Rest L.P.	NY,Ch,Ph	Family style restaurant svc	B+	No	24	267	35.6	...	10390	2.46	12.9	23.9	9-30-93	Q0.32½	2-15-94	12-27	1.3	1.3	1.3
11	PBT	√Permian Basin Try Tr55	NY,B,Ch,P,Ph	Royalty oil interests, Texas	NR	No	24	1098	...	...	46609	Southland Royalty (prop)				0.031	1-14-94	12-27	0.40¾	0.4	0.456
#12	PRGO	√Perrigo Co	NMS	Mfr store brand pharmac'l prd	NR	No	186	29307	77.0	...	75266	0.35	236	111	9-30-93	None Since Public			...	Nil	...
13	PDS	√Perry Drug Stores	NY,B,Ch,P,Ph	Drug chain in Michigan	#C	5¢	41	3914	94.4	...	12027	3.80	157	78.0	7-31-93	0.05½	9-14-87	8-24	...	Nil	...
14	PCPI	√Personal Computer Prod	NSC	Dvlp. mkt laser printers/prod	"B-	.005¢	4	414	1.20	3	12121	0.54	6.05	2.82	9-30-93	None Since Public			...	Nil	...
◆ 15	PT	√Pet Inc	NY,B,Ch,P,Ph	Specialty food & confections prd	NR	1¢	259	59474	★720	...	104125	21.3	368	316	9-30-93	Q0.08	1-1-94	12-13	0.28	0.32	0.24

(continued)

FIGURE 5-9 (Continued)
Hypothetical excerpt from a stock guide.

S&P 500 # MidCap Options Index	Ticker Symbol	Price Range 1971–91 High	Low	1992 High	Low	1993 High	Low	Dec. Sales in 100s	December, 1993 Last Sale or Bid High	Low	Last	% Div. Yield	P-E Ratio	Earnings $ Per Share End	1989	1990	1991	1992	1993	Last 12 Mos.	Interim Earnings Period	1992	1993	Index
1	PTEL	7	2	8⅞	5½	13¼	7⅞	24570	11½	9¾	9¾	...	28	Dc	△0.19	0.14	0.25	0.28	...	0.35	9 Mo Sep	0.21	0.28	1
2	PSFT	...	...	32	17	40½	23⅜	40064	33½	27⅞	31¼	...	51	Dc	d0.07	0.07	0.2	0.48	...	0.61	9 Mo Sep	0.29	0.42	2
◆3,¹	PBY	19½	⅓	27⅞	15⅛	27⅜	19⅛	25809	27⅞	25½	26¼	0.6	25	Ja	0.63	0.67	0.69	0.9	E1.05	1.01	9 Mo Oct	0.7	0.81	3
◆4,²	PEP	35⅜	1⅓	43⅜	30½	43⅜	34½	227685	42⅜	39⅜	40⅞	1.6	20	Dc	1.13	1.35	1.35	☐1.61	E2.00	1.73	36 Wk Sep	☐1.29	1.41	4
5	PRCP	...	...	8¼	5⅜	13¼	5¼	9248	13¼	10¾	13¼	...	38	Dc	d8.87	0.38	d0.57	0.57	...	0.35	9 Mo Sep		0.2	5
6	PFGC	...	...	...	...	24¾	14	3683	24¾	18¾	24½	...	31	Dc	0.41	0.28	0.16	☐0.54	...	0.79	9 Mo Sep	☐0.38	0.63	6
7	PCR	44	3	18¾	10	18⅜	9⅞	1279	11⅞	10⅛	11⅝	...	d	Dc	3.11	d1.20	0.27	d4.69	...	d5.38	9 Mo Sep	0.88	0.19	7
8	Pr	28⅜	11½	24⅜	16½	25⅞	21	117	23¼	22¼	22⅝	9.4	...	Dc	b1.94	b0.31	b0.91	bd0.94	...	...	3 Mo Sep			8
◆9,³	PFR	41⅛	7¼	36	27¼	39¾	28½	31149	39	33¾	38½	1.8	...	Je	d0.56	1.1	d0.47	p540.81	☐0.54	0.26	3 Mo Sep	☐0.30	0.02	9
10	PKN	18⅞	7⅜	21½	15⅞	23⅜	17¼	1086	22¼	21¼	21⅝	6.1	14	Dc	1.14	1.31	1.47	1.48	...	1.55	9 Mo Sep	1.23	1.3	10
11	PBT	25	3¾	5⅛	3⅞	5	3½	5998	4⅞	4½	4¾	8.4	11	Dc	0.46	0.53	0.51	0.45	...	0.45	9 Mo Sep	0.31	0.31	11
#12	PRGO	15⅜	8	22⅝	12	34⅞	19⅛	49075	34⅞	30	34¾	...	54	Je	...	...	p0.26	0.41	0.57	0.63	3 Mo Sep	0.13	0.19	12
13	PDS	20⅞	½	11⅛	7⅞	9⅜	5⅜	10269	6¼	5⅞	6⅞	...	d	Oc	0.7	☐0.06	0.3	0.75	Pd1.54	d1.54				13
14	PCPI	6⅛	¼	1⅛	⅜	1⅞	⅞	22634	1⅜	⅞	1⅛	...	24	Je	d0.33	d0.30	d1.14	0.01	0.05	0.05	3 Mo Sep	Nil	Nil	14
◆15	PT	23¾	15	23¾	14⅜	18⅜	14⅜	54540	17¾	16½	17½	1.8	25	Je	...	p560.39	p570.39	p0.96	☐0.68	0.69	9 Mo Sep	☐0.19	0.2	15

5.5 ESTIMATING A STOCK'S REQUIRED RETURN: THE CAPITALIZATION RATE

In our section on bonds, we asked why anyone would go to the trouble of valuing a bond that is trading regularly in a capital market? The same question can be asked about valuing stocks. And our answer is the same: The Principle of Capital Market Efficiency applies. For a stock that is publicly traded, the most recent price paid is the best available estimate of its value. As with bonds, we can observe market prices but not required returns. And like the bond valuation model, the stock valuation model provides a good way to estimate a required return: Compute the expected return, and under the Principle of Capital Market Efficiency, that equals the required return. For a stock, the required return is sometimes called its **capitalization rate**.

Rearranging Equation (5.4) with $t = 0$ provides a model for computing a stock's expected return, which in turn is a good estimate of its required return, or capitalization rate:

$$r = \frac{D_1}{P_0} + g \tag{5.6}$$

Earlier, we referred to the two components of a stock's value: income and capital gains. You can see these in Equation (5.6). The income component is also called the **dividend yield**, which is the dividend divided by the price, as we noted earlier in discussing the PepsiCo stock quote. The capital gains component, or **capital gains yield**, is g. The total return is simply the sum of the two.

Suppose you look in today's *Wall Street Journal* and see the following stock quote for International Paper in the New York Stock Exchange quote section:

Estimating International Paper's Capitalization Rate (Required Return)

EXAMPLE

52 WEEKS		STOCK	DIV	YLD %	PE	VOL 100s	HI	LO	CLOSE	NET CHG
HI	LO									
33½	54⅝	IntPpr	1.52	3.0	10	3616	51¼	50⅝	51	−¼

Suppose further that the Value Line Investment Survey estimates International Paper's dividend growth rate to be 5.25% per year forever. What is the capitalization rate on its common stock?

First, note that next year's dividend, D_1, is expected to be $1.60 (= 1.52 × 1.0525). Then, with the closing price of 51 for P_0, $D_1 = 1.60$, and $g = 0.0525$ in Equation (5.6), the expected return is

$$r = \frac{D_1}{P_0} + g = \frac{1.60}{51.00} + 0.0525 = 0.084$$

Thus the implied capitalization rate, our estimate of International Paper's required return, is 8.4%. This rate consists of a 5.25% capital gains yield plus a 3.15% dividend yield. ∎

In future chapters, we will show you other methods of estimating a required return. Although the other methods are more widely used than the one we have shown here, they are also more complex. The method shown in this section enabled us to introduce you to the concept in a more "friendly" environment.

Self-Check Questions

1. Explain in your own words the meaning of a stock's capitalization rate.
2. What are the two components of a stock's total return?
3. How is a stock's dividend yield calculated?
4. What is a stock's capital gains yield?

5.6 THE SOURCE OF DIVIDEND GROWTH: RETAINED EARNINGS

Arriving at the 8.4% capitalization rate in the International Paper example is straightforward as long as we don't ask how g was estimated. When we introduced the topic of stock valuation, we said that estimating the future cash flows was a difficult task. Using g in the Dividend Growth Model simply shifts the difficulty from estimating the dividends themselves to estimating g!

If the payout ratio (POR) is constant, growth in a firm's dividends depends directly on growth in the firm's earnings. In turn, growth in earnings depends on (1) the amount of money retained and (2) the return earned on that money. The more money retained and reinvested (meaning the less paid out), the larger the future earnings. The retained proportion is the amount not paid out, so the retention rate is 1 minus the payout ratio, or $(1 - \text{POR})$. Similarly, the higher the return on the reinvested money, the larger the future earnings. Let i represent the expected return on the retained and reinvested money. POR and i are constant, and g is the product.

$$g = (1 - \text{POR})i \qquad (5.7)$$

This relationship provides a way to break down further the process of estimating future dividends. To estimate g, we can estimate the firm's expected future payout ratio and the firm's expected return on its future investments. Breaking down g may make the task easier, because firms tend to follow certain patterns in their payout ratios, and expected returns tend to fall into groups for particular types of investments. However, in some sense, separating g into an expected return and a POR simply shifts, once more, the difficulty of what must be estimated. This time it is shifted from g to the expected return on future investments.

EXAMPLE

U.S. Hair's Capitalization Rate

Although it owns no airplanes, U.S. Hair (USH) is a fly-by-night distributor of barber shop supplies. USH has had earnings totaling $20 million over the last 6 years. It has paid a total of $8 million in dividends over the same time period, for a payout ratio of 40%. USH expects to have an EPS next year of $3.00 and expects to pay $1.20 dividend per share. USH stock is currently selling for $24.00 per share. If USH expects to earn 15% on its future investments, what is the required return on USH's stock?

With POR = 0.4 and i = 0.15, from Equation (5.7), g = 0.09. Then, with D_1 = 1.2,

$P_0 = 24.00$, and $g = 0.09$ in Equation (5.6),

$$r = \frac{D_1}{P_0} + g = \frac{1.20}{24.00} + 0.09 = 0.14 = 14\%$$

Thus USH has a required return of 14%. But USH is expected to have future investments that have positive NPVs, because its expected return is 15%, which exceeds the 14% required return.

Now go through the same computations again with the same values, except with the expected return on future investments, i, set equal to 10%. You'll find that, with $i = 10\%$, r is equal to 11%. In this case USH has a required return of 11%, which exceeds its 10% expected return. Therefore, in this case, USH is expected to have future investments that have negative NPVs.

Finally, go through the computations one more time, with $i = 12.5\%$. This time you'll find that the required return, r, equals the 12.5% expected return. The implication for this last case is that USH is expected to have future investments that have NPVs equal to zero.

In each case, the value of the stock was assumed to be $24.00 per share, and we examined the impact of various assumptions about the expected return on future investments on the estimated required return on the stock. Even though the *estimate* of r depends on the expected return on future investments, we want to remind you that in fact the stock has only *one* required return—in spite of the problems associated with estimating its actual value. ■

You may breathe a sigh of relief to know that the buck stops here! The value of the stock depends on the expected return on the firm's current and future investments. The task facing the firm is to earn a return on its investments that equals or exceeds the required return on those investments. Value is increased by positive-NPV investments. Value is decreased by negative-NPV investments. In short, the problem is to figure out which is which. This is called capital budgeting, and it is the focus of Part III, Chapters 10 through 13.

Self-Check Questions

1. What is the relationship among the capital gains yield, the payout ratio, and the expected return on retained earnings?
2. Explain why separating the capital gains yield into two components shifts the problem of estimating the required return for a stock to estimating the firm's expected return on its future investments.

5.7 THE PRICE-EARNINGS RATIO

Like participants in conversations about football and the weather, many investors will join into a discussion concerning the investment potential of a stock and feel good about their contribution, regardless of whether they know anything about the stock. In this type of conversation,

EXAMPLE

Estimating NPVFI: McHandy

A financial analyst has just told you that she has analyzed the fast-hardware industry and estimated that the capitalization rate for the industry is currently 15%. You are thinking of buying stock in McHandy, a firm that is invested solely in this industry. McHandy expects to earn $4.20 per share next year (which you feel represents a good estimate of the firm's long-run prospects). McHandy's stock is selling for $30\frac{1}{2}$. What is the expected NPV of McHandy's future investments?

From Equation (5.9), McHandy's stock is worth $28.00 ($= 4.20/0.15$) on the basis of its current operations alone. Because the market value of the stock is $30.50, NPVFI is positive and equals $2.50. Therefore, McHandy is expected to increase its value in the future by making good future investments, ones that are expected to earn more than their required returns and thus have a positive NPV. ■

Self-Check Questions

1. How is the price-earnings ratio computed? What does it signify?
2. Explain why a high P/E ratio doesn't always imply good future investment opportunities.
3. When is the NPV of future investments positive? When is it negative?
4. How does the expected NPV of the firm's future investments (NPVFI) affect the value of its shares (P_0)?

5.8 LIMITS TO USING THE STOCK VALUATION MODEL

A few words of caution about using the stock valuation model are in order. In some ways the model is true by definition. Mathematically, the value of a share of stock can be represented as the present value of its expected future dividends. Unfortunately, there will always be an infinite number of combinations of parameter values that will produce a particular P_0 when they are inserted into one of the valuation equations. The problem of estimating parameters so that we can use the model is especially difficult. We can never be sure that any *one* of the parameter estimates is correct, and each one depends on the others.

For example, suppose D_1 = $2.16, r = 15.75%, POR = 0.55, and i = 20%. By Equation (5.7), g = 9%. Then Equation (5.4) implies a fair price of $32.00 for the stock. But the same estimates for D_1 and POR, with r = 16% and i = 20.556%, also imply a fair price of $32.00. If we observe a market value of $32.00, which set of parameter values is correct? Or is there yet a third set of values that are the "true" values? The quality of an estimate of a stock's value ultimately depends on the quality of the information you can get.

A major constraint on the use of any model is the ability to estimate the parameter values. If the necessary information cannot be obtained, the model will not be useful. Computing historical growth rates and looking at other firms in the industry are two examples of methods of obtaining additional information. However, care must be taken because even though an application of the model may appear to be valid, an "answer" will be obtained whether it is valid or not. That is, you get some kind of answer no matter what parameter values you use.

A second major obstacle to using the stock valuation model is the cost of obtaining information. The value of any answer must be weighed against the cost of using the model. If the cost of obtaining sufficiently accurate information is too high, the model is not worth using.

Of course, such obstacles to valuing a stock easily are exactly why the process is challenging—and interesting. As we said in connection with estimating capitalization rates, the approach provides a good starting point for understanding the process. In later chapters we will build on this understanding as we examine more complex methods.

Self-Check Questions

1. What are two major obstacles to using the stock valuation model?
2. What sources of information are available to help you estimate the parameter values needed to apply the stock valuation model?

SUMMARY

In this chapter we described the typical features of bonds and stocks and explored the relationships among the factors that affect their values. The fair price of a bond or share of stock can be expressed as the present value of its expected future cash flows. Conversely, given its market price, we can compute the expected return for a bond or stock. The expected return is called the yield to maturity for a bond and the capitalization rate for a stock. Applying the Principle of Capital Market Efficiency, we can estimate the required return for a bond or stock with its expected return.

An estimate of the value of a stock is much more uncertain than an estimate of the value of a bond. In the final analysis, the value of a share of stock depends on the firm's expected return on its investments. This is a very simple, and also a very powerful, statement. However, estimating a firm's expected return by predicting the future cash flows from its investments is a difficult task. But then, predicting the future is always difficult!

DECISION SUMMARY

- The value of any financial security is the present value of its expected future cash flows, discounted at its required return.
- The expected future cash flows are the bond's future coupon payments and terminal value. The terminal value may be a future sale price, the par value paid at maturity, or the call price paid at the firm's option.
- A bond's interest rate risk depends primarily on its remaining maturity.
- A call provision provides the firm with a valuable option that can limit a bond's value.
- A stock's expected future cash flows are more uncertain and are therefore more difficult to estimate than a bond's. They are the stock's future dividends and terminal sale price.
- The pattern of dividends will be determined by the firm's future earnings and the firm's dividend policy. For now, we characterized the firm's dividend policy as simply an average payout ratio.
- The firm's expected future earnings depend on the expected return on its investments. Therefore, the choice between growth and income depends on the NPV of the firm's investments. Growing with positive-NPV investments creates value, whereas growing with negative-NPV investments destroys value.

EQUATION SUMMARY

$$B_0 = PV(\text{coupon payments}) + PV(\text{par value})$$

(5.1)
$$= \left[\frac{CPN}{2}\right]\left[\frac{(1+r/2)^{2N}-1}{(r/2)(1+r/2)^{2N}}\right] + \frac{1000}{(1+r/2)^{2N}}$$

(5.2)
$$P_0 = \frac{D_1}{(1+r)} + \frac{D_2}{(1+r)^2} + \cdots + \frac{D_n}{(1+r)^n} + \frac{P_n}{(1+r)^n}$$

(5.3)
$$P_0 = \frac{D_1}{(1+r)} + \frac{D_2}{(1+r)^2} + \cdots = \sum_{t=1}^{\infty}\frac{D_t}{(1+r)^t}$$

(5.4)
$$P_t = \frac{D_{t+1}}{(r-g)}$$

(5.5)
$$P_0 = \frac{D_1}{(1+r)} + \frac{D_2}{(1+r)^2} + \cdots + \frac{D_n}{(1+r)^n} + \frac{(1+g)D_n}{(1+r)^n(r-g)}$$

(5.6)
$$r = \frac{D_1}{P_0} + g$$

(5.7)
$$g = (1 - POR)i$$

(5.8)
$$r = (POR)\left(\frac{EPS_1}{P_0}\right) + (1 - POR)i$$

(5.9)
$$P_0 = \frac{EPS_1}{r}$$

KEY TERMS

EXERCISES

PROBLEM SET A

A1. What is a required return?

A2. Define the term *expected return.*

A3. What are coupon payments, and what is a coupon rate?

A4. What is the maturity of a bond?

A5. RCA made a coupon payment yesterday on its "6.25s06" bonds that mature on October 9, 2006. The required return on these bonds is 9.2% APR, and today is April 10, 1997. What should be the market price of these bonds?

A6. Dow made a coupon payment yesterday on its "7.75s07" bonds that mature on April 9, 2007. The required return on these bonds is 8.4% APR, and today is April 10, 1997. What should be the market price of these bonds?

A7. Suppose Toyota has nonmaturing (perpetual) preferred stock outstanding that pays a $1.00 quarterly dividend and has a required return of 12% APR (3% per quarter). What is the stock worth?

A8. What does the term *payout ratio* mean?

A9. If Footlocker has perpetual preferred stock outstanding that pays a $0.60 quarterly dividend and has a required return of 13.2% APR (3.3% per quarter), what is the stock worth?

A10. Assume that IBM is expected to pay a total cash dividend of $5.60 next year and that dividends are expected to grow at a rate of 6% per year forever. Assuming annual dividend payments, what is the current market value of a share of IBM stock if the required return on IBM common stock is 10%?

A11. Let's say the Mill Due Corporation is expected to pay a dividend of $5.00 per year on its common stock forever into the future. It has no growth prospects whatsoever. If the required return on Mill Due's common stock is 14%, what is a share worth?

A12. Suppose Toshiba has a payout ratio of 55% and an expected return on its future investments of 15%. What is Toshiba's expected growth rate?

A13. Cite and explain three reasons why a P/E ratio may not be a reliable indicator of a stock's expected future performance.

A14. Cite and discuss two important factors that limit the usefulness of the stock valuation model.

A15. What is the realized return?

PROBLEM SET B

B1. DuPont's "8.45s12" bonds closed yesterday at 103. These bonds mature on October 9, 2012, and today is April 10, 1997. What is the YTM of these bonds?

B2. GMAC's "8 3/4s08" bonds closed yesterday at $95\frac{1}{4}$. These bonds mature on April 9, 2008, and today is April 10, 1997. What is the YTM of these bonds?

B3. IBM's "9 3/8s" bonds closed yesterday at $95\frac{1}{8}$. A coupon payment was made yesterday, April 9, 1997, and the YTM on these bonds is 10%. When do these bonds mature?

B4. ATT's "7 1/8s" bonds closed yesterday at $92\frac{3}{4}$. A coupon payment was made yesterday, April 9, 1997, and the YTM on these bonds is 8%. When do these bonds mature?

B5. Suppose Coca-Cola has a zero-coupon bond that will pay $1000 at maturity on May 9, 2001. Today is May 9, 1997, and the bond is selling for $790.09. What is its YTM?

B6. Assume J.C. Penney has a zero-coupon bond that will pay $1000 at maturity on April 9, 2022. Today is April 9, 1997, and the bond is selling for $98.24. What is its YTM?

B7. Let's say Daimler-Benz, the builder of Mercedes cars and trucks, is expected to pay $4.00 (or the equivalent in German marks) in cash dividends next year at the rate of $1.00 per quarter. The required return on Daimler-Benz stock is 14%. The stock is currently selling for the equivalent of $37.50 per share on the Frankfurt Stock Exchange. What is the expected growth rate in dividends for Daimler-Benz on the basis of the Dividend Growth Model?

B8. A quick look at a bond-quote section in the *Wall Street Journal* will tell you that GMAC has many different issues of bonds outstanding. Suppose that four of them have identical coupon rates of $7\frac{1}{4}$% but mature on four different dates. One matures in 2 years, one in 5 years, one in 10 years, and the last in 20 years. Assume that they all made coupon payments yesterday.

  a. GMAC's yield curve (term structure) is flat, and all four bonds have the same YTM of 9%. What is the fair price of each bond today?

b. Assume that during the first hour of operation of the capital markets today, the term structure shifts (but stays flat), and the YTM of all these bonds changes to 10%. What is the fair price of each bond now?

c. Assume that in the second hour of trading, the YTM of all these bonds changes once more to 8%. Now what is the fair price of each bond?

d. On the basis of the price changes in response to the changes in YTM, how is interest rate risk a function of the bond's maturity? That is, is interest rate risk the same for all four bonds, or does it depend on the bond's maturity?

B9. Philadelphia Electric has many publicly traded bonds. Suppose PhilEl's bonds have identical coupon rates of $9\frac{3}{8}$% but that one issue matures in 1 year, one in 7 years, and the third in 15 years. Assume that a coupon payment was made yesterday.

a. If the YTM for all three bonds is 8%, what is the fair price of each bond?

b. Suppose that the YTM for all these bonds changes instantaneously to 7%. What is the fair price of each bond now?

c. Suppose that the YTM for all these bonds changes instantaneously again, this time to 9%. Now what is the fair price of each bond?

d. On the basis of the fair prices at the various yields to maturity, is interest rate risk the same, higher, or lower, for longer-maturity compared to shorter-maturity bonds?

B10. Suppose Samsung has a bond that cannot be called today but can be called in 4 years at a call price of $1080. The bond has a remaining maturity of 16 years, has a coupon rate of 10%, and is currently selling for $1107.67. What is the bond's YTC?

B11. Assume MCI has a bond that cannot be called today. It can, however, be called in 2 years at a call price of $1050. The bond has a remaining maturity of 8 years, has a coupon rate of 14%, and is currently selling for $1112.05. What is the bond's YTC?

B12. Gehr's Gears, Inc. has bonds outstanding that mature in 14 years and 6 months from today. The bonds have an annual coupon rate of 15%. They pay interest every 6 months. The bonds are currently selling for $1100.

a. Assume that a coupon payment was made yesterday and that there are 29 more coupon payments remaining to be paid in the life of the bond. What is the YTM of this bond? What is the APY for this bond under these assumptions?

b. Assume that a coupon payment was made yesterday and that there are 28 more coupon payments remaining to be paid in the life of the bond. What is the YTM of this bond? What is the APY for this bond under these assumptions?

B13. Kay Patteris owns a bond that matures in 6 years and 6 months from today. The bond has an annual coupon rate of 6%. It pays interest every 6 months. Currently, the bond is selling for $825.

a. Assume that a coupon payment was made yesterday and that there are 13 more coupon payments remaining to be paid in the life of the bond. What is the YTM of this bond? What is the APY for this bond under these assumptions?

b. Assume that a coupon payment was made yesterday and that there are 12 more coupon payments remaining to be paid in the life of the bond. What is the YTM of this bond? What is the APY for this bond under these assumptions?

B14. Let's say Time Warner is expected to pay a dividend of $2.00 next year on its common stock, the required return is 14%, and dividend payments are expected to grow at a rate of 7% per year forever. What is the fair price for a share of Time Warner common stock?

B15. Suppose Logan has recently undertaken a major expansion project that is expected to provide growth in earnings per share of 400% within the coming year and 75% growth in each of the subsequent 3 years. After that time, normal growth of 3% per year forever is expected. The cash dividend was 10 cents per share this last year. It is expected to be that amount for each of the next 5 years. In the sixth year, it is expected that the payout ratio will be 80% of the earnings per share. The payout ratio is expected to remain at that level forever. The required return on Logan common stock is 32% per year, and the latest earnings per share were 25 cents. At what price should Logan Corp. common stock be selling in the market?

B16. Suppose Sears is currently in a building stage. It is not expected to change its annual cash dividend while new projects are being developed over the next 4 years. The dividend was $1.50 last year. It is expected to be $1.50 for each of the next 4 years. After the projects have been developed, earnings are expected to grow at a high rate for 3 years as the sales resulting from the new projects are realized. The higher earnings are expected to result in a 30% increase in dividends each year for 3 years. After these three extraordinary increases in dividends, the dividend growth rate is expected to be 2% per year forever. If the required return for Sears common stock is 11%, what is a share worth today?

B17. A stock is expected to pay a single cash dividend next year of $1.80, and its growth in dividend payments is expected to be 2% per year forever. The stock is selling for $25.00 per share. What is the capitalization rate according to the Dividend Growth Model?

B18. Assume Losh Key Corporation's common stock is selling for $25.00 per share. Its cash dividend next year is expected to be $1. Short-term prospects are excellent for Losh Key: A 25% annual growth rate in dividend payments is expected for the 3 years following next year's dividend. After that, a normal growth rate of 4% per year forever is expected. What required return is implied by the current $25.00 price?

B19. Let's say Stowe-Away Travel, Inc. (Stowe) has a required return of 18% and is expected to pay a dividend next year of $1.28. It has a payout ratio of 50% and is currently selling for $16.00 per share. What is Stowe's expected return on future investments?

PROBLEM SET C

C1. Managers of The Biden-Time Co., makers of Mickey Moose watches, are currently considering suspending the firm's cash dividends for the next 3 years to invest the money in a project they call Court Jesters. Biden-Time's current operations are expected to earn $0.85 per share next year. With a constant payout ratio of 75%, earnings are expected to grow at 5% per year forever. Under the Court Jesters plan, earnings are expected to grow at 17% per year for the investment years. After the investment, the firm expects to have a payout ratio of 70% and a growth rate in earnings of 6.5% forever. The required return on Biden-Time's stock is 20% per year. What is the NPV per share of the Court Jesters plan?

C2. The copy service Quick Quality in Quantity (Q3) has a payout ratio of 80% and a required return of 10%. It is expected to pay a dividend next year of $2.00. If Q3 is selling for $25 per share, what is its expected return? What is the expected market value of a share of Q3 4 years from now?

C3. Gin & Technic (G&T), a bar that caters to engineers, is about to issue new bonds. The bonds will make 10 coupon payments of $200 every other year, starting 1 year from today. G&T will pay a maturity value of $1200 with the last coupon payment. If you buy one of these bonds for $1100, what will be your expected APY return?

C4. Philip Quick, owner of a chain of self-service gas stations, has several investments. One of them is 2000 shares of Getty Oil. Getty is expected to pay a dividend next year of $2.38. The expected dividend growth rate is 6% per year forever. If Getty is selling for $19.45 per share, what is Phil's expected return on Getty Oil? Another of Phil's investments is 1200 shares of ConEdison. It has an expected growth rate in dividends of 4% per year forever. It sells for $41\frac{7}{8}$. It is expected to pay a dividend of $3.35 per share next year. What is Phil's expected return on ConEdison? Now the real question: How can Phil's expected returns be different for these two investments? Why doesn't Phil sell the one with the lower expected return and buy more of the one with the higher return?

Real-World Application: Calculating Yields for Johnson & Johnson's Debt

Johnson & Johnson is one of the leading pharmaceutical firms in the world. It is large and financially sophisticated. When it needs to borrow money, it sells bonds where it can get the best deal. Sometimes that means selling bonds to U.S. investors. Other times it means issuing Eurodollar bonds to investors outside the United States. (We discuss the Eurobond market in more depth in Chapters 24 and 29.)

You can use the techniques we've developed in this chapter to calculate the yields of either domestic bonds or Eurobonds. The main difference between the two is that domestic bonds pay interest semiannually, whereas Eurobonds pay interest annually. Due to this difference in the frequency of compounding, you must be careful to compare the APYs of domestic and Eurobonds when trying to find the lower cost alternative.

The following table provides information concerning five Johnson & Johnson debt issues:

ISSUE	MARKET	COUPON	FREQUENCY	MATURITY	PRICE (% OF PAR)
$7\frac{3}{8}$s 97	Eurobond	$7\frac{3}{8}\%$	Annual	11/09/97	101.9689
$7\frac{3}{8}$s 02	Domestic	$7\frac{3}{8}\%$	Semiannual	06/29/02	103.7711
$8\frac{1}{4}$s 04	Eurobond	$8\frac{1}{4}\%$	Annual	11/09/04	108.3751
6.73s 23	Domestic	6.73%	Semiannual	11/15/23	93.6594
8.72s 24	Domestic	8.72%	Semiannual	11/01/24	111.6299

1. Rewrite Equation (5.1) for a bond that makes annual coupon payments.

2. Suppose today is November 10, 1996. Calculate the YTM of the $7\frac{3}{8}$s 97.

3. Suppose today is June 30, 1996. Calculate the YTM of the $7\frac{3}{8}$s 02. Express the YTM as an APY.

4. Suppose today is November 10, 1998. Calculate the YTM of the $8\frac{1}{4}$s 04.

5. Suppose today is November 16, 1997. Calculate the YTM of the 6.73s 23. Express the YTM as an APY.

6. Suppose today is November 2, 1999. Calculate the YTM of the 8.72s 24. Express the YTM as an APY.

7. The 8.72s 24 are callable at 104.36 on November 2, 2004. Calculate the YTC and express it as an APY.

8. The 8.72s 24 are callable at par on November 2, 2014. Calculate the YTC and express it as an APY.

Suppose you would like to value a bond between interest payment dates. The bond pays interest semiannually. A fraction f of an interest period has elapsed since the last interest payment. (Thus, a fraction $1 - f$ remains until the next interest payment.) The fair price of the bond in this case is the sum of its quoted price, P, and the accrued interest, $f\left(\frac{CPN}{2}\right)$:[11]

$$B_0 = P + f\left(\frac{CPN}{2}\right).$$

The present value of the bond's coupon payments can be calculated by adjusting Equation (5.1) for the fractional period. The adjustment is the same as the one illustrated in Figure 4-13 on page 115. The basic annuity present value, Equation (5.1), is compounded forward by f, the fraction of the interest period. Setting this adjusted present value equal to the adjusted fair price (the quoted price plus accrued interest), we have

$$B_0 = P + f\left(\frac{CPN}{2}\right)$$

$$= \left(\left[\frac{CPN}{2}\right]\left[\frac{(1 + r/2)^{2N} - 1}{(r/2)(1 + r/2)^{2N}}\right] + \frac{1000}{(1 + r/2)^{2N}}\right)(1 + r/2)^f$$

(5.10)

Note that $2N$ is the actual number of remaining coupon payments, which is a whole number. Note also that solving for r, the YTM, using this equation requires tedious trial and error.

9. Suppose today is August 31, 1996. Consider the $7\frac{3}{8}$s 02. Verify that $f = \frac{1}{3}$. What is B_0? Calculate the YTM and express it as an APY.

10. Suppose today is October 15, 1998. Consider the 6.73s 23. What is f? What is B_0? Calculate the YTM and express it as an APY.

---

[11] The convention in the bond market is to quote the price of a bond *without* accrued interest. The buyer pays the seller the quoted price plus accrued interest, which is referred to as the *invoice price*.

BIBLIOGRAPHY

Fuller, Russell J., and Chi-Cheng Hsia. "A Simplified Common Stock Valuation Model," *Financial Analysts Journal*, 1984, 40(September-October):49–56.

Gordon, M. J., and L. I. Gould. "Comparison of the DCF and HPR Measures of the Yield on Common Shares," *Financial Management*, 1984, 13(4):40–47.

Siegel, Jeremy J. "The Application of the DCF Methodology for Determining the Cost of Equity Capital," *Financial Management*, 1985, 14(1):46–53.

Woods, John C., and Maury R. Randall. "The Net Present Value of Future Investment Opportunities: Its Impact on Shareholder Wealth and Implications for Capital Budgeting Theory," *Financial Management*, 1989, 18(2):85–92.

RISK AND RETURN: FINANCIAL SECURITIES

OBJECTIVES

After studying this chapter, you should be able to

1. Calculate average realized returns for a security.

2. Estimate the expected return to a portfolio from the expected returns of the securities that make up the portfolio.

3. Calculate a portfolio's standard deviation from the standard deviations of the securities that make up the portfolio and the correlation coefficients for the securities' returns.

4. Explain why diversification can be beneficial when one asset's returns are less than perfectly positively correlated with other asset returns.

5. Describe the efficient frontier and explain its significance to choosing which portfolio to invest in.

6. Determine the capital market line (CML) when given the riskless return and the expected return and risk of the market portfolio.

We learned about the concept of a rate of return in Chapter 4. Recall that we defined three different rates of return: required, expected, and realized. We also explained how to calculate expected returns and how an asset can be valued by discounting its expected future cash flows using a market-determined required return. We used these concepts in Chapter 5 to value securities. We showed how to rearrange the present-value formula to compute a particular required return, a stock's capitalization rate. Along the way, we said that the required return should reflect the risk of the cash flows, but we did not define risk.

In this chapter and the next, we'll tackle the problem of measuring risk, using realized returns on stocks. We will then use what we learn about risk to develop a model for calculating an asset's required return, one that is more general than a capitalization rate calculation.

Risk is something everyone knows about. Some people won't skydive because they think it's too risky. Others refuse to fly in an airplane because they find even that too risky. Most of us would say there is more risk in jumping out of a flying airplane (even if we are wearing a parachute) than there is in simply being up in the plane in the first place, but *how much more* risk? We can't measure the difference in risk between staying in the plane and jumping out. We can't even measure the amount of risk connected with getting in the plane in the first place. We have no way to measure this type of risk. Of course, you don't need to measure the risk precisely to decide whether you'll fly in an airplane— and, once you are flying, whether you will jump out.

Now think about investing in a security or other asset. We know it can be risky, but as in skydiving, you could make an investment without measuring the risk precisely. Most of us, however, would want to know about the risk and would consider an investment in terms of its opportunity costs. That is, we would ask, "Compared to what?" To do that, we must find a way to measure risk.

As we will see, measuring the variability of the returns on a single asset in isolation is not the best way to measure risk. Investors typically hold groups of assets called *diversified portfolios*. An investor is therefore concerned with each security's incremental contribution to the risk of the entire portfolio. For example, let's say the returns from a particular security are highly variable. Does such a security then have high risk? Suppose the security's returns tend to be high when the returns on the rest of the portfolio are low. Adding that security to the portfolio could actually reduce the risk of the portfolio because of the Principle of Diversification. We would say such a security has high *specific risk* when the security is considered in isolation but that it has low *market risk* when placed in the portfolio.

We will demonstrate that an asset's risk, and therefore its required return, depends on how the asset's expected future cash flows *covary* with the combined cash flow stream for all other assets. We will show you how to measure market risk on the basis of the correlation between a security's returns and the returns on the rest of the portfolio.

RISK AND RETURN AND THE PRINCIPLES OF FINANCE

◇ *Diversification*: Invest in a combination of assets, a *portfolio*, to reduce the total risk of your entire investment.

◇ *Risk-Return Trade-Off*: Invest in the combination of amounts of the risky *market portfolio* and the *riskless asset* that provides the investment risk level you choose.

◇ *Efficient Capital Markets*: Estimate the risk and required return for a security from its past realized returns.

◇ *Incremental Benefits*: Measure the incremental benefits from owning a financial security, which are its expected future cash flows.

◇ *Two-Sided Transactions*: Use the fair price of a financial security to compute its expected return, because the fair price does not favor either side of the transaction.

◇ *Time Value of Money*: Determine the value of a financial security by computing the present value of its expected future cash flows.

◇ *Valuable Ideas*: Look for innovative management or information services that might create a positve NPV by providing positive–NPV investment opportunities for capital market participants.

6.1 ALTERNATIVE MEASURES OF RETURNS

We will start our discussion by showing you how to measure the realized return from owning a security. To keep the discussion simple, we will use a share of common stock as the example, but the method of calculation applies to *any* asset.

Dollar Returns

Let's say a friend owns 100 shares of Merck common stock, which she purchased three months ago for $35 per share. The stock is listed on the New York Stock Exchange. It is now worth $40 per share on the basis of today's closing price. In addition, she has received one quarterly dividend of $0.50 per share. (You can congratulate her!)

Recall from Chapter 5 that a stock's value has two components: income from dividends and capital gain from changes in value. Let's analyze your friend's stock investment in these terms. She invested $3500 (= 35 × 100) and received $50 in dividends (= 0.50 × 100). Because the current share price exceeds the purchase price, she has also realized a capital gain of $500 [= (40 − 35)100].[1] Her total dollar return on the investment equals the sum of the two:

$$\text{Total Dollar Return} = \text{Dividends} + \text{Capital Gain (or Loss)} = 50 + 500 = \$550$$

Note that if she sold the shares for $40 each, then the total cash she realized would equal the sale proceeds plus dividends received. This would be the same as the amount of her investment plus her total dollar return.[2]

$$\text{Total Cash Realized} = \text{Sales Proceeds} + \text{Dividends} = 4000 + 50 = \$4050$$

$$\text{Total Cash Realized} = \text{Investment} + \text{Total Dollar Return} = 3500 + 550 = \$4050$$

It is important to understand that the $500 capital gain is part of the total dollar return whether or not the shares are sold.

Realized Returns

Suppose you did not know the history of your friend's investment or the number of shares she owned. And suppose she told you she earned a total dollar return of $550 on her investment in Merck stock and asked you what you thought of her investment performance. You would ask how much she had invested, and you would react differently depending on whether she had invested, say, $3500 or $10,500. In the first case she would have had a percentage total return of 15.7% (= 550/3500). In the second, it would have been only 5.2% (= 550/10,500).

The *realized return* is the rate of return per dollar invested. Let's generalize the calculation by drawing on what we learned in Chapter 5. D_t is the amount of dividends (in dollars) actually paid during period t.[3] P_t is the price of the stock at the beginning of period t, and P_{t+1} is the price of the stock at the beginning of period $t + 1$, or equivalently, at the end of period t.

The realized *dividend yield* your friend has earned on her Merck stock so far is 1.4% (= 0.50/35). The realized *capital gain yield* on the stock is 14.3% [= (40 − 35)/35]. Her realized return is 15.7%, the sum of these two yields. This is like our stock's capitalization rate in the previous chapter. It is also the sum of two yields. The difference between them is the difference between the future and the past. The stock's capitalization rate is a required return. Our estimate of it is based on an expected return. The expected return was computed on the basis of expected future cash flows and a current market price. Here we are simply computing the realized return, the one actually earned over a past time period.

Figure 6-1 illustrates the relationship between the total dollar return and realized return calculations for the three-month investment in Merck common stock. The investment is worth $4050 now, but $3500 represents the return of the original investment, referred to as the *return of capital*.

In many cases, we are more interested in the realized return than in the total dollar return. This is because we are interested in making comparisons of *rates* of return on alternative investments.

---

[1] Of course, if the current share price were less than the purchase price, then the difference would be a negative value, a capital loss.

[2] To keep the example simple, we have ignored income taxes and transaction costs. The $500 capital gain is more correctly termed the pretax capital gain; the $550 total return is the pretax total dollar return.

[3] Recall that in Chapter 5, D_t was an *expected* future dividend. Here it is a realized (past) dividend.

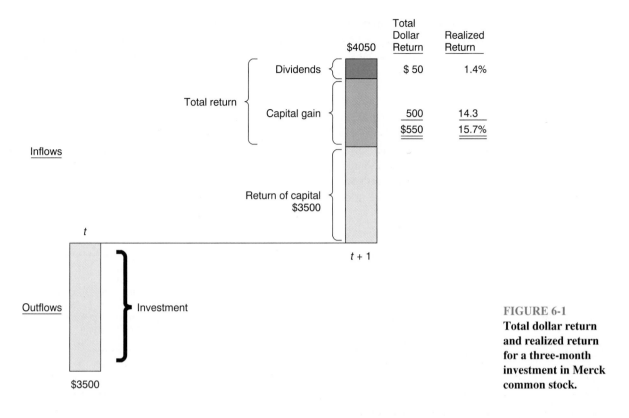

		$4050	Total Dollar Return	Realized Return
Dividends			$ 50	1.4%
Capital gain			500	14.3
			$550	15.7%

FIGURE 6-1
Total dollar return and realized return for a three-month investment in Merck common stock.

Self-Check Questions

1. Explain the difference between total dollar return and realized return. Why is the realized return often a more useful measure of the returns from an investment?

2. What are the two components of total return?

3. If the dividend yield is 4.1% and the capital gain yield is −7.5%, what is the realized return?

6.2 MEASURING REALIZED RETURNS

Let's consider another aspect of your friend's return on her investment in Merck stock. She realized $550 on a $3500 investment. But over what period? Realizing $550 over a one-year period would be better than realizing it over two years. The length of the *holding period* clearly makes a difference. If you invest $3500 and realize $4050 at the end of one year, your return is 15.7% per year (= 550/3500). But your friend earned the same rate in only a quarter of a year, so she earned an APR of 62.8% [= (4)15.7] and an APY of 79.2% [= $(1.157)^4 − 1$].

Reinvestment of Interim Cash Flows

In Chapter 4 we saw that cash flow timing is important. Money has a time value. Realized returns are expressed as percentages. By convention, they are normally expressed as average annual percentages to adjust for the length of the holding period. We also need to take into account the timing of interim cash flows. Interim cash flows are interest in the case of bonds, and dividends in the case of stocks.

Investment professionals often calculate realized returns by assuming that interim cash flows are reinvested in additional units of the same investment. For example, dividends would be used to buy additional shares of the same stock.

Calculating a Realized Return

Table 6-1 illustrates the calculation of the realized return on Merck stock over a one-year period. Dividends are paid quarterly at the rate of $0.50 per share. At the end of the first quarter, $50 in dividends (= 0.50 × 100) are received, and Merck's share price is $38.00. The realized return for the first 1-quarter holding period is 10% (= 350/3500). The dividends are used to purchase 1.3158 additional shares (= 50/38).[4] The investor now owns 100 + 1.3158 = 101.358 shares, worth $3850 (= 38 × 101.3158). This equals the original 100 shares valued at the current share price ($3800) plus the reinvested dividend ($50).

TABLE 6-1
Calculating a realized return.

TIME	EVENT	SHARE PRICE	CASH INFLOW[a]	CASH OUTFLOW[b]	NUMBER OF SHARES PURCHASED[c]	NUMBER OF SHARES OWNED[d]	VALUE OF INVESTMENT[e]
0	Purchase 100 shares	$35.00	—	$3500.00	100.0000	100.0000	$3500.00
0.25	Dividend of $0.50/share	38.00	$50.00	50.00	1.3158	101.3158	3850.00
0.50	Dividend of $0.50/share	40.00	50.66	50.66	1.2665	102.5823	4103.29
0.75	Dividend of $0.50/share	42.00	51.29	51.29	1.2212	103.8035	4359.75
1.00	Dividend of $0.50/share	40.00	51.90	51.90	1.2975	105.1010	4204.04

[a] Number of shares owned at the time the dividend is paid multiplied by the dividend per share.
[b] Dividends are fully reinvested by buying additional shares at the current share price.
[c] Number of shares purchased equals the amount of dividends reinvested (cash outflow) divided by the share price.
[d] Number of shares owned equals the number of shares purchased with the reinvested dividends plus the number of shares previously owned.
[e] Value of investment equals the number of shares owned multiplied by the share price.

At the end of the second quarter, the investor receives a dividend of $0.50 per share on each of 101.3158 shares, for a total of $50.66 (= 0.50 × 101.3158). The share price is $40, so the dividends will purchase 1.2665 additional shares (= 50.66/40). Following this latest purchase, the investor owns 101.3158 + 1.2665 = 102.5823 shares, worth $4103.29 (= 40 × 102.5823).

The calculations for the third and fourth quarters are similar. At the end of the fourth quarter the investment is worth $4204.04. Of this amount, $3500 is the return of capital. The realized return for the 1-year holding period is 20.1% [= (4204.04 − 3500)/3500]. ∎

REALIZED APY   The investor in the preceding example earned an annual return of 20.1% in a one-year holding period. Because holding periods can be of any length, the realized return for any particular holding period is usually converted to an annual equivalent rate, such as when we compute an APY. This *annual equivalent return,* called the **realized APY**, can be obtained by adapting Equation (4.7).

To compute the realized APY, the realized return for the holding period, r, must be compounded for one year. The realized APY is then

$$\text{Realized APY} = (1 + r)^m - 1 \tag{6.1}$$

---

[4] This calculation is hypothetical. Firms do not normally issue fractional shares. However, you can think of it as a dividend reinvestment plan (DRP). With a DRP, a stockholder can choose to be credited with fractional shares calculated to four decimal places instead of receiving cash.

where r is the realized return for the holding period, and m is the number of holding periods in one year. For example, there are 4.0 three-month holding periods (quarters) in one year $(= 12/3)$.[5]

What is the realized APY for Merck common stock for a 6-month holding period, assuming that the stock is purchased at time 0 and the share prices are those shown in Table 6-1?

After 6 months the investment is worth $4103.29, for a capital gain of $603.29 $(= 4103.29 - 3500)$ and a 6-month realized return of 17.24% $(= 603.29/3500)$. Using Equation (6.1) with $r = 0.1724$ and $m = 2$ $(= 1/0.5)$, we find that the realized APY is 37.45%.

$$\text{Realized APY} = (1.1724)^{1/0.5} - 1 = (1.1724)^2 - 1 = 37.45\%$$

[Put in PV = 1.00, $r = 17.24\%$, $n = 2$, and CF = 0, and then compute FV = 1.3745. The realized APY = (FV − 1) × 100 = 37.45%.] ■

Calculating a Realized APY

EXAMPLE

Holding Periods of More Than One Year

Suppose someone tells you that a particular investment produced a return r_1 the first year, r_2 the second year, . . . , and r_N in year N when it was finally sold. The N-year realized return, r, is simply the result of compounding the N annual returns:

$$r = (1 + r_1)(1 + r_2)\ldots(1 + r_N) - 1$$

But what is the realized APY in this case?

Normally, we think of compounding from the smaller period to the larger. Therefore, when the holding period is more than one year, we compound the APY for the number of years in the holding period to compute the realized return for the holding period. With a holding period of N years, we have

$$1 + r = (1 + \text{realized APY})^N \tag{6.2}$$

Suppose a friend told you he bought $12,000 worth of Hasbeen Corporation common stock 45 months (3.75 years) ago. Hasbeen has paid no dividends since he bought the stock. Your friend's stock is currently worth $13,680. What is his realized APY?

First, the realized return for the 3.75-year holding period is 14% $[= (13,680/12,000) - 1]$. Therefore, applying Equation (6.2) with $r = 0.14$ and $N = 3.75$ yields a realized APY of 3.56%. [Put in PV = 1.00, FV = 1.14, $n = 3.75$, and CF = 0, and then compute $r = 3.56\%$.]

$$1.14 = (1 + \text{realized APY})^{3.75}$$

Calculating a Realized APY for a 3.75-Year Holding Period

EXAMPLE

Self-Check Questions

1. What factors affect the size of the realized return?
2. What is meant by the term *annual equivalent return*?
3. If the investment of $1000 produces cash of $1250 when the investment is liquidated 1 year later, what is the realized return?
4. What are the realized return and the realized APY if the investment of $1000 is liquidated after 6 months, producing $1250?

---

[5] Another way to view m is that it is 1 over the holding period when it is measured in years or fractions thereof. For example, for a six-month holding period (0.5 year), $m = 2$ $(= 1/0.5)$.

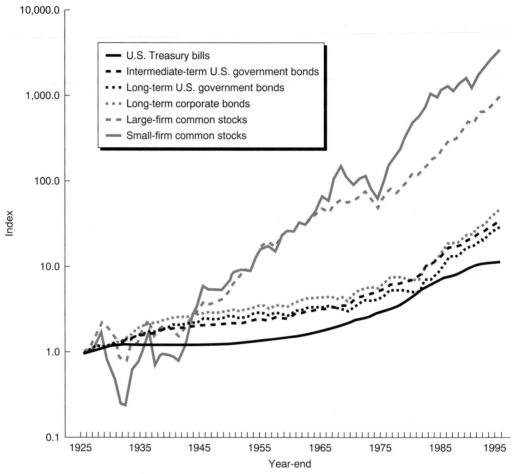

FIGURE 6-2
Cumulative returns from investing in different classes of securities, 1926–1995.
Source: *Stocks, Bonds, Bills, and Inflation 1996 Yearbook* (Chicago, Ill.: Ibbotson Associates, 1996), pp. 232–249.

▌6.3 HISTORICAL SECURITY RETURNS IN THE UNITED STATES

The history of security returns provides a useful backdrop for our discussion of risk and return. For now, we will assume that the things that affect value—the process that generated these realized returns—(1) has not changed and (2) will not change in the foreseeable future.[6]

An Historical Comparison

Figure 6-2 compares the cumulative realized returns since year-end 1925 from investing $1 in each of six classes of securities: large-firm common stocks, small-firm common stocks, long-term corporate bonds, long-term U.S. government bonds, intermediate-term U.S. government bonds, and U.S. Treasury bills. The vertical (*y*) axis shows the compound realized returns for all holding periods starting from the end of 1925. For example, if one dollar had been invested in large-firm common stocks at year-end 1925, with all dividends reinvested in additional

---

[6] A mathematician would say this statement assumes that the random process that generated these realized returns is *stationary*. The annual returns were all drawn from the same underlying distribution of possible returns.

TABLE 6-2
**Average annual
realized returns for
different classes of
securities, 1926–1995.**

CLASS OF SECURITY	ARITHMETIC MEAN	GEOMETRIC MEAN	STANDARD DEVIATION
Large-firm common stocks	12.5%	10.5%	20.4%
Small-firm common stocks	17.7	12.5	34.4
Long-term corporate bonds	6.0	5.7	8.7
Long-term U.S. government bonds	5.5	5.2	9.2
Intermediate-term U.S. government bonds	5.4	5.3	5.8
U.S. Treasury bills	3.8	3.7	3.3

Source: *Stocks, Bonds, Bills, and Inflation 1996 Yearbook* (Chicago, Ill.: Ibbotson Associates, 1996), p. 118.

shares of common stock, the investment would have grown to $1113.92 by year-end 1995. This is a 70-year holding period with a realized return of 111,292% [= (1113.92 − 1.00)/1.00] and a realized APY of 10.54%. [Put in PV = 1.00, FV = 1113.92, n = 70, and CF = 0, and then compute r = 10.54%.] Small-firm common stocks produced the greatest cumulative return, and Treasury bills produced the smallest. But the small-firm stock returns also appear to have been the most variable.

Table 6-2 gives the average annual realized returns. It also gives the standard deviations of these returns. We will explain later in the chapter how the standard deviation of returns serves as a measure of risk.

Common Stock Annual Realized Returns

Figure 6-3 shows average yearly realized APYs for common stocks in each year from 1926 to 1995. The highest (53.99%) occurred in 1933 and the lowest (−43.34%) in 1931. Figure 6-4 shows the frequency of these APYs. Note how the realized returns are spread out over a wide range.

FIGURE 6-3

Yearly realized APYs from investing in large-firm common stocks, 1926–1995.
Source: *Stocks, Bonds, Bills, and Inflation 1996 Yearbook* (Chicago, Ill.: Ibbotson Associates, 1996), pp. 180–181.

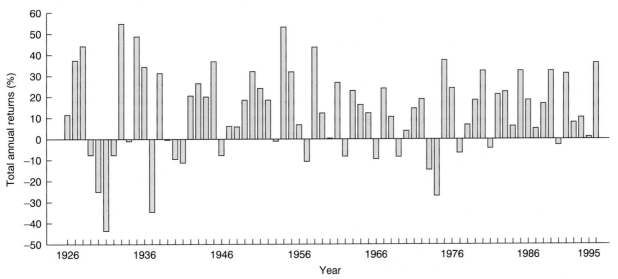

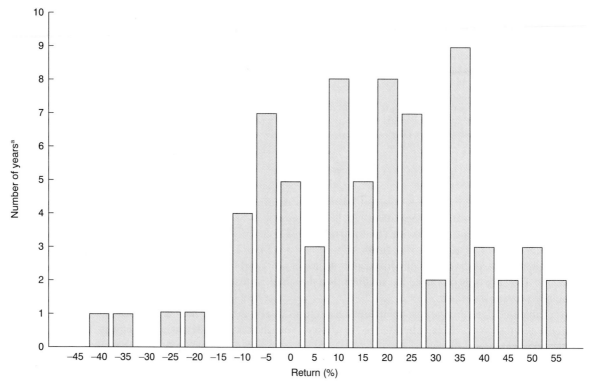

[a]Each interval is centered over the number that appears beneath it. For example, the height of the bar over the number 10 (meaning 10% return) indicates that 8 of the realized APYs were between 7.5% and 12.5%. The numbers beneath the horizontal axis are the midpoints of the indicated ranges.

FIGURE 6-4

The frequency of the APYs in Figure 6-3.

Source: *Stocks, Bonds, Bills, and Inflation 1996 Yearbook* (Chicago, Ill.: Ibbotson Associates, 1996), pp. 180–181.

Self-Check Questions

1. In how many years did the average realized APY for large-firm common stocks exceed 40%? In how many years was it below 30%?

2. For common stocks, what was the longest period without a negative annual return? What was the longest period of consecutive losing years?

3. How might you explain the fact that the highest percentage return occurred in 1933, just 2 years after the largest negative return in the entire 1926–1994 time period?

6.4 PROBABILITY CONCEPTS

Intuitively, we can think of the risk of an asset as the likelihood that its realized return will vary substantially from its expected return. That is, an important dimension of risk is the probability (chance) that a really bad outcome will occur. Here we will briefly develop two important concepts from probability and statistics that we will need later in the chapter.

Random Variables

Intuitively, a *random variable* is one whose value is subject to uncertainty. It is not perfectly predictable (there is a part that is random). For example, the amount of Exxon Corporation's earnings for next year is a random variable. We might have in mind some possible outcomes for this random variable, but we can't know the value for sure until the year ends and Exxon reports its earnings.

Probabilities

Because the value of a random variable is uncertain, we need a way to assess the relative likelihood of each possible value. We do this by assigning a **probability** to each possible value. Probabilities must satisfy two conditions: (1) A probability cannot be negative and (2) the probabilities of all possible outcomes must sum to 1.0.

The first condition says we are interested only in *possible* outcomes. The second ensures that the specified set includes all possible outcomes.

Consider a random variable X that can take on only N possible values. The respective probabilities are $p_1, p_2, \ldots, p_N$. Our two conditions are

$$p_n \geq 0 \quad \text{for all } n$$

$$\sum_{n=1}^{N} p_n = 1 \tag{6.3}$$

For example, heads and tails are equally likely for a fair coin, so the probability of heads is 1/2, and the probability of tails is 1/2. Similarly, for a fair die, the probability of each face occurring is 1/6. Note that both cases satisfy Equation (6.3).

The Great Jones Securities Service gathers securities analysts' forecasts and analyzes them for its subscribers. Ten analysts follow Exxon. Three predict earnings per share next year of $5.75, two forecast $5.90, one predicts $6.25, and four forecast $6.30. What are the probabilities associated with these forecasts?

EXAMPLE

Exxon's Next-Year Earnings Per Share

There are four values: $5.75, $5.90, $6.25, and $6.30. For simplicity, assume that at least one analyst will have a correct forecast. That way there are no other possible outcomes. Then Exxon's next-year earnings per share will be $5.75 with probability 0.3 (= 3/10), $5.90 with probability 0.2 (= 2/10), $6.25 with probability 0.1 (= 1/10), and $6.30 with probability 0.4 (= 4/10). ∎

The Mean

So far, we have talked about expected cash flows without really defining the term *expected*. An expected amount is the mean of the random variable. The **mean** of a random variable is its long-run average. It is the average value we would get if we repeated a random experiment a very large number of times. The mean is usually shown by writing a lower case letter with a bar over it. For example, $\bar{x}$ is the mean of X.

Suppose a random variable X can take on N possible values x_n. The probability associated with x_n is p_n. Then

$$\bar{x} = \sum_{n=1}^{N} p_n x_n \tag{6.4}$$

In words, Equation (6.4) says multiply each possible outcome x_n by its probability of occurrence p_n, and sum the products. The mean is the weighted average of the possible outcomes, where the probabilities p_n are the weights.

| EXAMPLE | *Calculating the Mean of Exxon's Earnings Per Share* | The expected value of Exxon's earnings per share for next year is |

$$\bar{x} = (0.3)(5.75) + (0.2)(5.90) + (0.1)(6.25) + (0.4)(6.30) = \$6.05$$

Graphically, the mean locates the "weighted center" of the probability distribution. You can see this by looking at Figure 6-5. The mean is like a fulcrum that balances the probability-weighted values on either side of it.

We have said that the mean is the average outcome when an experiment is repeated many times (actually, an infinite number of times). However, suppose we can have only a single outcome, such as one flip of a coin or realized earnings this year. The mean doesn't provide a complete picture of what might happen in a single trial. Any single outcome might vary tremendously from its mean. For example, consider a single flip of a coin, where no actual outcome *ever* equals the mean. (If the possible outcomes are 0 and 1, the mean is 0.5, which differs from both possible outcomes.) In spite of this and other limitations, the mean is very useful as a *summary statistical measure*.

Variance and Standard Deviation

As we have noted, an actual outcome may differ (perhaps substantially) from the mean. The **variance** is a measure of the dispersion of possible outcomes. It measures how much outcomes can vary above and below the mean. Variance is typically shown using a Greek letter, as σ^2, sometimes with an identifying subscript. The formula for variance is

$$\sigma^2 = \sum_{n=1}^{N} p_n(x_n - \bar{x})^2 \tag{6.5}$$

The **standard deviation** is simply the square root of the variance, sometimes with an identifying subscript. For example, σ_X is the standard deviation of X.

FIGURE 6-5
Mean value of Exxon's earnings per share.

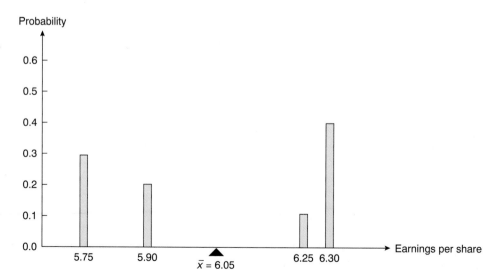

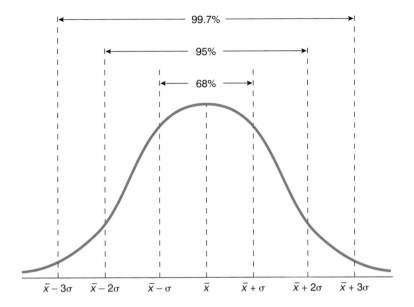

FIGURE 6-6
Distribution of possible outcomes for a normal random variable (normal pdf).

Figure 6-6 shows the bell-shaped probability density function for what is known as the *normal random variable* (normal pdf). The normal pdf is frequently encountered in finance. In such situations, we know that there is a 68% probability that any single outcome will fall within one standard deviation (plus or minus) of the mean, a 95% probability that it will be within two standard deviations of the mean, and a 99.7% probability that it will fall within three standard deviations of the mean.

Interpreting Variance and Standard Deviation

Let's say we know the variance (or standard deviation), but nothing else. Like a mean, variance provides limited insight unless we have additional information. For example, suppose we told you the variance of X is 100. That would mean little without more information. Suppose we told you the variance of television prices for all current models is 100, or the variance of prices for all fast food hamburgers is 100. In the first case, the variance would be small. In the second case, it would be large.

Variance measures the dispersion of possible outcomes around the mean, so once we know the mean, the variance is more meaningful.[7] Consequently, mean and variance are used *together* to furnish summary measures of possible outcomes. Look at Figure 6-6. Knowing $\bar{x}$ and σ would enable you to draw the normal pdf *exactly*.

The variance of Exxon's possible earnings per share next year is

$$\sigma^2 = (0.3)(5.75 - 6.05)^2 + (0.2)(5.90 - 6.05)^2 + (0.1)(6.25 - 6.05)^2 + (0.4)(6.30 - 6.05)^2$$

$$= 0.0605$$

The standard deviation is

$$\sigma = \sqrt{0.0605} = 0.2460$$

Calculating the Variance and Standard Deviation of Exxon's Earnings Per Share

EXAMPLE

---

[7] The pun wasn't intended. Honest.

Covariance and Correlation Coefficient

Covariance is a measure of how two random variables vary together, or "covary." Covariance can be positive, negative, or zero. A positive covariance indicates that when one random variable has an outcome above its mean, the other also tends to be above its mean. A negative covariance indicates the reverse—a higher outcome for one tends to be associated with a lower outcome for the other. A covariance of zero indicates that a simple pairing of outcomes does not reveal any regular pattern.

The covariance of two random variables, say X and Y, is usually shown as Cov(X,Y), or sometimes σ_{XY}. The formula for the covariance is

$$\text{Covariance} = \text{Cov}(X,Y) = \sum_{n=1}^{N} p_n(x_n - \bar{x})(y_n - \bar{y}) \tag{6.6}$$

The covariance is sensitive to the particular units of measurement. The **correlation coefficient** removes this sensitivity. Although covariance can take on any value, the correlation coefficient can be only between minus 1 and plus 1. The correlation coefficient is usually shown as Corr (X,Y). The formula for the correlation coefficient is

$$\text{Corr}(X,Y) = \frac{\text{Cov}(X,Y)}{\sigma_X \sigma_Y} \tag{6.7}$$

Dividing by the standard deviations cancels out the units of measurement, leaving Corr(X,Y) unit-free.

Standard Probability Distributions and Model Building

You probably recall from your past course work that there are quite a few "standard" probability distributions, in addition to the normal pdf shown in Figure 6-6. Others include the binomial, Student's t, exponential, chi-square, and poisson. These standard probability distributions are useful in building mathematical models.

If we wanted to model a particular stock's return, we could compute its realized returns to use as the basis for our model. In that case, each stock would have a slightly different return distribution. Each distribution would be based on the particular sample observed for that stock over the observation period.

Using a standard type of distribution to represent each stock's return is a better approach. Then we can model the returns simply by estimating the parameter values that characterize that distribution. We need no cumbersome samples. For example, mean and variance (or its square root, standard deviation) completely characterize the normal pdf. With just these two values, we can precisely draw the bell-shaped curve in Figure 6-6. Studies have shown that the normal pdf is a reasonable approximation of the true distribution in certain cases.[8] If stock returns follow a normal pdf, and we know the mean and variance, we know *all* there is to know about the stock's return.

In the rest of this chapter, we will take parameter values such as the mean and standard deviation as given. We will disregard the statistical work, often difficult and time-consuming, that goes into estimating such values in practice.

---

[8] More accurately, stock returns tend to follow what is called a *lognormal probability distribution*. The logarithm of the continuously compounded return (as well as the logarithm of the share price) follows a normal pdf.

Self-Check Questions

1. Explain the meaning of the terms *mean* and *standard deviation.*
2. A random variable X can take on five possible values: 5, 10, 15, 20, and 25. The respective probabilities are 0.2, 0.3, 0.15, 0.25, and 0.10. Calculate the mean, variance, and standard deviation of X.
3. Two random variables X and Y both have a mean of 5. The variances are $\sigma_X^2 = 10$ and $\sigma_Y^2 = 20$. Both random variables follow a normal pdf. Draw a figure like Figure 6-6 and compare the two distributions.
4. What does a positive correlation coefficient between two random variables signify? What does a negative correlation coefficient between them signify?

6.5 THE EXPECTED RETURN OF AN INVESTMENT

We have shown you how to compute an asset's realized return. However, in selecting investments, we are concerned with the *future* returns, which are uncertain. We are therefore interested in the expected return.

Measuring the Expected Return

One measure of the expected return is the mean of future possible returns. Remember, however, the drawback to using the mean. It represents the average outcome when the experiment is repeated many times. But suppose you can get only *one* of those outcomes?

Recall our discussion in Chapter 4 about how risk disconnects the expected and realized returns. If you own an asset for the next year, it will provide you with *one* realized return. That return may turn out to be positive, zero, or negative. More important, it can turn out to be very different from its mean. And once next year's outcome is realized, the experiment is not repeated. (The second year might be considered a repeat. However, conditions may have changed so much that the possible outcomes are quite different from those of the first year.) After the fact, when you have the outcome, it does not really matter what the mean was.

A Definition of Expected Return

In spite of this drawback, investment decisions must be made before the outcome is known. You may remember the *law of large numbers* from your statistics class. Applied to finance, it says that with a sufficient number of investments, the good and bad outcomes tend to cancel each other out. In that way, the average of the outcomes will approximate the mean of the group more and more closely as the number of investments increases.[9] In this sense, the mean is a good measure of the expected return when you have a large number of investments.

After five and a half chapters, we can finally give you a precise definition of expected return: An asset's **expected return** is the mean of its future possible returns.

---

[9] Literally, the law of large numbers states that the mean of the outcomes approaches the expected value in the limit (that is, as the number of trials increases without bound).

An Asset's Expected Return

While the two of you are working out, a friend recommends investing in IBM common stock. She has researched it for her finance class. She thinks it has a 0.35 probability of producing a 15% return, a 0.25 probability of a 25% return, and a 0.10 probability of a 40% return. However, she says a bad outcome of −10% is also possible, with probability 0.30. What is the expected return?

Applying Equation (6.4) yields

$$\text{Expected return} = (0.30)(-10) + (0.35)(15) + (0.25)(25) + (0.10)(40) = 12.5\%$$ ■

Self-Check Questions

1. What is the mean of a random variable?
2. Explain the drawbacks to using the mean return when evaluating the returns you might realize next year from holding 100 shares of AT&T common stock.
3. Explain why the mean is a good measure of expected return when you have a large number of different investments.
4. According to your broker, a share of Microsoft common stock might produce one of three possible returns next year: 15%, 25%, or 50%. The respective probabilities, again according to your broker, are 0.20, 0.45, and 0.35. What is the expected return?

6.6 THE SPECIFIC RISK OF AN INVESTMENT

The other aspect of risk-return trade-off that we need to quantify is risk. First, let's consider the riskiness of an asset by itself. Then we will generalize to the risk of an asset that belongs to a group, called a *portfolio*, of assets.

The Two Dimensions of Risk

When thinking about why an investment is risky, people usually come up with two notions: (1) uncertainty about the future return and (2) the possibility of a large negative return—that is, a bad outcome. By bad outcome we mean an outcome that is truly undesirable. Failing to win a lottery may not be a good outcome, but it's not a really negative outcome. Thus most people don't think of buying a lottery ticket as a risky investment. On the other hand, losing an entire investment—say your life savings of $80,000—because the firm went bankrupt would be a bad outcome!

A Definition of Risk

A good definition of risk, then, should include a measure of variability and a measure of the possibility of negative outcomes. Standard deviation reflects variability both above and below the mean return. Strictly speaking, the standard deviation captures only one dimension of risk. An asset with a return that has a very large standard deviation, such as a lottery ticket, may be interpreted as having a large degree of risk when it is not really very risky. However, suppose an asset has a return distribution that is approximately symmetrical around the mean (like the normal pdf in Figure 6-6). In such cases, the larger the standard deviation, the riskier the investment. When the return distribution is symmetrical, standard deviation captures both dimensions of risk.

In spite of its apparent shortcomings, the standard deviation of the return (just "standard deviation," for short) is actually a pretty good measure of risk. This is so for two reasons. First, return distributions tend to be approximately symmetrical. Second, evidence indicates that other conceptually superior measures do not perform any better. Therefore, as a practical matter, standard deviation is a useful measure of risk.

We will develop theoretical models of required returns using standard deviation as the risk measure. The **specific risk** of an asset is its standard deviation.

 *ie the diversifiable risk.*

Self-Check Questions

1. What are the two dimensions of risk? Explain the practical meaning of each.
2. Explain the drawback in using standard deviation to measure risk when the return distribution isn't symmetrical.
3. Explain why standard deviation is a relatively good measure of risk as long as the return distribution is approximately symmetrical.

6.7 INVESTMENT PORTFOLIOS

An investment made up of a group of assets is called a **portfolio**. Combining securities into portfolios reduces risk. This follows from the Principle of Diversification. Stocks with "good" returns tend to cancel out those with "bad" returns. Rational investors hold a portfolio of stocks rather than putting all their eggs in one basket.

Efficient Portfolios

According to the Principle of Risk-Return Trade-Off, investors want high return and low risk. Therefore, investors will want to invest only in efficient portfolios. An **efficient portfolio** is one that provides the highest expected return for any given degree of risk. Viewed from the other dimension, an efficient portfolio provides the lowest risk for any given expected return.

Now let's see how the expected returns and risks of individual assets combine to create the portfolio's expected return and risk.

Two-Asset Portfolios

Let's show the return to asset 1 as R_1 with expected return $\bar{r}_1$ and specific risk σ_1. The return to asset 2 is R_2 with expected return $\bar{r}_2$ and specific risk σ_2. Suppose a proportion w_1 of portfolio value is invested in asset 1, and the remainder $(1 - w_1)$ is invested in asset 2. The **portfolio expected return**, $\bar{r}_p$, is

$$\bar{r}_p = w_1\bar{r}_1 + (1 - w_1)\bar{r}_2 \tag{6.8}$$

Equation (6.8) says the portfolio expected return is simply the weighted average of the expected returns to the individual assets. The weights are the proportions of money invested in each asset. Therefore, the portfolio's expected return is a linear function of the expected returns to the individual assets. However, the portfolio's risk is related to the risk of the individual assets in a more complex way.

Portfolio risk, represented as σ_p, is the standard deviation of the portfolio's return:

$$\sigma_p = \{w_1^2\sigma_1^2 + (1 - w_1)^2\sigma_2^2 + 2w_1(1 - w_1)\text{Corr}(R_1,R_2)\sigma_1\sigma_2\}^{1/2} \tag{6.9}$$

where $\text{Corr}(R_1, R_2)$ stands for the correlation coefficient between the returns on the two assets. As you can see, the standard deviation of the portfolio is not a simple weighted average of the standard deviations of the individual assets. (There is an exception to this statement, which we will explore later.)

EXAMPLE

Calculating a Portfolio's Expected Return and Risk

Table 6-3 provides the possible returns and their probabilities for two assets, "mature stock" and "growth stock," in each of four scenarios. Equation (6.4) is used to calculate the expected return. Equation (6.5) is used to calculate the variance, the square root of which is the standard deviation, σ. Suppose equal amounts are invested in the two stocks. What will be the portfolio's expected return and risk?

TABLE 6-3
Return estimates for two stocks.

STATE OF THE ECONOMY	PROBABILITY OF OCCURRENCE	MATURE STOCK	GROWTH STOCK
Recession	0.10	−3.0%	2.0%
Stable	0.30	3.0	4.0
Moderate growth	0.40	7.0	10.0
Boom	0.20	10.0	20.0
	1.00		
Expected return, $\bar{r}$		5.4%	9.4%
Standard deviation, σ		3.7%	6.1%
Correlation coefficient, Corr		0.90	

First, we calculate the correlation coefficient using Equations (6.6) and (6.7).

$$\text{Cov}(R_1, R_2) = 0.1(-8.4)(-7.4) + 0.3(-2.4)(-5.4) + 0.4(1.6)(0.6) + 0.2(4.6)(10.6) = 20.24$$

$$\text{Corr}(R_1, R_2) = 20.24/[(3.7)(6.1)] = 0.90$$

Next, because the stocks are weighted equally, $w_1 = 0.5$. Then, using Equation (6.8), we find that the portfolio expected return is

$$\bar{r}_p = 0.5(5.4) + 0.5(9.4) = 0.074 = 7.4\%$$

Finally, we use Equation (6.9) to find the portfolio's standard deviation:

$$\sigma_p = \{(0.5)^2(3.7)^2 + (0.5)^2(6.1)^2 + 2(0.5)(0.5)(0.90)(3.7)(6.1)\}^{1/2} = 4.8\%$$ ■

ASSET-PORTFOLIO RISK-RETURN INTERACTIONS Our portfolio example looked at an equally weighted two-asset portfolio. But what about other, unequal combinations? Figure 6-7 graphs the expected return and risk for each asset. Expected return is measured along the vertical (y) axis, and risk (standard deviation) along the horizontal (x) axis. Suppose all the money is invested in either asset 1 or asset 2. Then the risk-return combinations are at A_1 and at A_2, respectively. But we are more interested in "true" portfolios involving both assets. These are cases where money is invested in each asset.

Equation (6.8) shows the relationship between the assets' expected returns and the portfolio's expected return. Equation (6.9) shows the relationship between the assets' risks and the portfolio's risk. We can explore the combined effect of Equations (6.8) and (6.9) by substituting a value for the correlation coefficient, Corr, and looking at all possible values for w_1 be-

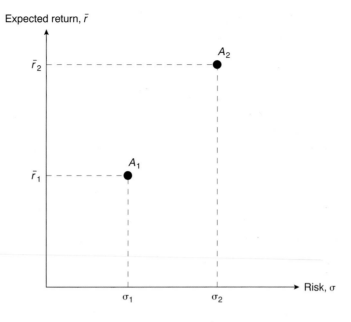

FIGURE 6-7
**Expected return and
risk of asset 1 and
asset 2.**

tween 0 and 1. In general, we want to find the portfolio with the smallest σ_p for any particular expected return $\bar{r}_p$. We have to do this mathematically.[10]

First, let's consider three special cases: perfect negative correlation (Corr = −1.0), perfect positive correlation (Corr = +1.0), and zero correlation (Corr = 0).

PERFECT NEGATIVE CORRELATION   Figure 6-8 graphs the portfolio risk-return combinations given by Equations (6.8) and (6.9) for $0 \le w_1 \le 1.0$ when Corr = −1.0. Note in Figure 6-8 that it is possible to combine investments in the two risky assets so that the portfolio

---

[10] Take the derivative of the equation with respect to w_1, set it equal to zero, and solve for w_1. To check that you have determined a minimum (as opposed to a maximum), show that the second derivative is positive at that point.

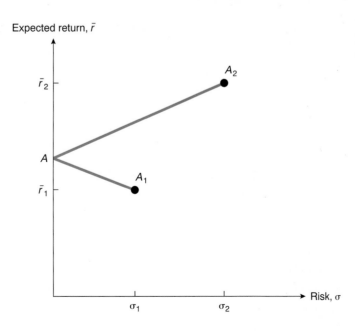

FIGURE 6-8
**Perfect negative
correlation
(Corr = −1.0).**

risk is zero. This result is a direct consequence of the perfect negative correlation. When asset 1's realized return is high, asset 2's is low, and vice versa. When asset 1 has a "medium return," so does asset 2. Therefore, when the two assets are combined in the proportions represented by portfolio A in Figure 6-8, high and low returns always cancel each other out *exactly*. The portfolio earns the same return every period.

The idea that you might be able to invest in two assets, both of which are risky, and yet have your total investment be riskless is not at all intuitive. Harry Markowitz pointed out this phenomenon in 1952 and launched a revolution in the way people think about investing.

Figure 6-8 illustrates the special case in which the minimum value of portfolio risk is $\sigma_p = 0$. When Corr $= -1.0$, we can determine analytically the exact proportions to invest in the two risky assets, w_1 and $(1 - w_1)$, so that the portfolio is riskless. These proportions can be derived simply by setting Equation (6.9) equal to zero and solving for w_1.

EXAMPLE

Perfect Negative Correlation

Consider two stocks whose possible future returns are as indicated in Table 6-4. The five scenarios are equally likely to occur. What are the investment weights that will create a two-asset portfolio with zero standard deviation, such as point A in Figure 6-8?

TABLE 6-4
Future returns for two stocks (Corr $= -1.0$).

SCENARIO	1	2	3	4	5	AVERAGE	STANDARD DEVIATION
Stock A return	20%	−10%	15%	−5%	25%	9.0%	13.9%
Stock B return	15	51	21	45	9	28.2	16.7

First, the correlation coefficient is

$$\text{Corr} = \frac{0.2(11.0)(-13.2) + 0.2(-19.0)(22.8) + 0.2(6.0)(-7.2) + 0.2(-14.0)(16.8) + 0.2(16.0)(-19.2)}{(13.9)(16.7)} = -1.00$$

Next, with Corr $= -1.0$, Equation (6.9) reduces to

$$\sigma_p = w_1(\sigma_1 + \sigma_2) - \sigma_2$$

Therefore, putting in the known values yields

$$0 = w_1(13.9 + 16.7) - 16.7$$

Solving, we get

$$w_1 = 0.54575$$

With this value for w_1,

$$\sigma_p = \{(0.54575)^2(13.9)^2 + (0.45425)^2(16.7)^2 - 2(0.54575)(0.45425)(13.9)(16.7)\}^{1/2} = 0.0 \quad \blacksquare$$

What can we say in general about how to invest in two risky securities when Corr $= -1.0$? Individuals may have specific preferences about investments, but would you invest all your money in asset 1? Of course not. By investing at least some of your money in asset 2, you can earn a higher expected return with less risk.

Look again at Figure 6-8. The line AA_2 *dominates* the line AA_1 because there is a point on AA_2 that has the same risk but higher return for every point on AA_1. Therefore, we have our first generalization about how to invest:

GENERALIZATION 1
When Corr = −1.0 *never* invest all your money in the lower-return-less-risky asset.

Of course, people who are willing to take more risk may want to invest all their money in the higher-return-riskier asset. Because of this, our generalization may seem somewhat limited. But Generalization 1 is a first step in building *general rules for investment* that apply to *everyone*.

Are there two securities to invest in that are perfectly negatively correlated? No, not that we know of, so let's consider some other cases that are more interesting because they are more realistic. But keep our starting point in mind. We're going to build on it.

PERFECT POSITIVE CORRELATION   Unlike the first case, it is both realistic and easy to find two assets with perfect positive correlation. A simple example is two shares of common stock in the same firm. Figure 6-9 shows the possible expected returns to portfolio combinations for values of w_1 between 0.0 and 1.0, when Corr = +1.0.

When Corr = +1.0, Equation (6.9) reduces to

$$\sigma_p = w_1\sigma_1 + (1 - w_1)\sigma_2$$

In this case, the risk of the portfolio is the weighted average of the risks of the individual securities. This is a simple linear function, as can be seen in Figure 6-9. This is the single exception to our earlier statement that the risk of the portfolio is not a simple linear function of the risk of the individual assets.

ZERO CORRELATION   Figure 6-10 shows the case where Corr = 0.0. It is somewhat like the perfect negative correlation case. We can make the same generalization here, even though it is not possible to create a riskless portfolio with just these two assets. Once again, the line of possible combinations moves from A_1 up and to the left (the "hook"). There is a set of combinations that is dominated by other possible combinations. Again, Generalization 1 holds for *everyone*: Never invest all your money in the lower-return–less-risky asset.

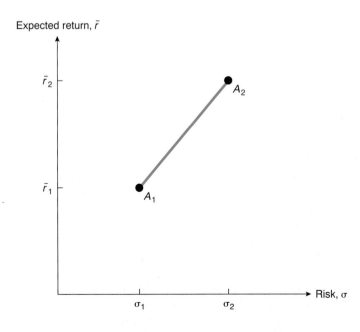

FIGURE 6-9
Perfect positive correlation (Corr = +1.0).

FIGURE 6-10
Zero correlation
(Corr = 0.0).

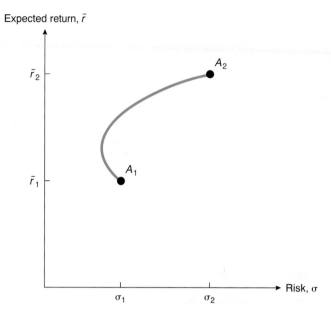

FIGURE 6-10
Zero correlation
(Corr = 0.0).

POSITIVE CORRELATION   We have looked at three special cases. Now let's see what happens to the portfolio risk-return combinations when the correlation coefficient is positive but less than 1.0. This is the most common case. It leads us to more interesting generalizations about how you should invest your money.

Figure 6-11 shows the curve linking all possible combinations of portfolio risk and return for assets 1 and 2 when Corr = 0.4. It is not a straight line. Compare portfolios with w_1 = 1.0 (all the money invested in asset 1) and w_1 = 0.5. A portfolio (call it portfolio B) with

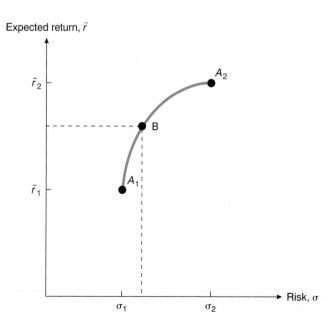

FIGURE 6-11
Positive correlation
(Corr = 0.4).

$w_1 = 0.5$ has an expected return exactly halfway between the expected returns of assets 1 and 2. However, it has a standard deviation that is only about one-fifth of the way toward asset 2 from asset 1. Think about that. The trade-off between how much expected return you get and how much risk you take on is more favorable to the investor in the area where w_1 is greater than 0.5 than it is where w_1 is less than 0.5. In mathematical terms, the slope is greater when w_1 is close to 1.0 and smaller when w_1 is close to zero.

We can also look at the investment possibilities by starting with $w_1 = 0.0$ (all the money invested in asset 2): When half the money is invested in asset 1, risk is decreased 80% of the way toward σ_1, but expected return decreases only half the way toward $\bar{r}_1$.

Some people might be so risk-averse that they would not invest anything in asset 2. Others might have such little risk aversion that they would invest all their money in asset 2. But we believe most people will find it attractive to diversify. This leads us to our second generalization.

GENERALIZATION 2
When asset returns are not perfectly positively correlated, diversification can increase the ratio of the portfolio's expected return to its risk.

In other words, when asset returns are not perfectly positively correlated, diversification can change the risk-return trade-off among our set of possible investments as we move along the curve in Figure 6-11. Note that although risk is reduced by combining stocks into portfolios when $0 < \text{Corr} < 1$, it *cannot* be completely eliminated.

Figure 6-12 shows how the set of all possible combinations for two-asset portfolios depends on Corr. It is important to understand that each specific case has only one value for Corr. The set of all possible combinations for each specific case is represented by one line.

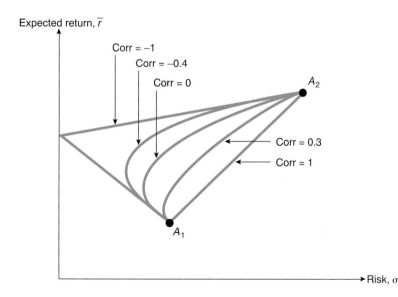

FIGURE 6-12

How the set of all possible combinations for two-asset portfolios depends on Corr. The higher Corr is, the straighter the curve.

Portfolios with More Than Two Assets: An Expanded Framework

Now let's expand our thinking from two assets. Consider all the stocks that are publicly traded on the NYSE, on the AMEX, or through the National Association of Securities Dealers Automated Quotation (NASDAQ) system. That gives us more than 10,000 assets. In addition, we can form an infinite number of portfolios containing different proportions of these stocks.

It is impossible to list all of the possible asset combinations. Nevertheless, we can show you, in a figure, what the set of risk-return combinations looks like on the basis of numerical estimations of actual returns from stocks. Figure 6-13 illustrates the returns of all possible portfolios of stocks. (It reminds us of an umbrella without a handle.)

As before, the important concern is what we can say about how investors should invest their money when they face this set of investment alternatives. Should they invest in portfolio N, which lies in the middle of the umbrella in Figure 6-13? No, because they can instead invest in portfolio E_1. It has the same expected return but lower risk. Or they can invest in portfolio E_2, which has the same risk but a higher expected return.

The set of *efficient portfolios* consists of the ones on the curve between points E and F. Clearly, they are more "interesting" than the others. This set is called the efficient frontier. The

FIGURE 6-13
The expected returns to all possible combinations of risky assets.

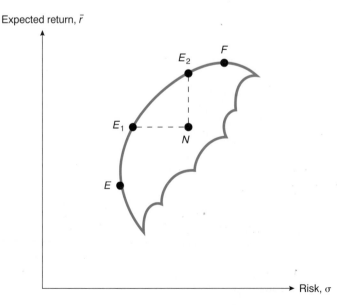

efficient frontier is the set of efficient portfolios. These portfolios have the highest expected return for a given level of risk (or, equivalently, the lowest risk for a given expected return). Regardless of how much or how little risk you are willing to take, you should never invest below the efficient frontier. Why? Because you can do better.

This leads us to our third important generalization.

GENERALIZATION 3
Never invest your money in a portfolio that lies below the efficient frontier.

Self-Check Questions
1. What is an efficient portfolio?
2. What is the efficient frontier?
3. Explain why a rational investor would never knowingly invest money in a portfolio that is below the efficient frontier.

6.8 CHOOSING THE BEST RISKY PORTFOLIO

We need one more element to finish building our model. It is called the *riskless asset*. Using the riskless asset, we will show you how investors choose risky portfolios. This will lead us to the risk-return relationship we are looking for.

A Riskless Asset

What traits would a riskless asset have? A **riskless asset** is simply an asset with a zero standard deviation. That is to say, there is no uncertainty about the asset's future return. The realized return will always equal the expected return.

Is there such an asset? Literally, no. Among other possibilities, there is some chance of a late or missed payment, regardless of who owes it—even the U.S. government.[11] But for practical purposes, some investments have a small enough standard deviation to be considered riskless. Most financial economists think of U.S. government 90-day Treasury bills as riskless investments. The risk of default by the U.S. Treasury in the next 90 days is negligible. Although such investments are not *literally* riskless, we will go along with the majority and assume them to be essentially without risk.

Investing in the Riskless Asset

Surprisingly, the fact that a "riskless" asset exists makes it possible to generalize further about how everyone should invest their money in *risky* assets. Combining our investment in a risky portfolio of assets with investment in a riskless asset resembles the two-asset portfolio problem we have already examined. Thus we can draw on what we have already learned about two-asset portfolios. However, please carefully identify the items we refer to: asset 1 is the riskless asset, asset 2 is a risky portfolio, and the total portfolio is a combination of asset 1 (the riskless asset) and asset 2 (the risky portfolio).

---

[11] You might recall the "federal budget battle" late in 1995 and early in 1996. There was genuine concern that the federal government might default because Congress delayed raising the debt ceiling.

FIGURE 6-14
**Combinations of
risky portfolios and
the riskless asset.**

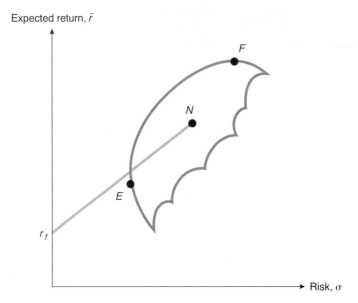

Equations (6.8) and (6.9) again provide us with expressions for the expected return and standard deviation of the return from the total portfolio. Let's simplify Equation (6.9) further. With $\sigma_1 = 0.0$, Equation (6.9) reduces to

$$\sigma_p = \{(1 - w_1)^2\sigma_2^2\}^{1/2} = (1 - w_1)\sigma_2 \tag{6.10}$$

Equation (6.10) shows that the risk of the total portfolio (the combination of the riskless asset and the risky portfolio), σ_p, is a simple linear function of the risk of asset 2 (the risky portfolio), σ_2. Therefore, whatever risky portfolio we choose for asset 2, the set of all possible total portfolio risk-return combinations of asset 1 and asset 2 forms a straight line between the riskless asset and the chosen risky portfolio. Figure 6-14 shows this relationship for an arbitrarily chosen risky portfolio, N, from among our "umbrella set" of all possible portfolios.

Note that some of the possible combinations along the line from the riskless return, r_f,[12] to N dominate a part of the efficient frontier. The problem is further complicated because how much of the efficient frontier is dominated depends on our choice of N. This brings us to the next logical question: Is there a "best" risky portfolio? Yes. Now let's see why, and what that portfolio is.

Choosing the Best Risky Portfolio

Figure 6-14 suggests the following decision rule: Choose the risky portfolio that dominates the largest portion of the efficient frontier. If we follow this rule, the *best* risky portfolio is the one that produces a line of combinations that is tangent to the efficient frontier. This best risky portfolio is denoted M. Figure 6-15 shows combinations of M and the riskless asset. It takes us to our next generalization.

> **GENERALIZATION 4**
> Always invest part of your money in the tangent portfolio M and the rest in the riskless asset unless you are willing to take on more risk than the risk of M.

---

[12] The f in r_f is to indicate that the return is *f*ree of risk.

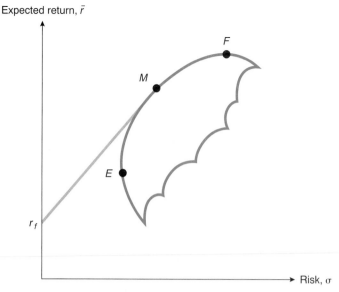

Expected return, $\bar{r}$

Risk, σ

FIGURE 6-15
Combinations of M
and the riskless asset.

As with the other generalizations, the important thing about Generalization 4 is that it applies to everyone. Under the conditions we have modeled thus far, you should invest *your* money this way. The proportions you invest in the riskless asset and M are determined by your willingness to take on risk. Nevertheless, the choice of M is the same for everyone (except those willing to take on more risk than M). That means that a large number of people will want to invest some of their money in the risky portfolio, M. Further generalizations about how everyone should invest are possible if we introduce the opportunity to borrow money to invest.

Self-Check Questions

1. What is a riskless asset?

2. In what sense is a 90-day Treasury bill a riskless asset? In what sense is a 30-year Treasury bond *not* a riskless asset?

3. Explain how the existence of a riskless asset alters an investor's set of investment opportunities.

6.9 BORROWING AND PORTFOLIO SEPARATION

The idea of borrowing can be introduced into the model by representing the borrowed amount as a *negative* proportion invested in the riskless asset (asset 1). That is, in our two-asset portfolio model of M and the riskless asset, the investor is borrowing money to invest when w_1 is negative. This is like saying that what we owe you is negative to us but positive to you. The person who lends the money is investing in the borrower, so the borrowed amount is simply a negative investment. (The Principle of Two-Sided Transactions strikes again!)

One problem with using negative values for w_1 to represent a borrowed amount is that the implied borrowing rate of interest is the same as the lending rate of interest. At first, this may seem troublesome. We know that when we go to a bank, we find that it demands a higher rate for borrowing than it offers for lending (the rate paid on deposits).

Different borrowing and lending rates are certainly a fact of life for most of us. However, consider large firms. Many large firms invest and borrow in the commercial paper market. One day a firm is a lender, but the next day that same firm may be a borrower. The commercial paper rate is generally quoted as a single rate.

The main difference between the bank's borrowing and lending rates in practice is the charge for transacting in small amounts. In other words, the bank is simply charging (a transaction cost) for separating large amounts into small amounts or putting small amounts together to make large amounts. Therefore, using a single rate for borrowing and lending is essentially equivalent to assuming costless transactions. On the basis of the Principle of Capital Market Efficiency, costless transactions are a good starting point for our model.

The Capital Market Line

Allowing w_1 to be negative requires no change in Equations (6.8) and (6.9). With the possibility of borrowing (a negative investment in asset 1), the line of investment possibilities simply extends past M and continues to climb with the same slope. Figure 6-16 shows the line that links possible investment combinations when borrowing at the riskless rate is possible. It is called the **capital market line (CML)**. The CML touches the efficient frontier at M and dominates the efficient frontier everywhere else. Figure 6-16 leads to another important generalization.

> **GENERALIZATION 5**
> Invest your money in the best risky portfolio M and set your portfolio's return and risk levels by lending or borrowing.

Portfolio Separation Theorem

Generalization 5 is a very powerful statement. In fact, one implication of Generalization 5 is so important that, like other important concepts, it has its own name. This implication is called the **portfolio separation theorem**: *The composition of the best risky portfolio does not depend on the investor's attitude toward risk.*

FIGURE 6-16

The capital market line (CML): Alternative combinations of the best risky portfolio and lending and borrowing at the riskless rate.

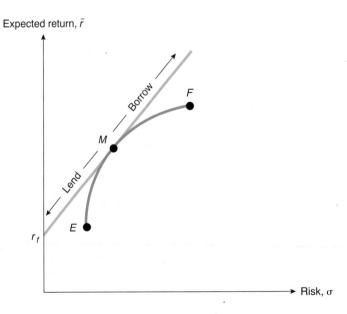

Don't choose risky assets on the basis of your attitude toward risk. Instead, you should invest your money in M and the riskless asset. Your levels of risk and expected return are determined by the mixture of the two. This is very different from what people did before the development of modern portfolio theory.

When you really think about it, this is a startling approach to picking investments. It is extremely unlikely that anyone would arrive at such an approach intuitively. A careful modeling of the world of stock investments has produced surprising conclusions that led to a revolution in the way the world thinks about investing. And there is more. Generalization 5 states that everyone should invest in the risky portfolio M. But what is M?

The Market Portfolio

In the model derived so far, everyone invests in the same set of risky assets. Thus everyone owns a portion of every asset that is in this special portfolio M (for "market"). Any asset available in the market that is not in M cannot have an owner. This is because everyone owns a part of the same set of assets. But every asset that is available in the market must have an owner. Thus every asset must be included in M. Because M includes every asset that is available in the market, it is called the **market portfolio**.

In this model of the world, all investors diversify their ownership of risky assets by owning some of everything. But what proportion of your money should you invest in each asset? This question is more easily analyzed by examining a simple example of a market, rather than the stock market with its more than 10,000 stocks.

Consider a market with three risky assets: 1, 2, and 3. They are worth $100, $200, and $300, respectively, for a total market value of $600. Suppose there are two investors, A and B. Investor A owns $450 worth of the market portfolio, M, and B owns $150 worth. They invest the rest of their money in the riskless asset. Because Investor A owns 75% of M, A will own 75% of each asset. Similarly, B owns 25% of M and 25% of each asset. The investors own identical mixes of risky assets. But what proportion of each investor's portfolio is invested in asset 1?

The answer is one-sixth, because asset 1 is one-sixth ($= 100/600$) of the total market value. If an Investor C decides to invest in this market, she should invest one-sixth of her money in asset 1, one-third ($= 200/600$) in asset 2, and one-half ($= 300/600$) in asset 3. In this way, C would also be investing in this market portfolio. ∎

Composition of the Market Portfolio

EXAMPLE

The Market Portfolio in Practice

If we translate our three-asset example into a large market of risky assets such as the stock market, the principle for determining the market portfolio is the same. However, identifying the value of each asset can be tricky. An asset's value is not the market value *per share*. Instead, it is the market value of all the firm's stock.

That is, the asset value to use in determining the proper investment proportions is the market value per share times the number of shares the firm has outstanding. For example, if IBM is selling for $100 per share and there are 200 million shares of IBM, the stock market value of IBM is $20 billion.

We determine the proportion of money to invest in each stock in the following manner. First, sum the total stock market values of all the firms in the market. Then divide the firm's total stock market value by the sum of all the values. The resulting fraction is the proportion of the portfolio to invest in the stock. Continuing our hypothetical example of IBM, suppose the sum of the values for all stocks is $3 trillion. Then M would contain 0.67% (= 20 billion/3 trillion) invested in IBM stock.

If determining the proportions to invest in each stock sounds tedious, that is because it would be! Fortunately, when such information is valuable to one set of people, other people apply the Principle of Valuable Ideas. They recognize the potential to make a positive NPV by producing the information for a profit or by creating investment funds that approximate the market portfolio.

Currently, information about the composition of the market portfolio can be purchased from a variety of information services. In addition, a number of investment managers and mutual fund providers have created so-called stock index funds. They invest in a portfolio of common stocks that matches the composition of the Standard & Poor's 500 Index, a diversified collection of common stocks that is generally accepted as a good proxy for the (common stock) market. For example, the oldest and largest of the S&P 500 mutual funds, the Vanguard Index Trust-500 Portfolio, had approximately $9.4 billion under management at year-end 1994. The 43 S&P 500 mutual funds tracked by Lipper Analytical Services had $20.5 billion under management at year-end 1994.

Looking Ahead

The real value of deriving this portfolio model, in our opinion, is to identify the determinants of the value of an asset. With that in mind, it may be somewhat surprising to learn that the major determinant of the value of a stock (or any asset) is the correlation between its return and the market portfolio's return. Other determinants of value include market imperfections, such as tax or informational asymmetries, and innovative ideas that have positive or negative NPV (the Principle of Valuable Ideas). We will explore these determinants of value in the next chapter.

Self-Check Questions

1. Describe in your own words what the capital market line (CML) is.

2. Why does the capital market line intersect the efficient frontier at just one point?

3. Explain the meaning of the term *market portfolio*.

SUMMARY

In this chapter we demonstrated the Principle of Diversification by showing the benefits of diversification to investors. Combining assets into portfolios reduces risk. The "good" returns tend to offset the "bad" ones. Consequently, rational investors hold portfolios of stocks. Because most investors are rational, the proper measure of a stock's risk is its *market risk*, not its specific risk. Thus a stock's required return will generally be based on its market risk, that is, on how much it contributes to the riskiness of the market portfolio.

In Chapter 7 we will build on these basic risk-return and investment concepts. We'll develop a model that expresses an asset's required return in terms of its market risk.

DECISION SUMMARY

- Investors purchase securities only if they expect a return that fully compensates for the security's risk. The Principle of Risk-Return Trade-Off says the greater the expected return, the higher the risk.

- A realized APY is the annual equivalent of a realized return for a particular holding period.

- An asset's expected return is the mean of its future possible returns.

- There are two dimensions to risk: (1) uncertainty concerning the future outcome and (2) the possibility of a negative outcome. As long as the distribution of future returns is at least approximately symmetrical around the mean, the standard deviation captures both dimensions. On this basis, we use standard deviation to measure risk.

- A portfolio's expected return is the weighted average of the expected returns of the individual securities. The weights are the proportions of portfolio value invested in each security.

- A portfolio's risk (the standard deviation of its return) depends primarily on the correlation coefficients between the returns of the securities that compose the portfolio. A portfolio's risk is *not* simply a weighted average of the standard deviations of the component securities.

- When asset returns are not perfectly positively correlated, the Principle of Diversification says that diversification can be beneficial. This is because it can increase the ratio of the portfolio's expected return to its risk. That is, diversification improves the risk-return trade-off.

- The efficient frontier is the set of portfolios that provide the highest expected return for a given risk or, equivalently, the lowest risk for a given expected return. Investors should never invest all their money in a portfolio that is below the efficient frontier.

- The capital market line (CML) shows the risk-return trade-off for portfolio investments. The CML is a line that starts at the riskless return and is tangent to the best risky portfolio M.

- The market portfolio includes all assets. In practice, a stock market index, such as the S&P 500, is used as a proxy for the market portfolio.

- Investor decisions about which risky assets to invest in do not depend on investor attitude toward risk.

- Investors should always have their investment portfolio on the CML by investing their money in M and then setting their expected return and risk levels by lending or borrowing in the riskless asset.

EQUATION SUMMARY

(6.1) $$\text{Realized APY} = (1 + r)^m - 1$$

(6.2) $$1 + r = (1 + \text{realized APY})^N$$

$$p_n \geq 0 \quad \text{for all } n$$

(6.3) $$\sum_{n=1}^{N} p_n = 1$$

(6.4) $$\bar{x} = \sum_{n=1}^{N} p_n x_n$$

(6.5) $$\sigma^2 = \sum_{n=1}^{N} p_n (x_n - \bar{x})^2$$

$$(6.6) \qquad \text{Covariance} = \text{Cov}(X,Y) = \sum_{n=1}^{N} p_n(x_n - \bar{x})(y_n - \bar{y})$$

$$(6.7) \qquad \text{Corr}(X,Y) = \frac{\text{Cov}(X,Y)}{\sigma_X \sigma_Y}$$

$$(6.8) \qquad \bar{r}_p = w_1 \bar{r}_1 + (1 - w_1)\bar{r}_2$$

$$(6.9) \qquad \sigma_p = \{w_1^2\sigma_1^2 + (1 - w_1)^2\sigma_2^2 + 2w_1(1 - w_1)\text{Corr}(R_1,R_2)\sigma_1\sigma_2\}^{1/2}$$

$$(6.10) \qquad \sigma_p = \{(1 - w_1)^2\sigma_2^2\}^{1/2} = (1 - w_1)\sigma_2$$

KEY TERMS

realized APY...174

probability...179

mean...179

variance...180

standard deviation...180

covariance...182

correlation coefficient...182

expected return...183

specific risk...185

portfolio...185

efficient portfolio...185

portfolio risk...185

efficient frontier...193

riskless asset...193

capital market line (CML)...196

portfolio separation theorem...196

market portfolio (M)...197

EXERCISES

PROBLEM SET A

A1. An investment produces annual returns of 12% the first year, 7% the second, and 10% the third. Calculate the average realized APY.

A2. An investment of $700 produces total cash proceeds of $1070 a year later. What is the realized return?

A3. What are the two dimensions of risk?

A4. How is risk defined in the models contained in this chapter? What are the shortcomings of this definition? Why is this definition useful as it is applied to investment models, in spite of these shortcomings?

A5. Explain how it is possible to invest in two risky assets that are perfectly negatively correlated (Corr = −1.0) and earn a riskless return.

A6. In your own words, state the portfolio separation theorem. Explain why it is such an important finding.

A7.

a. Suppose you own $1 million worth of 30-year Treasury bonds. Is this asset riskless?

b. Let's say you own $1 million worth of 90-day Treasury bills. You "roll over" this investment every 90 days by reinvesting the proceeds in another issue of 90-day Treasury bills. Is this investment truly riskless? Is it riskless for practical purposes?

c. Can you think of an asset that is truly riskless?

A8. Your roommate asks why you would not invest off the efficient frontier if you had the opportunity to do so. How do you respond?

A9. Define the CML. What information does it convey?

A10. Consider a market with four risky assets, 1, 2, 3, and 4, worth $1000, $2500, $1500, and $5000, respectively. What proportion of each investor's portfolio should be invested in each risky asset?

A11. What is the market portfolio? What practical problems are involved in trying to measure the value of and returns on the market portfolio?

A12. The dividend yield is 6.2%, and the capital gain yield is 15.1%. What is the realized return?

PROBLEM SET B

B1. Explain the fallacy in the following statement: "I bought the stock for $30 per share. It's now selling for $20 per share. But I haven't lost anything because I haven't sold it yet."

B2. Solve Equation (6.9) for the proportion of investment in each asset, w_1 and $(1 - w_1)$, that makes the investment in a two-asset portfolio riskless when the correlation coefficient Corr equals -1.0.

B3. Calculate the realized APY for the investment illustrated in Table 6-1, assuming a holding period that consists of the first quarter only.

B4. Calculate the realized APY, assuming the investment illustrated in Table 6-1 is purchased at time 0 and is held for 3 quarters.

B5.

  a. Calculate each of the quarterly percentage returns for the investment illustrated in Table 6-1.

  b. Show how these quarterly returns can be used to calculate the 1-year return.

B6. Given the probability distribution for returns for stock X and stock Y, compute (a) the expected return for each stock, $\overline{r}_X$ and $\overline{r}_Y$; (b) the variance for each stock; (c) the covariance between X and Y; and (d) the correlation coefficient between X and Y.

	Returns	
Probability	**Stock X**	**Stock Y**
0.1	-10%	4%
0.3	0	8
0.3	6	0
0.2	10	-5
0.1	20	15

B7. Given the probability distribution of returns for stock A and stock B, compute (a) the expected return for each stock, $\overline{r}_A$ and $\overline{r}_B$; (b) each stock's variance; (c) the covariance between the stocks; and (d) the correlation coefficient between the stocks.

	Returns	
Probability	**Stock A**	**Stock B**
0.25	-15%	-10%
0.15	5	-5
0.20	10	0
0.30	25	15
0.10	40	35

B8. The following table provides the monthly returns for Microsoft Corp. (symbol MSFT) common stock and the S&P 500 Index during 1994. Compute (a) the average monthly return for the market and for MSFT over these 12 months; (b) the variance of the monthly return for each over these 12 months; (c) the covariance between the market and MSFT over these 12 months; and (d) the correlation coefficient between the market and MSFT for these 12 months.

Month	S&P 500	MSFT	Month	S&P 500	MSFT
JAN	3.25	5.58	JUL	3.15	−0.24
FEB	−3.00	−3.08	AUG	3.76	12.86
MAR	−4.58	2.73	SEP	−2.69	−3.44
APR	1.16	9.14	OCT	2.08	12.25
MAY	1.24	16.22	NOV	−3.95	−0.20
JUN	−2.68	−3.95	DEC	1.23	−2.78

✓ B9. Consider two securities whose expected returns are $\bar{r}_1 = 0.10$ and $\bar{r}_2 = 0.12$ and whose returns have standard deviations $\sigma_1 = 0.07$ and $\sigma_2 = 0.09$. The correlation coefficient between their returns is $\text{Corr} = -1.0$. Find the portfolio combination that produces a zero-risk portfolio.

B10. A share of common stock has the end-of-year market prices and pays the cash dividends per share shown in the following table.

Year	Share Price	Cash Dividend
0	$25	
1	40	$1.00
2	35	$1.50
3	50	$1.75
4	75	$2.25

a. Calculate the realized returns.

b. Calculate the realized 4-year return.

c. Calculate the realized APY for the 4-year holding period.

B11. The following table provides the monthly returns for Home Depot Inc. (symbol HD) common stock and the S&P 500 Index during 1995. Compute (a) the average monthly return for the market and for HD over these 12 months; (b) the variance of the monthly return for each over these 12 months; (c) the covariance between the market and HD over these 12 months; and (d) the correlation coefficient between the market and HD for these 12 months.

Month	S&P 500	HD	Month	S&P 500	HD
JAN	2.43	1.63	JUL	3.18	7.98
FEB	3.61	−4.01	AUG	−0.03	−9.09
MAR	2.73	−1.39	SEP	4.01	−0.31
APR	2.80	−5.65	OCT	−0.50	−6.58
MAY	3.63	−0.30	NOV	4.10	19.13
JUN	2.13	−2.10	DEC	1.74	7.61

B12. The Great Jones Securities Service has gathered securities analysts' forecasts of next year's earnings per share for the Southern Company. Three analysts predict $2.75, two forecast $2.85, ten predict $3.00, six forecast $3.10, and three predict $3.15.

a. Describe the probabilities associated with these forecasts.

b. What is the expected value of Southern Company's earnings per share for next year?

c. What are the variance and standard deviation of Southern Company's earnings per share for next year?

B13. Consider the following information, which has three securities and three possible economic scenarios:

State of the Economy	Probability of Occurrence	Security 1	Security 2	Security 3
Recession	0.20	5.0%	−3.0%	−7.0%
Stable	0.50	9.0	4.0	−1.0
Boom	0.30	15.0	20.0	13.0

a. Calculate the expected return and standard deviation for each security.

b. Calculate the correlation coefficient for each pair of securities.

c. Suppose a portfolio contains (by market value) 25% each of Securities 1 and 2 and 50% of Security 3. Calculate the portfolio's expected return and standard deviation.

B14. Discuss the implications that the portfolio separation theorem has for the job of a corporate financial manager.

B15. Calculate the expected return and standard deviation for the next year on a stock that is selling for $30 now and has probabilities of 0.2, 0.6, and 0.2 of selling 1 year from now at $24, $33, and $39, respectively. Assume that no dividends will be paid on the stock during the next year, and ignore taxes.

B16. Consider the following information, which has four securities and five possible economic scenarios:

State of the Economy	Probability of Occurrence	U.S. T-bills	Government Bonds	Corporate Bonds	Common Stock
High growth	0.10	6.0%	8.0%	10.0%	25.0%
Moderate growth	0.25	6.0	7.5	9.0	15.5
Slow growth	0.35	6.0	7.0	8.5	11.5
Stagnation	0.15	6.0	6.0	6.0	−1.0
Recession	0.15	6.0	4.0	−2.0	−11.5
	1.00				

a. Calculate the expected return and standard deviation for each security.

b. Calculate the correlation coefficient for each pair of securities.

c. Assuming the four securities are weighted equally, calculate the portfolio's expected return and standard deviation.

d. Assuming that 20% of the portfolio is invested in U.S. T-bills, 20% in government bonds, 30% in corporate bonds, and 30% in common stock, calculate the portfolio's expected return and standard deviation.

B17. General Eclectic Corporation is considering three possible investment projects. The projected returns depend on the future state of the economy.

State of the Economy	Probability of Occurrence	Projected Return		
		1	2	3
Recession	0.20	10%	8%	12%
Stable	0.60	15	13	10
Boom	0.20	21	25	8

    a. Calculate each project's expected return, variance, and standard deviation.

    b. Rank the projects on the basis of (1) expected return and (2) risk. Which project would you choose?

B18. Suppose General Eclectic decides to invest equal amounts in each of the three projects in Problem B17.

    a. Calculate the portfolio's expected return.

    b. Calculate the portfolio's variance and standard deviation.

    c. Calculate the correlation coefficients (1) between projects 1 and 2 and (2) between projects 2 and 3.

B19. Suppose a portfolio consists of two securities, Security 1 and Security 2, whose returns are given in Problem B13. Graph the efficient frontier, assuming these are the only two securities that exist in the world.

B20. Consider a market with five risky assets: 1, 2, 3, 4, and 5. They are worth $1200, $5000, $3400, $2300, and $7200, respectively. Consider also two investors, X and Y. They invest $1000 and $2000, respectively. What proportion of each investor's portfolio is invested in each asset?

B21. Explain why *M must be* the "market portfolio,"—that is, why *M* must include some of every possible asset.

PROBLEM SET *C*

C1. Consider a two-stock portfolio consisting of stocks that are less than perfectly positively correlated. Show that the portfolio will have less risk than the lower-risk stock only if Corr $< \sigma_1/\sigma_2$ where $\sigma_1 < \sigma_2$.

C2. Discuss the following statement: Because capital markets are so efficient, developing new information about the value of a firm must be a worthless undertaking.

C3. Figure 6-13 shows what the group of all possible portfolio combinations for stocks in the stock market looks like. Is it possible that any two of these portfolios have a correlation coefficient between them that is equal to *minus* 1.0? If it is possible, give an example. If it is not possible, explain why.

C4. Using calculus, find the value of w_1 (as a function of the correlation coefficient, Corr, and the standard deviations of the returns, σ_1 and σ_2) that provides the two-asset investment portfolio with the minimum risk possible, assuming that $0.0 \leq w_1 \leq 1.0$.

Real-World Application: Realized APYs for Stocks and Bonds

Smart investors, including corporate pension fund managers, regularly monitor their stock and bond investments and compare the realized returns to broader measures of stock and bond returns. For example, Ibbotson Associates has calculated realized APYs for different types of stocks and bonds all the way back to 1926. You can use these APYs to calculate the average realized return and standard deviation of returns for stocks and bonds. Comparing the average APY and standard deviation for different bonds and stocks illustrates the Principle of Risk-Return Trade-Off. Also, the correlation coefficient between the APYs tells you how Treasury bond returns covary with Treasury bill returns, stock returns covary with bond returns, and so on.

    The following table provides annual stock and bond APYs for the period 1975–1994.

YEAR	SMALL-FIRM STOCKS	LARGE-FIRM STOCKS	LONG-TERM CORPORATE BONDS	LONG-TERM GOVERNMENT BONDS	TREASURY BILLS
1975	52.82%	37.20%	14.64%	9.20%	5.80%
1976	57.38	23.84	18.65	16.75	5.08
1977	25.38	−7.18	1.71	−0.69	5.12
1978	23.46	6.56	−0.07	−1.18	7.18
1979	43.46	18.44	−4.18	−1.23	10.38
1980	39.88	32.42	−2.76	−3.95	11.24
1981	13.88	−4.91	−1.24	1.86	14.71
1982	28.01	21.41	42.56	40.36	10.54
1983	39.67	22.51	6.26	0.65	8.80
1984	−6.67	6.27	16.86	15.48	9.85
1985	24.66	32.16	30.09	30.97	7.72
1986	6.85	18.47	19.85	24.53	6.16
1987	−9.30	5.23	−0.27	−2.71	5.47
1988	22.87	16.81	10.70	9.67	6.35
1989	10.18	31.49	16.23	18.11	8.37
1990	−21.56	−3.17	6.78	6.18	7.81
1991	44.63	30.55	19.89	19.30	5.60
1992	23.35	7.67	9.39	8.05	3.51
1993	20.98	9.99	13.19	18.24	2.90
1994	3.11	1.31	−5.76	−7.77	3.90

Source: *Stocks, Bonds, Bills, and Inflation 1995 Yearbook* (Chicago, Ill.: Ibbotson Associates, 1995), p. 39.

1. Calculate the average realized APY for a. small-firm stocks, b. large-firm stocks, c. long-term corporate bonds, d. long-term government bonds, and e. Treasury bills.

2. Calculate the standard deviation of returns for a. small-firm stocks, b. large-firm stocks, c. long-term corporate bonds, d. long-term government bonds, and e. Treasury bills.

3. Draw the following graph. Label the horizontal axis risk (standard deviation), and label the vertical axis expected return (average APY). Plot the points corresponding to the pairs (standard deviation, average realized APY) for small-firm stocks, large-firm stocks, long-term corporate bonds, long-term government bonds, and Treasury bills. Do you see a pattern?

4. The annual equity risk premium, ERP, is defined by the equation:

    ERP = (1 + Large Stock APY)/(1 + T Bill APY) − 1,

    where Large Stock APY is the large-firm stock APY and T Bill APY is the Treasury bill APY. Calculate the average annual ERP for 1975 to 1994. How do you interpret this number?

5. The annual small stock premium, SSP, is defined by the equation:

    SSP = (1 + Small Stock APY)/(1 + Large Stock APY) − 1,

    where Small Stock APY is the small-firm stock APY. Calculate the average annual SSP for 1975 to 1994. How do you interpret this number?

6. The annual bond default premium, BDP, is defined by the equation:

    BDP = (1 + LT Corporate Bond APY)/(1 + LT Government Bond APY) − 1,

    where LT Corporate Bond APY is the long-term corporate bond APY and LT Government Bond APY is the long-term government bond APY. Calculate the average annual BDP for 1975 to 1994. How do you interpret this number?

7. Calculate the correlation coefficient between the small-firm stock and large-firm stock APYs. How do you interpret this number?

8. Calculate the correlation coefficient between the long-term corporate bond and long-term government bond APYs. How do you interpret this number?

9. Calculate the correlation coefficient between the long-term government bond and Treasury bill APYs. How do you interpret this number?

10. Are the results of your analysis consistent with the Principle of Risk-Return Trade-Off? Explain.

BIBLIOGRAPHY

Amihud, Yakov, and Haim Mendelson. "Liquidity and Asset Prices: Financial Management Implications," *Financial Management*, 1988, 17(1):5–15.

Bremer, Marc, and Richard J. Sweeney. "The Reversal of Large Stock-Price Decreases," *Journal of Finance*, 1991, 46(2):747–754.

Chan, K.C., and Nai-Fu Chen. "Structural and Return Characteristics of Small and Large Firms," *Journal of Finance*, 1991, 46(4):1467–1484.

Chan, Kalok. "Imperfect Information and Cross-Autocorrelation among Stock Returns," *Journal of Finance*, 1993, 48(4):1211–1230.

Chan, Louis K.C., Yasushi Hamao, and Josef Lakonishok. "Fundamentals and Stock Returns in Japan," *Journal of Finance*, 1991, 46(5):1739–1764.

Chang, Eric C., and J. Michael Pinegar. "A Fundamental Study of the Seasonal Risk-Return Relationship: A Note," *Journal of Finance*, 1988, 43(4):1035–1039.

Conine, Thomas E., Jr., and Maurry Tamarkin. "Implications of Skewness in Returns for Utilities' Cost of Equity Capital," *Financial Management*, 1985, 14(4):66–71.

Conrad, Jennifer S., Allaudeen Hameed, and Cathy Niden. "Volume and Autocovariances in Short-Horizon Individual Security Returns," *Journal of Finance*, 1994, 49(4):1305–1330.

Davis, James L. "The Cross-Section of Realized Stock Returns: The Pre-COMPUSTAT Evidence," *Journal of Finance*, 1994, 49(5):1579–1593.

Donaldson, R. Glen, and Harald Uhlig. "The Impact of Large Portfolio Insurers on Asset Prices," *Journal of Finance*, 1993, 48(5):1943–1955.

Dubofsky, David A. "Volatility Increases Subsequent to NYSE and AMEX Stock Splits," *Journal of Finance*, 1991, 46(1):421–432.

Easley, David, and Maureen O'Hara. "Order from and Information in Securities Markets," *Journal of Finance*, 1991, 46(3):905–928.

Fama, Eugene F. "Stock Returns, Expected Returns, and Real Activity," *Journal of Finance*, 1990, 45(4):1089–1108.

Fama, Eugene F., and Kenneth R. French. "Size and Book-to-Market Factors in Earnings and Returns," *Journal of Finance*, 1995, 50(1):131–155.

Glosten, Lawrence R., Ravi Jagannathan, and David E. Runkle. "On the Relation Between the Expected Value and the Volatility of the Nominal Excess Return on Stocks," *Journal of Finance*, 1993, 48(5):1779–1801.

Harris, Robert S., and Felicia C. Marston. "Estimating Shareholder Risk Premia Using Analysts' Growth Forecasts," *Financial Management*, 1992, 21(2):63–70.

Haugen, Robert A., Eli Talmor, and Walter N. Torous. "The Effect of Volatility Changes on the Level of Stock Prices and Subsequent Expected Returns," *Journal of Finance*, 1991, 46(3):985–1008.

Jegadeesh, Narasimhan. "Seasonality in Stock Price Mean Reversion: Evidence from the U.S. and the U.K.," *Journal of Finance*, 1991, 46(4):1427–1444.

Jones, Steven L., Winson Lee, and Rudolf Apenbrink. "New Evidence on the January Effect Before Personal Income Taxes," *Journal of Finance*, 1991, 46(5):1909–1924.

Kothari, S.P., Jay Shanken, and Richard G. Sloan. "Another Look at the Cross-section of Expected Stock Returns," *Journal of Finance*, 1995, 50(1):185–224.

Loderer, Claudio, John W. Cooney, and Leonard D. Van Drunen. "The Price Elasticity of Demand for Common Stock," *Journal of Finance*, 1991, 46(2):621–652.

Longstaff, Francis A. "How Much Can Marketability Affect Security Values?" *Journal of Finance*, 1995, 50(5):1767–1774.

Markowitz, Harry M. "Foundations of Portfolio Theory," *Journal of Finance*, 1991, 46(2):469–478.

Markowitz, Harry M. "Portfolio Selection," *Journal of Finance*, 1952, 7(1):77–91.

Markowitz, Harry M. *Portfolio Selection: Efficient Diversification of Investments*. New York: Wiley, 1959.

McQueen, Grant, and Steven Thorley. "Are Stock Returns Predictable? A Test Using Markov Chains," *Journal of Finance*, 1991, 46(1):239–264.

Roll, Richard. "Industrial Structure and the Comparative Behavior of International Stock Market Indexes," *Journal of Finance*, 1992, 47(1):3–42.

Roll, Richard, and Stephen A. Ross. "On the Cross-Sectional Relation Between Expected Returns and Betas," *Journal of Finance*, 1994, 49(1):101–121.

Sarig, Oded, and Arthur Warga. "Some Empirical Estimates of the Risk Structure of Interest Rates," *Journal of Finance*, 1989, 44(5):1351–1360.

Seyhun, H. Nejat. "Overreaction or Fundamentals: Some Lessons from Insiders' Response to the Market Crash of 1987," *Journal of Finance*, 1990, 45(5):1363–1388.

RISK AND RETURN: ASSET PRICING MODELS

We know investors purchase risky assets only if they expect to get a return that makes the risk worth taking. And we know from the Principle of Risk-Return Trade-Off, the greater the risk, the higher the required return. But what required return is necessary to compensate for a particular amount of risk? As we have learned, a required return can be thought of as an opportunity cost. But suppose there is no comparable opportunity from which to estimate the required return. What factors determine a required return? In other words, how does the market set a required return?

In this chapter we present a model for determining a required return where return is expressed as a function of risk. You would expect that the required return for any asset could be expressed as a "base" return to a riskless asset plus an added return to compensate for risk. This simplifies the problem a little. We can determine the required return if we can figure out what the risk premium should be. But what determines a risk premium?

The model we'll develop, the *capital-asset-pricing model* (CAPM), expresses the required return as the riskless return plus a risk premium. It looks like this:

$$\text{Required Return} = \text{Riskless Return} + \text{Beta} \left[\begin{array}{l} \text{Market Portfolio's} \\ \text{Expected Return} \end{array} - \text{Riskless Return} \right]$$

The risk premium is a function of two variables. Beta (pronounced "bay-tah") measures the asset's incremental contribution to the risk of a diversified portfolio. Building on Chapter 6, beta is a measure of the asset's market risk. Beta reflects the correlation between an asset's returns and those of the market portfolio. The market portfolio's expected return minus the riskless return can be thought of as the price per risk unit. That is, it is the (additional) required return the market will pay you for bearing one unit of risk.

This very simple structure for the risk premium is what distinguishes the CAPM from other models. In this chapter, we will examine both the strengths and the shortcomings of this model and show you how to use it in practical situations.

O B J E C T I V E S

After studying this chapter, you should be able to

1. Explain the importance of asset pricing models.

2. Demonstrate how to choose an investment position on the capital market line (CML).

3. Explain the relationship between the CML and the security market line (SML).

4. Describe the relationship between expected return and risk within the CAPM.

5. Use the CAPM to calculate the required return for a proposed investment.

6. Cite the three critical assumptions that underlie the CAPM.

7. Describe the arbitrage pricing theory and explain the principal differences between the CAPM and arbitrage pricing theory.

RISK AND RETURN AND THE PRINCIPLES OF FINANCE

◆ *Efficient Capital Markets*: Estimate a security's risk and required return from its past realized returns.

◆ *Two-Sided Transactions*: Use a security's fair price to compute its expected return, because the fair price does not favor either side of the transaction.

◆ *Risk-Return Trade-Off*: Invest in the combination of amounts of the risky *market portfolio* and the *riskless asset* that provides the investment risk level you choose.

◆ *Diversification*: Invest in a group of assets, a *portfolio*, to reduce the total risk of your entire investment.

◆ *Incremental Benefits*: Measure the incremental benefits from owning a financial security, which are its expected future cash flows.

◆ *Time-Value-of-Money*: Determine the value of a financial security by computing the present value of its expected future cash flows.

◆ *Self-Interested Behavior*: Recognize that prices will be set by the highest bidder, because owners will sell to the highest bidder.

7.1 ASSET PRICING MODELS

In the previous chapter we showed how to construct portfolios and calculate their returns. Now we will take a closer look at how to evaluate returns from individual securities that make up the market portfolio. That effort will lead to a model we can use to compute an asset's required return on the basis of its risk.

Why Asset Pricing Theory Is Important

Asset pricing theory plays an important role in corporate financial management. Its main use is to estimate a required return for calculating an NPV. This is especially critical for major corporate decisions, such as capital budgeting and the evaluation of possible acquisitions.

Estimating an asset's required return is easiest when there are close economic substitutes for it that are traded in a liquid capital market. But some assets have no close substitutes.[1] In such cases, asset pricing theory is a necessary part of the valuation process. It tells us which asset characteristics affect value.

The CML Reconsidered

Generalization 5 (in Chapter 6) prescribes how to invest in risky assets. The prescribed line of investment possibilities, the CML (capital market line), is shown again in Figure 7-1. The CML defines the market risk-return trade-off. But where should you be in that trade-off?

Figure 7-1 includes three *utility curves*.[2] Each represents risk-return combinations that make an investor equally well off. According to the Principle of Risk-Return Trade-Off, investors require a higher return to compensate for greater risk. Moreover, most investors are risk-averse. The more risk-averse an investor is, the greater will be the curvature in that in-

---

[1] Shanken and Smith (1996) cite the example of COMSAT Corporation. At the time it was considering launching its first communications satellite, it could not look to the market to see how comparable projects were being valued; there weren't any.
[2] Economists use the term *utility* to describe the level of investor well-being.

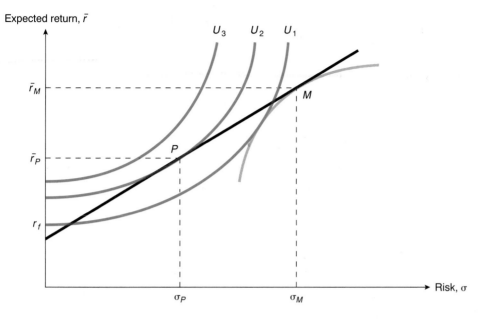

Expected return, $\bar{r}$

Risk, σ

FIGURE 7-1
The capital market line (CML) shows the risk-return combinations that are attainable by combining the market portfolio and lending or borrowing at the riskless return. The best combination for an investor is the one that achieves the investor's highest utility curve.

vestor's utility curves. The curvature means that a doubling of risk requires more than a doubling of expected returns for the investor to be equally well off.

Because investors prefer more return to less return and prefer less risk to more risk, U_2 is preferred over U_1, and U_3 is preferred over U_2. An investor selects the place on the CML that achieves the highest utility curve. U_2 is the best the investor can do in Figure 7-1. It is achieved at P. The highest attainable utility curve is the one tangent to the CML.

Suppose P lies to the left of M, as it does in Figure 7-1. In that case, the investor lends part of her funds at the riskless return. Suppose instead that the shape of the utility curves is such that P lies to the right of M. Then the investor borrows at the riskless return. What does he do with the borrowed funds? He increases his investment in the market portfolio.

In the mid-1960s, several scholars, working independently, asked whether the CML could be used to determine the required return for an individual security.[3] The answer is yes. The CML can be used to identify the determinants of a security's required return. The resulting model is a particularly simple one. In it, the risk premium depends only on the covariance (or, equivalently, on the correlation coefficient[4]) between the security's return and the return on the market portfolio.

Self-Check Questions

1. What does the CML (capital market line) represent?

2. Explain why the CML can be used to determine the required return for an individual security.

---

[3] William Sharpe, John Lintner, and Jan Mossin published papers on the question in 1964, 1965, and 1966, respectively, and Jack Treynor wrote an article in the same period that never appeared in a journal. The published papers are included in the references at the end of the chapter.
[4] Recall from Chapter 6 that covariance and correlation coefficient are directly related. Rearranging Equation (6.7), $Cov(X,Y) = Corr(X,Y)\sigma_X\sigma_Y$.

7.2 THE CAPITAL-ASSET-PRICING MODEL (CAPM)

In Chapter 5 we applied the Principle of Capital Market Efficiency: The capital markets are efficient, so the expected returns must equal the required returns. We do so again here. Remember what we said about required and expected returns. There is no better estimate of the market value, or required return, of a particular stock than the one we observe in the market. However, if we can identify the determinants of an asset's required return, then we can estimate any asset's required return—even one that is *not currently observable*.

Inverting the CML

The capital-asset-pricing model rests on three critical assumptions. The assumptions box lists them. It provides an easy reference. These assumptions are critical in the sense that the model may not work properly if they don't hold.

ASSUMPTIONS UNDERLYING THE CAPM

It will help to be explicit about the formal assumptions underlying the CAPM, so we are going to list them. The list may cause you to wonder if the model has any relevance, because the assumptions do not seem very realistic. We split them into two groups according to how they are viewed by experts. The first group consists of critical assumptions. They must hold for us to believe the insights of the model. The second group consists of assumptions that are less problematic. Some appear to hold in the real world. Others in the second group, though not very realistic, can be violated without destroying the model's conclusions.

Critical Assumption 1

The derivation of the CAPM assumes that investors all have the same expectations and that the mean and standard deviation of a sample of observations are what statisticians call *sufficient statistics* for describing the probability distribution of the asset's return. All investors have identical assessments of expected returns, variances, and covariances. This implies that the mean and standard deviation contain *all* the relevant information that exists about the security.

There are several more specific assumptions that will cause this very broad assumption to hold. For example, the mean and standard deviation are sufficient statistics for the normal pdf and others that seem to approximate asset returns. Thus this broad assumption holds if asset returns follow any of several distributions. Of course, the mean and standard deviation are not sufficient statistics for *all* possible return distributions. Therefore, the "bottom line" is that if there is important information about returns that isn't in the mean and standard deviation, CAPM may be missing one or more significant determinants of an asset's required return.

Critical Assumption 2

The capital market is in equilibrium. That is, the Principle of Capital Market Efficiency applies.

On the one hand, this assumption reflects a widely held belief. On the other hand, if this assumption is violated, the CAPM cannot be tested because the model is formulated on the assumption that the capital markets *are* efficient. Therefore, any test of the CAPM is really a joint test of the model *and* of market efficiency. If a test of the CAPM fails, then we cannot say for sure whether the model is somewhat incorrectly specified or the market is not exactly efficient. Most people believe that the model identifies a major determinant of an asset's return and that the capital markets are very efficient. Therefore, although it is unlikely that the model is a perfect representation of reality, the model is useful in a practical way. It approximates reality and identifies an important determinant of an asset's return.

Critical Assumption 3

The CAPM is a one-period model. Asset returns are defined to be realized over the next period. The length of the period is not specified. However, no relationship with a subsequent period is assumed. Therefore, it is possible that investors with differing investment horizons should be acting in different ways to maximize their benefit from their wealth. That is, what if investors have different "utilities" from wealth, depending on when it is received? Then it is possible that a more complex model is necessary to describe required returns.

Implications and Other Assumptions

The three critical assumptions can be challenged as unrealistic. Consequently, the validity of the CAPM is ultimately an empirical question.

The validity of the CAPM is further challenged by its other, noncritical assumptions: The CAPM is derived in a perfect market environment, which has the following implications. All investors can borrow or lend at the riskless return without limitation. There are no restrictions on selling *short*. All assets are perfectly divisible and perfectly liquid. There are no transaction costs or taxes. All investors are what economists call *price takers*.

This set of assumptions sometimes makes people doubt whether the CAPM can have any relevance. Researchers have extensively investigated the impact of relaxing each of these assumptions on the conclusions of the model. They have found that very similar conclusions are reached with considerably more complex models. Therefore, the benefits from such increased complexity do not appear to be worth the increased effort it takes for people to understand and apply the more complex models.

We can invert the CML to obtain the CAPM, which specifies an individual asset's required return. That is, we ask, "Given the CML, what must be the expected return and risk of a particular security?"

Consider an individual security *j*. Its impact on investors' risk-return combinations can be gauged by comparing the location of the CML when the market includes security *j* with its location when the market excludes security *j*. Define a portfolio, *M'*, which is identical to the market portfolio *M* except that *M'* doesn't have any investment in security *j*.

What two-asset combinations can be made by combining *M'* and *j*? We know that the curve linking all possible combinations of *M'* and *j* must include, at one point, the market portfolio *M*. Why? Because the market portfolio *M* includes every security, including *j*.

Figure 7-2 shows all the possible combinations of *j* and *M'*. At the point *M*, the slope of the line of possible combinations of *j* and *M'* must equal the slope of the CML. This is because the market portfolio *M* includes security *j* and lies on the efficient frontier. Thus the curve *M'Mj* (joining *M'*, *M*, and *j*) cannot lie outside the curve *EMF* (joining *E*, *M*, and *F*). Also, the curves *M'Mj* and *EMF* can intersect only at *M*, because at that point portfolio *M* contains the best mix of *M'* and *j*. Other combinations of *M'* and *j* are less valuable and are below the efficient frontier.

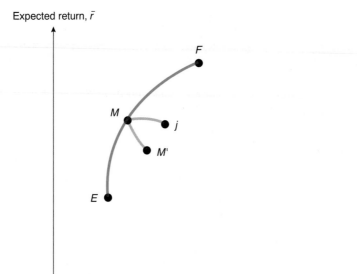

FIGURE 7-2

All possible combinations of portfolios M' and security j.

Deriving the Security Market Line

The slope of the CML is the amount of return per unit of risk. A slope is the rise over the run. For the CML, the rise is $\bar{r}_M - r_f$. The run is $\sigma_M - \sigma_f$. But $\sigma_f = 0$, so $\sigma_M - \sigma_f = \sigma_M$. Therefore,

$$\text{CML slope} = \frac{\bar{r}_M - r_f}{\sigma_M} \qquad (7.1)$$

The amount $\bar{r}_M - r_f$ is called the **market risk premium**.

EXAMPLE

Calculating the Slope of the CML

Let's say that $\bar{r}_M = 15\%$, $r_f = 7\%$, and $\sigma_M = 16\%$. What is the slope of the CML? From Equation (7.1), it is

$$\text{CML slope} = (15\% - 7\%)/16\% = 0.50$$

The slope of the curve $M'Mj$ at the point M is[5]

$$\text{Slope of } M'Mj \text{ at the point } M = \frac{(\bar{r}_j - \bar{r}_M)\sigma_M}{\text{Cov}(j,M) - \sigma_M^2} \qquad (7.2)$$

where $Cov(j,M)$ is the covariance between security j and the market portfolio's return.

Our objective is to express the expected return $\bar{r}_j$ as a function of the risk of security j. Both curves in Figure 7-2 pass through the point M. Thus they have identical slopes at M. Therefore, we can set Equation (7.1) equal to Equation (7.2) and solve for $\bar{r}_j$. This is the required/expected return to security j that is implied by the CML:

$$\bar{r}_j = r_f + \beta_j (\bar{r}_M - r_f) \qquad (7.3)$$

where

$$\beta_j = \frac{\text{Cov}(j,M)}{\sigma_M^2} = \frac{\text{Corr}(j,M)\sigma_j\sigma_M}{\sigma_M^2} = \frac{\text{Corr}(j,M)\sigma_j}{\sigma_M} \qquad (7.4)$$

β is the Greek letter beta. We referred to beta briefly in the introduction to this chapter.

---

[5] Equation (7.2) is obtained by taking the derivative of the function $\bar{r} = f(\sigma)$ at the point M.

Equation (7.4) is the formula for beta, shown in three equivalent forms.

Equation (7.3) is the formula for what is called the **security market line (SML)**. It is important to understand that the SML is based on the capital market being in equilibrium (required return = expected return).

For this example, $r_f = 7\%$, $Cov(j,M) = 250$, $\sigma_M^2 = 225$, and $\bar{r}_M = 15\%$. What is the expected return on security j?

Applying Equation (7.4), β_j is 1.11:

$$\beta_j = \frac{Cov(j,M)}{\sigma_M^2} = \frac{250}{225} = 1.11$$

Then, from Equation (7.3), security j's expected return is

$$\bar{r}_j = 7\% + 1.11(15\% - 7\%) = 15.89\%$$

Calculating the Expected Return on Security j

EXAMPLE

The SML, Equation (7.3), expresses the expected return on security j as the sum of the riskless return and a risk premium. The risk premium is the product of two factors. The first is β_j (beta), which is the ratio of $Cov(j,M)$ and σ_M^2. The second is the market risk premium, $\bar{r}_M - r_f$, which is the slope of the SML. It reflects the market price of risk.[6] The greater the market's aversion to risk, the higher the market risk premium, and the steeper the slope of the SML.

Figure 7-3 shows the SML at May 31, 1995. The riskless return—the yield on 3-month Treasury bills is used as the proxy—was 5.8%. The market risk premium, estimated from historical data, was 8.4%. Note that the expected return on the market portfolio (which corresponds to the point M) was

$$\bar{r}_M = 5.8\% + 8.4\% = 14.2\%$$

---

[6] It is especially important for you to recognize that beta is *not* the slope of the SML. It is the variable that is plotted along the horizontal axis in Figure 7-3.

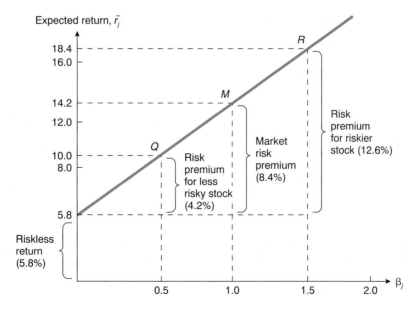

Expected return, $\bar{r}_j$

FIGURE 7-3
The security market line at May 31, 1995. The expected risk premium on the market portfolio (Ibbotson Associates's estimated short-horizon expected equity risk premium for 1926–1994) is 8.4%.
Sources: Bloomberg, L.P. and *Stocks, Bonds, Bills, and Inflation 1995 Yearbook* (Chicago, Ill.: Ibbotson Associates, 1995), p. 157.

The Risk-Return Trade-Off

What is the risk-return trade-off that is reflected in Figure 7-3?

Riskier (higher-covariance) stocks have higher required returns. Consider point R, where $\beta_j = 1.5$. Applying Equation (7.3), we find that

$$\bar{r}_R = 5.8 + 1.5(8.4) = 18.4\%$$

Next consider point Q. Less risky (lower-covariance) stocks have a lower beta and therefore a lower required return:

$$\bar{r}_Q = 5.8 + 0.5(8.4) = 10.0\%$$

In more general terms, a stock is a **capital asset**. The SML prices stocks by specifying a required/expected return. Can we generalize and use it to specify a required return to *any* capital asset? Yes, if the model is appropriate to the situation. When we use the more general concept that *j* is a capital asset, rather than specifically a stock, Equation (7.3) becomes one form of what is called the **capital-asset-pricing model (CAPM)**. Just as the name implies, it is a model for pricing capital assets.

As we just saw, the CAPM says that an asset's required return can be expressed as the sum of (1) the riskless return and (2) a risk premium to compensate for the risk of the particular asset. In other words, any asset's required return is the riskless return adjusted for the asset's risk.

This statement is very appealing. It might make you wonder why we have gone to such great lengths to derive this model. The reason is that it shows that the appropriate risk adjustment is not immediately obvious. The risk adjustment is based on how an asset's return *covaries* with the market portfolio's return. This adjustment is appropriate. It shows how an individual asset contributes to the risk of an investor's total portfolio.

Self-Check Questions

1. Explain why the curve $M'Mj$ in Figure 7-2 cannot lie outside the curve EMF.
2. What is the security market line (SML)? What does it specify?
3. Explain the meaning of Equation (7.3).

7.3 BETA AND THE SML

Suppose we knew (1) the exact return distribution of all assets in the market and (2) the covariance of each asset's return with the market portfolio's return. Then we could specify a required return using Equation (7.3). In practice, we don't have all this information.

In applying the CAPM in real-world situations, we are taking it out of the perfect capital market environment in which it was derived. Nevertheless, the CAPM is still useful in estimating individual stock returns. We can measure how they vary with respect to the market portfolio's return by applying a statistical method called *linear regression*. We can express stock j's realized return r_j as a linear function of the realized market risk premium $(r_M - r_f)$, so that

$$r_j = r_f + \tilde{\beta}_j (r_M - r_f) \qquad (7.5)$$

We use the tilde (~) to indicate that $\tilde{\beta}$ is a random variable.

We can then use linear regression to estimate β_j from historical data. First we collect a sample of simultaneous observations of r_j, r_M, and r_f. Then we use Equation (7.5) to estimate the regression coefficient β_j.

Interpreting Beta

Equation (7.5) is why the coefficient β_j came to be called the common stock's **beta**. Beta plays a critical role in asset pricing. It is a *linear measure* of how much an individual asset contributes to the standard deviation of the market portfolio. Thus the beta of an asset is a simple, well-behaved measure of an asset's risk.

Table 7-1 shows the monthly returns for Merck common stock (symbol MRK) and the market (using the Standard & Poor's 500 Index as a market portfolio proxy). MRK's beta is calculated by applying linear regression to estimate Equation (7.5).

$$r_{\text{MRK},t} - r_{f,t} = \beta(r_{M,t} - r_{f,t}) + \epsilon$$

where $r_{\text{MRK},t}$ is the realized return (including dividends) on Merck common stock during month t, $r_{f,t}$ is the realized return on Treasury bills during month t, $r_{M,t}$ is the realized return on the S&P 500 Index during month t, β is the regression coefficient, and ϵ is a linear regression error term. Note that the y intercept is constrained to equal zero.

TABLE 7-1
Monthly returns on Merck common stock, the S&P 500 Index, and Treasury bills during 1994.

MONTH	MRK	MARKET (S&P 500)	RISKLESS SECURITY	MONTH	MRK	MARKET (S&P 500)	RISKLESS SECURITY
JAN	6.18%	3.25%	0.25%	JUL	−1.35%	3.15%	0.28%
FEB	−11.30	−3.00	0.21	AUG	15.19	3.76	0.37
MAR	−7.24	−4.58	0.27	SEP	5.27	−2.69	0.37
APR	−1.35	1.16	0.27	OCT	−0.84	2.08	0.38
MAY	2.95	1.24	0.32	NOV	4.56	−3.95	0.37
JUN	−1.54	−2.68	0.31	DEC	3.15	1.23	0.44

Sources: Bloomberg, L.P. and *Stocks, Bonds, Bills, and Inflation 1995 Yearbook* (Chicago, Ill.: Ibbotson Associates, 1995), p. 203.

We applied ordinary least-squares regression analysis (using Lotus 1-2-3's data regression function). The estimated β coefficient for Merck common stock, on the basis of monthly 1994 data, is 1.05.

Figure 7-4 plots the regression equation. This plot is called the stock's **characteristic line**. A security's beta is thus the slope of the stock's characteristic line.

Most experts prefer to use a larger number of observations in order to reduce the likelihood that temporary factors will affect the beta estimate. It is customary to use at least 3 years' but not more than 7 years' data. We used 12 months' data to simplify the example. ■

Calculating a Beta

EXAMPLE

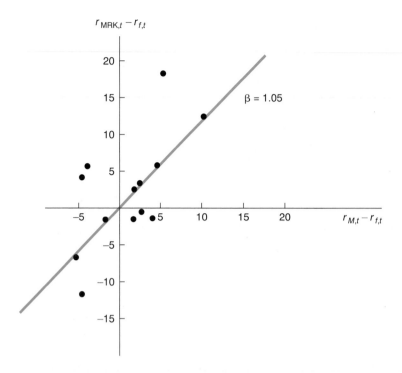

FIGURE 7-4
A stock's
characteristic line.

Table 7-2 shows the beta coefficients for twenty firms, many of which are familiar to you. (Having lunch at McDonald's this week? Had a Pepsi lately?)

Beta indicates how sensitive a security's returns are to changes in the market portfolio's returns. If a security's beta is 1.0, its returns tend to track the market portfolio. If the market portfolio increases or decreases by 10%, the stock also tends to move up or down by 10%.

If a stock has a beta less than 1.0, it tends to rise or fall less than the market. For example, suppose a stock has a beta of 0.5. If the market portfolio increases or decreases by 10%, the stock will tend to move up or down only about 5%.

A stock with a beta greater than 1.0 tends to rise or fall more than the market. For example, a stock with a beta of 1.5 will tend to rise or fall by about 15% when the market portfolio increases or decreases 10%. Most common stock betas are between 0.75 and 1.50.

TABLE 7-2
Beta coefficients for
selected firms.

COMMON STOCK	BETA	COMMON STOCK	BETA
Alex. Brown	1.90	Boeing	1.00
Magma Copper "B"	1.65	Berkshire Hathaway	0.95
NIKE, Inc. "B"	1.50	Minnesota Mining & Mfg.	0.95
Microsoft Corp.	1.40	Quaker Oats	0.90
ITT Corp.	1.20	AT&T Corp.	0.85
J. P. Morgan & Co.	1.15	Gibson Greetings	0.85
PepsiCo, Inc.	1.10	Boston Edison	0.75
General Electric	1.10	Florida Progress Corp.	0.65
McDonald's Corp.	1.05	Exxon Corp.	0.60
Neiman Marcus	1.00	Idaho Power	0.60

Source: The Value Line Investment Survey (June 16, 1995).

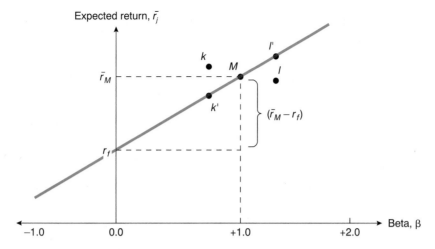

FIGURE 7-5
The security market line: expected return as a function of beta.

Figure 7-5 is a graph of the SML. It expresses expected return as a function of β. Note that the beta of the market portfolio equals 1.0. The value-weighted average of all common stock betas equals 1.0. Also note that the beta of the riskless asset equals 0. Therefore, it is possible to create an artificial riskless asset. The SML is the graphical representation of Equation (7.3). The riskless return is the vertical intercept of this line. The slope of the line is $\bar{r}_M - r_f$, the market risk premium.

Finally, note that beta can be negative. Accordingly, an asset can have a required return that is *less* than the riskless return. At first glance, this seems counterintuitive: How can any asset have an expected return that is less than the riskless return?

Remember, these are assets held in a fully diversified portfolio, the market portfolio. Therefore, an individual asset's risk depends on what it contributes to the market portfolio's standard deviation. When a negative-beta asset is added to the market portfolio, it actually lowers the market portfolio's standard deviation. Thus, although the notion of negative risk seems counterintuitive, it makes sense in this context.

Arbitrage and the SML

As the name *security market line* suggests, the (beta, expected return) combinations of all securities in the market portfolio must lie along the SML. Consider a security *l* whose (beta, expected return) combination lies below the SML. This is represented by the point *l* in Figure 7-5. Would anyone want to invest in asset *l*? No.

There is an asset whose (beta, expected return) combination, located at *l′* on the SML, is superior. Asset *l′* has the same β as asset *l*. Thus both contribute identically to portfolio risk. However, *l′* has a higher expected return. In a perfect capital market, *l* would create an *arbitrage opportunity*. Investors could earn an *arbitrage profit*, without changing their portfolio's risk, by selling *l* short and buying asset *l′*.

Selling short involves borrowing a security and selling it with the expectation that you will be able to buy it back later at a lower price (to make a profit). The expected profit is $\bar{r}_{l'} - \bar{r}_l$.

How long would such an arbitrage opportunity continue to exist? Until the price of asset *l* had been driven down to such an extent that the (beta, expected return) combination for asset *l* shifted up to the SML. That is, until the (beta, expected return) combinations for assets *l* and *l′* are equal.

Can a security whose (beta, expected return) combination lies above the SML, such as security k in Figure 7-5, exist for long? Again, not in a perfect capital market. Investors would purchase asset k and sell asset k' short, thereby earning an arbitrage profit without changing their portfolio's risk. The expected profit is $\bar{r}_k - \bar{r}_{k'}$. Arbitrage activity would continue until the market value of asset k had been driven up to such an extent that the (beta, expected return) combination for asset k shifted down to the SML.

In a perfect capital market environment, one with no barriers to arbitrage (no restrictions on short selling, for example), the (beta, expected return) combinations for all securities *and* for all portfolios of securities must lie along the SML.

Portfolio Beta

A **portfolio beta** equals the weighted average of the betas of the portfolio's assets:

$$\beta_p = w_1\beta_1 + w_2\beta_2 + w_3\beta_3 + \cdots + w_n\beta_n \tag{7.6}$$

where w_i is the proportion of value invested in security i, β_i is the beta of security i, and there are n securities in the portfolio. The beta of the market portfolio is 1.0.

EXAMPLE

Calculating a Portfolio Beta

A portfolio contains three securities. Security 1 has a beta of 1.20, and it is 25% of the portfolio. Security 2 has a beta of 0.75, and it is 50% of the portfolio. Security 3 has a beta of 1.05, and it is the balance of the portfolio, 25%. What is the portfolio's beta?

Applying Equation (7.6),

$$\beta_p = 0.25(1.20) + 0.50(0.75) + 0.25(1.05) = 0.9375$$

Self-Check Questions

1. Define the term *arbitrage*.
2. Explain the significance of beta in asset valuation. What does beta measure?
3. Can a security have a negative beta? How would such a security's expected return compare to the riskless return?
4. Why must the (beta, expected return) combinations of all securities lie on the SML?
5. Explain why a (beta, expected return) combination such as k in Figure 7-5 could not persist in a perfect capital market.

7.4 APPLYING THE CAPM

The main conclusion that modern portfolio theory has reached is Generalization 5 (in Chapter 6). Investors should put their investment on the CML by investing in a mix of the market portfolio and the riskless asset.

This is an inconvenient prescription in the real world. Not only are transactions costly, but they are much more so when one is buying or selling a small number of shares. Fortunately, the market portfolio's return can be accurately approximated with a relatively small number of assets. We can restate the main conclusion of portfolio theory as the Principle of

Diversification: Diversification is beneficial. The remaining question is one we raised when we discussed that principle: How much diversification is necessary to get "all" the benefits?

Approximating the Market Portfolio

In discussing an asset's expected return (in Chapter 6), we cited the law of large numbers as a justification for using the mean to represent a portfolio's expected return. The concept of large numbers, and more specifically random samples, can also be used here. The law of large numbers can help determine an accurate approximation of the market portfolio.

Remember the procedure for estimating the unknown mean of some probability distribution. Compute the sample mean for a reasonably large random sample. The definition of "large" does not necessarily depend on the size of the underlying population. A large sample in statistics may contain only 25–30 observations.

Accordingly, we can predict that the realized return to a portfolio of approximately equal investments in 25–30 *randomly* chosen stocks will be consistently close to the market portfolio's realized return. This result has also been shown empirically countless times. On this basis, therefore, we know that the expected return to a randomly chosen portfolio of 25–30 stocks will be very close to the market portfolio's expected return. Its accuracy is a function of the portfolio's number of stocks. Figure 7-6 graphs portfolio standard deviation as a function of the number of randomly selected securities in the portfolio.

Using a technique called *stratified random sampling*, we can accurately approximate the market portfolio with fewer securities. Stratified random sampling breaks the population to be sampled into "key" segments. Then a random sample is drawn from each segment. This technique is widely used in opinion polls to reduce the cost of taking the poll. Stratifying the random sample reduces the sample size that is needed for a given level of accuracy.

With stocks, the key segments might be the major industries that make up the stock market. Using stratified random sampling, it is possible to use a sample of between seven and ten stocks to approximate the market portfolio accurately. With prices per share averaging $25 to $30, and purchasing 100 shares of each stock, it takes about $25,000 to $30,000 to construct such a portfolio. But what if you do not have that much money to invest?

In Chapter 6 we noted that there are numerous stock index funds. Many of these funds are based on the Standard & Poor's 500 Index, which approximates the market portfolio. An investor can invest as little as perhaps $1000 in such a *mutual fund*. And there are many, many

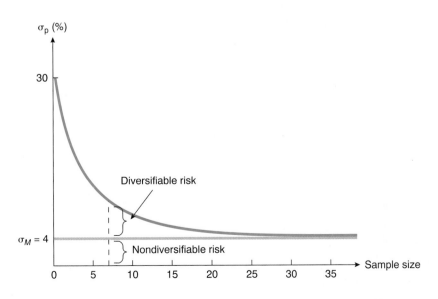

FIGURE 7-6
Portfolio standard deviation as a function of portfolio size.

other mutual funds. Mutual funds give all investors the opportunity to diversify inexpensively. In fact, this is a primary reason why they were created.

Diversifiable and Nondiversifiable Risk

Beta measures the risk an individual asset adds to the market portfolio. The portfolio is fully diversified; it includes every security. Hence the risk that beta measures cannot be diversified away. It is the part of a security's risk that is systematically related to the market portfolio's risk. As you can see in Equation (7.4), beta is essentially the covariance (or, equivalently, the correlation coefficient), because that is the part that makes the value unique to the asset. The denominator, σ_M^2, is the same for every asset.

If investors hold well-diversified portfolios, security j's expected return satisfies Equation (7.3). The expected return depends only on the part of the risk that cannot be diversified away. But suppose an investor does not fully diversify his portfolio. Such an investor faces additional, unnecessary risk. Total risk can be expressed as two parts, nondiversifiable risk and diversifiable risk.

$$\text{Total risk} = \text{Nondiversifiable risk} + \text{Diversifiable risk} \qquad (7.7)$$

Nondiversifiable risk (or **systematic risk**) is risk that cannot be eliminated by further diversification. **Diversifiable risk** (or **unsystematic risk**) is risk that can be eliminated by diversification. Diversifiable risk is firm-specific. It is caused by significant events such as successes or failures in launching a new product, getting a contract, or settling a strike or lawsuit. Such events are essentially random across firms. Diversification can eliminate their effects: Good events at one firm tend to offset bad events at another.

Nondiversifiable risk is caused by events that affect the stock market as a whole. Such events include recession, a sharp change in monetary policy, and the outbreak of war. This element of risk reflects the degree to which a particular stock's returns tend to move *systematically* with the returns on all other stocks.

From this perspective, the two different parts of risk in Equation (7.7) present another way of showing how diversification reduces portfolio risk. People who invest in a nondiversified portfolio, such as a single security, take on more risk than those who invest in that security as part of a well-diversified portfolio. Figure 7-6 illustrates this point. Adding securities can reduce diversifiable risk but not nondiversifiable risk.

The market compensates investors for taking on nondiversifiable risk. However, it will not pay them for taking on diversifiable risk. This makes sense. In a market that contains a large number of risky assets, as the U.S. stock market does, it is both easy and relatively inexpensive to diversify. U.S. investors are thus not able to require payment for it, even though it is negative to them. This is because it can be easily (and almost costlessly) eliminated. In other words, investors have a choice of whether to take on diversifiable risk. Consequently, when they invest, they cannot require payment for taking it on.

What Happens If You Do Not Diversify?

The Dividend Growth Model (Chapter 5) offers a method of converting a stock's required return into its market value. Let's use the Dividend Growth Model to value security j for two prospective buyers. One investor will add this security to a diversified portfolio. The other invests solely in security j. The value of security j to the diversified investor, denoted V_d, can be expressed as

$$V_d = \frac{D_1}{\bar{r}_j - g}$$

where D_1 is the next period's expected cash dividend and g is the expected growth rate of dividends forever. Similarly, the value of security j to the nondiversified investor, denoted V_n, can be expressed in terms of his required return for security j, $\bar{r}_{jn}$, as

$$V_n = \frac{D_1}{\bar{r}_{jn} - g}$$

The relationship between V_n and V_d can be determined from the relationship between their respective required returns, $\bar{r}_{jn}$ and $\bar{r}_j$. Equation (7.3) expresses $\bar{r}_j$ in terms of nondiversifiable risk. Because $\bar{r}_{jn}$ has all that risk *plus* security j's diversifiable risk, its risk premium will be larger. As a consequence, $\bar{r}_{jn}$ is virtually always greater than $\bar{r}_j$. Therefore, with g and D_1 identical in either case, V_n is less than V_d.

Suppose $\bar{r}_j = 10\%$, $\bar{r}_{jn} = 14\%$, $D_1 = \$2$, and $g = 5\%$. How would diversified and nondiversified investors value this stock?

From the dividend growth model formula, $V_d = \$40$ and $V_n = \$22.22$. The value of the security to the diversified investor is always greater than it is to the nondiversified investor. ■

What Happens When You Don't Diversify?

EXAMPLE

$$V_d = \frac{2}{10-5} = \frac{2}{5} = .4 = \$40$$

$$V_n = \frac{2}{14-5} = \frac{2}{9} = .22 = \$22$$

We have established the relative value of the stock to diversified and nondiversified purchasers. But there are two sides to a transaction. What about the value to the seller of the stock? Following the Principle of Self-Interested Behavior, current owners of the shares will sell to the highest bidder. In a bidding competition between diversified and nondiversified purchasers, diversified investors can "afford to" bid a higher price. Therefore, observed stock prices reflect the higher value that diversified investors are willing to pay for the shares. Nondiversified investors who are going to purchase shares must pay the higher (diversified) price.

A nondiversified investor, then, faces three alternatives: (1) do not invest in the stock, (2) receive a lower return (by paying a higher price) than is appropriate for the risk, or (3) diversify. We need to emphasize that under the second alternative, nondiversified investors *must* pay the higher prices appropriate for a diversified investor. Otherwise, they will be outbid. And this holds even if there are a sizable number of nondiversified investors.

This is a striking example of the robustness of the conclusions of the CAPM. It is assumed that all investors invest in the market portfolio. However, even if that assumption is violated, competition ensures that *prices will be set as though all investors did invest in the market portfolio*.

Self-Check Questions

1. What are the principal assumptions underlying the CAPM? How realistic are they?

2. Explain the difference between diversifiable risk and nondiversifiable risk.

3. Why are investors not compensated for taking on diversifiable risk?

4. Explain why nondiversified investors will have to pay the same price as diversified investors in a competitive market. Is that fair?

7.5 MULTIFACTOR MODELS

The first critical assumption underlying the CAPM is that the mean and standard deviation contain all relevant information about an asset's future return. But suppose there is more to an asset's expected return. Essentially, the CAPM says an asset's expected return depends on a single factor: the market portfolio's expected return. But what if other factors affect required returns?

Consider the return on the common stock of a firm, GIOC (for Great Investment Opportunity Corporation). The return on GIOC stock can be expressed as the sum of two components, the riskless return r_f, plus an uncertain, or risky, component that we will call R (for risky). Letting r_G represent the return on GIOC stock, we have

$$r_G = r_f + R$$

The uncertain component R is affected by a variety of factors. Some affect all firms, whereas others are specific to GIOC (and perhaps a handful of similar firms). To be perfectly general, suppose that there are K independent factors that contribute to nondiversifiable risk. In that case, the stock return would be a *multifactor model*:

$$r_G = r_f + R(F_1, F_2, ..., F_K) + \epsilon \tag{7.8}$$

where F_k denotes factor k $(k = 1, 2, \ldots, K)$, $R(F_1, ...)$ is some function of the factors, and ϵ denotes the incremental return due to diversifiable risk.

Self-Check Questions
1. What is critical assumption 1 underlying the CAPM?
2. How does a multifactor model differ from the CAPM?

7.6 ARBITRAGE PRICING THEORY

Equation (7.8) is a more general model of a required return than the CAPM. But exactly what do the F_k values consist of? And what does the function $R(F_1, \cdots)$ look like? There is considerable debate about these questions. For example, are multiple factors being approximated by the market portfolio's expected return in the CAPM, thereby masking the *true* determinants of a required return? At this point, no single opinion has emerged triumphant.

There is, however, one model that has received considerable attention because it relaxes the assumption of a single determinant. This alternative model is called the **arbitrage pricing theory (APT)**. As the name implies, the APT relies on the concept of arbitrage. It is a model based on a market that is in equilibrium and free of arbitrage opportunities.

A Multifactor Linear Model
Like the CAPM, the APT is built on the Principle of Capital Market Efficiency. The APT simply represents an alternative approach to securities valuation within the same framework. The APT relates asset returns within a multivariate framework in which the return relationships are linear.

Although the APT takes the Principle of Capital Market Efficiency as its starting point, it does not attempt to specify any particular set of determinants on the basis of conceptual arguments. Instead, the APT *asserts* that an asset's expected return depends on a linear combination of some set of factors. The factors must be identified empirically.

Thus far, in empirical tests of the APT, a variety of different factors have emerged as possible determinants of actual common stock returns. A statistical method called *factor analysis* has been used to attempt to identify relevant factors.[7]

The APT model looks strikingly like an "extended" CAPM. However, it is derived in a very different way. We will not derive the APT model here, but we will show you its operational form:

$$\bar{r}_j = r_f + \beta_{j1}(\bar{r}_{f1} - r_f) + \beta_{j2}(\bar{r}_{f2} - r_f) + \cdots + \beta_{jK}(\bar{r}_{fK} - r_f) \qquad (7.9)$$

where K is the number of factors that affect an asset's return; $\bar{r}_{f1}, \bar{r}_{f2}, \ldots, \bar{r}_{fK}$ are the expected returns to factors $1, 2, \ldots, K$, respectively; and $\beta_{j1}, \beta_{j2}, \ldots, \beta_{jK}$, are the asset's sensitivities to factors $1, 2, \ldots, K$, respectively. APT formulations typically include the market risk premium, the sole factor in the CAPM, as an explanatory variable.

The APT, then, is a multifactor model of the general form of Equation (7.8). The F_K values are identified empirically, by assuming $R(F_1, \ldots)$ is a simple linear function.

Applications

To illustrate the APT, let's assume there are three relevant factors: the market risk premium, $F_1 = \bar{r}_M - \bar{r}_f$; the growth rate of real gross domestic product (GDP) relative to the riskless return, $F_2 = \bar{r}_{GDP} - r_f$; and the rate of consumer price inflation (CPI) relative to the riskless return, $F_3 = \bar{r}_{CPI} - r_f$. Note that the respective impacts of the second and third factors must be incremental to the impact of the market risk premium. If the impact of F_2 can be explained completely in terms of the impact of F_1, then $\beta_2 = 0$. In that case F_2 is not a necessary part of the model, even though it does exist. A similar statement holds for F_3. Again, the significant factors are identified empirically.

EXAMPLE

Applying the APT

Suppose the riskless return is 6% and the beta coefficients for security j are $\beta_1 = 1.2$, $\beta_2 = 0.2$, and $\beta_3 = 0.3$. The market portfolio's expected return is 12%. The expected growth rate of real GDP is 3%. The expected rate of consumer price inflation is 4%. What is security j's expected return?

Substituting into Equation (7.9), we find that the required return is

$$\bar{r}_j = 6\% + 1.2(r_M - 6\%) + 0.2(r_{GDP} - 6\%) + 0.3(r_{CPI} - 6\%)$$

$$= 6\% + 1.2(12\% - 6\%) + 0.2(3\% - 6\%) + 0.3(4\% - 6\%) = 12.0\% \blacksquare$$

APT versus CAPM

As a practical matter, the APT is simply an alternative model that describes actual stock returns about as well as the CAPM. The CAPM endures, probably because it is simpler and it was the first one put forth. Alternatives have not provided significantly better descriptions of realized returns. Neither have they provided such an increase in understanding that one of them is clearly superior in a conceptual sense. Perhaps the market risk premium adequately in-

---

[7] One of the difficulties that arise with this research is that in some cases, the quantified factors have not appeared to be associated with identifiable real-world factors. That is, some quantified factors cannot be identified as something familiar, such as a measure of inflation or unemployment.

corporates the effect of the plausible alternative factors. Perhaps additional factors are yet to be identified. Or maybe the return relationships are significantly nonlinear. Future research may eventually answer these important questions.

✓ **Self-Check Questions**
1. Describe the meaning and significance of the arbitrage pricing theory (APT).
2. How does the APT differ from the CAPM?
3. How is the APT applied in practice?

7.7 INTERNATIONAL CONSIDERATIONS

There are many mulitnational firms. These firms make investments in more than one country. Such investments are often called *projects*. Should the required return on a foreign project be greater than the required return on an otherwise identical domestic project?

Many believe we should add a risk premium when evaluating foreign projects. This reflects a perception of higher economic and political risks. You may be surprised to learn that the required return for an international project may actually be *less* than it is for an otherwise identical domestic project.

International Diversification

Just as firms invest internationally, investors purchase both domestic and foreign securities. Suppose there is a single world capital market. In it, all investors hold well-diversified international portfolios.

We know that the appropriate measure of an asset's risk is its incremental contribution to the risk of a well-diversified portfolio. In such a market, most of the economic and political risk specific to a particular foreign project could be eliminated through diversification. Consequently, the firm's shareholders would face the same nondiversifiable risk on a foreign project as on an otherwise identical domestic project. Therefore, the required return for the two projects would be the same. We could still use the CAPM, but the market portfolio would be a **world market portfolio**. It would literally include all the assets in the world. Beta would be measured relative to world market portfolio returns.

Now let's consider the extreme opposite of a single world market. Suppose the various national capital markets are perfectly separated. In each one, all investors hold well-diversified domestic portfolios. However, American investors can purchase only American stocks. Japanese investors can only purchase Japanese stocks, and so on. In that case, a project's beta is measured against the firm's domestic market portfolio, because that is where the firm's investors are located.

Imagine an American firm that is considering investing in two identical projects. One would be located in Columbus, Ohio, and would serve the U.S. market. The other would be located in Manchester, England, and would serve the U.K. market. The U.K. project would be exposed to the fortunes of the U.K. market. Nevertheless, the Principle of Diversification does not depend on national boundaries. Therefore, as long as the U.K. project's returns were not perfectly correlated with the returns on any subset of the American market portfolio, diversi-

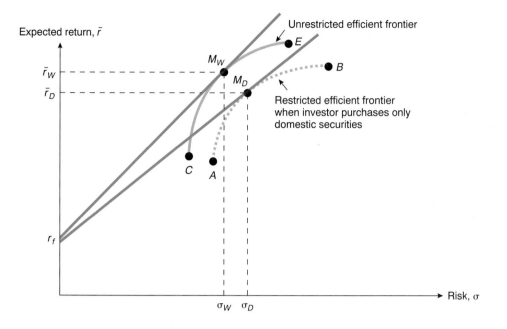

FIGURE 7-7
**The benefit from
international
diversification.**

fication could be beneficial.[8] Because of this benefit, U.S. investors could actually earn a lower return on the U.K. project and still be better off.

To see this, recall what happens when you add a negative-beta stock to the market portfolio. The risk-reducing benefits overcome the negative effect that the stock's lower-than-riskless return has on the portfolio.

Consequently, we can view the firm's U.K. project as having two benefits: (1) the "basic" returns that would be like those from an otherwise identical domestic project, and (2) the risk-reducing benefits from international diversification. With perfectly separated capital markets, the investors cannot get these benefits in any other way. Thus the firm can earn a little less on the first part (which is the required return on an otherwise identical domestic project) if it more than makes it up with the extra benefit of the second part. In that way, the *net* benefit would make investors better off. Therefore, with separated national capital markets, the foreign project's required return is actually less than that of an otherwise identical domestic project.

Figure 7-7 shows how international diversification can benefit investors. Suppose investors are restricted to domestic securities. The curve AM_DB is the restricted efficient frontier that exists when investors are limited to domestic securities. The constrained-to-domestic optimal portfolio is M_D in that case.

Removing international investing restrictions makes additional investments possible. The unrestricted efficient frontier is the curve CM_WE in Figure 7-7. The world market portfolio is M_W. Note that investors are clearly better off: M_W provides a higher expected return and entails lower risk than M_D.

---

[8] Note that such imperfect correlation is not sufficient for international diversification to be beneficial. A foreign project's nondiversifiable risk could nevertheless be the same as that of a comparable domestic project if the outputs from both are sold in a single worldwide product market. For example, gold mines in two different countries could have the same nondiversifiable risk.

You can also see in Figure 7-7 how international investment can change the risk-return trade-off. The CML using M_W has a steeper slope. When international investment is possible, M_D is no longer on the efficient frontier and therefore would not be used to make the CML.

Should the Required Return Be Adjusted?

In reality, the world capital markets are not fully integrated. Certain countries have restrictions on foreign investors purchasing voting securities in home-country firms. Therefore, national capital markets may well be somewhat separated. Also, although American investors can own foreign securities, they have generally invested only a small portion of their portfolios overseas.

No one knows why American investors have been so reluctant to purchase foreign securities. Potential factors include difficulties in obtaining financial information on foreign firms,[9] foreign withholding taxes on dividends, the cost of converting foreign currencies, higher transaction costs, the risk of expropriation, the possibility of adverse changes in laws, and other forms of political risk.

A 1986 study concluded that American investors were behaving as though investing in foreign common stocks added costs of between 2% and 4% per year.[10] For example, there may be higher transaction costs associated with purchasing foreign shares. There may also be added monitoring costs as a result of more lax foreign financial disclosure standards. Such costs reduce the return on direct investments in foreign common stocks. But investor behavior seems to be changing. The introduction and recent accelerating expansion of international investing have reduced the effect of these costs.

In recent years, U.S. financial institutions have increased their foreign investing. In addition, many foreign firms have listed their shares on the NYSE. Mutual funds have been created that invest in firms located in a specific region (for example, there are several Latin American funds) or in a particular country (there are dozens of country funds, including funds investing in Argentina, India, Korea, Mexico, and Spain). These changes have made it easier and less expensive for Americans to make foreign investments.

Unfortunately, all this does not tell us exactly how to determine the required return for a particular foreign project. On the one hand, if there are benefits to be had from additional international diversification by a firm, then a foreign project's required return may actually be less than that of an otherwise identical domestic project. On the other hand, it may be that all required returns should reflect the *world market portfolio*, without differentiation.

The "bottom line" is that we do not have an exact formula for a foreign project's required return. However, we can say that it is *not* the required return for an otherwise identical domestic project plus a "tacked-on" risk premium.

Self-Check Questions

1. Describe what is meant by the term *world market portfolio.*
2. Suppose the world capital markets were fully integrated. Explain why a foreign project would have the same required return as an otherwise identical domestic project.
3. In practice, don't foreign projects entail greater risk than domestic projects? Shouldn't a firm that is considering a foreign project estimate the required return as if the project were domestic and then tack on a risk premium to compensate for this greater risk?

---

[9] Foreign countries generally impose less exacting disclosure requirements than exist in the United States.
[10] Cooper and Kaplanis (1986).

SUMMARY

In the capital-asset-pricing model (CAPM), the risk of an individual asset depends on the covariance (or, equivalently, the correlation coefficient) between the asset's return and the market portfolio's return. The covariance is reflected in the asset's beta. Beta measures how much the individual asset contributes to a well-diversified portfolio's standard deviation.

Current models of required returns, such as the CAPM, are not perfect representations of asset valuation. There are empirical tests that reveal imperfections in even the most complex forms of the CAPM, as well as the arbitrage pricing theory (APT). However, the CAPM identifies a very important and nonintuitive determinant of an asset's required return, namely the market risk premium. The APT broadens our view of asset pricing by allowing for the inclusion of other significant factors. However, the APT does not itself identify these other factors.

As a practical matter, the market risk premium can be viewed as the principal determinant of an asset's required return. Like many models, the CAPM provides a good starting point for understanding and action.

DECISION SUMMARY

- The capital-asset-pricing model (CAPM) expresses an asset's required return as the riskless return plus a risk premium.

- The riskless return is the expected return on an asset with a zero standard deviation. The 3-month Treasury bill rate is often used to approximate the riskless return.

- An asset's risk premium is the product of the asset's beta and the market risk premium. The market risk premium is the difference between the market portfolio's expected return and the riskless return.

- Beta measures a security's nondiversifiable (systematic) risk. That is, beta measures how much the individual asset contributes to a well-diversified portfolio's standard deviation. Beta can be estimated by using linear regression. Many analytical services provide beta estimates for actively traded common stocks.

- The market portfolio includes all assets. In practice, a stock market index, such as the S&P 500, is often used as a proxy for the market portfolio.

- The CAPM shows that the market pays only for nondiversifiable (systematic) risk. This is because investors can easily and cheaply diversify their investments. Therefore, investors who fail to diversify bear more risk without enjoying a corresponding increase in expected return.

- The CAPM appears to work reasonably well in most situations. However, as we discuss in the appendix to this chapter, there is evidence that it tends to *understate* the required return for the shares of firms that are *small* and of firms that are *highly leveraged* (those with a large proportion of debt financing).

- Stock prices depend on the value of the stock to diversified investors. People who invest without diversifying are not receiving as much return as possible for the risk they are taking. Therefore, you should invest without diversifying *only* if you have valuable information about a stock that is not already reflected in its price. This is an extremely rare occurrence in an efficient capital market. Otherwise, apply Generalization 5 (in Chapter 6). You should put your investment on the CML by investing in a mix of the market portfolio and the riskless asset. Use this mix to set your expected return and risk according to your willingness to take on risk.

- When using the CAPM to determine the required return for a foreign project, it is *incorrect* simply to calculate the required return for an otherwise identical domestic project and "tack on" an additional risk premium. Because of the potential benefits of international diversification, the required return might actually be lower than for such a domestic project.

EQUATION SUMMARY

(7.1)
$$\text{CML slope} = \frac{\bar{r}_M - r_f}{\sigma_M}$$

(7.2)
$$\text{Slope of } M'Mj \text{ at the point } M = \frac{(\bar{r}_j - \bar{r}_M)\sigma_M}{\text{Cov}(j,M) - \sigma_M^2}$$

(7.3)
$$\bar{r}_j = r_f + \beta_j(\bar{r}_M - r_f)$$

(7.4)
$$\beta_j = \frac{\text{Cov}(j,M)}{\sigma_M^2} = \frac{\text{Corr}(j,M)\sigma_j}{\sigma_M}$$

(7.5)
$$r_j = r_f + \tilde{\beta}_j(r_M - r_f)$$

(7.6)
$$\beta_p = w_1\beta_1 + w_2\beta_2 + w_3\beta_3 + \cdots + w_n\beta_n$$

(7.7)
$$\text{Total risk} = \text{Nondiversifiable risk} + \text{Diversifiable risk}$$

(7.8)
$$r_G = r_f + R(F_1, F_2, ..., F_K) + \epsilon$$

(7.9)
$$r_j = r_f + \beta_{j1}(\bar{r}_{f1} - r_f) + \beta_{j2}(\bar{r}_{f2} - r_f) + \cdots + \beta_{jK}(\bar{r}_{jK} - r_f)$$

KEY TERMS

market risk premium...212

security market line (SML)...213

capital asset...214

capital-asset-pricing model
(CAPM)...214

beta...215

characteristic line...215

selling short...217

portfolio beta...218

nondiversifiable risk...220

diversifiable risk...220

systematic risk...220

unsystematic risk....220

arbitrage pricing theory (APT)...222

world market portfolio...224

EXERCISES

PROBLEM SET A

A1. What is the beta of a stock whose covariance with the market portfolio return is 0.0045 if the variance of the return on the market portfolio is 0.002?

A2. Define the term *market risk premium.*

A3. Common stock A has a 10% expected return, a standard deviation of 25%, and a beta of 1.25. Common stock B has a 12% expected return, a standard deviation of 15%, and a beta of 1.50. Which stock is riskier? Explain.

A4. General Electric's beta in May 1995 was approximately 1.10, according to the Value Line Investment Survey. The riskless return at the time was 5.75%. The market risk premium was 8.4%. Graph the SML for May 1995, and plot General Electric's required return.

A5. What is the difference between the CML and the SML?

A6. Explain how nondiversifiable risk differs from diversifiable risk.

A7. Why is it that the market will pay an investor for taking on nondiversifiable risk but will not pay an investor for taking on diversifiable risk?

A8. The market portfolio's expected return is 12% and the riskless return is 7%. According to the CAPM, what is an asset's required return if it has a beta of 1.35?

A9. Suppose an investor's degree of risk aversion increases. How is the investor's required return on a particular stock affected? Does it matter whether the stock's beta is high or low?

A10. Explain why a foreign investment project might have a lower required return than an otherwise identical domestic project.

PROBLEM SET B

B1. The following table provides the monthly returns for Exxon common stock (symbol XON) and the market as proxied by the S&P 500 Index, both during 1994. Compute the following:

a. The average monthly return for the market and for XON over these 12 months.

b. The variance of the monthly return for each over these 12 months.

c. The covariance between the returns for the market and XON over these 12 months.

d. The correlation coefficient between the returns for the market and XON for these 12 months.

e. The beta for XON, using linear regression for these 12 months.

Month	Market (S&P 500)	XON	Riskless Security	Month	Market (S&P 500)	XON	Riskless Security
JAN	3.25%	5.35%	0.25%	JUL	3.15%	4.85%	0.28%
FEB	−3.00	−1.36	0.21	AUG	3.76	1.21	0.37
MAR	−4.58	−4.15	0.27	SEP	−2.69	−4.52	0.37
APR	1.16	0.00	0.27	OCT	2.08	9.35	0.38
MAY	1.24	−1.64	0.32	NOV	−3.95	−2.78	0.37
JUN	−2.68	−8.24	0.31	DEC	1.23	−0.61	0.44

B2. Suppose $r_f = 5\%$, $\text{Cov}(j,M) = 155$, $\sigma_M^2 = 125$, and $\bar{r}_M = 12\%$. What is the expected return on the asset?

B3. The following table provides the monthly returns for Procter & Gamble common stock (symbol PG) and the market as proxied by the S&P 500 Index, both during 1995. Compute the following:

a. The average monthly return for the market and for PG over these 12 months.

b. The variance of the monthly return for each over these 12 months.

c. The covariance between the returns for the market and PG over these 12 months.

d. The correlation coefficient between the returns for the market and PG for these 12 months.

e. The beta for PG, using linear regression for these 12 months.

Month	Market (S&P 500)	PG	Riskless Security	Month	Market (S&P 500)	PG	Riskless Security
JAN	2.43%	5.04%	0.35%	JUL	3.18%	−4.17%	0.31%
FEB	3.61	2.11	0.41	AUG	−0.03	0.73	0.26
MAR	2.73	−0.38	0.32	SEP	4.01	10.99	0.25
APR	2.80	5.47	0.37	OCT	−0.50	5.19	0.33
MAY	3.63	2.86	0.39	NOV	4.10	6.79	0.36
JUN	2.13	0.00	0.28	DEC	1.74	−4.05	0.39

B4. It has been said that asset pricing models do not work very well because the actual monthly returns are often considerably larger or smaller than the return specified by the model. Explain why this is or is not a valid criticism of asset pricing models.

✓B5. What is the beta of an asset whose correlation coefficient with the market portfolio's returns is 0.62 and whose variance is 0.1 if the variance of the market portfolio's return is 0.0025?

B6. Discuss the differences and similarities between the CAPM and the APT.

✓B7. Respond to the following remark: "First you say σ measures the risk of investing. Then you say β measures the risk of investing. Which is right?"

B8. According to the CAPM, an asset with a beta of zero has a required return equal to the riskless return, r_f. Does this mean that the asset is riskless? Can an asset with a positive standard deviation of return, σ, have a beta of zero?

B9. The required return on an asset with a beta of 1.4 is 17%, and the riskless return is 7%. What is the expected return on the market portfolio?

B10. The Principle of Diversification states that diversification is beneficial. However, in an efficient capital market, the value of a share of stock does not reflect whether the share's owner is diversified. Why is this the case?

B11. Suppose the expected return and variance of the market portfolio are 0.11 and 0.0016, respectively. If the riskless return is 0.06, what will be the required return on a stock whose return variance is 0.12 and whose correlation with the market portfolio's returns is 0.46?

B12. What is the beta of a stock when its expected return is 15%, its standard deviation of return is 25%, its correlation coefficient with the market is 0.2, and the return to the market portfolio is 14% with a standard deviation of 4%? Assuming the market for this stock is in equilibrium, what is the riskless return that is implied by the information given?

B13. Stock A has a beta of 2.0 and a required return of 15%. The market return is 10%. What will be the required return on stock B, which has a beta of 1.4?

B14. Refer to Figure 7-1.

a. How would the utility curves look for a highly risk-averse investor? Explain why such an investor would wind up at a point on the CML to the left of M.

b. How would the utility curves look for a slightly risk-averse investor? Explain why such an investor would wind up at a point on the CML to the right of M.

B15. Refer to Figure 7-3. Suppose the securities market's collective degree of risk aversion increases. How would you expect the market risk premium to change? How would you expect the SML to shift?

B16. A portfolio contains five common stocks. The following table provides their respective betas and the percentages of the portfolio invested in each. Calculate the portfolio beta.

Stock	1	2	3	4	5
Beta	1.15	0.85	1.00	1.30	0.80
Percentage of portfolio	20%	10%	15%	25%	30%

B17. Chicago Gear has estimated the following contingent returns:

State of the Market	Probability That State Occurs	Return Stock Market	Return Chicago Gear
Stagnant	0.20	(10%)	(15%)
Slow growth	0.35	10	15
Average growth	0.30	15	25
Rapid growth	0.15	25	35

The riskless return is currently 6%.

a. Calculate the expected returns on the stock market and on the project.

b. What is Chicago Gear's beta?

c. What is Chicago Gear's required return according to the CAPM?

B18. I. Will Eatem, a portfolio manager for the Conservative Retirement Equity Fund (CREF), is considering investing in the common stock of Big Caesar's Pizza (stock symbol PIES). His analysts have compiled the following data:

Year	Return on the S&P 500	Return on PIES
1	(10.2%)	(5.3%)
2	5.8	13.2
3	12.2	6.1
4	(7.3)	2.1
5	(1.5)	(8.8)
6	10.5	15.7
7	8.3	3.9
8	15.7	12.6
9	(2.1)	(7.3)
10	8.6	10.2

a. Calculate the beta coefficient for PIES.

b. The riskless return is 6% and the market risk premium is 8.4%. Plot the SML.

c. You have recently met with the management of PIES. You are favorably impressed, and you estimate that the stock will earn a return of 19% over the next 12 months. Should you invest in PIES?

B19. Suppose Swift Meat Processors is considering building a new meat processing facility in Omaha, Nebraska. Swift has 75 million common shares outstanding. The share price is $25. Assume $r_f = 6.5\%$, $\beta = 0.95$, and $\bar{r}_M - r_f = 8.4\%$. Estimate Swift's required return on its equity investment in the new facility.

B20. Suppose $\bar{r}_j = 15\%$, $\bar{r}_{jn} = 18\%$, $D_1 = \$1.50$, and $g = 10\%$. What is the value per share (a) assuming the shares are added to a well-diversified portfolio and (b) assuming they are held as part of a very poorly diversified portfolio?

B21. Suppose the riskless return is 6% and the beta coefficients are $\beta_1 = 1.15$, $\beta_2 = 0.5$, $\beta_3 = 0.75$, and $\beta_4 = 0.25$. The expected return on the market portfolio is 14%. The expected rate of growth of real GDP is 4%. The expected rate of consumer price inflation is 3%. The expected rate of growth of personal disposable income is 5%.

a. What is the required return according to the CAPM?

b. What is the required return according to the APT model?

PROBLEM SET C

C1. Suppose that r_f is 5% and $\bar{r}_M$ is 10%. According to the SML and the CAPM, an asset with a beta of -2.0 has a required return of *negative* 5% $[= 5 - 2(10 - 5)]$. Is this possible? Does it mean the asset has negative risk? Why would anyone ever invest in an asset that has an expected and a required return that are negative? Explain.

C2. The Principle of Capital Market Efficiency states that the capital markets are so efficient that market prices for securities reflect all available information about the security. In other words, a security's market price is the best estimate of the value of the security. If we believe this is true, why do we bother to try to create models that accurately value a security? Why not simply use the latest trading price as the best possible estimate?

C3. Respond to the following statement: "Because all I can expect to earn from investing in a security that is on the SML is a zero NPV, I don't see why it's worth my trouble to invest in financial securities that are traded in an efficient capital market."

C4. Plot the following 10 investment portfolio risks and returns.

Portfolio	1	2	3	4	5	6	7	8	9	10
Expected return	10.0	12.0	7.5	8.3	6.1	13.2	14.1	7.9	9.2	13.1
Risk	15.5	18.7	14.3	17.2	22.3	23.0	25.2	17.1	16.7	23.4

a. Identify the efficient portfolios and plot the efficient frontier.

b. Suppose the riskless return is 10%. Which is the best portfolio?

c. Suppose you can accept a standard deviation of up to 10%. What is your best investment strategy? What is your expected return?

d. Suppose you can accept a standard deviation of up to 30%. What is your best investment strategy? What is your expected return?

Real-World Application:
Estimating Microsoft's Required Return

Microsoft Corporation (stock symbol MSFT) is one of the leading providers of computer software in the world. Its common stock is traded in the over-the-counter market and listed in NASDAQ. The following table shows MSFT's monthly closing share price during 1991–1995.

MONTH	MSFT CLOSING PRICE	MARKET RETURN	T-BILL RETURN	MONTH	MSFT CLOSING PRICE	MARKET RETURN	T-BILL RETURN	MONTH	MSFT CLOSING PRICE	MARKET RETURN	T-BILL RETURN
1/91	$21.81	4.42%	0.52%	9/92	$40.25	1.15%	0.26%	5/94	$53.75	1.63%	0.32%
2/91	23.06	7.16	0.48	10/92	44.38	0.36	0.23	6/94	51.63	−2.47	0.31
3/91	23.58	2.38	0.44	11/92	46.56	3.37	0.23	7/94	51.50	3.31	0.28
4/91	22.00	0.28	0.53	12/92	42.69	1.31	0.28	8/94	58.13	4.07	0.37
5/91	24.39	4.28	0.47	1/93	43.25	0.73	0.23	9/94	56.13	−2.41	0.37
6/91	22.71	−4.57	0.42	2/93	41.69	1.35	0.22	10/94	63.00	2.29	0.38
7/91	24.50	4.68	0.49	3/93	46.25	2.15	0.25	11/94	62.88	−3.67	0.37
8/91	28.42	2.35	0.46	4/93	42.75	−2.45	0.24	12/94	61.13	1.46	0.44
9/91	29.67	−1.64	0.46	5/93	46.31	2.70	0.22	1/95	59.38	2.60	0.42
10/91	31.29	1.34	0.42	6/93	44	0.33	0.25	2/95	63.00	3.88	0.40
11/91	32.42	−4.04	0.39	7/93	37	−0.47	0.24	3/95	71.13	2.96	0.46
12/91	37.08	11.43	0.38	8/93	37.56	3.81	0.25	4/95	81.75	2.91	0.44
1/92	40.00	−1.86	0.34	9/93	41.25	−0.74	0.26	5/95	84.69	3.95	0.54
2/92	41.17	1.28	0.28	10/93	40.06	2.03	0.22	6/95	90.38	2.35	0.47
3/92	39.50	−1.96	0.34	11/93	40.00	−0.94	0.25	7/95	90.50	3.33	0.45
4/92	36.75	2.91	0.32	12/93	40.31	1.23	0.23	8/95	92.50	0.27	0.47
5/92	40.33	0.54	0.28	1/94	42.56	3.35	0.25	9/95	90.50	4.19	0.43
6/92	35.00	−1.45	0.32	2/94	41.25	−2.70	0.21	10/95	100.00	−0.35	0.47
7/92	36.00	4.03	0.31	3/94	42.35	−4.35	0.27	11/95	87.13	4.40	0.42
8/92	37.13	−2.02	0.26	4/94	46.25	1.30	0.27	12/95	87.75	1.85	0.49

Sources: Bloomberg, L.P., and *Stocks, Bonds, Bills, and Inflation 1996 Yearbook* (Chicago, Ill.: Ibbotson Associates, 1996), pp. 181, 207. MSFT Closing Price is adjusted for stock splits in June 1991 (3-for-2), June 1992 (3-for-2), and May 1994 (2-for-1).

1. Calculate the monthly excess returns, $r_M - r_f$, on the market portfolio.

2. MSFT is not currently paying a dividend. The closing price in December 1990 (adjusted for stock splits) was $16.72. Calculate the monthly excess returns, $r_{MSFT} - r_f$, on Microsoft common stock.

3. a. Estimate the β for MSFT using the linear regression model

$$r_{MSFT} - r_f = \alpha + \beta\,(r_M - r_f)$$

   b. What is the adjusted R^2 for the regression model (that is, what proportion of the variation in $r_{MSFT} - r_f$ is explained by variation in $r_M - r_f$)?

   You can use the CAPM to estimate Microsoft's required return. You calculated Microsoft's beta in question 3. You will need the following additional information:

	RISKLESS RATE AT YEAR-END 1995	MARKET RISK PREMIUM $(r_M - r_f)$
Short-term	5.13%	8.40%
Intermediate-term	5.50	7.40
Long-term	6.00	7.00

4. Estimate MSFT's required return (r_e) using the CAPM and the short-term riskless rate.

5. Estimate r_e using the CAPM and the intermediate-term riskless rate.

6. Estimate r_e using the CAPM and the long-term riskless rate.

7. Compare your answers to questions 4, 5, and 6. Can you explain why they differ?

8. Why is it important to be consistent in choosing the riskless rate and the market risk premium when you use the CAPM?

APPENDIX: EMPIRICAL TESTS OF THE CAPM

The CAPM provides a precise relationship for the risk-return trade-off. The model is simple in form and easy to apply. It follows logically from a set of basic assumptions. However, if one of these assumptions is violated, the CAPM may not exactly represent reality.

As we have noted, the three critical underlying assumptions can be challenged as unrealistic. Before placing much reliance on any model, we must validate it empirically. Unfortunately, the CAPM's empirical record is mixed. Research has produced results that do not match the predictions of the CAPM. The literature is too extensive to permit a comprehensive treatment here, so we will just highlight some of the important findings.

Testing the CAPM involves two problems. First, the CAPM addresses *expected* returns. But we can't observe expected returns, so researchers have to work with realized returns. Unfortunately, realized stock returns reflect the various surprises that cause them to have standard deviations of 30% per year or more. Second, the market portfolio includes *all* risky assets, including bonds, real estate, and commodities as well as all common stocks. But virtually all tests of the CAPM have used a subset of common stocks as a proxy for the market portfolio.

These two problems raise an important question: Have the various tests of the CAPM been properly specified? In practice, measuring expectations is impossible. Also, there is no practical way of measuring "true" market portfolio returns because of the large number of assets that do not trade in liquid markets.

The Early Evidence

A classic 1973 study by Eugene Fama and James MacBeth furnished early support for the CAPM. They based their study on common stocks traded on the NYSE between 1926 and 1968. They performed a series of regression tests. On the basis of their tests, they drew the following conclusions.

• The behavior of average returns on NYSE-listed stocks was consistent with attempts by risk-averse investors to hold efficient portfolios. On average, there appears to be a positive relationship between risk and expected return, with risk being measured in a portfolio context.

- An investor making a portfolio decision could reasonably assume that the relationship between a security's expected return and its contribution to portfolio risk is linear, as implied by the CAPM.

- There was no evidence that any measure of risk, other than beta, had systematically affected average security returns.

- The behavior of security returns was consistent with what one would expect to find in an efficient capital market.

Size Effect

The CAPM predicts that (1) expected returns are a positive linear function of beta, and (2) security betas are sufficient to describe the cross section of expected security returns. However, a 1981 study by Rolf Banz found that the aggregate stock market value (ME) of the firm (share price times the number of shares outstanding) played a significant role, incremental to beta, in explaining a cross section of realized common stock returns. He found a strong negative relationship between size and average return. He found that the average returns on small (low-ME) stocks were higher than the CAPM predicted and that the average returns on large (high-ME) stocks were lower than the CAPM predicted.

A more recent 1992 study by Eugene Fama and Kenneth French analyzed realized stock returns for the period 1963 through 1990 for a large sample of common stocks of nonfinancial firms that were listed on the NYSE, AMEX, or NASDAQ. First, they sorted firms into ten deciles on the basis of size (ME). Then they divided each size decile into ten portfolios on the basis of beta coefficients estimated using the trailing five years of monthly returns (or a shorter period, depending on data availability).

Fama and French found that when the common stock portfolios were formed on size alone, average return appeared to be positively correlated with beta, as the CAPM predicts and as illustrated in Figure 7A-1. But they also found that the portfolio betas and size were almost perfectly negatively correlated. When they subdivided the size portfolios on the basis of historical betas, they found a strong relationship between average returns and size *but no significant relationship between average realized returns and beta*. Figure 7A-2 illustrates this lack of a significant relationship. In an appendix, they repeated the tests on NYSE-listed stocks for the period 1941–1990 and obtained similar results.

It appears that size proxies for risk. A relationship between size and risk seems plausible. Larger firms tend to have more information available about them, to have longer operating histories, to be more well-established, and to be better diversified (across product lines, geographical regions, and so on) than smaller firms. But the precise linkage between firm size and required return is unclear. Empirical evidence of a linkage exists, but we do not have an asset pricing model that specifies the relationship.

Leverage Effect

A 1988 study by Laxmi Bhandari documented a positive relationship between a firm's leverage (the firm's proportion of debt financing) and average return. Higher leverage entails greater financial risk. However, beta in the CAPM should capture the effect of higher leverage. But Bhandari found that leverage helped explain the cross section of average stock returns when measures of firm size (ME) and leverage were included as well as beta.

Other Measures of Risk

A number of studies have concluded that a firm's book-to-market-equity ratio or its earnings-price ratio helps explain the cross section of equity returns in empirical tests that include beta.

BOOK-TO-MARKET-EQUITY RATIO   Several studies have found that the average returns on common stock are positively related to the ratio of the book value of the firm's com-

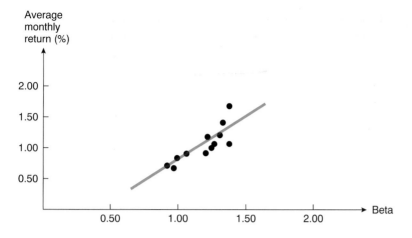

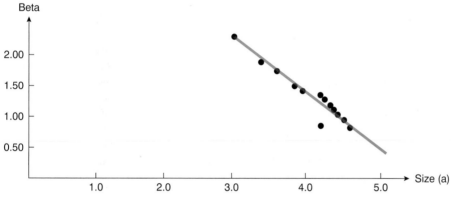

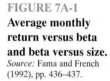

FIGURE 7A-1
Average monthly return versus beta and beta versus size.
Source: Fama and French (1992), pp. 436–437.

FIGURE 7A-2
Average monthly return versus beta for different size classes.
Source: Fama and French (1992), pp. 434–435.

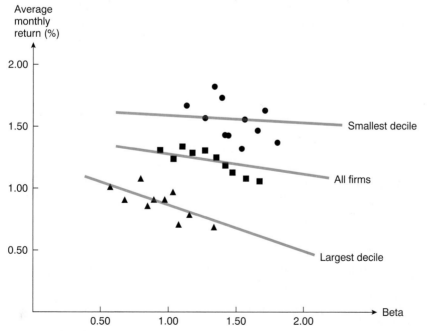

mon equity (BE) to its market value (ME).[11] It is possible that the BE/ME ratio proxies for the degree of risk of financial distress.[12] Firms that appear to have poor financial prospects, as indicated by a high BE/ME ratio (that is, a low ratio of market value to book value), have higher-than-average realized stock returns. Put somewhat differently, because of the greater risk involved, they have a higher required return than firms with more favorable prospects. However, Fama and French (1992) note that the BE/ME ratio might merely capture the "regression toward the mean" of irrational, or uninformed, market whims concerning the firm's prospects.

EARNINGS-PRICE RATIO   A 1983 study by Sanjoy Basu shows that the earnings-price ratio (E/P) helps explain the cross section of average returns on U.S. common stocks in empirical tests that include a size variable and beta. Ball (1978) notes that E/P is likely to be higher for riskier stocks. Ball's argument could also apply to size (ME), leverage, and BE/ME as proxies for risk. Unfortunately, none of these studies on alternative measures explains the linkage between the risk proxy and the required return.

Tests of the Slope of the SML

Fama and French (1992) concluded that there was a relationship between size and average return but no relationship between β and average return when size was controlled for. Surprisingly, they found that the regression coefficient on the beta variable was not significantly different from zero when beta was used as the sole independent variable explaining common stock returns for the 1963–1990 period. One must interpret these results carefully.

In 1993, Fischer Black criticized the Fama–French study. He argued that the statistical tests employed were not sufficiently powerful to rule out the possibility that the slope of the SML is positive. The slope of the SML may be smaller than the CAPM predicts, but we do not have enough evidence to conclude that it is zero. Black pointed out that with thousands of researchers studying roughly the same data, nonmeaningful chance relationships are bound to occur from time to time. This is the result of what he referred to as *data mining*. Data mining is the process of examining data to identify patterns without having a theoretical basis for the patterns. "I especially attribute their results to data mining when they attribute them to unexplained 'priced factors,' or give no reasons at all for the effects they find (Black, 1993, p. 10)."

The Fama–French study, and many others, suggest that the SML is linear but that it is flatter than the one shown in Figure 7-5. Figure 7A-3 illustrates the relative position of the "theoretical" SML and the empirically observed SML. However, the empirical results to date leave the precise position of the SML unclear.

Adjusting for Firm Size

Ibbotson Associates (1995) has compiled data measuring the effect of firm size. The U.S. operating firms whose shares are listed on the NYSE are divided into deciles of equal size. The decile portfolios are rebalanced quarterly. Table 7A-1 reports the annual returns of the ten deciles over the 1926–1994 period. The inverse relationship between firm size and realized return is clearly evident. Table 7A-1 also reports the size premium (discount if negative) implicit in these realized returns.

Ibbotson Associates recommends modifying the CAPM by appending a size premium to Equation (7.3):

$$\bar{r}_j = r_f + \beta_j(\bar{r}_M - r_f) + s_j \tag{7A.1}$$

where s_j denotes the *size premium*. The size premium is one of three empirically estimated values: 1.31% for mid-cap stocks (equity capitalization between $617 million and $2.57 billion),

---

[11] Stattman (1980); Rosenberg, Reid, and Lanstein (1985); and Fama and French (1992):among others. Chan, Hamao, and Lakonishok (1991) find that the BE/ME ratio also has a strong effect on the returns of Japanese stocks.
[12] Chan and Chen (1991).

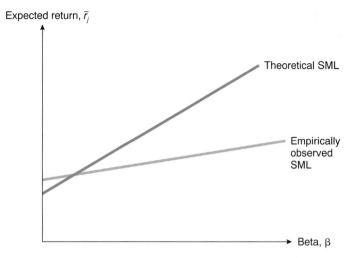

2.12% for low-cap stocks (equity capitalization between $149 million and $617 million), and 4.02% for micro-cap stocks (equity capitalization below $149 million). The following example illustrates how to use the size-premium adjustment to CAPM.

TABLE 7A-1
The relationship between firm size and realized return for common stocks listed on the New York Stock Exchange during the period 1926 through 1994.

	DECILE	BETA	ARITHMETIC MEAN RETURN	RETURN IMPLIED BY CAPM	SIZE PREMIUM (RETURN IN EXCESS OF CAPM)
	1 (largest)	0.90	11.01%	11.45%	−0.44%
	2	1.04	13.09	12.46	0.63
Mid-cap stocks[a] {	3	1.09	13.83	12.82	1.01
	4	1.13	14.44	13.11	1.33
	5	1.17	15.50	13.24	2.16
Low-cap stocks[b] {	6	1.19	15.45	13.50	1.95
	7	1.24	15.92	13.87	2.05
	8	1.29	16.84	14.17	2.67
Micro-cap stocks[c] {	9	1.36	17.83	14.69	3.14
	10 (smallest)	1.47	21.98	15.45	6.53
Mid-cap		1.12	14.32	13.01	1.31
Low-cap		1.23	15.87	13.75	2.12
Micro-cap		1.39	18.92	14.90	4.02

[a] Equity capitalization between $617 million and $2.57 billion.
[b] Equity capitalization between $149 million and $617 million.
[c] Equity capitalization below $149 million.
Source: Stocks, Bonds, Bills, and Inflation 1995 Yearbook (Chicago, Ill.: Ibbotson Associates, 1995), p. 135.

Adjusting the CAPM for the Size Effect

EXAMPLE

Northern Bearings, Inc. has 10 million common shares outstanding. The current price is $31.50 per share. It is considering building a new gear plant in Allentown, Pennsylvania. What is the new plant project's required return?

Mary Rivera, Northern's CFO, has gathered the following information to calculate the required return. The riskless return is 8%. Beta is 1.25. The market risk premium is 8.4%.

Rivera knows she needs to allow for Northern's size in the return calculation. Northern's equity capitalization is $315 million (= 31.50 × 10 million). The low-cap risk-premium adjustment applies. Applying Equation (7A.1), she finds that the project's required return is

$$r = 8\% + 1.25(8.4\%) + 2.1\% = 20.6\%$$

The precise form of the size-premium adjustment is somewhat arbitrary. It is a force-fitted empirical estimate. It is an attempt to "tweak" the CAPM to accommodate the empirically observed size effect. We do not have an alternative to the CAPM that explicitly incorporates a size effect and indicates precisely how it operates. Therefore, we cannot be certain that the size effect will not disappear someday. Nevertheless, we think the size adjustment is a reasonable approach to handle the firm-size effect that afflicts the CAPM.

Status of the CAPM

The CAPM is appealing: It is logically consistent and simple. But it rests on certain assumptions that can be challenged. Moreover, a number of studies have produced potentially troubling empirical results.

At this point, we feel that the studies to date do not invalidate CAPM, but they issue a warning. Nondiversifiable risk may not be the only dimension of risk that affects required returns—even when investors hold well-diversified portfolios. In particular, firm size seems to be important. But are there other dimensions of risk that are relevant?

The observed significance of various measures of leverage (proportion of debt financing) suggests the possibility that the CAPM tends to understate a firm's required return when the firm is in financial distress. If other dimensions of risk are important, how should we measure them, and how do they affect required returns? Only more research will answer these questions.

APPENDIX EXERCISES

PROBLEM SET A

A1. What questions have empirical tests raised about the validity of the CAPM?

A2. What is the relationship between firm size and average return?

A3. Describe how to adjust the CAPM to reflect the effect that firm size has on common stock returns.

A4. What might explain the observed correlation between measures of leverage and common stock returns?

PROBLEM SET B

B1. Suppose Northern Bearings had 50 million common shares outstanding. Calculate the required return on its common stock.

B2. Suppose $\bar{r}_j = 15.7\%$, $r_f = 6\%$, $\beta_j = 1.20$, and $\bar{r}_M = 13\%$.

  a. What is the implied value of s_j?

  b. In what size range does the firm's equity capitalization lie?

PROBLEM SET C

C1. How might the size adjustment that Ibbotson Associates recommends be improved on?

BIBLIOGRAPHY

Affleck-Graves, John and Bill McDonald. "Nonnormalities and Tests of Asset Pricing Theories," *Journal of Finance*, 1989, 44(4):889–908.

Ball, Ray. "Anomalies in Relationships Between Securities' Yields and Yield-Surrogates," *Journal of Financial Economics*, 1978, 6(2/3):103–126.

Banz, Rolf W. "The Relationship Between Return and Market Value Of Common Stocks," *Journal of Financial Economics*, 1981, 9(1):3–18.

Basu, Sanjoy. "The Relationship Between Earnings' Yield, Market Value and Return for NYSE Common Stocks: Further Evidence," *Journal of Financial Economics*, 1983, 12(1): 129–156.

Bhandari, Laxmi Chand. "Debt/Equity Ratio and Expected Common Stock Returns: Empirical Evidence," *Journal of Finance*, 1988, 43(2):507–528.

Black, Fischer. "Estimating Expected Return," *Financial Analysts Journal*, 1993, 49(5):36–38. Reprinted in *Financial Analysts Journal*, 1995, 51(1):168–171.

Black, Fischer. "Return and Beta," *Journal of Portfolio Management*, 1993, 20(1):8–18.

Boquist, John A., and William T. Moore. "Estimating the Systematic Risk of an Industry Segment: A Mathematical Programming Approach," *Financial Management*, 1983, 12(4):11–18.

Breeden, Douglas T., Michael R. Gibbons, and Robert H. Litzenberger. "Empirical Tests of the Consumption-Oriented CAPM," *Journal of Finance*, 1989, 44(2):231–262.

Brennan, Michael J. "The Optimal Number of Securities in a Risky Asset Portfolio When There Are Fixed Costs of Transaction: Theory and Some Empirical Evidence," *Journal of Financial and Quantitative Analysis*, 1975, 10(3):483–496.

Brigham, Eugene F., Dilip K. Shome, and Steve R. Vinson. "The Risk Premium Approach to Measuring a Utility's Cost of Equity," *Financial Management*, 1985, 14(1):33–45.

Brown, Stephen J. "The Number of Factors in Security Returns," *Journal of Finance*, 1989, 44(5):1247–1262.

Burmeister, Edwin, and Marjorie B. McElroy. "Joint Estimation of Factor Sensitivities and Risk Premia for the Arbitrage Pricing Theory," *Journal of Finance*, 1988, 43(3):721–733.

Chan, K. C. and Nai-Fu Chen. "Structural and Return Characteristics of Small and Large Firms," *Journal of Finance*, 1991, 46(4):1467–1484.

Chan, K. C., and Nai-Fu Chen. "An Unconditional Asset-Pricing Test and the Role of Firm Size as an Instrumental Variable for Risk," *Journal of Finance*, 1988, 43(2):309–325.

Chan, Louis K. C., Yasushi Hamao, and Josef Lakonishok. "Fundamentals and Stock Returns in Japan," *Journal of Finance*, 1991, 46(5):1739–1764.

Cho, D. Chinhyung, Cheol S. Eun, and Lemma W. Senbet. "International Arbitrage Pricing Theory: An Empirical Investigation," *Journal of Finance*, 1986, 41(2):313–330.

Connor, Gregory, and Robert A. Korajczyk. "A Test for the Number of Factors in an Approximate Factor Model," *Journal of Finance*, 1993, 48(4):1263–1291.

Cooper, Ian A., and Evi Kaplanis. "Cost to Crossborder Investment and International Equity Market Equilibrium." In *Recent Developments in Corporate Finance*, J. Edwards, Julian Franks, C. Mayer, and Stephen Schaefer. ed. Cambridge, England: Cambridge University Press, 1986:209–240.

Crum, Roy L., and Keqian Bi. "An Observation of Estimating the Systematic Risk of an Industry Segment," *Financial Management*, 1988, 17(1):60–62.

Ehrhardt, Michael C., and Yatin N. Bhagwat. "A Full-Information Approach for Estimating Divisional Betas," *Financial Management*, 1991, 20(2):60–69.

Fama, Eugene F., and Kenneth R. French. "The Cross-Section of Expected Stock Returns," *Journal of Finance*, 1992, 47(2):427–466.

Fama, Eugene F., and Kenneth R. French. "Multifactor Explanations of Asset Pricing Anomalies," *Journal of Finance*, 1996, 51(1):55–84.

Fama, Eugene F., and James D. MacBeth. "Risk, Return and Equilibrium: Empirical Tests," *Journal of Political Economy*, 1973, 81(May):607–636.

Ferson, Wayne E., and Campbell R. Harvey. "Seasonality and Consumption-Based Asset Pricing," *Journal of Finance*, 1992, 47(2):511–552.

Gehr, Adam K., Jr. "Some Tests of the Arbitrage Pricing Theory," *Journal of the Midwest Finance Association*, 1978, 7: 91–105.

Glosten, Lawrence R., Ravi Jagannathan and David E. Runkle. "On the Relation Between the Expected Value and the Volatility of the Nominal Excess Return on Stocks," *Journal of Finance*, 1993, 48(5):1779–1801.

Gombola, Michael J., and Douglas R. Kahl. "Time-Series Processes of Utility Betas: Implications for Forecasting Systematic Risk," *Financial Management*, 1990, 19(3):84–93.

Gultekin, Mustafa N., and N. Bulent Gultekin. "Stock Return Anomalies and the Tests of the APT," *Journal of Finance*, 1987, 42(5):1213–1224.

Handa, Puneet, S. P. Kothari, and Charles Wasley. "Sensitivity of Multivariate Tests of the Capital Asset-Pricing Model to the Return Measurement Interval," *Journal of Finance*, 1993, 48(4):1543–1551.

Harris, Robert S., and Felicia C. Marston. "Estimating Shareholder Risk Premia Using Analysts' Growth Forecasts," *Financial Management*, 1992, 21(2):63–70.

Ibbotson Associates. *Stocks, Bonds, Bills, and Inflation 1995 Yearbook*. Chicago, Ill.: Ibbotson Associates, 1995.

Jagannathan, Ravi, and Zhenyu Wang. "The Conditional CAPM and the Cross-Section of Expected Returns," *Journal of Finance*, 1996, 51(1): 3–53.

Lintner, John. "The Valuation of Risk Assets and the Selection of Risky Investments in Stock Portfolios and Capital Budgets," *The Review of Economics and Statistics*, 1965, 47(1):13–37.

Longstaff, Francis A. "Temporal Aggregation and the Continuous-Time Capital Asset Pricing Model," *Journal of Finance,* 1989, 44(4): 871–888.

MacKinlay, A. Craig. "Multifactor Models Do Not Explain Deviations from the CAPM," *Journal of Financial Economics*, 1995, 38(1):3–28.

Maddox, Farris M., Donna T. Pippert, and Rodney N. Sullivan. "An Empirical Study of Ex Ante Risk Premiums for the Electric Utility Industry," *Financial Management*, 1995, 24(3):89–95.

Mossin, Jan. "Equilibrium in a Capital Asset Market," *Econometrica*, 1966, October:768–783.

Pettengill, Glenn N., Sridhar Sundaram, and Ike Mathur. "The Conditional Relation Between Beta and Returns," *Journal of Financial and Quantitative Analysis*, 1995, 30(1):101–116.

Roll, Richard. "A Critique of the Asset Pricing Theory's Tests; Part I: On Past and Potential Testability of Theory," *Journal of Financial Economics*, 1977, 4(2):129–176.

Rosenberg, Barr, Kenneth Reid, and Ronald Lanstein. "Persuasive Evidence of Market Inefficiency," *Journal of Portfolio Management*, 1985, 11(3):9–17.

Ross, Stephen A. "The Arbitrage Theory of Capital Asset Pricing," *Journal of Economic Theory*, 1976, 13(December):341–360.

Shanken, Jay. "The Current State of the Arbitrage Pricing Theory," *Journal of Finance*, 1992, 47(4):1569–1574.

Shanken, Jay, and Clifford W. Smith, Jr. "Implications of Capital Market Research for Corporate Finance," *Financial Management*, 1996, 25(1):98–104.

Sharpe, William F. "Capital Asset Prices: A Theory of Market Equilibrium Under Conditions of Risk," *Journal of Finance*, 1964, 19(3):425–442.

Sharpe, William F. "Capital Asset Prices with and without Negative Holdings," *Journal of Finance,* 1991, 46(2):489–510.

Shukla, Ravi, and Charles Trzcinka. "Sequential Tests of the Arbitrage Pricing Theory: A Comparison Of Principal Components and Maximum Likelihood Factors," *Journal of Finance*, 1990, 45(5):1541–1564.

Stattman, Dennis. "Book Values and Stock Returns," *The Chicago MBA: A Journal of Selected Papers*, 1980, 4, 25–45.

Stulz, Rene M., and Walter Wasserfallen. "Foreign Equity Investment Restrictions, Capital Flight, and Shareholder Wealth Maximization: Theory and Evidence," *Reveiw of Financial Studies,* 8(4):1019–1057.

Trzcinka, Charles. "On the Number of Factors in the Arbitrage Pricing Model," *Journal of Finance*, 1986, 41(2):347–368.

Wei, K. C. John. "An Asset-Pricing Theory Unifying the CAPM and APT," *Journal of Finance*, 1988, 43(4):881–892.

OPTIONS: VALUING CONTINGENCIES

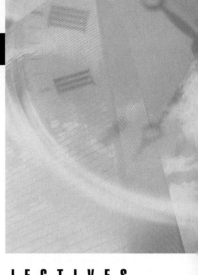

Options are everywhere. People often use the term *option* to refer to a choice or alternative. For example, they might say they have a lot of options or that they don't have any options. We all know the first situation is good and the second is bad. That's because we understand the Options Principle: Options are valuable.

People like options because options provide a measure of control over uncertain events. Insurance is an option that you purchase to provide protection against bad events such as death or fire. At the heart of an option is a contingency—something that may or may not happen. An option is a *contingent claim* to particular outcomes; it comes into play only when certain conditions occur, such as an accident or winning the lottery.

Of course, most options don't come with a tag attached that says "option." Many of the options we focus on in this chapter are subtle or even hard to recognize. They are implicit options inherent in a situation, such as the examples of "hidden" options we cited in our discussion of the Options Principle (Chapter 3).

Now, having told you that options are valuable, we must also say that options can be extremely complex. In some situations, measuring the exact value of an option can be very difficult. This can be the case even with obvious and explicit options, such as those traded in the capital markets. (We will discuss market-traded options in Chapter 26.)

In this chapter we will explore what an option means in terms of rights to the possible outcomes in a situation. We will tell you about the factors that determine an option's value and explain how changes in those factors alter an option's value. Then, armed with some generalizations about options, we will identify both explicit and hidden options. Finally, we will present a simple model for valuing options.

OBJECTIVES

After studying this chapter, you should be able to

1. Summarize the importance of options, and demonstrate how they can dramatically affect value.

2. Identify "hidden" options in business situations.

3. Describe the dramatic effect a contingency can have on a situation.

4. Calculate payoffs under various possible outcomes.

5. Cite the determinants of the value of an option.

6. Describe how changes in those determinants affect the value of an option.

◆ *Options*: Look for options that can significantly affect value.

◆ *Two-Sided Transactions*: Always consider both sides. The option buyer has the right, but the option seller has the obligation.

◆ *Incremental Benefits*: Measure the impact of options on an incremental basis.

◆ *Time Value of Money*: Include the time value of money's impact on the value of an option.

◆ *Risk-Return Trade-Off*: Evaluate the change in risk and expected return when an asset owner buys or sells an option on the asset.

8.1 OPTIONS

An **option** is the right to do something without the obligation to do it. In this book we use the term in its broadest sense: An option is *any* right that has no obligation attached to it. However, there are also specific types of options. A **call option** is the right to buy an asset. A **put option** is the right to sell an asset. In both cases the asset on which the option is written is known as the **underlying asset**. The **strike price** is the price at which the optionholder may buy or sell the underlying asset when the option is exercised. When you **exercise** an option, you make the exchange specified in the option contract.

When exercising an option would provide an advantage over buying or selling the underlying asset in the open market, the option is **in-the-money**. For example, an option to sell (put) an asset for $100 when you can sell it for only $80 in the market is in-the-money. This option would allow the optionholder to sell the asset for $20 more than it is currently worth. When exercising an option would *not* provide an advantage over buying or selling the underlying asset currently in the market, the option is **out-of-the-money**. For example, an option to buy (call) an asset at a strike price of $100, when you could buy it for $80 in the market, is out-of-the-money. Exercising this option contract, the optionholder would pay $20 more for the asset than it is currently worth. Out-of-the-money options are not exercised because it would be a disadvantage, but they are frequently sold to others who believe the option might become in-the-money in the future.

The **exercise value** (also called *intrinsic value*) is the amount of advantage an in-the-money option provides over buying or selling the underlying asset currently in the market. For example, the $20 just noted in the in-the-money example is its exercise value. An out-of-the-money option has a zero exercise value. After all, optionholders have the right without the obligation, so they will "walk away from the option" rather than exercise an out-of-the-money option.

Like most things, options do not live forever. An option's **expiration** is the point in time when the option contract ceases to exist, the point at which the option expires or dies. Options are also of two types. An **American option** is an option that can be exercised at any time prior to its expiration. In contrast, a **European option** can be exercised only at the end of the contract, not before.

The complexity of an option stems from its very nature. It is a contingency that creates a discontinuity in the possible outcomes. Because the outcome is contingent, it may not matter at all or it may matter a lot. Sometimes a seemingly small difference in conditions makes a *big* difference in the outcome. Alternatively, a seemingly big difference in conditions may make little or no difference in the outcome. The set of possible outcomes is cut off, or trun-

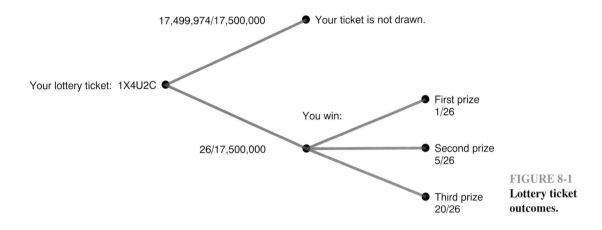

cated. Let's start by viewing an everyday item through "option glasses." Consider an example of something you might not think of as an option, a lottery ticket.

An Option View of a Lottery Ticket **EXAMPLE**

Suppose you bought a lottery ticket for $2.00. The first prize is $5000 a week for life. There are 5 second prizes of $1000 a week for life, and 20 third prizes of $250 a week for life. You, of course, would like to win the first prize. But you also understand that this outcome is not very likely; 17.5 million tickets will have been sold. Upon reflection, you decide the condition that you win *first* prize isn't critical. You would rather win than not win—if you could choose. This is because the difference between winning one prize and winning another is relatively small compared to the difference between not winning anything and winning any of the prizes.

Your ticket is marked 1X4U2C. Watching the big drawing on TV, you see the 26 winning numbers. Your heart jumps, one of the second prizes is 1X4U2B. (None of the others are close.) Sooooo close! If only the last letter had been the next one in the alphabet. A small difference in the one drawn—a C rather than a B in that last place—would have made a *big* difference in your outcome. At the same time, a big difference in the one drawn—an outcome of 9A8B7C—would not have changed your outcome at all. You would still not have been a winner. This is what we mean by a discontinuity in the outcomes. The outcomes for your lottery ticket are shown in Figure 8-1.

Your lottery ticket is a contingent claim. A **contingent claim** can be made only if particular conditions occur. You can claim a prize only if your ticket is drawn a winner. In most cases (17,499,974 of the 17.5 million possible outcomes, to be precise), your ticket is worthless and you get nothing. But if one of the 26 tickets that gets drawn happens to be yours, you can claim a prize in exchange for your lottery ticket. A contingent claim is an option in its broadest sense: the right, without the obligation, to do something.

Your lottery ticket is a European call option on a prize, which is the *underlying asset*. It is a *call option* because it gives you the right to "buy" the underlying asset for a *strike price* of zero. You would *exercise* your option by turning in your ticket if it has a winning number. It is a *European option* because you can do this only at its *expiration*, the end of the option's life just after the big drawing. The $2 price you paid for the ticket is the value of the option when you purchased it. Your option had an *exercise value* of zero during its life, because it gave zero advantage to claiming the prize before the drawing and so was *out-of-the-money*. As it turned out, your option was still out-of-the-money after the drawing when it *expired*. ■

A Call Option on an Asset

The lottery ticket example shows how something you do not think of as an option can be implicitly an option. Now let's look at an explicit call option on an asset.

Suppose Alice buys some land for $100,000 and immediately sells Carl a *European call option* on the same piece of land with a *strike price* of $110,000 and *expiration* one year from today. Both of their outcomes with respect to this land (the *underlying asset*) now include a contingency. While the call option exists, the most Alice can sell the land for is $110,000; she might get less. The most Carl will have to pay for the land is $110,000; he might be able to buy it for less. We can express this contingency for Alice as

$$\text{Alice's value} = \min[\text{market value; } 110,000]$$

The **min function** expresses the contingency in the situation mathematically. Its value is whichever is smaller, the market value *or* $110,000.

Basic Option Value: The Exercise Value

The Principle of Two-Sided Transactions reminds us to consider the other side of the transaction. Carl's situation is the mirror image, or opposite, of Alice's because he is on the other side of the transaction. We can show the "basic" value of Carl's call option, its *exercise value*, by using a mirror image of the min function, the **max function**, which takes the largest of a set:

$$\text{Exercise value of Carl's call option} = \max[(\text{market value} - 110,000); 0]$$

We know Carl's option is never worth less than zero, because an option cannot have a negative value. That is represented by the zero inside the max function. If the option is *out-of-the-money*, the exercise value is zero, and the option provides no advantage over an open market purchase. If the option is *in-the-money*, it provides an advantage of (market value − 110,000) over an open market purchase.

Note that the strike price is a break point in the outcomes for both sides of the transaction. If the market value is below the strike price on a call option at expiration, it does not matter how much below. Being just a little less is the same as being a great deal less. Whether the market value of the land is $109,000 or only $1, the option is out-of-the-money and will not be *exercised*. But if the market value is above the strike price on a call option at expiration, the option is in-the-money and will be exercised. And the farther the market value is above the strike price, the larger the exercise value is.

The exercise value changes dollar-for-dollar with the market value whenever the market price is above the call option's strike price. This is shown in Figure 8-2, which graphs the exercise value of a call option against the market value of the underlying asset. The line going up from the strike price at a 45° angle shows the one-for-one relationship as the asset's market value increases and the option becomes deeper in-the-money. The flat line to the left of the strike price shows that the exercise value is zero everywhere in the out-of-the-money area.

There is an important point to keep in mind when you look at a figure such as Figure 8-2. *There will be only one outcome.* At expiration, the underlying asset will have a single value, represented as one point on the horizontal axis. But before expiration, we don't know which point will represent its value. That is the nature of a risky—that is, uncertain—outcome. This is just like the distinction between a realized return and an expected return. If we knew ahead of time what the outcome was going to be, we would know which side of the transaction was going to "win." And if we knew that, we wouldn't need a complex analysis of option value. We would already know the exact value of the option!

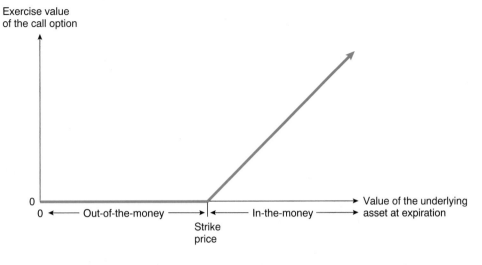

FIGURE 8-2
How the exercise value of a call option depends on the value of the underlying asset.

Self-Check Questions

1. What is an option?

2. What is the difference between an American option and a European option?

3. What is the difference between a call option and a put option?

4. What does it mean to say that an option is in-the-money?

8.2 BUYING AND SELLING PARTS OF AN ASSET'S RETURN DISTRIBUTION

We can think of an asset as a probability distribution of possible realized returns. Let's continue our example of Alice's land purchase. If she sells the land a year later for $126,000, she will have a realized return of 26% [= (126 − 100)/100]. Now consider the impact of Carl's option on Alice's realized return.

A Call Option

Suppose Alice sold Carl the call option for $4000. Figure 8–3 shows the net gain or loss to Alice and Carl a year later, at the option's expiration, as a function of the market value of the land. Note once again that neither Alice nor Carl can choose the outcome. There will be only one value for the land a year later, and they do not know what it will be.

Having sold the call option, a next-year market value outcome of $126,000 would give Alice a realized return of about 14.6%.[1] Carl would exercise his option and buy the land for $110,000 (the strike price) because it is worth $126,000. As you can see, with any market value outcome greater than $110,000, Carl will exercise his option and Alice will have a realized return of 14.6% on her land investment and option sale. Carl has a claim on all of her possible realized returns above 14.6%. When Alice sold the call option to Carl, she effectively sold him all her outcomes above a 14.6% realized return. Thus an option can be described as

---

[1] Alice spent $100,000 for the land and sold the option for $4000, so her net investment is $96,000. Thus her net gain of $14,000 provides a return of 14.6% (= 14/96).

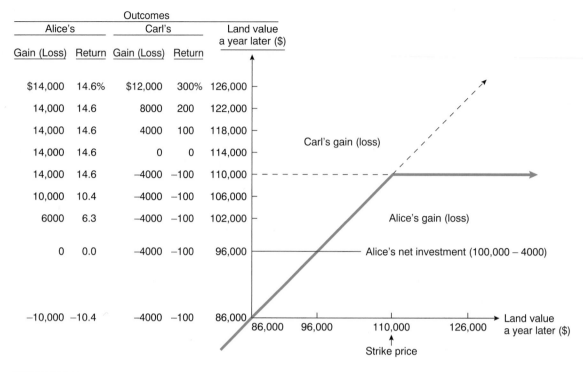

FIGURE 8-3

The gain or loss to Carl and Alice at the option's expiration, depending on the land's value. Remember, there will be only one outcome for the land value (one point on the *x* axis), which creates all of the *y* axis outcomes. Alice's net investment is $96,000.

a claim to some of the possible realized returns on the underlying asset. Figure 8-4 presents the probability distribution of Alice's realized returns in terms of the sale value of the land.

We can divide the outcome distribution into two parts: one part above and the other part below $110,000. Alice would prefer the higher possible outcomes (those to the right of $110,000) over the lower possible outcomes (those to the left of $110,000). Of course, knowing that people prefer higher return to lower return (Principle of Risk-Return Trade-Off), we can make this same statement if we partition the distribution into two parts at any point. On this basis, we can view outcomes to the right of *any* split point as good outcomes and those to the left as bad outcomes, because all asset owners like Alice want the good outcomes but do not want the bad. As a result, asset owners must be paid to give up their claim to the good possible outcomes. This is why Carl had to pay Alice for the call option.

The split point between the good and bad outcomes is the strike price for the option. When an asset owner is paid for giving up good outcomes, the owner has sold a call option on the asset.

Figure 8-5 illustrates the claim portion of the return distribution for Carl's call option. A call option gives the optionholder the right to claim all of the good outcomes (the highlighted portion above the strike price) by exercising the option. Carl can avoid bad outcomes (those below the strike price) by simply not exercising his option. But if the outcome is more than $110,000—say $118,000—Carl can claim the return by buying the land from Alice for $110,000 and reselling it to someone else for $118,000, thereby gaining the $8000 exercise

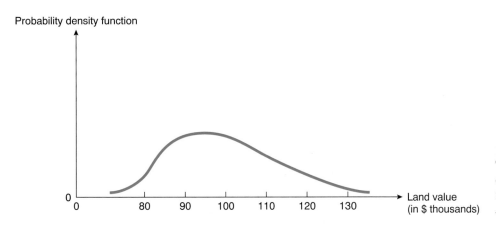

FIGURE 8-4
**The probability
distribution of the
future value of
Alice's land.**

value. You can see in Figure 8-3 that his net gain would then be $4000 ($8000 minus the $4000 he paid for the call option).

Barb Wyre purchased a building in downtown San Francisco for $2.3 million. Right after this, she sold a 1-year European call option on the building, with a strike price of $2.5 million, for $150,000 to Bob N. Weave. Thus Barb's net investment is $2.15 million. What are Barb's and Bob's outcomes, in terms of the land's possible value when the option expires?

Computing Outcomes for a Call Option

EXAMPLE

They will be as follows (in $ millions):

Land Value	Barb's Gain (Loss)	Barb's Return	Bob's Gain (Loss)	Bob's Return
$3.00	$0.35	16.28%	$0.35	233.33%
2.75	0.35	16.28	0.10	66.67
2.50	0.35	16.28	−0.15	−100.00
2.25	0.10	4.65	−0.15	−100.00
2.00	−0.15	−6.98	−0.15	−100.00
1.75	−0.40	−18.60	−0.15	−100.00

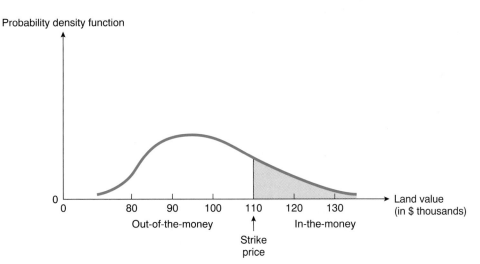

FIGURE 8-5
**Carl's call option
claim.**

A Put Option

Now consider the bad outcomes. Naturally, an asset owner like Alice would have to *pay* someone to get rid of the bad outcomes. When an asset owner pays someone else to take the bad outcomes, the asset owner has purchased a *put option* on the asset. The split point is again the (put) option's strike price. Figure 8-6 shows how the exercise value of a put option (the savings from not having to keep the bad outcomes) depends on the value of the underlying asset.

If you look back at Figure 8-2, you can see how the exercise value of a put option is simply a mirror image of that of a call option. The 45° line going up and to the left from the strike price shows the one-for-one relationship between exercise value and asset value as the asset's market value decreases and the option becomes deeper in-the-money. The flat line shows how the exercise value is zero everywhere in the out-of-the-money area.

Buying a put option is like purchasing insurance on an asset. For example, automobile collision insurance is like a put option on a car, exercisable only in the event of an accident. In the event of an accident, the insurance company covers your loss (in an agreed-upon way, such as all but $100 if you have "$100 deductible" insurance). In effect, you had a bad outcome (an accident), so you "sell" the destroyed car to the insurance company for the strike price (typically, the car's market value before it was destroyed).

Let's return to Alice's land situation. Suppose for now that Alice has lost interest in selling a call option. However, she has just heard about put options and has decided she does not want to have outcomes below $90,000. Because the outcomes below this $90,000 split point are bad outcomes, Alice would have to pay a person to take responsibility for those outcomes, should one of them occur. In other words, Alice buys a put option from Paul (the put option writer) with a strike price of $90,000. The put option gives Alice the right to sell the land to Paul for $90,000.

Figure 8-7 illustrates Paul's put option obligation. The put option gives Alice the right to avoid all the bad outcomes (the highlighted portion below the strike price) by exercising her option should one of them occur. Alice can claim the good outcomes simply by failing to exercise her put option. Therefore, if the land is worth more than $90,000, Alice will accept the outcome and let the put option expire without exercising it. If the land is worth less than $90,000, Alice will sell the land to Paul for $90,000, thereby gaining the exercise value of the put option—the difference between $90,000 and the market value of the land. Her net gain will then be the exercise value minus whatever she paid Paul for the option.

FIGURE 8-6

How the exercise value of a put option depends on the value of the underlying asset.

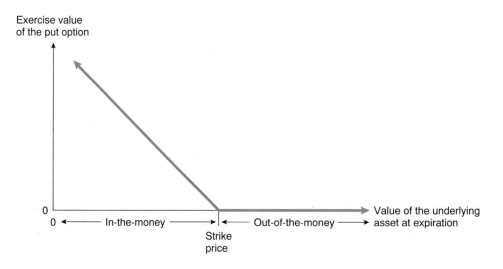

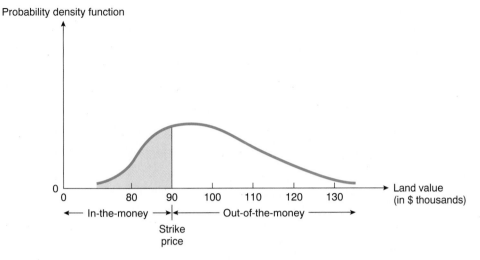

FIGURE 8-7

**Paul's put option
obligation (Alice's
put option claim).**

Barb Wyre purchased a building in downtown San Francisco for $2.3 million. Right after this, she bought a 1-year European put option on the building, with a strike price of $2.1 million, for $150,000 from Peter N. Da'Wolfe. Thus Barb's net investment is $2.45 million. What are Barb's and Peter's outcomes in terms of the land's possible value when the option expires?

*Computing
Outcomes
for a Put
Option*

    They will be as follows (in $ millions):

Land Value	Barb's Gain (Loss)	Barb's Return	Peter's Gain (Loss)	Peter's Return[2]
$3.00	$0.55	22.45%	$0.15	100.00%
2.75	0.30	12.24	0.15	100.00
2.50	0.05	2.04	0.15	100.00
2.25	−0.20	−8.16	0.15	100.00
2.00	−0.35	−14.29	0.05	33.33
1.75	−0.35	−14.29	−0.20	−133.33
1.50	−0.35	−14.29	−0.45	−300.00

Equivalent Claims or Put-Call Parity

Sometimes the same claim can be made in different ways. Suppose that after Carl approached Alice about wanting all the good outcomes above $110,000 and offered to buy a call option, Alice reconsidered her situation. She decided Carl's idea of claiming only the good outcomes above $110,000 sounded better than all the other possibilities we have talked about. Therefore she purchased a put option from Paul with a strike price of $110,000. What does her claim look like? Think about it. She has claim to all the good outcomes above $110,000, but the put option allows her to avoid all the bad outcomes below $110,000. If you think this sounds familiar, you are right. Alice's claim portion will be the same as Carl's would have been with the call option, the one shown in Figure 8-5.

    The equivalence between this new claim of Alice's and Carl's claim is called **put-call parity**. Put-call parity expresses the relationship between the values of put and call options.

---

[2] Peter's return is expressed as a percentage of the initial option value. Peter is taking risk, but he gets money at the start rather than investing money. Thus his return is not "normal" in an economic sense.

Put-call parity is interesting, but it can also be confusing: *Every situation that can be described in terms of a call option has a parallel description in terms of a put option.* In this book, we try to use the description that seems easiest to grasp in the situation. However, because a situation can always be described in terms of *either* a call or a put option, we sometimes simply talk about the "optionality" in the situation.

Self-Check Questions

1. How does buying a call option let you benefit from the really good outcomes?

2. Why is buying a put option like purchasing insurance?

3. Suppose you do not want to sell a particular stock you own right now, because of tax reasons. But you are afraid its value may decline before you do sell it. Should you buy a call option or a put option?

4. What sort of relationship does put-call parity express?

8.3 VALUING AN OPTION

So far we have not said much about the prices paid for options, except that Carl would have paid $4000 for his call option. But where did that price come from? We referred to the exercise value of an option as the *basic* value of an option. But would Alice sell the call option to Carl for its exercise value? Of course not. In fact, the exercise value of Carl's call option was zero when he bought it—the option was out-of-the-money. The land was worth $100,000 (Alice just bought it for that price) and the strike price was $110,000. Alice would require more than the exercise value because she would be taking on an obligation. Carl would have the right to buy the land for $110,000, because he would own the option (the right without the obligation). However, if Alice sold the option, she would have the obligation to sell the land for $110,000 if Carl decided to exercise his right. Thus there is more to an option's value than its exercise value.

Additional Option Value: The Time Premium

The **time premium of an option** (*time premium* for short) is the value of its "optionality." That is, the time premium is the extra value (above the exercise value) provided by having control. Control is the right without the obligation. It allows the optionholder to claim good outcomes and avoid bad ones. We call this part the time premium because it decreases as the option approaches expiration and becomes zero when the option is just about to expire. The time premium is determined by three factors: *time until expiration*, *risk of the underlying asset*, and market *riskless return*.

TIME UNTIL EXPIRATION   It is easy to see why time is a determinant of option value. If you have a choice between two options, where the only difference between them is their time until expiration, which option would you prefer to own? You can never be worse off with the option that has the longer time until expiration. Another way to think about this is to say that more time allows more chance for the option to be more in-the-money.[3]

---

[3] Some cynics might point out that it also allows more chance for the option to be more out-of-the-money. But remember that the optionholder can avoid bad outcomes—at least those that lie beyond the strike price in the out-of-the-money direction.

RISK OF THE UNDERLYING ASSET   Less obvious is how the *risk* (potential variation of the realized return) of the underlying asset affects the time premium. Figure 8-8 demonstrates the effect of risk on a call option. It illustrates the claim portions for identical call options on assets with identical market values and strike prices but different risk levels. Asset A has an outcome distribution with a relatively small variation, whereas Asset B has an outcome distribution with a relatively large variation. As you can see, Asset B's claim portion is much larger. It has a much greater probability (the area under the curve) of having a good outcome than Asset A. Therefore, the call option for Asset B is worth more than the call option for Asset A. Although we illustrated this with a call option, the same concept holds for a put option. That is, greater asset risk also enlarges the value of a put option.

Here are two other ways to see the impact of asset risk on option value. First, the greater the risk, the more the underlying asset value can change in a given amount of time. And because the optionholder has control (can claim the good outcomes but leave the bad), if everything else is the same, the greater the possible change is, the more the option is worth.

Finally, note that an increase in risk (a flatter probability distribution) increases the number of outcomes at the extremes of the distribution. That means there are more extremely good outcomes to be claimed and also more extremely bad outcomes to be avoided. Again, with optionholder control, the more outcomes that are covered, the more valuable is the option.

RISKLESS RETURN   The final determinant of the value of an option is the riskless return. We can think of this market return as the pure, or base, market required return. It is the basic, or benchmark, opportunity cost of money. The effect of the riskless return depends primarily on who has to pay the strike price if the option is exercised. The higher the riskless return is, the lower will be the present value of this payment, because the payment will not take place until the future when the option is exercised. A complexity of the riskless return is that its effect is reversed for call and put options. This is because the owner of a call option *pays* the strike price to obtain the underlying asset, whereas the owner of a put option *receives* the strike price to give the asset up. So an increase in the riskless return increases the value of a call option, but decreases the value of a put option.

Total Option Value

You can see now that an option's value has two parts: (1) its exercise value and (2) its time premium. We have just described the time premium. Let's review the option's exercise value. It contains the cutoff, or contingency, in the option. It is zero for an out-of-the-money option.

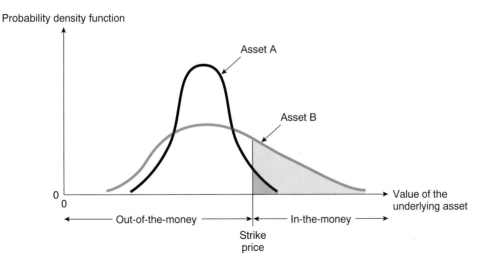

FIGURE 8-8
The effect of risk on the value of a call option.

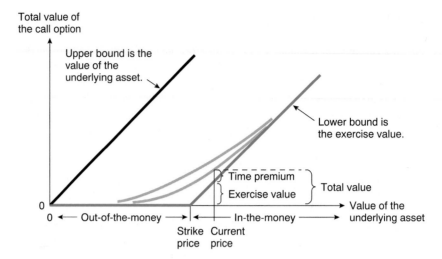

FIGURE 8-9

Total call option value as a function of underlying asset value.

For an in-the-money option, it is the difference between the strike price and the market value of the underlying asset. Thus the exercise value is itself determined by two factors: the *underlying asset's current market value* and the option's *strike price*. The larger the difference for an in-the-money option, the larger the exercise value and the more the option is worth. In other words, the deeper in-the-money an option is, the more it is worth.

MAXIMUM OPTION VALUE   Although Alice may require Carl to pay more than the exercise value for the call option, there is a natural limit to what Carl will be willing to pay. In the extreme, that limit is the value of the land. After all, if he paid any more, he would be better off simply buying the land now. Thus the extreme upper limit on the value of a call option is the value of the underlying asset. In fact, except in the most extraordinary of situations, a call option's value never even approaches this limit.

We can now show you the boundaries of an option's value and what the total value of a typical call option looks like as a function of the value of the underlying asset. Figure 8-9 illustrates the value of two call options. As you can see, the options are worth more than their exercise values. The additional amount is the time premium. You can also see that one option is worth more than the other. Such a higher value can be due to a longer time until expiration, to greater risk in the underlying asset, or to an increase in the riskless return.

Figure 8-10 illustrates the value of a put option as a function of underlying asset value. As with exercise value, you can see that the total value of a put option is a mirror image of a call option's total value.

Self-Check Questions

1. Why is there more to an option's value than its exercise value?

2. What is an option's time premium?

3. What three factors determine an option's time premium?

4. Why does greater asset risk increase the value of call options *and* put options?

5. What determines an option's exercise value?

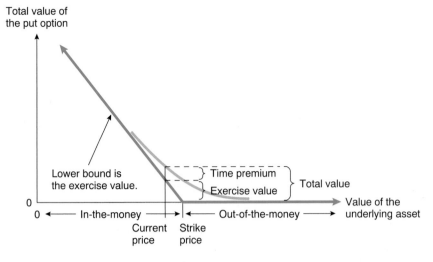

FIGURE 8-10
Total put option value as a function of underlying asset value.

8.4 SOME IMPORTANT GENERALIZATIONS ABOUT OPTIONS

Using the determinants of an option's value, we can establish some generalizations about option valuation. Applying these generalizations can tell us a great deal about the options, their values, and how the determinants affect value in a given situation. The generalizations we discuss here are extremely important, because they provide ready insight into many real-world situations we will describe in the rest of the book.

We start by looking at the determinants of option value. Table 8-1 summarizes these factors and indicates how an increase in each affects the value of an option.

THE LARGEST TIME PREMIUM FOR AN OPTION OCCURS WHEN THE UNDERLYING ASSET'S VALUE EQUALS THE STRIKE PRICE   You can see this for the options illustrated in Figure 8-9. The time premium is at its maximum here because the asset's value could go either way. That is, at the split point, when the underlying asset value exactly equals the strike price, the uncertainty is greatest about whether the option will expire in- or out-of-the-money.

AN OPTION'S TIME PREMIUM DECREASES AS THE OPTION BECOMES MORE IN- OR OUT-OF-THE-MONEY   This phenomenon is also illustrated in Figure 8-9, and we note it in Table 8-1 as well. It occurs because there is less uncertainty about whether the

TABLE 8-1
The determinants of option value.

AN INCREASE IN THIS FACTOR	HAS THIS EFFECT ON THE OPTION'S VALUE
The option's exercise value	
depth in-the-money	increases it
depth out-of-the-money	has no effect on it
The option's time premium	
time until expiration	increases it
risk of the underlying asset	increases it
increase in riskless return	increases the value of a call option
increase in riskless return	decreases the value of a put option
depth in-the-money	decreases it
depth out-of-the-money	decreases it

option will expire in- or out-of-the-money when the underlying asset is *already* worth more or less than the strike price. Quite simply, an option that is already in- or out-of-the-money is more likely to stay that way than it is to change. (This is not to say it *can't* change—only that the likelihood is smaller. We are dealing with probabilities.)

AN AMERICAN OPTION IS NEVER WORTH LESS THAN A COMPARABLE EUROPEAN OPTION

This is easy to understand. Essentially, there is more optionality in an American option. Consider two options that are comparable except that one is American and the other is European. The American option has everything the European option has, but in addition it provides the option of allowing exercise prior to expiration. Like any option, this added option cannot have a negative value. Therefore, the American option is never worth less than the comparable European option. Of course, the added optionality has positive value in some situations, so in those cases the American option would be worth more than the comparable European option.

AN OPTION'S TIME PREMIUM IS GENERALLY POSITIVE

This always holds for an out-of-the-money option because an option cannot have a negative value. (This is our Corollary to the Options Principle.) For an in-the-money American option, if the time premium were negative, a person could buy and immediately exercise the option for an arbitrage profit. Thus market competition naturally enforces a positive time premium. This generalization does not hold strictly, because in-the-money European options cannot be exercised during their life. It is therefore possible (although not at all common) to have a case where we know the asset's value is going down in the future, and the time premium becomes somewhat negative.

For example, consider a high-coupon bond that is currently selling above par value because of low interest rates. In the future, at maturity, the asset (bond) will be worth only its par value. In such a case, we know the asset's value is going down in the future. We illustrated this in Figure 5-6.

IT IS GENERALLY BETTER TO SELL THAN TO EXERCISE AN OPTION PRIOR TO ITS EXPIRATION

Although this follows directly from the previous generalization, it is a very important insight. Quite simply, if you exercise an option, you give up its time premium. If you exercise the option, you only get its exercise value. If you sell the option, you get the exercise value *plus* the time premium. (This generalization also breaks down in the unlikely case of a negative time premium.)

THE FURTHER AN OPTION IS OUT-OF-THE-MONEY, THE LESS IT IS WORTH

This principle follows directly from two previous observations. First, an out-of-the-money option is worth only its time premium because its exercise value is zero. Second, the time premium decreases as the option gets further out-of-the-money.

But remember our lottery ticket example. Even a very unlikely event *can* happen. Whenever one does, it can dramatically change things. When an option is far out-of-the-money, it is not worth very much and its existence seems insignificant. But if an unlikely event occurs and that option becomes in-the-money, the option's claim and value suddenly become very important. In the next chapter, we will show you how such things can happen with contingent stakeholder claims when a firm falls into financial distress.

Self-Check Questions

1. Which underlying asset value leads to the largest time premium?
2. What happens to an option's time premium as the option becomes more in-the-money? What about when it becomes more out-of-the-money?
3. Can an American option ever be worth less than a comparable European option? Explain.
4. Is it generally better to sell or to exercise an option prior to its expiration?

8.5 PLACES TO LOOK FOR OPTIONS

We have said that options exist in many forms. To help you develop insight into their pervasive existence, the following sections describe a number of places to look for options.

INSURANCE   As we noted earlier, in its simplest form, insurance is a put option. For complex insurance contracts, a put option is also the best starting point for understanding and valuing the insurance.

REAL ESTATE OPTIONS   Options have been used for many years in real estate. For example, consider a person trying to develop a new shopping mall. The development depends on many things, such as buying several pieces of real estate, obtaining financing, and gaining commitments from retailers to lease shops. The development can proceed only if *all* the parts come together. Rather than invest in each piece of land sequentially, the developer can purchase call options from the landowners with agreed-upon strike prices. Then, *if* everything comes together, the developer has claim to the land for a particular price. Without the call option, the later landowners could hold out for extraordinary prices. The last landowner could require a price of almost the total positive NPV of the project!

To see this point, suppose that, on the basis of estimates for purchasing all the pieces, the NPV of the project is $5 million at the start of the development. Also assume that everything has happened exactly according to plan—so far. Only one last piece of land, which was expected to cost $100,000, remains to be purchased. If the investment project *must* have this parcel of land to be completed, then the owner of the land can refuse to sell for the expected $100,000 price. How much will the developer be willing to pay?

The developer will be better off as long as the price for the land is less than the $5 million in positive NPV. That, of course, is considerably more than what the land was worth before the project was this far along. Now, however, if the landowner sets a price of $4 million for the land, the developer will be $1 million ahead even after paying the "inflated" price. A call option can keep the developer from being caught in the position of having to give up a substantial portion of the value created—positive NPV of the project—to a holdout.

CONVERTIBLES   Convertible bonds and convertible preferred stock can be converted into shares of common stock at the securityholder's option. Such securities can be viewed as combinations of other securities. For example, a convertible bond can be seen as a "straight" corporate bond *plus* a call option on shares of the firm's common stock.

WARRANTS   A **warrant** is a long-term call option on a stock. Warrants generally have very long lives when they are issued, such as ten years or longer. They are issued by a firm on its own stock. Warrants differ from many other call options in that if they are exercised, the firm typically issues new shares of stock so that it actually creates new equity. Often, new warrants are issued together with new "straight" bonds. In effect, the package is like a convertible bond, except that the two parts are independent and can be bought and sold separately. Sometimes warrants are referred to as "sweeteners" that are added to the bond to make it more attractive to buy.[4]

CALL PROVISIONS   Many corporate bonds include a call provision that allows the *firm* to redeem the bond for a preset amount prior to maturity. A call provision is a call option. As with any option, it increases the firm's flexibility. More specifically, if interest rates decline, it

---

[4] It seems to us that the "sweetener" concept must have to do with a psychological marketing notion, like a rebate for buying a car. The rebate is simply a cut in the purchase price. Likewise, rather than adding the warrants, the issuer could have offered the bonds for a lower price—lower by the value of the warrants!

allows the firm to save money: The firm can replace its high-interest-rate loan with a new lower-interest-rate loan. In simple terms, this call option is a formal contract provision that says the firm can pay off the money it owes sooner than was originally expected. (As we said in Chapter 5, it may seem odd to have to be "allowed" to pay back the money you owe, but there it is!) Therefore, even the typical corporate bond is not a simple security. It is a combination of even more basic securities. The bondholder owns the asset (a "straight" bond) but also has written a call option on that asset. The firm is on the "other side of the transaction." It has sold the bond but has also purchased a call option.

EXAMPLE

The Option in Gibson Greetings's Treasury-Linked Swap

In April 1994, Gibson Greetings, Inc. announced that it had lost approximately $20 million on a series of "swap" transactions with a major bank.[5] One of them was a "Treasury-linked swap."

At the end of eight months, Gibson was to pay the bank $30 million in principal plus interest on that amount. Interest was to be charged at a well-known and regularly published variable market rate called LIBOR.[6] The "swap" (exchange) called for the bank to pay Gibson interest on $30 million at LIBOR *plus* 2%. (For example, if LIBOR turned out to be 8%, the bank would pay 10%). In addition, the bank was to pay a principal amount equal to the smaller of either (1) $30.6 million or (2) a contingent amount P determined by a complex formula. P depended on future yields on 2-year Treasury notes and 30-year Treasury bonds. The higher the yields, the lower P would be.[7]

Figure 8-11 shows the bank's savings on the principal amount (payoff) on the swap in terms of Treasury yields. The Treasury-linked swap contained an option. Compare Figures 8–6 and 8–11. In effect, Gibson had sold the bank a put option in exchange for the extra 2% interest. (The bank was paying Gibson 2% above LIBOR, whereas Gibson was paying the bank LIBOR.)

FIGURE 8-11
The bank's payoff on the Treasury-linked swap.

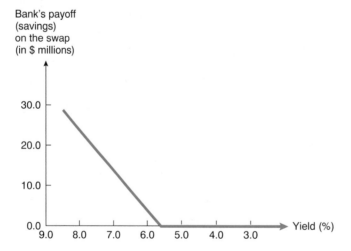

---

[5] The swaps are described in Overdahl and Schachter (1995).
[6] London Interbank Offer Rate.
[7] However, in the formula for P, the input variable representing the 30-year yield was the market *price* of the 30-year Treasury bond. This increased the complexity of the formula and apparently caused Gibson to misunderstand the deal. Problem C5 at the end of the chapter gives the formula for P.

Unfortunately for Gibson, Treasury yields rose during the spring and summer of 1994. As they did, the contingent amount P fell farther and farther below the $30.6 million. This resulted in a large loss for Gibson. The bank, being on the other side of the transaction, did quite well, thank you, realizing an equally large gain. ■

PUBLICLY TRADED OPTIONS   In addition to the Chicago Board Options Exchange, standardized puts and calls are also traded on the American and Philadelphia Stock Exchanges, among others. Warrants are also sometimes traded on the stock exchanges. Other publicly traded options, such as stock index options, interest rate options, commodity options, and currency options are listed in the "Money & Investing" section (Section C) of the *Wall Street Journal*.

"Hidden" Options

As we have noted before, the importance of options extends well beyond those cases where they can be easily identified. Many assets contain implicit, or "hidden," options. Whenever a claim is contingent on particular outcomes, there is probably a hidden option involved. For example, being able to claim a tax loss on an asset requires that you sell the asset for a loss. Thus the "option" to claim the tax loss is contingent on having incurred the loss. Hidden options dramatically complicate the valuation process. This may seem an obvious statement because the option is hidden. However, even in cases that are known to contain an option, identifying it can pose a significant analytical puzzle. The difficulties are dramatically illustrated in the Gibson Greetings example.

Common Stock as an Option

In our overview of the Options Principle, we pointed out that **limited liability** creates the option to default and not repay a debt fully. When a debt contract is created, it is as though the debtholders have written the stockholders a sequence of European call options on the firm. Each required debt payment represents a strike price. Whenever *any* payment is due (interest or principal), the shareholders must in effect decide whether they should "exercise" their call option.[8] If the firm is worth more than the payment that is due, the shareholders will exercise their option and "buy back" the firm from the debtholders by making the required payment. If the firm is ever worth less than the strike price (the required payment), the stockholders will simply refuse to exercise their call option, and the debtholders will "keep" the firm. Therefore, when a firm has one or more debts, it is as though the shareholders have a call option on the firm.

We said earlier in our discussion of the concept of put-call parity that we would try to use the description that is easiest to grasp in the situation. Here is a case where it might be easier to see this idea from the alternative viewpoint, so let's look at the optionality in this situation by trying on our "put option glasses."

The stockholders' option can also be viewed as a put option with a strike price of $0. If the stockholders do not want to make the required debt payment, they can "sell" the firm's assets to the debtholders for $0—and the debtholders have no choice but to accept the "sale." You might say the stockholders are "putting" it to the debtholders!

Although common stock can be described *exactly* as an option only under certain restrictive conditions, it is a very good approximation. More important, it can provide key insights into a situation. For example, we will show you in the next chapter how the stock-as-

---

[8] Of course, the smaller the required payment, the less likely it is that the assets will not be worth the "strike price." So default is much more likely when a large payment is due, such as when a $200 million loan comes due.

an-option view provides insights into stakeholder relationships and into the practical management of a firm.

It is interesting to note that the hidden default option adds further to the complexity of the typical corporate bond. We pointed out that many corporate bonds include a call provision. Now you can see that they also include a hidden default option. Thus not only is the typical corporate bond not a simple security, but determining the makeup of its exact value is also much more complex than it appeared to be in Chapter 5.

Other "Hidden" Options

There are many other situations that contain hidden or implicit options that are not obvious. Here are a few.

STAKEHOLDER RELATIONSHIPS IN FINANCIAL CONTRACTING   In the next chapter, we will use our generalizations about option valuation to study the contingent claims that the firm's various stakeholders—such as the employees, stockholders, bondholders, and customers—have on the firm's assets and on each other.

REFUNDING A HOME MORTGAGE   When a mortgage on a home permits prepayment of the loan (mortgage), the borrower can refinance the home loan at a lower interest rate if interest rates go down. In effect, the right to refinance the loan involves a hidden call option; the homeowner can take out a new (lower-interest) loan and use the proceeds to prepay the original high-interest loan. The option to prepay the home mortgage loan is analogous to the call provision we noted on a corporate bond. Some banks charge the customer extra for prepaying a home mortgage. This additional charge can be viewed as the price for the hidden call option of prepayment. Of course, the larger such a charge is, the larger the interest savings would have to be to make refinancing attractive.

TAX-TIMING OPTIONS   Tax laws include many contingencies. Some of them create valuable options. For example, one of them involves capital gains. Suppose a taxpayer purchased two stocks last year. Since then, one has increased and the other has decreased in value. Thus our taxpayer has earned "income" on one and lost "income" on the other. If this were regular income, the taxpayer would pay taxes on the gain and save taxes on the loss. But because this income is subject to the capital gains tax rules, the taxes apply only when the taxpayer sells the stock, which is his "option." The taxpayer can use this option to his advantage: Keep the first stock, thereby continuing to postpone the tax liability, and sell the second stock, thereby claiming the tax savings on the loss right away.

OPTIONS CONNECTED WITH CAPITAL INVESTMENTS   In Chapter 13, we will discuss options the firm has in connection with its capital investment projects. Such options include product price setting and postponing, expanding, or abandoning an investment project.

VARIABLE REDUCTION IN COSTS   In Chapter 10, we will talk about operating leverage, which is how much a firm spends on fixed costs versus how much it spends on variable costs. Firms sometimes have choices about these proportions. For example, firms have increased their use of robotic equipment in manufacturing as technology has advanced. Overall, firms determined that the robotic equipment would produce the product more cheaply. However, compared to human labor, robotic equipment has a higher fixed cost (it is more costly to buy) and lower variable costs (it is cheaper to use). Consider what happens if production is temporarily suspended. Variable costs are no longer incurred then, but fixed costs must still be paid. Under these conditions, the firm would have had the option of reducing its costs more if it had not invested in robotic equipment. Thus, a production process with relatively more variable costs and less fixed cost provides a hidden option to reduce total cost should production ever have to be suspended temporarily.

Self-Check Questions

1. What is the relationship between a convertible bond and a straight bond?
2. What is a warrant? How are warrants used as "sweeteners" in bond financing?
3. Why is a bond's call provision valuable to the firm that issued the bonds?
4. How can the common stock of a firm be described as an option on the firm's assets?
5. What type of option does the right to prepay a home mortgage involve?

8.6 A SIMPLE MODEL OF OPTION VALUATION

Determining the exact value of an option can be difficult. There are firms that sell complex mathematical models for valuing options. Unfortunately, then, we are not going to be able to make you a wiz at valuing options in the space available here. We will, however, illustrate the basic relationships by using a simplified valuation method. This model determines the value of an option by computing the present value of the option's expected outcomes. The model has four steps:

1. Compute the probabilities of possible price changes on the basis of what an investor can earn on the riskless asset.
2. Calculate the possible exercise values at expiration.
3. Determine the expected outcome as the probability-weighted average of the outcomes.
4. Compute the present value of the expected outcome by discounting at the riskless return.

The Value of Carl's Call Option

EXAMPLE

Let's take a final look at Carl's call option on Alice's land. Suppose that Alice's land can have only one of two possible values next year: $120,000 or $94,138. In other words, the land can go up 20% or down 5.862% in value, from its current $100,000 price. There are no other possibilities. Also assume that the riskless return is 5% per year. What is Carl's call option worth?

Our first step is to compute the probabilities of the two possible outcomes if the return on the land must equal the riskless return of 5%. Recall that the probabilities of all possible outcomes have to sum to 1.0. Because there are only two possible outcomes, the probability of a decrease is 1 minus the probability of an increase. Thus

$$5\% = (\text{probability of an increase})(+20\%) + (1 - \text{probability of an increase})(-5.862\%)$$

Solving for the probability of an increase, we get 0.42, or 42%. The probability of a decrease is 1 minus this, so it is 0.58, or 58%.

We now move on to the second step, which is to compute the call option's possible exercise values at expiration. Recall that

$$\text{Exercise value of Carl's call option} = \max[(\text{market value} - 110,000); 0]$$

Because the land has only two possible values, Carl's call option can have only two possible exercise values as well. These are 0 and $10,000. (With the decrease, the out-of-the-money option has an exercise value of 0. With the increase, the exercise value is $120,000 − $110,000.)

Armed with the probabilities and exercise values, we can compute the expected value of Carl's outcome. It is simply the outcomes times their probabilities, or

$$(0.42)(10,000) + (0.58)(0) = \$4200$$

Finally, the value of Carl's call option is the present value of the expected value of his outcome, or

$$(4200)/(1.05) = \$4000$$

Under these conditions, then, Carl's call option is worth $4000. ■

Self-Check Questions
1. Why is it difficult to determine the exact value of an option?
2. What are the four steps in the simple option valuation model described in this section?

8.7 COMBINING OPTION VALUES

Another important issue is how option values combine. For traded options, this is straightforward: The value of owning multiple options is simply the sum of the values of the individual options. But it is not always this simple.

In some cases, exercising one option can affect the value of another option. This is more likely when the options exist on the same asset. Such complex situations arise most often in connection with "hidden" options. This is because hidden options often do not require an incremental payment to create them. They occur naturally. Frequently, outside forces create them. In the case of the default option, it exists because of the bankruptcy laws.

Overlapping "Hidden" Options

Here is another useful generalization: *The value of two or more hidden options may be less than the sum of their individual option values.* This often occurs when the options provide "coverage" for some of the same outcomes.

Think about buying car insurance. Suppose you buy car insurance and then have an accident. Your "put option" (insurance) contract will require the insurance company to reimburse you for most, but not all, of your loss. Now consider buying car insurance from two different firms on the same car at the same time. If you did this and then had an accident, you could be reimbursed for all of your loss. However, you would not get more than your total loss. The firms would split the repair bill. Although you might be reimbursed more with two insurance policies than you would with one, the incremental cost for the second policy does not add enough value to be worth it. In short, if you are covered by one policy, the second policy does not add very much.

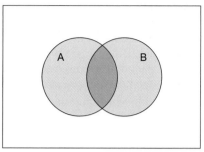

FIGURE 8-12
A Venn diagram of outcomes for choices of price and production quantity.

Consider two hidden options a firm has in connection with the manufacture and sale of a product: the option to set the selling price and the option to choose the quantity produced. These options exist without action on the firm's part. They cannot be separated from the ownership of the underlying asset, the manufacturing process.

The Price-Setting and Production-Quantity Options

EXAMPLE

Figure 8–12 is a Venn diagram of outcomes for choices of price and production quantity. The circle marked A contains the "in-the-money outcomes" for the price-setting option. That is, the circle includes the price choices where the firm would make more money than it does now. (This can be a higher price if demand has been exceeding production, or it can be a lower price, with more sold, if inventory has been accumulating.) The price-setting option is out-of-the-money for all other price choices, and its value is $12,000. The choices in the circle marked A, and option value, are based on the quantity the firm is currently producing.

Of course, the firm can choose a different production quantity. The circle marked B in Figure 8-12 contains the "in-the-money outcomes" for the production-quantity option. That is, circle B includes the production-quantity choices where the firm would make more money a than it does now. (This can be a larger quantity if demand has been exceeding production, or it can be a smaller quantity if inventory has been accumulating.) The production-quantity option is out-of-the-money for all other quantity choices, and its value is $10,000. Once again, these choices and values are based on current conditions, which in this case include the price the firm is now charging.

Now look again at Figure 8-12. Given that the firm already has the price-setting option, what additional value does the production-quantity option offer? The price-setting option "covers" the firm for all the outcomes in circle A, and the production-quantity option covers it for all the outcomes in circle B. Because the firm owns the price-setting option, however, the production-quantity option adds coverage *only* for those outcomes that are not also in circle A. In other words, the intersection of circles A and B is redundant as long as the firm has either one of the options. If the firm is not selling all that it is producing, it can *either* lower its price *or* reduce the quantity it is producing. And even if it couldn't do one of these, the other could take care of the problem.

Suppose the value of the overlap of the option coverage of outcomes is $6000. In this case, the combined value of the price-setting and production-quantity options, $V(A + B)$, is the sum of the values of the individual options, $V(A) + V(B) = \$22,000 (= 12,000 + 10,000)$, minus the value of the intersection, $V(A \cap B) = \$6000$. That is,

$$V(A + B) = V(A) + V(B) - V(A \cap B) = 22,000 - 6000 = \$16,000$$

Thus the value of having these two options is not equal to the sum of the separate values of the individual options. This lack of simple additivity is typically the case with overlapping options. ■

A similar situation can occur when exercising one option affects the value of another option. The simplest case is where exercising one option eliminates another. Suppose a firm has an investment opportunity to build a new plant with a positive NPV. Then, just before it starts to build, an alternative site becomes available. Building the plant on the newly discovered, alternative spot is also a positive-NPV investment opportunity. In effect, the firm now has two options. But if the firm exercises one of the options, the other will become worthless. You may recognize this situation as an option view of an *opportunity cost*: Taking one action eliminates the possibility of taking other desirable actions. Although they can be difficult to determine accurately, such costs can be very significant. Therefore, it is important to include the lost value of options that are eliminated by exercising another option.

A Portfolio of Options

Consider two ways of holding options on a set of assets. You could buy an option on each asset individually, or you could buy a single option on the whole set of assets. In the first case, you would have a portfolio of options. In the second case, you would have a single option on a portfolio of assets. Would one way of holding options always be more valuable than the other? We just demonstrated that sometimes an option does not add its entire stand-alone value. Still, we have told you options are valuable, so an additional option never decreases your wealth.

The effects of diversification can help us understand the relative values of the two alternatives. An option is a claim on the good outcomes without the obligation to take the bad. Therefore, an option on each asset enables you to claim every good outcome, and avoid every bad outcome, among all the assets. In a portfolio of assets, good and bad outcomes are netted out. (This is, after all, the basis for saying that diversification is beneficial.) Thus a single option on the portfolio allows you to claim only the *net* of all the outcomes if that net is good and to avoid claiming it if it is bad.

We have discovered another important generalization about options: *The value of an option on a portfolio of assets is always less than or equal to the value of a portfolio of comparable options on the individual assets.*

EXAMPLE

A Portfolio of Options

Suppose you can invest in two different assets using call options. Each asset can have a future value of $400, $600, or $800. You can have either a single call option on a portfolio of the two assets, with a strike price of $1000, or two separate call options, one on each asset, each with a strike price of $500. Which is worth more?

Table 8-2 shows the values of the assets, options, and combinations for each of the possible outcomes. As you can see, the portfolio of two separate options has a higher value in four of the nine possible outcomes, and it has the same value as the single option on the portfolio of assets for all the other outcomes.

The portfolio of options, then, is worth more than the single option on the portfolio of assets. ■

TABLE 8-2
The value of a portfolio of options (O_1 and O_2) versus the value of a single option on a portfolio of assets (O_p).

ASSET$_1$	O_1	ASSET$_2$	O_2	PORTFOLIO	O_p	$O_1 + O_2$	$(O_1 + O_2) - O_p$
400	0	400	0	800	0	0	0
400	0	600	100	1000	0	100	100
400	0	800	300	1200	200	300	100
600	100	400	0	1000	0	100	100
600	100	600	100	1200	200	200	0
600	100	800	300	1400	400	400	0
800	300	400	0	1200	200	300	100
800	300	600	100	1400	400	400	0
800	300	800	300	1600	600	600	0

Self-Check Questions
1. Can the value of two options ever be less than the sum of their separate option values?
2. Why is it that a firm's price-setting option may not add its entire stand-alone value when it is considered in addition to the firm's production-quantity option?
3. What is the relationship between the value of an option on a portfolio of assets and the value of a portfolio of comparable options on the individual assets?

SUMMARY

An option is the right to do something without the obligation to do it. An option is often referred to as a contingent claim because its use depends on the occurrence of some event. When an option is exercised, it creates a discontinuity in the outcome of returns. In fact, an option can be viewed as a claim on a portion of an asset's return distribution. It gives its owner the ability to claim good outcomes and avoid bad ones.

An option is valuable because it gives the optionholder control of specific situations. It takes real precision to determine the *exact* value of an option. We set much of that precision aside for now. Instead, we established several useful generalizations about options. We will use these throughout the rest of the book.

"Hidden" options can significantly affect the value of an asset. Such options can be especially important because they are not always included in other valuation models. The accurate inclusion of option values can be tricky when there are multiple options, especially when their values are interdependent. We will use the concepts established in this chapter to help understand the capital budgeting process discussed in Part III.

Because of "hidden" options, many contractual relationships are much more complicated than they seem at first. By recognizing the "optionality" in a situation from a financial perspective, we can gain significant insight into explicit and implicit contractual relationships. These insights will help us examine the nature of financial contracts in the next chapter. Together, options and financial contracting constitute a very important perspective from which we will analyze business situations in the rest of the book.

DECISION SUMMARY

- An option's value is the sum of its exercise value and its time premium.
- An option's exercise value is the difference between the underlying asset's market value and the strike price for in-the-money options. It is zero for out-of-the-money options.
- An option's time premium (1) increases with the option's time until expiration, (2) increases with the risk of the underlying asset, and (3) decreases with the option's depth in- or out-of-the-money (how far the underlying asset's value is from the strike price). A call (put) option's time premium (4) increases (decreases) with the market riskless return.
- It is generally better to sell, rather than exercise, an option prior to expiration, because an option's value includes both the exercise value and a time premium. Exercising an option eliminates its time premium.

- The value of a put option is a mirror image of the value of a call option.
- The "optionality" in a situation can always be described either in terms of a put option *or* in terms of a call option. This relationship is referred to as put-call parity.
- Stock can be viewed as an option on the firm. Stockholders have the right to "sell" the firm to the debtholders for a strike price of $0.
- The value of two or more "hidden" options may be less than the sum of the values of the individual options.
- The value of a portfolio of options is greater than or equal to the value of a comparable single option on a portfolio of the assets.

KEY TERMS

option...242
call option...242
put option...242
underlying asset...242
strike price...242
exercise...242
in-the-money...242

out-of-the-money...242
exercise value...242
expiration...242
American option...242
European option...242
contingent claim...243

min function...244
max function...244
put-call parity...249
time premium of an option...250
warrant...255
limited liability...257

EXERCISES

PROBLEM SET A

A1. Define the terms *option*, *call option*, and *put option*.

A2. Define the terms *strike price*, *exercise value*, *in-the-money*, and *out-of-the-money*.

A3. Cite three situations that involve "hidden" options.

A4. In your own words, explain how limited liability makes shares of common stock like an option.

A5. Explain how auto insurance can be viewed as a put option.

A6. Why would an American call option traded in an efficient capital market never be worth less than its exercise value?

PROBLEM SET B

B1. Tom Smith purchased a building in uptown Indianapolis for $50,000. Right after this, he sold a one-year European call option on the building, with a strike price of $54,000, for $2200 to Sarah Smyth. What are Tom's and Sarah's outcomes, in terms of the land's possible value when the option expires?

B2. The value of an option includes (a) its exercise value and (b) its time premium. Name the parameters that determine each of these two parts, and explain how each parameter affects the option's value.

B3. Jenny Johnson purchased a building in New York's lower east side for $1.5 million. Right after this, she bought a 1-year European put option on the building, with a strike price of $1.6 million, for $350,000 from Jimmy Johnsen. What are Jenny's and Jimmy's outcomes, in terms of the land's possible value, when the option expires?

B4. Why does the maximum time premium for an option occur when the underlying asset's value equals the strike price? Why does the time premium decrease as the option becomes more in- or out-of-the-money?

B5. Why is the time premium for an American option never negative?

B6. Explain how shares of stock can be viewed as a put option on the firm's assets.

B7. Why is it generally better to sell rather than exercise an American option?

B8. Explain how shares of stock can be viewed as a series of European call options on the firm's assets.

B9. What is the relationship between the value of an American option and the value of a comparable European option? For example, is it always greater or less, or does the relationship depend on some parameter? Explain why this relationship exists.

B10. Consider the following statement: "A call option is a great way to make money. If the asset goes up in value, you get the increase, but if the asset goes down in value, you do not exercise the option and don't lose any money. Therefore, everyone should invest in call options." Is this statement true, false, or partly true and partly false? Explain.

B11. Suppose you can buy a call option on a business that is currently worth $10,000,000 but will be worth either 25% more or 15% less 1 year from today. The option's strike price is $11,000,000, and the riskless return is 6% per year. What is this call option worth today?

B12. We pointed out that common stock in a firm that has some debt can be viewed as a call option. Can common stock in a firm that has no debt also be viewed as a call option? If so, explain how. If not, explain why.

B13. Explain why an option on a portfolio of assets is never worth more than a portfolio of comparable options on the individual assets.

B14. Suppose you can buy a call option on a parcel of land that is currently worth $200,000 but will be worth either 15% more or 8% less 1 year from today. The option's strike price is $215,000, and the riskless return is 7% per year. What is this call option worth today?

PROBLEM SET C

C1. A particular type of bond that has actually been issued from time to time allows for the bond to be redeemed, at the option of the bondholder, at either of two future points in time. Suppose such a bond can be redeemed for its face value after either 10 or 20 years. That is, at the 10-year point, the bondholder makes a one-time decision to redeem or not. Clearly there is an option in this contract. Describe this complex bond in terms of one or more (a) option contracts and (b) bonds that are otherwise identical but do not have the two-points-of-redemption option.

C2. Why is an American put option necessarily worth more than a comparable European put option when both options are certain to be in-the-money during the entire remaining time until maturity?

C3. An investor is considering investing $5 million to acquire a thrift institution that currently has $1 billion of assets and zero net worth on its balance sheet. The thrift's liabilities consist principally of federally insured deposits. Its assets are principally real estate loans, which were recently written down to their supposed "fair market value" by the thrift's regulators to enhance the thrift's salability. What does option theory tell you about how the investor should view the prospective $5 million investment?

C4. Suppose you live in a state that has a usury law prohibiting interest charges above 9% APR. Current market interest rates are 18% APY for a project for which you have the opportunity to provide 6-year debt financing. Show how you can use option contracts on an asset that is connected with the project to provide it with a 6-year "loan" of $250,000, from which you will earn the market rate 18% APY with interest payments of $45,000 per year and a principal repayment of $250,000 at the end of 6 years.

C5. The Gibson Greetings example referred to a contingent amount P. The formula for P was

$$P = \left[1 - \frac{\dfrac{103(2\text{-year yield})}{0.0488} - 30\text{-year T price}}{100} \right][\$30 \text{ million}]$$

where 2-year yield is the yield to maturity (YTM) on a 2-year Treasury note (expressed in decimal form), and 30-year T price is the market price of a 30-year Treasury bond (expressed as a percentage of face amount). Assume that (1) the 30-year Treasury bond has a coupon rate of 7%,

(2) there is a flat term structure so that the 2-year *yield* and the 30-year *yield* are always equal (they vary together), and (3) bonds make semiannual coupon payments.

  a. Calculate the 30-year T price, assuming its yield is 6%.

  b. Calculate *P*, assuming yields are 6%.

  c. Calculate the bank's principal obligation when the yield is 6%.

  d. Calculate the bank's principal obligation when the yield is 8%.

  e. Why does the bank's principal obligation decrease when yields increase?

  f. Explain why this swap can be described as a put option.

Real-World Application:
McDonald's Corporation's Executive Stock Options

An April 17, 1996 article in the *Wall Street Journal* remarked that the professional managers of the McDonald's Corporation had recently digested the stock market equivalent of a "happy meal."[1] In a two-month period, they had exercised options on 490,119 shares and sold 470,119 of them. For example, McDonald's chairman exercised and sold 135,000 shares, worth about $6.9 million, on January 30, 1996. The profit represented nearly seven times his annual base salary.

    According to McDonald's 1994 shareholder proxy, its board of directors believes the stock option program is "the best vehicle by which to link employees' interests with those of shareholders."[2] The stock option program covers more than 22,000 employees. The number of options each employee is given depends on the individual's responsibilities and the "potential for influencing the firm's future results." The highest-level managers receive the greatest numbers of options.

    The following table provides information from the 1994 proxy concerning compensation and stock options for McDonald's five highest-paid executives.[3]

MANAGER	SALARY, BONUS, AND OTHER 1994 COMPENSATION	OPTIONS GRANTED IN 1994	PERCENTAGE OF OPTIONS FIRM GRANTED	EXERCISE PRICE	EXPIRATION
Chairman & CEO	$2,115,930	350,000	2.6%	$30	10 years
President-USA	1,325,893	176,000	1.3	30	10 years
President-International	1,307,319	176,500	1.3	30	10 years
Vice Chairman & CFO	1,263,290	176,000	1.3	30	10 years
Senior Executive VP	855,273	72,600	0.5	30	10 years

1. Calculate the option value for each manager at the end of 10 years assuming McDonald's share price grows at a 5% APY for 10 years.

2. Calculate the option value for each manager at the end of 10 years assuming McDonald's share price grows at a 10% APY for 10 years.

3. What is the present value of each manager's option if the required return is 7.35% APY?

4. a. What percentage of each manager's total 1994 compensation would the options provide under the assumption that McDonald's share price grows at a 5% APY for 10 years?

    b. What percentage of each manager's total 1994 compensation would the options provide under the assumption that McDonald's share price grows at a 10% APY for 10 years?

---

[1]"McDonald's Executives Feast on Options, Sell Shares Amid Recent 52-Week High," *Wall Street Journal* (April 17, 1996), p. C1.
[2]McDonald's Corporation, *Proxy Statement* (May 26, 1995), p. 11.
[3]*Ibid.*, p. 15.

5. What are the options worth if McDonald's share price does not exceed $30 when the options are exercisable?

6. Why would you expect McDonald's stock option program to link the firm's professional managers' financial interests with those of the firm's shareholders?

7. McDonald's 1994 proxy noted that McDonald's stockholders' equity would increase by $13.2 billion over 10 years if its share price grows at 5% APY and would increase by $33.5 billion over 10 years if its share price grows at 10% APY.

   a. How much of the increase in stockholders' equity would each manager realize assuming a 5% compound growth rate?

   b. How much of the increase in stockholders' equity would each manager realize assuming a 10% compound growth rate?

8. Do you think the option payoffs would give the professional managers a "fair share" of the increase in shareholder value?

BIBLIOGRAPHY

Adams, Paul D., Steve B. Wyatt, and Yong H. Kim. "A Contingent Claims Analysis of Trade Credit," *Financial Management*, 1992, 21(3):95–103.

Biger, Nahum, and John Hull. "The Valuation of Currency Options," *Financial Management*, 1983, 12(1):24-28.

Black, Fischer. "Fact and Fantasy in the Use of Options and Corporate Liabilities," *Financial Analysts Journal,* 1975, 31(July-August):36–41:61–72.

Black, Fischer, and Myron Scholes. "The Pricing of Options and Corporate Liabilities," *Journal of Political Economy*, 1973, 81(May/June):637–654.

Block, Stanley B., and Timothy J. Gallagher. "The Use of Interest Rate Futures and Options by Corporate Financial Managers," *Financial Management*, 1986, 15(3):73–78.

Bodnar, Gordon, Greg Hayt, Richard Marston, and Charles Smithson. "Wharton Survey of Derivatives Usage by U.S. Non-Financial Firms," *Financial Management*, 1995, 24(2):104–114.

Brown, Keith C., and Scott L. Lummer. "A Reexamination of the Covered Call Option Strategy for Corporate Cash Management," *Financial Management*, 1986, 15(2):13–17.

Carr, Peter. "The Valuation of Sequential Exchange Opportunities," *Journal of Finance,* 1988, 43(5):1235–1256.

Carter, Richard B. and Frederick H. Dark. "The Use of the Over-Allotment Option in Initial Public Offerings of Equity: Risks and Underwriter Prestige," *Financial Management*, 1990, 19(3):55–64.

Chatfield, Robert E., and R. Charles Moyer. "'Putting' Away Bond Risk: An Empirical Examination of the Value of the Put Option on Bonds," *Financial Management*, 1986, 15(2):26–33.

Chung, Kee H., and Charlie Charoenwong. "Investment Options, Assets in Place, and the Risk of Stocks," *Financial Management*, 1991, 20(3):21–33.

Cook, Douglas O., and John C. Easterwood. "Poison Put Bonds: An Analysis of Their Economic Role," *Journal of Finance,* 1994, 49(5):1905–1920,

De, Sankar, and Jayant R. Kale. "Contingent Payments and Debt Contracts," *Financial Management*, 1993, 22(2):106–122.

Dufey, Gunter, and S. L. Srinivasulu. "The Case for Corporate Management of Foreign Exchange Risk," *Financial Management*, 1983, 12(4):54–62.

Eckbo, B. Espen, and Ronald W. Masulis. "Adverse Selection and the Rights Offer Paradox," *Journal of Financial Economics,* 1992, 32(3):293–332.

Emery, Douglas R., and Adam K. Gehr, Jr. "Tax Options, Capital Structure, and Miller Equilibrium: A Numerical Illustration," *Financial Management*, 1988, 17(2):30–40.

Fleming, Jeff, and Robert E. Whaley. "The Value of Wildcard Options," *Journal of Finance,* 1994, 49(1):215–236.

Flood, Eugene, Jr., and Donald R. Lessard. "On the Measurement of Operating Exposure to Exchange Rates: A Conceptual Approach," *Financial Management*, 1986, 15(1):25–36.

Galai, Dan, and Ronald W. Masulis. "The Option Pricing Model and the Risk Factor of Stock," *Journal of Financial Economics*, 1976 3(1/2):53–81.

Grenadier, Steven R. "Valuing Lease Contracts: A Real-Options Approach," *Journal of Financial Economics*, 1995, 38(3):297–332.

Grundy, Bruce D. "Option Prices and the Underlying Asset's Return Distribution," *Journal of Finance,* 1991, 46(3):1045–1070.

Hansen, Robert S., Beverly R. Fuller, and Vahan Janjigian. "The Over-Allotment Option and Equity Financing Flotation Costs: An Empirical Investigation," *Financial Management*, 1987, 16(2):24–32.

Jacob, David P., Graham Lord, and James A. Tilley. "A Generalized Framework for Pricing Contingent Cash Flows," *Financial Management*, 1987, 16(3):5–14.

Jameson, Mel, and William Wilhelm. "Market Making in the Options Markets and the Costs of Discrete Hedge Rebalancing," *Journal of Finance*, 1992, 47(2):765–780.

Kalotay, Andrew, and Bruce Tuckman. "Sinking Fund Prepurchases on the Designation Option," *Financial Management*, 1992, 21(4):110–118.

Kemna, Angelien G. Z. "Case Studies on Real Options," *Financial Management*, 1993, 22(3):259–270.

Kim, In Joon, Krishna Ramaswamy, and Suresh Sundaresan. "Does Default Risk in Coupons Affect the Valuation of Corporate Bonds? A Contingent Claims Model," *Financial Management*, 1993, 22(3):117–131.

Kulatilaka, Nalin. "The Value of Flexibility: The Case of a Dual-Fuel Industrial Steam Boiler," *Financial Management*, 1993, 22(3):271–280.

Laber, Gene. "Bond Covenants and Managerial Flexibility: Two Cases of Special Redemption Provisions," *Financial Management*, 1990, 19(1):82–89.

Laughton, David G., and Henry D. Jacoby. "Reversion, Timing Options, and Long-Term Decision-Making," *Financial Management*, 1993, 22(3):225–240.

Longstaff, Francis A. "Pricing Options with Extendible Maturities: Analysis and Applications," *Journal of Finance*, 1990, 45(3):935–958.

Mason, Scott P., and Robert C. Merton. "The Role of Contingent Claims Analysis in Corporate Finance." In *Recent Advances in Corporate Finance*, ed. Edward I. Altman and Marti G. Subrahmanyam. Homewood, Ill.: Irwin, 1985.

McLaughlin, Robyn, and Robert A. Taggart, Jr. "The Opportunity Cost of Using Excess Capacity," *Financial Management*, 1992, 21(2):12–23.

Merton, Robert C. "Theory of Rational Option Pricing," Bell *Journal of Economics and Management Science*, 1973, 4(Spring):141–183.

Mozes, Haim A. "An Upper Bound for the Firm's Cost of Employee Stock Options," *Financial Management*, 1995, 24(4):66–77.

Overdahl, James, and Barry Schachter. "Derivatives Regulation and Financial Management: Lessons from Gibson Greetings," *Financial Management*, 1995, 24(1):68–78.

Phillips, Aaron L. "1995 Derivatives Practices and Instruments Survey," *Financial Management*, 1995, 24(2):115–125.

Rendleman, Richard J., Jr., and Brit J. Bartter. "Two-State Option Pricing," *Journal of Finance*, 1979, 34(5):1093–1110.

Ritchken, Peter L. Sandarasubramanian, and Anand M. Vijh. "Averaging Options for Capping Total Costs," *Financial Management*, 1990, 19(3):35–41.

Smit, Han T. J., and L. A. Ankum. "A Real Options and Game-Theoretic Approach To Corporate Investment Strategy Under Competition," *Financial Management*, 1993, 22(3):241–250.

Sprenkle, Case. "Warrant Prices as Indications of Expectations," *Yale Economic Essays*, 1961, 1:179–232.

Sterk, William Edward. "Option Pricing: Dividends and the In- and Out-of-the-Money Bias," *Financial Management*, 1983, 12(4):47–53.

Triantis, Alexander J., and James E. Hodder. "Valuing Flexibility as a Complex Option," *Journal of Finance*, 1990, 45(2):549–566.

Trigeorgis, Lenos. "Real Options and Interactions with Financial Flexibility," *Financial Management*, 1993, 22(3):202–224.

Winton, Andrew. "Limitation of Liability and the Ownership Structure of the Firm," *Journal of Finance*, 1993, 48(2):487–512.

Woods, John C., and Maury R. Randall. "The Net Present Value of Future Investment Opportunities: Its Impact on Shareholder Wealth and Implications for Capital Budgeting Theory," *Financial Management*, 1989, 18(2):85–92.

Yermack, David. "Do Corporations Award CEO Stock Options Effectively?" *Journal of Financial Economics*, 1995, 39(2&3):237–270.

Zivney, Terry L., and Michael J. Alderson. "Hedged Dividend Capture with Stock Index Options," *Financial Management*, 1986, 15(2):5–12.

FINANCIAL CONTRACTING

The modern corporation is exceedingly complex. We touched on a little of that complexity in our fictionalized account of Henry Ford's car company in Chapter 1. A lot of the complexity occurs because in addition to all the explicit contractual relationships, there are so many implicit ones.

Financial contracting describes the business world in terms of *both* types of contracts, implicit and explicit. The purpose is to identify important practical considerations, such as the implicit aspects of the "stake," or contingent claim, that each stakeholder has in the firm. In this chapter, we will apply the options concepts developed in the previous chapter to determine the impact on firm value of the many contingencies we encounter.

The main question in financial contracting is how to minimize the costs of having someone else make decisions that affect you. This really refers to the cost of managing a situation in which you have a stake *through* other people. The answer lies in (1) creating incentives, constraints, and punishments; (2) having reasonable monitoring procedures; and (3) identifying and using contracts that minimize the *possibility* of conflicts of interest at the outset.

Costs associated with financial contracting occur throughout the corporate decision-making process, and they can be very significant. Therefore, these costs play an important role in many of the topics covered in the rest of the book.

OBJECTIVES

After studying this chapter, you should be able to

1. Understand the complexity of the modern corporation as a network of many implicit as well as explicit contractual relationships.

2. Identify the most significant implicit contractual relationships.

3. Understand how many situations can be described as though they were a principal-agent relationship.

4. Analyze situations in a principal-agent framework in terms of decision-making authority and control to identify the incentives for each side of a contract, and determine the impact of those incentives.

5. Identify areas of naturally occurring conflicts of interest where incentives diverge.

◆ *Self-Interested Behavior*: Look for the incentives that can bias an agent's decision making.

◆ *Incremental Benefits*: Measure the incentives on an incremental basis.

◆ *Signaling*: Interpret the information contained in the actions of others. Recognize the incentive value of building and maintaining a good reputation.

◆ *Options*: Include all of the contingencies and their impact on incentives and value.

◆ *Diversification*: Recognize that human capital, a person's unique capabilities and expertise, is extremely difficult to diversify.

◆ *Two-Sided Transactions*: Consider every situation from both the principal's and the agent's point of view.

◆ *Risk-Return Trade-Off*: Require a higher return from unique (as opposed to generic) assets because of their higher risk.

◆ *Valuable Ideas*: Beware of free riders who might illegally copy your valuable ideas.

9.1 PRINCIPAL-AGENT RELATIONSHIPS

The **set-of-contracts model** of the firm highlights the complexity of the modern corporation. The model was developed by using **agency theory**, which is the analysis of principal-agent relationships. Stakeholder claims on a firm can be described as principal-agent relationships, where an **agent** is acting on behalf of a **principal**.

Many situations involve a principal-agent relationship. Some of the more visible *explicit* principal-agent relationships are those that principals enter into with money managers, lawyers, and real estate, travel, and insurance agents. Many other situations can be described in the principal-agent framework *as though* the two parties were principal and agent, even though one party is not literally an agent for the other. In fact, virtually any situation wherein one person or group has decision-making authority that affects another can be described in terms of a principal-agent relationship. For example, even though most employees are not explicitly classified as agents for the employer, most act as agents at some point.

EXAMPLE

A Principal-Agent Conflict

Seldon C. Fish is the CEO of a large financial firm. While looking over the firm's financial reports, he found that the latest quarter was great. A large change in interest rates provided a windfall for the firm. Although the extra income was not caused by anything the firm did, Sel was of course delighted. However, he knew competition would not allow his firm to have the same big margins next year, so the extra income was only a one-time bit of luck.

Now the firm must decide what to do with the extra income. Sel will be making a recommendation on this matter to the firm's board of directors. He has narrowed it down to two possibilities: (1) extra-large employee bonuses as a reward for having such a successful year, or (2) a one-time "extra" cash dividend to the stockholders for getting lucky.

Suppose you are a stockholder (part owner) of this firm, but you are not also an employee. As a principal in this example, which alternative do you want Sel to recommend?

Now suppose you are an employee who gets part of the employee bonuses, but you are not also a stockholder. As an agent in this example, which alternative do you want Sel to recommend?

Finally, consider the CEO, Mr. Fish. He is both a stockholder (principal) and a bonus-earning employee (agent). How would he fare under each alternative? In other words, what are his incentives? Here are some additional facts to help you decide which alternative you think he might like. (1) The CEO will himself get 4% of this year's employee bonus money. (2) If paid, the extra dividend would be split equally among the 9 million shares of the firm's stock. Sel owns 27,000 of these shares, so he would get 0.3% of the extra dividend. If you consider only these one-time financial incentives, what do you think Sel Fish is likely to recommend?

You can see that the CEO's incentives in this example favor the extra-large employee bonuses. Regardless of how much the extra is, Sel Fish will get more of this one-time extra if it is paid out in employee bonuses (4% versus 0.3%). Note that for other bonus-earning employees who are stockholders, the employee bonus is also likely to be larger than their share of the dividend. Although they would get a smaller portion of the bonus, most own much less stock and would get less in dividends as well. Compared to other stockholders and employees, the CEO has a large stake. You might say he is a "big fish." ∎

A potential conflict between the interests of the agent and those of the principal creates an **agency problem**. Such conflicts can be as simple as the agent not putting forth "full effort." From the Principle of Self-Interested Behavior, we know that agents may be tempted to put their own self-interest ahead of those of the principal. As a result, an agent's decision making becomes suspect when the interests of agent and principal compete.

For example, is it okay for an employee traveling on behalf of the firm to enjoy a side-trip vacation along the way? Answering this question can be difficult or even impossible. On the one hand, if travel is necessary for the employee to do the job, what is wrong with the employee getting personal benefit from the trip? That is, if the employee benefits at no cost to the firm, why not allow the employee to take the side trip? The problem lies in making sure it is truly costless to the firm. It may be impossible to make sure the employee's travel decision was not influenced by the lure of a personal side benefit.

Agency problems occur because of asymmetric information. If the principal knew everything the agent knows, the agent would never be able to take actions that were not in the best interest of the principal. Thus if it were possible and not unreasonably costly for the principal to **monitor** the agent's actions perfectly, there would be no agency problems. Obviously, even if perfect monitoring were possible, it would be exorbitantly expensive. Most people would quickly conclude that "it's easier to do it myself." Therefore, contracts rarely have perfect monitoring, and the problem of **moral hazard** can arise. Moral hazard occurs whenever agents can take unobserved actions in their own interest to the detriment of the principal.

The amount of monitoring is important with respect to efficient resource allocation. The more monitoring there is, the harder it is for an agent to misbehave—but the extra monitoring costs money. And because not all agents will take self-interested actions at the principal's expense, spending too much on monitoring agent behavior is wasteful. For any specific situation, there is a trade-off between the resources spent on monitoring and the possibility of agent misbehavior.

Alternatives to monitoring include constraints, incentives, and punishments that encourage an agent to act in the principal's best interest. Managerial stock options and performance share plans are incentives designed for this purpose. Another common incentive is a sales commission.

If it were possible to create a contract that paid agents in perfect accord with the best interests of the principal, the need for monitoring would be eliminated. This is because when the agents acted in their own best financial interest, they would also be acting in the principal's best interest. But our world is not characterized by perfect accord or perfect information. Consequently, we need to search for better contracts, ones that minimize the *possibility* of conflicts of interest.

Self-Check Questions
1. What is a principal-agent relationship?
2. Why do principal-agent relationships give rise to agency problems?
3. How can monitoring reduce agency problems? Is there a cost involved?
4. What are some alternatives to monitoring an agent's behavior?

9.2 AGENCY COSTS

Monitoring, constraints, incentives, and punishments are designed to encourage agents to act in the principals' best interests, but they are costly. The costs of doing these things are called **agency costs**. Agency costs are the extra costs of having an agent act for a principal—those in excess of what it would cost the principals to "do it themselves." These costs are like friction in a machine—the more there is, the less efficient the machine, and the more energy that will be wasted.

Agency costs are defined in terms of the Principle of Incremental Benefits: The agency cost is the *incremental* cost of working *through* others, who serve as agents. In a perfect world, the agent would be paid exactly the fair amount without any waste. In our imperfect world, agency costs are a waste that is lost to the system.

Agency costs are of three types:

1. Direct contracting costs, which include
   a. The transaction costs of setting up the contract, such as the selling commissions and legal fees of issuing bonds.
   b. The opportunity costs imposed by constraints that preclude otherwise optimal decisions (for example, an inability to make a positive-NPV investment because of a restrictive bond covenant).
   c. The incentive fees, such as employee bonuses, paid to the agent to encourage behavior consistent with the principal's goals.
2. The costs to the principal of monitoring the agent (for example, auditing costs).
3. The loss of wealth the principal suffers as a result of misbehavior in spite of monitoring, such as unidentified excessive employee expense accounts.

A major goal is to find the contract that minimizes the relationship's total agency costs. The optimal contract transfers the decision-making authority in the most efficient way. It is the one that provides the smallest waste. Note that in some cases, the cost of periodic misbehavior is less than the cost of monitoring. In most cases, the optimal solution involves some attention to each of the three component costs.

In our search for better contracts, it is important to identify those situations wherein conflicts of interest arise naturally. In the following sections, we examine several important relationships and conditions that are prone to such conflicts. Of course, no set of contracts can cover all possible contingencies. Therefore, it is impossible to eliminate all potential for conflict. This is an especially good reason to keep the Principles of Self-Interested Behavior and Two-Sided Transactions in your mind as you interact in the business world.

Self-Check Questions

1. What are agency costs, and how do they arise?

2. What are the three types of agency costs? Give an example of each.

3. How can financial contracting deal with agency costs?

9.3 STOCKHOLDER–MANAGER CONFLICTS

The stockholder–manager relationship is created by separating ownership and control. In simple firms, the owners are the managers. In more complex firms, many stockholders have nothing to do with the daily operation of the firm. Still, in theory, the managers work for all the stockholders. If managers do not do a good job, the stockholders can fire them and hire new managers. But as you might guess, such a process is cumbersome and difficult to accomplish in practice.

Strictly speaking, the common stockholders of a publicly held corporation do not even own the firm; they own shares of common stock that entitle them to voting rights and certain other rights. Such corporations are operated by professional managers, who may or may not own shares themselves. The firm's board of directors hires the managers. Although the directors serve as the shareholders' elected representatives and have a legal responsibility to the shareholders, they are typically nominated for election by top management. You can see the problem right away. It seems almost circular if you ignore the obligation to the shareholders.

Managers, therefore, are the primary decision makers. They have considerable control over the firm and its assets. In some cases, managers have even been accused of using the firm's assets against the owners. Thus two important questions arise: Are the managers' interests different from the nonmanagement shareholders' interests? And if they are, whose interests are the managers really promoting?

How Stockholders' and Managers' Goals May Diverge

In accordance with the Principle of Self-Interested Behavior, the theory of finance holds that the goal of the stockholders is to maximize the present value of their investment.

Also on the basis of the Principle of Self-Interested Behavior, the theory of finance allows managers' goals to differ from the stockholders' goal of maximizing stockholder wealth. Managers are alleged to favor growth and large size for a variety of reasons. Managers appear to value salary, power, and status, all of which are positively correlated with the size of the firm. Larger size, it is argued, provides management with (1) greater job security and (2) larger compensation. Faster growth creates more opportunities for the internal promotion of lower- and middle-level managers. Growth also creates opportunities to distinguish oneself as a productive member of the organization, one who is worthy of promotion. Other potential managerial objectives include greater prestige and discretionary expense accounts.

A FEW WORDS ABOUT ETHICS

The goal of stockholder wealth maximization should be pursued subject to a fundamental restriction: Corporate managers should take only steps that are legal and ethically sound.

You may encounter situations in your career that tempt you to "play it close to the edge" or even cross over the line that separates ethical from unethical behavior in order to enhance your firm's—and your own—position. But modest transgressions tend to lead to more serious transgressions and eventually to serious legal difficulties.

Corporate history offers many examples of price fixing, insider trading, market manipulation, and similar activities that people undertook after convincing themselves that it was somehow in their firms' best interests to do so. We explicitly exclude such behavior when we talk about maximizing stockholder wealth.

We have also said that managers may act in their own self-interest at the stockholders' expense. These actions may sometimes not be illegal, or even explicitly prohibited, but they are not good for the corporation. Managers who abuse their positions set a bad example for everyone else. Still, as a practical matter, we must acknowledge that such behavior does exist.

For example, empirical evidence shows that administrative costs (including management benefits) tend to be lower when managers are monitored more closely. The most important benefit you can derive from this acknowledgement is probably an increase in awareness. And such awareness can help protect you from unethical behavior.

Differences in the goals of stockholders and managers lead to several specific points where goals can diverge, which we will discuss in the following section. In this relationship, the stockholders are the principals who are trying to get the managers to act in their best interest.

Employee Perquisites

One of the most obvious examples of moral hazard (the possibility of agent misbehavior) involves employee decisions that affect personal benefits, or **perquisites.** These include direct benefits, such as the use of a company car or expense account for personal business, and also indirect benefits such as excessively fancy office decorations. When excessive money is spent on such things, it is money lost to the stockholders.

Employee Effort

Some employees would like to get paid without having to put forth any effort. It has been said that 20% of the people do 80% of the work.[1] The problem of an agent putting forth less than full effort is referred to as **shirking**.

The Nondiversifiability of Human Capital

The unique capabilities and expertise of individuals are referred to as **human capital**. Typically, human capital is tied to employment, and employees devote most of their efforts to a single firm. Therefore, employees cannot easily diversify their human capital. They become specialists in the firm they serve and in the role they play. This creates a problem called the **nondiversifiability of human capital**.

---

[1] Shareholders would of course like to have only "20%-type" employees, in which case—conceptually—the shareholders would need only one-quarter as many employees: $x/100\% = 20\%/80\%$ implies that $x = 25\%$.

We know about the benefits of diversification from the Principle of Diversification. Still, even if a person wants to, it is extremely difficult to diversify human capital. Professionals, such as corporate managers, engineers, physicians, accountants, and lawyers, simply do not have the time to become proficient in several areas—and certainly not in a sufficient number to provide reasonable diversification. The nondiversifiability of human capital leads to yet other goal divergences between managers and stockholders.

CAPITAL INVESTMENT CHOICES   The stockholders of large, publicly traded firms typically hold many different stocks in their financial investment portfolio. Therefore, they are not overly concerned with random fluctuations in the value of one particular firm. This is because the random fluctuations in the many different stock values tend to cancel each other out. In marked contrast, managers can be "wiped out" by a random fluctuation in the value of their firm. As a result, the stockholder and manager incentives for making investments can be quite different. But, of course, it is the managers who routinely make the firm's investment decisions.

To see this divergence of incentives, compare the impact of bankruptcy on a well-diversified stockholder with its impact on an employee. Let's take the extreme bankruptcy case where the firm becomes worthless. Despite the lost stock value, the bankruptcy has no effect on the value of the stockholder's other investments, nor does it affect his job. Employees, however, lose their jobs—even though their financial investments are unaffected. The important question is one of differential impact: Is the loss of a job worse than the loss of, say, 5% of one's financial investments? In the overwhelming majority of cases, job income is much larger than 5% of one's financial investments. Therefore, the impact of bankruptcy is much greater on the employee than it is on the stockholder.

This divergence of incentives results in an investment decision-making bias. Because employees have more to lose from a really bad outcome, they have a bias against the firm making high-risk investments. And because the bias is based on risk (rather than on return), it can still exist even if the investment has a large positive NPV.

ASSET UNIQUENESS   Another impact of the nondiversifiability of human capital on agency costs involves the firm's products and services. If the products and/or services are unique (as opposed to generic), the employee's human capital will have even less than normal diversification. Highly specialized employees may be able to sell their services *only* to this firm, because no one else is in exactly this business. In such cases, the stockholders will have to pay the employees extra to compensate them for the lack of job alternatives. After all, employees doing more generic work have options to work for other firms (and we know options are valuable!).

The problems of capital investment choices and asset uniqueness impose their costs at different points. The agency cost with capital investment choices is the possibility of passing up positive-NPV investments; hence the effect is on the choice of *new* investments. The agency cost of unique assets is the higher wages paid to employees to induce them to work for the firm; hence the effect is on *existing* investments.

Self-Check Questions

1. How can stockholders' and managers' goals diverge?
2. What is shirking? Why is it an agency problem?
3. How does the nondiversifiability of human capital give rise to a stockholder-manager conflict?
4. How does asset uniqueness intensify the problem of the nondiversifiability of human capital?

9.4 DEBTHOLDER-STOCKHOLDER CONFLICTS

In the previous chapter we explained how, in a general sense, the stockholders can be viewed as having an option against the debtholders (bondholders): The stockholders have limited liability. That is, the stockholders have the option to default. Consequently, there is always some possibility (even if it is extremely small) that the contractually required payments to corporate debtholders will not be the full amount promised on or before the specified due date. For this reason, the debt is called **risky debt**.

Incentive conflicts occur between the debtholders and the stockholders because the debt is risky. These conflicts lead to several specific problems that we will discuss in this section. First, let's get the roles straight. In the previous section, the stockholders are principals with respect to their corporate managers (agents). In this section, the stockholders reverse their role. Here, we are examining them in their role as agents in their relationship with debtholders (principals). The debtholders want to protect themselves against actions taken by the agent stockholders, who in turn make their decisions through the firm managers.

The Asset Substitution Problem

Firms routinely make decisions that result in the substitution of assets. In the simplest and most common instance, cash is used to buy equipment or materials. In fact, for every investment, some assets are substituted for others. Prudent managers weigh the risks and returns of these investments. But with risky debt, stockholders may be motivated to substitute riskier assets for the firm's existing assets. The **asset substitution** problem occurs when riskier assets are substituted for the firm's existing assets, thereby expropriating value from the firm's debtholders.

Here is how the asset substitution problem arises. The total value of a firm is the market value of all its assets. The debtholders have a claim that is secured by this total value. The stockholders have the residual claim to the remaining firm value. But the debtholders' claim is a fixed promised amount. What can change is the likelihood that they will actually get the amount they have been promised. With the promised payment fixed, an increase in the risk of the assets decreases the value of the debtholders' claim. After all, with higher risk there is more chance that the debtholders will not be repaid the promised amount. This lowers the expected value of the payment.

As we said, the asset substitution problem arises because of the stockholders' valuable default option. Thus we can view the problem in terms of options (contingent claims). Recall that the value of an option increases and decreases with the risk of the underlying asset. In this case the "underlying asset" is all of the firm's assets. Therefore, if the firm (that is, the stockholders) increases the risk of its assets through substitution, the value of this option goes up. This lowers the expected value of the debt payment, as we just noted. Expropriating this value from the debtholders distorts the stockholders' incentives. In fact, it can even cause a negative-NPV investment to *increase* stockholder wealth.

Consider the case where the asset substitution does not change the total value of the firm's assets. This is illustrated in Figure 9-1. With the same total value—the same-sized "pie"—and only the debtholders and stockholders as claimants, a decrease in the value of the debtholders' claim must cause an exactly offsetting increase in the value of the stockholders' claim. It is a zero-sum game played between the debtholders and the stockholders. After making the risky asset substitution, the stockholders could sell their shares for more than before. If the debtholders sold their bonds, however, they would get equivalently less, because the marketplace would factor in the increased risk of default.

Figure 9-1 is a useful way of illustrating the debtholder-stockholder conflict. We use the same framework in Figures 9–2 through 9–6 to illustrate other aspects of this conflict. It is

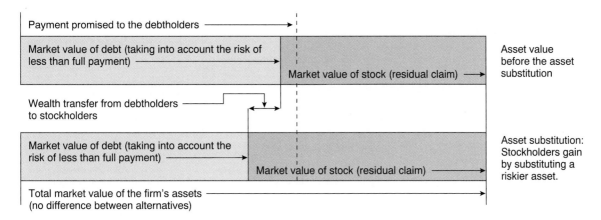

FIGURE 9-1
The asset substitution problem. Stockholders gain at the expense of the debtholders.

therefore "worth your while" to spend enough time with Figure 9-1 to understand and become familiar with it.

The idea behind the asset substitution problem might seem puzzling at first. It *is* tricky. But examining its potentially dramatic implications in the following detailed example will enhance your understanding. It may even amaze you!

The Hunt brothers' Green Canyon oil and gas drilling project illustrates the asset substitution problem.[2] Placid Oil Co. defaulted on its bank loan agreement in March 1986 after oil prices plummeted. The firm was owned by trusts of the three Hunt brothers of Dallas, sons of the legendary H.L. Hunt. Placid filed for bankruptcy protection from its creditors in September 1986. Placid wanted to stretch out its loan payments in order to fund its Green Canyon Project. Understandably, the banks wanted Placid to pay them off before undertaking new investments—especially highly risky ones.

The Hunt brothers had embarked on the highly risky $340 million Green Canyon Project in the hope that a massive oil and gas discovery would save their business. (At one time the Hunts contended that they might find a 70-million-barrel oil reserve worth upwards of $1 billion.) At that time they apparently had debts they were unable to repay. These debts included Placid's debt, debts of Placid's sister firm Penrod Drilling Co., and personal debts that grew out of their unsuccessful, very expensive attempt to corner the world silver market in 1979–1980.

The Green Canyon Project entailed drilling for oil and gas in very deep water in the Gulf of Mexico. One well, drilled through 2243 feet of water, set a world water-depth record for drilling. This is a very hostile operating environment. Hurricane gusts can reach 150 miles per hour. Also, they used an untested technology, a one-of-a-kind floating drilling and production system. The Hunts were "betting the ranch" on one of the world's riskiest ventures. Many industry experts questioned the project's economic viability. Understandably, the banks went to

The Green Canyon Project

EXAMPLE

---

[2] "Hunts' Empire May Unravel in U.S. Court," *Wall Street Journal*, September 2, 1986, A3, A18; "Hunts' Plan to Drill in the Gulf Runs into Stiffer Opposition from Lenders," *Wall Street Journal*, December 23, 1986, A4; "Hunts' Legal Victory on Drilling Project Exposes Their Lenders to Greater Risks," *Wall Street Journal*, April 16, 1987, A18; "Hunt Brothers Pin Hopes for Comeback on 'Crapshoot' in Oil," *Wall Street Journal*, July 12, 1988, A1, A14; "Placid Oil's Bank Settlement Outlines Hunts' Severe Moves to Save Company," *Wall Street Journal*, July 25, 1988, A20; and "Hunt for Black Gold at Green Canyon Ends in Red Ink," *Wall Street Journal*, April 25, 1990, A6.

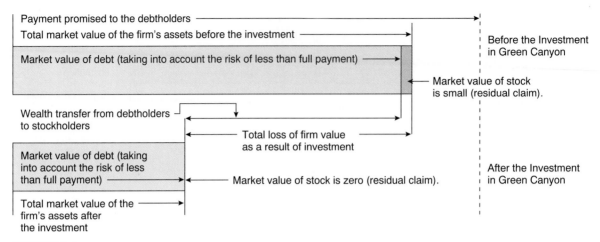

FIGURE 9-2

The effect of the Green Canyon Project on Placid Oil Co. The debtholders bore the risk of the investment made by the stockholders.

extraordinary lengths in their efforts to stop the project, arguing that if the project failed, there would be little left of Placid for them to collect toward their loans.

Consider the situation in terms of one of the hidden options we discussed in the previous chapter: Common stock can be viewed as an option on the firm's assets. When the firm's assets are worth less than its debt obligations, the stock is like an out-of-the-money call option and so is not worth much. To risk such a relatively small equity value on an unlikely chance of the firm earning a lot of money is sort of like buying a lottery ticket: The stockholders have a lot to gain but not much to lose. This is the essence of the asset substitution problem in a financially distressed firm. Increasing the risk of the underlying asset (the firm's total assets), by using cash to invest in highly risky assets, increases the value of the call option (the firm's common stock). The gamble may not be very likely to pay off, but hey, you never know!

Afterward: Eventually, all three Hunt brothers' trusts and two of the Hunt brothers and their wives wound up in bankruptcy as their financial woes mounted. The Green Canyon Project did not pay off, and Placid abandoned it in April 1990. The banks didn't do so badly after all. They got back their principal and some of the interest they were owed.

The effect of the Green Canyon Project on Placid Oil Co. is illustrated in Figure 9-2. It is important to note that even though "everyone lost," it could have turned out differently. Winning this big gamble would have provided enough for everyone. The problem, of course, was that the debtholders put up all the money for the gamble—even though they didn't want to. The stockholders chose the gamble without putting up any additional money. Perhaps more of us would play the lottery if we could get other people to purchase the tickets for us! ■

Now let's consider a more general asset substitution situation where the increase in risk changes the total value of the firm. New investments may have either a positive or a negative NPV. Let's look at the good investments first. Because the debt claim is fixed, the stockholders get the positive NPV (increase in "pie" size). If the value of the debtholders' claim is also reduced by a simultaneous increase in risk, the stockholders get that value as well. This is because it is a zero-sum game.

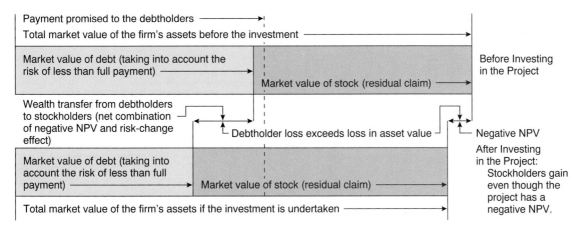

FIGURE 9-3
The problem of asset substitution with a negative-NPV investment. The stockholders gain more in wealth transfer from the debtholders than they lose in negative NPV.

What happens with bad investments? Even with a smaller-sized "pie" (a smaller firm value as a result of the negative NPV), if the decrease in the debtholders' claim value is *more* than the loss in the size of the pie, then the value of the stockholders' claim *increases*. That is, if the wealth transfer dominates the negative NPV, the stockholders still gain. The debtholders suffer the entire negative NPV and then some.[3] The asset substitution problem is illustrated with a negative-NPV investment in Figure 9-3.

Let's summarize. The asset substitution problem occurs when the stockholders substitute riskier assets for the firm's existing assets and expropriate value from the debtholders. This can be accomplished in the process of new investment (growth) or through the sale of some existing assets and the purchase of new ones. Although the total value of the firm may stay the same, increase, or decrease, the value of the debtholders' claim goes down because of the greater chance of default. The decrease in debtholder value causes an exactly offsetting increase in stockholder value because of the zero-sum-game condition between the two claimants.

The Underinvestment Problem

Underinvestment is essentially the mirror image, or reverse, of the asset substitution problem. With risky debt outstanding, the stockholders may *lose* value if the firm makes a low-risk investment. And this can happen even if the investment has a positive NPV. As we saw in the asset substitution problem, with a neutral (zero-NPV) investment, the stockholders gain with an increase in risk. Logically, under the same conditions, the stockholders will lose with a decrease in risk. With asset substitution, stockholders may undertake a bad (negative-NPV), but high-risk, investment to expropriate wealth from the debtholders. With underinvestment, stockholders refuse to undertake a good (positive-NPV), but low-risk, investment so as not to shift wealth away from themselves to the debtholders. Despite the loss from such a risk change, of course, stockholders can gain from an investment—if it has a sufficiently large positive NPV. However, if the decrease in stockholder value from lowering the asset risk outweighs the positive NPV of an investment, stockholders will refuse to undertake the investment. Figure 9-4 illustrates the underinvestment problem.

---

[3] You can see right away why the debtholders don't like this game!

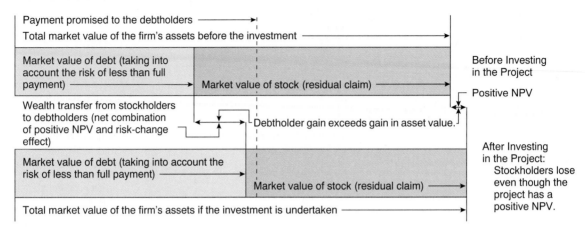

FIGURE 9-4

The underinvestment problem. The stockholders would lose more in wealth to the debtholders than they would gain in positive NPV.

Claim Dilution via Dividend Policy

Paying out a large cash dividend may dilute the existing debtholders' claim. The dividend simultaneously reduces the firm's cash and its stockholders' equity. The equity reduction enlarges the firm's proportion of debt financing, thereby increasing the risk of the debt and reducing the value of its claim. This is simply a different form of asset substitution. The substituted assets are the same except for having a smaller amount of cash. Because cash is a riskless asset, removing some of it (paying it out to the stockholders) raises the average risk of the remaining assets. As you now know, this increase in risk will decrease the value of the firm's outstanding debt. Figure 9-5 illustrates the problem of claim dilution via dividend policy.

Claim dilution via dividend policy is why many bond issues (and virtually all "junk," or high-yield, issues) have some form of dividend restriction. Such a restriction typically limits

FIGURE 9-5

The problem of claim dilution via dividend policy. Because cash is a riskless asset, paying it out to stockholders as a dividend increases the firm's risk, based on the remaining assets. The value of the stock declines because of the drop in assets, but by less than the value of the dividend.

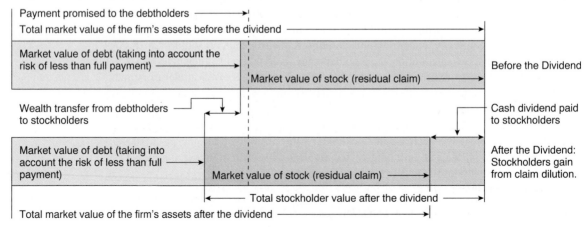

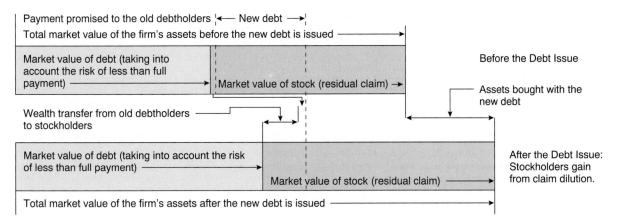

FIGURE 9-6

The problem of claim dilution via new debt. The stockholders gain from a wealth transfer from the old debtholders.

cash dividends to a certain fraction of earnings or cash flow. For firms with a large portion of debt financing, it may prohibit the payment of cash dividends altogether until long-term debt is repaid to some specified level.

Claim Dilution via New Debt

A substantial increase in debt may also dilute the existing debtholders' claim on the firm's assets. Claim dilution occurs if the new debt increases the chance that the existing debtholders will not be repaid the promised amount. As with asset substitution, the increased risk decreases the value of the firm's outstanding debt. And once again, because of the nature of the zero-sum game and the contingent claim, the stockholders get the benefit of the debtholders' loss in value. Figure 9-6 illustrates the problem.

The leveraged buyout of RJR Nabisco, Inc. illustrates how claim dilution can be caused by new debt.[4] The buyout increased the firm's outstanding debt from about $5.7 billion to about $23.2 billion. Following the announcement of the bid, existing RJR Nabisco bonds plunged roughly 20% in market value. The pre-existing debt did not have a legal restriction preventing a large amount of new debt. Existing bondholders had expected the firm to continue to use similar amounts of debt. But the bondholders were rudely awakened: Once the debt was issued, the firm limited its actions *only* by the explicit legal debt contract.

Following the RJR Nabisco experience, there was near turmoil in the market for high-grade bonds issued by consumer products firms. After things settled down, many investors had learned a lesson from this incident. Since then, investors have required additional restrictions to try to prevent other firms from doing what RJR Nabisco did. ■

RJR Nabisco's Leveraged Buyout

EXAMPLE

We have just explained how a firm may engage in claim dilution by paying a large dividend, or by deliberately changing its financial makeup (its mix of liabilities and stockholders' equity) by taking on a significant amount of new debt.[5] A significant economic downturn can

---

[4] RJR Holdings Capital Corp., prospectus, May 12, 1989, 11; Margaret A. Elliott, "Rating the Debt Raters," *Institutional Investor*, December 1988, 109; "Takeover Fears Rack Corporate Bonds," *Wall Street Journal*, October 25, 1988, C1, C23; and "A Bruising Battle Over Bonds," *New York Times*, November 27, 1988, F1, F21.

[5] A firm's financial makeup is called its capital structure. We defer for now an extensive discussion of this important topic. Chapters 15 and 16 are devoted to capital structure.

also cause claim dilution. This is because poor economic conditions increase the probability of default. In such cases the claim dilution may not have been the firm's choice!

Asset Uniqueness

In general, when a firm's assets are unique, as opposed to generic, there is more risk associated with the disposal of those assets, should disposal become necessary. Thus the collateral provided by the assets to the debtholders is of lower value. Although the assets might be highly sought after because of their uniqueness, they also might become worthless (or perhaps even costly to dispose of). Of course, this is the essence of a risk-return trade-off. Therefore, if everything else is equal, a firm with unique assets has to pay a higher interest cost to compensate the debtholders for the increased risk.

EXAMPLE

The Effect of Asset Uniqueness on Making a Loan

Suppose you are a banker considering two different loan applications. Each loan would enable its respective firm to build a business facility that would be almost entirely controlled by robotic equipment. The new facility would be the collateral for the loan. One is a storage facility that can be used for virtually anything that does not need specialized treatment such as refrigeration. The other is a facility for manufacturing a new kind of home entertainment product, such as a video laser disc player. The costs of building the facilities are identical. What would be the comparative risk of lending money to these two firms?

The storage facility would be built by one firm for a specific use, but at little extra cost, it could easily be used for something different. The manufacturing facility would also be built for a specific use, but using it for something else would require considerable additional cost. Therefore, if the second firm defaulted, it is likely that the facility would be worthless for its intended purpose. That is, if the product was unsuccessful, the robotic facility would require extensive and costly modifications to make it useful for another purpose. But if the first firm defaulted, the bank would stand a better chance of reselling the collateral to another business without having to spend much money to modify it.

As the banker, would you be willing to lend the same amount of money to the two firms? We wouldn't. Even if the likelihood of default were identical, the bank's risk would be greater with the manufacturing facility, because the value of the facility would be considerably less if it had to be used for something else. Therefore, for the manufacturing firm, we would either not lend as much money or charge a higher interest rate on a loan of the same amount as the loan for the storage facility. ∎

Just as the manager of a firm in a unique business would charge more for her labor, so a lender would charge such a firm more. If the unique business defaulted, the manager would need to become re-educated to recover the value of her human capital. The lender would have to reinvest to make the value of the collateral assets equal their original value. When a firm heads for uncharted waters, the increased risk has its costs.

Self-Check Questions

1. Why is corporate debt risky?
2. What is the asset substitution problem, and how are debtholders hurt by it?
3. What is the underinvestment problem, and how are the debtholders hurt by it?
4. What does claim dilution mean? How does paying a cash dividend give rise to claim dilution? How does a new debt issue lead to claim dilution?
5. How does an asset's uniqueness affect its value as collateral for a loan?

9.5 CONSUMER-FIRM CONFLICTS

Even some consumer-firm interactions can be viewed as principal-agent relationships. Of course, it is important to keep in mind who the players are. In the first situation we discuss, the firm is the agent and the consumer is the principal. In the second situation, the firm is the principal and the consumer is the agent.

Guarantees and Service After the Sale

In its agent role, the firm promises future service, should it become necessary. The fundamental question is whether the consumer can "trust" the firm to fulfill its future obligations. If the consumer (principal) is confident that the firm will live up to its promise, the firm can get full value for its products and services. The level of confidence is the essence of the firm's reputation. A good reputation is the assurance that promises will be fulfilled to the consumer's satisfaction. Needless to say, a firm in financial distress—even one with a great reputation—may not be able to provide adequate assurance of future service. When it comes time for service, the firm may be long gone!

Several years ago Chrysler Corporation experienced financial distress. This led the federal government to provide more than $1.5 billion of loan guarantees. It stands as one of the few times the federal government has stepped in to "bail out" a private firm.

    Warranties were a critical factor that compounded Chrysler's trouble. As Chrysler's financial woes mounted, consumers grew more concerned that Chrysler might not be around to honor its warranties and sell replacement parts. Sales plummeted, which led to greater losses. Even the cars that were sold brought much lower prices than competitors' comparable models. The federal government loan guarantees came just before Chrysler would have had to file for bankruptcy. ■

Consumer-Firm Conflicts and Chrysler's Financial Distress

EXAMPLE

The Free-Rider Problem

What a customer does with a firm's product can in some cases significantly affect the firm. For example, a firm may be hurt by a customer who duplicates and sells the firm's products and/or services without proper agreement. (The customer's "option" to do this is yet another hidden option.) Accordingly, this relationship also can be viewed in a principal-agent framework. Recall the concept of a free rider, one who receives the benefit of someone else's expenditure (money, effort, or creativity) simply by imitation. The potential for consumers (the agents in this case) to duplicate and sell the firm's (the principal's) products and/or services without proper agreement is another example of the free-rider problem.

    Consider the copying of books (photocopying or plagiarism), computer software, videotapes, audiotapes, and so on. Copyright laws make such misuse illegal. Similarly, patent laws make certain kinds of copying of a valuable idea illegal. The purpose of such laws is to provide incentives for people to be creative. In other words, our society has recognized the Principle of Valuable Ideas and encourages people to create value in this manner. In many cases these laws work well. However, new products and technologies sometimes require the modification of existing laws. Such a modification was deemed necessary with respect to video-movie rentals. During the 1980s, royalties for movie rentals became mandated by law.

    Another free-rider problem area involves international law. Making and enforcing copyright, patent, and royalty laws are important to international trade and relations. As markets become truly international, countries that do not recognize and enforce such laws become places where pirated material can be created easily. Alleged blatant violations are a major bone of contention in international talks, as they were recently in U.S.-China trade negotiations. Such pirated material can inflict a significant loss on the creators.

How can the firm protect itself from unscrupulous consumers who exercise the hidden option to free-ride? It is rumored that the Coca-Cola Company has employed people to order "Coke" in establishments that do not sell its product. If such establishments fail to make it clear that the drink served was not actually Coke, Coca-Cola is said to have sued the establishment for violation of its trademark. Although this may sound like a harsh measure, it may be one of the few methods available to protect a valuable trademark.[6]

Self-Check Questions

1. Describe two consumer-firm conflicts.

2. How does financial distress affect the consumer-firm conflict that revolves around promises of future service?

3. What is the free-rider problem, and how does it involve a hidden option?

9.6 WORKING IN CONTRACTUAL RELATIONSHIPS

There are a number of other practical considerations in ongoing explicit and implicit contractual relationships.

Financial Distress

Financial distress can intensify the problem of goal divergence. As an example, consider again the debtholder-stockholder relationship. After a debt contract has been made, stockholders make firm decisions (through the managers) within the constraints of the contract. But the incentives to "push the edge of the contract" and engage in asset substitution and underinvestment increase dramatically if a firm becomes financially distressed. We saw this in practice in the Placid Oil Green Canyon Project example.

In Figure 9-7, we illustrate two firms that are facing the same two alternative investments: a positive-NPV, low-risk investment and a negative-NPV, high-risk investment. Firm A is financially healthy, but firm B is financially distressed. As you can see, the incentives differ for the two firms' stockholders. The stockholders of the financially distressed firm are better off engaging in asset substitution and underinvestment, taking the negative-NPV investment and leaving the positive-NPV investment. In contrast, the financially healthy firm has incentives to take the positive-NPV investment and leave the negative-NPV one.

CLAIMANT COALITIONS   Financial distress can distort other situations as well. It can create incentives for the firm's various claimants (stakeholders) to form coalitions and "gang up" on one another. For example, suppose a firm is in financial distress, and liquidation would produce the largest total value. Despite this, the managers might contract with a bank for a loan to continue operations. Each claimant will favor or oppose liquidation on the basis of its own outcome, not on the basis of maximizing total firm value. The loan provides the managers with another chance to save their jobs (an option!), even though continuing hurts the stockholders. But the stockholders might support the loan, even though it hurts the debtholders. This can

---

[6] Perhaps Coca-Cola has reason to worry. Many years ago Bayer lost its trademark name, aspirin, after the term became commonly used to refer to the drug, regardless of the manufacturer.

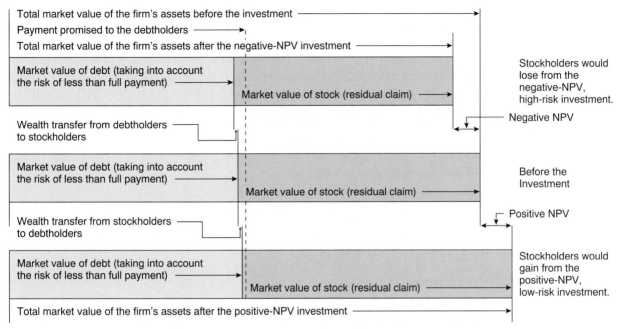

Panel A: The case of the financially healthy firm. Default is unlikely in either case, so the amount of wealth transfer is small in either case, and the NPV dominates the "hidden" stockholder incentives.

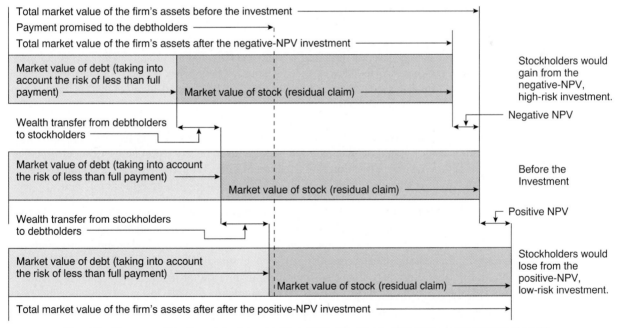

Panel B: The case of the financially distressed firm. Default is already fairly likely, so the amount of wealth transfer is large in either case, and the "hidden" stockholder incentives dominate the NPV.

FIGURE 9-7

The potential effect of financial distress on investment choice.

happen if the stockholders will get little from liquidation but might get a lot if the firm recovers. If you ever played the board game "Monopoly" with several players until only one player was left, you probably saw, or even engaged in, a claimant coalition game. Of course, the play is considerably more intense when there is real money at stake!

The dramatic shift in incentives brought on by financial distress in each case occurs because the contingent claim—the option—inherent in the situation falls in value and becomes out-of-the-money. At that point, the optionholder has little more to lose—perhaps only the time premium. The downside risk is limited, because an option cannot have a negative value. At the same time, the option is worthless if it expires out-of-the-money, so the possibility of its coming back into the money can make fighting to keep the option alive worthwhile. You can't lose much and you might win. This combination can create powerful incentives to take risks and engage in protracted legal battles.

Information

A financial contract is complex because it involves imperfect information. In a perfect capital market, complete information is available to all participants at no cost. In a real capital market, you can apply the Signaling Principle to interpret actions. Although it would be nice if the meaning of all actions were absolutely clear, this is not the case. Interpretation can be complex and difficult. For example, when is a "sale" really a sale? Some retailers have essentially continuous sales. When is such a claim or any other advertising claim credible?[7] This represents a significant and ongoing asymmetric information problem.

Even when the meaning of an action is clear, other problems can arise. For example, to avoid being taken advantage of, one might choose to camouflage some actions. Suppose a firm always reduced its price on a model that was about to be discontinued. If you knew this, you would not think the sale was such a good deal. After all, the item might not be worth much after a new model came out. Thus the firm faces the problem of adverse selection: Offering the reduced price is a negative signal indicating imminent model discontinuation. How can the firm reduce this problem?

One approach to this problem is to deliberately add uncertainty. The firm could occasionally (randomly) offer a lower price on items not being discontinued—a "real" sale. In that way, the firm plants the idea that a reduced price can be a good deal rather than an obvious signal of a model discontinuation.

Incentives also play an important role. Ideally, an agent would have incentives to send accurate signals. But consider managers whose earnings depend on the firm's performance. Such managers might be tempted to mislead, or even falsely report better firm performance, unless they face penalties for being found out later. Properly structured, penalties lead to more credible signals by making it unattractive to mimic the activities of a "better" agent.

AGENT REPUTATION   The many factors that contribute to an agent's incentives include rewards, punishments, ethical attitudes, the likelihood of being caught misbehaving, and the agent's reputation. As with firms, agents with good reputations can demand higher prices for their products and/or services. An agent's good reputation carries with it an implicit guarantee of satisfactory performance. Therefore, building and/or maintaining a good reputation is valuable. Conversely, its loss is costly. The opportunity cost of a lost good reputation increases the cost of being caught misbehaving. Therefore, an agent with a good reputation has a greater incentive to behave properly.

---

[7] You have probably wondered about particular advertising claims. Our own risk aversion toward lawsuits keeps us from citing specific examples.

Management Contracts

Beyond the separation of ownership and control that we noted earlier, stockholders can be a widely dispersed group. For example, at year-end 1995, AT&T and GM had more than 2.2 and 1.3 million common stockholders, respectively. This tremendous diffusion of ownership appears to intensify stockholder-manager conflicts. There are some who cite large executive salaries as evidence that the managers are winning the conflict, at least in the instances cited. However, empirical studies have yielded conflicting conclusions about whether manager-controlled firms differ significantly from stockholder-controlled firms.

Even with widely diffused share ownership—and managerial control—there are several ways in which stockholders can help align managerial goals with their own. These devices include designing incentive compensation plans for managers, the right to sell their own shares, the right to replace managers, and the right to elect directors.

INCENTIVE COMPENSATION PLANS   Management contracts often include stock options, performance shares, and bonuses. Because accounting measures can sometimes be manipulated, it is generally preferable to base bonuses on appreciation in the firm's share price.

Lee Iacocca's First-Year Compensation Package — EXAMPLE

When Chrysler Corporation hired Lee Iacocca, he insisted on taking only $1 in salary the first year. In place of the typical salary, he chose an incentive package that included options to purchase approximately 350,000 shares of Chrysler common stock. These options were far out-of-the-money. He argued that if he was successful in turning the firm around, he would be well paid; if he wasn't successful, he would appropriately get nothing.

Eight years later, Iacocca cashed in his options for a gain of roughly $20 million. Unfortunately, it was incorrectly reported that the $20 million was his pay for the single year in which he cashed in his options. Understandably, others have since cited this payment as evidence that corporate executives are being paid too much.

We take no position on the issue of whether executive compensation is fair. However, we believe the starting place for such a debate must be accurate facts and a complete understanding of the contract. ■

THE STOCKHOLDERS' RIGHT TO SELL THEIR SHARES   Except in special cases, stockholders can sell the shares they own. This can create the threat of a takeover. When many stockholders offer to sell their shares, and the market price per share falls, others may buy up the shares and take over the firm if the price is low enough.

The right to tender shares to a prospective acquiror, or sell them in the market, is potentially the most effective (although a last-resort) measure open to shareholders. However, many recently introduced anti-takeover measures may have reduced the threat of takeover. So-called poison pills are an example of an anti-takeover measure. They typically take the form of an option to purchase shares in the target firm at a bargain price. The option becomes exercisable in the hands of the target firm's stockholders once an "unfriendly" suitor (one not approved by the firm's board of directors) acquires some specified percentage of the outstanding shares, often just 20%. The poison pill provision gets its name from the pill of cyanide a spy is given to swallow when capture is imminent. Although such a poison pill does prevent the spy from talking after being captured, it has some other striking side effects!

EXAMPLE

Chrysler's Poison Pill

In November 1994, Chrysler Corporation's largest stockholder, billionaire Kirk Kerkorian, demanded action from Chrysler. He owned about 9% of Chrysler's stock and felt it was undervalued. He wanted the firm to raise its dividend and buy back some of its shares.

At the time, Chrysler had a poison pill that prevented a shareholder from controlling 10% or more of Chrysler's shares without board approval. Kerkorian wanted to increase his ownership proportion to 15%. He asked Chrysler's board to modify the poison pill. Several large investors went even further. They urged Chrysler to eliminate the poison pill.

Within a few weeks, Chrysler took action. The dividend was boosted 60%. A $1 billion stock buy-back program was announced. Finally, Chrysler modified its "shareholder-rights plan" to permit a shareholder to own up to 15% of the stock. Chrysler's board diluted the poison pill but didn't discard it. ■

REPLACING MANAGERS   Managers, like all agents, have significant incentives to build and/or maintain a good reputation. On average, executives who lose their jobs in connection with a financially distressed firm do not subsequently get comparable or better-paying jobs. In contrast, when people are recruited away from an existing job into a higher-paying job, their past success is almost always cited as the basis for their being hired.[8]

EXAMPLE

How Much Will Michael Ovitz Make at Disney?

In August 1995, The Walt Disney Company hired Michael Ovitz as president and a director of Disney. Ovitz had co-founded Creative Artists Agency and was very highly regarded in Hollywood. It was rumored that MCA Inc. had tried to hire him just a few months before. To get Ovitz to leave Creative Artists, Disney offered 10-year options on 5 million of its shares. Compensation experts valued the option package at between $107 million and $140 million. ■

THE STOCKHOLDERS' ELECTION OF DIRECTORS   Unhappy stockholders can elect new directors or even mount a *proxy fight*.[9] However, this is difficult. Further, the recently adopted practice of staggering directorships (such as electing one-third each year) makes winning a proxy fight even harder.

EXAMPLE

Sallie Mae's Proxy Fight

The Student Loan Marketing Association (nicknamed Sallie Mae) buys and services student loans under federally sponsored student loan programs. In 1995, a group of shareholders, led by former Sallie Mae chief operating officer Albert Lord, started a proxy fight. They said Sallie Mae was poorly managed and blamed current management for not paying enough attention to the firm's profit margin and stock price.[10] Earnings had slumped in 1994 for the first time in the firm's 21-year history.

The proxy fight succeeded. At the 1995 annual meeting, the dissidents elected 8 new directors to the 21-member board. (Of the other 13, 6 were management candidates, and the other 7 were appointed by President Clinton.) Management started a legal battle to keep the new directors from serving but gave up after a month. Meanwhile, Sallie Mae announced that it was considering changes in the way it ran its business. ■

---

[8] Sadly, we must point out that there are also many people who are quite successful but never get hired away for "big bucks"!

[9] Sometimes one or more shareholders lead a takeover attempt by asking other shareholders to make a precommitment to vote with them. This precommitment is called a *proxy*.

[10] Apparently, the market agreed. The firm's stock jumped 30% in value when the proxy fight was announced.

Available empirical evidence indicates that, on average, there is not a sharp divergence between managers' and stockholders' interests. Still, we recommend the continued use of monitoring, because effective monitoring may be a critical ingredient of this general consistency!

Debt Contracts

How will debtholders react to the risks of asset substitution, underinvestment, and claim dilution? They will try to restrict the firm's ability to engage in these behaviors. For example, debt contracts may include specific limits on the firm's activities, such as preventing the firm from issuing new bonds without first paying off, or otherwise protecting, existing bonds. As we noted earlier, restrictions of this sort became much more widely used after the RJR Nabisco leveraged buyout. The debtholders may also initiate legal action with respect to an existing contract, as in the case of Placid Oil's Green Canyon Project.

Despite all attempts at restriction, some possibility remains that stockholders will be able to expropriate wealth from the debtholders. The essential question is how large that possibility is. The larger it is, the higher the rate of interest the debtholders will require to compensate them for that risk. Such a higher rate is part of the agency costs borne by the stockholders. Also, contractual limitations may restrict more than just the targeted activities. Therefore, another part of the agency cost is reduced decision-making flexibility that might unintentionally prevent the firm from making a positive-NPV investment.

The explicit legal contract for a publicly traded bond is called the **bond indenture**. The structure of this explicit contract affects the incentives by detailing responsibilities, constraints, punishments, and required monitoring. For example, such contracts specify the timing and amounts of all interest and principal payments. They also appoint a particular agent, called the *trustee*, who has a legal responsibility to look after the bondholders' interests.

Certain contractual provisions within a bond indenture are called **bond covenants**. These are designed to protect the interests of the bondholders. They are of two types. A *negative* covenant *limits* certain actions, such as incurring more debt or paying dividends. A *positive* covenant *requires* certain actions, such as regularly making tax payments and providing periodic financial statements.

Bond covenants are a form of monitoring. They provide a warning system that is triggered when a firm fails to comply with a covenant. Of course, the warning system is activated only with a failure to comply. This can save resources because more complete monitoring — such as a monthly review of the firm's actions — is more costly and time-consuming. Further, even when a covenant is violated, corrective action can often be taken before the problem becomes more severe and the firm falls into financial distress. Thus a bond covenant can be an *early* warning device.

Bond covenants provide value by lowering the risk of the bonds. The bondholder gets increased protection against certain events and therefore agrees to a lower interest rate. This benefits the firm. Of course, the value of a specific covenant depends on the particular situation. This is quite similar to the overlapping options problem discussed in the previous chapter.

With hidden options, the addition of an option may not add much value if the contingency it "covers" is already covered by other options. If the bondholder is protected in other ways, a covenant may not add much value. Generally, covenants are more valuable to bondholders in a higher-risk firm, because the likelihood of running into a problem there is greater.

However, bond covenants are also costly. They restrict the firm's operating flexibility and can eliminate positive-NPV investment opportunities. In short, they can eliminate valuable options for the firm. It is possible to solicit consent from the bondholders to relax a restrictive covenant. But such a process is cumbersome, time-consuming, and often expensive.

Bondholders normally demand some form of payment—either an immediate cash payment or an increase in the coupon rate—in exchange for their consent. Even when the firm does go to the trouble and cost of eliminating a covenant that is constraining it, the lost time it takes to do so adds to the opportunity cost of that covenant. As with so many other things, there is a trade-off between the benefits and costs of bond covenants.

<table>
<tr><td>**EXAMPLE**</td><td>*Removing a Restrictive Covenant*</td><td>In April 1988 the owners of The Seven-Up Company offered a group of its bondholders incentives to agree to changes in the bond indenture: (1) an immediate one-time payment of $25 per $1000 bond, (2) an increase in the coupon rate from $12\frac{1}{8}\%$ to $12\frac{3}{8}\%$ for the period from November 15, 1989, through May 14, 1992, and (3) a further increase in the coupon rate to $12\frac{5}{8}\%$ for the period from May 15, 1992, through May 15, 1997.[11] At the same time, the Dr. Pepper Company offered a similar financial incentive to a group of its bondholders.[12] The offers were in exchange for a consent to allow a leveraged buyout of each firm to form a single merged firm. The cost of the cash payment if all bondholders consented (a majority was required in each case) was $9.3 million. The increase in coupon rate, which would benefit every bondholder as long as a majority consented, amounted to $934,000 per year for the first increase and a further $934,000 per year for the second.

This is a particularly interesting example of managing *implicit* stakeholder claims. Both solicitation statements pointed out that the bondholder consents were not *legally* required for the planned leveraged buyout. Did this mean that the firm was paying something and getting nothing? Of course not. The firm offered a financial incentive in exchange for *explicit* consent to preempt potential legal action from the bondholders. This was important because even if no protesting bondholders prevailed in their legal complaints, they could have caused a costly, or even disastrous, delay in the firm's plans.[13] ■</td></tr>
</table>

One alternative to an extensive array of restrictive bond covenants is the use of a conversion option to create a **convertible bond**. A convertible bond can be exchanged for a preset number of shares of the firm's common stock at the bondholder's option. The option in a convertible bond allows the securityholder to share in the upside if the investments the firm makes are especially successful. Smaller, younger firms often issue convertible bonds, rather than bonds without the conversion option, for precisely this reason.

Optimal Contracts

An **optimal contract** balances the three types of agency costs (contracting, monitoring, and misbehavior) against one another to minimize the total cost. In some cases, the optimal contract involves a fixed wage and some degree of monitoring, as is typically the case for employees. In other cases, the cost of monitoring is not worth it. When its cost exceeds the expected cost of agent misbehavior, the optimal contract is a simple bonus based on the outcome. An example is a salesperson who earns only a commission, which is a percentage of sales.

Some of the decisions connected with the choice of a financial contract are similar to trade-offs an agent might make in an effort to earn a good reputation: Agents may forgo profiting from misbehaving in the short run to earn more in the long run. Demonstrating good be-

---

[11] The Seven-Up Company, Solicitation Statement for $12\frac{1}{8}\%$ Senior Subordinated Notes Due 1997, April 25, 1988, with $155.8 million outstanding principal amount.
[12] Dr. Pepper Company, Solicitation Statement for $12\frac{3}{4}\%$ Senior Subordinated Debentures Due 2001, April 25, 1988, with $218 million outstanding principal amount.
[13] This can be viewed as one more hidden option—the option to "make trouble" by suing, even though you don't expect to win!

havior can increase the value of their services. Similarly, agents may agree to "severe" monitoring to earn more for their services. The principal agrees to the higher price because the severe monitoring reduces the chance of agent misbehavior. Again, it is a cost trade-off.

Choosing the Best Contract

EXAMPLE

Suppose the Nintendo Corporation can choose one of four managerial contracts. The estimated annual total and component contracting costs (in millions of dollars) of these alternatives are given in the following table. Which managerial contract should Nintendo choose?

	DIRECT	MONITORING	MISBEHAVIOR	TOTAL
Contract 1	1.4	0.1	5.0	6.5
Contract 2	1.1	2.4	0.1	3.6
Contract 3	2.2	0.4	0.4	3.0
Contract 4	2.6	0.1	0.7	3.4

Contract 3 is the best choice because it provides the lowest *total* costs among the alternatives. On the basis of the firm's estimates, it is the best game in town. ■

Unfortunately, a financial contract cannot cover every possible contingency; beforehand, you can't conceive of everything that might go wrong. In any case, dealing with every possible situation would involve tremendous time and expense. Each party must take reasonable precautions but must ultimately rely on the other parties to behave ethically and responsibly in those situations not explicitly covered by the agreement. If either party behaves unethically, the contractual provisions may not prove very effective anyway.

Self-Check Questions
1. Why does financial distress intensify the problem of goal divergence?
2. What devices do stockholders have for aligning managerial goals with their own?
3. What is a poison pill, and how does it help current managers keep their jobs in the face of a takeover threat?
4. What is the purpose of bond covenants?
5. Describe an optimal contract in your own words.

9.7 MONITORING

As we noted earlier, a financial contract is complex because it involves imperfect information. Despite this complexity, there are a number of potentially cost-effective monitoring devices.

New External Financing

Whenever a firm seeks new external financing, it is exposed to special scrutiny, which is a form of monitoring. The firm must reveal new information. If this information is made public, existing investors can look more closely at the firm. Even if the new information is not made public, the new investors provide a form of monitoring. They provide reassurance to existing investors by their willingness to invest their own money.

This reassurance concept is quite broad. Suppose a firm has a valuable new idea that would be damaged if it were made public, because of the free-rider problem. That is, others would copy the idea. In such cases, the firm may be able to issue new securities through investment bankers who underwrite the issue.

Here is how it works. The firm explains the idea to the investment bankers now but does not make the idea public until it is marketed. With an underwritten issue, the investment bankers actually purchase the securities before reselling them to the public. Taking ownership, even for a short time, is much riskier than simply marketing the securities for a commission. Presumably, investment bankers would not take on this risk if they thought it was large. The investment banker's purchase signals the market about the value of the new idea. As a reputable middleman, it can profit from its role as third-party monitor.

Other Monitoring Devices

Many elements of the financial environment serve as monitoring devices. People openly offer and seek information in the normal course of business. They also signal information through their actions. Information is revealed through government enforcement of laws and regulations. Even a firm's reputation and structure convey information. Common monitoring devices include

- **Financial statements**   Audited accounting statements are a monitoring device for stockholder-manager, debtholder-stockholder, and consumer-firm relationships. They provide an early warning system.

- **Cash dividends**   Cash dividends can be a monitoring device in two ways. First, the failure to declare a cash dividend in the expected amount provides a warning. Although it may or may not be negative information, it prompts investors to look further. They must determine the meaning of the failure. Second, paying cash dividends may force the firm to seek new external financing more frequently, the benefits of which we just noted.

- **Bond ratings**   Bond ratings by agencies such as Moody's or Standard & Poor's provide monitoring at issuance and, to a lesser extent, over the bonds' life.

- **Bond covenants**   As we discussed earlier in the chapter, bond covenants provide a warning system.

- **Government regulation**   Government monitoring devices in the public interest continue to evolve. For example, numerous federal agencies, such as the IRS, SEC, and FDA, monitor firms for various legal violations.

- **The entire legal system**   Theft, fraud, and many other forms of agent misbehavior are illegal. The legal system provides various forms of monitoring for everyone.

- **Reputation**   Reputation and the general information it contains are a form of monitoring. As we noted earlier, building and/or maintaining a good reputation is valuable. This creates incentives for providing accurate information, which also facilitates monitoring.

- **Multilevel organizations**   A firm that uses many levels of authority to review and evaluate decisions also provides a structural form of monitoring. Misbehavior is more difficult when you need a large number of people to do it. To get approval in such a firm, a plan must be widely discussed. Large groups are more likely to include honest people, braggarts, and blabbermouths. Not everyone can keep a secret.

Throughout the rest of the book we will examine information from these and other sources to understand better the motivations contained in implicit and explicit financial contracts.

The ***Barings Bankruptcy***

EXAMPLE

Barings PLC was a venerable 233-year-old British investment bank. It had helped Britain reopen trade with the United States after the Revolutionary War. In 1803 it helped the United States double in size by financing the purchase of the Louisiana Territory from France. Yet despite the bank's long and distinguished history, early in 1995 it took a single 28-year-old trader just a month of undetected trading to create a $1 billion loss, which caused the firm to go bankrupt.

Nicholas Leeson had been an arbitrage trader at Barings Securities. He was trading futures contracts in Singapore and Japan. He simultaneously bought in one market and sold the same contract in the other to exploit price differences. Profits were small but so were the risks.

One day in late January 1995, Leeson decided that "plain vanilla" arbitrage was too tame, so he changed tactics. He stopped matching buy and sell orders. He became a gambler who thought he knew which way Japanese stock prices and interest rates were headed. Without authorization, he bet big.

By the time Leeson's betting was finally discovered, he had bought stock futures contracts representing $7 billion worth of Japanese shares and interest rate futures contracts representing $22 billion worth of Japanese government bonds. (That's right, we said *billion*.) Unfortunately, Leeson didn't know as much as he thought he did. He racked up about a $1 billion loss.

The regulators found there had been a "failure of control." Apparently, the firm didn't really understand what Leeson was doing. It was reported that someone at a Barings risk committee meeting asked whether the high level of trading by Leeson was "safe." Barings's head of derivatives assured the group that it was. This is particularly surprising in light of press reports that Leeson's trading was large enough to generate comment throughout the Asian markets about his aggressive strategy.[14] As it turned out, the derivatives head's belief was based on reports filed by Leeson! Leeson's superiors thought he was trading on behalf of clients rather than for the firm's own account.

Barings's lack of controls surprised Wall Street risk managers. Unlike most sales representatives, Leeson was allowed to go to the trading floor to trade. Barings didn't limit the size of Leeson's trading positions. In contrast to industry practice, he was both head derivatives trader and head of the back-office settlement department. He was therefore monitoring himself. This enabled him to withhold information from the head office and send in falsified reports. And that, of course, crippled the monitoring process.

It would be reassuring to think that Barings's monitoring problem was unique, but it isn't! Kidder, Peabody & Co. said its head government bond trader racked up $350 million in fake profits by entering false trades into its computer system. Daiwa Bank Ltd. suffered $1.1 billion of losses over an 11-year period as a result of questionable trading by a lone trader. Like Leeson, he headed a back-office department responsible for monitoring trading (including his own).

As these examples vividly illustrate, monitoring isn't very effective when the individual being monitored is the one doing the monitoring! ■

Self-Check Questions

1. Describe three external monitoring devices. How cost-effective is each?

2. How do investment bankers function as monitors when they underwrite a new issue of securities?

3. How do audited financial statements assist in monitoring?

---

[14] At one point, his trades accounted for *half* the outstanding positions in the Nikkei-225 futures contract.

SUMMARY

This chapter described many of the problems connected with financial contracting in a principal-agent framework. Many times, the interests of principals and agents diverge. For example, managers operate the firm but may own only a tiny fraction of it. Therefore, the firm's various stakeholders (such as employees, stockholders, debtholders, and customers) may not have identical interests. The divergence of interests among stakeholders creates agency problems: Each stakeholder tends to be self-interested. Therefore, incentives, constraints, punishments, and monitoring are necessary to ensure that an agent acts in the principal's best interest. Such things impose agency costs. Agency problems and costs arise in many of the relationships that compose the set of contracts making up the modern corporation. Financial distress is an important complicating factor that intensifies most agency problems and costs.

Figure 9-8 shows the contractual relationships we examined in this chapter, each in a separate principal-agent framework.

The contingent-claim view of the firm's various stakeholders provides important insights into how the incentives can shift dramatically if the contingent claim (option) comes to be at, or out-of-the-money. Because the option cannot have a negative value, the downside risk is limited. In this respect, it is rather like a lottery ticket. The agent has little to lose, but the upside potential can be tremendous. Placid Oil's Green Canyon Project is one example of such a shift in incentives.

In future chapters we will encounter agency issues repeatedly. Agency theory has been used to an increasing extent to explain financial contracting phenomena that were not previously well understood. Agency cost considerations are important to the capital budgeting process (Part III), and they help explain the choice of capital structure (Chapters 15 and 16), the choice of dividend policy (Chapters 17 and 18), many of the day-to-day decisions firms make

FIGURE 9-8

Important implicit principal-agent relationships connected with a firm.

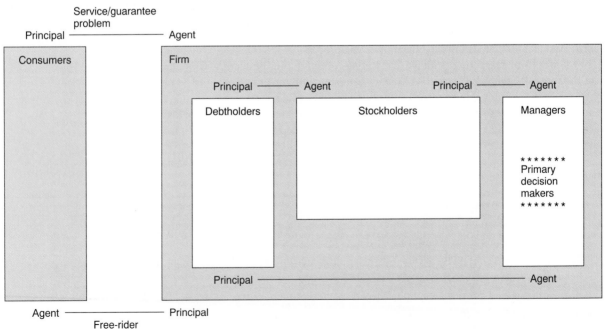

(Part V), the design of new securities issues (Chapter 23), the choice between leasing and buying an asset (Chapter 25), and the design of merger or acquisition financing arrangements (Chapter 28).

DECISION SUMMARY

- The modern corporation involves a large number of both explicit and implicit contracts.
- Both implicit and explicit contracts frequently involve contingent claims.
- An agency cost is the incremental cost of working through agents. The agency cost is the amount above whatever cost would be incurred in a perfect market environment.
- Financial distress complicates and intensifies many agency problems and costs.
- The existence of agency problems adds agency costs to the cost of financial contracting.
- An optimal financial contract minimizes the total agency cost, which is made up of financial contracting costs (transaction costs, opportunity costs, and incentive fees), monitoring costs, and misbehavior costs.
- Conflicts of interest can arise naturally between stockholders and managers because of employee perquisites, employee effort, and the nondiversifiability of an employee's human capital, among other things.
- Ultimately, if stockholders are dissatisfied, they can sell their shares. If the market value of a poorly run firm falls sufficiently, another firm or investor can purchase enough shares to gain control and fire inept managers.
- Conflicts of interest between debtholders and stockholders can arise naturally because of the possibility of asset substitution, underinvestment, and claim dilution, among other things.
- Debt contracts typically include provisions designed to control agency costs.
- Conflicts of interest between consumers and the firm can arise naturally because of guarantees and product imitation, among other things.
- The value of building and maintaining a good reputation provides important long-term incentives that help reduce some agency problems.

KEY TERMS

set-of-contracts model...270
agency theory...270
agent...270
principal...270
agency problem...271
monitor...271
moral hazard...271

agency costs...272
perquisites...274
shirking...274
human capital...274
nondiversifiability of human capital...274
risky debt...276
asset substitution...276

underinvestment...279
bond indenture...289
bond covenants...289
convertible bond...290
optimal contract...290

EXERCISES

PROBLEM SET A

A1. In your own words, describe a principal-agent relationship. Cite two examples of explicit principal-agent relationships and two others that are not explicit but can be viewed as such.

A2. Describe and discuss the asset substitution problem.

A3. Describe and discuss the underinvestment problem.

A4. Define the term *moral hazard.*

A5. Define the term *free rider* and explain why this phenomenon causes problems. Cite an example of the free-rider problem and a contract form that is typically used to reduce or eliminate the problem.

A6. Define the concept of agency problems and cite three examples of such problems.

A7. Cite three goals managers might have that are not necessarily consistent with the goal of maximizing shareholder wealth.

A8. What is an agency cost? What are its three components? Cite an example of each one.

A9. Cite and describe two ways in which the uniqueness of assets creates agency costs for shareholders.

A10. How can employee perquisites create a conflict between the shareholders and the employees?

A11. How can product and service guarantees create an agency problem between the firm and its consumers?

A12. Cite and briefly discuss four devices that naturally monitor agent behavior for the principal.

Problem Set B

B1. Perfect monitoring in a perfect market environment always provides an optimal contract. Explain why monitoring is not always the best choice, even in a well-functioning market environment with low transaction costs.

B2. How does having a manager who is also a stockholder reduce potential conflicts of interest?

B3. Describe the problem of claim dilution, using the stock-as-an-option view.

B4. Explain the problem of the nondiversifiability of human capital.

B5. How does the nondiversifiability of human capital cause a conflict of interest between the managers and the stockholders regarding the firm's choice of investments?

B6. Explain how an agent's desire to maintain the ongoing value of a good reputation can facilitate shareholder monitoring of the agent.

B7. Explain why the stock price of a firm that is undergoing bankruptcy proceedings is virtually always positive and never negative.

B8. Explain how covenants in a bond indenture help to reduce a firm's agency costs, thereby reducing the firm's cost of financing.

B9. Using the stock-as-an-option view, explain why stockholders might choose not to undertake a low-risk investment, even if the expected NPV of the investment is positive. What group is on the other side of this transaction?

B10. Explain why debtholders typically require, in the bond indenture, covenants that restrict the firm's ability to take on additional debt. Cite two such covenants that are common, and relate them to your explanation.

B11. Define and explain in your own words the concept of an optimal contract.

B12. Using a contingent-claim view, describe in your own words how financial distress can intensify conflicts of interest among the firm's claimants. Cite three specific examples of situations in which this can occur.

B13. What methods do shareholders have at their disposal for aligning managers' goals with their goals?

B14. Using the stock-as-an-option view, explain why stockholders might choose to undertake a high-risk investment, even if the NPV of the investment is negative. What group is on the other side of this transaction?

Problem Set C

C1. Respond to the following statement: "Because a firm can lower its interest cost by including more restrictive covenants in its bond indentures, a firm should use the most restrictive set of covenants it can in order to achieve the lowest interest cost." (Obviously, there is the trade-off between lower interest cost and reduced decision-making flexibility. The subtle point here is the possibility of overlapping restrictions that don't add much protection for the debtholders but can be quite costly for the firm. For this reason, they are truly wasted costs.)

C2. Is it possible to have an agency problem if there is no asymmetric information? If so, cite an example. If not, explain why not.

C3. In some bankruptcy settlements, the debtholders accept less than full payment on the claim and at the same time agree to the stockholders getting a payment as well. Because the stockholders are only the *residual* claimants (after the debtholders get what they have been promised), why do the debtholders agree to let the stockholders get something? (*Hint*: Consider our example of the "unnecessary" payment The Seven-Up Company and Dr. Pepper Company made to their debtholders in exchange for their consent to the leveraged buyout—the hidden option to sue.)

C4. Suppose you were a firm's debtholder. Would you be concerned about the firm's dividend policy? Explain why or why not.

C5. How can employee perquisites create an agency problem between managers and the *debtholders*?

C6. Explain in your own words how a complex multilevel organization provides a natural form of agent monitoring.

C7. How does convertible debt help to reduce the agency problem between the shareholders and the debtholders?

C8. We have said that in cases of financial distress, various claimant coalitions can form. Is it possible to predict what those coalitions will be when the firm is healthy? If so, explain how. If not, explain why.

Real-World Application:
RJR Nabisco's Bond-Swap Plan

In March 1995, RJR Nabisco, Inc. (RJRN) announced a plan to restructure its debt. At the time, the firm had 32 issues of bonds with an aggregate principal amount of $5.5 billion. RJRN would swap 13 new debt issues of its Nabisco, Inc. food products subsidiary for equal principal amounts of 13 of the outstanding issues of RJRN (the parent firm) debt. The 13 new issues had an aggregate principal amount of $1.9 billion. The new debt would rank senior to the old debt with respect to the food business's assets and cash flow, and it would also have slightly less restrictive debt covenants than the old debt.[1] The other 19 issues, with an aggregate principal amount of $3.6 billion, would remain with the parent. The swap was widely seen as a preliminary step in what would eventually lead to the complete separation of RJRN's food and tobacco businesses into entirely separately owned corporations.

RJRN offered to swap bonds on the following basis.

	OLD ISSUE				NEW ISSUE		
Issuer	Principal Amount ($Millions)	Coupon	Maturity	Issuer	Principal Amount ($Millions)	Coupon	Maturity
RJRN	$600	8.30%	1999	Nabisco	$600	8.30%	1999
RJRN	441	8⅝%	2017	Nabisco	441	8⅝%	2017
RJRN	750	8%	2000	Nabisco	750	8%	2000
RJRN	10 issues aggregating $127 million			Nabisco	10 issues aggregating $127 million		

[1]The new debt would give RJRN's subsidiaries greater flexibility to borrow money.

In addition, RJRN offered holders of the 19 bond issues not subject to the exchange offer cash incentives for their *consents* to allow Nabisco, Inc. to make the swap: $2.50 per bond (0.25% of face amount) for the shortest maturities to $25.00 per bond (2.5% of face amount) for the longest maturity.

1. Suppose the food and tobacco businesses are broken into separately owned corporations. The food corporation has $1.9 billion of debt, the tobacco corporation has the other $3.6 billion, and the two corporations get assets in exactly the same proportions as the debt. Explain how *each* set of bondholders could experience claim dilution. (*Hint*: Consider the value of a portfolio of options on assets compared to the value of a comparable single option on the portfolio of assets. The options are the option to default.)

2. If both sets of bondholders experience claim dilution, does anyone benefit? Who, and how much?

3. Nabisco was a subsidiary of RJRN at the time of the exchange offer. Explain how shifting $1.9 billion of debt from RJRN "down" to Nabisco could benefit the holders of the bonds that are shifted but hurt the holders of the bonds that remain behind.

4. Explain how one set of bondholders might benefit at the expense of the other, depending on how the assets of RJRN are divided between the two corporations. (Nabisco had total assets of $11.8 billion and total debt of $5.6 billion. RJRN, its parent, had total assets of $31.4 billion and total debt of $11.1 billion.)

5. Following the announcement of the swap offer, RJRN's 8⅝% notes due December 1, 2002, which would remain with RJRN, rose in yield to maturity to 9.00% from 8.75% previously. How great a loss of wealth did the holders of that issue suffer? (Assume an April 1, 1995 valuation date.)

6. Following the announcement of the swap offer, RJRN's 9¼% debentures due August 15, 2013, which would also remain with RJRN, rose in yield to maturity to 9.60% from 9.50% previously. How great a loss of wealth did the holders of that issue suffer? (Assume an April 1, 1995 valuation date.)

7. How large a cash incentive would be needed to compensate the holders of the bonds in questions 5 and 6 for their loss of wealth?

8. Can you think of an alternative to making cash payment to compensate the holders of the bonds in questions 5 and 6 for their loss of wealth?

9. Following the announcement of the swap offer, RJRN's 8.30% notes due April 15, 1999, which could be exchanged, rose in price from 98 to 100. Holders of the bonds that would remain with RJRN argued that they should be paid at least 2 points per bond ($20) to consent to the restructuring. Do you agree?

10. RJRN required the approval of a majority of holders of some issues and of at least two-thirds of the other issues to complete the restructuring. That is, so long as the required (by the particular indentures) percentages of bondholders approved, all the bond indentures would be modified so as to permit the exchange offer to proceed. The changes would have the same effect on all holders of the 19 debt issues that would remain with RJRN. However, only those bondholders who had granted their consents would receive the cash incentive fees. How might this affect a bondholder's voting strategy?

BIBLIOGRAPHY

Admati, Anat R., and Paul Pfleiderer. "Robust Financial Contracts and the Role of Venture Capitalists," *Journal of Finance*, 1994, 49(2):371–402.

Agrawal, Anup, and Nandu J. Nagarajan. "Corporate Capital Structure, Agency Costs, and Ownership Control: The Case of All-Equity Firms," *Journal of Finance*, 1990, 45(4):1325–1331.

Agrawal, Anup, and Ralph A. Walkling. "Executive Careers and Compensation Surrounding Takeover Bids," *Journal of Finance*, 1994, 49(3):985–1014.

Bagnani, Elizabeth Strock, Nickolaos T. Milonas, Anthony Saunders, and Nickolaos G. Travlos. "Managers, Owners, and the Pricing of Risky Debt: An Empirical Analysis," *Journal of Finance*, 1994, 49(2): 453–477.

Baker, George P., Michael C. Jensen, and Kevin J. Murphy. "Compensation and Incentives: Practice vs. Theory," *Journal of Finance*, 1988, 43(3):593–616.

Barnea, Amir, Robert A. Haugen, and Lemma W. Senbet. *Agency Problems and Financial Contracting.* Englewood Cliffs, N.J.: Prentice-Hall, 1985.

Barry, Christopher B., Chris J. Muscarella, and Michael R. Vetsuypens. "Underwriter Warrants, Underwriter Compensation, and the Costs of Going Public," *Journal of Financial Economics*, 1991, 29(1):113–136.

Barton, Sidney L., Ned C. Hill, and Srinivasan Sundaram. "An Empirical Test of Stakeholder Theory Predictions of Capital Structure," *Financial Management*, 1989, 18(1):36–44.

Bergman, Yaacov Z., and Jeffrey L. Callen. "Opportunistic Underinvestment in Debt Renegotiation and Capital Structure," *Journal of Financial Economics*, 1991, 29(1):137–172.

Berkovitch, Elazar, and Stuart I. Greenbaum. "The Loan Commitment as an Optimal Financing Contract," *Journal of Financial and Quantitative Analysis*, 1991, 26(1):83–96.

Berkovitch, Elazar, and E. Han Kim. "Financial Contracting and Leverage Induced Over- and Under- Investment Incentives," *Journal of Finance*, 1990, 45(3): 765–794.

Berlin, Mitchell, and Jan Loeys. "Bond Covenants and Delegated Monitoring," *Journal of Finance*, 1988, 43(2):397–412.

Bessembinder, Hendrik. "Forward Contracts and Firm Value: Investment Incentive and Contracting Effects," *Journal of Financial and Quantitative Analysis*, 1991, 26(4):519–532.

Boot, Arnoud W. A., and Anjan V. Thakor. "Security Design," *Journal of Finance*, 1993, 48(4): 1349–1378.

Booth, James R., and Daniel N. Deli. "Factors Affecting the Number of Outside Directorships Held by CEOs," *Journal of Financial Economics*, 1996, 40(1):81–104.

Born, Jeffrey A. "Insider Ownership and Signals—Evidence from Dividend Initiation Announcement Effects," *Financial Management*, 1988, 17(1):38–45.

Born, Jeffrey A., and Victoria B. McWilliams. "Shareholder Responses to Equity-for-Debt Exchange Offers: A Free-Cash-Flow Interpretation," *Financial Management*, 1993, 22(4): 19–20.

Borstadt, Lisa F., and Thomas J. Zwirlein. "The Efficient Monitoring Role of Proxy Contests: An Empirical Analysis of Post-Contest Control Changes and Firm Performance," *Financial Management*, 1992, 21(3):22–34.

Brickley, James A., Frederick H. Dark, and Michael S. Weisbach. "An Agency Perspective on Franchising," *Financial Management*, 1991, 20(1):27–35.

Brickley, James A., and Kathleen T. Hevert. "Direct Employees Stock Ownership: An Empirical Investigation," *Financial Management*, 1991, 20(2):70–84.

Brook, Yaron, and Ramesh K. S. Rao. "Shareholder Wealth Effects of Directors' Liability Limitation Provisions," *Journal of Financial and Quantitative Analysis*, 1994, 29(3):481–497.

Bulow, Jeremy I., and John B. Shoven. "The Bankruptcy Decision," *The Bell Journal of Economics*, 1978, 9(Autumn):437–456.

Byrd, John W., and Kent A. Hickman. "Do Outside Directors Monitor Managers? Evidence from Tender Offer Bids," *Journal of Financial Economics*, 1992, 32(2):195–222.

Campbell, Tim S., and William A. Kracaw. "Corporate Risk Management and the Incentive Effects of Debt," *Journal of Finance*, 1990, 45(5):1673–1686.

Cannella, Albert A., Jr., Donald R. Fraser, and D. Scott Lee. "Firm Failure and Managerial Labor Markets: Evidence from Texas Banking," *Journal of Financial Economics*, 1995, 38(2):185–210.

Carter, Richard B., and Roger D. Stover. "Management Ownership and Firm Compensation Policy: Evidence from Converting Savings and Loan Associations," *Financial Management*, 1991, 20(4):80–90.

Chan, Yuk-Shee, Stuart I. Greenbaum, and Anjan V. Thakor. "Is Fairly Priced Deposit Insurance Possible?" *Journal of Finance*, 1992, 47(1): 227–246.

Chang, Chun. "Capital Structure as an Optimal Contract Between Employees and Investors," *Journal of Finance*, 1992, 47(3):1141–1158.

Chang, Saeyoung. "Employee Stock Ownership Plans and Shareholder Wealth: An Empirical Investigation," *Financial Management*, 1990, 19(1):48–58.

Choi, Yoon K. "The Choice of Organizational Form: The Case of Post-Merger Managerial Incentive Structure," *Financial Management*, 1993, 22(4):69–81.

Clayton, Ronnie J., and William Beranek. "Disassociations and Legal Combinations," *Financial Management*, 1985, 14(2): 24–28.

Conte, Michael A., and Douglas Kruse. "ESOPs and Profit-Sharing Plans: Do They Link Employee Pay to Company Performance?" *Financial Management*, 1991, 20(4):91–100.

Cook, Douglas O., John C. Easterwood, and John D. Martin. "Bondholder Wealth Effects of Management Buyouts," *Financial Management*, 1992, 21(1):102–112.

Cornell, Bradford, and Alan C. Shapiro. "Corporate Stakeholders and Corporate Finance," *Financial Management*, 1987, 16(1):5–14.

Cornett, Marcia Millon, and Nickolaos G. Travlos. "Information Effects Associated with Debt-for-Equity and Equity-for-Debt Exchange Offers," *Journal of Finance*, 1989, 44(2): 451–468.

Cotter, James F., and Marc Zenner. "How Managerial Wealth Affects the Tender Offer Process," *Journal of Financial Economics*, 1994, 35(1):63–97.

Crabbe, Leland. "Event Risk: An Analysis of Losses to Bondholders and 'Super Poison Put' Bond Covenants," *Journal of Finance*, 1991, 46(2):689–706.

Crutchley, Claire E., and Robert S. Hansen. "A Test of the Agency Theory of Managerial Ownership, Corporate Leverage, and Corporate Dividends," *Financial Management*, 1989, 18(4):36–46.

DeFusco, Richard A., Thomas S. Zorn, and Robert R. Johnson. "The Association Between Executive Stock Option Plan Changes and Managerial Decision Making," *Financial Management*, 1991, 20(1):36–43.

Denis, David J. "Organizational Form and the Consequences of Highly Leveraged Transactions: Kroger's Recapitalization and Safeway's LBO," *Journal of Financial Economics*, 1994, 36(2):193–224.

Denis, David J., and Diane K. Denis. "Performance Changes Following Top Management Dismissals," *Journal of Finance*, 1995, 50(4):1029–1057.

Denning, Karen C., and Kuldeep Shastri. "Changes in Organizational Structure and Shareholder Wealth: The Care of Limited Partnerships," *Journal of Financial and Quantitative Analysis*, 1993, 28(4):553–564.

Diamond, Douglas W. "Optimal Release of Information by Firms," *Journal of Finance*, 1985, 40(4):1071–1094.

Diamond, Douglas W. "Reputation Acquisition in Debt Markets," *Journal of Political Economy*, 1989, 97(August):828–862.

Donaldson, Gordon. *Managing Corporate Wealth: The Operations of a Comprehensive Financial Goals System*. New York: Praeger, 1984.

Fields, L. Paige, and Eric L. Mais. "Managerial Voting Rights and Seasoned Public Equity Issues," *Journal of Financial and Quantitative Analysis*, 1994, 29(3):445–457.

Finnerty, John D. "Stock-for-Debt Swaps and Shareholder Returns," *Financial Management*, 1985, 14(3): 5–17.

Fischer, Paul E. "Optimal Contracting and Insider Trading Restrictions," *Journal of Finance*, 1992, 47(2):673–694.

Fridson, Martin S. "Do High-Yield Bonds Have An Equity Component?" *Financial Management*, 1994, 23(2): 82–84.

Furtado, Eugene P. H., and Vijay Karan. "Causes, Consequences, and Shareholder Wealth Effects of Management Turnover: A Review of the Empirical Evidence," *Financial Management*, 1990, 19(2):60–75.

Giammarino, Ronald M., Tracy R. Lewis, and David E. M. Sappington. "An Incentive Approach to Banking Regulation," *Journal of Finance*, 1993, 48(4):1523–1542.

Gilson, Stuart C. "Bankruptcy, Boards, Banks, and Blockholders: Evidence on Changes in Corporate Ownership and Control When Firms Default," *Journal of Financial Economics*, 1990, 27(2):355–388.

Gilson, Stuart C., and Michael R. Vetsuypens. "CEO Compensation in Financially Distressed Firms: An Empirical Analysis," *Journal of Finance*, 1993, 48(2):425–458.

Gombola, Michael J., and George P. Tsetsekos. "The Information Content of Plant Closing Announcements: Evidence from Financial Profiles and the Stock Price Reaction," *Financial Management*, 1992, 21(2):31–40.

Gupta, Atul, and Leonard Rosenthal. "Ownership Structure, Leverage, and Firm Value: The Case of Leveraged Recapitalizations," *Financial Management*, 1991, 20(3):69–83.

Handa, Puneet, and A. R. Radhakrishnan. "An Empirical Investigation of Leveraged Recapitalizations with Cash Payout as Takeover Defense," *Financial Management*, 1991, 20(3):58–68.

Harris, Milton, and Artur Raviv. "Capital Structure and the Informational Role of Debt," *Journal of Finance*, 1990, 45(2):321–350.

Hasbrouck, Joel. "Measuring the Information Content of Stock Trades," *Journal of Finance*, 1991, 46(1):179–208.

Hermalin, Benjamin E., and Michael S. Weisbach. "The Effects of Board Composition and Direct Incentives on Firm Performance," *Financial Management*, 1991, 20(4):101–112.

Hertzel, Michael, and Richard L. Smith. "Market Discounts and Shareholder Gains for Placing Equity Privately," *Journal of Finance*, 1993, 48(2):459–485.

Hirshleifer, David. "Managerial Reputation and Corporate Investment Decisions," *Financial Management*, 1993, 22(2):145–160.

Jensen, Michael C., and William H. Meckling. "Theory of the Firm: Managerial Behavior, Agency Costs and Ownership Structure," *Journal of Financial Economics*, 1976, 3(4): 305–360.

Jordan, James V., and George Emir Morgan. "Default Risk in Futures Markets: The Customer-Broker Relationship," *Journal of Finance*, 1990, 45(3):909–934.

Kaplan, Steven N., and David Reishus. "Outside Directorships and Corporate Performance," *Journal of Financial Economics*, 1990, 27(2):389–410.

Kumar, Raman, and Parvez R. Sopariwala. "The Effect of Adoption of Long-Term Performance Plans on Stock Prices and Accounting Numbers," *Journal of Financial and Quantitative Analysis*, 1992, 27(4):561–574.

Laber, Gene. "Bond Covenants and Forgone Opportunities: The Case of Burlington Northern Railroad Company," *Financial Management*, 1992, 21(2):71–77.

Lippert, Robert L., and William T. Moore. "Monitoring versus Bonding: Shareholder Rights and Management Compensation," *Financial Management*, 1995, 24(3):54–62.

Loderer, Claudio P., and Dennis P. Sheehan. "Corporate Bankruptcy and Managers' Self-Serving Behavior," *Journal of Finance*, 1989, 44(4):1059–1076.

Logue, Dennis E., James K. Seward, and James P. Walsh. "Rearranging Residual Claims: A Case for Targeted Stock," *Financial Management*, 1996, 25(1):43–61.

Long, Michael S. "The Incentives Behind the Adoption of Executive Stock Option Plans in U.S. Corporations," *Financial Management*, 1992, 21(3):12–21.

Mahajan, Arvind. "Pricing Expropriation Risk," *Financial Management*, 1990, 19(4):77–86.

Maksimovic, Vojislav. "Product Market Imperfections and Loan Commitments," *Journal of Finance*, 1990, 45(5):1641–1654.

Maksimovic, Vojislav, and Josef Zechner. "Debt, Agency Costs, and Industry Equilibrium," *Journal of Finance*, 1991, 46(5):1619–1644.

Malitz, Ileen. "On Financial Contracting: The Determinants of Bond Covenants," *Financial Management*, 1986, 15(2):18–25.

McLaughlin, Robyn M. "Does the Form of Compensation Matter? Investment Banker Fee Contracts in Tender Offers," *Journal of Financial Economics*, 1992, 32(2):223–260.

Mehran, Hamid. "Executive Compensation Structure, Ownership, and Firm Performance," *Journal of Financial Economics*, 1995, 38(2):163–184.

Merton, Robert C., and Zvi Bodie. "On the Management of Financial Guarantees," *Financial Management*, 1992, 21(4):87–109.

Michel, Allen, and Israel Shaked. "Airline Performance Under Deregulation: The Shareholders' Perspective," *Financial Management*, 1984, 13(2):5–14.

Murphy, J. Austin. "Analyzing Sub-Classes of General Motors Common Stock," *Financial Management*, 1989, 18(1):64–71.

Netter, Jeffry, and Annette Poulsen. "State Corporation Laws and Shareholders: The Recent Experience," *Financial Management*, 1989, 18(3):29–40.

Park, Sangsoo, and Moon H. Song. "Employee Stock Ownership Plans, Firm Performance, and Monitoring by Outside Blockholders," *Financial Management*, 1995, 24(4):52–65.

Perotti, Enrico C., and Serhat E. Guney. "The Structure of Privatization Plans," *Financial Management*, 1993, 22(1):84–98.

Persons, John C. "Signaling and Takeover Deterrence with Stock Repurchases: Dutch Auctions versus Fixed Price Tender Offers," *Journal of Finance*, 1994, 49(4):1373–1402.

Petersen, Mitchell A., and Raghuram G. Rajan. "The Benefits of Lending Relationships: Evidence from Small Business Data," *Journal of Finance*, 1994, 49(1):3–37.

Rosen, Corey. "The Record of Employee Ownership," *Financial Management*, 1990, 19(1):39–47.

Rosenstein, Stuart, and Jeffrey G. Wyatt. "Outside Directors, Board Independence, and Shareholder Wealth," *Journal of Financial Economics*, 1990, 26(2):175–192.

Roy, Asim. "Partial Acquisition Strategies for Business Combinations," *Financial Management*, 1985, 14(2):16–23.

Sanders, Ralph W., Jr., and John S. Zdanowicz. "Target Firm Abnormal Returns and Trading Volume Around the Initiation of Change in Control Transactions," *Journal of Financial and Quantitative Analysis*, 1992, 27(1):109–130.

Schwartz, Eduardo S., and Salvador Zurita. "Sovereign Debt: Optimal Contract, Underinvestment, and Forgiveness," *Journal of Finance*, 1992, 47(3):981–1004.

Slovin, Myron B., and Marie E. Sushka. "Ownership Concentration, Corporate Control Activity, and Firm Value: Evidence from the Death Of Inside Blockholders," *Journal of Finance*, 1993, 48(4):1293–1321.

Slovin, Myron B., Marie E. Sushka, and John A. Polonchek. "The Value of Bank Durability: Borrowers as Bank Shakeholders," *Journal of Finance*, 1993, 48(1):247–266.

Smith, Clifford W., Jr., and Ross L. Watts. "The Investment Opportunity Set and Corporate Financing, Dividend, and Compensation Policies," *Journal of Financial Economics*, 1992, 32(3):263–292.

Spatt, Chester S., and Frederic P. Sterbenz. "Incentive Conflicts, Bundling Claims, and the Interaction Among Financial Claimants," *Journal of Finance*, 1993, 48(2):513–528.

Szewczyk, Samuel H., and George T. Tsetsekos. "State Intervention in the Market for Corporate Control: The Case of Pennsylvania Senate Bill 1310," *Journal of Financial Economics*, 1992, 31(1):3–22.

Thakor, Anjan V. "Game Theory in Finance," *Financial Management*, 1991, 20(1):71–94.

Thakor, Anjan V. "Strategic Issues in Financial Contracting: An Overview," *Financial Management*, 1989, 18(2):39–58.

Williamson, Oliver E. "Corporate Finance and Corporate Governance," *Journal of Finance*, 1988, 43(3):567–591.

Part III

CAPITAL BUDGETING: STRATEGIC ASSET ALLOCATION

Capital budgeting is the process of choosing a firm's long-term capital investments. This includes investments in such things as land, plant, and equipment. Capital budgeting is fundamental, because a firm is essentially defined by its assets and the products and services those assets produce. For example, Ford is a car maker, regardless of how it is financed. A firm's choices of which products to produce and which services to offer, then, are capital budgeting decisions—and those choices are intertwined with all the other decisions facing the firm.

A firm has an almost limitless number of possible investments, but past and current choices constrain its future choices. This is why we have added the phrase "strategic asset allocation" to the title of Part III. The strategic nature of these choices can be seen in the time horizons of capital assets, which may span years or even decades. In some cases, such as forest product management, capital assets may not produce returns for generations.

Regardless of their time horizons, capital investments are judged on the value they create. When you buy a stock or bond that is worth more than it costs—one with a positive NPV—your wealth increases by the amount of the difference. When a firm undertakes a capital investment project with a positive NPV, the value of the firm's stock increases by that amount. And, of course, a negative-NPV project decreases the value of the firm's stock. You can see why we say capital budgeting decisions are the most important decisions facing the firm. Capital budgeting has a direct link to shareholder wealth. The more successful a firm's capital budgeting decisions, the higher the value of the firm's stock.

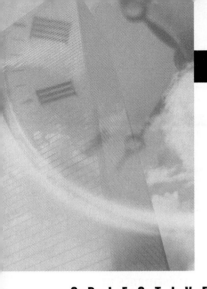

COST OF CAPITAL

O B J E C T I V E S

After studying this chapter, you should be able to

1. Describe the process of capital budgeting and the purpose and importance of each of its aspects.

2. Explain why the cost of capital is based on the concept of an opportunity cost, not on the historical cost of funds.

3. Distinguish among the cost of capital, the required return to equity, and the required return to debt, and identify the major determinants of each.

4. Distinguish between business risk and financial risk, and identify the important differences between operating leverage and financial leverage.

5. Estimate the cost of capital for a capital budgeting project.

The required return for a capital budgeting project is called the *cost of capital*. The cost of capital can be thought of as an opportunity cost. If a firm invests the money in the project, it creates an opportunity cost: It gives up the chance to invest in other, essentially comparable financial securities. Thus one way to view the cost of capital is as the required return on essentially comparable publicly traded securities.[1]

Recall that corporate financial management can be broken down into two parts: (1) the financing decision and (2) the investment decision. The financing, or capital structure, decision involves the components of the right-hand side of the balance sheet. In simple terms, it is the firm's choice between liabilities and stockerholders' equity. The investment decision involves the components of the left-hand side of the balance sheet. It is the firm's choice of assets. We use the fact that the two sides must be equal to help us understand how the cost of capital (financing) is related to the firm's choice of assets (investment).

In Chapter 4, we defined the required return as the minimum return an investor must expect to earn to be willing to undertake the investment. In a sense, then, the required return is related to the financing decision, because the investor must earn that return to be willing to provide financing.

The expected return is the return that the investor actually expects to earn if the investment is undertaken. The expected return for a capital budgeting project is called its *internal rate of return* (IRR). The expected return is related to the investment decision. It is what investors expect to earn if they invest.

Recall that in a perfect capital market environment, the expected and required returns are equal. For example, an investment in a security that is traded in a perfect capital market is a zero-NPV investment: The investor expects to earn exactly the required return.

Based on the Principle of Capital Market Efficiency, a perfect capital

---

[1] Such comparability is admittedly difficult to define in some cases. In Chapter 7 we noted the example of COMSAT's communications satellite. In that case there was nothing comparable. However, recall that nondiversifiable risk is the primary dimension. As a practical matter, then, investments are considered comparable when they have identical nondiversifiable risk.

market environment is a good starting point for determining a required return, just as it was in our discussions in Chapters 5 through 8. However, the firm's investment decision often involves purchases and sales of real (physical) assets in markets that are not always efficient or well behaved. This is because of differences in the similarity of assets, transaction costs, and the degree of competition. We will discuss the important differences between capital markets and real asset markets in Chapter 14.

Because real asset markets are not generally as efficient as our capital markets, prices are less likely to be consistently *fair*. We therefore compute the present value of an investment to determine its value and thus help us decide whether to undertake the investment. The required return, which we will estimate from the capital markets, is a necessary—and critical—input to measuring the NPV of an investment. It is critical because the present value of a future cash flow is inversely related to the discount rate, r. The higher the discount rate, the lower the present value of the future cash flow. Clearly, then, using the wrong value for r can cause the NPV of an investment to be incorrectly measured, which may in turn cause poor investment decisions.

In Chapters 5 through 8, we determined required returns for investing in financial securities such as bonds, stocks, and options. In this chapter we will apply these concepts to determine required returns for corporate investments in real assets. We continue to assume that the firm is operating in an essentially perfect capital market environment. Later, in Chapters 14 through 16, we will examine the effect of capital market imperfections on the cost of capital and on required returns in general.

COST OF CAPITAL AND THE PRINCIPLES OF FINANCE

◇ *Valuable Ideas:* Look for new ideas to use as a basis for capital budgeting projects that will create value.

◇ *Comparative Advantage:* Look for capital budgeting projects that use the firm's comparative advantage to add value.

◇ *Risk-Return Trade-Off:* Consider the risk of a capital budgeting project when determining the project's *cost of capital:* its required return.

◇ *Time Value of Money:* Measure the value a capital budgeting project will create: its NPV.

◇ *Incremental Benefits:* Identify and estimate the incremental expected future cash flows for a capital budgeting project.

◇ *Options:* Recognize the value of options, such as the options to expand, postpone, or abandon a capital budgeting project.

◇ *Two-Sided Transactions:* Consider why the other party to a transaction is willing to participate.

◇ *Signaling:* Consider the actions and products of competitors.

10.1 THE CAPITAL BUDGETING PROCESS

Let's begin by looking at how **capital budgeting** works in practice. The overall process can be broken down into five steps as a project moves from idea to reality:

1. Generating ideas for capital budgeting projects.
2. Preparing proposals.
3. Reviewing existing projects and facilities.
4. Evaluating proposed projects and creating the **capital budget**, the firm's set of planned capital expenditures.
5. Preparing appropriation requests.

We will look at each step in turn.

Idea Generation

Generating new ideas is the first—and most important—part of the capital budgeting process. Its critical importance is obvious from the Principle of Valuable Ideas. Unfortunately, we cannot teach people how to come up with valuable new ideas. If we could, we would already be wealthy from having followed the procedure ourselves! However, although we do not have a process that ensures the creation of new ideas, it is important to stress their value. Such an emphasis increases the likelihood that the ideas that do occur to us and to others will be given serious consideration.

Where do new ideas come from? Ideas for capital budgeting projects come from all levels within an organization. Figure 10-1 diagrams the typical flow of capital budgeting ideas within a firm. Often plant managers are responsible for identifying potential projects that will enable their plants to operate on a different scale or on a more efficient basis. For instance, a plant manager might suggest adding 10,000 square feet of production space to a plant or replacing a piece of equipment with a newer, more efficient machine. After screening out the less advantageous or less attractive ideas, the manager would send the ones that appear to be attractive along to the divisional level, with supporting documentation.

FIGURE 10-1
The typical flow of capital budgeting ideas within a firm.

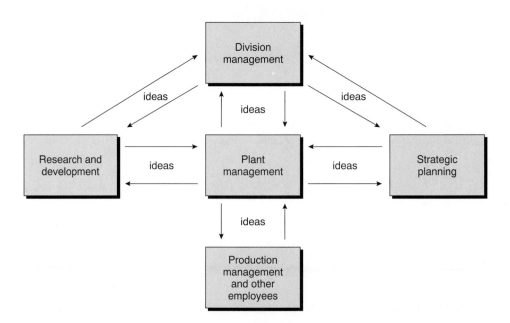

TABLE 10-1
Development and approval stages for a proposed capital budgeting project.

1. Approve funds for research that may result in a product *idea*.
2. Approve funds for market research that may result in a product *proposal*.
3. Approve funds for product development that may result in a usable *product*.
4. Approve funds for plant and/or equipment for the *production* and sale of the new product.

Division management not only reviews such proposals but also adds ideas of its own. For example, division management may propose introducing a new product line or combining two plants and eliminating the less efficient one. Such ideas are less likely to come from the plant managers!

This "bottom-up" process results in ideas percolating upward through the organization. At each level, ideas submitted by lower-level managers are screened, and some are forwarded to the next level. In addition, the managers at successively higher levels, who are in a position to take a broader view of the firm's business, add ideas that might not occur to lower-level managers.

At the same time, there can be a top-down process. Strategic planners can generate ideas about new businesses the firm should enter, other firms it might acquire, and ways to modify its existing businesses to achieve greater profitability. Strategic planning is a critical element in the capital budgeting process. The processes complement one another. The top-down process generates ideas of a broader, more strategic nature. The bottom-up process generates ideas of a more project-specific nature.

In addition, some firms have a research-and-development group, either within a production division or as a separate department. A research-and-development group often provides new ideas for products, and these ideas are sent on to a marketing research department. Table 10-1 lists the typical stages in the development and approval of a capital investment proposal.

Each stage in Table 10-1 involves a capital budgeting decision at one or more levels of the firm. Therefore, at each stage the firm re-estimates the NPV of going ahead. With this kind of sequential appropriation of funds, an automatic progress review makes possible the early cancellation of unsuccessful projects. Thus each stage includes options to abandon, postpone, change, or continue.

Boeing Corporation is the world's leading maker of commercial aircraft. Just a few years ago, the firm faced a critical capital budgeting decision: whether to develop a new generation of passenger aircraft, the 777. Developing new aircraft is very expensive, as Boeing well knows. The firm estimated that research and development, testing, and evaluation for the 777 would cost between $4 billion and $5 billion. Placing the new aircraft into production would require new manufacturing facilities costing about $1.5 billion, plus an additional $0.5 billion in personnel training costs. An aggregate investment of between $6 billion and $7 billion was large enough that the project's success or failure would have a profound effect on Boeing's fortunes for years to come. An unprofitable project of that size could threaten Boeing's very survival, whereas its success would strengthen Boeing's leadership in commercial aviation. Therefore, correctly analyzing the 777 project was critical to Boeing's future and to the value of its shareholders' investment. ■

Boeing's Strategic Decision: Will the 777 Project Fly?

EXAMPLE

Classifying Capital Budgeting Projects

Analysis costs money. Therefore, certain types of projects receive only cursory checks before approval, whereas others are subjected to extensive analysis. Generally, less costly and more routine projects are subjected to less extensive evaluation. As a result, firms typically categorize projects and scrutinize them to the level judged appropriate for their category.

MAINTENANCE EXPENDITURES   At a most basic level, a firm must make certain investments to continue to be a healthy, profitable business. Replacing worn-out or damaged equipment is a necessity. Therefore, the major questions concerning such investments are "Should we continue in this business?" and if so, "Should we continue to use the same production process?" Because the answers to these questions are so frequently "yes," an elaborate decision-making process is not a good use of resources, and typically such decisions are approved with only routine review.

COST SAVINGS/REVENUE ENHANCEMENT   Projects in this class include improvements in production technology to realize cost savings and marketing campaigns to achieve revenue enhancement. The central issue is increasing the difference between revenue and cost; the result must be sufficient to justify the investment. Cost-reducing investments require not only that purchase and installation of the equipment be profitable but also that taking immediate action be better than waiting until a later time—the firm may have a valuable option that will have to be postponed.

CAPACITY EXPANSION IN CURRENT BUSINESSES   Deciding to expand the current business is inherently more difficult than approving maintenance or cost-savings proposals. Firms have to consider the economics of expanding or adding new facilities. They also must prepare demand forecasts, and the Principle of Two-Sided Transactions reminds us to consider competitors' likely strategies. Marketing consultants may help, but the cash flow projections for this type of project have naturally greater uncertainty than do maintenance or replacement projects.

NEW PRODUCTS AND NEW BUSINESSES   Projects in this category, which include research-and-development activities, are among the most difficult to evaluate. Their newness and generally longer lead times make it very difficult to forecast product demand accurately. In many cases, the project may be of special interest because it would give the firm an option to break into a new market. For example, consider a firm that possesses an exclusively controlled technology, such as one involving a patented process. Such a firm might spend additional research-and-development funds trying to develop new products based on this technology. If successful, these new products could pave the way for profitable future investment opportunities. Access to such follow-on opportunities represents an important option for the firm, and we know options are valuable.

MEETING REGULATORY AND POLICY REQUIREMENTS   Government regulations and firm policies concerning such things as pollution control and health or safety factors are viewed as costs. Often, the critical issue in such projects is meeting the standards in the most efficient manner—at the minimum present-value cost—rather than realizing the value added by the project. Engineering analyses of alternative technologies often provide critical information in such cases. Of course, the firm must also consider the possibility that the option to abandon the business is worth more than making the required investments and continuing.

Capital Budgeting Proposals

Small expenditures may be handled informally, but in general, the originator presents a proposal in writing. Sometimes proposals are not formally written in smaller privately owned firms, which tend to have relatively informal organizational structures. Most firms use standard forms, and these are typically supplemented by written memoranda for larger, more complex projects. Also, there may be consulting or other studies prepared by outside experts, such as forecasts from economic consultants.

For a healthy firm, a maintenance project might require only limited supporting information. In contrast, a new product would require extensive information gathering and analysis. At the same time, within a category, managers at each level typically have upper limits on their authority regarding both expenditures on individual assets and the total expenditure for a budgeting period. This ensures that larger projects require the approval of higher authority. For example, at the lowest level, a department head may have the authority to approve $25,000 in total equipment purchases for the year. However, that same person might have to obtain specific approval from higher authority to spend more than $5000 for any single piece of equipment. A plant manager might have authorization limits of $250,000 per year and $50,000 per piece of equipment, and so on. Such a system requires that larger expenditures get more extensive review and have a greater number of inputs to approve them. Multiple reviews make sense, because a firm wishes to avoid making a negative-NPV decision. The hierarchical review structure reflects the obvious fact that misjudging a larger project is potentially more costly than misjudging a smaller one.

Self-Check Questions

1. List the five steps in the capital budgeting process. Which is most important?

2. Where do new ideas for capital budgeting projects come from?

3. What are the four development and approval stages for a proposed capital budgeting project?

4. List the five categories in which firms classify capital budgeting projects. What distinguishes each from the others?

10.2 HISTORICAL VERSUS INCREMENTAL COST OF CAPITAL

Unfortunately, the term **cost of capital** can be very misleading. The cost of capital is the required return for a capital budgeting project. It is *not* the firm's historical cost of funds, such as coupon payments on existing bonds, that determines the cost of capital. The relevant cost of funds is an *opportunity cost*. It is the return at which investors would provide financing for the capital budgeting project under consideration *today*. If the firm's historical cost of capital were used to evaluate capital budgeting projects, the analysis would be wrong if market rates had changed.

Observing capital markets for just a short time will convince you that market rates are not constant. However, at any one time, there is only *one* return for a given risk level in an efficient capital market. Any differential in the expected returns for comparable investments will be eliminated quickly by arbitrage activity.

A second problem with the historical perspective involves differences in risk. The cost of capital also is *not* the required return on the firm's existing operations. This is because the firm's current cost of capital reflects the average risk of *all* the firm's existing assets, and the project's risk may be very different from this average.

The required return for any investment is the minimum return that investors must expect to earn in order to be willing to finance the investment today. When management acts in the shareholders' best interest, the cost of capital reflects the return that investors could earn today on comparable capital market investments—that is, those that have the same risk.

Self-Check Questions

1. What is the cost of capital? Why is it *not* the firm's historical cost of funds?

2. Why is the required return from an investment the minimum return investors must expect to earn in order to be willing to finance that investment today?

10.3 CORPORATE VALUATION

In a perfect capital market environment, a firm's market value is not affected by the way the firm is financed. The value of a firm depends only on the size of its expected future cash flows and the required return on those expected future cash flows. The firm's value does not depend on how those cash flows must be divided between the debtholders and the shareholders. Therefore, a firm's capital structure—how the firm is financed—is irrelevant to the firm's value in a perfect capital market environment.

The Financing Decision

If the financing decision does not affect the value of the firm, you might wonder why we have any interest in it. There are at least three reasons. First, even if the financing decision does not affect the firm's value, it can provide us with important insight into how to estimate the cost of capital. Second, as a practical matter, even in an efficient capital market, mistakes can be made. It is important to understand the financing decision, if only to avoid making stupid mistakes in operating the firm. Finally, examining the financing decision in a perfect capital market environment provides a good foundation for understanding, later on, why and how certain capital market imperfections cause the financing decision to affect the firm's value after all.

The value of a firm can be expressed as the value of the claims on its assets. That is, the firm's value equals the total market value of its liabilities plus the total market value of its stockholders' equity:

$$\text{Firm Value} = \text{Equity} + \text{Debt}$$

Although this may look suspiciously like the balance sheet equation, it is important to emphasize that it is given in market values rather than book values. Equity is the current value of all the firm's outstanding shares of stock. This value is often estimated by multiplying the current market value per share times the number of outstanding shares.

For example, suppose CBS's stock is currently selling for $48.25 and there are 20 million shares outstanding. CBS's equity would be estimated to be $965 million (= 20 × 48.25). Similarly, debt is the market value of all the firm's outstanding liabilities.

The Investment Decision

We can also express the value of a firm in terms of its assets. That is, firm value is also the sum of the market values of its assets, shown as $A_1, A_2, \ldots$:

$$\text{Firm value} = A_1 + A_2 + A_3 + \cdots$$

This representation is also a market value expression, but in this case it is for the asset (left-hand) side of the balance sheet. Here, the firm's value is represented as a portfolio of its real assets.[2] The firm's investment decision consists of choosing which assets to add to, or remove from, its portfolio. That choice is based on earning at least the required return on each asset.

---

[2] Note that to equate these two expressions for firm value is to see a firm as an intermediary between its investors and the real asset markets. This is essentially the investment-vehicle model of the firm we outlined in Figure 1-4.

This view of firm value as a portfolio of assets is important. It shows how each asset must "rest on its own bottom." That is, each asset (or group of interrelated assets) has its own unique value, required return, and expected return. The expected return for a capital budgeting project is called its **internal rate of return (IRR)**.

An asset must be expected to earn at least its cost of capital (required return) to justify its inclusion in the firm's asset portfolio. In simple terms, then, the IRR must equal or exceed the cost of capital. As the next chapter will show, this rule can break down in some situations. For now, however, the simple notion that the expected return must equal or exceed the required return provides us with the intuition we need to understand the concept of cost of capital.

The Market Line for Capital Budgeting Projects

Our derivation of the Capital-Asset-Pricing Model (CAPM) in Chapter 7 was based on shares of common stock. However, the concept can be extended to include all real assets as well. We can build on the idea of the security market line (SML) and create what might be called the capital budgeting project market line (PML). The cost of capital for capital budgeting project j, r_j, can then be expressed as a function of the nondiversifiable risk of the project, its beta:

$$r_j = r_f + \beta_j(r_M - r_f)$$

where r_f is the riskless return, β_j is the beta for project j, and r_M is the required return on the market portfolio. Capital budgeting projects are then evaluated on the basis of the PML in the same way securities are evaluated using the SML.

Suppose Kmart Corporation is considering five capital budgeting projects. Undertaking any single project does not preclude, or require, undertaking any of the others. Each project costs the same ($1 million), but each has a unique beta (and therefore its own cost of capital) and promises a unique perpetual annual cash flow. The required return on the market portfolio is 15%, and the riskless return is 7%.

Capital Budgeting for Kmart

EXAMPLE

Table 10-2 shows the beta, cost of capital, annual cash flow, IRR, and NPV of each project. For example, the beta for project A is 1.30, so its cost of capital is 17.4% [= 7 + 1.30(15 − 7)]. Project A's annual cash flow is $200,000 making its IRR 20% (= 200,000/1,000,000). Finally, the NPV for project A is $149,430, which is the present value of the expected future cash flows, $1,149,430 (= 200,000/0.174), minus its initial cost of $1,000,000.

PROJECT	BETA	REQUIRED RETURN	ANNUAL CASH FLOW	EXPECTED RETURN	NPV
A	1.30	17.4%	$200,000	20%	$149,430
B	1.75	21.0	220,000	22	47,620
C	.95	14.6	140,000	14	− 41,100
D	1.50	19.0	170,000	17	− 105,260
E	.60	11.8	140,000	14	186,440

TABLE 10-2
Kmart's capital budgeting projects.

Figure 10-2 graphs the costs of capital and IRRs for the projects Kmart is considering, along with the PML. The costs of capital fall on the PML, because they were determined by the PML equation. As with the SML, investments that are above the line have a positive NPV. Thus projects A, B, and E have positive NPVs, whereas projects C and D have negative NPVs. ■

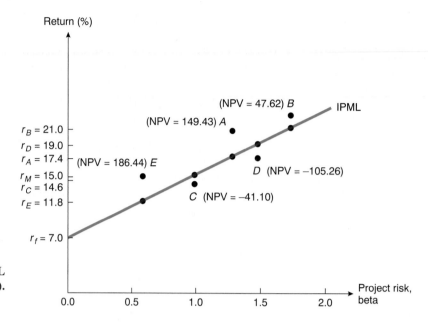

FIGURE 10-2
Kmart's alternative capital budgeting projects and the PML (NPV in $ thousands).

Self-Check Questions

1. True or false? A firm's capital structure does not affect its value in a perfect capital market environment.

2. Why should we be interested in how a firm finances itself?

3. Cite two alternative bases for the equation Firm value = Equity + Debt. Which basis is the one that interests us in finance?

4. What is the internal rate of return for a capital budgeting project?

5. What is the capital budgeting project market line (PML)? How is it like the security market line (SML)?

10.4 VALUE AND THE RISK-RETURN TRADE-OFF

It is very important to keep in mind the relationship among the cost of capital, expected cash flows, and present value. Present value depends on both the cost of capital *and* the expected cash flows. When any one of these three things changes, at least one of the others must also change.

For example, when the cost of capital increases, present value decreases if the expected cash flows do not also change. We have seen this in the case of a bond. With constant coupon payments, the market value of a bond changes whenever market interest rates change.

Similarly, an increase in the expected cash flows increases present value if the cost of capital (and therefore risk) has not changed. The relationship most easily forgotten with respect to this concept is that *present value can remain constant even when there are changes in both the expected cash flows and the cost of capital (required return)*. The changes can exactly offset each other. This is precisely what the Principle of Risk-Return Trade-Off means. Present value is constant, even though the required return and expected cash flows change.

Consider the following simple example.

Assume you have an asset that has an expected cash payment of $100 per year forever. Some years the cash payment may be more, and other years less. The risk of this asset makes its required return 10%, so the asset's value is $1000 (= 100/0.1). Now suppose you can exchange this asset for some other asset that has an expected cash payment of $200 per year forever. However, because of higher risk, its required return is 20%. The alternative asset's cash flow can be much smaller or larger than the expected $200 per year. Should you make the exchange?

A Pure Risk-Return Trade-Off

EXAMPLE

The value of the alternative asset is also $1000 (= 200/0.2). Therefore, your choice depends *only* on your attitude toward risk. In other words, your choice represents a pure risk-return trade-off. Even though the other asset's expected cash flows are larger, *there is no difference in value*. Such is the case when an investor moves along the SML or a firm moves along the PML. Value is enhanced only when the increase (decrease) in expected cash flows exceeds (is less than) the increase (decrease) in risk. ■

Self-Check Questions

1. What happens to present value when the expected cash flows all increase and the cost of capital does not change?

2. What happens to present value when the cost of capital decreases and the expected cash flows do not change?

3. How can the present value remain constant if the expected cash flows and the cost of capital are changing?

10.5 LEVERAGE

According to the CAPM, the required return depends only on the nondiversifiable risk of an investment. However, nondiversifiable risk borne by the shareholders can be split into two parts. The main part is often called **business risk** or **operating risk**. The secondary part is referred to as **financial risk**. It is important to distinguish between these two types of risk, because they affect required returns in different ways.

In many cases a firm cannot control its business risk. It is simply the inherent risk of an investment. In contrast, a firm's financial risk is determined by the amount of debt it has—its financial leverage or simply **leverage**. More leverage increases risk.

The term *leverage* is derived from the mechanical lever that enables you to lift more weight than you could by yourself. Financial leverage allows shareholders to control (lift, so to speak) more assets than would be possible if they used only their own money. In addition to (financial) leverage, there is a second type of leverage called operating leverage. We turn to it now.

Operating Leverage

Operating leverage is the relative mix of fixed versus variable costs in the process used to produce a product or service. Multiple methods of producing a product or service may exist, whereby a firm spends more on fixed costs and less on variable costs, or vice versa. A decrease in the variable cost per unit creates an increase in the contribution margin (the selling price minus the variable cost). With a larger contribution margin, the firm's profit is more sensitive to changes in sales. That is, a smaller change in sales makes a larger change in profit, because the variable costs are smaller whereas the fixed costs are incurred in either case.

In contrast, an increase in the variable cost per unit causes a decrease in the contribution margin. With a smaller contribution margin, the change in profit caused by a change in the sales level will not be so large. Therefore, lowering the variable cost per unit (by increasing fixed costs) increases the sensitivity of the firm's profit to changes in the level of sales. Such an increase in fixed cost is referred to as an increase in operating leverage.

EXAMPLE

Eastern Mountain Apparel Ski Cap Production

Eastern Mountain Apparel will purchase one of two alternative production methods for manufacturing ski caps. Method A costs $30,000 to install and $6 to make one cap. Method B costs $54,000 to install and $4 to make one cap. Eastern sells caps for $11 apiece. Which production method should Eastern purchase?

The answer, of course, depends on how many ski caps will be sold. For simplicity, let's ignore taxes and the time value of money. Profit will be the contribution margin times the number of caps sold, N, minus the fixed cost. The profit will be $5N - \$30,000$ for method A and $7N - \$54,000$ for method B. Figure 10–3 illustrates Eastern's profit as a function of the number of ski caps sold for both methods.

As you might predict from our foregoing discussion, method B with its higher operating leverage (larger fixed cost and smaller variable cost) will make Eastern's profit more sensitive to the number of units sold. The slope of the profit line for method B is steeper. If the number sold turns out to be more than 12,000 (the point where the profit functions are equal, $5N - 30,000 = 7N - 54,000$), then method B would be the better choice. On the other hand, if sales turn out to be less than 12,000 units, then method A would be the better choice. Of course, the best choice may not be obvious if the sales amount is highly variable or if it is expected to be about 12,000. ■

FIGURE 10-3
Eastern Mountain Apparel's operating leverage alternatives.

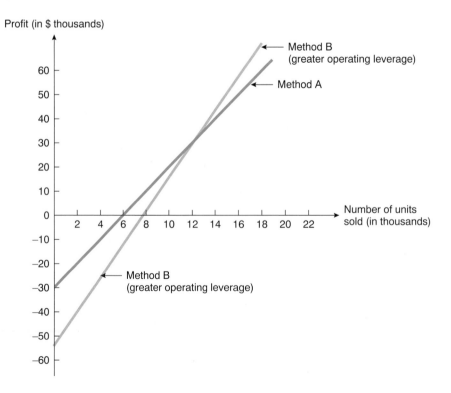

Operating leverage is important because of its impact on the risk of the investment. However, a firm's choice of operating leverage is limited by the number of possible different methods of producing a product and/or service. In some cases, a firm has no choice because there is a single (or significantly most efficient) method of production.

There are two important things to remember about operating leverage. First, operating leverage is generally unique for each investment rather than identical for all the firm's investments. Second, operating leverage affects the total risk of the capital budgeting project, both diversifiable and nondiversifiable risk. Because operating leverage affects nondiversifiable risk, it also affects both the beta and the project's cost of capital.

Financial Leverage

Operating risk depends principally on the nature of the investment and to a lesser extent on the firm's choice of operating leverage. In contrast, financial risk depends mostly on financial leverage. When a firm has some debt financing, the debt portion of its financing costs are fixed rather than variable. Although we would expect a larger return to shareholders than to debtholders, shareholder return can vary from one period to the next without affecting the operation of the firm. However, failure to make required debt payments can result in bankruptcy. We could say, then, that financial leverage substitutes fixed payments to debtholders for variable payments to shareholders.

Graphically, financial leverage looks similar to operating leverage. The shareholders' (owners') realized return in an all-equity-financed firm is the same as the firm's realized return. The shareholders' realized return in a leveraged firm is the return realized *after* the fixed payment to the debtholders has been taken out. The shareholders are the *residual* owners.

Figure 10-4 illustrates the shareholders' realized return as a function of the firm's realized return with and without leverage. The leverage alternative assumes 50% debt financing. Figure 10-4 ignores taxes and assumes that the firm pays a 10% interest rate on its debt.

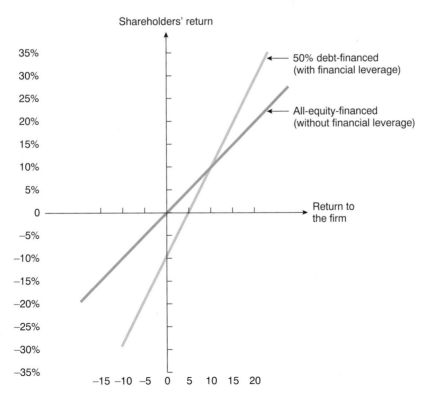

FIGURE 10-4
The effect of (financial) leverage on shareholder return.

We have come across the concept of financial leverage before. Recall that all investors in a perfect capital market should invest in the same risky portfolio—the market portfolio. Investors set their risk and return levels by lending or borrowing. This kind of lending and borrowing is simply *personal financial leverage*. There is a very important fact that we learned about personal leverage: The choice of lending or borrowing (personal financial leverage) does not alter the *total* value of an investment. It is just like our example of a pure risk-return trade-off. Any change in the expected cash flows is exactly offset by a change in risk and required return.

Thus the choice of personal leverage is yet another pure risk-return trade-off. It is the investor's choice of personal capital structure that puts the investor at a particular point on the capital market line (CML). We will see that this same conclusion holds for a firm's choice of capital structure in a perfect capital market environment. Financial leverage does not affect value. It involves a risk-return preference, subject to a market-determined risk-return trade-off.

As with operating leverage, there are two important corresponding (and almost opposite) things to remember about financial leverage. First, a firm's choice of leverage is for the most part made for the entire firm rather than separately for each of the firm's investments. Second, leverage affects the risk borne by each class of investor (debt, equity, and so on) but does not affect the cost of capital for the investment in a perfect capital market environment.

Self-Check Questions

1. What are the two parts of nondiversifiable risk?

2. What is operating leverage? How does it differ from financial leverage? How is it similar?

3. How does a firm's choice of financial leverage affect its cost of capital in a perfect capital market environment?

10.6 LEVERAGE AND RISK BEARING

In a perfect capital market environment, leverage does not affect a firm's value or the cost of capital. However, even in a perfect capital market environment, leverage does affect the required returns for the debtholders and shareholders. This is because leverage affects how the risk of the firm is borne by each group. To see this point, consider the following simple scenario.

EXAMPLE

Leveraging Per-Pet, Inc.

Per-Pet, Inc. is financed only with equity. It has a perpetual expected cash inflow each year of $150, which can be larger or smaller but is never less than $50 per year. Per-Pet's cost of capital is 15%, so Per-Pet is worth $1000 (= 150/0.15). Recently, the shareholders heard the old adage that "the way to get rich is to use someone else's money." The manager pointed out that the firm could borrow $500 at 10% per year and give the $500 to the shareholders. Then the shareholders' expected return on their remaining $500 investment would increase to 20% per year. If $500 of financing were converted into debt, the firm would be taking on leverage and would have a capital structure that was half debt and half equity.

First of all, why would the debtholders accept a return of only 10% when the firm's cost of capital is 15%? The answer, of course, is the risk-return trade-off: The debtholders will get their 10% return *every* period without fail—their return is riskless. But the shareholders are the *residual* claim holders. They get what is left after the debtholders have been paid. Their risk will increase with leverage.

When the firm is all-equity-financed, the shareholders bear all the firm's risk, spread out over an investment of $1000. With the proposed 50% debt capital structure, Per-Pet's shareholders also bear all the firm's risk, but the risk is spread out over an investment of only $500. Thus the risk *per dollar invested* for the shareholders will be twice as large with the leverage as it is currently. Thus the shareholders "pay" for their increased expected return with an increase in risk. ■

What conclusions can we draw from the Per-Pet example? First, we can see that the expected $150 coming into Per-Pet each year is not affected by how much it must pay out to those financing the firm. In other words, the return distribution for a capital budgeting project is not altered by a change in leverage in a perfect capital market environment.

Second, the shareholders' expected return increases with an increase in leverage—but so does their required return. The shareholders' increased risk from leverage exactly offsets their increase in expected return, so there is no change in the shareholders' collective wealth. Without leverage, shareholders have $1000 invested. Under the proposed leveraging, shareholders will have $500 in cash to invest as they wish and $500 of invested value ($= 100/0.2$) in Per-Pet stock, for an unchanged *total* value of $1000.

Finally, with the proposed leverage, debtholders provide $500 in cash for promised future payments worth *exactly* $500 ($= 50/0.1$).

This example also demonstrates that because of financial risk, not all investors bear the same amount of risk. The shareholders bear more risk per dollar invested than do the debtholders, because they are the residual claim holders. At the same time, leverage does not affect the firm's cost of capital (required return). The cost of capital, when it is all-equity-financed, is 15%. The weighted average of the debt and equity required returns with the proposed leverage is also 15% $[= 0.5(0.2) + 0.5(0.1)]$. This is not an accident. It must hold in all cases in a perfect capital market environment.

Self-Check Questions

1. As a firm's leverage increases, how is each of the following affected in a perfect capital market environment? required return for debtholders, required return for shareholders, and cost of capital
2. How does an increase in a firm's leverage affect its shareholders' collective wealth in a perfect capital market environment?

10.7 THE WEIGHTED AVERAGE COST OF CAPITAL

We always come back to opportunity cost. The **weighted average cost of capital (WACC)** can be described in terms of financing rates. Therefore, it can *always* be represented as the weighted average cost of the components of *any* financing package that allows the project to be undertaken. For example, such a financing package could be 20% debt plus 80% equity,

55% debt plus 45% equity, and so on. Or it could be 30% 30-year debt, 10% 180-day debt, 10% preferred stock, 15% 20-year convertible debt, and 35% common stock.

The cost of capital is the return required by a group of investors to take on the risk of the project. But the investors can share the burden of that risk in any way they agree on. In a perfect capital market environment, each investor requires the fair return for the amount of risk borne. However, the *average* will always be the same, regardless of the components.

Certain capital market imperfections, such as asymmetric taxes, asymmetric information, and transaction costs, might cause the package to have an impact on the average cost, but we leave that part of the story for later. For now, it is most important to understand that the required return for each participant depends on the proportion of risk being borne by that participant.

Before proceeding, we need to say exactly what we mean by the components of a financing package. For simplicity, we will restrict the analysis to the proportions of financing provided by debt and equity. Let L be the ratio of debt financing to total investment value. For example, suppose a capital budgeting project has a total present value of $10,000, and suppose $4000 of debt will be used to finance the project. Then $L = 0.4$. It is important to note that L does not depend on the initial cost of the project; it depends on the total value of the project.

Suppose our example project has an initial cost of $8000 and an NPV of $2000, making up its present value of $10,000. Then the shareholders of this project will be putting up $4000 and getting $6000 in value, because they get the NPV. Thus the shareholders own 60% of the value, even though they will be putting up only 50% of the initial cost ($4000 of the $8000). The project is referred to as 40% debt-financed and 60% equity-financed, because those proportions reflect the distribution of the *market* value of the project among the claimants. Proportions of the initial cost are not relevant because to consider them would be to disregard the project's NPV.

The Per-Pet example illustrates that the shareholders' required return depends on leverage. The same phenomenon occurs with respect to the debtholders' required return. It also depends on leverage. This might not be obvious, because as long as there is no chance of default, the debtholders' required return is the riskless return. However, when default is possible, the debtholders' required return must increase to reflect the risk that debtholders will not receive full payment.[3]

A Cost-of-Capital Formula

The WACC (weighted average cost of capital) can be expressed as the weighted average of the required return for equity, r_e, and the required return for debt, r_d, in the same way as in the Per-Pet example:

$$\text{WACC} = (1 - L)r_e + L(1 - T)r_d \tag{10.1}$$

where T represents the marginal corporate tax rate on income from the project.

Note that the WACC is expressed as the after-corporate-tax return. Because the returns to equity investors are paid after corporate taxes, r_e is also an after-corporate-tax return (to equity). The return to debt, r_d, is a pretax return and must be multiplied by $(1 - T)$ to convert it to an after-tax basis.[4]

---

[3] Note that full payment includes the time value of money. That is, late payments reduce the value that debtholders receive.

[4] We first described this difference in tax treatment in Section 2.4 of Chapter 2, in "Tax Treatment of Interest Expense and Dividends Paid."

General Patent, Inc. makes innovative military equipment. It has only long-term debt and common equity financing. Both securities are traded regularly on a securities exchange. What is
the WACC for General Patent?

To begin, we gather the following information:

General Patent's Cost of Capital

EXAMPLE

Current market value of General Patent's common stock	$33.25/share
(5 million shares outstanding)	
Total market value of equity (= 5 × 33.25)	$166.25 million
Next year's expected cash dividend	$2.83/share
Expected constant annual dividend growth rate	10%
Current market value of General Patent's bonds	$800.00/bond
(70,000 bonds outstanding, 7.5% coupon rate, maturing in 17 years)	
Yield to maturity on General Patent's bonds	10%
Total market value of debt (= 70,000 × 800)	$56.00 million
Current total market value of General Patent (= 166.25 + 56.0)	$222.25 million
General Patent's marginal corporate income tax rate	34%

On the basis of this information, we can use the dividend growth model from Chapter 5
to estimate r_e. From Equation (5.6),

$$r_e = [D_1/P_0] + g = [2.83/33.25] + 0.10 = 0.185 = 18.5\%$$

The yield to maturity on the long-term bonds, 10%, provides an approximation of r_d.[5] The proportion of debt financing, L, is 0.252 (= 56/222.25). From Equation (10.1), then, our estimate
of General Patent's WACC is 15.5%:

$$\text{WACC} = (1 - L)r_e + L(1 - T)r_d = (0.748)(0.185) + (0.252)(0.66)(0.10) = 0.155 = 15.5\%$$ ■

The estimated 15.5% WACC in the General Patent example can be used as a cost of capital for capital budgeting projects that essentially duplicate (with respect to operating risk level
and financing mix) the firm's current operations. But how can we estimate a cost of capital for
projects that are significantly different from the firm's current operations?

Conceptually, a firm could offer a financing package in the capital market to determine
a project's cost of capital. For projects that differ in risk level or financing package, this would
be ideal. However, it would also be cumbersome, to say the least. The transaction costs would
probably outweigh the benefits from such a strategy.

In practice, a firm looks at existing market-traded securities of comparable risk to estimate the cost of capital, rather than incurring the transaction costs of actually offering a potential financing package in the capital market. The project's cost of capital is then derived
from such market rates. We'll get back to this later in the chapter.

Self-Check Questions

1. What is the weighted average cost of capital? How is it calculated?

2. How is the ratio L of debt to total value calculated?

3. Suppose a project costs $10,000. Its NPV is $5000. Shareholders put up $5000, and
debtholders lend $5000. What is L?

4. In the WACC formula, why do we multiply only r_d by $1 - T$?

5. Suppose a firm wants to estimate the cost of capital for a project that differs from its current
operations. Shouldn't it just offer a financing package in the capital market to determine the
project's cost of capital? Explain.

---

[5] The yield to maturity is only an approximation because of tax considerations.

10.8 A POTENTIAL MISUSE OF THE WEIGHTED AVERAGE COST OF CAPITAL

We have said that a project's cost of capital must reflect its own risk, *not* the risk of a firm's existing operations. But what happens if a firm incorrectly uses its weighted average cost of capital (WACC) for existing operations to evaluate all capital budgeting projects, regardless of risk? Figure 10-5 graphs the risk (beta) versus the IRR for some capital budgeting projects.

Assume that the firm's existing operations have a risk equal to the average risk of the set of capital budgeting projects and that the return w correctly reflects the WACC of the firm's current operations. The horizontal line wc in Figure 10-5 represents the use of the firm's WACC to evaluate the projects. All projects with an IRR above w are accepted, and all those with an IRR below w are rejected.

If this decision rule is followed, the new projects undertaken will be riskier than the firm's existing operations. This is because, taken as a group, the projects that would be accepted using this decision rule are riskier than the remaining set that would not be undertaken. (You can see this by visually estimating the center point of the groups, above and below wc, and comparing the two points.) Therefore, following such a decision rule will cause the risk of the firm to increase over time as new projects are undertaken. Of course, the firm's WACC will also increase to reflect the greater investor risk.

Taken to the extreme, misusing a firm's WACC to evaluate new projects could lead a firm with low operating risk, such as a utility, to take on high-risk projects, such as drilling exploratory oil wells. The incorrect low return could make the projects appear to be very desirable by incorrectly computing the project's NPV. Other firms that regularly undertake such projects would find the projects to have a (correctly computed) negative NPV! Note also that in addition to undertaking bad projects, the firm would be incurring opportunity costs by passing up good projects.

Alternatively, consider what happens when a firm applies the PML concept and uses risk-adjusted costs of capital, such as those depicted by the line connecting r_f and j in Figure 10-6. As with the single-cost-of-capital decision rule, projects above the line will be accepted, whereas projects that fall below the line are rejected. In this case, the average risk of accepted and rejected projects is approximately the same. Thus the application of project-specific risk-adjusted costs of capital does not, as a matter of course, cause the risk of a firm to increase over

FIGURE 10-5
Misapplication of the WACC concept to capital budgeting project selection.

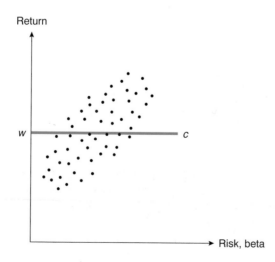

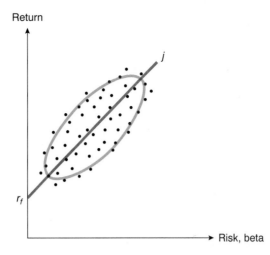

FIGURE 10-6
Proper capital budgeting project selection.

time. Of course, in other cases, the total risk could change. However, a change in total risk will not matter as long as the firm earns the returns sufficient to compensate for the risk.

You might recall that we have previously run across implications associated with increased firm risk in connection with the *asset substitution* problem. Asset substitution is a technique that shareholders can use to expropriate wealth from the debtholders. The firm deliberately undertakes riskier investments to reduce the value of the firm's outstanding debt. The value of the debt is reduced because of the increased risk of default. The present situation differs from the asset substitution problem in one major respect. In cases of asset substitution, shareholders are exhibiting knowledgeable self-interested behavior. The present case is simply the result of a misapplication of the concept of the cost of capital.

In practice, a firm can define various risk classes on the basis of the amount of nondiversifiable risk. It can then calculate a cost of capital for each risk class. Each project being considered is assigned to a particular **risk class**. Each risk class, then, is a group of projects that all have approximately the same amount of nondiversifiable risk. A "naturally occurring" risk class might be a division of a firm.

Risk class assignments take into account risk differences among capital budgeting projects. Each risk class has its own cost of capital, which is appropriate to the risk of the projects in that class.

In practical terms, firms should use from three to five different risk classes. At least three are needed to account sufficiently for differences in risk. Using five risk classes generally eliminates virtually all of the problem of shifting risk created by the misuse of a single cost of capital. Using more than five is unnecessarily cumbersome.

Suppose American Airlines has a beta of 1.3. It is considering issuing stock to raise money for a project that has a beta of 1.0. The project has an IRR (internal rate of return) of 18%. The riskless return is 5%, and the expected return on the market is 10%. Should American go ahead with the project?

The project's cost of capital from the PML (project market line) is 10% [= 5 + 1.0(10 − 5)]. Because the project's expected return, its IRR, of 18% is greater than its required return, its cost of capital, of 10%, American should go ahead with the project. Note that the firm's current beta of 1.3 is not relevant to the investment decision. Note also that how American will finance the project does not change the answer. ■

A Capital Budgeting Project at American Airlines

EXAMPLE

Self-Check Questions

1. What happens to the firm if it uses its (overall) WACC for existing operations to evaluate all capital budgeting projects?

2. Why does using the firm's WACC to evaluate all capital budgeting projects lead to incorrect investment decisions? Might doing so cause the firm to accept some negative-NPV projects? Might it cause the firm to reject some positive-NPV projects?

3. Explain why applying the PML concept should lead to correct capital budgeting decisions.

4. How can a firm use risk classes to evaluate its capital budgeting projects? How many risk classes are usually sufficient?

10.9 FINANCIAL RISK

The operating risk of a firm is determined by the characteristics of the individual assets in the firm's portfolio of assets. Therefore, as a portfolio, the betas of the individual assets combine to determine the operating risk of the entire firm.

In contrast to operating risk, financial risk depends on firm rather than individual asset characteristics. In some sense, an asset or new project undertaken by an ongoing firm has no financial risk; only the firm itself has financial risk. This is because financial risk is created by a financial obligation.

If a firm is *all*-equity-financed (no money owed at any time, no matter what), then the firm has no financial risk. Such a firm has not even one creditor. All the risk of this hypothetical firm is its operating risk, because the firm never owes anyone anything. In such a case there is no possibility of, or option to, default. In effect, the shareholders' limited liability has no effect on value.

Of course, such a firm could go bust. But although the shareholders could lose everything they invested in the firm, no wealth can be transferred because no loss can ever be inflicted on anyone other than the shareholders. Thus, although such shareholders still cannot lose more than they have invested in the firm, they also cannot benefit from limited liability and the default option.

Because financial risk depends on financial leverage, adjusting for the impact of financial risk must be done on the basis of whatever unit has responsibility for that financial obligation. Except in very special cases, the shareholders' obligation is not limited by the results of one capital budgeting project. Rather, each financial obligation extends to the entire firm.

When one project does poorly, the firm is still obligated to pay debts from the proceeds of all its other projects. This reflects the firm's diversification. Only when the firm's total performance from all its operations is inadequate to meet its promised obligations will the shareholders be relieved of their obligation—that is, exercise their option to default.

Thus, in marked contrast to considerations of operating risk, financing considerations cannot generally be accounted for on a project-by-project basis. Instead, because financial obligations exist at the level of the firm, the impact of leverage on required returns is determined by the capital structure of the whole firm.

Another difference between financial risk and operating risk is the extent to which a firm can control each type of risk. A firm can control its financial risk to a reasonable extent (and typically at reasonable cost) by its choice of capital structure and the maturities of its financial obligations. As previously noted, in theory a firm could have zero financial risk if it was financed entirely with equity. By contrast, the firm's operating risk is not so easily controlled.

Although a firm's choice of assets affects its operating risk via operating leverage (commitments to fixed as opposed to variable costs), the choice of assets is often constrained in some way. Technological considerations may force a firm to use certain processes that have a large component of either fixed or variable expense. For example, some products can be produced by one method only. Thus we point out again that operating risk is not easily manipulated, whereas financial risk is controlled by the firm's financial policy.

Subsidiaries

Whenever a firm splits into separate units, with each unit having limited liability with respect to its financing, the capital structure of each unit becomes the relevant consideration for the cost of capital. For example, suppose a firm is considering a capital budgeting project wherein the financing will be obtained by creating a subsidiary for which the firm has limited liability. Then the cost of capital for financing that project must reflect the capital structure of the subsidiary.

How Leverage Affects the Cost of Capital

In a perfect capital market environment, capital structure (the choice of leverage) is a pure risk-return trade-off. It does not affect value. We saw this in the Per-Pet example earlier in the chapter. This fact enables us to draw some important conclusions about the various required returns in Equation (10.1).

Most important, if capital structure is irrelevant, then the value of a capital budgeting project is unaffected by how the project is financed. This means that WACC *does not* vary with L; WACC is constant for *all* values of L because changes in L do not affect the total value of the project or its expected cash flows. If the present value and the expected cash flows are constant, the third parameter in the present value equation, WACC, must also be constant. Of course, as we saw in the Per-Pet example, changes in leverage alter how the risk of the project is borne by the debtholders and shareholders. Therefore, leverage *does* affect r_e and r_d, even in a perfect capital market environment.

On the basis of the fact that WACC is constant across all possible values of L, we can determine the values of r_e and r_d when L takes on either of its extreme possible values. When the firm is all-equity-financed, $L = 0.0$. The second term in Equation (10.1) drops out, so that WACC $= r_e$. At the other extreme, when the firm is all-debt-financed, the first term drops out because $(1 - L) = 0.0$, and WACC $= (1 - T)r_d$.[6]

The result that r_e (with $L = 0.0$) $= (1 - T)r_d$ (with $L = 1.0$) makes intuitive sense. The debtholders of a firm that is financed totally with debt would bear all of the firm's business risk. Accordingly, the debtholders' risk would be the same as the risk borne by the shareholders if the firm were all-equity-financed. Therefore, these two returns must be equal because the risks are equal. The only difference between the all-debt and the all-equity alternatives is due to taxes—assuming an otherwise perfect capital market: An all-debt-financed firm that is just earning its required return would not pay any income taxes because interest would offset its taxable income; the all-equity-financed firm would pay corporate income taxes because all its income would be taxable.

A second implication to be drawn from a perfect capital market analysis involves the return that debtholders will require for financing only an infinitesimal fraction of the investment—r_d when L is tiny. We have already established that a firm that is truly 100%-equity-financed has no chance of default. Such a hypothetical firm can borrow a *very small* amount of money in our assumed environment at the riskless return. Of course, the amount of money such a firm can borrow at the riskless return may be only 1 cent for 1 minute. Still, conceptu-

[6] We know of no firm that is literally all-debt-financed ($L = 1.0$). Strictly speaking, L is always less than 1.0. For convenience, rather than continue to indicate that L is as close to 1.0 as possible, we will simply refer to $L = 1.0$.

ally, the return on the first fraction of debt in a perfect capital market environment *must be* the required return for the riskless asset, r_f.

On the basis of these two implications from a perfect market analysis (and hypothetical functions for r_e and r_d), Figure 10-7 illustrates the relationships that would hold in a perfect capital market environment.

EXAMPLE

Toshiba's Leveraged Investment

Let's say Toshiba plans to invest $1 million in a one-year capital budgeting project. The firm will borrow $500,000 from a bank and put up $500,000 in cash. The bank is charging 9% interest. Assume Toshiba pays no taxes and operates in a perfect capital market environment. With this arrangement, Toshiba expects a return of 16% on its equity investment. What would Toshiba's return be without the leverage?

Toshiba expects a dollar return (above its return of capital) of $80,000 (= 0.16 × 500,000) after paying interest (above its repayment of capital) of $45,000 (= 0.09 × 500,000). Thus the project is expected to have a total dollar return of $125,000 (= 80,000 + 45,000). Without leverage, therefore, the project has an expected return of 12.5% (= 125,000/1,000,000).

Another way to answer the question is to calculate the weighted average of the returns. The project's expected return is 12.5% [= (0.5)16% + (0.5)9%]. ■

How Leverage Affects Beta

We now know that leverage entails a pure risk-return trade-off. But how does leverage affect beta?

An investor's risky portfolio, the market portfolio, is made up of individual stocks. Each has its own beta. Each stock contributes to the beta of the market portfolio. The investor then makes a choice about personal leverage (lending or borrowing). That leverage choice puts the

FIGURE 10-7
Weighted average cost of capital (WACC), required return for equity (r_e), and required return for debt (r_d) as hypothetical functions of the leverage ratio (L) in a perfect capital market environment.

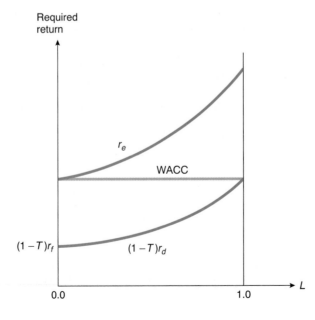

investor's total investment at one point on the CML and determines the investor's risk-return trade-off.

The process is similar for the firm's choice of leverage, but here it actually occurs *before* the investor makes the personal leverage choice. Thus the stock's beta already has embedded in it the effect of the firm's leverage choice.

As we noted previously, the firm can be viewed as a portfolio of assets. Therefore, the asset beta for the firm, β_A, is simply the weighted average of its separate asset betas, or

$$\beta_A = \sum_{j=1}^{J} w_j \beta_j \tag{10.2}$$

where J is the firm's total number of assets and w_j is the proportion of firm value invested in asset j ($j = 1, 2, \ldots, J$). The firm's WACC can then be expressed in terms of β_A as

$$\text{WACC} = r_f + \beta_A(r_M - r_f) \tag{10.3}$$

This expression is based on the asset (left-hand) side of our market-value-balance-sheet view of the firm. In contrast, Equation (10.1) is based on the liabilities and stockholders' equity (right-hand) side of our market value balance sheet. Comparing the two expressions points out once again that the required return for equity, r_e, is not necessarily the WACC to use for measuring the NPV of a capital budgeting project, even if the risk of the project is identical to the risk of the firm as a whole. The difference is the firm's leverage. As shown in Figure 10-7, WACC and r_e are equal only if the firm has no leverage ($L = 0.0$).

We can now draw the parallel between the firm's leverage and the shareholder's personal leverage. After choosing its assets, and therefore β_A, the firm then chooses its leverage, which determines the stock's beta, β.

What must be the relationship between the asset beta for the firm, β_A (which is a weighted average of asset betas), and the shareholders' beta? β_A can be thought of as the shareholders' beta if the firm were all-equity-financed. But now we need to add the effect of debt. Just as there are equity betas and asset betas, there are also debt betas.

A portfolio's beta is simply the weighted average of the betas of its components. Although the idea for a firm is the same, the equity and debt components are taxed in different ways. Corporate interest payments are tax-deductible. Therefore, we must adjust the asset beta for this taxation difference, just as we have in other situations.[7] The adjustment requires multiplying the asset beta by an adjustment factor that includes the debt ratio, L, and the corporate tax rate, T. The factor TL is simply adjusting for the tax-deductibility of the interest on the proportion L of project cost that is debt-financed.

Equating the adjusted asset beta with the weighted average of the betas of the financing components, the debt and equity betas, we have

$$(1 - TL)\beta_A = L\beta_d + (1 - L)\beta \tag{10.4}$$

where β_d is the debt beta for the given L, and β is the equity beta.[8] Equation (10.4) expresses β_A in terms of the liabilities and stockholders' equity (right-hand) side of our market value balance sheet. Equation (10.2) expresses β_A in terms of the asset (left-hand) side of our market value balance sheet.

---

[7] As we noted in footnote 4, this difference was first described in Section 2.4 of Chapter 2, in "Tax Treatment of Interest Expense and Dividends Paid."

[8] Sometimes people add a subscript e to make it clear that it is the equity beta. In order to emphasize that it is the same β we used to derive the CAPM in Chapter 7, we have not added the subscript e.

Self-Check Questions

1. True or false? Operating risk exists project by project. Financial risk exists for the firm as a whole.

2. How can a firm control its financial risk? Is operating risk easier to control?

3. Suppose a firm will finance a project through a subsidiary for which it will have only limited liability. Which capital structure should it use to calculate the WACC for the project?

4. True or false? A firm's asset beta, β_A, is simply the weighted average of its separate asset betas.

5. How is a firm's WACC related to its asset beta in a perfect capital market environment?

10.10 A PRACTICAL PRESCRIPTION FOR ESTIMATING A COST OF CAPITAL

When a firm takes on financial leverage, the risk borne by the debtholders is generally quite low.[9] If the debtholders bear no risk, β_d is zero. In such a case the debtholders will earn the riskless return, r_f. Even when the debtholders bear some of the firm's risk, the amount is typically small compared with other investment opportunities. As a practical matter, if we approximate β_d as zero and solve for β_A, we can rewrite Equation (10.4) as

$$\beta_A = \frac{(1 - L)\beta}{(1 - TL)} \tag{10.5}$$

We can now use this expression to approximate β_A.

EXAMPLE

Calculating Officemate's β_A

Suppose Officemate International Corporation is contemplating an expansion of its current operations. To evaluate the proposed expansion, the financial vice president has asked you to estimate the cost of capital for the project. How do you proceed?

First, you look in an investor's guide and find that the beta for shares of common stock in Officemate is estimated to be 1.30. Second, you note that the current market value of a share of Officemate is $8.25 and that there are 2 million shares outstanding. Thus the market value of Officemate's equity is $16.5 million (= 8.25 × 2 million). From Officemate's balance sheet you determine that the total book value of all of Officemate's liabilities is $8.5 million.[10] On the basis of these figures, L is approximately 0.34 [= 8.5/(8.5 + 16.5)]. From Officemate's income statement, you estimate a marginal corporate tax rate of $L = 0.37$. Then, using Equation (10.5), we find that β_A is about 0.981:

$$\beta_A = \frac{(1 - L)\beta}{(1 - TL)} = \frac{(1 - 0.34)1.3}{1 - (0.37)(0.34)} = 0.981$$

Finally, you estimate that r_f and r_M are 5% and 13%, respectively. Therefore, on the basis of Equation (10.3), Officemate should use a cost of capital for its expansion of about 12.8%:

$$\text{WACC} = r_f + \beta_A(r_M - r_f) = 0.05 + 0.981(0.13 - 0.05) = 0.128 = 12.8\%$$ ■

---

[9] An exception is a so-called "junk" (or high-yield) bond.
[10] Theoretically, the market value of the liabilities should be used rather than the book value. In practice, the book value is often used for simplicity and because the difference is typically not very significant.

Estimating the Cost of Capital for a Capital Budgeting Project

In the Officemate example, the capital budgeting project was of the same risk class as the firm's overall current operations. Now let's consider how to estimate the cost of capital for a project that is significantly different, such as one either in an area where the firm has no experience, or one that has significantly different risk from the firm's average.

Poly-brands, Inc. is a multinational conglomerate with worldwide operations involving products and services that range from a ski resort in Vail, Colorado, to a high-tech ball-bearings manufacturing plant located in Bonn, Germany. The audio division of Poly is considering an expansion of its compact-disk player manufacturing facilities located just outside of Tokyo. Poly needs to estimate the cost of capital for the project.

Expanding Compact-Disk Player Production at Poly-Brands

EXAMPLE

Poly's stock and bonds are publicly traded on major exchanges. We can use this market information to estimate Poly's WACC. In this case, however, Poly's WACC is not a good estimate of the project's cost of capital, because the manufacture of compact-disk players has greater operating risk than the average risk of all of Poly's assets.

The steps for estimating the beta for this project are

1. Obtain estimates of stock betas for a sample of firms whose primary business is the manufacture of audio products, especially compact-disk players.

2. Estimate β_A for each of the firms in the manner illustrated in the Officemate example.

3. The average of all the firm's betas is the estimate of beta for Poly's project.

Table 10-3 summarizes the foregoing procedure. It estimates beta to be 1.31.

TABLE 10-3
Estimating the beta of Poly-brands, Inc.'s capital budgeting project.

SAMPLE FIRM	β	L	T	$\dfrac{(1-L)\beta}{(1-TL)}$
A	1.70	0.29	0.42	1.37
B	1.85	0.45	0.31	1.18
C	1.95	0.37	0.34	1.41
D	1.90	0.43	0.28	1.23
E	2.00	0.42	0.34	1.35
F	1.60	0.35	0.38	1.20
G	1.65	0.26	0.42	1.37
H	1.80	0.34	0.37	1.36
			Average asset beta =	1.31

The riskless return is 5%, and r_M is 13%. The cost of capital for Poly's project is then calculated using Equation (10.3):

$$\text{WACC} = 0.05 + 1.31(0.13 - 0.05) = 0.155 = 15.5\%$$

How Operating Leverage Affects Beta and the Cost of Capital

We said earlier that operating risk is the primary determinant of a project's cost of capital. We also noted that a firm often has little control over a project's operating leverage because of technological, efficiency, or other production considerations. However, for those projects where a firm has a choice of operating leverage, how does operating leverage affect the project's beta and cost of capital?

Unlike financial leverage, operating leverage affects β_A and therefore affects the WACC. Its effect is similar to the effect of leverage on r_e—an increase in operating leverage increases β_A and the WACC. Changes in the WACC then in turn affect both r_e and r_d.

The Cost of Capital with a Choice of Operating Leverage

Because operating risk affects the beta of a capital budgeting project, the estimation method we have outlined must include one more condition when there is a choice of operating leverage. If there are significant differences in operating risk among potential production methods, the sample of representative firms must be restricted to those firms that are using a set of assets and production methods that are approximately equivalent to those in the proposed project.

EXAMPLE

Estimating the Cost of Capital with a Choice of Operating Leverage

Let's re-examine Poly-brands, Inc.'s capital budgeting project. A technological advance in the production process for manufacturing compact-disc players has recently occurred. Poly's project will use this new process. Assume that firms B, D, and F in Table 10-3 are using the new process. The other firms are more established and have not yet upgraded their production process. What cost of capital should Poly use?

In this case, the subsample of only firms B, D, and F is used to estimate beta. These firms have an average implied firm beta of about 1.20, so the estimated project beta would be 1.20, rather than the 1.31 average for all eight firms. This produces a slightly lower WACC of 14.6% [= 0.05 + 1.20(0.13 − 0.05)]. ∎

Self-Check Questions

1. Describe a three-step procedure for estimating the beta for a project whose risk differs from that of the firm considering it.
2. How does operating leverage affect a project's beta and its cost of capital?
3. How do differences in operating risk affect the choice of firms to use in estimating the beta for a project?

SUMMARY

This chapter considered the capital budgeting process and the cost of capital. The capital budgeting process typically involves the simultaneous exchanges of ideas depicted in Figure 10–1. Firms use a hierarchical review structure with limits on expenditure authorization to screen capital budgeting proposals. This helps ensure a more extensive review of larger capital budgeting projects and greater potential for their improvement.

The cost of capital depends on the risk of the capital budgeting project—not on the firm that undertakes the project. The value of the project is based on its ability to generate future cash flows, just as the value of a share of stock is based on its expected future cash dividends. If a particular firm can generate higher expected future cash flows using the project's assets than can other firms, then the project will add more value to that firm than to the other firms. However, the risk of the asset is the same, regardless of which firm owns it. Therefore, the project's cost of capital must be the same for all firms; differences in the value of a project among firms are reflected in the expected cash flows, not in the cost of capital (required return). In the next three chapters, we will examine in detail the process of evaluating proposed capital budgeting projects.

In practice, you might be tempted to "add a few points" to a cost of capital "just for insurance." Ad hoc adjustments for "judgmental" factors should be avoided. This is not to belittle the valuable role that specialized judgment can play in a firm's choice of assets. But there are better methods of incorporating those important "other" factors into the decision-making process.

This chapter outlined a method for estimating a cost of capital on the basis of the required returns on equity and debt. It provides a good "back-of-the-envelope" estimate of a cost of capital, because operating risk is by far the most important determinant of the cost of capital. The adjustment for risk must reflect the risk of the capital budgeting project rather than the risk of the firm's current operations. Adjustments for the particular financing package will matter only to the extent that there are capital market imperfections. Chapter 15 examines the effect on the firm's financing decision of capital market imperfections such as asymmetric taxes, asymmetric information, and transaction costs. Adjusting for these imperfections, which we do in Chapters 15 and 16, leads to return calculations that are more complex than those involved in the method developed in this chapter.

Accurately estimating a cost of capital is so complicated that it is not usually done separately for each capital budgeting project under consideration. Instead, firms use risk classes. Costs of capital for various risk classes are established and reviewed periodically. Each capital budgeting project is assigned to the appropriate risk class as part of its evaluation.

DECISION SUMMARY

- Idea generation is the first and most important part of the capital budgeting process. Sources of potentially valuable ideas include production employees, managers at all levels, sales and marketing staff, research and development groups, and the strategic planning process.

- The cost of capital is based on the concept of an opportunity cost. It is estimated from the expected return on comparable capital market investment alternatives. Therefore, it is important to disregard the historical cost of funds. Market rates change regularly because of changes in expected inflation and in the supply of and demand for money. Investment decisions must be based on the alternatives that are *currently* available. The relevant question is "What else can be done with the money *now*?"

- The cost of capital depends on the operating risk of the capital budgeting project. Theoretically, each project has its own cost of capital. In practice, however, projects are typically categorized by risk classes, each of which has a different cost of capital.

- The cost of capital for a capital budgeting project is the same as the cost of capital for the firm's current operations *only* if the nondiversifiable risk of the project is identical to the nondiversifiable risk of the existing firm taken as a whole.

- Present value is a function of both expected cash flows and the required return. With a pure risk-return trade-off, present value is constant, and changes in the other two parameters offset one another.

- Except for capital market imperfections, changes in financial leverage involve a pure risk-return trade-off. Therefore, a capital budgeting project's cost of capital does not vary as the degree of financial leverage changes—in a perfect capital market environment.

- A capital budgeting project's cost of capital does not equal either of the required returns on debt or leveraged equity. The cost of capital is the *weighted average* of the current required returns on debt and equity, where the weights are the market-value proportions of debt and equity in the firm's capital structure. In a perfect capital market environment, this weighted average is constant across alternative financing packages and is equal to the required return for an all-equity-financed firm.

- The leverage ratio, L depends on the market values of the firm's debt and equity.
- A capital budgeting project's cost and market value differ by its NPV.
- Potential differences between the value of a project to one firm and its value to another that might undertake it are reflected in the expected cash flows rather than in the cost of capital.

EQUATION SUMMARY

(10.1)
$$\text{WACC} = (1 - L)r_e + L(1 - T)r_d$$

(10.2)
$$\beta_A = \sum_{j=1}^{J} w_j \beta_j$$

(10.3)
$$\text{WACC} = r_f + \beta_A(r_M - r_f)$$

(10.4)
$$(1 - TL)\beta_A = L\beta_d + (1 - L)\beta$$

(10.5)
$$\beta_A = \frac{(1 - L)\beta}{(1 - TL)}$$

KEY TERMS

capital budgeting...306

capital budget...306

cost of capital...309

internal rate of return (IRR)...311

business risk...313

operating risk...313

financial risk...313

leverage...313

operating leverage...313

weighted average cost of capital (WACC)...317

risk class...321

EXERCISES

PROBLEM SET A

A1. Explain what we mean by the firm's financing decision and the firm's investment decision. What entities are on the "other side" of these decisions?

A2. What is the NPV of a project that has an IRR exactly equal to its cost of capital?

A3. Exxon's required return for equity, r_e, is 14%. Its required return for debt, r_d, is 8%, its debt-to-total-value ratio, L, is 35%, and its marginal tax rate, T, is 40%. Calculate Exxon's WACC.

A4. Assume that the expected return on the market portfolio is 15% and the riskless return is 9%. Also assume that all the projects listed here are perpetuities with annual cash flows (in $) and betas as indicated. None of the projects requires or precludes any of the other projects, and each project costs $2000.

Project	A	B	C	D	E	F
Annual cash flow	310	500	435	270	385	450
Beta	1.00	2.25	2.22	0.65	1.37	2.36

a. What is the NPV of each project?

b. Which projects should the firm undertake?

A5. Stowe-Away Travel, Inc. is a diversified conglomerate with six different projects. The projects, their betas, and the proportion of the firm's value invested in each project follow.

Project	A	B	C	D	E	F
Proportion of firm value	20%	10%	12%	10%	34%	14%
Beta	1.00	2.25	2.22	0.65	1.37	2.36

a. What is β_A for this firm?

b. If Stowe is 20% debt-financed, what is Stowe's equity beta, β?

A6. What are the two factors on which present value depends?

A7. If Goodyear has a debt-to-total-value ratio, L, of 43% and its common stock has a beta of 1.32, what is the approximate value of Goodyear's firm beta, β_A?

A8. Distinguish between operating leverage and financial leverage.

A9. Give an example of a case where the expected future cash flows increase but the present value of the cash flows remains unchanged.

A10. A firm used a single discount rate to compute the NPV of all its potential capital budgeting projects, even though the projects had a wide range of nondiversifiable risk. The firm then actually undertook all those projects that appeared to have a positive NPV. Briefly explain why such a firm would become riskier over time as it undertook the projects.

PROBLEM SET B

B1. You are considering three stocks for investment purposes. The required return on the market portfolio is 14%, and the riskless return is 9%. On the basis of the information that follows, in which (if any) of these stocks should you invest?

Stock	Beta	Current Price	Last Dividend	Growth Rate
A	1.3	$15	$1.2	5%
B	0.9	28	1.3	10
C	1.1	31	2.4	8

B2. What are the important differences in the ways in which operating risk and financial risk enter into the consideration of a capital budgeting project?

B3. The following information has been gathered about O'ryan Swim-Where, Ltd. On the basis of this information, estimate O'ryan's WACC.

Current market value of common shares (10 million outstanding)	$23.63/share
Next year's expected cash dividend	$1.92/share
Expected constant annual dividend growth rate	8%
Current market value of bonds (100,000 bonds outstanding, 8.5% coupon, maturing in 21 years)	$835.00/bond
Corporate tax rate	34%

B4. The treasurer of a large firm is considering investing $50 million in 10-year Treasury notes that yield 8.5%. The firm's WACC is 15%. Is this a negative-NPV investment? Explain.

B5. Suppose a loan pays $200 now and requires only a single repayment of principal and all accrued interest after 4 years in the amount of $295.49. Ignore taxes.

a. What is the yield to maturity on this loan, assuming semiannual compounding?

b. Create an amortization schedule showing the semiannual period-by-period accrued interest charges for this loan.

B6. Yukon, Etiquette, Inc. has a beta of 1.85 and is deciding whether to issue stock to raise money for a project that has the same risk as the market and an IRR of 20%. The riskless return is 10% and the expected return on the market is 15%. Under what conditions should the firm go ahead

The following market data were available at year-end 1995:

PepsiCo's beta	1.00		
PepsiCo's long-term borrowing rate	6.75%		
Riskless returns:		Market risk premium:	
Short-term	5.13%	Short-term	8.40%
Intermediate-term	5.50	Intermediate-term	7.40
Long-term	6.00	Long-term	7.00

1. Calculate the market value of PepsiCo's debt at year-end 1995.

2. Calculate the market value of PepsiCo's stockholders' equity at year-end 1995.

3. PepsiCo subtracts the value of its portfolio of short-term investments, which is held outside the United States and is not required to support day-to-day operations, from its total debt when calculating its "net debt ratio." Calculate PepsiCo's net debt ratio.

4. Calculate PepsiCo's overall WACC.

The following table provides year-end 1995 information concerning publicly traded restaurant firms. Note that NPC International is the largest franchisee of Pizza Hut restaurants.

FIRM	STOCK LISTED	BETA	TOTAL DEBT ($ MILLIONS)	PREFERRED STOCK ($ MILLIONS)	COMMON SHARES (MILLIONS)	CLOSING STOCK PRICE
Applebee's International	NASDAQ	1.30	28.5	–	31.0	$22¾
Bob Evans Farms	NASDAQ	0.95	54.7		42.3	19
Brinker International	NYSE	1.70	104.7		72.1	15⅛
CKE Restaurants	NYSE	1.15	86.7		18.4	16
McDonald's	NYSE	1.00	4820.1	411.1	694.0	45⅛
NPC International	NASDAQ	0.80	81.4		24.5	7¼
Shoney's	NYSE	0.90	440.4		41.5	10¼
Wendy's International	NYSE	1.15	147.0	–	103.4	21¼

Sources: Bloomberg, L.P., and *Value Line Investment Survey* (March 22, 1996).

5. Should PepsiCo use its overall cost of capital to evaluate its restaurant capital investments? Under what circumstances would it be correct to do so?

6. Estimate the unleveraged beta for PepsiCo's restaurant business.

7. Estimate the cost of capital for PepsiCo's restaurant business.

8. Explain why there is a difference between PepsiCo's overall cost of capital and the cost of capital for its restaurant business.

BIBLIOGRAPHY

Booth, Laurence. "The Influence of Production Technology on Risk and the Cost of Capital," *Journal of Financial and Quantitative Analysis,* 1991, 26(1):109–128.

Brigham, Eugene F., Dilip K. Shome, and Steve R. Vinson. "The Risk Premium Approach to Measuring a Utility's Cost of Equity," *Financial Management*, 1985, 14(1):33–45.

Brown, Keith C., W. V. Harlow, and Seha M. Tinic. "The Risk and Required Return of Common Stock Following Major Price Innovations," *Journal of Financial and Quantitative Analysis*, 1993, 28(1):101–116.

Butler, J. S., and Barry Schachter. "The Investment Decision: Estimation Risk and Risk Adjusted Discount Rates," *Financial Management*, 1989, 18(4):13–22.

Chambers, Donald R., Robert S. Harris, and John J. Pringle. "Treatment of Financing Mix in Analyzing Investment Opportunities," *Financial Management* 11(2):24–41.

Conine, Thomas E., Jr., and Maurry Tamarkin. "Divisional Cost of Capital Estimation: Adjusting for Leverage," *Financial Management*, 1985, 14(1):54–58.

Diamond, Douglas W., and Robert E. Verrecchia. "Disclosure, Liquidity, and the Cost of Capital," *Journal of Finance*, 1991, 46(4):1325–1360.

Durand, David. "Afterthoughts on a Controversy with MM, Plus Thoughts on Growth and the Cost of Capital," *Financial Management*, 1989, 18(2):12–18.

Ehrhardt, Michael C., and Yatin N. Bhagwat. "A Full-Information Approach for Estimating Divisional Betas," *Financial Management*, 1991, 20(2):60–69.

Fama, Eugene F. "Risk-Adjusted Discount Rates and Capital Budgeting Under Uncertainty," *Journal of Financial Economics*, 1977, 5(1):3–24.

Harris, Robert S. "Using Analysts' Growth Forecasts to Estimate Shareholder Required Rates of Return," *Financial Management*, 1986, 15(1):58–67.

Harris, Robert S., Thomas J. O'Brien, and Doug Wakeman. "Divisional Cost-of-Capital Estimation for Multi-Industry Firms," *Financial Management*, 1989, 18(2):74–84.

Kale, Jayant R., Thomas H. Noe, and Gabriel G. Ramirez. "The Effect of Business Risk on Corporate Capital Structure: Theory and Evidence," *Journal of Finance*, 1991, 46(5):1693–1716.

Krueger, Mark K., and Charles M. Linke. "A Spanning Approach for Estimating Divisional Cost of Capital," *Financial Management*, 1994, 23(1):64–70.

Linke, Charles M., and J. Kenton Zumwalt. "Estimation Biases in Discounted Cash Flow Analyses of Equity Capital Cost in Rate Regulation," *Financial Management*, 1984, 13(3):15–21.

Linke, Charles M., and J. Kenton Zumwalt. "The Irrelevance of Compounding Frequency in Determining a Utility's Cost of Equity," *Financial Management*, 1987, 16(3):65–69.

Mehta, Dileep R., Michael D. Curley, and Hung-Gay Fung. "Inflation, Cost of Capital, and Capital Budgeting Procedures," *Financial Management*, 1984, 13(4):48–54.

Modigliani, Franco, and Merton H. Miller. "The Cost of Capital, Corporation Finance, and the Theory of Investment," *The American Economic Review*, 1958, 48(June):261–297.

Myers, Stewart C. "Determinants of Corporate Borrowing," *Journal of Financial Economics*, 1977, 5(2):147–175.

O'Brien, Thomas J., and Paul A. Vanderheiden. "Empirical Measurement of Operating Leverage for Growing Firms," *Financial Management*, 1987, 16(2):45–53.

Prezas, Alexandros P. "Effects of Debt on the Degrees of Operating and Financial Leverage," *Financial Management*, 1987, 16(2):39–44.

Ravid, S. Abraham. "On Interactions of Production and Financial Decisions," *Financial Management*, 1988, 17(3):87–99.

Siegel, Jeremy J. "The Application of the DCF Methodology for Determining the Cost of Equity Capital," *Financial Management*, 1985, 14(1):46–53.

Sundem, Gary L. "Evaluating Capital Budgeting Models in Simulated Environments," *Journal of Finance*, 1975, 30(4):977–991.

Taggart, Robert A., Jr. "Consistent Valuation and Cost of Capital Expressions with Corporate and Personal Taxes," *Financial Management*, 1991, 20(3):8–20.

Yagil, Joseph. "Divisional Beta Estimation Under the Old and New Tax Laws," *Financial Management*, 1987, 16(4):16–21.

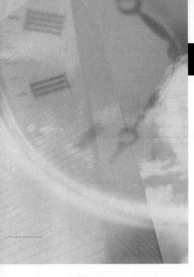

CAPITAL BUDGETING: THE BASICS

O B J E C T I V E S

After studying this chapter, you should be able to

1. Calculate the incremental after-tax cash flows for a capital budgeting project.

2. Calculate various investment criteria for a capital budgeting project, including its net present value, its expected return (internal rate of return), and its profitability index.

3. Explain why net present value is the most reliable investment criterion, and describe the problems that can arise when other investment criteria are used.

4. Explain why the NPV profile is the single most useful item of capital budgeting project analysis.

When making capital budgeting decisions, a firm evaluates the expected future cash flows in relation to the required initial investment. The objective is to find capital budgeting projects that will add value to the firm. These are projects that are worth more to the firm than they cost—projects that have a positive NPV.

Capital budgeting is concerned with problems ranging from purchasing a piece of replacement equipment to developing a totally new business or product line. For example, IBM Corporation's decision to develop a new personal computer operating system was a capital budgeting decision. Capital assets include tangible assets such as land, plant, and machinery, and intangible assets such as patents, trademarks, and technologies. One special case of capital budgeting, mergers, is saved for later discussion. Mergers represent mega-capital budgeting decisions. They are discussed in Chapter 28 along with the strategic, legal, tax, accounting, and other factors that make them so special.

You can see the pivotal role of capital budgeting, and the risks associated with capital investments, by comparing the initial cash outflow—which can be huge—to the much smaller expected periodic future cash inflows. The risk is especially obvious if you consider the tremendous uncertainty associated with the timing and size of the future cash flows. A firm might invest $200 million now, *hoping* to net $30 million per year *after* several years of development!

A firm's evaluation of a long-term investment, a capital budgeting project, is like an individual's investment decision. The steps are the same:

1. Estimate the expected future cash flows from the project. This is like estimating the coupon payments for a bond, or the dividend stream for a stock, and a maturity value or terminal sale price.

2. Assess the risk, and determine a required return (cost of capital) for discounting the expected future cash flows.

3. Compute the present value of the expected future cash flows.

4. Determine the cost of the project and compare it to what the project is worth. If the project is worth more than it costs—if it has a positive NPV—it will create value.

In Chapter 10, we looked at what determines the required return for a capital budgeting project, its cost of capital. In this chapter, we will develop a framework for using the cost of capital to make capital budgeting decisions. We will examine the ways in which managers measure the attractiveness of projects. As you will see, some badly flawed methods remain in use and can lead to poor decisions. But we will show you how sound methods of evaluating business investments can be applied both to proposed projects and to current operations. When combined with reasonable estimates of future outcomes, these methods support good decisions.

CAPITAL BUDGETING AND THE PRINCIPLES OF FINANCE

◇ *Incremental Benefits*: Identify and estimate the incremental expected future cash flows for a capital budgeting project.

◇ *Time Value of Money*: Measure the value the capital budgeting project will create—its NPV.

◇ *Risk-Return Trade-Off*: Consider the risk of the capital budgeting project when determining the project's *cost of capital*, its required return.

◇ *Valuable Ideas*: Look for new ideas to use as a basis for capital budgeting projects that will create value.

◇ *Comparative Advantage*: Look for capital budgeting projects that use the firm's comparative advantage to add value.

◇ *Options*: Recognize the value of options, such as the options to expand, postpone, or abandon a capital budgeting project.

◇ *Two-Sided Transactions*: Consider why the other party to a transaction is willing to participate.

◇ *Signaling*: Consider the actions and products of competitors.

11.1 CALCULATING INCREMENTAL CASH FLOWS

The initial step in measuring the value of a capital budgeting project is estimating the expected incremental after-tax cash flows. There are three important concepts involved.

First, as with any investment, the costs and benefits associated with a capital budgeting project are measured in terms of cash flow rather than earnings. This distinction is critical. Earnings calculations also reflect certain noncash items. But ultimately, only cash flow can be paid to the shareholders, either immediately or through reinvestment and later disbursement. And the *timing* of a cash flow affects its value because of the time value of money. In addition, it is cash, not earnings, that is required to meet the firm's financial obligations. Failure to meet them can cause the firm to pay penalty fees and can even lead to bankruptcy. Also, including indirect noncash benefits leads to ambiguity and subjective (nonfinancial) choices that might hide any principal-agent problems between management and the shareholders.[1]

The second important concept is embodied in the Principle of Incremental Benefits: Cash flows must be measured on an *incremental*, or *marginal*, basis. They are the difference between the firm's cash flows with and without the project. That is, if a cash flow will occur regardless of whether the project is undertaken, it is not relevant.

For example, consider a sequential set of capital budgeting decisions concerning the research and development of a new product. Initial funds are appropriated for research; subsequent funds may or may not be approved for product development, test marketing, and production. At each stage, previous expenditures are sunk costs. Therefore, at each stage of the decision-making process, only *future* expenditures and revenues are relevant to the decision of whether to proceed with product development.

Third, the Principle of Incremental Benefits further requires that expected future cash flows be measured on an after-tax basis. A firm is concerned with after-tax cash flows in the same way in which you as an individual are interested in take-home pay: Ultimately, that's what you can spend. Shareholders are interested in the *net* gain in wealth, and taxes diminish the wealth gain.

Also, remember that cash flows are always assumed to occur at the end of the period unless it is explicitly stated otherwise. This assumption is made simply for convenience in making computations.

Tax Considerations

Some sections of the tax code are complex and change periodically. Still, we can generalize about the effect of a capital budgeting project on a firm's tax liability. In addition to statutory rates, three things affect the firm's taxes: revenues, expenses, and how and when those revenues and expenses are recognized for tax purposes.

An important tax affect occurs whenever there is a discrepancy between cash flow timing and recognition of the cash flow for tax purposes. The present value of taxes paid is less on a revenue item the further into the future that the tax payment actually occurs. Similarly, the present value of taxes saved is greater on an expense item the sooner the reduction in taxes paid actually occurs.

For example, suppose a firm takes in a cash advance of $1000 on goods yet to be manufactured that will be delivered one year from today. If the tax will be $100, the firm will earn $900. But if the tax doesn't have to be paid until the goods are delivered, the present value of the tax is only $92.59 at 8% (= 100/1.08). Therefore, it is as though the firm actually earned $907.41 (= 1000 − 92.59) rather than $900.

The discrepancy that occurs most often between cash flow timing and tax recognition concerns depreciation. Depreciation plays an important role in determining cash flow. Over time, machines wear out. The accounting treatment of depreciation expense, where it is deducted each period, reflects this wear. For capital budgeting decisions, the important impact of depreciation is on the timing of the firm's tax payments. Recall that depreciation is a noncash expense. The cash was expended to acquire the asset. Depreciation is simply the recognition of the expense as the asset is used over time. Because depreciation is deducted from revenue when net income is calculated, it affects the timing of the firm's tax payments.

Depreciation arises when assets are **capitalized**. Capitalizing allocates the cost of the asset to two or more time periods. The entire cost is not an immediately recognized expense. In-

---

[1] Nonquantified items can be a very important component of a capital budgeting project. However, such items should be introduced into the evaluation only *after* the direct cash flows have been identified and incorporated. This is so that the nonquantified items get proper consideration. It is also necessary to minimize potential principal-agent conflicts by making the nonquantified items explicit.

stead, the expenditure is recognized as a prespecified series of expenses at various times in the future. By contrast, cash expenditures for items that are not required to be capitalized can be expensed immediately. Cash expenditures that are **expensed** are recognized for tax purposes entirely at the time of expenditure. Expensed items do not have any *subsequent* tax consequences, because they do not involve the process of depreciation. To contrast these two different tax treatments, consider the following example.

Suppose the Boeing Corporation is going to purchase an asset that costs $1 million. Let's say Boeing's marginal tax rate is 40%. How does the pattern of expenses recognized for tax purposes differ between (1) capitalizing the asset on a straight-line basis over 4 years and (2) expensing the $1 million right now?

Capitalizing Versus Expensing at Boeing

EXAMPLE

    The pattern of expenses recognized over time for expensing versus capitalizing the expenditure for the asset is (in $ millions)

Time:	0	1	2	3	4	Total
Expensed:	1.0	0	0	0	0	1.0
Capitalized:	0	0.25	0.25	0.25	0.25	1.0

Note that the *total* amount of expenses claimed in both cases is $1 million. The only difference is the time at which the expense is claimed.

    Taxes are paid on the basis of revenue minus expenses. If the tax rate is T, revenue is R, and expenses are E, then we can express the tax liability as

$$\text{Tax liability} = T(R - E) = TR - TE$$

In this form, it is easy to see that expenses reduce the tax liability and revenue increases it. Of course, it is important to remember that because revenue also adds to cash inflow, more revenue is always preferred to less revenue, unless T is greater than or equal to 1.0. Likewise, because expense adds to cash *out*flow (in addition to reducing taxes), less expense is always preferred to more expense unless T is greater than or equal to 1.0.

    The reduction in taxes due to an expense is expressed in the far-right term of the tax liability equation, TE. The pattern of alternative reductions in tax liabilities for expensing versus capitalizing Boeing's expenditure is (in $ millions)

Time:	0	1	2	3	4	Total
Expensed:	0.40	0	0	0	0	0.40
Capitalized:	0	0.10	0.10	0.10	0.10	0.40

All of these tax reductions are cash flows (as opposed to expenses claimed). The total is the same in either case. Therefore, because of the time value of money, Boeing would clearly be better off if it expensed rather than capitalized its expenditure—it will get the cash sooner. ■

    As the Boeing example demonstrates, then, firms do not generally choose to capitalize rather than expense an asset. However, the tax code *requires* that certain assets be capitalized.[2]

---

[2] We are assuming the firm has sufficient income to use the tax credit or that loss carryforwards work properly. Exceptions to this assumption (and therefore to this generalization) occur only very infrequently. When they do, it is often a unique situation that requires careful analysis.

Incremental Cash Flows

The cash flows associated with a capital investment project fall into four basic categories:

1. Net initial outlay.
2. Future net operating cash flows from operating the asset.
3. Nonoperating cash flows required to support the initial outlay, such as those necessary for a major overhaul.
4. Net salvage value, which is the after-tax total amount of cash received and/or spent upon termination of the project.

Note that we didn't include financing charges in the list. This is because the cost of capital implicitly includes the financing cost. Therefore, only extraordinary financing costs, such as special transaction costs explicitly tied to the project, are included in the incremental cash flow computations. Such costs are most often included in the net initial outlay.

NET INITIAL OUTLAY   The net initial outlay can be broken down into cash expenditures, changes in net working capital, net cash flow from the sale of old equipment, and investment tax credits.

As we have said, capitalized expenditures do not affect taxes at the start of the project, but expensed items have an immediate tax effect. Let the net expenditure to be capitalized be I_0, and the net expenditure to be expensed immediately be E_0. Then the first component of the initial outlay is

$$\text{Cash expenditure} = -I_0 - E_0 + TE_0 = -I_0 - (1 - T)E_0$$

The negative signs indicate cash outflows.

Changes in net working capital at the start of an investment project are also part of the initial outlay for the project. For example, additional cash might be needed to open up an expansion outlet. Additional inventory and accounts receivable might also be needed to process the greater level of production and sales. The additional net working capital requires funding. Similarly, if a project reduces the firm's net working capital, then those funds are freed up to be invested elsewhere.

The third component of the initial outlay is the net cash flow from the sale of old equipment. When an asset is sold, there is revenue and maybe an expense. There may also be a tax effect. A tax effect occurs if the asset is sold for a net sale price that is different from the tax basis of the asset at the time of its sale (its net, or depreciated, book value).

For example, suppose an asset was purchased 5 years ago for $2000 and $300 of depreciation expense has been claimed for tax purposes for each of the 5 years. The net book value of that asset is currently $500 [= 2000 − 5(300)]. If the asset is sold today for more than $500, then "too much" depreciation was claimed. In such a case, the government will "recapture" the excess depreciation by taxing the amount above the net book value.

In the same way, if the asset is sold today for less than $500, then "too little" depreciation was claimed, and the firm now claims the rest of the depreciation. The firm gets a tax credit by claiming the amount below the net book value as an expense. Let the net sale price (revenues minus expenses) be S_0 and the net book value be B_0. Then the after-tax cash flow from selling the old equipment is[3]

$$\begin{array}{l}\text{Net cash flow from the} \\ \text{sale of old equipment}\end{array} = S_0 - T(S_0 - B_0) = S_0(1 - T) + TB_0 \qquad (11.1)$$

---

[3] The gain is taxed at ordinary income tax rates until all prior depreciation deductions have been fully "recaptured." If—as, for example, a result of inflation—the asset is sold for more than was initially paid for it, all prior depreciation deductions are recaptured, and the excess above the original purchase price is taxed as a capital gain.

Finally, the purchase of certain capitalized assets may create an investment tax credit. This part of the tax law changes frequently, so check the tax code at the time the project is to be undertaken. Let the investment tax credit be I_c and the change in net working capital be ΔW. Then the net initial outlay, C_0, can be expressed as

$$C_0 = -I_0 - \Delta W - (1 - T)E_0 + (1 - T)S_0 + TB_0 + I_c \tag{11.2}$$

NET OPERATING CASH FLOW

Let ΔR be the change in periodic revenue and ΔE be the change in periodic expense connected with undertaking the project in each period. The net operating cash flow, CFAT (cash flow after tax), can then be expressed as $\Delta R - \Delta E$ minus the tax liability on this amount.

$$\text{Net operating cash flow} = \text{CFAT} = \Delta R - \Delta E - \text{tax liability}$$

The tax liability depends in part on the incremental change in depreciation. For simplicity, we assume that all depreciation is on a straight-line basis. The change in depreciation expense is therefore identical for each period. If ΔD stands for depreciation change, the tax liability will be $T(\Delta R - \Delta E - \Delta D)$, and

$$\text{CFAT} = \Delta R - \Delta E - T(\Delta R - \Delta E - \Delta D)$$

Rearranging this equation, we get

$$\text{CFAT} = (1 - T)(\Delta R - \Delta E) + T\Delta D \tag{11.3}$$

In this form, CFAT is represented as the after-tax revenue minus expenses plus the "tax shield" from the depreciation expense. We can also rearrange the expression like this:

$$\text{CFAT} = (1 - T)(\Delta R - \Delta E - \Delta D) + \Delta D \tag{11.4}$$

In this alternative form, CFAT can be thought of as net income plus depreciation. This is because $(1 - T)(\Delta R - \Delta E - \Delta D)$ would be the net income from the project if the firm were all-equity-financed.

NONOPERATING CASH FLOWS

Nonoperating cash flows, such as the cost of repairing or upgrading equipment, are treated the same way as cash expenditures for the initial outlay. Nonoperating cash flows either are required to be capitalized or are allowed to be expensed immediately. Therefore, their effect on net cash flow is like initial cash expenditures. Multiply the expensed nonoperating cash flows by $(1 - T)$ to adjust for taxes. Capitalized nonoperating cash flows create a cash outflow when they occur and depreciation expenses that follow.

NET SALVAGE VALUE

The **net salvage value** is the after-tax net cash flow for terminating the project. It can be broken into three parts: sale of assets, cleanup and removal expenses, and release of net working capital.

The adjustment for the sale of assets was described earlier in our discussion of the net initial outlay. When we drop the zero subscripts from Equation (11.1), the adjustment is $(1 - T)S + TB$. Cleanup and removal expenses are generally expensed immediately. Therefore, they are multiplied by $(1 - T)$ to adjust for taxes. The release of net working capital is unaffected by tax considerations. Tax law treats it as an internal transfer of funds, such as exchanging inventory and accounts receivable for cash. Therefore, the release of net working capital is simply an added cash flow. With cleanup and removal expenses shown as REX, net salvage value is

$$\text{Net salvage value} = (1 - T)S + TB - (1 - T)\text{REX} + \Delta W \tag{11.5}$$

The term **salvage value** typically refers to the before-tax difference between the sale price (S) and the cleanup and removal expense (REX). That is, salvage value $= S -$ REX.

A Simple Example of Working Capital

The importance of working capital considerations is often overlooked. This may result from confusion about exactly what working capital is. In your accounting class (and in Chapter 2), you learned that net working capital equals current assets minus current liabilities. But exactly what is working capital? To get a better understanding, consider the following simple (even silly) example about an entrepreneurial child named Terry.

It is a hot summer afternoon, and after watching people walk uncomfortably through the neighborhood because of the heat, Terry decides there is money to be made selling lemonade. Terry makes some lemonade and a sign, *Lemonade: 25 cents.*[4] After Terry has made several trips to the curb in front of the house—taking the sign, a table, a chair, some cups, and the lemonade—a customer walks by and asks Terry for a glass of lemonade. Terry pours the glass and says, "That will be 25 cents, please." The customer hands over a $1 bill, to which Terry responds, "Would you like to buy four glasses?" The customer is not that thirsty and asks for change. Terry puts the customer on hold, runs into the house, and borrows $3 worth of change from Mom. After returning and making change for the customer, Terry settles into selling lemonade all afternoon.

That evening at the dinner table, Dad asks about everyone's day. Terry proudly reports making $11 selling lemonade. This prompts Mom to ask about the $3 in change. Terry hands $3 to Mom and revises the profit figure down to $8. Mom, however, points out that money has a time value and that Terry had the use of her money all afternoon. Terry agrees and pays Mom the loan-shark rate of 5 cents interest on the $3 loan.

Terry's working capital was the $3 in change. It was put in at the start, and when operations were shut down, it was there in the bottom of the cash register at the end. The only cost of having the working capital was the time value of money. However, Terry could not operate the lemonade stand without the working capital. And although the time value of money is trivial for $3 for an afternoon, it *can* be a substantial cost, as in the case of a 10-year project that requires $5 million in working capital.

When we analyze a capital budgeting project, the cost of the time value of money associated with working capital is typically accounted for by the incremental cash flows: Increases in working capital are outflows. Decreases in, and releases of, working capital are inflows. The difference in the timing of these cash flows accounts for the time-value-of-money cost of using the working capital through a difference in the present values of cash flows. We will deal with working capital management in Chapters 19 through 21.

An Example of Incremental Cash Flow Analysis

Rocky Mountain Chemical Corporation (RMC) is thinking of replacing the packaging machines in its Texas plant. Each packaging machine currently in use has a net book value of $1 million, and each will continue to be depreciated on a straight-line basis to a net book value of zero over the next 5 years. The plant engineer estimates that the old machines will have a total remaining life of 10 years. The purchase price for the new machines is $5 million apiece. Each machine would be depreciated over a 10-year period on a straight-line basis to a net book value of $500,000. Each new machine is expected to produce a pretax operating savings of $1.5 million per year over the machine it would replace.

---

[4] Terry thought about charging $25 per glass. That way, selling only one glass would make a successful afternoon. Then Terry remembered the price-elasticity of demand: Such a high price would probably eliminate any demand for the lemonade.

RMC estimates that it could sell the old packaging machines for $250,000 each. Installation of each new machine would be expected to cost $600,000 in addition to the purchase price. Of this amount $500,000 would be capitalized in the same way as the purchase price, and the remaining $100,000 will be expensed immediately. Because the new machines are so much faster than the ones they would replace, the firm's average raw materials inventory account would need to be increased by $30,000 for each new machine. Simultaneously, because of trade credit, accounts payable would increase by $10,000. Finally, management believes that even though the new machines would have a net book value of $500,000 at the end of 10 years, it would only be possible to sell them for $300,000, with additional removal and cleanup cost of $40,000.

If RMC has a marginal tax rate of 40%, what would be the after-tax incremental expected future cash flows associated with each new machine?

The cash expenditures for the initial outlay in this case would be the $5 million purchase price, the $500,000 capitalized installation cost, and the $100,000 expensed installation cost, so $I_0 = \$5.5$ million and $E_0 = \$100,000$. The increases in inventory and accounts payable would require an increase in net working capital of $\Delta W = \$20,000$.[5] The sale of the machine currently in use would have two effects on future cash flows.

The effect in the current period is given by Equation (11.1), with $S_0 = \$250,000$, $B_0 = \$1$ million, and $T = 0.4$, for a total of $550,000. The second effect occurs in the depreciation expenses that would *not* be claimed for the old machine in each of the next five years. This effect would be accounted for in the expected future annual cash flows. No investment tax credit has been specified. The net initial outlay can now be computed via Equation (11.2):

$$C_0 = -I_0 - \Delta W - (1 - T)E_0 + (1 - T)S_0 + TB_0 + I_c$$
$$C_0 = -5,500,000 - 20,000 - 0.6(100,000) + 0.6(250,000) + 0.4(1,000,000) + 0$$
$$= -\$5,030,000$$

Note that the original purchase price of the old machine does not enter into this calculation. The original cost is a *sunk cost*. It was incurred in the past and therefore cannot be affected by the decision to replace the old machine. Similarly, care must be taken to treat in the correct manner sunk costs that have been incurred more recently. Dollars that have already been spent—for example, on feasibility studies, prior research and development, and site preparation—are irrelevant for purposes of capital budgeting analysis. They are also sunk costs. Whether or not the firm proceeds with the project, the timing and levels of prior capital expenditures cannot change, because these expenditures have already been made.

The net operating cash flows that result from purchasing the new machine can be calculated using either Equation (11.3) or Equation (11.4). The change in revenue, ΔR, is zero. The change in expenses, ΔE, is −$1.5 million. Depreciation would increase $500,000 per year [$= (5,500,000 - 500,000)/10$] for the next 10 years because of the new machine. It would decrease $200,000 per year ($1,000,000/5$) for the next 5 years because of the sale of the old machine. Therefore, ΔD is $300,000 (= $500,000 - 200,000$) for years 1 through 5. Using Equation (11.3) yields

$$CFAT = (1 - T)(\Delta R - \Delta E) + T\Delta D$$
$$CFAT(1 \text{ through } 5) = (1 - 0.4)(0 - (-1,500,000)) + (0.4)(300,000) = \$1,020,000$$

For years 6 through 10, $\Delta D = \$500,000$ and

$$CFAT(6 \text{ through } 10) = (1 - 0.4)(0 - (-1,500,000)) + (0.4)(500,000) = \$1,100,000$$

---

[5] Note that we have assumed the project will not cause a change in any other current asset or liability account. If changes in other accounts (such as accounts receivable) were expected, such changes must also be taken into account.

There are no nonoperating cash flows anticipated over the life of this project, so no additional adjustments are necessary.

Even though these machines would be depreciated to a book value of $500,000 over 10 years, they are expected to have a market value of $300,000 at the end of the project's life. A removal and cleanup expenditure of $40,000 is expected. From Equation (11.5), the net salvage value is

$$\text{Net salvage value} = (1 - T)S + TB - (1 - T)\text{REX} + \Delta W$$

$$= 0.6(300,000) + 0.4(500,000) - 0.6(40,000) + 20,000 = \$376,000$$

The incremental after-tax cash flows for this project are then (in $ millions)

Year	0	1	2	3	4	5	6	7	8	9	10
Cash flows	−5.03	1.02	1.02	1.02	1.02	1.02	1.1	1.1	1.1	1.1	1.476

Self-Check Questions

1. Why is it important to use cash flow rather than earnings to measure the costs and benefits connected with a capital budgeting project?
2. What is the difference between capitalizing an expenditure and expensing it for tax purposes? Which is more advantageous to the firm?
3. What are the four basic categories of cash flows connected with a capital budgeting project? Where do the financing charges fit in?
4. What is the net salvage value, and how is it calculated?

11.2 NET PRESENT VALUE (NPV)

As we saw in Chapter 4, the net present value (NPV) is the difference between what a capital budgeting project costs and what it is worth (its market value).

Can something be worth more than it costs? Yes, it happens. But being the skeptical and insightful person you are, you know we are not going to give you a list of such opportunities—we would rather keep it for ourselves. In fact, the main thing that makes finding a project's NPV so hard is the need to see situations differently from other people. That translates into an assumption of risk on the basis of special knowledge or valuable ideas. At best, we can *estimate* a project's NPV in advance. We will not know its true market value—what it is *really* worth—until the project is completed and the returns are collected.

The NPV of a capital budgeting project is the present value of *all* the cash flows connected with the project, all its costs and revenues, now and in the future:

$$\text{NPV} = \text{CF}_0 + \frac{\text{CF}_1}{(1 + r)} + \frac{\text{CF}_2}{(1 + r)^2} + \text{L} + \frac{\text{CF}_n}{(1 + r)^n}$$

$$= \sum_{t=0}^{n} \frac{\text{CF}_t}{(1 + r)^t}$$

(11.6)

▶ **DECISION RULE** for net present value: Undertake the capital budgeting project if the NPV is positive.

Assume you have noticed a run-down office building in downtown Chicago that you think has possibilities. You decide to buy it for $420,000, and you have to invest $300,000 more in renovations over the next six months. After this, you offer the building for sale and sell it to the highest bidder for $910,000. Because the building turned out to be worth more than you paid for it—that is, its market value of $910,000 exceeded its cost of $720,000 (= 420,000 + 300,000)—your management has created about $190,000 (= 910,000 − 720,000) in value.

Discovering a Positive-NPV Opportunity

EXAMPLE

Although it is delightful to contemplate the money you made in this example, think about how you could have known enough to undertake this project in the first place. To estimate the market value after renovation, you might have looked at other buildings in good repair to see what they were worth and then adjusted for differences between these buildings and the run-down one you were thinking of buying. You would also have estimated the cost of the needed renovations, and added that to the cost of buying the building, to determine the total cost. Finally, you would have compared your market value estimate to your total cost estimate.

If the estimates tell you the project creates value, and your estimates turn out to be correct, then you get the value that is created. You can see right away how important accurate estimates are! ■

Let's generalize from our building renovation example. You could find the market value of the building by offering it for sale—the highest offer you get is its market value. However, that is possible only after doing the renovations. Although you might be able to offer the building before undertaking the renovations by describing your plans, this would be awkward, time-consuming, and expensive. Furthermore, keep in mind the Principle of Two-Sided Transactions: Once you pointed out the potential value of renovating the building to other people, some of them might decide to bid on the building now for more than the $420,000 you had hoped to pay for it.

As an alternative, the example mentioned a method of estimating market value without offering it for sale: Find the market value of another asset just like it, and adjust for whatever differences there are between the two.

Yet another way to determine value is to use **discounted cash flow (DCF) analysis** and compute the present value of all the cash flows connected with ownership. This is like discounting the interest payments on a bond or the dividends on a stock. DCF analysis is the essence of the net-present-value method, which we illustrate in our next example.

Let's continue our earlier example of RMC's replacement of packaging machines. If the project's cost of capital is 12%, what is the NPV?

Applying Equation (11.6) to the project's annual incremental cash flows, we have

Computing the NPV of Rocky Mountain's Packaging Machine

EXAMPLE

$$NPV = \sum_{t=0}^{n} \frac{CF_t}{(1+r)^t}$$

$$= -5.03 + \sum_{t=1}^{5} \frac{1.02}{(1.12)^t} + \sum_{t=6}^{9} \frac{1.10}{(1.12)^t} + \frac{1.476}{(1.12)^{10}}$$

$$= \$1,017,925$$

[a. Put in CF = 1.02, r = 12%, n = 5, and FV = 0, and compute PV = 3.677 for the second term. b. Put in CF = 1.10, r = 12%, n = 9, and FV = 0, and compute PV = 5.861. Then put in CF = 1.10, r = 12%, n = 5, FV = 0, and compute PV = 3.965. The difference between these two PVs, 1.896, is for the third term. c. Put in FV = 1.476, r = 12%, n = 10, and CF = 0, and compute PV = 0.475, for the last term. d. Sum these three values and subtract the initial outlay to get $1.018 million = −5.03 + 3.677 + 1.896 + 0.475.] The project should be accepted because the NPV is positive. ■

It is important to note that the uncertainty associated with the firm's assumptions about costs and selling price are included in the cost of capital (required rate). That is to say, calculating the NPV does not reduce the risk. If the assumptions work out, however, RMC's shareholders will be richer for accepting the project.

Adding Value per Share

How much value would undertaking the packaging-machine replacement project add to a share of RMC's stock? Each share of stock has a claim on the firm. Typically, this is $1/N$, where N is the number of outstanding shares, and the claim would extend to the NPV of the new project. Assuming such a claim, then, if RMC has 1,000,000 shares of common stock outstanding, and our estimates are correct, the project would simply add the proportional share of its NPV to the stock's price. The stock price would therefore increase by $1.02 per share (= 1,017,925/1,000,000).

A More Convenient Computation Procedure

Our computation of the NPV for the packaging machine is partitioned by years. That is, $CFAT_t$ for each year is computed, and then the NPV is given by the sum of the present values of the $CFAT_t$s.

An alternative to this procedure is to compute the CFAT for each item (for example, the initial cost, the change in working capital, and so on), in which case the NPV is given by the sum of the present values of the CFATs for the items. Most people make fewer mistakes grouping by item because we think in terms of items rather than annual cash flows.

Naturally, the total discounted cash flows will be the same, regardless of whether we group them by year or by item. In the previous example we totaled the cash flows in each year, discounted their values, and summed them. The column totals in Table 11-1 show these cash flows by year before discounting. The row totals in Table 11-1 show them undiscounted by item. Table 11-2 then shows the NPV calculation for the example, using item cash flow groupings. In Table 11-2, CFBT refers to the item's before-tax cash flow, and the formulas for each item's CFBT and CFAT are shown below the amount.

Self-Check Questions

1. What is the net present value of a capital budgeting project?
2. State the decision rule for net present value.
3. What is discounted cash flow analysis?
4. Describe two procedures for grouping the incremental after-tax cash flows for a project. Why are they equivalent?

TABLE 11-1

Alternative groupings of cash flows for RMC's packaging-machine replacement, by years and by items (in $ millions).

ITEM	0	1	2	3	4	5	6	7	8	9	10	TOTAL BY ITEM	
Capitalized installation and equipment cost	−5.50											−5.50	$t = 0$
Expensed installation cost	−0.06											−0.06	$t = 0$
Change in net working capital	−0.02											−0.02	$t = 0$
Sale of old equipment	0.55											0.55	$t = 0$
Investment tax credit	0.00											0.00	$t = 0$
Lost depreciation from sale of old equipment		−0.08	−0.08	−0.08	−0.08	−0.08						−0.08/yr	$t = 1–5$
Depreciation		0.20	0.20	0.20	0.20	0.20	0.20	0.20	0.20	0.20	0.20	0.20/yr	$t = 1–10$
Change in revenues minus expenses		0.90	0.90	0.90	0.90	0.90	0.90	0.90	0.90	0.90	0.90	0.90/yr	$t = 1–10$
Sale of equipment											0.38	0.38	$t = 10$
Removal expense											−0.024	−0.024	$t = 10$
Return of net working capital											0.02	0.02	$t = 10$
Total by year	−5.03	1.02	1.02	1.02	1.02	1.02	1.10	1.10	1.10	1.10	1.476		

TABLE 11-2

Alternative NPV calculation for RMC's packaging-machine replacement, with the cash flows grouped by item.

TIME	ITEM	CFBT[a]	CFAT	PV AT 12%
0	Capitalized installation and equipment cost	−5,500,000 $-I_0$	−5,500,000 $-I_0$	−5,500,000
0	Expensed installation cost	−100,000 $-E_0$	−60,000 $-(1-T)E_0$	−60,000
0	Change in net working capital	−20,000 $-\Delta W$	−20,000 $-\Delta W$	−20,000
0	Sale of old equipment	250,000 S_0	550,000 $S_0(1-T) + TB_0$	550,000
0	Investment tax credit	0	0 I_c	0
1–5	Lost depreciation from sale of old equipment	0	−80,000/yr $-TD_{old}$	−288,382
1–10	Depreciation	0	200,000/yr TD_{new}	6,215,245
1–10	Change in revenues minus expenses	1,500,000/yr $\Delta R - \Delta E$	900,000/yr $(1-T)(\Delta R - \Delta E)$	
10	Sale of equipment	300,000 S	380,000 $S(1-T) + TB$	121,062
10	Removal expense	−40,000 $-REX$	−24,000 $-(1-T)REX$	
10	Return of net working capital	20,000 ΔW	20,000 ΔW	
			NPV =	$1,017,925

[a] Note that noncash items have zero before-tax cash flow.

11.3 INTERNAL RATE OF RETURN (IRR)

Another method of evaluation is called the internal-rate-of-return method. Recall from Chapter 10 that the **internal rate of return (IRR)** is a capital budgeting project's expected return. If the cost of capital (required return) equals the IRR (expected return), the NPV equals zero. Because of the uncertainty connected with risky cash flows, the realized return will almost surely be different from the IRR. In Chapter 5, we showed you how to find the expected return for a bond—its yield to maturity. In this chapter, we apply those same time-value-of-money techniques to compute IRRs, the expected returns for capital budgeting projects.

▶ **DECISION RULE** for internal rate of return: Undertake the capital budgeting project if the IRR exceeds r, the project's cost of capital.

In its simplest form, the IRR rule is intuitively appealing. In essence, it asks whether the expected return on the investment exceeds the required return. In other words, will the investment create value?

At first glance, this seems to be saying the same thing the NPV rule does. As we will see, this is generally true—but not always. The intuitive appeal of the IRR rule, however, probably accounts for its widespread use (some analysts even prefer it).

Like other expected returns, the IRR must be calculated by trial and error. Although some calculators and spreadsheets can solve for the IRR, they employ trial and error to do so.[6] Let's work through a detailed trial-and-error calculation here to help you understand the problem.

EXAMPLE		
Computing an IRR for Reebok	Suppose Reebok has an investment opportunity that has a 12% cost of capital. The expected future net cash flows for the project are shown in Table 11-3. What is the IRR of Reebok's project?	

TABLE 11-3
Expected future net cash flows for Reebok's project (in $ thousands).

Year	0	1	2	3	4
Cash flows	−800	300	300	300	150

When in doubt, start by trying 10%. At a discount rate of 10%, the NPV of this project would be

$$NPV_{10\%} = -800 + \frac{300}{(1.10)^1} + \frac{300}{(1.10)^2} + \frac{300}{(1.10)^3} + \frac{150}{(1.10)^4} = +48.51$$

Because $NPV_{10\%}$ is positive, we must try a larger discount rate. Let's try 12%. It is the cost of capital in this example, anyway.

$$NPV_{12\%} = -800 + \frac{300}{(1.12)^1} + \frac{300}{(1.12)^2} + \frac{300}{(1.12)^3} + \frac{150}{(1.12)^4} = +15.88$$

This is still too low. Let's try 14%.

---

[6] When it seems the calculator is taking time to "think," it is going through a trial-and-error calculation. Its answer is actually an estimate that is accurate to within some prespecified degree, such as nine decimal places.

$$NPV_{14\%} = -800 + \frac{300}{(1.14)^1} + \frac{300}{(1.14)^2} + \frac{300}{(1.14)^3} + \frac{150}{(1.14)^4} = -14.70$$

Because 14% would make the NPV negative, it must be too high. Let's try 13%:

$$NPV_{13\%} = -800 + \frac{300}{(1.13)^1} + \frac{300}{(1.13)^2} + \frac{300}{(1.13)^3} + \frac{150}{(1.13)^4} = +0.34$$

That is pretty close, but you could keep going with this process and find that, to four-decimal-place accuracy, the IRR is 13.0225%. With a cost of capital of 12%, then, the IRR decision rule would tell us to undertake this project. That is the same advice the NPV decision rule offers. ■

Self-Check Questions

1. What is the internal rate of return of a capital budgeting project?

2. State the decision rule for internal rate of return. What does it mean in practical terms?

3. Does the IRR rule usually lead to the same investment decisions as the NPV rule?

11.4 WHEN THE IRR AND NPV METHODS AGREE: INDEPENDENT, CONVENTIONAL PROJECTS

In the example just given, the IRR and NPV methods agree. This happens whenever the projects are both independent and conventional. An **independent project** is one that can be chosen independently of other projects. That is, undertaking it neither requires nor precludes any other investment. A project that requires other investments is simply part of a larger project, which must be evaluated together with all of its parts. When undertaking one project prevents investing in another project, and vice versa, the projects are said to be **mutually exclusive**.

A **conventional project** is a project with an initial cash outflow that is followed by one or more expected future cash inflows. That is, after the investment is made, the total cash flow in each future year is expected to be positive. Purchasing a stock or bond is a simple example of a conventional project: You buy the security (a negative cash flow), and the terminal sale price and any dividends or interest payments you get while you own it will not be negative (you have limited liability).

NPV Profile

Another way to look at this problem is to graph NPV as a function of the discount rate. This graph is called an **NPV profile**. The NPV profile is the most useful tool of discounted cash flow analysis.

The NPV profile includes both NPV and IRR. It also shows the value of the project at different possible costs of capital. Therefore, if you are unsure about the project's cost of capital, you can use the NPV profile to identify costs of capital at which the project would and would not add value.

Figure 11-1 shows an NPV profile for our IRR computation example. To construct this profile, we used the calculations in the example and a couple more. One of the additional cal-

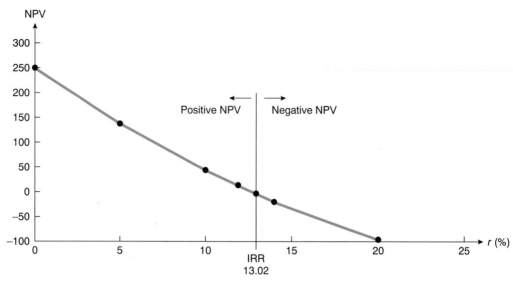

FIGURE 11-1
An NPV profile.

culations assumes a cost of capital of 0%, in which case the NPV would be +250. This calculation is straightforward because it is simply the undiscounted sum of all the cash flows. We also calculated what the NPV would be at discount rates of 5% and 20% to fill in the graph.

The NPV profile in Figure 11-1 shows the general relationship between IRR and NPV for independent, conventional projects. If the IRR exceeds the cost of capital, the NPV is positive. If the IRR is less than the cost of capital, the NPV is negative.

Self-Check Questions
1. What is the difference between mutually exclusive projects and independent projects?
2. What is a conventional project?
3. What is an NPV profile?
4. When do the NPV and IRR methods agree?

11.5 WHEN THE IRR AND NPV METHODS CAN DIFFER: MUTUALLY EXCLUSIVE PROJECTS

So far, we have looked only at the question of whether to undertake an independent project. But often we have to choose from a set of mutually exclusive projects. If we undertake one, we cannot undertake any of the others.

For example, a firm that plans to build a new assembly plant might have three possible locations and four possible plant configurations. But the firm needs only *one* plant. Therefore, it has to choose one configuration in one location, and the alternatives are mutually exclusive. In such cases, the IRR and NPV methods can yield conflicting recommendations.

Conflicting recommendations can occur because there is a difference in (1) the *size* of the projects or (2) the *cash flow timing*. An example of the latter occurs when cash flows from one project come in mainly in the beginning and cash flows from the other project come in later. We will look at each of these types of differences in turn.

Size Differences

When one project is larger than the other, the smaller project can have a larger IRR but a smaller NPV. For example, let's say that project A has an IRR of 30% and an NPV of $100 and that project B has an IRR of 20% and an NPV of $200. The choice between these two projects—and therefore the resolution of such conflicts—is fairly straightforward. You need only decide whether you would rather have more wealth or a larger IRR. Like you, we'll take the wealth, thank you. Therefore, the NPV decision rule is the better rule to follow when mutually exclusive projects differ in size.

Cash Flow Timing Differences

The problem of cash flow timing can arise because of **reinvestment rate assumptions**. The question is "What will the cash inflows from the project earn when they are subsequently reinvested in other projects?" The IRR method assumes the future cash inflows will earn the IRR for this project. The NPV method assumes they will earn the project's cost of capital.

The following example illustrates the reinvestment rate assumption conflict that results from a difference in cash flow timing. As you will see, the NPV profiles diverge at a **crossover point**, a cost of capital where the two projects have equal NPV.

Suppose Guess, Inc. can invest in only one of two projects, S (for short-term) and L (for long-term). The cost of capital is 10%, and the projects have the expected future cash flows shown in Table 11-4. Which is the better project?

Comparing IRR with NPV at Guess, Inc. **EXAMPLE**

TABLE 11-4
Alternative short-term (S) and long-term (L) projects for Guess.

YEAR	0	1	2	3	4	5	6	IRR	NPV
Project S	−250	100	100	75	75	50	25	22.08%	76.29
Project L	−250	50	50	75	100	100	125	20.01%	94.08

Project S has an IRR of 22.08%, and project L has an IRR of 20.01%. But project S has an NPV of $76.29, and project L has an NPV of $94.08. Thus the IRR method tells us to choose S, but the NPV method says choose L.

Take a look at Figure 11-2. It compares NPV and IRR. You can see there that project S will have a higher NPV than project L whenever the cost of capital is higher than 15.40%, the crossover point.[7] Both projects would have an NPV of $37.86 if the cost of capital were 15.40%. You can also see that project L has a steeper NPV profile than project S. This is because the present values of cash flows further in the future are more sensitive to the discount rate. We saw this in the case of bond values, where the market value of a long-term bond changes more than that of a short-term bond in response to a given change in interest rate. ■

---

[7] You can compute the crossover point by finding the rate that makes the present value of the cash flow *differences* equal zero. For this example, the yearly differences are as follows:

Year	0	1	2	3	4	5	6
Cash flow difference	0	50	50	0	−25	−50	−100

You can verify that 15.3985% will make the present value of this cash flow stream equal zero.

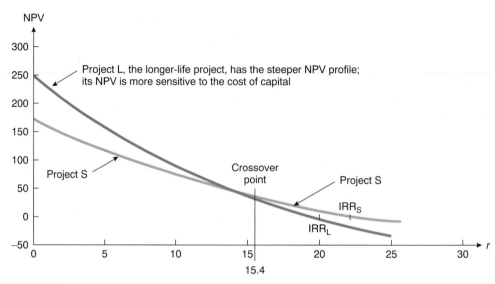

FIGURE 11-2
A comparison of NPV and IRR.

Which method makes the better assumption about what the reinvested cash flows will earn? If the cost of capital is computed correctly, it is the required return for the capital budgeting project. In equilibrium, the required return equals the expected return, and over time, competitive forces drive investment returns to equilibrium. Although new ideas can be very valuable, after a while most people will be using them, and they will no longer command a positive NPV. Thus the NPV from future projects based on the same sort of idea will tend toward zero. In the long run, then, reinvested cash flows can earn the cost of capital, but not the extra, positive NPV. The NPV method's assumption that the reinvestment rate will equal the cost of capital is the better assumption. Again, the NPV decision rule is superior to the IRR decision rule.

Self-Check Questions

1. Give an example of a set of mutually exclusive projects.

2. Under what circumstances can the IRR and NPV methods differ?

3. How do the IRR and NPV methods differ in their reinvestment assumptions? Which assumption is more reasonable?

4. Which of the two methods, IRR or NPV, is the superior decision rule?

11.6 ANOTHER CASE WHERE THE IRR AND NPV METHODS CAN DIFFER: NONCONVENTIONAL PROJECTS

We defined a conventional project earlier in the chapter. Nonconventional projects have a cash flow pattern that is different in some way from those of conventional projects. Nonconventional projects can create a conflict between the NPV and IRR decision rules.

In some cases, a nonconventional project is simply the reverse of a conventional project, one for which the initial cash flow is positive and the subsequent flows are all negative. A life-

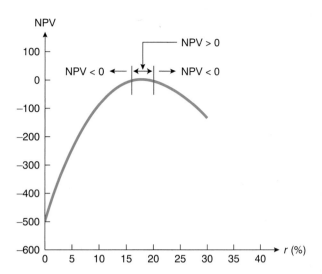

FIGURE 11-3
A capital budgeting project with multiple IRRs.

time annuity, which insurance companies sell to retired persons, is an example. From the insurance company's point of view, it receives a lump-sum amount at the start of the investment. It then makes monthly payments to the annuity's owner for the rest of that person's life. Analyzing such cases using IRR is straightforward: Simply reverse the IRR decision rule. That is, for a reverse conventional project, undertake the project if the IRR is *less than* the cost of capital. Of course, if you forget to reverse the IRR rule in such cases, you will make exactly the wrong decision.

Unfortunately, complications can arise. When some future cash flows are expected to be positive and others negative, there can be multiple IRRs. Such cases can occur, for example, when an environmental cleanup is necessary at the end of the project. The firm makes an initial investment, receives positive cash flows while the project is operating, and then must make a cash outlay to clean up when the project is terminated. Another example is a project that requires one or more major renovations during its life. Let's take a look at the kinds of conflicts that can arise in these more complex situations.

Let's say that Triborg Inc. can invest in a project that has an initial cost of −$15,625, with expected future cash flows of $36,875 after 1 year and −$21,750 after 2 years. Thus the net expected cash flows are negative, positive, and negative. Is this a problem? It can be.

The best way to see the problem is to look at the NPV profile for the project, which is shown in Figure 11-3. You can spot the problem right away. With possible discount rates from 0 to 30%, the NPV goes from negative to positive and back to negative again. The project has two IRRs: 16% and 20%. That is, there are two points where the NPV would be zero if that were the cost of capital.[8]

In this case, the IRR decision rule breaks down completely. If we applied the IRR rule blindly to this choice, we could make a serious mistake. For example, if the cost of capital were 10%, we would undertake the project because both IRRs exceed this. However, at a 10% cost

Multiple IRRs for Triborg Inc.

---

[8] The number of IRRs is never more than the number of sign reversals in the stream of cash flows. Thus conventional projects and reverse conventional projects have only one IRR, because they have only one sign reversal—a negative followed by all positives, or a positive followed by all negatives. In this example, there can be at most two IRRs because there are two reversals. The flows go from negative to positive and back to negative.

of capital, the project has a negative NPV. Reversing the rule as we did with reverse conventional projects doesn't help either. In cases where the cost of capital exceeded 20%, the rule would again lead to an incorrect decision. Moreover, to the extent that we do not know the project's cost of capital, 16% to 20% is a small "window" to hit. Finally, even in the range where the NPV is positive, it is not very large, and the project would not make an exciting addition to wealth, anyway. ■

To make matters worse, calculators and available computer software generally are not equipped to handle the problem of multiple IRRs. They tend to report the first IRR they stumble on. But you can use a calculator or PC to create an NPV profile, which will give you a much more nearly complete view of the project you are analyzing. Besides, all of these procedures require an NPV calculation, and the NPV decision rule is superior anyway.

Self-Check Questions
1. Give an example of a nonconventional project.
2. What happens to the IRR decision rule when it is applied to a reverse conventional project?
3. Which decision rule, IRR or NPV, should you use for a project that has multiple IRRs?

11.7 INTERNAL RATE OF RETURN, ON BALANCE

At this point you may ask, "Why use the IRR rule, when you may have to make several NPV calculations in the course of computing the IRR?" Our answer is that you should not use the IRR rule. Use NPV, instead.

In practice, however, the IRR rule is more widely used than the NPV rule. Many people prefer the intuitive feel of the IRR method. If the expected return is big *enough*, it will surely exceed the required return, and the project is a good investment. Such straightforward simplicity is appealing. For example, in cases where the cost of capital is especially uncertain, as in the case of an entirely new product, using the IRR rule gets around having to compute the cost of capital carefully.

Also, if the IRR for a conventional project is large enough, say 78%, it is probably not worth the trouble to estimate the cost of capital accurately. Because the cost of capital would almost never be that high, we can simply undertake the project without wasting additional resources on analysis. Those resources can be spent instead on making the project successful!

Self-Check Questions
1. If the NPV rule is superior, why is the IRR rule more widely used?
2. Give an example of a situation where using the IRR rule would be sufficient for deciding whether to undertake a project.

11.8 INFERIOR ALTERNATIVES TO THE NPV METHOD

Several other methods are sometimes used in practice. We will describe them here as background in case you encounter them.

Profitability Index

Another time-value-of-money-adjusted method that can be used to evaluate capital budgeting projects is the **profitability index (PI)**, or **benefit-cost ratio**, as it is sometimes called. The PI for a project equals the present value of the future cash flows divided by the initial investment. One way to view the PI is that it is 1 plus the NPV divided by the initial investment:

$$\text{Profitability index} = \text{PI} = \frac{\text{PV(future cash flows)}}{\text{initial investment}} = 1 + \frac{\text{NPV}}{\text{initial investment}} \quad (11.7)$$

If a project had an NPV of $240 and required an initial cash flow of $-$1000, the PI of the project would be 1.24 (= 1 + 240/1000).

▶ **DECISION RULE** for the profitability index: Undertake the capital budgeting project if the PI is greater than 1.0.

You probably wonder why we bother to introduce this method, because it is obvious that the NPV decision rule will give you the identical recommendation.[9] The idea underlying the PI is to measure the project's "bang for the buck." By scaling (dividing) the present value of the future cash flows by the amount of the initial outlay that is necessary to get the return, you can see how much return is obtained *per dollar* invested. Thus with a PI of 1.24, you get $1.24 of present value back for each $1 invested, or an NPV of $0.24 for each $1 invested.

Although PI works fine for independent projects, the scale problem of mutually exclusive projects that we saw with IRR also occurs with PI. For example, suppose that project A has a PI of 1.6 and an NPV of $100 and that project B has a PI of 1.3 and an NPV of $200. Again, the choice between these two projects is straightforward: Would you rather have more wealth or a larger PI? (Again, like you, we'll take the wealth.) Therefore, the NPV decision rule is the better rule to follow when mutually exclusive projects differ in size.

PROFITABILITY INDEX, ON BALANCE   Although it offers a perspective on "bang for the buck," the PI method is best used in conjunction with NPV rather than in place of NPV. PI gets some use in practice, but less than IRR. Its most beneficial application is in situations where the firm is restricting the amount of investment it makes, rather than investing in all worthwhile projects. (We will discuss such capital *rationing* in Chapter 13.)

Payback

An appealing investment concept is that of "getting your money back." Of course, risk may intervene, but investors often want an estimate of the time it will take to recover the initial cash outflow. When this amount of time is calculated without regard to the time value of money, it is called the **payback** of a project. Payback is found by simply summing all of the expected cash flows (without discounting them) in sequential order until the sum equals the initial outflow.

▶ **DECISION RULE** for payback: Undertake the capital budgeting project if the payback is less than a preset amount of time.

---

[9] In fact, some people define the PI as simply the NPV divided by the initial investment. Such a definition changes the scale to center on zero, rather than 1.0. There is no substantive difference, because such a definition simply changes the cutoff for the PI rule to zero from 1.0.

EXAMPLE

Computing Payback

Let's turn again to the building renovation example we used earlier in the chapter to illustrate the NPV method. We expected to purchase the building for $420,000 and spend $300,000 on renovations, for an initial cost of $720,000. Let's say that instead of selling the building after renovation, we expect to be able to lease it out for $110,000 per year. Ignoring taxes, this would give the cash flows shown in Table 11-5. What is the payback for the project?

The payback is 6.55 years, because $110,000 per year for 6.55 years equals $720,000, the initial investment. ■

TABLE 11-5
Payback for the building renovation project.

YEAR	0	1	2	3	4	5	6	7	8
Cash flows	−720	110	110	110	110	110	110	110	110
Cumulative	−720	−610	−500	−390	−280	−170	−60	+50	
Payback:								↑ 6.55 years	

Shorter

The idea underlying the payback method is simple: The shorter the payback the better. But there are serious deficiencies in the payback method. You are probably already saying "But, but, but—it ignores the time value of money!" This is true. And it also ignores risk differences. In fact, the cutoff is entirely arbitrary, and all cash flows beyond the cutoff are effectively ignored. Let's compare the payback method with the NPV method.

EXAMPLE

Comparing Payback with NPV for Projects at Nike

Suppose Nike requires a 2-year payback. The cost of capital is 15% for two projects it is considering, S (for short-term) and L (for long-term). These projects have the expected future cash flows given in Table 11-6. What would the payback rule advise in this case?

Project S has a 2-year payback, and project L has a 3-year payback. Therefore, the payback rule would tell us to invest in project S but not in project L. But is this good advice? Frankly, no. First, consider the projects' NPVs:

$$NPV_S = -1000 + \frac{500}{(1.15)^1} + \frac{500}{(1.15)^2} + \frac{150}{(1.15)^3} + \frac{100}{(1.15)^4} = -31.34$$

$$NPV_L = -1000 + \frac{300}{(1.15)^1} + \frac{300}{(1.15)^2} + \frac{400}{(1.15)^3} + \frac{500}{(1.15)^4} + \frac{500}{(1.15)^5} = +285$$

TABLE 11-6
Short-term and long-term investment alternatives for Nike.

Year	0	1	2	3	4	5
Project S	−1000	500	500	150	100	0
Project L	−1000	300	300	400	500	500

Is this a problem? Of course it is. Project S will actually decrease shareholder wealth, even though it has the shorter payback; and the opposite holds for project L. Although we would urge the firm to undertake L and "pass" on S, in practice most firms require that projects meet multiple tests. In this case, a firm that used both NPV and a 2-year payback rule might decide not to invest in either project. ■

As we have seen, payback ignores the time value of money. In effect, it assumes the cost of capital is 0%. This underestimates the time required to recover the true (present) value of the initial investment. It can even lead to recommending projects that actually decrease wealth. In addition, managers who use payback set an arbitrary cutoff for project profitability. If the payback exceeds the maximum time, the project is rejected—period. Furthermore, it is impossible to estimate the value of projects through payback alone, because all cash flows beyond the payback cutoff are ignored. Obviously, this method has major deficiencies: It can rule out attractive long-term opportunities.

PRACTICAL VALUE   Despite the drawbacks of the payback method, the gut reaction of wanting to "at least get your money back" is a powerful feeling to overcome. Moreover, payback provides a control on liquidity, offers a different type of risk control, is easy to compute, and is simple to understand. Payback is biased toward liquidity because it rejects long-term projects. This may be important for a smaller, less liquid firm, because it favors investments that will return cash sooner. That cash can be reinvested in other profitable projects or used to meet liabilities that will come due.

Cash flows further in the future are arguably more risky. As a risk control device, payback addresses this harshly by simply ignoring cash flows beyond the payback period, which is an arbitrary cutoff. Finally, we would add two other practical considerations: First, most investments with a short payback, and additional benefits beyond that, also have a positive NPV. Second, for relatively small investments, the cost of extensive analysis can exceed the potential loss from a mistake. This can make the simplicity of payback attractive.

PAYBACK, ON BALANCE   Probably because of the practical considerations just noted, the payback rule is widely used in practice despite its serious deficiencies. However, very few firms use payback by itself. Most firms require that investments also be acceptable on the basis of other rules, such as NPV. Because of its weaknesses, payback should be viewed as a supplement to the discounted-cash-flow techniques, at best.

Discounted Payback

If a firm wants to use the payback method, a better measure is a variation of payback called **discounted payback**. The discounted payback is the amount of time it takes for the project's discounted cash flows to equal the project's initial cost. The idea underlying the discounted payback period is to incorporate the time value of money into the basic notion of getting your money back.

▶ **DECISION RULE** for discounted payback: Undertake the capital budgeting project if the discounted payback is less than a preset cutoff.

Computing Discounted Payback   **EXAMPLE**

Let's look again at Nike's two alternative projects that we used to compare payback and NPV, with a discounted payback cutoff of 4 years. What are the discounted paybacks for these investments? What investment decisions would the discounted payback rule imply?

Calculations of discounted payback for the projects are shown in Table 11–7. Project S has an infinite discounted payback, whereas project L has a 3.87-year discounted payback. The prorated portion of the fourth year is determined by the amount of the year-4 benefit needed to sum to the initial cost. In this case, it is 0.87 [= (286 − 37)/286]. Therefore, the discounted payback rule would tell us to invest in project L but not in project S. ■

TABLE 11-7		PROJECT S					
Discounted payback for Nike's alternative short-term and long-term projects.	**YEAR**	**0**	**1**	**2**	**3**	**4**	**5**
	Cash flows	−1000	500	500	150	100	0
	PV	−1000	435	378	99	57	0
	Cumulative	−1000	−565	−187	−88	−31	−31
	Discounted payback: infinite because the initial investment is not returned						

	PROJECT L					
YEAR	**0**	**1**	**2**	**3**	**4**	**5**
Cash flows	−1000	300	300	400	500	500
PV	−1000	261	227	263	286	248
Cumulative	−1000	−739	−512	−249	+37	+285
Discounted payback:					↑ 3.87 years	

Is this good advice? We know from the past calculations that NPV$_S$ is negative and NPV$_L$ is positive, so this advice matches that of the NPV rule. In fact, you can probably see that for conventional projects, which are the most common type, a project that meets a discounted payback cutoff will always have a positive NPV. This is because the present value of the future cash flows during the discounted payback period alone cover the initial cost. The project's NPV, then, is the present value of the remaining cash flows—those ignored by the discounted payback period calculation. You can see this by noting that the cumulative sum for all the project cash flows equals the NPV of the project, $285. Figure 11-4 illustrates the cumulative present values of the cash flows for project L.

The discounted payback method is superior to the payback method because it incorporates the time value of money. However, it too is arbitrary, and it too suffers from the weakness of ignoring all cash flows beyond the cutoff. This can be a significant problem when there are negative expected future cash flows. The rule can break down in such cases.

For example, let's say that project L had a year-6 cash flow of −$700, such as might be connected with cleaning up an environmental hazard after the project was done. If that were

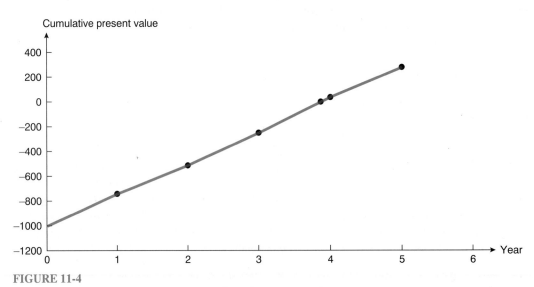

FIGURE 11-4
The cumulative present values of the cash flows for Nike's project L.

the case, the project would have an NPV of −$18, but the discounted payback rule would still favor undertaking the project because the discounted payback period would still be 3.87 years, less than the 4-year cutoff. Thus the discounted payback rule can break down with nonconventional projects.

DISCOUNTED PAYBACK, ON BALANCE   Though it is better than payback, the discounted payback method is still not an adequate indicator by itself. It too should be viewed as, at best, a supplement to the NPV method. Discounted payback is neither as conceptually correct as NPV nor as simple as payback. If you can understand the idea of discounted payback, you can understand and use net present value, so why bother with discounted payback? This is probably why discounted payback is not very widely used in practice.

Average Rate of Return

The **average rate of return on investment (ARR)** is the ratio of the average cash inflow to the average amount invested:

$$\text{Average rate of return} = \text{ARR} = \frac{\text{average cash inflow}}{\text{average amount invested}}$$

For example, consider a project requiring an initial cost of $2 million and providing a cash inflow of $250,000 per year for five years. The average cash inflow is then simply $250,000. The average investment is the average over the life of the project. For the typical case of a constant rate of decline over its life, this is simply the average of the initial and final values (the sum of the two divided by 2). If the project is worthless at the end of the five years, the average investment is $1,000,000 [= (2,000,000 + 0)/2]. Therefore, ARR in this example is

$$\text{ARR} = \frac{250,000}{1,000,000} = 25\%$$

The ARR method contains a fatal flaw that makes it completely unacceptable as a decision method. It averages cash flows across time periods, actually *distorting* the representation of the cash flows. After all, a project may offer an attractive cash flow for a year or two and then end without repaying the initial investment. The ARR considers only the average cash flow per period, not the total over the project's life. Note that in the example we just gave, the payback period is infinite. That is, the project is not even expected to return the initial investment, without regard to the time value of money. You can see that the 25% is indeed an odd measure of return. In fact, it has no economic meaning whatsoever.

AVERAGE RATE OF RETURN, ON BALANCE   It has no redeeming features. Don't use it.

Return on Investment

Another investment criterion is called **return on investment (ROI)**. This term is used by many firms to refer to their own measure of a project's profitability. Unfortunately, different firms define ROI in different ways. Some define ROI to be much like IRR. Others define ROI to be much like ARR. Still others have definitions unique unto themselves. Some firms make the mistake of using accounting income rather than cash flow for investment returns to compute ROI. (We will discuss the problems associated with this last mistake in the next chapter.)

RETURN ON INVESTMENT, ON BALANCE   You must carefully examine the definition of ROI that is used in each situation you encounter. Only after determining how it is defined can you assess its usefulness as an evaluation method. Whenever the definition differs from IRR, it may be an inappropriate method that should not be used.

Urgency

The final method we will look at can be described by inverting Ben Franklin's advice and asking, "Why do today what you can put off until tomorrow?" The corollary to this perverse statement as applied to capital budgeting is "Let's not replace it until we *absolutely* have to." No need for replacement studies. Wait until the machine breaks down, and then air-freight in a new one. At that point, the specter of costly downtime will be sufficient to convince management to skip the analysis and simply order the replacement equipment.

Such a policy has obvious disadvantages, yet stories of plants that have critical equipment held together by "chewing gum and baling wire" loom large in industrial folklore. Capital budgeting projects and key pieces of equipment should be reviewed at regular intervals. A firm should develop a program of preventive maintenance and should estimate a probable replacement date each time it acquires a significant piece of equipment. This will help to ensure that the assets are used with maximum efficiency and that equipment is replaced when it is most advantageous to do so—rather than when the baling wire finally snaps and the equipment stops working!

Urgency, on Balance

Urgency is a frequently used but extremely poor basis for decision making, and it should be avoided. Firms should instead plan ahead. Drawing on Ben Franklin again, and quoting him accurately this time, "An ounce of prevention is worth a pound of cure."

Self-Check Questions

1. What is the profitability index, and how is it calculated?
2. State the decision rule for the profitability index.
3. Explain how the profitability index rule breaks down when there is a size difference between mutually exclusive projects.
4. What is the payback rule? Why is it inferior to NPV? Does it have any practical value? Does using the discounted payback method avoid the shortcomings of the simple payback method?
5. What is the average rate of return on investment? Should it ever be used to evaluate a capital budgeting project?

11.9 CAPITAL BUDGETING IN PRACTICE

In this section, we will look at some other practical aspects of capital budgeting and provide some perspective on how it's actually done.

Methods of Evaluation

Just about all firms use the evaluation methods we have discussed, in one form or another. *The single most useful item is the NPV profile.* This is because it provides the most nearly complete view of the project. It incorporates both NPV and IRR, and it also sheds light on the problem of an uncertain cost of capital.

Understandably, however, ~~most firms use more than one evaluation technique.~~ Over the last 30 years, the use of techniques based on the time value of money, especially the NPV method, has increased substantially. We hope this means that when you finish school and apply the things you have learned here, you will be able to convince your employer to use the better discounted-cash-flow techniques available for capital budgeting if it's not already using them.

Appropriations

A decision to include an investment in the capital budget seldom means automatic approval of the expenditures required. Most firms require that plant managers or division heads submit detailed appropriation requests before funds can be released for a project. Firms often create manuals that specify how the appropriations request should be prepared. This helps maintain managerial control over investments and their associated costs. Conducting a review of budgeted capital expenditures just before releasing funds provides one last check before the expenditure is made. This can be valuable in cases where new information has come to light that might make one or more changes advantageous.

Review and Performance Measurement

As we have said, capital budgeting plays a critical role in the firm's strategic plan. Therefore, firms must systematically review the status of all projects. Such a process is sometimes called a **post-audit**. Managers should examine projects that are not yet completely underway to determine whether development should continue. They also must assess the performance of the firm's existing assets. Consideration should be given to whether projects should, for example, be expanded, contracted, liquidated, sold off, reconfigured, or simply continued. The basic techniques of capital budgeting discussed in this chapter can be applied to the review and performance-measurement process.

The main goal of a post-audit is improvement. Improvements can come primarily in two areas: (1) forecasting and (2) operations. When people know that records of estimates, either forecasts or operational goals, will be maintained and later compared to the actual outcomes, they tend to make their estimates more carefully in the first place. The fact that they are being monitored and will be evaluated and held accountable for their work tends to motivate people to seek better methods and to resist both conscious and unconscious biases. This kind of process is sometimes referred to as *continuous improvement*, and it is part of the concept of *total quality management (TQM)*.

Although very difficult in some situations, post-audits are extremely important because of their potential impact on value. In Chapter 13, we will discuss post-audits further.

Self-Check Questions

1. What is the single most useful investment criterion?

2. Why are appropriation requests useful in the capital budgeting process?

3. What is a post-audit? Why are post-audits useful in the capital budgeting process?

SUMMARY

This chapter described the basics of capital budgeting: analyzing and choosing long-term investments. Firms are effectively defined by the products and services they produce, so capital budgeting decisions are critical.

We presented and discussed five different decision rules for capital budgeting. Of the five, the NPV method is superior. However, the IRR method is the most widely used. In practice, almost all firms use more than one evaluation method. The NPV profile is the single most useful tool, because it provides the project's NPV, IRR, and sensitivity to the cost of capital at a glance.

We want to leave you with one final observation. *The accuracy of the estimates used in capital budgeting is critically important.* Bad estimates will not lead to good decisions, regardless of what evaluation methods are used or how well they are applied. Having said that, however, we must sadly note that nobody ever has completely accurate estimates of investment outcomes.

DECISION SUMMARY

- The method known as **net present value** (NPV) discounts all cash flows at the project's required return—its *cost of capital*. The NPV measures the difference between what the project is worth and what it will cost to undertake it. The NPV method recommends that all independent projects with a positive NPV be undertaken. This method is widely used in practice.

- The **internal rate of return** (IRR) is the project's expected return. It is the return that would make the NPV zero if it were the project's cost of capital. The IRR method recommends that every independent conventional project with an IRR greater than its cost of capital be undertaken. Caution is needed because the IRR decision rule can break down when projects are mutually exclusive or nonconventional. IRR is widely used in practice, probably because of its "intuitive feel."

- The **profitability index** (PI) is defined as 1 plus the project's NPV divided by its initial cost. The idea is to measure the project's "bang for the buck." The PI rule can break down when projects are mutually exclusive.

- The **payback** method determines how long it will take to recover the initial investment, without regard to the time value of money. It recommends acceptance of projects that "return the investment" quickly. The payback method has several serious deficiencies that can cause it to make bad recommendations, but it may have some practical value. In particular, it can provide a liquidity screen, which can be desirable in some situations. Although widely used in practice in conjunction with other methods, payback is rarely used alone.

- The **discounted payback** method is like payback but incorporates the effect of the time value of money. The discounted payback is the time it takes the project to earn a present value equal to its initial cost. Although this method is superior to the payback method, it is still inferior to NPV, because it ignores the value of cash flows after the payback point. Discounted payback is not widely used in practice, probably because it is neither as conceptually correct as NPV nor as simple as payback.

- The **average rate of return** (ARR) method is fatally flawed and should not be used to evaluate a capital budgeting project. Fortunately, its use has substantially declined over the last 30 years.

- The **return on investment** (ROI) does not have a consistent definition. You must find out which definition is being used to determine the potential usefulness of the ROI method.

- **Urgency** is a dangerous but widely used method of allocating resources. Its use is always shortsighted. Many potential crises can be avoided through good planning.

- The **NPV profile** is the single most useful tool. It provides the project's NPV, IRR, and sensitivity to the cost of capital at a glance.

- The **post-audit** is a critical and ongoing part of capital budgeting. It offers a significant opportunity to create value through *continuous improvement* in forecasting outcomes and in choosing and operating projects.

EQUATION SUMMARY

(11.1) $\text{Net cash flow from the sale of old equipment} = S_0 - T(S_0 - B_0) = S_0(1 - T) + TB_0$

(11.2) $C_0 = -I_0 - \Delta W - (1 - T)E_0 + (1 - T)S_0 + TB_0 + I_c$

(11.3) $\text{CFAT} = (1 - T)(\Delta R - \Delta E) + T\Delta D$

(11.4) $\text{CFAT} = (1 - T)(\Delta R - \Delta E - \Delta D) + \Delta D$

(11.5) $\text{Net salvage value} = (1 - T)S + TB - (1 - T)\text{REX} + \Delta W$

$$\text{NPV} = \text{CF}_0 + \frac{\text{CF}_1}{(1 + r)} + \frac{\text{CF}_2}{(1 + r)^2} + \cdots + \frac{\text{CF}_n}{(1 + r)^n}$$

(11.6)

$$= \sum_{t=0}^{n} \frac{\text{CF}_t}{(1 + r)^t}$$

(11.7) $\text{Profitability index} = \text{PI} = \dfrac{\text{PV(future cash flows)}}{\text{initial investment}} = 1 + \dfrac{\text{NPV}}{\text{initial investment}}$

KEY TERMS

EXERCISES

PROBLEM SET A

A1. Describe the four basic steps involved with evaluating an investment for an individual or for a corporation.

A2. Suppose the Caltron Corporation is going to purchase an asset that costs $0.5 million. Caltron's marginal tax rate is 35%. How does the pattern of expenses recognized for tax purposes differ between (1) capitalizing the asset on a straight-line basis over 5 years and (2) expensing the $0.5 million right now?

A3. Briefly explain why the Principle of Incremental Benefits is so important to the process of evaluating a capital budgeting project.

A4. Why are *current* tax laws very important to the proper evaluation of a capital investment project?

A5. Why is it important to recognize and exclude sunk costs from a capital budgeting analysis?

A6. How are financing charges normally accounted for in a capital budgeting analysis?

A7. Suppose GAF Corporation is contemplating a capital budgeting project with capital assets that will be depreciated to a book value of $10,000 but that GAF expects to have a salvage value of $18,000. GAF's marginal tax rate is 34%. Cleanup and removal expenses are expected to be $1000, and there will be no return of working capital. What is the net salvage value?

A8. What is an internal rate of return (IRR)?

A9. Define the term *mutually exclusive.*

A10. Define the term *profitability index,* and describe the concept.

A11. Define the term *payback,* and describe the concept.

A12. Why is the Principle of Valuable Ideas of critical importance to the capital budgeting process?

A13. Briefly explain why net present value is the most reliable investment criterion, and cite some potential problems with using other investment criteria.

A14. Suppose you were restricted to using only one method of analysis to evaluate a capital budgeting project. Briefly explain why the NPV profile is the best method to use.

PROBLEM SET B

B1. A Wendy's franchisee is considering replacing his kitchen equipment. The equipment currently has a net book value of $60,000, and will continue to be depreciated on a straight-line basis to a net book value of zero over the next 3 years. The franchisee estimates that the current equipment could be used for up to an additional 6 years. The purchase price for the new equipment is $300,000, and it would be depreciated over a 6-year period on a straight-line basis to a net book value of $50,000. The new equipment would produce pretax operating savings of $80,000 per year as compared to the replaced equipment. The old equipment can be sold for $25,000. Installation would cost $30,000 in addition to the purchase price, all of which would be expensed immediately. The franchisee believes the equipment would have a net salvage value of $40,000 at the end of 6 years.

   a. If the franchisee has a marginal tax rate of 30%, what would be the after-tax incremental expected future cash flows associated with the new equipment by year and by item?

   b. Approximately what is the IRR for the project?

   c. If the cost of capital for the project is 12%, what is the NPV?

   d. Compute the NPV assuming costs of capital of 0%, 4%, 8%, 12%, and 16%. Prepare an NPV profile for the project.

B2. Let's say Johnson & Johnson currently has a machine that has 5 years of useful life remaining. Its current net book value is $50,000, and it is being straight-line depreciated to its expected zero salvage value in 5 years. It generates $60,000 per year in sales revenue, requiring $30,000 in operating expenses, excluding depreciation. If the firm sells the machine now, it could get $30,000 for it. The firm is considering buying a new machine to replace this one. The new machine will have a useful life of 5 years and a salvage value of $5000. It costs $65,000. It is expected to generate $70,000 in sales revenue and require $25,000 in operating expenses annually, excluding depreciation. The project's cost of capital is 10%, the firm uses straight-line depreciation, and the relevant tax rate is 40%. Compute the NPV from replacing the old machine.

B3. Suppose a firm can either expense or capitalize an asset it has just purchased for $9000. If it capitalizes the asset, it will depreciate the asset to a book value of zero on a straight-line basis over 3 years. The firm has a marginal tax rate of 38%, and the cost of capital for this asset is 12%. What is the present-value difference to the firm between expensing and capitalizing the asset? Assume the firm will have sufficient income over the next 3 years to use all possible tax credits.

B4. You are considering two mutually exclusive projects. Both require an initial investment of $80,000. Project A will last for 6 years and has expected net future cash flows of $40,222 per year. Project B will last for 5 years and has expected net future cash flows of $44,967 per year. The cost of capital for this project is 12%.

   a. Calculate the NPV for each project.

   b. Calculate the IRR for each project.

c. Graph the NPV of the projects as a function of the discount rate, including solving for the crossover point.

d. Assuming these projects cannot be repeated in the future, which one should you undertake?

B5. The NSF-Grant Co. is considering a project that has a 5-year useful life and costs $2500. It would save $500 per year in operating cost and increase revenue by $300 per year. It would be financed with a 5-year loan that has an APR of 8%. The salvage value for the newly purchased equipment is expected to be zero. It will be depreciated to a zero book value at the end of 5 years. The project's cost of capital is 12%. If Grant has a 40% tax rate, what is the NPV of the project?

B6. Reebok is considering a capital budgeting project with a cost of capital of 10% and the following expected cash flow pattern:

Time	0	1	2	3	4	5
Cash flow	−100	25	50	50	25	10

a. Calculate the NPV. Should the firm accept the project?

b. Calculate the IRR. According to this criterion, should the firm accept the project?

c. Calculate the payback.

d. What does payback tell you about the project's acceptability?

e. How would your answers to parts a and b change if you were told that the project is one of two mutually exclusive projects the firm has under consideration?

B7. Texaco has a capital budgeting project with a cost of capital of 12%, and the following expected cash flow pattern:

Time	0	1	2	3
Cash flow	50	100	−20	−50

a. Calculate NPV. According to this criterion, should the firm accept the project?

b. Calculate IRR. According to this criterion, should the firm accept the project?

c. Explain the meaning of the answer you obtained to part b.

d. How would you resolve the inconsistency between the answers to parts a and b?

B8. Sperry is considering two mutually exclusive capital budgeting projects with a cost of capital of 14% and the following expected cash flow patterns:

Time	0	1	2	3	4	5
Project A	−100	30	40	50	40	30
Project B	−150	45	60	75	60	60

Which project, if either, should Sperry undertake? Justify your answer.

B9. Suppose Kodak is considering two mutually exclusive capital budgeting projects with the following expected cash flow patterns:

Time	0	1	2	3	4	5	6
Project A	−350	140	140	100	100	65	30
Project B	−350	65	65	100	140	140	175

    a. Compute the IRR for each project.

    b. Compute the NPV for each project, assuming the cost of capital is 10%.

    c. Compute the NPV for each project, assuming costs of capital of 14%, 18%, and 22%. Create NPV profiles comparing the projects.

    d. If the cost of capital is precisely 12%, which project should Kodak undertake?

B10. Nassau Manufacturing Corporation is considering two capital budgeting projects with a cost of capital of 15% and the following expected cash flow patterns:

Time	0	1	2	3	4	5
Project A	−100	25	30	40	30	25
Project B	−50	10	15	25	15	15

    a. Calculate the NPV and IRR for each project.

    b. Which project(s) should Nassau accept, if they are independent?

    c. Which project(s) should Nassau accept, if they are dependent (both or neither are required)?

    d. Which project(s) should Nassau accept, if they are mutually exclusive?

B11. Let's say Fuji is considering a capital budgeting project with the following expected cash flow pattern:

Time	0	1	2	3	4	5
Cash flow	−500	100	150	150	200	200

    If this project has a cost of capital of 12%, what is its discounted payback?

B12. A staff analyst has just brought you an incomplete capital budgeting analysis that only shows you that the discounted payback of this conventional project is 5.24 years. A moment later, before you can fully collect your thoughts and ask the analyst any questions, the Marketing Vice President calls you and asks if the project analysis shows a positive NPV. You answer yes. Explain how you know this.

B13. The Howe Fix-It Corp. is considering buying a new machine called a TX2 that costs $60,000. The TX2 requires $10,000 in setup costs that are expensed immediately and $10,000 in additional working capital. The TX2's useful life is 10 years, after which it can be sold for a salvage value of $20,000. The TX2 requires a maintenance overhaul costing $30,000 at the end of year 7. The overhaul is fully expensed when it is done. Howe uses straight-line depreciation, and the machine will be depreciated to a book value of zero on a 6-year basis. Howe has a tax rate of 40% and the project's cost of capital is 15%. The TX2 is expected to increase revenues minus expenses by $17,500 per year. What is the NPV of buying the TX2?

B14. Why is a change in net working capital an important and necessary part of the incremental cost of a capital budgeting project?

B15. The Miller Corporation is considering a new product. An outlay of $6 million is required for equipment to produce the new product, and additional net working capital of $500,000 is required to support production and marketing. The equipment will be depreciated on a straight-line basis to a zero book value over 8 years. Although the depreciable life is 8 years, the project is expected to have a production life of only 6 years, and it will have a salvage value of zero at that time (removal cost = scrap value). Revenues minus expenses for the first 2 years of the project will be $5 million per year, but, because of competition, revenues minus expenses in years 3 through 6 will be only $3 million. The cost of capital for this project is 16%, and the relevant tax rate is 35%. Compute the NPV of Miller's new product.

PROBLEM SET C

C1. Respond to the following statement: Capital budgeting analysis is all about numbers; noncash, nonquantified items are irrelevant.

C2. The Doug E. Nuff Construction Company is considering a 33-year project that the government wants it to undertake. Development and construction will take 3 years, and the project will operate for 30 years. The riskless rate is 5%; the rate of return on the market portfolio is 12%; the project's beta is 1.3. Doug's firm has no debt. Doug expects to spend $250,000 for land, 1 year from the date the contract is awarded ($t = 1$). Construction of the building will cost $2 million, and the equipment will cost $3 million, both of which will be cash outflows at $t = 2$. There is a 5% investment tax credit on the building and a 7% investment tax credit on the equipment that can be claimed when operations begin ($t = 3$). The life of the building is 30 years, with a salvage value of $50,000, while the equipment has a 5-year useful life with no salvage value. The equipment will be replaced at 5-year intervals at a cost of $3 million upon each replacement. Straight-line depreciation will be used (over years $t = 4$ through $t = 8$, initially). To support operations, Doug expects to need $20,000 additional cash, to invest $60,000 in accounts receivable and $80,000 in inventory, and to maintain $60,000 in accounts payable. The investment in net working capital occurs at the start of operations ($t = 3$). The revenues from the project will amount to $800,000, fixed cost will be $100,000, and variable costs will be $150,000—all on an annual basis. At the end of the project, the firm is expected to restore the surrounding area at a cost of $420,000. The tax rate is 40%. The value of the land is expected to be constant over the life of the project, and the building can be sold for its net book value at the end of the project. What is the minimum amount that the government would have to pay Doug at the time the contract is awarded ($t = 0$) to get him to undertake the project?

C3. Brenda's Place (BP) is a national chain of short-order restaurants that has been very successful over the past 15 years. However, the growth potential in this market has declined and therefore BP's management is contemplating investing in a new line of business—publishing. BP can enter this new field by purchasing and renovating a small building in downtown Chicago at a cost of $80,000, which will be depreciated on a straight-line basis to a zero book value over 10 years. Although the depreciable life is 10 years, the entire project is expected to be sold off for a salvage value of $50,000 at the end of 8 years. It is estimated that the project would increase sales by $100,000 per year during the next 2 years and by another $50,000 ($150,000 above current sales) in years 3 through 8. Variable costs (including all labor and material) will be 60% of sales, and an increase of $10,000 per year in other annual operating expenses is expected. About $80,000 of added receivables and inventories will be needed. Accounts payable are expected to increase by $20,000. BP is completely equity-financed and has a current cost of equity capital of 15%, which corresponds to a beta of 2.0. The publishing business has an unleveraged beta of 1.4. The rate of return on the market portfolio is 10%. BP's tax rate is 40%. What is the NPV of this project?

Real-World Application:
The Boeing 777 Project

In October 1990, Boeing announced the newest addition to its fleet, the Boeing 777. It would fit in the medium-to-large-passenger-capacity niche. It would carry between 350 and 390 passengers up to 7600 nautical miles (roughly the distance from Los Angeles to Frankfurt).

Deliveries would begin in 1995 (and they eventually did).

The 777 was an enormous undertaking. Research and development, begun two and a half years earlier, would cost between $4 billion and $5 billion. Production facilities and personnel training would require an additional investment of $2.0 billion, and $1.7 billion in working capital would be required in 1996. The table below furnishes cash flow projections for the 777 project as of year-end 1990.

Cash Flow Projections for the Boeing 777 Project
(Dollar Amounts in Millions)

YEAR	AFTER-TAX PROFIT[a]	DEPRECIATION	CAPITAL EXPENDITURES[b]	YEAR	AFTER-TAX PROFIT[a]	DEPRECIATION	CAPITAL EXPENDITURES[b]
1991	(597.30)	40.00	400.00	2008	1691.19	129.20	178.41
1992	(947.76)	96.00	600.00	2009	1208.64	96.99	627.70
1993	(895.22)	116.40	300.00	2010	1954.39	76.84	144.27
1994	(636.74)	124.76	200.00	2011	2366.03	65.81	100.51
1995	(159.34)	112.28	182.91	2012	2051.46	61.68	(463.32)
1996	958.62	101.06	1741.42	2013	1920.65	57.96	(234.57)
1997	1718.14	90.95	2.12	2014	2244.05	54.61	193.92
1998	1503.46	82.72	(327.88)	2015	2313.63	52.83	80.68
1999	1665.46	77.75	67.16	2016	2384.08	52.83	83.10
2000	1670.49	75.63	(75.21)	2017	2456.65	52.83	85.59
2001	1553.76	75.00	(88.04)	2018	2531.39	52.83	88.16
2002	1698.99	75.00	56.73	2019	2611.89	47.52	90.80
2003	1981.75	99.46	491.21	2020	2699.26	35.28	93.53
2004	1709.71	121.48	32.22	2021	2785.50	28.36	96.33
2005	950.83	116.83	450.88	2022	2869.63	28.36	99.22
2006	1771.61	112.65	399.53	2023	2956.28	28.36	102.20
2007	1958.48	100.20	(114.91)	2024	3053.65	16.05	105.26

[a] Includes expenditure for research and development.
[b] Includes changes in working capital. Negative values are caused by reductions in working capital.
Source: Robert F. Bruner, *Case Studies in Finance*, 2nd ed. (Burr Ridge, Ill.: Irwin, 1994), pp. 209–213.

Consider also the following information:

Boeing's beta	1.06
Boeing's market-value debt ratio	0.02
Boeing's new issue rate for long-term debt	9.75%
Riskless return	8.75%
Market risk premium	8.00%
Boeing's marginal income tax rate	34%

Use this information to determine whether Boeing should continue with the 777 project.

1. Explain why you should ignore the research and development expenditures made prior to October 1990 when you evaluate the project.

2. Calculate the annual CFATs.

3. Estimate Boeing's cost of equity capital.

4. Boeing derived about 25% of its revenues from the U.S. defense and space programs and the remainder from its commercial aircraft business. Suppose you analyze other aircraft manufacturers and find that the unleveraged beta for the commercial aircraft business is 1.20. Estimate the cost of equity capital for Boeing's commercial aircraft business.

5. Estimate the WACC for the 777 project.

6. What is the NPV of the 777 project?

7. What is the IRR of the 777 project?

8. What is the payback period for the 777 project? Is this figure useful in determining whether to continue with the project?

9. On the basis of your analysis, do you think Boeing should have continued with the 777 project? Explain.

BIBLIOGRAPHY

Bathala, Chenchuramaiah T., and Steven J. Carlson. "Repeal of the Investment Tax Credit and Firms' Investment Spending," *Financial Management*, 1994, 23(1):13.

Brick, Ivan E., and Daniel G. Weaver. "A Comparison of Capital Budgeting Techniques in Identifying Profitable Investments," *Financial Management*, 1984, 13(4):29–39.

Brigham, Eugene F., and T. Craig Tapley. "Financial Leverage and Use of the Net Present Value Investment Criterion: A Reexamination," *Financial Management*, 1985, 14(2):48–52.

Flannery, Mark J., Joel F. Houston, and Subramanyam Venkataraman. "Financing Multiple Investment Projects," *Financial Management*, 1993, 22(2):161–172.

Golbe, Devra L., and Barry Schachter. "The Net Present Value Rule and an Algorithm for Maintaining a Constant Debt-Equity Ratio," *Financial Management*, 1985, 14(2):53–58.

Greenfield, Robert L., Maury R. Randall, and John C. Woods. "Financial Leverage and Use of the Net Present Value Investment Criterion," *Financial Management*, 1983, 12(3):40–44.

Howe, Keith M. "A Note on Flotation Costs and Capital Budgeting," *Financial Management*, 1982, 11(4):30–33.

Howe, Keith M. "Perpetuity Rate of Return Analysis," *Engineering Economist*, 1991, 36(3):248–257.

Kasanen, Eero. "Creating Value by Spawning Investment Opportunities," *Financial Management*, 1993, 22(3):251–258.

McCarty, Daniel E., and William R. McDaniel. "A Note on Expensing versus Depreciating Under the Accelerated Cost Recovery System: Comment," *Financial Management*, 1983, 12(2):37–39.

Pohlman, Randolph A., Emmanuel S. Santiago, and F. Lynn Markel. "Cash Flow Estimation Practices of Large Firms," *Financial Management*, 1988, 17(2):71–79.

Pruitt, Stephen W., and Lawrence J. Gitman. "Capital Budgeting Forecast Biases: Evidence from the Fortune 500," *Financial Management*, 1987, 16(1):46–51.

Statman, Meir, and Tyzoon T. Tyebjee. "Optimistic Capital Budgeting Forecasts: An Experiment," *Financial Management*, 1985, 14(3):27–33.

Viswanath, P. V. "Adjusting Capital Budgeting Rules for Information Asymmetry," *Financial Management*, 1993, 22(4):22–23.

Vogt, Stephen C. "The Cash Flow/Investment Relationship: Evidence from U.S. Manufacturing Firms," *Financial Management*, 1994, 23(2):3–20.

CAPITAL BUDGETING: SOME COMPLICATIONS

OBJECTIVES

After studying this chapter, you should be able to

1. Explain the problems of erosion and enhancement that are created by a project's interaction with a firm's existing products.

2. Calculate equivalent annual costs and determine optimal replacement cycles in cases of routine asset replacement.

3. Incorporate the effects of inflation into an NPV calculation.

4. Explain the importance of using *current* tax laws to estimate after-tax cash flows and to value a project.

5. Describe alternative methods of project analysis, including break-even and sensitivity analysis, decision trees, and Monte Carlo simulation, and explain their potential pitfalls.

In this chapter, we will apply the concepts from Chapter 11 and introduce some factors that complicate the capital budgeting decision. One such factor is economic independence. Projects are generally formulated to be independent of one another. However, this is not always possible. A proposed project may interact with a firm's current operations or with other projects. We will examine such a situation in this chapter.

We will also look at optimal replacement cycles, taxes, and inflation. These too can complicate capital budgeting. We will show, however, that proper treatment of these considerations in a capital budgeting analysis simply means applying time-value-of-money mechanics carefully.

The chapter ends with a look at alternative ways to analyze a capital budgeting project that may give us some additional insight into project value. These methods can be useful when it is impossible to determine a market-based estimate of the project's cost of capital.

CAPITAL BUDGETING AND THE PRINCIPLES OF FINANCE

◇ *Time Value of Money*: Measure the value the capital budgeting project will create—its NPV.

◇ *Incremental Benefits*: Identify and estimate the incremental expected future cash flows for a capital budgeting project.

◇ *Risk-Return Trade-Off*: Consider the risk of the capital budgeting project when determining the project's *cost of capital*, its required return.

◇ *Options*: Recognize the value of options, such as the options to expand, postpone, or abandon a capital budgeting project.

◇ *Two-Sided Transactions*: Consider why the other party to a transaction is willing to participate.

◇ *Signaling*: Consider the actions and products of competitors.

◇ *Valuable Ideas*: Look for new ideas to use as a basis for capital budgeting projects that will create value.

◇ *Comparative Advantage*: Look for capital budgeting projects that use the firm's comparative advantage to add value.

12.1 NEW-PRODUCT SIDE EFFECTS

An innovation can cause what is called **erosion** of one or more existing products. A sales reduction may be an obvious consequence of an innovation. Perhaps less obvious is the decline, caused by the innovation, in the market value of the production facilities for existing products. Because of reduced or eliminated sales opportunities, the value of plant and equipment used by *other firms*, as well as that of the firm introducing the innovation, declines. Therefore, as perverse as it might seem, a firm may be best served by delaying introduction of an innovation until it can be incorporated into the firm's natural replacement of equipment. Of course, as a defensive move against competitors, a firm might also introduce the innovation sooner than it might otherwise have done.

Headcleaner, Inc. manufactures a product called Clean-e-z, which is used to clean magnetic tape heads on a videocassette recorder (VCR). Recently, the research lab at Headcleaner developed a new method for cleaning VCR heads. The new process is being referred to by its laboratory name, Q-10. Q-10 is superior to Clean-e-z in every way. Consequently, the firm expects Q-10 to overtake, and ultimately eliminate, Clean-e-z sales.

In the meantime, continuing to make and sell Clean-e-z would allow differential pricing of the two products. It would also make use of existing facilities that will eventually have to be scrapped because they cannot be used to produce Q-10. Therefore, there are dependencies between Q-10 and Clean-e-z that cannot be ignored. In addition, there are sunk costs in Clean-e-z production facilities that *must be* ignored.

One big question facing Headcleaner is how long it can enjoy monopolistic pricing for Q-10. Although the product can be patented, competitors will be able to imitate it. As a result, Headcleaner's price premium for Q-10 has a limited life. The firm estimates that an equivalent product could be developed in about two years. If a competitor discovers the idea while

TABLE 12-1

Present-value calculation for Headcleaner, Inc.'s new product, Q-10.

TIME	ITEM	CFBT	CFAT	PV AT 16%
0	Equipment	−6.0	−6.0	−6.000
0	Δ Working capital	−0.5	−0.5	−0.500
1–6	Depreciation	0	0.263/yr	0.967
1–2	$\Delta R - \Delta E$	5.0/yr	3.25/yr	5.217
3–6	$\Delta R - \Delta E$	3.0/yr	1.95/yr	4.055
6	Salvage	0	0.525	
		$(B = 1.5)$	$(1 - T)S + TB$	0.421
6	Δ Working capital	0.5	0.5	
				PV = \$4.160 million

Headcleaner is still working out the production and marketing details for Q-10, the price premium will last even less than two years.

Let's first look at the Q-10 project by itself. An outlay of \$6 million is required for equipment to produce the new product, and additional net working capital of \$500,000 is required to support production and marketing. The equipment will be depreciated on a straight-line basis to a zero book value over eight years, so depreciation will be \$750,000 per year (= six million/8). Although the depreciable life is eight years, the expected production life is only six years.[1] After the six years, the salvage value is estimated to be zero because of continuing technological innovations.

Revenues minus expenses for the first two years of Q-10 production are expected to be \$5 million per year. Because of competition, however, revenues minus expenses in years 3 through 6 are expected to be only \$3 million per year. The project's cost of capital is 16%, and the relevant marginal tax rate is 35%. The project's present value, without regard to its effects on current operations, is given in Table 12-1.

The calculation in Table 12-1 ignores the value of Clean-e-z sales, which are expected to continue for the next two years, although at a substantially reduced level. Specifically, revenues minus expenses for Clean-e-z are expected to be \$1.3 and \$0.8 million per year before taxes for the next two years, respectively. Production equipment for Clean-e-z currently has a book value of \$3.0 million, six more years of straight-line depreciation at \$500,000 per year to a zero book value, and an expected scrap value in two years of \$250,000. Finally, \$500,000 in net working capital will be released when the production of Clean-e-z is discontinued. The present value of Clean-e-z production for the next two years, assuming that Q-10 is introduced now, is given in Table 12-2.

TABLE 12-2

Present-value calculation for 2 more years of Clean-e-z production.

TIME	ITEM	CFBT	CFAT	PV AT 16%
1–2	Depreciation	0	0.175/yr	0.281
1	$\Delta R - \Delta E$	1.3	0.845	0.728
2	$\Delta R - \Delta E$	0.8	0.520	0.386
2	Salvage	0.25	0.863	
		$(B = 2.0)$	$(1 - T)S + TB$	1.013
2	Δ Working capital	0.5	0.5	
				PV = \$2.408 million

---

[1] It is important to note once again that the useful life of an asset is not necessarily equal to its depreciable life. The Internal Revenue Code specifies one depreciable life for an asset for tax purposes. The useful life depends on the specific use of the asset, among other things.

TIME	ITEM	CFBT	CFAT	PV AT 16%
1–6	Depreciation	0	0.175/yr	0.645
1–6	$\Delta R - \Delta E$	2.6/yr	1.690/yr	6.227
6	Salvage	0	0	
		$(B = 0)$	$(1 - T)S + TB$	0.205
6	ΔWorking capital	0.5	0.5	
			PV =	$\overline{\$7.077}$ million

TABLE 12-3
Present-value calculation for 6 more years of Clean-e-z production.

The total present value of the Q-10 project, then, appears to be the sum of the two present values, or $6.568 million. Although this looks good, we must also determine the value of continuing to produce Clean-e-z without introducing Q-10. The facilities for producing Clean-e-z could be used for another six years. Revenues minus expenses for Clean-e-z are currently $2.6 million per year. Suppose this sales level continues for six years and the equipment has a zero salvage value. Then the present value of continuing Clean-e-z production—without introducing Q-10—is as given in Table 12-3.

The continued production of Clean-e-z appears to be more valuable than the immediate introduction of Q-10. However, this determination ignores the interaction of Clean-e-z sales with competing products. Future Clean-e-z sales depend on competitors not developing and introducing a product like Q-10. Once a competitor comes up with the idea, not only will Clean-e-z sales be hurt, but Headcleaner's projected two years of monopolistic price premium will also be eroded or even eliminated. Therefore, Headcleaner must consider postponing the introduction of Q-10 *temporarily,* rather than putting it off until the Clean-e-z production facilities have been completely worn out. The firm estimates that there is a 20% chance of a competitor discovering the idea within the next year, a 25% chance in the year after, and a 50% chance in the third year. If the idea has not been discovered before then, it is virtually certain that a competitor will discover the idea in the fourth year.

Although a painstakingly complete analysis would contain every possible introduction time, the decision facing Headcleaner is whether *any* postponement yields a greater NPV. Therefore, we need only compare the results of introducing Q-10 now (PV = $6.568 million) with those of introducing it later—say 1 year from now.[2] Figure 12-1 presents a comparison of the two alternatives. The subsequent PVs (8.304 and 7.193) are given without present-value tables. Problems B2 and B4 in the "Exercises" section at the end of the chapter ask you to verify these numbers.

The present value of waiting a year is the discounted expected value of having either 1 or 2 years of monopolistic pricing power. If Headcleaner waits a year, there is a 0.20 probability that it will have only 1 year of monopolistic price premium and therefore a 0.80 probability it will have 2 years of monopolistic price premium. The expected value is then $8.082 million [= 0.8(8.304) + 0.2(7.193)], and the present value is $6.967 million (= 8.082/1.16). Therefore, the present value of waiting a year is $399,000 more than the present value of introducing it now.

Although the largest present value, of those examined, appears to be achieved by continuing Clean-e-z production until the equipment is worn out, it is important to reiterate that this NPV is illusory. Competition eliminates this alternative. Although Headcleaner could continue to produce only Clean-e-z, sales of Clean-e-z would not continue as they had been projected if a product like Q-10 were introduced by a competitor.

Also, note that we do not have to consider other waiting strategies at this time. We have

---

[2] The choice of 1 year from now is of course somewhat arbitrary. "Later" is simply the next possible point at which introducing the product would be "reasonable."

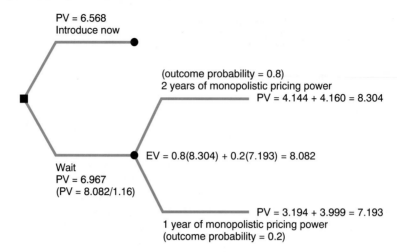

FIGURE 12-1
Diagram of Headcleaner's decision whether to wait to introduce its new product, Q-10 (in $ millions).

shown that waiting 1 year is better than introducing now (6.967 versus 6.568). Headcleaner can still decide later to postpone longer than 1 year. Headcleaner can use any new information it acquires during the next year to help make that subsequent decision.

Erosion and Enhancement

The Q-10 example illustrates an important interaction between innovation and existing products. Just as one interaction among products may cause a decrease in value, another interaction may cause an increase in value. Such an increase is called **enhancement**. Enhancement occurs when the production and/or sales of one product increases the value of another. For example, an innovation that causes a reduction in the cost of making or installing a home swimming pool may cause an increase in the sales of swimming pool maintenance equipment.

EXAMPLE

New Computer Game Systems at Nintendo

What if Nintendo discovered a computer graphics innovation that would require a new type of machine, such as when Sega introduced its Genesis system? The firm would face the problems of erosion and enhancement. Sales of existing products and the value of existing production facilities, for Nintendo and its competitors, would probably be eroded by a superior system. At the same time, a new system might provide Nintendo with an enhancement of some existing and potential future products. The firm could develop the new system to facilitate such enhancement. ■

It is vital to include dependencies that cause significant erosion or enhancement in order to correctly measure a project's NPV. If you don't include them, you won't have measured the NPV, even though you may think you have!

Self-Check Questions

1. How can an innovation cause erosion of an existing product?

2. How can an innovation cause enhancement of an existing product?

3. Why is it important to consider the effects of erosion and enhancement in capital budgeting analysis?

12.2 EVALUATING REPLACEMENT CYCLES

The packaging-machine example in the last chapter involved replacing specialized equipment that is subject to periodic technological design improvements. In such cases, the replacement decision is basically a one-time decision. Later, when the chosen machine becomes worn out or technologically outmoded, its replacement is essentially an entirely new project. Such a replacement decision is, in effect, a decision whether to continue producing a product and even whether to remain in that line of business.

But many replacement decisions are not like the packaging-machine example. Instead, they are routine, involving machinery and equipment that does not change very much over time. The asset is replaced or overhauled because of worn-out parts rather than technological improvement. Essentially, the new asset is identical to the one it replaces. In such cases, there is a routine pattern, or **replacement cycle**. The asset is purchased, maintained, and replaced on a regular basis. A delivery vehicle for Federal Express is an example.

A problem arises because of differing useful lives. When alternatives in a routine replacement decision do not have identical life cycles, the asset with the largest single-cycle NPV is not necessarily the best choice. Instead, the choice must be made on a comparable basis. For example, if a firm is choosing between two assets, one with a 5-year life and the other with a 10-year life, then two sequential 5-year assets would be needed to do the job of one 10-year asset.

One way to choose among alternatives in a replacement cycle decision, then, is to find a common horizon where some number of sequential replacements of one asset equals that for the alternative. This approach can be cumbersome, however.

For example, comparing a 6-year type A asset with a 7-year type B asset would involve a horizon of 42 years: seven sequential purchases of A types versus six of B types. If there was a C-type alternative with an 8-year life, the process would become even more tedious. A more convenient method of choosing among alternatives in such situations is on the basis of equivalent annual cost.

Equivalent Annual Cost

Equivalent annual cost (EAC) is the *equivalent* cost per year of owning an asset over its entire life. The method is a simple two-step application of time-value-of-money mathematics. The first step is to compute the present value of all costs associated with owning the asset over its entire life. These costs include the purchase price, maintenance costs, and operating costs over the period of expected ownership. Let the net initial outlay be C_0 and the yearly CFAT costs be $C_1, C_2, \ldots, C_n$, where n is the length of the asset's life. The cost of capital is r. The total present value of costs over the life of the asset, TC, is

$$\text{TC} = C_0 + \sum_{t=1}^{n} \frac{C_t}{(1 + r)^t} \tag{12.1}$$

The second step is to determine the cash flow that, if it was paid out each year, would have the same present value, TC. This cash flow is the equivalent annual cost (EAC). It is given by the formula for determining the payments of an ordinary annuity, Equation (4.3). With the equivalent annual cost notation, it is

$$\text{EAC} = \text{TC} \left[\frac{r(1 + r)^n}{(1 + r)^n - 1} \right] \tag{12.2}$$

EXAMPLE

Changing Inventory Equipment at Hoover

Let's say the Hoover Corporation is considering the replacement of a machine used for its inventory storage. Hoover can buy one of two alternative machines, A or B. Which machine should Hoover buy?

Hoover should choose the machine with the lower equivalent annual cost, so we must calculate each machine's EAC. Machine A costs $49,000 to purchase and install, has a 5-year life, and will be depreciated over 5 years on a straight-line basis to a book value of $4000, so depreciation will be $9000 per year for 5 years [$= (49,000 - 4000)/5$]. At the end of the 5 years, Hoover expects to be able to sell machine A for $10,000. For the expected production level, it will cost $25,000 per year to operate machine A. The relevant tax rate is 40%, and the project's cost of capital is 12%.

The present value of all of machine A's costs is $-\$85,783$, as given in Table 12-4. The EAC can then be calculated using Equation (12.2). [Put in PV $= -85,783$, $r = 12\%$, $n = 5$, and FV $= 0$, and compute CF $= -23,797$].

$$EAC = TC\left[\frac{r(1 + r)^n}{(1 + r)^n - 1}\right] = -85,783\left[\frac{0.12(1.12)^5}{(1.12)^5 - 1}\right] = -\$23,797$$

TABLE 12-4
Present value of the total cost for Hoover's machine A.

TIME	ITEM	CFBT	CFAT	PV AT 12%
0	I_0	−49,000	−49,000	−49,000
1–5	$-\Delta E$	−25,000/yr	−15,000/yr	−54,072
1–5	Depreciation	0/yr	3,600/yr	12,977
5	Salvage	10,000	7,600	4,312
		($B = 4,000$)	$(1 - T)S + TB$	
				TC $= -\$85,783$

Machine B has a 10-year life but costs $72,000 to purchase and install. It will be depreciated over 8 years on a straight-line basis to a book value of zero, so depreciation will be $9000 per year for the first 8 years ($= 72,000/8$) and zero for the last 2 years of use. Machine B is expected to require an overhaul at the end of year 6 that will cost $18,000 and will be expensed rather than capitalized. At the end of the 10 years, Hoover expects to be able to sell machine B for a scrap value that will equal the cost of removal and cleanup. Machine B is slightly less expensive to run than machine A, costing $24,000 per year to operate.

The present value of all the costs for machine B is $-\$140,952$, as given in Table 12-5. The EAC can then be calculated using Equation (12.2). [Put in PV $= -140,952$, $r = 12\%$, $n = 10$, and FV $= 0$, and compute CF $= -24,946$].

$$EAC = TC\left[\frac{r(1 + r)^n}{(1 + r)^n - 1}\right] = -140,952\left[\frac{0.12(1.12)^{10}}{(1.12)^{10} - 1}\right] = -\$24,946$$

TABLE 12-5
Present value of the total cost for Hoover's machine B.

TIME	ITEM	CFBT	CFAT	PV AT 12%
0	I_0	−72,000	−72,000	−72,000
1–10	$-\Delta E$	−24,000/yr	−14,400/yr	−81,363
1–8	Depreciation	0/yr	3,600/yr	17,883
6	Overhaul	−18,000	−10,800	−5,472
				TC $= -\$140,952$

Judging by the EACs, then, Hoover should buy machine A with its lower EAC. Note that we disregarded the revenues, because both alternatives have the same revenues and risk. ■

| EAC$_A$ = | 23,797 | 23,797 | 23,797 | 23,797 | 23,797 | 23,797 | 23,797 | 23,797 | 23,797 | 23,797 |
| EAC$_B$ = | 24,946 | 24,946 | 24,946 | 24,946 | 24,946 | 24,946 | 24,946 | 24,946 | 24,946 | 24,946 |

| 0 | 1 | 2 | 3 | 4 | 5 | 6 | 7 | 8 | 9 | 10 |

85,782   85,782

48,675 ◄

134,457 = Present value of total costs for machine A over a 10-year horizon

140,952 = Present value of total costs for machine B over a 10-year horizon

FIGURE 12-2
Comparison of equivalent annual cost and common horizon methods.

Figure 12-2 compares the costs over 10 years of using the two machines. The comparison shows both the EACs and the present values of total cost outlays over a common 10-year horizon. Figure 12-2 illustrates how comparing EACs is equivalent to comparing costs over a common horizon, which happens in all cases. However, as we noted earlier, the EAC method is more convenient, especially when there are more than two alternatives.

Replacement Frequency

The preferred shorter replacement cycle in the Hoover example has an additional option associated with it. Because of the shorter life cycle, there is less chance that a mechanically sound machine will be made useless by a technological advance. In essence, the firm has the option to change production technologies more often when it purchases the machine with the shorter life cycle. Therefore, if the two machines had identical EACs (including removal costs), the machine with the shorter life cycle would be preferred. Although we do not have an option pricing model for conveniently determining an estimate for the value of more frequent replacement, it is nevertheless a valuable option. Other capital budgeting options will be discussed in the next chapter.

The Hoover example compared two alternative machines. It is also useful to consider alternative replacement cycles for a given machine. The optimal replacement cycle is the one that minimizes the EAC. Salvage values and maintenance costs vary with the type and usage of a machine. (Salvage value is also a function of the potential future uses of the equipment.) One life cycle is not necessarily optimal for *all* situations. Let's investigate replacement cycle frequency by extending the Hoover example to consider various life cycles for machine A. Note that the depreciation schedule does not change, despite the change in usage.

Let's say that instead of replacing it after 5 years, Hoover could replace machine A early at the end of 4 years. Or machine A could be used an extra year and replaced after 6 years. With less use, the machine would have an expected $16,000 resale value at the end of 4 years. With more use, the machine would require maintenance costing $1000 at the end of year 5 and would be expected to have a zero salvage value at the end of year 6. Which replacement cycle is best?

The total cost over one 4-year life cycle is −$74,220, as given in Table 12-6. From Equation (12.2), the EAC for a 4-year cycle is −$24,436.

Replacement Cycle Frequency at Hoover

EXAMPLE

TIME	ITEM	CFBT	CFAT	PV AT 12%
0	I_0	−49,000	−49,000	−49,000
1–4	ΔE	−25,000/yr	−15,000/yr	−45,560
1–4	Depreciation	0/yr	3,600/yr	10,934
4	Salvage	16,000	14,800	9,406
		$(B = 13,000)$	$(1 - T)S + TB$	
			TC =	−$74,220

TABLE 12-6
Present value of the total cost for machine A if it is replaced after 4 years.

The total cost over one 6-year life cycle is −$97,223, as given in Table 12-7. From Equation (12.2), the EAC for a 6-year cycle is −$23,647.

TABLE 12-7
Present value of the total cost for machine A if it is replaced after 6 years.

TIME	ITEM	CFBT	CFAT	PV AT 12%
0	I_0	−49,000	−49,000	−49,000
1–6	ΔE	−25,000/yr	−15,000/yr	−61,671
1–5	Depreciation	0/yr	3,600/yr	12,977
5	Maintenance	−1,000	−600	−340
6	Salvage	0	1,600	811
		$(B = 4,000)$	$(1 - T)S + TB$	
				TC = −$97,223

Thus the 6-year replacement cycle is best. ∎

As we pointed out earlier, the choice of machine A (over B), with its shorter replacement cycle, provides more flexibility with respect to technological innovations. Similarly, flexibility in a machine's replacement cycle is also valuable because even if one cycle is projected at one point in time, the firm has the option to change when replacement will occur, depending on conditions that develop.

In the replacement cycle frequency example, the alternative EACs are very similar. Therefore, the firm can purchase machine A, run it for 4 years, and reevaluate the replacement decision then. The reevaluation would include technological considerations, the condition of the machine, replacement cost, salvage values, maintenance experience over the 4 years, and more accurate maintenance cost projections for its continued use, among other things.

Equivalent Annual Annuities

The EAC calculation annualizes the total cost of a project over its life. The same type of calculation can be used to annualize *any* amount, such as a project's NPV, its total revenue, and so on. In such cases, the amount is called an *equivalent annual benefit*. The general term for an annualized amount is **equivalent annual annuity (EAA)**. The EAA is a useful measure whenever the project horizon is indefinitely long, so that the assumption of an infinite, or permanent, stream is a good characterization of the situation.

EXAMPLE

Computing an Equivalent Annual Annuity (EAA)

Suppose one 5-year cycle of a machine has an NPV of $2800. Assuming a required return of 11%, the EAA for this project's NPV would be $757.60. With an infinite horizon of sequential replacement, the NPV from the sequence would be the present value of a perpetuity of EAA inflows, or $6887.27 (= 757.60/0.11). ∎

Other Replacement Scenarios

In Chapter 11 we looked at one-time replacement decisions. Such decisions should be made by using the one-time NPV decision criterion: Choose the asset with the largest NPV. Here, we assumed that a project would be replaced periodically, with an infinitely long horizon. The choice of replacement cycle for the *routine* like-for-like replacement of assets is made on the basis of equivalent annual cost: *Choose the asset with the lowest EAC.*

When future significant technological advances are likely, the replacement cycle decision becomes more complex. Among other things, the decision must include the option connected with a shorter replacement cycle to make technological change sooner. In practice, technological advances can be difficult to predict. Nevertheless, their possible occurrence can materially affect a firm's choice of asset.

Self-Check Questions

1. How do periodic replacement decisions differ from one-time replacement decisions? What is the best way to handle assets with replacement cycles in capital budgeting analysis?

2. What is the equivalent annual cost of owning an asset? How is it related to an ordinary annuity?

3. How is the EAC approach used to decide which of two machines to purchase?

4. What is an equivalent annual annuity? How can it be used in capital budgeting analysis?

12.3 INFLATION

Expectations about inflation affect required returns. Thus a project's cost of capital depends on inflation uncertainty. Even U.S. government bonds are not truly riskless because of inflation uncertainty, as we saw in Chapter 6.[3] We showed that with fixed payments, changes in the bond's required return cause changes in the value of the bond. This phenomenon follows directly from the present value equation.

But as we stressed in Chapter 10, asset value is a function of *both* the required return *and* the expected future cash flows. And inflation affects the project's expected future cash flows as well as its cost of capital. The effect of inflation can be complex.

Yet it is possible for project value to be unchanged, even though a change in inflation expectations has caused both future cash flows and the cost of capital to change. The effects can cancel each other out, leaving the project's NPV unchanged.

To analyze a capital budgeting decision, either include inflation in all the estimates of expected future cash flows and the cost of capital, or exclude inflation everywhere. When an estimate includes inflation, it is said to be stated in *nominal* terms. When an estimate excludes inflation, it is said to be stated in *real* terms.[4] For proper measurement, then, all of the parts must be stated either entirely in real terms or entirely in nominal terms.

To explore the effects of inflation, let's look first at its effect on the cost of capital. Let the cost of capital in real terms be r_r, the cost of capital in nominal terms be r_n, and the expected inflation rate be i. The nominal rate can be obtained by simply compounding the real rate and the inflation rate:

$$(1 + r_n) = (1 + r_r)(1 + i)$$

---

[3] It is very important to note that the relevant measure is the *expected* future inflation rate. This can be quite different from the inflation rate actually realized, even though recent realized inflation rates are often highly correlated with expected future inflation rates.

[4] Recall from Chapter 4 that the term *nominal* means that the value is a value "in name only." Cash flows that are expressed in nominal dollar terms are not comparable in purchasing power to today's dollars. This is the reason why the phrase *in dollars of constant purchasing power* is often used in place of the phrase *in real terms*.

Multiplying the right-hand side and rearranging, we get:

$$r_n = r_r + i + ir_r \tag{12.3}$$

This relationship may surprise you. You may have seen the nominal rate expressed simply as the sum of the real and inflation rates, without the cross-term, ir_r, being included. Because the cross-term is relatively small compared to the other terms, the sum is a good approximation and is often used in practice. However, Equation (12.3) is the correct expression.

A subtle problem that occurs with inflation is that although revenues and expenses inflate, the depreciation tax credits do not. This is because depreciation expense is based on the historical cost of the equipment. Thus either the depreciation tax credits must be converted into real terms, or the expected revenue and expense cash flows must be converted into nominal terms. You can see the problem in the following example, in which the NPV of the project is computed in both real and nominal terms. The example shows that we can state all items in today's dollars (real terms) and use the real cost of capital (Table 12-8). Alternatively, we can state all items in inflated dollars (nominal terms) and use the nominal cost of capital (Table 12-9).

EXAMPLE

Monogramming at Christian Dior

Suppose Christian Dior is thinking of buying a monogramming machine. The machine of interest has a 4-year useful life. It would require an initial outlay of $100,000. The machine would be depreciated to a zero book value over 4 years on a straight-line basis, so depreciation would be $25,000 per year. The machine would generate an incremental increase in operating income of $50,000 per year before taxes. The relevant tax rate is 40%. Inflation is expected to be 8% per year, and the project's cost of capital in real terms would be $r_r = 10\%$. What is the NPV of purchasing this machine?

First, let's compute the NPV of Christian Dior's project in real terms. To do this, we must convert the depreciation tax credits into real terms. The tax credit for the first year would be $TD = 0.4 \times 25,000 = 10,000$. With 8% inflation, this would be worth $9260 (= 10,000/1.08) in real terms, or dollars of constant purchasing power. The tax credit for the second year would be worth $8570 (= 10,000/[1.08]^2). The other tax credits would be determined in a similar manner, by discounting them for the appropriate number of years at the inflation rate. Table 12-8 gives the NPV calculation for the project in real terms.

TABLE 12-8
NPV calculation in real terms.

TIME	ITEM	CFBT	CFAT (REAL)	PV AT 10%
0	I_0	−100,000	−100,000	−100,000
1–4	$\Delta R - \Delta E$	50,000/yr	30,000/yr	95,090
1	Depreciation	0	9,260	8,420
2	Depreciation	0	8,570	7,090
3	Depreciation	0	7,940	5,960
4	Depreciation	0	7,350	5,020
				NPV = $21,580

To compute the NPV in nominal terms, we need the nominal required return. From Equation (12.3), this is

$$r_n = r_r + i + ir_r = 0.10 + 0.08 + (0.08)(0.10) = 18.8\%$$

In nominal dollars, the first year's $\Delta R - \Delta E$ would be \$54,000 (= 50,000 × 1.08). The second year's $\Delta R - \Delta E$ would be \$58,320 [= $50,000(1.08)^2$], and the subsequent flows would be computed in a similar manner, by compounding them forward at the inflation rate. Table 12-9 gives the NPV calculation for the project in nominal terms.

TIME	ITEM	CFBT	CFAT (NOMINAL)	PV AT 18.8%
0	I_0	− 100,000	− 100,000	− 100,000
1	$\Delta R - \Delta E$	54,000	32,400/yr	27,270
2	$\Delta R - \Delta E$	58,320	34,990	24,790
3	$\Delta R - \Delta E$	62,990	37,790	22,540
4	$\Delta R - \Delta E$	68,020	40,810	20,490
1–4	Depreciation	0	10,000/yr	26,490
				NPV = \$21,580

TABLE 12-9
NPV calculation in nominal terms.

As you can see, the two calculations produce exactly the same NPV. ■

If inflation affects various component cash flows differently—for example, if revenues are expected to increase 6% per year but expenses are expected to increase 9%—those differences must be incorporated into the analysis. Differences in inflation rates among cash flows can cause complexity, as can differences in the effect of inflation on the cost of capital and the expected cash flows. Still, this merely complicates the problem. Such complexity does not change the way we incorporate the effects of inflation. Whatever the case, the analysis should be cast in a consistent manner, *entirely in real terms or entirely in nominal terms.*

Self-Check Questions

1. Explain why it is important, when analyzing a capital budgeting decision, either to include inflation in all the estimates of expected future cash flows and the cost of capital, or else to exclude it everywhere.
2. Why is the nominal cost of capital not simply the sum of the real cost of capital and the expected inflation rate?
3. True or false? A capital budgeting analysis must be cast entirely in real terms.

12.4 A FEW WORDS ABOUT THE TAX ENVIRONMENT

Early in this century, Congress instituted a procedure for collecting taxes, now familiar to most Americans, called the income tax. Since that time, income tax has come to provide the primary source of tax revenue for the federal government. Income tax provisions and rates have changed frequently. Table 12-10 shows the statutory federal tax rates on corporate income from 1909 through 1995.

Another way in which tax laws have changed over the years is in the provisions for capitalizing equipment expense—depreciation—and for claiming an investment tax credit. In the last three decades there have been no fewer than five major changes in the depreciation rules,

TABLE 12-10

Statutory corporate income tax rates from 1909 through 1995.

YEAR	RATE BRACKETS OR EXEMPTIONS	RATE[a] (PERCENT)
1909–1913	$5000 exemption	1
1913–1915	No exemption after March 1, 1913	1
1916	None	2
1917	None	6
1918	$2000 exemption	12
1919–1921	$2000 exemption	10
1922–1924	$2000 exemption	12.5
1925	$2000 exemption	13
1926–1927	$2000 exemption	13.5
1928	$3000 exemption	12
1929	$3000 exemption	11
1930–1931	$3000 exemption	12
1932–1935	None	13.75
1936–1937	Graduated normal tax	
	First $2000	8
	Over $40,000	15
	Graduated surtax on undistributed profits ranging from—	7–27
1938–1939	First $25,000	12.5–16
	Over $25,000	19[b]
1940	First $25,000	14.85–18.7
	$25,000 to $31,964.30	38.3
	$31,964.30 to $38,565.89	36.9
	Over $38,565.89	24
1941	First $25,000	21–25
	$25,000 to $38,461.54	44
	Over $38,461.54	31
1942–1945	First $25,000	25–29
	$25,000 to $50,000	53
	Over $50,000	40
1946–1949	First $25,000	21–25
	$25,000 to $50,000	53
	Over $50,000	38
1950	First $25,000	23
	Over $25,000	42
1951	First $25,000	28.75
	Over $25,000	50.75
1952–1963	First $25,000	30
	Over $25,000	52
1964	First $25,000	22
	Over $25,000	50
1965–1967	First $25,000	22
	Over $25,000	48
1968–1969	First $25,000	24.2[c]
	Over $25,000	52.8[c]
1970	First $25,000	22.55[c]
	Over $25,000	49.2[c]
1971–1974	First $25,000	22
	Over $25,000	48
1975–1978	First $25,000	20
	Next $25,000	22
	Over $50,000	48

(continued)

YEAR	RATE BRACKETS OR EXEMPTIONS	RATE[a] (PERCENT)
1979–1981	First $25,000	17
	$25,000 to $50,000	20
	$50,000 to $75,000	30
	$75,000 to $100,000	40
	Over $100,000	46
1982	First $25,000	16
	$25,000 to $50,000	19
	$50,000 to $75,000	30
	$75,000 to $100,000	40
	Over $100,000	46
1983–1986	First $25,000	15
	$25,000 to $50,000	18
	$50,000 to $75,000	30
	$75,000 to $100,000	40
	Over $100,000	46
1987–1990[d]	First $50,000	15
	$50,000 to $75,000	25
	Over $75,000[e]	34
1991–1992	First $50,000	15
	$50,000 to $75,000	25
	$75,000 to $100,000	34
	$100,000 to $335,000	39
	Over $335,000	34
1993–1995	First $50,000	15
	$50,000 to $75,000	25
	$75,000 to $100,000	34
	$100,000 to $335,000	39
	$335,000 to $10,000,000	34
	$10,000,000 to $15,000,000	35
	$15,000,000 to $18,333,333	38
	Over $18,333,333	35

[a] In addition to the rates shown, certain types of ''excess profits'' levies were in effect in 1917–1921, 1933–1945, and 1950–1953.
[b] Less adjustments: 14.025% of dividends received and 2.5% of dividends paid.
[c] Includes surcharge of 10% in 1968 and 1969 and 2.5% in 1970.
[d] Rates shown effective for tax years beginning on or after July 1, 1987. Income in taxable years that include July 1, 1987 (other than as the first date of such year) is subject to a blended rate.
[e] An additional 5% tax is imposed on a corporation's taxable income in excess of $100,000. Maximum additional tax is $11,750; this provision phases out the benefit of graduated rates for corporations with taxable income between $100,000 and $335,000; corporations with income above $335,000, in effect, pay a flat tax at a 34% rate.
Source: Treasury Department, Office of Tax Analysis.

in addition to numerous minor changes. *Modified* ACRS (accelerated cost recovery system, pronounced "acres") is the latest provision. ACRS was originally introduced to replace the asset depreciation range (ADR) method. ADR had been an attempt to specify carefully (once and for all!) the rules for using the three allowable depreciation methods, which were, at that time, *double-declining-balance, sum-of-the-years'-digits*, and *straight-line*. The designation of these three depreciation methods as the allowable methods for federal income tax purposes had occurred many years earlier, but the rules governing their use had changed often during the intervening years.

Looking at this history of change, we see little reason to assume that the modified ACRS procedure is permanent.

Because changes in the tax laws, including the federal corporate income tax, occur often, it is important to *use the current tax laws to determine after-tax cash flows* for a capital budgeting decision (or for any financial decision for that matter). However, because of the frequency of changes, there is little point in memorizing all of the tax provisions. When you make a financial decision, determine exactly what the treatment for each item will be under current tax law by consulting current tax guides (federal, state, or private) or tax experts within or outside your organization.

Even though the federal corporate income taxes are the largest part of a corporation's total tax bill, there are other tax provisions. Most states have an income tax. A corporation may also face other taxes that are not directly related to its income.[5] So although they are closely tied to its income, a corporation's total taxes are not necessarily in exact proportion to income. Furthermore, because of the variety of taxes a corporation faces, its marginal tax rate usually is not the federal income tax rate but is rather a higher rate.

Because of the complexity of the tax laws, we do not attempt to model taxes perfectly. In our presentations, we follow the convention of using a single marginal tax rate that people often think of as the federal income tax rate. To remind us that normally the rate is higher than the federal rate, we generally use in our examples a tax rate that is different from the current peak federal corporate income tax rate (before surtax) of 35%.

Depreciation

Throughout our examples and problems, we use straight-line depreciation, even though few if any firms actually use it for tax purposes or capital budgeting analysis. (Most firms *do* use it for financial reporting purposes.) Straight-line depreciation is not used for tax purposes because of the time value of money. As long as a firm has enough income to use fully all of its tax credits and deductions, the sooner it claims them, the sooner it can put the money to work earning more money. Over the life of an investment, the total amount of depreciation tax deductions will be the same, regardless of what depreciation schedule is used.

What depreciation method is best for a firm to use? This question can be answered by determining which allowable method provides the most advantageous time-value-of-money treatment for the tax credits (the product of the depreciation deduction times the marginal tax rate). The answer is not necessarily the same from year to year, because the allowable methods and procedures change with disturbing regularity. Therefore, there's no point in memorizing the fact that a particular method is optimal now, because it probably will not be optimal by the time you get around to using it.

There is considerable value, however, in describing a general method for identifying the optimal depreciation schedule from whatever schedules are allowable at the time you have to choose one. Despite the changes in allowable depreciation methods and procedures for using them, the way to determine the optimal method has not changed since the income tax laws first began requiring firms to capitalize equipment costs. *A firm should use the depreciation method that provides the largest present value of depreciation tax credits.*

EXAMPLE

Alternative Depreciation Methods at General Electric

Let's say that General Electric has been given a choice of methods to use to depreciate an asset that cost $110,000 down to a book value of $20,000 at the end of 5 years. GE can use either the straight-line method or what is called the sum-of-the-years'-digits method. GE's cost of capital is 10%, and its marginal tax rate is 40%. Which method provides the more advantageous time-value-of-money treatment?

The sum-of-the-years'-digits method specifies the depreciation expense each year as a proportion of the difference between the purchase price and the salvage value. The procedure is as follows. First, sum the numbers 1, 2, 3, up to and including the number of years over

---

[5] For example, federal and state excise taxes and state and local sales taxes. These taxes do not alter our analysis, because in the case of excise and sales taxes, the tax amount is typically added directly onto the price of a product at the time the product is sold to a customer and consequently does not directly affect the corporation's incremental revenues and costs. In effect, such taxes are "taken off the top."

which the asset will be depreciated. For depreciating an asset over 5 years, the sum of the years' digits is 15 (= 1 + 2 + 3 + 4 + 5).

To determine what proportion to use each year, reverse the order of the digits, and divide each digit by the sum of all the digits. For a 5-year asset, the first year's depreciation expense would be 5/15 of the difference between the purchase price and the salvage value. The proportions to apply in years 2 through five would be 4/15, 3/15, 2/15, and 1/15, respectively.

The difference between the cost and the salvage value in this case is $90,000. The straight-line method would specify a depreciation expense of $18,000 per year in each of the 5 years (= 90/5). This creates a CFAT of $7200 (= TD = 0.4 × 18,000) per year for each of the 5 years, which has a present value of $27,294 at a 10% cost of capital. The sum-of-the-years'-digits method would specify depreciation expenses of $30,000 [= (5/15)90,000], $24,000 [= (4/15)90,000], $18,000, $12,000, and $6000, which yield CFATs of $12,000 (= 0.4 × 30,000), $9600 (= 0.4 × 24,000), $7200, $4800, and $2400 in years 1 through 5, respectively. These CFATs have a present value of $29,021 at a discount rate of 10% [= (12,000/1.1) + (9600/1.1) + ⋯].

The sum-of-the-years'-digits method, then, will provide a $1727 larger present value of depreciation tax credits. Therefore, GE should use the sum-of-the-years'-digits method to depreciate its machine. ∎

On the basis of the general superiority of expensing over capitalizing (which we illustrated in the Boeing example in Chapter 11), we could have predicted the superiority of the sum-of-the-years-digits method in the GE example. The comparison in the General Electric example was between straight-line and an "accelerated" method. Although not as quick as expensing, an accelerated method allows depreciation to be claimed more quickly than straight-line. As long as a firm can use the tax credits, accelerated depreciation provides the more advantageous treatment. Of course, for alternative accelerated depreciation rules, the best choice may not be so obvious.

Self-Check Questions

1. Why is a firm's marginal tax rate often different from the peak statutory federal income tax rate?

2. When conducting a capital budgeting analysis, why is it important to check how the most current tax law will affect a project?

3. What rule should a firm follow in selecting a depreciation method when more than one method is available?

4. How do the straight-line and the sum-of-the-years'-digits methods differ? Which method is more advantageous to the firm?

12.5 OTHER METHODS OF PROJECT ANALYSIS

In our discussion of the cost of capital in Chapter 10, we specified one method of incorporating the risk of a project into our analysis. In that method, risk, as measured by the nondiversifiable business risk of the project, is fully reflected in the choice of discount rate. When the cash flows are discounted at the risk-adjusted cost of capital, the effect of risk is thereby included in the calculation of the project's NPV. As we said in Chapter 10, firms use risk classes, with a different cost of capital for each class, to adjust for differences in risk among projects. In some cases, the risk classes are represented by various divisions or groups of divisions of the firm.

Although this is the most widely used method of incorporating risk into the capital budgeting decision, other methods are also used. Let's look at a few of them now: break-even analysis, sensitivity analysis, decision trees, and Monte Carlo simulation.

There is a problem with using the methods we will describe: The distinction between diversifiable and nondiversifiable risk can easily be lost in the analysis. In other words, special care is necessary to ensure that the risk measure excludes diversifiable risk. As we learned in Chapter 9, diversifiable risk is not relevant to shareholders, but it can be very relevant to managers personally because of the difficulty of diversifying the managers' human capital.

The use of some of the methods discussed in this section, then, presents a particular problem because managers have an incentive to use them improperly. By deliberately including diversifiable risk, managers may be able to use risk as a basis for rejecting projects that have a large amount of diversifiable risk. Thus these methods may provide managers with a justification for rejecting projects that are undesirable from their viewpoint, even though the projects may be desirable from the shareholders' perspective. This aspect of capital investment analysis represents another example in which divergent interests can cause a conflict between shareholders and managers.

Despite this problem, the methods presented here can be useful when it is not possible to determine a market-based estimate of a project's cost of capital. Generally, using these techniques takes more expertise than you will acquire here. However, it is important to know of their existence and to understand the benefits and problems associated with using them. Additional expertise can be obtained from further study or from support staff who are well versed in such quantitative methods. You have probably encountered (or will encounter) some or all of these methods in other course work.

Break-Even

The **break-even point** is where the total contribution margin exactly equals the total fixed cost of producing a product or service. Recall that the contribution margin is the difference between revenue and variable cost. For example, if revenue is $15 per unit for a product, and the variable cost of producing a unit of the product is $10, the contribution margin is $5 per unit. With a total fixed cost of $500,000, break-even is 100,000 units ($= 500,000/5$).

Break-even is the point at which the accounting income is zero. But accounting income ignores the opportunity cost associated with the time value of money (among other problems), so break-even is *not* the point at which the NPV equals zero. In spite of this, break-even is commonly used as a point of analysis, so it is important to understand the pitfalls of using break-even as part of the decision criteria.

It is easy for people to believe that as long as sales stay above the break-even point, the firm is "making money." But this is true only in the sense that accounting income will be positive. If sales were to continue essentially at the break-even point forever, it is most likely that the firm would have been better off if it had exercised its abandonment option on the project.

Consider the break-even example just given. Suppose that the firm could sell off the entire project and everything connected with it for an after-tax net salvage value of $1.2 million. Then selling the project would be a positive-NPV decision if sales would fall exactly at the break-even point forever into the future. With sales forever at the break-even point, the firm's net cash flow from the project each year would equal the tax credit from the depreciation. The firm could sell the project and create value by investing the money elsewhere.

The actual point of indifference is the level of sales at which the NPV from selling or abandoning the project is zero. We need more information to determine that point. The following example illustrates this calculation.

Suppose that our project has 6 more years of useful life, after which it will have a net salvage value of zero. Also assume that depreciation would be $150,000 per year for the next 4 years and zero for the last 2 years, that the relevant tax rate is 40%, and that the project's cost of capital is 12%. The level of sales for which the NPV of selling the project equals zero can be determined by first setting the NPV from selling equal to zero. Next, work backward to the present value of the CFATs it would require, which must result from a particular value of $\Delta R - \Delta E$. Finally, you can solve for the zero-NPV sales level by using the necessary $\Delta R - \Delta E$ and the contribution margin per unit.

Determining the Zero-NPV Sales Level

EXAMPLE

TIME	ITEM	CFBT	CFAT	PV AT 12%
0	Salvage	1,200,000	1,200,000	1,200,000
1–6	$\Delta R - \Delta E$	?	?	?
1–4	Depreciation (lost)	0	−60,000/yr	−182,241
			NPV =	0

TABLE 12-11
NPV calculation for the production amount that will yield a zero NPV.

The NPV calculation with these unknowns is given in Table 12-11. To have a zero NPV, the project must produce a present value of $1,017,759 (= 1,200,000 − 182,241). Solving for the corresponding annuity payment implies that the CFAT is $247,545 per year. Therefore, the CFBT equals $412,575 per year [= 247,545/(1 − 0.4)]. The CFBT per year for $\Delta R - \Delta E$ is the total contribution margin minus the fixed cost. If the number of units sold is Q, the contribution margin per unit is c, and the fixed cost per year is F, CFBT is given as

$$\text{CFBT} = cQ - F \tag{12.4}$$

Solving for Q yields

$$Q = \frac{\text{CFBT} + F}{c} = \frac{412,575 + 500,000}{5} = 182,515$$

Therefore, the indifference point—which we might call the "true" break-even point—is a sales level of 182,515 units per year for the next 6 years. This sales level is almost twice the 100,000 units at which accounting income is zero. Although the relationship between the indifference point and the break-even point is specific to each situation, in most cases the indifference point is much larger than what is commonly referred to as the break-even point. ■

Determining the indifference point of the project—the unit sales level per period at which the NPV of the project is zero— provides one with a feel for the project by putting the NPV in terms of the number of units that must be sold per year to have a worthwhile investment. This principle applies to possible new, as well as ongoing, projects. And you can get still more of a feel for a project by determining how sensitive the project's NPV is to variations in sales. This is called sensitivity analysis, which we turn to next.

Sensitivity Analysis

Sensitivity analysis varies key parameters to determine the sensitivity of outcomes to the variation. The question sensitivity analysis addresses is "What happens if things don't go as predicted?" Sensitivity analysis can provide insight into a project's operating leverage. And as we saw in Chapter 10, project risk depends on operating leverage.

Essentially, operating leverage refers to how changes in sales affect profit. A high level of operating leverage means that a relatively small change in sales will cause a relatively large change in profit. A low level of operating leverage means that a relatively large change in sales

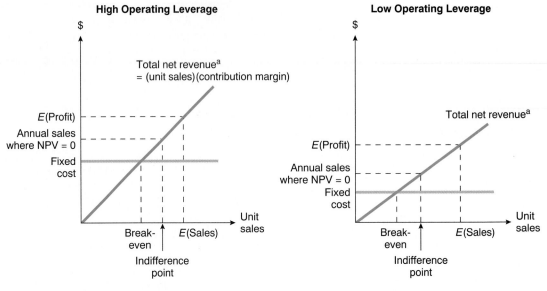

aNet revenue = revenue − variable cost

FIGURE 12-3
Comparison of high and low operating leverage.

will cause a relatively small change in profit. Therefore, one way to get a feel for how much operating leverage a project has is to examine the sensitivity of its NPV to variations in sales.

NPV sensitivity—the operating leverage—is characterized by the relative steepness of the slope that expresses the relationship between profit and sales in a graph. This slope is in turn determined by the contribution margin. A large contribution margin makes a steep slope, in which case profits are very sensitive to changes in sales. A small contribution margin makes a flatter slope, and profits are less sensitive to changes in sales. Increasing the contribution margin, then, increases the operating leverage and magnifies the sensitivity of profit to changes in sales.

Figure 12-3 shows how two different operating leverage functions affect a firm's profit. Hypothetical values are shown that illustrate the typical relationships among the break-even point, indifference point, and expected sales levels for a positive-NPV project. Note the difference in the slopes of the total net revenue lines. Also note that although the expected level of sales is identical for the two cases, the break-even point, indifference point, and expected profit are all higher for the high-operating-leverage case. These differences, of course, are due to the difference in risk between high and low leverage. They simply represent another risk-return trade-off that the firm can make.

EXAMPLE

Sensitivity Analysis

A common way to get a feel for the operating leverage of a project—its profit sensitivity—is to estimate optimistic, expected, and pessimistic levels for future annual sales. Extending our break-even example, suppose that optimistic, expected, and pessimistic estimates for future sales levels are 250,000, 200,000, and 150,000, respectively. At the expected sales level, yearly CFBT for $\Delta R - \Delta E$ is given by Equation (12.4):

$$\text{CFBT} = cQ - F = 5(200{,}000) - 500{,}000 = \$500{,}000$$

The NPV calculation for keeping the project, given the expected sales level, is shown in Table 12-12. Similar calculations for $Q = 250{,}000$ and $Q = 150{,}000$ show that the NPVs range from −\$401,048 to \$832,374. ∎

TIME	ITEM	CFBT	CFAT	PV AT 12%
0	Salvage (foregone)	−1,200,000	−1,200,000	−1,200,000
1–6	$\Delta R - \Delta E$	500,000/yr	300,000/yr	1,233,422
1–4	Depreciation	0	60,000/yr	182,241
				NPV = $215,663

TABLE 12-12
NPV calculation for keeping the project at the expected sales level.

The range of NPV outcomes found through sensitivity analysis provides an estimate of the operating leverage of the project. If the optimistic and pessimistic sales estimates had been 75,000 and 400,000 instead of 150,000 and 250,000, respectively, the variation in the NPVs would have been much larger, ranging from −$1,326,115 to $2,682,508. Comparisons such as these provide further insight into the nature of a project. But as we said earlier in the chapter, great care is necessary to exclude diversifiable risk from the analysis. When the variation in the sales level is due to economy-wide or industry-wide factors, such as total market size, it represents mostly nondiversifiable risk. In contrast, when the variation is due to factors that are specific to the firm, such as market share, the risk is mainly diversifiable.

Obviously, you can perform sensitivity analysis with respect to any parameter in the NPV computation. However, special care is also necessary when combining optimistic and pessimistic estimates for multiple parameters, because the parameter values may be positively correlated, negatively correlated, or not at all correlated with one another. It is also important to avoid the tendency to view the combinations of parameter outcomes as equally likely. For example, a high variable cost per unit, which causes the industry to set a high selling price, affects the total market size. Thus a pessimistic market size is more likely to occur with a pessimistic variable cost.

Decision Trees

You may have encountered decision trees in other course work.[6] A *decision tree* is a visual aid that can help you identify all relevant cash flows and their probabilities, thereby enhancing your understanding of a situation. In fact, we used a decision tree at the start of the chapter for Headcleaner's Q-10 postponement decision.

In a decision tree, outcomes are represented by sequences of "forks" for decisions and for possible outcomes. All outcomes result from following a path along what looks like the-branch of a tree. In most cases, the possible outcomes of a fork of a decision tree are called **subjective probabilities**. These are educated guesses that we give probability numbers to.[7] Let's see show how a decision tree works in an example.

Woody's Hazing, Inc. manufactures a line of window film called Buckeye Vision for blocking out the sun. Recently, the research-and-development laboratory at Woody's came up with a promising new idea. Management at Woody's (in fact, Woody herself) wonders whether to develop the idea further in the hope that it will lead to a new product. The first decision, then, is whether to spend $600,000 further developing the idea, which creates a fork in the decision tree. Figure 12-4 shows the tree. The forks (boxes) represent choices. The probabilities of outcomes (circles) then stem from those choices. This first fork is shown at the bottom left of the figure.

A Decision Tree at Hazing, Inc.

EXAMPLE

---

[6] Particular analytical techniques you might encounter in other course work that also use the "decision tree" approach include the critical path method (CPM) and the program evaluation and review technique (PERT).
[7] Although estimating such subjective probabilities can be a very difficult process, as with model building, the process often adds greatly to one's understanding of a situation.

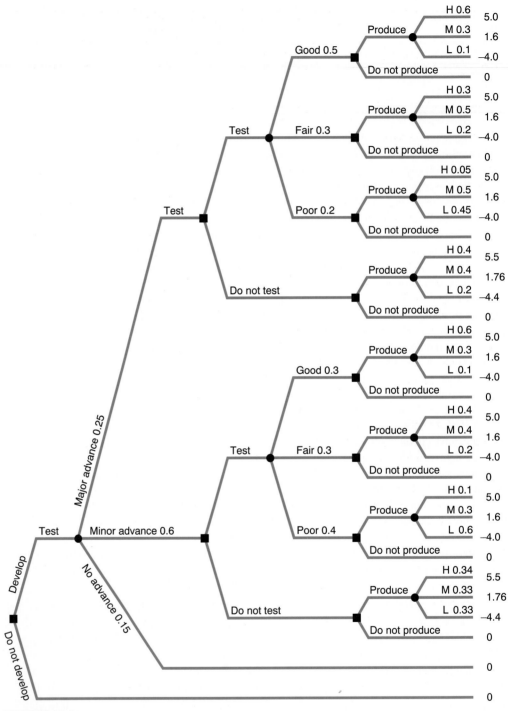

FIGURE 12-4

A decision tree.[a]

[a] Terminal NPVs (in $ millions) are given without supporting computations, to simplify the analysis.

If the development is undertaken, there is another fork showing possible outcomes. The outcome can be a major advance, a minor advance, or a bad idea (no advance). If it turns out to be a major or a minor advance, Woody's is faced with yet another decision fork, concerning whether to conduct a marketing research study (test) of the new product at a cost of $250,000.

The outcome from the test marketing is an estimate of the demand for the new product as good, fair, or poor. Depending on what the demand forecast is, Woody's can decide to start production of the new product or to abandon it.[8]

Finally, if production is undertaken (produce), we reach one of the forks at the far right in Figure 12-4. Actual sales for the product can then turn out to be high, medium, or low.

Woody estimates that further development has a 25% chance of producing a major advance, a 60% chance of producing a minor advance, and a 15% chance of producing no advance at all. If a major advance occurs, the probabilities for good, fair, and poor outcomes from the marketing research are 50%, 30%, and 20%, respectively. Similarly, with a minor advance, good, fair, and poor outcomes from marketing research have probabilities of 30%, 30%, and 40%, respectively.

The NPV of each outcome is given at the end of its branch at the far right of the figure. For simplicity's sake, let's take the terminal NPVs as being given and not go into how they were estimated. However, note that arriving at a terminal NPV depends on the decision fork leading to that outcome. For example, the decision not to undertake production has a zero NPV. This is because at the point where *that* decision must be made, any development and marketing research costs are sunk costs. The NPVs also reflect timing differences when production is postponed to undertake test marketing. ■

As with any model-building exercise, it is often helpful to approach the process in stages to avoid being overwhelmed by the problem. We actually constructed the decision tree in Figure 12-4 in stages, fitting it together by trial and error, although the figure shows it in its entirety.[9]

You solve a decision tree in a backward fashion, from end to beginning, starting with each final outcome. The procedure is similar to solving for the indifference level of annual sales in our break-even example. The optimal choice at each decision fork is the path with the highest expected NPV. For example, with a major advance and a good outcome predicted by the marketing research, the expected NPV of production is $3.08 million [= 0.6(5.0) + 0.3(1.6) + 0.1(−4.0)]. Therefore, with those outcomes, Woody would choose to produce the product, because the expected NPV of $3.08 from producing exceeds the zero NPV from not producing at that point. Figure 12-5 illustrates this computation.

In contrast, with a minor advance and a poor outcome predicted by marketing research, the expected value of production is −$1.42 million [= 0.1(5.0) + 0.3(1.6) + 0.6(−4.0)]. Therefore, with this second example of outcomes, Woody's would choose not to produce the new product.

---

[8] Of course, the interaction of the new product with the sales and production of existing products must be considered. Also, the postponement option, which was illustrated in the Headcleaner expansion example and which will be further explored in Chapter 13, is available at various points. We left these considerations out of the example to reduce its complexity.

[9] Sometimes it causes frustration (and perhaps confusion) when an instructor presents a solution to a problem that makes it appear very straightforward. The frustration occurs because it is not obvious that solving the problem from scratch takes a great deal of time. The student sees the instructor solve problems effortlessly and yet takes hours to slog through similar problems alone. We are sure your instructor is bright and capable, but remember that you don't know how much time the instructor spent making it look easy! You might also find it comforting to know how much trouble it has taken to write this book, but frankly, we'd be embarrassed to tell you.

FIGURE 12-5
The production decision (in $ millions).

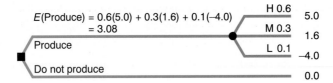

$E(\text{Produce}) = 0.6(5.0) + 0.3(1.6) + 0.1(-4.0)$
$= 3.08$

H 0.6 5.0
M 0.3 1.6
L 0.1 −4.0

Produce

Do not produce   0.0

By indicating what decision paths should be followed on the basis of probabilistic outcomes, we can "prune" the decision tree so that the decision forks are eliminated and the presentation is simplified. For this example, the first round of decisions to be solved for is the final set of decisions—to produce or not produce.

Following the production decisions, the next round to address is the set of decisions whether to test market the new product if the idea has led to an advance. As with the decision to produce, we compute expected values to determine the optimal choice. If the decision is to produce, then regardless of the outcome from the marketing research, the test marketing should not be undertaken. The information is not relevant because it will not alter the decision. In effect, the money would be wasted because the cost of $250,000 spent on the study would exceed the benefit derived from having the information it would provide.

EXAMPLE

Using a Decision Tree to Make a Choice

To decide whether to undertake the test marketing, we can examine the subparts dealing with that decision. Figure 12-6 illustrates the marketing research decision for the minor-advance outcome of the decision tree, including the expected values from the "pruned" production decisions. The total expected value from test marketing the new product is the expected value from the production decisions, based on the test outcome, minus the cost of test marketing the product. The computation of the total expected value from test marketing is illustrated in Figure 12-6. The expected value is $1.226 million.

To compute the expected value from producing the new product without first test marketing it, we need the probabilities of having high, medium, and low demand, respectively. We can get these by multiplying the probabilities of sequential outcomes and summing common final outcomes. For example, because high demand could occur whether the outcome from the market test was good, fair, or poor, the probability of high demand is the sum of the probabilities under each possible outcome. A 30% chance of a good market test result followed by a 60% chance of high demand produces an 18% (30% times 60%) chance of that particular high-demand outcome. The total probability of all the possible high-demand outcomes is then $(0.3)(0.6) + (0.3)(0.4) + (0.4)(0.1) = 0.34$, or 34%. The calculations for the probabilities of medium and low demand are also given in Figure 12-6. On the basis of the probabilities for high, medium, and low demand, the expected value for producing the new product without first test marketing it equals $0.9988 million.

FIGURE 12-6
The test marketing decision if the development leads to a minor advance (in $ millions).

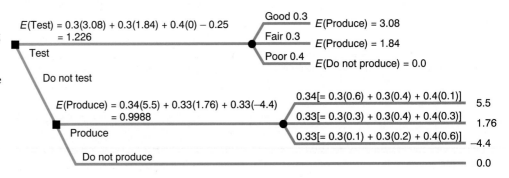

$E(\text{Test}) = 0.3(3.08) + 0.3(1.84) + 0.4(0) - 0.25$
$= 1.226$

Test

Good 0.3 $E(\text{Produce}) = 3.08$
Fair 0.3 $E(\text{Produce}) = 1.84$
Poor 0.4 $E(\text{Do not produce}) = 0.0$

Do not test

$E(\text{Produce}) = 0.34(5.5) + 0.33(1.76) + 0.33(-4.4)$
$= 0.9988$

Produce

Do not produce

$0.34[= 0.3(0.6) + 0.3(0.4) + 0.4(0.1)]$ 5.5
$0.33[= 0.3(0.3) + 0.3(0.4) + 0.4(0.3)]$ 1.76
$0.33[= 0.3(0.1) + 0.3(0.2) + 0.4(0.6)]$ −4.4

0.0

Because the expected value from test marketing exceeds the expected value from producing the new product without the test, Woody's should test market the new product if product development has led to a minor advance. The test marketing decision is also relevant if product development has led to a major advance. ■

EXPECTED VALUE OF ADDITIONAL INFORMATION   An extension of the test market decision is to ask what the value is of the additional information to be obtained from the test. This value can be determined from the expected values calculated in Figure 12-6. The expected value without the test is $0.9988 million. If the test marketing is costless, the expected value with the test is $1.476 million. As long as the cost of running the test is less than the difference between the two, the test is valuable. Therefore, the value of the additional information from the test is

$$\text{Information value} = \text{EV(test)} - \text{EV(no test)} + \text{cost of test}$$

where EV indicates expected value. In this case, then,

$$\text{Information value} = 1.226 - 0.9988 + 0.25 = \$0.4772 \text{ million}$$

EXPECTED VALUE OF PERFECT INFORMATION   The idea of information value can be further extended to consider the **expected value of perfect information (EVPI)**. Suppose a test exists that would provide a perfect prediction of high, medium, or low demand. The probabilities of high, medium, and low demand are calculated in Figure 12-6 as 0.34, 0.33, and 0.33, respectively. If low demand is forecast, Woody will choose not to produce the new product and will realize an NPV of zero. Otherwise, Woody will produce the product and earn an NPV of either 5.0 or 1.6. Therefore, the expected value of this perfect test, if it is costless, is $2.228 million [$= 0.34(5.0) + 0.33(1.6) + 0.33(0)$], and the expected value of perfect information (EVPI), is

$$\text{EVPI} = \text{EV(perfect test)} - \text{EV(no test)} \tag{12.5}$$

which in this case is

$$\text{EVPI} = 2.228 - 0.9988 = \$1.2292 \text{ million}$$

Therefore, if perfect test information were available, Woody's would increase the expected value of the project by spending up to $1.2292 million to get it. Knowing the EVPI is especially useful when a variety of alternative tests, each with a different cost, are being considered—because any test with a cost that exceeds the EVPI can be immediately eliminated without further consideration. After all, a test cannot provide better than perfect information, so it cannot be worth more than perfect information!

Now, by analyzing the pruned decision tree (Figure 12-7), we can decide whether Woody's should spend $600,000 to develop the new idea. The expected value of developing the idea equals the outcomes weighted by their probabilities minus the $0.6 million cost of developing the idea, which is $0.6416 million, as shown in Figure 12-7. Thus the development project has a positive NPV and should be undertaken.

Even in this simple example, the decision tree becomes quite complicated. Analysis of a more complex, real-world decision could overwhelm the decision maker. Computer software packages are available to help construct and solve decision tree problems, but such packages rarely deal successfully with the question of risk. In our example, we "finessed" the question

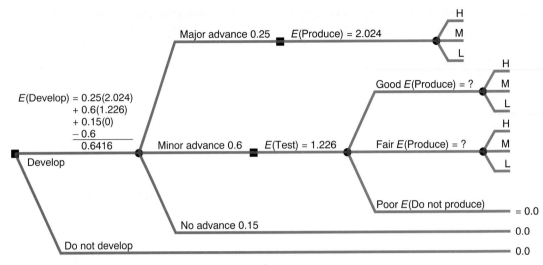

FIGURE 12-7
The development decision and the "pruned" decision tree (in $ millions).

of differential risk and the cost of capital by simply providing the NPVs. In such situations, it can be argued that a variety of discount rates should be used to reflect risk differences among the various decisions.

We have no general solution to this problem. However, keep in mind our warning about diversifiable risk. Also, this kind of analysis should be kept as simple as possible by discarding pieces that are no longer relevant. Finally, we offer the following advice: As you build the model, apply the basic concepts developed in this chapter *carefully* to be sure you have not overlooked anything that could have a significant bearing on the decision.

Monte Carlo Simulation

Airline pilots receive some of their training on flight simulators. A flight simulator is a physical model that simulates or imitates (as realistically as possible) what it is like to fly an airplane in a variety of circumstances. Physically, the pilot sits in the model, which is an exact replica of the cockpit of the plane being simulated. Video equipment provides a visual scene that appears for the pilot through the cockpit windows. The model is mounted on a complex construction of hydraulic equipment that creates motion like that of flying. Although expensive, flight simulators help train pilots in a variety of situations. Inexpensive computer programs are also available that can make a PC seem like a flight simulator, minus the physical movement.

Monte Carlo simulation, or more simply **simulation**, is a technique that uses a mathematical model to represent a financial decision or other phenomenon. As with a flight simulator, the intention is to "take a spin" on the model without having to risk life and limb actually flying the thing in the air (or in this case, making the financial decision).

A simulation model is similar to sensitivity analysis in that it can be used to attempt to answer "what-if" questions. The model relies on random sampling from probability distributions of outcomes. Using a computer, a simulation model can assess the likelihood of particular outcomes by trying out a large number of outcomes.

Often, in statistics courses, a coin is flipped a number of times to illustrate that the number of resulting heads actually does turn out to be very close to the 50% that is estimated via probability theory. This is a simple simulation experiment. Flipping two coins and observing that both are heads about 25% of the time is a slightly more complex simulation experiment. With two coins, of course, the probability of two heads can be calculated by multiplying the probabilities of the individual outcomes together: 0.5 for the occurrence of heads on the first coin times 0.5 for heads on the second coin equals 0.25 for the combined event. Although we can use probability theory to determine the probabilities of combined outcomes in simple cases like these coin examples, it is not hard to imagine situations too complex to derive the probabilities of all possible outcomes mathematically. But by making assumptions about the joint probability distributions of the random variables, we can determine outcome probabilities for complex situations by using a simulation model.

We are not going to illustrate an application of simulation because of the complexity of such examples. However, as with the other methods discussed in this section, let's look at the major benefits and pitfalls of using simulation.

There are two major benefits, both of which result from the model-building process. First, the process of building the simulation model can provide useful insights. The very framework that must be built requires extensive understanding. The model-building process fosters such an understanding, and insights are a valuable by-product. The second benefit is that a simulation model can describe a situation that may be indescribable in simple terms. That is, although we may not be able to determine the answer immediately, by breaking the problem down into smaller parts and evaluating each part, we can develop a reasonable estimate.

For example, the distance between two points can be estimated by summing the distances of subsections. So too with simulation models: A solution can be obtained by combining many simple parts.

The main problem associated with using simulation is the difficulty of specifying the interrelationships among the parts. In the case of two coins, we can reasonably assume that the two flips are independent. But in modeling real-world phenomena, we do not usually know exact relationships.

A second problem, related to the first, is that often the model becomes so complex so quickly that the decision maker gives up and employs someone else, such as support staff or a consultant, to build it. If the major value to be obtained from using simulation is that building the model enhances understanding of the problem, having someone else build the model reduces, or even eliminates, that value. The only way to minimize this problem is to work closely with the model builder and extract as much understanding as possible.

Finally, among all the methods discussed in this section, the problem of eliminating diversifiable risk from the analysis is probably most severe for simulation. It may be impossible to identify diversifiable risk and remove it from the analysis.

Self-Check Questions

1. What is a firm's break-even point? How is it different from the indifference point, or "true" break-even point, the zero-NPV sales level?

2. What is sensitivity analysis? Why is there a danger that sensitivity analysis will allow diversifiable risk considerations to creep into the decision-making process?

3. What is a decision tree? How does it help identify all relevant cash flows and their probabilities? How can it aid in the capital budgeting process when developing a project might involve a sequence of decisions?

4. What is Monte Carlo simulation? How is simulation similar to sensitivity analysis?

5. What side-effect benefits can result from building a simulation model?

SUMMARY

In this chapter, we pointed out a number of factors that complicate capital budgeting decisions. Admittedly, some (such as erosion and enhancement) can pose a serious challenge. However, others may increase the complexity of the analysis, and yet their inclusion is fairly straightforward from a conceptual viewpoint. For example, using equivalent annual cost (EAC) to find the optimal replacement cycle or to choose among equipment alternatives is simply an application of time-value-of-money mathematics.

Alternative methods of incorporating risk into a capital budgeting analysis were presented: break-even analysis, sensitivity analysis, decision trees, and simulation. All of these methods are more complex mathematically than using an estimated risk-adjusted cost of capital. All four methods have certain deficiencies—in particular, difficulty in eliminating diversifiable risk—that make them inappropriate as the sole method of incorporating risk into a capital budgeting analysis. Despite this drawback, you should be aware of them because they may provide additional insights into a project, especially when it is not possible to obtain a good capital-market-based estimate of the risk-adjusted cost of capital.

DECISION SUMMARY

- Be sure to include the effects of all economic dependencies that cause erosion or enhancement in the value of existing or other potential projects.

- The minimum equivalent annual cost (EAC) can be used to find an asset's optimal replacement cycle. It can also be used to find the best choice among alternative assets. Do not use EAC for choosing one-time projects or for choosing among assets that are subject to substantial technological change.

- Be sure to use the *current* tax laws to determine after-tax cash flows.

- For tax and capital budgeting purposes, a firm should use the depreciation method that provides the largest present value of depreciation tax credits.

- Include the effect of inflation by representing all parameters, cash flows, and discount rates for a decision on a consistent basis—either in real terms *or* in nominal terms.

- Be sure to distinguish between the accounting break-even point and the level of sales for which the NPV would be zero.

- Sensitivity analysis can provide insight into a project's operating leverage by examining "what-if" questions.

- A decision tree is an excellent visual aid for understanding critical relationships. Among other things, a decision tree can be used for estimating the value of additional information.

- The expected value of perfect information (EVPI) specifies a maximum value that can be gained from additional information.

- Be careful to exclude diversifiable risk when using break-even analysis, sensitivity analysis, decision trees, and (especially) simulation.

EQUATION SUMMARY

(12.1)
$$TC = C_0 + \sum_{t=1}^{n} \frac{C_t}{(1 + r)^t}$$

(12.2)
$$EAC = TC\left[\frac{r(1 + r)^n}{(1 + r)^n - 1}\right]$$

(12.3)
$$r_n = r_r + i + ir_r$$

(12.4)
$$CFBT = cQ - F$$

(12.5)
$$EVPI = EV(\text{perfect test}) - EV(\text{no test})$$

KEY TERMS

erosion...371

enhancement...374

replacement cycle...375

equivalent annual cost (EAC)...375

equivalent annual annuity (EAA)...378

break-even point...386

sensitivity analysis...387

subjective probabilities...389

expected value of perfect information (EVPI)...393

simulation...394

EXERCISES

PROBLEM SET A

A1. Define the terms *erosion* and *enhancement* as they are related to the firm's capital investment decisions.

A2. Explain in your own words the concept of an equivalent annual cost (EAC).

A3. The total present value of all costs associated with an asset over a 7-year life is $73,285. If the asset has a cost of capital of 11%, what is the EAC of using this asset?

A4. Verify that the NPV for the optimistic and pessimistic sales levels in the sensitivity example are $832,374 and −$401,048, respectively.

A5. A firm is considering a capital investment project that has the following expected cash flows:

Time	0	1	2	3	4	5	6
Cash flow	−70	20	30	30	20	20	10
Abandonment	—	40	35	30	20	10	10

a. If the cost of capital for this project is 13%, should the project be undertaken?

b. If the firm accepts the project, at what point in time should it expect to abandon the project?

A6. Suppose the expected value of a decision is $734,500. Suppose further that additional information about the likelihood of various outcomes from the decision could be gathered at a cost of $87,000 and that if such information was gathered, the expected value of the decision would increase to $853,225. If perfect information was gathered, the expected value of the decision would be $1,010,000.

a. What is the expected value of perfect information (EVPI) in this case?

b. What is the information value of gathering the additional information?

A7. Define the term *simulation*.

A8. Define the term *sensitivity analysis*.

A9. The Canton Sundae Corporation is considering the replacement of an existing machine. The new machine, called an X-tender, would provide better sundaes, but it costs $120,000. The X-tender requires $20,000 in setup costs that are expensed immediately and $20,000 in additional working capital. The X-tender's useful life is 10 years, after which it can be sold for a salvage value of $40,000. Canton uses straight-line depreciation, and the machine will be depreciated to a book value of zero on a 6-year basis. Canton has a tax rate of 45% and requires a 16% return on projects like this one. The X-tender is expected to increase revenues minus expenses by $35,000 per year. What is the NPV of buying the X-tender?

A10. A machine that costs $10,000 new can be replaced after being used from 4 to 7 years. Annual maintenance costs are identical for all possible replacement cycles. If the machine has a cost of capital of 12% and the net salvage values at the end of 4 to 7 years of use are those given below, what is the optimal replacement cycle? Ignore taxes and inflation.

Number of years of use	=	4	5	6	7
Net salvage value	=	$3800	$2800	$1000	−$1000

PROBLEM SET B

B1. In the section on replacement frequency in this chapter, the example considered Hoover's inventory equipment. Suppose that machine A could be used for a seventh year if $18,000 is spent for maintenance at the end of year 6. This is in addition to $1000 necessary at the end of year 5 to use the machine a sixth year. The net salvage value will be zero. What is the EAC for a 7-year replacement cycle?

B2. Verify that the NPV of $7.193 million shown in Figure 12-1 is correct. This is the value associated with 3 years of production of Clean-e-z and only 1 year of monopolistic pricing power for Q-10.

B3. Y.B. Blue Corporation is considering two alternative machines. Machine A will cost $50,000, will have expenses (excluding depreciation) of $34,000 per year, and will have a useful life of 6 years. Machine B will cost $70,000, will have a useful life of 5 years, and will have expenses (excluding depreciation) of $26,000 per year. Y.B. uses straight-line depreciation and pays taxes at the rate of 35%. The cost of capital for this project is 13%. Net salvage value is zero for each machine at the end of its useful life. Assuming that the project for which the machine will be used is profitable, which machine should be purchased?

B4. Verify that the NPV of $8.304 million shown in Figure 12-1 is correct. This is the value associated with 3 years of production of Clean-e-z and 2 years of monopolistic pricing power for Q-10.

B5. Suppose Federal Express is considering which of two delivery trucks to purchase. The German model will cost $75,000, will have expenses (excluding depreciation) of $250,000 per year, and will have a useful life of 3 years. The Japanese model will cost $100,000, will have expenses (excluding depreciation) of $240,000 per year, and will have a useful life of 4 years. Suppose Federal Express uses straight-line depreciation and pays taxes at a 40% rate. The cost of capital for the project is 12%. The salvage values are $15,000 for the German model and $12,000 for the Japanese model. Which model of delivery truck should Federal Express purchase?

B6. Suppose Federal Express in Problem B5 could refit either model of delivery truck at the end of its estimated useful life. An expenditure of $5000 would extend either truck's useful life by 1 year. Operating expenses would be $10,000 higher in the extra year for either truck. Alternatively, spending $10,000 would extend either truck's original estimated useful life by 2 years. Operating expenses would be $20,000 per year higher in the extra years under this alternative. The depreciation schedules would remain as given in B5. Estimated salvage values for the 1- and 2-year extensions are, respectively, $12,000 and $10,000 for the German truck, and $10,000 and $8000 for the Japanese truck.

a. What is the optimal replacement cycle for each truck?

b. Which one should Federal Express purchase?

B7. A project's initial investment is $40,000, and it has a 5-year life. At the end of the fifth year, the equipment is expected to be sold for $12,000 when its book value is $5000. The actual (including inflation and net salvage value) after-tax cash flows for the next 5 years are expected to be (000's omitted)

Year	1	2	3	4	5
CFAT	20	25	10	10	10

The following rates are in real terms: The cost of capital for this project is 10%, the riskless rate is 7%, and the return on the market portfolio is 9%. The tax rate is 46%, and the inflation rate is 3%.

a. What is the implied beta of the project?

b. What is the NPV of the project?

c. What is the equivalent annual annuity of the project?

B8. Compare and contrast the concepts of break-even and net present value. Why is NPV the correct measure of project value? What insights concerning the choice of a capital budgeting project might the break-even point provide?

B9. Suppose Starter, makers of athletic wear, is considering purchasing a new knitting machine that will cost $250,000. It will have an 8-year useful life. It can be depreciated to a $10,000 book value on a straight-line basis. Incremental operating income will be $100,000 per year before taxes. Starter's marginal tax rate is 40%. Inflation is expected to average 5% per year, and the project's cost of capital in real terms is 8%. The salvage value will be $10,000.

a. Calculate the NPV in real terms.

b. Calculate the NPV in nominal terms.

B10. Suppose Starter in Problem B9 believes the inflation rate will be 10%, rather than 5%. How does that affect the NPV?

B11. In what way does a decision tree differ from the simple model of option valuation developed in Chapter 8?

B12. What are the potential benefits and pitfalls associated with using sensitivity analysis?

B13. A new product called AW-SUM is being considered by Egg Streams, Unlimited. An outlay of $16 million is required for equipment to produce the new product, and additional net working capital in the amount of $3.2 million is also required. The project is expected to have an 8-year life, and the equipment will be depreciated on a straight-line basis to a zero book value over 8 years. Although the equipment will be depreciated to a zero book value, it is expected to have a salvage value of $2 million. Revenues minus expenses for the project are expected to be $5 million per year. The cost of capital for this project is 16%, and the relevant tax rate is 35%. Compute the NPV of the AW-SUM project.

B14. How does nondiversifiable risk create a pitfall in the use of simulation?

B15. Depreciation provides a sort of shield against taxes. If there were no taxes, there would be no depreciation tax shields.

a. Does this mean that the NPV of the AW-SUM project in Problem B13 would be less if there were no taxes?

b. Compute the NPV of the AW-SUM project in Problem B13, assuming a tax rate of 0% and that the cost of capital is 16%.

B16. Discuss the importance of the concept of economic dependence to a firm such as IBM when it considers introducing a new product.

B17. Calculate the relevant expected values and determine the optimal choice for the test marketing decision in the Woody's Hazing example, assuming that product development has led to a major advance.

B18. Suppose the Denis and Denis Corporation has a project with a useful life of 10 years, at the end of which it will have a net salvage value of zero. Depreciation amounts to $100,000 per year. The firm's tax rate is 40%, and the project's cost of capital is 15%. Suppose the firm could sell off the entire project for an after-tax net salvage value of $2.5 million.

a. What is the break-even annual CFAT?

b. Suppose Denis and Denis can realize a (pretax) contribution margin of $25 per unit. What is the zero-NPV sales level?

B19. Suppose the optimistic, expected, and pessimistic annual unit sales levels for the project in problem B18 are 75,000, 50,000 and 25,000, respectively.

a. What is the range of NPVs?

b. Suppose this variation is due entirely to factors that are specific to the firm. Should Denis and Denis sell the project, or retain it?

B20. Suppose Denis and Denis expects the project in Problem B18 to sell 100,000 units per year for 10 years with a pretax contribution margin of $30 per unit. The firm also expects to be able to sell what's left of the project (including the exclusive right to produce the item) at the end of the 10th year for $1,000,000 net of taxes. What is the minimum price the firm should be willing to accept from someone who offers to buy the project today?

PROBLEM SET C

C1. A machine has an NPV of $1500 for one 4-year replacement cycle. The cost of capital for this machine is 12%.

a. What is the EAA (equivalent annual annuity) for the NPV of this machine?

b. What would be the NPV from an infinite series of EAAs in part a?

c. Show that the total NPV from earning an NPV of $1500 on this project at the start of every 4-year cycle, with an infinite series of future replacements, is equal to the NPV computed in part b. [*Hint*: First compute the 4-year rate, and then apply it to compute the present value of an infinite *annuity due* (payments at the *start* of the period) of $1500.]

C2. An increase in net working capital is an important and necessary part of the incremental cost of a capital budgeting project. The method we used to account for the impact of an increase in net working capital on the value of a project is to treat the increase as an outflow at the start of the project and as an inflow at the end of the project.

a. Compute the cost in present value terms of a change in net working capital of $100,000 for a 10-year project if the cost of capital for the project is 12%.

b. Illustrate that this cost can also be accounted for by computing the yearly opportunity cost associated with the increase in net working capital. That is, 12% of $100,000 is $12,000 per year. Compute the present value of $12,000 per year for 10 years at 12%.

c. Explain why these two methods of accounting for the cost of an increase in net working capital are equivalent.

C3. Letter-Fly, Unlimited, a conglomerate corporation with investments in overnight mail service and skeet-shooting franchises, is contemplating a 5-year investment project that requires an initial investment of $200,000 for equipment (depreciated over 5 years on a straight-line basis to a zero salvage value). The project also requires $25,000 in additional net working capital and is expected to have a salvage value of zero. The revenues from the project are expected to be $100,000 in the first year and to grow with inflation at 3.5% per year over the life of the project. Expenses are expected to be $25,000 in the first year and to grow at a different inflation rate of 6% per year. The general level of inflation for the economy is expected to be 5% per year. If the cost of capital on this project in real terms is 8% and taxes are paid at the rate of 32%, should Letter-Fly undertake the investment project?

C4. From one point of view, inflation does not create a problem in the evaluation of a capital budgeting project. From another point of view, inflation creates tremendous problems in the evaluation of a capital budgeting project. What are these two points of view?

C5. J. Hopkins, Inc. has decided to produce a new product. The product is most likely (probability = 0.75) to generate $700,000 per year in new revenues. If revenues are at or above this figure and this product is accepted by the public, its product life is permanent into the foreseeable future. However, although expected sales are high, there is a 25% chance that the product will not be well received by the public, in which case the project will be shut down after 1 year. Even if it is shut down after 1 year, it is expected that the project will produce revenues of $180,000. This product can be produced using either of two methods. Method A requires an initial investment in equipment of $200,000 and annual expenses of $305,000. The equipment will be depreciated over 5 years to a zero book value on a straight-line basis, but it has an expected useful life of 10 years with a salvage value of zero. If the project fails, it will cost $50,000 to shut down. Method B requires an initial investment in equipment of $815,000 but annual expenses of only $75,000. The equipment for method B will also be depreciated over 5 years to a zero book value on a straight-line basis, but it has an expected useful life of 7 years with a salvage value of minus $50,000, (because of removal costs). If the project fails, the salvage value for the project will be $75,000 if method B has been used. J. Hopkins has a tax rate of 37%, and this project has a cost of capital of 18%. How should J. Hopkins proceed with this project?

C6. What level of revenues per year in the previous problem would make J. Hopkins, Inc. indifferent to the project using method A?

C7. Stephenson's Orchards, Inc., Kansas City, MO, has always sent its payroll out to a local CPA firm for processing. Recently, Stephenson's has been considering the purchase of a computer and necessary associated hardware to process the payroll itself. The CPA firm Stephenson's currently uses charges $3050 per year to process the payroll. Stephenson's has investigated computer hardware and software and has found out that it can purchase the necessary hardware for $2500 and a software package for $750 plus a $75-per-year charge to update the package, starting next year. To set the process up will take about 2 weeks of one employee's time (at $1000 per week) and will cost $4000 for a consultant. After the procedure is set up, supplies and the employee's time will amount to $480 per year. The hardware, software, and consultant cost will be depreciated on a 4-year straight-line basis, but the useful life is expected to be 8 years with a salvage value of zero. Stephenson's tax rate is 30% and the cost of capital for this project is 15%. Should Stephenson's undertake doing the payroll itself?

Real-World Application:
The Indiantown Cogeneration Project

The Indiantown Cogeneration Project involved the construction and operation of a coal-fired plant in Martin County, Florida, that produces electricity and steam. The capital cost (including interest during construction) was approximately $770 million. Completed in 1996, it has an electric generating capacity of 330 megawatts (net) and a steam capacity of 175,000 pounds per hour. The project sells the electric power to Florida Power & Light Company (FPL) under a 30-year contract and the steam to Caulkins Indiantown Citrus Company under a 15-year contract. FPL's electricity payments have two parts: one for electric capacity and the other for the electric energy that it receives.

The project's financing consisted of $630 million of 9% APR interest rate debt and $140 million of equity. The debt matures in 2024 (30 years from the date it was issued) and requires equal annual sinking fund payments of $31.5 million beginning in 2005 (year 11).

Use the following operating data to estimate the CFATs for the project:

OUTPUT/INPUT		
Electricity	2,500,000	megawatt-hours per year
Steam	525,000,000	pounds per year
Coal consumption	1,000,000	tons per year

PRICES IN 1996 AND ANNUAL ESCALATION RATES (IN PARENTHESES)

Electric capacity payment	$375,000.00	per megawatt (1% per year)
Electric energy payment	24.00	per megawatt-hour (4% per year)
Steam price	0.20	per thousand pounds (7% per year)
Coal price	29.00	per ton (4.5% per year)

OPERATING COSTS IN 1996 AND ANNUAL ESCALATION RATES

Fuel delivery and waste disposal	$20	per ton of coal (4.5% per year)
Operations and maintenance	$15	million (3% per year)
Other operating expenses	$15	million (3% per year)

OTHER ASSUMPTIONS

Income tax rate	40%
Depreciation	straight-line over 20 years

1. Calculate the estimated total operating revenues for each year in the period 1996 through 2024 assuming there is a full year of production in 1996.

2. Calculate the estimated total operating expenses for each year in the period 1996–2024.

3. Calculate the estimated CFAT for each year in the period 1996–2024.

4. Assume a required return on equity of 15%. Calculate the WACC.

5. Calculate the NPV for the project assuming the assets are worthless at the end of 2024. What does the

NPV criterion indicate about the project in this case?

6. Calculate the IRR for the project. What does the IRR criterion indicate about the project in this case?

7. The debt was issued at the end of 1994. Calculate the interest coverage ratio for each year in the period 2006–2015.

8. Calculate the debt service coverage ratio for each year in the period 2006–2015.

9. Will the project be able to meet its annual debt service obligations?

BIBLIOGRAPHY

Angell, Robert J. "Depreciable Basis/ITC Decisions When the ITC Is Deferred," *Financial Management*, 1985, 14(2):43–47.

Cason, Roger L. "Leasing, Asset Lives and Uncertainty: A Practitioner's Comments," *Financial Management*, 1987, 16(2):13–16.

Flannery, Mark J., Joel F. Houston, and Subramanyam Venkataraman. "Financing Multiple Investment Projects," *Financial Management*, 1993, 22(2):161–172.

Gaumnitz, Jack E., and Douglas R. Emery. "Asset Growth, Abandonment Value and the Replacement of Like-for-Like Capital Assets," *Journal of Financial and Quantitative Analysis*, 1980, 15(2):407–419.

Howe, Keith M. "Does Inflationary Change Affect Capital Asset Life?" *Financial Management*, 1987, 16(2):63–67.

Howe, Keith M., and George M. McCabe. "On Optimal Asset Abandonment and Replacement," *Journal of Financial and Quantitative Analysis*, 1983, 18(3):295–305.

Hubbard, Carl M. "Flotation Costs in Capital Budgeting: A Note on the Tax Effect," *Financial Management*, 1984, 13(2):38–40.

Kwan, Clarence C. Y., and Yufei Yuan. "Optimal Sequential Selection in Capital Budgeting: A Shortcut," *Financial Management*, 1988, 17(1):54–59.

Marcus, Alan J. "Depreciation Rules and Rate Shock in Rate of Return Regulation," *Financial Management*, 1986, 15(4):61–68.

Mehta, Dileep R., Michael D. Curley, and Hung-Gay Fung. "Inflation, Cost of Capital, and Capital Budgeting Procedures," *Financial Management*, 1984, 13(4):48–54.

Prezas, Alexandros P. "Effects of Depreciation and Corporate Taxes On Asset Life Under Debt-Equity Financing," *Financial Management*, 1992, 21(2):24–30.

Rappaport, A., and R. A. Taggart, Jr. "Evaluation of Capital Expenditure Proposals Under Inflation," *Financial Management*, 1982, 11(1):5–13.

Sick, Gordon A. "A Certainty-Equivalent Approach to Capital Budgeting," *Financial Management*, 1986, 15(4):23–32.

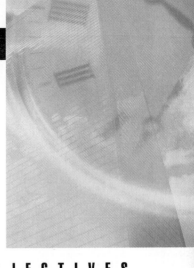

CAPITAL BUDGETING IN PRACTICE

In this chapter, we focus on actually making capital budgeting decisions. The principles and techniques we have learned so far provide an excellent framework. However, using that framework can become complex because of practical realities.

For example, the principle that options are valuable is straightforward, but applying it in valuing a capital budgeting project can be challenging. Similarly, opportunity costs play a very important role in determining the value of a project, but first we have to identify them. This chapter suggests places to look for options and opportunity costs that result from interaction among existing operations and new projects.

Another kind of interaction among projects comes from *capital rationing*. Capital rationing places limits on what a firm spends, such as placing a cap on the amount available to spend on projects this year. On the one hand, such limits can seem bad, because they might eliminate positive-NPV projects. On the other hand, there are good reasons for such limits, and what is called *"soft" capital rationing* can be a practical tool for planning and coordinating a firm's capital budget. Control over managerial responsibility and incentives are two other useful tools for managing a firm's capital budgeting decisions.

The chapter ends with a discussion of additional practical considerations in the capital budgeting process. We examine several factors that can be subtle and difficult to deal with in practice. Finally, we provide an overview, with practical reminders of the importance of the Principles of Finance.

OBJECTIVES

After studying this chapter, you should be able to

1. Describe the critical role of capital budgeting options, and the opportunity costs they create, in properly valuing capital budgeting projects.

2. Explain the pitfalls of "hard" capital rationing, and cite the benefits of "soft" capital rationing as a tool for planning and controlling a firm's capital budget.

3. Describe the practice of capital budgeting, including important practical considerations that are difficult to quantify, such as the role of managerial responsibility and incentives.

4. Explain why a set of simple mechanical rules cannot consistently win out in complex and competitive capital budgeting situations.

5. Apply the Principles of Finance to capital budgeting decisions.

CAPITAL BUDGETING AND THE PRINCIPLES OF FINANCE

◆ *Options*: Recognize the value of options, such as the options to expand, postpone, or abandon a capital budgeting project.

◆ *Two-Sided Transactions*: Consider why the other party to a transaction is willing to participate.

◆ *Signaling*: Consider the actions and products of competitors.

◆ *Valuable Ideas*: Look for new ideas to use as a basis for capital budgeting projects that will create value.

◆ *Comparative Advantage*: Look for capital budgeting projects that use the firm's comparative advantage to add value.

◆ *Incremental Benefits*: Identify and estimate the incremental expected future cash flows for a capital budgeting project.

◆ *Risk-Return Trade-Off*: Consider the risk of the capital budgeting project when determining the project's *cost of capital*, its required return.

◆ *Time Value of Money*: Measure the value the capital budgeting project will create—its NPV.

13.1 A PROPOSAL FOR CAPACITY EXPANSION

Remember Rocky Mountain Chemical Corporation's packaging-machine proposal, which we analyzed in Chapter 11? Well, let's assume that besides the new packaging-machine proposal, RMC has several other projects under consideration. If undertaken, these projects will be financed with funds from a new bond issue that RMC sold earlier this month.

One project is an expansion of RMC's production capacity for a consumer product produced at its Colorado plant, a specialty facial soap called Smooooth. This year's sales are running substantially ahead of last year's and are currently just about at the plant capacity of 10 million bars per year. Next year's sales might top 11 million bars if RMC had the production capacity to produce that much soap. Furthermore, management estimates that if RMC spent an additional $500,000 per year on advertising in each of the next 3 years, sales would rise to 12 million bars next year, to 13 million the year after, and then to 14.5 million per year for the foreseeable future.

The proposal under consideration is to increase RMC's production capacity for Smooooth soap by 65%. Before-tax initial outlays for the project are expected to total $1.85 million. Of this amount, $50,000 would be an increase in working capital. Capitalized space and equipment costs would be $1.45 million, installation costs that would have to be capitalized would be $250,000, and costs associated with the installation that could be expensed immediately would be $100,000.

This last amount could be expensed immediately because it would stem from the tem-

TIME	ITEM	CFBT	CFAT	PV	
0	Capitalized installation and equipment cost	$-1,700,000$ $-I_0$	$-1,700,000$ $-I_0$	$-1,700,000$	**TABLE 13-1** **NPV calculation for Smooooth production capacity expansion.**
0	Expensed installation cost	$-100,000$ $-E_0$	$-60,000$ $-(1-T)E_0$	$-60,000$	
0	Change in net working capital	$-50,000$ $-\Delta W$	$-50,000$ $-\Delta W$	$-50,000$	
1–3	Additional advertising expense	$-500,000/\text{yr}$ $-\Delta E$	$-300,000/\text{yr}$ $-(1-T)\Delta E$	$-673,767$	
1–8	Depreciation	0 0	$85,000/\text{yr}$ TD	$369,205$	
1	Changes in revenues minus expenses	$450,000/\text{yr}$ $\Delta R - \Delta E$	$270,000/\text{yr}$ $(1-T)(\Delta R - \Delta E)$	$232,759$	
2	Change in revenues minus expenses	$675,000/\text{yr}$ $\Delta R - \Delta E$	$405,000/\text{yr}$ $(1-T)(\Delta R - \Delta E)$	$300,981$	
3–10	Change in revenues minus expenses	$1,012,000/\text{yr}$ $\Delta R - \Delta E$	$607,500/\text{yr}$ $(1-T)(\Delta R - \Delta E)$	$1,961,007$	
6	Overhaul expense	$-200,000$ $-\Delta E$	$-120,000$ $-(1-T)\Delta E$	$-49,253$	
10	Return of net working capital	$50,000$ ΔW	$50,000$ ΔW	$11,334$	
				NPV $= \$342,266$	

porary reassignment of current employees.[1] The capitalized expenses would be depreciated to a zero book value on a straight-line basis over 8 years. However, the additional facility is expected to be able to produce for 10 years if a substantial overhaul of the equipment is done at the end of the sixth year. The overhaul would be expected to cost $200,000 and would be expensed (rather than capitalized) when it was done. Depreciation, therefore, would be $212,500 per year $[= (1.45 + 0.25)/8]$ for the first 8 years and zero for the last 2 years of the project. The salvage value of the new equipment (scrap value minus the cost of removal and cleanup) would be zero at the end of the 10 years.

The wholesale price for Smooooth is $0.612 per bar, and the variable cost of production is $0.387 per bar. Thus RMC earns a contribution margin of $0.225 per bar on Smooooth. The additional 4.5 million bars sold in years 3 through 10 would therefore generate an increase of $1,012,500 $(= 0.225 \times 4.5$ million) in revenue minus expenses each year. The increases for years 1 and 2 would be $450,000 and $675,000, respectively. RMC's marginal tax rate is 40%, and the project's cost of capital is 16%. What is the project's NPV?

Table 13-1 shows the NPV calculation for the proposed expansion. Note once again that financing charges do not appear explicitly anywhere in the analysis, even though we know the funds for the project will come from RMC's recent bond issue. The financing opportunity costs are part of the project's cost of capital. The NPV is $342,266. By trial and error, the IRR is found to be about 19.7%, which exceeds the 16% cost of capital. Finally, because the NPV is positive, the profitability index is also positive and equals 1.189 $[= 1 + 342,266/(1,700,000 + 60,000 + 50,000)]$.

At this point it would be easy to say, "Let's do it!" However, although the project looks good so far, we have left an important option out of the analysis.

---

[1] Although these employees will be paid anyway, their wages become an opportunity cost if the project is undertaken. This is because the firm will lose the work normally done by these employees while they help with the installation process. This phenomenon can also occur with respect to managerial time.

The Price-Setting Option

What we did not consider in the NPV calculation shown in Table 13-1 is the alternative of raising the wholesale price for Smooooth soap. That option creates a significant opportunity cost.

What if we raised the price less than 2 cents, from $0.612 to $0.629 per bar? If this price increase reduced next year's demand to 10.2 million bars, then the current plant's entire capacity of 10 million bars could be sold at the higher price. And this would be possible without *any* additional cash outflows!

Judging by the sales projections, demand at a wholesale price of $0.629 is expected to exceed 10 million bars per year for the next 10 years. With an increase of $0.017 over the current price, RMC would have additional before-tax revenues of $170,000 (= 0.017 × 10 million) per year. This translates into an increase in after-tax revenues of $102,000 [= 170,000(1 − 0.4)] per year.

As an alternative to the expansion plan, then, RMC could increase its wholesale price and obtain an increase of $102,000 in its annual net CFAT—*with no other changes whatsoever in its after-tax cash flows*. You can verify that the present value of $102,000 per year for 10 years at 16% is $492,989, which exceeds the $342,266 from the expansion plan. Therefore, although the expansion plan is better than the status quo, the alternative of increasing the price is even better than expansion.

Let's say that on the basis of extensive marketing research, RMC determines that the demand curve for Smooooth soap is

$$\text{Demand} = \frac{2.538 \text{ million}}{(\text{price})^3}$$

RMC can optimize its price setting on the basis of its *current* production capacity. Set the demand equal to the maximum production (10 million bars) and solve for price, which is $0.633. This price is the highest possible price that will produce the desired 10 million in demand.

Of course, estimating a demand curve is not easy. Many dimensions must be taken into account, such as consumers substituting other products and the likelihood that a competing product will become available. But in spite of the cost and difficulty of obtaining it, an estimate of the demand curve for a product may be very valuable. In any case, the analysis for a proposed expansion should always include consideration of the price-setting option, and the opportunity costs associated with it.

Something else to think about is the cost of capital. The cost of capital for RMC's proposed change in wholesale price would probably be less than the cost of capital for the capacity expansion proposal. That is because it is a less risky alternative. The firm would have more operating leverage, and hence more business risk, if it undertook the expansion. If demand were to decline in the future, the price could be reduced under either alternative to stimulate demand. However, the firm's fixed costs would be higher under the expansion alternative. Using a cost of capital that is less than 16% would, of course, raise the NPV of the price increase alternative.

Flexibility in product pricing is another illustration of the importance of hidden options, and it demonstrates once again the value of options. Price flexibility is a very valuable tool. Automobile manufacturers have exercised this option, popularizing cash rebates as a form of price reduction to stimulate demand. Similarly, firms should consider price *increases* among their alternative actions. Of course, in some cases, keeping a constant price can have benefit as well.

Self-Check Questions

1. Explain how the price-setting option works.
2. Explain why expanding production facilities involves greater business risk than raising the price of the product.
3. Why might the cost of capital for a proposed price change be less than the cost of capital for a proposed capacity expansion?

13.2 CAPITAL BUDGETING OPTIONS

Many options are connected with any investment a firm might make. In the expansion example just given, we saw the value of the price-setting option. In Chapter 11, we analyzed the replacement decision and noted that a replacement option is always open to the firm. When an option is ignored, the firm may be incurring an opportunity cost. Therefore, we must consider the value of all options connected with a capital budgeting project in order to measure the project's NPV correctly.

How does a firm value capital budgeting options? An option is the right to do something without any obligation to do it. When the option is costless, it simply adds to the project's value. Not all options are costless. Therefore, a project's NPV can be expressed as its "basic" net present value from discounted cash flows (DCF-NPV) *plus* the value of all options associated with the project *minus* any costs connected with obtaining or maintaining those options:

$$NPV = DCF\text{-}NPV + \text{value of options} - \text{cost of options} \qquad (13.1)$$

Unfortunately, we do not have an option pricing model for many options, so we cannot readily get the "value of options" to use in Equation (13.1). However, a decision tree is often useful for estimating the value of a capital budgeting option. In any case, it is important to understand that the lack of a convenient option pricing model does not diminish the importance of an option.

Managerial options have been shown to have substantial value. For example, consider mineral mining operations. A mining firm has the option to suspend mining operations during times when the price of the mineral is too low to make extraction profitable. The firm can then restart operations whenever extraction becomes profitable again. This option substantially increases the value of the mine.

Options are valuable, but recall from Chapter 8 that there are certain problems associated with combining option values. When a capital budgeting option is exercised, other options are often precluded. In effect, when one option is exercised, other options are eliminated, and simultaneously many costs become sunk costs. Thus the decision to exercise an option must include the value of all alternative actions in the analysis. Otherwise, a firm may incur an opportunity cost by choosing an alternative that was not the best.

We will now discuss three other capital budgeting options: (1) future investment opportunities, (2) the abandonment option, and (3) the postponement option.

Future Investment Opportunities

Future investment opportunities are options to identify additional, more valuable investment possibilities in the future that result from a current opportunity or operation.

For example, manufacturing and distributing a product now puts a distribution and marketing network in place. This creates an option to sell additional products, should they be developed from valuable new ideas.

Money is spent on research and development in the hope of discovering a new idea first and thus securing the option of developing it into a product, production technique, or service.

Chapter 5 presented a dividend growth method of valuing stock. We found that probably the most important, as well as the most difficult, factor in determining the value of a stock is estimating the NPV of a firm's future investments (NPVFI). Managers often say that the largest part of a project's value comes from its future investment opportunities. Unfortunately, we must emphasize that accurately measuring such future investment opportunities can be a difficult, if not impossible, task.

The Abandonment Option

When a firm makes a capital budgeting decision, one option to consider is the possibility of stopping the project earlier than originally planned. This is the **abandonment option**. The abandonment value of a project is simply the NPV from terminating the project by selling or scrapping its assets.

The abandonment value of a project or asset depends on a number of things, but it is enhanced by the existence of an active used-equipment market. Generic and widely used brands of tangible assets are more likely to have such markets, as in the case of cars and trucks. Intangible assets—such as special production processes, patents, and copyrights—are less likely to have organized secondary markets. Therefore, intangible assets tend to involve higher transaction costs to find buyers. They are more difficult to sell than generic, tangible assets. Of course, there are rarely any cleanup or removal costs associated with disposing of an intangible asset. Consequently, highly specialized tangible assets subject to technological obsolescence tend to have even higher transaction costs than intangible assets.[2]

When we discussed the capital budgeting process in Chapter 10, we considered the importance of deciding whether to *continue to develop* an investment project. This is simply the abandonment option during the development stage of a project. In addition to its importance during development, the abandonment option should be considered periodically after a project is actually under way. It is possible that abandonment of part, or even all, of its operations could have a positive NPV (keep in mind that sunk costs should be ignored).

To Sell or Not to Sell Joe's Diner

Joe's Diner has been operating for about as long as anyone can remember. Pete has run it for the last 18 years since taking it over from his father, Jack. Last month, Pete was approached by a developer about selling the place. Diane, the developer, would not say exactly what she had in mind, except that Pete could move the diner if he wanted to. She was interested only in the land. At the end of their conversation, Diane offered Pete $350,000 for the land.

Pete was confident that this was a fair price—indeed, the most he could hope to get for the place at this time. Pete thought about moving the diner, but he found that it was not feasible to move the physical structure. Besides, there was nowhere he could put it that was close

---

[2] Mainframe computers in the 1970s are an example of such highly specialized equipment subject to technological obsolescence. Many universities were offered mainframe computers as "gifts" if the university would pay the cost of removal and reinstallation. Several universities made the mistake of accepting such "gifts," only to discover that they could have gotten greater computing capability for less money by purchasing a new machine! Corporations were sorry when universities began refusing such "gifts," because not only did the firm then have to pay the removal cost, but in some cases it also lost a significant tax benefit that would have accrued from having made a "gift" to a not-for-profit organization.

enough to keep the clientele and good name of Joe's Diner. If he sold, he would have no choice but to abandon the business.

To analyze his decision whether to sell the diner, Pete gathered the following information. The sale price of $350,000 would provide an after-tax amount of $280,000. The equipment could be sold at auction for about $30,000, on which he would have to pay $5000 in taxes. The building needed renovation about every 10 years. The before-tax equivalent annual cost (EAC) of this periodic maintenance was $24,000, and the after-tax EAC, including the effect of depreciation, was $18,000. The annual revenues minus expenses from running the diner were $100,000 per year, and Pete paid taxes at the rate of 25% on this amount. Pete determined that his cost of capital is 12%. The one thing Pete almost forgot to include in the analysis was the opportunity cost for his time.

Recently, a friend offered Pete $35,000 per year, including retirement and other benefits, to come and work for him. Pete figured that it would not be exactly a 40-hour work week, but it would average less than his 55-hour work week in the diner. With the change in income sources, Pete's tax specialist estimated that the $35,000 per year would be taxed at a rate of 20%. Finally, Pete had been planning for quite a while to sell the diner and retire 12 years from now. He estimated that the land would sell for the same price then as now, after adjusting for the effect of inflation.

From this information, with the help of a friend who had taken a finance course. Pete created the NPV calculation for abandoning his investment in the diner (Table 13-2). Note that the positive and negative signs are reversed from what they would normally be, because Pete is selling, rather than undertaking, the project.

As you can see from the table, the "basic" NPV—the DCF-NPV—of abandonment was positive, $53,494. But in spite of this, Pete turned Diane down, because he decided that he enjoyed what he was doing more than he would enjoy increasing his wealth by $53,494.

We want to emphasize that this was *not* necessarily an irrational choice on Pete's part. For him, the nonmonetary values he received from owning the diner exceeded $53,494. Pete said he was just relieved that his opportunity cost of continuing with the diner was no larger. At some price, he would have had to sell the diner, because the nonmonetary values would not have been large enough to overcome the opportunity cost.

Postscript: 2 years later, Diane came back and offered Pete $600,000 for the diner. He took it. ■

TIME	ITEM	CFBT	CFAT	PV AT 12%
0	Land sale	350,000	280,000	280,000
0	Equipment sale	30,000	25,000	25,000
1–12	EAC-building (saved)	24,000/yr	18,000/yr	
1–12	$\Delta R - \Delta E$ (forgone)	−100,000/yr	−75,000/yr	−179,637
1–12	Wages	35,000/yr	28,000/yr	
12	Land sale (forgone)	−350,000	−280,000	−71,869
				NPV = $53,494

TABLE 13-2 NPV calculation for abandoning Joe's Diner.

An important point to understand in the foregoing example is that Pete needed to have an accurate estimate of the monetary opportunity cost of continuing to own the diner in order to make a rational decision about whether the nonmonetary values exceeded that cost. The nonmonetary values are not irrelevant, but it is simply more accurate to consider them *after* including all other costs that are more easily quantified.

The Postponement Option

We illustrated the price-setting option earlier in the chapter. A logical next step is to consider the **postponement option**, which is the option to postpone, rather than cancel, an expansion. A price increase now, followed by an expansion in production capacity, additional advertising, and perhaps even a price *decrease* later, might be superior to a simple price increase now. Of course, because of interactions among the various alternatives, the analysis can become very complex when such additional alternatives are included. In Chapter 12 we analyzed a postponement option for introducing a new type of VCR-head cleaner and showed that decision trees (see Chapter 12) are useful for dealing with this kind of complexity.

A Warning About Capital Budgeting Options

In Chapter 11, we discussed many different rules and analyses used in making capital budgeting decisions. Often, people in practice talk about the "gut feel," or special expertise, that enables them to say a project should be undertaken even though it does not appear to have a positive NPV. Options are frequently at the heart of the matter. It is difficult to quantify their value, so the "gut feel" approach is often simply to "guesstimate" that the project is profitable and then to go ahead with it. Although this approach is not without redeeming merit, it has to be applied with extreme care. Otherwise, the value of one or more vague options can be used to justify undertaking *any* project, no matter how unprofitable it might appear or actually be.

It is best to quantify the additional value for the options that would be necessary to justify the project. Then you can see whether that additional value is at all reasonable.

EXAMPLE

Follow-On Markets at Hess, Inc.

Suppose Hess, Inc. has a project with a DCF-NPV of −$1 million before the value of a significant option is added to the NPV calculation. If that option is worth more than $1 million, then the project will actually have a positive NPV and should be undertaken.

The option that exists for Hess consists of a 25% chance of gaining entry into a new market 5 years from now. The project's cost of capital is 20%. What does the future value of the follow-on market entry have to be in order to make the current project's NPV positive?

For the present value of the option to exceed $1 million, the expected future value (5 years from now) must be greater than about $2.5 million [$= (1.2)^5 1,000,000 = 2,488,320$]. With a 25% chance of achieving market entry, the future project within the option must then be expected to produce almost $10 million [$= 0.25(10) + 0.75(0) = 2.5$ million] in additional NPV (5 years from now) for the current project to have a positive total NPV. That's a lot of NPV! ■

Self-Check Questions

1. Why is it important to consider all options connected with a proposed capital budgeting project?

2. What is the relationship among the "basic" NPV of a project, its DCF-NPV, and the value and cost of project-related options?

3. List three capital budgeting options and describe each one.

4. What is the major pitfall that can result from hidden options?

13.3 PROBLEM DEFINING INCREMENTAL CASH FLOWS: THE CASE OF RISK DIFFERENCES

In Chapter 10 we introduced the concepts of operating risk and operating leverage. We noted that in some cases, a firm can choose among different levels of operating leverage.

For example, a choice between using robots and using humans in manufacturing typically represents a choice between two levels of operating leverage. Robotic manufacturing has higher fixed costs to install, but lower variable costs to operate, than human manufacturing. Therefore, robotic manufacturing has a higher level of operating leverage. This difference in operating leverage creates a difference in the business risk of the alternative processes, and consequently there will be a difference in the costs of capital for the processes.

Consider two alternative manufacturing processes with different levels of operating leverage. Let's say that the total production capacity is the same for the two processes and that the production process does not affect the sales for the product.[3] Because the sales revenue will be the same in either case, it would appear that sales revenue is not incremental and can therefore be excluded from the analysis. However, this is not so. Even though the expected revenues are the same in either case, because of the difference in risk between the two processes, the revenues *must* be included in the analysis.

This problem stems from how we define *incremental.* The increment for each alternative is measured from the status quo, *not* with respect to the other alternative. Consequently, the contribution margin—the difference between the selling price and the variable cost per unit—is the incremental amount, not the difference in costs. Therefore, the process should not be chosen on the basis of the lowest present value of costs, because that approach will not always yield the correct decision. The process chosen must be the one that produces the largest NPV, as in the following example.

Stephenson's Orchards, Inc., Kansas City, MO, manufactures apple cider. The level of production is limited by its production facilities, so Ron Stephenson is considering an expansion of the firm's production capacity. There are two types of processes that can be installed for the expansion. One process is considerably more automated than the other, and therefore the operating leverage would be higher. The total production capacity would be the same for the two processes, and the expected value of the additional sales of cider is $100,000 per year. Stephenson's marginal tax rate is 30%.

Cider Production at Stephenson's Orchards, Inc.

EXAMPLE

Process A would cost $120,000 to install and would have variable costs of $57,000 per year. Process B would cost $30,000 to install and would have variable costs of $72,000 per year. Both processes would be depreciated on a straight-line basis to a zero book value over 8 years, but both have a 10-year useful life and expected salvage values of zero at the end of 10 years. Therefore, the depreciation tax credits would be $4500 for A [= 0.3(120,000/8)] and $1125 for B [= 0.3(30,000/8)] per year for the first 8 years and zero for the last 2 years of the project. Process A has a 15% cost of capital, process B 12%.

Which project, if either, should Stephenson's undertake?

First, consider the present values of the total *cost* of each process over the 10-year life. As shown in Table 13-3, these present values are $300,056 for A and $309,182 for B. Al-

---

[3] This, of course, is not always the case. An example of a case where the production process apparently might affect the sales level is furnished by a Coors beer marketing campaign that claimed the process of continuous refrigeration of the beer improves its quality.

though project A appears to have the lower total cost, *it is the wrong choice* because the NPV of the net cash flows (revenues minus expenses) depends on which process is used to generate them. Process A is riskier, so the present value of the revenues depends on which process is used.

With process A, the firm would be spending much more now, but less later, to earn those revenues. With process B, the firm would spend less now, but more later, to earn the same revenues. Even though the revenues are expected to be the same in either case, if there was a downturn in demand and the revenues turned out badly, many of the expenses of process A would already have been incurred. With process B, if the revenues turned out badly, the expenses would be lower because a larger portion of the expenses for process B are variable and are thus incurred only if needed to produce the product. Therefore, the revenues, which are the same in either case, would be riskier if process A were chosen.

Now consider the NPV of each process, *including the revenues*, over the 10-year horizon. As shown in Table 13-4, the NPV for process A is only $51,258, whereas for process B it is $86,333. Process B should be installed, because it has the larger positive NPV of these mutually exclusive projects. ■

TABLE 13-3
Present value of costs calculations for Stephenson's cider production alternatives.

		PROCESS A		
Time	Item	CFBT	CFAT	PV At 15%
0	$-I_0$	120,000	120,000	120,000
1–8	Depreciation	0/yr	−4500/yr	−20,193
1–10	ΔE	57,000/yr	39,900/yr	200,249
			Total cost =	$300,056

		PROCESS B		
Time	Item	CFBT	CFAT	PV At 12%
0	$-I_0$	30,000	30,000	30,000
1–8	Depreciation	0/yr	−1125/yr	−5,589
1–10	ΔE	72,000/yr	50,400/yr	284,771
			Total cost =	$309,182

TABLE 13-4
NPV calculations for Stephenson's alternative cider production processes, including revenues.

		PROCESS A		
Time	Item	CFBT	CFAT	PV At 15%
0	$-I_0$	−120,000	−120,000	−120,000
1–8	Depreciation	0/yr	4500/yr	20,193
1–10	$\Delta R - \Delta E$	43,000/yr	30,100/yr	151,065
			NPV =	$51,258

		PROCESS B		
Time	Item	CFBT	CFAT	PV At 12%
0	$-I_0$	−30,000	−30,000	−30,000
1–8	Depreciation	0/yr	−1125/yr	5,589
1–10	$\Delta R - \Delta E$	28,000/yr	19,600/yr	110,744
			NPV =	$86,333

Self-Check Questions

1. A firm can use either of two production processes to manufacture a product. One has much greater operating leverage than the other. Which one might have a higher cost of capital? Why?

2. Suppose two alternative processes differ in cost of capital but not in sales revenue. Why is it necessary to take revenue into account in the capital budgeting analysis?

13.4 CAPITAL RATIONING

Just as the name implies, **capital rationing** limits (rations) the firm's capital expenditures. A firm can impose such limits in a number of different ways, but two are widely employed. One is to use a discount rate that exceeds the project's cost of capital by, for example, 3%. Although this is a form of rationing, the use of a "higher" rate can be subtle, because in many cases it is not explicitly acknowledged. Often management argues on the basis of "conservatism," and "a few points" are added or the number is "rounded up" when a cost of capital is established.

Another method of capital rationing is to set a maximum on parts of the capital budget or on the total. For example, a firm may decide it will invest a maximum of $1.2 million in new projects this year. This second method of capital rationing is the more visible method, because rationing is explicitly acknowledged. And because of this explicit acknowledgement, it appears to be the more widely used of the two methods.

Pitfalls of Capital Rationing

One obvious consequence of using a higher discount rate is that for conventional projects (an outflow followed by one or more inflows), the project's NPV will be understated. Some financial managers are not bothered by this fact, because they like the idea that value is being "conservatively" measured. Likewise, limiting the total amount of money spent on new capital budgeting projects can be viewed as being "conservative." This conservatism, however, can inflict opportunity costs if the firm passes up positive-NPV projects.

Unfortunately, management may be eager to incur this opportunity cost because of an agency cost. In Chapter 9, we described the nondiversifiability of human capital and showed how it causes a divergence of incentives between shareholders and managers over the choice of capital investments. Shareholders hold diversified investment portfolios and are concerned only about nondiversifiable risk. But because managers' human capital is not well diversified, managers can be "wiped out" if the firm goes bankrupt, and so managers are concerned about the firm's total risk (diversifiable plus nondiversifiable).

Therefore, managers may want to choose project NPVs "conservatively" so that projects with a greater margin of safety will be chosen. In this way, managers reduce the likelihood of bankruptcy, the firm's total risk, and the chance that they will lose their jobs. When managers choose projects "conservatively" to reduce their personal risk, such choices create opportunity costs that add to the firm's agency costs.

Capital Rationing and Capital Market Efficiency

Capital rationing has been widely criticized because the efficiency of the capital markets should make rationing unnecessary. In a perfect capital market, a firm could *always* obtain the funds needed to undertake a positive-NPV project, because the project would be better than other capital market opportunities. Therefore, given that existing capital markets are very efficient, firms should simply obtain whatever additional funds are needed to undertake all positive-NPV projects. In practice, however, firms regularly ration their capital expenditures. And, as it turns out, there can be some practical benefits from capital rationing.

Benefits of Capital Rationing

In Chapter 14, we will identify three persistent capital market imperfections: tax asymmetries, information asymmetries, and transaction costs. We show here how two of these imperfections, information asymmetries and transaction costs, can make capital rationing beneficial for a firm.

To obtain funds from the capital market, a firm must convince investors that they can expect to earn at least their required return. However, recall from our discussion of the Signaling Principle the problem of *adverse selection*, wherein offering something for sale appears to be a negative signal. Adverse selection leads investors to ask, "If this investment is so good, why is the firm willing to let me in on it? Why doesn't the firm want to keep all of the positive NPV for itself?"

Of course, only the managers know the answer. This creates what is called **asymmetric information** between investors and the firm. Asymmetric information exists when information is known to some participants but not to others. Investors will raise their required return to protect themselves from the risk of being "taken." The higher required return lowers the amount of funds obtained from selling new securities to the outside investors. As a result, the firm must have "special circumstances" to make the sale of new securities attractive.

Two such special circumstances are a "really great" new investment opportunity and a "really bad" set of current operations. The benefits from really great new investment opportunities are obvious, but let's examine the second case to see how additional funds can help a troubled firm.

When people learn that a firm's current operations are worth less than was previously believed, the market value of the firm declines, and investors incur a loss in value. When new investors are brought in prior to such a decline in market value, the new investors help the existing investors by sharing in the value loss, so the existing investors' loss is smaller than it would otherwise have been.

Without going on to explain this idea fully, this brief discussion should help you to appreciate the importance of problems of asymmetric information. Capital rationing can be beneficial because it is a way in which a firm can manage the problems and costs of asymmetric information connected with getting additional financing for new projects. It reduces the need for external financing and thus reduces these agency costs.

The direct transaction costs of obtaining additional financing, such as the issuance costs of new bonds, provide another way in which capital rationing can benefit a firm. Simply stated, the cost of obtaining additional financing is a declining function of the amount of new financing. That is, the cost, as a percentage of the amount of new financing, is lower when more funds are obtained. For example, the total flotation costs for $200 million worth of bonds might be only 1% of the value of the new bonds. In contrast, $10 million worth of bonds might have total flotation costs of 6% or more of the value of the bonds.

Let's say a firm has a project with a "basic" NPV that is positive but has insufficient funds to undertake it. If the transaction costs of obtaining the needed funds exceed the project's NPV, the project's true NPV is negative and the project is undesirable after all. A capital rationing process can help avoid such situations.[4]

---

[4] It might be argued that in such cases, the firm would not really be capital rationing. It would simply be measuring the project's NPV more accurately by considering all the costs, including those of obtaining the needed financing. As a practical matter, however, the process used would look like capital rationing.

Another market imperfection that can make capital rationing beneficial takes place in the labor, as opposed to the capital, markets. When a firm invests, it must have a manager for the project. Existing managers can often manage additional small projects without too much difficulty. However, a large new project may require managerial expertise beyond what the firm's existing employees can provide.[5] Although a firm may be confident of the high quality of its current employees, it cannot be so confident of being able to hire similar employees "off the street."

Many current employees have been extensively trained and have grown into their current positions over time. Others were not promoted because they were less qualified. Just as there is information asymmetry between investors and the firm's managers, there is an information asymmetry between the firm and potential new employees who could be hired so that the firm could undertake a positive-NPV project. That information asymmetry causes an increase in the transaction costs associated with undertaking the proposed project and thus decreases the NPV. As with capital market transaction costs, a capital rationing process provides a way to include otherwise ignored costs and thereby measure the project's NPV more accurately.

Capital Rationing, on Balance

Agency costs create pitfalls in the use of capital rationing. But other market imperfections can make capital rationing beneficial. We suspect that both factors contribute to the fact that almost all firms engage in some sort of capital rationing process.

We will build on this later in the chapter and will show how capital rationing can also be beneficial in planning and managing capital expenditures.

Self-Check Questions

1. What is capital rationing?
2. How do firms impose capital rationing? Which method is more widely used?
3. What are some of the pitfalls of capital rationing?
4. Explain why capital rationing would be unnecessary in a perfect capital market environment.
5. Are there any practical benefits to capital rationing? Explain.

13.5 PROJECT CHOICE UNDER CAPITAL RATIONING

How can a firm choose the best projects under capital rationing? Although NPV is still the best criterion, the rule must be modified for use under capital rationing. The problem is that a firm needs to choose the best *set* of new projects. That is, it should choose the set of projects that provides the largest *total* NPV.

The problem is somewhat like a jigsaw puzzle, because fractions of a project cannot usually be undertaken. Normally, a firm either undertakes or rejects a whole project. Consequently, a firm must fit together a total capital budget that is less than or equal to the maximum amount of funds available. Each project can cause the firm to over- or underspend its budget, because it comes as a lump amount. The profitability index (PI) can be a useful tool

---

[5] Of course, new employees may be assigned to current operations to allow existing employees to manage the new operations. Whatever the distribution of assignments, however, the firm must hire additional qualified managers.

Capital Rationing as a Planning Tool

The capital rationing example just given illustrates **"hard" capital rationing**. The word *hard* refers to how the maximum total expenditure is viewed, implying that under no circumstances can that maximum be exceeded. When a set of projects is particularly attractive, management may decide to exceed its self-imposed capital expenditure limit. In fact, firms often establish a condition called **"soft" capital rationing**: The firm sets a target for its total amount of capital expenditures. Then, depending on project desirability and on the firm's condition at the time decisions are actually made, the firm may over- or underspend relative to that target.

The techniques we have described for hard capital rationing are also useful for soft capital rationing. The firm can get a good picture of the trade-offs among alternative projects by using sensitivity analysis, which entails varying the maximum somewhat. For example, a firm may find that a small increase in the total expenditure would enable it to undertake the next most desirable project, and management may consider that small increase a worthwhile trade-off. Computer software is particularly useful for soft capital rationing and sensitivity analysis. Once the problem has been formulated, analysts can use the computer to obtain alternative solutions simply by changing the constraint values.

Managerial Authority and Responsibility

Cooperation is a prerequisite to good decision making. This holds for capital budgeting as well. Interpersonal relationships can play a key role. Feuds between people and/or divisions hurt the firm. Members of any one functional area, such as marketing research, obviously must be able to work together successfully. And cooperation among the various decision making *levels* also plays a critical role.

Perhaps somewhat more subtle is the need for members of different functional areas to work together successfully. For example, marketing research and finance must exchange information to estimate project cash flows. Procedures that provide authority by area and amount, with a hierarchy of amounts, are designed to minimize problems among individuals, levels, and areas. Unfortunately, although such procedures generally provide a net gain by reducing or eliminating certain kinds of problems, they may create others.

In Chapter 10 we described a typical budgetary authority system in which a manager could approve capital expenditures—but only within certain limits. However, a manager can circumvent such constraints by breaking up expenditures that exceed the limit into smaller ones that do not require additional approval, spread them out over time, or both. In this way, a manager can undertake a project without having to obtain prior approval from a higher decision-making level. This may sound extreme, yet cases have been cited where a division of a firm actually built and equipped a whole new plant using plant expense orders. In one such case, headquarters discovered the new plant only after its managers submitted an expenditure request for a chimney. They had to. They couldn't figure out how to break a key component of the chimney expense into smaller amounts!

The problem illustrated by this example is that the division thought the firm needed the new plant but felt that headquarters would turn down the project. In essence, the division thought it knew better than headquarters. The division managers probably felt that corporate-level managers lacked the hands-on viewpoint. Of course, they might have been right, but they might just as easily have been wrong. The responsibility for that decision was not theirs. The perspective from the division level does not encompass the breadth of the higher level of decision-making authority.

This example illustrates a tremendous breakdown of the system of authority and responsibility. The division's responsibility was to communicate its viewpoint to higher levels. Headquarters had the responsibility of trying to understand that viewpoint, weighing it along with other information, and deciding on the best course of action.

At the other extreme, having top management review all decisions could lead to the absurd case where the CEO has to approve a salesperson's purchase of a new pencil. In essence, budgetary authority is designed to reduce transaction costs. Lowering the level of decision-making authority within a firm may reduce the net cost of making the decision, including the opportunity cost of delay when time is critical.

The problems just cited emphasize the need to balance decision-making authority against transaction costs. In spite of these and other problems that can arise, recall from Chapter 9 that multiple layers of decision-making authority provide a monitoring function that can reduce agency costs. The multiple layers and divisions of authority make collusion among employees more difficult, and it is less likely that employees will take self-interested actions at the expense of the shareholders. Therefore, the multiple layers may provide a form of agency cost reduction that also enters into the choice of decision-making authority for each level of the firm.

In practice, the procedures outlined in Chapter 10, along with intelligent and honest employees best using their abilities, provide methods of coping with the complexities encountered in practice. And thankfully, they generally produce sensible capital budgeting decisions.

Managerial Incentives and Performance Evaluation

As we have seen, capital rationing can provide additional opportunities for managers to engage in self-interested behavior, thus increasing the firm's agency costs. This highlights once again the value of managerial incentives that reduce agency costs.

A typical example of poor incentives is the case where managers are evaluated on the basis of the firm's or the division's return on the book value of assets. This rate is often called a return on investment (ROI).[9] Unfortunately, this measure doesn't have a consistent relationship with NPV. Therefore, it does not measure managerial success in choosing projects that create value.

When managers are evaluated and rewarded for a measure of performance, self-interested behavior leads them to actions that will increase it. Consequently, it is important to choose performance measures that are consistent with the firm's goals. Otherwise, the firm might get exactly what it asked for—even though that was not at all what it wanted!

Post-audits

A **post-audit** is a set of procedures for evaluating a capital budgeting decision after the fact. Although post-audits can be valuable, some words of caution are in order. Post-audits can pose practical challenges and must be done carefully. Sometimes the opportunity costs of forgone alternatives and options are simply impossible to measure. Also, as the cliche "hindsight is better than foresight" points out, using hindsight to evaluate foresight is not reasonable. Outcomes can occur that were not even thought possible, let alone predicted. In some cases, as in the following example, identifying and measuring the incremental cash flows that actually resulted from a decision can be impossible.

---

[9] Recall that ROI has several different definitions.

<table>
<tr><td>

EXAMPLE

Kroger's Optical Scanners

</td><td>

Let's say Kroger installed optical scanners in its grocery checkout counters 6 years ago. The scanners were installed for a variety of reasons. It was argued that they would dramatically improve the store's inventory management by reducing the chance of over- and understocking, reducing the time to take inventory, and reducing the cost of ordering. In addition, the scanners were expected to improve customer service by reducing the time for customers to check out. If Kroger is now interested in determining whether installing the scanners was a good decision, what can be determined from a post-audit?

The current costs of ordering and taking inventory can be compared to such costs before the scanners were installed to measure any savings. Also, it might be possible to establish a cost savings for any reduction in overstocking. However, estimating the incremental revenues associated with a reduction in the number of stockouts would be very difficult at best: How can we determine how many sales would have been lost?

An observed increase in sales could have been caused by many things, such as improved economy-wide conditions. Similarly, connecting the sales level to an improvement in the customer service level is not possible. Although Kroger could survey its customers to measure improvement in customer service, suppose total sales have not increased. We cannot establish what the sales level would have been if the scanners had not been installed. After all, competitors may also have put in scanners, so the store might have experienced a substantial drop in sales had the scanners *not* been installed.

In this case, it is not possible to measure precisely the incremental cash inflows that were generated by installing the optical scanners. At this point, only the financial condition of the entire store can be meaningfully established. ■

</td></tr>
</table>

In spite of the problems of evaluating a decision after the fact, post-audits made up of sensible evaluation procedures can be useful, and they are often undertaken in practice. One valuable and typical procedure is to evaluate some or all of the expected future cash flow estimates. This process is often aimed more at improving the analysts' ability to forecast expected future cash flows on current and future projects than at simply evaluating the analyst's performance. Some analysts have relatively consistent biases in their estimates (either optimistically above or pessimistically below). It might be possible to correct such a bias over time through the review and evaluation of the analyst's work.

A second form of post-audit is conducted to determine the value of abandonment of an entire project versus its continued operation. Often, as in the optical-scanner example, determining the value of the entire operation is the only reasonable method of evaluating the project. Of course, although this may determine the project's current value, it does not indicate whether a particular decision was good or bad. The current value provides a measure of the outcome from the entire set of past decisions, but that outcome could be more the result of good or bad luck than the result of good or bad decision making.

The Capital Budgeting Framework

The capital budgeting/NPV framework is a useful decision-making tool that is based on sound principles and techniques. However, practical realities can significantly complicate its use. In practice, there can be a great deal of "squish" in the decision-making process. Without a rationally based system for making decisions as a guide, however, managers could justify self-interested choices with enough "subjective add-ons." Recall our warning about this problem in our discussion of the value that options add to a project's DCF-NPV.

Do not be swayed by the following kind of argument: Because estimating and planning are complex, difficult, and uncertain, in the final analysis, decisions are subjective. Therefore, forget all the complex analysis and "just take your best shot." Although the first statement is true, the conclusion does not follow. A decision is certainly easier to make if it is simply the result of a coin flip or a "gut-feel best guess," but such a decision can lead to disaster.

If a decision is worth considering and can benefit from additional information, gather the most cost-efficient information set and base the decision on that information. Sometimes the most cost-efficient information is what you already have. In such cases, choose the optimal alternative on the basis of that information. But often, gathering extra information is a cost-effective method of making a better decision, even if the information is not perfect.

Remember that if capital budgeting decisions were trivial, there would not be much reason to study the process. Framing the analysis and decision properly enhances subjective judgments and puts them in the proper context. Of course, using the NPV framework will not save you from the effects of inaccurate forecasts of incremental cash flows or from the effects of using the wrong cost of capital.

Self-Check Questions

1. What is hard capital rationing? How is soft capital rationing different?

2. Are different analytical techniques required to apply the two types of capital rationing?

3. Why is soft capital rationing a useful managerial tool for planning?

4. What is the purpose of having multiple layers of decision-making authority within a firm?

5. What is a post-audit? How is it useful in capital budgeting?

13.7 OTHER FACTORS THAT ARE DIFFICULT TO QUANTIFY

We have already mentioned several factors that are difficult to quantify in a capital budgeting analysis, such as options, incorporating the effects of erosion and enhancement, predicting the likelihood of technological advances, and hiring qualified managers.

On the one hand, overlooking such factors that create opportunity costs can lead to bad decision making. On the other hand, we have emphasized the importance of taking care in performing incremental analysis to reflect such factors (when they are important), while avoiding double-counting and/or overestimating the impact of these factors, particularly with respect to options.

Here we will list some other factors that can also increase or decrease project value. For the most part, these factors have a much smaller impact on project value than those we have already mentioned.

1.   *Working relationships with suppliers*—either good or bad. The importance of interpersonal relationships within a firm that we noted earlier extends to relationships with individuals and departments in other firms. An individual who works for a supplier can cause a costly delay because of a personal vendetta.

2.   *Particular expertise* concerning a project, or the lack of it, among current employees. In our discussion of capital rationing, we pointed out the problems of information asymmetry in the labor markets and noted the difficulty of identifying high-quality employees. When transaction costs must be incurred to identify and hire additional employees, those costs decrease the project's NPV. Similarly, when existing employees have expertise that can be used for a project, transaction costs associated with undertaking the project (such as training) will be lower, which in turn increases the project's NPV.

3.   *Experience* with the quality of machines and/or service from particular manufacturers. As with relationships with suppliers, good or bad service or parts availability from a manufacturer can decrease

or increase the firm's expenses. Likewise, when a machine is known to have a better or worse "cost/quality" relationship, it will increase or decrease the project's NPV. Also, improved knowledge of the expenses connected with using a machine may increase the accuracy of the forecast of cash flows. Such improved knowledge is more likely to be available for machines that use existing technology than for machines that use innovative technology.

The same warning we gave about options applies to these and similar factors: As long as no one insists on specific values that can be carefully examined, a proponent of a project can always find a long enough list of vague add-ons with which to "shout down" an opponent of the project. Don't be fooled. *A long list is not a substitute for a large NPV!*

Self-Check Questions
1. Name three factors that can affect the NPV of a capital budgeting project but are difficult to quantify.
2. Explain why it is important to describe thoroughly the benefits that you expect to result from a factor that cannot be readily quantified. What problem do vague add-ons present?

13.8 SOME PRACTICAL ADVICE

Making decisions in a complex world is particularly difficult because no single approach *always* works best. As with earning extraordinary returns in the stock market, if it were that easy, everyone would already be doing it. At one extreme, the analyst-manager could gather *all* the relevant information needed to make the optimal choice. But of course there is always more information that could be gathered in just about every situation, and so with that strategy, the decision maker would never make a decision.

At the other extreme, gathering information costs money and takes time. Therefore, in order to minimize cost, one could conclude that the analyst-manager should never gather more information.

Either approach may in fact be best in a particular situation, but both are too extreme to be applied to every situation. Extreme solutions involving "always" or "never"—such as always wait (or never wait) and always purchase more information (or never purchase more information)—are too simplistic to be consistently successful in complex situations. Our advice is to be wary of simplistic decision-making procedures that are like cure-all medicines, claimed to be appropriate for all situations.

Despite the need to be wary, the capital budgeting/NPV framework for decision making described in Chapter 11 is *always* correct! The problem is that following the framework is sometimes extremely difficult because of a variety of complicating factors, such as opportunity costs, options, erosion, and enhancement. The tools we have described provide methods of coping in an environment where it is not only impossible to predict future outcomes but it is often impossible even to describe the possible outcomes. In other words, in some cases, we cannot even imagine some of the outcomes.

When your investment depends on unknown future events, you simply do the best you can. We can talk about the possibility of a technological advance, but often we cannot say anything more about it than to make some general statements about rendering an existing product obsolete. Also, some possible outcomes are so unlikely that they have no significant effect on the analysis, yet if such an outcome occurs, its effect will be catastrophic. We discussed this phenomenon in Chapter 8 in connection with contingent claims.

As we said in Chapter 10, we know of no way to teach a person how to generate new ideas. Our ability to teach a person to assimilate information is also limited.

Applying the Principles of Finance

In spite of all the difficulties, several Principles of Finance are especially important to remember with respect to capital budgeting decisions.

VALUABLE NEW IDEAS   Bad financing decisions can destroy a firm. On the other hand, although good financing decisions can contribute to a firm's profitability, the possibility of extraordinary success lies primarily in investment decisions. Because of capital market efficiency, great financing rarely makes a firm extraordinarily profitable. The Principle of Valuable Ideas is alive and well. ***Pursuing valuable ideas is the best way to achieve extraordinary returns.***

Valuable new ideas are not necessarily limited to new products. A valuable new idea can be related to many dimensions of the business. An improved management technique can be valuable. Ray Kroc employed valuable new management procedures in helping to make McDonald's a profitable corporation. He had many new ideas in addition to his idea of serving hamburgers quickly. For example, McDonald's introduced fast food in a family restaurant, a substantive change from the take-out hamburger joint.

Introducing new ideas in the form of products, services, management, and/or technology can reduce the value of current ideas or even render current ideas worthless. This was pointed out in the Headcleaner example in Chapter 12, but it can be seen in many places. For example, what are typewriters worth today, compared with what they were worth when new?

COMPARATIVE ADVANTAGE   Beyond new ideas, a firm should look for ways to make good use of its comparative advantages or current expertise. Promising places to look for opportunities include the use of patents and marketing or distribution networks.

MARKET EFFICIENCY   In Chapter 5, we asked why we should bother with a model for valuing a bond when the bond's value can be easily determined by looking at the latest trading price. The main reason is that the model established a required return. We have also noted that the physical asset markets are not as efficient as the capital markets. In the next chapter, we will explore the reasons for this fact. In spite of lower efficiency, there is useful information contained in a physical asset's market-traded price.

If you are not going to trust a market price, you should have a very good reason. This is true in the physical asset markets as well as the capital markets. Beware of an analysis that places a value on an asset that is very different from prices observed in a competitive market. Even if the market is less efficient than the capital markets, you need to have one or more good reasons why it should be different, such as a new idea or comparative advantage.

When there is a market for an asset, ***you should think long and hard before you conclude that a market price is "wrong."*** Ask yourself what value you are bringing to the asset. That is, how will your use of the asset be different, so that the asset is worth more to you than it is to other people? Alternatively, if an asset will be used more profitably by others because, say, they hold a critical patent, it is probably not good to compete with them for the use of that asset.

TWO-SIDED TRANSACTIONS   Why is the other party to the transaction willing to sell the asset to you or purchase it from you? For example, why is the other party willing to sell you the asset for less than you think it is worth? Remember that the party on the other side of the transaction is acting in his self-interest. Establishing reasons for the difference will help you understand the project you are analyzing.

SIGNALING   Watch the competition. Try to understand competitors' actions. Often, but not always, their actions contain information. The question is what information the actions contain. The actions could simply be blind application of the Behavioral Principle, which can lead to a "herd" mentality. If you are the first to recognize such behavior, you can profit from your alertness.

Finally, *plan ahead.* Undertaking a major project is not as simple as discounting cash flows. It requires management. The capital budgeting/NPV framework is useful for making decisions. It is always correct. The difficulty is in correctly estimating the parameter values. But just because it is difficult or the process becomes complex, don't get discouraged and flip a coin. Use the information you have in the best way you can to decide whether to go ahead, quit, or seek additional information.

Self-Check Questions
1. Which capital budgeting decision criterion is always correct?
2. What is the most promising way to achieve extraordinary returns?
3. True or false? You should *always* think long and hard before concluding that the market price of an asset is wrong.

SUMMARY

In this chapter we focused on actually making capital budgeting decisions. We discussed additional factors that complicate the process. A major topic was interactions among capital budgeting projects, with respect to both investment and financing decisions. The inclusion of some factors, such as options and opportunity costs, can dramatically alter a project's true NPV.

Capital rationing has both potential pitfalls and potential benefits. In its broader application, soft capital rationing is a useful managerial tool for planning.

Use all the relevant information that is available. From one point of view, the capital budgeting process is "not as easy as NPV." However, the decision-making process based on maximizing NPV provides a *framework* for making the best possible capital budgeting decisions.

DECISION SUMMARY

- Options and the opportunity costs they create play a very important role in capital budgeting decisions. We identified the following options:

Expansion option	Postponement option
Price-setting option	Replacement option
Abandonment option	Future investment opportunities

- A decision tree can often be useful for estimating the value of a capital budgeting option.
- "Soft" capital rationing is a useful framework for the planning process. It can be conveniently accomplished by using zero-one integer programming, which is available in many business software packages.

- The profitability index may provide insight into trade-offs under capital rationing.

- Pursuing valuable new ideas and using the firm's comparative advantages are the best ways to achieve extraordinary returns.

- Factors such as the level of expertise among employees, working relationships with other firms, and past experience with machines and/or service can play valuable roles in capital budgeting decisions.

- Watch how other people and firms act—the competition and those on the other side of your transactions.

- Have good reasons why you should be able to get a positive NPV from a project, especially if there is no innovative idea or comparative advantage involved.

- The framework presented in this chapter for making capital budgeting decisions helps structure the decision and can enhance one's understanding of complex situations, even though its application is not as simple as hastily calculating an NPV.

EQUATION SUMMARY

(13.1) $NPV = DCF\text{-}NPV + \text{value of options} - \text{cost of options}$

KEY TERMS

future investment opportunities...404

abandonment option...408

postponement option...410

capital rationing...413

asymmetric information...414

zero-one integer programming...417

"hard" capital rationing...420

"soft" capital rationing...420

post-audit...421

EXERCISES

PROBLEM SET A

A1. Cite and briefly discuss six areas in which to look for options that might be connected with a firm's capital investment opportunities.

A2. Define the term *capital rationing*.

A3. Contrast the concepts of "soft" and "hard" capital rationing.

A4. Briefly describe the technique of zero-one integer programming.

A5. How can capital rationing be used as a tool for managerial planning?

A6. Why might it be important to review and assess (via post-audit) a firm's decisions? What are some of the pitfalls associated with such a task?

A7. Briefly explain how the pricing of a product can interact with a firm's decision whether to expand production capacity.

A8. Why might the consideration of abandonment value be more important for a firm engaging in capital rationing than for firms that simply take on all positive-NPV projects?

A9. With respect to the Smooooth soap expansion example, at what price would RMC be indifferent between the expansion and an increase in the price? Assume that sales will be 10 million bars per year for 10 years at this price.

A10. Cite and briefly discuss six factors that can be especially difficult to quantify for inclusion in a capital budgeting NPV calculation.

PROBLEM SET B

B1. The current level of production for Adam's Gears, Inc. (the original gear) is limited by its production facilities, so Adam is considering an expansion of the firm's production capacity. Because the product has become essentially generic, raising the price is not an option for Adam. There are two types of processes that can be installed for the expansion. One process is considerably more automated than the other, so the operating leverage of the expansion project would be higher if the more automated process were chosen. The total production capacity is the same for the two processes, as is the expected value of the additional gear sales ($1.3 million per year). Process A costs $1.56 million to install and has variable costs of $740,000 per year. Process B costs $390,000 to install and has variable costs of $935,000 per year. Both investments would be depreciated on a straight-line basis to a zero book value over 8 years, but both have a 10-year useful life and expected salvage values of zero at the end of 10 years. Required returns are 15% for process A and 12% for process B. Adam's Gears has a marginal tax rate of 30%. Which, if either, project should Adam undertake?

B2. What is the internal rate of return of a project that has an initial net outflow of 100, a $t = 1$ cash flow of $+250$, and a $t = 2$ cash flow of -156?

B3. On the basis of the Principle of Two-Sided Transactions, what would you tell a firm that has "discovered" a large positive-NPV project that requires the firm to purchase the assets (which are necessary to undertake the project) from another firm?

B4. Billy Bob's Big Eat'n Place has decided to purchase a new cornhusker. Billy Bob will buy one of two machines. Both machines cost $1500. Machine A has a 4-year life, a salvage value of $1000, and expenses of $475 per year. Machine B has a 5-year life, a salvage value of $500, and expenses of $460 per year. Whichever machine is used, revenues for this project are $1200 per year, and machines will be replaced at the end of their lives. Under conditions of straight-line depreciation to the salvage value, a tax rate of 35%, and a discount rate of 20%, which machine should Billy Bob buy? Why?

B5. Cite an example of a situation in which "hard" capital rationing would be appropriate for at least a limited time.

B6. Rework the capital rationing example in the chapter with a constraint of $0.8 million.

B7. Respond to the following comment: "First you tell us the value of a project is its NPV. Now you say that the project's value is its NPV plus the value of its options minus the cost of those options. Which is right?"

B8. Rework the capital rationing example in the chapter with a constraint of $1.8 million.

B9. Consider the following projects (data in thousands):

Project:	A	B	C	D	E	F	G
Initial cost:	10	20	20	15	30	40	20
NPV:	1.1	3.6	0.8	1.6	4.0	3.0	1.4

a. Compute the profitability index for each project.

b. If you were rationed to $115,000 for the initial investment, which projects should you choose?

c. If you were rationed to $95,000 for the initial investment, which projects should you choose?

B10. Suppose you are a section head considering a capital budgeting project. You have examined the proposed project, and having "factored in" every relevant piece of information you can find, you feel the project should be undertaken. After you submit your analysis, the division head informs you that the project has not been approved for funding. Briefly discuss the possible causes of the difference between your opinion of the project and that of upper management.

B11. The owners of Egg Sauce, Ltd. are tired of their business. In fact, they are so *exhausted* that they are considering abandoning the business. The building and land could be sold for $700,000 and would provide an after-tax amount of $640,000. The equipment could be sold at auction for about $55,000, and at that price, they could also claim a tax credit of $5000. The building needs renovation about every 10 years, the before-tax EAC of this periodic maintenance is $40,000, and the after-tax EAC (including the effect of depreciation) is $30,000. The annual revenues minus expenses (including all employee costs) from running Egg Sauce are $200,000 per year, and the firm pays taxes at the rate of 35% on this amount. The owners have determined that the investment's cost of capital is 15%. What is the NPV from abandoning Egg Sauce?

B12. Cite and briefly discuss potential pitfalls encountered in estimating the value of future investment opportunities, in the context of our warning about capital budgeting options.

B13. Ivan's Onion-Brick Restaurant has been very successful for 10 years. However, the growth potential in Ivan's area has declined, and therefore Ivan is contemplating investment in a new business line: consulting. Ivan can enter this new field by purchasing and renovating a small building in downtown Newark at a cost of $100,000, all of which will be depreciated on a straight-line basis to a zero book value over 10 years. Although it will be depreciated to a zero book value, the entire project is expected to be sold off for a salvage value of $65,000 at the end of 8 years. It is estimated that the revenues from the project will be $100,000 per year during the next 2 years and $150,000 in years 3 through 8. Variable costs (including all labor and material) will be 65% of revenues. At the expected revenue levels, Ivan expects to average about $30,000 in receivables, and accounts payable are expected to average $5000. Ivan has determined that the project's cost of capital is 17.31%, and the tax rate is 35%. What is the NPV of this project?

B14. Suppose Upjohn's research team would like to spend $50 million on final development and testing of a new kidney drug. The DCF-NPV is −$10 million. Production cannot begin until testing has been completed, which will take several years, and success is not assured. There is a 40% chance that the research might also give Upjohn the option to produce a related drug that could stimulate hair growth and eliminate baldness.

a. Suppose the hair growth stimulant could be marketable within 3 years and yield CFATs of $5 million per year forever. If the cost of capital for the research project is 15%, should Upjohn proceed with it?

b. What's the minimum option value necessary to justify the research project?

c. What's the minimum level of perpetual annual CFATs needed to justify the research project?

B15. Suppose Chrysler Corporation is considering which of two emission testing devices to buy. Machine A costs $100,000, has a 5-year useful life, and has operating expenses of $40,000 per year. Machine B costs $36,000, has a 6-year useful life, and has operating expenses of $62,000 per year. Both machines will have zero salvage value and revenues of $85,000 per year, and both will be replaced at the end of their lives. Chrysler's tax rate is 35%.

a. Assume a 12% cost of capital for each machine. Which one should Chrysler buy?

b. Suppose instead that Machine A requires a higher cost of capital, 15%, because of its greater operating leverage. Machine B's cost of capital is still 12%. Which machine should Chrysler buy?

B16. Explain how self-interested behavior by Upjohn's research team in Problem B14 could result in an overestimate of the value of the option. What steps could Upjohn take to prevent this from happening?

PROBLEM SET C

C1. We have said that abandonment should always be considered with respect to a firm's current operations. Suppose a firm has the opportunity to sell one of its subsidiaries that is doing poorly. As a general rule, why would a firm *not* be likely to be able to "limit its losses" by selling off such subsidiaries?

C2. How might the agency costs associated with the separation of ownership and control contribute to a tendency for firms to expand rather than raise the prices of their products?

C3. Cite and discuss four broad factors that can cause the NPV of a capital budgeting project to be incorrectly measured.

C4. Use Figure 8-12 (in Chapter 8) to explain why a large number of options connected with a capital budgeting project might not necessarily be any more valuable than a single option on the project.

C5. Rework the capital rationing example with a constraint of $1.2 million.

C6. Capital rationing would not be a shareholder wealth-maximizing strategy in a perfect capital market. How might capital market imperfections (tax asymmetries, information asymmetries, and transaction costs) make capital rationing into a value-enhancing tool?

C7. RMC's Smooooth soap has a marginal cost of $0.387 per bar. Given the demand function we used in the chapter (Demand = 2.538 million/price^3), express total revenue as a function of the quantity demanded. Show that marginal revenue equals marginal cost when the quantity demanded is 12,974,330. Demonstrate that, without production limitations, the optimal price is $0.5805 per bar.

Real-World Application: The Eurotunnel Project

The Eurotunnel Project was begun in 1984 and completed in 1994. It involved the construction of a twin-bore rail tunnel with associated infrastructure, rolling stock ("railroad cars"), and terminals. It joined the United Kingdom's rail system with those of France and the rest of continental Europe. It provides comfortable, fast, frequent, and reliable rail service that is competitive with air travel between London and Paris.

The project was technically straightforward from an engineering standpoint. It was initially expected to cost £4.8 billion (£ stands for British pounds.) The cost estimate was later increased to £6.0 billion. This construction cost was spread more or less evenly over 1986–1993. The sponsors raised £1.0 billion of equity and £5.0 billion of debt. Most of the debt was floating rate (the rate is reset regularly to current market rates).

In return for building the project, the sponsors received authority to operate it through 2041. They would receive all the revenues and pay all the costs. At the end of 2041, the governments of Great Britain and France would become the owners without any further compensation to the project sponsors.

Table 13-8 provides a set of projections for the project.

1. Assume that each item increases by equal annual amounts between 2003 and 2013. Calculate the projected amounts for each year in the period 2004–2012.

2. Make the same assumption as in 1 for the periods 2013–2023, 2023–2033, and 2033–2041. Project the annual CFATs for the period 1994–2041.

3. Assume an average interest cost of 10% APY, a required return on equity of 18% APY, and a marginal income tax rate of 40%.

   a. Calculate the WACC for the project.

   b. Calculate the project's NPV.

   c. Calculate the project's IRR.

   d. Is the project expected to create value?

TABLE 13-8

Cash flow projections for the Eurotunnel Project (millions of pounds sterling).

	1994	1995	1996	1997	1998	1999	2000	2001	2002	2003	2013	2023	2033	2041
Revenue:														
Shuttle	£384	£423	£463	£505	£551	£599	£652	£709	£770	£836	£1763	£3527	£6,682	£10,650
Rail	314	341	368	396	430	459	493	530	569	612	1191	2105	3,641	5,526
Ancillary	64	71	77	85	91	100	109	117	127	138	282	552	1,033	1,648
Total Revenue	762	835	908	986	1072	1158	1254	1356	1466	1586	3236	6184	11,356	17,824
Operating Costs:														
Fixed expenses	88	92	99	107	117	126	137	148	161	174	314	562	1,006	1,604
Variable expenses	57	63	69	76	89	90	98	107	116	130	317	645	1,240	2,000
Total Operating Costs	145	155	168	183	206	216	235	255	277	304	631	1207	2,246	3,604
Depreciation	158	159	160	162	167	169	171	173	176	184	234	271	328	383
Interest, net	351	322	307	291	277	265	234	212	190	171	39	173	370	616
Profit before taxes	108	199	273	350	422	508	614	716	823	927	2410	4879	9,152	14,453
Income taxes	18	38	53	69	88	198	240	279	321	361	934	1893	3,547	5,573
Profit after taxes	£90	£161	£220	£281	£334	£310	£374	£437	£502	£566	£1476	£2986	£5,605	£8,880

Source: Eurotunnel P.L.C./Eurotunnel S.A., *Offer for Sale of 220,000,000 Units with New Warrants* (November 16, 1987), pp. 54–55.

4. What is the impact on the CFATs and the NPV if the project's construction cost increases by
   a. 10% each year, 1986–1993.
   b. 25% each year, 1986–1993.

5. What is the impact on the CFATs and the NPV if the project's total annual revenues decrease by
   a. 10%.
   b. 25%.

6. What is the impact on the CFATs and the NPV if the project's total annual operating costs increase by
   a. 10%.
   b. 25%.

7. What is the impact on the CFATs and the NPV if the construction cost increases by 25%, total annual revenues decrease by 10%, and total annual operating costs increase by 10%?

BIBLIOGRAPHY

Bebchuk, Lucian Arye, and Chaim Fershtman. "Insider Trading and the Management Choice Among Risky Projects," *Journal of Financial and Quantitative Analysis*, 1994, 29(1):1–14.

Berkovitch, Elazar, and E. Han Kim. "Financial Contracting and Leverage Induced Over- and Under-Investment Incentives," *Journal of Finance*, 1990, 45(3):765–794.

Bjerksund, Petter, and Steinar Ekern. "Managing Investment Opportunities Under Price Uncertainty: From 'Last Chance' to 'Wait And See' Strategies," *Financial Management*, 1990, 19(3):65–83.

Blackwell, David W., M. Wayne Marr, and Michael F. Spivey. "Plant-Closing Decisions and the Market Value of the Firm," *Journal of Financial Economics*, 1990, 26(2):277–288.

Brennan, Michael J. "Presidential Address: Latent Assets," *Journal of Finance*, 1990, 45(3):709–730.

Brennan, Michael J., and Eduardo S. Schwartz. "A New Approach to Evaluating Natural Resource Investments," *Midland Corporate Finance Journal*, 1985, 3(Spring):37–47.

Butler, J. S., and Barry Schachter. "The Investment Decision: Estimation Risk and Risk Adjusted Discount Rates," *Financial Management*, 1989, 18(4):13–22.

Campbell, Tim S., and William A. Kracaw. "Corporate Risk Management and the Incentive Effects Of Debt," *Journal of Finance*, 1990, 45(5):1673–1686.

Chan, Su Han, John D. Martin, and John W. Kensinger. "Corporate Research and Development Expenditures and Share Value," *Journal of Financial Economics*, 1990, 26(2):255–276.

Chauvin, Keith W., and Mark Hirschey. "Advertising, R&D Expenditures and the Market Value of the Firm," *Financial Management*, 1993, 22(4):128–140.

Chung, Kee H., and Charlie Charoenwong. "Investment Options, Assets in Place, and the Risk of Stocks," *Financial Management*, 1991, 20(3):21–33.

Cooper, Kerry, and R. Malcolm Richards. "Investing the Alaskan Project Cash Flows: The Sohio Experience," *Financial Management*, 1988, 17(2):58–70.

Copeland, Thomas. "Improving Capital Efficiency," *Financial Management*, 1993, 22(4):25–26.

Denis, David J. "Corporate Investment Decisions and Corporate Control: Evidence from Going-Private Transactions," *Financial Management*, 1992, 21(3):80–94.

Flannery, Mark J., Joel F. Houston, and Subramanyam Venkataraman. "Financing Multiple Investment Projects," *Financial Management*, 1993, 22(2):161–172.

Harris, Milton, and Artur Raviv. "The Capital Budgeting Process, Incentives and Information," *Journal of Finance*, 1996, 51(4):1139–1174.

Hearth, Douglas, and Janis K. Zaima. "Voluntary Corporate Divestitures and Value," *Financial Management*, 1984, 13(1):10–16.

Heinkel, Robert, and Josef Zechner. "The Role of Debt and Preferred Stock as a Solution to Adverse Investment Incentives," *Journal of Financial and Quantitative Analysis*, 1990, 25(1):1–24.

Hirshleifer, David. "Managerial Reputation and Corporate Investment Decisions," *Financial Management*, 1993, 22(2):145–160.

John, Kose, and BaniKanta Mishra. "Information Content of Insider Trading Around Corporate Announcements: The Case of Capital Expenditures," *Journal of Finance*, 1990, 45(3):835–856.

Kasanen, Eero. "Creating Value by Spawning Investment Opportunities," *Financial Management*, 1993, 22(3):251–258.

Kemna, Angelien G. Z. "Case Studies on Real Options," *Financial Management*, 1993, 22(3):259–270.

Kulatilaka, Nalin. "The Value of Flexibility: The Case of a Dual-Fuel Industrial Steam Boiler," *Financial Management*, 1993, 22(3):271–280.

Laber, Gene. "Bond Covenants and Managerial Flexibility: Two Cases of Special Redemption Provisions," *Financial Management*, 1990, 19(1):82–89.

Laughton, David G., and Henry D. Jacoby. "Reversion, Timing Options, and Long-Term Decision-Making," *Financial Management*, 1993, 22(3):225–240.

Long, Michael S., Ileen B. Malitz, and S. Abraham Ravid. "Trade Credit, Quality Guarantees, and Product Marketability," *Financial Management*, 1993, 22(4):117–127.

Maksimovic, Vojislav. "Product Market Imperfections and Loan Commitments," *Journal of Finance*, 1990, 45(5):1641–1654.

McLaughlin, Robyn, and Robert A. Taggart, Jr. "The Opportunity Cost of Using Excess Capacity," *Financial Management*, 1992, 21(2):12–23.

Merton, Robert C., and Zvi Bodie. "On the Management of Financial Guarantees," *Financial Management*, 1992, 21(4):87–109.

Opler, Tim C., and Sheridan Titman. "Financial Distress and Corporate Performance," *Journal of Finance*, 1994, 49(3):1015–1040.

Sicherman, Neil W., and Richard H. Pettway. "Wealth Effects for Buyers and Sellers of the Same Divested Assets," *Financial Management*, 1992, 21(4):119–128.

Smit, Han T. J., and L. A. Ankum. "A Real Options and Game-Theoretic Approach to Corporate Investment Strategy Under Competition," *Financial Management*, 1993, 22(3):241–250.

Smith, Clifford W., Jr., and Ross L. Watts. "The Investment Opportunity Set and Corporate Financing, Dividend, and Compensation Policies," *Journal of Financial Economics*, 1992, 32(3):263–292.

Statman, Meir, and James F. Sepe. "Project Termination Announcements and the Market Value of the Firm," *Financial Management*, 1989, 18(4):74–81.

Thakor, Anjan V. "Corporate Investments and Finance," *Financial Management*, 1993, 22(2):135–144.

Triantis, Alexander J., and James E. Hodder. "Valuing Flexibility as a Complex Option," *Journal of Finance*, 1990, 45(2):549–566.

Trigeorgis, Lenos. "The Nature of Option Interactions and the Valuation of Investments with Multiple Real Options," *Journal of Financial and Quantitative Analysis*, 1993, 28(1):1–20.

Trigeorgis, Lenos. "Real Options and Interactions with Financial Flexibility," *Financial Management*, 1993, 22(3):202–224.

Trigeorgis, Lenos, and Scott P. Mason. "Valuing Managerial Flexibility," *Midland Corporate Finance Journal*, 1987, 5(Spring):14–21.

Viswanath, P. V. "Adjusting Capital Budgeting Rules for Information Asymmetry," *Financial Management*, 1993, 22(4):22–23.

Vogt, Stephen C. "The Cash Flow/Investment Relationship: Evidence from U.S. Manufacturing Firms," *Financial Management*, 1994, 23(2):3–20.

Woods, John C., and Maury R. Randall. "The Net Present Value of Future Investment Opportunities: Its Impact on Shareholder Wealth and Implications for Capital Budgeting Theory," *Financial Management*, 1989, 18(2),85–92.

Williams, Joseph. "Efficient Signalling with Dividends, Investment, and Stock Repurchases," *Journal of Finance*, 1988, 43(3):737–747.

Part IV

CAPITAL STRUCTURE AND DIVIDEND POLICY

Whether a firm's choice of *capital structure* (its mix of debt and equity) and dividend policy can affect its value—and if so, how it can—is controversial. Practitioners certainly behave as though these decisions were important. However, the relative significance of the factors involved continues to be debated. What we do know is that how a firm implements these policies can convey useful information to investors and thus affect the firm's value, even in an otherwise *efficient capital market.*

In an efficient capital market, the prices of securities reflect all available information and adjust fully and quickly to new information. Chapter 14 explains why it makes sense that capital markets should be efficient. We will see that competition to profit from new information lies at the heart of capital market efficiency. We will also explain how three persistent *capital market imperfections* interfere with capital market efficiency.

Chapters 15 through 18 explore how firms choose their capital structure and dividend policy in an efficient capital market. We will show how capital market imperfections can cause a firm's capital structure to affect its value and will outline a practical method of managing capital structure.

However, also as with capital structure, there are conflicting viewpoints about dividend policy in practice. We will explain why capital market imperfections make dividend policy matter and will outline a practical method of managing dividend policy.

CAPITAL MARKET EFFICIENCY: EXPLANATION AND IMPLICATIONS

OBJECTIVES

After studying this chapter, you should be able to

1. Explain why it makes sense that capital markets should be efficient.

2. Describe how the Principles of Self-Interested Behavior, Two-Sided Transactions, Signaling, and Risk-Return Trade-Off combine with the similarity among financial assets, low transaction costs, and intense competition to make capital markets efficient.

3. Describe a perfect capital market in terms of seven formal conditions, or more simply as a market that has no *arbitrage* opportunities.

4. Cite and explain the impact of the three most significant ongoing capital market imperfections: asymmetric taxes, asymmetric information, and transaction costs.

Capital market efficiency means that the prices of securities traded in capital markets reflect all available information and that they adjust fully and quickly to new information. We described this concept in Chapter 3 but postponed an explanation of why it makes sense that capital markets *should be* efficient. This chapter explains why. You will see how the Principle of Capital Market Efficiency is a by-product of many people applying other principles of finance to the capital market environment.

Capital markets evolved to perform several important functions. To explain capital market efficiency, we must first examine these functions and see how capital markets should operate. We can then understand how (1) new information becomes reflected in securities prices, (2) transaction costs can inhibit this process, and (3) information about differences in value can create opportunities for profit. The first person to recognize and take advantage of such an opportunity can indeed profit but will, at the same time, eliminate the difference (*and* the opportunity). The competition to find and take advantage of such opportunities lies at the heart of capital market efficiency.

CAPITAL MARKET EFFICIENCY AND THE PRINCIPLES OF FINANCE

◆ *Self-Interested Behavior*: Self-interested capital market transactions force market prices toward being fair prices.

◆ *Two-Sided Transactions*: Intense capital market competition to get and use information to take advantage of arbitrage opportunities eliminates such opportunities.

◆ *Signaling*: Information in the transactions of others can be valuable, such as providing an accurate measure of current market value or information about expected future value.

◆ *Risk-Return Trade-Off*: Differences between financial assets are measured primarily in terms of risk and return. Investors choose the highest return for a given risk level.

◆ *Capital Market Efficiency*: The fact that people apply the Principles of Self-Interested Behavior, Two-Sided Transactions, and Signaling to an environment characterized by similar financial assets, low transaction costs, and intense competition leads to capital market efficiency.

◆ *Valuable Ideas*: New ideas can provide value when first introduced, even in an efficient capital market.

◆ *Comparative Advantage*: Capital market efficiency enables a firm to concentrate its primary efforts on its comparative advantage, rather than on its day-to-day financing.

14.1 AN ANALOGY

The idea that the capital markets are so efficient that they can be thought of as *perfect* can be hard to accept at first. But it is a very useful way of looking at the world, because it yields a number of important insights. One is that investors cannot consistently earn abnormally high risk-adjusted returns, other than through extraordinarily good luck. This rather surprising implication has led to a great deal of criticism of the idea of perfect capital markets and to much doubt about the theory even though extensive evidence suggests that capital markets are efficient. We hope the following analogy will help you see the logic of capital market efficiency.

Efficiency refers to the amount of wasted energy. Efficient machines do not waste much energy. Friction—the "stickiness" between things—is the main reason for the waste of energy in a machine. Lubricants, such as oil, are used to increase the efficiency of machines by reducing friction that wastes energy. The more efficient a machine is, the better it is. So too for capital markets.

We can think of a capital market as being like a machine. In a capital market, **frictions** are the "stickiness" in making transactions. They are the total "hassle," including the time, effort, money, and associated tax effects of gathering information and making a transaction such as buying stock or borrowing money. As with machines, efficiency is critical. Perfect efficiency represents an ideal, because unavoidable frictions keep a system (machine or market) from being perfectly efficient.

Energy Conservation

An important law in the physical sciences, the law of energy conservation, states that energy is neither created nor destroyed. Instead, energy is transformed from one form into another within a system. This law implies that no machine can be more than 100% efficient. That is, the energy output from a machine can never exceed the energy input to the machine. Simply stated, you can't get something for nothing! In the financial world, schemes that seem to provide more output than input are known as scams. They are illegal, yet they persist. We will talk more about them later.

Refrigeration provides an example of the limits of efficiency. Suppose it's a hot summer day and you are a poor graduate student who can't afford the electric bills for running an air conditioner, let alone its initial cost. But on this particular day it is so hot you can't stand it. You go into the kitchen and open the refrigerator door to feel a blast of cool, refreshing air across your face. Thinking you have solved the problem, you decide to stay in the kitchen with the refrigerator door open. What will happen?

A refrigerator works much like an air conditioner, so why shouldn't it be able to cool the kitchen? A refrigerator takes heat from inside itself and puts that heat outside itself. But outside itself is still *inside* the kitchen, so the kitchen will not be cooled at all. In fact, because a refrigerator is substantially less than 100% efficient, energy escapes in the form of heat with each transfer. Thus the kitchen will actually heat up if you leave the refrigerator door open!

The law of energy conservation prevents a machine's efficiency from exceeding 100%. Machines with an efficiency equal to 100% don't exist either, because energy is lost to friction. If the refrigerator were 100% efficient, we could say that the transaction (leaving the door open) was costless (made no difference) in terms of increased temperature. But as we have said, transactions are not costless.

Frictions in the Capital Markets: Transaction Costs

Our analogy with the capital markets is that the transfer of assets from one party to another is like a transfer of heat from one area to another within the kitchen. The total wealth of the parties is like the temperature in the kitchen, with lower temperature corresponding to greater wealth. It makes no more sense to say that the total wealth of a group of people can be increased by the simple transfer of assets among them than it does to say that opening the refrigerator door can cool the kitchen! The only thing involved is a transfer from one to another.

It is certainly possible to make one individual better off at the expense of another individual, just as it is possible to decrease the temperature inside the refrigerator by increasing the temperature outside it. In other words, it is possible to make unbalanced transfers between people. (For example, we would not protest if you paid us $1000 for an asset that is worth only $800.) But the wealth of the two individuals, taken together, cannot be increased by a transfer between them, any more than the kitchen can be cooled by a transfer of heat within its boundaries.

To press our analogy a little further, just as the kitchen will heat up as a result of wasted energy from many heat transfers, the total wealth of two parties will be wasted by many transfers of assets between them. The waste occurs because of factors that we classify as transaction costs, asymmetric taxes, or asymmetric information. **Transaction costs** are the time, effort, and money necessary to make a transaction, including such things as commission fees and the cost of physically moving an asset from seller to buyer. We will describe and discuss the other two later in the chapter. These three factors are very much like friction: They slow down the process and waste resources (energy).

Self-Check Questions

1. True or false? Investors cannot consistently earn abnormally high risk-adjusted returns in an efficient capital market.
2. True or false? Transferring assets from one party to another cannot increase the parties' combined wealth.
3. What are transaction costs? How can they reduce the combined wealth of the two parties to a transaction?

14.2 EFFICIENCY, LIQUIDITY, AND VALUE

The concept of **capital market efficiency** is linked to the concept of wasted wealth. An efficient capital market allows the transfer of assets with little loss of wealth. Capital market efficiency results from market prices reflecting all available information so that prices are *fair*. But what does it mean to reflect all available information?

Three forms of capital market efficiency have been defined. The **strong form of capital market efficiency** requires that prices reflect *all* information that exists about the asset's value. This includes every bit of information known to anyone in the world that has any relevance whatsoever to the asset's value. The **semi-strong form of capital market efficiency** requires only that prices fully reflect *publicly available* information. Publicly available information is a subset of all the information that exists about an asset's value. The **weak form of capital market efficiency** requires only that prices fully reflect the information *contained in past asset market prices*, the prices at which assets have been exchanged. Past asset prices are a small subset of the publicly available information about an asset's value.

Figure 14-1 shows the relationships among various sets of information pertaining to the strong, semi-strong, and weak forms of capital market efficiency. Figure 14-1 illustrates how the information sets are nested, or contained within one another.

The Principle of Capital Market Efficiency refers to the semi-strong form of capital market efficiency. Thus when we use the phrase *all available information*, we mean all publicly available information. It seems to us that infamous insider-trading scandals over the years provide sufficient evidence to conclude that the capital markets are not efficient in the strong form.

The Reason for Capital Markets: Liquidity

Historically, society has evolved by developing new ideas and procedures that facilitate life, retaining the best and discarding the rest. In ancient times, individuals were responsible for meeting all their own needs. Over time, cooperative societies developed, and individuals specialized in certain tasks. This change embodied the initial recognition and application of the Principle of Comparative Advantage. Still later, a barter society developed, in which individuals exchanged goods and services to meet their needs. Finally, money was used to *represent* the goods and services—to collect and store resources—because it is so easily exchanged. Money has proved so useful that today its logic is rarely questioned.

To make a physical comparison again, money allows for the easy transfer of resources, much as liquids can flow through a tube better than solids. The rate at which a liquid flows through a tube depends on how thick the liquid is. This analogy leads to the idea of asset *liquidity*, which we discussed in Chapter 2. Liquidity reflects how easily assets are transferred without loss of value. Cash is the most liquid asset, because it is most easily transferred from

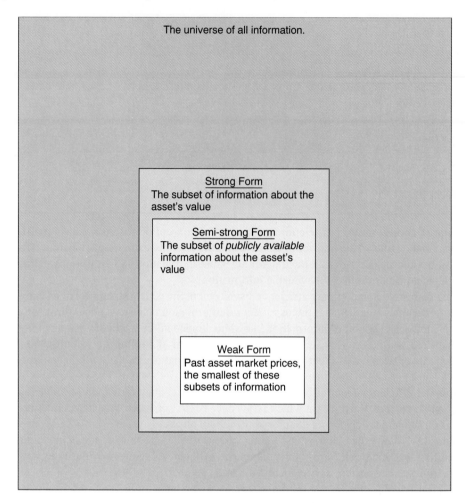

The universe of all information.

Strong Form
The subset of information about the asset's value

Semi-strong Form
The subset of *publicly available* information about the asset's value

Weak Form
Past asset market prices, the smallest of these subsets of information

FIGURE 14-1

The universe of relevant information and, within it, the nested subsets of information about an asset's value that are required by the strong, semi-strong, and weak forms of capital market efficiency.

one entity to another without loss of value. Real property, such as a building, is a less liquid type of asset. Considerable time, effort, and money can be spent in finding a buyer willing to pay a fair price for a building. Alternatively, a substantially reduced price may attract a buyer quickly. Either way, it can be costly.

Liquidity is the primary reason why money is used. Money enables us to exchange our efforts for another person's efforts without having to trade our services directly. Money also makes it possible to exchange one asset for another readily.

EXAMPLE

Exchanging Shares of Exxon for GM Stock

Imagine that you own 100 shares of Exxon. You would rather have your money invested in GM stock (perhaps because you believe that oil and gas prices are about to drop). Although you might be open to the possibility of trading the Exxon shares for General Motors shares, it is generally much easier to sell the Exxon shares for cash and then to use that cash to buy the GM shares. This saves your having to find a trading partner who wants exactly what you are offering (100 Exxon shares) and who offers exactly what you want (GM shares of corresponding value). ■

The stock market makes the stocks more liquid. Without that market, you would have to incur higher transaction costs—extra time, effort, and money. The stock market reduces the total transaction cost. In many markets, such as the New York Stock Exchange (NYSE), there is a **market maker** who increases liquidity by handling transactions in a particular asset. For example, when your order to sell 100 Exxon shares and your order to buy GM stock are carried out on the NYSE, a **specialist** (market maker) handling each stock, rather than another individual investor like yourself, may be on the other side of the transaction.

Most markets are set up to increase liquidity by reducing the transaction costs of asset transfer. Think about what you would do if there were no stock market and you wanted to sell your 100 Exxon shares. One possibility is to consider the Principle of Valuable Ideas: Set up a stock market yourself, provide a service to other people, and earn money. If you were the first to set up such a market, you might earn a positive NPV. Setting up a new market to provide liquidity for particular assets may be a valuable idea. Creating a viable new market provides a service that might earn a positive NPV. Creating a viable market can also make the Principle of Capital Market Efficiency come true.

Of course, this is exactly why capital markets exist. There are real benefits to the participants, which can be exploited for profit by those clever enough to do so.

An Unexpected Benefit: A Measure of Value

Although markets are created in response to the need for liquidity, there is an additional benefit when market transactions are made public. Such transaction prices provide a measure of value that is visible to everyone.

Pricing Treasury Bills

EXAMPLE

Suppose you are going to invest in a 3-month "$10,000" U.S. Treasury bill. Such securities are sold on a discount basis. This means that they make no interest payments but simply pay their stated amount at *maturity*. Your return is the difference between what you pay and the maturity value.

Knowing this, what price should you be willing to pay for the Treasury bill? There are a couple of ways to establish a fair price. You could call a broker and ask for the latest trading price. Or you could look in the finance or business section of a newspaper, such as the *Wall Street Journal*, to find yesterday's closing price. Which price would be likely to be more accurate? The latest price is the more accurate one, because it reflects any new information that has come to light since yesterday's close. Of course, yesterday's closing price is generally a very good approximation of the security's current fair price. ■

Most capital market transactions are reported publicly, and the information is conveniently available shortly after the transactions take place. This means that fair market prices for many securities are freely observable at any time.

Thus if you want to know what a share of IBM is worth, find out the most recent actual transaction price, and you will have an accurate estimate of a share's value. After all, two parties actually transferred a share at that price. They didn't just talk about it or *offer* to buy or sell it. Moreover, the price isn't an average of many transactions from the last few weeks or months. The parties actually transferred shares within the last few minutes, and either one of them would have been willing for *you* to have been the other party in the transaction. (In most cases, they would not have known the difference if you had been!)

The result is that even though liquidity is the main reason to create a market, a "spin-off" benefit of a public market is that it provides an inexpensive, fast, and accurate method of estimating fair prices: current market values.

14.3 ARBITRAGE: STRIVING FOR EFFICIENCY

In the last section we saw why capital markets were created. Now let's turn to their operation. In this and the next section, we will present two concepts that are very important to the operation of the capital markets: arbitrage and signaling.

Arbitrage: Get Rich Quick?

Let's assume that the current price of a security in one market differs from the current price of that same security in a different market. Assume too that this information is available to one or more market participants. Someone who possesses this information can exploit it for profit by engaging in what is called arbitrage. As we said in Chapter 3, **arbitrage** refers to buying an asset in one market for the purpose of immediately reselling it, at a higher price, in another market.[1]

Arbitrage is an important factor in the efficient operation of any market, but especially a capital market. When people first learn about arbitrage, their usual reaction is to say that it sounds wonderful but that they are skeptical about the existence of such opportunities. In spite of their (very healthy) skepticism, market prices do in fact differ between two markets for short periods.

For example, consider an asset that is traded in two markets, such as shares of Exxon common stock. If Exxon shares were trading at a higher price on the Pacific Stock Exchange than on the NYSE, it would be possible to buy Exxon shares on the NYSE and resell them on the Pacific Stock Exchange for more than you paid for them.

When there is a price differential, arbitrage is possible by simply buying at the lower price and selling at the higher. The transactions, taken together, "lock in" a profit equal to the price differential multiplied by the number of shares simultaneously purchased and sold. This profit is "riskless," because the shares purchased and sold offset one another exactly. There are people who earn a living exploiting arbitrage opportunities that they observe while watching different capital markets that trade the same asset.

A DEFINITION OF A PERFECT MARKET Later in the chapter, we will list seven conditions that create a **perfect capital market**. But without getting into detail now, a convenient

---

[1] We start by using the dictionary definition of *arbitrage*, or what may be termed "riskless arbitrage." The term *arbitrage* is also used in the sense of "risk arbitrage" to describe the purchase of shares of firms that are expected to increase in value in the future for reasons such as becoming a takeover target. Such purchases involve a large element of speculation. We compare arbitrage and speculation later.

way to define a perfect capital market is simply to say it is a market in which there are never any arbitrage opportunities.

Competition: If It's That Easy . . .

Now that you know what arbitrage is and that opportunities for earning a riskless arbitrage profit do exist, if you are like many of us, you may be considering applying the Principle of Self-Interested Behavior to participate in such a delightful process. You're not alone. Consequently, how often do you think trading price differences exist for the same asset between two markets? And when they exist, how large do you think the price differences are?

That's right—not very often, and not very large. And the larger the difference you are looking for, the less likely it is to occur. Rather than thinking this one through, we could have used a shortcut, the Principle of Capital Market Efficiency. Perhaps you were already applying it with your skepticism when we first told you about arbitrage.

There is an important implication of investor arbitrage. Suppose one investor discovers an arbitrage opportunity and trades securities to take advantage of it. When other investors become aware of this opportunity, the competition will eventually eliminate it.

A few years ago, Edward O. Thorp, a "onetime university professor and mathematical whiz" who had developed strategies for exploiting price discrepancies between a firm's common stock and securities that were convertible into its common stock, closed his money management business after more than 20 years in the business and returned $200 million of his clients' money. Mr. Thorp had published some of his ideas in a book entitled *Beat the Market* and had set up a successful investment partnership that traded securities using his arbitrage strategies. Mr. Thorp said he was withdrawing from the money management business because his ideas had become so widespread that only those investors with the lowest transaction costs could still use his arbitrage strategies profitably.

Competition among people engaged in arbitrage is actually an important contributing factor to capital market efficiency. The very existence of people, **arbitrageurs**, who are constantly looking for arbitrage opportunities ensures that prices for a particular asset will not differ very much among the various markets where the asset is traded. If it is easy to access both markets, then there is not much need for arbitrageurs. People making a transaction would buy or sell their assets for the best price provided by the two markets. When two markets are not easily accessed simultaneously, then it is worthwhile for arbitrageurs to incur the cost of accessing them. In doing so, they make transactions that push the two markets toward identical prices for a given asset. Of course, in time, competition among arbitrageurs will drive their NPV to zero. (Careful now—that doesn't mean the arbitrageur has a zero profit.) *When the NPV is zero, participants are getting exactly a fair return for the effort they are expending and an appropriate positive return for the risk they are taking on, and capital market efficiency is enforced.*

Another important factor that contributes to the competitive environment of the capital markets is the similarity of financial assets. Financial assets are very similar. For example, consider a simple financial asset, a $10 bill. Would you exchange one $10 bill for another? Of course. Would you exchange a $10 bill for two $5 bills? Certainly. For the most part, people are indifferent to such exchanges. Forms of money are very homogeneous. Almost any positive incentive (such as additional money) will induce people to exchange one form of money for another.

Similarity applies to securities as well as money. Let's say there are two securities that are exactly alike except for their expected future return. The Principle of Risk-Return Trade-Off says that investors will choose the alternative with the higher expected return. Investors are fairly indifferent to owning shares in one firm versus another, except for differences in return and risk. For example, most people do not have strong feelings, beyond the financial considerations of return and risk, about whether they own shares of stock in IBM or in Xerox. Corporate bonds are also similar to government bonds, except that corporate bonds are riskier. For that matter, bonds are relatively similar to stocks, except that stocks are riskier.

When you think about it, you can see that financial assets are more similar to one another than are physical assets such as, say, houses. As a result, investors in financial assets can concentrate on the risk and return of an asset. When investors find two identical (or even very similar) investment opportunities, they will make transactions to increase the return on their investments, just as arbitrageurs do. Therefore, even though not all investors are primarily pursuing arbitrage opportunities, arbitrageurs must compete with the investing population as well as with each other.

Limits to Arbitrage: Transaction Costs

We need to reconcile the occasional arbitrage opportunities that do exist with capital market efficiency. How far apart do prices have to be for arbitrage opportunities to exist?

Conceptually, any difference in price is an opportunity. In practice, however, transaction costs are not zero. Therefore, if the difference between the prices is too small, arbitrageurs will not make a transaction because it will not be profitable. As you have probably already guessed, an arbitrage transaction is worth making only if the benefit exceeds the cost of the transaction.

As with any business, arbitrageurs have two types of transaction costs: fixed and variable. Variable transaction costs are specific to a particular arbitrage opportunity. For example, suppose a stock sells for 31⅛ in London and 31⅜ in New York, and that it will cost you $\frac{1}{16}$ to buy in London, $\frac{1}{16}$ to sell in New York, and $\frac{1}{16}$ for transfer and communications costs. Consequently, it will cost you $\frac{3}{16}$ to make ¼ point. If you can buy and sell 1000 shares, you make $62.50. Sounds good, because you will have more than covered your variable costs. You will have earned a riskless arbitrage profit.

But what about the cost of setting up your office and communication lines, educating yourself, and paying your support staff? These are fixed transaction costs, and they must be considered, too.

When two or more markets for the same asset exist, the differential between trading prices for the asset will exceed the variable cost of making a transaction only for a brief period. This period will be only as long as it takes arbitrageurs to buy and sell enough assets to reduce the price differential to less than the variable costs of making another transaction.

Because of arbitrage, *the price differential between markets is generally smaller than the variable transaction costs* for an asset traded in two markets.

How do variable transaction costs compare among different assets? How do the transaction costs of buying a used car in Los Angeles, transporting it to Chicago, and selling it there compare with the costs of buying, transporting, and selling a share (or 1000 shares) of stock? Unless you have someone who wants to drive across the United States from Los Angeles to Chicago, getting a car between those points can be costly in time (yours or that of someone you pay) as well as in gas and vehicle wear. In contrast, the ownership of shares of stock can be transferred quickly and easily via telecommunications, and all at a fairly low cost.

For several reasons, transaction costs for buying and selling financial assets are low compared to transaction costs for physical assets. The most important reason is simply the physical difference. A few sheets of paper, or instructions typed at a computer keyboard, are much easier to transport than 3000 pounds of automobile. A second important reason is market size. An enormous number of financial assets change hands every day. When many transactions take place, the fixed transaction costs are less on a per-transaction basis, because they can be spread over more transactions.

Because the transaction costs for financial assets are so low (in both relative and absolute terms), price differentials for financial assets in different markets are tiny compared with price differentials for physical assets in different markets. Even on a percentage basis, price differentials for financial assets are relatively small because of low transaction costs and high competition among arbitrageurs. The low price differentials among markets reflect capital market efficiency.

Arbitrage versus Speculation

Let's return to our car example. Could we risklessly arbitrage used cars between areas of the country that have different market values for the same type of car?[2] Probably not, because the cars might have to be at both the purchase and the sale points for careful inspection. This would eliminate the possibility of simultaneous purchase and sale. Literally speaking, a transaction that involves holding an asset for any length of time is not riskless arbitrage.

We cannot be specific about the time that determines where arbitrage leaves off and speculation begins. But we can say that when the asset is held for any positive time, risk is introduced into the transaction. The longer the time between purchase and sale, the greater the risk. People who buy and sell a particular asset are not arbitrageurs but traders. **Traders** are people who engage in short-term speculation.

The importance of the continuum from arbitrage to speculation is that in many cases, traders anticipate price changes using less than perfect information. Traders are involved in "small gambles." But these gambles are investments, because they average a positive return. After all, if the average return were not positive, the trader could not continue to do business while sustaining losses.

"Slightly" speculative transactions, which anticipate price changes, smooth the transition from one price level to another. New information does not generally occur in a complete and correct form. The first inkling of new information may come as a rumor. One trader's talent for determining more quickly than other traders which rumors are true and which are false is valuable, because facts can translate directly into price changes that can be turned into profit.

Some talents cannot be taught, and interpreting information may be one of them. But we can point out that some actions carry with them subtle implications about a firm's current condition or its prospects for the future. This brings us to the topic of the next section.

Self-Check Questions

1. What is arbitrage? How does it contribute to capital market efficiency?
2. How long do arbitrage opportunities exist in an efficient capital market?
3. What is a perfect capital market? How long do arbitrage opportunities exist in such a market?
4. For an asset traded in two markets, what is the relationship between the price differential and the variable transaction costs?
5. Which type of asset has a smaller price differential between markets, common stocks or used motor homes?
6. What is the difference between arbitrage and speculation?

14.4 SIGNALING AND INFORMATION GATHERING

Underlying the Principle of Capital Market Efficiency is an important concept: Market participants react quickly to events that convey useful information. This quick reaction is due in part to the Signaling Principle, which states that actions convey information.

---

[2] This is not a hypothetical example. Auto brokers are extensively involved in this process.

Recall that *signaling* refers to using actual behavior to infer things you cannot observe directly or find out in other ways. Signaling involves inferences concerning asymmetric information. **Asymmetric information** is information that is known to some people but not to others. Actions convey the asymmetric information and in so doing eliminate it. Asymmetric information is a second imperfection, another one of the significant frictions in the capital markets.

In Chapter 17 we will discuss the signaling aspects of dividend announcements. In an efficient market, participants react to the information signals contained in such announcements by making buy and sell decisions. Executing the purchase and sale transactions will cause securities prices to change, which is the mechanism by which the information content of the signals is reflected in securities prices.

What Is Signaling?

In our discussion of the Signaling Principle in Chapter 3, we introduced the concept of *adverse selection*. Adverse selection is a process of inferring negative information about a product or service. Adverse selection can discourage offering "good-quality" products or services, because doing so may give an apparently negative signal. Consider the following example.

EXAMPLE

Selling a Used Car

Let's say you decide to sell your used car. The question for a buyer is *why* you want to sell the car. One possible reason for selling it is that it does not run well. In that case, buyers would be foolish to buy it. If the car is in fact a good car that buyers would like to buy, why should you want to sell it?

This line of reasoning leads to the problem of adverse selection. Simply offering the car for sale can be a negative signal. How negative the signal is depends on how often sellers voluntarily sell good cars. And used-car prices will reflect this frequency.

If the only reason for selling a car were that it is not worth fixing, all used cars would be worthless. Of course, we have all heard stories about used cars turning out to be exceptionally good as well as exceptionally bad. Because there are reasons for selling a car other than it's not being worth the trouble to repair, and because people have different levels of tolerance for car trouble, not all used cars are worthless. There is a chance that buying a used car will turn out well, and there is a chance that it will turn out poorly.

Many people who are not skilled in determining the quality of used cars always buy new cars to protect themselves from this problem. Others, skilled in evaluating the quality of a used car, put that skill to use and pay less for their dependable transportation. The savings represent the difficulty and cost—in time, effort, and money—of obtaining and using this valuable skill. ∎

There have been many applications of the concept of signaling to financial transactions. Most applications are too technical to be detailed here, but it should be obvious that many daily events can be thought of as information signals.

Firms make decisions nearly every day that provide an almost continuous flow of information about their current operations and intended future direction. For example, decisions about new equipment and raw materials, such as how much to buy and from whom to buy, occur regularly. Other less frequent but telling information signals concern financing, such as decisions to issue new stock or bonds or to change the quarterly dividend paid to stockholders. Still other signals are decisions made not by the firm itself but by people outside the firm, such as decisions to buy the firm's products.

Conditional Signals: Watching Management

An important thing to note about information signals is that some are sent intentionally and others inadvertently. Suppose you are listening to a chief executive officer (CEO) of a corporation speak about the firm's prospects for the future. The CEO paints a rosy picture, outlining plans for expanded production facilities to handle the projected increase in sales that will result in "big profits" for the next several years. The CEO is dynamic, enthusiastic, and persuasive. But a week later, you find out that the CEO sold 10,000 of the 15,000 shares she owned just 3 days after you heard the better-things-are-coming speech. How would it make you feel to learn that the CEO sold that stock? After hearing about the stock sale, what do you think the CEO really believed about the firm's prospects for the next several years?

Now, it is possible that the CEO merely sold the 10,000 shares to pay for a new yacht and that the sale did not reflect negatively on the firm's prospects. However, most of us would consider it a negative signal if a person sold an asset while telling everyone else to buy it because of its investment value. Share sales by insiders are often regarded as a leading indicator of an imminent worsening of a firm's profitability.

That negative signal was fairly easy to read, but there are many other signals that can be positive or negative, depending on additional facts or decisions. For example, when a firm announced that it planned to borrow money, you would want to know why. Without any further information, that announcement cannot be considered positive or negative. Borrowing can be a positive signal of new investment opportunities, a negative signal of low sales or poor management, or a neutral signal of the scheduled replacement of worn-out equipment.

Interpreting Signals: A Very Valuable Talent

Most information is easily and costlessly available if you just wait long enough. IBM's sales data for last year are easily obtained from the library. But knowing what IBM's sales were for last year is not going to help you determine whether shares of IBM's stock will sell for more or less in the future than they do now. Some information, such as the number of shares owned by management and how much money a firm has borrowed, is published on a regular basis (every quarter or year), as required by the Securities and Exchange Commission (SEC). However, just like the sales figure from the library, it is unlikely that this information can be profitably used *after* it is published.

Traders, as well as "speculators," who own stock for longer periods, are constantly searching for new information that will tell them whether shares of a stock are going to increase or decrease in value in the future so that they will know whether to buy or sell the shares now. Competition is intense to obtain information before prices reflect that information. The more often a trader or speculator obtains valuable new information first, the more money he makes. (Such competition has led some people to breach ethical and legal standards, creating insider-trading scandals.)

Of course, the more current that information is, the more difficult and costly it is to obtain. For example, a trader dealing in shares of Wal-Mart's stock might pay someone to check local stores for the number of customers at various times and to make statistical estimates of current sales, so that by the time Wal-Mart announces the latest sales figures, the trader has already anticipated any change in share price that is due to higher- or lower-than-expected sales. Profits that a trader earns result from her having incurred the cost—in time, effort, and money—of gathering information and using it to make informed trades.

When considering information like recent sales figures or levels of borrowing, we are dealing with "hard facts." However, just as there is a continuum from arbitrage to speculation, there is a continuum for the quality of information. That continuum might be described, from one end to the other, as starting with hard information and moving through interpretive information, speculation, and intuition to blind guess.

We interpret information by using inductive reasoning. Most of us are familiar with **deductive reasoning**, wherein a *general* fact provides accurate information about a *specific* situation. For example, if a friend tells you he just got a new cat, you can predict that the animal has four legs and a tail with a high probability of being correct.

In contrast, **inductive reasoning** attempts the reverse: to use a *specific* situation to make *general* conclusions. Therefore, accuracy depends on having sufficient information. For example, suppose a friend tells you he has just brought home an animal that has four legs and a tail. Without more information, making an accurate prediction of what kind of animal your friend got is virtually impossible. The pieces of information that are uncovered for use with inductive reasoning may be obvious, such as the fact that your friend had planned to visit a person whose cat recently had kittens. However, the missing pieces of information are often quite subtle, such as a few cat hairs on your friend's knee.

Because information can be drawn from truly obscure facts and can be interpreted in many different ways, a person's talent for dealing with new or uncertain information is like any other talent a person might have—say in music, sports, or art. To some extent it is possible to teach people how to go about interpreting new or uncertain information. But as with other activities, there are differences in ability among people despite identical training. Exceptional talent for dealing with new or uncertain information and for interpreting information signals correctly has great value. And even for those of us who do not possess that unusual talent, it is still important to understand the process.

Self-Check Questions

1. What does the term *signaling* refer to? How does the information that signaling conveys get reflected in securities prices?
2. What is asymmetric information? How is signaling useful in eliminating asymmetric information?
3. Why is new information about a firm whose shares are actively traded unlikely to create profitable opportunities after it is published?

14.5 COLLECTIVE WISDOM

In this section we will learn how competition for information can make stock prices good predictors of the future. With many different ways to interpret new and uncertain information, and with so many people competing for information, could one person be consistently right? The answer is no. But we can obtain information from the **collective wisdom**. The collective wisdom is the combination of all the individual opinions about a stock's value. It is the *net* opinion that results from intense competition, and it is more accurate than any single assessment.

Available Information and Stock Price Movement

We have said that market prices reflect all available information. A logical implication of this statement is that any transaction you make in an efficient market has a zero NPV (that is, the cost equals the value). So why bother to invest? The answer is that a zero NPV includes a profit that is appropriate for the risk of the investment. The reason one bothers to invest, then, is to earn a profit (and perhaps a large profit, if you are willing to take on considerable risk).

Another important implication of market prices reflecting all available information concerns the movement of prices. *Price movements are random in an efficient market.* If you think about it, this *must* be the case. If price movements could be predicted before new information arrived, the information would already be here! Instead, price movements take place only after someone can better assess an asset's value on the basis of new information. Thus, because price movements depend on the arrival of information and because information arrives randomly, price movements must reflect that randomness.

It is important to distinguish between anticipated and unanticipated new information. Some information, such as earnings and dividend announcements, is available at regular intervals, such as quarterly. It is therefore anticipated by market participants, who will use whatever other information is available to formulate expectations and may then enter into securities transactions in anticipation of the release of the new information. As a result, in an efficient market, if traders were skilled enough to anticipate the new information perfectly, market prices would fully reflect the new information even *before* the official announcement. When the new information is not perfectly anticipated—as when market participants expect an earnings increase but a decrease occurs instead—there will be price adjustments both before and after the announcement.

Other information cannot be anticipated. An example is a tornado that destroys a firm's production facilities; another is the discovery of a revolutionary product. The occurrence of such events is essentially random in nature. In such cases, the market can react only after the event occurs and is disclosed.

In between the two extremes, there are varying degrees of anticipation. For example, a tender offer for a firm may be anticipated if there have recently been tender offers for other firms in the same industry. After the leveraged buyout of Northwest Airlines, similar offers for United Airlines and American Airlines quickly followed. We frequently observe such "industry effects." How effectively market participants anticipate new information determines how market prices react to the information.

Over time, information can arrive that causes the likelihood of a particular outcome to increase from unlikely to likely and then from likely to actual occurrence. Securities analysts generate earnings forecasts and keep revising them up to the time of the actual earnings announcement. Although each securities analyst may have perfectly valid reasons for each revision to the earnings forecast, the series of earnings forecasts and revisions, taken collectively, behaves as though it were a random process. With each tiny change in the likelihood of an outcome, the value of that stock changes. Because new information arrives almost continuously, and because its interpretation goes on continuously, there will be many price changes, and they will be random. In fact, stock prices change almost constantly for precisely this reason.

At first glance, all the movements of stock prices appear to occur because we are not sure what a stock is worth. At this point in the chapter, however, we hope you can see that the movement in stock prices is the result of constantly *reassessing* what a stock is worth. Price changes are the result of competition in the ongoing interpretation of all available information, so random stock price movement can result from *rational* behavior.

The amount of time it normally takes for a market price to adjust to new information is a measure of capital market efficiency. As we have said, in an efficient market, prices adjust quickly and fully (within hours) to new information. The process can be shown visually.

Figure 14-2 illustrates alternative price reactions to new information that indicates a stock is worth less than was previously thought. Three reactions are shown: The perfect-market reaction, in which the price adjusts instantaneously; an overreaction, in which the price drops too much and then increases during the adjustment period to the correct level; and an underreaction, in which the price does not react immediately but declines during the adjustment period to the correct level. The smaller the adjustment period, the more efficient the market.

The Stock Market as an Important Leading Economic Indicator

Random stock price movement implies that no single person can consistently predict future stock prices correctly. Although traders use information that lies somewhere along the continuum we mentioned earlier (ranging from hard facts to blind guesses), as a general rule many of their decisions are educated guesses.

FIGURE 14-2

Alternative price reactions to new information indicating that a stock is worth less than was previously thought.

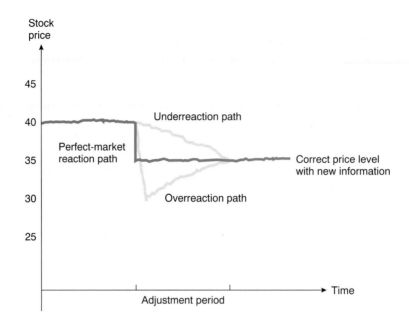

Now, if one trader has extraordinary talent in interpreting information and predicting future stock prices with great accuracy, she will very quickly amass a fortune. People observing this talent will value that trader's opinion more highly than the opinions of others. These people, then, by watching, would be interpreting the information available to them. They would have another signal to watch: the expert trader.

No single trader, analyst, or firm has yet been consistently accurate enough to convince the rest of the world that he, she, or it is *the* expert. As a group, however, their work and competition create prices that reflect the chances of future events more accurately than does any single trader, analyst, or firm. In fact, stock prices are so accurate at assessing the probabilities of future events that stock market indexes such as the Standard & Poor's 500 Index of common stock prices are among the most accurate leading economic indicators known. Traders, or their representatives (who provide a valuable service for which traders are willing to pay), expend a lot of resources doing things like counting customers at Wal-Mart stores so they can translate those statistics into sales estimates, the sales into profit estimates, the profit estimates into dividend estimates, the dividend estimates into predicted stock value, and (finally) the predicted stock value into decisions to buy or sell.

The important point is that the collective wisdom that a competitive price embodies, generally provides a much more accurate assessment of value than any single assessment. Of course, it is always possible to find an assessment that at a particular point in time turns out to be more accurate than the market's assessment. However, we can establish this only after the fact. What has not yet been observed is an individual's assessment that is consistently, over a long period, more accurate than the market's competitive price. There have been many temporary successes—people who appear better than the market. But even random guesses achieve some successes. For example, if you always pick heads when a coin is flipped, you will choose correctly 50% of the time. Think about the following example.

Let's say there are 4096 market prognosticators and their predictions are evaluated quarterly. Every quarter each forecaster is just as likely to pick the stock market's direction correctly as incorrectly. With a 0.5 probability of being correct each time, we can use the binomial probability distribution to show that during an average year, 256 will be correct in every quarter [= $(0.5)^4 = 6.25\%$; 6.25% of 4096 = 256]. Over a typical 2-year period, 16 will have correctly predicted the stock market's movement each quarter. Even over a 3-year period, on average, one of the prognosticators will be exactly right *every* quarter. In spite of the equal likelihood of being right or wrong in any one quarter, 1 out of 4096 prognosticators, on average, will make 12 correct predictions in a row ($2^{12} = 4096$).

This shows us that someone can have a good run of luck, even if he doesn't possess any extraordinary predictive powers. Perhaps that is why any individual's standing as a market guru tends to be short-lived! A review of the financial press reveals that different forecasters from time to time have appeared unusually prescient. But each one's period in the limelight has been limited. (Note that 4096 is a very small number of prognosticators when compared with the number of market participants.)

In any case, the competitive market price reflects the collective wisdom about the probabilities of all the possible outcomes, taking into account the cost of being wrong as well as the benefit of being right. ■

Stock Market Prediction Experts

EXAMPLE

Self-Check Questions

1. Any transaction you make in an efficient market has a zero NPV. So why bother to invest?
2. How do prices behave in an efficient market? Why must this be so?
3. Explain how random stock price movement results from rational investor behavior. When stock prices behave this way, can any single trader expect to be able consistently to predict future stock prices correctly?
4. How do you explain the stock market's role as an important leading economic indicator?
5. Explain why a string of correct forecasts does not necessarily prove that a particular forecaster is smarter than the collective wisdom.

14.6 VALUE CONSERVATION

We said at the beginning of the chapter that perfect—meaning entirely frictionless—markets are perfectly efficient. Another important, and startling, implication of perfect markets is the concept of value additivity. **Value additivity** means that the value of the whole (a group of assets) exactly equals the sum of the values of the parts (the individual assets). Value additivity holds in a perfect capital market. If this were not the case, there would be a profitable arbitrage opportunity. As we noted earlier, people would exploit this opportunity until further profits were no longer possible, at which point value additivity would have been restored.

The Law of Value Conservation

The law of value conservation in finance is like the law of energy conservation in physics. If value is conserved across transactions, as it is in a perfect market, value additivity will exist among assets. In the case of two assets, value additivity can be stated in this way: The value of two assets combined equals the sum of their two individual values. Algebraically, if V

stands for value, A stands for one asset, and B stands for the other, value additivity can be represented as

$$V(A + B) = V(A) + V(B) \qquad (14.1)$$

Note that this equation describes the process of separating assets as well as combining them. Also note that the equation can easily be generalized to apply to more than two assets.

The two people most responsible for introducing the concept of value conservation into finance are Franco Modigliani and Merton Miller, commonly referred to as MM (pronounced "M 'n' M"). Both have won the Nobel Prize for their work, which changed the way people think about finance.

In Chapter 3, we defined a zero-sum game as a situation wherein one person's gain (loss) is always another person's loss (gain). In the absence of any new information, an efficient market represents a *zero-sum-game* environment at a specific point in time. Value additivity results from competition within such an environment. It is an implication of the combined effect of capital market efficiency and two-sided transactions.

A word of caution is in order. As we also said in Chapter 3, the one significant factor that can cause capital markets to deviate from being a zero-sum-game environment is taxes. (We also pointed out, however, that even in the presence of taxes, the capital markets still represent a zero-sum-game environment when we include the government in the game.) Taxes are another imperfection, the last of our set of three significant frictions in the capital markets.

It sounds so simple to say that value is neither created nor destroyed when assets are exchanged, and yet countless hours of work have gone into debate over this issue. The fundamental question is whether an asset can be worth different amounts, depending on whether it is attached to another asset. The Principle of Valuable Ideas says, in effect, that it may be possible to combine assets in value-increasing ways. But the Principle of Capital Market Efficiency says that doing so is not possible if people are already aware of the value-increasing possibility. How do we resolve this apparent contradiction?

A financial asset is really only a set of expected cash flows. If we combine cash flows from various sources, can they be worth more in total after they are combined than before? *Only if we are the first ones to think of making this valuable combination.* If the owners of the separate cash flow streams know that the cash flows are worth more when combined, they will either make the combination themselves or charge us the equivalent combined value for the assets because they *could* combine the cash flows themselves.

We could also ask the opposite question: Can cash flows be worth more if they are split up? Again, only if we are the first ones to think of a value-increasing breakup.

To appreciate the concept underlying the law of value additivity, consider once again our example of that simple financial asset, a $10 bill. Would you exchange a $10 bill for nine $1 bills? Of course not. But how about exchanging it for eleven of them? More interested? Value additivity says that breaking a $10 bill into several smaller assets does not change the total value—you will still have $10 worth of assets.

Similarly, suppose you have two $5 bills. Can combining the two bills by exchanging them for one $10 bill make the total worth more than the sum of the two taken separately? No.

But what if a $10 bill has been torn into four equal pieces and each piece given to a different person. Individually, the pieces are all worthless—or are they? Suppose you know the four people who each hold a piece. You point out to each individual that their piece is worthless but that you will be happy to take it off their hands at no cost to them. If they all give you their pieces, you will have an asset worth $10. If each person knows that the other three pieces are obtainable, however, the holders are not likely to *give* their pieces to you. The holders would be willing to *sell* their pieces to you for $2.50 each, but then there would be no reason for you to bother with the transaction, because it would cost you $10 for an asset worth $10. If the four individuals did not want to bother spending the time, effort, and money to get together and make the deal themselves, however, you might get them to sell their pieces for less than $2.50 each. If they sold you the pieces for $2 each, you would make a "commission" of $2 on the transaction, and they would be paying a transaction cost of 50 cents each.[3]

The capital markets are just a more sophisticated application of this example. Value additivity holds exactly when all the parts are included. That is, when the loss due to frictions is included, there is perfect conservation of value. More important, however, value additivity is the best approximation of a situation with relatively low transaction costs. And this is the case with the capital markets.

A Chance for a Bigger Pie to Split: Lowering Your Taxes

We have already mentioned that taxes can create a situation in which the environment is no longer a zero-sum game. This can happen when two parties pay taxes at different rates. When one records a dollar of revenue and the other records a dollar of expense in a single transaction, an asymmetry in taxes occurs if the two parties pay taxes at different rates. This is true because the revenue increases taxes collected, and the expense decreases taxes collected. But because the increase and decrease are at different rates, the tax amounts are not equal. Thus the government may collect more or less taxes on the revenue than it gives up on the expense. This means there can be an advantage if the transaction reduces their combined tax bill.

For the most part, because people understand this phenomenon, the government generally collects fewer tax dollars when such asymmetries occur. Of course, in many of these cases people are doing exactly what the government is encouraging them to do. For example, the government uses the tax code to encourage saving for retirement by creating special advantages for such things as Individual Retirement Accounts. The goal is to reduce the future burden on social programs. And the government has sometimes encouraged investment in new capital equipment to spur the economy by providing an investment tax credit.

An example of a tax asymmetry that Congress may not have intended involves zero-coupon bonds. Recall that a zero-coupon bond (sometimes called a pure-discount bond) is like a Treasury bill except that it has a much longer life. A zero-coupon bond sells on a discount basis because it makes no interest payments between the time it is issued and the time it matures. For example, a zero-coupon bond might be sold for $100 when issued and pay $1000 at maturity 20 years later. The interest is effectively compounded over the life of the bond. That is, the discount ($900 in the example) is the total amount of interest over the bond's entire life.

At one point, the Internal Revenue Code permitted the issuer and the holders to allocate equal amounts of the discount to each year of the bond's existence, rather than allocating the discount on the basis of how interest would truly compound. This straight-line treatment is like straight-line depreciation. The tax treatment issue here is like the choice of depreciation method we illustrated in Chapter 12. There we showed that claiming the expense sooner (ac-

The Tax Treatment of Zero-Coupon Bonds

EXAMPLE

---

[3] Note that an interesting sunk-cost problem could arise. If you bought three of the pieces for $2.50 each and the holder of the fourth piece discovered that information, he could bargain for a higher price. How much higher? The $7.50 you have already paid is a sunk cost. If your three pieces are not worth anything without the fourth piece, the fourth person could demand up to $9.99, and you would be better off making the transaction, in spite of the $7.50 you have already spent! (Of course, you might take nothing rather than let the fourth person "fleece" you. Acting out of frustration would be due to emotional rather than financial considerations.) To avoid this problem, you could bargain with each person separately and purchase options from them before making any transactions. Although the options would complicate the valuation problem by creating more "pieces," the whole would still be worth exactly $10.

celerated depreciation) lowered the present value cost of taxes. Here, by using the straight-line allocation of interest expense, the firm lowers its present value cost of taxes if it claims the interest sooner, even though the total amount claimed over the life of the security is the same.

Continuing our example, interest would be allocated as $45 for each of the 20 years (= 900/20). This amount was both claimed by the firm and recorded as income by each bond-holder. As we know, interest actually compounds slowly at first but accelerates over time. That is, the interest earned on past interest grows from one year to the next. The actual interest accrued is $12.20 in the first year and $108.75 in the last year. Thus the firm is overstating its interest expense for tax purposes in the early years (45 versus 12.20 in the first year) and understating its interest expense in the later years.

This "incorrect" allocation of the interest expense causes a shift in the firm's tax payments: Lower taxes are paid in the early years, and higher taxes are paid in the later years, than would be paid under the "correct" allocation. Although the total underpayment in the early years exactly equals the total overpayment in the later years, this shift is valuable to the firm because of the time value of money. The firm can invest the tax underpayments in the early years so that it will have more than enough money to cover the added cost of the tax overpayments in the later years.

The shift in tax payments is good for the firm, but the Principle of Two-Sided Transactions reminds us to look at the other side of the transaction: the bondholders' position in the scheme of things. And sure enough, the shift in tax payments is bad for the bondholders. However, in spite of the apparently bad position for the bondholders, several billion dollars worth of zero-coupon bonds were issued. The buyers were primarily tax-exempt investors, such as pension funds. Such investors pay no taxes, so that the shift in interest payments for tax purposes is irrelevant to them. The decrease in taxes collected from the issuing firms was not being offset by an increase in taxes collected from the bondholders.

As more firms learned about this opportunity, the number of new zero-coupon bonds being issued each month began to increase dramatically. When the IRS realized that this tax asymmetry was occurring on a large scale and was significantly affecting the taxes being collected, it asked Congress to change the tax law. Congress agreed, and the rule for allocating interest expense/income for a zero-coupon bond was changed to how it actually compounds, to reflect accurately each year's interest cost. ∎

Zero-coupon bonds are only one example of many tax asymmetries that have occurred or that currently exist. A lot of attention has been given to tax asymmetries connected with leasing. For example, a significant reduction in the tax deductibility of personal interest substantially increased the attractiveness of leasing to many individuals. Although most tax asymmetries exist by Congressional design, many people spend considerable effort looking for others to exploit for profit.

Apparent Exceptions to Value Additivity

People are often reluctant to believe that value conservation holds in capital markets. To some extent, this skepticism may rest on the hope for an easy way to riches or on what people perceive as exceptions to the conservation of value.

And there are some apparent exceptions worth mentioning. The first concerns a privately owned firm that issues its stock publicly for the first time. Frequently, the value of the shares is larger after the firm goes public. This situation looks like a clear violation of the law of value conservation and therefore a violation of value additivity as well. However, it is not necessarily a violation of value additivity, because going public increases the liquidity of the shares.

Consider the owners of a privately held firm who have decided they want to sell shares of stock in their firm. The first step in the process is to find potential buyers for the stock. It can take substantial time, anxiety, and money to locate buyers. In many markets there are specialists paid to *search* for potential buyers. After locating one or more potential buyers, each of the parties (the firm and each buyer) must assess the value of the firm. This is a second task that takes time, effort, and money. After assessing the value of the firm, negotiations are necessary to reach agreement for the sale to one or more parties.

When a potential buyer is thinking about buying shares, she must consider resale, especially that necessitated by unforeseen future events. Purchasers in a private transaction face significant restrictions on their ability to resell their shares unless they register them under the U.S. securities laws. Assume for the moment that the shares in question are unregistered. What would happen if it becomes necessary to resell the shares? Who would buy them? Realistically, "sophisticated purchasers" (high-net-worth individuals and financial institutions) would be the only potential buyers for the unregistered shares, unless the holder could convince the firm to go to the time, trouble, and expense of registering the shares before the resale. What would these *other* investors be willing to pay for the shares? They would have an awareness of the resources used to get this far in the negotiations for *this* sale. These contingencies increase the buyer's risk. The Principle of Risk-Return Trade-Off tells us that buyers will lower the price they are willing to pay in order to raise their expected return to compensate for the higher risk.

Now consider the same scenario except that the resources the current owners put into finding potential buyers go instead into registration for public sale. In this second case, when potential buyers consider the purchase of shares, one aspect of risk and transaction costs has been removed. With shares registered for public sale, there is a much higher likelihood that a resale could be transacted quickly and at low cost. Shareholders can sell in the public market. They are not restricted to selling to sophisticated investors, as they are in the case of a private transaction. (Of course, registration does nothing to guarantee the resale price.)

The process of going public appears to add value to the firm. However, we hope you can see that value has not actually been created. Rather, transaction costs have been reduced: There is a broader market, so the time and cost of locating buyers have been reduced. Investment risk has also been reduced because of increased liquidity and the greater valuation accuracy that comes from public prices and more people valuing the firm. Finally, the costs of transferring ownership have been reduced. In short, the increased liquidity of the shares, which results from their public registration and their being traded in the stock market, is valuable.

Let's look at one other apparent exception to value additivity. The **pyramid scheme** is a scam in which a con artist tells victims they can earn an extraordinary return on their money, such as 10% per quarter, with no risk. The con artist takes the money, returns the investment with the promised interest one quarter later, and then inquires about reinvesting. The soon-to-be victim is pleased because he has got the money back with tremendous interest, as promised. Usually people reinvest their money and can be called on to cajole some friends into investing, too. The con artist takes in the invested money, using the new money coming in to pay off any investors who want to quit. Of course, most people want to keep their money invested in such a great investment, so the outflow for "quitters" is small for quite a while. In the meantime, a lot of money comes in. From the start, the amount of promised money exceeds the amount of money actually held by the con artist. Then, over time, the difference between promised returns and the funds available grows. It eventually becomes enormous. At some point the con artist disappears, along with the accumulated money.

This may seem to be an unlikely scenario because of the difficulty of pulling it off. The scheme is illegal, and there are many checks to prevent its occurrence. However, in each of the last four decades there have been one or more pyramid schemes that have been at least partially successful for the con artist. The pyramid scheme is not an exception to value additivity, because the cash to pay interest to those who wish to withdraw is obtained from others who have been sucked in. Value is not created; it is simply transferred from one group of participants to another, with a sizable "commission" being taken by the unscrupulous promoter.

Self-Check Questions

1. What is value additivity? What does it imply about the relationship between the value of two assets X and Y and their combined value? Must value additivity hold in a perfect capital market?

2. How can a tax asymmetry benefit both parties to a transaction?

3. True or false? Value conservation is a good approximation of value for assets traded in capital markets.

4. Is the increase in value of the shares of a firm that goes public an exception to value conservation? Why or why not?

5. Why are pyramid schemes not an exception to value additivity?

14.7 PERFECT CAPITAL MARKETS

We have spoken about how market imperfections such as transaction costs can limit market efficiency, chiefly by interfering with the arbitrage process. Earlier in the chapter we defined a perfect capital market simply as a market in which there are never any arbitrage opportunities. More formally, a perfect capital market is one in which

1. There are no barriers to entry that would keep any potential suppliers or users of funds out of the market.

2. There is perfect competition—that is, each participant is sufficiently small that its actions cannot affect prices.

3. Financial assets are infinitely divisible.

4. There are no transaction costs, including no bankruptcy costs.

5. All existing information is fully available to every capital market participant without charge.

6. There are no tax asymmetries.

7. There are no government or other restrictions on trading.

The idea of a perfect capital market is an excellent starting point for analysis. For example, we used it in Chapter 10.

Do our perfect market conditions describe existing capital markets? The answer is yes, very well, but not *perfectly* (contradiction—and pun—intended). How far a market deviates from these seven conditions determines how "imperfect" the market is. For example, suppose there are few participants in the market for a common stock, and the flow of information to investors is very poor because there are no securities analysts who monitor the stock and prepare research reports on it. In that case, the market for the stock may not always behave efficiently.

The Principle of Capital Market Efficiency states that the capital markets are efficient, but how far is "efficient" from perfect? We do not have a precise way of separating the two concepts, but our seven conditions provide us with guidance in looking for important exceptions to a perfect capital market. If you think back over the present chapter, you might see that we have already told you how the capital markets are imperfect. We have identified three significant frictions in the capital markets: three persistent capital market imperfections. Let's summarize.

Asymmetric Taxes

One significant market imperfection is the existence of asymmetric taxes. Because tax laws change quite frequently, we don't get into too much detail about them in this book. Later on, we will point out some tax asymmetries that have existed for quite a while and that are relevant to major corporate decisions. However, even those tax asymmetries might be changed by Congress. It is important to remember to check for tax asymmetries as a potential explanation for transactions that would otherwise appear to be a "zero-sum game."

Asymmetric Information

A second significant market imperfection concerns the availability of information. In our discussion on speculation, we pointed out the importance and cost of obtaining information. New information relevant to pricing a security is not costless and available to everyone. However, because competition incorporates new information into prices so quickly and because information is published almost as quickly, it is a good approximation of the environment to say that information is freely available to everyone. Signaling is an important component of the flow and interpretation of information. As with tax asymmetries, information flow—sending signals—is a potential explanation for transactions that would otherwise appear to be a "zero-sum game."

Transaction Costs

Transaction costs are the third imperfection we discussed. Unbelievable as this may sound, transaction costs may be less important than asymmetric taxes and asymmetric information. Transaction costs affect transactions in a way that is fundamentally different from the effects of asymmetric taxes and asymmetric information. Transaction costs are usually symmetric. Although they may inhibit arbitrageurs, traders, and speculators from making transactions, transaction costs don't bias prices upward or downward, nor do they provide an incentive for making a transaction. That is, they do not create profit in and of themselves, except for the financial intermediary collecting a commission or finding a way to structure a transaction that reduces transaction costs.

The significant effect that transaction costs can have is to favor one *type* of transaction over another. For example, the existence of fixed transaction costs favors less frequent, larger transactions over more frequent, smaller ones. Note that price discounts because of a lack of liquidity are transaction costs.

Despite the existence of these imperfections, perfect is a very good approximation for most segments of the capital markets. Value conservation—value is neither created nor destroyed through splitting or combining cash flows—is the best starting point for financial analysis. This is why we so often use this approach of starting with a "clean slate" in our analyses.

Self-Check Questions

1. List the seven characteristics of a perfect capital market.

2. Describe three significant capital market imperfections.

3. Are transaction costs likely to be more important or less important than asymmetric taxes and asymmetric information in inhibiting capital market efficiency?

4. Why does a perfect capital market serve as the best starting point from which to analyze capital market transactions?

SUMMARY

In this chapter we explained how the Principles of Self-Interested Behavior, Two-Sided Transactions, Signaling, and Risk-Return Trade-Off combine with the similarity of financial assets, low transaction costs, and large size in a very competitive market environment and lead us to the Principle of Capital Market Efficiency. This fundamental principle is a critical part of the fabric that underlies finance. It states that at any point in time, capital market prices reflect all available information and adjust fully and quickly to new information. Although disparities in valuation can occur, these will prove temporary when transaction costs are low, because arbitrage activity will tend to eliminate them quickly and restore fair pricing.

DECISION SUMMARY

- Price movements in an efficient market are random, because market participants react to each new piece of information, and the events that generate this new information occur randomly.

- Market prices at any point in time will reflect the up-to-date collective wisdom of the market participants about the "correct" value of each asset.

- Market participants will interpret each new event and respond with buy and sell decisions. This involves the interpretation of many events, such as dividend or new-product announcements, as signals regarding possible changes in the firm's financial condition or prospects.

- Conservation of value across transactions leads to value additivity. In the special case of a perfect capital market, where there are no frictions such as asymmetric taxes or transaction costs, and information is fully and costlessly available to everyone, the value of combined assets exactly equals the sum of their individual values. As a result, the law of value conservation holds: Value is neither created nor destroyed when assets are combined or separated.

- Asymmetric taxes can cause the capital markets to deviate from being a zero-sum-game environment. Thus tax-related factors might be responsible for transactions that would otherwise seem to be "zero-sum games." In practice, tax-related factors are often the driving force behind a transaction.

- Asymmetric information is an important capital market imperfection. Individuals can temporarily benefit from superior information, but their actions will signal others to respond. Efficient capital markets incorporate new information into prices very quickly.

- Transaction costs do not generally cause a bias in prices. In most cases, both parties to a transaction must pay approximately equivalent transaction costs. However, as we show in later chapters, transaction costs can have important effects on decisions.

- In spite of capital market imperfections, perfect is a good approximation of the capital markets and serves as the best starting point from which to analyze capital market transactions.

KEY TERMS

efficiency...435

frictions...435

transaction costs...436

capital market efficiency...437

strong form of capital market efficiency...437

semi-strong form of capital market efficiency...437

weak form of capital market efficiency...437

market maker...439

specialist...439

arbitrage...440

perfect capital market...440

arbitrageurs...441

traders...443

asymmetric information...444

deductive reasoning...445

inductive reasoning...446

collective wisdom...446

value additivity...449

pyramid scheme...453

EXERCISES

PROBLEM SET A

A1. For what reason were capital markets originally created?

A2. Show that the first and last year's implied interest in our zero-coupon bond example are in fact $12.20 and $108.75, respectively.

A3. Explain how public securities prices provide a measure of value.

A4. Define the term *riskless arbitrage*.

A5. How can arbitrage be used to define a perfect market?

A6. Respond to the following: "Why should I invest in the capital markets when I don't earn any money—that is, when I get a zero NPV?"

A7. What do we mean when we say that financial assets are very similar?

A8. What does the term *collective wisdom* mean?

A9. Why is it important to distinguish between anticipated and unanticipated new information?

A10. What is value additivity?

A11. Describe what we mean by the term *asymmetric taxes*.

A12. What is asymmetric information?

A13. Cite and briefly discuss three types of capital market imperfections that may affect corporate decision making.

PROBLEM SET B

B1. Originally, the capital markets were created to bring users and suppliers of capital together. In addition to this important purpose, we now find that there are important side benefits. Cite and discuss three benefits that capital markets provide for society.

B2. Explain the importance of arbitrage to the efficiency of the capital markets.

B3. Is the following statement true or false? Because arbitrageurs sell assets for more than they paid for them, arbitrageurs must make a lot of money. Justify your answer.

B4. Explain how an increase in the liquidity of a financial security can appear to be a violation of value additivity.

B5. Explain how the similarity of assets contributes to the efficiency of the capital markets.

B6. Describe in your own words the problem of adverse selection.

B7. Applying the Signaling Principle involves inductive reasoning. Cite an important aspect of inductive reasoning that can make some applications of this principle extremely difficult.

B8. Evaluate the following statement. The evidence suggests that price movements are random; this clearly implies that the capital markets are not functioning well.

B9. Describe in your own words the law of value conservation.

B10. Use algebraic representation to explain how a continuing violation of value additivity would create an arbitrage opportunity.

B11. Explain how the effect of transaction costs on market prices is fundamentally different from the effects of asymmetric taxes and asymmetric information.

B12. Comment on the following statement: If *all* markets were perfect, it would be both a blessing and a curse.

B13. Using our Principles of Finance, explain why a market return is often referred to as an opportunity cost of capital (or an opportunity cost discount rate).

B14. If payments for a $20,000 five-year car loan are $300.99 twice a month, what is the APR for the loan? What is the APY for this loan?

B15. Both fixed and variable transaction costs for arbitrageurs inhibit capital market efficiency. How would the effect of relatively large fixed and small variable transaction costs differ from that of relatively small fixed and large variable transaction costs?

PROBLEM SET C

C1. Smiling John's Retirement Service offers the following deal: "You pay us $10,000 a year for 12 years, with the first payment today, and we'll pay you $1000 a month forever after." What APY is Smiling John offering? (This can be approximated via an algebraic solution, but the exact solution will be obtained using trial and error. If you do not see how to get the exact answer, try to make a good approximation.)

C2. Suppose you will receive $10,000 once a year forever, and the first payment will be made 3 months from today. What is the present value of this stream if the APY is 20%?

C3. Transaction costs are often cited as definite proof that capital markets are not perfect.

   a. Explain why although this is literally true, transaction costs do not generally cause actual capital market prices to be a bad approximation of perfect capital market prices.

   b. Explain how the magnitude of the bid-ask spread and the proportionate transaction costs purchasers and sellers must pay affect your answer to part a.

C4. Define the term *opportunity cost*, and explain why it is an important concept in the process of determining the value of an asset.

C5. In our discussion of the Principle of Self-Interested Behavior, we said that it is important to take opportunity costs into account. How is the opportunity cost of alternative investments accounted for in an NPV calculation?

C6. Explain how the Behavioral Principle is related to the Principle of Capital Market Efficiency.

Real-World Application: The Inefficient Market Fund

The Inefficient Market Fund (IMF) is a closed-end management investment firm that was formed in January 1990. (A closed-end investment firm is a mutual fund that has a fixed number of common shares outstanding.) The IMF seeks long-term capital appreciation through investments in firms that meet the following criteria: (1) a total capitalization no greater than $500 million, (2) the IMF believes the firm is undervalued, and (3) the stock is "underowned" by financial institutions and "underfollowed" by Wall Street (that is, relatively few institutions own it and few securities analysts follow it).

Table 14-1 compares changes in the IMF share price to the total returns on large-firm common stocks and small-firm common stocks for the period 1990–1995.

1. What's the rationale behind the IMF? Does it make sense? Explain. (*Hint:* Recall the size effect discussed in Chapter 6 and the Appendix to Chapter 7.)

2. Calculate the monthly total returns on the IMF for the period February 1990 through December 1995.

3. Calculate the annual returns for 1990 (11 months annualized) through 1995 on

   a. The IMF.

   b. Large-firm common stocks.

   c. Small-firm common stocks.

4. Calculate the average monthly return on

   a. The IMF.

   b. Large-firm common stocks.

   c. Small-firm common stocks.

5. Calculate the standard deviation of the monthly returns on

   a. The IMF.

   b. Large-firm common stocks.

   c. Small-firm common stocks.

6. On a sheet of graph paper, plot the monthly returns on the IMF, large-firm common stocks, and small-firm common stocks. Do the three sets of returns move together?

7. Do a difference-of-means test between

   a. Monthly returns on the IMF and large-firm common stocks.

TABLE 14-1

Market price study for the Inefficient Market Fund.

MONTH	IMF CLOSING PRICE	IMF CASH DISTRIBUTIONS	TOTAL RETURN Small Firms	TOTAL RETURN Large Firms
1/90	$12⅛	—	−7.64%	−6.71%
2/90	11	—	1.87	1.29
3/90	11⅝	—	3.68	2.63
4/90	10¾	—	−2.66	−2.47
5/90	10¼	—	5.61	9.75
6/90	11	$0.10	1.44	−0.70
7/90	10⅜	—	−3.82	−0.32
8/90	8¾	—	−12.96	−9.03
9/90	7¾	—	−8.29	−4.92
10/90	7⅞	—	−5.72	−0.37
11/90	8⅛	—	4.50	6.44
12/90	8⅜	0.27	1.94	2.74
1/91	9½	—	8.41	4.42
2/91	9⅜	—	11.13	7.16
3/91	9⅛	—	6.80	2.38
4/91	9	—	0.34	0.28
5/91	9½	—	3.34	4.28
6/91	9⅜	0.30	−4.85	−4.57
7/91	9⅛	—	4.07	4.68
8/91	9¼	—	2.61	2.35
9/91	9⅜	—	0.32	−1.64
10/91	9⅛	—	3.17	1.34
11/91	8⅞	0.632	−2.76	−4.04
12/91	8⅞	—	6.01	11.43

MONTH	IMF CLOSING PRICE	IMF CASH DISTRIBUTIONS	TOTAL RETURN Small Firms	TOTAL RETURN Large Firms
1/92	$10	—	11.28%	−1.86%
2/92	10½	—	4.52	1.28
3/92	10½	—	−2.49	−1.96
4/92	10¼	—	−4.03	2.91
5/92	9⅞	—	−0.14	0.54
6/92	9¼	$0.04	−5.19	−1.45
7/92	9⅝	—	3.70	4.03
8/92	9¼	—	−2.28	−2.02
9/92	9¼	—	1.31	1.15
10/92	9¼	—	2.59	0.36
11/92	9⅝	—	8.85	3.37
12/92	9⅞	0.01	4.41	1.31
1/93	10	—	5.43	0.73
2/93	10⅛	—	−1.80	1.35
3/93	10	—	2.89	2.15
4/93	9½	—	−3.06	−2.45
5/93	10	—	3.42	2.70
6/93	9⅝	0.01	−0.38	0.33
7/93	9¾	—	1.66	−0.47
8/93	10	—	3.39	3.81
9/93	10⅜	—	3.16	−0.74
10/93	10¾	—	4.71	2.03
11/93	10⅜	—	−1.75	−0.94
12/93	10½	—	1.94	1.23

MONTH	IMF CLOSING PRICE	IMF CASH DISTRIBUTIONS	TOTAL RETURN Small Firms	TOTAL RETURN Large Firms
1/94	$11	—	6.18%	3.35%
2/94	10⅝	—	−0.23	−2.70
3/94	10¼	—	−4.46	−4.35
4/94	9⅞	—	0.60	1.30
5/94	9⅞	—	−0.12	1.63
6/94	9½	—	−2.62	−2.47
7/94	9⅝	—	1.84	3.31
8/94	9⅞	—	3.37	4.07
9/94	9⅝	—	1.05	−2.41
10/94	9⅝	—	1.15	2.29
11/94	9¼	—	−3.26	−3.67
12/94	9½	$0.1372	0.02	1.46
1/95	9⅜	—	2.83	2.60
2/95	9¾	—	2.52	3.88
3/95	9⅝	—	1.45	2.96
4/95	9¹³⁄₁₆	—	3.52	2.91
5/95	9¾	—	2.98	3.95
6/95	10⅛	—	5.68	2.35
7/95	10⅜	—	6.45	3.33
8/95	10⅜	—	3.58	0.27
9/95	10¾	—	1.95	4.19
10/95	10½	—	−4.87	−0.35
11/95	11	—	1.92	4.40
12/95	9¹³⁄₁₆	2.0424	2.39	1.85

Sources: Bloomberg, L. P., and *Stocks, Bonds, Bills, and Inflation 1996 Yearbook* (Chicago, Ill. Ibbotson Associates, 1996), pp. 181, 187.

b. Monthly returns on the IMF and small-firm common stocks.

8. Fit the equation $Y = a + bX$

a. Where Y = monthly return on IMF and X = monthly return on large-firm common stocks.

b. Where Y = monthly return on IMF and X = monthly return on small-firm common stocks.

9. Compare the three sets of monthly returns in terms of risk and average return.

10. How well has the IMF done?

BIBLIOGRAPHY

Ackert, Lucy F., and Brian F. Smith. "Stock Price Volatility, Ordinary Dividends, and Other Cash Flows to Shareholders," *Journal of Finance*, 1993, 48(4):1147–1160.

Affleck-Graves, John, Shantaram P. Hegde, and Robert E. Miller. "Trading Mechanisms and the Components of Bid-Ask Spreads," *Journal of Finance*, 1994, 49(4):1471–1488.

Affleck-Graves, John, and Richard R. Mendenhall. "The Relation Between the Value Line Enigma and Post-Earnings-Announcement Drift," *Journal of Financial Economics*, 1992, 31(1):75–96.

Akerlof, George A. "The Market for 'Lemons': Quality Uncertainty and the Market Mechanism," *Quarterly Journal of Economics*, 1970, 84(August):488–500.

Ariel, Robert. "High Cost Returns Before Holidays: Existence and Evidence on Possible Causes," *Journal of Finance*, 1990, 45(5):1611–1626.

Baker, H. Kent, and Richard B. Edelman. "AMEX-to-NYSE Transfers, Market Microstructure, and Shareholder Wealth," *Financial Management*, 1992, 21(4):60–72.

Balvers, Ronald J., Thomas F. Cosimano, and Bill McDonald. "Predicting Stock Returns in an Efficient Market," *Journal of Finance*, 1990, 45(4):1109–1128.

Bathala, Chenchuramaiah T., Kenneth P. Moon, and Ramesh P. Rao. "Managerial Ownership, Debt Policy, and the Impact of Institutional Holdings: An Agency Perspective," *Financial Management*, 1994, 23(3):38–50.

Benveniste, Lawrence M., Alan J. Marcus, and William J. Wilhelm. "What's Special About the Specialist?," *Journal of Financial Economics*, 1992, 32(1):61–86.

Berry, Thomas D., and Keith M. Howe. "Public Information Arrival," *Journal of Finance*, 1994, 49(4):1331–1346.

Best, Ronald, and Hang Zhang. "Alternative Information Sources And The Information Content Of Bank Loans," *Journal of Finance*, 1993, 48(4):1507–1522.

Bhardwaj, Ravinder K., and LeRoy D. Brooks. "The January Anomaly: Effects of Low Share Price, Transaction Costs, and Bid-Ask Bias," *Journal of Finance*, 1992, 47(2):553–576.

Bhide, Amar. "The Hidden Costs of Stock Market Liquidity," *Journal of Financial Economics*, 1993, 34(1):31–51.

Black, Fischer. "Presidental Address: Noise," *Journal of Finance*, 1986, 41(3):529–544.

Blume, Lawrence, David Easley, and Maureen O'Hara. "Market Statistics and Technical Analysis: The Role Of Volume," *Journal of Finance*, 1994, 49(1):153–181.

Brennan, Michael J., and Patricia J. Hughes. "Stock Prices and the Supply Of Information," *Journal of Finance*, 1991, 46(5):1665–1692.

Brous, Peter A., and Omesh Kini. "The Valuation Effects of Equity Issues and the Level of Institutional Ownership: Evidence from Analysts' Earnings Forecasts," *Financial Management*, 1994, 23(1):33–46.

Campbell, Cynthia J., Louis Ederington, and Prashant Vankrudre. "Tax Shields, Sample-Selection Bias, and the Information Content of Conversion-Forcing Bond Calls," *Journal of Finance*, 1991, 46(4):1291–1324.

Chan, Kalok, Y. Peter Chung, and Herb Johnson. "Why Option Prices Lag Stock Prices: A Trading-Based Explanation," *Journal of Finance*, 1993, 48(5):1957–1967.

Chatterjea, Arkadev, Joseph A. Cherian, and Robert A. Jarrow. "Market Manipulation and Corporate Finance: A New Perspective," *Financial Management*, 1993, 22(2):200–209.

Christie, William G., Jeffrey H. Harris, and Paul H. Schultz. "Why Did NASDAQ Market Makers Stop Avoiding Odd-Eighth Quotes?" *Journal of Finance*, 1994, 49(5):1841–1860.

Christie, William G., and Paul H. Schultz. "Why Do NASDAQ Market Makers Avoid Odd-Eighth Quotes?" *Journal of Finance*, 1994, 49(5):1813–1840.

Conrad, Jennifer, and Gautam Kaul. "Long-Term Market Overreaction or Biases in Computed Returns?" *Journal of Finance*, 1993, 48(1):39–64.

Conroy, Robert M., Robert S. Harris, and Bruce A. Benet. "The Effects of Stock Splits on Bid-Ask Spreads," *Journal of Finance*, 1990, 45(4):1285–1295.

Copeland, Thomas E., and Won Heum Lee. "Exchange Offers and Stock Swaps—New Evidence," *Financial Management*, 1991, 20(3):34–48.

Cornell, Bradford, and Erik R. Sirri. "The Reaction of Investors and Stock Prices to Insider Trading," *Journal of Finance*, 1992, 47(3):1031–1060.

Cox, Don R., and David R. Peterson. "Stock Returns Following Large One-Day Declines: Evidence on Short-Term Reversals and Longer-Term Performance," *Journal of Finance*, 1994, 49(1):255–268.

Daves, Phillip R., and Michael C. Ehrhardt. "Liquidity, Reconstruction, and the Value of U.S. Treasury Strips," *Journal of Finance*, 1993, 48(1):315–330.

DeBondt, Werner F. M., and Richard H. Thaler. "Further Evidence on Investor Overreaction and Stock Market Seasonality," *Journal of Finance*, 1987, 42(3):557–581.

Dezhbakhsh, Hashem, and Asli Demirguc-Kunt. "On the Presence of Speculative Bubbles in Stock Prices," *Journal of Financial and Quantitative Analysis*, 1990, 25(1):101–112.

Dubofsky, David A. "A Market Microstructure Explanation of Ex-Day Abnormal Returns," *Financial Management*, 1992, 21(4):32–43.

Easley, David, and Maureen O'Hara. "Time and the Process of Security Price Adjustment," *Journal of Finance*, 1992, 47(2):577–606.

Ederington, Louis H., and Jae Ha Lee. "How Markets Process Information: News Releases and Volatility," *Journal of Finance*, 1993, 48(4):1161–1192.

Fama, Eugene F. "Efficient Capital Markets: II," *Journal of Finance*, 1991, 46(5):1575–1618.

Froot, Kenneth A., David S. Scharfstein, and Jeremy C. Stein. "Herd on the Street: Informational Inefficiencies in a Market with Short-Term Speculation," *Journal of Finance*, 1992, 47(4):1461–1484.

Furbush, Dean. "Program Trading and Price Movement: Evidence from the October 1987 Market Crash," *Financial Management*, 1989, 18(3):68–83.

Glosten, Lawrence R. "Is the Electronic Open Limit Order Book Inevitable?" *Journal of Finance*, 1994, 49(4):1127–1161.

Golec, Joseph, and Maurry Tamarkin. "The Degree of Inefficiency in the Football Betting Market," *Journal of Financial Economics*, 1991, 30(2):311–324.

Gombola, Michael J., and George P. Tsetsekos. "The Information Content of Plant Closing Announcements: Evidence from Financial Profiles and the Stock Price Reaction," *Financial Management*, 1992, 21(2):31–40.

Gosnell, Thomas, Arthur J. Keown, and John M. Pinkerton. "Bankruptcy and Insider Trading: Differences Between Exchange-Listed And OTC Firms," *Journal of Finance*, 1992, 47(1):349–362.

Griffiths, Mark D., and Robert W. White. "Tax-Induced Trading and the Turn-of-the-Year Anomaly: An Intraday Study," *Journal of Finance*, 1993, 48(2):575–598.

Harlow, W. V., and John S. Howe. "Leveraged Buyouts and Insider Nontrading," *Financial Management*, 1993, 22(1):109–118.

Harris, Milton, and Artur Raviv. "Capital Structure and the Informational Role of Debt," *Journal of Finance*, 1990, 45(2):321–350.

Hasbrouck, Joel, and George Sofianos. "The Trade of Market Makers: An Empirical Analysis of NYSE Specialists," *Journal of Finance*, 1993, 48(5):1565–1593.

Haugen, Robert A. "Finance from a New Perspective," *Financial Management*, 1996, 25(1):86–97.

Haugen, Robert A. *The New Finance: The Case Against Efficient Markets*. Englewood Cliffs, N.J.: Prentice-Hall, 1995.

Hertzel, Michael G. "The Effects of Stock Repurchases on Rival Firms," *Journal of Finance*, 1991, 46(2):707–716.

Hirshleifer, David, Avanidhar Subrahmanyam, and Sheridan Titman. "Security Analysis and Trading Patterns When Some Investors Receive Information Before Others," *Journal of Finance*, 1994, 49(5):1665–1698.

Hochman, Shalom J., Oded Palmon, and Alex P. Tang. "Tax-Induced Intra-Year Patterns in Bonds Yields," *Journal of Finance*, 1993, 48(1):331–344.

Holden, Craig W., and Avanidhar Subrahmanyam. "Long-Lived Private Information and Imperfect Competition," *Journal of Finance*, 1992, 47(1):247–270.

Holthausen, Robert W., Richard W. Leftwich, and David Mayers. "Large-Block Transactions, the Speed of Response, and Temporary and Permanent Stock-Price Effects," *Journal of Financial Economics*, 1990, 26(1):71–96.

Jarrow, Robert A., and Maureen O'Hara. "Primes and Scores: An Essay on Market Imperfections," *Journal of Finance*, 1989, 44(5):1263–1288.

Jegadeesh, Narasimhan, and Sheridan Titman. "Returns to Buying Winners and Selling Losers: Implications for Stock Market Efficiency," *Journal of Finance*, 1993, 48(1):65–92.

Jones, Charles M., Gautam Kaul, and Marc L. Lipson. "Information, Trading, and Volatility," *Journal of Financial Economics*, 1994, 36(1):127–154.

Kadlec, Gregory B., and John J. McConnell. "The Effect of Market Segmentation and Illiquidity on Asset Prices: Evidence from Exchange Listings," *Journal of Finance*, 1994, 49(2):611–636.

Krueger, Thomas M., and William F. Kennedy. "An Examination of the Super Bowl Stock Market Predictor," *Journal of Finance*, 1990, 45(2):691–698.

Kryzanowski, Lawrence, and Hao Zhang. "The Contrarian Investment Strategy Does Not Work in Canadian Markets," *Journal of Financial and Quantitative Analysis*, 1992, 27(3):383–396.

Kumar, Raman, Atulya Sarin, and Kuldeep Shastri. "The Behavior of Option Price Around Large Block Transactions in the Underlying Security," *Journal of Finance*, 1992, 47(3):879–890.

Lakonishok, Josef, Andrei Shleifer, and Robert W. Vishny. "Contrarian Investment, Extrapolation, and Risk," *Journal of Finance*, 1994, 49(5):1541–1578.

Lee, Chun I., Stuart Rosenstein, Nanda Rangan, and Wallace N. Davidson, III. "Board Composition and Shareholder Wealth: The Case of Management Buyouts," *Financial Management*, 1992, 21(1):58–72.

Lee, D. Scott. "Management Buyout Proposals and Inside Information," *Journal of Finance*, 1992, 47(3):1061–1080.

Lee, Winson B., and Elizabeth S. Cooperman. "Conglomerates in the 1980s: A Performance Appraisal," *Financial Management*, 1989, 18(1):45–54.

Lin, Ji-Chai, and John S. Howe. "Insider Trading in the OTC Market," *Journal of Finance*, 1990, 45(4):1273–1284.

Liu, Pu, Stanley D. Smith, and Azmat A. Syed. "Stock Price Reactions to the *Wall Street Journal*'s Securities Recommendations," *Journal of Financial and Quantitative Analysis*, 1990, 25(3):399–410.

Lockwood, Larry J., and Scott C. Linn. "An Examination of Stock Market Return Volatility During Overnight and Intraday Periods, 1964–1989," *Journal of Finance*, 1990, 45(2):591–602.

Long, Michael S. "The Incentives Behind the Adoption of Executive Stock Option Plans in U.S. Corporations," *Financial Management*, 1992, 21(3):12–21.

Loughran, Tim. "NYSE vs. NASDAQ Returns: Market Microstructure or the Poor Performance of Initial Public Offerings," *Journal of Financial Economics*, 1993, 33(2):241–260.

Maloney, Michael T., and J. Harold Mulherin. "The Effects of Splitting on the Ex: A Microstructure Reconciliation," *Financial Management*, 1992, 21(4):44–59.

McInish, Thomas H., and Robert A. Wood. "An Analysis of Intraday Patterns in Bid/Ask for NYSE Stocks," *Journal of Finance*, 1992, 47(2):753–764.

McQueen, Grant, and Steven Thorley. "Are Stock Returns Predictable? A Test Using Markov Chains," *Journal of Finance*, 1991, 46(1):239–264.

Merton, Robert C. "Presidential Address: A Simple Model of Capital Market Equilibrium with Incomplete Information," *Journal of Finance*, 1987, 42(3):483–510.

Michaely, Roni. "Ex-Dividend Day Stock Price Behavior: The Case of the 1986 Tax Reform Act," *Journal of Finance*, 1991, 46(3):845–860.

Miller, Merton, and Franco Modigliani. "Dividend Policy, Growth, and the Valuation of Shares," *Journal of Business*, 1961, 34(October):411–433.

Miller, Merton H., Jayaram Muthuswamy, and Robert E. Whaley. "Mean Reversion of Standard & Poor's 500 Index Basis Changes: Arbitrage-Induced or Statistical Illusion?" *Journal of Finance*, 1994, 49(2):479–513.

Mitchell, Mark L., and J. Harold Mulherin. "The Impact of Public Information on the Stock Market," *Journal of Finance*, 1994, 49(3):923–950.

Modigliani, Franco, and Merton Miller. "The Cost of Capital, Corporation Finance, and the Theory of Investments," *American Economic Review*, 1958, 48(June):261–297.

Moyer, R. Charles, Ramesh Rao, and Phillip M. Sisneros. "Substitutes for Voting Rights: Evidence from Dual Class Recapitalizations," *Financial Management*, 1992, 21(3):35–48.

Netter, Jeffry M., and Mark L. Mitchell. "Stock-Repurchase Announcements and Insider Transactions after the October 1987 Stock Market Crash," *Financial Management*, 1989, 18(3):84–96.

Pearce, Douglas K., and V. Vance Roley. "Firm Characteristics, Unanticipated Inflation, and Stock Returns," *Journal of Finance*, 1988, 43(4):965–981.

Persons, John C. "Signaling and Takeover Deterrence with Stock Repurchases: Dutch Auctions versus Fixed Price Tender Offers," *Journal of Finance*, 1994, 49(4):1373–1402.

Pound, John. "Proxy Voting and the SEC: Investor Protection versus Market Efficiency," *Journal of Financial Economics*, 1991, 29(2):241–286.

Pruitt, Stephen W., and K. C. John Wei. "Institutional Ownership and Changes in the S&P 500," *Journal of Finance*, 1989, 44(2):509–514.

Rosen, Corey. "The Record of Employee Ownership," *Financial Management*, 1990, 19(1):39–47.

Schall, Lawrence D. "Asset Valuation, Firm Investment, and Firm Diversification," *Journal of Business*, 1972, 45(January):11–28.

Schwert, G. William. "Stock Returns and Real Activity: A Century of Evidence," *Journal of Finance*, 1990, 45(4):1237–1257.

Seguin, Paul J., and Gregg A. Jarrell. "The Irrelevance of Margin: Evidence from the Crash of '87," *Journal of Finance*, 1993, 48(4):1457–1473.

Shanken, Jay, and Clifford W. Smith. "Implications of Capital Markets Research for Corporate Finance," *Financial Management*, 1996, 25(1):98–104.

Shefrin, Hersh, and Meir Statman. "The Disposition to Sell Winners Too Early and Ride Losers Too Long: Theory and Evidence," *Journal of Finance*, 1985, 40(3):777–782.

Sivakumar, Kumar, and Gregory Waymire. "Insider Trading Following Material New Events: Evidence from Earnings," *Financial Management*, 1994, 23(1):23–32.

Young, Philip J., James A. Millar, and G. William Glezen. "Trading Volume, Management Solicitation, and Shareholder Voting," *Journal of Financial Economics*, 1993, 33(1):57–72.

WHY CAPITAL STRUCTURE MATTERS

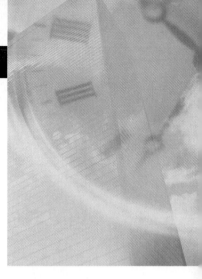

How a firm finances itself is called its **capital structure**. In simple terms, capital structure refers to the firm's proportion of debt financing, its leverage ratio. The leverage ratio was represented by L in Equation (10.1). In Chapter 10, we said that capital structure does not affect firm value—*in a perfect capital market environment*. The choice of capital structure is a pure risk-return trade-off. We then showed that this is equivalent to saying that leverage does not affect the cost of capital—in a perfect capital market environment.

The question of whether capital structure affects firm value in real capital markets has been called the *capital structure puzzle*. And *puzzle* is a particularly appropriate term, because our understanding has evolved in much the same way in which a puzzle is pieced together. Pieces are still being added, and we still don't have the complete picture.

In practice, capital structure matters if for no other reason than that firms behave as though it does. The empirical evidence shows consistent patterns of leverage ratios. These patterns occur both across industries and for individual firms over time. This suggests that managers have definite reasons for following certain policies. Some argue that firms are simply following the Behavioral Principle of Finance—just copying each other—and that these patterns are "neutral mutations" that do not affect firm value but, once started, continue from habit and imitation. We believe this interpretation is too simplistic.

In Chapter 14, we identified three persistent capital market imperfections: tax asymmetries, information asymmetries, and transaction costs. In this chapter, we will show how such capital market imperfections cause a firm's capital structure to affect its value and, therefore, how they cause capital structure to matter.

In the next chapter, we will outline a practical method of managing capital structure that is consistent with this conceptual framework. We will also explain further how to adjust for the effect of capital structure on firm value under some other conditions.

OBJECTIVES

After studying this chapter, you should be able to

1. Describe six different views of capital structure: perfect market, corporate tax, personal tax, agency cost, bankruptcy cost, and pecking order.

2. Describe how these views depend on asymmetric taxes, asymmetric information, and transaction costs, and combine to create an environment in which a firm's capital structure can affect its total value.

3. Explain how the capital market imperfections view of capital structure leads to preferences among new financing alternatives in which retained earnings are the preferred source, debt is next, and new external equity is the least preferred source.

4. Explain why adjusting a firm's weighted average cost of capital is an equivalent alternative to adjusting the expected cash flows and required returns on equity and debt.

5. Adjust the cost of capital for the effect of capital structure on total firm value.

CAPITAL STRUCTURE AND THE PRINCIPLES OF FINANCE

◆ *Incremental Benefits*: Consider the possible ways to minimize the value lost to capital market imperfections, such as asymmetric taxes, asymmetric information, and transaction costs. At the same time, be sure to include all the transaction costs of making potentially beneficial financing transactions, because they reduce the *net* benefit from such transactions.

◆ *Capital Market Efficiency*: Recognize that the potential to increase firm value through capital structure is limited. The potential to increase firm value through the introduction of valuable new ideas and through wise use of the firm's comparative advantages is much larger.

◆ *Signaling*: Consider any possible change in capital structure carefully, because financing transactions and changes in capital structure convey information to outsiders and can be misunderstood.

◆ *Time Value of Money*: Include any time-value-of-money tax benefits from capital structure choices.

◆ *Valuable Ideas*: Look for opportunities to create value by issuing securities that are in short supply, perhaps because of changes in tax laws.

◆ *Behavioral*: Look to the information contained in the capital structure decisions and financing transactions of other firms for guidance in making decisions.

◆ *Risk-Return Trade-Off*: Recognize that capital structure changes made at fair market security prices, which also change equity-debt risk bearing, are simply a risk-return trade-off. Such transactions do not affect firm value (except for possible information effects).

15.1 THE PERFECT MARKET VIEW

In Chapter 10, we asserted that a firm's capital structure is irrelevant to its value in a perfect capital market environment. We demonstrated in the Per-Pet example that leverage is a pure risk-return trade-off in such an environment. This result is called the **perfect market view** of capital structure.

In Chapter 14, we discussed the concept of value conservation, which is the fundamental concept underlying the perfect market view. In a perfect capital market environment, the value of a firm depends only on the size of its expected future operating cash flows and on the cost of capital, not on how those cash flows are divided between the debtholders and the shareholders.

Let's review our Chapter 10 Per-Pet example. With or without leverage, the total value of the firm is $1000. With leverage, the shareholders get $500 in exchange for half their claim on the firm. Figure 15-1 illustrates these cases in terms of "pies." The total size of the pie is the same whether the firm is leveraged or all-equity-financed. The only difference is in the claims on that pie. Figure 15-1 expresses the perfect market view in terms of total firm value, the present value of the expected future cash flows.

Figure 15-2 is a reproduction of Figure 10-7. Figure 15-2 also illustrates the perfect market view, but it does so in terms of the cost of capital, WACC, and the required returns on the expected future cash flows.

Recall that present value depends on both the cost of capital and the expected cash flows. If the cash flows do not change and one of the other parameters does not change, then the third

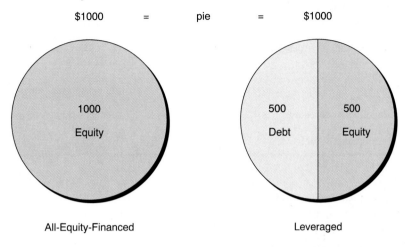

$1000 = pie = $1000

1000
Equity

500
Debt

500
Equity

All-Equity-Financed

Leveraged

FIGURE 15-1
A "pie" representation of the perfect market view of capital structure.

must also remain constant. However, also recall that even though the leverage ratio (L) does not affect WACC, it does affect how the risk of the firm is borne by the shareholders and debtholders. Therefore, the required returns on equity and debt (r_e and r_d, respectively) depend on the leverage ratio (L). The required return for both stockholders and debtholders rises as L increases, because the risk of default also increases.

Finally, recall that the WACC can always be expressed as the weighted average cost of any financing package. With only equity and debt, the WACC is the weighted average of r_e and r_d adjusted for taxes,[1] or

$$\text{WACC} = (1 - L)r_e + L(1 - T)r_d \tag{15.1}$$

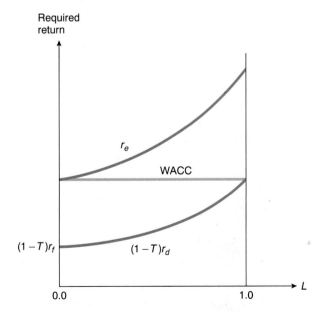

Required return

r_e

WACC

$(1 - T)r_f$

$(1 - T)r_d$

0.0

1.0

L

FIGURE 15-2
Weighted average cost of capital, WACC, required return for equity, r_e, and required return for debt, r_d, as hypothetical functions of the leverage ratio, L, under the perfect market view of capital structure.

[1]As we discussed in Chapter 2 and again in Chapter 10, the tax adjustment is necessary because interest payments are paid out *before* corporate taxes are levied on the firm's income, but dividends are not paid out until after. See Figure 15-6 for a visual representation of this process that includes personal taxes.

	FIRM L	FIRM U
Leverage ratio [= debt/(debt + equity)]	50%	0
Operating income	$10,000,000	$10,000,000
−Interest expense[a]	3,600,000	0
Net income	$ 6,400,000	$10,000,000
Market value of equity	$30,000,000	$50,000,000
Market value of debt	30,000,000	0
Total market value	$60,000,000	$50,000,000

TABLE 15-1
An illustration of capital structure arbitrage.

[a] At a 12% interest rate.

Note that L in Equation (15.1) and Figure 15-2 is the proportion of debt and $(1 - L)$ is the proportion of equity. Also, once again, the weighted average stays constant even though the rates both increase, as shown in Figure 15-2. This is because the weight is shifting from the higher to the lower return as L increases and $(1 - L)$ simultaneously decreases.

Another way of illustrating the irrelevance of capital structure is with an arbitrage argument. In the following argument, we show that if two firms have identical operating profitability but different capital structures, arbitrage among investors will ensure that the two firms have equal market values.

An Arbitrage Argument for the Irrelevance of Capital Structure

Consider two firms operating in a perfect capital market environment. Each will generate $10,000,000 of operating income. They are identical in every respect except for their capital structures. Firm L is leveraged; it has debt in its capital structure. Firm U is unleveraged; it has an all-equity capital structure. The two firms have the market values shown in Table 15-1. Firm L has a higher market value, supposedly because of its leverage.

According to the perfect market view, the situation shown in Table 15-1 cannot persist because of a profitable arbitrage opportunity. Shareholders of firm L can realize a greater return on their investment, with no increase in either their investment risk or the amounts of funds they have invested, by making the following transactions. First, sell their shares of firm L. Second, borrow and create their own personal 50% leverage to duplicate firm L's capital structure. Third, use all the resulting cash to purchase shares of firm U. To illustrate this opportunity, consider the following example.

EXAMPLE

Arbitraging Differences in Leverage Valuation

An investor owns 1% of the shares of firm L. The first step in the arbitrage process is to sell these shares at their market value of $300,000 (1% of $30,000,000). The second step is to borrow an identical amount, $300,000, at an interest rate of 12% per year. This creates a personal capital structure that is 50% debt and 50% equity—exactly firm L's capital structure. The final step is to use the total funds to purchase $600,000 (= 300,000 + 300,000) of firm U shares, which happens to be 1.2% (= 600,000/50,000,000) of firm U.

Now let's compare the return before and after. Before the three-step transaction, the investor's return per year is 1% of firm L's expected net income, $64,000. Afterward, the return per year is $120,000 (1.2% of firm U's expected net income) minus an interest charge of $36,000 (12% of $300,000), or $84,000. Thus, after completing the arbitrage transaction, and without adding any funds, our investor has an investment with an identical amount of leverage (and therefore identical risk) that earns $20,000 (= 84,000 − 64,000) per year more. ■

With self-interested behavior, arbitrage activity by investors will continue until the market prices of the shares make the total values of the two firms equal. Only when the total firm values are equal will there be no further profitable arbitrage opportunity.

In our example, the firm's choice of capital structure cannot affect its value. This is because we assumed a perfect capital market environment. Let's relax this assumption now. We will find that capital market imperfections can forge a link between capital structure and total firm value.

Self-Check Questions
1. What is the perfect market view of capital structure?
2. What is the formula for the WACC? Identify each variable and explain how it contributes to the WACC.
3. What is the shape of the WACC curve, according to the perfect market view?

15.2 CORPORATE INCOME TAXES

In Chapter 14, we identified three persistent capital market imperfections: tax asymmetries, information asymmetries, and transaction costs. Thus an important place to look for possible value-changing market imperfections is in the tax code. Whenever tax rates differ for the two sides of a transaction, there is a tax asymmetry that might be used to enhance firm value.

We have noted at various points in earlier chapters that interest payments are tax-deductible to the firm, whereas dividend payments are not. This tax asymmetry gives rise to the **corporate tax view** of capital structure. In this view, capital markets are efficient enough to make capital structure essentially irrelevant, except that the corporate tax asymmetry causes debt to be a cheaper source of financing than equity.

The corporate tax view of capital structure concludes that the maximum firm value results from being essentially all-*debt*-financed.

In the following example, we illustrate the corporate tax view. The illustration extends our leveraging Per-Pet, Inc. example, given in Chapter 10, where the hypothetical firm has a simple perpetual yearly cash inflow.

Corporate Taxes at Per-Pet, Inc.

EXAMPLE

As in our Chapter 10 example, we will start with an all-equity firm and examine the effect of leverage on firm value. We assume that Per-Pet must pay corporate taxes on its net income at the rate of 37.5%. However, it operates in an otherwise perfect capital market environment. What is Per-Pet worth if it is all-equity-financed, and what is it worth with leverage?

Per-Pet has a perpetual expected cash inflow each year of $150, which can be larger or smaller but is never less than $50 per year. Therefore, its expected after-tax net income is $93.75 per year $[= (1 - 0.375)150]$. Per-Pet's all-equity-financed $(L = 0)$ cost of capital is 15%, so Per-Pet is worth $625 $(= 93.75/0.15)$, compared to a $1000 value without corporate taxes $(= 150/0.15)$.

Now suppose the firm borrows $500 and gives the money to the shareholders. The debtholders will lend the money at the rate of 10% per year. Therefore, this debt will require $50 per year in interest payments. The debtholders charge less than the 15% all-equity rate because the loan is riskless. The debtholders will get their money each period without fail.

From the firm's viewpoint, the interest payments are made *before* corporate taxes are assessed. Therefore, they cost only $31.25 $[= (1 - 0.375)50]$ in after-tax cash flow. After the change in capital structure, then, the residual expected future cash flow to be paid out to shareholders each year is $62.50 (= $93.75 − 31.25).[2] This is a smaller but riskier cash flow stream.

When the firm is all-equity-financed, the shareholders bear all the firm's risk, spread out over an investment of $625. With the proposed 50% debt capital structure, the shareholders also bear all the firm's risk, but the risk is spread out over a smaller investment. Thus the risk *per dollar invested* for the shareholders is larger, and the shareholders must "pay" for their increased expected return with an increase in risk. As we said in the Chapter 10 example, the shareholders' required return increases to 20% to offset their higher risk.

Under the proposed leveraging, then, shareholders would get $500 from the debtholders in cash to invest as they wish and would have a remaining investment worth $312.50 (= $62.50/0.20), for a total value of $812.50. Thus in this environment, the proposed leveraging increases shareholder value by $187.50 (= 812.50 − 625.00).

Simultaneously, the total value of Per-Pet would increase by the same $187.50. With no leverage, the firm is worth $625.00 (= 93.75/0.15). Under the proposed leveraging, total firm value is the value of the debt (500) plus the value of the equity (312.50), for a total value of $812.50. ∎

---

[2] This amount can also be computed by starting with the firm's expected income of $150 per year. Subtract the $50 interest payment and apply the corporate tax rate: (1 − 0.375)(150 − 50) = $62.50.

The extra value for the Per-Pet shareholders can be traced directly to the tax asymmetry. The expected after-tax cash flows to investors increase because the government collects fewer tax dollars from the leveraged firm. Specifically, with the all-equity capital structure, the firm pays an average of $56.25 (= 0.375 × 150) per year. It pays an average of only $37.50 [= (0.375)(150 − 50)] per year with the leveraged capital structure.

Figure 15-3 illustrates the corporate tax view of capital structure, showing the Per-Pet alternatives in terms of "pies." Once again, the total size of the pie is the same whether the firm is leveraged or all-equity-financed: $1000. The only difference is in the claims on the pie. However, this time, under the corporate tax view, there are three claimants: shareholders,

FIGURE 15-3
A "pie" representation of the corporate tax view of capital structure.

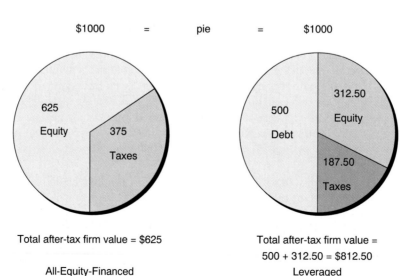

$1000   =   pie   = $1000

625
Equity

375
Taxes

500
Debt

312.50
Equity

187.50
Taxes

Total after-tax firm value = $625

Total after-tax firm value =
500 + 312.50 = $812.50

All-Equity-Financed

Leveraged

debtholders, and the government. By selling part of the cash flow to the debtholders in this assumed environment, the government collects less in taxes. This shrinks its claim and leaves more for investors. Leverage increases the total after-tax value of the firm from $625 to $812.50.

The Cost of Capital with Corporate Income Taxes

Although leverage actually changes the after-tax cash flows, the effect can be equivalently accounted for by adjusting the cost of capital. Let $\bar{I}$ represent the expected perpetual cash inflow per year. Then the unleveraged firm pays taxes of $T\bar{I}$ each year and the shareholders get the rest, an expected yearly after-tax cash flow of $\bar{I}(1 - T)$. The value of the unleveraged firm, V_U, is then

$$V_U = \frac{\bar{I}(1 - T)}{r} \tag{15.2}$$

where r is the unleveraged cost of capital (15% in the Per-Pet example).

In the Per-Pet example, we adjusted the after-tax cash flows and the required returns for equity (20%) and debt (10%) to find the value of the leveraged firm. Alternatively, we can represent the value of the leveraged firm, V_L, in terms of the "basic" after-tax cash flow to the firm and an appropriately adjusted cost of capital. The "basic" cash flow is the cash flow to the shareholders if the firm were unleveraged, $\bar{I}(1 - T)$. This flow is what we called CFAT in capital budgeting (see Chapter 11). Then

$$V_L = \frac{\bar{I}(1 - T)}{\text{WACC}} \tag{15.3}$$

where WACC is the weighted average cost of capital, which has been adjusted for the effect of corporate taxes. Now we need to determine just what that adjustment is.

To avoid having to adjust the required returns on equity and debt, r_e and r_d, for differences in risk, we will use a little "trick." We will assume the firm uses an amount of debt, $D = LV_L$, with interest payments that are a specified proportion of the firm's cash inflow, $\bar{I}$. Therefore, this debt has the same risk as unleveraged equity and must also have the same required return, r. Thus the debtholders earn a *risky* (rather than a riskless) amount each period, which has an expected value of rD. The only difference between this debt and unleveraged equity is that the debt payments are tax-deductible.[3]

The firm pays taxes on all its income that is not paid out as interest, so the firm's annual taxes are expected to be

$$T(\bar{I} - rD)$$

The combined after-tax cash flow expected to be paid out to debtholders and shareholders is a yearly perpetuity of

$$\bar{I} - T(\bar{I} - rD) = \bar{I}(1 - T) + TrD$$

We can use this perpetuity to value the leveraged firm because of our risk "trick." The after-tax cash flows to equity and debt have the same risk and therefore the same required return.

---

[3] This is somewhat hypothetical, but it simplifies the analysis so that we can focus on how financial risk affects the cost of capital. A more complex analysis using a more typical debt instrument produces the same result after adjusting for risk differences. (Actually, our debt instrument is not as artificial as it sounds. Income bonds could have been used to create the hypothetical debt instrument in this example up until about 1980, when such securities were essentially eliminated by an IRS ruling that interest on them is not tax-deductible.)

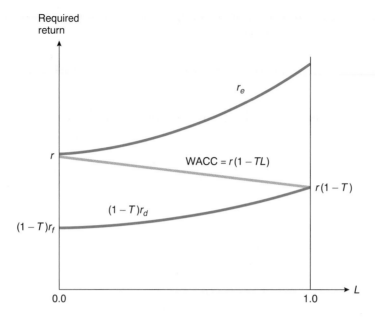

FIGURE 15-4
Weighted average cost of capital, WACC, shown under the corporate tax view of capital structure in terms of hypothetical functions for the required return for debt, r_d, and the required return for equity, r_e.

Thus

$$V_L = \frac{\bar{I}(1-T)+TrD}{r} = \frac{\bar{I}(1-T)}{r} + TD \qquad (15.4)$$

The fraction in the expression on the far-right-hand side of this equation equals the right-hand side of Equation (15.2), so we can rewrite V_L as

$$V_L = V_U + TD \qquad (15.5)$$

This is the most common way of mathematically expressing the corporate tax view.

We can build on this result. A value for WACC can be derived by setting Equations (15.3) and (15.4) equal to each other and solving for WACC.[4]

$$WACC = r(1 - TL) \qquad (15.6)$$

Figure 15-4 illustrates the corporate tax view of capital structure in terms of the WACC and hypothetical functions for the required returns on equity and debt. Note that the function for WACC is a straight line. WACC decreases as L increases. The lowest value for WACC, $r(1 - TL)$, occurs when the firm is financed entirely with debt—that is, when $L = 1.0$. Under

---

[4] Setting the equations equal, we have

$$\frac{\bar{I}(1-T)}{WACC} = \frac{\bar{I}(1-T)}{r} + TD$$

Cross-multiplying, rearranging, and substituting LV_L for D, we get

$$WACC = r - \frac{rTLV_L WACC}{\bar{I}(1-T)}$$

From Equation (15.3) we can see that $WACC/\bar{I}(1-T)$ is the inverse of V_L, so it cancels out V_L and

$$WACC = r - TLr = r(1 - TL)$$

the corporate tax view, then, the optimal capital structure—the one that creates the most valuable firm—is the one that contains as much debt as possible.

EXAMPLE

The Cost of Capital at Per-Pet, Inc.

Now we can check our work by applying the adjusted cost of capital given in Equation (15.6) to our Per-Pet example with corporate taxes. Under the proposed leveraging, the firm borrows $500 and leveraged firm value is $812.50. This means that Per-Pet's leveraged capital structure would be $L = 0.61538 \, (= 500/812.50)$. (Remember that L, the leverage ratio, is based on market values.) What is Per-Pet's cost of capital under the proposed leveraging?

From Equation (15.6), we have

$$\text{WACC} = r(1 - TL) = (0.15)[1 - (0.375)(0.61538)] = 0.115385 - 11.5385\%$$

Alternatively, we can find the WACC using Equation (15.1):

$$\text{WACC} = (1 - L)r_e + L(1 - T)r_d$$
$$= (1 - 0.61538)(0.20) + (0.61538)(1 - 0.375)(0.10) = 0.115385 = 11.5385\%$$

We can now verify that our adjustment produces the correct value for V_L by using this WACC and Per-Pet's CFAT of $93.75 in Equation (15.2):

$$V_L = \frac{\bar{I}(1 - T)}{\text{WACC}} = \frac{93.75}{0.115385} = \$812.50$$

Before moving on, we want to emphasize the equivalence between (1) adjusting the WACC and (2) adjusting the after-tax cash flows and required returns on equity and debt. Adjusting the WACC has become more commonly used, probably because of convenience. It involves only a single adjustment.

Also, once again, we feel it is important to emphasize that *the leverage ratio is based on market values*.

Where does the corporate tax view leave us? Corporate borrowing involves a tax advantage. From this perspective, firms should use 100% debt financing because that minimizes the WACC or, equivalently, maximizes total firm value. What a surprising result! But it is also troubling, because firms do not do this in practice. There must be more to the capital structure puzzle. Let's continue our investigation of the impact of market imperfections.

Self-Check Questions

1. What is the corporate tax view of capital structure?
2. Why does the U.S. corporate tax system seem to favor debt financing over equity financing?
3. According to the corporate tax view, what is the relationship between the leveraged value of the firm, V_L, and its unleveraged value, V_U?
4. What is the shape of the WACC curve, according to the corporate tax view?

15.3 PERSONAL INCOME TAXES

From an income tax perspective, our Per-Pet corporate tax example is incomplete. There are other significant taxes besides corporate income taxes. The corporation pays taxes on its income, but investors then pay personal income taxes on their income from the corporation. And the rates investors pay are not all the same. The rates depend on the form of the investment—in particular, on whether it is equity or debt.

Interest and dividends are taxed when they are received, but capital gains are not taxed until the asset is sold. Therefore, a shareholder can postpone the tax on a gain by not selling the shares. At the same time, there is a mirror image treatment of losses. The shareholder can claim the tax shield resulting from a loss right away by selling the asset. This creates the valuable tax-timing option we described in Chapter 8. The capital gain tax-timing option lowers the effective tax rate on shareholder income. In turn, this lower effective rate leads to the **personal tax view** of capital structure. According to this view, the firm is still operating in a perfect capital market environment, except for corporate *and* personal income taxes.

The personal tax view concludes that the differential between tax rates on personal income from equity and from debt cancels out the corporate tax asymmetry. The outcome is that leverage has no effect on firm value in this environment and that, once again, capital structure is irrelevant.

To illustrate the personal tax view of capital structure let's extend our Per-Pet example one more time.

EXAMPLE

Personal Taxes at Per-Pet, Inc.

Once again, we will start with an all-equity firm and examine the effect of leverage on firm value. Suppose Per-Pet's debtholders' tax rate is 50%, whereas the shareholders' rate is 20%. Per-Pet's corporate tax rate is the same 37.5%, and it operates in an otherwise perfect capital market environment. What is Per-Pet worth if it is all-equity-financed, and what is it worth with leverage?

After paying 20% in personal taxes, the shareholders get to keep 80% ($= 1.0 - 0.20$) of their cash flow from the firm, which after corporate taxes is expected to be $93.75 [$= (1 - 0.375)150$]. With an all-equity capital structure, then, the shareholders' expected cash flow after corporate *and* personal taxes is $75.00 ($= 0.8 \times 93.75$). On the basis of Per-Pet's 15% unleveraged cost of capital, Per-Pet is worth $500 ($= 75.00/0.15$).

Now suppose the firm borrows $250 at an after-personal-taxes required return of 10%. Thus the debtholders must receive 10% of $250, or $25, after taxes. Therefore, the interest payment from the firm must be $50 [$= 25/(1 - 0.5)$] per year. This interest payment and corporate taxes leave an expected amount for the shareholders of $62.50 [$= (1 - 0.375)(150 - 50)$], on which they must pay personal taxes. Under the proposed leveraging, the shareholders have an expected annual cash flow after corporate and personal taxes of $50 [$= (1 - 0.2)62.50$]. Again, the leverage would increase the shareholders' required return to 20%. Under the proposed leveraging, then, shareholders would get $250 from the debtholders in cash to invest as they wish and would have a remaining investment in Per-Pet worth $250 ($= 50/0.20$). Thus shareholders will have the same total value of $500 whether or not the firm is leveraged.

The total value of Per-Pet is not changed, and capital structure is irrelevant in this environment. In both cases, the firm is worth $500—either $500 worth of equity, or $250 worth of equity plus $250 worth of debt. ∎

Figure 15-5 illustrates the personal tax view of capital structure, showing the alternatives in our personal taxes Per-Pet example in terms of "pies." In this case, the total size of the pie is the same and the total taxes paid are the same. The only difference is the amounts paid of each type of tax. With all-equity financing, more corporate taxes and less personal taxes are paid than under the proposed leveraging, but the total after-tax value is $500 either way.

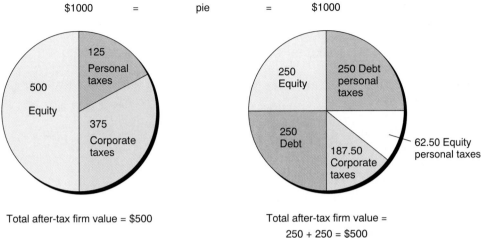

Total after-tax firm value = $500

All-Equity-Financed

Total after-tax firm value =
250 + 250 = $500

Leveraged

FIGURE 15-5
A "pie" representation of the personal tax view of capital structure.

If it occurs to you that the results illustrated in Figure 15-5 depend on the personal tax rates we use, you are right. The critical issue is the amount that reaches the investor after corporate and personal taxes. Let T_d, T_e, and T represent the tax rates for debtholders, equityholders, and the corporation, respectively. The difference in personal taxes for equity and debt exactly cancels out the corporate tax asymmetry *only* when

$$(1 - T_d) = (1 - T_e)(1 - T) \tag{15.7}$$

When this condition holds, the after-corporate-and-personal-taxes portion of the firm's cash flow that "reaches" an investor is the same, whether the investor has an equity or a debt claim. That is, a before-tax dollar taxed at T_d provides the same net amount to an investor as a before-tax dollar taxed at T and then taxed again at T_e.

If $T_e = 10\%$, $T = 30\%$, and $T_d = 37\%$, then Equation (15.7) is satisfied:

$$(1 - 0.37) = (1 - 0.1)(1 - 0.3) = 0.63$$

Figure 15-6 illustrates the tax process using these tax rates. Note once again how the cash flows to the shareholders are taxed twice, whereas those to the debtholders are taxed only once, but at a higher rate. Despite this difference, the net amount received is the same with these tax rates. ■

Neutral Tax Rates

EXAMPLE

FIGURE 15-6
An example of corporate and personal taxation of cash flows going to shareholders and debtholders.

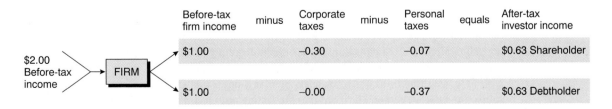

	Before-tax firm income	minus	Corporate taxes	minus	Personal taxes	equals	After-tax investor income
$2.00 Before-tax income → FIRM →	$1.00		−0.30		−0.07		$0.63 Shareholder
	$1.00		−0.00		−0.37		$0.63 Debtholder

It is very important to understand that the personal tax view that capital structure is irrelevant depends on having tax rates that satisfy Equation (15.7).

Self-Check Questions

1. What is the personal tax view of capital structure?
2. Explain why the personal tax view depends on the personal tax rates on debt and equity income.
3. If $T = 0.3$ and $T_d = 0.35$, what tax rate on equity income, T_e, leads Equation (15.7) to hold?
4. How is it that the personal tax view reaches the same conclusion as the perfect market view concerning the irrelevance of capital structure?

15.4 THE COMBINED EFFECT OF CORPORATE AND PERSONAL INCOME TAXES

If the corporate tax view of capital structure ignores personal taxes, it takes an extreme position. Similarly, when the effect of personal taxes is analyzed by using tax rates that satisfy Equation (15.7), the personal tax view takes an extreme position. Now let's consider some of the "fertile ground" between these two extremes.

Suppose tax rates are such that (1) personal taxes do not *exactly* cancel out the corporate tax asymmetry and (2) the single tax rate on debt income is smaller than the combined tax rate on corporate income and equity returns. Then the conclusion of the corporate tax view of capital structure still holds: More leverage increases firm value by reducing the net loss to taxes. But the benefit to leverage is significantly less than if we ignore personal taxes. Therefore, even if personal taxes don't eliminate the corporate tax asymmetry, they significantly reduce it, along with the net benefit to leverage.

The Tax Reform Act of 1986 provides evidence of the effect on capital structure of the interaction between corporate and personal tax rates. The act reduced the maximum tax rates, but the reduction was larger for personal than for corporate income. Thus the new rates increased the difference between the left- and right-hand sides of Equation (15.7). The act also eliminated the investment tax credit, reduced the degree of acceleration in depreciation tables, and eliminated or reduced many other non-debt-related tax deductions. It also reduced the rate of personal taxation on interest income, but it eliminated the personal dividend exclusion and increased the rate of personal taxation on the capital gain component of equity returns.

The net result of all these tax changes was to make corporate leverage relatively more attractive, compared with personal leverage, than it had been. And, in fact, corporate leverage ratios did increase, on average, in the years following passage of the legislation. This observed change in leverage is evidence of the importance of taxes to capital structure.

Tax-Timing Options

In addition to lowering the effective tax rate on shareholder income, tax-timing options have another, secondary effect, on a firm's value. We described the capital gain tax-timing option on shareholder income, but debt also has such an option. Because bond values change, debtholders can also have a capital gain or loss. They too can postpone the tax on a gain by not selling their bond or can claim the tax shield resulting from a loss right away by selling it. Thus there is a tax-timing option attached to both stocks and bonds.

When a firm is all-equity-financed, there is a single tax-timing option on the firm's portfolio of assets. A leveraged firm has two tax-timing options on its portfolio of assets, one connected to the equity and a second to the debt. Recall from Chapter 8 that the value of a port-folio of options on individual assets can be greater (and is never less) than a single option on a portfolio of those same assets. This creates the possibility that total firm value may be larger when it is financed with both equity and debt.

We believe—and we think we have the support of most of our colleagues in the finance profession—that there is a net tax benefit to leverage. If so, however, why do firms not use 100% leverage? To answer this, let's continue our investigation of capital market imperfections.

Self-Check Questions

1. Suppose there is a single tax rate on debt income that is smaller than the combined tax rate on corporate income and equity returns. Suppose also that personal taxes do not exactly can-cel out the corporate tax asymmetry. How would leverage affect firm value under these con-ditions?
2. How do personal taxes modify the conclusion of the corporate tax view of capital structure?
3. What are tax-timing options?
4. Name the two tax-timing options that a leveraged firm has.

15.5 AGENCY COSTS

In Chapter 9 we described certain conflicts among the debtholders, shareholders, and man-agers. These conflicts give rise to the **agency cost view** of capital structure. In this view, cap-ital market imperfections resulting from agency cost considerations create a complex envi-ronment in which capital structure affects a firm's value. We will discuss a few of these conflicts here to illustrate the potential role of agency costs. (Our discussion in Chapter 9 is more thorough.) The agency cost view concludes that firm value is maximized by some mix-ture of debt and equity.

Agency Costs of Debt

A major conflict that arises from using debt financing is the possibility that shareholders will expropriate wealth from the debtholders. Recall the problem of *asset substitution*. Suppose debtholders lend money to the firm assuming that the firm will invest in a low-risk project; ac-cordingly, they agree to a low interest rate on the loan. If the firm then invests in a high-risk project, the risk of the loan increases. This increases the required return on the loan and low-ers its present value.

As a second example, recall the problem of *claim dilution*. Let's assume the firm bor-rows money to invest in its business and immediately thereafter, the firm's managers do a leveraged buyout. That is, they take over ownership of the firm with a very small amount of equity financing and a tremendous amount of debt. What happens to the value of the original debt? The present value of the original debt decreases, and the decrease is lost to those debtholders but gained by the shareholders. Other debtholder-stockholder conflicts that are relevant to a firm's capital structure include the underinvestment problem and the effect of as-set uniqueness.

Agency conflicts among the firm's various claimants must be resolved in some way. When possible, contracts that eliminate these conflicts are created. For example, restrictive covenants, such as a restriction on leverage, are used to limit potential conflicts.[5] When it is

---

[5] As we said in Chapter 9, for the most part, debt covenants have provided protection against this sort of claim dilu-tion, following the RJR Nabisco leveraged buyout.

not possible to create a contract that eliminates a particular conflict, investors solve the problem in their own way. They reduce the price they are willing to pay for the debt to protect themselves from the risk of future expropriation of wealth. When a firm issues new securities, the agency cost of the securities is the sum of all the costs of a special contract (such as restrictive covenants for a bond, which are costly because they eliminate some of the firm's options) plus any reduction in price that is due to potential conflicts that remain.

A firm's capital structure may also affect the firm's agency costs with respect to its labor contracts. Recall the problem of the nondiversifiability of human capital. Employees are more likely to incur search costs for getting a new job when they work for a firm that is more likely to go bankrupt, and those costs are not consistent across all firms. The expected costs of the employees' job searches depend on the uniqueness of the firm's product or service. Employees who perform more generic tasks have lower expected job search costs than do employees who perform more specialized tasks. Labor costs reflect this difference. Therefore, when all else is equal, agency costs connected with labor are higher for firms that provide more specialized products or services. Higher agency costs resulting from greater leverage are likely to mean that the degree of specialization of a firm's product or service affects its choice of capital structure.

There is also an aspect of debt financing that reduces the firm's agency costs: the costs of the debtholders monitoring the shareholders, and of the shareholders monitoring the managers. Whenever the firm issues new debt, prospective debtholders will analyze the firm very carefully to determine a fair price to offer for the debt. Each time new debt is issued, then, existing debtholders and shareholders are provided with a free outside "audit" of the firm. This outside audit reduces the cost of monitoring to ensure that agents (managers) are acting responsibly.

Another way the use of debt can involve a monitoring function is with a sinking fund provision. With a sinking fund, the firm must be able to meet the periodic required payments in addition to the interest payments. Difficulty in doing so can provide a relatively early warning that the firm is in trouble. Inability to make the required sinking fund payments can trigger default. Obviously, this monitoring function is beneficial for debtholders, but it also provides further monitoring of the managers for the benefit of the shareholders.

Securing debt by using specific tangible assets as collateral can play a role in reducing the agency costs of debt. Secured debt limits the potential for debtholder loss in case of bankruptcy, thereby limiting the amount of wealth shareholders can expropriate from the debtholders. Assets securing a debt instrument cannot be sold without the permission of the debtholders or the Bankruptcy Court.

Total Agency Costs

Our discussion has so far focused primarily on the agency costs of debt. However, there are agency costs associated with obtaining *any* additional financing, debt or equity. When a firm seeks additional financing to undertake a desirable capital budgeting project, total transaction costs (including the agency costs) of the alternative methods must be compared.

There are also agency costs associated with other firm claimants, such as the employees, customers, and society. The trade-off among the agency costs of *all* the firm's various claimants leads to a theory of optimal capital structure that involves the use of multiple types of securities to balance the various classes of agency costs against one another. Figure 15-7 illustrates the relationships among the various agency costs and the total agency costs.

A particularly appealing implication of this theory is that the optimal capital structure it implies involves multiple types of securities but does not depend on the existence of income taxes. This is appealing because firms were being financed with combinations of debt and equity securities before income tax laws existed.

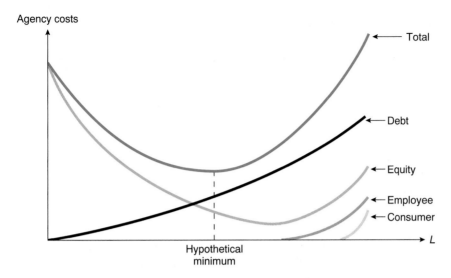

FIGURE 15-7
**The agency cost view
of capital structure.**

Self-Check Questions

1. What is the agency cost view of capital structure?

2. How does increased leverage provide incentives for asset substitution?

3. How does increased leverage lead to claim dilution?

4. In what sense can debt financing *reduce* the firm's agency costs?

5. Why are there agency costs associated with obtaining *any* additional financing?

15.6 FINANCIAL DISTRESS AND BANKRUPTCY

Several important effects of financial distress and bankruptcy are relevant to the capital structure question. These effects give rise to the **bankruptcy cost view** of capital structure. In this view, capital market imperfections associated with financial distress and bankruptcy offset the other benefits from leverage created by such things as taxes and agency costs.

Expected Cost of Bankruptcy

With debt in its capital structure, a firm has an expected cost of bankruptcy. This cost includes *direct costs* such as notification costs, court costs, and legal fees. And it includes the possible need to have virtually every major decision approved by the Bankruptcy Court. It also includes the significant *indirect costs* of management's attention being diverted from the day-to-day operation of the business in order to deal with the financial distress and bankruptcy process. And it includes lost tax credits and other indirect costs, such as suppliers refusing to ship goods other than on a COD basis (or refusing to ship altogether) as financial distress sets in. For example, at one point, the owners of Macy's Department Stores experienced financial difficulties that led many suppliers to halt shipments of goods.

The direct transaction costs of bankruptcy are paid only if bankruptcy actually occurs. Therefore, it is important to note that with an ongoing firm that is not in financial distress, the cost is a mathematical expectation. This expected value is considerably less than the actual cost when there is only a small chance of bankruptcy.

The expected bankruptcy costs depend in part on the uniqueness of the firm's assets. The more unique the asset, the lower the degree of liquidity and the greater the sales transaction costs. In the extreme case, a specially designed piece of equipment that is unique to a single firm's production process might be worth only its scrap value if the firm goes bankrupt.

An argument similar to the argument concerning uniqueness is based on a firm's type of assets: A firm with primarily tangible assets can borrow more than an otherwise comparable firm with primarily intangible assets (such as patents and trademarks). Intangible assets are less liquid and have higher sales transaction costs than tangible assets, and their value may be more firm-specific. The values of patents and trademarks depend on how they are used and on past conditions. Another firm may not be able to realize as much value from some of them. For example, the good-service reputation of a trademark product may be damaged or even destroyed by bad service resulting from otherwise unrelated financial distress. As a consequence, firms with more intangible assets have larger expected bankruptcy costs.

The effect on capital structure of possible financial distress and bankruptcy costs is as follows. Suppose that all other factors combined—such as personal and corporate taxes, agency costs, and other transaction costs—create a net value benefit to leverage, thereby making leverage desirable. But it will be desirable only up to a certain point, because as the firm increases its leverage, expected bankruptcy costs also increase and offset that benefit. Thus bankruptcy costs reduce the net value benefit of leverage and make "too much" leverage undesirable. (Of course, if there were no net benefit to leverage from all the other factors combined, expected bankruptcy costs would mean that even the first dollar of leverage would reduce a firm's value and therefore be undesirable.)

The bankruptcy effect produces an "optimal" capital structure that balances the expected bankruptcy cost against the other benefits. This is similar to the net effect of the various agency costs. And as with agency costs, a solution is hard to quantify. The bankruptcy view, however, is more satisfying than the corporate tax view, because it does not call for the extreme of 100% debt financing.

Indirect Costs of Financial Distress

The most significant potential cost of financial distress and bankruptcy is an indirect cost that can be difficult to measure but should not be underestimated. It arises because of the possibility that the firm will not continue as a going concern. This likelihood is important, because it can dramatically affect the value of the firm's products. In Chapter 9 we discussed this problem as a consumer-firm conflict. Consider the case where consumers believe the firm may not be able to honor warranties, provide service, or even supply replacement parts in the future. Such a belief can dramatically hurt sales, as it would with a car manufacturer in financial distress.[6]

When potential customers fear product discontinuation, they will force the firm to sell its product for a lower price than what it would otherwise be worth. The lower price reduces and can easily eliminate the manufacturer's profit margin on the product. This forgone profit can be very substantial. In fact, even though it is an opportunity cost that is difficult to measure, *this loss is the largest cost of financial distress/bankruptcy by a wide margin.*

More generally, financial distress dramatically intensifies many of the financial contracting conflicts of interest. As we discussed in Chapter 9, the incentives for agents to "push

---

[6] This possibility helped convince the U.S. Congress to provide loan guarantees for the Chrysler Corporation when it was in financial distress. The loan guarantees made Chrysler's warranties and promises of future service and parts availability believable.

the edge of the contract" and engage in bad behavior, such as asset substitution and underinvestment, can become tremendous. This is because of the contingent claim—the option—inherent in the situation. The agent may have virtually nothing to lose but a lot to gain. In some instances, the temptation to create claimant coalitions to enforce self-interested behavior can be overwhelming. It can lead to devastating risk taking, and lengthy and costly legal battles. These tendencies during financial distress substantially increase the firm's agency costs.

Possible Loss of Tax Shields

The possible loss of a firm's tax shields during periods of financial distress is another tax asymmetry that can affect a firm's value.[7] Loss carryforwards and loss carrybacks are sometimes limited, so that some of the corporate tax shields resulting from leverage may be lost during a period of financial distress. Even if all current losses can be fully carried forward and eventually deducted from future income, the firm still loses the time value of money on the tax shields.

Lost tax shields are not limited to those that result from debt financing. Other expenses, such as depreciation, also provide tax deductions. Therefore, such "nondebt" tax shields are a sort of substitute for leverage. And nondebt tax shields do not have the default risk that is connected with debt payments. This creates the possibility of boosting total firm value from a given total amount of tax shields by using proportionately more nondebt tax shields. This greater total firm value is due to the lower likelihood of bankruptcy connected with nondebt tax shields—and the resulting lower expected bankruptcy costs.

For the moment, we will restrict our view to taxes. Then the effect of the possibility of lost tax shield value is similar to that of other financial distress and bankruptcy costs: Suppose that personal taxes only partially offset the corporate tax benefit to leverage, and so there is a net tax benefit to leverage. Then increasing leverage is desirable, but only up to a certain point. Beyond that point, the loss in expected tax shield value also increases and offsets the other tax benefit. Thus the possibility of lost tax shield value limits the net tax benefits of leverage and makes "too much" leverage undesirable.

Once again, this time with respect to taxes, the bankruptcy effect produces an "optimal" capital structure—one that balances the expected tax shield value loss against the net corporate/personal tax benefit to leverage. And again, it leads to a solution that may be hard to quantify but is still somewhat satisfying because it is not the extreme of 100% debt financing prescribed by the corporate tax view.

Continuing with only the tax effect just a little longer, it is interesting to consider what would happen if the personal tax view's severe version were correct. Suppose the personal tax asymmetry entirely canceled out the corporate tax asymmetry. Then leverage would be neutral with respect to firm value *except* for the expected tax shield value loss in financial distress. Therefore, in such a case, leverage would actually be undesirable. The possibility of lost tax shields would make leverage decrease value.

Direct Bankruptcy Costs

The direct costs of bankruptcy—such as legal fees, court costs, and notification costs—are relatively small when compared to the indirect costs of bankruptcy and the total value of the firm. Therefore, they simply add to the firm's total expected bankruptcy costs. They do not change the basic conclusion of the bankruptcy view that the benefits of leverage stop before the firm is 100% debt-financed.

---

[7] This loss includes lost tax deductions and lost tax credits. Tax credits are the more valuable of the two. Tax credits offset taxes owed dollar for dollar. Tax deductions reduce taxable income; their value equals the tax rate times the reduction in the amount of taxable income.

15.7 EXTERNAL FINANCING TRANSACTION COSTS

The transaction costs associated with obtaining new external financing can play an important role in a firm's capital structure decisions. As in the case of bankruptcy, there are both direct and indirect costs. These costs lead to the **pecking order view** of capital structure. In the pecking order view, firms use internally generated funds as much as possible for financing new projects. New debt is less preferred than internal funds but is preferable to other sources. Debt-equity combinations, such as convertible debt, are third in the pecking order, with securities that have smaller proportions of equity being preferred to those with larger proportions of equity. Last in the pecking order comes new external equity.

The cost of obtaining new financing affects the firm's management of its capital structure in similar ways to other factors we have discussed, but also in a way that is different. In addition to affecting the desirability of the proportion of debt and equity at a particular point in time, these costs also affect capital structure decisions over time, in a dynamic way. We touched on this dynamic dimension in Chapter 13, when we said that the direct transaction costs of obtaining additional financing are a legitimate reason for capital rationing.

The combined (direct and indirect) cost per dollar of additional financing declines with increases in the size of the issue. This is because of a fixed-versus-variable-cost problem, and it affects how the firm should manage its capital structure over time. The transaction costs associated with obtaining new external financing make it much more costly for a firm to sell a series of small issues than to issue a single large amount when it needs to obtain additional external funds. Thus, to reduce the net transaction costs of new external financing, the firm should sell larger issues, less often.

EXAMPLE

Goodyear's Capital Structure

Let's say that Goodyear's optimal capital structure is 42% debt. Goodyear's stock has recently increased in value, and as a result, Goodyear's L is now 0.39. Despite the fact that Goodyear now appears to be at a suboptimal capital structure, the firm takes no action. Why?

Goodyear determines that the transaction costs required to restore its capital structure to 42% debt (for example, by issuing new debt and buying back some of its shares) exceed the benefits. Therefore, its current capital structure is not suboptimal. When these transaction costs are included in the analysis, it is actually more beneficial for Goodyear to tolerate a debt ratio that is lower than 42%—for now. If Goodyear's debt ratio moved enough, the benefits of returning to 42% debt could overcome the costs. ■

Our conclusion about issuing a relatively larger amount of a security when the firm does obtain new external financing is not limited to the use of debt, and it does not imply a preference for any particular method of financing. However, it does imply that the dynamic management of the firm's capital structure is important to the value of the firm. A firm can waste resources on issuance expenses if it does not manage its capital structure carefully.

Concerning particular methods, the total cost of new debt (the cost of negotiating private debt, or the combination of underwriting spread and direct issuance expenses connected with public debt) is typically lower than the total cost of obtaining other new external financing. Therefore, whether or not other factors create a net value benefit to leverage, debt is generally attractive *relative* to equity when a firm has already decided that it is going to obtain additional outside financing.

Of course, frequently firms with existing publicly traded stock issue additional new shares. Apparently, therefore, there are cases where managers believe a new project is desirable enough to justify the potential loss connected with issuing new equity.

Signaling and Capital Structure Decisions

A firm's decision about how to finance a project reflects its choice of capital structure. It also conveys information about the project and about how the firm's managers view its current market value.

Consider two examples. The first illustrates how the choice between internal (equity) and external financing can convey information about project value. The second illustrates how the choice between debt and equity can convey information about any perceived under- or overvaluation of the firm's shares.

Two firms, G and N, are identical except for new projects they are about to undertake. G has a good project that has a large positive NPV, whereas N has a neutral project that has a zero NPV. The owners of G are eager to provide the financing for the new project themselves, using personal funds so that they alone will earn the large expected NPV. In contrast, the owners of N are indifferent to allowing outside investors to invest in the new project, because it has a zero NPV. Generalizing the argument, then, we conclude that the percentage of owner financing may provide a signal of the owners' opinion of investment opportunities. ■

Adverse Selection: Internal Versus External Financing

EXAMPLE

Suppose shareholders know the firm is currently overvalued. Then they would like to have partners to share in the decline in market value that will take place in the future when others realize the firm is overvalued. Suppose instead that they know the firm is currently undervalued. Then they don't want to have new partners who will get a share of the increase in market value that will take place in the future when others realize the firm is undervalued. Shareholders of properly valued firms are indifferent to having new partners.

This leads to the idea that if additional financing is to be obtained, the firm will choose debt or equity depending on whether or not it wants new partners. That is, undervalued firms will issue new debt, whereas overvalued firms will issue new equity. Of course, in this simple world we have just described, shareholders of overvalued firms may not want to be identified as such. Therefore, they may try to imitate undervalued firms by issuing debt instead of equity. In such situations investors require other information to help them to understand the firm's actions. ■

Adverse Selection: External Debt Versus Equity Financing

EXAMPLE

These examples of adverse selection can be further generalized by considering new-project value and the current market value of a firm simultaneously. A simple description of combinations can be constructed by classifying each as good, OK, or bad. For example, the firm is OK (correctly valued) and the new project is good (has a large positive NPV). Let's also add that the firm has some ability to finance new projects with currently available funds.

The interactions among currently available funds, the NPV of the new project, and any current under- or overvaluing of the firm makes various types and amounts of new financing more, or less, attractive to the firm's shareholders. Although we won't do it here, with this kind of a classification scheme, we could analyze the conditions under which firms will or will not obtain additional financing. And if new financing would be sought, we could predict the conditions that will lead the firm to issue debt or equity.

One way in which firms may try to overcome the adverse selection problem is to use underwriters, rather than selling securities themselves. This can be especially useful if there is a need to maintain proprietary information. The underwriter may be able to certify the value of the firm and its new projects by standing ready to purchase all the shares without revealing (and therefore destroying the value of) certain types of private information.

Self-Check Questions
1. What is the pecking order view of capital structure?
2. Why do transaction costs make it more costly to sell a series of small issues than to sell a single large issue?
3. Where do retained earnings, a new debt issue, and a new issue of common stock appear in the pecking order for most firms?
4. Explain how using underwriters might enable a firm to overcome the adverse selection problem.

15.8 FINANCIAL LEVERAGE CLIENTELES

The personal tax view of capital structure says that both personal tax and corporate tax considerations affect the desirability of a particular capital structure. It also points to the fact that investors will take their own tax situations into account in deciding whether to invest in a particular firm. The idea that investors "sort" themselves into groups, where each group prefers the firms it invests in to follow a certain type of policy, is called the **clientele effect**.

When applied to financial leverage, the clientele effect refers to those investors who prefer a particular type of security or capital structure. A similar concept in marketing is called *market segmentation*. A market segment is an identifiable group of consumers who purchase a product with particular attributes that are distinct from the attributes of alternative products. One example is a market segment that buys luxury cars as distinct from one that buys economy cars.

The existence of various leverage clienteles mitigates some, but not all, of the arguments in favor of the relevance of capital structure. With respect to taxes, some securities may be a more attractive or a less attractive investment for certain investors. For example, investors with a high marginal income tax rate may find debt securities less attractive, whereas tax-exempt investors may find debt securities more attractive. Investors who prefer a firm with a particular capital structure strictly because of their own risk preferences are able to avoid the transaction costs of personal leverage by simply investing in a firm that already has their preferred amount of leverage.

Arguments concerning personal marginal tax rates lead to the hypothesis that an investor's marginal tax rate is a major determinant of the investor's preference for investing in firms with more or less leverage. According to these arguments, investor preferences for corporate financial leverage should be inversely related to the investor's marginal tax rate. The preference is based on whether the firm or the investor will get more tax benefit from the interest deduction. The one with the higher marginal tax rate will realize the greater tax savings. Therefore, investors with a low marginal tax rate should prefer to invest in firms with high leverage, and vice versa. Note that confirmation of this hypothesis would verify the important role of taxes, and yet there may be no implications for firm valuation. In other words, the existence of leverage clienteles would not lead firms to choose a particular capital structure consistently. And yet investor preference may make it more advantageous for a firm to issue one type of security than others at particular times.

Opportunities to Profit from Adjusting Corporate Leverage

Taxes and transaction costs reduce the return to shareholders. Therefore, investors should, and do, invest in securities that minimize their aggregate taxes and transaction costs for any particular combination of risk and return. The result of taking taxes and transaction costs into account is that a particular clientele group may pay a premium for a certain type of security. (Note that the premium is measured relative to the prices of securities that are equivalent.) Such a premium gives firms an incentive to follow particular policies that appeal to various clientele groups. Of course, this is simply another application of the Principle of Valuable Ideas: Being the first to have the idea has the potential to create value.

Over time, however, competition among firms will drive such premiums to zero, and market equilibrium will return. In the aggregate, firms will supply just enough of each type of security and eliminate the positive-NPV opportunities from capital structure choices. What remains after the premiums are gone is clientele groups and firms that are comfortable with one another.

In equilibrium, patterns can remain indefinitely, because neither the clientele groups nor the firms have any incentive to change. Such patterns have been referred to as "neutral mutations." However, whenever there are changes in laws (tax laws or any law affecting investments), it may be possible to "play the game" all over again as the market attains a new equilibrium. Each change creates the potential for new opportunities.

The result is that it may be possible to earn a premium for supplying a security or capital structure policy that is in short supply. (Note that this gain must be weighed against the transaction costs of investors' rearranging their security holdings.) Whenever a law is changed that affects the taxes and transaction costs for a particular financial leverage clientele, opportunities may arise for a firm to earn a positive NPV by changing its capital structure.

The Tax Reform Act of 1986 reduced the personal tax rate relative to the corporate tax rate and imposed a constraint on personal leverage. Investors may deduct interest expense on debt incurred to support investments, but only to the extent that such interest expense does not exceed investment income by more than $5000 per year. This constraint on personal leverage affects those financial leverage clienteles who have the most personal leverage. Firms whose shareholders belonged predominantly to such clienteles thus had an opportunity to increase corporate leverage. ■

The 1986 Tax Reform Act's Limit on Personal Leverage

EXAMPLE

Industry Patterns

Despite the possibility of periodic opportunities to profit from adjusting capital structure, such opportunities may not occur uniformly across different industries. There are systematic interindustry differences in the availability of tax shelters from depreciation and other sources besides interest deductions. Also, considerations of asymmetric information do not apply equally to every industry. For example, when product reliability and follow-up service are important concerns, as in the home appliance industry, we can expect the industry to have relatively low leverage. Why? Because the indirect costs of financial distress are potentially much greater in such cases.[8] In addition, external financing transaction costs can also differ among industries.

The result of these differences is that we can expect to find, and do in fact observe, systematic interindustry differences in leverage. In Chapter 16 we will explore the implications of this statement for the way firms choose their capital structures in practice.

Practical Limitations

Opportunities to profit from changes in capital structure have natural limitations. First, direct transaction costs to the firm reduce the potential benefit from a change in capital structure. Second, shareholder transaction costs make it expensive for investors to buy and sell shares, and this can affect the market price of the firm's stock.

When a firm's shareholder mix changes in response to a change in its capital structure, the new shareholders may wonder whether more transaction costs are in store for them as yet another subsequent change causes them to sell their shares in the same way they are now purchasing previous owners' shares. This leads to a potential indirect cost. Market participants may discount a firm's value in purchasing shares to protect themselves from future selling transaction costs.

Third, a series of changes in capital structure may create one other indirect cost. Market participants may discount a firm's value because they conclude that the firm's managers are incompetent.

These factors make sudden or frequent shifts in a firm's capital structure generally undesirable. Too sudden a shift may be disruptive to the firm's stock price in the near term, and frequent major shifts may be disruptive over the longer term.

In practice, most firms try to maintain a stable capital structure. It appears, then, that firms depart from a stable capital structure only when the managers believe there are valid reasons to do so. Such reasons include significant changes in the firm's investment opportunities, its earnings, or its own or shareholders' tax position.

Self-Check Questions

1. Explain what is meant by the clientele effect.
2. According to the clientele effect, investors with low marginal income tax rates should prefer to invest in firms with high leverage. Do you agree? Explain.
3. How might a firm profit when a change in tax law causes a particular financial leverage clientele to change its investment preferences?
4. Why might a sudden shift in a firm's capital structure be disruptive to its share price?

15.9 THE CAPITAL MARKET IMPERFECTIONS VIEW OF CAPITAL STRUCTURE

We have identified five views of capital structure beyond the perfect market view. Each view depends on certain aspects of the three persistent capital market imperfections we have described. The rationale for each view draws on one or more of these imperfections. For example, the agency cost view depends on problems of asymmetric information and transaction costs. The tax views focus on asymmetric tax considerations. The bankruptcy view involves all three imperfections.

The overall view that emerges is that of a dynamic process that involves various trade-

---

[8] The Chrysler example mentioned in footnote 6 also applies here.

offs and results in a general preference order among a firm's financing alternatives. We call this view the **capital market imperfections view** of capital structure. In this view, debt is generally valuable. With relatively low leverage, where there is little chance of incurring the transaction costs associated with financial distress, the expected value of the costs of financial distress are low. Therefore, for small amounts of leverage, the value-enhancing considerations of leverage that result from taxes and agency costs (including asymmetric information considerations) dominate the expected costs of financial distress. At some point, the expected costs of financial distress become large enough to overcome the other value-enhancing considerations. Along the way, transaction costs, asymmetric information considerations, and monitoring benefits also affect the attractiveness of the various alternative types of financing at particular points in time.

The firm's choice of capital structure, then, is a dynamic process that involves all these various considerations in conjunction with its investment opportunities and the amount of internal funds it is able to generate. The firm "factors them all in" when deciding how much and how often it will obtain new external financing.

The optimal capital structure is the one that maximizes the firm's total value. Figure 15-8 is a conceptual picture of the effect on firm value of all the various factors involved with all five of the views we have examined. Total firm value V_L reaches its maximum at the point where (1) the net tax benefits V_T from additional leverage are just offset by (2) the increase in the expected financial distress and bankruptcy costs V_B and (3) the change in total agency costs (including asymmetric information considerations) V_A from additional leverage.

It is important to understand that Figure 15-8 is only a "snapshot"; it cannot include the dynamic considerations that transaction costs, asymmetric information considerations, and monitoring benefits connected with external financing introduce into the picture. These managerial considerations mean that the "optimal" capital structure may not be a simple fixed proportion of debt financing.

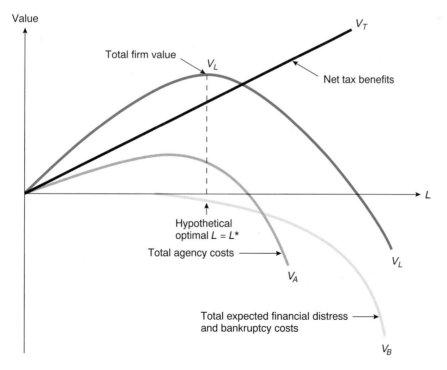

FIGURE 15-8
The capital market imperfections view of capital structure.

The Cost of Capital and Market Imperfections

Figure 15-8 illustrates the capital market imperfections view in terms of a firm's total value. Once again, the view can be represented in a corresponding way in terms of the firm's WACC, its weighted average cost of capital. According to this view, the optimal capital structure occurs at the point L^* where the firm's WACC reaches a minimum or, equivalently, the firm's value reaches a maximum.

Figure 15-9 illustrates the capital market imperfections view of capital structure that takes into account all of the factors we have discussed. In Figure 15-9, WACC is expressed in terms of hypothetical functions of r_d and r_e. The optimal capital structure occurs at L^*. To the left of L^*, increasing leverage reduces the WACC and increases firm value. To the right of L^*, increasing leverage has the opposite effects.

Figure 15-9 is a "snapshot" like Figure 15-8. It also cannot include the dynamic considerations that transaction costs, asymmetric information considerations, and monitoring benefits connected with external financing introduce. Thus the firm's optimal capital structure is really more complex than these figures indicate. Although Figure 15-9 provides a visual aid to understanding the impact of capital structure on the WACC and on firm value, we need an equation for WACC in order to determine more precise values.

To capture the impact of *all* the relevant dimensions connected with debt financing, define T^* as the **net-benefit-to-leverage factor**. T^* is assumed to be derived from a linear approximation to the actual net-benefit-to-leverage relationship over some relevant range of values for L. T^* enables us to operationalize the total impact of leverage on firm value in the capital market imperfections view. We can use the same sort of mathematics we used with the corporate tax view to adjust the WACC for all the relevant factors. In this more general case, we can express the value of the leveraged firm as

$$V_L = V_U + T^*D = \frac{\bar{I}(1-T)}{r} + \frac{T^*r_d D}{r_d} \tag{15.8}$$

which is a generalization of Equation (15.5).

Once again, V_L can be viewed as being made up of two components. The first compo-

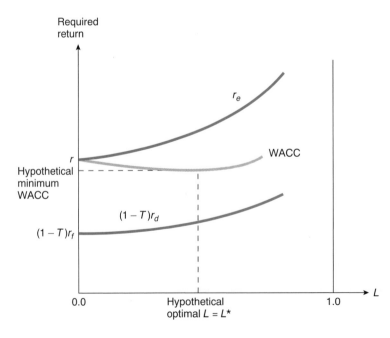

FIGURE 15-9
Weighted average cost of capital, WACC, shown under the capital market imperfections view of capital structure in terms of hypothetical functions for the required return for debt, r_d, and the required return for equity, r_e.

nent is the basic value of the firm if it is unleveraged, V_U. The second component is the net benefit from leverage. Each component represents the present value of a stream of expected future cash flows. The first stream is $\bar{I}(1 - T)$, the firm's after-tax income each period, its CFAT. The second stream is the net benefit from maintaining an amount D of debt. This net benefit can be expressed as T^* times the interest payment each period, or T^*r_dD.

For the perpetuity case, the present value is simply these cash flow amounts divided by their required returns. In this more general case, the risks of the two streams are different, so their required returns are different (recall that to derive Equation 15.5, we used "trick" debt that had the same required return as the equity). The required return for the firm's (unleveraged) after-tax income stream, its CFAT, is r. Because of lower risk, the required return for the net-benefit-to-leverage stream is r_d, which is lower than r.

Finally, the parallel is completed by expressing the impact on firm value in terms of the firm's WACC (the firm's required return). We will not prove it,[9] but the result is

$$WACC = r(1 - T^*L) \qquad (15.9)$$

The usefulness of Equation (15.9) is based on how easily it fits into our framework for making capital budgeting decisions. It is simply an adjustment made to the project's cost of capital, which accounts for the effect of leverage on project value. The adjusted rate is then used to compute the present value of the project's CFATs, its NPV.

You need an estimate for T^* to use Equation (15.9) to calculate the WACC. Assessing this factor requires professional judgment. We will show you how to estimate a reasonable value in Chapter 16.

Total Firm Value and Capital Market Imperfections

There is one final point we want to make. All of the views of capital structure, beyond that of a perfect capital market, are based on minimizing the value lost to one or more imperfections.

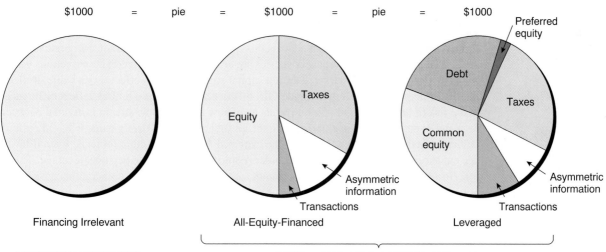

FIGURE 15-10

These three "pie" views of capital structure illustrate the loss of firm value from all the various capital market imperfections and the minimization of that loss through the choice of capital structure.

---

[9] The proof is similar to the one we used in footnote 4 to derive Equation (15.6).

Thus even though we talk about using leverage to increase firm value, in fact we are actually describing ways to use leverage to *reduce the loss* connected with various imperfections. What this means is that the total value of the firm is never more than what it would be in a perfect capital market. We illustrate this point in Figure 15-10 by using three "pie" views of a $1000 firm.

In Figure 15-10, the far-left "pie" shows the perfect market view. In it, there is no loss in value from imperfections. A firm's value does not depend on its capital structure. The other two pies reflect the capital market imperfections view of capital structure. In them, a dynamic optimal capital structure minimizes the total loss from all the various imperfections. In the middle pie, the firm is all-equity-financed. In the far-right pie, the firm has multiple types and amounts of financing that might typically be found in the practice of corporate financial management.

The net benefit to leverage can be seen in Figure 15-10. It is the difference between the value of the firm on the far right (the combined values of common equity, preferred equity, and debt) and the value of the firm in the middle pie (equity). However, despite this positive net benefit to leverage, the total value of the firm on the far right is substantially less than the firm value would be in a perfect capital market. This is because of losses to capital market imperfections.

Self-Check Questions

1. What is the capital market imperfections view of capital structure?
2. What is the shape of the WACC curve, according to the capital market imperfections view?
3. What is the net-benefit-to-leverage factor?
4. Suppose the net-benefit-to-leverage factor is $T^* = 0.15$. How would you interpret this value?

SUMMARY

The critical issue concerning capital structure is whether it affects the value of the firm. We described seven different views that address this question: the perfect market, corporate tax, personal tax, agency cost, bankruptcy cost, pecking order, and capital market imperfections views.

In a perfect capital market, a firm's capital structure has no effect on its value. Reflecting the Principle of Risk-Return Trade-Off, differences in required returns reflect differences in the risk of the investment—*not* differences in how the cash flow stream is divided between debt and equity claims—in a perfect market. In such a world, a firm's value is based entirely on the profitability of its assets and on the expected NPVs of its future projects. Even if leverage enhanced investment value, shareholders could borrow to create personal leverage. Therefore, in a perfect capital market, firms cannot capture any value due to leverage, because shareholders can do it themselves just as cheaply as the firm.

But our financial system contains some important persistent imperfections. Information is not costless and freely available to everyone, so the Signaling Principle (actions contain information) is a very important consideration. Choice of capital structure and changes in capital structure may provide information about the firm to the public. Thus a firm should be careful to choose the best method of financing, taking all costs into account—including the information that investors will infer from the firm's financing transactions. The problem of adverse selection is especially important in this connection.

There are other market imperfections. The system of corporate income taxation imposes a bias in favor of debt over equity, as do issuance costs. However, the system of individual income taxation, as well as direct and indirect financial distress/bankruptcy costs, impose an opposite bias. Aggregate agency costs and tax-timing options both favor having a mix of debt and equity rather than using one or the other exclusively. Taken together, these market imperfections lead to a view that there is some dynamic optimal capital structure that maximizes the value of a firm and that a general preference order among financing alternatives exists.

The clientele effect, wherein personal investments are made in firms that have adopted capital structures that are best for the individual investors, may mitigate some of these considerations. Changes in laws, particularly the tax code, sometimes create a demand for new types of securities or alter the demand for existing ones. Such changes in demand may in turn create profitable opportunities for a firm to supply a particular type of security to satisfy this new demand, thereby making one type of financing relatively more attractive to both issuer and investor. These opportunities are eliminated as the supply of new securities fulfills the demand for them.

There is not yet complete agreement about how capital structure affects the value of the firm. We expect future research to provide more insight into this issue. In the meantime, we will try to offer some guidance in the next chapter about how firms can, and currently do, manage their capital structure in light of the many considerations relevant to it.

DECISION SUMMARY

A firm should establish its capital structure with a view to maximizing the wealth of its shareholders. Important considerations are

- *Tax consequences*, both the firm's current and projected corporate tax rate and the personal tax positions of its investors, and also the possible loss of tax shield value in case of financial distress.

- *Total agency costs* associated with the firm, including those connected with debt, equity, and all other forms of financing, but also those connected with employees, customers, and society.

- *Financial distress and bankruptcy costs*, which include many indirect costs, such as reductions in product prices because of the firm's potential inability to honor warranties and provide service and replacement parts in the future and costs arising from the distortion of incentives caused by financial distress because of contingent claims—options—inherent in the situation, as well as more direct bankruptcy costs.

- *External financing transaction costs* such as direct selling and commission costs, but also indirect asymmetric information costs created by the problem of adverse selection. These add a dynamic dimension to the capital structure decision that makes it attractive to issue fewer and larger amounts of securities rather than more frequent but smaller amounts.

- *Market reaction* based on information perceived to be contained in the firm's choice of capital structure and in any changes that are made to it.

- *Demand-supply imbalances* for securities, especially those that result when changes in laws create profitable issuance opportunities.

- *Transaction costs associated with the firm's investors rearranging their security holdings* because of a change in the firm's capital structure policy.

- Any *legal or policy restrictions* on the firm and its shareholders that might affect the firm's choice of capital structure.

EQUATION SUMMARY

(15.1) $$\text{WACC} = (1 - L)r_e + L(1 - T)r_d$$

(15.2) $$V_U = \frac{\bar{I}(1 - T)}{r}$$

(15.3)
$$V_L = \frac{\bar{I}(1-T)}{\text{WACC}}$$

(15.4)
$$V_L = \frac{\bar{I}(1-T) + TrD}{r} = \frac{\bar{I}(1-T)}{r} + TD$$

(15.5)
$$V_L = V_U + TD$$

(15.6)
$$\text{WACC} = r(1 - TL)$$

(15.7)
$$(1 - T_d) = (1 - T_e)(1 - T)$$

(15.8)
$$V_L = V_U + T^* D = \frac{\bar{I}(1-T)}{r} + \frac{T^* r_d D}{r_d}$$

(15.9)
$$WACC = r(1 - T^*L)$$

KEY TERMS

EXERCISES

PROBLEM SET A

A1. Briefly compare the corporate tax view and the personal tax view of capital structure.

A2. Briefly explain how the personal tax view of capital structure mitigates the corporate tax view.

A3. Give an example of a tax-timing option and explain why it is valuable.

A4. How can restrictive debt covenants reduce agency costs?

A5. How can a new debt issue serve a monitoring function for a firm's shareholders?

A6. Cite two examples of how transaction costs might affect a firm's choice of financing.

A7. Why might potential new equity investors be leery of buying newly issued stock in a firm?

A8. How does the existence of financial leverage clienteles reduce the impact of tax asymmetries on the firm's choice of capital structure?

A9. True or false: The *direct* transaction costs connected with financial distress and bankruptcy are large as a proportion of the value of the firm.

A10. True or false: The *direct* transaction costs connected with financial distress and bankruptcy are much larger than the indirect, implicit opportunity costs such as lost sales, depressed product price, and lost tax credits.

A11. Briefly explain why taxes would not be asymmetric if Equation (15.7) held.

A12. Why might a firm that manufactures a unique product by using specialized employee expertise tend to finance with less debt than an otherwise identical firm that manufactures a generic product?

PROBLEM SET B

B1. You invest $12,000 in Joe's Garage, Inc., borrowing $5000 of the money at 10%. If you expect to earn 24% on your investment under this arrangement, what would you expect to earn if you put up the entire $12,000 from your own money? Ignore taxes.

B2. Consider two firms operating in a perfect capital market environment. Each will generate $10 million of operating income, and they are identical in every other respect, except that firm A has debt in its capital structure and firm B has an all-equity capital structure. Suppose that investors currently value firm A the same as firm L indicated in Table 15-1 but that the market value of the equity in B is $65 million. According to the perfect market view, this situation cannot persist. Suppose an investor owns 1% of the shares of B. Show how this owner can profit from arbitrage.

B3. Show how financial distress can affect the value of the firm through its tax credits, even when a firm is able to use all tax credits completely via loss carryforwards.

B4. Respond to the following statement: "Because a firm can lower its interest cost by including more restrictive covenants in its bonds, a firm should use the most restrictive set of covenants it can in order to achieve the lowest interest cost."

B5. Miles's Manor, an unassuming resort in midstate Pennsylvania, currently has an all-equity capital structure. Miles's Manor has an expected income of $10,000 per year forever and a required return to equity of 16%. There are no personal taxes, but Miles's pays corporate taxes at the rate of 35%, and all transactions take place in an otherwise perfect capital market.

a. What is Miles's Manor worth?

b. How much will the value of the firm increase if Miles's Manor leverages the firm by borrowing half the value of the unleveraged firm at an interest rate of 10% and the leverage causes the required return on equity to increase to 18.89%?

B6. What is the basis for the view that a firm's total market value is not affected by its choice of capital structure? Cite three broad types of capital market imperfections that can cause the capital structure of a firm to have an effect on the value of that firm. Give three examples (one for each type) where such an imperfection would cause a firm's capital structure to affect the value of that firm. Explain *how* each of the three examples you gave would cause a firm's capital structure to have an effect on the value of that firm.

B7. Dick's Pet-Way Corporation (DPC) is a chain of pet stores that has an expected cash inflow of $1000 each year forever. DPC's required return is 20% per year. Assume that all of DPC's income is paid out to the firm's investors.

a. If DPC is all-equity-financed and there are no taxes, what would DPC be worth in a perfect capital market?

Now suppose that DPC's corporate tax rate is 30%.

b. If DPC is all-equity-financed and there are no personal taxes, what would DPC be worth in an otherwise perfect capital market?

In addition to assuming corporate taxes at 30%, now suppose that DPC borrows $1400 at a required return on the debt of 10%. (*Note*: Because of risk, the required return on equity increases to 23.89%.)

c. If there are no personal taxes, what would DPC be worth in an otherwise perfect capital market? What would be DPC's leverage ratio, L?

d. If there are personal taxes on debt income at a rate of 37%, and personal taxes on equity income at a rate of 10%, what would DPC be worth in an otherwise perfect capital market?

e. If there are personal taxes on debt income at a rate of 25%, and personal taxes on equity income at a rate of 10%, what would DPC be worth in an otherwise perfect capital market?

f. Finally, compute the value of DPC as a 35.7% leveraged firm, with a 10% interest rate on the debt, when there are no taxes at all in a perfect capital market.

B8. Suppose that a firm is operating with corporate and personal taxes in an otherwise perfect capital market and that Equation (15.7) currently holds. In such a world, a firm would never take on any risky debt. Why not? (*Hint*: Consider what would happen in financial distress.)

B9. Describe the capital market imperfections view of capital structure.

PROBLEM SET C

C1. The operating head of your division approaches you, as division controller, and poses the following question: "If our firm issues bonds that bear a 10% coupon and sells them at par, and then the firm pays $100 per year in cash on the bonds, the cash yield is 10% and the firm's cost of debt is 10%. Our firm's share price is $50, and each share pays $2.50 per year in dividends. If the firm were to sell stock at the current market price, the firm would have to pay $2.50 per year in cash on the stock, the cash yield would be 5%, and therefore the firm's cost of common equity would be 5%, wouldn't it?"

  a. Is the operating head correct in his reasoning?

  b. Help the operating head resolve his confusion.

C2. Leverage increases the risk (and therefore the required return) of the equityholders. Above some point, an increase in leverage also increases the risk (and required return) of the debtholders. How is it possible, then, that in a perfect capital market environment the weighted average of the two is constant?

C3. A journalist commented that the trouble with U.S. corporations was obvious from reading their balance sheets: They owed more money than they had! His conclusion was based on the firm's debt being larger than its equity. How would you respond to such a comment? (Think about it before responding.)

C4. The good fairy has decided to smile on you and has offered you a choice between two "great" outcomes. The alternatives concern an investment that has the same risk as the market portfolio and requires an initial investment of $10 million. The alternatives are (1) the cost of financing for the investment will be three standard deviations less than the current average market required return for financing such investments, but the investment will have an otherwise zero NPV or (2) the expected future cash inflows from the investment will be three standard deviations larger than those that would make the investment have a zero NPV, but the cost of financing for the investment will be at the current average market required return for financing such investments. Therefore, either alternative will provide you with a positive-NPV investment. Alternative 1 does so by virtue of "great" financing, whereas alternative 2 does so by virtue of "great" investing. Which alternative should you choose, and why?

Real-World Application:
PepsiCo's Capital Structure Choice

PepsiCo, Inc. manufactures soft drinks and snack foods and operates three nationwide restaurant chains. PepsiCo has established a long-term target range of 20% to 25% for what it calls its "net debt ratio."[1] PepsiCo measures its net debt ratio on a market-value basis. Net debt equals total debt, including the present value of its operating lease commitments, minus the cash and marketable securities it holds outside the United States (it does so mainly for tax reasons). The net debt ratio is defined as

$$L^* = (D + PVOL - CMS)/(NP + D + PVOL - CMS)$$

where D is the total market value of debt, PVOL is the present value of operating lease commitments, CMS is cash and marketable securities (net of the cost of remitting these funds to the United States), N is the number of common shares, and P is the common stock price.

PepsiCo's 1995 annual report provides the following information as of December 31, 1995:

Total debt	$9215 million ($9453 approximate market value)
Annual rental expense	$479 million
Cash and marketable securities	$1498 million (approximate market value)
Number of common shares	788 million
Closing share price	$55⅞

Table 15-2 provides information regarding comparable firms as of year-end 1995.

1. Calculate PepsiCo's net debt ratio at year-end 1995. (Assume that the present value of operating leases is 5 times the 1995 annual rental expense and that remitting the cash and marketable securities to the United States reduces them by 25% due to taxes and transaction costs.)

2. Calculate each firm's interest coverage ratio.

3. Calculate each firm's fixed charge coverage ratio.

4. Calculate each firm's long-term debt ratio.

5. Calculate each firm's ratio of total debt to adjusted

---

[1]PepsiCo, Inc., *1995 Annual Report to Shareholders,* p. 29.

TABLE 15-2
Selected information concerning PepsiCo and comparable firms (dollar amounts in millions).

FIRM	DEBT RATINGS (MOODY'S/ S&P)	ANNUAL EBIT	ANNUAL RENTAL EXPENSE	ANNUAL INTEREST	CASH AND MARKETABLE SECURITIES	MARKET VALUE OF LONG-TERM DEBT	MARKET VALUE OF TOTAL DEBT	ANNUAL CASH FLOW
PepsiCo	A1/A	$3114	$479	$682	$1498	$8747	$9453	$3742
Cadbury Schweppes	A2/A	661	25	135	129	864	1490	492
Coca-Cola	Aa3/AA	4600	—	272	1315	1141	1693	3115
Coca-Cola Enterprises	A3/AA−	471	31	326	8	4138	4201	644
McDonald's	Aa2/AA	2509	498	340	335	4258	4836	2296

Source: *Value Line Investment Survey* and Annual Reports to Shareholders.

total capitalization. (Recall that adjusted capitalization includes short-term debt.)

6. Calculate each firm's ratio of cash flow to long-term debt.

7. Calculate each firm's ratio of cash flow to total debt.

8. Suppose PepsiCo's real objective is to maintain a single-A senior debt rating. Does its net debt ratio target seem reasonable, or would you recommend a different target?

BIBLIOGRAPHY

Agrawal, Anup, and Nandu J. Nagarajan. "Corporate Capital Structure, Agency Costs, and Ownership Control: The Case of All-Equity Firms," *Journal of Finance*, 1990, 45(4):1325–1331.

Barton, Sidney L., Ned C. Hill, and Srinivasan Sundaram. "An Empirical Test of Stakeholder Theory Predictions of Capital Structure," *Financial Management*, 1989, 18(1):36–44.

Baskin, Jonathan. "An Empirical Investigation of the Pecking Order Hypothesis," *Financial Management*, 1989, 18(1):26–35.

Ben-Horim, Moshe, Shalom Hochman, and Oded Palmon. "The Impact of the 1986 Tax Reform Act on Corporate Financial Policy," *Financial Management*, 1987, 16(3):29–35.

Bergman, Yaacov Z., and Jeffrey L. Callen. "Opportunistic Underinvestment in Debt Renegotiation and Capital Structure," *Journal of Financial Economics*, 1991, 29(1):137–172.

Bradley, Michael, Greg A. Jarrell, and E. Han Kim. "On the Existence of an Optimal Capital Structure: Theory and Evidence," *Journal of Finance*, 1984, 39(3):857–878.

Castanias, Richard P. "Bankruptcy Risk and Optimal Capital Structure," *Journal of Finance*, 1983, 38(5):1617–1635.

Chang, Chun. "Capital Structure as an Optimal Contract Between Employees and Investors," *Journal of Finance*, 1992, 47(3):1141–1158.

Chang, Rosita P., and S. Ghon Rhee. "The Impact of Personal Taxes on Corporate Dividend Policy and Capital Structure Decisions," *Financial Management*, 1990, 19(2):21–31.

Chatrath, Arjun, Mukesh Chaudhry, Sanjay Ramchander, and Jandhyala L. Sharma. "Gains from Leverage," *Financial Management*, 1993, 22(4):21–22.

Dann, Larry Y., and Wayne H. Mikkelson. "Convertible Debt Issuance, Capital Structure Change and Financing-Related Information: Some New Evidence," *Journal of Financial Economics*, 1984, 13(2):157–186.

DeAngelo, Harry, and Ronald W. Masulis. "Optimal Capital Structure Under Corporate and Personal Taxation," *Journal of Financial Economics*, 1980, 8(1):3–30.

Easterwood, John C., and Palani-Rajan Kadapakkam. "The Role of Private and Public Debt in Corporate Capital Structures," *Financial Management*, 1991, 20(3):49–57.

Emery, Douglas R., and Adam K. Gehr, Jr. "Tax Options, Capital Structure, and Miller Equilibrium: A Numerical Illustration," *Financial Management*, 1988, 17(2):30–40.

Fischer, Edwin O., Robert Heinkel, and Josef Zechner. "Dynamic Capital Structure Choice: Theory and Tests," *Journal of Finance*, 1989, 44(1):19–40.

Friend, Irwin, and Larry H. P. Lang. "An Empirical Test of the Impact of Managerial Self-Interest on Corporate Capital Structure," *Journal of Finance*, 1988, 43(2):271–281.

Harris, John M., Jr., Rodney L. Roenfeldt, and Philip L. Cooley. "Evidence of Financial Leverage Clienteles," *Journal of Finance*, 1983, 38(4):1125–1132.

Harris, Milton, and Artur Raviv. "Capital Structure and the Informational Role of Debt," *Journal of Finance*, 1990, 45(2):321–350.

Harris, Milton, and Artur Raviv. "The Theory Of Capital Structure," *Journal of Finance*, 1991, 46(1):297–356.

Haugen, Robert A., and Lemma W. Senbet. "Bankruptcy and Agency Costs: Their Significance to the Theory of Optimal Capital Structure," *Journal of Financial and Quantitative Analysis*, 1988, 23(1): 27–38.

Hodder, James E., and Lemma W. Senbet. "International Capital Structure Equilibrium," *Journal of Finance*, 1990, 45(5):1495–1516.

Hull, Robert M., and Richard Moellenberndt. "Bank Debt Reduction Announcements and Negative Signaling," *Financial Management*, 1994, 23(2):21–30.

Jensen, Gerald R., Donald P. Solberg, and Thomas S. Zorn. "Simultaneous Determination of Insider Ownership, Debt, and Dividend Policies," *Journal of Financial and Quantitative Analysis*, 1992, 27(2):247–264.

John, Kose. "Risk-Shifting Incentives and Signalling Through Corporate Capital Structure," *Journal of Finance*, 1987, 42(3):632–641.

John, Kose, Lemma W. Senbet, and Anant K. Sundaram. "Cross-Border Liability of Multinational Enterprises, Border Taxes, and Capital Structure," *Financial Management*, 1991, 20(4):54–67.

John, Teresa A., and Kose John. "Top-Management Compensation and Capital Structure," *Journal of Finance*, 1993, 48(3):949–974.

Kale, Jayant R., Thomas H. Noe, and Gabriel G. Ramirez. "The Effect of Business Risk on Corporate Capital Structure: Theory and Evidence," *Journal of Finance*, 1991, 46(5):1693–1716.

Kang, Joseph C., and Ira Horowitz. "Insider Equity Ownership and Financial Leverage," *Financial Management*, 1993, 22(4):20–21.

Leland, Hayne E. "Corporate Debt Value, Bond Covenants, and Optimal Capital Structure," *Journal of Finance*, 1994, 49(4):1213–1252.

Long, Michael S., and Ileen Malitz. "Investment Patterns and Financial Leverage." In *Corporate Capital Structure in the United States*, ed. Benjamin Friedman. Chicago, Ill.: University of Chicago Press, 1985:325–348

MacKie-Mason, Jeffrey K. "Do Taxes Affect Corporate Financing Decisions?" *Journal of Finance*, 1990, 45(5):1471–1494.

Masulis, Ronald W. "The Effects of Capital Structure Change on Security Prices: A Study of Exchange Offers," *Journal of Financial Economics*, 1980, 8(2):139–178.

Masulis, Ronald W. "The Impact of Capital Structure Change on Firm Value, Some Estimates," *Journal of Finance*, 1983, 38(1):107–126.

Miller, Merton H. "Debt and Taxes," *Journal of Finance*, 1977, 32(2):261–275.

Miller, Merton H. "Leverage," *Journal of Finance*, 1991, 46(2):479–488.

Modigliani, Franco, and Merton H. Miller. "Corporate Income Taxes and the Cost of Capital: A Correction," *American Economic Review*, 1963, 53(June):433–443.

Modigliani, Franco, and Merton H. Miller. "The Cost of Capital, Corporation Finance and the Theory of Investment," *American Economic Review*, 1958, 48(June):261–297.

Myers, Stewart C. "Presidential Address: The Capital Structure Puzzle," *Journal of Finance*, 1984, 39(3): 575–592.

Myers, Stewart C., and Nicholas S. Majluf. "Corporate Financing and Investment Decisions When Firms Have Information That Investors Do Not Have," *Journal of Financial Economics*, 1984, 13(2):187–221.

Opler, Tim C., and Sheridan Titman. "Financial Distress and Corporate Performance," *Journal of Finance*, 1994, 49(3):1015–1040.

Pilotte, Eugene. "The Economic Recovery Tax Act of 1981 and Corporate Capital Structure," *Financial Management*, 1990, 19(4):98–107.

Rogers, Ronald C., and James E. Owers. "Equity for Debt Exchanges and Stockholder Wealth," *Financial Management*, 1985, 14(3):18–26.

Ross, Stephen A. "The Determination of Financial Structure: The Incentive Signalling Approach," *Bell Journal of Economics*, 1977, 8(Spring):23–40.

Scott, David F., Jr., and John D. Martin. "Industry Influence on Financial Structure," *Financial Management*, 1975, 4(1):67–73.

Shleifer, Andrei, and Robert W. Vishny. "Liquidation Values and Debt Capacity: A Market Equilibrium Approach," *Journal of Finance*, 1992, 47(4):1343–1366.

Shrieves, Ronald E., and Mary M. Pashley. "Evidence on the Association Between Mergers and Capital Structure," *Financial Management*, 1984, 13(3):39–48.

Taggart, Robert A., Jr. "A Model of Corporate Financing Decisions," *Journal of Finance*, 1977, 32(5):1467–1484.

Titman, Sheridan, and Roberto Wessels. "The Determinants of Capital Structure Choice," *Journal of Finance*, 1988, 43(1):1–19.

Williams, Joseph. "Perquisites, Risk, and Capital Structure," *Journal of Finance*, 1987, 42(1):29–48.

CHAPTER 16

MANAGING CAPITAL STRUCTURE

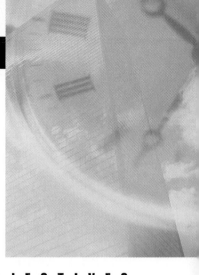

Corporations manage their capital structure carefully. As we described in the preceding chapter, the factors involved with choosing a capital structure are complex, and the impact of each factor on the value of the firm is not clear-cut. In principle, a firm should balance the incremental advantage of more financial leverage against the incremental costs. Unfortunately, we don't have methods to measure precisely such things as the expected costs of financial distress, agency costs, and the cost of reduced financing flexibility.

A number of methods exist for analyzing the impact of alternative capital structures, but in the end, the choice of capital structure requires expert judgment. The analytical models give us a range of reasonable capital structures, rather than pinpointing the absolute best.

In this chapter, we describe how a firm can take into account the various relevant factors to select an appropriate capital structure. We then show how to incorporate the effect of that choice of capital structure on the cost of capital for a firm or one of its capital budgeting projects. The method is very practical because it simply adjusts the WACC (weighted average cost of capital), which is then used in a "standard" NPV calculation without any other changes.

OBJECTIVES

After studying this chapter, you should be able to

1. Apply the concepts discussed in Chapter 15 to choose a firm's capital structure.

2. Explain why a firm's senior debt rating serves as a useful indicator of the firm's exposure to default risk.

3. Use a firm's choice of senior debt rating to help it choose and manage its capital structure.

4. Calculate the adjusted present value of a capital budgeting project.

5. Calculate the cost of capital for a firm or capital budgeting project when the firm follows a policy of *leverage rebalancing* each period on the basis of realized market value.

◆ *Behavioral*: Use the information contained in the capital structure decisions of other firms.

◆ *Risk-Return Trade-Off*: Recognize that there are risk differences between equity and debt and that fair market transactions that change the risk borne by each involve risk-return trade-offs but do not affect the value of the firm.

◆ *Incremental Benefits*: Include in your analysis ways to minimize the value lost to capital market imperfections, such as asymmetric taxes, asymmetric information, and transaction costs. At the same time, be sure to identify all the transaction costs when considering seemingly beneficial financing transactions, because they reduce the *net* benefit from such transactions.

◆ *Valuable Ideas*: Look for opportunities to create value by supplying securities that have a temporary demand-supply imbalance, as in the case of those resulting from changes in laws.

◆ *Signaling*: Consider any possible change in capital structure carefully, because financing transactions convey information to outsiders, and this information can be misunderstood.

◆ *Time Value of Money*: Include any time-value-of-money tax benefits from capital structure choices.

◆ *Capital Market Efficiency*: Recognize that the potential to increase firm value by optimizing capital structure is limited. Managers have a greater chance to increase firm value through the introduction of *valuable new ideas* and the wise use of the firm's *comparative advantages*.

16.1 INDUSTRY EFFECTS

We have a fair understanding of several factors that affect a firm's choice of capital structure. But financial theory does not tell us *precisely* how they determine a firm's *optimal* capital structure. In practice, firms usually apply the Behavioral Principle to select an *appropriate* capital structure. They look to the capital structure choices of comparable firms for guidance. This is a reasonable approach. Studies show systematic differences in capital structures across industries. These are due largely to differences in

1. The degree of operating risk.
2. The availability of tax shelter provided by things other than debt, such as accelerated depreciation, investment tax credits, and operating tax loss carryforwards.
3. The ability of assets to support borrowing.

Debt Ratings

Differences among average industry capital structures, however, are only part of the story. A firm should not simply adopt the industry average debt ratio. Significant differences exist among firms in any particular industry with respect to tax position, size, competitive position, operating risk, business prospects, and other factors. Firms also differ in their willingness to bear financial risk and in their desire to maintain access to the capital markets.

In practice, a firm's bond rating has important implications for the choice of capital structure. Table 16-1 shows the debt rating definitions of two major rating agencies: Moody's Investors Service, Inc. and Standard & Poor's Corporation. The highest four rating categories are known as **investment-grade ratings**. For Moody's, the investment-grade ratings are Aaa, Aa, A, and Baa. For Standard & Poor's, the investment-grade ratings are AAA, AA, A, and BBB. Ratings lower than investment grade are called **speculative-grade ratings**.

Each rating agency further distinguishes among different levels of credit quality within each rating category below triple-A. Moody's attaches the numbers 1 (high), 2 (medium), and 3 (low). Standard & Poor's attaches a plus sign for the highest and a minus sign for the lowest. For example, a medium-grade single-A credit would be rated A2 by Moody's and A by Standard & Poor's, and it would be of somewhat higher quality than one rated A3 by Moody's and A- by Standard & Poor's.

As you can see by reading Table 16-1, the ratings are indicators of the likelihood of financial distress, as judged by the rating agencies. Bonds in the top three investment-grade cat-

---

TABLE 16-1
Bond rating definitions.

MOODY'S INVESTORS SERVICE[a]	STANDARD & POOR'S[b]
Investment Grade Ratings	
Aaa	**AAA**
Bonds rated Aaa are judged to be of the best quality. They carry the smallest degree of investment risk and are generally referred to as "gilt edged." Interest payments are protected by a large or by an exceptionally stable margin, and principal is secure. Although the various protective elements are likely to change, such changes as can be visualized are most unlikely to impair the fundamentally strong position of such issues.	Debt rated AAA has the highest rating assigned by Standard & Poor's. Capacity to pay interest and repay principal is extremely strong.
Aa	**AA**
Bonds rated Aa are judged to be of high quality by all standards. Together with the Aaa group, they comprise what are generally known as high-grade bonds. They are rated lower than the best bonds because margins of protection may not be as large as in Aaa securities, fluctuation of protective elements may be of greater amplitude, or there may be other elements present that make the long-term risk appear somewhat larger than the Aaa securities.	Debt rated AA has a very strong capacity to pay interest and repay principal and differs from the higher-rated issues only in small degree.
A	**A**
Bonds rated A possess many favorable investment attributes and are to be considered as upper-medium-grade obligations. Factors giving security to principal and interest are considered adequate, but elements may be present that suggest a susceptibility to impairment some time in the future.	Debt rated A has a strong capacity to pay interest and repay principal, although it is somewhat more susceptible to the adverse effects of changes in circumstances and economic conditions than debt in higher-rated categories.
Baa	**BBB**
Bonds rated Baa are considered medium-grade obligations (they are neither highly protected nor poorly secured). Interest payments and principal security appear adequate for the present, but certain protective elements may be lacking or may be characteristically unreliable over any great length of time. Such bonds lack outstanding investment characteristics and in fact have speculative characteristics as well.	Debt rated BBB is regarded as having an adequate capacity to pay interest and repay principal. Whereas it normally exhibits adequate protection parameters, adverse economic conditions or changing circumstances are more likely to lead to a weakened capacity to pay interest and repay principal for debt in this category than in higher-rated categories.

(continued)

TABLE 16-1
Bond rating definitions *(continued).*

Speculative Grade Ratings

Ba

Bonds rated Ba are judged to have speculative elements; their future cannot be considered as well-assured. Often the protection of interest and principal payments may be very moderate, and thereby not well safeguarded during both good and bad times over the future. Uncertainty of position characterizes bonds in this class.

BB

Debt rated BB has less near-term vulnerability to default than other speculative issues. However, it faces major ongoing uncertainties or exposure to adverse business, financial, or economic conditions that could lead to inadequate capacity to meet timely interest and principal payments. The BB rating category is also used for debt subordinated to senior debts that is assigned an actual or implied BBB− rating.

B

Bonds rated B generally lack characteristics of the desirable investment. Assurance of interest and principal payments or of maintenance of other terms of the contract over any long period of time may be small.

B

Debt rated B has a greater vulnerability to default but currently has the capacity to meet interest payments and principal repayments. Adverse business, financial, or economic conditions are likely to impair capacity or willingness to pay interest and repay principal. The B rating category is also used for debt subordinated to senior debt that is assigned an actual or implied BB or BB− rating.

Caa

Bonds rated Caa are of poor standing. Such issues may be in default, or elements of danger with respect to principal or interest may be present.

CCC

Debt rated CCC has a currently identifiable vulnerability to default and is dependent on favorable business, financial, and economic conditions to meet timely payment of interest and repayment of principal. In the event of adverse business, financial or economic conditions, it is not likely to have the capacity to pay interest and repay principal. The CCC rating category is also used for debt subordinated or senior debt that is assigned an actual or implied B or B− rating.

Ca

Bonds rated Ca represent obligations that are speculative in a high degree. Such issues are often in default or have other marked shortcomings.

CC

The rating CC is typically applied to debt subordinated to senior debt that is assigned an actual or implied CCC rating.

C

Bonds rated C are the lowest-rated class of bonds, and issues so rated can be regarded as having extremely poor prospects of ever attaining any real investment standing.

C

The rating C is typically applied to debt subordinated to senior debt that is assigned an actual or implied CCC− debt rating. The C rating may be used to cover a situation where a bankruptcy petition has been filed but debt-service payments are continued.

CI

The rating CI is reserved for income bonds on which no interest is being paid.

D

Debt rated D is in payment default. The D rating category is used when interest payments or principal payments are not made on the date due even if the applicable grace period has not expired, unless S&P believes that such payments will be made during such grace period. The D rating also will be used upon the filing of a bankruptcy petition if debt-service payments are jeopardized.

[a] Moody's applies numerical modifiers 1, 2, and 3 in each generic rating classification from Aa through B in its corporate bond rating system. The modifier 1 indicates that the security ranks in the higher end of its generic rating category; the modifier 2 indicates a mid-range ranking; and the modifier 3 indicates that the issue ranks in the lower end of its generic rating category.

[b] The ratings from "AA" to "CCC" may be modified by the addition of a plus or minus sign to show relative standing within the major rating categories.
Sources: Moody's Bond Record (New York: Moody's Investors Service, April 1996), p. 3, and *Standard & Poor's Bond Guide* (New York: Standard & Poor's, April 1996), p. 12.

egories are judged from "favorable" to "gilt edge." They have a capacity to pay interest that ranges from "strong" to "extremely strong." Bonds in the fourth category (Baa or BBB) offer investors less protection than higher-rated bonds. The risk of financial distress is greater for lower-rated bonds.

The distinction between investment-grade and speculative-grade ratings is important because of institutional investment restrictions. Various state laws impose minimum rating standards and other restrictions that bonds must meet to qualify as **legal investments** for savings banks, trust firms, public pension funds, and insurance firms. Bonds rated speculative-grade fail to qualify as legal investments for many financial institutions, as is the case for commercial banks. A firm's bond rating is very important, then, to maintaining access to the capital markets on acceptable terms.

The National Association of Insurance Commissioners (NAIC) has established six bond rating categories. The amount of reserves an insurance company must maintain for each bond investment depends on the bond's rating. Bonds rated NAIC-3 or below are speculative-grade. They require significantly more capital reserves.[1] With the introduction of this new rating system and capital-maintenance standards, speculative-grade bonds have become much less attractive to insurance companies. And of course, the yields a firm requires from speculative-grade bonds are significantly higher, to compensate for the greater amount of capital the firm must maintain.

Choosing a Bond Rating Objective

A firm can choose a bond rating objective. Such a choice involves a decision about (1) the chance of future financial distress and (2) the desire to maintain access to the capital markets. When it looks as though a firm would gain value from raising its proportion of debt financing, but the firm chooses not to (by having a higher rating objective), the value that is missed can be viewed as a "margin of safety." The desired margin of safety is determined by how much risk of future financial distress, or restricted market access, the firm is willing to bear.[2] A single-A rating would seem to be a reasonable rating target, but some firms are either more or less risk-averse than this standard implies.

Bond Ratings and Financial Ratios

Once a firm has chosen its rating target, what financial steps should the firm take to hit the target? The rating agencies use many criteria to rate a bond. For example, in the case of industrial firms, Standard & Poor's evaluates (1) operating risk, (2) market position, (3) margins and other measures of profitability, (4) management quality, (5) conservatism of accounting policies, (6) fixed-charge coverage, (7) leverage (including off-balance-sheet debt) compared to liquidation value of assets, (8) adequacy of cash flow to meet future debt service obligations, and (9) future financial flexibility in light of future debt service obligations and planned capital expenditure requirements.

Each factor bears on the risk of future financial distress. The rating agencies weigh their assessments of relevant factors and reach a decision. There is no all-purpose formula. In fact,

---

[1] NAIC-2 corresponds to Moody's Baa (and to Standard & Poor's BBB). NAIC-3 corresponds to Moody's Ba (and to Standard & Poor's BB). Life insurance companies' reserve requirements for NAIC-3 bonds are five times as high as for NAIC-2 bonds. Property and casualty insurance companies can account for bonds rated NAIC-2 or higher (investment grade) on the basis of their historical cost but must account for bonds rated NAIC-3 or lower (speculative grade) on the basis of their current market value

[2] Note that this decision contains an agency problem and can be a source of agency costs for the shareholders. The conflict is due to the nondiversifiability of human capital, which causes managers to avoid diversifiable risk even though shareholders do not object to it. See Chapter 9 for a discussion of this concept.

TABLE 16-2

Senior debt ratings as indicators of credit quality.

	KEY FINANCIAL RATIOS[a]					
Senior Debt Rating[b]	**AAA**	**AA**	**A**	**BBB**	**BB**	**B**
Interest coverage ratio	21.39x	10.02x	5.67x	2.90x	2.25x	0.74x
Fixed-charge coverage ratio[c]	6.96	5.31	3.42	2.22	1.62	0.85
EBITDA/Interest[d]	31.68	14.78	8.25	5.02	3.46	1.56
Funds from operations/Total debt	109.8%	75.4%	49.1%	30.3%	20.2%	9.8%
Free operating cash flow/Total debt	53.8	27.9	19.5	3.9	0.7	(1.7)
Pretax return on permanent capital	25.1	19.1	16.0	11.8	10.2	6.2
Operating income/Sales	21.2	17.1	14.6	12.3	11.9	8.7
Long-term debt/Capitalization	9.7	18.9	28.8	40.7	50.2	62.2
Total debt/Adjusted capitalizaztion (including short-term debt)	22.6	28.3	36.7	45.3	55.6	71.4
Total debt/Adjusted capitalization (including short-term debt and 8x rents)	36.1	40.1	46.8	56.1	65.5	76.5

[a] Median of the 3-year simple arithmetic averages for the period 1992–1994 for firms whose senior debt had the indicated rating.
[b] As assigned by Standard & Poor's.
[c] Based on full rental charges, rather than the one-third of rental charges used in the SEC fixed-charge-coverage calculation.
[d] EBITDA = earnings before interest, taxes, depreciation, and amortization.
Source: Global Sector Review (New York: Standard & Poor's, October 1995), p. 10.

several factors are difficult to quantify. Nevertheless, certain key credit statistics for comparable firms whose debt carries the target rating offer useful guidance.

Table 16-2 shows how the values of ten key credit statistics vary across the six highest rating categories assigned by Standard & Poor's. Note that all the ratios are progressively better, the higher the firm's senior debt rating. Taken together, they go a long way toward distinguishing a stronger credit rating from a weaker one.

Having selected a rating target, a firm can use the values of the key credit statistics of comparable firms with that target rating as a rough guide to the ratio targets it should set for itself. We will show you how to do that in this chapter. For now, three points of caution should be emphasized:

1. Quantitative factors are not the entire story. A deteriorating market position, or perceived weaknesses in management, will require above-average credit statistics.

2. Achieving an improved credit rating requires a proven track record. Improving credit statistics do not themselves guarantee a higher credit rating unless the firm demonstrates that it can maintain the improvement.

3. The averages may change over time.

Self-Check Questions

1. What three factors might explain the systematic differences in capital structure across industries?

2. What are investment-grade ratings, and what are speculative-grade ratings? Why is this distinction important?

3. Cite three factors that Standard & Poor's evaluates to determine a bond rating for an industrial firm.

4. What do bond ratings indicate about the likelihood of default?

16.2 FACTORS AFFECTING A FIRM'S CHOICE OF CAPITAL STRUCTURE

There are five basic considerations involved in a firm's choice of capital structure:

1. Ability to service debt
2. Ability to use interest tax shields fully
3. Protection against illiquidity
4. Desired degree of access to capital markets
5. Dynamic factors and debt management over time

Let's look at each of these factors in turn.

Ability to Service Debt

A careful financial manager does not recommend that a firm take on more debt unless she is confident that the firm will be able to service the debt—that is, to make the contractually required payments on time, even under adverse conditions. Many firms appear to maintain a margin of safety, or unused debt capacity, to control the risk of financial distress and maintain access to the capital markets.

There are various measures of debt-servicing capacity. One is the **interest coverage ratio**:

$$\text{Interest Coverage Ratio} = \frac{\text{EBIT}}{\text{Interest Expense}} \tag{16.1}$$

where EBIT is the earnings before interest and income taxes. Rental (including lease) payments include an interest component.

Fixed charges, which include interest expense and one-third of rental expense, represent a better indicator of true interest expense. To take these factors into account, we can calculate a **fixed-charge coverage ratio**:[3]

$$\text{Fixed-Charge Coverage Ratio} = \frac{\text{EBIT} + \frac{1}{3}\text{ Rentals}}{\text{Interest Expense} + \frac{1}{3}\text{ Rentals}} \tag{16.2}$$

The $\frac{1}{3}$ rentals is an attempt to approximate the interest component of rental expense.

To avoid default, a firm must meet its principal repayment obligations as well as its interest obligations on schedule. A more comprehensive measure of a firm's ability to service its debt obligations is its **debt-service coverage ratio**:

$$\text{Debt-Service Coverage Ratio} = \frac{\text{EBIT} + \frac{1}{3}\text{ Rentals}}{\text{Interest Expense} + \frac{1}{3}\text{ Rentals} + \dfrac{\text{Principal Repayments}}{1 - \text{Tax Rate}}} \tag{16.3}$$

The amount of principal repayments is divided by 1 minus the tax rate, because principal repayments are not tax-deductible. They are paid with after-tax dollars, whereas interest expense and rental expense are tax-deductible.

Coverage ratios can be used in *pro forma* analysis to gauge the impact of a new issue. Pro forma simply means forecast, estimated, or projected.

---

[3] The fixed-charge coverage ratio in Equation (16.2) is the one specified by the Securities and Exchange Commission. However, some analysts prefer to use total rentals rather than one-third of this amount. For example, see *Debt Ratings Criteria*, 50. The measure we presented in Chapter 2 used total rentals.

***Pro Forma
Credit
Analysis***

A firm has EBIT of $25 million and interest expense of $10 million. It is considering issuing $50 million of 10% debt. Calculate its pro forma interest coverage ratio assuming that the entire proceeds are invested in plant under construction. Then recalculate it assuming that the investment produces additional EBIT of $10 million per year.

In the first case,

$$\text{Interest Coverage Ratio} = \frac{25}{10 + (50)(0.1)} = 1.67x$$

In the second case,

$$\text{Interest Coverage Ratio} = \frac{25 + 10}{10 + (50)(0.1)} = 2.33x$$

A firm can evaluate the impact of alternative capital structures by using *sensitivity analysis*. The firm calculates the interest coverage ratio, fixed-charge coverage ratio, and debt-service coverage ratio for each capital structure under a variety of projected business scenarios. Then it compares the calculated values to benchmarks that reflect its desired credit rating. Table 16-2 suggests the following rough benchmarks. If a firm's industry has average operating risk, and the firm wishes to meet minimum investment-grade standards, it should strive for an annual interest coverage ratio of at least 3.05 and for an annual fixed-charge coverage ratio of at least 2.30 under reasonably conservative "expected case" assumptions, and it should strive for a debt-service coverage ratio of at least 1.00 under pessimistic assumptions.[4]

A firm in a highly cyclical industry should set higher interest coverage and fixed-charge coverage ratio standards to compensate for the higher level of operating risk, whereas a firm in a noncyclical industry can safely set lower standards. For example, an electric utility firm can set lower coverage ratio standards than a manufacturer of rollerblades.

A firm that wishes to maintain single-A-type ratios would aim toward an interest coverage ratio of at least 5.53 and a fixed-charge coverage ratio of at least 2.93 if it is in an industry of average operating risk. Higher (or lower) standards would be appropriate for firms in industries that have more (or less) operating risk. You could obtain more precise benchmarks by calculating ratios for firms in the same industry that have the target rating.

Ability to Use Interest Tax Shields Fully

As we said in Chapter 15, one of the principal benefits of debt is the tax-deductibility of interest payments. But firms that use debt financing must generate sufficient income from operations to claim the interest deductions.

A firm that does not pay income taxes and does not expect to become a taxpayer has less incentive to incur additional debt. The tax shields would go unused, and that would raise the after-tax cost of the debt. Also, the additional debt would increase the risk of incurring the costs of financial distress. And although a firm can carry tax losses forward, the added debt will be beneficial only if the expected present value of these tax shields exceeds the increase in the expected present value of financial distress costs and agency costs.

Most firms regularly estimate their future tax positions. It is important for a firm to test alternative capital structures in light of the firm's estimated taxpaying position under a variety of possible business scenarios.

---

[4] The particular minimums chosen for the debt-service coverage ratio depend, to a certain extent, on the firm's confidence in its ability to refinance its debt.

A firm's capital structure should probably contain no more debt than its future tax position will allow it to use. For example, firms in industries with other substantial tax shelter opportunities, such as oil and gas companies (with their depletion allowances) and steelmakers (with their depreciation and loss carryforwards), should have lower leverage ratios than firms in other industries.

As we have said, changes to the tax code occur frequently. Such changes complicate this analysis and can cause the firm's target capital structure to change over time.

The actual tax advantage of additional leverage is difficult to estimate for any particular firm. As the personal tax view of capital structure suggests, the tax benefits from an additional dollar of borrowing are substantially less than the statutory tax rate. Also, the tax value of incremental interest deductions varies significantly across industries because of differences in nondebt tax shields. Note that the smaller the tax advantage accruing to leverage, the smaller the cost of maintaining any particular margin of safety.

Ability of Assets to Support Debt

A firm should not incur additional debt if doing so would involve a significant chance of insolvency. The risk of insolvency depends not only on the projected debt-service coverage but also on the firm's ability to generate cash through additional borrowing, the sale of equity securities, or the sale of assets.

Assets vary in their ability to support debt. Lower-risk, more generic, more tangible assets with more stable market values provide better collateral for debt. This allows a firm to borrow a larger proportion of such assets' market value. For example, a real estate firm or a credit firm can generally support a relatively large amount of leverage.

The market values of assets also change because of new information. Firms can sometimes borrow more, and sometimes must reduce the amount of their debt, in response to such changes in market value.

EXAMPLE

Leverage and Discovering Oil

Say you bought 200 acres of land on which to create a catfish ranch. You paid $100,000 for the land and have an $80,000 mortgage on it. You plan to use an additional $60,000 of your own money to develop the ranch. You figure the project has an NPV of $40,000, so the total value of the project is $200,000 (= 100 + 60 + 40) at a cost of $160,000. Therefore, your ranch project has a 40% leverage ratio (its proportion of debt financing is $L = 80/200$).

In the process of digging a pond for the catfish, you discover oil on your land. An analysis of the discovery puts the new value of your land at $15.25 million. Now your project is only about $L = 0.5\%$ debt financed! But don't worry. You can, of course, increase your leverage by borrowing against the increased market value of your land. ■

Firms can do the same when the value of their assets increases. They can borrow against that additional value. On the other hand, when the value of a firm's assets declines, perhaps because of reduced ability to generate future cash flow, the firm will be at increased risk of default after its leverage has increased.

Desired Degree of Access to Capital Markets

A firm that is planning a substantial capital expenditure program will want to maintain access to the capital markets on acceptable terms. This requires adequate credit strength. Historically, a firm large enough to sell debt publicly could be reasonably confident of maintaining such access by maintaining a senior debt rating of single-A or better. In 1983, the "junk bond" market expanded rapidly and appeared to lessen the need to have such a high credit standing for maintaining market access. In 1990, however, the junk bond market all but collapsed, emphasizing the risk inherent in increasing leverage to such an extent that a firm's debt rating falls below investment grade.

We think the junk bond market collapse was due at least in part to bond investors and thrift insurance regulators finally recognizing that the Principle of Risk-Return Trade-Off also applied to junk bonds: The high rates of interest paid on junk bonds did not provide a free lunch. Rather, they compensated for the higher default rate on junk bonds than on investment-grade bonds.

Corporate Debt Management Over Time

The four factors just discussed all affect a firm's capital structure target. The capital market imperfections view of capital structure (Chapter 15) also plays a role. A firm might appear to deviate from the normal financing preference order. This could be, for example, because one large issue has proportionally lower transaction costs than two or more smaller issues. Similarly, a firm that needs only a relatively small amount of external funds would tend to use bank lines of credit rather than issue securities, even if issuing securities would appear to be better. Another apparent deviation can occur when a firm decides to pursue a capital budgeting project that costs more than the retained earnings available but does not wish to reduce the cash dividend to common stockholders.

The dynamic process can even make it appear that a firm has *no* target capital structure. For example, if a firm takes advantage of an attractive but temporary financing opportunity (say, the opportunity to issue tax-exempt securities prior to the date the authority to issue such securities expires), its capital structure may move away from its "target." Such apparent deviations in a firm's capital structure policy simply reflect the dynamic nature of an optimal capital structure.

Self-Check Questions

1. What are the five basic considerations involved in a firm's choice of capital structure?
2. What are coverage ratios? What do they measure? Why should a firm and its investors be concerned with the values of the firm's coverage ratios?
3. How would a firm in a highly cyclical industry compensate for that feature of its environment in selecting its financial ratio targets?
4. Explain why some assets provide better collateral value than others.

16.3 CHOOSING AN APPROPRIATE CAPITAL STRUCTURE

In this section we will tie together the five considerations just discussed into a single framework for determining an appropriate capital structure. To do this we will use comparative credit analysis and pro forma capital structure analysis. A **comparative credit analysis** suggests a range of target capital structures that might be appropriate. A **pro forma capital structure analysis** shows the impact of the alternatives within the target range on the firm's credit statistics and reported financial results, and it indicates whether the firm will be able to use tax shield benefits fully. This enables the firm to select a specific target capital structure.

Comparative Credit Analysis

A comparative credit analysis is the most widely used technique for selecting an appropriate capital structure. This approach is an application of the Behavioral Principle. It bases a firm's choice of capital structure on the capital structures of other comparable firms whose senior debt carries the desired bond rating. It involves the following steps:

- Select the desired rating objective.
- Identify a set of comparable firms that also have the target senior debt rating.
- Perform a comparative credit analysis of these firms to define the capital structure (or range of capital structures) most consistent with this rating objective.

Earlier in the chapter, we discussed five considerations that enter into the capital structure decision. Choosing a target debt rating actually encompasses three of the five. The only two not covered are the ability to use tax benefits and debt management considerations, such as issuance expenses, which affect the immediate preference order of the various sources of funds. We must evaluate these two factors separately.

As we said before, a single-A rating offers a compromise between maintaining capital market access and getting more tax savings from additional leverage. However, more conservative firms, and firms with very heavy future financing programs, might strive for a higher rating. Other firms, willing to bear greater financial risk, might set a lower rating target.

Table 16-3 illustrates a comparative credit analysis of specialty chemicals firms that are comparable to the firm being analyzed, Washington Chemical Corporation. There are six specialty chemicals firms with rated debt. The senior debt ratings (Moody's/Standard & Poor's) range from a low of Ba1/BB to a high of A2/A.

Choosing Financial Target Ratios Using Comparative Credit Analysis

EXAMPLE

Washington Chemical has decided on a target senior debt rating "comfortably within" the single-A range. Three of the firms in Table 16-3 have at least one senior debt rating in the single-A category, and Johnson Chemical and Wilson Chemical are rated in the middle of the single-A category by both agencies.

Washington Chemical is significantly more profitable than one of the A2/A issuers and only slightly less profitable than the other. Washington Chemical's debt-to-capitalization, funds-from-operations-to-debt, and fixed-charge coverage ratios fall between the higher and lower of the two values for each ratio exhibited by the two A2/A specialty chemicals firms. Washington Chemical's ratios are substantially better than those of Myers Chemicals, which is a borderline triple-B/single-A. Washington Chemical concluded from this analysis that its financial condition is of medium-grade single-A quality.

We need to clarify one point regarding the ratios in Table 16-3. We have emphasized the importance of basing financial decisions on market values, but the financial ratios in Table 16-3 contain some book value items. This is because it is simply not practical to include current market values in every case. The rating agencies consider the market value of a firm's assets in assessing its leverage. But they view these assets on a liquidity basis rather than on a going-concern basis. The most significant, practical, and common adjustment is the use of the market value (based on the common stock price) in place of the book value of equity.

The actual debt-to-capitalization ratio should value the common equity component on the basis of the liquidation value of the assets rather than on the basis of even the firm's prevailing share price (which reflects the value of the firm on a going-concern basis). Assets such as proven oil and gas reserves, which are relatively liquid, will support a higher degree of leverage than less liquid assets. New plant and equipment will tend to support greater leverage than old plant and equipment of equal book value. But determining these liquidating values is necessarily subjective. There are few liquid markets for fixed assets, and appraisals normally are not available. Still, the quality of assets will tend to vary systematically from one

TABLE 16-3

A comparative credit analysis of specialty chemicals firms.

	WASHINGTON CHEMICAL CORPORATION	MYERS CHEMICALS CORP.	NORTHWEST CHEMICALS INC.	DELAWARE CHEMICALS CORP.	WESTERN INDUSTRIES	JOHNSON CHEMICAL INC.	WILSON CHEMICAL CORP.
Senior debt rating (Moody's/Standard & Poor's)	—	A3/BBB+	Ba1/BBB−	Baa2/BBB−	Ba1/BB	A2/A	A2/A
Profitability							
Operating profit margin	7.4%	5.9%	1.9%	4.5%	8.9%	4.1%	9.2%
Net profit margin	3.9	2.6	1.0	2.3	2.2	2.3	4.1
Return on assets	4.8	3.2	2.2	4.9	2.8	4.3	4.9
Return on common equity	10.3	9.2	5.0	13.9	8.8	10.8	10.0
Capitalization							
Short-term debt	$ 16	$ 60	$ 10	$ 10	$ 16	$ 8	$ 36
Senior long-term debt	$158	$144	$ 49	$163	$110	$140	$245
Capitalized lease obligations	—	22	10	20	—	—	1
Subordinated long-term debt	—	—	—	13	80	8	—
Total long-term debt	158	166	59	196	190	148	246
Minority interest	—	—	3	2	—	—	—
Preferred equity	—	2	35	5	—	—	—
Common equity	321	253	165	334	162	278	659
Total capitalization	$479	$421	$262	$537	$352	$426	$905
Long-term debt ratio	33%	39%	23%	36%	54%	35%	27%
Total-debt-to-adjusted-capitalization ratio	35	47	25	38	56	36	30
Funds-from-operations-to-long-term-debt ratio	60	42	45	35	27	51	63
Funds-from-operations-to-total-debt ratio	55	31	39	33	25	49	55
Liquidity							
Current ratio	2.4x	1.9x	2.7x	2.1x	1.9x	2.2x	2.6x
Fixed-Charge Coverage Ratio							
Last 12 months	3.5x	2.3x	2.4x	3.3x	2.0x	3.3x	3.7x
Latest fiscal year	4.3	4.0	3.8	2.9	2.3	4.4	4.2
One year prior	5.6	3.0	3.2	2.7	2.8	5.4	5.7
Two years prior	6.3	4.0	2.8	2.2	3.8	7.9	4.9

industry to another. Thus, for a particular rating category, the debt-to-capitalization ratios for firms in one industry, when compared to the debt-to-capitalization ratios for firms in another industry whose debt bears the same rating, will reflect interindustry differences in liquidating asset value.

Similarly, rating agencies evaluate the issuer's accounting methods to adjust the reported profit measures to a reasonably comparable basis for the issuers in each industry. They also use information reported in the footnotes to the financial statements to adjust long-term debt to include off-balance-sheet liabilities. These items include noncapitalized leases, take-or-pay contract obligations, and other liabilities related to project financing. These obligations tend to be greater in some industries than in others.

An analysis like the one in Table 16-3 is necessarily imperfect. But if comparable firms are chosen carefully, and if differences between the comparable firms and the firm being analyzed are carefully weighed, the comparative credit analysis can produce useful guidelines.

As we have said, however, in the final analysis the choice of capital structure requires judgment. Before reaching a decision, Washington Chemical also consulted its investment bankers and evaluated its expected profitability. Washington Chemical believed that its profitability would exceed that of its single-A competitors. Thus it might be a little more aggressive than its single-A competitors in its use of leverage. On the other hand, it might decide to issue debt publicly (rather than continuing to borrow exclusively from banks), which would argue for conservatism. Having carefully considered all these factors and the averages of key financial ratios given in Table 16-2, Washington Chemical decided to try to stay within the following ranges:

Annual fixed-charge coverage ratio: 3.50x to 4.00x

Annual funds-from-operations-to-total-debt ratio: 50% to 60%

Long-term debt ratio: 30% to 35%

In applying the third of these tests, Washington Chemical included the permanent component of short-term debt as part of long-term debt. ■

Pro Forma Analysis

Before choosing where to aim within each of these ranges, Washington Chemical decided to

- Confirm its ability to use the estimated tax shield benefits fully, particularly under somewhat adverse conditions.
- Assess the impact of these obligations on its future financing requirements.
- Determine what impact, if any, this capital structure policy might have on its dividend policy.

Table 16-4 contains a pro forma capital structure analysis. In its evaluation, Washington Chemical realized the importance of considering a reasonably pessimistic case as well as its expected case. Consequently, there are four cases considered in Table 16-4. They correspond to two degrees of leverage (long-term debt ratios of 30% and 35%) and two operating scenarios (10% growth and 5% growth).

It is evident from cases 1 and 2 that Washington Chemical could justify a 35% long-term debt ratio in the expected case. Both the fixed-charge coverage and the funds-from-operations-to-total-debt ratios increase steadily and remain comfortably within their target ranges. Moreover, Washington Chemical could fully use the tax benefits of ownership and fully claim all interest deductions. Washington Chemical has established a policy of paying out one-third of its earnings as cash dividends. Continuing both that policy and its target capital structure would require a modest amount of external equity financing ($46 million over 5 years if the long-term debt ratio is 35% and $56 million if it is only 30%). Thus Washington Chemical might have to compromise on one of its objectives.[5]

Under a more pessimistic scenario, cases 3 and 4 show that Washington Chemical's fixed-charge coverage and funds-from-operations-to-total-debt ratios would eventually fall below their target ranges. The deterioration is less severe in case 4, because the long-term debt ratio is only 30%. However, the external equity financing requirement is greater. To be conservative, Washington Chemical decided to finance itself with a leverage ratio of 33%. Because Washington Chemical could fully use the tax benefits even in the pessimistic case, it did

---

[5] We discuss dividend policy in the next two chapters.

TABLE 16-4
A pro forma capital structure analysis.

			PROJECTED AHEAD			
	Initial	1 Year	2 Years	3 Years	4 Years	5 Years
Case 1: Leverage at upper end of range/expected case operating results						
Pre-interest taxable income[a]	$ 61	$ 67	$ 74	$ 81	$ 89	$ 98
Interest	18	20	22	24	26	28
Surplus (Deficit)[b]	$ 43	$ 47	$ 52	$ 57	$ 63	$ 70
Earnings before fixed charges and income taxes[c]	$ 70	$ 77	$ 85	$ 93	$102	$113
Fixed charges[d]	20	22	24	26	28	30
Fixed-charge coverage	3.5x	3.5x	3.5x	3.6x	3.6x	3.8x
Net income	$ 30	$ 33	$ 36	$ 42	$ 45	$ 51
Noncash expenses	65	72	79	84	94	102
Funds from operations[c]	95	105	115	126	139	153
Dividends	(10)	(11)	(12)	(14)	(15)	(17)
Internal cash generation	85	94	103	112	124	136
Capital expenditures	(125)	(125)	(125)	(135)	(150)	(160)
Cash required	$ 40	$ 31	$ 22	$ 23	$ 26	$ 24
External debt requirement	$ 20	$ 17	$ 14	$ 15	$ 17	$ 17
External equity requirement[e]	$ 20	$ 14	$ 8	$ 8	$ 9	$ 7
Funds from operations to total debt[f]	55%	55%	56%	57%	59%	60%
Case 2: Leverage at lower end of range/expected case operating results						
Pre-interest taxable income[a]	$ 61	$ 67	$ 74	$ 81	$ 89	$ 98
Interest	18	19	21	23	25	26
Surplus (Deficit)[b]	$ 43	$ 48	$ 53	$ 58	$ 64	$ 72
Earnings before fixed charges and income taxes[c]	$ 70	$ 77	$ 85	$ 93	$102	$113
Fixed charges[d]	20	21	23	25	27	28
Fixed-charge coverage	3.5x	3.7x	3.7x	3.7x	3.8x	4.0x
Net income	$ 30	$ 33	$ 36	$ 42	$ 45	$ 51
Noncash expenses	65	72	79	84	94	102
Funds from operations[c]	95	105	115	126	139	153
Dividends	(10)	(11)	(12)	(14)	(15)	(17)
Internal cash generation	85	94	103	112	124	136
Capital expenditures	(125)	(125)	(125)	(135)	(150)	(160)
Cash required	$ 40	$ 31	$ 22	$ 23	$ 26	$ 24
External debt requirement[g]	$ 17	$ 15	$ 12	$ 13	$ 15	$ 15
External equity requirement[g]	$ 23	$ 16	$ 10	$ 10	$ 11	$ 9
Funds from operations to total debt[f]	55%	56%	57%	59%	61%	63%

(continued)

TABLE 16-4
A pro forma capital structure analysis *(continued)*.

	Initial	1 Year	2 Years	3 Years	4 Years	5 Years
		PROJECTED AHEAD				
Case 3: Leverage at upper end of range/pessimistic case operating results						
Pre-interest taxable income[a]	$ 61	$ 64	$ 67	$ 71	$ 74	$ 78
Interest	18	20	22	24	27	30
Surplus (Deficit)[b]	$ 43	$ 44	$ 45	$ 47	$ 47	$ 48
Earnings before fixed charges and income taxes[c]	$ 70	$ 74	$ 78	$ 82	$ 86	$ 90
Fixed charges[d]	20	22	24	26	29	32
Fixed-charge coverage	3.5x	3.4x	3.3x	3.2x	3.0x	2.8x
Net income	$ 30	$ 30	$ 33	$ 33	$ 33	$ 33
Noncash expenses	65	70	72	77	82	88
Funds from operations[c]	95	100	105	110	115	121
Dividends	(10)	(10)	(11)	(11)	(11)	(11)
Internal cash generation	85	90	94	99	104	110
Capital expenditures	(125)	(125)	(125)	(135)	(150)	(160)
Cash required	$ 40	$ 35	$ 31	$ 36	$ 46	$ 50
External debt requirement	$ 20	$ 18	$ 17	$ 19	$ 23	$ 25
External equity requirement[e]	$ 20	$ 17	$ 14	$ 17	$ 23	$ 25
Funds from operations to total debt[f]	55%	52%	50%	48%	46%	44%
Case 4: Leverage at lower end of range/pessimistic case operating results						
Pre-interest taxable income[a]	$ 61	$ 64	$ 67	$ 71	$ 74	$ 78
Interest	18	19	21	23	26	28
Surplus (Deficit)[b]	$ 43	$ 45	$ 46	$ 48	$ 48	$ 50
Earnings before fixed charges and income taxes[c]	$ 70	$ 74	$ 78	$ 82	$ 86	$ 90
Fixed charges[d]	20	21	23	25	28	30
Fixed-charge coverage	3.5x	3.5x	3.4x	3.3x	3.1x	3.0x
Net income	$ 30	$ 30	$ 33	$ 33	$ 33	$ 33
Noncash expenses	65	70	72	77	82	88
Funds from operations[c]	95	100	105	110	115	121
Dividends	(10)	(10)	(11)	(11)	(11)	(11)
Internal cash generation	85	90	94	99	104	110
Capital expenditures	(125)	(125)	(125)	(135)	(150)	(160)
Cash required	$ 40	$ 35	$ 31	$ 36	$ 46	$ 50
External debt requirement[g]	$ 17	$ 16	$ 15	$ 17	$ 20	$ 22
External equity requirement[g]	$ 23	$ 19	$ 16	$ 19	$ 26	$ 28
Funds from operations to total debt[f]	55%	53%	51%	50%	48%	46%

[a] As computed for federal income tax purposes. Estimated to grow at 10% per annum in the "expected case" and 5% per annum in the "pessimistic case."
[b] Calculated as pre-interest taxable income minus interest.
[c] Estimated to grow at 10% per annum in the "expected case" and 5% per annum in the "pessimistic case."
[d] Assumes rental expense of $6 million per year. Under the SEC method, one-third of this amount is included in fixed charges.
[e] Calculated to preserve a ratio of 35% long-term debt financing to 65% additional common equity.
[f] The amount of total debt at the end of the initial year is $174 (= 16 + 158 from Table 16-3). The debt level for any single year projected ahead is the initial amount plus the sum of the annual external debt requirements up to the year in question. The debt level projected ahead 2 years is $205 (= $174 + 17 + 14) so that funds from operations to total debt equals 56% (= 115/205).
[g] Calculated to preserve a ratio of 30% long-term debt financing to 70% additional common equity.

not plan to use leveraged lease or preferred stock financing. Thus its financing ratios would be 33% conventional long-term debt and 67% common equity.

Other Aspects of the Capital Structure Decision

Washington Chemical's target capital structure contains only long-term debt and common equity. Firms often adopt more complex capital structures that include one or more layers of subordinated debt, convertible debt, capitalized lease obligations, or preferred equity. Let's take a quick look at each of these.

SUBORDINATED DEBT   Subordinated debt ranks below senior debt in case of default. If strict priority held in bankruptcy, a layer of subordinated debt would be just as beneficial to senior debtholders as more equity. In addition, the interest payments to subordinated debtholders are tax-deductible, whereas payments to shareholders are not, which benefits the issuer. However, interest payments and principal repayments must be made in a timely fashion on subordinated debt, as well as on senior debt, for the issuer to avoid default.

In view of the greater exposure to default risk, the rating agencies usually rate subordinated debt one step below senior debt if the senior debt is rated investment grade and rate it two steps below if the senior debt is rated speculative grade.[6] The rating differential increases the cost of a new debt issue (consistent with the Principle of Risk-Return Trade-Off). Moreover, because strict priority is not always preserved in bankruptcy, the rating agencies generally add nonconvertible subordinated debt to senior debt for purposes of their ratio calculations. In view of the higher interest cost, $1 of subordinated debt has a more severe impact than $1 of senior debt on a firm's coverage and funds-from-operations-to-debt ratios. Consequently, investment-grade manufacturing firms seldom find it attractive to issue nonconvertible subordinated debt.

In contrast, finance companies often issue subordinated debt. Because of the comparatively close matching of the maturity structures of their assets and their liabilities, credit firms can support a high degree of leverage. The bulk of their business consists of lending funds at a favorable spread over their funding costs. Thus a well-run finance company will have the capacity to use the interest tax shields fully, even when it is very highly leveraged. The subordinated debt, like equity, will provide comfort to senior lenders and tax deductions to the issuer, which equity would not provide.

CONVERTIBLE DEBT   Firms usually issue convertible debt on a subordinated basis. Both issuers and investors expect the issue to be converted into common equity within a few years. It is thus appropriate that convertible debt be junior to nonconvertible debt with respect to bankruptcy priority.

CAPITALIZED LEASE OBLIGATIONS   Firms that cannot fully use the tax benefits of ownership often find it attractive to lease assets from entities that can claim these tax deductions and are willing to pass on the tax benefits in the form of reduced lease payments. But failure to make a timely lease payment places a firm in default under the lease agreement. Consequently, leases are really a form of secured debt. Rating agencies customarily include capitalized leases, which are reported on the face of the balance sheet, in long-term debt. The decision whether to take on capitalized leases or conventional debt thus hinges principally on tax considerations, as we will discuss in Chapter 25.

---

[6] For example, a senior debt rating of A2/A would imply a subordinated debt rating of A3/A−. Conversely, a senior debt rating can be inferred from a subordinated debt rating when a firm has only rated subordinated debt outstanding. For example, Western Industries has convertible subordinated debt outstanding that is rated Ba3/B+. This implies the senior debt rating of Ba1/BB (up two notches because it is speculative grade), as indicated in Table 16-3.

PREFERRED EQUITY   Preferred stock is a hybrid security. It incorporates certain debt features and certain equity features. Failure to make a timely preferred dividend or preferred sinking fund payment will not put the issuer into default. Consequently, substituting preferred stock for a portion of a firm's debt enhances the position of debtholders in case of default. However, firms normally treat their preferred stock payment obligations as though they were fixed. If a firm issues a significant amount of preferred stock, particularly if it contains a sinking fund, these payment obligations can impair the credit standing of the firm's debt securities.[7]

Making a Change in Capital Structure

What should a firm do when it finds that its desired capital structure differs significantly from its current capital structure? There are two basic choices: change its capital structure slowly or change it more quickly. A firm can alter its capital structure slowly by adjusting its future financing mix appropriately.

For example, suppose a firm's target capital structure consists of 35% long-term debt and 65% common equity, and its current capital structure contains 25% long-term debt and 75% common equity. The firm could cure this underleveraged condition by using long-term debt for all new external financing until the long-term debt ratio reached 35%. However, this means that the firm's capital structure would continue to be "suboptimal" while the firm changed it over time.

Alternatively, the firm could change its capital structure quickly through an exchange offer, recapitalization offer, debt or share repurchase, or stock-for-debt swap. Of course, such a quick change is not without cost either. The firm will incur transaction costs, and there will be signaling effects associated with the change.

If the difference between a firm's actual capital structure and its target corresponds to one full rating category or more, some type of one-time transaction to make an immediate change in capital structure is probably warranted. A leverage increase for a significantly underleveraged firm is likely to increase the firm's share price. If the firm is less than one full category away from its rating objective (for example, it is a weak single-A and wants to become a strong single-A), altering its retention ratio and its external financing mix is probably more cost-effective.

Self-Check Questions

1. What are the three steps in a comparative credit analysis?

2. How can a firm select an appropriate rating objective?

3. Why is it useful to consider different economic scenarios when conducting a pro forma analysis?

4. What is subordinated debt? Why do firms usually issue convertible bonds in that form rather than as senior debt?

5. Suppose a firm's capital structure is different from its target capital structure. Explain how it could bring its capital structure gradually back into line with the target. How might it do so quickly?

---

[7] The use of preferred equity financing is not likely to impair the firm's senior debt rating, as long as preferred equity represents no more than 5% of a firm's capitalization if it is nonregulated, 10% if it is a natural gas or telephone utility, or 15% if it is an electric utility.

16.4 ADJUSTING PRESENT VALUE AND REQUIRED RETURNS FOR CAPITAL STRUCTURE EFFECTS

In Chapter 10 we described a basic method of estimating a cost of capital. We treated the investment and financing decisions independently of one another. But in Chapter 15 we saw that capital structure can affect a firm's value and therefore the value of an investment it undertakes. Because of this interaction, the investment and financing decisions cannot be completely separated. In the balance of this chapter, we will show you how to account for the valuation impact of capital structure.

In practice, the cost of capital, WACC, is simply adjusted to reflect the impact of capital structure on firm value. In many cases, the adjustment is only an estimate of a complex process. Yet this method is particularly useful. After adjusting WACC, we can use it directly in our valuation procedure without any other changes. The only difference is that the (adjusted) WACC reflects the firm's capital structure *in addition* to the project's risk.

A Capital Budgeting Project's Cost of Capital

Before going any further, we need to review a few things. First, recall that the required return is an *opportunity cost of capital*. It is not a historical cost of funds. The required return is the rate at which investors would provide financing for the project under consideration *today*. Theoretically, then, each project has its own cost of capital.

Second, remember that value is a function of both expected future cash flows and the required return. Value can remain unchanged even though both the expected future cash flows and the required return change, if the changes offset each other. Third, because of the risk-return trade-off, there is a single return for each level of risk in an efficient capital market.

Recall that a firm's WACC can always be described in terms of financing rates. This also holds for a capital budgeting project's cost of capital. We can think of the project as a "mini" firm. Therefore, a project's WACC can always be represented as the weighted average of the market value proportions of any debt and equity financing package that will allow the project to be undertaken. That is,

$$\text{WACC} = (1 - L)r_e + L(1 - T)r_d \tag{16.4}$$

where T is the relevant corporate tax rate, r_d is the required return on debt, and r_e is the required return on equity. Both r_d and r_e are specific to the project. You may recognize that Equation (16.4) is identical to both Equation (15.1) and Equation (10.1).

As we have said, this equation is always correct. However, it can be difficult to apply in some situations. As we saw in Chapter 15, r_e and r_d depend upon tax laws, asymmetric information considerations, and transaction costs associated with a given capital structure. If accurate functions for r_e and r_d did exist, they could simply be substituted into Equation (16.4), and our job would be done. Unfortunately, we cannot do this without making assumptions that are only an approximation of the firm and the world in which it operates.

The Basis for Adjusting for Capital Structure Effects

The effect of capital structure on value is based on the entire firm's financing. Therefore, the project's cost of capital must be adjusted on the same basis. This means that adjusting the project cost of capital is fundamentally different from adjusting for risk. In a sense, a project undertaken by an ongoing firm has no financial risk. Still, the firm itself does have financial risk.

Financial risk is created by issuing financial obligations, such as long-term debt. The shareholders' obligation is not limited by the results of one investment. Rather, the financial obligation extends to the results of the whole firm. When one investment does poorly, the firm must still pay whatever debts come due from the proceeds of all its other investments. Thus financing considerations cannot be accounted for on a project-by-project basis. Instead, the impact of financing on the project's cost of capital is determined by the capital structure of the whole firm.

In the event that a firm finances an investment through a separate corporate subsidiary, the parent firm has no direct liability for any of the subsidiary's financial obligations. The parent is a shareholder. The corporate form thus limits its liability to what it has invested in the subsidiary. In such cases, the subsidiary's capital structure is the one on which to base the project's cost of capital.

When Capital Structure Effects Are Important

There are two situations in which it is particularly important to adjust explicitly for capital structure effects. The first is when the repayment of a loan is tied to one or more specific assets. Leverage will change as the loan is repaid and as the asset is used up and its value declines.[8] This planned reduction in leverage makes it *both* inappropriate to assume a constant debt ratio (as the procedure developed in Chapter 10 assumes) and impractical to assume some sort of time-weighted average debt ratio. The *adjusted-present-value* (APV) approach discussed in this chapter can handle this situation.

The second case occurs in practice when firms adjust their leverage to coincide with their target capital structures. A firm's total amount of debt (as distinguished from the proportion, *L*) at any point in time therefore depends on the firm's profitability. More profitable firms accumulate retained earnings more quickly and can add debt faster. The reverse is true for less profitable firms. *Leverage rebalancing* thus adds an element of risk to the firm's financial situation, which affects its cost of capital. Later in the chapter, we will explain how to incorporate this factor when calculating a firm's WACC.

Self-Check Questions

1. Explain why each capital investment project has its own cost of capital.
2. Describe two situations wherein it is important to adjust the cost of capital for capital structure effects.

16.5 ADJUSTED PRESENT VALUE

The value of a leveraged firm, or of any investment, is given by Equation (15.8):

$$V_L = V_U + T^*D = \frac{\bar{I}(1 - T)}{r} + \frac{T^*r_d D}{r_d} \qquad (15.8)$$

The right-hand side expresses the total present value as the present value of two perpetuities (the cash flow divided by the discount rate). The first is the present value of the firm's operating cash flow stream, calculated as though the firm had no debt. The second is the present

---

[8] An example is a leveraged buyout, which we will discuss in Chapter 28. It involves an asset-specific capital structure. By design, the leverage will decrease over time. Cash flows from asset sales and operations are dedicated to repay debt. The owners of the firm intend to restore its capital structure to one that is more "normal," typically within five to seven years.

value of the stream of interest tax shields. Equation (15.8) implies the required return given by Equation (15.9):

$$\text{WACC} = r(1 - T^*L) \tag{15.9}$$

which is appropriate for investments that are level perpetuities.[9] But most investments are not level perpetuities. We could still use Equation (15.9) as a less accurate estimate, but more accurate ones are available.

Suppose a firm's loan is tied to one or more specific assets by an agreement such as a mortgage or lease. In such cases, the interest and principal payments are prespecified to occur within the asset's life. Over that payment period, the value of the asset declines with its use because the project (asset) has a finite life. Finite-life projects with contractually specified debt payment schedules are fundamentally different from perpetual investments. In these cases, we know at the start the exact pattern of the "capital structure" of such projects (the remaining debt at any point) because of the repayment contract. Such a project's cost of capital can then be adjusted for the effects of this capital structure over the project's life. **Adjusted present value (APV)** is a method that can account for such patterns.

Equation (15.8) expresses the firm's value as the sum of two components. We can rewrite this equation to approximate a project's value as the sum of two components, each of which is the present value of a *finite* cash flow stream. The first is the "basic" project income, its CFATs, and the other is the net benefit from debt financing. Thus the value of the project—its APV—is

$$\text{APV}_0 = \sum_{t=1}^{n} \frac{\text{CFAT}_t}{(1 + r)^t} + \sum_{t=1}^{n} \frac{T^*\text{INT}_t}{(1 + r_d)^t} \tag{16.5}$$

where n is the number of periods in the life of the project and INT_t is the interest payment in period t. Each sum is the present value of a finite stream, which corresponds to the present value of a perpetuity in Equation (15.8).

EXAMPLE

Calculating an APV at Borden

Let's say that Borden, Inc. is evaluating an investment in a new type of soy bean processing plant. The investment would be set up as a wholly owned subsidiary called SBP. SBP would be financed with $2.5 million of debt and $1.5 million of cash, provided by Borden as equity. The (unleveraged) after-tax cash flows, the CFATs, expected to result from SBP are $1 million per year for 6 years. After that time, the project is expected to be sold off for a net after-tax $2 million in cash. SBP will have 6-year debt at an interest rate of 13.2% per year. Principal repayments will be $200,000 per year for 5 years and $1.5 million at the end of year 6. Suppose the net-benefit-to-leverage factor, T^*, for this investment is 0.25 and the (unleveraged) required return for the project, r, is 20%. What is the incremental value of the project to Borden? In other words, what is the project's *net* APV?

Table 16-5 gives an amortization schedule for SBP's loan. It identifies the interest pay-

---

[9] We say *level* perpetuity to emphasize that the expected cash flow is constant and to distinguish it from a *growing* perpetuity. We first encountered growing perpetuities in Chapter 5 in the dividend growth model.

YEAR:	0	1	2	3	4	5	6
(a) Loan balance at start of period	0	2.5000	2.3000	2.1000	1.9000	1.7000	1.5000
(b) Interest for the period (13.2% of loan balance)	0	0.3300	0.3036	0.2772	0.2508	0.2244	0.1980
(c) Principal repayment	0	0.2000	0.2000	0.2000	0.2000	0.2000	1.5000
(d) Loan balance at end of period, (a)–(c)	2.5000	2.3000	2.1000	1.9000	1.7000	1.5000	0

TABLE 16-5
Loan amortization schedule for SBP (dollar amounts in millions).

ments that SBP must make over the life of the loan. From Equation (16.5), we have

$$APV_0 = \sum_{t=1}^{6} \frac{1.0}{(1.2)^t} + \frac{2.0}{(1.2)^6}$$

$$+ \left[\frac{0.3300}{1.132} + \frac{0.3036}{(1.132)^2} + \frac{0.2772}{(1.132)^3} + \frac{0.2508}{(1.132)^4} + \frac{0.2244}{(1.132)^5} + \frac{0.1980}{(1.132)^6} \right] [0.25]$$

$$= 3.325510 + 0.669796 + 0.271775 = \$4.267 \text{ million}$$

The net APV (APV_0 minus the initial cost) is then $0.267 million (= 4.267 − 4.0). ■

Self-Check Questions

1. What are the two components of the adjusted present value of a project?

2. Explain why Equation (16.5) for a particular project is analogous to Equation (15.8) for the whole firm.

3. What is the difference between the APV and the net APV?

16.6 MANAGING CAPITAL STRUCTURE AND ITS IMPACT ON FIRM VALUE

APV is very useful in situations where the financing and investment are tied together, such as leases and leveraged buyouts.[10] However, capital budgeting decisions usually do not involve financing that is tied to the project. Nevertheless, even when the firm's financing decisions are separate from its capital budgeting decisions, if T^* is positive, capital structure affects the value of the firm's investments. To include that value effect, we must know the *pattern* of debt payments.

Leverage Rebalancing

A firm generally establishes a capital structure policy that involves a target debt ratio, L^*. The firm's actual debt ratio, L, might be above or below L^* at any point in time. Although the firm

---

[10] We will discuss leasing in Chapter 25 and leveraged buyouts in Chapter 28.

does not maintain $L = L^*$ at all times, periodically the firm adjusts its capital structure back to $L = L^*$. Such adjustments are especially common when a firm has additional reasons for making a major financial transaction, such as issuing new bonds or paying off old ones. When a firm adjusts its capital structure back to L^*, it is referred to as **leverage rebalancing**.

Unintended changes in a firm's capital structure may necessitate leverage rebalancing. These unintended changes can occur for a number of reasons. Most often such changes occur because new information arrives. For example, an innovation in technology can cause an increase or a decrease in the value of a firm. Because L is the ratio of debt to the *total market value* of the firm, a change in the firm's value causes L to change.

A General Pattern for Debt Payments

Suppose a firm has a target leverage ratio and periodically rebalances its leverage to that target. In particular, suppose leverage is rebalanced each period on the basis of the project's realized market value. This sounds much more complex than it is. Under such a policy, there is a simple adjustment to the unleveraged required return, r, to get the cost of capital for correctly computing the value of an investment. And this works even when the project's CFAT stream is not a level perpetuity.

When leverage is rebalanced each period on the basis of the realized market value, the net benefit to leverage in future periods will vary with the value of the project. Thus the net benefit to leverage in future periods is riskier with leverage rebalancing than it is with a fixed debt payment schedule. In fact, the actual debt pattern will vary in the same way project value varies.

With leverage rebalancing, the present value of the net benefits to leverage is not determined by r_d. Only the net benefit from the first period is discounted at r_d, because only the first period's debt is known at the start ($t = 0$). The net benefit to leverage in later periods must be discounted at r, the project's unleveraged required return, because this net benefit will vary as the project value varies in future periods.

Adjusting WACC for Capital Structure Valuation Effects

We will derive the adjustment to r that gives the project's correct cost of capital assuming income that is a level perpetuity, because it is easier to understand. However, the answer also applies to projects that have finite lives.

With level perpetual income, there is a "basic" expected after-tax cash flow, CFAT, of $\bar{I}(1 - T)$ each period. There is also an expected (mathematical expectation) net benefit to leverage each period of $T^*Lr_dE(V_L)$, where $E(V_L)$ is the expected value of the project. Note that the actual value of the project at each future time is a *realization*. It will almost surely differ from the expectation, just as the realized return differs from the expected return.

According to Equation (15.8), the total value of the investment is the sum of the two present values. However, to compute these present values, we need to know the required return for each income stream. The required return for the first stream is straightforward. It is the unleveraged required return, r. Thus the present value, V_U, is

$$V_U = \frac{\bar{I}(1 - T)}{r} \tag{15.2}$$

Determining the required return for the second stream is more complex. V_L is the value of the project at $t = 0$. The net benefit to leverage in the first period is $T^*Lr_dV_L$, because the debt level is LV_L. This amount has the same risk as the debt. However, the net benefits to leverage in later periods are based on the expected value $E(V_L)$. They are therefore riskier. The

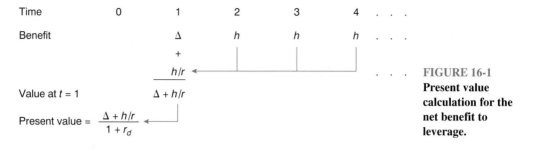

FIGURE 16-1
Present value calculation for the net benefit to leverage.

amount of debt in each future period depends on what the project's value turns out to be at that time. The risk of those tax benefits is therefore comparable to the risk of the unleveraged cash flows.

Let the net benefit to leverage in the first period be $\Delta = T^*Lr_dV_L$. Let the expected net benefit to leverage in all periods after the first be $h = T^*Lr_dE(V_L)$. The stream of net benefits to leverage and the present value calculation for them are illustrated in Figure 16-1.

At time $t = 1$, the stream of future net benefits to leverage is a level perpetuity with an expected value of h each period. Thus the value, at $t = 1$, of future benefits in periods 2, 3, 4, .. . is simply h/r—the present value of a perpetuity. The total value attributable to leverage, then, at $t = 1$, equals $\Delta + h/r$. To get the total value at $t = 0$, we must discount the value at $t = 1$ back one period. We discount it at r_d because it belongs to the same risk class as the debt itself. The present value of all the net benefits to leverage over the life of the project is then

$$\text{PV(net benefit to leverage)} = \frac{\Delta + h/r}{1 + r_d} \tag{16.6}$$

The total value of the leveraged investment, V_L, equals the sum of V_U and the PV(net benefit to leverage):

$$V_L = \frac{\bar{I}(1 - T)}{r} + \frac{\Delta + h/r}{1 + r_d} \tag{16.7}$$

$\bar{I}$ is a level expected perpetuity. Its expected value at any future point in time is the same as its current expected value. Therefore $E(V_L) = V_L$ and $h = \Delta$. Thus we can substitute $T^*Lr_dV_L$ for both Δ and h in Equation (16.7). Making these substitutions and rearranging terms (which we will not show in detail here) give the following expression for the total value of the leveraged investment:

$$V_L = \frac{\bar{I}(1 - T)}{r - T^*Lr_d\left(\dfrac{1 + r}{1 + r_d}\right)} \tag{16.8}$$

Equation (16.8) expresses V_L as the present value of a perpetuity of CFAT $= \bar{I}(1 - T)$. Therefore, the denominator must be the required return for this perpetuity, so

$$\text{WACC} = r - T^*Lr_d\left(\frac{1 + r}{1 + r_d}\right) \tag{16.9}$$

Equation (16.9) shows a firm's or project's (weighted average) cost of capital, assuming the firm follows a policy of leverage rebalancing each period on the basis of the investment's realized market value.

Calculating Bausch & Lomb's WACC

Let's say the unleveraged required return, r, for Bausch & Lomb's entire portfolio of assets is 18%. Suppose $T^* = 0.25$ and Bausch & Lomb rebalances its leverage each year to a target of $L = 0.35$. Bausch & Lomb can borrow currently at a rate of $r_d = 11.5\%$. What is Bausch & Lomb's WACC?

From Equation (16.9) we have

$$\text{WACC} = 0.18 - 0.25(0.35)(0.115)\left(\frac{1.18}{1.115}\right) = 0.1694, \text{ or } 16.94\%$$

■

Estimating the Unleveraged Required Return

Equation (16.9) shows the WACC for a firm or project on the basis of the unleveraged required return, r. Often we need to reverse this process and estimate r on the basis of the WACC.

We know that Equation (16.4) is always correct. And we have said that the debt management pattern assumed in Equation (16.9) represents typical corporate policy quite well. Therefore, we can use Equation (16.4) to estimate the WACC and use that value to calculate r. To simplify the notation (if you can imagine it), we will use a variable, H:

$$H = \frac{T^*Lr_d}{1 + r_d} \tag{16.10}$$

Then, expressing Equation (16.9) in terms of H and solving for r, we get the following expression for the unleveraged required return:[11]

$$r = \frac{\text{WACC} + H}{1 - H} \tag{16.11}$$

Estimating Conoco's Unleveraged Required Return

Suppose DuPont wants to estimate the unleveraged required return for a project that its subsidiary, Conoco Oil and Gas, is considering. DuPont's finance staff has identified Prairie Oil and Gas, a publicly traded firm in the same industry as the Conoco project. Prairie's operating risk profile should therefore be similar to the project's. Prairie's leverage ratio is $L = 0.40$. DuPont estimates that Prairie's new-issue debt rate is $r_d = 12\%$ and calculates that Prairie's WACC = 15%. It also estimates that $T^* = 0.25$.

Substituting into Equation (16.10) yields

$$H = \frac{(0.25)(0.40)(0.12)}{1.12} = 0.01071$$

Substituting into Equation (16.11) yields

$$r = \frac{0.15 + 0.01071}{1 - 0.01071} = 0.1625$$

Thus the unleveraged required return for the Conoco project is estimated to be 16.25%. ■

---

[11] Equation (16.9) becomes WACC $= r - (1 + r)H$. Then solving for r yields Equation (16.11).

Self-Check Questions

1. What does it mean to say that a firm follows a capital structure policy of periodically rebalancing its leverage?

2. Explain why r, not r_d, is the appropriate discount rate for calculating the present value of the future interest tax shields when the firm regularly rebalances its leverage.

3. As long as T^* can never be negative, explain why the WACC can never exceed the unleveraged required return, r.

16.7 ESTIMATING THE WACC FOR A CAPITAL BUDGETING PROJECT

Now let's see how to calculate the WACC for a project when the firm regularly rebalances its leverage. We will combine the procedure outlined in the previous section with the other basic steps we have discussed previously. That will give you the complete set of steps you need to follow.

The process for estimating a WACC is as follows:

1. Choose one or more comparable firms that are similar to the project in risk and industry characteristics and have publicly traded securities.

2. For each comparable firm:

   a. Estimate L. L can be estimated as the total market value of the firm's debt divided by the sum of the total market values of the firm's debt and equity.

   b. Estimate r_d. r_d can be estimated as the yield to maturity on the firm's outstanding debt.

   c. Estimate r_e. Estimating r_e is more difficult and requires professional judgment. The Dividend Growth Model (Chapter 5) or the Capital-Asset-Pricing Model (Chapter 7) can be used to estimate r_e.[12]

   d. Estimate the firm's marginal tax rate, T, using publicly reported data.

   e. Estimate the net-benefit-to-leverage factor for the firm, T^*. T^* is the most difficult parameter to estimate. Estimating T^* involves considering the firm's marginal tax rate, the uniqueness of its products, and the amount of nondebt tax shields, among other factors discussed in Chapter 15. The estimate of T^* is ultimately based on subjective professional judgment. Empirical research suggests that most estimates for a healthy firm fall somewhere between 0.05 and 0.25.

3. For each comparable firm, use the parameter estimates from step 2 to estimate H using Equation (16.10) and the WACC using Equation (16.4). Then use Equation (16.11) to estimate r.

4. On the basis of the set of one or more estimates of r from comparable firms, make a single estimate of r. Generally, an average can be used. However, judgment is necessary when the variation in the estimates is large or some of the estimates are very different from each other. r reflects the project's business risk.

5. The estimate of the project's WACC (which includes both business risk and the effects of capital structure) can now be computed by using Equation (16.9), the single estimate of r derived in step 4, and the following estimates for the firm that is considering the investment:

   a. The target capital structure, L^*, that the firm plans to maintain

---

[12] If you do not have enough information to use one of these analytical methods, "Emery's rule" says that r_e is normally about 1.5 times r_d.

b. The firm's current r_d based on L^*

c. The firm's net-benefit-to-leverage factor, T^*

EXAMPLE

Estimating a Project's WACC for PepsiCo

Suppose PepsiCo is considering an investment opportunity in laser printers, an area in which it has no previous experience. PepsiCo has identified several firms that are primarily in this business. One of these firms is H-P, whose common stock and bonds are traded publicly on the NYSE. Currently, the market value of H-P common stock is $27 per share. H-P has 10 million shares outstanding. H-P's latest earnings were $3.40 per share. Next year's dividend is expected to be $1.60 per share. Five years ago, H-P paid a dividend of $0.73 per share. H-P has long-term bonds with a total market value of $120 million. Its 9% coupon bonds maturing in 2009 are currently selling for $860. In addition to long-term bonds, H-P has $20 million in notes payable and $40 million in other current liabilities.

H-P has total liabilities of $180 million consisting of long-term bonds and current liabilities ($= 120 + 20 + 40$). Current liabilities mature soon enough that the book and market values are sufficiently close for us to ignore the difference and simply use the book value in our calculations. Total equity is $270 million ($= 27 \times 10$ million). The total market value of H-P is $450 million ($= 120 + 60 + 270$), and $L = 0.40$ ($= 180/450$). H-P's 9% coupon bonds have a 10.8% yield to maturity [put in PV $= 860$, FV $= 1000$, CF $= 45$ ($= 90/2$), and $n = 36$ (semiannual for 18 years), and compute the semiannual rate as $r = 5.4\%$, which times 2 equals the YTM] and an 11.09% APY. Because the bonds are selling at a discount and will incur lower taxes as a consequence of capital gains tax deferral, we estimate that new debt for H-P has a required return that is slightly higher than the 11.09% APY. We estimate r_d to be 11.25% APY.

Lasser Financial Services estimates that H-P's beta is 1.25. Short-term U.S. government securities are currently earning 7%, so we estimate the riskless rate, r_f, to be 7%. The required return on the market portfolio, r_M, is estimated to be 15%. The CAPM estimate of H-P's required return on equity is $r_e = 0.07 + 1.25(0.15 - 0.07) = 0.17$, or 17%. During the 6-year period from 5 years ago until next year, H-P's cash dividend grew from $0.73 to $1.60, which represents an annual growth rate of $g = 14\%$. The current market value is $P_0 = \$27$, and expected next year's dividend is $D_1 = \$1.60$. The dividend growth model estimate of the required return for equity is $r_e = (1.6/27) + 0.14 = 0.20$, or 20%.

The estimate obtained from the dividend growth model is based on a growth rate that is almost as large as the return to the market portfolio and is considerably larger than the return on the riskless asset. It is unlikely that growth of this magnitude could be maintained indefinitely. Thus the dividend growth model estimate of r_e is probably too large. However, it is plausibly close to the CAPM estimate. Therefore, the two estimates do not appear to contradict one another significantly. Because the CAPM estimate is more reliable, we will use it as our estimate of H-P's required return on equity.

PepsiCo's financial staff estimates that H-P's net-benefit-to-leverage factor is $T^* = 0.2$. Applying Equation (16.10), with $T^* = 0.20$, $L = 0.40$, and $r_d = 11.25\%$, yields

$$H = \frac{T^* L r_d}{1 + r_d} = \frac{(0.2)(0.4)(0.1125)}{1.1125} = 0.00809$$

The relevant marginal tax rate is estimated as $T = 35\%$. Therefore, with $r_e = 17\%$, applying Equation (16.4) we get

$$\text{WACC} = (1 - L)r_e + L(1 - T)r_d = 0.6(0.17) + 0.4(0.65)(0.1125) = 0.13125$$

Finally, putting $H = 0.00809$ and WACC $= 13.125\%$ into Equation (16.11), we have

$$r = \frac{\text{WACC} + H}{1 - H} = \frac{(0.13125 + 0.00809)}{(1 - 0.00809)} = 0.1405$$

Assume that the foregoing procedure was followed for other comparable firms in addition to H-P and that the single estimate of r based on the set of comparable firms is 14%. We can now estimate the WACC for the project on the basis of this "best" estimate of r and the following estimates of PepsiCo's financial parameters: $r_d = 11\%$, $L^* = 0.3$, and (because of its unique tax situation) $T^* = 0.15$. From Equation (16.9),

$$\text{WACC} = r - T^* L r_d \left(\frac{1 + r}{1 + r_d} \right) = 0.14 - (0.15)(0.3)(0.11)\left(\frac{1.14}{1.11} \right) = 0.135, \text{ or } 13.5\%$$

Thus PepsiCo should use a 13.5% WACC to compute the NPV of its proposed investment in laser printers. ■

Self-Check Questions

1. List the steps in the five-step process for estimating the WACC for a capital budgeting project.

2. Explain why the estimate of r calculated at step 4 reflects the operating risk of the project under consideration and *does not* reflect any financial risk.

3. Explain how step 5 adjusts for financial risk on the basis of the project sponsor's capital structure.

4. Which factor is most difficult to estimate: r, T^*, L, or r_d? Why?

SUMMARY

The method of financing can affect the value of a firm and its investments because of capital market imperfections. Therefore, firms choose and manage their capital structures carefully. Choosing an appropriate capital structure involves balancing the net tax advantage and agency cost reduction against the increase in the expected cost of financial distress and the cost of reduced financial flexibility that result from additional leverage. Transaction costs and information effects must also be considered. Unfortunately, these costs cannot be measured precisely. As a result, the "best" capital structure cannot be pinpointed.

This chapter described and illustrated a practical procedure that a firm can use to select and manage an appropriate capital structure. The procedure involves two important steps. First, the firm conducts a comparative credit analysis of comparable firms. The values of key financial ratios for each firm are then calculated to determine the relationship between senior debt rating and capital structure.

A bond rating provides estimates for both the relative risk of financial distress and the relative access to the capital markets. A single-A senior debt rating suggests a very modest risk of financial distress. This rating is usually sufficient to maintain capital market access on acceptable terms. The rating choice and the results of the comparative credit analysis allow a firm to specify reasonable target ranges for its key financial ratios.

The second step in the procedure involves conducting a pro forma capital structure analysis. This tests, among other things, the firm's ability to use fully the tax shields from its target capital structure. If it cannot use all the tax shields, it should reduce its target leverage ratio and substitute preferred equity and/or lease financing for conventional debt financing. The result of this two-step process is a target capital structure that balances the advantages of a change in financial leverage against the costs.

We also described a method for including the effect of capital structure on investment value, adjusted present value (APV). APV has two parts. The first part is the basic value without regard to financing—the unleveraged value, V_U. The second part "adjusts" that basic value by adding the value obtained from leverage.

We illustrated two ways to use APV. In the first (the general form), the added value from leverage is computed as the present value of a series of cash flow adjustments. This form can be used with fixed debt payment patterns, such as leases and leveraged buyouts. It can also be used for any unique debt pattern.

An easier way to use APV is based on a presumed general debt pattern of leverage rebalancing on the basis of realized market value. Such leverage rebalancing is a capital structure management policy that is widely used in practice. This debt pattern leads to an adjustment of the unleveraged required return, r, to get a firm's or capital budgeting project's WACC. Although the adjustment is really only an estimate of a more complex process, this method is particularly useful. Its simplicity results from our being able to use the (adjusted) WACC directly in our valuation procedure without any other changes. The only difference is that the "standard NPV calculation" gives the *adjusted* NPV (net APV), which reflects the value from the firm's capital structure *in addition* to the project's basic value.

DECISION SUMMARY

- Risk is by far the most important determinant of a WACC. Capital structure, however, is an important secondary determinant. It results from capital market imperfections, including asymmetric taxes, asymmetric information, and transaction costs.

- In most cases, the valuation effect of capital structure can be included by adjusting the WACC that is used to calculate present value.

- The general form of APV can be used to measure investment value for cases with a fixed debt payment pattern.

The following procedure is useful for choosing and managing capital structure:

- Determine the *rating objective*. It reflects the desired margin of safety for the risk of financial distress and for maintaining access to the capital markets.

- Conduct a *comparative credit analysis* of comparable firms to determine the capital structure that is consistent with the chosen rating. It is particularly important to select firms with similar asset portfolios, because asset type affects the costs of financial distress and the amount of leverage for a particular rating. It is also important to select firms that are comparable in size, because other things being equal, the larger a firm, the greater the amount of debt the rating agencies will tolerate for a given rating.

- Determine the values of the *key financial ratios that characterize leverage*. Three such ratios that are particularly meaningful are the annual fixed-charge coverage ratio, the annual funds-from-operations-to-total-debt ratio, and the long-term debt ratio. However, three simple ratios usually do not tell the whole story, so many analysts use additional ratios to define the target capital structure.

- Conduct a *pro forma financial analysis* to test the firm's ability to use fully both the depreciation tax benefits under its planned capital expenditure program and the interest tax shields if it finances in accordance with its target capital structure. Also test the impact on financial ratios of different future operating scenarios to determine what adjustment to the target capital structure is appropriate in light of the firm's expected future operating environment.

- Determine the need for, and desirability of, a *share repurchase or other form of transaction* to adjust capital structure quickly.

EQUATION SUMMARY

(16.1) $\text{Interest Coverage Ratio} = \dfrac{\text{EBIT}}{\text{Interest Expense}}$

(16.2) $\text{Fixed-Charge Coverage Ratio} = \dfrac{\text{EBIT} + \frac{1}{3}\,\text{Rentals}}{\text{Interest Expense} + \frac{1}{3}\,\text{Rentals}}$

(16.3) $\text{Debt-Service Coverage Ratio} = \dfrac{\text{EBIT} + \frac{1}{3}\,\text{Rentals}}{\text{Interest Expense} + \frac{1}{3}\,\text{Rentals} + \dfrac{\text{Principal Repayments}}{1 - \text{Tax Rate}}}$

(16.4) $\text{WACC} = (1 - L)r_e + L(1 - T)r_d$

(16.5) $\text{APV}_0 = \displaystyle\sum_{t=1}^{n} \frac{\text{CFAT}_t}{(1 + r)^t} + \sum_{t=1}^{n} \frac{T^*\text{INT}_t}{(1 + r_d)^t}$

(16.6) $\text{PV(net benefit to leverage)} = \dfrac{\Delta + h/r}{1 + r_d}$

(16.7) $V_L = \dfrac{\bar{I}(1 - T)}{r} + \dfrac{\Delta + h/r}{1 + r_d}$

(16.8) $V_L = \dfrac{\bar{I}(1 - T)}{r - T^*Lr_d\left(\dfrac{1 + r}{1 + r_d}\right)}$

(16.9) $\text{WACC} = r - T^*Lr_d\left(\dfrac{1 + r}{1 + r_d}\right)$

(16.10) $H = \dfrac{T^*Lr_d}{1 + r_d}$

(16.11) $r = \dfrac{\text{WACC} + H}{1 - H}$

KEY TERMS

investment-grade ratings...497

speculative-grade ratings...497

legal investments...499

interest coverage ratio...501

fixed-charge coverage ratio...501

debt-service coverage ratio...501

comparative credit analysis...504

pro forma capital structure analysis...504

adjusted present value (APV)...514

leverage rebalancing...516

EXERCISES

PROBLEM SET A

A1. Why is a pro forma analysis an important prerequisite to choosing a capital structure?

A2. What is the major reason why subordinated debt is typically rated lower than senior debt?

A3. A firm's latest 12 months' EBIT is $30 million, and its interest expense for the same period is $10 million. Calculate the interest coverage ratio.

A4. The firm in Problem A3 also had $15 million of rental expense during the latest 12 months. Calculate the firm's fixed-charge coverage ratio.

A5. The firm in Problems A3 and A4 also had $6 million of principal repayments during the latest 12 months. Its marginal tax rate is 40%. Calculate the debt-service coverage ratio.

A6. Explain why selecting a target senior debt rating is a reasonable approach to choosing a capital structure. Explain why a target senior debt rating of single-A is a prudent objective when there is only a very limited new-issue market for non-investment-grade debt and when investor willingness to purchase triple-B-rated debt is likely to be highly sensitive to the state of the economy.

A7. A firm's capital structure consists solely of debt and common equity. What form would an exchange offer take if the firm believes it is (a) overleveraged? (b) underleveraged?

A8. William Bates is contemplating starting a new firm that will provide background music for elevators, dentists' offices, and the like. He estimates a positive NPV of $270,000 for the investment. Mr. Bates plans to call the firm Tarry-Tune, Unlimited. He estimates that the initial investment needed to start Tarry-Tune is $325,000. He plans to borrow $200,000 of the initial investment. What is the expected leverage ratio, L, for Tarry-Tune?

A9. Because the weighted average given in Equation (16.4) is always a correct measure of a required return, why don't firms create securities to finance each project and offer them in the capital market in order to accurately determine the required return for the project?

A10. Suppose a firm is unleveraged and has an unleveraged required return, r, of 15%. The firm borrows 30% of the value of the firm at $r_d = 8\%$. Because of the financial leverage, r_e becomes 18%. What is the firm's WACC under each of the following conditions.

  a. The firm is operating in a perfect capital market (including no taxes).

  b. There are only corporate taxes at a rate of 35% in an otherwise perfect capital market.

A11. Nathan's Catering is a gourmet catering service located in Southampton, New York. It has an unleveraged required return of $r = 43\%$. Nathan's rebalances its leverage each year to a target of $L = 0.52$. $T^* = 0.20$. Nathan's can borrow currently at a rate of $r_d = 26\%$. What is Nathan's WACC?

A12. Maxicomputer Corporation is considering building a new manufacturing facility in Taiwan. Maxicomputer's debt ratio is $L = 0.5$. Maxicomputer's cost of debt is $r_d = 10\%$. Maxicomputer estimates that the leveraged cost of equity capital for the project is $r_e = 16\%$. $T^* = 0.25$. Maxicomputer's marginal ordinary income tax rate is 40%. Calculate the project's unleveraged required return, r.

A13. Suppose a firm currently has an unleveraged required return of 10% and perpetual unleveraged after-tax income of $140,301 per year. The firm has come up with an investment opportunity that would alter the firm's asset makeup so that it would increase its perpetual unleveraged after-tax income to $170,650 per year. Because the new asset mix is riskier, the firm's unleveraged required return would also increase to 12.165%. Should the firm undertake this investment opportunity?

A14. Reconsider the PepsiCo example. PepsiCo has identified a second company that is closely comparable to H-P. Epson has a debt ratio of $L = 0.60$, a cost of debt of $r_d = 12\%$, a leveraged required return to equity of $r_e = 20\%$, a 40% marginal tax rate, and a net-benefit-to-leverage factor of $T^* = 0.20$.

  a. Calculate Epson's unleveraged required return, r.

  b. Recalculate the estimate of r for PepsiCo to use by averaging H-P's and Epson's.

  c. What is the required return that PepsiCo should use to compute the (adjusted) NPV of the capital budgeting project?

A15. Why should a firm's ability to use tax credits affect its capital structure?

PROBLEM SET B

B1. Bixton Company's new chief financial officer is evaluating Bixton's capital structure. She is concerned that the firm might be underleveraged, even though the firm has larger-than-average research and development and foreign tax credits when compared to other firms in its industry. Her staff prepared the following industry comparison:

Rating Category	Fixed-Charge Coverage	Funds from Operations/ Total Debt	Long-Term Debt/ Capitalization
Aa	4.00–5.25x	60–80%	17–23%
A	3.00–4.30	45–65	22–32
Baa	1.95–3.40	35–55	30–41

a. Bixton's objective is to achieve a credit standing that falls, in the words of the chief financial officer, "comfortably within the A range." What target range would you recommend for each of the three credit measures?

b. Before settling on these target ranges, what other factors should Bixton's chief financial officer consider?

c. Before deciding whether the target ranges are really appropriate for Bixton in its current financial situation, what key issues specific to Bixton must the chief financial officer resolve?

B2. How does a firm's size (as measured by total assets or total sales, for example) affect its choice of capital structure under the comparable-firms approach?

B3. Sanderson Manufacturing Company would like to achieve a capital structure consistent with a Baa2/BBB senior debt rating. Sanderson has identified six comparable firms and calculated the following credit statistics:

Firm	A	B	C	D	E	F
Senior debt rating	Baa2/BBB	Baa3/BBB−	Baa2/BBB	Baa1/A−	Baa1/BBB−	Baa2/BBB+
Return on assets	5.2%	5.0%	5.4%	5.7%	5.2%	5.3%
Long-term debt/ capitalization	38%	41%	45%	40%	25%	43%
Total capitalization ($millions)	425	575	525	650	210	375
Cash flow/long-term debt	39%	43%	28%	46%	57%	43%
Fixed-charge coverage	2.57	2.83	2.75	2.38	3.59	2.15

a. Sanderson's return on assets is 5.3%. It has a total capitalization of $600 million. What are reasonable targets for long-term debt/capitalization, cash flow/long-term debt, and fixed-charge coverage?

b. Are there any firms among the six who are particularly good or bad comparables? Explain.

c. Suppose Sanderson's current ratio of long-term debt to total cap is 60% but its fixed-charge coverage is 3.00. What would you recommend?

B4. Why would lenders be willing to lend a larger proportion of the market value of tangible assets such as plant and equipment than of the market value of intangible assets such as "special" formulas and goodwill?

B5. Show that of the interest coverage ratio, fixed-charge coverage ratio, and debt-service coverage ratio, (1) the interest coverage ratio will always have the greatest value and (2) the debt-service coverage ratio will always have the smallest value, as long as interest coverage exceeds 1. Under what circumstances will all three ratios have the same value?

B6. Suppose the investment banking firm Dewey, Cheetem & Howe wishes to maintain a capital structure that is consistent with an A senior debt rating. Under what circumstances would the firm maintain a lower degree of leverage than a cross section of single-A-rated firms?

B7. A firm has $100 million of earnings before interest and taxes and $40 million of interest expense.

  a. Calculate this firm's interest coverage ratio.

  b. Calculate the pro forma interest coverage ratio, assuming the issuance of $100 million of 10% debt with the issue proceeds to be invested fully in a plant under construction.

  c. Calculate the pro forma interest coverage ratio, assuming the issuance of $100 million of 10% debt with the proceeds to be invested temporarily in commercial paper that yields 8%.

B8. Suppose Quaker Oats Corp. is evaluating a potential new investment. The investment will be financed with $100,000 of debt and $100,000 of equity. The (unleveraged) after-tax cash flows, the CFATs, expected to result from the investment are $150,000 per year for 4 years. At that time Quaker Oats expects to be able to sell the project for a net after-tax $100,000 in cash. The debt financing will be 4-year debt with interest payments of 14% per year on the remaining balance. Principal payments will be zero in year 1, $20,000 in year 2, $30,000 in year 3, and a final principal payment of $50,000 at the end of year 4. The net-benefit-to-leverage factor, T^*, is 0.20. The (unleveraged) required return for the project is 20%. What is the project's net APV?

B9. The Query Company has identified two alternative capital structures. If the firm borrows 15% of the value of the firm, it can borrow the money at $r_d = 10\%$, and the shareholders will have a required return of $r_e = 18\%$. If the firm borrows 45% of the value of the firm, it can borrow the money at $r_d = 12\%$, and the shareholders will have a required return of $r_e = 23.21\%$. Query pays corporate taxes at the rate of 35%. Which capital structure should Query adopt? Suppose Query is operating in an essentially perfect capital market except for taxes. Are the taxes approximately symmetric, or are they asymmetric?

B10. Rusty-Sell, Inc., a midstate Pennsylvania recycling facility, is $L = 27\%$ debt-financed. It pays corporate taxes at the rate of 35%. The firm's (leveraged) beta is 1.45. $T^* = 0.21$, $r_d = 12\%$, $r_f = 8\%$, and $r_M = 15\%$. Assume annual capital structure rebalancing.

  a. What is Rusty-Sell's required return to (leveraged) equity, r_e?

  b. What is Rusty-Sell's WACC?

  c. What is Rusty-Sell's unleveraged required return, r?

  d. What unleveraged beta is implied by r?

B11. The RTE Corporation expects to pay a dividend next year of $2.22. It expects its cash dividends to grow 5% per year forever. RTE has a debt ratio of $L = 35\%$. Its borrowing rate is $r_d = 9\%$. RTE pays corporate taxes at the rate of 30%, $r_f = 6\%$, $r_M = 12\%$, and RTE's common stock is currently selling for $20 per share.

  a. What is the current (leveraged) required return, r_e, on RTE's common stock?

  b. What is RTE's WACC?

  c. What is RTE's unleveraged required return, r?

  d. What unleveraged beta is implied by r?

  e. What would you say about the estimates in parts a through d if you learned that the market model estimated a (leveraged) beta of 2.2 for RTE's common stock?

B12. Both the common stock and the long-term bonds of Crib-Tick, Inc., makers of baby furniture, are traded publicly. Currently, the market value of Crib-Tick common stock is $14 per share, and there are 4 million shares outstanding. Crib-Tick's latest earnings were $2.09 per share. Next year's dividend is expected to be $1.02 per share. Five years ago, Crib-Tick paid a dividend of $0.72 per share. Crib-Tick has long-term bonds with a total market value of $30 million. The bonds mature in 2006 and have an 8% coupon. They are currently selling for $880. (Assume the bonds have 22 more coupon payments until maturity.) In addition to long-term bonds, Crib-Tick has $5 million in notes payable and $10 million in other current liabilities. Current market conditions are $r_f = 6\%$ and $r_M = 13.75\%$. Crib-Tick has a beta of 1.1. It pays corporate taxes at a rate of 30%. It has estimated $T^* = 0.18$. What would you estimate are Crib-Tick's unleveraged required return, r, and its WACC? What unleveraged beta does r imply?

B13. Managers of the Stan Lee Martin Corporation are considering a capital budgeting project that is unrelated to their current investments. The proposed project will be 40% debt-financed at $r_d = 11.25\%$. They have identified three firms that they believe are basically comparable to the capital budgeting project under consideration, and they have collected the following information about those comparable firms:

Firm	Stock Beta	Stock Price	Number of Shares	Bond Price	Coupon	Number of Bonds
A	1.10	$25	1 million	$1100	12%	10,700
B	1.20	30	2 million	900	10	67,000
C	1.15	22	5 million	850	8	32,350

Assume that for all firms $r_M = 15\%$, $r_f = 7\%$, $T = 0.35$, $T^* = 0.2$, and the total debt is the number of bonds indicated, each with a par value of $1000 and 10 years to maturity. What required return would you recommend the managers of Stan Lee Martin Corporation use to evaluate the proposed capital budgeting project?

B14. Cans-R-Us, Inc. (CRU) is a recycling company located in the suburbs of Missouri City, Kansas. CRU is currently evaluating a potential new investment. The investment will be financed with $700,000 of debt and $1,200,000 of equity. The (unleveraged) after-tax cash flows, the CFATs, expected to result from the investment are $1 million per year for 3 years, after which time the project is expected to be sold off for a net after-tax $1 million in cash. The debt financing will take the form of 3-year debt with interest payments of 15% per year on the remaining balance. Principal payments will be $100,000 in year 1, $200,000 in year 2, and $400,000 at the end of year 3. The net-benefit-to-leverage factor, T^*, is 0.25 for this investment. The (unleveraged) required return for the project is 25%. The corporate tax rate is 30%.

a. What is the project's net APV?

b. On the basis of the net APV computed in part a, what is L for this project?

c. Also on the basis of the net APV computed in part a, what is the project's WACC? (*Hint*: You will need to use trial and error to solve for WACC.)

d. On the basis of the WACC computed in part c, what is the leveraged required return to equity, r_e, for this project?

B15. Why is it so important to note that the required return is not a historical cost of funds? Cite two factors that can render the use of a firm's historical cost of funds (to evaluate a new investment) potentially damaging to the firm.

B16. In what sense is subordinated debt advantageous to senior debtholders, and in what sense is it disadvantageous to them?

PROBLEM SET C

C1. Explain why you might expect to observe a negative correlation between financial leverage and operating leverage.

C2. Firms A and B are identical except for their capital structures. Firm A has a debt ratio of 25%. Firm B has a debt ratio of 33.33%. Suppose that the interest rate on both firms' debt is 10% and that investors can also borrow at a 10% interest rate.

   a. An investor owns 5% of the common stock of firm A, half of which is financed through borrowings. What investment-loan package involving firm B will produce identical returns?

   b. An investor owns 10% of the common stock of firm B, none of which is financed through borrowings. What investment-loan combination involving firm A will produce identical returns?

C3. Using agency theory concepts, explain how restrictive covenants that forbid leases and liens on a firm's assets might cause the firm to achieve a higher rating on its bonds than would be possible without such covenants.

C4. The development of the new-issue junk bond market had important implications for capital structure choice. The existence of a viable junk bond market means that firms can comfortably maintain higher degrees of leverage than they could prior to the development of this market. Do you agree or disagree? Justify your answer.

C5. A balance sheet sometimes includes something called minority interest, which appears below long-term debt and above preferred stock. Discuss whether minority interest should be treated as debt or equity under each of the following conditions.

   a. It consists of outstanding common stock of a subsidiary, and the parent firm has no intention of repurchasing or otherwise retiring that common stock.

   b. It consists of redeemable preferred stock of a subsidiary, which the firm is obligated to redeem in equal annual amounts over the next 5 years. What is your conclusion regarding whether minority interest is really debt or equity?

C6. Ida Rather's Knot Corporation, a modest rope manufacturing firm in the northeast corner of the Yukon, has been contacted by Wile E. Coyote. He has offered her an investment opportunity that would pay her $2500 per month for 60 months. Ida must invest $10,000 now and borrow $90,000 from Wile E. at 16% APR, for a total initial investment of $100,000. However, the entire loan must be paid back at the end of the 60 months (principal and interest will total $199,242.62). No prepayment is allowed. There are no taxes. Assume that this investment is riskless, as Wile E. Coyote has claimed. Under what conditions would you recommend that Ida undertake it?

C7. Alpha Manufacturing is considering building a new distribution center that would cost $1 million. Alpha would finance the investment with $250,000 of equity and $750,000 of debt. The (unleveraged) after-tax cash flows, the CFATs, expected to result from the investment are $400,000 per year for 10 years, after which time the distribution center will be sold off for a net after-tax amount of $200,000 cash. The loan will bear interest at a rate of 12% payable annually. It will be repaid in equal annual installments of $75,000, beginning at the end of year 1. The corporate tax rate is 35%, $T^* = 0.30$, and the unleveraged cost of equity for the project is 17%.

   a. Calculate the project's net APV.

   b. Calculate the WACC and the leveraged required return to equity, r_e, for the project.

   c. Calculate the (adjusted) NPV of the project.

   d. Reconcile your answers to parts a and c.

Real-World Application:
AMR's Debt-for-Equity Exchange Offer

In 1994, AMR Corporation (AMR), the parent firm of American Airlines, found that its profitability had improved. A few years earlier, AMR had issued privately about $1.1 billion of convertible preferred stock. As you know, interest is tax-deductible whereas dividends are not. AMR decided to offer the preferred stockholders the chance to exchange their shares for a new issue of convertible Quarterly Income Capital Securities ("QUICS").[1] AMR offered to exchange $1000 face amount of 6⅛% convertible QUICS for $1000 face amount of 6% convertible preferred stock. All $1.1 billion of preferred stock could be exchanged if holders wanted to do that.

The QUICS would carry a slightly higher yield and would rank senior to the preferred stock. But QUICS include an interest deferral feature: AMR can defer interest payments from time to time for up to 20 consecutive quarters. It was reported that because of this feature, the rating agencies view QUICS as "virtually identical to the preferred."[2]

AMR's main purpose in offering to exchange convertible QUICS for convertible preferred was to improve the firm's after-tax cash flow because of the tax-deductibility of interest. Table 16-6 compares the QUICS and the preferred stock.

AMR's capitalization just prior to the exchange offer was (dollar amounts in millions):

	JUNE 30, 1994
Long-term debt:	
Current maturities	$189
Long-term debt, less current maturities	7,710
QUICS	—
Total long-term debt	7,899
Convertible preferred stock	1,081
Common stock	3,318
Total stockholders' equity	4,399
Total capitalization	$12,298

1. Describe the QUICS. Are they debt, or are they equity? How do they differ from the convertible preferred stock?

2. What would be the effect on AMR's capitalization if holders of 50% of the convertible preferred stock exchanged them for QUICS?

---

[1] AMR Corporation, *Offer to Exchange* (October 14, 1994).
[2] "AMR Wraps Up Exchange Offer, Will Issue $1 Bil of 'QUICS'," *Investment Dealers' Digest* (November 21, 1994), pp. 11–12.

	QUICS	PREFERRED	
Interest/Dividend Rate	6⅛% APR; payable quarterly; interest payments can be deferred for up to 20 calendar quarters; at the end of the deferral period, all accrued and unpaid interest must be repaid, together with interest on the unpaid amount compounded quarterly at the 6⅛% APR.	6% APR; payable quarterly out of funds legally available therefor.	**TABLE 16-6** **Comparison between convertible QUICS and convertible preferred.**
Conversion	At $79.00 per common share.	At $78.75 per common share.	
Subordination	Subordinated to all existing and future senior debt of AMR and its subsidiaries but senior to AMR's preferred stock.	Subordinated to all debt of AMR.	
Market	Registered for public trading; listed on the New York Stock Exchange.	Privately placed; not registered for public trading.	

3. What would be the effect on AMR's capitalization if holders of 100% of the convertible preferred stock exchanged them for QUICS?

4. Calculate the increase in net income available for common stock that would result from 50% of the convertible preferred stock being exchanged for QUICS.

5. Calculate the increase in net income available for common stock that would result if all the convertible preferred stock is exchanged.

6. Why does this debt-for-equity exchange increase the risk of the common stock?

7. How does the interest-deferral feature affect your interpretation of the QUICS? The risk of the common stock?

8. What trade-off did AMR have to evaluate as it considered whether to proceed with the exchange offer?

BIBLIOGRAPHY

Arzac, Enrique R. "On the Capital Structure of Leveraged Buyouts," *Financial Management*, 1992, 21(1):16–26.

Ashton, D., and D. Atkins. "Interactions in Corporate Financing and Investment Decisions—Implications for Capital Budgeting: A Further Comment," *Journal of Finance*, 1978, 33(5):1447–1453.

Bar-Yosef, Sasson. "Interactions of Corporate Financing and Investment Decisions—Implications for Capital Budgeting: Comment," *Journal of Finance*, 1977, 32(1):211–217.

Bruner, Robert F., and E. Richard Brownlee, II. "Leveraged ESOPs, Wealth Transfers, and 'Shareholder Neutrality': The Case of Polaroid," *Financial Management*, 1990, 19(1):59–74.

Chaplinsky, Susan, and Greg Niehaus. "The Tax and Distributional Effects of Leveraged ESOPs," *Financial Management*, 1990, 19(1):29–38.

Collins, J. Markham, and William S. Sekely. "The Relationship of Headquarters Country and Industry Classification to Financial Structure," *Financial Management*, 1983, 12(3):45–51.

Cordes, Joseph J., and Steven M. Sheffrin. "Estimating the Tax Advantage of Corporate Debt," *Journal of Finance*, 1983, 38(1):95–105.

Davis, Alfred H. R. "Effective Tax Rates as Determinants of Canadian Capital Structure," *Financial Management*, 1987, 16(3):22–28.

Debt Ratings Criteria: Industrial Overview. New York: Standard & Poor's, 1986.

Denis, David J. "Organizational Form and the Consequences of Highly Leveraged Transactions: Kroger's Recapitalization and Safeway's LBO," *Journal of Financial Economics*, 1994, 36(2):193–224.

Ezzell, John R., and William A. Kelly, Jr. "An APV Analysis of Capital Budgeting Under Inflation," *Financial Management*, 1984, 13(3):49–54.

Ezzell, John R., and James A. Miles. "Capital Project Analysis and the Debt Transaction Plan," *Journal of Financial Research*, 1983, 6(1):25–31.

Froot, Kenneth A., David S. Scharfstein, and Jeremy C. Stein. "Risk Management: Coordinating Corporate Investment and Financing Policies," *Journal of Finance*, 1993, 48(5):1629–1658.

Janjigian, Vahan. "The Leverage Changing Consequences of Convertible Debt Financing," *Financial Management*, 1987, 16(3):15–21.

Kester, W. Carl. "Capital and Ownership Structure: A Comparison of United States and Japanese Manufacturing Corporations," *Financial Management*, 1986, 15(1):5–16.

Lewellen, Wilbur G., and Douglas R. Emery. "Corporate Debt Management and the Value of the Firm," *Journal of Financial and Quantitative Analysis*, 1986, 21(5):415–426.

Long, Michael, and Ileen Malitz. "The Investment-Financing Nexus: Some Empirical Evidence." In *The Revolution in Corporate Finance,* ed. Joel M. Stern and Donald H. Chew, Jr., pp. 112–118. New York: Basil Blackwell, 1986.

MacKie-Mason, Jeffrey K. "Do Taxes Affect Corporate Financing Decisions?" *Journal of Finance*, 1990, 45(5):1471–1494.

Masulis, Ronald W. "The Impact of Capital Structure Change on Firm Value, Some Estimates," *Journal of Finance*, 1983, 38(1):107–126.

Mauer, David C., and Wilbur G. Lewellen. "Debt Management Under Corporate and Personal Taxation," *Journal of Finance*, 1987, 42(5):1275–1291.

Mauer, David C., and Alexander J. Triantis. "Interactions Of Corporate Financing and Investment Decisions: A Dynamic Framework," *Journal of Finance*, 1994, 49(4):1253–1277.

Mehran, Hamid. "Executive Incentive Plans, Corporate Control, and Capital Structure," *Journal of Financial and Quantitative Analysis*, 1992, 27(4):539–560.

Miles, James A., and John R. Ezzell. "Reformulating Tax Shield Valuation: A Note," *Journal of Finance*, 1985, 40(5):1484–1492.

Miles, James A., and John R. Ezzell. "The Weighted Average Cost of Capital, Perfect Capital Markets, and Project Life: A Clarification," *Journal of Financial and Quantitative Analysis*, 1980, 15(3):719–730.

Myers, Stewart C. "Interactions in Corporate Financing and Investment Decisions—Implications for Capital Budgeting," *Journal of Finance*, 1974, 29(1):1–25.

Myers, Stewart. "The Search for Optimal Capital Structure." In *The Revolution in Corporate Finance*, ed. Joel M. Stern and Donald H. Chew, Jr., pp. 91–99. New York: Basil Blackwell, 1986.

Patterson, Cleveland S. "The Effects of Leverage on Revenue Requirements of Public Utilities," *Financial Management*, 1983, 12(3):29–39.

Ravid, S. Abraham. "On Interactions of Production and Financial Decisions," *Financial Management*, 1988, 17(3):87–99.

Taggart, Robert A., Jr. "Consistent Valuation and Cost of Capital Expressions with Corporate and Personal Taxes," *Financial Management*, 1991, 20(3):8–20.

Viswanath, P. V. "Strategic Considerations, the Pecking Order Hypothesis, and Market Reactions to Equity Financing," *Journal of Financial and Quantitative Analysis*, 1993, 28(2):213–234.

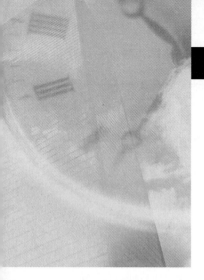

WHY DIVIDEND POLICY MATTERS

O B J E C T I V E S

After studying this chapter, you should be able to

1. Describe four different views of dividend policy: perfect market, traditional, tax differential, and signaling.

2. Explain how these views depend on the three capital market imperfections we described in Chapter 14—asymmetric taxes, asymmetric information, and transaction costs—and how they combine to create an environment in which a firm's dividend policy can affect its total value.

3. Explain why the existence of dividend clienteles significantly lessens the effect of tax differentials on dividend policy.

4. Explain how share repurchases and dividend payments are substitutes for one another.

5. Calculate the value of transferable put rights, and describe the advantages of transferable put rights over a fixed-price tender offer.

Don't you think it is reasonable that a firm should give its owners part of the profit? Why not share the wealth? Recall what we said in Chapter 5 about income versus growth. Suppose the firm has positive-NPV projects it can invest the money in. Might the shareholders be better off if the firm puts the money there and forgoes dividends? These questions are central to dividend policy, which addresses the question "What part of available cash should the firm pay out as dividends, and what part should it retain and reinvest?"

A firm's **dividend policy** is its decision to pay out a portion of its earnings to its shareholders as dividends. Can a firm's dividend policy affect its value? We know from value conservation (Chapter 14) that splitting or combining cash flows cannot alter their total value—*in a perfect capital market environment*. In that case, dividend policy would not matter. But as we noted in Chapter 14, taxes, information asymmetries, and transaction costs are important imperfections in the operation of capital markets. Those imperfections provide the basis for our conclusions about dividend policy.

Thus far, for simplicity, we have characterized a dividend policy simply as a constant *payout ratio* (the ratio of dividends paid to earnings; see Chapter 5). But a firm's payout ratio typically varies over the firm's life. For example, a small and rapidly growing firm may retain all its earnings for many years to help finance its growth. As a firm matures, typically it begins to pay dividends at some point and then, over time, increases the proportion of its earnings that are paid out in dividends. About 50% of the earnings of all U.S. corporations over the past half-century have been paid out as dividends.

As with capital structure, there are conflicting viewpoints about dividend policy. But also like capital structure, dividend policy is relevant in practice, because firms certainly behave as though it matters. The empirical evidence shows consistent patterns of dividend policy, and it shows significant average stock price reactions to dividend changes. In this chapter, we will explain why dividend policy matters. In the next chapter we will outline a practical method of managing dividend policy.

DIVIDEND POLICY AND THE PRINCIPLES OF FINANCE

◆ *Capital Market Efficiency*: Recognize that the potential increase in value a firm can get through dividend policy is smaller than what it can get through capital structure policy. Most important to the firm's value, however, are the introduction of valuable new ideas and wise use of the firm's comparative advantages.

◆ *Risk-Return Trade-Off*: Recognize that the trade-off between dividends and capital gains with fair market transactions is simply a risk-return trade-off. It does not affect firm value.

◆ *Signaling*: Consider any possible change in dividend policy carefully, because it conveys information to outsiders and can be misunderstood.

◆ *Time Value of Money*: Include any time-value-of-money tax benefits from dividend policy choices.

◆ *Valuable Ideas*: Look for opportunities to create value by supplying a dividend policy that has a demand-supply imbalance, such as may result from changes in tax laws.

◆ *Behavioral*: Use the information contained in the dividend policies of other firms.

◆ *Options*: Consider transferable put rights as an alternative method of repurchasing shares.

CHRYSLER'S DIVIDEND DILEMMA

Chrysler Corporation chairman Robert J. Eaton was concerned. Financier Kirk Kerkorian—Chrysler's largest single shareholder, who controlled 9% of the firm's stock—publicly demanded that Chrysler's board take specific steps to boost Chrysler's sagging share price. Kerkorian said the board should raise the dividend rate, authorize a share repurchase program, and declare a stock split. Although Chrysler had already raised its dividend rate twice in the last 12 months, he noted that Ford had just increased its dividend rate 12.5% and split its common stock 2-for-1. And even though Chrysler was the auto industry's low-cost producer and was reporting record earnings, its stock price was only about 5 times its annual earnings (versus Ford's stock price, which was about 7 times Ford's annual earnings), and its dividend yield was about 2.2% (versus 3.6% for Ford). Chrysler's stock price had fallen by about 20% since the beginning of the year.

Chrysler currently had cash and cash equivalents amounting to $6.6 billion. Profits were robust. Yet Eaton, a long-time veteran of the automobile industry, believed Chrysler would need to have at least $7.5 billion on hand—and perhaps as much as $10 billion—to carry out its ambitious product-development plans through the next recession. Chrysler had skirted financial disaster several times in the past.

The *Wall Street Journal* wrote that Kerkorian's move raised a fundamental issue: "During a boom, how much of its profits should a corporation such as Chrysler return to its shareholders in the form of higher dividends and stock buybacks?"

Several large institutional owners of Chrysler stock supported Kerkorian's proposals. One said "a buyback is needed to signal Chrysler's strength to Wall Street." Another said

Chrysler should double its dividend rate, because "Chrysler is the most undervalued major stock today" and "the low dividend was one reason for that." Moreover, Chrysler's stock price rose $3.125, or 6.8%, from $45.875 to $49, the day Kerkorian's letter was released to the media. It climbed a further $0.875, or 1.8%, the next day.

As you read this chapter, think about how the main ideas apply to the situation confronting Mr. Eaton. At the end of the chapter, we'll return to Chrysler's dilemma.

17.1 THE PERFECT MARKET VIEW

As we have said, the perfect market environment is the logical starting place for any discussion of corporate financial policy. First we examine the significance of a particular financial policy decision in such an environment. This leads us to the **perfect market view** of dividend policy. The perfect market view of dividend policy concludes that dividend policy does not matter. Because the capital markets are so efficient, a firm's value is relatively insensitive to its dividend policy.

After establishing the perfect market view, we'll relax our assumptions and see how that affects dividend policy.

What is Dividend Policy?

Although we have characterized dividend policy as simply a payout ratio, it is more than that. Dividend payments are generally made in cash. Because a firm has alternative uses for cash, confusion can occur among the dividend, capital budgeting, and capital structure policies. For example, if making a capital expenditure will reduce the firm's cash dividends by the amount of the expenditure, then the dividend decision would simply be the result of the investment decision.[1] We could not distinguish the valuation effect of a dividend change from that of a change in capital budget. The two policies would simply mirror each other. Similarly, if the capital budget is held constant, and the firm issues new shares to finance the dividend, dividend policy would simply be a result of the capital structure policy.

If we maintain constant capital budgeting and capital structure policies, we may have too little or too much cash for dividends. In a strict sense, then, a pure dividend policy decision involves only a trade-off between retaining earnings on the one hand and selling new shares to obtain the cash to pay dividends on the other. Although some firms (mostly utilities) have maintained a high payout ratio of regular quarterly cash dividends and *simultaneously* sold new issues of common stock, they are not typical.

To understand the role of dividends, then, we must isolate the effect of a change in cash dividends from the firm's choices of investments and capital structure. Otherwise, we would not be analyzing dividend policy exclusively.

Another complication is the method of payment. There are different ways to distribute cash to shareholders. A firm can make regular payments (say, quarterly) or it can make larger irregular payments of "special" dividends. Or instead of paying any dividends, it can use the cash to repurchase shares, which may have tax advantages.

Dividends in a Perfect Market Environment

Once again we call on the concept of value conservation. In a perfect capital market environment, if a firm maintains constant capital budgeting and capital structure policies, it cannot af-

---

[1] Even the "high and mighty" have made this mistake. Martin Feldstein, at the time chairman of the Council of Economic Advisers, and a colleague tried to explain dividend policies in Feldstein and Green (1983). But their model made dividend policy a mirror image of capital budgeting policy. See Bortz and Rust (1984).

fect the wealth of its existing shareholders by paying out either more or less than its residual cash flow. The crux of the argument is that fair market transactions are neutral and don't transfer wealth. Let's look at the transactions involved with a dividend and examine how it is financed.

When a firm pays a dividend, money is simply transferred from one form to another. Before payment of the dividend, the money is in the form of a shareholder claim on the firm's assets. After payment of the dividend, the shareholder has cash. But as long as the transfer is a fair market transaction in a perfect capital market environment, the value is the same.

Another transaction we need to consider is selling new shares. Again, this is simply a transfer of money from one form to another. Before the transaction, the new investors have cash. After exchanging the cash for new shares, the new investors have an equal-value claim on the firm's assets. And again, as long as the transfer is a fair market transaction in a perfect capital market environment, the value is the same.

Now let's consider a dividend under three different cases. In the first case, the firm has the necessary cash and simply reduces its cash account to pay the dividend. The "offsetting" amount in the double-entry system is an equal reduction in the shareholder equity account. This is the transfer of money from one form, a claim on the firm, to another form, cash in the shareholder's "hand."

In the second case, the firm does not have the cash to pay the dividend, so it issues new shares in exchange for cash, which temporarily increases the total value of the firm. Then the firm makes the dividend payment, which reduces total firm value back to its pre-new-share value. Because both transactions are simply fair market transactions that transfer money from one form to another, each party's value is the same, and after both transactions, firm value is unchanged.

Figure 17-1 illustrates the second case. The firm pays out 20% of its value as a cash dividend. It then raises an equal amount of cash by selling new shares. The new shareholders own 20% of the firm.

Think about what happened in this second case. In effect, existing shareholders—through the firm's transactions—sold part of their claim on the firm to the new investors.

FIGURE 17-1

The transfer of value when a firm pays a cash dividend and finances it with a new share issue.

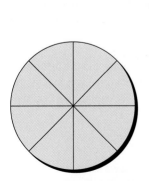

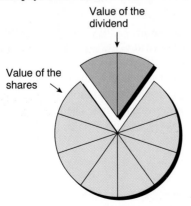

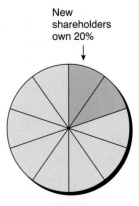

Before the dividend the original stockholders own 100% of the firm's shares.

A 20% dividend reduces the value of the firm by 20% but leaves shareholder wealth unchanged.

After the dividend and new share issue the original stockholders own 80% of the firm's shares.

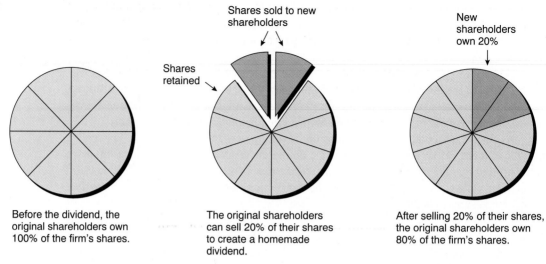

Before the dividend, the original shareholders own 100% of the firm's shares.

The original shareholders can sell 20% of their shares to create a homemade dividend.

After selling 20% of their shares, the original shareholders own 80% of the firm's shares.

FIGURE 17-2

The transfer of value when the original shareholders sell some of their shares to create a homemade dividend.

③ In our third case, a shareholder wants a cash dividend and thus wants the firm to make the transactions in Figure 17-1. But the firm has decided not to pay the dividend because it does not want to go to the trouble of making the two transactions. The existing shareholder can go out and find a new investor and sell some shares directly to that new investor in exchange for cash. The net effect of this direct sale is the same as the firm's two transactions in the second case. Part of the existing shareholder's claim would go to the new investor in exchange for cash. And as long as it is a fair market transaction in a perfect market environment, neither party gains nor loses value. This direct transaction—a shareholder selling some shares to get cash—is called a **homemade dividend**.

Figure 17-2 illustrates a homemade dividend. Let's compare alternatives. When the firm pays a cash dividend and sells additional shares to pay for it, total value is unchanged. But the number of shares outstanding increases, and the value per share (the stock price) declines. The original shareholders are just as well off, because even though their shares are worth less and they have the same number of shares, they have cash that is equal to their decline in share value. With a homemade dividend, the original stockholders sell some of their shares, and the number of outstanding shares does not change, so the stock price does not change. The original stockholders are just as well off, because even though they have fewer shares worth the same per share, they have cash that is equal to their decline in share value.[2]

Therefore, despite the differences in the number of shares outstanding and the difference in stock (per-share) price, value is maintained. The two alternatives leave the original shareholders equally well off. Thus dividend policy is irrelevant—in a perfect capital market environment.

---

[2] The original shareholders sell 20% of their holdings (which corresponds to 2 of the 10 slices in the pie chart). Problem B3 at the end of the chapter provides a numerical example consistent with the pie charts in Figures 17-1 and 17-2.

Consider a firm that has decided to undertake, but has not yet announced, a major new capital budgeting project. The project costs $10 million and has a positive NPV of $20 million. The firm has the cash to finance the project. The firm also has 10 million shares of stock currently outstanding, selling for $24 each, and no debt. Thus the firm's total value is $240 million (= 24 × 10 million) before the project announcement and $260 million (= 240 + 20) after.

To determine whether paying dividends affects shareholder wealth, let's look at two alternatives facing the firm. The alternatives are (1) pay no cash dividend and finance the project with cash, or (2) pay a cash dividend of $1 per share and obtain $10 million in new external financing for the project. To make a fair comparison of alternatives, the firm must sell $10 million in new shares with the dividend alternative. Otherwise, any difference could be due to factors other than the difference in dividend policy. The sale of new stock finances the project by replacing the $10 million in equity that the firm pays out as dividends.

With no dividend, the firm simply uses the cash to finance the project. In that case, each share would be worth $26 (= 260/10). If all the shareholders want the $10 million dividend, they can sell 384,615 (= 10,000,000/26) of their shares to get it.

With a dividend, the firm pays out $10 million cash and sells $10 million worth of new shares. After payment of the dividend, each share will be worth the predividend share price ($26) minus the dividend ($1), or $25. Note that paying the dividend does not affect shareholder wealth; it is $26 before and 25 + 1 = $26 after.

To get the $10 million to finance the project, the firm must sell 400,000 (= 10,000,000/25) fair-priced new shares. Then the firm will have 10.4 million shares outstanding worth $25 each, for a total firm value of $260 million (= 25 × 10.4 million). And $260 million is exactly what the firm's total value was before the dividend–new-share transactions. Therefore, the dividend does not change the firm's total value or the wealth of its shareholders. In effect, it simply allows original shareholders to "cash in" part of their equity in the firm. ■

But Aren't Capital Gains Riskier than Dividends?

Even though dividend policy should be irrelevant to firm value in a perfect capital market, many investors seem to believe that current dividends are less risky than future capital gains. A cash dividend now reduces the potential for future capital gain, because less money is invested. The **traditional view** of dividend policy therefore advocated a high payout ratio. It held that "within reason," investors prefer larger to smaller cash dividends.[3] Dividends represent cash in hand, which involves no risk. Reinvesting the money by forgoing the dividend involves risk. The realized return may be quite different from the expected return. Thus capital gains really are riskier than dividends. Then aren't shareholders better off getting the dividend now—even in a perfect capital market?

At this point, we hope you recognize an opportunity to apply the Principle of Risk-Return Trade-Off and answer, "No, not necessarily." The difference between the dividend now and the potential future capital gains is, of course, risk and the time value of money. Therefore, because of the risk-return trade-off, if we want the dividend now, we must accept a lower return on the investment in those shares. (Investors are still free to choose a different risk-re-

---

[3] This conclusion is based on what is often referred to as the bird-in-the-hand fallacy. The term *fallacy*, of course, reveals what most people think of the traditional view.

turn level, depending on how they reinvest the dividends.) Looking back at our dividend-irrelevance example, the issue is whether the existing shareholders or some "new" shareholders are going to invest the $10 million in the firm's operations, including the new capital budgeting project.

Shareholders who decide that future dividends and capital gains are *excessively* risky (as opposed to being in accordance with the risk-return trade-off) can sell some or all of their shares. This involves transaction costs, but it enables shareholders to make their own risk-return choices. Moreover, if the firm can reinvest funds profitably, and if the firm's capital budgeting and capital structure policies are held constant, merely paying a dividend does not alter the firm's risk profile or the risk to its shareholders. Therefore, the risk difference between a dividend now and an uncertain future return does not affect value either—in a perfect capital market environment.

Capital Market Imperfections

Of course, the perfect market view leaves out taxes, transaction costs, and information asymmetries. If capital gains are taxed at a lower rate than dividends, shareholders paying taxes on both types of income should prefer getting the income as capital gains rather than as dividends.

There are also psychological theories that provide a rationale for some individuals' preferring cash dividends over capital gains. These theories argue that for psychological reasons, dividends and capital gains are not perfect substitutes for one another. For example, a lack of self-control provides a reason for an investor to prefer regular cash dividends. If the investor had to sell stock to get income, he might sell more and spend too much, thereby using up his capital too quickly for his own good. These psychological reasons are additional capital market imperfections that can make dividend policy relevant.

Finally, it may be that dividend policy can be used, less expensively than other methods, to convey information to the public.

All of these concerns are valid. Capital market imperfections, including asymmetric information considerations, contribute to the relevance of dividend policy.

Self-Check Questions

1. What does the term *dividend policy* mean?

2. What do we mean by the term *homemade dividend*?

3. Why are homemade dividends and firm dividends perfect substitutes in a perfect capital market?

4. What sort of dividend policy does the traditional view of dividend policy recommend?

17.2 THE ROLE OF INCOME TAXES

Tax laws change with some regularity. As in the case of capital budgeting projects, you must know the relevant tax laws before making decisions on dividend policy. Currently, personal taxes are higher on dividends than on capital gains. The maximum tax rate on capital gains is 28% versus 36% in the top bracket for ordinary income.[4] In addition, there is the valuable cap-

---

[4] In addition, there is a surcharge for incomes in excess of $250,000, which raises the marginal tax rate on ordinary income to 39.6%.

ital gains tax-timing option—postpone the tax on a gain, and claim the tax reduction on a loss.[5] The capital gains tax-timing option further lowers the *effective* tax rate on capital gains. Previous versions of the Internal Revenue Code have also included such a tax differential.

The **tax differential view** of dividend policy argues that shareholders prefer capital gains over dividends, and hence low payout ratios, because capital gains are effectively taxed at a lower rate than dividends. Therefore, shareholders who are paying taxes on both types of income may prefer capital gains rather than dividends. But transaction costs to create a homemade dividend offset the tax gain. Thus other shareholders who want liquidity and face large enough transaction costs can still be better off with the dividend. And even if transaction costs to create a homemade dividend are not very high, tax-exempt shareholders who want liquidity will prefer dividends as long as transactions are not costless. This is because they can save the transaction costs, but they cannot save taxes because they do not pay taxes.

Corporate shareholders actually have a "reversed" tax preference. Currently, corporate shareholders pay income tax at a 35% maximum marginal rate and are not taxed on 70% of the dividends received (see Chapter 2). A corporate shareholder would therefore pay tax on dividend income at a rate no greater than 10.5% $[= (1 - 0.70)0.35]$, because only 30% of the dividends it receives are taxable. In contrast, corporate shareholders pay tax on long-term capital gains at rates up to 35%. Thus corporate investors may prefer dividends over capital gains from the tax perspective.

EXAMPLE · *The Effect of Personal Taxes*

Suppose dividends are taxed at a 36% rate and capital gains are not taxed. We can show that a dividend-paying firm will have a lower value than an otherwise identical non-dividend-paying firm.

Firm A has a $50 share price. It pays no dividend. Investors expect its share price to be $57.50 after 1 year. Shareholders thus expect a capital gain of $7.50 per share. The expected return is 15% $(= 7.50/50)$ both pretax and after-tax.

Firm B is identical except that it will pay a $5.00 dividend per share at the end of the year. The ex-dividend price (the price right after the point when a new shareholder would not get the dividend) will be $52.50 $(= 57.50 - 5.00)$. Its shares and those of firm A are equally risky. Thus firm B's shares must also provide a 15% after-tax return.

What is firm B's share price? The tax on the dividend is $1.80 $(= 0.36 \times 5.00)$. The after-tax dividend is $3.20 $(= 5.00 - 1.80)$. An investor will have $55.70 $(= 52.50 + 3.20)$ per share of firm B. To provide a 15% return, each share of firm B must be worth, today, the present value of its expected future value. That is,

$$\text{Share price} = \frac{55.70}{1.15} = \$48.43$$

What is the pretax return on firm B's shares? It is

$$\text{Pretax return} = \frac{57.50 - 48.43}{48.43} = 18.73\%$$

Therefore, firm B's shares must provide a higher pretax expected return (18.73% versus 15%). This higher return is to compensate for the tax liability. ∎

---

[5] We described the capital gains tax-timing option in Chapter 8. Recall that capital gains are taxed at the time of the sale of the asset, not as they accrue. Thus the tax liability for a capital gain is reinvested and earns the time value of money until the tax payment is actually made.

Clientele Effect

The *clientele effect* (discussed in Chapter 15) is also important in the study of dividend relevance. The clientele effect refers to investors "sorting" themselves into groups, each of which prefers the firms it invests in to follow a particular type of policy. When applied to dividend policy, the clientele effect refers to those investors who prefer one dividend policy over another for a particular reason.

The clientele effect lessens, and may even eliminate, the rationale for the tax differential view of dividend policy. As you might guess from our foregoing discussion, there are natural clienteles for high-cash-dividend stocks and low-cash-dividend stocks. And considerable empirical evidence supports the existence of investor clienteles. On the basis of their tax positions, investors choose stocks with high or low cash dividends. A firm's dividend policy simply appeals to different tax clienteles. Each tax clientele can invest in the shares of firms whose dividend policies best suit that clientele's tax posture. Of course, as long as there is a sufficient supply of investment opportunities for each group, no premium is needed to buy a preferred investment instrument. With no premium, dividend policy would again be irrelevant—in spite of the apparent tax asymmetry.

An International Perspective

Shareholders' returns are taxed twice in the United States. Corporate profits are taxed, and after-tax profits distributed to investors as dividends are taxed again. This method of taxation is known as a **two-tier tax system**. Table 17-1 compares the systems of corporate and individ-

TABLE 17-1
Corporate and individual taxation in selected countries.[a]

COUNTRY	SYSTEM OF CORPORATE TAXATION	CORPORATE TAX RATE APPLIED TO		INDIVIDUAL TAX RATE APPLIED TO	
		Dividends	Retained Earnings	Dividends	Capital Gains[b]
Australia	Imputation	33%	33%	—[c]	47[d]%
Austria	Two-tier	34	34	50%	—
Belgium	Two-tier	40.17	40.17	55	—
Canada	Imputation	39.52[e]	39.52[e]	31.32	23.49[f]
France	Imputation	33.33	33.33	56.8	33.33
Germany	Split-rate	30[g]	45[g]	53[g]	—
Ireland	Imputation	38	40	48	40[d]
Italy	Imputation	37	37	51	51[h]
Japan	Two-tier	37.5	37.5	50	20
Netherlands	Two-tier	35	35	60	—
New Zealand	Imputation	33	33	33	—
Spain	Imputation	35	35	56	56[i]
Sweden	Two-tier	28	28	30	25
United Kingdom	Imputation	33	33	40	40[d]
United States	Two-tier	35	35	39.6	28

[a] Peak marginal federal income tax rate.
[b] On sales of equity securities.
[c] Dividends are exempt from taxation to the extent that they are paid out of profits that have been taxed at the full corporate rate.
[d] Cost basis is indexed for inflation.
[e] The national rate of 38% is reduced to 28% if the income is also subject to provincial taxation. For example, income earned in the province of Ontario is subject to a 15.5% income tax. There is also a 4% national surtax which brings the peak federal tax rate to 39.52% [= 38 × 1.04]. The effective tax rate on income earned in Ontario is thus 44.62% [= 28 + (0.04) (28) + 15.5].
[f] Only 75% of the capital gain is included in taxable income.
[g] In addition, there is a "reunification surcharge" equal to 7.5% of total tax due.
[h] Under certain circumstances, capital gains tax can be paid in installments over 5 years.
[i] The rate of capital gains tax is reduced for each year over two that the asset is held. The gain is tax-exempt on listed shares held 10 years or longer.
Sources: Corporate and Withholding Tax Rates, Deloitte Touche Tohmatsu International, New York, April 1995; and Deloitte Touche Tohmatsu International, ed., *Executives Living Abroad,* Kluwer, Netherlands, 1994.

ual taxation in 15 countries. Of these, Austria, Belgium, Japan, the Netherlands, Sweden, and the United States have two-tier tax systems.

Germany has a **split-rate tax system**. Retained earnings are taxed at a higher rate (45%) than earnings that are distributed as dividends (30%). In such a system, tax-exempt investors would prefer a very high payout ratio. The lower corporate income tax rate applied to dividends favors dividends over retained earnings/capital gains for these investors. However, taxable investors pay income taxes only on dividends. Nevertheless, very wealthy investors might still prefer capital gains over dividends, depending on their tax rate on dividends and the value of their tax-timing options.

Eight of the countries in Table 17-1 have an **imputation tax system**. In such a system, shareholders' returns are not fully taxed twice. Shareholders are taxed on the dividends they receive, but they get a credit for the tax the corporation paid on the profits it distributed. In some countries, such as Australia, shareholders get a full credit for the amount of corporate tax paid. In other countries, such as Canada, they receive only a partial credit.

A Canadian firm earns C\$4.00 per share. It pays income tax at a 38% rate, or C\$1.52 per share. Suppose it pays a dividend of C\$1.24 per share. Canadian shareholders are required to "gross up" the dividend by 25% and to include the grossed-up amount in their taxable income. They are permitted to claim the 25% gross up as a tax credit. | *Imputation Tax System*   **EXAMPLE**

Suppose a shareholder pays federal income tax at a 29% rate. The amount of the gross up is C\$0.31 (= 0.25 × 1.24). The shareholder is treated as having received a dividend equal to C\$1.55 (= 1.24 + 0.31). The tax is C\$0.45 (= (0.29 × 1.55) minus a credit of C\$0.31, for a net tax of C\$0.14 per share. If the shareholder were in a 17% tax bracket instead, she would be entitled to a *refund* of C\$0.05 [= 0.31 − (0.17)1.55] per share. ■

Tax-exempt shareholders prefer high payout ratios under an imputation tax system. They receive a check for the amount of the tax credit. High-tax-rate investors are usually in the opposite position. They have to write a check to cover the amount of tax owed in excess of the credit. So, they prefer a low-payout policy.

Therefore, the specific tax procedures and rates on dividends, retained earnings, and capital gains can influence the choice of dividend policy. As a consequence, dividend policy's effect on shareholder wealth may differ from one country to another.

Where does all this leave us concerning taxes? Income taxes can affect the sort of dividend policy shareholders want. But the clientele effect reduces the importance of taxes. Changes in the tax system are probably more important than the level of taxes existing at any particular time. They can create profitable opportunities for a firm to offer a dividend policy that has become attractive because of the change in law but is in short supply.

Self-Check Questions

1. Which are usually taxed more favorably in the United States, dividends or capital gains?

2. What is the tax differential view of dividend policy?

3. How does the existence of tax clienteles affect our conclusion that the differential taxation of dividends and capital gains can affect dividend policy?

17.3 TRANSACTION COSTS

We have said that tax systems create preferences for certain dividend policies. But investor clienteles can lessen the impact of those differences. Transaction costs introduce additional considerations.

Flotation Costs and Commission Charges

Although shareholders can create homemade dividends or reinvest the dividends they receive, they will incur brokerage commissions. Likewise, if a firm issues shares to pay a cash dividend, it will incur direct transaction costs in the form of flotation costs. Therefore, the effect of such transaction costs depends on your point of view.

In general, brokerage commissions and flotation costs both vary inversely with the size of the transaction. These economies of scale make it cheaper for the firm to sell a large block of shares than for individual shareholders to make small sales. Consequently, it is generally cheaper for the firm to pay dividends than for shareholders to create homemade dividends. Regular dividend checks relieve investors of the inconvenience and significant brokerage charges involved in making frequent small sales.

Two trends have affected the difference between flotation costs and brokerage commissions. The growth of the discount brokerage industry has reduced brokerage commissions. The greatest reductions in commissions, however, have occurred in connection with larger transactions—those involving several hundred shares or more. In addition, new-issue *dividend reinvestment* plans have permitted firms to reduce issuance costs substantially, to as little as 2% (versus 4% to 5% for normal-size public offerings). Dividend reinvestment plans offer shareholders the option to reinvest their dividends with little or no brokerage commission.[6] This reduces the penalty a high-dividend-payout policy would otherwise impose on shareholders who want their dividends to be reinvested. However, it does not eliminate the tax bias in favor of capital gains, because shareholders must declare the reinvested dividends as income. Nevertheless, by reducing flotation costs, dividend reinvestment plans may have led to increased payout ratios for those firms, such as electric utilities, whose dividend clientele groups want relatively high dividend income.

Legal and Policy Restrictions

Some institutions are prohibited, by law or policy, from investing in the common stocks of firms that have not established a history of regular dividend payments over a sufficiently long period. Other investors, such as many trust and endowment funds, can spend only dividend income as a matter of policy. These investors show a preference for at least some minimum level of regular dividend income, so that they can maintain some institutional decision-making flexibility. Legal and policy restrictions are forms of indirect transaction costs.

Net Effect of Taxes and Transaction Costs

We believe that the tax bias favoring capital gains exerts a stronger influence than transaction costs on what a firm's dividend policy ought to be. We think the majority of our colleagues in the finance profession would agree. Consequently, the combined effect of taxes, direct transaction costs, and the legal and policy restrictions that are responsible for some investors having a dividend preference favors retentions over dividends. The extent of this bias depends largely on the shareholder mix and on the tax positions and liquidity preferences of share-

---

[6] Dividend reinvestment plans are discussed in Chapter 23.

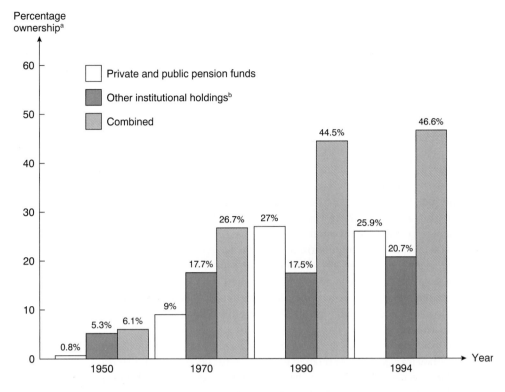

Percentage ownership[a]

Legend:
- Private and public pension funds
- Other institutional holdings[b]
- Combined

Year	Private and public pension funds	Other institutional holdings	Combined
1950	0.8%	5.3%	6.1%
1970	9%	17.7%	26.7%
1990	27%	17.5%	44.5%
1994	25.9%	20.7%	46.6%

[a]Equity assets as a percentage of the aggregate market value of common stocks in the United States.
[b]Insurance companies, open-end investment companies, and foreign institutions.
Source: New York Stock Exchange Fact Book 1994 (New York: New York Stock Exchange, 1994), p. 83.

FIGURE 17-3
Growth in institutional ownership of U.S. common stocks.

holders, all of which may change. For example, Figure 17-3 shows that between 1950 and 1994, the percentage of U.S. common stocks owned by institutional investors increased from about 6% to 47% (on the basis of total market value).[7]

If individual shareholders are the largest group, and if they consist chiefly of higher-marginal-tax-rate individuals, there is likely to be a *net* preference for capital gains over dividends. This is due to the time value of money connected with postponing the tax liability. Conversely, for the same reason, if shareholders consist primarily of older retired individuals, other corporations, and tax-exempt institutions, there is likely to be a *net* preference for dividends. These considerations reflect the importance of market imperfections to the relevance of dividend policy. In turn, we can conclude that when setting dividend policy, a firm must understand its shareholder mix and its shareholders' probable preferences.

Opportunities to Profit from Clientele Disequilibrium

We know from the Principle of Valuable Ideas that new ideas can be valuable when they are first applied. But the Principle of Capital Market Efficiency says that after others recognize the same opportunity and competition enters the picture, the possibility of earning extraordinary returns is eliminated. We can apply these principles to dividend clienteles.

Taxes and transaction costs reduce the return to shareholders. Therefore, investors

---

[7] *New York Stock Exchange Fact Book 1994* (New York: New York Stock Exchange, 1994), p. 83. Private and public pension funds collectively owned 26% of U.S. common stocks at year-end 1994 (versus 0.8% in 1950). Nontaxable institutions' collective percentage ownership has increased more or less steadily over the past two decades.

should invest in a firm with dividend policies that minimize investor taxes and transaction costs, holding all else (risk and return) constant. This is the very basis for dividend clienteles. In fact, because of taxes and transaction costs, a dividend clientele will be better off paying up to some maximum premium for shares of firms that follow its optimal policy.[8] As long as a premium is offered, firms will have an incentive to change their policy and sell shares to the clientele group offering the premium.

As with capital structure, over time, competition among firms drives the premium to zero, and capital market equilibrium and efficiency return. In the aggregate, firms will supply enough of each type of stock so that all the positive NPVs resulting from dividend policy choices have been gotten, and the premiums have been driven to zero. What remains after the premiums are gone are clientele groups and firms that are very comfortable with each other. In equilibrium, the patterns can remain indefinitely, because neither the clientele groups nor the firms have any incentive to change. However, whenever there are changes in laws (tax laws or any laws affecting investments), it may be possible to "play the game all over again" as the market attains a new equilibrium. Each change represents a potential new opportunity.

This is another reason why dividend policy matters: It may be possible to earn a premium for supplying a dividend policy that is in short supply. Thus whenever a law is changed that affects the optimal dividend policy for a particular clientele, there may be opportunities for firms to earn a positive NPV by altering their dividend policy decisions to take advantage of the opportunity.

For example, following the passage of the Tax Reform Act of 1986, which raised the effective tax rate on capital gains relative to the effective tax rate on dividends, Teledyne, which had used excess cash to repurchase shares and had not declared a cash dividend in 26 years, declared its first cash dividend on its common stock.[9]

The following example illustrates how a firm might benefit by altering its dividend policy in response to a change in tax law, in this case an increase in the rate of taxation of dividends.

EXAMPLE

Changing Dividend Policy at Kodiak

Let's say Kodiak pays $3.00 per share annually in dividends. Its current share price is $50.00. Investors require an 18.2% after-tax return. They expect the share price a year from now to be $60.00.

Table 17-2 illustrates the effect of a change in tax law that raises the tax rate on dividends to 50% from 30% currently but leaves the tax rate on capital gains unchanged. If Kodiak does not change its dividend policy, its share price falls to $49.32 per share. The stock must provide a higher pretax return (27.74% versus 26.00%) to compensate for the higher rate at which the dividend is now taxed.

But suppose Kodiak eliminates its dividend and reinvests the cash. This change effectively converts the dividend into a capital gain. The gain is taxed at an effectively lower rate than the dividend would be.

Kodiak avoids the reduction in share price by altering its dividend policy. If it chooses this course of action, of course, it should clearly articulate its reason for doing so. Otherwise,

---

[8] The maximum premium is determined by the opportunity cost: It is the additional cost if the investors invest in the next best firm that is otherwise identical but does not follow their optimal policy.

[9] Between 1972 and 1986, Teledyne purchased 71 million shares of its common stock, reducing its common shares by 86% to 12 million.

	CURRENT DIVIDEND POLICY		NEW DIVIDEND POLICY
	Effect of Old Tax Law	Effect of New Tax Law	Effect of New Tax Law
Tax rate on dividends	30%	50%	50%
Tax rate on capital gains	30	30	30
Share price next year	$60.00	$60.00	$63.00[b]
Current share price[a]	50.00	49.32	50.00
Pretax capital gain	10.00	10.68	13.00
Dividend per share	3.00	3.00	—
Pretax dollar return	$13.00	$13.68	13.00
Pretax percentage return	26.00%	27.74%	26.00%
Tax on dividend	$ 0.90	$ 1.50	—
Tax on capital gains	3.00	3.20	$ 3.90
Total income tax	3.90	4.70	3.90
After-tax dollar return	$ 9.10	$ 8.98	$ 9.10
After-tax percentage return	18.2%	18.2%	18.2%

TABLE 17-2
Effect of a change in dividend policy in response to a change in tax law.

[a] The current share price solves the equation

$$[(1 - T_g)(P_1 - P_0) + (1 - T_d)D]/P_0 = R$$

where P_0 and P_1 are the share prices currently and 1 year hence, respectively; T_d and T_g are the tax rates on dividends and capital gains, respectively; D is the annual pretax dividend per share; and R is the after-tax required return.
[b] The expected share price 1 year hence is adjusted upward because no dividend is paid.

investors might misinterpret the dividend cut as a negative signal regarding the firm's earnings prospects. ■

Self-Check Questions

1. How do brokerage commissions affect the choice between homemade dividends and cash dividends?

2. What sorts of legal and policy restrictions give firms an incentive to pay at least a small dividend?

3. What is the net effect of taxes and transaction costs on dividend policy?

4. How can the existence of dividend clienteles lead to profitable opportunities to make changes in dividend policy when tax laws change?

17.4 SIGNALING

Dividend changes can affect the price of a firm's stock if investors believe that such changes convey useful information. For example, suppose a firm has rarely changed its dividend rate, and each time the rate was changed, the firm's earnings also subsequently changed in the same direction. Investors would then interpret future changes in the dividend rate as a signal that management believes the firm's earnings prospects have changed. A dividend increase would be a positive signal of greater future earnings. A dividend decrease would be a negative signal of lower future earnings.

This reasoning gives rise to the **signaling view** of dividend policy. According to the signaling view, dividend changes are important signals to investors of changes in management's expectations about the firm's future earnings.

Significance of the Signaling Effect

The signaling view differs from the traditional and tax differential views with respect to clienteles. Whereas the clientele effect softens the implications of the traditional and tax differential views, it does not lessen the signaling view. Even in a capital market environment that is perfect except for information asymmetries (and the connected problems of a lack of available information or cost to obtain information), dividend policy can affect firm value. Because of the informational content of dividend changes, simply paying out residual cash flow on a year-by-year basis may not be in the shareholders' best interest. Such a policy would lead to a dividend level and a payout ratio that could fluctuate wildly, depending on year-to-year changes in the availability of attractive investment projects. Generally, firms manage their dividend policies so that dividend changes are orderly and consistent with changes in earnings prospects. In the next chapter, we describe an operational approach to dividend policy based on this guiding principle.

A major insight into why dividend policy matters comes when we stop assuming that information is freely available and costless. If it is costly to gather information, it is possible that dividend policy may be the least expensive, and/or most accurate, method of conveying information to shareholders. If this is the case, then dividend policy is an important tool that can be used to benefit a firm's shareholders.

Table 17-3 summarizes the dividend changes that U.S. firms announced from 1970 to 1994. Fewer than 3% [= (2583 + 4168)/248,600] of the dividend actions taken during this period involved either dividend decreases or *dividend omissions* (reducing the dividend rate to zero). Dividend increases and *dividend resumptions* (paying dividends once again after having previously cut the dividend rate to zero) outnumbered decreases and omissions by more than 7 to 1 [= (45,999 + 1859)/6751]. And lack of changes in the dividend rate outnumbered decreases and omissions by almost 29 to 1 (= 193,991/6751)!

You will not be surprised to learn that, on average, stock prices increase in response to a dividend-increase announcement and that they decline in response to dividend-decrease announcements. This pattern is consistent with the signaling view that dividend increases (decreases) are positive (negative) signals of better (worse) future earnings.

Dividend Adjustment Model

Managers frequently believe the firm should aim toward some long-term *target* payout ratio in order to give shareholders a "fair share" of the firm's earnings. The following model describes this process in mathematical terms:

$$DPS_{t+1} - DPS_t = ADJ[POR(EPS_{t+1}) - DPS_t] \qquad (17.1)$$

where DPS is the dividend per share, ADJ is the adjustment to dividends, POR is the payout ratio, and EPS is earnings per share. Let's see what these terms mean.

According to this model, a firm that is currently paying dividends at the rate of DPS_t per share, and that has a target payout ratio of POR, will adjust (ADJ) its dividend rate, but less than fully, as its earnings per share (EPS) changes. If a firm always paid out its target ratio of earnings, then its dividends per share in the coming period would be $DPS = POR(EPS_{t+1})$. But firms manage their dividend payments to produce a smooth progression in dividends. Accordingly, the value of ADJ is less than 1, so that dividends progress toward the target over several periods rather than all at once. This, of course, reduces the likelihood that a dividend

YEAR	NUMBER OF FIRMS TAKING DIVIDEND ACTION	DIVIDEND INCREASED	DIVIDEND RESUMED	DIVIDEND DECREASED	DIVIDEND OMITTED	EXTRA OR SPECIAL DIVIDEND DECLARED
1970	About 9,800	828	75	201	284	910
1971	About 9,800	885	111	154	213	841
1972	About 9,800	1,563	107	73	103	980
1973	About 9,800	2,197	116	37	114	1,105
1974	About 9,800	2,120	139	86	228	1,097
1975	About 9,800	1,648	129	186	266	1,013
1976	About 9,800	2,624	137	74	117	1,047
1977	Over 10,000	2,984	120	68	138	968
1978	Over 10,000	3,211	105	46	105	997
1979	Over 10,000	2,968	71	46	131	829
1980	Over 10,000	2,445	51	88	160	719
1981	Over 10,000	2,160	45	103	198	640
1982	Over 10,000	1,590	46	258	315	515
1983	Over 10,000	1,833	66	106	126	480
1984	Over 10,000	1,774	58	65	116	435
1985	Over 10,000	1,560	35	68	139	428
1986	Over 10,000	1,513	46	96	189	359
1987	Over 10,000	1,590	54	74	104	403
1988	Over 10,000	1,705	38	62	117	501
1989	Over 10,000	1,658	41	85	160	524
1990	Over 10,000	1,263	39	143	266	385
1991	Over 10,000	1,086	50	187	250	322
1992	Over 10,000	1,333	53	131	146	317
1993	Over 10,000	1,635	75	87	106	368
1994	Over 10,000	1,826	52	59	77	384
Total	Over 248,600	45,999	1859	2583	4168	16,567

Source: Standard & Poor's, *Annual Dividend Record,* 1974–1995.

increase will have to be rolled back in the future. And this is why dividend changes serve as a signaling device: A firm increases its dividend rate when it believes it can sustain the increase through higher expected earnings.

Suppose Snapple Corporation has historically paid out 40% of its earnings as dividends. Snapple's treasurer believes it appropriate to adjust the dividend rate in a gradual manner. She applies the dividend adjustment model with ADJ = 2/3. Snapple earned $5.00 per share last year and paid dividends of $0.50 per quarter, or $2.00 per year. She believes that earnings will reach $6.00 per share this year and will stay at that level into the foreseeable future. According to our model, how would the dividend rate change this year and the next four?

Adjusting Dividends for a Change in Earnings Per Share

EXAMPLE

Equation (17.1) becomes

$$DPS_1 - DPS_0 = ADJ[POR(EPS_1) - DPS_0]$$
$$DPS_1 - 2.00 = (2/3)[0.4(6.00) - 2.00]$$
$$DPS_1 = 2.266667 \cong 2.27$$

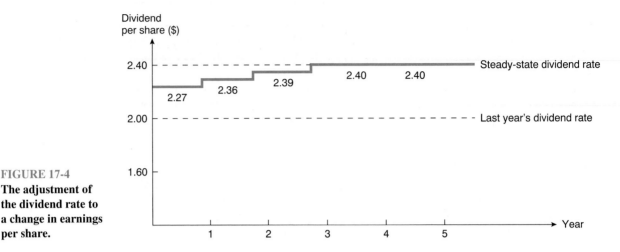

FIGURE 17-4

The adjustment of the dividend rate to a change in earnings per share.

The following year, Equation (17.1) becomes

$$DPS_2 - 2.266667 = (2/3)[0.4(6.00) - 2.266667]$$

$$DPS_2 = 2.355556 \cong 2.36$$

Figure 17-4 shows the pattern of dividend changes. The dividend rate moves to the steady-state dividend rate $2.40 per annum (= 0.4 × 6.00), each year closing two-thirds of the remaining gap. ■

Effect of Inflation

During periods of inflation, it is not enough for a firm simply to sustain a particular dividend level, because inflation would erode the value of the dividend in real terms. Many firms try to raise the amount of their dividend at least fast enough to keep pace with inflation. This became evident during the 1970s and early 1980s when inflation was high. However, a firm can afford to raise the dividend, whatever the inflation rate, only when the increases are in line with its earnings prospects and other financial policies.

Suppose a firm follows such a policy of trying to preserve the purchasing power of its dividend. Investors might then use the dividend growth rate evident in the historical pattern—provided they believe the pattern is sustainable—to gauge the likelihood that the future rate of dividend growth will at least keep pace with inflation.

Self-Check Questions

1. What is the signaling view of dividend policy?

2. How do investors usually interpret a dividend increase? A dividend decrease?

3. How do stock prices usually react to a dividend increase? To a dividend decrease? Why?

4. Explain the dividend adjustment model.

17.5 SHARE REPURCHASES

Firms that want to distribute cash to their shareholders usually do so by declaring cash dividends. A **share repurchase** is an alternative to a cash dividend, in which the firm repurchases shares of its common stock. For example, some years ago IBM announced a tender offer for up to 4 million shares of its common stock. At the time, IBM had more than $6 billion in cash and marketable securities on its balance sheet. The tender offer resulted in IBM reacquiring 2,546,000 shares at a cost of $280 per share, an aggregate cost of approximately $713 million.

Share Repurchase Versus Dividends

We have demonstrated that in a perfect capital market environment, shareholders are indifferent between (1) dividend payout with the issuance of new shares and (2) retention of earnings. Similarly, shareholders are indifferent between (1) dividend payout and (2) the repurchase of outstanding shares. In a perfect capital market environment, these events do not affect shareholder wealth either. The following examples illustrate this point.

Suppose that International Paper (IP) has determined that it has $50 million cash available for distribution. IP has 10 million shares outstanding. It expects to earn $2.50 per share. The current market value per share is $25, giving IP a current P/E (price-earnings) ratio of 10 (= 25/2.50). IP could pay a cash dividend of $5 per share, implying an ex-dividend value of $20 per share. This would reduce the P/E ratio to 8 (= 20/2.50). Alternatively, IP could use the $50 million to repurchase 2 million (= 50 million/25) shares. After the share repurchase, each share would be worth

Illustration of Equivalence of Dividends and Share Repurchases

$$\frac{10,000,000(25) - 50,000,000}{10,000,000 - 2,000,000} = \$25$$

Thus, as long as IP repurchases shares at the current market price of $25, a shareholder who does not sell will have the same wealth per share as a shareholder who does sell, namely $25 per share. The only difference is that one person has the wealth in the form of cash and the other has it in the form of stock. Moreover, each shareholder would have the same $25 per share in wealth if IP paid the $5 dividend. In that case, every shareholder would have wealth in the same form: $5 in cash plus a share of stock worth $20. ■

Note that to the extent that IP pays a repurchase price in excess of the market price, there is a wealth transfer to the shareholders who sell from those who do not.

Let's continue our IP example. Suppose IP decides to spend $50 million to buy shares for $30 each from one of its shareholders. IP can purchase 1,666,667 (= 50 million/30) shares. After the share repurchase, each share will be worth

Illustration of Wealth Transfer

$$\frac{10,000,000(25) - 50,000,000}{10,000,000 - 1,666,667} = \$24$$

There is a transfer of wealth *to* the selling shareholder of $8,333,333.33 [= (30 −

25)1,666,667], and there is a transfer of wealth *from* the remaining shareholders amounting to the same $8,333,333.33 [= (25 − 24)8,333,333].

In the past, many firms have paid a premium to buy back shares from a takeover raider. When they do, the takeover raider effectively expropriates a portion of the other shareholders' collective wealth. This expropriation of wealth has come to be known by the colorful name **greenmail**. ■

Impact on EPS

The effect of a share repurchase on shareholder wealth can be misunderstood by people who judge the impact in terms of EPS (earnings per share). In the first example, the firm's shares should trade at a P/E ratio of 8 after the distribution of the $50 million in cash, regardless of whether the cash is distributed as a dividend or through share repurchase. This is because of the risk-return trade-off—the same amount of equity is invested in either case. Neither the firm's capital structure nor its capital budgeting policies are affected by the method of cash distribution. The share repurchase results in projected EPS of

$$\frac{\$2.50(10,000,000)}{8,000,000} = \$3.125$$

However, although EPS is higher with the share repurchase, each share is still worth $25 (= 3.125 × 8). The increase in projected EPS is just offset by the decline in the P/E ratio (from 10 to 8). The confusion over the impact of share repurchases results from the mistaken belief that share repurchases do not alter the P/E ratio. But if the P/E ratio remained unchanged, the risk-return relationship would differ between the alternatives. This would be inconsistent with the Principles of Capital Market Efficiency and Risk-Return Trade-Off.

Advantages of Repurchasing Shares

In the first IP example, the share repurchase program did not affect shareholder wealth. But this conclusion depends on our assumption of a perfect capital market environment. Asymmetric taxes can alter this conclusion. Because of lower effective taxes on capital gains, taxable individual shareholders would generally prefer that the firm repurchase shares instead of paying a dividend. Suppose dividends are taxed at a 50% rate and capital gains at a 20% rate. Shareholders would have to pay $25,000,000 (= 0.5 × 50,000,000) in total taxes on the dividend distribution, but no more than $10,000,000 (= 0.2 × 50,000,000) in total taxes on the share repurchase (depending on the tax basis of the shares).

On the other hand, dividends paid to other corporations are taxed at a lower rate than capital gains because of the 70% dividends-received deduction. Consequently, corporate shareholders usually prefer dividends over capital gains. The overall net tax advantage (or disadvantage) of share repurchase versus dividends thus depends on the shareholder mix. In the next section, we will consider a strategy that combines the two alternatives by offering shareholders an option.

Why Do Firms Repurchase Their Shares?

Firms have different motives for repurchasing shares. When considering the reason a firm gives when it announces a share repurchase, you should keep in mind that there are potential agency problems. Firms may not want to announce that they have excess cash available (implying they have no good investment opportunities) or that they are actually using cash in inappropriate ways. Consequently, the stated objective may mask the truth.

The reason most widely cited by firms for repurchasing shares is that their stock is "undervalued" and is therefore a positive-NPV investment. Another possible reason is to eliminate small shareholdings. It costs about the same to service an account with few shares (printing and mailing annual and quarterly reports, proxy materials, and dividend checks) as a large-share account. Therefore, the cost of servicing small shareholder accounts is proportionately greater.

Other possible reasons for share repurchases are to increase leverage, to increase reported earnings per share, and to consolidate insiders' control position. (Insiders are management and certain large shareholders.) Note that these last two reasons (as well as others that we have not mentioned) are not necessarily consistent with shareholder wealth maximization. Thus agency problems should be considered in connection with share repurchases.

Firms that repurchase their shares are generally less leveraged, less profitable, and slower-growing than other firms, which is generally consistent with the view that such firms lack positive-NPV investment opportunities. But the stock market's reaction to a share repurchase announcement depends on *how* the firm decides to implement the share repurchases.

The two most often used share repurchase methods are an open-market purchase program and a tender offer. An **open-market purchase program** is a systematic program of repurchasing shares of the firm's stock in market transactions at current market prices, in competition with other prospective investors. A **fixed-price tender offer** is a one-time offer to purchase a stated number of shares at a price above the stock's current market price.[10]

On average, the stock market reacts more positively to tender offers than to open-market repurchases. However, this does not mean a firm should always choose the tender offer, because it is typically more expensive and can have other disadvantages, particularly if too many people try to take advantage of the offer. Of course, these are probably just the reasons why the tender offer is interpreted as the more positive signal!

Self-Check Questions

1. What is a share repurchase?
2. Why is a share repurchase a substitute for a dividend?
3. Explain why a share repurchase does not affect shareholder wealth in a perfect capital market.
4. How does a share repurchase usually affect the firm's P/E ratio? Doesn't that mean the share price should rise?
5. What tax advantage may result from repurchasing shares?

17.6 TRANSFERABLE PUT RIGHTS

A firm cannot force its shareholders to sell their shares. It can only offer to repurchase them. As we will see in Chapter 18, firms often use a fixed-price tender offer to repurchase shares, offering shareholders the opportunity to sell their shares back to the firm for a tender price that is above the market price.

Typically, the firm sets a maximum number of shares it is willing to repurchase at the tender price. Each shareholder is free to tender shares (accept the offer and sell shares to the firm) or to reject the offer (and keep the shares). But if the aggregate number of shares tendered exceeds the maximum, the firm can repurchase a prorated (a proportionately reduced)

---

[10] Methods of share repurchase are discussed at greater length in Chapter 18.

number of shares from each shareholder. Thus shareholders may sell fewer shares than they had intended.

A fixed-price tender offer gives shareholders a put option. The tender price is the strike price. When the tender price exceeds the market price, the put option is in-the-money. We know from the Options Principle that this option is valuable. But shareholders cannot sell this option separately from their shares. They can get the value of this option *only* if they exercise it.

If shareholders do not exercise the option, it expires and they get nothing for it. This means that the premium over market price that is paid to the selling shareholders transfers wealth from the shareholders who "remain behind" (do not exercise their option by tendering). But because of taxes, the *net* value of this put option is not the same for all shareholders.

Shareholders with a low tax basis in their shares would trigger a large capital gains tax liability if they tendered the shares. Tendering would eliminate their tax-timing option to continue to postpone the tax on their capital gain. Triggering this tax liability then reduces the incentive for low-tax-basis shareholders to sell their shares. Higher-tax-basis shareholders do not face this problem. Therefore, if the tender offer is proportionately distributed, there is a tax inefficiency: Some investors with low tax bases, and hence greater tax liabilities as a result of tendering, will sell shares, whereas investors with higher tax bases, and hence smaller potential tax liabilities, will not sell all their shares.

Transferable put rights are designed to minimize these deficiencies. A **transferable put right** is the right to sell the firm one share of its common stock at a fixed price (the strike price) within a stated period (the time to maturity). This security is called transferable because, after being created, it is separated from its "birth" share (our analysis assumes that one put right is attached to each share). After being separated, it becomes transferable. The put right can be bought and sold in the capital markets. In this way, shareholders can get the option value by selling the put right if they do not want to exercise it (perhaps because of a capital gains tax liability).

In Chapter 23, we will discuss *rights offerings*, which distribute call options to a firm's shareholders. Such call options give the right to buy (from the firm) one share of the firm's common stock at a fixed price within a stated period. Transferable put rights and a rights offering are symmetrical: The former provides the proportional right to sell shares; the latter provides the proportional right to buy shares. Exercising a transferable put right triggers a share repurchase, which shrinks the firm's total amount of equity in the same way as a dividend. A rights offering creates new shares that increase the firm's total amount of equity.

EXAMPLE	*Gillette's Transferable Put Rights*

The Gillette Company issued 1 transferable put right for each 7 shares held as of 3 days earlier. Each put right entitled the holder to sell 1 share of stock to the firm anytime in the next 35 days at a price of $45, a significant premium above the market price of $34⅞. Gillette had 112,100,227 shares outstanding and would repurchase 16,014,318 shares (one-seventh of the shares outstanding) at a cost of approximately $721 million if all the put rights were exercised.■

Valuing Transferable Put Rights

As we explained in Chapter 8, the value of an option—and therefore that of a put right—is a function of (1) the strike price, (2) the value of the underlying asset, (3) the time to expiration,

(4) the variance of the return on the underlying asset, and (5) the riskless return. In addition, the value of a put right depends on the decrease in the number of shares outstanding.

Put rights are issued in-the-money to encourage shareholders to exercise them, as in the Gillette example. That is, the issuer sets a positive *exercise value* by setting the repurchase (strike) price above the stock's current market price. Because of the short time to expiration, the option's time premium is small and is therefore a relatively insignificant determinant of the value of the put right.

The initial value of a put right just after the offering is announced, and while the put right is still attached to the share, is approximately

$$R_P = \frac{S - P_R}{N - 1} \tag{17.2}$$

where R_P is the value of one put right, P_R is the market value of a share with the put right attached, S is the strike price, and N is the number of rights to sell 1 share (assuming that one put right is created for each outstanding share).[11]

The initial value of one of Gillette's transferable put rights, on a per-share basis, was

$$R_P = \frac{45.00 - 34.875}{7 - 1} = \$1.6875$$

Because Gillette issued 1 put right per 7 common shares, the value on a per-put-right basis is 7 times the per-share value, $11.8125 ($= 7 \times 1.6875$). ∎

Gillette's Transferable Put Rights (Continued)

EXAMPLE

After the put right is separated from the stock, the share price decreases by the value of the right. Therefore, P_E, the share price alone (after separation), is

$$P_E = P_R - R_P \tag{17.3}$$

Thereafter, the value of the put right varies with the price of the firm's shares:

$$R_P = \frac{S - P_E}{N} \tag{17.4}$$

The closing price for put rights on the day trading began was $10⅝, and the stock closed at $33¾ per share. Substituting into Equation (17.3), we find that the value of each put right, on a per-share basis, would be

$$R_P = \frac{45.00 - 33.75}{7} = \$1.6071$$

Because Gillette issued one put right per 7 common shares, the value on a per-put-right basis is 7 times the per-share value, $11.2497 ($= 7 \times 1.6071$). This is *more than* the market price. Surprised? ∎

Gillette's Transferable Put Rights (Continued)

EXAMPLE

---

[11] Compare Equations (17.2) and (23.2). Note the symmetry. Transferable put rights eliminate 1 share for every N shares the firm has outstanding; a rights offering issues 1 new share for every N that are outstanding.

Taxes

One additional factor that can affect the value of a put right does not appear in Equations (17.2) and (17.4): taxes. Put rights enable low-tax-basis shareholders to realize the value of the option by selling the put right, thereby avoiding the capital gains tax liability they would incur if they sold their shares. Avoiding (or at least deferring) this tax liability is valuable. Depending on the supply of put rights offered by low-tax-basis shareholders and on the demand for put rights by high-tax-basis shareholders, the put price can be bid up above the sum of its exercise value plus its time value. To the extent that it is bid up above the sum of these values, low-tax-basis shareholders effectively get a greater proportion of the value of the tax savings relative to a fixed-price tender offer.

The following generalized version of Equation (17.4) reflects these tax considerations.

$$R_P = \frac{(1 - T_g)S + T_g B - P_E}{(1 - T_g)N} \qquad (17.5)$$

where T_g stands for the capital gains tax rate and B is the tax basis of the marginal purchaser of put rights.

EXAMPLE

Gillette's Transferable Put Rights (Concluded)

Here we conclude the Gillette example. Suppose the marginal purchaser has a tax rate of 18% and a tax basis of $30 per share. Then the value of the Gillette transferable put rights, on a per-share basis, is

$$R_P = \frac{(1 - 0.18)45 + (0.18)30 - 33.75}{(1 - 0.18)7} = 1.4895$$

which is $10.4265 on a per-put-right basis ($= 7 \times 1.4895$). This implies a time premium of $0.1985 ($= market value minus exercise value $= 10.625 - 10.4265$) for the put right (with the assumed tax rate and tax basis). This example shows clearly that tax factors can affect option valuation. ■

Advantages of Transferable Put Rights

Transferable put rights offer at least three potentially significant advantages over a fixed-price tender offer.

1. Low-tax-basis shareholders are able to get the value for their rights without having to incur the tax liability that the sale of their shares would trigger.

2. There is no risk of oversubscription.

3. There is a "tax-efficiency" gain (at the expense of the U.S. Treasury), because low-tax-basis shareholders sell their rights rather than their shares.

Transferable put rights are an innovative share repurchase strategy. The only potential drawback we can see is that because of the complexity of the tax laws, shareholders may be forced to incur significant transaction costs in the form of effort (or cost of tax advice) necessary to determine the correct tax treatment of the receipt and exercise of the put rights. This problem should prove relatively minor in the long run, as investors become more familiar with put rights, and we expect that transferable put rights will become more widely used in the future because of their inherent advantages.

17.7 POLICY IMPLICATIONS

Some investors prefer high-payout stocks, and others prefer capital gains. As you would expect, dividend-oriented investors tend to invest in high-payout stocks, such as utilities. Capital-gain-oriented investors tend to invest in rapidly growing firms that distribute low or no dividends, such as younger high-technology firms. Thus a significant change in dividend policy can cause a shift in shareholder mix. After a period of transition, the firm's stock value may exhibit little change from its value before the change in dividend policy. This is because former shareholders who objected to the new dividend policy have simply sold out to new shareholders who like the new policy. In this way, changes in shareholder mix can lessen any longer-term impact of a change in dividend policy on share price.

However, dividend policy can be an important signaling device. Thus firms should not simply pay out residual earnings year by year, because the dividend rate could fluctuate wildly and lose its information value. For dividend changes to serve as an effective signaling mechanism, a firm must prevent excessive variation in its dividend rate. A firm can smooth out fluctuations by building cash surpluses in times of smaller capital budgets to use in times of larger capital budgets.

Even though shareholder mix is likely to change in response to a change in dividend policy, a sudden shift may be disruptive in the near term. And frequent major changes or a significantly misunderstood change may be disruptive over the longer term for two reasons. Most important, asymmetric information can cause the market to conclude, on the basis of misunderstanding a dividend policy change, that the firm's management is incompetent. Secondarily, transaction costs make it expensive for investors to buy and sell shares. Consequently, a series of changes can frustrate investors and decrease the price they are willing to pay for the firm's stock. Such a price decrease would be to cover anticipated extra buying and selling transaction costs.

Therefore, a firm should strive to maintain a stable dividend policy. Reasons for departing from an established dividend policy include (1) significant changes in a firm's investment opportunities, (2) significant changes in its earnings prospects, and (3) passage of a law that creates a temporary chance to profit from a particular policy.

RESOLUTION OF CHRYSLER'S DIVIDEND DILEMMA

After it received Kirk Kerkorian's letter, Chrysler Corporation reassessed its cash position. It determined that it was "on track" to meet its goals of building a cash reserve of at least $7.5 billion *and* fully funding its pension plan by year-end.

Then, a mere 17 days after Kerkorian issued his demand, Chrysler announced (1) an increase in the quarterly dividend rate to 40 cents per share from 25 cents and (2) a $1 billion share repurchase program. (The firm also loosened its shareholder-rights plan to allow Kerkorian to increase his ownership percentage. We will discuss such plans in Chapter 28.) The 60% increase in the dividend rate would raise Chrysler's annual cash payout to $600 million from $360 million. Robert J. Eaton, Chrysler's chairman, noted, "We fully expect that this dividend level is sustainable over the course of the business cycle."

Eaton said that Chrysler had been considering the dividend increase and share repurchase program for some time and that the board had decided that "the time is right to take such actions." Stock market investors agreed. Right after the announcement, Chrysler's share price rose from $47¾ to $48¾.

SUMMARY

The critical issue in dividend policy is whether the dividend decision should be made actively or passively. If passively, a firm simply pays out any funds that it cannot invest profitably. We recommend that a firm use its dividend policy to maximize shareholder wealth. The policy should be determined primarily by the firm's investment opportunities and internal needs for funds. But also important are

1. Anticipating how the market will interpret the firm's changes, or *lack* of changes, in its dividend policy.
2. Taking advantage of changes in laws that create a demand for innovative dividend policies that might be profitable.
3. Balancing shareholder preferences for capital gains and dividends.
4. Taking shareholder preferences for liquidity into account.
5. Balancing the transaction costs of selling shares for the firm against the costs of the shareholders selling them.
6. Taking into account any legal or policy restrictions on the firm and its shareholders concerning dividend policy.

In a perfect capital market environment, a firm's choice of dividend policy does not affect firm value and is therefore irrelevant. But our financial system contains some important persistent imperfections. Information is not costless and freely available to everyone. Dividend policy can be an efficient signaling device.

Other market imperfections exist. The tax system creates biases that, depending on the participants and their particular circumstances, can favor capital gains over dividends, or dividends over capital gains. Transaction costs also affect the preferences of the participants. However, the clientele effect lessens the impact of some of these considerations.

When a firm has cash available for distribution to its shareholders, it can repurchase shares instead of paying cash dividends. Other potential reasons for repurchasing shares include eliminating small shareholdings, increasing leverage, buying back "undervalued" shares, increasing reported earnings per share, and consolidating insider control. Some reasons involve agency problems. When a share repurchase is planned, a firm should consider using transferable put rights.

We believe dividend policy is relevant. However, it is important to keep in mind that its relevance may be very small, because it is a relatively minor piece of the valuation puzzle! An optimal dividend policy can contribute to the profitability of a firm, but it is more "fine tuning" than a major source of value. The possibility of extraordinary success rests primarily on the firm's investment decisions. Remember: *Pursuing valuable new ideas is the best way to achieve extraordinary returns.*

DECISION SUMMARY

- First and foremost, strive to maintain a stable dividend policy.
- Before making a change in a firm's dividend rate or policy, be sure to take into account the potential information content of the change, and seek to minimize any disruptive effects.
- Recognize that the appropriate dividend action depends primarily on the firm's future earnings prospects and anticipated funds requirements.
- Consider repurchasing shares instead of paying out cash dividends when the firm has a large amount of cash to distribute.
- If the firm has decided to repurchase shares, consider doing so through a transferable put rights offering.
- Monitor changes in laws, especially tax laws, to identify opportunities to profit from a particular dividend policy.

EQUATION SUMMARY

(17.1) $$\text{DPS}_1 - \text{DPS}_0 = \text{ADJ}[\text{POR}(\text{EPS}_1) - \text{DPS}_0]$$

(17.2) $$R_P = \frac{S - P_R}{N - 1}$$

(17.3) $$P_E = P_R - R_P$$

(17.4) $$R_P = \frac{S - P_E}{N}$$

(17.5) $$R_P = \frac{(1 - T_g)S + T_g B - P_E}{(1 - T_g)N}$$

KEY TERMS

dividend policy...532

perfect market view...534

homemade dividend...536

traditional view...537

tax differential view...539

two-tier tax system...540

split-rate tax system...541

imputation tax system...541

signaling view...545

share repurchase...549

greenmail...550

open-market purchase program...551

fixed-price tender offer...551

transferable put right...552

EXERCISES

PROBLEM SET A

A1. Briefly explain the tax differential view of dividend policy.

A2. Briefly explain the signaling view of dividend policy.

A3. Explain how the existence of dividend clienteles mitigates the tax differential view of dividend policy.

A4. True or False: The empirical evidence shows that on average, a dividend decrease affects the firm's stock price negatively, but a dividend increase has no effect on the stock price.

A5. True or False: A large majority of firms follow a dividend policy that specifies a fixed payout ratio, so that the dollar amount each quarter fluctuates according to the firm's earnings.

A6. Cite two examples of how transaction costs might affect a firm's choice of dividend policy.

A7. Briefly explain how a change in law might create a positive-NPV opportunity for a firm with respect to its dividend policy.

A8. What is meant by the phrase "bird-in-the-hand fallacy" when it refers to the traditional view of dividend policy? Briefly explain how the counterargument invalidates the traditional view that shareholders benefit from a large dividend payout.

A9. In what sense are share repurchases and dividend payments substitutes for one another? Under what circumstances, if any, are they perfect substitutes?

A10. Common stock of the I. M. Wright Company has a current market value of $47. Suppose Wright issues transferable put rights to its shareholders, and 5 put rights are required to sell 1 share back to the firm for $55. What would you expect a put right to be worth (ignoring taxes)?

PROBLEM SET B

B1. What is the basis for the view that a firm's total market value is unaffected by its choice of dividend policy? Cite three broad types of capital market imperfections that might cause the dividend policy of a firm to have an effect on the firm's value. Give three examples (one for each type) where such an imperfection would cause a firm's dividend policy to have an effect on the firm's value. Explain *how* each of the three examples you gave would cause a firm's dividend policy to have an effect on the firm's value.

B2. How might the cost of issuing new stock affect a firm's choice of dividend policy?

B3. Refer to Figures 17-1 and 17-2. A firm currently has 8000 shares outstanding that are worth $100 each. Shareholders want a dividend of $20 per share. Assume a perfect capital market.

a. Suppose the firm pays a dividend of $20 per share and sells new shares to raise $160,000 to replace the cash it paid out. Show that these steps do not alter the wealth of the original shareholders. What percentage of the firm do they end up owning?

b. Suppose instead that the shareholders raise $160,000 by selling some of their own shares. How many shares must they sell? Show that the two dividend alternatives leave them equally well off.

B4. Regional Software has made a great deal of money selling spreadsheet software and has begun paying cash dividends. The firm's chief financial officer would like the firm to distribute 25% of its annual earnings (POR = 0.25) and adjust the dividend rate to changes in earnings per share at the rate ADJ = 0.75. Regional paid $1.00 per share in dividends last year. It will earn at least $8.00 per share this year and each year in the forseeable future. Use the dividend adjustment model to calculate projected dividends per share for this year and the next four.

B5. Common stock of New Mexico Fruit Beverages has a current market value of $23. New Mexico is planning to issue transferable put rights to its shareholders, with 4 put rights required to sell 1 share back to the firm for $30. I.M. Confused has a tax basis of $17.50 per share for his shares in New Mexico. If I.M.'s capital gain tax rate is 14%, what would you expect a put right to be worth to him?

B6. Cite three broad reasons why an unexpected cut in a firm's dividend rate might cause a severe drop in the market price of the firm's stock.

B7. Explain why a firm's share price falls on the ex-dividend date. By how much would you expect it to fall? Does it matter whether the dividend is paid in cash or additional stock?

B8. If the price of a share of common stock can be expressed as the present value of the future dividend stream, how could dividend policy be irrelevant?

B9. Under what circumstances might the introduction of a dividend reinvestment plan increase shareholder wealth?

B10. Consider a firm that has decided to make, but has not yet announced, a large "bonus" cash dividend, in total $5 million. The firm has 1 million shares outstanding that sell for $20 each. The firm has no debt, there are no taxes, and all transactions take place in a perfect capital market. Using calculations like those in the illustration of dividend irrelevance in a perfect capital market, show that it will not matter to shareholders whether the firm pays out the "bonus" as a dividend or uses the money to buy back $5 million of its shares.

B11. Suppose Eddie Bauer has a choice of paying out a cash dividend or reinvesting the money in projects that are expected to earn their required return of 16.5% over the next 7 years. If the riskless rate is 8%, will the shareholders be better off with one or the other alternatives, or are the alternatives equally beneficial?

B12. How can a consistent policy of never decreasing the per-share dollar amount of the cash dividend that a firm pays each period facilitate monitoring (a) the firm's managers as agents by the firm's shareholders (as principals) and (b) the firm's shareholders as agents by the firm's debtholders (as principals)?

B13. In July 1995 International Paper Co. announced a 2-for-1 stock split. At the same time, it announced that the quarterly dividend rate, which had been 42 cents per presplit share, would become 25 cents a share after the stock split.

a. Did International Paper increase its dividend rate? Explain.

b. How would you expect the market to react to this dual announcement?

B14. A firm's common stock is trading at a P/E ratio of 12. Its projected earnings per share are $2.00, and its share price is $24. All its shareholders are tax-exempt.

a. An open-market purchase would result in projected earnings per share of $2.30. How would you expect the announcement of the share repurchase program to affect the firm's share price?

b. How might your answer to part a change if the firm instead announced a tender offer?

B15. A firm recently paid out $10 million in cash dividends. Within the same month, the firm announced the issue of $20 million in new 20-year debentures to raise capital for an expansion. Discuss why a firm might decide to pay a dividend in spite of the need for expansion capital and the flotation costs associated with the new issue.

B16. Cardinal Computer Corporation has developed a phenomenally successful software package that makes it very easy to combine spreadsheet modeling and basic financial calculations. As a result, Cardinal has $20 million of excess cash that is available for distribution to its shareholders. All of Cardinal's shareholders invested at the firm's inception and consequently have a negligible tax (cost) basis in their Cardinal shares. Cardinal has 10 million shares outstanding.

a. Assuming that dividend income is taxed at a 40% rate and that capital gains income is taxed at a 20% rate, calculate the impact on shareholder wealth of a $20 million cash dividend distribution and of a $20 million share repurchase.

b. Under what circumstances, if any, would Cardinal's shareholders be better off having Cardinal retain the cash and reinvest it in short-term financial instruments rather than pay it out to shareholders?

B17. Suppose the tax code was changed so that capital gains were taxed at a fixed and constant rate of 10% on the gain at the time the asset was sold. What impact do you think such a change in tax law would have on the average payout ratio of firms traded on the NYSE?

B18. In January 1996, the *Wall Street Journal* ("Daimler Won't Rule out 1995 Dividend Despite Loss") reported that Daimler-Benz AG was considering paying a cash dividend for 1995 even though the firm lost 6 billion marks ($4 billion). The article noted that Daimler's chairman said he expects Daimler to post a "very positive" result for 1996. How would you interpret the subsequent dividend announcement in light of the chairman's remark?

B19. Our discussion in this chapter leads to a less than completely satisfying conclusion. We do not provide a prescription that specifies *exactly* how to maximize shareholder wealth through dividend policy. If you recall, our prescription concerning capital structure was similar. Now the question: Suppose the good fairy can tell you exactly how to optimize both your firm's capital structure policy and your firm's dividend policy. Although the good fairy wants to be good to you, he does not want to be *too* good to you and has offered to provide you with the optimal prescription for your firm's capital structure policy *or* your firm's dividend policy, but not both. On the basis of what you now know of the potential gains to be had from each policy, which one would you choose to optimize? Explain your reasoning.

PROBLEM SET C

C1. An article in the *Wall Street Journal* ("Payouts Become Crucial Weapon in Appeasement," January 31, 1989) argues that cash dividends have become a "crucial weapon in corporate America's war of appeasement with raiders and other demanding investors."

  a. When might an increase in the dividend rate lead to an increase in a firm's share price?

  b. Under what circumstances would a firm prefer to pay out the cash in the form of a "special" or "extra" dividend?

  c. Does this renewed interest in cash dividends imply that the bird-in-the-hand argument for increased cash payouts is valid after all?

C2. Respond to the following comment: "Thirty years ago, the traditional view held that dividend policy mattered. The current view also holds that dividend policy matters. I guess they had it right in the first place."

C3.

  a. How does the stock market normally react to the announcement of a dividend reduction?

  b. How would you explain the reaction in part a?

  c. Suppose you were told that a firm announced a cut in its dividend rate to 25 cents per quarter from 50 cents per quarter but that the price of the firm's shares closed $1 higher on the announcement date than it did the previous day (up from $61 to $62 per share). Is this inconsistent with your answer to part b?

  d. Under what circumstances might the events in part c occur simultaneously?

C4. Explain why firms exhibit a reluctance to cut their dividend rate.

C5. It has been argued by a journalist that utilities should not be allowed to pay cash dividends because such a prohibition would (a) reduce their need to raise external capital, thus (b) reducing their transaction costs, so that (c) they would have a lower cost of capital, and consequently (d) lowering utility rates and (e) making consumers better off. Do you think a legal restriction preventing utilities from *ever* paying a cash dividend would result in this chain of events? If not, where does the logic break down?

C6. Dividend policy interacts with a firm's investment and capital structure policies. In Chapter 15 we said that issuing new equity is considered a negative signal. The logic of this empirical observation is that if the project is "really good," the shareholders would rather borrow than take on additional partners. In light of this, how might a firm's dividend policy give rise to an opportunity cost with respect to its investment opportunities if its capital structure is held constant?

C7. A firm plans to issue 1 put right for each outstanding share of common stock. N put rights will entitle the holder to tender 1 share of common stock to the firm at a price of S. The current share price (with the rights attached) is P_R. Ignore shareholder income taxes.

a. Assuming that all the put rights are exercised, develop an expression for the share price ex-rights (after the rights have been detached) in terms of N, S, and P_R.

b. Use the expression developed in part a, together with Equation (17.3), to obtain Equation (17.2).

c. Develop Equation (17.4) using the reasoning applied in part a.

C8. Repeat Problem C7 without ignoring shareholder income taxes. Let T_g be the marginal investor's capital gains tax rate and B her tax basis in the shares to be tendered. Note that the rights are taxed when they are issued.

a. Assuming that all the put rights are exercised, develop an expression for the share price ex-rights.

b. Show that if the marginal investor buys a put right and tenders it to the firm, the following condition must be satisfied for the transaction to have zero arbitrage profit:

$$(1 - T_g)S + T_g B - (1 - T_g)NR_P = P_E$$

c. Use the expression developed in part b to obtain Equation (17.5).

d. Obtain an expression analogous to Equation (17.2) for the case in which $T_g > 0$.

Real-World Application: Citicorp's Dividend Decision

Citicorp, the parent firm of Citibank, suspended its dividend in 1991 following huge real estate loan losses and other problems. Press reports indicated that bank regulators had begun close regulatory supervision of the bank and had pressured Citicorp into suspending dividend payments until it could shore up its capital. By the end of 1993, Citicorp's situation had improved significantly. Between the end of 1990 and the end of 1993, Citicorp's regulatory capital had increased from $16 billion to $23.5 billion and its *tier one leverage capital ratio* had doubled to 6.8% (versus the minimum required 4%).[1] Citicorp was considering whether to begin paying dividends again.

Citicorp's dividend actions during the two years before the dividend suspension were

QUARTER	DIVIDEND ACTION		QUARTER	DIVIDEND ACTION	
1990 I	$0.405	cash dividend	1991 I	$0.25	cash dividend
1990 II	$0.445	cash dividend	1991 II	$0.25	cash dividend
1990 III	$0.445	cash dividend	1991 III	$0.25	cash dividend
1990 IV	$0.445	cash dividend	1991 IV		dividend suspended (10/15/91)

Citicorp's historical and forecasted (marked by an F) earnings per share as of April 1994 were

Year	1988	1989	1990	1991	1992	1993	1994F	1995F	1996F
EPS	$4.87	$1.16	$0.57	($3.22)	$1.35	$3.53	$6.00	$6.50	$7.50

Citicorp reviewed the dividend policies of comparable banks as it decided whether to reinstate a cash dividend. Table 17-4 provides some of the information it considered.

1. What was Citicorp's payout ratio in 1990?

2. Why did Citicorp cut its dividend in the first quarter of 1991? Should it have suspended the dividend at that time?

[1]The tier one leverage capital ratio is the ratio of tier one capital (mainly common stockholders' equity) to average assets.

TABLE 17-4
Information concerning Citicorp and comparable firms.

BANK	NET WORTH/ASSETS			PAYOUT RATIO			DIVIDEND YIELD[a]
	1991	1992	1993	1991	1992	1993	
Citicorp	4.4%	5.2%	6.5%	NMF[b]	—	—	—
Bank of New York	7.4	8.6	8.9	131%	36%	32%	1.7%
BankAmerica	7.0	8.6	9.2	25	31	29	4.1
Bankers Trust	5.3	5.3	4.9	34	33	26	5.1
Chase Manhattan	5.5	6.8	8.0	38	35	63	4.1
Chemical	5.2	7.1	7.4	955	31	24	4.2
J.P. Morgan	5.9	6.9	7.4	36	32	29	4.3
Nations Bank	5.9	6.6	6.3	195	33	33	4.0

[a] At March 31, 1994. Four times the latest quarterly dividend divided by the share price.
[b] Not meaningful.
Sources: Bloomberg, L. P., and *Value Line Investment Survey.*

3. What was the average payout ratio for the comparable banks in 1992? What was the average in 1993?

4. Explain why Citicorp's net worth/assets ratio would suggest that its payout ratio should be below the average for the other banks.

5. How do you think the market would react to Citicorp declaring a cash dividend in the spring of 1994? Would the signal be credible?

6. What payout ratio would you recommend to Citicorp on the basis of the information available? What additional information would you like to have to make a firmer recommendation?

7. Assume Citicorp's share price is $39. If Citicorp wanted its stock to provide an "average dividend yield," what quarterly dividend should it declare?

8. Should Citicorp declare a cash dividend? If so, what dividend would you recommend?

BIBLIOGRAPHY

Ambarish, Ramasastry, Kose John, and Joseph Williams. "Efficient Signalling with Dividends and Investments," *Journal of Finance*, 1987, 42(2):321–343.

Ang, James S. *Do Dividends Matter? A Review of Corporate Dividend Theories and Evidence.* Monograph 1987-2, Graduate School of Business Administration, New York University, New York, 1987.

Bajaj, Mukesh, and Anand M. Vijh. "Dividend Clienteles and the Information Content of Dividend Changes," *Journal of Financial Economics*, 1990, 26(2):193–220.

Black, Fischer. "The Dividend Puzzle," *Journal of Portfolio Management*, 1976, 2(Winter):5–8.

Bortz, Gary A., and John P. Rust. "Why Do Companies Pay Dividends?: Comment," *American Economic Review*, 1984, 74(December):1135–1136.

Brennan, Michael J., and Anjan V. Thakor. "Shareholder Preferences And Dividend Policy," *Journal of Finance*, 1990, 45(4):993–1019.

Chang, Rosita P., and S. Ghon Rhee. "The Impact of Personal Taxes on Corporate Dividend Policy and Capital Structure Decisions," *Financial Management*, 1990, 19(2):21–31.

Dann, Larry Y. "Common Stock Repurchases: An Analysis of Returns to Bondholders and Stockholders," *Journal of Financial Economics*, 1981, 9(2):113–138.

Denis, David J., Diane K. Denis, and Atulya Sarin. "The Information Content of Dividend Changes: Cash Flow Signaling, Overinvestment, and Dividend Clienteles," *Journal of Financial and Quantitative Analysis*, 1994, 29(4):567–587.

Eades, Kenneth M. "Empirical Evidence on Dividends as a Signal of Firm Value," *Journal of Financial and Quantitative Analysis*, 1982, 17(4):471–500.

Feldstein, Martin, and Jerry Green. "Why Do Companies Pay Dividends?" *American Economic Review*, 1983, 73(March):17–30.

Gordon, Myron J. "Dividends, Earnings, and Stock Prices," *Review of Economics and Statistics*, 1959, 41(May):99–105.

Hansen, Robert S., Raman Kumar, and Dilip K. Shome. "Dividend Policy and Corporate Monitoring: Evidence from the Regulated Electric Utility Industry," *Financial Management*, 1994, 23(1):16–22.

Jensen, Gerald R., Donald P. Solberg, and Thomas S. Zorn. "Simultaneous Determination of Insider Ownership, Debt, and Dividend Policies," *Journal of Financial and Quantitative Analysis*, 1992, 27(2):247–264.

Kalay, Avner. "Signaling, Information Content, and the Reluctance to Cut Dividends," *Journal of Financial and Quantitative Analysis*, 1980, 15(4):855–869.

Kale, Jayant R., Thomas H. Noe, and Gerald D. Gay. "Share Repurchase Through Transferable Put Rights," *Journal of Financial Economics*, 1989, 25(1):141–160.

Lewellen, Wilbur G., Kenneth L. Stanley, Ronald C. Lease, and Gary G. Schlarbaum. "Some Direct Evidence on the Dividend Clientele Phenomenon," *Journal of Finance*, 1978, 33(5):1385–1399.

Lintner, John. "Distribution of Incomes of Corporations Among Dividends, Retained Earnings, and Taxes," *American Economic Review*, 1956, 46(May):97–113.

Litzenberger, Robert H., and K. Ramaswamy. "The Effects of Dividends on Common Stock Prices: Tax Effects or Information Effects," *Journal of Finance*, 1982, 37(2):429–443.

Litzenberger, Robert H., and K. Ramaswamy. "The Effect of Personal Taxes and Dividends on Capital Asset Prices: Theory and Empirical Evidence," *Journal of Financial Economics*, 1979, 7(2):163–195.

Maloney, Michael T., and J. Harold Mulherin. "The Effects of Splitting on the Ex: A Microstructure Reconciliation," *Financial Management*, 1992, 21(4):44–59.

Miller, Merton H., and Franco Modigliani. "Dividend Policy, Growth, and the Valuation of Shares," *Journal of Business*, 1961, v34(October), 411–433.

Miller, Merton H., and Myron S. Scholes. "Dividends and Taxes," *Journal of Financial Economics*, 1978, 6(4):333–364.

Miller, Merton H., and Myron S. Scholes. "Dividends and Taxes: Some Empirical Evidence," *Journal of Political Economy*, 1982, 90(6):1118-1141.

Ofer, Aharon R., and Daniel R. Siegel. "Corporate Financial Policy, Information, and Market Expectations: An Empirical Investigation of Dividends," *Journal of Finance*, 1987, 42(4):889–911.

Ofer, Aharon R., and Anjan V. Thakor. "A Theory of Stock Price Responses to Alternative Corporate Cash Disbursement Methods: Stock Repurchases and Dividends," *Journal of Finance*, 1987, 42(2), 365–394.

Papaioannou, George J., and Craig M. Savarese. "Corporate Dividend Policy Response to the Tax Reform Act of 1986," *Financial Management*, 1994, 23(1):56–63.

Shefrin, Hersh M., and Meir Statman. "Explaining Investor Preference for Cash Dividends," *Journal of Financial Economics*, 1984, 13(2):253–282.

Talmor, Eli, and Sheridan Titman. "Taxes and Dividend Policy," *Financial Management*, 1990, 19(2):32–35.

Vermaelen, Theo. "Common Stock Repurchases and Market Signalling: An Empirical Study," *Journal of Financial Economics*, 1981, 9(2):139–183.

MANAGING DIVIDEND POLICY

O B J E C T I V E S

After studying this chapter you should be able to

1. Describe the most common characteristics of corporate dividend policies.

2. Explain the timing of the dividend declaration date, ex-dividend date, record date, and payment date.

3. Apply the three-step approach to the dividend decision outlined in the chapter to determine an appropriate dividend action.

4. Distinguish "special" dividends from regular cash dividends.

5. Explain why a stock dividend is not a perfect substitute for a cash dividend.

6. Describe five alternative methods of repurchasing shares.

In the previous chapter we saw why a firm's dividend policy might affect the wealth of its shareholders. In this chapter, we explain how firms can select an appropriate dividend policy and determine how best to implement it. This chapter lays out a three-step approach for making a dividend decision.

We will also explain why striving for *the* optimal dividend policy at any particular time is usually not cost effective. Therefore, in practice, firms try to maintain a stable dividend policy. Such a policy includes paying at least some dividends on a regular basis once the firm is well established, having a relatively consistent target payout ratio, avoiding a reduction in an established dividend, using share repurchases to shareholder advantage whenever possible, and making dividend changes in a deliberate and orderly way.

We explained in Chapter 17 why a share repurchase program is an alternative to a dividend distribution. In this chapter we will discuss the factors affecting the share repurchase decision and describe five basic methods firms have available for repurchasing shares along with the advantages and disadvantages of each technique.

We begin our discussion with a brief review of the common characteristics of corporate dividend policies. This review will give you some practical insights that we hope will make our dividend policy guidelines more meaningful.

DIVIDEND POLICY AND THE PRINCIPLES OF FINANCE

◇ *Signaling*: Consider any possible change in dividend policy carefully, because it conveys information to outsiders and can be misunderstood.

◇ *Behavioral*: Use the information contained in the dividend policies of other firms.

◇ *Valuable Ideas*: Look for opportunities to create value by supplying a dividend policy that has a demand-supply imbalance, perhaps resulting from changes in laws.

◇ *Capital Market Efficiency*: Recognize that the potential increase in value a firm can get through dividend policy is smaller than what it can get through capital structure policy. Most important to the firm's value, however, are the introduction of valuable new ideas and wise use of the firm's comparative advantages.

◇ *Risk-Return Trade-Off*: Recognize that the trade-off between dividends and capital gains with fair market transactions is simply a risk-return trade-off. It does not affect firm value.

◇ *Options*: Consider transferable put rights as an alternative method of repurchasing shares.

◇ *Time Value of Money*: Include any time-value-of-money tax benefits from dividend policy choices.

MAJOR PHARMACEUTICAL COMPANY'S DIVIDEND PROBLEM

At its coming meeting, the board of directors of Major Pharmaceutical Company will discuss whether to increase its quarterly dividend. In preparation for that meeting, Major's chairman of the board has asked the treasurer to study the firm's dividend policy and to recommend appropriate dividend action to the board.

Table 18-1 presents Major's 10-year dividend history. Major's payout ratio decreased slightly over the 10-year period (note the difference between the 5-year averages), as did the average payout ratio of comparable pharmaceutical firms.

Major's financial forecast predicts earnings per share of $5.00, $6.00, and $7.20 in the next three years, respectively. It also predicts funds from operations amounting to $6.20, $7.40, and $8.80 per common share in the next three years, respectively. These funds would be available for reinvestment or cash dividends. However, Major expects to have a substantially larger capital budget in two of these years, to complete development of its new arthritic painkiller, and to purchase additional plant and equipment for producing the new drug.

Major's treasurer must analyze this historical and projected financial information, taking into account any other considerations that may have a bearing on the dividend decision, and make a recommendation. The treasurer's questions include the following:

Is an increase in the dividend likely to increase shareholder wealth?

Is Major's current payout ratio appropriate?

What should Major's payout ratio be, compared to that of other firms?

TABLE 18-1
Ten-year dividend history for Major Pharmaceutical Company.

YEAR	DIVIDEND PER SHARE	EARNINGS PER SHARE	PAYOUT RATIO		RANGE FOR COMPARABLE FIRMS		QUARTERLY COMMON DIVIDEND INCREASED		
			Major	Index for Comparable Firms	High	Low	In Qtr.	From	To
1987	$0.40	$1.20	33.3%	39.4%	57.3%	21.9%	I	$0.09	$0.10
1988	0.46	1.32	34.8	41.0	51.2	20.7	II	0.10	0.12
1989	0.54	1.50	36.0	40.9	48.3	24.8	II	0.12	0.14
1990	0.64	1.85	34.6	41.7	44.2	27.9	I	0.14	0.16
1991	0.72	2.07	34.8	43.2	46.1	22.2	I	0.16	0.18
5-year growth rate	15.1%	14.3%							
5-year average			34.7	41.2					
1992	$0.84	$2.45	34.3	35.2	51.1	23.6	I	0.18	0.21
1993	0.96	3.10	31.0	37.2	48.6	24.7	I	0.21	0.24
1994	1.12	3.73	30.0	38.2	54.1	25.3	I	0.24	0.28
1995	1.28	4.01	31.9	44.2	52.9	22.1	I	0.28	0.32
1996	1.44	4.25	33.9	40.6	53.7	18.6	I	0.32	0.36
5-year growth rate	13.7%	13.6%							
5-year average			32.2	39.1					
10-year growth rate	14.4%	15.4%							
10-year average			33.5	40.2					

Would repurchasing shares benefit Major's shareholders more than a cash dividend?

In view of Major's large capital budget, should the dividend be cut temporarily? Or should a stock dividend be paid instead of a cash dividend in order to conserve cash?

The responses to these and related questions will determine the firm's dividend policy. In what forms should it distribute the cash? How should it time these distributions? Later in the chapter, we will help Major's treasurer prepare her recommendation.

18.1 INDUSTRY DIFFERENCES

Payout ratios vary systematically across industries. What might explain this? We suspect that it is due primarily to the comparable investment opportunities within an industry and to differences across industries.

Table 18-2 lists the 5-year-average payout ratios for 13 industries. They are calculated for three 5-year periods beginning in 1980 and ending in 1994. Electric utilities had the highest payout ratios by a wide margin. The building materials and the drugs and health care industries generally had the lowest payout ratios. Because of these systematic differences in payout ratio, Major's treasurer can apply the Behavioral Principle and use the payout ratios of firms in the same industry as a guide. Of course, by taking significant firm-specific information into account, Major can do better than blind imitation.

Self-Check Questions

1. Why do payout ratios vary systematically across industries?

2. How can we make use of this systematic variation when selecting an appropriate payout ratio?

TABLE 18-2

Payout ratios in selected industries.

INDUSTRY	FIVE-YEAR INDUSTRY AVERAGE 1980–1984	1985–1989	1990–1994	OVERALL 1980–1994
Building materials	29.9%	13.3%	19.1%	20.8%
Drugs and health care	16.4	23.4	25.6	21.8
Life insurance	30.6	25.8	21.6	26.0
Textiles	28.4	39.7	15.5	27.9
Foods	28.0	26.4	31.3	28.6
Metals and mining	20.0	21.1	45.5	28.9
Paper and paper products	26.7	30.3	40.3	32.4
Business equipment	32.0	31.4	34.8	32.7
Steel	24.1	30.7	49.9	34.9
Aerospace and aircraft	33.5	59.8	18.5	37.3
Oil	14.3	75.8	29.1	39.7
Chemicals	33.0	72.2	50.1	51.8
Electric utilities	72.7	84.8	81.9	79.8
Average	29.9%	41.1%	35.6%	35.5%

Source: Compustat.

18.2 DIVIDEND POLICY IN PRACTICE

Actual dividend policies provide a useful backdrop for our discussion of how a firm can select an appropriate dividend policy. We will begin by describing several common characteristics. Then we will discuss the mechanics of implementing a dividend policy.

Characteristics of Corporate Dividend Policies

In practice, publicly traded firms prefer to (1) pay at least *some* dividends on a regular basis, (2) maintain a stable payout ratio and dividend, (3) make orderly changes in the dividend, and (4) avoid cutting the dividend.

PREFERENCE FOR PAYING COMMON DIVIDENDS   Smaller and younger firms generally do not pay cash dividends. But at some point in its life cycle, a firm decides that it is sufficiently "mature" to begin paying dividends. This may be due to a desire to demonstrate the firm's stability, a decline in profitable investment opportunities, investor preference for at least some cash distributions, a desire to broaden the market for the firm's stock to include investors prohibited from buying non-dividend-paying stocks, or other factors. Among NYSE-listed firms, in any given year since World War II, from 75% to 90% paid cash dividends.

STABILITY OF DIVIDENDS COMPARED TO EARNINGS   Figure 18-1 shows the pattern of corporate earnings and dividends for about the last 50 years and the corresponding movement in the average annual payout ratio. Dividends are more stable than earnings. This is true for most individual firms, such as Exxon (shown in Figure 18-2), as well as in the aggregate. Dividends follow the trend in cash flow per share much more closely than the trend in earnings per share.

REGULAR PAYMENTS   Dividend-paying firms usually make quarterly payments. Some firms make semiannual or annual payments, and a handful do it monthly. Once they begin paying dividends, firms try to continue making regular payments. Table 18-3 will give you a sense

FIGURE 18-1
Corporate dividends and earnings from World War II to the present.

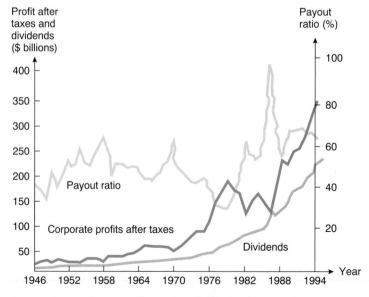

Source: Economic Indicators (Washington, D.C.: Government Printing Office, various issues).

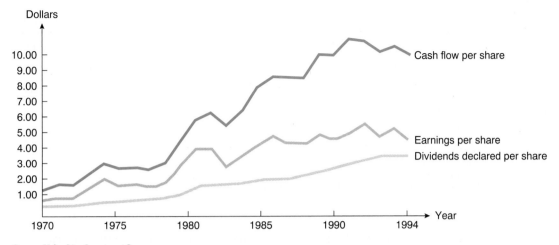

Source: Value Line Investment Survey.

FIGURE 18-2

Earnings, cash flow, and dividends per share for Exxon Corporation, 1970–1994.

of the length-of-dividend-payment records of firms listed on the New York Stock Exchange as of the end of 1983 (the last year the NYSE compiled such data). Roughly half made quarterly payments on an uninterrupted basis for 20 years or more. Firms frequently stress the length of their uninterrupted dividend records when declaring a dividend.

RELUCTANCE TO CUT THE DIVIDEND   Beyond the regularity of dividends, firms strongly dislike cutting their dividend (that is, the dollar amount per share). This is probably because a dividend cut is most often interpreted as a negative signal. Looking back at Table 17-3 in the last chapter, you can see that the numbers of dividend decreases and omissions increased sharply—and the numbers of dividend increases and resumptions decreased sharply—during the recession periods of 1974 to 1975 and 1980 to 1982. Investors generally interpret dividend reductions as a signal that the firm's earnings prospects have worsened. This can adversely affect a firm's share price and, in some cases, the share prices of other firms in the same industry.

For example, Consolidated Edison Company of New York once announced that it would omit its next quarterly dividend. Its share price fell by 43% over the next three weeks. During the same period, many other electric utility stocks decreased in value as investors feared that other firms would also reduce their dividends.[1]

EXTRA OR SPECIAL DIVIDENDS   Table 17-3 also shows that a minority of firms declared **extra or special dividends** during the period 1970 to 1994. In addition to a "regular" quarterly dividend, a firm may pay an extra dividend, possibly at regular intervals—say at each year-end. Such dividends tend to be considerably more variable in amount than regular dividend payments. They are generally paid during periods of temporarily higher earnings to bring the firm's payout ratio up to its target level.

Extra dividends usually occur near the end of the firm's fiscal year, which is the October-to-December quarter for most firms. Firms seem to pay extra dividends when the year-end review reveals unusually high earnings for the year. The firm wants to pay out its target per-

---

[1] Interestingly, a later dividend reduction by General Public Utilities did not affect many other firms in the industry. This was probably because the cause of the reduction, the Three Mile Island nuclear accident, was so specific.

TABLE 18-3
Number of firms that have paid dividends on New York Stock Exchange-listed common stocks for various periods of consecutive years.

	NUMBER OF CONSECUTIVE YEARS								NUMBER OF FIRMS LISTED AT YEAR-END
	100 or More	75–99	50–74	25–49	20–24	20 or More	10–19	Fewer Than 10[a]	1983
Quarterly payments	6	41	134	448	86	715	201	602	1518
Annual payments	37	85	232	403	84	841	201	476[b]	1518

[a] Includes stocks that have not paid dividends.
[b] Includes stocks that do not make quarterly dividend payments.
Source: New York Stock Exchange Fact Book 1984 (New York: New York Stock Exchange, 1984), p. 35.

centage of earnings but does not want falsely to signal higher sustainable earnings. Many firms in cyclical businesses, such as GM, have declared extra dividends during periods when earnings were at a cyclical peak. They increase the regular dividend only when they believe they have reached a higher level of sustainable earnings.

Special dividends are often declared when a firm finds itself with substantial excess cash that it wants to distribute to its shareholders.[2] Consequently, on a dollar-for-dollar basis, special dividends contain less information than regular dividends about a firm's future earnings prospects.

REGULAR DECISIONS   Most firms review their dividend policies at least annually, and they typically do so about the same time each year.

Dividend Mechanics

A dividend must be declared by the firm's board of directors. A firm can pay cash dividends only out of legally available funds. Similarly, stock dividends and stock splits must be declared by the board.

When a firm's board of directors declares a dividend, it specifies a **record date** and a **payment date**. The record date is established to determine who will actually get the dividend check for a share of stock if the share is sold between when the dividend is declared and when it is paid. The time line presented in Figure 18-3 shows the key dividend-related dates. The payment date is the date on which the firm will send a check to each shareholder of record. The **shareholder of record** is the owner as determined by the record date.

Since July 3, 1995, stock transactions must be settled by the third business day following the transaction. Consequently, the major stock exchanges and securities dealers (in the over-the-counter market) establish an **ex-dividend date** two business days prior to the record date. On that date the shares begin *trading ex-dividend*—that is, without dividend rights. Con-

---

[2] For example, Western Pacific Industries Inc. declared a $23 special dividend following the sale of its Western Pacific Railroad unit. An interesting question is whether shareholders would have been better off if the firm had repurchased some of its common stock instead of paying a special dividend.

FIGURE 18-3
A time line for dividend-related events.

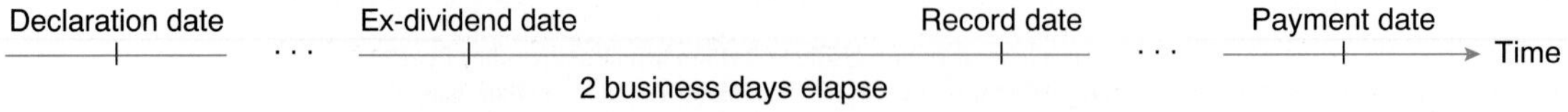

sequently, a stock normally opens for trading on the ex-dividend date at approximately the preceding day's closing price less the amount of the dividend per share.

					Dividend-Related Events for General Electric Company in 1994

General Electric Company established the following declaration, ex-dividend, record, and payment dates for the dividends it declared during 1994. In 1994, stock transactions had to be settled by the fifth business day following the transaction. Note the regularity in the pattern of dates.

EXAMPLE

QUARTER	DECLARATION DATE	EX-DIVIDEND DATE	RECORD DATE	PAYMENT DATE	DIVIDEND PER SHARE
1	2/11/94	3/2/94	3/8/94	4/25/94	$ 0.36
2	6/24/94	6/28/94	7/5/94	7/25/94	0.36
3	9/16/94	9/26/94	9/30/94	10/25/94	0.36
4	12/16/94	12/23/94	12/30/94	1/25/95	0.41

Legal Limitations on Dividend Payments

Two forms of legal restrictions on dividend payments are important. With the possible exception of the financially strongest firms, bond indentures, loan agreements, and preferred stock agreements usually contain restrictions on the amount of common dividends a firm can pay. You may recall from Chapter 9 that such limitations are designed to minimize the firm's agency costs.

State laws also impose dividend restrictions. They are designed to prevent excessive cash distributions to common stockholders. Most states have laws prohibiting firms from paying dividends if doing so would make the firm insolvent. Many states also prohibit firms from making dividend payments out of accounts that fall outside a legally defined "surplus." In some cases, this surplus includes only retained earnings. In other cases, it includes paid-in capital as well. And in still other cases, a firm is permitted to distribute current earnings, even though prior losses eliminated its surplus.

These limitations are seldom troublesome to a healthy firm. But a firm that has experienced large operating losses must ensure that its dividend policy will not cause it to violate existing dividend restrictions, even if this is otherwise contrary to the shareholders' best interest.

Self-Check Questions

1. List four characteristics of corporate dividend policies.
2. Which are more stable, dividends or earnings?
3. Why are firms reluctant to cut the dividend?
4. What are extra dividends, and when do firms pay them?
5. What happens on the ex-dividend date?

18.3 DIVIDEND POLICY GUIDELINES

Establishing a dividend policy involves a variety of conflicting and sometimes confusing considerations. In Chapter 17 we described factors that often lead to competing dividend policy preferences among shareholders. Thus almost any policy can disappoint some shareholders. Moreover, as with capital structure, we have no way to measure many of these factors precisely. Therefore, although a firm should strive to balance the needs of all of its shareholders against one another, the complexity of considerations makes managing dividend policy more an art than a science.

The Behavioral Principle provides a good starting point for establishing a target payout range. After factoring in its own specific firm-related and investor-related considerations (discussed in Chapter 17), a firm can choose an appropriate long-term target payout ratio.

A Three-Step Approach to the Dividend Decision

Determining an appropriate dividend policy for a firm involves a three-step approach. The firm must forecast its future residual funds, determine an appropriate target payout ratio, and then decide on the quarterly dividend.

PROJECT FUTURE RESIDUAL FUNDS Start with the firm's earnings and cash flow projections. Usually these are prepared for a period of approximately five years. Estimated capital expenditures and funds from operations are most important. At a minimum, a firm should pay out cash it cannot invest in positive-NPV projects. After considering investor-related factors, it might decide to pay out more than this minimum. However, because of flotation costs, it is usually unwise to pay out so much more than the minimum as to trigger the need for a new equity issue.

Many factors complicate this analysis. Capital budgeting projects often come in large units, and they can vary substantially from their expected timing and cost. As economic and business conditions change, so will the desired portfolio of capital budgeting projects. Similarly, future funds from operations are not entirely predictable. Analyzing even the most carefully prepared cash flow projections will suggest a *range* of distributable amounts, a *range* of needs for funds, and hence a *range* of *feasible target payout ratios*.

DETERMINE AN APPROPRIATE TARGET PAYOUT RATIO An analysis of the payout ratios of comparable firms—firms in the same industry and of similar size, product mix, and operating characteristics—will suggest a range of *customary payout ratios*. A firm should consider the range of feasible target payout ratios, together with the range of customary payout ratios and the shareholder mix, in setting its long-term target payout ratio.

SET THE QUARTERLY DIVIDEND Because of the informational content of dividend changes, a fluctuating regular dividend is usually unwise. Investors would find the dividend signals confusing. Such confusion would make the asymmetric information problem worse. And this would lead to higher perceived risk and therefore to a decline in the firm's share price.[3] Such a policy might also lead to shifts in the shareholder clientele, which would be costly to shareholders.

A firm should increase its dividend, then, only if it believes it can sustain the higher rate. On the other hand, suppose earnings prospects worsen significantly. At some point it will have to cut its dividend, compromise its capital budgeting plans, alter its capital structure policy, or issue additional equity.

---

[3] There is at least one situation in which a fluctuating regular dividend rate would not be confusing to investors. If a firm paid out a fixed percentage of its earnings each quarter and if investors understood this policy, the dividend changes would not be confusing. But in that case, dividend policy would be passive; dividend changes would mirror earnings changes, and dividend changes would have no informational content beyond the information conveyed by the latest earnings announcement. You should be able to see why such a myopic dividend policy would be ill-advised: Not only would it rob dividend policy of its potential signaling value, but it would also tie the dividend rate to short-run earnings rather than to the long-run availability of residual cash flow. We should stress that using a target payout ratio as we are recommending involves projecting a feasible average payout ratio over the firm's planning horizon. The projected annual payout ratios will deviate around this average, and the actual payout ratios are likely to deviate even more, depending principally on the profitability of the firm's operations.

Given its target payout ratio and its earnings projections, a firm should establish its quarterly dividend at the highest *comfortably sustainable* level. That is, the firm should be able to keep paying that dividend at least over the planning horizon. Caution dictates setting the actual rate somewhat below the expected maximum in order to compensate for the uncertainty of the earnings and funds forecasts. In addition, when a firm wants to increase its dividend, it is usually better to make one significant increase (at least 5%), rather than several tiny ones, to serve as an effective signal.

A Word to the Wise

It is important to recognize that the informational value of dividend changes is necessarily transitory. The information conveyed is either confirmed or denied by later events. The main goal with respect to the informational content of dividends should be to reinforce management's public statements about the firm's prospects. In this regard, it seems advantageous to select a particular quarter in which to review the dividend policy every year, thus creating a predictable pattern.

Self-Check Questions

1. What are the three steps in the recommended approach to the dividend decision?

2. How can you use comparable firms to determine an appropriate target payout ratio?

3. Why is a fluctuating regular dividend undesirable?

4. Why is it desirable to select a particular quarter in which to review the dividend policy every year?

18.4 APPLYING THE DIVIDEND POLICY GUIDELINES

This section applies the dividend policy guidelines just developed to the dividend decision confronting Major Pharmaceutical Company. Major's Financial Planning Group prepared a 5-year plan, which Major's board of directors tentatively approved. Table 18-4 provides the projected values of some financial variables drawn from the 5-year plan.

Estimated Future Residual Funds

The 5-year capital budgeting plan tentatively approved by Major's board calls for expenditures of $335 million on positive-NPV projects. The plan provides for capital investment of $45.0 million in 1997, $54.0 million in 1998, $74.0 million in 1999, $72.0 million in 2000, and $90.0 million in 2001. Over the 5-year period, Major projects total residual funds of $115.0 million.

Target Payout Ratio

The projected residual funds of $115.0 million represent about one-third of projected earnings available for common. These amount to $367.0 million for the 5-year period. A detailed analysis of Major's shareholder group would be expensive and time-consuming. However, Major's treasurer realizes that as long as their dividend policies are clearly articulated and stable, particular industries and particular firms tend to attract certain shareholder clienteles.

As Table 18-1 illustrates, Major's payout ratio has averaged 33.5% over the past 10 years and 32.2% over the past 5 years. Major's financial staff has also analyzed the payout policies of its 10 closest competitors. The average payout ratio for these firms for the preceding year was 40.6%. The range of payout ratios was 18.6% to 53.7%. Major's treasurer con-

TABLE 18-4
Selecting an appropriate dividend action for Major Pharmaceutical Company.

		PROJECTIONS					
	INITIAL	1997	1998	1999	2000	2001	TOTALS
Earnings per common share	$4.25	$ 5.00	$ 6.00	$ 7.20	$ 8.50	$ 10.00	
Number of common shares (millions)		× 10	× 10	× 10	× 10	× 10	
Earnings available for common		$50.0	$60.0	$ 72.0	$ 85.0	$ 100.0	$367.0
Depreciation and other noncash charges		12.0	14.0	16.0	19.0	22.0	83.0
Funds from operations available for reinvestment or dividends		62.0	74.0	88.0	104.0	122.0	450.0
Capital investment requirement		45.0	54.0	74.0	72.0	90.0	335.0
Residual funds		$17.0	$20.0	$14.0	$ 32.0	$ 32.0	$115.0
Assuming No Change in the Dividend							
Dividend per share	$1.44	$ 1.44	$ 1.44	$ 1.44	$ 1.44	$ 1.44	
Payout ratio	33%	29%	24%	20%	17%	14%	
Residual funds		$17.0	$20.0	$ 14.0	$ 32.0	$ 32.0	$115.0
Dividend requirements		14.4	14.4	14.4	14.4	14.4	72.0
Surplus (deficit)		$ 2.6	$ 5.6	$ (0.4)	$ 17.6	$ 17.6	$ 43.0
One Possible Dividend Policy Alternative A							
Dividend per share	$1.44	$ 1.70	$ 1.70	$ 1.70	$ 2.70	$ 3.70	
Payout ratio	33%	34%	28%	24%	32%	37%	
Residual funds		$17.0	$20.0	$ 14.0	$ 32.0	$ 32.0	$115.0
Dividend requirements		17.0	17.0	17.0	27.0	37.0	115.0
Surplus (deficit)		—	$ 3.0	$ (3.0)	$ 5.0	$ (5.0)	$ 0.0
Another Possible Dividend Policy Alternative B							
Dividend per share	$1.44	$ 1.68	$1.88	$ 2.00	$ 2.64	$ 3.30	
Payout ratio	33%	34%	31%	28%	31%	33%	
Residual funds		$17.0	$20.0	$ 14.0	$ 32.0	$ 32.0	$115.0
Dividend requirements		16.8	18.8	20.0	26.4	33.0	115.0
Surplus (deficit)		$ 0.2	$ 1.2	$ (6.0)	$ 5.6	$ (1.0)	$ 0.0

cluded that a payout ratio of 30% to 40% would be appropriate. But because of Major's expected heavy capital budgeting requirements beginning in 1999, she feels that Major's payout ratio should remain below the industry average.

Analyzing the Impact of Alternative Dividend Policies

Table 18-4 also illustrates how to evaluate alternative dividend policies. A firm would normally examine several such alternatives before deciding on a particular action.

The current annual dividend is $1.44 per share. Suppose Major were to keep this rate through 2001. Its payout ratio would fall steadily, and it would retain substantial funds.

Major is considering two alternative policies. Under both alternatives, Major would pay out all the estimated residual funds to shareholders. Alternative B provides for increases each year. It avoids the very large increases in 2000 and 2001 that alternative A calls for. Also, the payout ratio is less variable and closer to the long-run target under alternative B.

Major reassesses its dividend policy each year and so is more concerned about 1997 than the later years. It appears that Major can sustain a 24-cent increase in its dividend to $1.68 per share per year. Such an increase seems appropriate in light of Major's improved earnings prospects. Of course, other considerations might indicate that a dividend other than $1.68 is more appropriate. But Major's projection of residual funds is the best starting place for such an analysis.

What about the years 2000 and 2001? The policy alternatives in Table 18-4 suggest very large dividend increases. Such increases will necessarily be reconsidered in the future. Major would implement them only if it continued to find them sustainable.

Special Considerations for the Privately Held Firm

The preceding example applies only to publicly traded firms. In most cases, *privately held* firms do not have informational effects to worry about. However, tax considerations and the owners' liquidity needs are of great importance.

Because of taxes, the owners of a privately held firm normally benefit from capital gains more than from cash dividends. For this reason, Internal Revenue Service regulations prohibit excessive earnings retention. But the definition of "excessive" is not clear. Privately held firms are generally smaller than publicly traded firms. They consequently have less financial flexibility and somewhat more variable liquidity requirements. Greater retentions are therefore warranted to compensate for the higher liquidity risks of privately held firms. Minimizing dividend payouts—especially until a surplus has been built up—may therefore be financially prudent as well as beneficial from a tax standpoint.

Self-Check Questions

1. Why is it useful to consider more than one dividend policy alternative?

2. What special dividend policy considerations apply to privately held firms?

18.5 EXTRA DIVIDENDS

As we noted earlier, firms in cyclical businesses often pay extra (or special) dividends during periods when earnings are at a cyclical peak. Such a policy is prudent. It preserves the integrity of changes in the regular dividend as a signaling device. At the same time, it enables the firm to pay out a stable percentage of its earnings, which corresponds to the longer-term ratio of residual earnings to total earnings.

Alternatively, a firm could set a higher regular dividend to achieve the same total dividend payout over time. This would require either (1) additional *borrowing* during low-income periods, the borrowings being repaid during high-income periods, or (2) the buildup of *excess cash balances* during high-income periods, the cash balances being drawn down to pay dividends during low-income periods. The first policy would worsen a firm's liquidity position during low-income periods, when it might already be strained for other reasons. The second policy requires excess cash balances. Therefore, for firms in highly cyclical businesses, supplementing regular dividends with occasional extra dividends is a less risky policy from a financial standpoint than paying regular dividends exclusively. It is also more efficient from a cash management standpoint.

EXAMPLE

Alcoa's Special Dividends

Aluminum Company of America (Alcoa), the world's largest aluminum producer, declared regular quarterly cash dividends of $0.20 each in 1989 and 1990. Alcoa earned $5.34 per share in 1989 and declared a special dividend of $0.70 per share on January 19, 1990. In view of the proximity to Alcoa's December 31st year-end, it seems appropriate to add the special dividend to 1989's regular cash dividends in calculating the payout ratio for 1989:

$$\text{Payout ratio} = \frac{4(0.20) + 0.70}{5.34} = 28\%$$

In 1990 Alcoa earned $3.30 per share. It declared a special dividend of $0.09 per share on January 18, 1991. The implied payout ratio for 1990 is

$$\text{Payout ratio} = \frac{4(0.20) + 0.09}{3.30} = 27\%$$

Between 1991 and 1994, Alcoa's earnings per share varied between $0.40 and $1.64 (before extraordinary items). Alcoa did not declare any special dividends subsequent to those year-ends. However, it continued to pay $0.20 per quarter in regular cash dividends. During 1995, Alcoa earned $4.43. It paid a regular quarterly dividend of $0.225. Just after year-end it declared an extra dividend of $0.1075. That brought 1995's payout ratio to

$$\text{Payout ratio} = \frac{4(0.225) + 0.1075}{4.43} = 23\%$$

Self-Check Questions

1. Why do firms in cyclical businesses often pay extra dividends?
2. How does a special dividend "preserve the integrity" of the regular dividend?
3. Why is a policy of paying a special dividend during peak earnings periods efficient from a cash management standpoint?

18.6 STOCK DIVIDENDS AND STOCK SPLITS

Firms do not always pay dividends in cash. Frequently firms pay **stock dividends**. A stock dividend is a bookkeeping reapportioning of the claim size of a share of stock so that there are more shares and each share has a proportionally smaller claim. Suppose a firm declares a 5% stock dividend. Then a shareholder will receive 5 new shares for every 100 shares owned.

A firm can achieve much the same financial effect as a stock dividend through a **stock split**. Although there is a technical difference between the two, stock dividends and stock splits represent alternative ways to rearrange a firm's capital accounts on its balance sheet. Neither affects the net worth of the firm or the proportional ownership interest of any of its shareholders.

Stock Dividends

A stock dividend proportionally increases the number of shares each shareholder owns. The fair market value of the shares distributed in the stock dividend is transferred from the "Retained earnings" account to the "Paid-in capital" and "Capital contributed in excess of par value" accounts.

Table 18-5 illustrates the balance sheet impact of a 100% stock dividend for a firm whose shares are selling at $30. The $30 million fair market value of the 1 million shares that constitute the dividend is transferred out of retained earnings. The declaration of the stock dividend does not affect each share's par value, which is $10 in this case. Thus $10 million (1 million shares at $10 par value each) is added to paid-in capital. The $20 million balance is added to capital contributed in excess of par value. The firm's common stockholders' equity remains $100 million. ■

A 100% Stock Dividend and a 2-for-1 Stock Split

EXAMPLE

Stock Splits

Table 18-5 (the bottom part) also illustrates the balance sheet impact of a comparable stock split (a 2-for-1 stock split). A stock split alters the par value of the shares but does not involve any transfer of balances between the components of common stockholders' equity. In the case of a 2-for-1 split, the par value of each share is halved. Thus paid-in capital is unchanged.

TABLE 18-5
Comparison of the balance sheet impact of a 100% stock dividend and that of a 2-for-1 stock split.

COMMON STOCKHOLDERS' EQUITY INITIALLY	
Paid-in capital ($10 par value; 1,000,000 shares)	$ 10,000,000
Capital contributed in excess of par value	20,000,000
Retained earnings	70,000,000
Common stockholders' equity	$100,000,000
COMMON STOCKHOLDERS' EQUITY FOLLOWING 100% STOCK DIVIDEND	
Paid-in capital ($10 par value; 2,000,000 shares)	$ 20,000,000
Capital contributed in excess of par value	$ 40,000,000
Retained earnings	$ 40,000,000
Common stockholders' equity	$100,000,000
COMMON STOCKHOLDERS' EQUITY FOLLOWING 2-FOR-1 STOCK SPLIT	
Paid-in capital ($5 par value; 2,000,000 shares)	$ 10,000,000
Capital contributed in excess of par value	$ 20,000,000
Retained earnings	$ 70,000,000
Common stockholders' equity	$100,000,000

EXAMPLE

General Electric Company's 1994 Stock Split

General Electric Company announced a 2-for-1 stock split on March 17, 1994. Holders of record on April 28, 1994 received 1 additional share on May 13, 1994 for each share that they held on the record date. (Sounds a lot like a stock dividend, doesn't it?) Prior to the stock split, GE had about 926,564,000 shares outstanding. Following the split, it had about twice that number, or 1,853,128,000 shares, outstanding. GE did not alter its per-share dividend. Thus the stock split effectively doubled the dividend from $0.36 per quarter to $0.72 per quarter. ■

Stock Dividends versus Stock Splits

Table 18-5 shows the difference in accounting impact between stock dividends and stock splits. There is also an important difference in practice. Firms generally use stock dividends for small stock distributions and use stock splits for larger ones. For example, the rules of the New York Stock Exchange prescribe that firms should make share distributions of less than 25% through stock dividends rather than stock splits.

Financial Impact of Stock Dividends and Stock Splits

Both the 100% stock dividend and the 2-for-1 stock split doubled the number of shares outstanding. They did not affect the firm's liquidity position, capital expenditure program, leverage, or any operating variable, however. Consequently, apart from any informational effects, a stock dividend or split should leave the stock market value of a firm unchanged. Hence, a proportional reduction in the firm's share price should occur.

Suppose the firm in Table 18-5 earned $5.00 per share prior to the stock dividend or stock split, earning $5 million in total. Suppose the shares were trading at $30. A 100% stock dividend or 2-for-1 stock split would double the number of shares outstanding but would not alter the $5 million total earnings. Thus earnings per share would be $2.50 per share following the dividend or split. Barring informational effects, the market value of a share would be halved to $15.00. The same earnings pie has simply been sliced into a greater number of pieces. What, then, is the value to shareholders of a stock dividend or of a stock split?

According to the Signaling Principle, actions convey information. The principal benefit of a stock dividend or stock split is probably the information it conveys. About half the shares listed on the NYSE, for example, tend to trade in the range between $10 and $30 per share in any particular year (Table 18-6). Stock dividends and stock splits are therefore typically associated with firms that have (or at least believe they have) excellent growth prospects. A stock split, in particular, may signal management's expectation that in the absence of the split, the firm's share price would move out of, or further above the top end of, this customary trading range. If so, investors ought to react favorably to the news of an impending stock split. In connection with a stock split, firms often announce their desire to reduce the price of a share to a more popular trading range. More important, there is evidence that investors react positively to this signal. A stock split, which normally involves a greater reduction in share price than a stock dividend, is likely to have the greater informational content of the two.[4]

Following a stock dividend, firms often maintain the cash dividend per share. Following a stock split, firms typically either reduce the per-share cash dividend less than proportionally, or else maintain it, as GE did. These actions increase the cash dividend payout. Such increases are generally interpreted as positive signals.

---

[4] Correspondingly, a reverse stock split, which reduces the number of shares outstanding and raises the share price proportionally, usually elicits a negative reaction.

TABLE 18-6
Distribution of prices of New York Stock Exchange-listed common stocks, 1967–1994.

PRICE GROUP	AS OF JANUARY 6, 1967		AS OF JANUARY 7, 1972		AS OF FEBRUARY 3, 1978		AS OF DECEMBER 31, 1984		AS OF DECEMBER 31, 1990		AS OF DECEMBER 30, 1994	
	Number of Firms	Percentage of Total	Number of Firms	Percentage of Total	Number of Firms	Percentage of Total	Number of Firms	Percentage of Total	Number of Firms	Percentage of Total	Number of Firms	Percentage of Total
Under $10	77	6.1%	105	7.4%	283	18.0%	219	14.5%	604	35.6%	487	28.1%
$10–$19⅞	282	22.3	350	24.8	561	35.7	448	29.6	589	34.7	704	40.7
$20–$29⅞	327	25.8	355	25.2	457	29.0	384	25.3	283	16.7	51	2.9
$30–$39⅞	251	19.9	241	17.0	163	10.4	238	15.7	111	6.6	258	14.9
$40–$49⅞	139	10.9	173	12.3	64	4.1	112	7.4	56	3.3	102	5.9
$50–59⅞	73	5.8	71	5.1	22	1.4	56	3.7	26	1.5	67	3.9
$60–99⅞	102	8.0	91	6.5	18	1.1	50	3.3	21	1.2	52	3.0
$100 and over	14	1.2	25	1.7	4	0.3	8	0.5	7	0.4	11	0.6
Total	1265	100.0%	1411	100.0%	1572	100.0%	1515	100.0%	1697	100.0%	1732	100.0%
Closing value of Dow Jones Industrial Average	808.74		910.37		770.96		1211.57		2633.66		3834.44	

By reducing the share price to a more popular trading range, a stock split—and to a lesser degree a stock dividend—may increase trading activity in a stock and thus improve its liquidity. By increasing the number of shares outstanding (and increasing the volume of trading activity), a stock split—and to a lesser degree a stock dividend—may broaden the ownership of a firm's shares. However, the evidence on both points is not conclusive.

Stock Dividend versus Cash Dividend

Firms sometimes declare a stock dividend instead of a cash dividend to conserve cash and yet convey information. Do you think investors miss the significance of the switch? When a firm substitutes a stock dividend for a cash dividend because of financial difficulty, investors will probably view this as negative rather than positive information.[5] Also, a stock dividend is more expensive administratively than a cash dividend.

Self-Check Questions

1. What is a stock dividend, and what is a stock split? How do they differ?
2. Do you think investors consider stock dividends and cash dividends perfect substitutes? Why, or why not?
3. How does a stock dividend work?
4. What is the value to shareholders of a stock dividend or a stock split?

18.7 REPURCHASING COMMON STOCK

Can a corporation increase shareholder wealth by reacquiring shares? This is a controversial subject. In Chapter 17, we showed that in a perfect capital market environment, shareholders are indifferent not only between dividend payout and retention but also between a dividend distribution and a share repurchase program. We also noted that shareholder wealth may be affected by the way a firm implements a share repurchase program.

Factors Affecting the Share Repurchase Decision

A firm should weigh several important factors before deciding on a share repurchase program.

TAX ADVANTAGE TO REPURCHASING SHARES FROM INDIVIDUALS   As we said in Chapter 17, there is a tax asymmetry between dividend and capital gains income. It causes individual investors to favor capital gains over dividends but causes corporate shareholders to have the opposite preference. This difference is the basis for the tax differential view of dividend policy. Because of the tax asymmetries, taxable individual shareholders generally have a reduced tax liability, and hence realize greater wealth, when the firm repurchases shares rather than pays a cash dividend. Thus if the shareholders are mostly individuals, there will be a net tax advantage to repurchasing shares.

REACTION OF INVESTORS   The effect of a share repurchase program on a firm's share price depends chiefly on two factors: (1) how investors react to the information that the firm intends to repurchase shares and (2) how execution of the share repurchase program affects the

---

[5] A series of small stock dividends may also distort downward a firm's perceived growth in earnings per share. Securities analysts usually adjust earnings-per-share comparisons for stock splits and large stock dividends but may fail to adjust for small stock dividends.

market value of the repurchaser's stock. Concerning the second point, it is important to note that Securities and Exchange Commission rules governing share repurchase programs are intended to minimize the market impact of such programs.

The reaction of investors to the announcement of a share repurchase program is influenced by the firm's public statements about the program and by the method adopted to effect the share repurchase. When a firm has a valid business purpose for undertaking a repurchase program, announcing this purpose increases the likelihood that the stock market will react favorably. In addition (as we noted in Chapter 17), tender offers generally have a more significant and lasting impact on shareholder wealth than open-market repurchase programs.

A repurchase announcement might also signal that the firm lacks attractive investment opportunities. If such a reduction has not yet been reflected in the share price, then the share price would probably fall. This would probably be the case if a so-called growth stock firm announced a large repurchase program and said simply that it thought purchasing its stock represented a "good investment." However, the firm might avoid this negative reaction by demonstrating a purpose for the program that the investment community would find acceptable—perhaps repurchasing shares to have them available upon the conversion of securities.

Among the positive signals, a share repurchase might demonstrate management's confidence in the future. Suppose significant improvements in profitability followed previous stock repurchases by the firm. In that case, we might expect an increase in the share price when the repurchase is announced, unless there are other negating factors. Liquidity is another factor. Suppose analysts believe that institutional holders of the firm's stock want to sell but are unwilling to accept the discount necessary to liquidate a major position. The announcement of a tender offer would signify additional liquidity to help facilitate the sale of large blocks. That might help eliminate a portion of the "overhang" from the market.

A careful review of recent securities analysts' reports on a firm will provide some clue to how the investment community might react to the announcement of a repurchase program. For example, if people generally believe a firm has substantial excess liquid assets, the announcement is less likely to elicit a negative reaction than would otherwise be the case. This remains true even if the firm is regarded as a "growth stock." In any case, it is important for a firm to explain its rationale to minimize the risk of an adverse reaction.

POSSIBLE IMPACT ON DEBT RATINGS Most stock repurchase programs do not affect the firm's credit statistics. However, a large repurchase program might have an adverse effect if the firm's debt rating is already in jeopardy. Suppose a firm is already on S&P's Credit Watch List for a possible downgrading. Then the leverage increase from a large share repurchase would increase the chance of a rating downgrade.

EFFECT ON ACCOUNTING FOR ACQUISITIONS A repurchase program might prevent a firm from accounting for an acquisition on a *pooling-of-interests basis*. (The pooling-of-interests and purchase methods of accounting for acquisitions will be discussed in Chapter 28.) Not being able to use pooling-of-interests accounting reduces the firm's accounting flexibility. However, the difference affects only the financial statements. The operating characteristics and tax position of the combined firms are not affected. Accordingly, the choice of accounting method should not affect the stock price of the combined entity. Accounting considerations are probably less important than firms generally believe.

Implementing a Share Repurchase Program

Once a firm decides to undertake a share repurchase program, it must choose a method of doing so. There are five basic methods of share repurchase: open-market purchases, cash tender offers, transferable put rights, privately negotiated block purchases, and exchange offers. We will discuss each in turn.

OPEN-MARKET PURCHASES   A firm can repurchase shares of its common stock in market transactions at current market prices. An *open-market repurchase program* averages the firm's repurchase prices during the repurchase period. More than 90% of the shares repurchased in the United States are bought in open-market purchases. Firms typically use such programs to satisfy their needs for shares—for example, for stock option and other employee benefit programs and to have them available upon conversion of convertible securities. Open-market repurchases are subject to SEC regulations governing the timing, price, volume, and coordination of share purchases. These rules are designed to minimize the impact of the share repurchase program on the firm's share price.

CASH TENDER OFFERS   The offer can be either an offer to purchase a stated number of shares at a fixed price or a Dutch auction. To repurchase a relatively large number of its shares quickly, a firm can announce a *fixed-price tender offer*. It specifies the number of shares it seeks and the price it is willing to pay. Such an offer has the advantage of giving all shareholders an equal opportunity to sell their shares back to the firm. However, transaction costs for tender offers are generally higher than for open-market repurchase programs (primarily due to the premium paid to induce tendering). At the same time, probably because of the premium, tender offers are generally a more positive signal than open-market repurchase programs.

The **Dutch auction tender offer** is a variation that gives a firm greater flexibility in determining the price at which it repurchases the shares. A Dutch auction "reverses" the tender process. Shareholders can offer to sell shares at prices within a specified range.

EXAMPLE

Holiday Inns, Inc.'s Dutch Auction Tender Offer

Holiday Inns, Inc. used a Dutch auction tender offer to buy up to 8 million shares. Table 18-7 shows the details: A minimum of 2.5 million and a maximum of 8 million shares at a minimum price of $46 and a maximum price of $49. Shareholders specified the minimum price (within the range) they were willing to accept. If fewer than 2.5 million shares were tendered (offered to sell back), the firm would pay $49 per share. Otherwise, the firm would pay a price within the specified range and buy all shares tendered at that or a lower price (up to the stated maximum).

Holiday Inns purchased all of the 6.3 million shares that were tendered at $49 per share. Note that the Dutch auction provides the chance that the firm might get the shares at a price lower than the maximum it is willing to pay. ■

There are two important considerations with a tender offer: (1) how to set the **tender offer premium** and (2) whether to use a soliciting dealer or group of dealers. The tender offer premium is the amount offered above the current market price. In general, the premium should be just large enough to attract the desired number of shares. In most cases, the tender offer premium is between 10% and 25%. A smaller premium (perhaps 5% or less) is possible if a block[6] holder wants to sell shares anyway. On the other hand, a larger premium (perhaps 20% or greater) would normally be needed for a low-trading-volume, widely held stock.

On the second question, it is usually beneficial to use dealers. Without their solicitation efforts, a larger tender premium would normally be required.

---

[6] A *block* is generally defined in terms of some minimum number of shares or some minimum market value. The NYSE defines a block (of shares sold in a single transaction) as consisting of the lesser of (a) 10,000 (or more) shares or (b) shares (regardless of the number) with a market value of $200,000 or more.

TABLE 18-7
**Holiday Inns, Inc.'s
tender offer for up to
8 million shares of its
common stock.**

Length of tender period	17 days
Tender method	Dutch auction
Purpose for the offer	The firm's board believes the firm's stock represents an ''attractive investment.''
Number of shares sought	
Maximum:	8,000,000 (The firm reserved the right to increase the maximum to 10,000,000 shares.)
Minimum:	2,500,000
Number of shares outstanding	34,786,931
Percentage of shares sought	
Maximum:	23.0% (up to 28.7% if the maximum is increased)
Minimum:	7.2
Pre-tender closing share price	$44.00
Tender offer price	
Maximum:	$49.00
Minimum:	46.00
Tender offer premium	
Maximum:	11.4%
Minimum:	4.5
Dollar value of tender	
At maximum price:	$392 million ($490 million if maximum increased)
At minimum price:	368 million ($460 million if maximum increased)
Number of shares tendered	6,300,000
% of outstanding tendered	18.1%
Success ratio	78.8%
Source of funds	$500 million bank credit agreement
Expenses	
Dealer/manager fee:	$0.15 per share purchased
Soliciting dealer fee:	None

TRANSFERABLE PUT RIGHTS   As explained in Chapter 17, a fixed-price tender offer conveys to shareholders nondetachable put options. Shareholders can get the value of their options only by tendering shares to the firm, which might create a tax liability. Instead, a firm can issue *transferable put rights* to its shareholders. Those who do not want to sell shares can sell the put rights. Put rights are thus more "tax efficient" than a fixed-price tender offer. Also, there is no risk of oversubscription, because the number of puts issued limits the number of shares that shareholders can tender.

PRIVATELY NEGOTIATED BLOCK PURCHASES   Privately negotiated block purchases are most often made in connection with, rather than as a substitute for, an open-market purchase program. Large blocks can often be purchased for less than the current market price, particularly when the transaction is initiated by the seller. Firms also frequently purchase large blocks, often at substantial premiums, from contentious or potentially threatening minority shareholders. As noted in Chapter 17, there are agency problems associated with such repurchases, so it is not clear that the repurchases are always in the *collective* shareholders' best interest.[7]

EXCHANGE OFFER   Instead of offering cash to repurchase shares, a firm might offer bonds or preferred stock in an **exchange offer**. One problem with an exchange offer is the difference in liquidity of the two securities. A larger premium might be necessary to compensate

---

[7] See Chapter 9 for a discussion of agency problems.

for the lower liquidity of the replacement security. Probably for this reason, most common stock repurchase programs involve cash purchases.

Table 18-8 summarizes the advantages and disadvantages of the five repurchase methods. Regardless of the method chosen, a publicly traded firm must comply with SEC regulations. These involve certain disclosure requirements and restrictions on a firm's simultaneously engaging in both a share repurchase program and a sale or other distribution of its common stock or of securities that are convertible into its common stock.

Self-Check Questions

1. Name four factors that can affect the share repurchase decision. How important is each?
2. If a firm's shareholders are all individuals, will tax considerations favor dividends or share repurchases? What if all the shareholders are corporations?
3. Why is it important for a firm to explain its rationale for a share repurchase program?
4. Describe five methods of repurchasing shares.
5. Which usually conveys a more favorable signal, announcing an open-market purchase program or announcing a tender offer?

18.8 WHEN IN DOUBT . . .

Let's review what we know and what we do not know about dividend policy. We know that in a perfect capital market environment, dividend policy does not matter. In such an environment, each shareholder could costlessly tailor the firm's dividend policy to suit her own preferences, so dividend policy would not affect value.

But the world is not perfect. Information is costly to gather, and there are taxes, transaction costs, and legal and policy restrictions. All of these may cause dividend policy to affect a firm's value. Just how much dividend policy really matters we do not know. Studies have provided evidence that dividend policy matters to at least a modest degree, but they offer no clear guidelines on how a firm can select the *best* dividend policy. Thus, although our understanding of dividend policy has come a long way, we are not ready to celebrate just yet.

Where does this leave us? In practice, the best a firm can do is try to find a reasonable dividend policy, communicate that policy clearly, and then make orderly changes in its dividend as its earnings and cash flow prospects change. What constitutes a "reasonable" dividend policy? The method illustrated in this chapter represents an important application of the Behavioral Principle: When in doubt, look at the dividend policies of comparable firms for guidance.

To return to our dinner analogy in our description of the Behavioral Principle (Chapter 3), the firms in the industry are sitting around the table, and the first course arrives. Some of the guests reach for the small fork, some for one of the larger forks, and some for a spoon (and there always seems to be at least one that reaches for a knife and cuts its dividend). That is, the firms exhibit a range of payout ratios and a variety of dividend policies. You check to see what the majority of guests are doing (what is the average payout ratio?), but you pay most attention to those you think will provide the most reliable guide (because of either their expertise or their similarity to you). You ignore those you decide are not competent and comparable (the poor fellow who is served soup and immediately grabs a fork). Then you select the utensil you decide is most appropriate.

It is important to keep in mind that you are not blindly imitating. The systematic differences across industries (in terms of investment opportunities, tax positions, and business and

ADVANTAGES	DISADVANTAGES

Open-Market Purchases
- No premium over market price
- Can extend over long period, thereby providing long-term support to the market
- Holders who desire liquidity receive cash
- Less market impact than tender offer or exchange offer if program is not completed successfully

- If blocks do not materialize, daily volume limitations make it difficult to complete program quickly
- Risk that market price can appreciate independent of the repurchase program before the program is completed
- Danger that buying can drive up market price, leading to a de facto premium

Private Block Purchases
- Blocks can often be purchased at a discount from market price
- Attracts less attention than other methods

- Success of program dependent on locating blocks (private block purchases are therefore normally used to supplement open-market purchase program)
- May provide less long-term support to the market
- Preferential treatment toward the selling shareholders may become an issue with other shareholders if blocks are purchased at a significant premium

Tender Offer
- Allows repurchase of significant number of shares quickly at a (maximum) price fixed at the outset of the program
- Provides an equal opportunity to all shareholders to sell their shares
- Evidence indicates that tender offers have more positive market impact after repurchase program is completed than open-market purchase program
- More effective than open-market purchase at drawing out "loose" shares
- Provides means of eliminating small holdings
- Holders who desire liquidity receive cash

- Normally requires premium of 10% to 25% over market price (Dutch auction may reduce this)
- Higher transactions costs than open-market purchase program
- Oversubscription or undersubscription can embarrass firm
- Oversubscription may indicate vulnerability to hostile takeover

Transferable Put Rights
- Allows repurchase of significant number of shares quickly at a (maximum) price fixed at the outset of the program
- Reduces agency costs by providing an equal opportunity to all stockholders to sell their shares
- More effective than open-market purchase at drawing out "loose" shares
- Holders who desire liquidity receive cash
- Transferability enables nontendering shareholders to receive value for their rights
- More tax efficient than a tender offer
- No risk of oversubscription
- Relatively low-tax-basis shareholders retain their shares, which will make the firm more costly to a takeover raider

- Higher transaction costs than open-market purchase program and than tender offer (for example, if fees are paid to list the put rights for trading on a stock exchange)
- Put rights taxed as a dividend upon distribution but give rise to a short-term capital loss if they expire worthless; a variety of additional tax consequences that are complex

Exchange Offer
- If preferred stock is offered in the exchange, there is a tax advantage to shareholders who exchange and hold the preferred
- Transaction cost savings to shareholders who exchange and hold

- Higher transaction costs than open-market purchase program
- Shareholders are offered a less liquid security that they may not wish to hold; therefore, an exchange offer may require a larger premium than a tender offer
- Oversubscription or undersubscription can embarrass firm

TABLE 18-8
Summary comparison of share repurchase methods.

other risks) provide a rationale for looking to the dividend policy choices of comparable firms for guidance.

SOLUTION TO MAJOR PHARMACEUTICAL COMPANY'S DIVIDEND PROBLEM

As we noted in the chapter, Major Pharmaceutical Company's treasurer concluded that a payout ratio between 30% and 40% would be appropriate for Major. On the basis of this analysis, she recommended an increase of 24 cents per share per year when Major's board reconsidered the dividend at the upcoming board meeting.

Such an increase exceeded the increases in prior years, but Major's treasurer felt that the larger increase was appropriate in view of Major's improved earnings prospects. After reading a number of securities reports prepared by analysts who follow Major, the treasurer also concluded that the recommended dividend increase was larger than analysts were expecting. And, because Major was also projecting higher-than-expected future earnings, she anticipated that the announcement of the dividend increase would probably have a favorable impact on Major's share price. And, in fact, it did.

SUMMARY

We outlined and illustrated a set of dividend policy guidelines. A firm should determine its expected residual earnings and set its dividend at a level consistent with its financial policies and its earnings and cash flow prospects. It can look at the payout ratios of comparable firms, and its expected residual earnings, to determine an appropriate long-term target payout ratio. Firms often supplement regular dividend payments with special dividends during high-earning periods to stabilize the payout ratio.

Five basic methods are available for repurchasing shares: open-market purchases, cash tender offers, transferable put rights, privately negotiated block purchases, and exchange offers. Any of the first four could be used by a firm that wanted to distribute excess cash. A firm that wanted to eliminate small shareholdings would use the tender offer method. A firm that wanted to buy a relatively large percentage of its outstanding shares would generally use either the tender offer or the put rights method. Probably because of their higher cost, tender offers generally have a more positive impact on a firm's value than open-market repurchase programs.

In the final analysis, striving for *the* optimal dividend policy and *the* optimal dividend at any particular time is probably not cost-effective, even if it were possible. Therefore, firms should—and do in practice—try to maintain a stable dividend policy by

1. Paying at least some dividends on a regular basis once the firm is well established
2. Having a relatively consistent target payout ratio
3. Avoiding a reduction in an established dividend
4. Using the additional tools of special dividends and/or share repurchases to shareholder advantage whenever possible
5. Making any deliberate changes in a careful and orderly way

As with many other aspects of financial policy, because of capital market efficiency, "satisficing" rather than "optimizing" in the near term often provides the best policy over the longer term when all things—including time and effort—are considered.

DECISION SUMMARY

How should a firm manage its dividend policy? Here are some useful guidelines:

- Determine how much cash is available for distribution.

- Decide how best to distribute the cash, keeping in mind tax and transaction cost considerations in light of the shareholder makeup.

- Keep in mind the information content of any method of distribution. A large dividend increase that the firm could not sustain would send a false signal to the market. A large dividend increase followed by a dividend reduction might harm the firm's credibility. Consequently, if the firm does not believe it can sustain the higher regular cash dividend, it should repurchase shares or make a special dividend.

- Evaluate the costs of each type of distribution. Share repurchase is generally more expensive than cash dividends, particularly if the firm pays a tender offer premium.

- If management believes the firm's shares are undervalued and wants to signal this belief, a tender offer is likely to be superior to a cash dividend.

- Note that a share repurchase (or a large special dividend) can have a negative impact on a firm's share price if it was previously believed that the firm had superior growth prospects. Firms may therefore be tempted to retain most of the excess cash and pay it out over time through increases in the regular dividend. However, this policy will prove harmful to shareholders if (1) they could have invested the funds more profitably themselves or (2) it is perceived that the cash buildup signals a decline in investment opportunities.

- Be aware that most common stock investors, particularly individuals, would prefer regular dividend payments over irregular cash distributions. There are at least three reasons for this. First, regular dividend payments aid individual financial planning by the shareowner, are paid on a regular basis, and are reduced or suspended only under adverse conditions. Second, certain institutions are limited by legal or policy constraints to stocks that pay regular dividends. For example, many university endowments are subject to rules that do not permit the use of capital gains to cover operating expenses. Third, the receipt of dividend income is a passive means of providing liquidity to a shareholder without the costs and inconvenience associated with selling shares to create a "homemade dividend."

- Consider a share repurchase program for eliminating small shareholdings.

KEY TERMS

extra or special dividends...569	ex-dividend date...570	Dutch auction tender offer...582
record date...570	stock dividends...576	tender offer premium...582
payment date...570	stock split...577	exchange offer...583
shareholder of record...570		

EXERCISES

PROBLEM SET A

A1. Consider the following four dates connected with a dividend: April 10, April 24, April 27, and May 5. Which is the ex-dividend date, which the record date, which the payment date, and which the declaration date?

A2. Among the following alternatives, which is the most common pattern of dividend policy? (a) A constant payout ratio where dividend payments vary with earnings. (b) A stable payment rate per share where dividend payments are more stable than earnings. (c) Dividend payments that vary each year according to the firm's capital investment opportunities. (d) A stable payment rate per share with a once-a-year "extra payment" based on the firm's earnings so that dividend payments are more stable than earnings.

A3. What is a record date for a dividend payment?

A4. Briefly describe our three-step approach to the dividend decision.

A5. True or False: Typically, a firm has a target payout ratio that it aims for over time, but the payout ratio for any particular quarter can be substantially different from this target.

A6. What is the difference between a stock dividend and a stock split? What conditions make one more likely to be used than the other?

A7. What are the major advantages of a share repurchase over a cash dividend?

A8. Why might a large share repurchase adversely affect a firm's debt rating?

A9. True or False: To pay a cash dividend, it is only necessary for the firm to have sufficient retained earnings to afford the dividend payment. If the statement is false, cite two factors that could preclude a firm from paying a dividend.

A10. True or False: Dividends are normally paid quarterly, whereas bond interest payments are normally made semiannually.

A11. With respect to a share repurchase program, describe the principal differences between an open-market purchase program and a tender offer.

A12. Describe how a Dutch auction tender offer works and how it differs from a fixed-price tender offer.

A13. What are the principal advantages of the transferable put rights method of share repurchase relative to the fixed-price tender offer method?

PROBLEM SET B

B1. The current share price of Milt's Multi-Media Mart is $25. M-Mart expects to earn $5.00 per share. It will pay a dividend of $2.00 per share next year. Investors expect a 10% dividend growth rate forever into the future. All transactions take place in a perfect capital market.

a. What return on the stock are investors expecting?

b. Suppose M-Mart announces that it is going to switch to a 100% payout policy. It will issue common stock whenever necessary to finance capital expenditures. What will happen to M-Mart's share price? Explain.

B2. Describe conditions under which a firm might find it advantageous to substitute a stock dividend for an increase in its cash dividend.

B3. Illustrate how a firm's repurchasing its own shares can be viewed as equivalent to the firm's paying a cash dividend. Ignore taxes and assume a perfect capital market environment.

B4. Illustrate how a firm's repurchasing its own shares will increase the firm's leverage. Ignore taxes and assume a perfect capital market environment.

B5. A firm has 20 million common shares outstanding. It currently pays out $1.50 per share per year in cash dividends on its common stock. Historically, its payout ratio has ranged from 30% to 35%. Over the next 5 years it expects the following earnings and discretionary cash flow:

	1	2	3	4	5	Thereafter
Earnings	100	125	150	120	140	150+ per year
Discretionary cash flow	50	70	60	20	15	50+ per year

a. Over the 5-year period, what is the maximum overall payout ratio the firm could achieve without triggering a securities issue?

b. Recommend a reasonable dividend policy for paying out discretionary cash flow in years 1 through 5.

B6. Aluminum Co. of America recently announced a new dividend policy. The firm said it would pay a base cash dividend of 40 cents per common share each quarter. In addition, the firm said it would pay 30% of any excess in annual earnings per share above $6.00 as an extra year-end dividend.

a. If Alcoa earns $7.50 per share in 1997, what percentage of its 1997 earnings will it pay out as cash dividends under the new policy?

b. For what types of firms would Alcoa's new dividend policy be appropriate? Explain.

B7. Gotham Manufacturing Corporation (GMC) pays quarterly cash dividends on its common stock at an annual rate of $1.00 per share. GMC's cost of common equity capital is 12% APR, compounded quarterly.

a. Calculate GMC's APY cost of common equity.

b. Suppose GMC's stockholders expect the firm to maintain the same dollar dividend forever. What should be the value of a share of GMC?

c. Suppose GMC changes its dividend policy so as to pay cash dividends at annual intervals, and the firm's stockholders expect it to pay $1.00 per share forever. What should be the value of a share of GMC? If your answer is different from what you computed in part b, why is it different and should this difference exist?

d. Suppose GMC projects earnings per share of $3.00 this year and of $2.70, $3.30, $3.90, and $3.60 over the next four years, respectively. It believes it can maintain a long-term payout ratio of 1/3. Which of the following dividend patterns would you recommend?

    1. $1.00, $1.00, $1.00, $1.30, $1.20

    2. $1.00, $0.90, $1.10, $1.30, $1.20

    3. $1.00, $1.00, $1.10, $1.20, $1.20

    4. $1.00, $0.90, $1.20, $1.20, $1.20

B8. Briefly describe a typical life cycle of dividend policy for a firm from its creation to its demise. (Penn Central Railroad might be considered typical of this pattern.)

B9. In October 1987, Allegis Corporation (now UAL Corporation) announced that it expected to declare a special dividend of not less than $50 per share to be paid out of the after-tax proceeds from the sale of its Hilton International and Westin Hotels & Resorts hotel subsidiaries and its Hertz Corporation car rental subsidiary. Its quarterly common dividend at the time was $0.25 per share.

a. What does the special dividend announcement tell you about Allegis Corporation's ability to reinvest profitably the after-tax proceeds from the sale of its subsidiaries?

b. Why do you suppose Allegis Corporation planned to pay a special dividend rather than increasing the regular dividend?

c. Allegis Corporation eventually used the after-tax proceeds to repurchase approximately $3 billion worth of its common stock. It acted at the behest of at least one large shareholder. What does the large shareholder's preference for a share repurchase rather than a special dividend suggest about that shareholder's tax position?

B10. Suppose a firm has $10 million available for distribution to its common stockholders. It has 5 million shares outstanding, which are worth $20 each.

a. How large a special dividend could the firm afford to pay? What would happen to its share price if it paid this dividend?

b. How many shares could the firm afford to purchase if it repurchases shares at the current market price instead of paying a special dividend?

c. Suppose the firm would earn $2.00 per share if it did not distribute the $10 million cash. How would the two methods of cash distribution in parts a and b affect earnings per share? How would an efficient market react to the change in EPS?

d. Show that in a perfect capital market, both methods of cash distribution leave shareholder wealth unchanged. What does this tell you about the dividend versus repurchase decision in a perfect capital market?

B11. Look again at Problem B10. Suppose that all shareholders must pay tax on dividend income at the rate of 50% and on capital gains at the rate of 25%. All shareholders have a tax basis (cost) of $10 per share.

a. Calculate the impact on shareholder wealth of the special dividend and the share repurchase, assuming that if there were no share repurchase, shareholders would continue to hold their shares forever.

b. Calculate the impact on shareholder wealth of the two cash distribution methods, assuming that if there were no share repurchase, shareholders would hold their shares for exactly 5 years. Assume a required after-tax return on the stock of 12% per year for the 5-year period.

c. How do tax considerations affect the decision to repurchase or pay a special dividend?

B12. Mega Electric Company has been denied its request for an electricity rate increase. Mega has continued to pay $2 per share per year in cash dividends in anticipation of receiving permission to increase electric rates. As a result of the denial, Mega's payout ratio will go over 100% within 12 months unless something is done quickly.

a. Mega Electric's chairman asks you, as the utility's chief financial officer, to study the advisability of paying a $1 cash dividend and a $1 common stock dividend in order to "preserve the dividend and not send a negative signal to the market." How would you respond to the chairman?

b. Mega Electric's president comes to you with a "better idea." He suggests paying a $1 cash dividend and distributing the "rest" of the dividend as $1 face amount of a new 12% debenture. (Assume the 12% interest rate would make the debenture worth its par value.) How would you respond to the president?

B13. When a firm repurchases shares of its common stock from a takeover raider, the payment for the shares is referred to as greenmail. The common stock of Trans-World-Dilemma (TWD) has a current price of $30 per share. Suppose TWD has 10 million shares outstanding. It buys back 1 million shares from Karl I. Can, paying Karl $35 per share for the block of shares.

a. What should be the firm's share price immediately following the buyback?

b. How has the payment of greenmail affected the holders of the other 9 million shares?

B14. Easy Mark, Inc. has a contentious minority shareholder who owns 10% of the firm's 50 million outstanding shares. Easy Mark's share price is $12 per share, but the minority shareholder wants the firm to repurchase her shares for $15 each. Assume all transactions take place in a perfect capital market (including no taxes).

a. How would such a repurchase affect the minority shareholder's wealth?

b. How would such a repurchase affect Easy Mark's share price?

c. How would such a repurchase affect the wealth of Easy Mark's other shareholders?

d. What do you conclude regarding the impact of greenmail on shareholder wealth?

B15. Why might transaction costs cause a firm to find it advantageous to repurchase small shareholdings that are outstanding?

B16. Can it *ever* happen that a person owns shares of stock but does not receive the same cash dividend per share paid to other shareholders or that a person no longer owns shares of stock but does receive a cash dividend?

B17. Shore Electronics Corporation's common stock is selling for $44 per share. Its common stockholders' equity is as follows:

Paid-in capital ($4 par value; 5,000,000 shares)	$ 20,000,000
Capital contributed in excess of par value	30,000,000
Retained earnings	50,000,000
Common stockholders' equity	$100,000,000

a. Show the impact of a 50% stock dividend.

b. Show the impact of a 3-for-2 stock split.

c. Describe how the stock market would react to each event. How would you explain this difference in reaction?

B18. In November 1994, Chrysler Corporation faced pressure from billionaire investor Kirk Kerkorian. Kerkorian urged Chrysler's board to take steps to build shareholder value, including increasing the dividend and repurchasing stock.

a. Kerkorian was concerned that Chrysler had excess cash. If it did, how would you expect the market to react to a dividend increase?

b. Chrysler's board announced a $1 billion share repurchase program. Would you recommend an open-market purchase program or a tender offer?

c. Why might both a dividend increase and a share repurchase make sense from the standpoint of investor taxes?

B19. The Dutch auction repurchase method has been criticized because it "lets the shareholders determine the repurchase price." Criticize this argument.

B20. Look again at Major Pharmaceutical's dividend decision. There is a third dividend policy alternative to consider. Call it alternative C. It calls for a dividend per share of $1.64 in 1997, $1.84 in 1998, $2.12 in 1999, $2.56 in 2000, and $3.34 in 2001.

a. Verify that the aggregate dividend requirements for 1997–2001 are $115.0 million.

b. Calculate the dividend per share, payout ratio, residual funds, dividend requirements, and surplus (deficit) for each year 1997–2001.

c. Compare alternative C to alternatives A and B.

d. What dividend action would you recommend to Major Pharmaceutical?

PROBLEM SET C

C1. Suppose a firm is facing the possibility of a necessary dividend cut because of poor economic conditions. Suppose further that you are a member of the firm's board of directors. How would you respond to the argument of another board member that the firm should publicly deny the possibility of such a cut until the board has decided that the cut is an unavoidable necessity? The other member's argument is that unless the firm denies the possibility of a dividend cut, its stock price will drop. If the cut can be avoided, the drop will have been unnecessary, and the firm's stockholders will have suffered needlessly.

C2. Suppose two firms, which you perceive to be equivalent, announce share repurchase programs. Both say the reason for the program is that the firm's stock is undervalued. Both stocks are selling in the capital market for $30 per share. Firm A's program is a tender offer at $33 per share. Firm B's program is an equivalent dollar amount of repurchase, but it will be accomplished over the next 6 months through open-market purchases.

a. Which firm do you believe is sending the more credible signal?

b. Suppose you have private information that the two firms have been, and will be in the future, identical in every aspect (except for their repurchase programs). Suppose further that you are contemplating the purchase of shares in one or the other firm and would expect to own those shares for at least 3 years. During that time, all investors will come to know that the two firms are indeed identical. Which firm's shares should you buy? Why?

C3. Belmar Iron & Steel currently pays an annual dividend of $4 per share on its common stock. Because of a shift in business strategy, it would like to eliminate the dividend entirely. The firm is concerned about adverse shareholder reaction.

a. Suggest how the firm could cushion the impact of the dividend elimination on an income-oriented class of investors that holds in the aggregate approximately 10% of the firm's common stock.

b. How would you go about implementing your solution?

Dhillon, Upinder S., and Herb Johnson. "The Effect of Dividend Changes on Stock and Bond Prices," *Journal of Finance,* 1994, 49(1):281–289.

Finnerty, John D. "The Behavior of Electric Utility Common Stock Prices Near the Ex-Dividend Date," *Financial Management*, 1981, 10(4):59–69.

Gay, Gerald D., Jayant R. Kale, and Thomas H. Noe. "Share Repurchases Mechanisms: A Comparative Analysis of Efficacy, Shareholder Wealth, and Corporate Control Effects," *Financial Management*, 1991, 20(1):44–59.

Grinblatt, Mark S., Ronald W. Masulis, and Sheridan Titman. "The Valuation Effects of Stock Splits and Stock Dividends," *Journal of Financial Economics*, 1984, 13(4):461–490.

John, Kose, and Larry H. P. Lang. "Insider Trading Dividend Announcements: Theory and Evidence," *Journal of Finance*, 1991, 46(4):1361–1390.

Lamoureux, Christopher G., and Percy Poon. "The Market Reaction to Stock Splits," *Journal of Finance*, 1987, 42(5):1347–1370.

Loderer, Claudio F., and David C. Mauer. "Corporate Dividends and Seasoned Equity Issues: An Empirical Investigation," *Journal of Finance*, 1992, 47(1):201–226.

McNichols, Maureen, and Ajay David. "Stock Dividends, Stock Splits and Signaling," *Journal of Finance*, 1990, 45(3):857–880.

Millar, James A., and Bruce D. Fielitz. "Stock-Split and Stock Dividend Decisions," *Financial Management*, 1973, 2(4):35–45.

Mohanty, Sunil K. "Returns from Hedged Dividend Capture Programs and Dutch Auction Rate Preferred Stock," *Financial Management*, 1994, 23(1):11–13.

Robin, Ashok J. "The Impact of the 1986 Tax Reform Act on Ex-Dividend Day Returns," *Financial Management*, 1991, 20(1):60–70.

Spudeck, Raymond E., and R. Charles Moyer. "Reverse Splits and Shareholder Wealth: The Impact of Commissions," *Financial Management*, 1985, 14(4):52–56.

Sterk, William Edward. "Option Pricing: Dividends and the In- and Out-of-the-Money Bias," *Financial Management*, 1983, 12(4):47–53.

Venkatesh, P. C. "Trading Costs and Ex-Day Behavior: An Examination of Primes and Stocks," *Financial Management*, 1991, 20(3):84–95.

Wansley, James W., William R. Lane, and Salil Sarkar. "Managements' View on Share Repurchase and Tender Offer Premiums," *Financial Management*, 1989, 18(3):97–110.

Woolridge, J. Randall, and Donald R. Chambers. "Reverse Splits and Shareholder Wealth," *Financial Management*, 1983, 12(3):5–15.

Zivney, Terry L., and Michael J. Alderson. "Hedged Dividend Capture with Stock Index Options," *Financial Management*, 1986, 15(2):5–12.

Part V

MANAGING THE FIRM

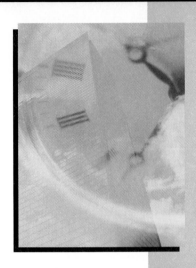

In Part V of the book, we will apply the principles of corporate financial management to the problems of managing a firm. Many of the problems we'll examine involve the day-to-day operation of the firm. Making correct management decisions is critical to maximizing stockholder wealth.

Chapter 19 deals with cash and working capital management. Working capital management refers to managing the firm's short-term assets and liabilities. These are assets and liabilities that the firm expects to receive and pay, respectively, in cash within a year. Managing them properly is important because it affects the firm's ability to meet its obligations as they come due.

Chapter 20 analyzes economic decisions about accounts receivable and inventories. A firm invests in both along with its investments in fixed assets. We'll show you how a firm can make sure that its investments in receivables and inventories are profitable.

Chapter 21 covers treasury management, which includes working capital management, pension fund management, investor and stockholder relations, risk management, and strategic or financial planning. In practice, these activities account for a large percentage of a financial manager's time. Learning how to manage these problems efficiently can make a financial manager's job a lot easier.

Finally, Chapter 22 deals with financial planning, the problems of coordinating the firm's various financial activities. Careful planning can be critical; a firm must be prepared to deal with problems as it meets them. A firm that doesn't plan for its future might find that it doesn't have one!

CASH AND WORKING CAPITAL MANAGEMENT

OBJECTIVES

After studying this chapter, you should be able to

1. Explain the composition of a firm's working capital accounts and calculate the cash conversion cycle.

2. Cite the motives for holding cash and marketable securities.

3. Describe and apply some of the popular cash management models.

4. Identify float and the methods that firms use to reduce float costs.

5. Describe the mechanics of short-term borrowing through accounts payable, short-term bank loans, and commercial paper.

6. Estimate the costs of the primary sources of short-term funds.

7. Describe the growing applications of electronic data interchange (EDI).

Most people use a checking account as a "collecting place" for their money between inflows and outflows. The account acts like a pool. It is useful because you can add money in any amount, say $139.24, and conveniently take it out in completely different amounts, say $22.39 and $41.78. The catch is that you cannot take out more than what is in the pool, so you have to manage the pool to make sure there is enough for the outflows. But you can arrange to have money added automatically, whenever you run short, by using "check-bouncing protection." Whenever money is added to your account to cover a check, you effectively take out a loan.

Many people also use a credit card. They can charge things and then get one bill for all their recent charges. They can pay the bill off entirely, or they may be able to pay only part of it, thereby effectively taking out a loan.

Checking accounts, check-bouncing protection, and credit cards are just a few of the many tools available for managing your money.[1] Firms use similar tools to manage their money. For example, firms create check-bouncing protection by establishing a credit line.

Suppose you have a choice. Which loan is cheaper, check-bouncing protection or credit card debt? The answer is to take the one with the lowest after-tax APY. In this chapter, we will tell you how a firm can answer such questions.

Firms make short-term financial decisions just about every day. Where should we borrow? Where should we invest our cash? How much liquidity should we have? The options come rapidly. Investment bankers want you to sell commercial paper, a bank wants to lend you money, and a supplier is willing to offer you trade credit. Which one is offering the best deal? Another bank wants you to purchase its lockbox services. Should you do it? After much complaining, your largest customer is threatening to stop doing business with you unless you immediately convert your ordering and invoicing systems over to EDI (electronic data interchange). How would that affect your costs and cash flow?

Working capital decisions are fast-paced because they reflect a firm's day-to-day operations. The principles of finance, along with hard work and imagination, provide guidance for sound, value-maximizing decisions.

---

[1]But if you're like most of us, even with all these tools it is a constant challenge to "balance" your checkbook.

WORKING CAPITAL MANAGEMENT AND THE PRINCIPLES OF FINANCE

◆ *Time Value of Money*: Compare the benefits and costs of alternative uses and sources of money by using APYs.

◆ *Incremental Benefits*: Calculate the incremental after-tax cash flows connected with a decision.

◆ *Risk-Return Trade-Off*: Recognize that risk-return trade-off decisions are part of a firm's choice of how to finance working capital.

◆ *Options*: Recognize the value of hidden options in a situation, such as the option to refinance long-term debt.

◆ *Capital Market Efficiency*: Periodically evaluate routine capital market alternatives to make sure they continue to be competitive. Also, be careful to distinguish between routine transactions made in an efficient capital market and unique transactions that are not subjected to such intense competition. For example, decisions to grant credit or to use a supplier are essentially private, so the prices and risks should be checked against those in a competitive marketplace.

◆ *Behavioral*: Use common industry practices as a good starting place for operating efficiently.

◆ *Comparative Advantage*: Consider subcontracting business activities to outside vendors if they can provide the services more cheaply and competently.

◆ *Two-Sided Transactions*: Do not act unethically to gain short-term profit at the expense of a supplier or a customer, because such behavior can damage or even destroy a profitable long-term relationship.

19.1 WORKING CAPITAL MANAGEMENT

Much of a financial manager's time is devoted to **working capital management**. Recall that a firm's working capital consists of its current assets minus current liabilities. *Current* refers to a horizon of a year or less. Working capital management includes all aspects of the administration of current assets and liabilities.

The goal of financial decisions is to maximize shareholder wealth, avoiding negative- and seeking positive-NPV decisions. Some methods of making working capital decisions in practice do not use the principles of finance. Rather, they use imprecise rules of thumb as approximations. Working capital decisions can and should be made in such a way as to maximize shareholder wealth.

Working capital management consists of choosing the levels of cash, marketable securities, receivables, and inventories, as well as the level and mix of types of short-term financing. Working capital management includes several basic business relationships.

- Sales impact. A firm must choose its levels of receivables and inventories. Granting easy credit and keeping high inventories may help boost sales and fill orders quickly, but these practices also raise costs.

- Liquidity. A firm must choose its levels of cash and marketable securities, taking into account needed liquidity and any required compensating balances.

	PERCENTAGE OF TOTAL ASSETS					DOLLARS INVESTED IN 1994
	1960	**1970**	**1980**	**1990**	**1994**	
Current Assets						
Cash	6.0%	4.3%	2.8%	2.4%	2.7%	$ 83.0 billion
Marketable securities	4.8	0.7	2.5	2.0	2.6	81.9
Accounts receivable	15.6	17.3	17.0	13.9	13.1	405.5
Inventory	23.6	23.0	19.8	14.3	12.8	391.3
Other current assets	2.3	3.5	2.8	3.4	4.0	124.9
Total current assets	52.3%	48.8%	44.9%	36.0%	35.2%	$1086.6 billion
Current Liabilities						
Notes payable	3.9%	6.3%	5.0%	6.2%	3.8%	$119.8 billion
Accounts payable	7.9	8.5	9.9	7.9	8.0	250.2
Accruals and other current liabilities	9.0	9.9	12.0	11.6	13.1	408.5
Total current liabilities	20.8%	24.7%	26.9%	25.7%	24.9%	$778.5 billion

Source: Quarterly Financial Report for Manufacturing, Mining, and Trade Corporations, U.S. Department of Commerce, various dates.

- Relations with stakeholders. Suppliers and customers are intimately affected by the management of working capital. Customers are concerned with the firm's ability to deliver high-quality products and service in a timely fashion at a competitive price. A firm has similar concerns about its suppliers. A firm's reputation in these dimensions depends mainly on how it manages its short-term assets and obligations.

- Short-term financing mix. A firm must choose its mix of types of short-term financing, as well as its proportions of short- and long-term financing, taking into account its profitability and risk objectives.

Table 19-1 shows the composition of the current assets and current liabilities for all U.S. manufacturing corporations in recent years. Note the sheer size of the investment in short-term assets. Manufacturers' current assets represented 35% of total assets—over $1 trillion. The current assets for other types of firms are similarly large. Also note that the percentage of short-term assets has declined substantially in recent years. Most of this decline has come from more efficient inventory management. Finally, notice that short-term debt of various types (total current liabilities) accounts for roughly 25% of the total financing of the firm.

Philosophies About Financing Working Capital

In its day-to-day operations, a firm must maintain adequate liquidity.[2] At the same time, it wants to operate as efficiently and profitably as possible. Cash is liquid but does not earn a return. Fixed assets are expected to earn a return. They may even have a positive NPV, but they are rarely very liquid. The need for liquidity to pay bills and meet emergencies results in a tension between risk and profitability. We can characterize a firm's philosophy about how it finances working capital, in terms of the risk-return trade-off, as the maturity-matching approach, the conservative approach, or the aggressive approach.

MATURITY-MATCHING APPROACH   In the maturity-matching approach, the firm hedges its risk by matching the maturities of its assets and liabilities (Figure 19-1, panel A). The firm finances seasonal variations in current assets with current liabilities of the same maturity. It finances long-term assets with long-term debt and equity securities. In addition, in most cases there is a permanent component of current assets. Inventories and receivables will

---

[2] Recall that liquidity refers to how quickly and easily assets can be bought or sold without loss of value. Cash is the most liquid asset.

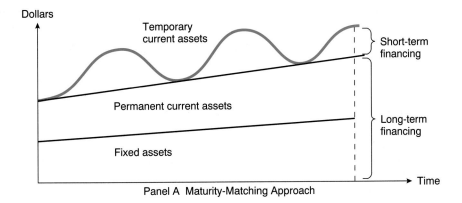

Panel A Maturity-Matching Approach

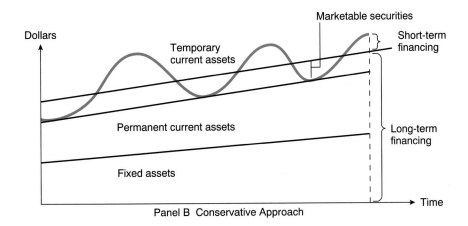

Panel B Conservative Approach

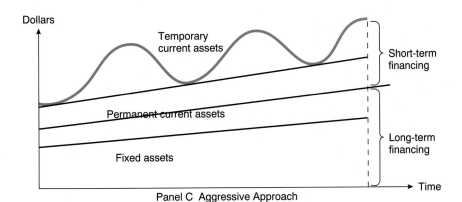

Panel C Aggressive Approach

FIGURE 19-1

Three philosophies of financing working capital.

remain above some minimum level. This permanent component of current assets is also financed with long-term capital. As panel A of Figure 19-1 illustrates, short-term borrowing (including temporary increases in payables as well as bank borrowings, commercial paper, and so on) mirrors the seasonal swings in current assets. Short-term borrowing under this sort of policy would fall to zero at seasonal low spots.

CONSERVATIVE APPROACH   Under the maturity-matching approach, a firm uses short-term financing for its temporary current assets. The firm assumes that funds will always be available. It also gambles that their cost will not rise dramatically. If general economic conditions worsen or if the firm's own circumstances deteriorate, the firm might have trouble getting the money it needs. Another possibility is that funds might be available, but at a much higher cost. To guard against the risks of a credit shutoff or a cost increase, the conservative approach uses more long-term and less short-term financing than the maturity-matching approach.

The conservative approach is shown in panel B of Figure 19-1. Long-term financing is used to finance all of the firm's long-term assets, all of its permanent current assets, and some of its temporary current assets. As you can see in the figure, only when asset needs are high does the firm use any short-term financing. At other times, when asset needs are low and in a trough, the firm actually has more long-term financing than total assets. At these times, the firm invests its excess funds in marketable securities. By financing a portion of its seasonal needs for funds on a long-term basis, the firm builds in a margin of safety.

AGGRESSIVE APPROACH   One problem with the maturity-matching and conservative approaches is that long-term funds generally cost more than short-term funds. The term structure is usually upward-sloping. Because of this, many managers prefer an aggressive approach to financing working capital (Figure 19-1, panel C). The aggressive approach uses less long-term and more short-term financing. The goal is to raise profitability. We know from the Principle of Risk-Return Trade-Off that without some sort of market imperfection, higher expected profitability comes only at the expense of greater risk.

COSTS OF THE THREE APPROACHES   We can think of the maturity-matching approach as the base-case scenario. If interest rates rise unexpectedly, a firm using the aggressive approach loses relative to less aggressive (maturity-matching and conservative) firms. This is because firms with more long-term financing locked in at the lower rate will have lower financing costs. But if interest rates fall, the situation is reversed and the aggressive firm is a winner. This is because firms with more long-term financing may be stuck with either higher interest costs or the cost of refinancing.

Therefore, because of the possibility that funds might become more expensive or even unavailable, a firm without ready access to capital markets should be more conservative. The availability of financing at a fixed cost can be ensured by locking in long-term financing. In contrast, a firm with ready capital market access can be more aggressive.

Some managers gamble on the direction of interest rates. A manager who expects a decline in interest rates will use the aggressive approach. The aggressive manager shortens the average maturity of the firm's debt by financing more with short-term and less with long-term debt. A manager who expects interest rate increases will use the conservative approach. This manager lengthens the average maturity of the firm's debt by financing more with long-term and less with short-term debt.

If interest rates in fact move in the direction that the manager forecasts, the firm will realize additional profits. However, if interest rates move in the "wrong" direction, the interest rate gamble will backfire and the firm will be less profitable. On the basis of the Principle of Capital Market Efficiency, we caution against such gambling. Our recommendation is that the firm apply the Principle of Comparative Advantage instead. For example, a shoe company might work on manufacturing higher-quality shoes at lower cost instead of guessing the direction of interest rate movement.

Self-Check Questions

1. What types of problems does working capital management deal with?
2. How can using rules of thumb in working capital management lead to poor decisions?
3. A firm must maintain adequate liquidity. What does this mean in practical terms?
4. Compare and contrast the maturity-matching, conservative, and aggressive approaches to financing working capital. Which approach benefits if interest rates rise? Which one benefits if interest rate fall?

19.2 CASH CONVERSION CYCLE

The **cash conversion cycle** is the length of time between the payment of cash for inventory and receipt of cash from accounts receivable.

Without credit, a firm's cash is tied up from the moment it purchases inventory until it collects its accounts receivable. Suppose a firm holds its inventory 50 days and collects its accounts receivable in 30 days. Then it would take 80 days for the original investment to be converted back into cash.

However, with supplier credit, the firm's money is not invested for the entire 80 days. Figure 19-2 illustrates this cycle with 20-day supplier credit. On day 0, goods are delivered from the supplier, go into inventory, and result in an account payable. In 50 days, the goods are sold for credit, and the accounts receivable are collected 30 days later, on day 80. However, the firm does not have to put up its own money until it pays its accounts payable on day 20. With 20-day supplier credit, the firm's cash is invested for 60 days, day 20 to day 80. Thus in this instance, the cash conversion cycle is 60 days.

The cash conversion cycle is equal to the inventory conversion period, plus the receivables collection period, minus the payables deferral period:

$$
\begin{array}{ccccc}
\text{Cash} & & \text{Inventory} & \text{Receivables} & \text{Payables} \\
\text{conversion} & = & \text{conversion} & + \;\; \text{collection} & - \;\; \text{deferral} \\
\text{cycle} & & \text{period} & \text{period} & \text{period}
\end{array}
\qquad (19.1)
$$

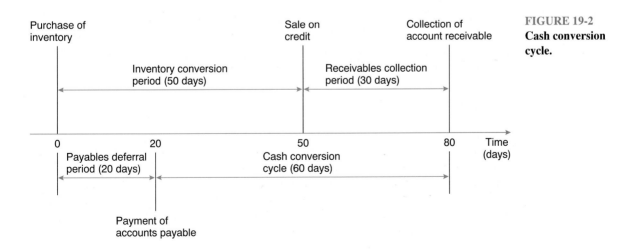

FIGURE 19-2
Cash conversion cycle.

The inventory conversion period is the average time between buying inventory and selling the goods:

$$\begin{array}{l} \text{Inventory} \\ \text{conversion} \\ \text{period} \end{array} = \frac{\text{Inventory}}{\text{Cost of sales}/365} = \frac{365}{\text{Inventory turnover}} \qquad (19.2)$$

The receivables collection period, or days' sales outstanding (DSO), is the average number of days that it takes to collect on accounts receivable:

$$\begin{array}{l} \text{Receivables} \\ \text{collection} \\ \text{period} \end{array} = \frac{\text{Receivables}}{\text{Sales}/365} = \frac{365}{\text{Receivables turnover}} \qquad (19.3)$$

The payables deferral period is the average length of time between the purchase of the materials and labor that go into inventory and the payment of cash for these materials and labor:

$$\begin{array}{l} \text{Payables} \\ \text{deferral} \\ \text{period} \end{array} = \frac{\text{Accounts payable} + \text{Wages, benefits, and payroll taxes payable}}{(\text{Cost of sales} + \text{Selling, general, and administrative expenses})/365} \qquad (19.4)$$

EXAMPLE

Cash Conversion Cycle at Parke-Davis

Suppose Parke-Davis has the following financial information. Find Parke-Davis's cash conversion cycle.

$1.40 million	Inventory
$1.70 million	Accounts receivable
$0.40 million	Accounts payable
$0.10 million	Wages, benefits, and payroll taxes payable
$20.0 million	Sales
$10.0 million	Cost of sales
$1.00 million	Selling, general, and administrative expenses

The inventory conversion period is

$$\begin{array}{l} \text{Inventory} \\ \text{conversion} \\ \text{period} \end{array} = \frac{1,400,000}{(10,000,000)/365} = 51.1 \text{ days}$$

The receivables collection period is

$$\begin{array}{l} \text{Receivables} \\ \text{collection} \\ \text{period} \end{array} = \frac{1,700,000}{20,000,000/365} = 31.0 \text{ days}$$

The payables deferral period is

$$\begin{array}{l} \text{Payables} \\ \text{deferral} \\ \text{period} \end{array} = \frac{(400,000 + 100,000)}{(10,000,000 + 1,000,000)/365} = 16.6 \text{ days}$$

The cash conversion cycle is

$$\text{Cash conversion cycle} = 51.1 + 31.0 - 16.6 = 65.5 \text{ days}$$

Self-Check Questions
1. What is the cash conversion cycle?
2. How is the cash conversion cycle related to the inventory conversion period, the receivables collection period, and the payables deferral period?
3. What happens to the cash conversion cycle (a) when inventory turnover increases, (b) when receivables turnover increases, and (c) when the payables deferral period increases?

19.3 CASH MANAGEMENT

Firms use increasingly sophisticated cash management systems to monitor their cash and marketable securities and to maintain their needed liquidity at minimum cost. Cash and marketable securities are managed together, because marketable securities are so liquid and the firm can move from one to the other quickly and cheaply. In fact, firms usually report only the total of cash and marketable securities on the balance sheet.

A firm's cash management decision can be broken into two parts. First, how much liquidity (cash plus marketable securities) should the firm have? Second, what should be the relative proportions of cash and marketable securities in maintaining that liquidity?

Demands for Cash

There are three basic motives for holding cash: (1) the transactions demand, (2) the precautionary demand, and (3) the speculative demand.

The **transactions demand** is simply the need for cash to make everyday payments for such things as wages, raw materials, taxes, and interest. The transactions demand for cash exists because of imbalances between cash inflows and outflows. The need for transactions balances depends on the size of the firm. The larger the firm, the more transactions it makes. The transactions demand also depends on the relative timing of cash inflows and outflows. The more closely they match, the less cash is needed to carry the firm until more inflow arrives.

The **precautionary demand** is essentially the margin of safety required to meet unexpected needs. The more uncertain the cash inflows and outflows, the larger the precautionary balance should be.

Finally, the **speculative demand** is based on the desire to take advantage of unexpected profitable opportunities that require cash. This motive accounts for a smaller percentage of corporate cash holdings than of individual cash holdings. For the most part, firms hold cash for transactions and precautionary reasons. Readily available bank borrowing can generally be used to meet the speculative demand for cash.

In addition to the three basic demands for cash, many firms hold cash in compensating balances. A **compensating balance** is an account balance that the firm agrees to maintain. It provides indirect payment to the bank for its loans or other services. Commercial banks may accept or require compensating balances in lieu of direct fees.

If a bank wants $1000 of compensation for a service, the bank can simply charge a fee of $1000. Alternatively, if the interest rate is 5%, a compensating balance of $20,000 left at the bank in a non-interest-bearing account for one year would provide the bank with the same $1000 (= $0.05 \times 20,000$) (indirect) compensation. Although direct fees are much more popular than they were in the past, a substantial amount of corporate cash balances is still made up of compensating balances.

Short-term Investment Alternatives

The following is a list of several types of marketable securities. They are shown in order of increasing level of risk and return.

- *U.S. Treasury securities.* *Treasury bills* (T-bills) have an original maturity of one year or less when they are issued. *Treasury notes* and *bonds* have an original maturity of one year or more. These securities have the lowest risk and greatest liquidity, but because of the risk-return trade-off, they also offer the lowest yield. Firms can buy and sell these securities directly. Firms can also invest in these securities for very short periods by using repurchase agreements, or *repos*, with securities dealers.

- *U.S. federal agency securities.* These securities are backed to varying degrees by the U.S. government. Many are nearly as liquid as U.S. Treasury securities but have slightly higher risk and return.

- *Negotiable certificates of deposit.* Negotiable CDs are time deposits issued by domestic or foreign commercial banks that can be sold to a third party.[3] *Eurodollar certificates of deposit* generally have higher risk and return than domestic CDs.

- *Short-term tax-exempt municipals.* *Munis* are short-term securities that are issued by state and local governments and are exempt from federal taxation. Several of these are short-term securities issued in anticipation of cash receipts. They are Tax Anticipation Notes (TANs), Revenue Anticipation Notes (RANs), and Bond Anticipation Notes (BANs).

- *Bankers' acceptances.* Bankers' acceptances are drafts that a commercial bank has "accepted." Their value is based on the accepting bank's credit standing.

- *Commercial paper.* These securities are unsecured promissory notes that corporations issue. Commercial paper seldom has an original maturity of more than 270 days.[4] Most commercial paper has an original maturity between 30 and 180 days and is generally issued only by very creditworthy corporations.

- *Preferred stock and money market preferred stock.* Preferred stock pays dividends that qualify for the 70% dividends-received deduction. Most preferred stock is a long-term security subject to market value fluctuations. Money-market preferred stock differs from other preferred stock. It is a short-term security that has a floating dividend rate that is reset frequently to reflect current interest rates. Therefore, it has lower risk and return, being much less subject to market value fluctuation, just like other short-term securities.

Transactions Demand Models

How much cash does a firm need to conduct its transactions? A simple and useful approach to answering this question treats cash management as an inventory management problem. In this approach, the firm manages its inventory of cash on the basis of the cost of holding cash (rather than marketable securities) and the cost of converting marketable securities to cash. The best policy minimizes the sum of these costs.

BAUMOL MODEL   The Baumol cash management model assumes that the firm can predict its future cash requirements with certainty, that cash disbursements are spread uniformly over the period, that the interest rate (the opportunity cost of holding cash) is fixed, and that the firm will pay a fixed transactions cost each time it converts securities to cash.

The Baumol model leads to a sawtooth pattern of cash balances (Figure 19-3). The firm sells C dollars worth of marketable securities and deposits the funds in its checking account. The cash balance decreases steadily to zero as the firm spends the cash. Then the firm sells C dollars of marketable securities and deposits the funds in the checking account, and the pat-

---

[3] Consumer CDs are usually non-negotiable. They can only be sold back to the issuing bank.
[4] So long as its maturity does not exceed 270 days, it does not have to be registered with the Securities and Exchange Commission (SEC).

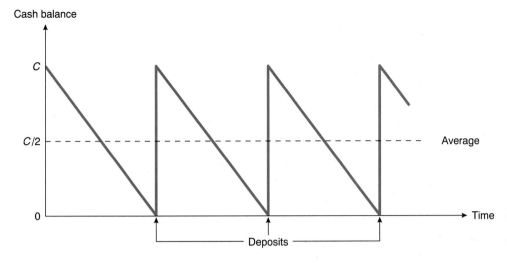

FIGURE 19-3
Cash balances with
the Baumol model.

tern repeats itself. Over time, the average (mean) cash balance will be $C/2$. The time value (opportunity cost) of funds is the interest rate, i, times the average balance, $iC/2$. Likewise, if each deposit is for C dollars and the firm needs to deposit a total of T dollars in its account during the year, the total number of deposits (and the number of sawtooths per year in Figure 19-3) equals T/C. The annual transactions cost will be the cost per deposit times the number of deposits, which is bT/C.

The annual cost of meeting the transactions demand is the transactions cost plus the opportunity (time value) cost:

$$\text{Cost} = b\frac{T}{C} + i\frac{C}{2} \tag{19.5}$$

where T = annual transactions volume in dollars (uniform through time)
       b = fixed cost per transaction
       i = annual interest rate
       C = size of each deposit

The decision variable is C, the deposit size. Increasing C increases the average cash balance and the opportunity cost as well. However, increasing C reduces the number of deposits, thereby lowering the annual transactions cost. Figure 19-4 demonstrates this trade-off between the two costs. The best or optimal deposit size, C^*, provides the minimum total cost, Cost.*

The optimal deposit size is given by

$$C^* = \sqrt{\frac{2bT}{i}} \tag{19.6}$$

The optimal deposit size is a function of the transactions cost b, the annual transactions volume T, and the annual interest rate i. The value of C^* is positively related to b and T and negatively related to i. Note that the optimal deposit size is not linearly related to these variables. For example, if T doubles, then the best deposit size will also increase, but it will not double.

Although the Baumol model makes many simplifying assumptions, it provides insight into the general relationships among the various factors.

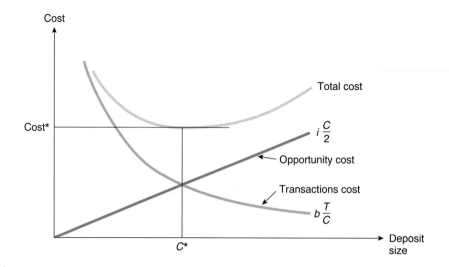

FIGURE 19-4
Annual costs for the Baumol model.

EXAMPLE

Using the Baumol Model at Fox

Let's say Fox, Inc. needs $12 million in cash next year. It believes that it can earn 12% per year on funds invested in marketable securities and that converting marketable securities to cash costs $312.50 per transaction. What does this imply for Fox?

Fox's optimal deposit size is

$$C^* = \sqrt{\frac{2bT}{i}} = \sqrt{\frac{2(312.50)(12,000,000)}{0.12}} = \$250,000$$

The annual cost is

$$\text{Cost} = b\frac{T}{C} + i\frac{C}{2}$$

The annual cost is $30,000. The parts of the solution follow.

$$\text{Cost} = 312.50\frac{12,000,000}{250,000} + 0.12\frac{250,000}{2} = 15,000 + 15,000 = \$30,000$$

$$T/C = 48 = \text{deposits per year}$$

$$bT/C = 312.50(48) = \$15,000 = \text{transactions cost per year}$$

$$C/2 = \$125,000 = \text{average cash balance}$$

$$iC/2 = 0.12(125,000) = \$15,000 = \text{annual opportunity cost of funds}$$

Fox would make about one deposit per week of $250,000. The average cash balance is $125,000, transactions costs are $15,000, opportunity costs are $15,000, and the total annual cost is $30,000. ■

MILLER-ORR CASH MANAGEMENT MODEL   The Miller-Orr cash management model is more realistic than the Baumol model. It allows the daily cash flows to vary according to a probability function. For example, suppose we can assume that the net cash flow (combined inflows and outflows) follows a normal distribution with a mean value of zero and a standard deviation of $50,000 per day. This incorporates the realistic uncertainty about future cash flows. Figure 19-5 illustrates the Miller-Orr model.

The Miller-Orr model uses two control limits and a return point. The lower control limit, LCL in the figure, is determined outside the model. The upper control limit, UCL, is 3Z above

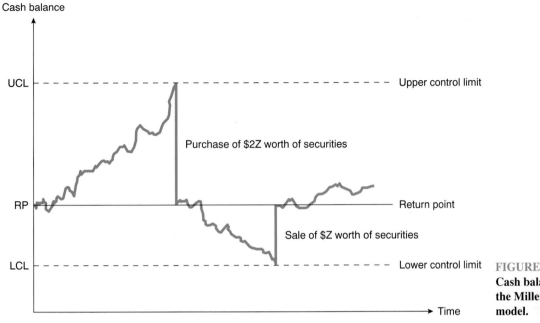

FIGURE 19-5
Cash balances with the Miller-Orr model.

the lower control limit. The model uses a return point that is Z above LCL. The return point is the target the firm returns to whenever it hits a control limit.

Whenever the cash balance hits the lower limit, the firm sells $\$Z$ worth of marketable securities and puts the money in the checking account. This brings the cash balance back to the return point. Whenever the balance hits the upper limit, $\$2Z$ worth of marketable securities are purchased with money from the checking account, putting the balance back to the return point. This procedure produces an average cash balance of LCL $+ \frac{4}{3}Z$.

Although the lower control limit is set outside the model, the upper control limit and the return point depend on LCL and Z. The return point is simply LCL $+ Z$, and UCL equals LCL $+ 3Z$. The variable Z depends on the cost per transaction, b, the interest rate per period, i, and the standard deviation of the net cash flows, σ. The interest rate and the standard deviation of cash flows are defined in the same unit of time, which is most often per day. Z is then

$$Z = \left(\frac{3b\sigma^2}{4i}\right)^{1/3} \tag{19.7}$$

As we have noted, the return point, the upper control limit, and the average cash balance are

$$RP = LCL + Z$$
$$UCL = LCL + 3Z$$
$$\text{Average cash balance} = LCL + \tfrac{4}{3}Z$$

A higher cost per transaction or greater variation in the cash flow results in a larger Z and a larger difference between LCL and UCL. Likewise, a higher interest rate results in a smaller Z and a smaller range.

The Miller-Orr model is a good example of *management by exception*. Managers allow the cash balance to fluctuate within specified limits. Only when these limits are violated do managers take action, and that action is planned ahead of time. The model is useful for managing transactions cash balances.

Using the Miller-Orr Model at KFC

Suppose KFC has estimated the standard deviation of its daily net cash flows (outflows minus inflows for the day) to be $\sigma = \$50,000$ per day. In addition, the cost of buying or selling marketable securities is $100. The annual interest rate is 10%. Because of its liquidity requirements and compensating balance agreements, the firm has a lower control limit of $100,000 on its cash balances. What would be KFC's upper control limit and return point in the Miller-Orr model?

First we find Z. We divide the annual interest rate by 365 to convert it to a daily rate, because the variability of cash flows is expressed on a daily basis.

$$Z = \left[\frac{3b\sigma^2}{4i} \right]^{1/3} = \left[\frac{3(100)(50,000)^2}{4(0.10/365)} \right]^{1/3} = \$88,125$$

Then we calculate the upper control limit and return point.

$$\text{UCL} = \text{LCL} + 3Z = 100,000 + 3(88,125) = \$364,375$$

$$\text{RP} = \text{LCL} + Z = 100,000 + 88,125 = \$188,125$$

If the cash balance falls to $100,000, KFC will sell $Z = \$88,125$ of securities and put the money in the cash account, thereby bringing the balance back to the return point of $188,125. If the cash balance climbs to $364,375, KFC will buy $2Z = \$176,250$ of securities from cash, thereby reducing the cash balance to the return point of $188,125 (= 364,375 − 176,250). KFC's average cash balance will be

$$\text{Average cash balance} = \text{LCL} + \tfrac{4}{3}Z = 100,000 + (4/3)(88,125) = \$217,500 \ \blacksquare$$

OTHER PRACTICAL CONSIDERATIONS IN CASH MANAGEMENT   The Baumol and Miller-Orr models deal with optimizing a firm's cash transactions balances. Other factors not included in these models also affect cash balances. For example, the firm may have a compensating balance requirement. In such a case, the firm's average cash balance is the greater of its balance needed for transactions and its compensating balance requirement. The compensating balance is costly, then, only if it raises the balance the firm would maintain anyway. Frequently, it is costly.

The optimal amount of marketable securities is the total liquidity desired minus cash balances. The firm invests in a variety of marketable securities, taking into account its possible future cash needs as well as the transactions costs, maturities, riskiness, and yields of the investments.

Some firms maintain unusually large portfolios of marketable securities. Although some of the portolios may be maintained for liquidity purposes, responding to special tax situations may also be the motive. Sometimes firms have foreign operations in countries with different tax laws, and they can benefit by investing the cash abroad rather than returning it to the United States and paying U.S. income taxes on it.

Float

When you write a check, there is a delay before the funds are taken out of your checking account. This delay occurs because of such things as the time your check is in the mail, the time needed to process the check, and the time it takes the banking system to remove the funds from your account. During this delay, you are benefiting from float. **Float** is the difference between the available or collected balance at the bank and the firm's book or ledger balance.

$$\text{Float} = \text{Available balance} - \text{Book balance} \tag{19.8}$$

Float arises from timing differences that occur when you pay your bills or collect from customers. Float, then, is between the firm and outsiders, such as customers or suppliers. There are two kinds of float, disbursement float and collection float.

DISBURSEMENT FLOAT   When you write a check, your book or ledger balance is reduced by the amount of the check, but your available or collected balance at the bank is not reduced until the check finally clears. This difference is **disbursement float**.

Disburse-ment Float at Coors   **EXAMPLE**

Suppose Coors has $50,000 for both its book balance and its bank balance. If Coors writes a $1000 check that takes 4 days to clear, during this period $1000 of disbursement float has been created. Coors's book balance declines by the amount of the check, from $50,000 to $49,000, but the bank balance is unchanged until the check clears.

$$\text{Float} = \text{Available balance} - \text{Book balance}$$
$$= 50{,}000 - 49{,}000 = \$1000$$

After the check clears, the book and bank balances are both $49,000 and there is no more disbursement float. ■

COLLECTION FLOAT   Of course, float can be either positive or negative. Suppose you receive a check and deposit it in your bank. Until the funds are credited to your account, your book balance will be higher than your actual balance. In this case, you are experiencing **collection float**.

Collection Float at Coors   **EXAMPLE**

Assume Coors has a $50,000 cash balance on both its ledger balance and its available balance at the bank. If Coors receives a $500 check and deposits it in its checking account, funds are not made available on this particular check for 2 days. Its book balance increases by $500, but the bank balance is unchanged until the funds are finally available. The float is then

$$\text{Float} = \text{Available balance} - \text{Book balance}$$
$$= 50{,}000 - 50{,}500 = -\$500$$

This negative float of $500 is Coors's collection float. ■

FLOAT MANAGEMENT TECHNIQUES   Firms use several devices and procedures to manage float.

- *Wire transfers* Large payments can be made with wire transfers instead of paper checks. Sending a wire transfer is more expensive than writing and mailing a paper check, but the wire transfer reduces the float because it is immediate.

- *Zero balance accounts (ZBAs)* These are special disbursement accounts that have a zero balance. They are funded out of a master account. Funds are automatically transferred into the ZBAs when checks are presented on them.

- *Controlled disbursing* This technique may use disbursing accounts at several banks in addition to the master account at the firm's lead bank. As with ZBAs, funds are put into the accounts on an as-needed basis. The banks notify the firm about what funds are needed. The firm then wires these funds to the banks. Conversely, the bank notifies the firm about excess funds and wires them out.

- *Centralized processing of payables* By centralizing payables, a cash manager knows when all bills must be paid and can make sure that funds are available and bills are paid on time. Prompt bill paying creates better relations with vendors. In addition, the firm avoids late penalties while reducing its cash balances.

- *Lockboxes* Lockboxes are post office boxes to which a firm directs its incoming checks. A bank is engaged to open the lockbox several times per day, process the checks, and collect them. Cash managers face two problems: the choice of lockbox locations and the assignment of customers to particular lockboxes. By strategically locating the lockboxes around the country and by using efficient banks, firms can reduce their float substantially. Float is reduced by shortening mail times (from customers to the lockbox), processing times (by using efficient banks), and availability times (the time it takes for funds to be made available on checks after they are presented to banks).

EXAMPLE

Cost of a Wire Transfer

You need to transfer $100,000 from Houston to Chicago. If you mail a check, it will cost $1.00 for postage and clearing the check, and it will take a total of 5 days for the funds to be transferred. During the money's 5-day travel, you are suffering an opportunity cost, because the $100,000 is not earning 3% APY interest. Alternatively, you could avoid the opportunity cost by sending a wire transfer that costs $12.00, which would instantaneously transfer the funds with no float. Which would be cheaper?

Cost = Fixed costs + Float costs

Cost of check = 1.00 + 100,000(0.03)(5/365) = 1.00 + 41.10 = $42.10

Cost of wire transfer = 12.00 + 0 = $12.00

The wire transfer would be substantially cheaper. ■

EXAMPLE

Using a Lockbox System at The Gap

Let's say The Gap currently collects all of its customer payments in Nashville. By going to a new lockbox system with boxes in Atlanta and St. Louis, The Gap expects to reduce the time from when customers mail their checks to when the funds are collected. Managers expect the time to fall from an average of 8 days to an average of 5 days, for a 3-day savings. The Gap collects $100,000 per day. The extra costs associated with the lockbox would be $12,000 per year. The Gap's opportunity cost of funds is 10% per year. What is the expected annual profit of using the new system?

Reduction in float = (100,000/day)(3 days)	=	$300,000
Value of float reduction = 300,000(0.10)	=	30,000
Less: Annual operating cost	=	12,000
Net before-tax profit of lockbox system	=	$18,000

The reduction in float of $300,000 permanently frees up this amount of cash. Invested at 10%, this cash is worth $30,000 per year. Subtracting the $12,000 yearly cost of operating the system gives an expected before-tax profit of $18,000 per year. ■

Self-Check Questions

1. What are the two parts of the firm's cash management decision?
2. What are the firm's three basic motives for holding cash?
3. Describe three short-term investment alternatives.
4. According to the Baumol model, how is the optimal deposit size, C^*, related to the transactions cost b, the annual transactions volume T, and the annual interest rate i? What two costs are traded off in the Baumol model? What is minimized in the Baumol model?
5. Why is the Miller-Orr cash management model more realistic than the Baumol model? How is it useful?
6. What is float? What causes float? What are the two kinds of float? What steps can firms take to control float?

19.4 SHORT-TERM FINANCING

The phrases *short-term funds* and *intermediate-term funds* refer to the original maturity of a debt obligation. Short-term funds are debt obligations scheduled for repayment within 1 year. Intermediate-term funds are debt obligations scheduled to mature between 1 and perhaps as many as 10 years from the date of issue. These time periods vary in practice.

Another useful distinction concerns the source of funds from which the loan is to be repaid. Firms usually arrange short-term loans to finance seasonal or temporary needs. Intermediate-term loans are to be repaid over a period of years. If the loan is short-term (due in a year or less), lenders are concerned mainly with the firm's working capital position and its ability to liquidate current assets—collecting on receivables and reducing inventories according to seasonal patterns—to generate cash to meet the firm's current debt service obligations. For an intermediate-term loan, lenders are more concerned with the longer-term profitability of the firm's operations.

There are three main sources of short-term funds: *trade credit* (borrowing from suppliers), *bank loans* (borrowing from banks), and *commercial paper* (selling short-term debt securities in the open market). This section discusses each of these sources of short-term funds, describes how to estimate the cost of funds from each source, and provides a framework for comparing the costs on a consistent basis.

Trade Credit

Trade credit is credit extended by one firm to another. Businesses routinely grant trade credit on the sales of their goods and services. Purchasers of raw materials, manufactured products, and services are generally permitted to wait until after the goods or services are delivered to pay for them. Trade credit is the largest single source of short-term funds for businesses, representing approximately one-third of the current liabilities of nonfinancial corporations. Because suppliers are often more liberal in extending credit than financial institutions, trade credit is a particularly important source of funds for small firms.

When extending trade credit, the seller specifies the period of time allowed for payment and often offers a *cash discount* if payment is made more quickly. For example, the terms "2/10, net 30" are frequently encountered; they mean the buyer can take a 2% cash discount if payment is made within 10 days (the *discount period*). Otherwise, the full amount is due within 30 days (the *net period*).

Trade credit can be a significant source of funds. For example, let's say a firm purchases $50,000 worth of supplies each day on terms of 2/10, net 30. The firm always pays in exactly 10 days. In this case, the firm will owe its suppliers 10 times $50,000, or $500,000, less the 2% discount. Its suppliers are providing almost $500,000 of funds that the firm can use in its business. If the firm pays at the end of 30 days, the total amount of trade credit is 30 days' worth of purchases, which is $50,000 times 30, or $1,500,000.

COST OF TRADE CREDIT   If no discount is offered, or if payment is made soon enough that the discount can be taken, there is no cost to the firm for use of the supplier's credit. When cash discounts are offered but not taken, however, there is an implicit cost to trade credit. When a firm offers a discount for early payment, the discounted price is the "real" price of the goods. That is, if the invoice is for $100 and a 2% discount is offered for early payment, the "real" price is $98. If the firm does not pay its bill within 10 days, it effectively borrows $98 and pays $2 interest for the loan by forgoing the discount.

Equation (4.6) is the formula for computing the APR (annual percentage rate). Similarly, the APR for trade credit is

$$\text{APR} = \left(\frac{\text{Discount\%}}{100\% - \text{Discount\%}} \right) \left(\frac{365}{\text{Total period} - \text{Discount period}} \right) \tag{19.9}$$

The APR is widely used, but of course it understates the true annual interest rate because it ignores compounding. The true interest cost is the APY (annual percentage yield), which for trade credit is

$$\text{APY} = -1 + \left(1 + \frac{\text{Discount\%}}{100\% - \text{Discount\%}} \right)^{\frac{365}{\text{Total period} - \text{Discount period}}} \tag{19.10}$$

Equation (19.10) is another version of Equation (4.7). You can use it to solve for the APY if you know the FV, the PV, and n.

<table>
<tr><td rowspan="5" style="vertical-align:middle">EXAMPLE</td></tr>
</table>

EXAMPLE

Trade Credit Cost at Radio Shack

What is the cost to Radio Shack when it skips the discount and pays at the end of the total credit period if credit terms are 2/10, net 30? The APR is

$$\text{APR} = \left(\frac{\text{Discount\%}}{100\% - \text{Discount\%}} \right) \left(\frac{365}{\text{Total period} - \text{Discount period}} \right)$$

$$= \left(\frac{2\%}{100\% - 2\%} \right) \left(\frac{365}{30 - 10} \right) = 37.24\%$$

This example can be visualized with the help of Figure 19-6. Radio Shack would pay $2 of interest on a $98 loan. The loan is for only 20 days, so the loan is rolled over $365/(30 - 10) = 365/20 = 18.25$ times per year.

For such a high interest rate, the difference between the APR and the APY can be substantial. The APY is 44.59% [put in PV = 98, FV = 100, $n = 0.05479$ (= 20/365), and CF = 0; then compute $r = 44.59\%$].

$$\text{APY} = \left(1 + \frac{\text{Discount\%}}{100\% - \text{Discount\%}} \right)^{\frac{365}{\text{Total period} - \text{Discount period}}} - 1$$

$$= \left(1 + \frac{2\%}{100\% - 2\%} \right)^{\frac{365}{30 - 10}} - 1 = 44.59\%$$

As the Radio Shack example illustrates, trade credit can be very expensive when a cash discount is offered but not taken. Thus it is important to evaluate the cost implicit in not taking the discount. Other sources of credit may be cheaper.

EFFECTIVE USE OF TRADE CREDIT   Trade credit offers some advantages as a source of short-term funds. It is readily available, at least to firms that regularly pay suppliers on schedule. And it is informal. If the firm is presently paying its bills within the discount period, the firm can get additional credit simply by delaying payment until the end of the net period or perhaps later (but at the cost of forgoing the discount). Trade credit is also more flexible

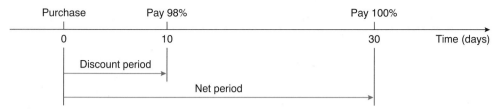

FIGURE 19-6
Cost of trade credit.

than other means of short-term financing. The firm does not have to negotiate a loan agreement, pledge collateral, or adhere to a rigid repayment schedule. In particular, the consequences of delaying a payment beyond the net period are much less onerous than those resulting from failure to repay a bank loan on schedule. For these and other reasons, trade credit is particularly valuable to smaller firms, which may have difficulty obtaining credit elsewhere.

STRETCHING ACCOUNTS PAYABLE   Firms may also "stretch" accounts payable by postponing payment beyond the end of the net period. Such stretching lowers the financing cost computed in Equation (19.9) or (19.10), because the loan period is extended without any increase in cost. For example, with credit terms of 2/10, net 30, paying in 40 rather than 30 days lowers the APR from 37.24% to 24.83%. It lowers the APY from 44.59% to 27.86%. Suppliers might tolerate such delinquencies during periods when the buyer has large seasonal requirements for funds. To minimize any adverse consequences, however, the buyer should keep the supplier fully informed of its situation. It should also try to keep current on its repayment obligations with the supplier over the rest of the year.

Stretching the payments on accounts payable is a good example of the Principle of Two-Sided Transactions. Paying late may be a zero-sum game, and what you save for yourself is a cost imposed on your supplier. The buyer must be careful to avoid excessive stretching of accounts payable. Excessive stretching may cause the firm to incur other implicit costs, such as a deterioration in the firm's credit rating, strained relations with suppliers, or both. These results can lead to less attractive repayment terms in the future and perhaps to higher prices as suppliers attempt to pass through to the buyer the cost of the buyer's delinquent payments. These implicit costs of trade credit, although difficult to estimate, should be carefully evaluated. In particular, smaller firms that may at times rely heavily on trade credit for short-term financing should assess the implicit as well as the explicit costs of trade credit.

BILLING ALTERNATIVES   In many business relationships, particularly where the number of purchases is small, the supplier sends a separate bill for each purchase. Obviously, this can result in a lot of paperwork.

Alternatively, several invoices are collected into a single statement, and the customer is asked to pay after the statement is presented. A common arrangement is monthly statements. The supplier's "month" might run from the 25th of one month until the 25th of the next. On the 25th day of the month, the supplier sends a bill for all the invoices from the last month, with credit terms for the total such as "2/10, net EOM." If the statement was prepared on, say, April 25, the customer can take a 2% discount if the bill is paid by the 10th of the next month, which is May 10th. If the discount is not taken, the net amount is due on EOM, the end of the month, which is May 31.

Self-Check Questions

1. What are the three main sources of short-term funds? Describe each. Which is the largest source of short-term funds for corporations?

2. What is trade credit? What are its advantages compared to other sources of short-term funds?

3. What does "3/10, net 20" mean?

4. What is the cost of trade credit when the borrower pays within the discount period?

5. Why does trade credit involve an implicit cost when a firm does not pay within the discount period?

Secured and Unsecured Bank Loans

Commercial bank lending is second to trade credit as a source of short-term financing. Commercial banks also provide intermediate-term financing (maturity between 1 and 10 years). Banks provide loans in a wide variety of forms that are tailored to the specific needs of the borrower. Banks generally lend to their most creditworthy customers on an unsecured basis. But when a borrower represents a significant credit risk, the bank may ask for some form of security, such as a lien on receivables or inventory. Finance firms also lend on a secured basis.

SHORT-TERM UNSECURED LOANS   Short-term unsecured bank loans take one of three basic forms: a specific *transaction loan*, a *line of credit*, or a *revolving credit*. Such loans are generally regarded as "self-liquidating": The lender expects that the assets purchased with the loan proceeds will generate sufficient cash to repay the loan within a year. Short-term unsecured loans are evidenced by a promissory note that specifies the amount of the loan, the interest rate, and the repayment terms. Short-term unsecured loans generally bear interest at a floating rate.

Banks make a **transaction loan** for a specific purpose. For example, a bank may lend funds to a house construction firm to pay for building houses. The loan agreement requires the firm to repay the bank when the houses are sold.

A **line of credit** is an arrangement between a bank and a customer concerning the maximum loan balance the bank will permit the borrower at any one time. Banks normally extend credit lines for a 1-year period, with 1-year renewals granted as long as the bank continues to find the borrower's credit acceptable. Banks generally do not like borrowers to use credit lines to cover their long-term needs for funds, so banks may require that a borrower be out of bank debt periodically for some specified amount of time (for example, 30 consecutive days each year). Inability to meet such a requirement gives the bank an early warning of potential trouble. If the firm is unable to meet this requirement, the bank will insist that the firm get additional long-term financing to be able to meet it. Most credit lines are informal arrangements. If the prospective borrower's credit deteriorates, the bank is not legally obligated to advance funds.

In contrast, a **revolving credit agreement** represents a legal commitment to lend up to a specified maximum amount any time during a specified period. In return for this legal commitment, the borrower must pay a commitment fee, usually between 0.25% and 0.5%, on the difference between the permitted maximum and the amount actually borrowed. This fee increases the firm's cost of borrowing and compensates the bank for committing itself to making extra funds available to the firm. Revolving credits are evidenced by short-term notes that usually mature in 90 days. The borrower can roll these over automatically as long as the notes mature no later than the date the revolving credit agreement expires. Revolving credits often extend beyond 1 year, and the borrower often has the option to convert the revolving credit to a term loan when the revolving credit expires.

TERM LOAN   Bank term loans represent intermediate-term debt, but the similarity between their pricing and the pricing of short-term bank loans makes it appropriate to discuss them in this chapter. A bank **term loan** is a loan for a specified amount that requires the borrower to repay it according to a specified schedule. A term loan generally matures in 1 to 10 years, but banks permit longer maturities under special circumstances. Repayment is normally at regular intervals in equal installments. In some cases, however, the loan may provide for a larger final payment, called a *balloon payment,* or simply for repayment at maturity in one lump sum, called a *bullet maturity.* A loan with a bullet maturity is like a typical corporate bond. The interest is paid periodically over the life of the loan, but the principal is repaid in one lump sum at the end. Banks often extend revolving credits that the borrower can convert into a term loan. A 3-year revolving credit convertible into a 5-year term loan at the end of the third year is not uncommon. Term loans usually carry a floating interest rate.

COST OF BANK FINANCING   Except for a rather small percentage of loans that bear interest at a fixed rate, commercial banks charge interest at a rate that floats. Generally the interest rate floats with the bank's **prime rate**, which is a benchmark rate that banks may use to price loans.[5] Banks often use other benchmark rates besides prime. These are usually based on the bank's cost of funding the loan. For example, commercial banks often offer their larger, more creditworthy customers the option of selecting interest rates based on (1) one of the London Interbank Offer Rates (LIBOR), the rates at which prime banks offer one another deposits in the London market, or (2) the interest rate the bank pays on large certificates of deposit. Nevertheless, the prime rate serves as the base lending rate in most cases.

A bank adjusts its prime rate to reflect changes in its cost of funds. In addition, commercial banks frequently offer loans at "money market rates" that are below prime to compete with the commercial paper market, which we will discuss in a moment. Banks charge less creditworthy customers a higher rate, usually expressed as a percentage over prime, depending on the customer's credit standing. For example, if a bank's prime rate is 12%, then it might lend to a local manufacturing firm at prime plus 0.5%, or 12.5%, and to a local merchant at prime plus 2%, or 14%. The interest rates on these loans would vary with changes in the bank's prime rate. If the bank raises its prime rate to 12.5%, the interest rate on the manufacturing firm's loan would automatically become 13%, and the interest rate on the merchant's loan would automatically become 14.5%.

A compensating balance requirement, generally between 10% and 20% of the size of the loan, is in addition to interest charges. This requirement may be a minimum, but more commonly it is a required *average* deposit balance during a particular interest period. Such an average gives the borrower greater flexibility, because a high balance one day can offset a low balance on another day. Compensating balance requirements are more common when credit is tight in the entire economy. In any case, a compensating balance adds to the cost of a loan in those instances where a firm has to maintain a higher cash balance than it otherwise would.

Despite the many differences in bank loan contracts, calculating the cost of a loan is not difficult. As with trade credit, we can calculate the APR. It is

$$\text{APR} = \left(\frac{\text{Net cost of loan}}{\text{Cash advance}} \right) \left(\frac{1}{f} \right) \tag{19.11}$$

---

[5] It used to be the interest rate banks charged their largest, most creditworthy customers. However, banks often lend to their best customers at below prime rate.

where f is the fraction of a year that the loan is outstanding. For example, for a 3-month loan, $f = 0.25$.

The APY is

$$\text{APY} = \left(1 + \frac{\text{Net cost of loan}}{\text{Cash advance}}\right)^{1/f} - 1 = \left(\frac{\text{Net repayment}}{\text{Cash advance}}\right)^{1/f} - 1 \qquad (19.12)$$

TRUE INTEREST COST WITH COMPENSATING BALANCES   When interest is paid in arrears (that is, at the end of an interest period) and compensating balances are required, the true interest cost of the loan is higher than the rate quoted on the principal amount of the loan. The compensating balance reduces the effective loan proceeds, raising the cost of the usable funds. The higher interest cost with a compensating balance is

$$\text{APR} = \left(\frac{\text{Net cost of loan}}{\text{Cash advance}}\right)\left(\frac{1}{f}\right)$$

$$= \left(\frac{\text{Interest charges}}{\text{Loan amount} - \text{Compensating balance}}\right)\left(\frac{1}{f}\right) = \left(\frac{rP}{P - B}\right)\left(\frac{1}{f}\right) \qquad (19.13)$$

where P = amount of the loan
B = increase in the firm's average cash balances as a result of the compensating balance requirement
f = fraction of a year the loan is outstanding
r = interest rate on the loan amount
rP = interest charges

The financing costs consist of interest expenses, and the net loan proceeds are the loan amount reduced by the amount of the compensating balance requirement.

The foregoing equation assumes the compensating balances do not earn interest, which is generally the case. But if the compensating balances earn some yield, y, the earned interest, yB, reduces the cost of the loan. In that case, the cost of the loan is

$$\text{APR} = \left(\frac{\text{Interest charges} - \text{Interest received}}{\text{Loan amount} - \text{Compensating balance}}\right)\left(\frac{1}{f}\right) = \left(\frac{rP - yB}{P - B}\right)\left(\frac{1}{f}\right) \qquad (19.14)$$

EXAMPLE

A Wendy's Franchise Loan with Compensating Balance Requirements

Suppose a Wendy's franchisee borrows $100,000 for 1 year. The bank charges interest at the prime rate plus 0.50%. It also requires a 10% compensating balance, which the franchisee would not otherwise have kept. If the prime rate averages 11.50%, the APR is

$$\text{APR} = \left(\frac{rP}{P - B}\right)\left(\frac{1}{f}\right) = \left(\frac{0.12(100,000)}{100,000 - 10,000}\right)\left(\frac{1}{1}\right) = \frac{12,000}{90,000} = 13.33\%$$

In the absence of any compensating balance requirements, the true interest cost would have been simply 12%. We can look at this problem another way.

The franchisee borrows $100,000 at the first of the year and repays the $112,000 at the end of the year. However, because $10,000 stays in the bank the whole year, the franchisee takes out only $90,000 at the first of the year and must pay $102,000 at the end. This produces a 1-year interest rate of 13.33% [put in PV = 90,000, FV = 102,000, $n = 1$, and CF = 0; then solve for $r = 13.33\%$].

Suppose the franchisee could deposit the compensating balance in a time deposit account earning 5% interest. Then the financing costs would be reduced by the amount of interest earned, which would be 5% of 10,000, or $500. The APR is now 12.78% [put in PV = 90,000, FV = 101,500 (= 102,000 − 500, because of the interest earned), $n = 1$, and CF = 0; then solve for $r = 12.78\%$].

$$\text{APR} = \left(\frac{rP - yB}{P - B}\right)\left(\frac{1}{f}\right) = \left(\frac{0.12(100,000) - 0.05(10,000)}{100,000 - 10,000}\right)\left(\frac{1}{1}\right) = \frac{11,500}{90,000} = 12.78\%$$

TRUE INTEREST COST OF DISCOUNT NOTES

Many loans are *discount loans*, which require the borrower to pay the interest in advance. The loan proceeds are reduced in advance by the interest cost. The stated loan amount is P, but the borrower gets only $P - rPf$, where f is the borrowing period expressed as a fraction of a year. Often, f is computed using a 360-day year. With an interest expense of rPf, with a "true" loan amount of $P - rPf$, and adjusting for a loan period of f, the APR is

$$\text{APR} = \left(\frac{rPf}{P - rPf}\right)\left(\frac{1}{f}\right) = \frac{r}{1 - rf} \tag{19.15}$$

As you would expect because of the time value of money, the true interest cost is higher when interest is paid in advance than when it is paid in arrears. If a compensating balance were also required, other adjustments would be needed as well.

Let's say Famous Amos is paying interest on a discount basis at the rate of 12% per year for a $100,000, 3-month loan. There is no compensating balance requirement. What is Famous Amos's true interest cost of this loan?

Using Equation (19.15) yields

$$\text{APR} = \frac{r}{1 - rf} = \frac{0.12}{1 - 0.12(0.25)} = \frac{0.12}{0.97} = 12.37\%$$

The APY is 12.96% [put in PV = 97,000, FV = 100,000, $n = 0.25$, and CF = 0; then compute $r = 12.96\%$]. ∎

Famous Amos's Cost for a Discounted Loan

EXAMPLE

SUMMARY OF COST OF SINGLE-PAYMENT LOANS

Figure 19-7 summarizes the costs of four types of single-payment $100 3-month loans at 12% APR. The types are based on whether interest is paid in arrears (at the end of the year, cases 1 and 2) or in advance (a discount loan, cases 3 and 4) and on whether a compensating balance is required (cases 2 and 4) or not (cases 1 and 3). Figure 19-7 shows how the loan's APY is increased by compensating balances, by paying interest on a discount basis, and by more frequent compounding.

THE APY FOR A DISCOUNTED INSTALLMENT LOAN

Instead of a single-payment loan, the bank may require the borrower to repay the loan on an installment basis. The APY of such loans is found by solving for the periodic interest rate and annualizing it.

Loan amount = $100, Interest rate = 12%, Loan term = 3 months

(1) Interest in arrears
    No compensating balance

```
100   −103
———————————————————————→ Time
0     0.25
```

APR = (3/100)4 = 12.00%

APY = (103/100)^4 − 1 = 12.55%

(2) Interest in arrears
    10% compensating balance

```
90    −93
———————————————————————→ Time
0     0.25
```

APR = (3/90)4 = 13.33%

APY = (93/90)^4 − 1 = 14.01%

(3) Discount loan (interest in advance)
    No compensating balance

```
97    −100
———————————————————————→ Time
0     0.25
```

APR = (3/97)4 = 12.37%

APY = (100/97)^4 − 1 = 12.96%

(4) Discount loan (interest in advance)
    10% compensating balance

```
87    −90
———————————————————————→ Time
0     0.25
```

APR = (3/87)4 = 13.79%

APY = (90/87)^4 − 1 = 14.52%

FIGURE 19-7
Costs of four types of single-payment loans.

EXAMPLE

Famous Amos's Cost for a Discounted Installment Loan

Suppose Famous Amos is borrowing another $100,000 at what the bank calls a 12% interest rate. In this case, the interest is discounted at 12% for 3 months (total discount of 3%). Famous Amos will repay the loan in three installments of $25,000 each at the end of the first 2 months and $50,000 at the end of 3 months. Thus Famous Amos gets $97,000 [= 100,000 − (0.12)(0.25)100,000], and its true interest cost is the r that solves

$$0 = -97,000 + \frac{25,000}{(1+r)} + \frac{25,000}{(1+r)^2} + \frac{50,000}{(1+r)^3}$$

Solving for r by using trial and error gives $r = 1.3658\%$ per month. Famous Amos's APR on this loan is 16.39% (= 12 × 1.3658%), and its APY is 17.68% (= $[1.013658]^{12} - 1$). ■

Famous Amos's "12%" discounted installment loan illustrates vividly, once again, why it is so critical to understand and account for the exact terms of a loan agreement. Two loans with the same quoted interest rate may have very different APYs because of differences in how interest is calculated or differences in the timing of repayment.

SECURITY   Commercial banks often ask lenders to provide security for their loans. When the bank is lending on a short-term basis, it may ask the borrower to pledge liquid assets such as receivables, inventories, or marketable securities. The pledge of collateral may take the form of a "floating lien" against one or more classes of short-term assets without specifying them in detail. More commonly, banks will ask the borrower to specify in detail the collateral for the loan (such as to provide a list of receivables it is pledging). Depending on the quality of the receivables, a firm can usually borrow between 70% and 90% of the face value of its pledged receivables. With inventories that are easily sold, a firm can probably borrow between 50% and 75% of the inventory's retail value.

For loans secured by receivables, commercial banks normally charge the prime rate plus a premium of up to 5 percentage points. The bank's cost of processing the receivables affects the rate it charges. The higher the processing cost, the higher the interest rate. However, there are normally no compensating balances on such loans. Interest rates on loans secured by inventory have a similar range. The premium is generally lower the higher the quality of the receivables or inventory pledged. Finance companies also make secured loans, but they usually do so at higher rates than commercial banks charge.

The main benefit from pledging is that a firm can borrow more than it could on an unsecured basis. In return, the firm incurs extra administrative and bookkeeping costs and sacrifices some degree of control over its receivables and inventories. In some cases, the borrower's customers repay their receivables directly to the bank. And pledged inventories are sometimes physically separated out and given special handling.

Commercial Paper

The largest, most creditworthy firms are able to borrow on a short-term basis by selling **commercial paper**. More than 4000 firms currently issue this form of security. Commercial paper consists of unsecured promissory notes that seldom have a maturity of more than 270 days. It is possible for commercial paper to have a maturity longer than 270 days, but such an issue must be placed privately or registered with the Securities and Exchange Commission.

MARKET FOR COMMERCIAL PAPER   Commercial paper is sold either directly or through dealers. Large industrial firms, utilities, and medium-size finance companies generally sell their paper through dealers, who usually charge a commission of $\frac{1}{8}$ of 1% on an annualized basis. Dealer-placed paper usually has a maturity between 30 and 180 days. The main buyers include other firms, insurance companies, pension funds, and banks.

Roughly 40% of all commercial paper is sold directly to investors. Large finance companies, such as General Motors Acceptance Corporation and General Electric Capital Corporation, usually sell their paper directly. They tailor the maturities and the amounts of the notes to fit the needs of investors, who consist mainly of corporations investing excess cash on a short-term basis. Maturities range from 1 to 270 days. In contrast to most industrial firms, the large finance companies use the commercial paper market as a permanent source of funds because of the finance companies' floating-rate assets and because commercial paper costs less than bank financing.

COMPUTING THE TRUE INTEREST COST OF COMMERCIAL PAPER   Interest on commercial paper is paid on a discount basis. For example, if 120-day prime commercial paper carries a 12% interest rate, then the APR interest cost (based on a 360-day year), using Equation (19.15), is

$$\text{APR} = \frac{r}{1 - rf} = \frac{0.12}{1 - 0.12(120/360)} = 12.5\%$$

Because of the many different ways to state interest rates, we remind you yet again to compute carefully the APY of each alternative. The one with the lowest APY is the lowest-cost alternative.

Firms that issue commercial paper generally maintain a backup line of credit to provide insurance against any problems selling commercial paper. If a firm cannot pay off its commercial paper at maturity, the backup line of credit is used. Banks generally charge an annualized fee of $\frac{1}{4}$ to $\frac{1}{2}$ of 1% for such backup lines, which increases the cost.

EXAMPLE

GMAC's Cost of Commercial Paper

Let's say General Motors Acceptance Corporation (GMAC) issues $50 million of 90-day commercial paper at 10%. The paper is discounted, so GMAC gets $48.75 million [= 50 − (0.10)(0.25)50]. From Equation (19.11), the APR is

$$\text{APR} = \left[\frac{1,250,000}{48,750,000}\right]\left[\frac{1}{0.25}\right] = \left[\frac{1,250,000}{48,750,000}\right][4] = 10.26\%$$

GMAC "rolls over" its paper four times per year, selling new commercial paper to replace each issue as it matures.

Assuming a backup line of credit costing 0.25% of the funds received and legal and other out-of-pocket costs amounting to another 0.50% per year, GMAC's total APR cost is

$$\text{Cost} = 10.26\% + 0.25\% + 0.50\% = 11.01\%$$ ■

RATING CONSIDERATIONS   The credit quality of commercial paper is rated by agencies such as Moody's Investors Service and Standard & Poor's Corporation. The agencies apply similar rating criteria. Moody's has two basic commercial paper rating categories: "Prime" and "Not Prime." The Prime category is subdivided into P-1 (highest quality), P-2, and P-3. Standard & Poor's has four basic commercial paper rating categories: A, B, C, and D. The A category corresponds to Moody's Prime category and is subdivided into A-1+ (highest), A-1, A-2, and A-3.

Paper with the highest rating, P-1/A-1+, carries the lowest cost of borrowing and the smallest chance of interrupted market access. At times the yield differential between P-1/A-1+ and P-3/A-3 rated paper has been more than two full percentage points. Furthermore, in market crises, the market for paper rated lower than P-1/A-1 can dry up. Even in the best of times, there is normally no market for commercial paper rated lower than P-3/A-3, and the market for commercial paper rated P-3/A-3 is very limited.

Firms with P-3/A-3 rated paper, and some firms with P-2/A-2 rated paper, may be able to lower their borrowing cost with an irrevocable letter of credit. The letter of credit is a form of insurance that raises the rating and lowers the interest rate. And, of course, if the present value of the interest savings exceeds the cost, this is a positive-NPV decision.

Contracting Costs, Agency Costs, and Short-term Debt

A variety of factors affect a firm's choice of amount and mix of short-term debt as well as the overall maturity structure of the firm's debt. These factors include (1) the cost of each source of funds, (2) the desired level of current assets, (3) the seasonal component of current assets, and (4) the extent to which a firm uses the maturity-matching approach to hedge its debt structure.

Beyond the basic factors just cited, several contracting costs and agency costs also affect the firm's use of short-term debt.

- *Flotation costs.* The costs of issuing long-term securities such as bonds and common stock are generally much higher than the costs of arranging short-term borrowings. Consequently, the firm issues these long-term securities infrequently. In the interim, firms borrow short-term from banks or issue commercial paper. As these short-term borrowings build up, they are eventually replaced with long-term securities.

- *Restricted access to sources of long-term capital.* Legal restrictions limit the types of loans that institutional investors can make. It may not be attractive for smaller firms, or for firms whose debt would be rated below investment grade, to sell debt securities. They may have to rely on trade credit, bank financing, or finance company borrowing.

- *Less restrictive terms.* Public and private debt normally carry penalties for early repayment. Such a penalty is simply the cost of the "hidden" option to refinance. Because of this cost, the more likely a firm is to want to repay early, the more attractive bank financing becomes, because bank financing generally does not have such a penalty.

- *Bankruptcy costs.* Bankruptcy costs create a bias in favor of longer maturities, because every time short-term financing comes due, there is the "hidden" option to default. Shareholders must decide whether it is worth it to "repurchase" the assets from the debtholders or to "walk away."[6]

- *The firm's choice of risk level.* The firm's attitude toward risk will help determine its philosophy about financing its working capital and, more generally, its choice of short- versus long-term financing. Because of possible increases in interest rates, firms whose shareholders are not well diversified, as is often the case with owner-managed businesses, frequently choose the conservative approach.

Self-Check Questions

1. Why do banks often require a borrower to pledge receivables or inventory as security for a loan?

2. Describe each of the three basic forms that a short-term unsecured bank loan can take. What are the main differences among them?

3. Do compensating balances always increase the cost of a bank loan? If not, when do they and when don't they?

4. Why is the true interest cost of a discounted loan always greater than the stated discount rate?

5. What is commercial paper? Who are the main issuers, and who are the main investors? What is responsible for the rapid growth of the commercial paper market?

19.5 ELECTRONIC DATA INTERCHANGE (EDI)

More and more, business transactions are using **electronic data interchange (EDI)**. EDI is the exchange of information electronically, directly from one computer to another. By moving the information in this way, firms save time, personnel costs, materials costs, and costs due to errors.

Let's follow a simple business transaction to see the potential value of EDI. First, assume you want to buy something using traditional paper documents and mail delivery. You contact a supplier about availability and price. You then place an order. The supplier acknowledges the purchase order. When the goods are shipped, the supplier also sends shipping documents and an invoice. When it is time to pay, you send a check along with remittance information through the mail. After getting the check, the supplier credits your account and deposits the check in its bank. Finally, the money is transferred from your bank account to the supplier's.

Now consider the same transaction using EDI. In North America, the American National Standards Institute (ANSI) sets EDI standards for such things as invoices, shipping information, purchase orders, customer account information, requests for quotations, and many others.

Each step in the traditional paper-based process causes time delays and labor costs. In addition, the paper-based system is prone to errors. There are also uncertainties in paper-based

---

[6] See Chapters 8 and 9 for more on this.

systems because participants do not know the status of the transaction. By simplifying the process and sending information almost instantaneously, EDI reduces labor costs, substantially reduces errors, and makes possible a much higher degree of control over the firm's resources.

Using EDI, some firms have been able to operate with much lower investments in inventories, to provide their customers with better service, and to be more price-competitive. In fact, the economic advantages of EDI are so compelling that some firms either require that all transactions be done with EDI or charge a fee, such as $50, for paper documents.

By increasing the availability and lowering the cost of high-quality information, EDI is changing the way firms manage their working capital assets. There are also some special kinds of EDI that can be considered a subset of the overall EDI architecture. Electronic funds transfer (EFT) is the transfer of money electronically from one bank to another bank. Financial EDI (FEDI) is the exchange of information between a bank and its customers (such as information about checks paid, account balances, lockbox information, and other things).

Self-Check Questions
1. What does EDI stand for? What is it, and what are its advantages?
2. How is EDI changing the way firms manage their working capital assets?

SUMMARY

This chapter covered working capital management, cash management practices, short-term financing sources, and electronic data interchange. These important aspects of business involve many day-to-day decisions. In making such decisions, the firm should take into account the time value of money and the importance of preserving the business relations that will maintain the firm's good reputation and facilitate its operations.

DECISION SUMMARY

- Working capital management is the management of the firm's short-term assets and liabilities.

- The cash conversion cycle is the length of time between when a firm pays its accounts payable and when it collects on its accounts receivable. The cash conversion cycle is equal to the inventory conversion period plus the receivables collection period minus the payables deferral period.

- Cash is needed for three reasons: to conduct ordinary transactions when cash flows are uneven (the transactions demand), to avert default on obligations (the precautionary demand), and to take advantage of investment opportunities (the speculative demand). Bank requirements for compensating balances also contribute to the demand for cash balances.

- The Baumol and Miller-Orr models can be useful in determining what cash balances a firm needs for transactions.

- Float is the difference between the checking account balance at the bank and the balance on the firm's books. It is the available balance minus the book balance. Firms use zero balance accounts, wire transfers, controlled disbursing, centralized processing of payables, and lockboxes to manage float.

- Trade credit, bank loans, and commercial paper are the main sources of short-term financing. The APYs of all sources are compared on the basis of the specific terms of each contract.
- Electronic data interchange is the direct exchange of data between the computers of two businesses. A wide variety of documents can be electronically exchanged with the structured formats in EDI.

EQUATION SUMMARY

(19.1)
$$\text{Cash conversion cycle} = \text{Inventory conversion period} + \text{Receivables collection period} - \text{Payables deferral period}$$

(19.2)
$$\text{Inventory conversion period} = \frac{\text{Inventory}}{\text{Cost of sales}/365} = \frac{365}{\text{Inventory turnover}}$$

(19.3)
$$\text{Receivables collection period} = \frac{\text{Receivables}}{\text{Sales}/365} = \frac{365}{\text{Receivables turnover}}$$

(19.4)
$$\text{Payables deferral period} = \frac{\text{Accounts payable} + \text{Wages, benefits, and payroll taxes payable}}{(\text{Cost of sales} + \text{Selling, general, and administrative expenses})/365}$$

(19.5)
$$\text{Cost} = b\frac{T}{C} + i\frac{C}{2}$$

(19.6)
$$C^* = \sqrt{\frac{2bT}{i}}$$

(19.7)
$$Z = \left(\frac{3b\sigma^2}{4i}\right)^{1/3}$$

(19.8)
$$\text{Float} = \text{Available balance} - \text{Book balance}$$

(19.9)
$$\text{APR} = \left(\frac{\text{Discount\%}}{100\% - \text{Discount\%}}\right)\left(\frac{365}{\text{Total period} - \text{Discount period}}\right)$$

(19.10)
$$\text{APY} = -1 + \left(1 + \frac{\text{Discount\%}}{100\% - \text{Discount\%}}\right)^{\frac{365}{\text{Total period} - \text{Discount period}}}$$

(19.11)
$$\text{APR} = \left(\frac{\text{Net cost of loan}}{\text{Cash advance}}\right)\left(\frac{1}{f}\right)$$

(19.12)
$$\text{APY} = \left(1 + \frac{\text{Net cost of loan}}{\text{Cash advance}}\right)^{1/f} - 1 = \left(\frac{\text{Net repayment}}{\text{Cash advance}}\right)^{1/f} - 1$$

(19.13)
$$\text{APR} = \left(\frac{\text{Interest charges}}{\text{Loan amount} - \text{Compensating balance}}\right)\left(\frac{1}{f}\right) = \left(\frac{rP}{P - B}\right)\left(\frac{1}{f}\right)$$

(19.14)
$$\text{APR} = \left(\frac{\text{Interest charges} - \text{Interest received}}{\text{Loan amount} - \text{Compensating balance}}\right)\left(\frac{1}{f}\right) = \left(\frac{rP - yB}{P - B}\right)\left(\frac{1}{f}\right)$$

(19.15)
$$\text{APR} = \left(\frac{rPf}{P - rPf}\right)\left(\frac{1}{f}\right) = \frac{r}{1 - rf}$$

KEY TERMS

working capital management...597

cash conversion cycle...601

transactions demand...603

precautionary demand...603

speculative demand...603

compensating balance...603

float...608

disbursement float...609

collection float...609

trade credit...611

transaction loan....614

line of credit...614

revolving credit agreement...614

term loan...615

prime rate...615

commercial paper...619

electronic data interchange (EDI)...621

EXERCISES

PROBLEM SET A

A1. Cite and describe three alternative approaches to working capital management.

A2. Describe the cash conversion cycle, and discuss its importance to working capital management.

A3. The Mennen Corporation is interested in examining its cash conversion cycle. Suppose a Mennen manager has assembled the following data for your use:

$1.00 million	Inventory
$0.80 million	Accounts receivable
$0.40 million	Accounts payable
$0.15 million	Wages, benefits, and payroll taxes payable
$25.0 million	Sales
$10.0 million	Cost of sales
$1.50 million	Selling, general, and administrative expenses

Estimate each of the following:

a. Inventory conversion period

b. Receivables collection period

c. Payables deferral period

d. Cash conversion cycle

A4. Cite and describe three basic motives for holding cash.

A5. Explain the concept of float.

A6. Suppose a Footlocker franchisee has $20,000 for both its book balance and its bank balance. If the franchisee writes a $2000 check that takes 4 days to clear, what is its disbursement float?

A7. Cite and describe five types of marketable securities.

A8. Say you need to transfer $250,000 from Houston to Chicago. If you mail a check, it will cost $1.00 for postage and clearing the check, and it will take a total of five days for the funds to be transferred. During the money's 5-day travel, you will suffer an opportunity cost, because the $250,000 is not earning 3% APY interest. Alternatively, you can avoid the opportunity cost by sending a wire transfer costing $12.00, which instantaneously transfers the funds with no float. Calculate the cost of each alternative. Which is cheaper?

A9. Cite and briefly describe five methods that corporations use to manage their float.

A10. Suppose you are offered trade credit terms of 1.5/15, net 50. What is the APR cost of this trade credit if you skip the discount and pay at the end of the net period? What would be the APR cost if you "stretched" the payable and paid after 75 days?

A11. Cite and describe three alternative types of short-term bank loans.

A12. What is the major advantage of using EDI (electronic data interchange)?

PROBLEM SET B

B1. Auburn Hair Products has an inventory turnover of six times per year, a receivables turnover of ten times, and a payables turnover of twelve times. What is Auburn Hair's inventory conversion period, the receivables collection period, and the payables deferral period? What is the cash conversion cycle?

B2. A firm uses the Baumol model and projects a need for $2 million cash per month. Its projected 30-day investment yield is 9% APR. The cost of converting securities into cash is $300 per transaction.

a. How much cash would the firm raise each time it sells securities?

b. How often should the firm plan to sell securities?

c. What will be the average cash balance?

d. What are the annual opportunity cost of funds, the annual transactions cost, and the annual total cost?

B3. Sturbens Electrical Systems uses the Baumol model and pays its $4,000,000 annual payroll expenses out of a Wyoming bank. The disbursements are roughly uniform throughout the year. Sturbens makes deposits into the account from its master account in a Chicago bank. Each deposit has a fixed cost of $200. The opportunity cost of funds is 4%, because the funds are earning 4% in Chicago and the corporate account in Wyoming receives no interest.

a. What is the optimal deposit size? What are the annual opportunity cost of funds, the annual transactions cost, and annual total cost?

b. Assume that interest rates have risen substantially and that Sturbens now has an opportunity cost of funds of 8%. If Sturbens continues to use the same deposit size that you determined in part a, what will be its annual opportunity cost of funds, its annual transactions cost, and its annual total cost?

c. Recompute the optimal deposit size assuming the new 8% opportunity cost. What are the annual opportunity cost, transactions cost, and total cost using the recomputed deposit size?

B4. Suppose a firm's cash flows are uncertain and have an estimated standard deviation of $100,000 per day. The interest rate is 9% APR, and the cost of converting securities into cash or vice versa is $300 per transaction. The lower control limit is zero. (*Hint*: do not forget to convert the annual interest rate into a daily rate.)

a. Calculate the return point and the upper control limit.

b. When and in what amounts should the firm buy and sell securities?

c. What is the average cash balance?

B5. Calculate the cost of skipping the discount and paying at the end of the net period for each of the following credit terms. Calculate the APR and APY cost of each.

a. 1/10, net 30

b. 6/10, net 70

c. 2/15, net 45

B6. Trade credit terms are 2/10, net 40.

a. What is the true interest cost of skipping the discount and paying on day 40. Estimate both the APR and the APY.

b. If payment is stretched to day 55 (15 days late), calculate the true interest cost of skipping the discount if the supplier accepts the payment without penalty at that time. Again, estimate both the APR and the APY.

B7. Dave Mauer writes a $100 check on Monday, a $200 check on Tuesday, and a $300 check on Wednesday. It takes exactly 2 days for the checks to be presented and funds taken from Dave's account and put into Peggy's account. What is Dave's disbursement float on each of Monday, Tuesday, Wednesday, Thursday, and Friday?

B8. Patin Risk Management Firm writes the checks and makes the deposits indicated in the table that follows. Assume that when Patin writes a check, it takes 3 days for the check to clear and funds to be removed from Patin's available balance at the bank. When Patin makes a deposit, it takes 1 day for the funds to be made available at the bank. Indicate for each day the amount of Patin's available balance at the bank, the disbursement float, the collection float, and the total float.

Day	Checks Written	Deposits	Book Balance	Available Balance	Disbursement Float	Availability Float	Total Float
1	0	0	10,000	10,000	0	0	0
2	500	1000	10,500				
3	800	0	9,700				
4	800	0	8,900				
5	0	0	8,900				
6	0	2000	10,900				
7	900	0	10,000				
8	0	0	10,000				
9	0	0	10,000				
10	0	0	10,000				

B9. For a 1-year loan of $100 with a 15% APR interest rate, determine the cash flows and the APY for each of the following loans.

a. Interest in arrears

b. Discount loan

c. Interest in arrears with a 10% compensating balance

d. Discount loan with a 10% compensating balance

B10. For a 3-month loan of $100 with a 15% APR interest rate, determine the cash flows and the APY interest rate for each of the following loans.

a. Interest in arrears

b. Discount loan

c. Interest in arrears with a 10% compensating balance

d. Discount loan with a 10% compensating balance

B11. A bank loan agreement calls for an interest rate equal to the prime rate plus 1%. If the prime rate averages 9% and non-interest-earning compensating balances equal to 10% of the loan must be maintained, what is the APR cost of the loan?

B12. Ray Brooks has discussed a $250,000 1-year loan with several different banks. Alternatives a, b, and c are described here. What are the APR and the APY of each alternative? Which alternative is the cheapest?

a. A 15% annual rate on a simple interest loan (interest in arrears), with no compensating balance. Interest is due at the end of the year.

b. An 11% annual rate on a simple interest loan (interest in arrears), with a 20% compensating balance requirement and interest due at the end of the year.

c. A 14% annual rate on a discount loan with no compensating balance. Interest is paid at the beginning of the year.

B13. Say Chemical Bank will give you an installment loan for $50,000 that will be repaid in 12 equal monthly installments. The loan is a 12% add-on loan, which means you must pay 12% on the original loan advance (not just the remaining balance). Your total payments will be $56,000 (the principal of $50,000 plus $6000 of interest) so your monthly payment is $4666.67. What APY are you paying on the loan?

B14. The discount rate for a 54-day issue of commercial paper is 8.50%. What is the APY? Assume a 360-day year.

B15. Suppose General Motors Acceptance Corporation sells commercial paper with a 180-day maturity. If GMAC sells the commercial paper at an annualized discount rate of 11%, calculate the APY. Assume a 360-day year.

B16. When you send money to firm headquarters with a wire transfer, it costs a fixed $10 and there is no float. On the other hand, when you write a check and mail it, the fixed cost is only $1.50 and the transfer of funds will occur in 5 days (the delay is due to mail times, processing times, and clearing times). The opportunity cost of funds is 8% APR. Assume a 365-day year.

  a. What are the cost of a wire transfer and the cost of sending a paper check if the amount being forwarded to headquarters is $5000?

  b. What are the cost of a wire transfer and the cost of sending a paper check if the amount being forwarded to headquarters is $25,000?

B17. The Denver Bakery Products Firm currently collects all of its customer payments in Denver. By going to a new lockbox system with boxes in Denver, Boston, and Atlanta, Denver Bakery Products can reduce the total time it takes to convert customer payments into available funds by an average of 2.50 days. The firm collects an average of $120,000 per day. The extra costs associated with the lockbox system are $7500 per year. The opportunity cost of funds is 6% APR. What is the expected annual profit of using the new system?

B18. Suppose Citibank has made a proposal to operate a lockbox for you. Checks cleared through the lockbox amount to $20,000 per day, and the lockbox will make these funds available to you 2.5 days faster.

  a. If Citibank will provide the lockbox services in exchange for a $30,000 compensating balance, is its proposal attractive?

  b. Instead of a compensating balance, the bank proposes to provide lockbox services on a fee basis, charging an annual fee of $1000 plus $0.10 per check. You expect 40,000 checks per year to be processed through the lockbox. If the opportunity cost of funds is 6% APR, what is the annual profit associated with accepting the fee-based proposal?

  c. Which is more profitable to you, the compensating balance proposal in part a or the fee-based proposal in part b?

PROBLEM SET C

C1. Let's say a McDonald's franchisee needs to borrow $100,000. The franchisee has two alternative loans. The first is a standard 5-year installment loan at 12% APR that will require equal monthly payments. The second is a 10% APR discount loan that requires a 15% compensating balance and has an additional $1500 setup cost. The second alternative requires interest plus principal payments of 20% of the loan at the end of each year. What is the APY of each loan? Which loan is cheaper? (*Hint*: Note that with the second alternative, the franchisee will have to borrow a larger stated amount to get the full $100,000 it needs.)

C2. In Problem C1, suppose there is a chance that the franchisee will want to repay the borrowed money after only 1 year, rather than after 5 years. How would this possibility affect the choice of loan?

C3. EDI reduces transaction costs for everyone, and yet it is coming into use fairly slowly. How can financial contracting considerations in a principal-agent framework explain the reluctance to change to EDI quickly? (Hint: Consider the two sides of float and the prisoner's dilemma.)

Real-World Application:
Kellogg's Cost of Short-Term Funds

Kellogg Company is the world's largest producer of ready-to-eat cereal products. It also produces toaster pastries, frozen waffles, cereal bars, and other convenience foods. Kellogg manufactures its products in 20 countries and distributes them in more than 150 countries.

Kellogg's capitalization at year-end 1995 is shown below.

CAPITALIZATION (dollar amounts in millions)	BOOK VALUE DECEMBER 31, 1995
Current maturities of long-term debt	$1.9
Commercial paper and other notes payable	188.0
Total short-term debt	$189.9
Long-term debt	$717.8
Stockholders' equity	1590.9
Total capitalization	$2308.7
Total capitalization (including short-term debt)	$2498.6

Kellogg is considering three borrowing alternatives:

1. 90-day commercial paper at a 6.50% discount rate
2. Commercial bank loan with three interest-rate alternatives:
   a. prime rate with interest payable quarterly
   b. 3-month London Interbank Offer Rate (LIBOR) plus 0.25%
   c. 3-month certificate of deposit (CD) rate plus 0.50%
3. Fixed-rate note maturing after 2 years and paying interest at the rate of 8% APR with interest payable semiannually.

Currently, the prime rate is 10% APR, 3-month LIBOR is 6% APR, and the 3-month CD rate is 6% APR.

1. Calculate the percentages of short-term debt and long-term debt in Kellogg's capitalization.
2. What is the true interest cost of the commercial paper alternative?

3. Kellogg has a policy of maintaining a backup line of credit for its commercial paper. The cost is 0.25% per year. What is the true interest cost of the commercial paper, including the cost of the backup line? Express this cost as an APY.

4. Assume the 90-day commercial paper rate is expected to increase to 6.75% after 90 days, to 7.00% 90 days thereafter, and to 7.50% 90 days thereafter. Calculate the APY of the commercial paper alternative, including the cost of the backup line.

5. Calculate the APY for each bank loan interest-rate alternative. Kellogg can pick the one that is the cheapest. What's the APY for the bank loan alternative?

6. In reading the "fine print," you notice that the bank would require a 10% compensating balance. Calculate the APY for the bank loan, including the cost of the compensating balance.

7. Suppose the prime rate is not expected to change over the next year, but 3-month LIBOR is expected to increase by 0.30% every 3 months, and the 3-month CD rate is expected to increase by 0.20% every 3 months. Calculate the APY for each bank loan interest-rate alternative. What is the APY for the bank loan?

8. Which is cheaper, issuing commercial paper or borrowing from the bank?

9. Are there any options that might affect the value of one alternative or the other?

10. How would you compare the fixed-rate alternative to the floating-rate alternatives?

11. Compare the APYs for the fixed-rate note and the floating-rate alternatives. Which alternative is cheapest on this basis? How might interest rate risk affect Kellogg's choice?

12. Find the average interest cost (APR) for year two for the cheapest floating-rate alternative in question 8 that would make Kellogg indifferent to choosing between that alternative and issuing the 2-year note. (This is called the *break-even rate*.)

BIBLIOGRAPHY

Anvari, M. "Efficient Scheduling of Cross-Border Cash Transfers," *Financial Management*, 1986, 15(2):40–49.

Aziz, Abdul, and Gerald H. Lawson. "Cash Flow Reporting and Financial Distress Models: Testing of Hypotheses," *Financial Management*, 1989, 18(1):55–63.

Baumol, William J. "The Transactions Demand for Cash: An Inventory Theoretic Approach," *Quarterly Journal of Economics*, 1952, 66(November):545–556.

Brown, Keith C., and Scott L. Lummer. "The Cash Management Implications of a Hedged Dividend Capture Strategy," *Financial Management*, 1984, 13(4):7–17.

Brown, Keith C., and Scott L. Lummer. "A Reexamination of the Covered Call Option Strategy for Corporate Cash Management," *Financial Management*, 1986, 15(2):13–17.

Gentry, James A. "State of the Art of Short-Run Financial Management," *Financial Management*, 1988, 17(2):41–57.

Gentry, James A., R. Vaidyanathan, and Hei Wai Lee. "A Weighted Cash Conversion Cycle," *Financial Management*, 1990, 19(1):90–99.

Gilmer, R. H., Jr. "The Optimal Level of Liquid Assets: An Empirical Test," *Financial Management*, 1985, 14(4):39–43.

Kallberg, Jarl G., and Kenneth K. Parkinson. *Current Asset Management*. New York: John Wiley, 1984.

Kamath, Ravindra R., Shahriar Khaksari, Heidi Hylton Meier, and John Winklepleck. "Management of Excess Cash: Practices and Developments," *Financial Management*, 1985, 14(3):70–77.

Miller, Merton H., and Daniel Orr. "A Model of the Demand for Money by Firms," *Quarterly Journal of Economics*, 1966, 80(August):413–435.

Pohlman, Randolph A., Emmanuel S. Santiago, and F. Lynn Markel. "Cash Flow Estimation Practices of Large Firms," *Financial Management*, 1988, 17(2):71–79.

Sartoris, William L., and Ned C. Hill. "A Generalized Cash Flow Approach to Short-Term Financial Decisions," *Journal of Finance*, 1983, 38(2):349–360.

Stone, Bernell K., and Tom W. Miller. "Daily Cash Forecasting with Multiplicative Models of Cash Flow Patterns," *Financial Management*, 1987, 16(4):45–54.

Winger, Bernard J., Carl R. Chen, John D. Martin, J. William Petty, and Steven C. Hayden. "Adjustable Rate Preferred Stock," *Financial Management*, 1986, 15(1):48–57.

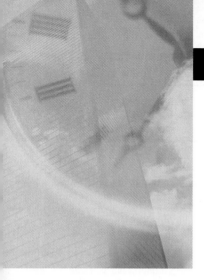

ACCOUNTS RECEIVABLE AND INVENTORY MANAGEMENT

OBJECTIVES

After studying this chapter, you should be able to

1. Explain the reasons for granting credit.

2. Evaluate credit-granting decisions using the NPV rule.

3. Describe and apply some important accounts receivable management tools.

4. Identify and calculate inventory management costs.

5. Apply inventory management models to the problem of optimizing the firm's inventories.

In this chapter we will discuss receivables and inventories, which are integral parts of working capital management. Receivables and inventories are important for several reasons. First, they make up a large investment in assets. Second, they represent a tremendous volume of transactions and decisions. Third, they involve a large proportion of jobs. Finally, receivables and inventories are important because if they are managed poorly, an otherwise healthy firm can actually be pushed into financial distress.

In practice, managing receivables and inventories often falls to new employees, including those who have just received their business degrees. From this vantage point, new managers apply the principles of finance to day-to-day decisions at the core of the business. Competent use of these resources is essential to the firm's short-term operation and long-term health. Therefore, inventory and receivables managers often work under close supervision. Employees who do well can earn promotion, and those who do poorly can find themselves out of work.

RECEIVABLES, INVENTORY, AND THE PRINCIPLES OF FINANCE

◇ *Incremental Benefits*: Calculate the incremental cash flows for receivables and inventories decisions.

◇ *Time Value of Money*: Compare the NPV of alternative receivables and inventories decisions.

◇ *Two-Sided Transactions*: Look for situations that are not zero-sum games; these may be profitable to you *and* your supplier or customer. Receivables and inventories decisions can be used to reduce both financial contracting costs and routine transaction costs.

◇ *Self-Interested Behavior*: Carefully evaluate and monitor the creditworthiness of your credit customers and the quality of the goods and services from your suppliers.

◇ *Comparative Advantage*: Consider subcontracting business activities to outside vendors if they can provide the services more cheaply and competently.

◇ *Behavioral*: Use common industry practices as a good starting place for operating efficiently.

20.1 ACCOUNTS RECEIVABLE MANAGEMENT

Credit sales create accounts receivable. There are two types of credit: trade credit and consumer credit. Between firms, **trade credit** occurs when one firm buys goods or services from another without simultaneous payment. Such sales create an account receivable for the supplier (seller) and an account payable for the buying firm. **Consumer credit**, or retail credit, is created when a firm sells goods or services to a consumer without simultaneous payment.

Most business transactions use trade credit. At the retail level, payment mechanisms include cash, checks, credit extended by the retailer, and credit extended by a third party (such as MasterCard, Visa, or American Express). The use of trade credit and consumer credit is so commonplace that we tend to take them for granted. If you ask why firms grant credit, managers often say they must because competitors do. Although true, this response is simplistic and does not address the fundamental reasons for the extensive use of credit.

Why Is Credit So Pervasive?

Trade credit is effectively a loan from one firm to another. But it is a loan that is tied to a purchase, like the "special-financing" offers we explored in Chapter 4. The product and loan (credit) are bundled together. Why does this bundling occur?

One answer is that bundling controls financial contracting costs that are created by market imperfections. By using trade credit, both sides of the transaction must be able to lower the cost or risk of doing business. Some specific market considerations follow.

1. *Financial intermediation.* Generally, the interest rate of a trade credit loan benefits both partners. It is lower than the customer's alternative borrowing rates but higher than short-term investment rates available to the supplier. A successful transaction makes the supplier a convenient and economical "bank" for the customer and makes the customer a reliable short-term investment for the supplier.

2. *Collateral.* Suppliers know how to handle the goods as collateral better than other lenders such as banks. When collateral is repossessed after a default on payment, the collateral is more valuable in the hands of a supplier, who has expertise in producing, maintaining, and marketing this collateral.

3. *Information costs.* A supplier may already possess the information needed to evaluate customer

creditworthiness. A firm accumulates important information about its customers in its normal business relations. This same information may be a sufficient basis on which to make credit-granting decisions. If a bank wants to lend to this same customer, making the credit-granting decision entails costs. Such costs give a supplier a cost advantage over a bank.

4. *Product quality information.* A supplier generally has better information than the customer about the quality of its products. If a supplier is willing to grant credit to customers who buy its products, this is a positive signal about product quality. Credit can provide a cheaply enforced product quality guarantee. If the product is of acceptable quality, the customer pays the trade credit on time. If the product is of low quality, the customer ships it back and refuses to pay. Of course, a supplier can offer a product quality guarantee, but this can be expensive and time-consuming for a customer to enforce if payment has already been made. (For a highly reputable supplier who readily honors all guarantees, the extension of credit adds little as a product quality signal.)

5. *Employee theft.* Firms try to protect themselves from employee theft in a variety of ways. One is to separate the employees who authorize transactions, who physically handle products, and who handle the payments. This segregation of duties makes it much more difficult for dishonest employees to steal merchandise or money without being caught. Trade credit helps separate the various functions.

6. *Steps in the distribution process.* If a supplier sells to a customer, but the goods must pass through the hands of shippers (such as rail, truck, sea, or air transporters), then it is simply impractical to have payments exchanged at each step in the distribution process. By granting credit to the ultimate buyer, the payments mechanism bypasses all of the agents in the distribution process, requiring only one payment from the ultimate buyer to the original seller.

7. *Convenience, safety, and buyer psychology.* Sometimes it is inconvenient to pay at the time of purchase. Carrying a lot of cash increases the likelihood of being robbed as well as the possibility of losing or misplacing cash. Convenience and safety are important for both business and retail customers, but psychology is also important, especially at the retail level. Most retailers know that their customers would probably buy less if they had to pay with cash or check instead of with credit. "Plastic money" just does not seem like real money. Credit can be an important part of marketing.

The Basic Credit-Granting Decision

The basic analysis for credit-granting decisions is the same as for other financial decisions. Credit should be granted whenever granting credit is a positive-NPV decision.

$$\text{NPV} = \text{PV of future net cash inflows} - \text{outlay}$$

For a simple credit-granting decision, the NPV is

$$\text{NPV} = \frac{pR}{(1 + r)^t} - C \tag{20.1}$$

At time zero, we invest C in a credit sale. The investment might be the cost of goods sold and sales commissions. The sale amount is R, the probability of payment is p, and the expected payment is pR. The customer's probability of payment is estimated subjectively or with the help of statistical models. The payment is expected at time t. The required return is r. If the NPV is negative, then credit should not be granted. Of course, we would like a positive NPV.

We can also calculate an indifference (zero-NPV) payment probability, p^*. If a credit customer has a payment probability exceeding p^*, then granting credit has a positive NPV. This indifference payment probability is found by setting the NPV in Equation (20.1) equal to zero and solving for p:

$$p^* = \frac{C(1 + r)^t}{R} \tag{20.2}$$

Boy Scouts of America (BSA) has a customer who wants to purchase $1000 of goods on credit. BSA estimates that the customer has a 95% probability of paying the $1000 in 3 months and a 5% probability of a complete default (paying no cash at all). Assume an investment of 80% of the amount, made at the time of the sale, and a required return of 20% APY. What is the NPV of granting credit, and what is the indifference payment probability?

Granting Credit at BSA

EXAMPLE

Using Equation (20.1) yields

$$\text{NPV} = \frac{pR}{(1+r)^t} - C = \frac{0.95(1000)}{(1+0.20)^{.25}} - 800 = 907.67 - 800 = \$107.67$$

The expected payment is $950, which has a present value of $907.67. [Put in FV = 950, r = 20%, n = 0.25, and CF = 0. Then compute PV = 907.67.] Thus the NPV is $107.67, credit is profitable, and it should be granted.

Using Equation (20.2) yields

$$p^* = \frac{C(1+r)^t}{R} = \frac{800(1+0.20)^{.25}}{1000} = \frac{837.31}{1000} = 83.7\%$$

This result is consistent with the NPV calculation, BSA's estimate of a 95% payment probability exceeds the indifference value of 83.7% and indicates that BSA should grant credit.

The NPV rule is the best method for evaluating credit-granting decisions. However, calculations can be quite complicated. The investment in the sale may not be made at time zero. In addition, the expected payments may occur at various times rather than at a single point in time. For example, with payment due in 30 days, the customer might have a 60% probability of paying in 30 days, a 30% probability of paying in 60 days, a 5% probability of paying in 90 days, and a 5% probability of never paying. No matter how complicated the situation, however, the NPV rule should be used.

Credit-Policy Decisions

Credit-policy decisions affect a firm's revenues and costs. For example, consider a policy of granting credit more easily. A more liberal credit policy should increase the cost of goods sold, gross profit, bad debt expenses, the cost of carrying additional receivables, and administrative costs. However, the more liberal policy might or might not increase net profit. A policy's profitability depends on the incremental benefits and incremental costs. These are the additional gross profits generated by the liberal policy minus the increase in costs, such as bad debt costs, carrying costs on increased receivables, and administrative costs.

Depending on the industry, credit policy can vary from being crucial to being irrelevant. A retail store may need a competitive policy to survive, whereas an electric utility must simply grant credit according to government regulation. Credit-policy decisions involve all aspects of receivables management. They include (1) the choice of credit terms, (2) setting evaluation methods and credit standards, (3) monitoring receivables and taking actions for slow payment, and (4) controlling and administering the firm's credit functions.

Credit Terms

Credit terms are the contract between the supplier and credit customer specifying how the credit will be repaid. In our discussion of accounts payable (Chapter 19), we used the term "2/10, net 30." As the seller, you are now *offering* such credit terms instead of *receiving* them.

For the 2/10, net 30 credit terms, you are offering a total **credit period** of 30 days from the date of the invoice, a **discount period** of 10 days, and a 2% **discount** if the bill is paid on or before the discount period expires.

The **invoice** is a written statement about goods that were ordered, along with their prices and the payment dates. In other words, the invoice is simply the bill for purchases. The **invoice date** is usually the date the goods are shipped. When a firm is using **invoice billing**, the invoice that accompanies shipment is a separate bill to be paid. When invoices are numerous, a firm may use statement billing instead of invoice billing. With **statement billing**, all of the sales for a period such as a month (for which a customer receives invoices, too) are collected into a single statement and sent to the customer as one bill.

Although any set of credit terms is possible, there tend to be only a few sets of terms used in a particular industry. These credit terms reflect the specific circumstances surrounding the industry and firm, as well as general economic conditions. The following box describes several basic types of credit terms that are in use.

TRADE CREDIT TERMS

CIA (cash in advance) and CBD (cash before delivery) Payment must be received before the order is shipped.

COD (cash on delivery) The shipper collects the payment (on behalf of the seller) upon delivery.

Cash Payment is due when the goods are delivered. Unlike COD, cash terms allow the buyer to mail payment. Effectively, cash terms allow the customer up to about 10 days to pay.

Standard terms: "net 30" or "net 60." Payment is due in full 30 or 60 days from the date of the invoice.

Discount terms: "2/10, net 30." Discount terms include a discount percent, discount payment date, and net date. The buyer can take a 2% discount if the payment is made by the tenth day following the invoice date. Otherwise, the full amount is due 30 days following the invoice date.

Prox terms: "10th prox," "25th prox," "2/10, prox net 30." Prox or proximate refers to the next month. All invoices dated prior to a cutoff are to be paid by a date in the next month. Invoices with "10th prox" must be paid by the 10th of the next month, and invoices with "25th prox" by the 25th of the next month. "2/10, prox net 30" means that invoices paid by the 10th of the next month receive a 2% discount. If payment is not made by the 10th, then the full amount is due by the 30th.

Seasonal Dating: "2/10, net 30, dating 120," or "2/10, net 30, 60 extra." For seasonal items such as sporting goods, some clothing, or Christmas items, payment is sometimes scheduled to be due near the buyer's selling season. The "dating 120" or "60 extra" means that the clock does not start until 120 or 60 days after the invoice date. Although seasonal dating gives buyers a longer time to pay, sellers benefit by encouraging buyers to make earlier purchase decisions. This lowers the seller's inventory costs by reducing the amount of time the goods spend in inventory.

Consignment: The seller ships the goods to the buyer, but the buyer is not required to pay until the goods have been sold or used.

Letter of credit: A letter of credit is an agreement wherein a financial institution (a bank or other financially strong party) substitutes its creditworthiness for that of the customer. The supplier can require a letter of credit when the payment risk is high. When terms specified in the letter of credit are met, such as delivery of the goods, the bank makes payment for the customer. Letters of credit are often used in international trade.

Electronic credit terms: The seller is paid directly from the buyer's bank account by an automated clearing house (ACH) transaction. Transfer usually occurs right after delivery. Electronic credit terms reduce administrative costs and uncertainties about payment dates. They also reduce supplier accounts receivable and buyer accounts payable.

Credit terms also specify the evidence of indebtedness. Most credit sales are made on an **open account** basis, which means that customers simply purchase what they want. The invoice they sign when receiving the shipment provides evidence that they received the goods and have accepted an obligation to pay. Suppliers usually establish a credit limit for each customer. It is the maximum total amount of outstanding invoices that the customer is permitted. If the cumulative bills reach the credit limit, further credit is denied until the customer makes some payment or gets the credit limit raised. Credit limits are an effective way to limit the amount that can be lost to default.

For large purchases or nonregular customers, a customer may be required to sign a promissory note. Because of time and expense and the low risk of default, promissory notes are not used for routine sales.

Self-Check Questions

1. What is trade credit? How is it different from consumer credit? Explain how both arise in the normal course of business transactions.
2. Why is credit so pervasive?
3. What should be the basis for credit-granting decisions?
4. What are the four main aspects of credit-policy decisions?

20.2 CREDIT STANDARDS AND CREDIT EVALUATION

Credit standards are the criteria used to grant credit. They depend on the variables that determine the NPV of the sale: investment in the sale, probability of payment, required return, and payment period. A higher probability of default, delayed payments, and the necessity of expensive collection efforts all reduce the NPV.

Table 20-1 gives three pairs of numerical examples of how each of these variables can cause a sale to be profitable or unprofitable. The first pair shows the effect of a lower probability of payment. A lower probability results in a negative NPV. The second pair shows the effect of delayed payment. The time value of money on a two-month payment delay more than eliminates the profit. The final pair emphasizes the role of collection costs. The present value of the collection costs is an added cost of the sale. Higher collection costs reduce the NPV and can even cause it to be negative. Collection costs have a fixed component, costs that are independent of the amount of the credit sale. These fixed administrative or collection costs often make small credit sales unprofitable.

TABLE 20-1
Effects of default risk, delayed payments, and collection costs.

SALE	INVESTMENT	PROBABILITY OF PAYMENT	COLLECTION PERIOD	PV OF COLLECTION COSTS	COST OF FUNDS	NPV
Effect of Default Risk						
$1000	$ 850	.99	1 month	0	20%	$125.07
$1000	$ 850	.85	1 month	0	20%	− 12.82
Effect of Delayed Payment						
$2000	$1925	.99	1 month	0	20%	$25.14
$2000	$1925	.99	3 months	0	20%	− 33.22
Effect of Collection Costs						
$ 100	$ 80	.95	1 month	$ 5	20%	$8.57
$ 100	$ 80	.95	1 month	$20	20%	− 6.43

Unfortunately, these individual factors that reduce the profitability of a credit sale often reinforce one another. For example, a customer who is likely to make late payments is also more likely to default and to require extra collection efforts. The management of credit policy, then, must include establishing credit standards and then evaluating individual customers against these standards. To do this, managers must know how to analyze creditworthiness.

Sources of Credit Information

There are several valuable internal and external sources of credit information. The primary *internal sources* are

1. A credit application, including references.

2. The applicant's previous payment history, if credit has previously been extended.

3. Information from sales representatives and other employees.

Several important *external sources* are

1. Financial statements for recent years. These financial statements can be analyzed to get insights into the customer's profitability, leverage, and liquidity.

2. Reports from credit rating agencies such as Dun & Bradstreet Business Credit Services (D&B). These agencies supply credit appraisals of thousands of firms and estimates of their overall strength. D&B appraises the credit of a firm relative to that of other firms of comparable financial strength and assigns composite credit appraisal ratings between 1 ("high") and 4 ("limited").

3. Credit bureau reports. These reports provide factual information about whether a firm's financial obligations are overdue. Credit bureau reports also give information about any legal judgments against the firm.

4. Industry association credit files. Industry associations sometimes maintain credit files. Industry associations and your direct competitors are frequently willing to share credit information about customers.

Two basic approaches to evaluating a credit application are the *judgmental* approach and the *objective* approach. The judgmental approach uses a variety of credit information, as well as specific knowledge and experience, to reach a decision. The objective approach uses numerical cutoffs or scores that must be reached for credit to be granted. The "five C's of credit" are used with the judgmental approach. Credit scoring is an example of an objective approach.

Five C's of Credit

The **five C's of credit** are five general factors that credit analysts often consider when making a credit-granting decision.

1. *Character.* The commitment to meet credit obligations. Character is best measured by a credit applicant's prior payment history.

2. *Capacity.* The ability to meet credit obligations with current income. Capacity is evaluated by looking at the income or cash flows on the applicant's income statement or statement of cash flows.

3. *Capital.* The ability to meet credit obligations from existing assets if necessary. Capital is evaluated by looking at the applicant's net worth.

4. *Collateral.* The collateral that can be repossessed in the case of nonpayment. Collateral value depends on the cost of repossessing and on the possible resale value.

5. *Conditions.* General or industry economic conditions. Conditions external to the customer's business affect the credit-granting decision. For example, improving or deteriorating general economic conditions can change interest rates or the risk of granting credit. Likewise, conditions in a particular industry can affect the profitability of granting credit to a firm in that industry.

Credit-Scoring Models

Assessing a firm's ability to pay its debts is a complex judgment, because many factors can affect creditworthiness. One tool that many firms use is credit scoring. **Credit scoring** combines several financial variables to create a single score, or index, that measures creditworthiness. The score is often a linear combination of several variables. A score based on four financial variables could be

$$S = w_1X_1 + w_2X_2 + w_3X_3 + w_4X_4 = 2X_1 - 0.3X_2 + 0.1X_3 + 0.6X_4$$

where X_1 = net working capital/sales (expressed as a percent)

   X_2 = debt/assets (%)

   X_3 = assets/sales (%)

   X_4 = net profit margin (%)

The w's are the coefficients (or weights) that are multiplied by the X's (financial characteristics) to create the overall credit score. The positive coefficients for X_1, X_3, and X_4 mean that a higher value results in a higher credit score. The negative coefficient for X_2 means that a higher debt/assets ratio reduces the credit score.

What are the credit scores for the two customers with the characteristics given here?

Calculating Credit Scores for a Business Customer

EXAMPLE

	CUSTOMER 1	CUSTOMER 2
X_1 = net working capital/sales (%)	15%	8%
X_2 = debt/assets (%)	40%	55%
X_3 = assets/sales (%)	105%	110%
X_4 = net profit margin (%)	12%	9%

The credit score for customer 1 is

$$S = 2.0(15) - 0.3(40) + 0.1(105) + 0.6(12) = 30 - 12 + 10.5 + 7.2 = 35.7$$

The credit score for customer 2 is

$$S = 2.0(8) - 0.3(55) + 0.1(110) + 0.6(9) = 16 - 16.5 + 11 + 5.4 = 15.9$$

If the firm estimates a zero NPV for customers that score 25, customer 1 should get credit and customer 2 should be denied credit. ■

Credit-scoring models are constructed by using sophisticated statistical methods to analyze the payment records of many past customers. Such models offer several advantages.

1. They enable the creditor to accept the clearly good customers and reject the clearly bad customers very quickly. The creditor then can devote costly evaluation talent to analyzing the "close calls."

2. They allow different loan processors to apply consistent standards across all credit applicants. They also make changing the standard easy. The firm could change the cutoff from 25 to, say, 28. This change would then apply equally to all loan applicants.

3. They are "objective" and can help the firm avoid bias or discrimination.

There are important disadvantages of credit-scoring models, too.

1. The models are only as good as the payment records used to construct the models. Many samples do not have a rich enough set of bad loans to build an effective scoring model. In addition, the models have to be updated occasionally. When the model is updated with a new sample, there is some "inbreeding" whereby the new model is built on data that eliminated many bad customers.

2. Credit-scoring models work best when applied to large populations of loan applicants. Consumer loan databases often include many thousands of loans, and credit-scoring models can be built readily. Unfortunately, the number of business loans in a database is often too small to be statistically reliable. Consequently, credit-scoring models are more often used for evaluating consumer loans than for evaluating business loans, which more often relies on judgmental methods.

Credit scoring is frequently used on consumer credit card applications and for personal loans and car loans. For a credit card application, the following scoring sheet (sometimes called a weighted application blank) is often used.

Telephone	Yes = 4 points, No = 0
Income	Above $40,000 = 3 points
	$20,000 - $40,000 = 2 points
	Below $20,000 = 0 points
Employment	More than 3 years with current employer = 3 points
	1–3 years with current employer = 2 points
	Less than 1 year with current employer = 1
	Self-employed = 1 point
	Unemployed = 0 points
Residence	Own = 3 points
	Rent = 1 point
	More than 3 years at current address = 2 points
	1–3 years at current address = 1 point
	0–1 year at current address = 0 points
Credit report	Good = 10 points
	Fair = 4 points
	Bad = −5 points
	None = 0 points

Credit Card Scoring

EXAMPLE

Suppose that Marcelle Welch is applying for a credit card. After graduating with her business degree, Marcelle has a new job earning $45,000 a year. She has just moved to her new job and has rented an apartment. Her telephone is connected, and she has a good credit report. What is her credit score?

Telephone	4 points
Income	3
Employment	1
Residence	1
Credit report	10
Total score	19 points

If the cutoff is 15, Marcelle will qualify for the credit card. ■

Self-Check Questions

1. What are the main sources of credit information? Which are internal and which are external sources?

2. What are the five C's of credit? Explain how credit analysts use them to decide whether to grant credit.

3. Explain how a firm can use a credit-scoring model to decide whether to grant credit. How is such a model constructed?

4. What are the main advantages and disadvantages of using credit-scoring models to evaluate customer creditworthiness?

20.3 MONITORING ACCOUNTS RECEIVABLE

Monitoring accounts receivable is critical because of the size of the investment. If the quality is surprisingly high or low, several relevant questions arise: Are the firm's credit standards too low or too high? Has a change in general economic conditions affected customer creditworthiness? Is something fundamentally wrong with the evaluation system?

In any case, a reliable, early warning about deterioration of receivables can make it possible to take action to prevent a worsening. Conversely, a reliable, early indication of improvement in the quality of receivables might inspire the firm to be more aggressive in its receivables policies.

Widely used techniques to monitor the quality of receivables include aging schedules, the average age of receivables, collection fractions, and receivables balance fractions. Let's take a look at each in turn.

Aging Schedules

An **aging schedule** is a table showing the total dollar amounts and the percentages of total accounts receivable that fall into several age classifications. It provides a picture of the quality of outstanding accounts receivable. Such schedules usually show those receivables that are 0 to 30 days old, 30 to 60 days old, 60 to 90 days old, and over 90 days old.

The following example shows how an aging schedule is prepared. All of the firm's outstanding invoices are collected and sorted according to their ages. These are then summarized on the aging schedule.

An Aging Schedule for Provo Palace

On September 30, Provo Palace prepares a list of all of its outstanding invoices from its database system and sorts them by their original dates. There are 25 invoices, as shown in Table 20-2.

The invoices for each month, up to the current date, are collected and totaled, as shown in Table 20-2. As you can see, the September invoices, which are 0 to 30 days old, are substantially more than for the previous months, because most of the older invoices have already been collected. Amounts are usually shown in both dollars and percentages. The percentage breakdown can be readily compared to previous aging schedule breakdowns to see whether the current situation is different from past experience. ■

TABLE 20-2

Aging schedule for Provo Palace.

OUTSTANDING INVOICES SEPTEMBER 30

Invoice Number	Invoice Date	Invoice Amount		
1041	7/7	$ 1,200		
1049	7/13	1,000	$ 3,400	Total for July
1060	7/27	800		
1061	7/27	400		
1063	8/5	1,500		
1066	8/12	1,000		
1067	8/12	500		
1072	8/15	800	$ 8,300	Total for August
1073	8/16	1,200		
1080	8/23	1,200		
1083	8/25	1,500		
1084	8/26	600		
1087	9/2	1,000		
1089	9/5	1,400		
1090	9/5	500		
1092	9/7	1,000		
1093	9/10	1,200		
1094	9/14	700		
1095	9/15	400	$11,800	Total for September
1096	9/18	900		
1097	9/20	1,000		
1098	9/22	800		
1099	9/25	1,000		
1100	9/25	500		
1101	9/28	1,400		
Total		$23,500	$23,500	

AGING SCHEDULE, SEPTEMBER 30

Age	Amount	Percent
0–30 days	$11,800	50.2%
30–60 days	8,300	35.3
60–90 days	3,400	14.5
over 90 days	0	0
Total	$23,500	100.0%

The aging schedule depends on the credit terms offered, customer payment habits, and trends in recent sales. For example, if a firm changes its credit terms, such as giving customers a longer credit period, the aging schedule will reflect this change. If customers are paying more quickly, the percentage in the youngest categories will increase and the percentage in the older categories will decrease. Likewise, a change in the firm's sales can affect the aging schedule. If sales increase during the current month, the percentage of 0 to 30 days receivables will increase. Conversely, a sales decrease tends to reduce the percentage of 0 to 30 days receivables.

Average Age of Accounts Receivable

In addition to an aging schedule, managers commonly compute an **average age of accounts receivable,** the average age of all of the firm's outstanding invoices. There are two common ways to make the computation. The first is to calculate the weighted average age of all individual outstanding invoices. The weights used are the percentages that the individual invoices represent out of the total amount of accounts receivable.

A simplified way to calculate the average age of accounts receivable is to use the aging schedule. Here, all receivables that are 0 to 30 days old are assumed to be 15 days old (the midpoint of 0 and 30), all receivables that are 30 to 60 days old are assumed to be 45 days old, and all receivables that are 60 to 90 days old are assumed to be 75 days old. Then the average age is computed by taking a weighted average of 15, 30, and 45. The weights are the percentages of receivables that are 0 to 30, 30 to 60, and 60 to 90 days old, respectively.

What is the average age of accounts receivable for Provo Palace? Using the aging schedule in Table 20-2, we estimate that the weighted average is

$$\text{Average age} = 0.502(15) + 0.353(45) + 0.145(75) = 7.53 + 15.89 + 10.88 = 34.30$$

Thus the average age is roughly 34 days. ■

Average Age of Accounts Receivable for Provo Palace

EXAMPLE

The same phenomena that affect an aging schedule affect its average age. Changes in credit terms, payment habits, or sales levels can increase or decrease the average age.

Collection Fractions and Receivables Balance Fractions

Two other measures used to monitor the quality of receivables are collection fractions and receivables balance fractions. **Collection fractions** are the percentages of sales collected during various months. For example, the collection fractions show the percentage of June's sales that are collected in June, as well as the percentage collected in each month thereafter (July, August, and September). After a month's billings have all been collected, the collection fractions sum to 100%. The pattern of the collection fractions is compared to an expected or budgeted collection pattern to see whether collections are faster or slower than expected.

Receivables balance fractions are the percentages of a month's sales that remain uncollected (and part of accounts receivable) at the end of the month of sale and at the end of succeeding months. For example, receivables balance fractions would include the percentage of June's sales that remain outstanding at the end of June and in the months of July, August, and September. The key point to notice about collection fractions and receivables balance fractions (compared to aging schedules) is that collections and receivables outstanding are always expressed as a *percent of original sales*.

If sales go up or down after the given month, collections and receivables are always compared to their original month of sale instead of to later sales figures. Data from each month's sales are always treated separately. June's collection fractions and balance fractions are never mixed in with those of another month. Hence collection fractions and receivables balance fractions are more reliable measures of quality than aging schedules, particularly when sales are increasing or decreasing. The following example illustrates how to use collection fractions and balance fractions to monitor the quality of receivables.

EXAMPLE

Collection Fractions and Receivables Balance Fractions for Connecticut Micro Systems

Connecticut Micro Systems, Inc., expects its collection fractions and receivables balance fractions to be as follows:

	COLLECTION FRACTION	BALANCE FRACTION
Original month	0.10	0.90
Month $t + 1$	0.50	0.40
Month $t + 2$	0.35	0.05
Month $t + 3$	0.05	0.00

These expected fractions are based on the firm's credit terms and on its best estimate of what the payment habits of its customers should be. Note that the expected collection fractions sum to 1.00, but the balance fractions do not. The balance fraction declines from its previous value by the amount collected during the month.

Table 20-3 is a schedule showing monthly sales and the pattern of collections over several months tied back to the original month's sales. What are the collection fractions, receivables balance fractions, and dollar amounts of receivables outstanding that go with these data. How would you assess the behavior of collections and receivables compared to the expected fractions?

Panel A of Table 20-3 shows how each month's sales are subsequently collected. For example, December's $1200 of sales were collected as follows: $110 in December, $550 in January, $420 in February, and $120 in March. Panel B shows the collection fractions that correspond to panel A. For example, December's sales collection fraction for December is 110/1200 = 0.092. For January it is 550/1200 = 0.458, for February 420/1200 = 0.350, and for March 120/1200 = 0.100.

Panel C shows this information in terms of receivables yet to be paid, the total and by age. For example, December's total accounts receivable of $1570 are made up of remaining receivables of $1090 from December sales, $420 from November sales, and $60 from October sales. The progression through panel C follows the diagonal, by subtracting the collections (panel A) according to the formula

$$\frac{\text{Receivables from one month previous}}{-\text{ Collections from two months previous}}$$
$$\overline{\text{Receivables from two months previous}}$$

For example, receivables in December from the previous month (420, in panel C) minus collections in January from two months previous (350, in panel A) equals receivables in January from two months previous (420 − 350 = 70, in panel C).

Panel D presents this information in terms of receivables balance fractions. The receivables balance fraction is the value in panel C divided by the original month's sales. For example, the receivables balance fractions in January are for the current month, one month previous, and two months previous: 0.910 (= 1365/1500), 0.450 (= 540/1200), and 0.070 (= 70/1000).

The collection fractions and receivables balance fractions are evaluated by comparing them to their expected sizes. In November, the collection fractions in panel B are exactly equal to the expected levels. Likewise, in November, the receivables balance fractions in panel D are equal to their expected levels. However, the quality of receivables then deteriorates. You can see that by the end of March, the collection fractions for the current month and the previous month are below expectations, and the collection fractions for late collections (from sales three months previous) are higher. It is taking longer to collect.

This collection slowdown also shows up in the receivables balance fractions for March in panel D. Because of delayed collections, the receivables balance fractions are higher than expected. Connecticut Micro Systems may have a receivables problem. If its credit terms were not changed, it could be that the firm is granting credit to less creditworthy customers or is managing collections poorly. ■

TABLE 20-3
Collection fractions and receivables balance fractions.

MONTH: SALES:	AUG 1000	SEPT 1000	OCT 1000	NOV 1000	DEC 1200	JAN 1500	FEB 1800	MAR 2000
Panel A								
Collections from:					↓			
Current month	100	100	100	100	110	135	160	175
Previous month		500	500	500	480	550	680	800
Two months previous			350	350	340	350	420	525
Three months previous				50	50	60	70	120
Total collections				1000	980	1095	1330	1620
								Collections of December sales
Panel B								
Collection fractions from:								
Current month	0.100	0.100	0.100	0.100	0.092	0.090	0.089	0.088
Previous month		0.500	0.500	0.500	0.480	+ 0.458	0.453	0.444
Two months previous			0.350	0.350	0.340	0.350	+ 0.350	0.350
Three months previous				0.050	0.050	0.060	0.070	+ 0.100 = 1.00
				↑				↑
				Collections fractions for the month				Fractions of December sales collected
Panel C								
Accounts receivable from:								
Current month	900	900	900	900	1090	1365	1640	1825
Previous month		400	400	400	420	540	685	840
Two months previous			50	50	60	70	120	160
Three months previous				0	0	0	0	0
Total accounts receivable				1350	1570	1975	2445	2825
Panel D								
Receivables balance fractions from:								
Current month	0.900	0.900	0.900	0.900	0.908	0.910	0.911	0.9125
Previous month		0.400	0.400	0.400	0.420	0.450	0.457	0.467
Two months previous			0.050	0.050	0.060	0.070	0.100	0.107
Three months previous				0.000	0.000	0.000	0.000	0.000
				↑				
				Receivables balance fractions for the month				

Pursuing Delinquent Credit Customers

Your best credit customers pay their bills promptly and are very easy to deal with. A few credit customers will prove to be complete deadbeats, and it will be difficult to recover anything from them no matter how hard you try. Other customers fall in between these two extremes, and dealing successfully with these marginal credit customers can be a key to profitability.

Businesses follow a number of specific steps in the collection process, depending on how long overdue the account is, the size of the debt, and other factors. A typical collection process can include the following steps.

1. *Letters.* When an account is overdue by a few days, a "friendly reminder" may be sent. If payment is not received, one or two more letters might be sent, the tone of the letters becoming progressively more severe and demanding.

2. *Telephone calls.* After the first couple of letters, the customer is phoned. If the customer is having financial troubles, a compromise might be worked out. A partial payment is better than no payment.

3. *Personal visits.* The salesperson who made the sale can visit the customer to request payment. Other special collectors besides the salesperson can be used.

4. *Collection agencies.* The account can be turned over to a collection agency that specializes in collecting past due accounts. Collection agencies usually charge a fee, such as half of whatever is recovered, and they recover only a fraction of the accounts they go after. Thus a firm's loss can be a very large proportion of the accounts turned over.

5. *Legal proceedings.* If the bill is large enough, legal action may be used to obtain a judgment against the debtor.

The collection process can be viewed as a capital budgeting process wherein the firm wants to use the collection procedures that generate the highest NPV. When collection is viewed this way, there are a few important principles to follow. The sequence of collection efforts begins with the least expensive and proceeds to increasingly more expensive techniques only after earlier methods have failed. Letters may cost the firm only $0.50, whereas telephone calls may average, say, $5.00, and personal visits can cost $20 to $100. Controlling the size of the investment in the collection effort can improve the NPV.

The early collection contacts are more upbeat and friendly, and the later contacts are not the least bit friendly. This is because many marginal customers will pay if asked and because future sales to these customers might be profitable. Once it becomes clear that there is limited potential for future profitable sales, collection efforts become much more aggressive.

Collection decisions follow capital budgeting principles. Sunk costs, which can be the uncollected investments made in goods sold, are eventually ignored. The collection sequence should be the one that results in the maximum NPV. Once the expected cash flow from continuing the collection effort is less than the additional cost of continuing, the correct decision is to stop pursuing the customer.

Changing Credit Policy

Credit policy can be changed by altering terms, standards, or collection practices. A change in credit policy can affect sales. It can also affect the cost of goods sold, bad debt expenses, carrying costs on accounts receivable, and other administrative costs. We can calculate the NPV of a credit policy change.

A firm currently uses credit terms of net 30. It is considering a switch to 2/10, net 30. The expected effects of this more liberal policy are summarized below:

	CURRENT POLICY	PROPOSED POLICY
Credit terms	net 30	2/10, net 30
Sales	$1,000,000	$1,050,000
Cost of sales (at time 0)	$600,000	$630,000
Bad debt losses	1.5% of sales	1.0% of sales
	0.015(1,000,000) = 15,000	0.01(1,050,000) = 10,500
Collection pattern	1.5 months (98.5% pay here on average) (1.5% never pay)	0.5 months (70%) 1.5 months (29%) (1% never pay)
Required return	1% per month	1% per month
Sales less bad debt	$985,000	$1,039,500
Discounts taken	$0	0.02(0.70)(1,050,000) = $14,700
Sales less bad debt and discounts	$985,000	$1,024,800

The expected cash flows under the current policy are

$$-600,000 \qquad\qquad 985,000$$

```
|---------------------------------------------->
0              1.5 months           Time
```

The current policy requires $600,000 at time zero and has an expected inflow of $985,000 (the sales of $1,000,000 less 1.5% bad debt) in 1.5 months. At a required return of 1% per month, the NPV of one year's sales under the current policy is

$$\text{NPV(current policy)} = \frac{0.985(1,000,000)}{(1.01)^{1.5}} - 600,000$$

$$= 970,408 - 600,000 = \$370,408$$

The expected cash flows under the proposed new policy are:

$$-630,000 \qquad 720,300 \qquad 304,500$$

```
|---------------------------------------------->
0          0.5 months    1.5 months     Time
```

The proposed policy results in a 5% increase in sales and cost of goods sold, an outlay of $630,000 at time 0. Here 70% of the customers pay early and take the 2% discount, resulting in a cash flow of 0.70(0.98)(1,050,000) = $720,300 at time 0.5 month. The balance of the customers who pay, 29% of sales, pay in 1.5 months. These customers pay 0.29(1,050,000) = $304,500. Thus the NPV of one year's sales under the proposed policy is

$$\text{NPV (proposed policy)} = \frac{0.70(0.98)(1,050,000)}{(1.01)^{0.5}} + \frac{0.29(1,050,000)}{(1+.01)^{1.5}} - 630,000$$

$$= 716,725 + 299,989 - 630,000 = \$386,714$$

Because the proposed policy has the greater NPV ($386,714 versus $370,408), the firm would be better off with the proposed change in credit policy. The tricky part of this kind of a decision is determining whether there is a third credit policy that would be even better than the proposed one we have just analyzed. This is essentially the same question we faced in capital budgeting. And our answer is still just as unsatisfying: You just have to do the best you can. ∎

Most firms in an industry use similar credit policies. Competitive pressures, as well as similar contracting cost structures, tend to cause credit policies to be strikingly similar. Therefore, the Behavioral Principle can be useful. When you are considering your own credit policy, a good starting point is the credit policies of other firms in the industry. Then, on the basis of your own strategic directions or changing economic conditions, you should consider credit policies that might be better for your firm.

Self-Check Questions

1. How do firms monitor the quality of their receivables?
2. What does an aging schedule show? How is one prepared?
3. Explain how a firm can use collection fractions and receivables balance fractions to monitor its accounts receivable. Are they more useful as measures of quality than aging schedules?
4. Describe the five steps that are typically part of the collection process.
5. How can information about your main competitors' current credit policies be useful to your firm in setting its credit policy?

20.4 INVENTORY MANAGEMENT

Inventories play a crucial role in a firm's purchasing-production-marketing process. Some inventories are a physical necessity for the firm. For example, partly built cars must be on the assembly line. Oil in transit must fill up oil pipelines. Other inventories are buffer stocks that are necessary at several points in the purchasing-production-marketing process. If the food is not in the grocery store when customers want it, the store cannot sell it. Likewise, if needed parts are delayed or out of stock, an assembly line can be shut down. Some goods, such as grain or coal, are shipped in such large quantities that it can take a year or more to use up one shipment.

Manufacturing firms generally carry three types of inventories: raw materials, work-in-process, and finished goods. The size of a firm's raw materials inventories depends on factors such as the anticipated level of production, production seasonality, and supply reliability. The size of the firm's work-in-process inventories depends mainly on the overall length of each production cycle and the number of distinct stages in the cycle. Finally, the size of the firm's finished goods inventories depends primarily on the rate of sales (units of product per unit of time), cost of carrying the inventory, cost of ordering replacement stocks, and cost of running out of an item (maybe losing the sale or even the customer). In general, larger inventories give the firm greater sales and operating flexibility, but they also cost more.

The Economic Order Quantity (EOQ) Model

A simple and useful inventory management model is the economic order quantity (EOQ) model. This model is derived in the following manner. Suppose that units are removed from inventory at a constant rate S (the rate at which goods are sold, in the case of finished goods inventories). Assume that there is a fixed reordering cost, F, per order regardless of the number of units reordered and that it costs C to carry a unit in inventory for an entire period. Note that the EOQ model assumes *constant* inventory usage or sales, and *instantaneous* inventory replenishment.

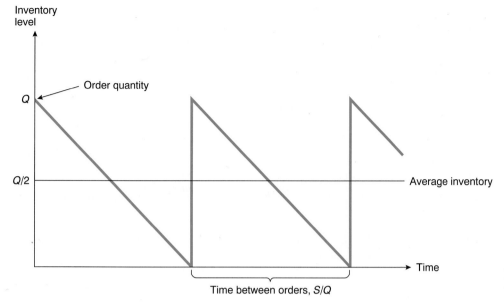

FIGURE 20-1
Inventory levels for the EOQ model.

Under these assumptions, the inventory level behaves as shown in Figure 20-1.[1] The inventory begins at Q units and is reduced at a constant rate until it reaches zero. At that point, the inventory is instantaneously replenished with another Q units, and the process starts over. Over the year, the inventory fluctuates between Q and zero, and the number of sawteeth in the figure is the number of orders per year.

The total annual cost is made up of two components, ordering costs and carrying costs. The ordering cost is the cost per order, F, times the number of orders per year. The number of orders per year is the annual usage (in units) divided by the order size, S/Q, so the annual ordering cost is $F(S/Q)$.

The annual carrying cost is the carrying cost per unit, C, times the average inventory, which is $Q/2$. Thus the annual carrying cost is $C(Q/2)$.

The total annual cost is the sum of these two components:

$$\text{Total cost} = \text{Ordering cost} + \text{Carrying cost} = F\frac{S}{Q} + C\frac{Q}{2} \qquad (20.3)$$

Figure 20-2 shows ordering costs and carrying costs as a function of Q, the order size, which is the decision variable. Note that an increase in Q increases the carrying cost but decreases the ordering cost. Total cost can be minimized by finding the order quantity that balances the two component costs. That order quantity is the **economic order quantity (EOQ)**, as shown in Figure 20-2. The formula for EOQ[2] is

$$\text{EOQ} = \sqrt{\frac{2FS}{C}} \qquad (20.4)$$

---

[1] If Figure 20-1 looks suspiciously familiar, that is probably because it is essentially identical to Figure 19-3, the Baumol cash management model. The two models have equivalent structures.

[2] The form of the model for the EOQ is identical to the one for C^*, the optimal deposit size in the Baumol cash management model. Thus we'll make your day and skip the mathematical derivation.

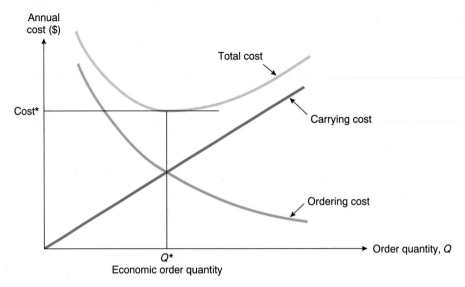

FIGURE 20-2
Annual costs for the EOQ model.

Officemax's EOQ

Suppose Officemax sells personal copying machines at the rate of 1800 units per year. The cost of placing one order is $400, and it costs $100 per year to carry a copier in inventory. What is Officemax's EOQ? Using the EOQ, find the average inventory, number of orders per year, time interval between orders, annual ordering cost, annual carrying cost, and annual total cost.

From Equation (20.4), the EOQ is

$$\text{EOQ} = \sqrt{\frac{2FS}{C}} = \sqrt{\frac{2(400)(1800)}{100}} = \sqrt{14,400} = 120 \text{ copiers}$$

Average inventory = Q/2 = 120/2 = 60 copiers

Number of orders per year = S/Q = 1800/120 = 15 times per year

Time interval between orders = Q/S = 120/1800 = 0.0667 years (0.0667 × 365 = 24.3 days)

Annual ordering cost = $F(S/Q)$ = 400(1800/120) = 400(15) = $6000

Annual carrying cost = $C(Q/2)$ = 100(120/2) = 100(60) = $6000

From Equation (20.3), Officemax's total annual cost is

$$\text{Total cost} = F\frac{S}{Q} + C\frac{Q}{2} = 400\frac{1800}{120} + 100\frac{120}{2} = 6000 + 6000 = \$12,000$$

Note that the carrying cost and the ordering cost are equal ($6000); this always holds for the EOQ. ■

Quantity Discounts

Many suppliers offer a quantity discount to encourage larger orders. For example, a supplier might offer a price discount for ordering 10,000 or more units. If your EOQ is currently more than the discount quantity, you get the discount without doing anything.

If your EOQ is less than the discount quantity, you have to increase your order size to get the discount. The trade-off is between higher inventory costs and a lower price for purchases. If the discounts exceed the cost of the extra inventory, then you should increase the order size to get the discounts. To analyze this decision, we can adjust the total cost function by adding in the price discounts:

$$\text{Total cost} = \text{Ordering cost} + \text{Carrying cost} - \text{Price discounts}$$

$$= F\frac{S}{Q} + C\frac{Q}{2} - dS \qquad (20.5)$$

where d is the price discount per unit.

The best order size is the one that provides the lowest total cost: either the result of using Equation (20.4) to find the EOQ without price discounts or the result of using Equation (20.5), which reveals the cost outcome of ordering the larger quantity and getting the price discounts.

The EOQ and Quantity Discounts at Officemax

EXAMPLE

Continuing our Officemax example, where the EOQ was 120, let's say the dealer offered a quantity discount of $3 per unit for orders of 200 or more. Should Officemax order 200 each time to get the discount?

Officemax must compare the total cost of ordering the larger quantity to get the discount with the total costs of ordering the EOQ. We calculated the total cost using the EOQ to be $12,000. Using Equation (20.5), we find that the total cost of ordering 200 units each time is

$$\text{Total cost} = F\frac{S}{Q} + C\frac{Q}{2} - dS$$

$$= 400\frac{1800}{200} + 100\frac{200}{2} - 3.00(1800) = 3600 + 10,000 - 5400 = \$8200$$

The order size of 200 increases the inventory costs from $12,000 per year (with the EOQ) to $13,600 ($= 3600 + 10,000$). The firm receives discounts of $3.00 per unit on *the entire year's purchases* (1800 units). The total discounts received ($5400) are more than the $1600 increase in ordering and carrying costs. The total costs decline by $3800 when the quantity discount is taken. Thus raising the order size to 200 is worth it. ■

Inventory Management with Uncertainty

The EOQ model makes simplifying assumptions: Future demand is known with certainty, inventory is used at a constant rate, and delivery is instantaneous (or equivalently, the lead time is known with certainty). Each factor, of course, actually has some uncertainty. A firm can protect itself from this uncertainty by having a **safety stock**—that is, a buffer inventory.

Figure 20-3 shows the firm's inventory level over time, with a safety stock and other more realistic assumptions. In the figure, the firm uses inventory down to the reorder point. At the reorder point, the firm orders its EOQ, but there is a lead time until the order arrives. During this lead time, the firm might have a *stockout* if demand is large. A stockout occurs when the firm cannot immediately make a sale because of lack of inventory. Stockouts can create customer badwill and/or cause lost sales. To guard against a stockout, the reorder point includes the expected lead-time demand plus a safety stock.

$$\text{Reorder point} = \text{Expected lead-time demand} + \text{Safety stock} \qquad (20.6)$$

With uncertainties, annual inventory cost has three components:

$$\text{Annual cost} = \text{Ordering cost} + \text{Carrying cost} + \text{Stockout cost} \qquad (20.7)$$

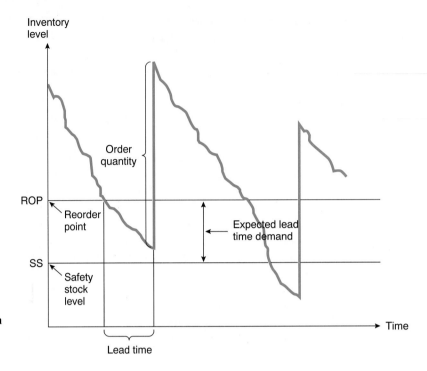

FIGURE 20-3
Inventory levels with uncertain demand and a safety stock.

The expected stockout cost is the probability of a stockout times the cost of a stockout. A larger safety stock reduces the expected stockout cost but raises the reorder point. Thus a larger safety stock increases the inventory carrying cost, because the average inventory level is equal to EOQ/2 *plus* the safety stock. Again, there is a trade-off between costs. But again, the optimal inventory policy provides the lowest total cost.

EXAMPLE

Order Quantity and Reorder Point at Oxford Arms

Oxford Arms sells bulletproof vests through mail orders. Oxford sells 5000 vests per year. The fixed cost is $60 per order, and the carrying cost is $15 per unit of average inventory. Thus Oxford's EOQ is

$$\text{EOQ} = \sqrt{\frac{2FS}{C}} = \sqrt{\frac{2(60)(5000)}{15}} = \sqrt{40,000} = 200 \text{ vests}$$

This order quantity implies 25 orders per year (= 5000/200) and an ordering cost of $1500 per year (= 25 × 60). What are Oxford's optimal safety stock and reorder point?

The average lead-time demand is 20 vests, so the reorder point will be the safety stock plus 20. The average inventory will be the safety stock plus EOQ/2 = 100. Oxford is considering several safety stock levels ranging from none to 30. Estimates of the expected stockout cost for various sizes of safety stock are given in Table 20-4.

Note in Table 20-4 that the expected stockout cost starts high and declines at a rapid but diminishing rate. Adding the first 5 units to the safety stock reduces the expected stockout cost by $500, from $1200 to $700. The annual carrying cost of the 5 units of safety stock is only $75 (= 5 × 15), so the total cost declines by $425 (= 500 − 75). As long as the expected

TABLE 20-4
**Finding the optimal
safety stock and
reorder point.**

REORDER POINT[a]	SAFETY STOCK	AVERAGE INVENTORY[b]	STOCKOUT COST[c]	CARRYING COST[d]	ORDERING COST[e]	TOTAL COST[f]
20	0	100	$1200	$1500	$1500	$4200
25	5	105	700	1575	1500	3775
30	10	110	450	1650	1500	3600
35	15	115	250	1725	1500	3475
40[g]	20[g]	120	150	1800	1500	3450[g]
45	25	125	90	1875	1500	3465
50	30	130	50	1950	1500	3500
55	35	135	30	2025	1500	3555
60	40	140	25	2100	1500	3625

[a] Reorder point = Lead time demand + Safety stock = 20 + Safety stock.
[b] Average inventory = $Q/2$ + Safety stock = 100 + Safety stock.
[c] Stockout costs are management's estimates for each safety stock level.
[d] Carrying costs = Average inventory times $15.
[e] Ordering costs = $F(S/Q) = \$60(25) = \$1500$.
[f] Total cost = Stockout cost + Carrying cost + Ordering cost.
[g] Indicates the cost-minimizing reorder point and safety stock.

stockout cost declines faster than the carrying cost increases, increasing the safety stock is beneficial. A safety stock of 20 and a reorder point of 40 provide the lowest total cost. This is the optimal safety stock and reorder point, because it balances the component costs off against each other. ■

ABC System of Inventory Control

The ABC system of inventory control categorizes inventory into one of three groups—A, B, or C—on the basis of critical need. The most important items are A items, and the least important are C items. For example, suppose 10% of inventory items make up 80% of the total inventory value. These might be the A items. The B items might compose 30% of the total *number* of items but only 15% of the total inventory value. The C items would be 60% of the number of items but would make up only 5% of total inventory value. Figure 20-4 shows the relationship between the number of items and their cumulative investment for the ABC inventory system.

Because they are the most critical, the A items are managed very carefully. The B items are managed with less care, and the C items are managed the least carefully. For example, for a car company, engines, transmissions, and in fact all of the components of the cars under production are A items and are managed very carefully. On the other hand, office supplies such as paper clips, pencils, and paper are ordered when needed without much supervision.

Materials Requirement Planning (MRP) Systems

Firms often produce or supply more than one product, and each product may have a large number of components. Typically, this means the firm has multiple suppliers. Coordinating and scheduling can become complex, so firms rely on **materials requirement planning (MRP) systems**. MRP systems are computer-based systems that plan backward from the production schedule to make purchases and manage inventory. These large software systems combine information about the production process and the supply process to determine when the firm should place purchase orders. Done properly, MRP assures that production proceeds smoothly without interruptions due to inventory stockouts.

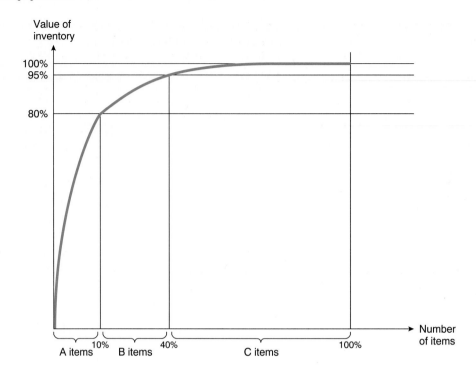

FIGURE 20-4
The ABC system of inventory control.

Just-In-Time (JIT) Inventory Systems

Just-in-time (JIT) inventory systems greatly reduce inventories. The philosophy of a JIT system is that materials should arrive exactly as they are needed in the production process. The system requires careful planning and scheduling, and extensive cooperation between suppliers and manufacturers is needed throughout the production process. All of this is facilitated by electronic data interchange (EDI), which we discussed in Chapter 19. A JIT system can reduce raw materials inventories, work-in-process inventories, and finished product inventories.

The success of a JIT system depends on several factors.

1. *Planning requirements*. JIT requires a coordinated, integrated plan for the entire firm. Recall that one of the basic functions of inventories is to serve as a buffer stock at various stages of the production process. By careful planning and scheduling, JIT systems practically eliminate these buffer stocks. The integrated operating environment of JIT can produce substantial savings. Of course, if a high degree of coordination and planning is impractical for a business, JIT does not work.

2. *Supplier relations*. The firm must work closely with its suppliers for JIT to work. Delivery schedules, quantities, quality, and instantaneous communication are all part of the system. The system requires frequent deliveries of the exact amounts needed and in the order required. Careful marking—often bar coding—is necessary. Therefore, there must be good relations.

3. *Setup costs*. The manufacturing process is redesigned to allow as much flexibility as possible by reducing the length of production runs. In manufacturing, there is often a fixed setup cost each time a production run begins. The optimal size of the production run is affected by the setup cost (much as inventory order costs are affected by the fixed order cost). By reducing these setup costs, the firm can use much smaller production runs and thus achieve more flexibility.

4. *Other cost factors*. Because JIT systems require careful monitoring and control, firms that employ JIT usually limit the number of their suppliers in order to reduce these costs. Many firms can reduce their inventory carrying costs and inventory setup costs by using a JIT system. However, nothing is free. Suppliers are asked to improve quality, provide more frequent deliveries, sequence and barcode

items in the shipments, and other such things. Suppliers' additional handling costs increase the price they charge. The trade-off has been very profitable, however, for many firms that have adopted JIT.

5. *Impact on credit terms*. JIT systems would be impossible without electronic data interchange (EDI). Because many aspects of the purchasing-production-marketing process are now handled electronically, trade credit is also becoming automated. When electronic credit terms are used, payment is not made, say, 30 days after an invoice date. Rather, payment can be made shortly—such as only a day—after delivery and use of materials. This essentially eliminates accounts payable for a firm, which was a major source of short-term financing. On the other hand, collecting electronically eliminates the supplier's accounts receivable. EDI also eliminates the costs and risks associated with paper-based payables and receivables systems.

Self-Check Questions

1. What is the economic order quantity? What cost does it minimize?
2. Explain how the economic order quantity is related to the rate at which items are removed from inventory, the fixed reordering cost, and the carrying cost.
3. What is safety stock, and what is its purpose?
4. Explain how a just-in-time inventory system works. What factors determine how well it works? What is the purpose of such a system?

SUMMARY

Accounts receivable and inventories are large investments in assets that support the firm's process of buying materials, transforming them into final products, and selling them. These investments, like capital budgeting projects, are measured in terms of their NPV. And, as with capital budgeting, a firm should avoid negative-NPV decisions and seek out positive NPVs.

DECISION SUMMARY

- Trade credit is used as a device to reduce the financial contracting costs created by market imperfections.

- The NPV of granting credit is the present value of all the expected cash flows that occur when credit is extended.

- An indifference payment probability can be derived where customers with a payment probability above this critical value are designated profitable (positive-NPV) customers.

- Credit policy includes the choice of (1) credit terms, (2) evaluation methods, and (3) credit standards, as well as the process of monitoring the quality of outstanding receivables, pursuing delinquent customers, and administering the credit functions.

- A variety of credit terms have been designed to allow suppliers and customers to carry on mutually profitable associations. See the "Trade Credit Terms" box for several examples.

- The five C's of credit are character, capacity, capital, collateral, and conditions. Subjective credit evaluation methods use the five C's.

- Credit-scoring models create a single credit score for a customer. This score is supposed to be an objective indicator of creditworthiness.

- Aging schedules, collection fractions, and receivables balance fractions are used to monitor the quality of outstanding accounts receivable.
- Pursuing delinquent credit customers is a balancing act between the cost of pursuit, the likelihood of maintaining a profitable relationship with a marginal customer, and the amount of cash that can be collected.
- Changing credit policies can be evaluated with the same discounted cash flow framework that is used for making basic credit-granting decisions. The optimal policy provides the largest NPV.
- The economic order quantity (EOQ) is the order size that minimizes the total inventory cost.
- When uncertainties in deliveries or demand exist, firms maintain safety stocks. The reorder point is the safety stock level plus the expected lead-time demand that provides the minimum total cost.
- The ABC system of inventory control categorizes inventory into three groups—A, B, and C—on the basis of critical need. The most important (A) items are managed the most carefully. The relatively less important (C) items are the least carefully managed.
- Computer-based materials requirement planning (MRP) systems plan backward from production schedules to make purchases and plan inventories.
- Just-in-time (JIT) inventory systems schedule arrivals of materials exactly when they are needed. JIT systems can greatly reduce inventories. When electronic data interchange (EDI) is used with JIT, firms often reduce both their payables and their receivables.

EQUATION SUMMARY

(20.1)
$$\text{NPV} = \frac{pR}{(1+r)^t} - C$$

(20.2)
$$p^* = \frac{C(1+r)^t}{R}$$

(20.3)
$$\text{Total cost} = \text{Ordering cost} + \text{Carrying cost} = F\frac{S}{Q} + C\frac{Q}{2}$$

(20.4)
$$\text{EOQ} = \sqrt{\frac{2FS}{C}}$$

$$\text{Total cost} = \text{Ordering cost} + \text{Carrying cost} - \text{Price discounts}$$

(20.5)
$$\text{Total cost} = F\frac{S}{Q} + C\frac{Q}{2} - dS$$

(20.6)
$$\text{Reorder point} = \text{Expected lead-time demand} + \text{Safety stock}$$

(20.7)
$$\text{Annual cost} = \text{Ordering cost} + \text{Carrying cost} + \text{Stockout cost}$$

KEY TERMS

EXERCISES

PROBLEM SET A

A1. Cite and discuss five reasons for the extensive use of trade credit.

A2. What is meant by the phrase *1/10, net 40*?

A3. Explain why trade credit is costless for the borrower when the funds are repaid before the end of the discount period.

A4. Cite and briefly describe the five C's of credit.

A5. Benny Baggins is applying for a credit card. After graduating with his business degree, Benny started at a job 2 years ago and now earns $41,000 a year. He has been renting an apartment near work since he started at the job. His telephone is connected, but he has only a fair credit report. Using the credit card application scoring sheet given in the chapter, and a cutoff of 15 points, determine whether Benny would qualify for the credit card.

A6. Describe the steps involved in a typical collection process.

A7. Explain the logic of an ABC system of inventory control.

A8. What is a materials requirements planning (MRP) system?

A9. What is meant by the term *safety stocks*? Why would a firm normally find it beneficial to maintain safety stocks in its inventory?

A10. What are the factors on which the success of a JIT system depends?

PROBLEM SET B

B1. Explain how financial contracting costs, created by market imperfections, can lead to the use of trade credit.

B2. The Salt Lake Ski Company wants to make a $200,000 credit purchase from your firm. Your investment in the credit sale is 70% of the amount of the sale. You estimate that Salt Lake has a 95% probability of paying you on time, which is in 3 months, and a 5% probability of paying nothing. If the opportunity cost of funds is 18% per year, what is the NPV of granting credit to Salt Lake?

B3. Squires Sports Equipment Company is selling $4000 rubber mats to the Springfield Fitness Center. Squires will invest $3400 in the sale. Squires has credit terms of 2/10, net 30, and it estimates that Springfield has a 50% probability of taking the discount and paying on day 10, a 40% probability of paying the net amount on day 30, and a 10% chance of defaulting. If Springfield Fitness defaults, Squires estimates that it will recover nothing. If the opportunity cost of funds is 12% compounded annually, what is the NPV of granting credit to Springfield Fitness? Assume a 365-day year.

B4. For each of the following items that are sold on credit, calculate the indifference (zero-NPV) payment probability.

Item	Sale Price	Investment in Sale	Collection Period	Required Return
Refrigerator	$1200	$1000	3 months	12%
Jewelry	300	150	12 months	14
Stereo	800	550	6 months	13

B5. The accounts receivable for the Boulder Skimobile Company include the following invoices.

Invoice	Invoice Date	Amount
522	March 3	$1200
530	March 12	1800
533	April 2	600
540	April 4	2400
544	April 12	1800
548	April 25	1200
550	May 5	1200
551	May 8	2400
552	May 12	1200
553	May 15	1800
554	May 16	2400
555	May 27	1200

Prepare an aging schedule as of May 31 for Boulder Skimobile in the following format:

Age	Accounts Receivable	Percent
0–30 days	$xx,xxx	xx.x%
30–60 days	xx,xxx	xx.x
60–90 days	xx,xxx	xx.x
Total	$xx,xxx	100.0%

B6. Wilson Licensing has the following aging schedule:

Age	Accounts Receivable	Percent
0–30 days	$400,000	53.33%
30–60 days	250,000	33.33
60–90 days	100,000	13.33
Total	$750,000	100.0%

Assume that the receivables in each age category have an age equivalent to the midpoint of the range. Calculate an average age of accounts receivables for Wilson Licensing.

B7. Texas Chili Products collects 20% of its sales in the month of the sale, 50% in the month following the sale, 25% in the second month following the sale, and 5% in the third month following the sale.

a. For a given month's sales, what percent of that month's sales should be outstanding at the end of the sale month, in the first month after the sale, in the second month after the sale, and in the third month after the sale.

b. Assume that collections proceed as predicted. Calculate the level of accounts receivable for January, February, and March from the following sales information:

Month	October	November	December	January	February	March
Sales	$500	$500	$500	$500	$700	$900

c. Provide an aging schedule for accounts receivable outstanding at the end of March.

B8. The Deep River Company is considering the liberalization of its credit terms and credit standards in order to increase sales and, it hopes, profits. The ad hoc management team charged with evaluating this credit liberalization has made the following estimates:

	Current Policy	Proposed Policy
Annual sales	$10 million	$11 million
Collection period	0.10 year	0.20 year
Bad debt/sales	1%	2%
Cost of goods sold/sales	85%	85%
Annual required return	15%	15%

Assume that the cost of goods sold is equivalent to an investment at time zero and that the expected sales (net of bad debt) are received at the predicted collection period.

a. What is the net present value of the current policy?

b. What is the net present value of the proposed policy?

c. Which policy is more profitable for the Deep River Company?

B9. Assume that annual usage is 12,000 units, that the fixed order cost is $60 per order, and that the carrying cost is $4 per unit average inventory. Find the average inventory, number of orders per year, carrying cost, ordering cost, and total cost for the order sizes indicated in the following table.

Order Size (units)	200	400	600	800	1000
Average inventory	____	____	____	____	____
Orders per year	____	____	____	____	____
Annual carrying cost	____	____	____	____	____
Annual ordering cost	____	____	____	____	____
Total annual cost	____	____	____	____	____

B10. Waters Printing Company orders six rolls of paper every week. The ordering and setup cost is $500, and the annual carrying cost is $1000 per unit average inventory. Assume a 52-week year.

a. What is the annual cost of ordering six rolls at a time?

b. What is the economic order quantity and the annual cost of using the EOQ?

c. Assume that Waters cannot order fractional rolls. If your EOQ in part b was not an integer value, what is the annual cost of using the next integer-valued order size above the EOQ? What is the annual cost of using the closest integer-valued order size below the EOQ? What order size do you recommend?

B11. The annual usage of toggle switches is 10,000 units per year, at a uniform rate through the year. The ordering cost is $50 per order, and carrying costs are $4.00 per unit average inventory per year.

a. What is the economic order quantity? What is the annual cost using the EOQ?

b. If the supplier offers a quantity discount of $0.10 per unit when you order in quantities of 250 or more, what should you do? What is the annual cost of following your recommendation?

c. If the supplier offers a quantity discount of $0.10 per unit when you order in quantities of 1000 or more, what should you do? What is the annual cost of following your recommendation?

B12. Alabama Central Hospital has established an economic order quantity for its obstetrics kits of 60 units. The lead time before orders arrive and are ready for use is 4 days. The average usage is 4 kits per day, and Alabama Central has determined that it would like to have a safety stock of 10 kits.

a. What is the expected lead time demand?

b. What should Alabama Central use as its reorder point?

B13. General Enzyme Company uses an average of 5 tons of beta medium per day. Because the lead time between a reorder and delivery is 4 days, expected lead time demand is 20 tons. The economic order quantity is 80 tons. Because the firm's usage is somewhat random, GE carries a safety stock to reduce the probability of a stockout. On the basis of the following estimated annual costs, which reorder point and safety stock would minimize total annual costs?

Safety Stock	Reorder Point	Ordering Cost	Carrying Cost	Stockout Cost
0	20	$10,000	$10,000	$12,000
5	25	10,000	12,500	7,000
10	30	10,000	15,000	4,000
15	35	10,000	17,500	2,000
20	40	10,000	20,000	1,000

B14. Brown Pontiac maintains an inventory of tires. The dealer uses tires at a constant rate of 1000 per month. The dealer's cost of placing a new order is $500 per order. The cost of carrying a tire in inventory for a year is $12.

a. Calculate the economic order quantity.

b. Brown Pontiac has found that if it is out of stock when a customer arrives, it will make the eventual sale only 20% of the time. For each lost sale, Brown Pontiac loses the net margin of $30 per tire. Lost sales as well as back orders cost $10 per stockout in record-keeping costs. Brown Pontiac has estimated the following benefit of maintaining safety stocks:

Safety stock	100	125	150	175	200
Stockouts per year	75	50	35	30	30

What level of safety stock should Brown Pontiac maintain?

PROBLEM SET C

C1. Explain how a firm's inventory and accounts receivable management problems are like a capital budgeting problem.

C2. Derive the EOQ model given in Equation (20.4).

a. Find an expression for the annual ordering cost.

b. Find an expression for the annual inventory carrying cost.

c. Find an expression for the total annual inventory cost.

d. Find the reorder quantity, EOQ, that minimizes the total annual inventory cost and show that it equals the formula for EOQ given in Equation (20.4).

C3. Create a spreadsheet model for the information given in Table 20-3. Use the model to create an extension for the months April, May, June, and July, using expected sales of 2200, 1400, 1700, and 1300, respectively. Assume the monthly collection fraction from current to three months previous are 0.09, 0.45, 0.36, and 0.10, respectively.

Real-World Application:
Ordering Inventory at Home Depot

The Home Depot, Inc. is the world's largest home improvement retailer and one of the ten largest retailers overall in the United States. At year-end 1995, the firm operated more than 400 full-service, warehouse-style stores. Each store stocks between 40,000 and 50,000 different kinds of building materials, home improvement supplies, and lawn and garden products. Its customers are primarily do-it-yourselfers. Perhaps you or a member of your family recently shopped at one of Home Depot's stores.

Home Depot is considering stocking a new deluxe toilet unit in its bathroom fixtures department. It's trying to broaden its product line to appeal to home-improvement contractors, and this item was recently featured in *Architectural Digest*. The toilet seat contains a special feature. When someone sits down, a system that sprays up a fine mist of air freshener and plays classical music is activated. The consumer has the option to specify musical selections.

The new toilet units have been test marketed successfully. Home Depot estimates that sales will average 1000 units per year. It will cost $100 to keep a unit in inventory for a year, and the fixed reordering cost is $80. Home Depot pays a purchase price of $500 per unit.

1. a. What is Home Depot's EOQ for the deluxe toilet units?
   b. What is the average inventory?

2. What would be the total annual cost of maintaining the inventory of deluxe toilet units?

3. How would the EOQ change assuming
   a. Sales double to 2000 units per year.
   b. Ordering cost doubles to $160 per order.
   c. Carrying cost doubles to $200 per year.

4. The average lead-time demand is 10 units. Table 20-5 shows how the expected annual stockout costs depend on the amount of safety stock. What's the optimal safety stock and reorder point?

5. The firm that supplies the deluxe toilet units has offered Home Depot a 5% discount if it orders 50 or more units each time. Should Home Depot order 50 units each time it buys?
   a. Solve the problem assuming zero stockout costs.
   b. Solve the problem assuming the expected annual stockout costs given in question 4.

6. The supplier also offers Home Depot a discount of 7% if it orders 60 or more units. Should Home Depot increase its order quantity to 60?

7. Home Depot can sell 1000 units per year at a price of $750 per unit. It estimates that it could sell 1100 units per year if it dropped the price to $700, but that it would sell only 900 units if it raised the price to $800 per unit. What is Home Depot's EOQ assuming no quantity discounts and
   a. $S = 900$ units/year.
   b. $S = 1100$ units/year.

8. Assuming the quantity discounts in questions 5 and 6 are available, how many units should Home Depot order assuming
   a. $S = 900$ units/year.
   b. $S = 1100$ units/year.

9. Specify the total annual cost of goods purchased, annual ordering cost, annual carrying cost, and expected annual stockout costs assuming
   a. $S = 900$ units/year.
   b. $S = 1000$ units/year.
   c. $S = 1100$ units/year.

10. Which price, $700, $750, or $800 per unit, maximizes the annual profit Home Depot can expect to earn from selling the deluxe toilet units?

REORDER POINT	SAFETY STOCK	EXPECTED STOCKOUT COSTS	REORDER POINT	SAFETY STOCK	EXPECTED STOCKOUT COSTS
10	0	$350	20	10	$200
12	2	290	22	12	192
14	4	255	24	14	186
16	6	225	26	16	182
18	8	210	28	18	180

TABLE 20-5
Safety stocks and expected annual stockout costs.

BIBLIOGRAPHY

Adams, Paul D., Steve B. Wyatt, and Yong H. Kim. "A Contingent Claims Analysis of Trade Credit," *Financial Management*, 1992, 21(3):95–103.

Ben-Horim, Moshe, and Haim Levy. "Management of Accounts Receivable Under Inflation," *Financial Management*, 1983, 12(1):42–48.

Brick, Ivan E., and William K. H. Fung. "The Effect of Taxes on the Trade Credit Decision," *Financial Management*, 1984, 13(2):24–30.

Brick, Ivan E., and William K. H. Fung. "Taxes and the Theory of Trade Debt," *Journal of Finance*, 1984, 39(4):1169–1176.

Emery, Gary W. "A Pure Financial Explanation for Trade Credit," *Journal of Financial and Quantitative Analysis*, 1984, 19(4):271–285.

Gallinger, George W., and A. James Ifflander. "Monitoring Accounts Receivable Using Variance Analysis," *Financial Management*, 1986, 15(4):69–76.

Gentry, James A., and Jesus M. De La Garza. "A Generalized Model for Monitoring Accounts Receivable," *Financial Management*, 1985, 14(4):28–38.

Lee, Yul W., and John D. Stowe. "Product Risk, Asymmetric Information, and Trade Credit," *Journal of Financial and Quantitative Analysis*, 1993, 28(2):285–300.

Long, Michael S., Ileen B. Malitz, and S. Abraham Ravid. "Trade Credit, Quality Guarantees, and Product Marketability," *Financial Management*, 1993, 22(4):117–127.

Mian, Shehzad L., and Clifford W. Smith, Jr. "Accounts-Receivable Management Policy: Theory and Evidence," *Journal of Finance*, 1992, 47(1):169–200.

Scherr, Frederick C. "Optimal Trade Credit Limits," *Financial Management*, 1996, 25(1):71–85.

Stowe, John D. "An Integer Programming Solution for the Optimal Credit Investigation/Credit Granting Sequence," *Financial Management*, 1985, 14(2):66–76.

TREASURY MANAGEMENT

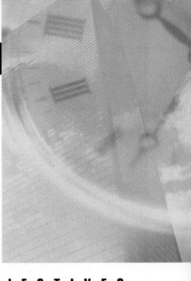

In this chapter, we will describe several financial responsibilities that are usually centralized and controlled at corporate headquarters or, for a small business, handled by the owner. In contrast, most other financial decisions are pervasive. That is, they occur to some degree in every decision made within a firm and at every level of the organization.

The centralized areas we will examine are pension fund management, risk management, and investor relations. Pension fund management includes designing the pension plan, choosing investment managers, selecting the level of funding, and making investment decisions. Risk management is the process of identifying and evaluating the risks the firm faces and developing strategies to manage these risk exposures. Investor relations involves communicating with the firm's debtholders and stockholders. We will explain why these functions are important and describe how well-managed firms perform them.

We'll start by looking at the corporate personnel charged with these concerns, the chief financial officer, the controller, and the treasurer. These are the highest ranking financial managers of the firm. We'll describe the main responsibilities of each so that you can appreciate how important their duties are.

OBJECTIVES

After studying this chapter, you should be able to

1. Explain the responsibilities of the corporate treasurer and controller.

2. Describe the two different types of pension fund plans.

3. Calculate pension benefits, and estimate total pension fund values.

4. Explain the economics of pension fund management for a firm and its employees.

5. Define risk management, and describe some common techniques for reducing risk.

6. Identify the potential benefits to be derived from an investor relations function, and provide an overview of how corporations typically handle investor relations.

TREASURY MANAGEMENT AND THE PRINCIPLES OF FINANCE

◆ *Self-Interested Behavior*: Carefully evaluate and monitor each stakeholder's incentives and potential reactions. Anticipating what to expect of other employees, investors, suppliers, and customers is a very valuable skill.

◆ *Two-Sided Transactions*: Look for situations that are not zero-sum games; such situations may be profitable to the firm *and* one or more of its stakeholders. Some decisions may be used to reduce both financial contracting costs and routine transaction costs. Be sure to consider how the firm's activities look to its investors.

◆ *Options*: Recognize the value of hidden options in a situation, such as the option to over- or underfund the firm's pension plan.

◆ *Risk-Return Trade-Off*: Recognize the critical importance of the firm's various choices concerning risk-return trade-off and, more generally, the role of risk management.

◆ *Incremental Benefits*: Calculate the incremental cash flows and other benefits and costs connected with treasury activities.

◆ *Time Value of Money*: Compare the NPVs of alternative actions.

◆ *Comparative Advantage*: Consider subcontracting business activities to outside vendors if they can provide the services more cheaply and competently.

◆ *Behavioral*: Use common industry practices as a good starting place for operating efficiently.

21.1 TREASURY MANAGEMENT

The principles of finance apply to all of the firm's decisions to some degree. Large corporations have a high-ranking corporate officer, often called the chief financial officer (CFO) or vice president of finance (VP-Finance), who oversees the financial aspects of a firm's decisions. Some financial decisions are the CFO's direct responsibility. Examples include issuing new securities, arranging a bank credit facility, and investing pension fund assets.

Other decisions are delegated but are indirectly supervised by the CFO. For example, the size, analytical methods, and final choices made in a manager's capital budget are subject to the CFO's approval. Figure 21-1 is an organizational chart showing the CFO's typical position and direct responsibilities. Many corporate presidents and chief executive officers (CEOs) have previously been CFOs.

The CFO's delegated responsibilities are often divided between two officers: the controller and the treasurer. The **controller** oversees the firm's accounting activities. The **treasurer** is responsible for designing and implementing many of the firm's financial activities. Because financial principles and accounting activities affect all of a firm's activities, both jobs require skills in accounting and finance, as well as a thorough understanding of the firm's operating and marketing activities. Both the controller and treasurer have staffs to support or, in many cases, carry out their responsibilities.

The Controller's Duties

As the chief accountant, the controller is responsible for the following activities:

1. *Financial accounting.* The firm prepares public financial statements and other accounting information, which are audited by an outside accounting firm usually at the end of each year.

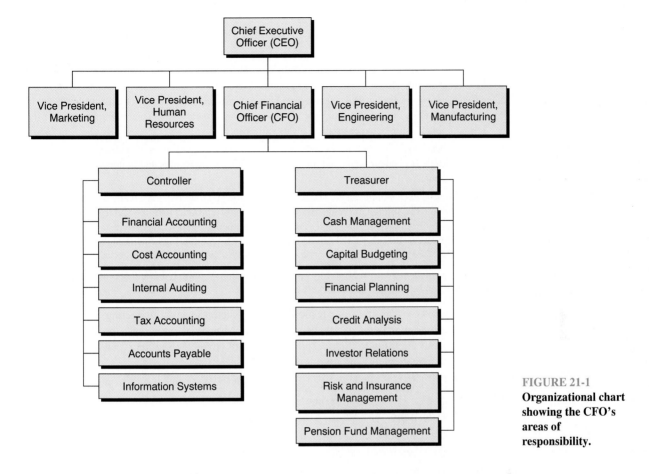

FIGURE 21-1
Organizational chart showing the CFO's areas of responsibility.

2. *Managerial/cost accounting.* The controller is responsible for developing and providing internal cost information for decision making.

3. *Internal auditing.* Internal auditors monitor the firm's transactions and assets to ensure accurate reporting and guard against dishonest activity.

4. *Tax accounting.* Corporations must pay a variety of taxes, including income, property, sales, excise, and social security taxes. The tax obligations are to numerous authorities, including one or more nations, states, counties, cities, school boards, and sewer districts. The controller is responsible for complying with the rules, regulations, and payment requirements of such obligations.

5. *Accounts payable.* The controller often verifies financial obligations and then disburses payments to employees, vendors, and others.

6. *Information systems.* In some firms, the controller has direct or indirect responsibility for the information system, because accounting is a major user of computing resources. In other firms, a chief information officer handles this job.

The Treasurer's Duties

The treasurer supervises several specialized financial activities.

1. *Cash and marketable securities management.* The treasury staff forecasts the firm's cash flows. When needed, they obtain funds from banks and other short-term lenders. They also invest any excess short-term funds.

2. *Capital budgeting.* The treasury office lays out the firm's capital budgeting methods and procedures.

Significant decisions are made, or at least approved, by the CEO or board of directors. Less critical decisions are made by others but must be consistent with the criteria and methods specified by the treasurer.

3. *Financial planning*. Forecasting models for short- and long-term financial planning are created and updated regularly.

4. *Credit analysis*. In many firms, the treasurer's staff grants credit and makes credit-line decisions. In other firms, these decisions are delegated to another department such as marketing, because of the intimate relationship between credit analysis and sales.

5. *Investor relations*. The firm must communicate with important outsiders, including institutional investors (such as pension funds and mutual funds), other stockholders and bondholders, and credit rating agencies.

6. *Risk and insurance management*. The firm's systematic and total risk have many components, such as operating risks, foreign exchange risks, interest rate risk, product liability, and regulatory risks. A firm can buy insurance against some risks, and it can hedge against others by using financial contracts. However, still other risks can be managed only by monitoring or avoiding particular activities.

7. *Pension fund management*. Most firms provide a pension of some type for their employees. A pension plan can be among a firm's largest commitments.

We discuss several treasurer responsibilities—such as capital budgeting, cash and marketable securities management, credit analysis, and financial planning—in other chapters. Here we turn our attention to three responsibilities not covered elsewhere: pension fund management, risk management, and investor relations.

Self-Check Questions
1. What are the controller's main areas of responsibility?
2. What are the treasurer's main areas of responsibility?

21.2 PENSION FUND MANAGEMENT

Pension funds are among a firm's most significant commitments for two reasons. First, pension contributions can be a large expense against income. Second, total future pension plan obligations are often a significant claim on the firm's assets. The pension fund assets, along with future contributions, are used to meet these claims. The size of the pension expense, and the magnitude of the pension fund assets and obligations, make it critical for the firm to manage its pension plan carefully so that the firm and its employees receive value for the resources committed.

Table 21-1 lists the pension fund assets and pension fund obligations of the 30 corporations in the Dow Jones Industrial Average. The table also shows each firm's pension fund surplus or deficit, the difference between its obligations and its assets. To put the pension fund accounts in perspective, the book and market values of equity are also shown. For 11 of the 30 firms, pension fund assets exceed the book value of equity. For three, pension fund assets exceed even the market value of equity.

TABLE 21-1

Defined benefit pension assets and obligations of the 30 DJIA corporations for fiscal year 1994 ($ billions).

FIRM	PENSION FUND ASSETS	PENSION FUND OBLIGATIONS	PENSION SURPLUS (DEFICIT)	TOTAL ASSETS	BOOK VALUE OF STOCKHOLDERS' EQUITY	MARKET VALUE OF STOCKHOLDERS' EQUITY
AlliedSignal	$ 4.744	$ 4.240	$ 0.504	$ 11.321	$ 2.972	$ 9.626
Alcoa	3.569	3.299	0.270	12.343	3.943	7.740
American Express	0.790	0.613	0.177	97.006	6.233	14.628
AT&T	45.150	28.778	16.372	79.006	17.921	78.843
Bethlehem Steel	3.276	4.394	−1.118	5.782	0.586	1.978
Boeing	9.290	7.473	1.817	21.463	9.700	16.021
Caterpillar	5.120	4.750	0.370	16.250	2.911	11.049
Chevron	3.626	2.874	0.752	34.407	14.596	29.084
Coca-Cola	0.944	0.957	−0.013	13.873	5.235	65.710
Disney	0.485	0.404	0.081	12.826	5.508	20.309
Du Pont	14.223	10.744	3.479	36.892	12.585	38.221
Eastman Kodak	5.263	5.077	0.186	14.968	4.017	16.223
Exxon	7.278	9.058	−1.780	87.862	37.474	75.451
General Electric	26.166	18.430	7.736	194.484	26.387	87.004
General Motors	54.624	64.273	−9.649	198.598	9.155	31.777
Goodyear	2.080	2.373	−0.293	9.123	2.803	5.091
IBM	44.204	40.929	3.275	81.091	22.288	43.197
International Paper	2.895	2.069	0.826	17.836	6.514	9.489
McDonald's	NA	NA	NA	NA	NA	NA
Merck	1.371	1.350	0.021	21.856	11.139	47.573
MMM	4.676	4.434	0.242	13.496	6.734	22.407
J.P. Morgan	1.029	0.718	0.311	154.917	9.074	10.535
Philip Morris	7.328	5.552	1.776	52.896	12.786	49.039
Procter & Gamble	0.806	1.125	−0.319	25.535	8.677	35.527
Sears	4.344	3.776	0.568	91.896	9.240	16.180
Texaco	1.822	1.690	0.132	25.505	9.216	15.539
Union Carbide	2.414	2.150	0.264	5.028	1.509	4.242
United Technologies	7.229	6.819	0.410	15.624	3.752	7.742
Westinghouse	3.557	4.731	−1.174	10.624	1.780	4.371
Woolworth	0.590	0.852	−0.262	4.173	1.353	2.087

NA: McDonald's Corporation reports no defined benefit pension plan.
Source: Standard & Poor's Compustat PC Plus.

Defined Benefit Pension Plans

There are two different types of pension plans: defined benefit and defined contribution. The names describe the firm's obligation, a *benefit* after retirement or a *contribution now* to a fund that will provide the future retirement benefit.

A **defined benefit pension plan** promises retirement payments that are based on the employee's years of service to the firm and salary. A common formula is the years of service times a percent factor (such as 1.5% or 2.0%) times the final salary:

$$\text{Annual pension payment} = (\text{Years of service})(\text{Percent factor})(\text{Final salary}) \qquad (21.1)$$

The amount is typically paid in monthly payments of one-twelfth of this amount.

The firm must estimate the obligation to fund it appropriately. The obligation depends on the specific terms. A common arrangement is a lifetime annuity, where pension payments continue until the person dies. Therefore, the firm must estimate the employee's final salary and life span after retirement. The obligation is then the present value of the expected future payments.

<table>
<tr>
<td>**EXAMPLE**

Defined Benefit Pension Calculation</td>
<td>Suppose Rae Dockweiler is retiring next month after 30 years of employment with UltraBank of Georgia. Her pension plan will provide a fixed yearly payment of 1.5% of her final salary times her years of service for the rest of her life. If Rae's final salary is $50,000, what will be her retirement benefit under this plan?

Using Equation (21.1) reveals that Rae's pension will be $22,500 per year ($1875 per month).

$$(0.015)(30)(50,000) = \$22,500$$

What is Ultrabank's pension fund obligation to Rae if the required return is 7% APR (0.5833% per month)?

Let's say that according to actuarial information used by insurance companies, Rae is expected to live 18 years (216 months) after retirement. (This is a mathematical expectation, where there is a certain probability of living 1 year after retirement, another probability of living 2 years after retirement, and so on.) The present value is $229,926. [Put in CF = 1875, $r = 0.5833\%$, $n = 216$, and FV = 0. Then compute PV = 229,926.]

$$PV = 1875\left[\frac{(1.005833)^{216} - 1}{0.005833(1.005833)^{216}}\right] = \$229,926$$

This is a substantial obligation. To ensure that they are able to meet such obligations, firms contribute funds to their pension plans on behalf of employees during their working years. These contributions are invested in such things as common stocks, bonds, mortgages, and real estate. ■</td>
</tr>
</table>

Corporate pension benefits are rarely indexed for inflation. Once an employee retires, the firm's obligation is fixed in nominal dollars, much like the obligation on other fixed-income instruments. Upon retirement, the retiree bears the inflation risk, which can be significant, as we show in the next example.

<table>
<tr>
<td>**EXAMPLE**

Inflation and the Value of a Pension Benefit</td>
<td>John Pascucci believes he can live comfortably in retirement on 80% of his working income. John makes $80,000 a year. If he retires, he will get $18,000 from social security and $48,000 from his firm's retirement plan, for a total of $66,000 per year. This is 82.5% of his current income (= 66/80).[1]

Suppose John retires, and over several years, inflation doubles the cost of living. John's social security income is indexed to inflation and becomes $36,000 a year. However, his pension income is fixed in nominal dollars at $48,000. Thus John's total annual income becomes $84,000 in current dollars. But with the cost of living doubled, keeping up his preretirement living standard would require $160,000 a year. Therefore, his retirement income now represents only 52.5% (= 84/160) of his preretirement income, instead of the 82.5% he had when he first retired. We would call that a significant drop in income. ■</td>
</tr>
</table>

---

[1] On the basis of the Principle of Self-Interested Behavior, we assume John wants the largest percentage possible. There is no amount that this ratio *should* be. However, many costs for such things as commuting and clothing are employment-related. These costs stop at retirement, which implies that you can have an equivalent living standard with a ratio below 1.0. On the other hand, some of us want even more income because of the added leisure time available in retirement.

Pension plans cover many employees. This includes people just beginning their careers, people who have been with the firm many years, and others who are already retired and are receiving their pension benefits. Current pension fund assets plus future contributions and earnings will be used to make the promised payments. A pension plan's condition depends on the amount of assets in the plan, the present value of the expected future contributions, and the present value of expected pension benefit payments. A pension plan is *underfunded* if the value of the pension fund assets is less than the present value of the accumulated pension benefit obligations. A pension plan is *overfunded* if the value of its assets is more than the present value of the accumulated pension benefit obligations. Note in Table 21-1 that of the 29 firms that have a defined benefit pension plan, 8 are underfunded and 21 are overfunded. Of the overfunded firms, about half have a surplus of more than 20%. We will discuss later in the chapter the advantages and disadvantages of overfunding and underfunding a firm's pension plan.

The present value of accumulated pension benefit obligation depends on the years of service that employees presently have, on assumptions about salary growth rates over the remaining working lives of working employees, on whether people quit before retirement age, and on life expectancies. The expected return on pension fund assets is used to calculate the present value of future contributions and future benefits. Because inflation affects salary growth rates *and* investment earnings, but perhaps differentially, assumptions about them must be carefully determined. Alternative assumptions can lead to very different conclusions about whether the pension is over- or underfunded.

Financial accounting standards require separate reporting for the firm's operating business and the pension fund. Pension fund assets and obligations are usually reported in the financial statement footnotes. An underfunded pension plan's deficit, based on its minimum accrued obligations, must be shown on the firm's balance sheet as a long-term debt obligation. However, an overfunded pension plan's surplus is not normally included on the balance sheet, but can be in certain circumstances.

Defined Contribution Pension Plans

The other major type of plan is the **defined contribution pension plan**. In this plan, each employee has an account to which the employer makes regular contributions. The contributions are frequently specified as a percent of salary. If the employer makes all of the contributions to the plan, it is called a *noncontributory plan* (from the viewpoint of the employee). If the employee makes some of the contributions, it is called a *contributory plan*. A defined contribution pension plan is essentially a tax-deferred retirement savings account. The employee gets the accumulated total contributions plus earnings at retirement. The employee can then choose either to take the total lump sum or to purchase an annuity that provides a monthly check until death.

The employee owns the retirement account and bears all of the investment risk. The sponsoring firm has no obligation beyond making the regular contributions to the plan. In Table 21-1, the pension fund assets and obligations reported were those associated with defined benefit pension plans. Those assets in defined contribution plans belong to the employees and were not included. In a defined contribution plan, the employee is the principal and makes the investment decisions, deciding how to allocate the contributions. The employer is an agent responsible for setting up the plan and making available an adequate range of investment vehicles.

For example, the firm might contract with one or more money management firms to provide investment choices of several classes of financial assets. These could include a money market fund, a bond fund, equity funds, and international funds. The employee's asset allocation decision greatly influences the terminal value of the pension account, because different classes of assets have different risks and returns. The following example illustrates this point.

EXAMPLE	**Final Values for Defined Contribution Plans with Differing Asset Allocations**

Every year, Chuck and Marcia contribute $10,000 each to their defined contribution pension plan. Let's say they do so for 20 years. Their employer has given them three investment choices: a money market fund, a bond fund, and an equity fund. The returns for these funds are not known ahead of time and can fluctuate considerably. Chuck is very cautious, fears risk, and has a deep suspicion of the stock market. He invests 30% in the money market fund, 50% in the bond fund, and 20% in the equity fund. What will be the total value of Chuck's retirement account after 20 years?

For simplicity, we will assume year-end contributions and expected returns of 5% for the money market fund, 7% for the bond fund, and 10% for the equity fund.

FUND	ANNUAL INSTALLMENT	EXPECTED RETURN	FUTURE VALUE AFTER 20 YEARS
Money market	$ 3,000	5%	$ 99,198
Bond	5,000	7%	204,977
Equity	2,000	10%	114,550
Total	$10,000		$418,725

Marcia believes Chuck is too conservative. She invests none of her contributions in the money market fund, 25% in the bond fund, and 75% in the equity fund. How much is in Marcia's retirement account after 20 years?

FUND	ANNUAL INSTALLMENT	EXPECTED RETURN	FUTURE VALUE AFTER 20 YEARS
Money market	$ —	5%	$ 0
Bond	2,500	7%	102,489
Equity	7,500	10%	429,562
Total	$10,000		$532,051

You can see that the asset allocation decision can be very important. But by now you also know that the choice is a risk-return trade-off.

Now let's translate the total into income. If Chuck and Marcia can purchase perpetuities (lifetime annuities) at retirement, what will be their incomes? Suppose they can earn a perpetuity return of 8.7% APR. The annuity firm would quote this as an annuity factor of 11.50 (= 1/0.087), the present value of the perpetuity. In other words, the annuity firm will pay $1.00 per year for an up-front investment of $11.50. This annuity factor depends on the purchaser's life expectancy and on current market conditions (expected returns). Chuck's annual income would then be $36,429 (= 0.087 × 418,725), and Marcia's annual income would be $46,288 (= 0.087 × 532,051). ■

Table 21-2 summarizes the main features of defined benefit and defined contribution pension plans and reiterates their similarities and differences.

Accounting and Economic Pension Plan Models

Two models are used in managing pension plans: the accounting model and economic pension plan model. The *accounting model* keeps separate balance sheets for a firm and its pension plan, although any underfunded liability is also a long-term liability on the firm's balance sheet.

TABLE 21-2
Defined benefit and defined contribution pension plans.

DEFINED BENEFIT PENSION PLAN	DEFINED CONTRIBUTION PENSION PLAN
Differences	
Pension benefits are based on a formula including salary and years of service.	Pension benefits are based on the amount of assets accumulated in a personal pension account.
The employer chooses the portfolio managers and investment policy.	The beneficiary has some choices of investment vehicles.
The pension fund obligation is a liability of the firm.	The firm has no obligation beyond making promised contributions to the plan.
Contributions are based on a balance of pension fund obligations and the current asset level.	Contributions are set as a percent of salary or a function of firm profits.
The pension plan is generally not portable if the employee changes employers.	The assets in the beneficiary's account can be held or transferred to another fund in the employee's name.
The beneficiary sometimes incurs a substantial penalty if employment ends before retirement.	There are no penalties for changing jobs.
Funds are often locked up until retirement.	Funds can be withdrawn under some circumstances and used for other purposes before retirement.

Similarities

Employer contributions are tax-deductible.

Earnings on pension assets accumulate tax-free.

The *economic model* combines these two balance sheets. The firm's assets are its combined operating assets and pension fund assets. The firm's liabilities are its combined operating financial liabilities and pension fund liabilities. The value of the firm's equity—the value of its common stock—is the total value of the firm's assets minus all of its liabilities:

$$
\begin{aligned}
\text{Value of equity} = \ & \text{Value of operating assets} \\
& + \text{Value of pension fund assets} \\
& - \text{Value of operating financial liabilities} \\
& - \text{Value of pension fund obligations}
\end{aligned}
\tag{21.2}
$$

Empirical evidence shows that pension plan overfunding or underfunding is reflected in stock market prices. Thus, to the extent that pension fund assets and obligations are large, they can have a correspondingly large impact on the firm's stock price.

Pension Fund Regulations

The landmark law in pension fund management is the Employee Retirement Income Security Act of 1974 (ERISA). This legislation has several major provisions:

1. *Minimum funding standards*. ERISA sets minimum required pension plan contributions for projected obligations. Prior to ERISA, many firms operated their pension plans on a pay-as-you-go basis, simply paying pension benefits out of current operations. Unfortunately, with these *unfunded* plans, if the firm went bankrupt, the beneficiaries lost their pensions.

2. *Fiduciary standards*. ERISA sets fiduciary standards for pension fund trustees. These are the standards a trustee must follow to avoid being held liable for something that goes wrong. They include

standards for loyalty, prudence, and diversification. Loyalty means that the plan must be managed for the sole benefit of plan participants, not for the benefit of the firm. Prudence requires that management meet the standards of a prudent expert familiar with the management of a pension plan. Diversification means that the plan must be diversified to minimize the chance of large losses.

3. *Minimum vesting standards.* Vesting is the process of conferring pension rights on employees. Typically, employees become vested after working for the firm for a specified amount of time, such as five years. ERISA requires that vesting occur much earlier than many pension plans had previously provided.

4. *Pension Benefit Guaranty Corporation (PBGC).* ERISA established the PBGC, a government agency that insures the vested benefits of defined benefit plans within certain limits.

The Department of Labor and the Internal Revenue Service are responsible for administering ERISA. Plan sponsors must make regular reports to these agencies and regular disclosures to plan participants. Violations of ERISA provisions can be dealt with forcefully because of the strength of these two federal agencies.

ERISA solidified and changed the rules for pension fund management. ERISA does not compel a firm to establish a pension plan, but if a firm chooses to have a defined benefit plan, it must comply with ERISA regulations. This important law makes a firm's pension promises much more secure.

Pension Fund Design

The firm is responsible for designing the pension plan. Since the passage of ERISA, most of the growth in pension fund coverage has been in defined contribution plans. In fact, because of the risky obligation of a defined benefit plan, many firms terminated these plans and replaced them with defined contribution plans. In addition, the majority of new employees who are being covered are in defined contribution plans.

The defined benefit plan differentially rewards older employees who have worked for the firm for more years. These plans are like golden handcuffs that tie workers to their employer after they have accumulated a substantial number of years of service.

Many employees, particularly young ones, prefer the defined contribution type of plan, because they have pension accounts in their own names and can keep their funds if they change employers. The most troubling aspect of the defined contribution type of plan is that employees very frequently liquidate their plans when they change jobs, spending their funds on such things as houses, cars, and college expenses, instead of holding them for retirement. From a societal perspective, these early liquidations of pension savings may create a poverty problem when these people retire.

If a firm chooses a defined benefit plan, it can make the plan contributory or noncontributory. Frequently, a defined benefit plan is supplemented with a defined contribution plan that is optional for employees. In the optional defined contribution plan, the employer may match employee contributions in some way. For example, the firm may contribute $0.50 for each $1.00 that the employee contributes.

If a firm establishes a defined contribution plan, the contributions can be a percent of each employee's salary. Alternatively, the contributions can be some fraction of the firm's income. Some defined contribution plans guarantee a minimum benefit even if the investments do not perform well. Such a "floor" plan is basically a defined benefit plan up to a point, but it is a defined contribution plan if investments perform reasonably well because it can pay higher benefits.

Choosing Investment Managers

The pension fund assets—for example, investments in domestic and foreign stocks, bonds, and real estate—are held apart from the firm by a trustee. However, the firm's pension fund manager can make decisions about investment categories, and even about specific investments. Such decisions can also be delegated to an outside management firm.

This is an opportunity to apply the Principle of Comparative Advantage. If a firm uses an outside manager, then it must hire and monitor the outside manager, but after that it need make only some broad strategic decisions about how to allocate investments. The outside manager makes the specific, day-to-day investment decisions. Making all such decisions internally requires much staff time. The trade-off, of course, is the total costs of one approach versus those of the other. Which is best depends on whether the outside manager has a comparative cost advantage.

The Funding Decision

The income tax system favors overfunding, because contributions are tax-deductible and pension fund earnings accumulate tax-free. No taxes are paid on the earnings until they are distributed to beneficiaries, at which time the beneficiaries must pay personal taxes on their pension payments.

In contrast, the hidden option to default favors underfunding. If a firm goes bankrupt, it simply defaults on its pension obligations much as it would default on other financial obligations, leaving its beneficiaries in jeopardy. The PBGC will step in to pay some of the insured pension benefits. High-risk firms may try to benefit by underfunding their pension plans and shifting their responsibility to their beneficiaries and the PBGC.

There is, then, a tax incentive for most firms to overfund their pension plans and a risk-shifting incentive for high-risk firms to underfund their plans. The Omnibus Budget Reconciliation Act (OBRA) of 1987 addresses these incentive problems. If a pension plan is underfunded (assets are less than 100% of obligations), the firm is required to increase its annual contributions until the plan is fully funded. At the other extreme, if the plan is overfunded by 50%, additional contributions to the plan become non-tax-deductible and therefore unattractive. Although OBRA sets some reasonable bounds on the level of fundedness (overfunding versus underfunding), the firm has considerable leeway in deciding how well to fund its plan.

Asset Allocation Decisions

The asset allocation decision is of great significance for firms with a defined benefit pension plan. (For employees covered by a defined contribution plan, this decision is equally important, and it is one they must make for themselves.) For retired employees whose pension payments are now fixed, the firm can hedge this obligation by investing in fixed-income securities. For active employees, the firm may choose to invest in a mix with equities because of inflation risk in salary growth and investment returns.

A tax strategy (which is consistent with overfunding) might be consistent with investing in bonds. The firm can borrow money by issuing its own bonds and then use the proceeds to purchase pension fund bonds. The interest the firm pays on its own bonds is tax-deductible, with a cost of $(1 - \text{tax rate})$ times the interest rate, but the fund's interest income is not taxed. This allows the firm to benefit from tax arbitrage. Of course, this is why OBRA limits the amount of overfunding. A high-risk underfunding strategy might be to invest in very high-risk pension assets. This shifts wealth to the stockholders at the expense of pension beneficiaries.

In reality, most firms behave as though they are going concerns and operate the firm and its pension plan in such a way as to fulfill their obligation to pension beneficiaries (as well as other stakeholders). These firms invest in a diversified portfolio of assets that controls the risk inherent in the pension obligations. This usually means making investments in other firms and in industries unrelated to their own operating businesses to obtain the greatest risk reduction from diversification.

Self-Check Questions

1. Why is prudent pension fund management so important to a firm and its employees?
2. Explain the main differences between defined benefit and defined contribution pension plans. Are there any similarities?
3. What does it mean to say that a pension plan is underfunded? That it is overfunded? Which of these conditions must be reported on the firm's balance sheet?
4. True or false? Pension plan overfunding or underfunding is reflected in the sponsoring firm's share price.
5. Explain why there is a tax incentive for most firms to overfund their pension plans and a risk-shifting incentive for high-risk firms to underfund their plans.

21.3 RISK MANAGEMENT

Recall that financial theory says that diversified investors value their investments on the basis of the nondiversifiable (systematic) risk rather than the total risk. This is because many firm-specific risks can be diversified away. Thus any practices that firms use to reduce diversifiable risks should be redundant and should fail to be rewarded by the financial marketplace.

In spite of this, firms engage in an extensive variety of risk-reducing behaviors. These include

1. Buying insurance against property and casualty losses and against product liability claims
2. Using financial futures and forward contracts to hedge against fluctuations in foreign currency exchange rates, interest rates, and commodity prices
3. Avoiding risky markets and risky products
4. Using low levels of financial leverage even when there are substantial tax advantages to using higher debt financing levels

Thus we have an apparent contradiction. Financial theorists argue that some risk-reducing activities are not profitable, and yet managers engage in precisely these activities. The key to understanding this paradox is financial contracting and various stakeholder incentives. Let's go back to the fundamental ideas of valuation and see what the financial theorists and business managers are really doing. The basic present value equation helps us see this:

$$PV = \sum_{t=1}^{n} \frac{CF_t}{(1 + r)^t}$$

where PV is the present value, CF_t is the cash flow at time t, n is the number of time periods, and r is the required return.

Financial theorists argue that for diversified investors, the required return is based on systematic risk, not total risk. If you do not change r, value is unaffected. Therefore, reducing unsystematic risk is a fruitless activity from the perspective of diversified investors.

Some financial managers argue that reductions in total risk (not just systematic risk) can increase the size of the firm's operating cash flows, because they are connected with the firm's customers, suppliers, employees, and other stakeholders—who are not fully diversified. Because total firm risk affects these stakeholders, managers rightly believe that the size of the operating cash flows in the numerator is affected by the risk of the firm. If reducing total firm risk can increase the cash flows without changing r, it will increase value. **Risk management,** which is the process of identifying and evaluating risks and selecting and managing techniques to adapt to risk exposures, has become an important function in modern corporations.

Effects of Risk on Operating Cash Flows

A lower-risk firm can be attractive to suppliers, customers, employees, managers, and others in many ways. Here are a few.

EFFECT ON CUSTOMERS   Customers are often wary of a high-risk supplier. Such a supplier cannot be depended on as a long-term source of supplies. To hedge the risk of a cutoff of needed supplies, a customer can find alternative suppliers and diversify its sources or can switch to one that has an acceptable risk level. Potential customers are also concerned that a distressed supplier might reduce the quality of its goods and services.

In response to high risk, a supplier may have to offer greater warranties on goods and services, sometimes using a third party to back the warranty. A risky firm will have to expend resources to advertise or upgrade its image, in order to persuade customers that it is a more dependable supplier than it appears to be. In addition to these costs, a risky supplier may lose potential new customers as well as existing customers, and salespersons and distributors may stop selling the firm's products and services.

EFFECTS ON SUPPLIERS AND EMPLOYEES   Just like customers, suppliers prefer not to deal with high-risk firms. A supplier that invests its resources in a profitable business relationship can suffer a loss if the trading partner goes out of business. Recruiting and retaining good employees are easier for a low-risk firm. If a firm ceases business, its employees will lose the value of many firm-specific skills they have acquired as well as incurring the substantial search costs of looking for a new job. When they find new employment, many employees will have to restart their careers at a lower level in terms of both pay and responsibility. Top managers may be shunned by the managerial marketplace, because their reputations can be sullied by their association with the failed enterprise.

ADVERSE MANAGERIAL INCENTIVES   When a firm is distressed, the firm's managers often make different business decisions than they would if the firm were a healthy going concern. In a distressed state, managers may seek short-term payoffs, sometimes in spite of the long-term consequences. The firm may sell off or liquidate promising lines of business to get cash. The firm may forgo investment opportunities that have good long-term payoffs. The managers may produce inferior products or tolerate a less safe work environment to improve near-term cash flows. The firm may invest in very high-risk projects, which will benefit stockholders if they are successful but are likely to reduce the wealth of bondholders. These incentives remind us of losing hockey or football teams toward the end of the game. The only way to win the game is to attempt desperate strategies (pulling the goalie, the "Hail Mary" pass) that are poor strategies on average but have become the only chance the team has of winning. A low-risk firm does not have an incentive to make so many bad business decisions as a high-risk firm.

EFFECTS ON OTHER STAKEHOLDERS   High risk can have an adverse effect on other stakeholders. For example, a community may give special preferences and special treatment to attract firms that are considered to be low-risk firms. Banks and other lenders will put more restrictions in their loan agreements in response to the perceived riskiness of their borrowers. If the firm has accumulated some tax-loss carryforwards or some tax credits, it can lose the value of these if it goes out of business.

The fact that many stakeholders are not diversified causes their interests to differ from those of diversified investors. In many cases, risk-reducing actions benefit these stakeholders because they improve the firm's cash flows. This, in turn, benefits the diversified stockholders.

Techniques for Reducing Risk

Although reducing unsystematic risk that can be diversified away does not benefit diversified investors, we have just discussed several examples where total risk affects the welfare of non-diversified stakeholders. Investors can reduce their risks by diversifying their portfolios across many investments. Businesses can reduce their total risk (although not necessarily their systematic risk) in several ways. These include buying insurance; using options, futures, and forward contracts; keeping their financial leverage low; and practicing risk avoidance.

RISK AVOIDANCE   Risk avoidance means refusing to engage in any new activity with a loss exposure or abandoning a current activity that entails a loss exposure. If the firm manufactures a product with a potential large liability, it can avoid the risk by getting out of this line of business. After the fact, some firms have ceased or curtailed some operations because of large risks. These firms include A. H. Robins with its Dalkon Shield, Johns-Manville with its asbestos, and Dow-Corning with its silicon gel breast implants. Huge financial losses could have been avoided if these firms had never manufactured the offending products. Because of product liability problems, many firms have left the private airplane manufacturing and swimming pool industries.

Of course, many risks are not avoidable and are a necessary part of being in business. Identifying risks and then estimating the potential losses associated with them is a step that management continually undertakes before entering a new business. Abandoning a risky business will not cause previous loss exposures to disappear, but it can reduce the exposures associated with future business.

RISK TRANSFER USING FINANCIAL CONTRACTING   There are several opportunities to transfer risks to another party through financial contracting. Futures contracts and forward contracts can be used to hedge the risks of foreign exchange rate movements, interest rate changes, stock market movements, and many commodity price changes. These futures and forward contracts can be used in the operating part of the business as well as in its financing and its pension fund. Option contracts can also be helpful. For example, an option to buy a piece of property that the firm might need would lock in a known purchase price for the life of the option. Chapter 26 describes these contracts and how firms use them.

RISK TRANSFER WITH OPERATING CONTRACTS   A firm can enter long-term contracts with critical suppliers to lock in prices and ensure a dependable supply. Likewise, a firm may seek long-term contracts with customers to protect its investment in serving the customers. A firm may lease equipment or real property instead of buying it if the firm believes that its needs are relatively short-term. The firm may apply the Principle of Comparative Advantage and subcontract some of its work to other firms rather than risking a large investment to manufacture the same components.

USING INSURANCE   Insurance companies pool the risks of a large number of parties. Each insured party pays a premium that is slightly more than the expected or average loss. The insurance premiums collected are used to pay the losses, to pay the insurance firm's operating expenses, and to provide a profit. There are many types of private insurance, including fire and related property insurance, marine (or transportation) insurance, automobile insurance, general liability insurance, burglary and theft insurance, workmen's compensation insurance, crop insurance, health insurance, credit insurance, life insurance, and fidelity and surety bonds.

By paying a firm when it sustains a loss, the effect of insurance is to leave the firm's financial position in substantially the same state as it would have been if the loss had not occurred. Large firms sometimes self-insure themselves against some perils. These firms are so large that their average losses are fairly predictable. If their expected loss is less than the cost of the insurance, they may profit by self-insuring. Interestingly, however, some large firms use insurance companies because of their comparative advantage in identifying and preventing perils and in handling the claims that arise.

Buying Insurance

EXAMPLE

Flex Fitness Center is a thriving business in Little Rock. The value of the business is estimated to be $500,000. Because it has $350,000 in debt, the value of equity is the residual $150,000. In case of a major fire, Flex's owners estimate that the loss would be $400,000. The probability of this loss is 0.25%, so the expected loss is $1000 (= 0.0025 × 400,000). The insurance premium is $1400, so the insurance costs $400 more than its expected value. Should Flex buy the insurance?

Most people buy insurance because the consequences of a large loss, even though its probability is small, are greater than the drawback of having to pay the insurance premium. Risk-averse individuals are willing to trade a certain small loss (the insurance premium) in exchange for eliminating even a small probability of a large loss. Thus Flex's owners might buy insurance because they are risk-averse. On the other hand, if the owners have substantial other wealth and are well diversified, they might self-insure and hope that, on average, they can save money by not buying insurance and paying for their own losses.

Let's look at this insurance proposal again from the viewpoint of Flex's creditors, the people who have lent $350,000 to the business. If the business is the only collateral for the loan and the business burns down, the creditors will lose a substantial amount of money. Assuming that the creditors can repossess remaining assets worth $100,000, the creditors can lose $250,000. The owners can lose all of their equity, which is $150,000. But because the probability of this loss to the owners is 0.25%, the expected loss for the owners is $375 (= 0.0025 × 150,000). The owners must pay $1400 for an insurance policy that has an expected payoff for them of only $375 (the rest of the expected payoff of the insurance goes to the creditors). Thus owners can have an incentive to underinsure when the insurance payoffs are shared with creditors. Because of this problem, most loan contracts require that the borrowers maintain enough insurance on the business to protect the lenders. ■

Self-Check Questions

1. How can risk management benefit a firm?

2. Why might customers, suppliers, or employees be reluctant to deal with a high-risk firm? Would your answer change if all the stakeholders were fully diversified?

3. What methods can a firm use to reduce its total risk?

4. Why do loan contracts require that the borrowers maintain adequate insurance on all collateral securing the loan? What is the agency cost involved here?

21.4 INVESTOR RELATIONS

Investor relations (IR) is the process that a firm uses to communicate with its investors. Investor relations officers explain their firm's performance, its future challenges and opportunities, and its present strategies to current and potential investors.

Why Is There an Investor Relations Function?

Why do many corporations spend money on investor relations? As with most decisions, an expenditure can be justified if its benefits exceed the costs incurred. However, in the case of investor relations, the specific benefits received are intangible and hard to quantify. The benefits sought through investor relations management are in the following areas.

1. *Recognition and credibility in the business community.* A good reputation can boost the morale and loyalty of employees and help recruit new employees. A good reputation can enhance sales to other business customers and can also contribute to positive relations with government officials, regulators, and the financial press.

2. *Fair valuation.* IR management can help a firm meet the obligation to ensure that market prices fairly and reasonably reflect fair value by providing full, complete, and accurate information on which the market will base prices. This reassures investors who are selling that they are selling at a fair value. Similarly, it reassures buyers that they are paying a fair price. If a firm ever caused an artificially high or low price by, for example, manipulating information, it should expect to face lawsuits. Unhappy stockholders, who were misled into buying the stock at an inflated price, or who sold their stock at less than its fair value, would be likely to sue.

3. *Well-informed constituency of professional investors.* A large group of knowledgeable investors should be able to assess new developments and incorporate them into their assessments of the value of the stock in an unbiased manner. This could help reduce distortions in the firm's stock price through time.

4. *Cost of capital.* IR management may help a firm raise new debt and equity capital more easily. A lower cost of capital might result from having investors who have full, fair, and complete information. Credibility and a good reputation with investors can translate into better valuations of the firm's stock.

5. *Compliance with securities laws.* Securities laws enforced by the Securities and Exchange Commission, other federal agencies, and state agencies require specialized knowledge and attention. One goal of IR management is to ensure that corporate officers comply with all applicable regulations.

6. *Information for nonfinancial corporate officers.* Many corporate executives do not have a finance background. The IR officer must interpret information from the marketplace (stock prices and trading), bond ratings, and other signals to help corporate officers understand the financial implications of their decisions.

In theory, you should always increase the investment in an activity as long as its incremental benefits exceed its incremental costs. This principle allows you to determine the optimal size of an investment. Although the benefits of IR are fairly intangible, you should continue to increase the resources committed to this function only up to the point where the incremental investment continues to be profitable. The example that follows reinforces this idea.

EXAMPLE

Cost-Benefit Analysis of Investor Relations

Claremont Holdings is considering increasing its expenditures on investor relations by $100,000 per year. Although the potential benefits are many and hard to assess precisely, the CFO estimates that an expanded IR program could reduce the cost of debt by 0.05% and the cost of equity by 0.15%. Claremont has $50 million of debt financing and $75 million of equity financing. The annual net savings should be

Savings on debt financing	0.05% of $50 million	$ 25,000
Savings on equity financing	0.15% of $75 million	112,500
Total savings		137,500
Minus:	Annual costs	100,000
Annual net savings		$ 37,500

If these estimates are correct, the incremental benefits of expanding the investor relations budget exceed the incremental costs by $37,500. ■

Investor Relations

The firm has contractual arrangements with many suppliers of capital. The suppliers include stockholders, banks and other financial institutions that supply short- and intermediate-term debt financing, and bondholders who supply long-term debt financing. The investor relations program will differ for each type of securityholder as well as for the various kinds of investors within each group. For example, specific programs for common stockholders might be called stockholder relations, and programs designed to communicate with commercial banks might be called bank relations.

Firms can communicate directly with current investors by mailing them information. For stockholders with certificates in their own names, the firm can mail information to their preferred mailing address. For stockholders whose shares are held in a street name (at their brokerage firms), the firm can mail information to the brokerage firms and ask them to forward it to individual stockholders. However, communicating with *potential* stockholders is especially difficult, because the number of potential investors is so large and because they are dispersed across the globe. You can imagine the inefficiency of many thousands of firms trying to communicate directly with millions of individual investors. As a result, much of financial communications is indirect, passing from the firm to stockholders indirectly through security analysts and the financial press.

Security analysts make earnings forecasts for the firms they cover. They also make buy/sell/hold recommendations for these firms. Security analysts often prepare research reports summarizing the marketing, financial, and operating prospects of individual firms. An analyst may limit her research to one or two industries and intensely study the firms in these industries. A good security analyst will know more about a firm and its prospects than almost everyone else, with the possible exception of a handful of top executives of the firm. An analyst provides her diligently acquired and interpreted information to clients and employers.

There are two primary groups of security analysts: "sell-side" analysts and "buy-side" analysts. The sell-side analysts work for brokerages firms such as Merrill Lynch, A. G. Edwards, Dean Witter Reynolds, and Smith Barney. They make recommendations that their firm's brokers use in dealing with the firm's customers. Their forecasts and recommendations are widely disseminated and used by the investing community. The buy-side analysts work for insurance companies, money managers, and other institutional investors. The buy-side analysts make recommendations mainly for their own employers to use. Thus, by disclosing a substantial amount of information that analysts, among others, can use, a corporation provides information to its potential and current stockholders.

Financial information is also reported by the financial press. The financial press includes the print media, such as the *Wall Street Journal*, *Value Line*, and *Barron's*. Information is also widely available through telecommunications. A number of vendors, such as Bloomberg, Bridge, and CompuServe, not only communicate financial information from firms but also provide analysis and other information useful to investors.

Investor relations also deals directly with individual investors. All publicly traded corporations have at least a few very large stockholders. These large investors—pension funds, wealthy individuals, trusts, or other firms—need to monitor the performance of their investments. The IR officer can provide timely information to large investors much as they would to security analysts.

It is unlikely that corporate officers will know very many of the small investors in their corporations. Small investors will receive the reports and information provided to analysts and large investors, but not the same personal attention.

Creditor Relations

As a practical matter, creditor relations takes less time and resources than stockholder relations. If a firm is financed with 50% equity and 50% debt, the firm may find that the demands for information from the IR officer come disproportionately from equityholders, say 90% from stockholders and the remaining 10% from all classes of creditors. Relations with creditors are simplified for two reasons. First, there may be fewer creditors than stockholders. Bonds and other short-term debt usually are concentrated in fewer hands than is the case for outstanding common stock. Second, because stockholders are the residual owners of the firm, they are more directly affected by changes in a firm's value than creditors are. Changes in the value of the firm have a muted effect on the value of debt instruments. Not only do creditors monitor the firm less closely than stockholders, but short-term creditors often monitor the firm less closely than long-term creditors. Short-term creditors such as bank lenders and commercial paper owners face the least risk of default, and they monitor their borrowers correspondingly less because of this. Bondholders and mortgageholders face higher levels of risk as a result of possible changes in the creditworthiness of the firm over a long time horizon, so they monitor the firm more closely.

Many loans from banks and pension funds are negotiated, rather than sold on the open market like many securities. These private placements involve fewer investors than a public offering of securities, and these loans are not very marketable by their owners. The banks and pension funds that hold the loans also hold them for a long time, usually until maturity. These private placements tend to require greater effort by the firm's officers than a similar quantity of publicly placed debt, because private lenders tend to monitor the borrower more closely than do public bondholders.

Creditors also rely heavily on rating agencies that evaluate the riskiness of the firm's commercial paper, bonds, and mortgages. In addition, because trustees are appointed to monitor the firm on behalf of public bondholders, the need for individual bondholders to monitor the firm is further reduced. The IR managers are charged with providing the credit rating agencies and bond trustees the information that they need to do their job fairly.

Forms of Financial Communications

Just about any form of communication is used, including written reports, speeches, computer and fax transmissions, telephone, and personal interviews.

1. *Computer and telecommunications technology.* There has been a rapid acceleration in the speed of communications through the use of modern computer and telecommunications technology. If there is some news to communicate, such as an earnings announcement or a possible merger, messages will be sent out within minutes to the major news services worldwide (such as Bloomberg, Dow Jones, and Reuters). Security analysts then alert their clients. The media used will include fax (facsimile) machines, computer-distributed reports (such as earnings reports on First Call), telephone conference calls, and recorded telephone messages.

   Securities trading responds to information within seconds. Thus it is important to disseminate information as rapidly as possible to as many clients and investors as possible. The fairness of the market is enhanced by these rapid communications. Some news, such as earnings announcements, is often released after the stock market has closed for the day or early in the morning before the market opens. This allows more time for all investors to receive the information and to assess its implications for the valuation of the firm's securities. Investors are usually advised ahead of time about when some announcements will be made and how to receive the information. If an important event happens during trading (while the stock market is open), the IR managers will try to distribute this information rapidly to allow trading to proceed with the best information possible.

2. *Written communications with stockholders.* The annual report is usually the most widely distributed piece of firm documentation. Its audience is wider than simply stockholders. It provides business and financial information for many other constituents, such as suppliers, customers, current employees, potential new employees, and the press.

   Firms issue interim reports such as quarterly financial reports. These are much briefer than the annual report. Stockholders can also request copies of a firm's 10-K and 10-Q, which are detailed annual and quarterly reports supplied to the SEC. IR managers often prepare an annual corporate/financial data book that supplements the regular annual report. This book provides information that is especially relevant for the particular firm or industry. It is designed to provide analysts with the information they want to do their evaluations. Firms also provide periodic institutional investor newsletters and communications. Both the corporate/financial data book and the institutional investor newsletters must be made available to individual investors on request.

Written copies of news releases or other announcements of events of significance to investors are mailed to investors. In addition, the text of speeches that top management has presented to financial analysts are often mailed.

3. *The annual meeting.* The annual meeting is a legal requirement. It provides a forum for shareholders and managers to get together. The importance or relevance of annual meetings varies across firms, but most institutional and professional investors find the annual meeting to be of very limited value. The annual meeting is a ritual that does generate some press coverage, but large investors often complain that these gatherings are too formal and that their value to the firm and to investors does not justify the expense.

4. *Communications with top management.* Top management presents the firm's story to a financial analyst society meeting once or twice a year. A firm often wants to have some news to give at these meetings. A firm that grabs the limelight but has nothing new to offer may irritate the financial community. Thus most firms take good advantage of this opportunity. As a result, analysts and the financial press follow these meetings very closely. Firms often publish and distribute the text of their top management presentation at an analyst society meeting.

Firms occasionally arrange field trips for security analysts. On a field trip, analysts spend one or two days touring facilities, becoming acquainted with management, and learning about the operations and marketing of the firm.

A firm may also host small groups of analysts or large investors recommended by brokerage firms at its headquarters. These meetings are briefer than field trips and sometimes focus on specific areas of the firm instead of on the firm as a whole. Hosted meetings provide an opportunity for investors and analysts to get to know management and to learn more about the firm.

Because the financial marketplace is globalized, U.S. firms now make presentations in major European and Pacific Rim financial centers. Before a significant financing event, such as the issuance of more common stock or new corporate bonds, the firm may have a "road show" to help sell the securities. These road shows include most of the firm's top managers and visit several financial centers within the United States as well as abroad. It is not unusual for road shows to keep top management traveling for a couple of weeks of intense, nonstop meetings to get the firm's story out.

Self-Check Questions

1. What is the purpose of the investor relations function? What benefits does a firm seek when it promotes investor relations?

2. Can good investor relations help promote capital market efficiency? Explain.

3. What are security analysts, and what is their function? How does investor relations help them perform their job?

4. Which of the three groups of investors (stockholders, long-term creditors, and short-term creditors) usually monitors a firm most closely? Which least closely? Explain why.

SUMMARY

This chapter described the typical responsibilities of a chief financial officer (CFO), a controller, and a treasurer. We then described three important treasury management functions for which they are responsible: pension fund management, risk management, and investor relations. Pension fund managerial functions include designing the plan, choosing investment managers, choosing the level of funding, and making asset allocation decisions.

Mitchell, Mark L., and J. Harold Mulherin. "The Stock Price Response to Pension Terminations and the Relation of Terminations with Corporate Takeovers," *Financial Management*, 1989, 18(3):41–56.

Petersen, Mitchell A. "Cash Flow Variability and Firm's Pension Choice: A Role for Operating Leverage," *Journal of Financial Economics*, 1994, 36(3):361–383.

Rajan, Raghuram G. "Insiders and Outsiders: The Choice Between Informed and Arm's-Length Debt," *Journal of Finance*, 1992, 47(4):1367–1400.

Strong, John S., and John R. Meyer. "Asset Writedowns: Managerial Incentives and Security Returns," *Journal of Finance*, 1987, 42(3):643–661.

Warshawsky, Mark J., H. Fred Mittelstaedt, and Carrie Christea. "Recognizing Retiree Health Benefits: The Effect of SFAS 106," *Financial Management*, 1993, 22(2):188–299.

FINANCIAL PLANNING

Financial planning creates a "blueprint" for the firm's future. Planning is necessary to (1) establish the firm's goals, (2) choose operating and financial strategies, (3) forecast operating results against which to monitor and evaluate performance, and (4) create contingent plans for dealing with unforeseen circumstances. Good financial planning involves all parts of the firm and its policies and decisions about such things as liquidity, working capital, inventories, capital budgeting, capital structure, and dividends.

A firm should not simply react to events as they unfold. It should be prepared to deal swiftly and effectively with both favorable and unfavorable developments. Competitive forces in the capital markets—and in other markets—make it difficult to find positive-NPV decisions. However, mistakes and poor planning make negative-NPV outcomes an ever-present possibility!

In this chapter, we will develop a framework for financial planning. We will look at both short- and long-term planning models, because the typical short-term plan is simply a more detailed part of a firm's long-term plan.

O B J E C T I V E S

After studying this chapter, you should be able to

1. Describe the financial planning process.

2. Construct a cash budget.

3. Use the simple percent of sales forecasting method to estimate a firm's future financing needs on the basis of sales growth.

4. Describe the usefulness of pro forma financial statements.

5. Create short- and long-term financial planning models using a spreadsheet.

6. Use the models you create to construct a cash budget, project pro forma financial statements, and estimate a firm's future financing needs.

FINANCIAL PLANNING AND THE PRINCIPLES OF FINANCE

◆ *Valuable Ideas*: Use both bottom-up and top-down processes to increase the chance of uncovering valuable ideas.

◆ *Self-Interested Behavior*: Carefully evaluate and monitor the financial plan's impact on the firm and its stakeholders.

◆ *Incremental Benefits*: Forecast the firm's cash flows, and analyze the incremental cash flows of alternative decisions.

◆ *Time Value of Money*: Compare the NPVs of alternative financial plans.

◆ *Two-Sided Transactions*: Look for situations that are not zero-sum games and thus may be profitable to you *and* your supplier or customer, perhaps by reducing financial contracting costs and routine transaction costs.

◆ *Comparative Advantage*: Consider subcontracting business activities to outside vendors if they can provide the services more cheaply and competently.

◆ *Behavioral*: Use common industry practices as a good starting place for the planning process.

22.1 THE FINANCIAL PLANNING PROCESS

A firm is a dynamic system. Decisions and policies about liquidity, working capital, inventories, capital budgeting, capital structure, and dividends (among other things) interact continually. Figure 22-1 illustrates this interaction in a flow-of-funds framework.

The main net source of funds is the firm's operations. The firm uses its fixed assets, together with labor, raw materials, and other inputs, to produce products and services to sell. Sales revenue minus cost of goods sold and operating expenses (such as selling, general, and administrative expenses) equals the firm's operating income. An important question in connection with financial planning is how operating income responds to increases in output. The answer depends on the firm's operating leverage. Recall from Chapter 10 that the higher the fixed-cost component of total costs, the greater is operating leverage.

Net income is left after interest expense and taxes are paid. Net income can be paid out as dividends, or it can be retained and reinvested. The firm's dividend policy determines the split between dividends and retained earnings. Dividend policy interacts with the firm's capital budget. A higher payout ratio increases the amount of external financing needed to meet the capital budget. Both of these policies in turn interact with the firm's capital structure policy. The combination of the firm's financing needs, its dividend policy, and its capital structure policy determines the mix of debt and equity in any required new external financing.

The firm's financing needs are determined mainly by its capital budget and internal cash generation. The capital budget is in turn affected by projected sales. Increased sales will eventually require expenditures for planned expansions and new equipment. In addition, higher production rates cause machines to wear out faster, so the need for replacement investment also increases. Higher sales levels will also require additional investment in working capital.

The firm's planned investment in current assets (net of increases in payables), along with its liquidity policy, determines the net increase or decrease in short-term borrowing. The

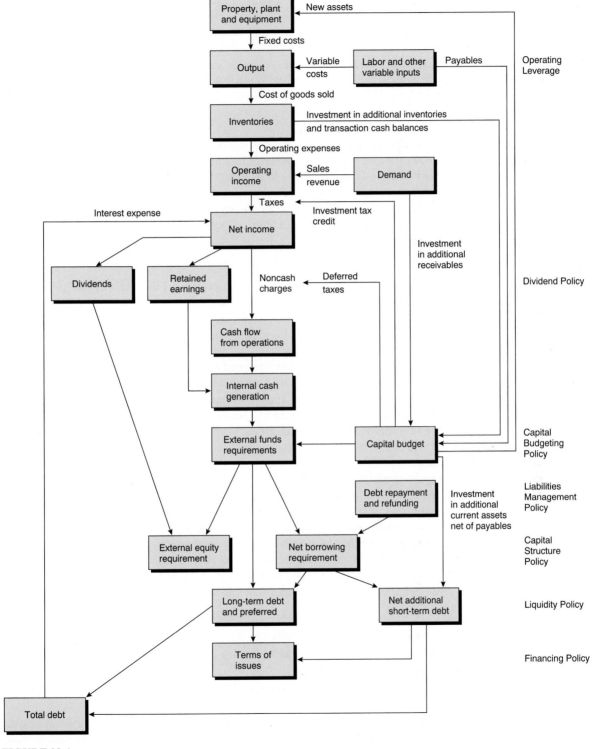

FIGURE 22-1
Interaction of financial decisions in a flow-of-funds framework.

rest of the firm's borrowing needs, the residual, should be on a long-term basis. The firm might issue some preferred stock in addition to (or in place of) long-term debt, depending on its tax position and capital structure objectives. The firm's tax position is essentially the amount of tax deductions and credits from depreciation, depletion allowance, and interest expense.

The total long-term borrowing requirement includes the residual just noted plus any required debt repayments and planned early refunding. Finally, the terms of the debt (and/or preferred stock) issues must be determined in light of the firm's financing policy. Any resulting debt issuance changes the firm's interest expense. This will affect net income—and the planning "circle" is complete.

The process illustrated in Figure 22-1 is a continuing one. Remember, the firm's total sources of funds must equal its total uses of funds in any finite planning period. For relatively short periods of time, this equality might require either unintended changes in cash balances or unplanned short-term borrowing. But the firm should strive to avoid these inefficiencies through good financial planning. All six of the basic financial policies must be determined simultaneously. This requires certain trade-offs. These trade-offs can be analyzed within a financial planning model.

The Financial Plan

Figure 22-1 provides a starting point for financial planning. **Financial planning** is a process of evaluating the impact of alternative investing and financing decisions. Decisions, such as the firm's capital budget or a debt restructuring, are then projected as part of a financial plan. Subsequently, outcomes are measured against the plan.

A financial plan has inputs, a model, and outputs. Examples of inputs include projections of sales, collections, costs, interest rates, and exchange rates. The firm's current position (cash balance, debt obligations, and so on) and alternative decisions are also inputs. The model is a set of mathematical relationships among the inputs and outputs.

The outputs of a financial plan are pro forma financial statements and a set of budgets. **Pro forma financial statements** are projected (forecasted) financial statements. A **budget** is a detailed schedule of a financial activity, such as an advertising budget, a sales budget, or a capital budget.

Firms use both short- and long-term financial planning models. Models are classified by their planning horizon. A model's **planning horizon** is the length of time it projects into the future. "Short-term" usually means a year or less. A five-year horizon is common for a long-term planning model, but some industries use a ten-year or longer horizon. For example, a forestry products firm might have a planning horizon of several decades.

Short-term models are detailed and very specific. Long-term models tend to be much less so.

A complete financial plan includes, at a minimum,

1. Clearly stated strategic, operating, and financial *objectives*.

2. The *assumptions* on which the plan is based.

3. Descriptions of the underlying *strategies*.

4. *Contingency plans* for emergencies.

5. *Budgets*, categorized and summarized in various ways, such as by time period, division, and type (for example, cash, advertising, and capital).

6. The *financing program*, categorized and summarized in various ways, such as by time period, sources of funds (for example, bonds, bank loans, and stock), and types of funds (for example, short-term versus long-term, and internal versus external).

7. A set of period-by-period *pro forma financial statements* for the entire planning horizon.

Planning Cycles

Financial plans are updated on a regular basis, according to a planning cycle. Each update adds the latest information and renews the planning horizon—that is, it projects into the future by the length of the cycle. Short-term models might be updated monthly, weekly, or even daily. Long-term plans might be updated once, twice, or perhaps four times a year. Updates also vary in how thorough they are.

For example, a firm might update its short-term model by adding the latest data each week but might extend another month (renew the planning horizon) only once a month. In addition, the firm might review and make any changes in the model itself only once a year. Similar procedures are typical for long-term models.

Bottom-Up and Top-Down Planning

Plans and ideas can be generated through either a bottom-up or a top-down process. A bottom-up planning process starts at the product or production level and proceeds upward through the plant and division levels to top management. At each level, ideas are added, modified, and/or deleted. Managers at successively higher levels, who are in a position to take a broader view, should be able to see things that are not visible to the lower levels. Higher management levels can also propose efficient combinations or eliminations that are unlikely to be suggested by the affected employees.

The top-down planning process starts with the firm's top management and its strategic plans and goals and proceeds downward through the organization's levels. Top management makes strategic decisions. These decisions often create, increase, shrink, or eliminate such things as the firm's products, divisions, and international marketing efforts. Managers describe how strategic decisions will be implemented. At each successively lower managerial level, the required actions become more specific.

Critics of the bottom-up process say it often fails to produce a coherent strategy for the firm as a whole and can cause the firm to appear chaotic and poorly managed. Critics of the top-down process say it tends to exaggerate the role of top managers and often results in bad investments and missed opportunities because top management may not be in touch with what is going on "in the field." But the bottom-up and top-down processes actually complement one another. Good planning requires both. Ideally, valuable new ideas are supported no matter where or how they originate.

Phases of the Financial Planning Process

Financial planning has three phases: *formulating* the plan, *implementing* the plan, and *evaluating* performance. Involvement in the three phases depends on the manager's specific role. For example, salespersons may have special insights into marketing forecasts, and engineers may have special expertise in developing cost estimates. A financial plan should be formulated by using the kinds of bottom-up and top-down processes we just described.

In the implementation phase, budgets with specific objectives, resource allocations, and operating policies are used to clarify each manager's responsibilities for contributing to the firm's goals. During implementation, circumstances change and opportunities evolve. A firm should alter its plans to adapt to, and take advantage of, changing circumstances. Consequently, a good budgeting system should be *flexible*. A budget is simply part of a financial plan, and plans need to be adapted to new opportunities and circumstances.

In the evaluation phase, the firm compares its overall performance to the financial plan. Managers and their units are evaluated in terms of how well their performance compares to the objectives. In this process the conditions that actually prevailed, which can be very different from those expected and forecasted, are taken into account.

Benefits of Financial Planning

Of course, the goal of the planning process is to help maximize the value of the firm. Toward this end, there are several benefits that a firm hopes to realize from the planning process:

1. *Standardizing assumptions.* The planning process can expose inconsistencies in decision-making methods. For example, when managers differ in their forecasts of future conditions, the more optimistic manager's plan will look better—even if there is no other difference between the plans. A similar problem occurs when managers use different required returns to evaluate the same project. Such differences bias the planning process in favor of one manager's proposals. Planning requires explicit assumptions that can themselves be evaluated and then must be agreed upon. Standardized assumptions then make it possible to compare the alternatives.

2. *Future orientation.* The planning process forces you to think about the future. Doing so generates new ideas and can eliminate bad ideas.

3. *Objectivity.* Because assumptions and models are made explicit, planning can expose decisions that are based on politics or emotions. Planning therefore increases the objective pursuit of organizational goals.

4. *Employee development.* The planning process includes input from many people. The ability to provide such input increases an employee's perceived stake in the firm. People who are empowered through the budgeting process may be better motivated to carry out the firm's plans. The planning process also educates participants about the firm. This fosters coordination and cooperation. It also helps prepare an employee for career advancement in the firm.

5. *Lender requirements.* Financial plans, sometimes very detailed, are necessary for borrowing—especially for the first time. Such plans indicate the use of the borrowed money and show the firm's expected future inflows and outflows, including the loan's interest and principal repayments.

6. *Better performance evaluation.* It is possible for a manager to make good decisions but to have bad performance because of an unexpected downturn in the economy. Similarly, bad decisions can have favorable outcomes as a result of just plain good luck. For example, when net income is higher than expected because interest rates and borrowing costs were lower than expected, the high performance is not due to superior managerial decision making. A financial plan provides a benchmark against which to identify reasons for the differences between outcomes and forecasts. Then the firm can avoid punishing good decisions because of bad outcomes or rewarding bad decisions because of good outcomes.

7. *Preparing for contingencies.* A good financial plan includes contingency plans for unlikely outcomes. The planning process can identify potential, if unlikely, conditions that would cause significant problems. This enables the firm to plan appropriate reactions should such an unlikely contingency occur. For example, the planning process might reveal a possible shortage of funds. The firm that has prearranged contingency financing will be able to continue to operate efficiently—regardless of its cash flow.

In the next section, we will discuss cash budgeting, which usually has a short-term planning horizon and focuses on the cash flows of the firm.

Self-Check Questions

1. What is financial planning? What benefits can a firm derive from it? Why is sound financial planning critical to a firm's success?

2. What are pro forma financial statements? How are they created?

3. What is a budget? How is it related to the firm's financial plan?

4. What is a financial plan? What should a complete financial plan include?

5. Describe the three phases of the financial planning process.

22.2 CASH BUDGETING

A **cash budget** projects and summarizes the cash inflows and outflows expected during the planning horizon. The cash budget also shows the monthly cash balances and any short-term borrowing used to cover cash shortfalls. Monthly cash budgets typically have a six- to twelve-month planning horizon. A positive net cash flow for a month can increase cash, reduce outstanding loans, or be used elsewhere in the business. Similarly, negative net cash flows can reduce cash or be offset with additional borrowing.

For the most part, cash budgets are used in short-term plans, so they include substantial detail. However, the amount of detail also depends on the size of the firm and on the present stage of projects in the planning horizon. Projections farther out in the planning horizon are less detailed. Small firms are less complex, and their cash budgets are less detailed. Because of the complexity of larger firms, more detail is required to take into account all of the factors that affect their cash flows.

Most cash budgets are based on sales forecasts, because so many cash flows are tied to sales. Inflows from sales depend on the amount of sales and also on the proportion that are cash versus credit sales. The time delays involved in collecting on credit sales depend on credit terms and payment patterns.

Several cash outflows also depend on sales. The cost of goods sold reflects raw materials purchases, wages, and production costs for inventories based on anticipated sales. Selling costs, including commissions, are often directly linked to sales.

Other cash expenditures do not fluctuate with current sales. These include capital expenditures; rent, lease, and debt payments; and some types of salaries and tax payments. Such fixed cash outflows are also included in the cash budget. Our next example shows how to create a cash budget.

The cash managers of Monet Paint are preparing a cash budget for the 6 months from April through September. Their cash management model is based on the following assumptions:

1. Recent and forecasted sales are

February (actual)	$400,000
March (actual)	500,000
April (forecast)	600,000
May	700,000
June	800,000
July	800,000
August	700,000
September	600,000
October	500,000

2. Twenty percent of sales are collected in the month of sale, 50% are collected in the month following the sale, and 30% are collected in the second month following the sale.

3. Purchases are 60% of sales, and purchases are paid for 1 month prior to sale.

4. Wages and salaries are 12% of sales and are paid in the same month as the sale.

5. Rent of $10,000 is paid each month. Additional cash operating expenses of $30,000 per month will be incurred for April through July. These will decrease to $25,000 for August and September.

6. Tax payments of $20,000 and $30,000 are expected in April and July, respectively. A capital expenditure of $150,000 will occur in June, and the firm has a mortgage payment of $60,000 due in May.

Cash Budgeting at the Monet Paint Company

EXAMPLE

7. The cash balance at the end of March is $150,000. Managers want to maintain a minimum balance of $100,000 at all times. The firm will borrow what it needs to achieve the minimum balance. Any cash above the minimum will be used to pay off any loan balance until it is eliminated.

The cash budget in Table 22-1 is based on these assumptions. The top part of the table presents the cash receipts, which reflect the sales predicted in assumption 1 and the collection pattern in assumption 2. The cash disbursements for each month reflect the checks that must be written to satisfy assumptions 3 through 6. April's beginning cash balance is the end-of-March cash balance in assumption 7. Monthly net cash flows are total receipts minus total disbursements for the month.

The lower portion of Table 22-1 projects the beginning and ending cash balances for each month, amounts borrowed or repaid on short-term loans, and the cumulative short-term loan balance. It is important to follow the logic in this section of the cash budget.

The monthly net cash flow plus the beginning balance for the month gives an available balance. The available balance is compared to the desired minimum $100,000 balance. If the available balance is too low, the firm borrows enough to bring the balance up to $100,000. Any amount above the minimum can be used to repay any outstanding short-term loans. The ending cash balance is the available balance plus the month's borrowing and minus the month's loan repayments. Finally, the cumulative loan balance is the previous month's loan balance plus any additional borrowing and minus any loan repayments this month. Note that Monet projects negative net cash flows for April, May, and June, which will require the firm to borrow each month and build up its loan balance. Beginning in July, the projected positive net cash flows will enable Monet to pay off its outstanding loan balance and to accumulate a substantial ending cash balance by the end of September. ■

TABLE 22-1

Cash budget for the Monet Paint Company.

	CASH BUDGET, APRIL–SEPTEMBER					
Sales	**April** **$600,000**	**May** **$700,000**	**June** **$800,000**	**July** **$800,000**	**August** **$700,000**	**September** **$600,000**
Cash Receipts:						
Collections (current) 20%	$120,000	$140,000	$160,000	$160,000	$140,000	$120,000
(previous month) 50%	250,000	300,000	350,000	400,000	400,000	350,000
(2nd month previous) 30%	120,000	150,000	180,000	210,000	240,000	240,000
Total cash receipts	490,000	590,000	690,000	770,000	780,000	710,000
Cash Disbursements:						
Purchases	420,000	480,000	480,000	420,000	360,000	300,000
Wages and salaries	72,000	84,000	96,000	96,000	84,000	72,000
Rent	10,000	10,000	10,000	10,000	10,000	10,000
Cash operating expenses	30,000	30,000	30,000	30,000	25,000	25,000
Tax installments	20,000			30,000		
Capital expenditure			150,000			
Mortgage payment		60,000				
Total cash disbursements	552,000	664,000	766,000	586,000	479,000	407,000
Ending Cash Balance:						
Net cash flow	− 62,000	− 74,000	− 76,000	184,000	301,000	303,000
Beginning cash balance	150,000	100,000	100,000	100,000	122,000	423,000
Available balance	88,000	26,000	24,000	284,000	423,000	726,000
Monthly borrowing	12,000	74,000	76,000			
Monthly repayment				162,000		
Ending cash balance	$100,000	$100,000	$100,000	$122,000	$423,000	$726,000
Cumulative loan balance	$ 12,000	$ 86,000	$162,000	$ 0	0	0

The purpose of a cash budget is to ensure a firm's smooth financial operation over the planning horizon. The cash budget identifies the amounts and timing of any surplus or needed funds and is the basis for planning the firm's uses and sources of funds. For example, there is often a benefit to maturity matching short-term investments to particular cash needs that are identified in the cash budgeting process. Once these needs have been quantified, the firm can select from among the short-term investment alternatives discussed in Section 19.3.

Monet's cash budget is a monthly budget. It could be further divided into weekly or daily flows. There are cash flow patterns within the month, which can be incorporated into the daily or weekly budgets. For example, wage and salary cash flows will occur on predictable days. Similarly, payments for rent, loans, and even trade credit are often known in advance. These more detailed daily and weekly cash budgets enable a firm to monitor its short-term finances very closely.

Self-Check Questions

1. What is a cash budget? What is the typical planning horizon for a cash budget?

2. What is the purpose of a cash budget?

3. How is a cash budget constructed?

22.3 PRO FORMA FINANCIAL STATEMENTS

Firms continually make decisions. For example, they choose the schedules, amounts, processes, innovations, and pricing connected with such things as their products, marketing, production, labor, and inventories. Before making such decisions—and to help them make the best ones—they want to know the effects of alternative choices. Although it is not possible to predict the future perfectly, the effects of many decisions can be predicted with reasonable accuracy.

Pro forma financial statements show the effects of the firm's decisions on its future financial statements. Firms use pro forma financial statements throughout the planning process to assess the effects of alternative decisions on various items of interest, such as sales and net income. In addition to helping in the decision-making process, pro forma statements also help the firm create contingent plans for responding to unexpected situations.

A complete financial plan includes a set of pro forma financial statements, which show the firm's planned financial position at regular points over the planning horizon. These statements are based on the actual decisions made as a result of the planning process, and on the agreed upon sales and other forecasts. Our next example illustrates the use of pro forma financial statements.

Bluestem Crafts operates several stores in medium-size towns in the Southwest. It has decided to expand into the Southeast. Pro forma financial statements for next year are shown in Table 22-2, along with the latest income statement and current balance sheet.

Bluestem forecasts increased sales and profits next year for existing stores. However, new stores are not expected to break even in their first year because of startup and extra promotional costs.

Cost of goods sold and the selling, general, and administrative expenses are expected to rise somewhat faster than sales. The result will be a small increase in earnings before interest

Pro Forma Financial Statements for Bluestem Crafts Stores

EXAMPLE

TABLE 22-2
Pro forma financial statements for Bluestem Crafts Stores.

	INCOME STATEMENT		
	Current	**Projected**	**Change**
Sales	$74,000,000	$95,000,000	$21,000,000
Less cost of goods sold	45,500,000	59,000,000	13,500,000
Less depreciation	500,000	600,000	100,000
Gross profit	28,000,000	35,400,000	7,400,000
Less selling & administrative expenses	21,000,000	28,000,000	7,000,000
Earnings before interest and taxes	7,000,000	7,400,000	400,000
Less interest	500,000	500,000	—
Earnings before taxes	6,500,000	6,900,000	400,000
Less taxes	3,000,000	3,200,000	200,000
Net income	3,500,000	3,700,000	200,000
Less cash dividends	—	—	—
Addition to retained earnings	$ 3,500,000	$ 3,700,000	$ 200,000
	BALANCE SHEET		
Assets:			
Cash and marketable securities	$ 3,000,000	$ 3,000,000	—
Accounts receivable	4,600,000	6,000,000	$ 1,400,000
Inventory	9,500,000	12,400,000	2,900,000
Total current assets	17,100,000	21,400,000	4,300,000
Net plant and equipment	6,500,000	8,000,000	1,500,000
Total assets	$23,600,000	$29,400,000	$ 5,800,000
Liabilities and Equity:			
Accounts payable	$ 3,400,000	$ 4,000,000	$ 600,000
Bank loans	1,700,000	3,200,000	1,500,000
Other short-term debt	3,000,000	3,000,000	—
Total current liabilities	8,100,000	10,200,000	2,100,000
Long-term debt	3,500,000	3,500,000	—
Stockholders' equity	12,000,000	15,700,000	3,700,000
Total liabilities and equity	$23,600,000	$29,400,000	$ 5,800,000

and taxes and a correspondingly modest increase in net income. Because of a recent decline in interest rates, Bluestem expects interest expense to be unchanged, even though total debt will increase. Bluestem is not planning any cash dividends during the next year.

Bluestem's balance sheet shows a $5.8 million increase in assets as receivables, inventories, and fixed assets all increase. This increase in assets is financed with $3.7 million from retained earnings, a $600,000 increase in accounts payable, and a $1.5 million increase in bank loans.

Income statements beyond next year are expected to show increased profitability as the new stores get over their "shakedown period" and become profitable. Of course, Bluestem may continue to expand, and future growth decisions will depend on the success of this year's new stores. ■

In addition to pro forma financial statements, firms create many specialized budgets that show in greater detail each unit's resources and responsibilities. Table 22-3 lists statements and budgets that are often created in the planning process. For example, a sales budget provides sales forecasts in units and total revenues, shown in various ways such as by product, division, geographical region, and store. The production budget shows the planned quantities of various items to be produced. Planned production equals forecasted sales plus the desired ending inventory minus the beginning inventory. The purchasing budget specifies the quantities

TABLE 22-3
Statements and budgets produced in the financial planning process.

FINANCIAL STATEMENTS	
Income statement	Projected revenues, expenses, net income, and additions to retained earnings
Balance sheet	Projected assets, liabilities, and equity
Statement of cash flows	Projected cash flows for operations, investing, and financing
SPECIALIZED BUDGETS	
Cash budget	Cash inflows, cash outflows, and cash balances
Sales budget	Planned sales in units and in dollar volume. Various sales budgets may be produced for different divisions, product lines, regions, and even individual stores and individuals
Production budget	Scheduled production (quantities and costs)
Purchasing budget	Planned purchases of the raw materials the firm uses in production, goods for resale, and supplies used in operating the firm
Advertising budget	Planned advertising campaigns and their cost
Capital budget	Purchase of long-term assets
R&D budget	Research-and-development plans for the period
Personnel training and recruiting budget	Planned expenses for training employees and recruiting new employees
Administrative budgets	Administrative expenses for each plant, store, department, or managerial unit in the organization

and costs of the necessary production input items. Of course, these and other budgets must be carefully coordinated.

Which budgets and statements managers are concerned with depends on their role in the firm. For example, top management and the board of directors often focus on the combined pro forma financial statements for the entire firm. These officials coordinate the firm's investing, financing, production, and liquidity; they must understand the entire firm's operations.

Middle managers need other kinds of information to do their specific jobs. Specialized budgets are provided for each managerial responsibility. For example, personnel managers are given training budgets for training current personnel and recruiting budgets for recruiting new employees. The recruiting budget has funds for advertising job opportunities, visiting college campuses, and hosting job candidates on visits to the firm.

Pro forma financial statements omit many details in order to provide a "big picture" of the firm. This big picture is important and is especially useful to the board of directors, CEO, CFO, and other top managers. But the many specialized budgets provide important detailed guidance to other employees. For example, a salesperson probably does not need to know the firm's leverage policy, liquidity objective, dividend policy, and the like. The salesperson, however, does need to know about the availability and prices of new and existing products and must be familiar with the resources available to help in selling them. Each of the firm's units and managers should have the budgets and parts of the financial plan that are relevant to their responsibilities.

Percent of Sales Forecasting Method

Although pro forma statements and budgets are very useful, they can be complex and time-consuming to produce. Consequently, managers often use a shortcut method to create them: the percent of sales forecasting method. This method is a crude but easy way to estimate the funds required to finance growth.

Sales growth requires additional investments in receivables, inventories, and fixed assets, so the firm must have financing to grow. Some short-term financing comes spontaneously from the additional sales, because accounts payable and accruals such as wages and taxes payable naturally increase with an increase in sales. Other financing can come from retained earnings. Any remaining necessary financing must come from other sources, such as additional borrowing.

The percent of sales forecasting formula is based on the following equation:

$$\begin{array}{c}\text{Additional} \\ \text{financing} \\ \text{needed}\end{array} = \begin{array}{c}\text{Required} \\ \text{increase} \\ \text{in assets}\end{array} - \begin{array}{c}\text{Increase} \\ \text{in liabilities}\end{array} - \begin{array}{c}\text{Increase in} \\ \text{retained} \\ \text{earnings}\end{array}$$

$$\text{AFN} = (A/S)gS_0 - (L/S)gS_0 - [M(1 + g)S_0 - D] \qquad (22.1)$$

where   AFN = additional financing needed
A/S = the increase in assets required per dollar increase in sales
L/S = the increase in liabilities provided per dollar increase in sales
S_0 = sales for the current year
g = growth in sales
M = net profit margin on sales
D = cash dividends planned for common stock

EXAMPLE

Forecasting Financing Needs at Cohen Energy Management Systems

Cohen Energy Management Systems is a small firm with excellent growth opportunities. Cohen's sales last year were $2 million. They are expected to grow 25% in the coming year to $2.5 million. Cohen believes that it has access to $250,000 of external capital and wants to know whether this is sufficient to finance its planned growth.

Cohen requires additional assets (receivables, inventories, and fixed assets) equal to 60% of the increase in sales. Short-term liabilities (accounts payable and other accruals) will increase by 10% of the sales increase. The net profit margin is 8%, and Cohen plans to pay a $50,000 cash dividend next year.

Using Equation (22.1) reveals that the additional financing required is

$$\text{AFN} = (A/S)gS_0 - (L/S)gS_0 - [M(1 + g)S_0 - D]$$
$$= (0.60)500,000 - (0.10)500,000 - [(0.08)2,500,000 - 50,000]$$
$$= 300,000 - 50,000 - 150,000 = \$100,000$$

From this, we can see that Cohen requires an additional $300,000 of assets to support its sales growth. Spontaneous financing from short-term liabilities that increase with sales provides $50,000 of the needed funds. After payment of the $50,000 dividend from the expected net income of $200,000, this year's retained earnings will provide $150,000 of funds. This leaves a need for only $100,000 more to finance the expected sales growth. Cohen will be fine, then, because it has access to up to $250,000 of additional financing. ∎

Cash Flow Break-Even Point

Knowing the firm's cash flow break-even point is helpful in interpreting the pro forma financial statements. In Chapter 12, we introduced the *break-even* concept with respect to accounting earnings. We noted that a firm faced with operating a project at its break-even point for a prolonged period would probably be better off exercising its abandonment option. However, even though the accounting-earnings break-even point is not a desirable target for performance, the break-even concept, applied to cash flow, can provide a pivotal point in connection with the planning process.

Over the planning horizon, the **cash flow break-even point** is the point below which the firm will need either to obtain additional financing or to liquidate some of its assets to meet its fixed costs (for example, salaries and administrative costs, interest and principal payments, and planned cash dividends). The existence of the cash flow break-even point is pivotal in that it "forces" the firm to address contingency plans for possible, but perhaps unlikely, bad outcomes.

Note that we are not suggesting that forecasting outcomes above this break-even point is all that is necessary to continue in business. Still, a temporary downturn in economic conditions may force a firm below the cash flow break-even point. Costly financial distress and eventually bankruptcy might result, even if the firm's portfolio of projects has a positive NPV.

The probability of falling below cash flow break-even during a planning horizon provides a measure of the firm's total risk. This probability depends both on the variability of sales and on how close the firm is to its cash flow break-even point when adversity begins to set in.

It is important to keep the possible effects of financial leverage and operating leverage in mind when preparing the financial plan for a firm. Both are sources of risk. Thus, to control the risk that it will be unable to meet, for example, its contractual debt payment obligations, a firm can, to whatever extent possible, (1) change its financial leverage, (2) change its operating leverage and, consequently, its break-even point, or (3) change some combination of the two. To the extent that a firm cannot control its operating leverage, the firm should use the planning process to control risk by creating contingency plans for dealing with bad outcomes.

Alternatives When Funds Are Inadequate

Many rapidly growing firms find themselves short of cash even though they are profitable. In such cases, the firm has the following alternatives:

1. *Reduce the growth rate.* The firm can choose to reduce its funds requirement to a manageable level by not fully meeting the demand for its product. One thing that might reduce demand is to raise the selling price. If implemented successfully, this approach has the added benefit of increasing the firm's income, which provides additional funds that can be reinvested to finance growth. (See our discussion of the price-setting option in Section 13.1.)

2. *Sell assets.* If there are any assets that are not required to run the firm, it can sell those assets and reinvest the proceeds. Such an alternative would need to be analyzed as a capital budgeting project under capital rationing. (See Chapters 10, 11, 12, and especially 13.)

3. *Obtain new external financing.* Among other things, a firm can issue new securities, arrange loans, lease or rent assets, or use venture capital financing. Because these choices can affect capital structure, they must be made in conjunction with the firm's capital structure policy. (See Chapters 15 and 16.)

4. *Reduce or stop paying dividends.* Cash dividends use funds that could otherwise be reinvested. However, there are many factors to consider before making this decision. (See our discussion of dividend policy in Chapters 17 and 18.)

Managers must weigh the benefits and costs of each alternative carefully before deciding on a course of action. Most important, the problem will not cure itself. Consider this simple rule: An unprofitable firm that does not have substantial unused production capacity cannot grow itself into profitability.[1]

Growth does not usually increase the firm's return on its existing assets. Growth in the

---

[1]A firm with substantial unused capacity might become profitable if it can grow. If it can expand sales, for example through better marketing, and earn a positive contribution margin on the increased sales, its *rate of return ratios* will improve. (See Chapter 2.)

form of a simple expansion of existing operations would normally have a lower *rate* of return than the rate of return on existing assets. Growth is attractive—in spite of this lower return—only when the growth has a positive NPV, that is, when the expected return exceeds the required return.[2] Growth can lead to disaster when it has a negative NPV. An unprofitable firm should consider the abandonment option if it is unable to move itself into profitability without growth.

It is also important to remember that rapid expansion is risky. Expansion often means sales in new markets or even sales of new products—both of which are likely to be riskier than the firm's current operations. Consequently, firms often limit their growth through capital rationing to control the firm's risk. (See our discussion of the potential benefits of capital rationing in Chapter 13.)

Internal Growth

How fast should the firm grow? The answer depends on several factors, including the amount of investment required for a given growth level, the firm's profit margin, its attitude toward risk, and its willingness and ability to obtain new external financing.

Equation (22.1) shows the additional financing needed for growth. Some short-term funds are generated naturally by payables and accruals, and other funds come from new retained earnings. The **internal growth rate** is the maximum rate of growth using *only* these funds.

We can find the internal growth rate from Equation (22.1) by assuming no additional funds are needed. Setting AFN = 0, we have

$$AFN = (A/S)gS_0 - (L/S)gS_0 - [MS_0(1 + g) - D] = 0$$

and solving for the growth rate, we get

$$g = \frac{MS_0 - D}{S_0[(A/S) - (L/S) - M]}$$

We can make a further simplifying assumption about cash dividends, the same one we used for the dividend growth model in Chapter 5. Let's assume the firm pays a cash dividend each year that is a fixed proportion, d, of its net income. Next year's net income is simply the profit margin times next year's sales, so the dividend next year will be

$$D = dMS_0(1 + g)$$

Substituting this expression for D, we find that the internal growth rate is

$$g = \frac{M(1 - d)}{(A/S) - (L/S) - M(1 - d)} \tag{22.2}$$

The internal growth rate (the maximum growth possible without using any external funds) is then directly related to the profit margin, M, and inversely related to the dividend payout ratio, d. A higher profit margin allows more growth, and a higher payout ratio restricts growth. The additional financing needed (AFN) for an additional dollar of sales is the denominator of Equation (22.2). It is the assets required, A/S, minus the natural increase in short-term liabilities, L/S, minus retained earnings, $M(1 - d)$. Let's look at an example of the relationship between AFN and the internal growth rate.

---

[2] We illustrated this point when we discussed growth versus income in Section 5.3 of Chapter 5.

EXAMPLE

The Internal Growth Rate at Tennessee Clay, Inc.

Tennessee Clay Inc. is currently doing $10 million per year in sales. The firm requires $0.75 in additional assets for each $1.00 increase in sales, and short-term liabilities go up $0.10 for each $1.00 increase in sales. Tennessee Clay's net profit margin on sales is 12%. Finally, the firm has a dividend payout ratio of one-third. What is the maximum amount of growth that Tennessee Clay can have without getting additional external financing?

Using Equation (22.2) reveals that Tennessee Clay's internal growth rate is

$$g = \frac{M(1-d)}{(A/S) - (L/S) - M(1-d)} = \frac{0.12(1 - 1/3)}{(0.75) - (0.10) - 0.12(1 - 1/3)}$$

$$= \frac{0.08}{0.75 - 0.10 - 0.08} = \frac{0.08}{0.57} = 14.04\%$$

Therefore, Tennessee Clay can finance internally up to 14.04% in growth. Growth above this level will require additional external financing.

Figure 22-2 shows the amount of external financing needed for various growth rates between zero and 40%. If Tennessee Clay's growth in sales is below 14.04%, the firm will have excess funds beyond what is required to finance its growth. ■

Sustainable Growth

If a firm finances its growth internally (with retained earnings and short-term, naturally occurring liabilities), then over time its retained earnings will grow, and because it is not raising long-term debt funds, its financial leverage will decline. If a firm wants to maintain its capital structure (proportion of debt financing), then it must issue new debt along with its increases in retained earnings. The **sustainable growth rate** is the maximum rate at which the firm can grow by using internal sources and new external debt, but without increasing its financial leverage. The sustainable growth rate is, of course, higher than the internal growth rate, because it includes new external debt in addition to the internal funds.

We can modify Equation (22.1) to include the effect of capital structure maintenance. We do this by subtracting the funds that come in from the new external debt. The new debt equals the debt-to-equity ratio, B/E, times the additional retained earnings, so

$$\text{AFN} = (A/S)gS_0 - (L/S)gS_0 - MS_0(1 + g)(1 - d) - (B/E)(MS_0)(1 + g)(1 - d)$$

$$= (A/S)gS_0 - (L/S)gS_0 - MS_0(1 + g)(1 - d)(1 + B/E)$$

The sustainable growth rate is then determined by again setting AFN = 0 and solving for g:

$$g = \frac{M(1-d)(1 + B/E)}{(A/S) - (L/S) - M(1-d)(1 + B/E)} \qquad (22.3)$$

The sustainable growth rate (the maximum rate at which the firm can grow by using internal and external new debt but without increasing financial leverage) is then directly related to the leverage ratio, B/E, and the profit margin, M, and inversely related to the dividend payout ratio, d. A higher leverage ratio allows more growth. A higher profit margin also allows more growth, but a higher payout ratio restricts growth. The additional financing needed, AFN, for an additional dollar of sales is the denominator of Equation (22.3). It is the assets required, A/S, minus the natural increase in short-term liabilities, L/S, minus retained earnings, $M(1 - d)$, and the new debt necessary for capital structure maintenance $(B/E)M(1 - d)$. The next example illustrates the relationship between AFN and the sustainable growth rate.

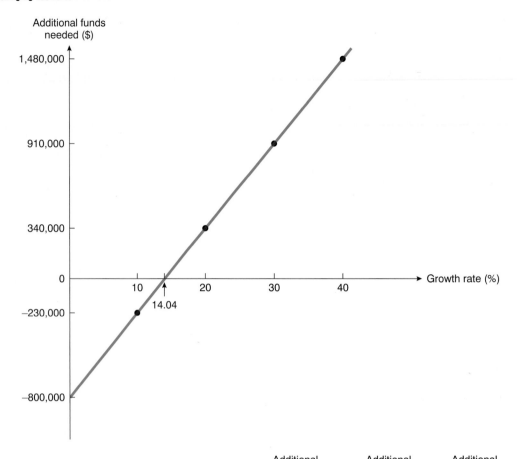

Growth Rate	Sales Increase	Additional Assets	Additional Spontaneous Funds	Additional Retained Earnings	Additional Financing Needed
0%	$0	$0	$0	$800,000	−$800,000
10	1,000,000	750,000	100,000	880,000	−230,000
14.04	1,404,000	1,053,000	140,400	912,320	280[a]
20	2,000,000	1,500,000	200,000	960,000	340,000
30	3,000,000	2,250,000	300,000	1,040,000	910,000
40	4,000,000	3,000,000	400,000	1,120,000	1,480,000

Sales increase = $g(S_0)$ = $g(10,000,000)$
Additional assets = (A/S)(sales increase) = 0.75(sales increase)
Additional spontaneous funds = (L/S)(sales increase) = 0.10(sales increase)
Additional retained earnings = $M(1−d)$(total sales) = 0.12(1−1/3)(10,000,000 + sales increase)
Additional financing needed = additional assets − additional spontaneous funds − additional
     retained earnings

FIGURE 22-2
External financing requirements and the internal growth rate for Tennessee Clay.

[a]This amount is not zero because the internal growth rate was rounded.

EXAMPLE

Tennessee Clay's Sustainable Growth Rate

Let's continue our Tennessee Clay example and calculate the sustainable growth rate. Tennessee Clay has a debt-to-equity ratio of 50%. To maintain this capital structure, the firm will take on additional debt capital at the rate of $0.50 for each additional $1.00 of retained earnings. What is the maximum amount of growth that Tennessee Clay can finance by using internal funds and new external debt but without raising its leverage ratio?

With B/E = 0.50, S_0 = $10 million, A/S = 0.75, L/S = 0.10, M = 0.12, and d = 1/3,

Tennessee Clay's sustainable growth rate is

$$g = \frac{M(1 - d)(1 + B/E)}{(A/S) - (L/S) - M(1 - d)(1 + B/E)} = \frac{0.12(1 - 1/3)(1 + 0.50)}{(0.75) - (0.10) - 0.12(1 - 1/3)(1 + 0.50)}$$

$$= \frac{0.12}{0.75 - 0.10 - 0.12} = \frac{0.12}{0.53} = 22.64\%$$

Therefore, Tennessee Clay can finance up to 22.64% in growth by using internal funds and new external debt but without raising its leverage ratio. Growth above this level will require external equity financing or an increase in Tennessee Clay's leverage ratio.

Figure 22-3 shows the amount of external equity financing needed for various growth rates between zero and 40%. Note that the two lines are not parallel because the amount of long-term debt that can be issued increases as the growth rate of sales increases. If Tennessee Clay's growth in sales is below 22.64%, then the firm will have excess funds beyond what is required to finance its growth. ■

Long-term Planning Models

Thus far we have focused on short-term planning models. Firms also use long-term planning models, where the planning horizon depends on the nature of the industry. Most firms use a five- or ten-year planning horizon. Some industries, such as electric utilities, have even longer horizons. Long-term planning models incorporate the firm's strategic commitments of resources. They are built around periodic pro forma financial statements over the planning horizon.

Whittaker Industries's Long-Term Planning Model — EXAMPLE

Whittaker Industries has a 7-year planning model that includes detailed financial statements for the next 7 years. Some of the data from Whittaker's pro forma income statements, statements of cash flows, and balance sheets are summarized and presented in Table 22-4. This table provides a good overview of several of the firm's strategic decisions.

The firm intends to expand from 1999 to 2001. You can see this in the large investing cash flow (the negative cash flow is an investment) for the first 3 years. Net fixed assets also increase substantially on the balance sheet in the early years of the plan. In the fourth year, 2002, some of the short-term debt expected to be accumulated to finance construction will be refinanced with long-term mortgages. Sales growth is expected to be slow for the first 3 years but much faster in years 4 through 6 of the plan. In year 7, sales growth is expected to taper off. The sales growth in years 4 through 6 is accompanied by planned increases in working capital. The firm plans to hold dividends constant for 4 years, until after the construction is completed and net income has begun increasing in response to the sales expansion. In years 5 and 6, if all goes well, the firm will be able to increase substantially the dividend on its common shares.

In the first 3 years of the plan, Whittaker's total asset turnover and current ratio fall slightly. Thereafter, these ratios improve. Late in the 7-year plan, the firm's overall financial health is expected to have improved to the point where other strategic decisions might be considered, such as additional growth, paying off debt, or repurchasing some common shares. ■

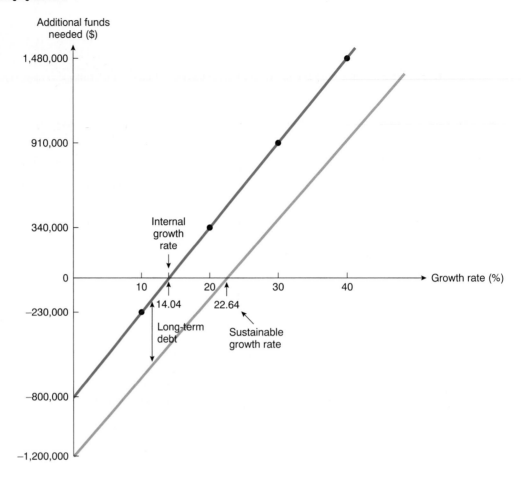

Growth Rate	Sales Increase	Additional Assets	Additional Spontaneous Funds	Additional Retained Earnings	Additional LT Debt Financing	Additional Financing Needed
0%	$0	$0	$0	$800,000	$400,000	−$1,200,000
10	1,000,000	750,000	100,000	880,000	440,000	−670,000
14.04	1,404,000	1,053,000	140,400	912,320	456,160	−455,880
20	2,000,000	1,500,000	200,000	960,000	480,000	−140,000
22.64	2,264,000	1,698,000	226,400	980,800	490,400	−400[a]
30	3,000,000	2,250,000	300,000	1,040,000	520,000	390,000
40	4,000,000	3,000,000	400,000	1,120,000	560,000	920,000

Sales increase = $g(S_0)$ = g(10,000,000)
Additional assets = (A/S)(sales increase) = 0.75(sales increase)
Additional spontaneous funds = (L/S)(sales increase) = 0.10(sales increase)
Additional retained earnings = $M(1-d)$(total sales) = 0.12(1−1/3)(10,000,000 + sales increase)
Additional long-term debt financing = (B/E)(additional retained earnings) = 0.50(additional retained earnings)
Additional financing needed = additional assets − additional spontaneous funds − additional retained earnings − additional long-term debt financing

[a]This amount is not zero because the sustainable growth rate was rounded.

FIGURE 22-3
External equity financing requirements and the sustainable growth rate for Tennessee Clay.

TABLE 22-4
Whittaker Industries's seven-year plan, 1999–2005.

	1999	2000	2001	2002	2003	2004	2005
Selected Income Statement Items							
Sales	60.00	62.00	65.00	80.00	95.00	105.00	110.00
Net income	3.00	3.10	3.25	4.00	4.75	5.25	5.50
Dividends	0.60	0.60	0.60	0.60	0.90	1.20	1.25
Statement of Cash Flow Summary							
Operating cash flow	6.50	6.25	6.50	7.50	6.50	7.50	8.00
Investing cash flow	−8.00	−9.00	−8.00	−2.00	−2.00	−4.00	−3.00
Financing cash flow	1.00	2.50	1.50	−4.00	−2.00	−2.00	−2.00
Total cash flow	−0.50	−0.25	0.00	1.50	2.50	1.50	3.00
Balance Sheet Summary							
Cash	4.00	3.75	3.75	5.25	7.75	9.25	12.25
Receivables	9.00	9.30	9.75	12.00	14.25	15.75	16.50
Inventory	7.20	7.45	7.70	9.60	11.40	12.60	13.20
Total current assets	20.20	20.50	21.20	26.85	33.40	37.60	41.95
Net fixed assets	35.00	42.00	48.00	50.00	52.00	54.00	56.00
Total assets	55.20	62.50	69.20	76.85	85.40	91.60	97.95
Payables and accruals	3.60	3.72	3.90	4.80	5.70	6.30	6.60
Other short-term debt	10.00	12.00	13.00	6.00	6.85	7.50	7.75
Total current liabilities	13.60	15.72	16.90	10.80	12.55	13.80	14.35
Mortgages	12.00	12.00	12.00	19.00	19.00	19.00	19.00
Other long-term debt	14.40	17.08	19.95	23.30	26.25	27.15	28.70
Stockholders' equity	15.20	17.70	20.35	23.75	27.60	31.65	35.90
Total liabilities and equity	55.20	62.50	69.20	76.85	85.40	91.60	97.95
Selected Financial Ratios							
Sales/total assets	1.09	0.99	0.94	1.04	1.11	1.15	1.12
Current assets/current liabilities	1.49	1.30	1.25	2.49	2.66	2.72	2.92
Dividends/net income	20.0%	19.4%	18.5%	15.0%	18.9%	22.9%	22.7%
Net income/stockholders' equity	19.7	17.5	16.0	16.8	17.2	16.6	15.3
Total debt/total assets	72.5	71.7	70.6	69.1	67.7	65.4	63.3

Self-Check Questions

1. How do firms use pro forma financial statements?

2. What role do business unit budgets play in the operation of the firm?

3. What is the relationship among the additional financing needed, the required increase in assets, the increase in liabilities, and the increase in retained earnings?

4. If a profitable but rapidly growing firm finds itself short of cash, what steps can it take to deal with the problem?

5. What are the internal growth rate and the sustainable growth rate? How are they different? Is one always higher than the other?

22.4 AUTOMATING FINANCIAL FORECASTING

Computer technology has greatly benefited cash budgeting and the entire planning process. Spreadsheet software lends itself to cash budgeting and pro forma financial statement analysis. You probably already know how to use a computer spreadsheet package. The main benefit of a spreadsheet is its flexibility. It can be updated very easily, which reduces the clerical burden. A spreadsheet is ideally suited to answer "what-if" questions. For example, changing the February sales projection would cause other changes that ripple through the entire annual cash budget. You can make such changes in seconds when you are using a spreadsheet.

An Example of an Automated Forecast

When Justin Case started his new job as treasurer of the You 'N' Me Toy Company (YN-MTC), he found the firm did not have a formal cash budgeting system. The owner said "Don't worry, we have plenty of money in the bank." However, Mr. Case wanted to create a cash management model for the firm's activities just the same. (Somewhat surprisingly, the owner agreed, saying, "We need this model, Justin Case.")

YNMTC is a small manufacturer with a stable customer base and stable supplier relationships. Accurate cash inflow and cash outflow data are available. Table 22-5 shows the information Justin Case gathered. Justin then had to decide on the form of the model, what period(s) it would cover, and how frequently it would be updated.

In his accounting classes, Justin learned that accountants go to great lengths to avoid having an account with a negative balance. For example, they create what are called contra accounts for dealing with negative amounts. We in corporate financial management do not feel so constrained. Therefore, we recognize that an account with a negative balance can be equivalently viewed as being a positive amount on the other side of the balance sheet. The two sides are mirror images: A negative asset is a liability, and a negative liability is an asset. We can recognize the Principle of Two-Sided Transactions in this relationship. For example, "nega-

TABLE 22-5

Information about the You 'N' Me Toy Company, compiled by Justin Case.

1. The payment pattern for revenues is estimated to be as follows: 40% of sales are for cash, 10% are paid for 1 month after the sale, 50% are paid for 2 months after the sale, and bad debt is negligible.
2. The treasury department believes that the cash account should be set to start each month in the amount of $10,000 plus 60% of next month's salaries and wages plus 70% of this month's accounts payable. It also believes YNMTC can earn 0.6% per month on its short-term investments. The model will adjust the cash account with the short-term investment (borrowing) account.
3. YNMTC appears to purchase raw materials each month in the amount of 30% of the predicted sales for the month after next plus 20% of next month's predicted sales plus 10% of this month's sales. Purchases are paid for in the month following their purchase, and there are no discounts available to YNMTC from its suppliers. The cost of raw materials averages 60% of sales.
4. YNMTC pays salaries and wages of $7000 plus 18% of this month's sales.
5. YNMTC is depreciating its net fixed assets at the rate of 1% of *net* fixed assets per month.
6. YNMTC pays a cash dividend of $2000 every month.
7. The long-term debt on the YNMTC balance sheet carries a 12% APR, and payments are made quarterly in December, March, June, and September.
8. Taxes for YNMTC are at the rate of 35% of taxable income (including rebates for negative taxes). Taxes are paid monthly.
9. Sales in October and November of this year were $40,000 and $60,000, respectively. Sales forecasts for the next 11 months ($ thousands) are

Dec.	Jan.	Feb.	Mar.	Apr.	May	Jun.	Jul.	Aug.	Sep.	Oct.
100.00	170.00	150.00	125.00	100.00	70.00	65.00	90.00	175.00	50.00	70.00

BALANCE SHEET AS OF NOVEMBER 30

Cash	$ 76.00	Accounts payable	$ 77.00
Short-term investment (borrowing)	70.00	Accrued interest	6.00
Accounts receivable	56.00	Long-term debt	300.00
Inventory	122.00	Common stock	70.00
Net fixed assets	391.00	Retained earnings	262.00
Total assets	$715.00	Liabilities + stockholders' equity	$715.00

tive debt" is money someone else owes you—so it is an asset. Similarly, a "negative marketable security" is simply money you owe someone else—so it is a liability.

Justin used this fact to simplify his short-term financial planning model of YNMTC. He created a short-term investment (borrowing) account to use as a "plug" for balancing the balance sheet. The account consists of marketable securities when it is positive, but it becomes a short-term bank loan whenever it must be negative to make the balance sheet balance. A negative balance in this account indicates that the firm needs to arrange for more short-term financing.

Justin's short-term investment (borrowing) account simplifies the model-building process. Letting the account be positive *or* negative avoids the problem of automating "conditional" accounts. Conditional accounts require a more complex set of equations. For example, with the short-term investment (borrowing) account, if YNMTC is investing money (the account is positive), then the amount invested is shown as a current asset. But if YNMTC is borrowing money (that is, if the account is negative), then the amount is normally shown in an entirely different account as a current liability with a positive balance.

Table 22-6 presents output from Justin Case's automated financial planning model, based on the information in Table 22-5. The short-term investment (borrowing) account is projected to be negative in January and February. Thus it seems that during January and February, YNMTC will have to either (1) obtain additional financing in the amounts indicated (the absolute value of the negative balance), to maintain its target level for the cash account, or (2) allow the cash account to fall below the target.

Table 22-7 presents the spreadsheet equations (or data) in Justin's model for the first month of the planning period, December, which is shown in column F. In principle, the general form of such equations is simple:

$$\text{Ending balance} = \text{Starting balance} + \text{Increases} - \text{Decreases} \qquad (22.4)$$

Of course the "trick" to building the model is to identify correctly all the potential increases and decreases for a given account. For example, the inventory account increases with the purchase of raw materials and decreases with the sale of finished goods. A purchase of raw materials also increases accounts payable or decreases cash. And a sale of finished goods increases accounts receivable or increases cash.

Account changes in double-entry accounting always maintain the "balance" of the balance sheet. When the offsetting accounts are on the same side of the balance sheet, an increase in one account causes a decrease in the other, and vice versa. For example, a cash purchase of raw materials causes an increase in inventory and a decrease in cash. When the offsetting accounts are on opposite sides of the balance sheet, the changes are in the same direction. An increase in one account causes an increase in the other, and a decrease in one causes a decrease in the other. For example, a credit purchase of raw materials causes an increase in inventory and an increase in accounts payable.

Once he had entered the equations into the December column, Justin *block-copied* them into subsequent columns for January through August. Then he put in "corrections" for two of the model's rows: (1) Each sales forecast was entered separately, and (2) he put in zeros in line 13 for the months in which YNMTC does not make a cash interest payment.[3]

---

[3] Note that unless you specify differently, the copy command maintains the relationships among the cells rather than maintaining specific cell identities. For example, if cell G6 has the equation [E5 + F4] in it, and you copy G6 to L12, the equation becomes [J11 + K10].

TABLE 22-6

Cash budget and pro forma income statements and balance sheets for the You 'N' Me Toy Company, based on the information in Table 22-5.

				CASH BUDGET FOR DECEMBER THROUGH AUGUST									
	Oct	Nov	Dec	Jan	Feb	Mar	Apr	May	Jun	Jul	Aug	Sep	Oct
SALES	40.00	60.00	100.00	170.00	150.00	125.00	100.00	70.00	65.00	90.00	175.00	50.00[a]	70.00[a]
A/R COLLECTIONS			66.00	108.00	127.00	150.00	127.50	100.50	83.00	77.50	111.50		
INTEREST INCOME			0.42	0.01	−0.13	−0.06	0.24	0.56	0.76	0.66	0.52		
CASH INFLOW			66.42	108.01	126.87	149.94	127.74	101.06	83.76	78.16	112.02		
PAYABLES PAID			77.00	89.00	84.50	70.00	53.50	43.50	47.00	77.00	59.00		
SALARIES & WAGES PAID			25.00	37.60	34.00	29.50	25.00	19.60	18.70	23.20	38.50	16.00[a]	
TAXES PAID			2.98	8.24	6.66	4.78	2.97	0.79	0.48	2.39	8.90		
INTEREST PAID			9.00	0.00	0.00	9.00	0.00	0.00	9.00	0.00	0.00		
DIVIDENDS PAID			2.00	2.00	2.00	2.00	2.00	2.00	2.00	2.00	2.00		
STARTING CASH			76.00	94.86	89.55	76.70	62.45	52.21	54.12	77.82	74.40		
ENDING CASH			94.86	89.55	76.70	62.45	52.21	54.12	77.82	74.40	53.55		
S-T INVESTMENT CHANGE (cash budget)			−68.42	−23.52	12.56	48.92	54.51	33.27	−17.12	−23.00	24.48		
S-T INVESTMENT CHANGE (balance sheet)			−68.42	−23.52	12.56	48.92	54.51	33.27	−17.12	−23.00	24.48		

			MONTHLY PRO FORMA INCOME STATEMENTS								
	Oct	Nov	Dec	Jan	Feb	Mar	Apr	May	Jun	Jul	Aug
SALES	40.00	60.00	100.00	170.00	150.00	125.00	100.00	70.00	65.00	90.00	175.00
COST OF RAW MATERIALS			60.00	102.00	90.00	75.00	60.00	42.00	39.00	54.00	105.00
SALARIES & WAGES			25.00	37.60	34.00	29.50	25.00	19.60	18.70	23.20	38.50
DEPRECIATION			3.91	3.87	3.83	3.79	3.76	3.72	3.68	3.64	3.61
INTEREST EXPENSE			3.00	3.00	3.00	3.00	3.00	3.00	3.00	3.00	3.00
INTEREST INCOME			0.42	0.01	−0.13	−0.06	0.24	0.56	0.76	0.66	0.52
TAXABLE INCOME			8.51	23.54	19.04	13.65	8.48	2.25	1.38	6.82	25.42
TAXES			2.98	8.24	6.66	4.78	2.97	0.79	0.48	2.39	8.90
NET INCOME			5.53	15.30	12.37	8.87	5.51	1.46	0.90	4.43	16.52
DIVIDENDS			2.00	2.00	2.00	2.00	2.00	2.00	2.00	2.00	2.00
CHANGE IN RETAINED EARNINGS			3.53	13.30	10.37	6.87	3.51	−0.54	−1.10	2.43	14.52

		CURRENT BALANCE SHEET AND MONTHLY PRO FORMA BALANCE SHEETS								
	Oct	Nov	Dec	Jan	Feb	Mar	Apr	May	Jun	Jul	Aug
CASH		76.00	94.86	89.55	76.70	62.45	52.21	54.12	77.82	74.40	53.55
S-T INVESTMENT (BORROWING)		70.00	1.58	−21.94	−9.38	39.53	94.04	127.31	110.19	87.19	111.66
ACCOUNTS RECEIVABLE		56.00	90.00	152.00	175.00	150.00	122.50	92.00	74.00	86.50	150.00
INVENTORY		122.00	151.00	133.50	113.50	92.00	75.50	80.50	118.50	123.50	67.00
NET FIXED ASSETS		391.00	387.09	383.22	379.39	375.59	371.84	368.12	364.44	360.79	357.19
TOTAL ASSETS		715.00	724.53	736.33	735.21	719.58	716.09	722.05	744.95	732.38	739.40
ACCOUNTS PAYABLE		77.00	89.00	84.50	70.00	53.50	43.50	47.00	77.00	59.00	48.50
ACCRUED INTEREST		6.00	0.00	3.00	6.00	0.00	3.00	6.00	0.00	3.00	6.00
LONG-TERM DEBT		300.00	300.00	300.00	300.00	300.00	300.00	300.00	300.00	300.00	300.00
COMMON STOCK		70.00	70.00	70.00	70.00	70.00	70.00	70.00	70.00	70.00	70.00
RETAINED EARNINGS		262.00	265.53	278.83	289.21	296.08	299.59	299.05	297.95	300.38	314.90
LIABILITIES + OWNERS' EQUITY		715.00	724.53	736.33	735.21	719.58	716.09	722.05	744.95	732.38	739.40

[a] Required for other computations.

TABLE 22-7
Spreadsheet equations for the output shown in Table 22-6. (The months of October through October are in columns D through P.)

LINE	COLUMN A	COLUMN F
4		DEC
5	SALES	100.00
6	A/R COLLECTIONS	0.4*F5 + 0.1*E5 + 0.5*D5
7	INTEREST INCOME	0.006*E42
8	CASH INFLOW	+ F6 + F7
9		
10	PAYABLES PAID	+ E48
11	SALARIES & WAGES PAID	7.0 + 0.18*F5
12	TAXES PAID	+ F32
13	INTEREST PAID	+ E49 + F28[a]
14	DIVIDENDS PAID	2.00
15	STARTING CASH	+ E41
16	ENDING CASH	+ F41
17	S-T INVESTMENT CHANGE (cash budget)	+ F15 − F16 + F8-F10-F11-F12-F13-F14
18	S-T INVESTMENT CHANGE (balance sheet)	+ F42-E42
19		
20		
21		
22	MONTHLY PRO FORMA INCOME STATEMENTS	
23		DEC
24	SALES	+ F5
25	COST OF RAW MATERIALS	0.6*F24
26	SALARIES & WAGES	+ F11
27	DEPRECIATION	0.01*E45
28	INTEREST EXPENSE	0.01*E50
29	INTEREST INCOME	+ F7
30	TAXABLE INCOME	+ F24-F25-F26-F27-F28 + F29
31		
32	TAXES	0.35*F30
33	NET INCOME	+ F30-F32
34		
35	DIVIDENDS	+ F14
36	CHANGE IN RETAINED EARNINGS	+ F33-F35
37		
38		
39	CURRENT BALANCE SHEET AND MONTHLY PRO FORMA BALANCE SHEETS	
40		DEC
41	CASH	10.0 + 0.6*G11 + 0.7*F48
42	SHORT-TERM INVESTMENT (BORROWING)	+ F53-F41-F43-F44-F45
43	ACCOUNTS RECEIVABLE	0.06*F5 + 0.5*E5
44	INVENTORY	E44 + F48-F25
45	NET FIXED ASSETS	+ E45-F27
46	TOTAL ASSETS	+ F41 + F42 + F43 + F44 + F45
47		
48	ACCOUNTS PAYABLE	0.1*F5 + 0.2*G5 + 0.3*H5
49	ACCRUED INTEREST	+ E49 + F28-F13
50	LONG-TERM DEBT	+ E50
51	COMMON STOCK	+ E51
52	RETAINED EARNINGS	+ E52 + F36
53	LIABILITIES + OWNERS' EQUITY	+ F48 + F49 + F50 + F51 + F52

[a] This equation repeats every 3 months, with zero for the intervening months.

In the cash budget, Justin put in two different equations for the short-term investment change as a check on the model. The first equation (cash budget) tracks the actual cash flows. This change is the sum of the increases and decreases in short-term investment (borrowing). The second equation (balance sheet) is the change in short-term investment (borrowing) that results from forcing the balance sheet to balance. This second change is the short-term investment (borrowing) ending balance minus its starting balance. If these two equations do not produce the same answer, then there is an error—the model is not internally consistent.

Before you build your own model, three warnings are in order. First, do not be alarmed if the values in the cells are incorrect or show ERR as you are entering the equations for a model. (Become alarmed only if such things remain when you *think* you are finished.) Second, even very simple errors can cause *many* of the spreadsheet cells to show nonsensical amounts or ERR or can cause the CIRC indicator to identify circular reasoning. (Circular reasoning is a situation where two or more cells are functions of one another, simultaneously.) This sometimes alarming result occurs because the model is a set of interwoven relationships. A single error can have an enormous ripple effect. Finally, remember that numbers can look okay but in fact be totally *wrong*! We do not mean to discourage you, but an impressively printed spreadsheet can be deceiving: There can be serious errors even though the numbers look fine. You should always check your model and its output very carefully to limit the possibility of errors.

"What-If" Questions: The Power of a Spreadsheet Package

After he had built the financial planning model shown in Tables 22-6 and 22-7, it occurred to Mr. Case that actual sales virtually never turn out to be what was expected. Therefore, he decided to consider the possibilities of higher- or lower-than-expected sales. Tables 22-8 and 22-9 present output from his model, assuming that sales are 80% and 120% of forecast levels, respectively.

Table 22-8 can be produced from Justin's model by following these steps:

1. Insert a blank row between lines 3 and 4 [the lotus spreadsheet command is /, W, I, A4 . . A4].

2. Copy line 6 (old line 5) to new line 4 [the lotus spreadsheet command is /, C, A6 . . P6, A4].

3. Enter 0.8 *F4 in cell F6 (old cell F5).

4. Copy cell F6 to G6 . . P6 [the lotus spreadsheet command is /, C, F6 . . F6, G6 . . P6].

Table 22-9 can then be produced from the model from Table 22-8 by following these steps:

1. Enter 1.2 *F4 in cell F6.

2. Copy cell F6 to G6 . . P6 [the lotus spreadsheet command is /, C, F6 . . F6, G6 . . P6].

Looking at Table 22-8, we see a case of "good news and bad news." The good news is that with lower-than-expected sales, YNMTC will not need to obtain additional financing to maintain its target level of cash; in none of the months is the short-term investment (borrowing) balance negative. The bad news is that total projected net income over the planning horizon declines from $70,890 to $41,130.

Similarly, Table 22-9 reveals that higher-than-expected sales will require an even greater amount of additional financing but that total projected net income increases from $70,890 to $100,660. Although growth can have its problems, You 'N' Me would be happy to have higher-than-expected sales, but, true to his name, Justin Case also considered lower-than-expected sales to help create contingency plans.

TABLE 22-8

Cash budget and pro forma income statements and balance sheets for the You 'N' Me Toy Company, with 80% of forecast sales.

	Oct	Nov	Dec	Jan	Feb	Mar	Apr	May	Jun	Jul	Aug	Sep	Oct
				CASH BUDGET FOR DECEMBER THROUGH AUGUST									
SALES	40.00	60.00	80.00	136.00	120.00	100.00	80.00	56.00	52.00	72.00	140.00	40.00[a]	56.00[a]
A/R COLLECTIONS			58.00	92.40	101.60	120.00	102.00	80.40	66.40	62.00	89.20		
INTEREST INCOME			0.42	0.09	0.01	0.06	0.28	0.54	0.69	0.60	0.48		
CASH INFLOW			58.42	92.49	101.61	120.06	102.28	80.94	67.09	62.60	89.68		
PAYABLES PAID			77.00	71.20	67.60	56.00	42.80	34.80	37.60	61.60	47.20		
SALARIES & WAGES PAID			21.40	31.48	28.60	25.00	21.40	17.08	16.36	19.96	32.20	14.20[a]	
TAXES PAID			1.44	5.65	4.40	2.89	1.44	−0.30	−0.54	0.98	6.19		
INTEREST PAID			9.00	0.00	0.00	9.00	0.00	0.00	9.00	0.00	0.00		
DIVIDENDS PAID			2.00	2.00	2.00	2.00	2.00	2.00	2.00	2.00	2.00		
STARTING CASH			76.00	78.73	74.48	64.20	52.80	44.61	46.14	65.10	62.36		
ENDING CASH			78.73	74.48	64.20	52.80	44.61	46.14	65.10	62.36	45.68		
S-T INVESTMENT CHANGE (cash budget)			−55.15	−13.59	9.29	36.57	42.83	25.83	−16.28	−19.20	18.78		
S-T INVESTMENT CHANGE (balance sheet)			−55.15	−13.59	9.29	36.57	42.83	25.83	−16.28	−19.20	18.78		

	Oct	Nov	Dec	Jan	Feb	Mar	Apr	May	Jun	Jul	Aug
				MONTHLY PRO FORMA INCOME STATEMENTS							
SALES	40.00	60.00	80.00	136.00	120.00	100.00	80.00	56.00	52.00	72.00	140.00
COST OF RAW MATERIALS			48.00	81.60	72.00	60.00	48.00	33.60	31.20	43.20	84.00
SALARIES & WAGES			21.40	31.48	28.60	25.00	21.40	17.08	16.36	19.96	32.20
DEPRECIATION			3.91	3.87	3.83	3.79	3.76	3.72	3.68	3.64	3.61
INTEREST EXPENSE			3.00	3.00	3.00	3.00	3.00	3.00	3.00	3.00	3.00
INTEREST INCOME			0.42	0.09	0.01	0.06	0.28	0.54	0.69	0.60	0.48
TAXABLE INCOME			4.11	16.14	12.58	8.27	4.13	−0.86	−1.55	2.79	17.67
TAXES			1.44	5.65	4.40	2.89	1.44	−0.30	−0.54	0.98	6.19
NET INCOME			2.67	10.49	8.17	5.38	2.68	−0.56	−1.01	1.82	11.49
DIVIDENDS			2.00	2.00	2.00	2.00	2.00	2.00	2.00	2.00	2.00
CHANGE IN RETAINED EARNINGS			0.67	8.49	6.17	3.38	0.68	−2.56	−3.01	−0.18	9.49

	Oct	Nov	Dec	Jan	Feb	Mar	Apr	May	Jun	Jul	Aug
			CURRENT BALANCE SHEET AND MONTHLY PRO FORMA BALANCE SHEETS								
CASH		76.00	78.73	74.48	64.20	52.80	44.61	46.14	65.10	62.36	45.68
S-T INVESTMENT (BORROWING)		70.00	14.85	1.26	10.55	47.12	89.95	115.78	99.50	80.29	99.07
ACCOUNTS RECEIVABLE		56.00	78.00	121.60	140.00	120.00	98.00	73.60	59.20	69.20	120.00
INVENTORY		122.00	145.20	131.20	115.20	98.00	84.80	88.80	119.20	123.20	78.00
NET FIXED ASSETS		391.00	387.09	383.22	379.39	375.59	371.84	368.12	364.44	360.79	357.19
TOTAL ASSETS		715.00	703.87	711.76	709.34	693.51	689.19	692.43	707.43	695.84	699.93
ACCOUNTS PAYABLE		77.00	71.20	67.60	56.00	42.80	34.80	37.60	61.60	47.20	38.80
ACCRUED INTEREST		6.00	0.00	3.00	6.00	0.00	3.00	6.00	0.00	3.00	6.00
LONG-TERM DEBT		300.00	300.00	300.00	300.00	300.00	300.00	300.00	300.00	300.00	300.00
COMMON STOCK		70.00	70.00	70.00	70.00	70.00	70.00	70.00	70.00	70.00	70.00
RETAINED EARNINGS		262.00	262.67	271.16	277.34	280.71	281.39	278.83	275.83	275.64	285.13
LIABILITIES + OWNERS' EQUITY		715.00	703.87	711.76	709.34	693.51	689.19	692.43	707.43	695.84	699.93

[a] Required for other computations.

TABLE 22-9

Cash budget and pro forma income statements and balance sheets for the You 'N' Me Toy Company, with 120% of forecast sales.

	Oct	Nov	Dec	Jan	Feb	Mar	Apr	May	Jun	Jul	Aug	Sep	Oct
					CASH BUDGET FOR DECEMBER THROUGH AUGUST								
SALES	40.00	60.00	120.00	204.00	180.00	150.00	120.00	84.00	78.00	108.00	210.00	60.00[a]	84.00[a]
A/R COLLECTIONS			74.00	123.60	152.40	180.00	153.00	120.60	99.60	93.00	133.80		
INTEREST INCOME			0.42	−0.07	−0.27	−0.18	0.19	0.59	0.83	0.73	0.56		
CASH INFLOW			74.42	123.53	152.13	179.82	153.19	121.19	100.43	93.73	134.36		
PAYABLES PAID			77.00	106.80	101.40	84.00	64.20	52.20	56.40	92.40	70.80		
SALARIES & WAGES PAID			28.60	43.72	39.40	34.00	28.60	22.12	21.04	26.44	44.80	17.80[a]	
TAXES PAID			4.52	10.83	8.92	6.66	4.49	1.87	1.51	3.79	11.60		
INTEREST PAID			9.00	0.00	0.00	9.00	0.00	0.00	9.00	0.00	0.00		
DIVIDENDS PAID			2.00	2.00	2.00	2.00	2.00	2.00	2.00	2.00	2.00		
STARTING CASH			76.00	110.99	104.62	89.20	72.10	59.81	62.10	90.54	86.44		
ENDING CASH			110.99	104.62	89.20	72.10	59.81	62.10	90.54	86.44	61.42		
S-T INVESTMENT CHANGE (cash budget)			−81.69	−33.45	15.83	61.26	66.19	40.70	−17.96	−26.81	30.18		
S-T INVESTMENT CHANGE (balance sheet)			−81.69	−33.45	15.83	61.26	66.19	40.70	−17.96	−26.81	30.18		

	Oct	Nov	Dec	Jan	Feb	Mar	Apr	May	Jun	Jul	Aug
			MONTHLY PRO FORMA INCOME STATEMENTS								
SALES	40.00	60.00	120.00	204.00	180.00	150.00	120.00	84.00	78.00	108.00	210.00
COST OF RAW MATERIALS			72.00	122.40	108.00	90.00	72.00	50.40	46.80	64.80	126.00
SALARIES & WAGES			28.60	43.72	39.40	34.00	28.60	22.12	21.04	26.44	44.80
DEPRECIATION			3.91	3.87	3.83	3.79	3.76	3.72	3.68	3.64	3.61
INTEREST EXPENSE			3.00	3.00	3.00	3.00	3.00	3.00	3.00	3.00	3.00
INTEREST INCOME			0.42	−0.07	−0.27	−0.18	0.19	0.59	0.83	0.73	0.56
TAXABLE INCOME			12.91	30.94	25.50	19.03	12.84	5.35	4.31	10.84	33.16
TAXES			4.52	10.83	8.92	6.66	4.49	1.87	1.51	3.79	11.60
NET INCOME			8.39	20.11	16.57	12.37	8.34	3.48	2.80	7.05	21.55
DIVIDENDS			2.00	2.00	2.00	2.00	2.00	2.00	2.00	2.00	2.00
CHANGE IN RETAINED EARNINGS			6.39	18.11	14.57	10.37	6.34	1.48	0.80	5.05	19.55

	Oct	Nov	Dec	Jan	Feb	Mar	Apr	May	Jun	Jul	Aug
		CURRENT BALANCE SHEET AND MONTHLY PRO FORMA BALANCE SHEETS									
CASH		76.00	110.99	104.62	89.20	72.10	59.81	62.10	90.54	86.44	61.42
S-T INVESTMENT (BORROWING)		70.00	−11.69	−45.14	−29.31	31.95	98.14	138.84	120.89	94.08	124.26
ACCOUNTS RECEIVABLE		56.00	102.00	182.40	210.00	180.00	147.00	110.40	88.80	103.80	180.00
INVENTORY		122.00	156.80	135.80	111.80	86.00	66.20	72.20	117.80	123.80	56.00
NET FIXED ASSETS		391.00	387.09	383.22	379.39	375.59	371.84	368.12	364.44	360.79	357.19
TOTAL ASSETS		715.00	745.19	760.90	761.07	745.64	742.99	751.67	782.47	768.91	778.87
ACCOUNTS PAYABLE		77.00	106.80	101.40	84.00	64.20	52.20	56.40	92.40	70.80	58.20
ACCRUED INTEREST		6.00	0.00	3.00	6.00	0.00	3.00	6.00	0.00	3.00	6.00
LONG-TERM DEBT		300.00	300.00	300.00	300.00	300.00	300.00	300.00	300.00	300.00	300.00
COMMON STOCK		70.00	70.00	70.00	70.00	70.00	70.00	70.00	70.00	70.00	70.00
RETAINED EARNINGS		262.00	268.39	286.50	301.07	311.44	317.79	319.27	320.07	325.11	344.67
LIABILITIES + OWNERS' EQUITY		715.00	745.19	760.90	761.07	745.64	742.99	751.67	782.47	768.91	778.87

[a] Required for other computations.

Self-Check Questions

1. Explain why spreadsheet software is useful in preparing financial plans.
2. In building a financial planning spreadsheet model, why is it convenient to use a single item to represent both short-term investments (when the amount is positive) and short-term borrowing (when the amount is negative)?

SUMMARY

Financial planning is an organized process of gathering information, analyzing alternative decisions, developing goals and plans, and evaluating performance against those plans. The financial plan is a firm's "blueprint" for the future. The purpose of planning and budgeting is to draw out the best of the units and the individuals. Therefore, good financial planning uses both bottom-up and top-down processes.

A financial plan has three phases. In the formulation phase, a firm forecasts and evaluates the impact of alternative decisions. In the implementation phase, the firm puts the plan into action. Outcomes are subsequently measured against the plan in the evaluation phase.

Financial plans should be updated on a regular basis, according to a planning cycle. Each update adds the latest information and renews the planning horizon. Short-term models might be updated monthly, weekly, or even daily. Long-term plans might be updated once, twice, or perhaps four times a year. Updates vary in how thorough they are, from merely adding certain recent data, to adding all the latest data, extending the planning horizon, and reviewing and changing the model itself.

Computer technology has greatly benefited cash budgeting and the entire planning process. Because of its flexibility, spreadsheet software lends itself to cash budgeting and to the analysis of pro forma financial statements. Changes can be made in minutes or even seconds, and "what-if" questions can be easily investigated.

DECISION SUMMARY

• A firm should prepare a financial plan on a regular basis, preferably at least annually. Any firm that does not plan for its future may not have one.

• A firm's financial plan should consist of (1) a long-term financial plan that covers a period of at least three to five years, (2) a short-term financial plan that covers the coming year and agrees with the first year of the long-term plan, and (3) a detailed cash budget for the coming year.

• A complete financial plan includes, at a minimum,

1. Clearly stated strategic, operating, and financial *objectives*.
2. The *assumptions* on which the plan is based.
3. Descriptions of the underlying *strategies*.
4. *Contingency plans* for emergencies.
5. *Budgets*, categorized and summarized in various ways, such as by time period, division, and type (for example, cash, advertising, and capital).
6. The *financing program*, categorized and summarized in various ways, such as by time period, sources of funds (for example, bonds, bank loans, and stock), and types of funds (for example, short-term versus long-term, and internal versus external).

7. A set of period-by-period *pro forma financial statements* for the entire planning horizon.

- The firm's business units should be intimately involved in the planning process, each unit preparing its own financial plan. The corporate staff must provide overall guidance by ensuring that all business units base their plans on a consistent set of assumptions (supplied by the corporate staff), checking the business unit plans for reasonableness, and consolidating the business unit plans into the overall financial plan for the firm.

- The firm should regularly (at least monthly) monitor its performance against the short-term plan and the cash budget.

- The cash flow break-even point over a planning horizon is a pivotal point for addressing contingency plans for possible, even if unlikely, bad outcomes.

- The probability of falling below cash flow break-even during a planning horizon provides a measure of the firm's total risk.

- Spreadsheet software is useful in building a financial planning model, because it is convenient for handling multiple cases and answering "what-if" questions.

EQUATION SUMMARY

	Additional financing needed	=	Required increase in assets	−	Increase in liabilities	−	Increase in retained earnings

(22.1) $$\text{AFN} = (A/S)gS_0 - (L/S)gS_0 - [M(1 + g)S_0 - D]$$

(22.2) $$g = \frac{M(1 - d)}{(A/S) - (L/S) - M(1 - d)}$$

(22.3) $$g = \frac{M(1 - d)(1 + B/E)}{(A/S) - (L/S) - M(1 - d)(1 + B/E)}$$

(22.4) $$\text{Ending balance} = \text{Starting balance} + \text{Increases} - \text{Decreases}$$

KEY TERMS

EXERCISES

PROBLEM SET A

A1. Steve Ferris has $6000 in the bank and has a part time job earning $500 per month. He estimates that his monthly college expenses for his senior year will be:

September	$4000	January	$4000
October	1000	February	1000
November	1000	March	1500
December	1500	April	1000
		May	1500

Steve has a loan agreement whereby his bank will simply lend him money when he runs out, such that he will eventually have a zero cash balance and will be accumulating a debt obligation. What is Steve's forecasted cash balance and loan balance for the 9 months? How much will he owe when he graduates in May?

A2. Tulsa Well Supply Company has a cash balance at the end of June of $1,200,000. It projects net cash flows of the following amounts for the next six months:

July	$220,000
August	205,000
September	−325,000
October	−625,000
November	100,000
December	360,000

If Tulsa must keep a cash balance of at least $1,000,000 at all times, when and how much will it need to borrow to maintain this minimum cash balance?

A3. Assume that you are working for a business and one of your colleagues is whining that the business is wasting resources on its financial planning. Because this person is your friend, outline for him some of the major benefits of the financial planning process that should justify its cost.

A4. In 1998, the sales for Amalgamated Meat Loaf Company were $12,000,000. Several balance sheet items varied directly with sales as follows:

Cash	3%
Accounts receivable	20%
Inventory	15%
Net fixed assets	25%
Accounts payable	10%
Other accruals	5%

The net profit margin for Amalgamated Meat Loaf is 6%, and the firm pays out an annual dividend equal to 25% of net income. The balance sheet for December 31, 1998 is

AMALGAMATED MEAT LOAF COMPANY
BALANCE SHEET, DECEMBER 31, 1998

Cash	$ 360,000	Accounts payable	$1,200,000
Accounts receivable	2,400,000	Accruals	600,000
Inventory	1,800,000	Short-term debt	800,000
Total current assets	4,560,000	Total current liabilities	2,600,000
Net fixed assets	3,000,000	Long-term debt	1,000,000
Total assets	$7,560,000	Stockholders' equity	3,960,000
		Total liabilities & equity	$7,560,000

If sales increase by 25% to $15,000,000 in 1999, what additional financing will be needed? Assume that the additional financing needed is acquired by increasing short-term debt. Create a balance sheet for December 31, 1999, showing the financial position of Amalgamated Meat Loaf at that time.

A5. Rodeo Supply Company is planning to increase its sales by 20% next year. The sales increase will require a total additional investment in receivables, inventory, and fixed assets of $750,000. Increases in liabilities such as accounts payable and other accruals will supply $175,000 of financing. Rodeo also expects total profits of $225,000 next year and will not pay any cash dividends. How much external financing is required to finance the sales increase?

A6. Chris Hughen is studying his firm's financing requirements for next year. Chris estimates that the firm must invest an additional $100 in assets and that short-term liabilities will increase spontaneously by $10. He also estimates that the firm will earn profits of $70 and that it has access to additional external financing of $50. What is the largest dividend that the firm can pay and still have adequate funds to finance its additional assets?

PROBLEM SET B

B1. At the beginning of January, the South Carolina Sportsplex has $150,000 of cash on hand. The firm forecasts the following cash flows for the first 6 months of the year:

			CASH FLOWS ($1000s)			
	Jan	Feb	Mar	Apr	May	June
Cash inflows	100	120	150	320	350	240
Cash outflows	150	180	200	290	240	180

The S. C. Sportsplex wants to maintain a cash balance of at least $100,000 at all times. If the balance falls below that level, the firm will borrow to bring its balance up to $100,000. If more than $100,000 of cash is available, it will use the excess to reduce its short-term borrowing. Show the monthly net cash flow, borrowing (if any), loan repayments, cash balance, and cumulative borrowing balance.

B2. Columbus Distributors has the following balance sheet:

	BALANCE SHEET, TODAY		
Cash	$ 500,000	Accounts payable	$ 1,000,000
Accounts receivable	3,500,000	Bank loan	1,500,000
Inventory	3,000,000	Long-term bond	2,000,000
Fixed assets	3,000,000	Stockholders' equity	5,500,000
Total assets	$10,000,000	Total liabilities & equity	$10,000,000

Next year, Columbus Distributors is planning for a major sales increase of 40%. Sales are currently $15,000,000, and they should increase to $21,000,000 next year. Cash, receivables, and inventory will increase proportionally to sales. Fixed assets will increase by $500,000. Payables will also increase proportionally to sales. The bank loan will increase to $2,000,000. Sinking fund payments will decrease the bond balance by $200,000. Columbus has a 6.0% profit margin and is expecting to pay a cash dividend of $100,000 to its common stockholders. Prepare a pro forma balance sheet for next year. Does the balance sheet show that extra external funds are needed or that excess funds are available for investment?

B3. Lafayette Oil Company has current sales of $50 million. Lafayette estimates that an additional dollar of sales requires an investment of $1.25 and generates spontaneous short-term financing of $0.15. Lafayette has an 8% net profit margin and expects to pay out dividends equal to 25% of net income.

a. How much additional financing is needed if Lafayette plans to expand sales by 10% next year?

b. How fast can Lafayette grow if it wants to finance all of its growth internally?

c. Assume that Lafayette will raise additional long-term debt equal to 60% of its additional equity. How much additional financing is needed now if Lafayette grows by 10%?

d. How fast can Lafayette grow if it wants to finance its growth internally and with additional debt capital equal to 60% of equity?

B4. Merrimack Resorts has projected the following cash flows for the 6 months of April through September:

	Apr	May	Jun	Jul	Aug	Sep
Cash inflows	100	100	175	250	300	250
Cash outflows	200	200	250	250	175	125

Prepare a schedule showing the monthly cash flow, borrowing, loan repayments, cash balance, and cumulative loan balance. Merrimack has a beginning cash balance of $150 and wishes to maintain a minimum cash balance of at least $100. If the firm has cash balances in excess of the minimum, the excess will be used to reduce any outstanding loan balances.

B5. The management team of Dark Adventures has asked you to prepare a monthly cash budget for the 6 months from October through March. Because the sales of Dark Adventures are seasonal, peaking around the turn of the year, cash budgeting is critical to the firm. To facilitate your preparation of the cash budget, the managers have supplied you with the following information:

1. The recent and forecasted sales are

August (actual)	$400,000
September (actual)	500,000
October (forecast)	600,000
November	700,000
December	800,000
January	800,000
February	700,000
March	600,000
April	500,000

2. Twenty-five percent of sales are collected during the month of sale, 50% are collected in the month following the sale, and 25% are collected in the second month following the sale.

3. Purchases are 50% of sales and are paid for 1 month prior to sale.

4. Wages and salaries are 24% of sales and are paid in the same month as the sale.

5. Rent of $4000 is paid each month. Additional cash operating expenses of $8000 per month will be incurred for October and November, $20,000 for December and January, and $8000 for February and March.

6. Tax installments of $10,000 are planned for October and January. A capital expenditure of $100,000 will occur in October, and the firm has a mortgage payment of $5000 due every month.

7. The cash balance at the end of September is $125,000, and managers want to maintain a minimum balance of $60,000 at all times. The firm will borrow the amounts necessary to ensure that the minimum balance is achieved. If the cash balance is above the minimum and there is still a loan balance from previous months, excess funds will be applied to the loan balance until it is eliminated.

B6. Kennesaw Leisure Products has the following balance sheet:

BALANCE SHEET, CURRENT DATE (THOUSANDS)			
Cash	$ 50	Accounts payable	$ 70
Accounts receivable	220	Bank loan	180
Inventory	300	Long-term mortgage	200
Fixed assets	210	Stockholders' equity	330
Total assets	$780	Total liabilities & equity	$780

In the year just completed, Kennesaw had sales of $600,000, with net income of $60,000 and a net profit margin of 10%. The firm expects the same profit margin on next year's sales. Kennesaw paid no dividend this year and does not plan to pay one next year. Next year, Kennesaw is planning on a substantial sales increase. Assume that cash, accounts receivable, inventory, and accounts payable will increase proportionally to the increase in sales. Furthermore, the existing level of fixed assets is sufficient to accommodate the planned sales increase, the mortgage loan will be amortized by $10,000, and the bank loan cannot be increased.

a. Assume that sales increase by 10%. Prepare a pro forma balance sheet showing the firm's financial position at the end of next year. If the balance sheet does not otherwise balance, indicate on the balance sheet the amount of additional external funds that are needed or the excess funds that are available for investment.

b. Assume that sales increase by 20%. Prepare a pro forma balance sheet showing the firm's financial position at the end of next year. If the balance sheet does not otherwise balance, indicate on the balance sheet the amount of extra external funds that are needed or the excess funds that are available for investment.

B7. Current sales of $1,000,000 are expected to increase by 20% next year. The investment in additional assets to finance this growth should be 150% of the sales increase. Short-term liabilities (such as accounts payable and other accruals) will provide financing equivalent to 15% of the sales increase. The firm's net income is predicted to be 20% of total sales, and the firm plans to pay a cash dividend equal to one-third of net income. How much additional financing is needed to finance the firm's growth?

B8. Scott Medical Supplies estimates that an additional dollar of sales requires an investment of $1.00 and generates spontaneous financing of $0.20. Scott Medical has a 9% net profit margin and expects to pay out dividends equal to 50% of net income.

a. How fast can Scott Medical Supplies grow if it wants to finance all of its growth internally?

b. Assume that Scott will raise additional long-term debt equal to 75% of its additional equity. How fast can Scott grow if it wants to finance its growth internally and with additional debt capital equal to 75% of equity?

B9. What sources of funds are available to finance growth when the firm is estimating its internal growth rate? What additional source of funds is available to the firm when it is estimating its sustainable growth rate?

B10. The maximum internal growth rate is estimated with the formula

$$g = \frac{M(1-d)}{(A/S) - (L/S) - M(1-d)}$$

Indicate whether an increase in each of the variables in this formula would increase ($+$) or decrease ($-$) the internal growth rate g.

_____ M (net profit margin)
_____ d (dividend payout ratio)
_____ A/S (asset requirement as a fraction of sales)
_____ L/S (spontaneous short-term financing as a fraction of sales)

PROBLEM SET C

C1. Mathew T. Box, III, grandson of the founder and currently CEO of the M. T. Box Company, has been concerned about the firm's short-term financial management. The treasurer of M. T. Box, Mary Hoover, has gathered the following information and is asking you to create a cash budget, monthly pro forma income statements, and monthly pro forma balance sheets for the next 6 months for M. T. Box.

1. The payment pattern for revenues is estimated to be as follows: 20% of sales are for cash, 15% are paid for 1 month after the sale, 55% are paid for 2 months after the sale, 9% are paid for in 3 months, and 1% are uncollectible.

2. The cash account should be set to start each month in the amount of $15,000 plus 65% of next month's salaries and wages plus 75% of this month's accounts payable. The cash account will be adjusted with the short-term investment (borrowing) account, and Mary Hoover believes M. T. Box can earn 9% APR on its short-term investments.

3. Purchases of raw materials each month are in the amount of 35% of the predicted sales for the month after next plus 25% of next month's predicted sales plus 8% of this month's sales. Purchases are paid for in the following month, and there are no discounts available from suppliers. The cost of raw materials averages 68% of sales.

4. The firm pays salaries and wages of $15,000 plus 14% of this month's sales.

5. Fixed assets are being depreciated at the rate of 1% of net fixed assets per month.

6. The firm pays a cash dividend of $2000 every month.

7. The long-term debt on the balance sheet carries a 15% APR, and payments are made quarterly in December, March, June, and September.

8. Taxes are at the rate of 35% of taxable income (including rebates for negative taxes). Taxes are paid monthly.

9. Mary Hoover is expecting the company to make a purchase of $150,000 in fixed assets at the end of April.

10. Sales for October, November, and December of this year were $60,000, $90,000, and $150,000, respectively. Sales forecasted for the next 8 months are (in thousands)

Jan.	Feb.	Mar.	Apr.	May	Jun.	Jul.	Aug.
250	235	190	160	110	90	135	260

BALANCE SHEET AS OF DECEMBER 31

Cash	$170	Accounts payable	$160
Short-term investments (borrowing)	90	Accrued interest	0
Accounts receivable	195	Long-term debt	600
Inventory	157	Common stock	120
Net fixed assets	615	Retained earnings	347
Total assets	$1227	Liabilities + stockholders' equity	$1227

C2. The following information has been gathered for Dunn Manufacturing, Inc. Ulysses R. Dunn, the founder, manager, and majority shareholder, is trying to get a "handle" on financial planning. Use the following information to create a cash budget, monthly pro forma income statements, and monthly pro forma balance sheets for the next 9 months for Dunn Manufacturing and U. R. Dunn.

1. The payment pattern for revenues is estimated to be as follows: 20% of sales are for cash, 10% are paid for 1 month after the sale, 50% are paid for 2 months after the sale, 18% are paid for 3 months after the sale, and 2% are uncollectible.

2. The cash account is targeted to start each month in the amount of $20,000 plus 70% of next month's salaries and wages plus 75% of this month's accounts payable. The cash account will be adjusted with the notes payable account, which currently costs 1.1% per month on the balance.

3. Dunn purchases raw materials each month in the amount of 40% of the predicted sales for the month after next plus 10% of next month's predicted sales plus 15% of this month's sales. Purchases are paid for in the following month, and there are no discounts available to Dunn from its suppliers. The cost of raw materials averages 65% of sales.

4. Dunn pays salaries and wages of $27,000 plus 10% of this month's sales.

5. Dunn is depreciating its net fixed assets at the rate of 0.9% of *net* fixed assets per month.

6. Dunn pays a cash dividend of $5000 every month.

7. The long-term debt on the Dunn balance sheet carries a 12% APR, and payments are made quarterly in December, March, June, and September.

8. Taxes for Dunn Manufacturing are at the rate of 34% of taxable income (including rebates for negative taxes). Taxes are paid quarterly (end of December, March, June, and September) on the basis of what the tax liability is *expected to be over the next quarter*. The model you build must be used in conjunction with trial and error to determine the correct tax payments to avoid encountering the problem of circular reasoning (CIRC). (*Hint*: Initially, just let the taxes "use up" what is currently in the prepaid tax account and go negative.)

9. Dunn expects to purchase $275,000 worth of fixed assets at the end of July.

10. Sales for January, February, and March of this year were $320,000, $345,000, and $365,000, respectively. Sales forecasted for the next 11 months are (in thousands)

Apr.	May	Jun.	Jul.	Aug.	Sep.	Oct.	Nov.	Dec.	Jan.	Feb.
410	430	350	325	300	220	265	290	375	350	370

BALANCE SHEET AS OF MARCH 31

Cash	$210	Accounts payable	$177
Accounts receivable	256	Notes payable	219
Inventory	437	Accrued interest	0
Prepaid taxes	43	Long-term debt	650
Other assets	15	Common stock	150
Net fixed assets	674	Retained earnings	439
Total assets	$1635	Liabilities + stockholders' equity	$1635

Real-World Application: Euro Disneyland's Financial Projections

The Walt Disney Company (Disney) is a diversified, international entertainment firm whose operations include theme parks and resorts, filmed entertainment, and consumer products. Disney is acknowledged as the world's leading theme park operator.

In the 1980s, Disney management had set a 20% growth target for the firm. Expansion of the theme park operations was an integral part of its strategy for achieving its growth target. With a well-penetrated American market, Disney realized that international expansion was crucial. The first international expansion took place in 1983 when the Tokyo Disneyland theme park opened. The success of this project prompted Disney to explore other international opportunities. Europe seemed to be an ideal site with the European Union taking shape.

Euro Disneyland would introduce to Europe a theme park and resort concept that Disney had developed—and seemingly perfected—in the United States and Japan during the preceding 35 years. The financing plan for Euro Disneyland included an initial public offering by the main project firm in 1989. The financing plan would change Euro Disneyland from an internally financed, privately owned project into a highly leveraged, publicly owned entity in which Disney would hold only a minority interest.

Disney planned to open Euro Disneyland in 1992. Table 22-10 provides financial projections for the period 1992–1996.

1. Project the annual revenues for 1997–2016 assuming that each class of revenue after 1996 grows at a 5% annual rate.

2. Project the annual operating expenses for 1997–2016 assuming that each class of expenses after 1996 grows at a 5% annual rate.

3. Calculate the operating income projected for each year between 1997 and 2016.

4. Project the annual other expenses (income) for 1997–2016 assuming that (a) royalties equal 5% of total revenues, (b) preopening amortization is zero after 1996, (c) annual depreciation, annual interest expense, annual interest and other income, and annual lease expense are constant after 1996, and (d) management incentive fees grow after 1996 at a 7.5% annual rate.

	1992	1993	1994	1995	1996
Revenues					
Magic Kingdom[a]	FF4246	FF4657	FF5384	FF5,853	FF6,415
Second theme park	0	0	0	0	3,128
Resort and property development	1236	2144	3520	5,077	6,386
Total revenues	5482	6801	8904	10,930	15,929
Operating expenses:					
Magic Kingdom	2643	2836	3161	3,370	3,641
Second theme park	0	0	0	0	1,794
Resort and property development	796	1501	2431	2,970	3,694
Total operating expenses	3439	4337	5592	6,340	9,129
Operating income	2043	2464	3312	4,590	6,800
Other expenses (income):					
Royalties	302	333	387	422	717
Preopening amortization	341	341	341	341	341
Depreciation	255	263	290	296	625
Interest expense	567	575	757	708	1,166
Interest and other income	(786)	(788)	(768)	(778)	(790)
Lease expense	958	950	958	962	975
Management incentive fees	55	171	477	963	1,820
Total other expenses (income)	1692	1845	2442	2,914	4,854
Profit before taxation	351	619	870	1,676	1,946
Taxation	147	260	366	704	818
Net profit	FF204	FF359	FF504	FF972	FF1,128

[a] Includes the Magic Kingdom Hotel.
Source: Euro Disneyland S.C.A., *Offer for Sale of 10,691,000 Shares* (October 5, 1989), p. 36.

TABLE 22-10
Financial projections for Euro Disneyland (millions of French francs).

5. Calculate the profit before taxation projected for each year between 1997 and 2016.

6. Calculate the net profit projected for each year between 1997 and 2016 assuming that Euro Disneyland's income tax rate is 42%.

7. Calculate the annual dividends assuming that Euro Disneyland pays out 75% of its net profit each year.

8. Calculate the present value of Euro Disneyland's equity as of the beginning of 1989 assuming that Euro Disneyland's cost of equity capital is 15% and its equity is worth 10 times the year's net profit at the end of 2016.

9. How much does the value estimated in question 8 change if the projected growth rate of annual revenue is 6% per year?

10. How much does the value estimated in question 8 change if the projected growth rate of annual operating expenses is 6% per year?

BIBLIOGRAPHY

Carpenter, Michael D., and Jack E. Miller. "A Reliable Framework for Monitoring Accounts Receivable," *Financial Management*, 1979, 8(4):37–40.

Elmer, Peter J., and David M. Borowski. "An Expert System Approach to Financial Analysis: The Case of S&L Bankruptcy," *Financial Management*, 1988, 17(3):66–76.

Emery, Gary W. "Some Empirical Evidence on the Properties of Daily Cash Flow," *Financial Management*, 1981, 10(1):21–28.

Fabozzi, Frank J., and Leslie N. Masonson, eds. *Corporate Cash Management: Techniques and Analysis.* Homewood, Ill.: Dow Jones-Irwin, 1985.

Ferguson, D. M., and Ned C. Hill. "Cash Flow Timeline Management: The Next Frontier of Cash Management," *Journal of Cash Management*, 1985, (May/June):12–22.

Finnerty, John D. *Corporate Financial Analysis.* New York: McGraw-Hill, 1986.

Francis, Jack Clark, and Dexter R. Rowell. "A Simultaneous Equation Model of the Firm for Financial Analysis and Planning," *Financial Management*, 1978, (1):29–44.

Maier, Steven F., and James H. Vander Weide. "A Practical Approach to Short-Run Financial Planning," *Financial Management*, 1978, 7(4):10–16.

Part VI

LONG-TERM FINANCING

We analyzed the firm's capital budgeting decisions in Part III. Making such investments requires capital. We discussed the cheapest and most readily available source of new equity capital, retained earnings, in Part IV. In this part, we will concentrate on the firm's external sources of long-term funds. Long-term financing alternatives include common stock, preferred stock, straight debt, leases, debt with options, and more.

A firm has a number of choices in connection with the securities it issues. It can sell securities to investors at large in a *general cash offer*. It can make *private placements* with large financial institutions. In the case of common stock, it can sell new shares to its existing shareholders through a *rights offering*. We will describe the features of each method and explain the advantages and disadvantages of each.

Firms also have a range of features to choose from when designing securities. We will describe the basic features of each class of securities. In the case of long-term debt, one of these features is a call option. As we said in Chapter 5, firms often include the option to call bonds and redeem them before the maturity date. We will explain and illustrate how firms can best use this valuable option. We will also discuss a special form of debt financing called *leasing* and show you why lease financing can be a tax-efficient alternative to conventional debt financing.

Sometimes debt includes a conversion option. Convertible debt gives the holder the option to convert it into shares of the issuer's common stock. Such debt is an example of securities known as derivatives. These securities have a variety of uses in corporate financial management, particularly in managing the firm's risk, through what is called *hedging*. We will describe the basic types of derivatives, explain how to value them, and show you how firms use them to raise funds and hedge risks.

EQUITY AND THE INVESTMENT BANKING PROCESS

OBJECTIVES

After studying this chapter, you should be able to

1. Describe the public offering and private placement methods of issuing securities.

2. Summarize the main features of common stock.

3. Explain the differences between the general cash offer and rights offering methods of selling common stock.

4. Describe the role of investment bankers in helping a firm raise funds externally.

5. Explain the difference between going public and going private, and cite some of the advantages and disadvantages of each.

6. Summarize the main features of preferred stock.

A firm needs capital to grow and acquire additional assets. Firms usually finance the purchase of long-term assets with long-term capital. Retained earnings are one source of long-term capital. But when capital requirements exceed the firm's ability to generate cash internally, it must raise funds externally.

Many firms, particularly smaller ones, issue debt securities directly to investors through a *private placement*. Privately placed securities are not registered for sale to the public. As a result, there are restrictions on resale. A private placement tends to be more expensive than a general cash offer because of the *illiquidity premium* investors demand on account of the resale restrictions.

In this chapter and the next, we examine alternative external sources of long-term capital. This chapter focuses on equity financing, the next on long-term debt financing. Because firms often sell securities (as opposed to borrowing money from banks), this chapter explains how firms issue securities and describes the markets in which they issue them. We also explain how the investment banking process helps firms raise funds.

EQUITY, INVESTMENT BANKING, AND THE PRINCIPLES OF FINANCE

◆ *Two-Sided Transactions*: Issuing securities requires setting a price and other terms that investors find acceptable.

◆ *Signaling*: Announcing a public offering of common stock usually leads to a negative stock market reaction because it suggests that managers think the firm's stock is over-valued.

◆ *Valuable Ideas*: Look for opportunities to develop new securities that reduce issuers' funding costs and raise investors' risk-adjusted after-tax returns.

◆ *Comparative Advantage*: Contracting with underwriters to bear the risk in pricing a new securities issue can be valuable if they can bear it more cheaply.

◆ *Options*: Value the rights distributed to shareholders in a rights offering just as you would any other call option.

◆ *Risk-Return Trade-Off*: Offering a new security that reduces the investors' risk will enable you to pay a lower interest rate than an otherwise identical conventional security would require.

◆ *Capital Market Efficiency*: Use the market price at which a firm's common shares are actively trading as the best measure of their value.

NORTHWEST AIRLINES CORPORATION'S NEW-ISSUE DECISION

Early in 1994 Alfred Checchi and Gary Wilson, co-chairmen of the board of directors of Northwest Airlines Corporation (Northwest), were studying Northwest's financing alternatives. Checchi and Wilson were financiers who in 1989 arranged a *leveraged buyout* of Northwest, the world's fourth largest passenger airline.[1] The leveraged buyout cost approximately $3.6 billion and left Northwest with a very high debt ratio.

By year-end 1993, Northwest's debt ratio remained high. Further, about $1.5 billion of its debt was scheduled to mature in 1997. Checchi and Wilson considered a range of financing alternatives, including a public offering of common stock. At first, investment bankers told Checchi and Wilson that Northwest could sell common stock at about $20 per share. But it soon became apparent that this price was unrealistic. Investors were concerned about the risk of further fare discounting and about the increasing age of Northwest's fleet of aircraft.

Investment bankers eventually told Northwest that it could sell 20 million common shares (roughly a one-third increase in the number of outstanding shares) at around $13 per share. Table 23-1 shows Northwest's capitalization with and without the common stock of-

---

[1] Chapter 28 discusses leveraged buyouts and how to structure them.

TABLE 23-1
Northwest Airlines Corporation's capitalization (at market value, dollar amounts in millions).

	DECEMBER 31, 1993[a]		PRO FORMA FOR THE COMMON STOCK OFFERING	
	Amount	Percent	Amount	Percent
Long-term debt and capital lease obligations[b]	$5211.2	74.4%	$5108.2[d]	71.5%
Preferred stock[b]	650.6	9.3	650.6	9.1
Common equity	1143.1[c]	16.3	1386.2[d]	19.4
Total	$7004.9	100.0%	$7145.0	100.0%

[a] As adjusted to reflect a $243 million aircraft financing, a $175 million receivables financing, a $350 million note offering, an exercise of stock options by employee unions that raised $54 million, and the use of a portion of the proceeds from these securities issues to pay down long-term debt.
[b] Assumes market value equals book value.
[c] 87,933,562 shares at $13 each. Includes 29,923,616 shares to be issued to employee trusts as part of the agreement struck with Northwest's labor unions at the time of the leveraged buyout (17,777,026 common shares and preferred stock convertible into an additional 12,146,590 shares).
[d] Pro forma the effect of selling 20,000,000 shares at $13 each to produce net proceeds of $243.1 million. Of these net proceeds, $103 million would be used to pay down long-term debt.
Source: Northwest Airlines Corporation, *20,000,000 Shares Common Stock,* prospectus (March 18, 1994), pp. 26–27.

fering. The stock offering would strengthen Northwest's balance sheet and raise net proceeds of $243.1 million, $103 million of which would be used to reduce long-term debt. The offering would increase Northwest's equity to about $1.4 billion and raise its equity ratio to 19.4% from 16.3%.

As you read this chapter, imagine you are Northwest's chief financial officer. How would you advise Checchi and Wilson concerning the advantages and disadvantages of a common stock offering? Bear in mind that both are major stockholders and that, as a result of their leveraged buyout, Northwest is privately held.

23.1 LONG-TERM FINANCING ALTERNATIVES

Each time a firm chooses to raise funds externally, it must decide what type of securities to issue and determine the size of the offering. Flotation costs play a role because they are proportionately smaller for larger issues. The fixed cost is spread out over a larger issue. The variable costs for small issues are greater because small issues are relatively illiquid.[1]

Debt, common stock, and preferred stock are the main sources of external long-term financing for firms. Table 23-2 shows the relative proportions of funds that U.S. firms raised from these sources between 1970 and 1994. Over that 25-year period, common stock, preferred stock, and debt accounted for 13.8%, 5.6%, and 80.6%, respectively, of the funds raised.

Figure 23-1 also shows that the aggregate sale of common stock is sensitive to stock market conditions. Firms try to take advantage of rising markets when the demand for common stock is relatively strong. New-issue activity tends to increase during periods of rising share prices, such as 1984–1986 and 1990–1993. By the same token, firms are usually reluctant to sell new issues of common stock when the share price is low by historical standards.

Figure 23-2 shows that the volume of debt issues tends to vary with the level of long-term interest rates. During periods of rising long-term interest rates, such as 1977–1981, firms

---

[1] We will give you the details later in the chapter.

TABLE 23-2
Main sources of domestic external long-term financing by U.S. firms, 1970–1994 (dollar amounts in millions).

YEAR	AGGREGATE DOMESTIC EXTERNAL FINANCING[a]	PERCENTAGE REPRESENTED BY			PERCENT CHANGE IN S&P 500 INDEX DURING YEAR	MOODY'S AVERAGE OF YIELDS ON Aa-RATED CORPORATE BONDS
		Common Stock	Preferred Stock[b]	Debt[c]		
1970	$ 38,945	18.6%	3.6%	77.8%	0.10%	8.32%
1971	45,084	20.6	8.1	71.3	10.79	7.78
1972	41,957	23.1	8.0	68.9	15.63	7.48
1973	33,390	23.2	10.1	66.7	−17.37	7.66
1974	38,313	10.4	5.9	83.7	−29.72	8.84
1975	53,619	13.8	6.4	79.8	31.55	9.17
1976	53,356	15.6	5.2	79.2	19.15	8.75
1977	53,792	14.6	7.3	78.1	−11.50	8.24
1978	47,230	15.9	6.0	78.1	1.06	8.92
1979	51,102	15.2	7.1	77.7	12.31	9.94
1980	73,694	22.9	4.9	72.2	25.77	12.50
1981	70,441	33.4	2.6	64.0	−9.73	14.75
1982	84,198	30.2	6.1	63.7	14.76	14.41
1983	119,949	37.0	6.0	57.0	17.27	12.42
1984	132,531	14.0	3.1	82.9	1.40	13.31
1985	201,269	14.4	3.2	82.4	26.33	11.82
1986	381,936	13.2	4.7	82.1	14.62	9.47
1987	367,863	11.8	6.3	81.9	2.03	9.68
1988	385,625	9.3	5.7	85.0	12.40	9.94
1989	325,034	8.0	4.1	87.9	27.25	9.46
1990	340,049	5.7	6.1	88.2	−6.56	9.56
1991	465,243	10.3	5.9	83.8	26.31	9.05
1992	559,827	10.2	5.6	84.2	4.46	8.46
1993	754,969	10.9	4.1	85.0	7.06	7.04
1994	582,569	8.2	6.4	85.4	−1.54	8.15
Total	$5,301,985	13.8%	5.6%	80.6%		

[a] Aggregate amount raised through the issuance of common stock, nonconvertible preferred stock, nonconvertible debt, and convertible securities.
[b] Includes convertible preferred and preference stock.
[c] Includes convertible debt.
Sources: Federal Reserve Bulletin, Board of Governors of the Federal Reserve System, Washington, D.C., various issues; *Daily Stock Price Record: New York Stock Exchange,* Standard & Poor's Corporation, New York, various issues; and *Moody's Bond Record,* Moody's Investors Service, Inc., New York, various issues.

tend to favor short-term borrowing in the hope that long-term interest rates will fall. When long-term interest rates do fall, as they did from 1981 to 1986 and from 1990 to 1993, firms begin to replace this short-term debt.

Self-Check Questions

1. Which among debt, common stock, and preferred stock provides the largest proportion of external long-term financing by firms? Which accounts for the smallest?

2. Why are the volumes of common stock and debt financing sensitive to market conditions?

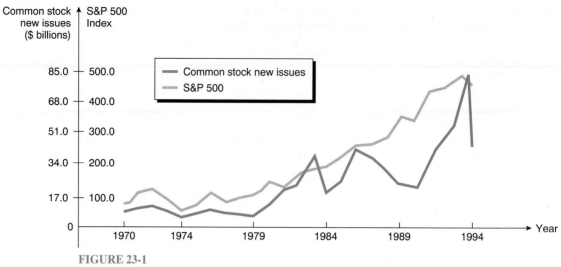

FIGURE 23-1
Volume of common stock new issues and changes in the S&P 500 Index, 1970–1994.
Sources: Securities Data Company, Inc., and Standard & Poor's Corporation.

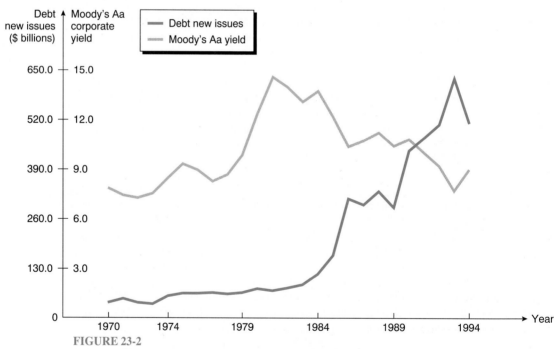

FIGURE 23-2
Volume of debt new issues and Moody's average yield on Aa-rated corporate bonds, 1970–1994.
Sources: Moody's Investors Service, Inc., and Securities Data Company, Inc.

23.2 PUBLIC OFFERINGS

A general cash offer, also referred to as a registered **public offering**, is much the same for debt and equity. The issuer must satisfy the securities laws, which are enforced by the Securities and Exchange Commission (SEC). In particular, securities sold in a public offering must be registered with the SEC.

Just as there are different financing alternatives, there is a choice of issue methods. Larger firms usually make a **general cash offer**. The firm offers the securities to investors at large, usually with the help of underwriters. Underwriters sell the securities, and in most cases, they also guarantee the price the issuer will receive. Alternatively, the firm can offer new common stock directly to existing holders through a *rights offering*. Rights offerings, which we will discuss later, differ from general cash offers in several ways.

There are foreign markets for securities, too. The **Eurodollar bond market** is the market outside the United States for U.S. dollar-denominated bonds. At times, the Eurodollar bond market provides more attractive new-issue terms than the U.S. market. It therefore pays a prospective bond issuer to keep an eye on the Eurodollar bond market.

General Cash Offers

When a firm issues securities in a general cash offer, it must register them with the SEC.[2] Making a general cash offer involves the following steps.

DECIDE WHAT TO ISSUE   Managers must first decide how much they need to raise and what type of security to issue. The firm's target capital structure will affect the decision. But other considerations, such as the specific terms available and management's view of how its common stock is priced, also play a role.

OBTAIN REQUIRED APPROVALS   Management must obtain board approval to issue new securities. Shareholder approval is required if the firm needs to increase the number of authorized shares of common or preferred stock.

FILE A REGISTRATION STATEMENT   The prospective issuer must prepare and file a *registration statement* with the SEC.[3] The registration statement contains a *preliminary prospectus*. The preliminary prospectus is also called a *red herring* because of a warning legend that must be printed on its cover in bold red letters. A prospectus describes the issuer's business, financial condition, and operating history; explains the terms of the security being offered; and provides other relevant information.

DETERMINE INITIAL PRICING AND FILE AN AMENDED REGISTRATION STATEMENT   The SEC reviews the registration statement and makes comments. Once this review process is complete, the issuer and the underwriters negotiate the terms of the offering and the underwriters' compensation. The issuer then files an amendment to the registration statement, which contains the terms of the offering and the *final prospectus*. Figure 23-3 shows the cover page and Figure 23-4 shows the summary page from a typical prospectus. (You may have used Microsoft's word processing package to prepare a paper for class.) After registration, the securities can be traded freely by investors.

CLOSE THE OFFERING   The offer for sale closes three business days later.[4] At the clos-

---

[2] The Securities Act of 1933 (the 1933 Act) and the rules issued thereunder regulate interstate issues of securities. All the states have their own laws to regulate *intra*state securities issues. An offering limited to one state is registered with the state securities department rather than the SEC. In addition, each state's "blue sky" laws regulate the sale of any securities (including SEC-registered securities) within that state.

[3] There are some exemptions from this requirement. In footnote 2 we mentioned the intrastate exemption. There is a commercial paper exemption for notes that will mature within 270 days of issue. There is also a small-issue exemption. Regulation A under the 1933 Act provides for an abbreviated offering statement when the issue will raise no more than $1.5 million.

[4] Corporate securities transactions customarily settle, or close, in the United States on the third business day following the transaction date.

2,795,000 Shares

MICROSOFT®

Microsoft Corporation

Common Stock

Of the 2,795,000 shares of Common Stock offered hereby, 2,000,000 shares are being sold by the Company and 795,000 shares are being sold by the Selling Stockholders. See "Principal and Selling Stockholders." The Company will not receive any of the proceeds from the sale of shares by the Selling Stockholders.

Prior to this offering, there has been no public market for the Common Stock of the Company. For the factors which were considered in determining the initial public offering price, see "Underwriting."

See "Certain Factors" for a discussion of certain factors which should be considered by prospective purchasers of the Common Stock offered hereby.

THESE SECURITIES HAVE NOT BEEN APPROVED OR DISAPPROVED BY THE SECURITIES AND EXCHANGE COMMISSION NOR HAS THE COMMISSION PASSED UPON THE ACCURACY OR ADEQUACY OF THIS PROSPECTUS. ANY REPRESENTATION TO THE CONTRARY IS A CRIMINAL OFFENSE.

	Initial Public Offering Price	Underwriting Discount(1)	Proceeds to Company(2)	Proceeds to Selling Stockholders(2)
Per Share	$21.00	$1.31	$19.69	$19.69
Total(3)	$58,695,000	$3,661,450	$39,380,000	$15,653,550

(1) The Company and the Selling Stockholders have agreed to indemnify the Underwriters against certain liabilities, including liabilities under the Securities Act of 1933.

(2) Before deducting expenses of the offering estimated at $541,000, of which $452,000 will be paid by the Company and $89,000 by the Selling Stockholders.

(3) The Company has granted to the Underwriters an option to purchase up to an additional 300,000 shares at the initial public offering price, less the underwriting discount, solely to cover overallotments. If such option is exercised in full, the total Initial Public Offering Price, Underwriting Discount and Proceeds to Company will be $64,995,000, $4,054,450 and $45,287,000, respectively.

The shares are offered severally by the Underwriters, as specified herein, subject to receipt and acceptance by them and subject to their right to reject any order in whole or in part. It is expected that the certificates for the shares will be ready for delivery at the offices of Goldman, Sachs & Co., New York, New York on or about March 20, 1986.

Goldman, Sachs & Co.   **Alex. Brown & Sons**
                                                                                            Incorporated

The date of this Prospectus is March 13, 1986.

FIGURE 23-3
Prospectus cover page.

PROSPECTUS SUMMARY

The following summary is qualified in its entirety by the more detailed information and Consolidated Financial Statements appearing elsewhere in this Prospectus. All information relating to the Company's Common Stock contained in this Prospectus, except as presented in the Consolidated Financial Statements, reflects the conversion of all outstanding shares of Preferred Stock into Common Stock on the date of this Prospectus.

The Company

Microsoft designs, develops, markets, and supports a product line of systems and applications microcomputer software for business and professional use. The Microsoft Software Product Line chart inside the front cover of this Prospectus illustrates the evolution and diversity of the Company's product line. Microsoft's systems software products include Microsoft® MS-DOS®, a 16-bit microcomputer operating system used on IBM PC and IBM compatible computers, and computer language products in six computer languages. The Company offers business applications software products in the following categories: word processing, spreadsheet, file management, graphics, communications, and project management. The Company's products are available for 8-bit, 16-bit, and 32-bit microcomputers, including IBM, Tandy, Apple, COMPAQ, Olivetti, AT&T, Zenith, Wang, Hewlett-Packard, DEC, Siemens, Philips, Mitsubishi, and NEC. Microsoft develops most of its software products internally using proprietary development tools and methodology. The Company markets and distributes its products domestically and internationally through the original equipment manufacturer ("OEM") channel and through the retail channel primarily by means of independent distributors and dealers and by direct marketing to corporate, governmental, and educational customers.

The Offering

Common Stock offered by the Company	2,000,000 shares(1)
Common Stock offered by the Selling Stockholders	795,000 shares
Common Stock to be outstanding after the offering	24,715,113 shares(1)
Proposed NASDAQ symbol	MSFT
Use of Proceeds	For general corporate purposes, principally working capital, product development, and capital expenditures.

Selected Consolidated Financial Information
(In thousands, except per share data)

	Year Ended June 30,				Six Months Ended December 31,	
	1982	1983	1984	1985	1984	1985
					(Unaudited)	
Income Statement Data:						
Net revenues	$24,486	$50,065	$97,479	$140,417	$62,837	$85,050
Income before income taxes	5,595	11,064	28,030	42,843	18,219	29,048
Net income	3,507	6,487	15,880	24,101	9,996	17,118
Net income per share	$ .17	$ .29	$ .69	$ 1.04	$ .43	$ .72
Shares used in computing net income per share	21,240	22,681	22,947	23,260	23,253	23,936

	December 31, 1985	
	Actual	As Adjusted(1)(2)
	(Unaudited)	
Balance Sheet Data:		
Working capital	$57,574	$96,502
Total assets	94,438	133,366
Total long-term debt	—	—
Stockholders' equity	71,845	110,773

(1) Assumes the Underwriters' over-allotment option is not exercised. See "Underwriting."
(2) Gives effect to the sale of shares offered by the Company hereby. The net proceeds have been added to working capital pending their use. See "Use of Proceeds."

FIGURE 23-4
Prospectus summary page.

ing, the issuer delivers the securities. The underwriters simultaneously deliver payment, net of their fees. The underwriters then deliver the securities to investors in return for payment.

<table>
<tr><td>**EXAMPLE**

GM's General Cash Offer of Common Stock</td><td>General Motors Corporation reported net losses of $2.0 and $4.5 billion in 1990 and 1991, respectively. It forecasted another operating loss in 1992. In addition, effective January 1, 1992, GM adopted Financial Accounting Standards Board Statement No. 106, *Employers' Accounting for Postretirement Benefits Other Than Pensions* (primarily postretirement medical, dental, vision, and life insurance benefits). This accounting change reduced GM's stockholders' equity by $20.6 billion.

GM decided to sell a new issue of common stock as one step in rebuilding its stockholders' equity. GM chose the general cash offer method. It filed a registration statement with the SEC on April 24, 1992. After receiving the SEC's comments, GM prepared the amendment. On May 20, 1992, GM filed the amended registration statement with the SEC, sold 57 million shares of its $1⅔ par value common stock at $39 per share, and realized net proceeds of $2.2 billion. ∎</td></tr>
</table>

Primary and Secondary Offerings

The GM common stock offering was a **primary offering**. In a primary offering, a firm sells newly issued shares to investors. Sometimes insiders or large institutional shareholders sell shares they hold in a registered public offering. Such an offering is known as a **secondary offering**. Shareholders sell previously issued shares that they purchased from the firm or from other investors. These offerings must also comply with SEC regulations.

<table>
<tr><td>**EXAMPLE**

GM Pension Funds' Secondary Offering</td><td>Firms sometimes find it advantageous to issue common shares to their pension funds in lieu of making cash contributions. The share issue augments the stockholders' equity without the stockholders having to pay the flotation costs they would incur in a public offering. At some point the pension funds might decide to sell some or all of these shares for diversification purposes. On March 13, 1995, General Motors Corporation contributed 173,163,187 shares of GM Class E Common Stock to its pension plans. The GM pension plans subsequently decided to sell 42,550,000 of these shares in a registered secondary offering. On June 8, 1995, the pension plans sold the shares for $42.375 each, realizing net proceeds of $1.75 billion. ∎</td></tr>
</table>

Role of the Underwriters

A firm can market its securities itself (as the U.S. government does), but most use investment bankers to underwrite the offerings because of their expertise and experience. Table 23-3 shows the ranking of the 15 leading managing underwriters in the United States during 1994. The ranking includes corporate debt and equity and taxable debt issued by government agencies but excludes tax-exempt municipal debt. Note that the five largest securities firms accounted for more than 55% of the underwriting volume.

Table 23-4 lists the 15 leading managing underwriters worldwide in 1994. It includes the same types of issuers as Table 23-3. Issues denominated in foreign currencies are ex-

ALL DOMESTIC ISSUES[a]
(FULL CREDIT TO LEAD MANAGER)
JANUARY 1, 1994–DECEMBER 31, 1994

Rank	Manager	Amount ($ millions)	%	Issues
1	Merrill Lynch	116,964.2	16.5	691
2	Lehman Brothers	77,284.7	10.9	557
3	CS First Boston	73,492.1	10.4	525
4	Goldman, Sachs	64,420.0	9.1	396
5	Morgan Stanley	58,675.9	8.3	434
6	PaineWebber	58,199.5	8.2	309
7	Salomon Brothers	57,238.0	8.1	482
8	Bear, Stearns	34,593.8	4.9	197
9	J.P. Morgan	26,472.5	3.7	177
10	Donaldson, Lufkin & Jenrette	23,284.4	3.3	220
11	Prudential Securities	16,380.2	2.3	137
12	Smith Barney	13,922.0	2.0	172
13	Citicorp	11,380.7	1.6	117
14	First Tennessee Bank	8,127.3	1.1	110
15	UBS	5,981.4	0.8	76
	Industry totals	708,555.5	100.0	6221

[a] Full credit is given to the lead managing underwriter.
Source: Investment Dealers' Digest, January 9, 1995, p. 16.

TABLE 23-3
Leading managing underwriters of general cash offers in the United States in 1994.

WORLDWIDE OFFERINGS[a]
(ALL DEBT AND EQUITY)
JANUARY 1, 1994–DECEMBER 31, 1994

Rank	Manager	Amount ($ millions)	%	Issues
1	Merrill Lynch	137,761.7	12.6	862
2	CS First Boston/Credit Suisse	96,895.6	8.9	647
3	Lehman Brothers	87,973.3	8.1	637
4	Goldman, Sachs	86,458.1	7.9	512
5	Morgan Stanley	74,775.4	6.8	556
6	Salomon Brothers	65,447.5	6.0	542
7	PaineWebber	61,743.7	5.7	344
8	J.P. Morgan	41,190.9	3.8	267
9	Bear, Stearns	35,499.0	3.3	209
10	Nomura Securities	23,666.6	2.2	151
11	Donaldson, Lufkin & Jenrette	23,586.4	2.2	226
12	UBS	21,699.9	2.0	153
13	Swiss Bank	17,066.5	1.6	113
14	Prudential Securities	16,506.9	1.5	142
15	Citicorp	15,182.9	1.4	222
	Industry totals	1,092,256.8	100.0	8972

[a] Full credit is given to the lead managing underwriter.
Source: Investment Dealers' Digest, January 9, 1995, p. 31.

TABLE 23-4
Leading managing underwriters of general cash offers worldwide in 1994.

pressed in an equivalent U.S. dollar amount. Again note the importance of the largest five underwriters. They accounted for more than 44% of the underwriting volume. Merrill Lynch is the leader both domestically and worldwide.

INVESTMENT BANKERS   The **investment banker** serves as an intermediary between the issuer and the purchasers. Investment bankers frequently serve as underwriters. They usually offer advice regarding the type of security to issue and the market that provides the most attractive terms. They also help prepare the documentation (such as the prospectus), and price and underwrite the new issue.

Investment bankers also devote much time and energy to designing new securities. They try to develop new securities that will reduce issuers' costs and increase investors' after-tax risk-adjusted returns. In keeping with the Principle of Valuable Ideas, they do so to create profitable securities-underwriting opportunities. The appendix to this chapter describes the benefits that securities innovation can provide.

UNDERWRITING   Underwriting is a form of insurance. In an **underwritten offering**, also referred to as a *purchase and sale*, the underwriters purchase the securities from the issuer at a fixed price. Then they reoffer them to investors at a specified price minus a specified *gross underwriting spread*. The underwriters bear the risk that the entire issue may not be salable at the initial offering price. If it is not, the underwriters sell the securities at the market clearing price and bear the loss.

SYNDICATED OFFERING PROCESS   In a **syndicated public offering**, an underwriting group, or *syndicate*, is formed to purchase the securities from the issuer and reoffer them to investors. The lead managing underwriter assembles a syndicate of securities firms it believes can best market the issue. Syndicating an offering spreads the underwriting risk among a group of securities firms.

EXAMPLE

A Syndicated Offering

Underwriters usually publish *tombstone advertisements* to advertise their role in connection with a public offering. (They are called tombstone advertisements because they look like tombstones.) The tombstone shown in Figure 23-5 is from the GM pension funds' secondary offering. It was a *global offering*. There were three *syndicates* of underwriters, one of U.S. underwriters (31.05 million shares), a second group identified as "international" (8.05 million shares), and a third, "Asian" syndicate (3.45 million shares). Merrill Lynch & Co. and Goldman, Sachs & Co. acted as joint global coordinators, coordinating the selling activity of the three syndicates and redistributing shares from one to another according to the demand for the offering. ■

UNDERWRITERS' COMPENSATION   For their services in an underwritten public offering, underwriters charge a **gross underwriting spread**. It is a percentage of the public offering price of the issue. This spread has three components. The *management fee*, usually 15% to 20% of the total spread, compensates the managing underwriters for their assistance in designing the issue, preparing the documentation, forming the syndicate, and directing the offering process. The *underwriting fee*, usually 15% to 20% of the total, compensates for the underwriting risk. The *selling concession*, generally 60% to 70% of the total, compensates for the selling effort.

June 8, 1995

42,550,000 Shares

General Motors Corporation

Class E Common Stock

Dividends are paid by General Motors Corporation on Class E Common Stock
based on the earnings of its wholly-owned subsidiary

Electronic Data Systems Corporation

Price $42.375 Per Share

Joint Global Coordinators

Merrill Lynch & Co.   **Goldman, Sachs & Co.**

Of the 42,550,000 shares sold, 40,550,000 shares were sold by the General Motors Special Hourly Employees
Pension Trust under the General Motors Hourly-Rate Employees Pension Plan and 2,000,000 shares were sold
by a trust under the General Motors Retirement Plan for Salaried Employees. United States Trust Company of
New York is the trustee for the General Motors Special Hourly Employees Pension Trust and Bankers Trust
Company is the trustee for a trust under the General Motors Retirement Plan for Salaried Employees.

Advisor to United States Trust Company of New York

Wasserstein Perella & Co.

Copies of the Prospectus may be obtained in any State or jurisdiction in which this announcement is circulated from only
such of the undersigned or other dealers or brokers as may lawfully offer these securities in such State or jurisdiction.

31,050,000 Shares
The above shares were underwritten by the following group of US Underwriters.

Merrill Lynch & Co.   **Goldman, Sachs & Co.**   **Lehman Brothers**

CS First Boston   **Morgan Stanley & Co.**   **Salomon Brothers Inc**

Bear, Stearns & Co. Inc.	Alex. Brown & Sons	Commerzbank Capital Markets Corporation
Dean Witter Reynolds Inc.	Dillon, Read & Co. Inc. A.G. Edwards & Sons, Inc.	Furman Selz
Hambrecht & Quist LLC	Invemed Associates, Inc.	Kemper Securities, Inc.
Lazard Freres & Co. LLC	Montgomery Securities J.P. Morgan Securities Inc.	Oppenheimer & Co., Inc.
PaineWebber Incorporated	Prudential Securities Incorporated	Robertson, Stephens & Company
Smith Barney Inc.	UBS Securities Inc.	Wertheim Schroder & Co.

Advest, Inc.   Sanford C. Bernstein & Co., Inc.   Cowen & Company   Dain Bosworth   Duff & Phelps Securities

First of Michigan Corporation   Janney Montgomery Scott Inc.   Edward D. Jones & Co.

C. J. Lawrence/Deutsche Bank   Legg Mason Wood Walker   Morgan Keegan & Company, Inc.

Needham & Company, Inc.   Principal Financial Securities, Inc.   Rauscher Pierce Refsnes, Inc.

Raymond James & Associates, Inc.   SoundView Financial Group, Inc.   Stephens Inc.

Sutro & Co. Incorporated   Wheat First Butcher Singer   M.R. Beal & Company   Doft & Co., Inc.

Ferris, Baker Watts   First Manhattan Co.   Luther, Smith & Small Inc.   Roney & Co.   Scott & Stringfellow, Inc.

Muriel Siebert & Co., Inc.   Stifel, Nicolaus & Company   Utendahl Capital Partners, L.P.   William K. Woodruff & Company

8,050,000 Shares
The above shares were underwritten by the following group of International Underwriters.

Merrill Lynch International Limited   **Goldman Sachs International**   **Lehman Brothers**

CS First Boston   **Morgan Stanley & Co.**   **Salomon Brothers International Limited**

ABN AMRO Hoare Govett	Cazenove & Co.	Credit Lyonnais Securities	Deutsche Bank
Dresdner Bank	NatWest Securities Limited	UBS Limited	S.G.Warburg Securities

3,450,000 Shares
The above shares were underwritten by the following group of Asian Underwriters.

Merrill Lynch International Limited   **Goldman Sachs (Asia) L.L.C.**   **Lehman Brothers**

HSBC Corporate Finance Limited   The Nikko Securities Co. (Asia) Limited   Nomura International (Hong Kong) Limited

Robert Fleming & Co. Limited   LG Securities Co., Ltd   Peregrine Capital Limited   J.B. Were & Son

FIGURE 23-5   Tombstone advertisement for GM pension funds' secondary offering.

Components of the Gross Underwriting Spread

GM pension funds' secondary offering involved a gross underwriting spread of $1.13 per share. The public offering price was $42.375 per share. The gross underwriting spread amounted to 2.67% (=1.13/42.375) of the public offering price. The management fee was $0.23 per share (20% of the gross underwriting spread). The underwriting fee was $0.25 (22%), and the selling concession was $0.65 (58%). ■

Underwriters' compensation represents a significant portion of the flotation expense. The other portion, *out-of-pocket expenses*, includes legal fees, accounting fees, printing costs, and so on. Table 23-5 shows gross underwriting spread and out-of-pocket expenses for public offerings of various types and sizes during the period 1975–1995. It is generally most expensive to float a common stock issue and least expensive to float an issue of (nonconvertible) bonds. This reflects differences in underwriting risks and the higher selling commissions required to distribute common stock issues. Large portions are usually marketed very broadly to individual investors. The significant economies of scale in issuing securities are also evident in Table 23-5.

Nonunderwritten Offerings

Securities issues sold through investment bankers are sometimes *nonunderwritten*. These are of two types.

BEST-EFFORTS OFFERING   In a *best-efforts offering*, investment bankers commit themselves only to use their best efforts to market the securities. There is no commitment to purchase—and therefore little financial risk to the investment bankers. Public offerings of the securities of smaller, lesser-known firms are often handled on a best-efforts basis. This may be

TABLE 23-5
Gross underwriting spread and out-of-pocket expenses as percentage of offering price for registered public offerings, 1975–1995.

ISSUE SIZE ($ MILLIONS)	COMMON STOCK			PREFERRED STOCK			CONVERTIBLE PREFERRED AND CONVERTIBLE DEBT			BONDS		
	Gross Under-writing Spread (%)	Out-of-Pocket Expense[a] (%)	Total (%)	Gross Under-writing Spread (%)	Out-of-Pocket Expense[a] (%)	Total (%)	Gross Under-writing Spread (%)	Out-of-Pocket Expense[a] (%)	Total (%)	Gross Under-writing Spread (%)	Out-of-Pocket Expense[a] (%)	Total (%)
Under 10.0	8.81	7.37	16.18	7.04	4.20	11.24	8.54	7.09	15.63	4.23	2.52	6.75
10.0 to 24.9	6.52	2.74	9.26	2.32	1.03	3.35	4.61	2.05	6.66	2.22	1.21	3.43
25.0 to 49.9	5.84	1.54	7.38	1.91	0.55	2.46	3.09	1.00	4.09	1.71	0.66	2.37
50.0 to 99.9	5.22	0.94	6.16	1.87	0.35	2.22	2.66	0.58	3.24	1.17	0.42	1.59
100.0 to 199.9	4.74	0.66	5.40	2.74	0.29	3.03	2.25	0.38	2.63	0.97	0.30	1.27
200 to 500	4.61	0.52	5.13	3.22	0.22	3.44	1.85	0.18	2.03	0.88	0.14	1.02
Over 500	4.79	0.29	5.08	3.17	0.14	3.31	1.22	0.09	1.31	0.96	0.18	1.14

[a] Includes legal fees, accounting fees, SEC filing fee, blue sky expenses, and printing, mailing, and miscellaneous out-of-pocket expenses.
Source: Securities Data Company, Inc.

because of the risk involved: The issuer is unable to find a securities firm willing to enter into a purchase-and-sale commitment (at least at an acceptable price).

DIRECT SALES OF SECURITIES   Some firms, including finance companies, may bypass the investment banks altogether and issue securities directly to investors. This approach reduces issuance expenses. The strategy can be cost-effective when the issuer has a natural market it can exploit, such as current securityholders.

In most cases, however, the investment banker has superior access to market information and to the channels of distribution. These advantages result from the investment banker's day-to-day interaction with prospective investors. Normally it is more economical for an issuer to sell securities through an investment banker.

Recently about 100 firms have begun to offer **direct stock-purchase programs.** Investors can buy shares of common stock directly from the issuer, usually without having to pay any transaction costs. They can usually telephone the firm to have their shares redeemed whenever they want to. Direct stock-purchase programs enable a firm to raise small amounts of new equity capital cheaply. But the syndicated offering process is still more appropriate when a firm wishes to raise a large amount of capital quickly.

Negotiated versus Competitive Offerings

A firm can offer securities publicly by using either competitive bidding or a negotiated offering. Under **competitive bidding**, the issuer specifies the type of securities it wishes to sell and invites securities firms to bid for the issue. It puts the securities up for bid, and the bidding process determines which investment bankers will market the issue and at what price.

In a **negotiated offering**, the issuer selects one or more securities firms to manage the offering and works closely with them to design the terms of the issue and determine the appropriate time to issue the securities. Until recently, registered public utility holding companies were required to offer securities competitively; like other firms they are now free to choose the offering technique.[5] Other electric utilities tend to offer debt and preferred stock by competitive bid (except during periods of high market volatility), but they generally sell common stock on a negotiated basis. Railroads frequently sell equipment trust certificates through competitive bidding. Until the introduction of *shelf registration*, other industrial firms seldom sold securities this way.

Are Competitive Offerings Cheaper?

Which offering method costs less? The question has been hotly debated, and the evidence is inconclusive. However, recent studies suggest that the competitive process usually does not lead to significant cost savings, except perhaps during stable market periods when strong competition among bidding groups results in lower costs. Competitive bidding generally results in lower underwriting spreads, but competitive underwritings may involve greater underwriting spreads than negotiated underwritings during periods of great market uncertainty.

Moreover, the negotiated offering process gives firms greater flexibility in the design of the securities and the timing of the issue. The issuer has not committed itself in advance to a specific set of terms (for example, maturity and redemption terms) or to a particular offering date (in competitive bidding, the date the bids are due). A negotiated offering also gives securities firms the opportunity to form the most effective selling group for the issue (rather than splitting into competing bidding groups). Securities firms also have a stronger incentive to as-

[5] Rule U-50 under the Public Utility Holding Company Act of 1935 required competitive bidding, although the SEC granted individual exemptions during volatile market periods. The SEC rescinded Rule U-50 in April 1994.

sess the demand for, and stimulate interest in, the issue before pricing a negotiated offering. Unlike the situation in competitive bidding, they know that they will have the securities to sell.

Shelf Registration

The SEC adopted Rule 415, commonly known as the *shelf registration rule*, in November 1983. Rule 415 allows a firm to register an inventory of securities of a particular type for up to two years. It can then sell the securities whenever it chooses during that time. The securities remain "on the shelf" until they are issued.

Shelf registration has improved firms' financing flexibility. A firm does not have to file a new registration statement each time it offers securities, which reduces flotation costs. Securities can be sold within minutes. Also, a single shelf registration statement can cover many types of debt securities. This enables issuers to design the security at the time they sell it to exploit any special investor preferences and minimize their cost of funds.

Rule 415 has effectively extended competitive bidding to issues of securities by the roughly 2000 large firms that qualify to use shelf registration. Securities firms and institutional investors can bid for securities that a firm has on the shelf. But the evidence is mixed on whether Rule 415 has had any impact on transaction costs.

Self-Check Questions

1. What are the steps involved in a general cash offer?
2. What is the difference between a primary offering and a secondary offering?
3. What is the role of the underwriters in a general cash offer?
4. What are the two types of nonunderwritten offerings?
5. What is shelf registration?

23.3 PRIVATE PLACEMENTS

As an alternative to selling securities to the general investing public, firms can sell securities directly to institutional investors through a **private placement**. Private placements must satisfy the requirements for exemption from registration under the Securities Act of 1933. These requirements limit the investors to whom unregistered securities may be offered for sale. There are also significant restrictions on resale to other investors, which makes such securities illiquid.

Investment bankers often assist with private placements. They serve as *agents* for the issuer. The issuer sells the securities directly to investors. The securities firms help negotiate the terms of sale but do not underwrite the issue. Such offerings are sold on a best-efforts basis.

Market for Private Placements

Because they are not registered, privately placed securities are not freely tradable. For this reason, securities regulations require firms to offer securities privately only to investors deemed sophisticated enough to make an independent determination of their investment merits. Such investors include insurance companies, credit companies, pension funds, commercial banks, college endowments, and wealthy individuals, among others.

Rule 144A Private Placements

In April 1990, the SEC adopted Rule 144A under the Securities Act of 1933. It has broadened the market for private placements in the United States, especially for foreign issuers. In a Rule 144A private placement, the issuer sells its unregistered securities to one or more investment banks, which then resell the securities to "qualified institutional buyers" (QIBs).[6] This process is much like an underwritten public offering.

Rule 144A has been a success. As of year-end 1995, more than half the private placements of debt were done under this rule.

Advantages of a Private Placement

A private placement offers the following advantages over a public offering:

1. *Lower issuance costs* for smaller issues. A private placement avoids the costs of registering the securities, printing prospectuses, and obtaining credit ratings. Also, the private placement agent's fee is generally a lot less than the underwriting expenses for a comparable public offering, and can be avoided altogether if the issuer negotiates directly with investors.

2. *Issues can be placed more quickly* for firms that do not qualify for shelf registration. Registering securities requires time to prepare the registration statement and have the SEC review it.

3. *Greater flexibility of issue size.* The private market is more receptive to smaller issues. Issues of only a few million dollars each are not uncommon. Public debt and preferred stock issues of less than $50 million principal amount are usually more costly because their small size decreases their liquidity and thus lessens their attractiveness to investors.

4. *Greater flexibility of security arrangements* and other terms. Private investors are capable of analyzing complex security arrangements, and it's easier to tailor the terms of an issue to suit both sides of the transaction. It's also easier to obtain lenders' consents to any subsequent changes in terms both because the debtholders are sophisticated and because there are fewer of them.

5. *More favorable share price reaction than a public offering.* Studies have found that the stock market usually reacts positively when a firm announces a private placement of debt, convertible debt, or equity. The larger private placements of debt tend to elicit the most positive market response. The positive impact tends to be especially large for firms that have never issued debt publicly. These results are consistent with the notion that private placement leads to reduced information asymmetries, permits better monitoring, and provides a certification of the issuer by investors. This contrasts with public offerings of equity and convertible debt, which generally have a negative announcement effect.

6. *Lower cost of resolving financial distress.* Private debt tends to be easier than public debt to restructure, because it generally involves fewer and more sophisticated investors. Empirical research has found that financial distress is more likely to be resolved outside bankruptcy when more of the firm's debt is owed to banks but is less likely to be resolved outside bankruptcy when the firm has more than one public debt issue outstanding. These findings are consistent with lower costs of resolving financial distress.

Private Placements versus Public Offerings

In connection with a public offering, investment bankers investigate the issuer on behalf of the investing public (the process is referred to as *due diligence*). In a private placement, the institutional investors make their own investigation. Private placement may therefore allow access to information about a firm that is not available to the general investing public. With respect

---

[6] A QIB generally is defined as a financial institution that invests on a discretionary basis at least $100 million in securities of unaffiliated firms or Treasury securities. QIBs can trade freely with each other in securities that have not been registered with the SEC.

TABLE 23-6
Comparison of the characteristics of the public bond, private placement, and bank-loan markets.

| | DEBT MARKET | | |
CHARACTERISTIC	Public Bond	Private Placement	Bank Loan
Maturity	Long	Medium to long	Short
Interest rate	Fixed	Fixed	Floating
Severity of information problems posed by the average borrower	Small	Moderate	High
Average loan size	Large	Medium to large	Small
Average borrower size	Large	Medium to large	Small
Average observable risk level	Lowest	Moderate	High
Covenants	Fewest	Fewer, looser	Many, tight
Collateral	Rare	Less frequent	Frequent
Renegotiation	Infrequent	Less frequent	Frequent
Lender monitoring	Minimal	Significant	Intense
Liquidity of loan	High	Low	Low
Principal lender	Various	Life insurance cos.	Banks

Source: Carey et al. (1993), p. 33.

to monitoring, private debt issues usually have more restrictive covenants than comparable public debt issues. The tighter covenants improve monitoring efficiency.

Finally, the purchasers—because they tend to be large, sophisticated institutional investors—are making a comment about the firm's quality in their very willingness to purchase and hold the firm's securities. A larger private placement, because of the accompanying increased commitment of funds, may intensify all of these considerations. This communicates greater confidence in the firm's quality.

Table 23-6 compares the public and private bond markets. It also compares these two markets to the bank-loan market. Bond investors in the public market are generally willing to accept longer maturities than are investors in the other two markets. Public debt issues tend to be larger on average than private debt issues, and they usually have less restrictive covenants. This is at least partly because registered securities are more liquid than privately placed securities or bank loans. Private investors require tighter covenants, are more likely to require collateral, and monitor borrowers more closely than do public investors. Lender reputation is very important in the private market. Private lenders seem to perceive that they have significant reputational capital at stake when they decide to lend funds. Hence, lending standards in the private market tend to be rigorous. This is consistent with the greater confidence communicated by private lenders' commitment of funds.

Compared to the public and private debt markets, the bank-loan market involves shorter maturities, tighter covenants, greater likelihood of collateral requirements, greater likelihood of covenant renegotiation, and closer monitoring. Also, banks prefer to lend at a floating interest rate.

Disadvantages of a Private Placement

A private placement has the following disadvantages compared to a public offering:

1. *Higher yield.* To compensate for the lack of liquidity, purchasers of privately placed securities require a yield premium relative to publicly traded securities.

2. *More stringent covenants and more restrictive terms.* Private purchasers insist on tighter covenant restrictions to compensate for the greater agency costs. Private issuers are often not public firms and thus not subject to the SEC's reporting requirements. The covenants alert investors when something "goes wrong," such as a significant reduction in net worth. Private lenders have also insisted on tighter protection against *event risk*, the risk that stockholders might initiate events such as a lever-

aged buyout that could expropriate bondholder wealth. These covenants can limit a firm's operating flexibility, possibly forcing it to pass up profitable investment opportunities.

Self-Check Questions
1. Who are the main purchasers of privately placed securities?
2. What are the advantages and disadvantages of a private placement as compared to a general cash offer?
3. What is a Rule 144A private placement?

23.4 COMMON EQUITY FINANCING

Large firms generally raise the bulk of new common equity internally—that is, by retaining a portion of earnings. But smaller or rapidly growing firms usually also issue new common stock to raise funds. Even large firms sometimes issue new common equity through sizable public offerings. In addition, many firms have instituted dividend reinvestment or employee stock purchase plans that generate additional common equity on a continuing basis.

Main Features of Common Stock

Common stock is a perpetual security. (Recall that this is the basis for the dividend growth model we described in Chapter 5.) Thus common stock is not redeemable by the issuer. However, the issuer can offer to repurchase shares, as we discussed in Chapters 17 and 18. And common stockholders are entitled to receive any dividends the firm's board of directors declares, although the board is not contractually obligated to declare any.

A firm's corporate charter specifies the features of its common stock. Many of these features are determined by the corporate laws of the state in which the firm is incorporated.

Rights and Privileges of Common Stock

The rights and privileges of common stock fall into four categories: voting rights, dividend rights, liquidation rights, and preemptive rights. These are the same rights of ownership we discussed in Chapter 1. Let's take another quick look at each.

DIVIDEND RIGHTS State laws usually require that all shares belonging to a single class of common stock must share pro rata in any distributions of dividends to that class of shares. Some firms have two or more classes of common stock with different dividend rights, although this is unusual in the United States.

VOTING RIGHTS Voting may be either cumulative or noncumulative. **Cumulative voting** allows a shareholder to target her votes to a subset of the directors up for reelection. For example, a holder of 100 shares could cast all 100 votes for a single director. State law usually requires an annual election of directors but many permit staggered elections. A popular structure is to have directors serve three-year terms, with one-third standing for reelection each year. Shareholders can vote in person or can transfer their vote to a second party who can vote it by proxy. Management solicits shareholder proxies and usually secures enough proxies to ensure the election of its nominated slate. However, dissident shareholders can also solicit proxies to mount a **proxy contest** for control. Although their chances of succeeding are small, dissidents have won some battles.

LIQUIDATION RIGHTS   Common stockholders are entitled to share pro rata in any distributions of assets by a firm when it winds up its affairs and liquidates. They get what is left over after all senior securityholders have been paid in full.

PREEMPTIVE RIGHTS   When common stockholders have *preemptive rights*, the firm must offer any new issue of common stock—or any new issue of other securities convertible into common stock—to existing shareholders before it can offer those securities to any other prospective investors.

Classification of Shares

A firm's corporate charter limits the number of *authorized shares* of common stock. A firm cannot issue shares unless it has authorized shares available. Increasing the number of authorized shares is usually noncontroversial, but it does require a shareholder vote.

Shares become *issued shares* when a firm sells them to investors. Issued shares consist of *outstanding shares* and *treasury shares*. Outstanding shares are held by investors. Treasury shares are those that the firm has repurchased from investors. It is the outstanding shares that are used in per-share calculations.

EXAMPLE

Du Pont's Earnings Per Share

Table 23-7 shows the stockholders' equity section of the 1994 balance sheet and the 1994 earnings-per-share calculation for E. I. du Pont de Nemours and Company. This firm had 900 million shares of common stock authorized at year-end 1994. There were 681,004,944 issued shares and none in the treasury. Du Pont had an average of 679,999,916 common shares outstanding during 1994 and an EPS of $4.00 (per average *outstanding* share). ■

TABLE 23-7
Stockholders' equity and earnings per share of E.I. du Pont de Nemours and Company for 1994 (dollar amounts in millions except per-share amounts).

	AT 12/31/94
Preferred stock, without par value:	
$4.50 Series—1,672,594 shares	$ 167
$3.50 Series— 700,000 shares	70
	237
Common stock, $0.60 par value:	
900,000,000 shares authorized;	
681,004,944 shares issued	408
Additional paid-in capital	4,771
Reinvested earnings	7,406
Common stockholders' equity	
	12,585
Total stockholders' equity	$ 12,822
Net income	$ 2,727
Preferred dividends	10
Available for common	$ 2,717
Average common shares outstanding	679,999,916
Earnings per common share	$ 4.00

Source: E.I. du Pont de Nemours and Company, *1994 Annual Report to Shareholders,* pp. 39 and 41.

Shares of common stock are issued with or without par value. Because some states do not permit firms to sell shares at a price below par value, par values are generally very small. Par value therefore has little significance.

Book Value per Common Share

Book value per common share is the ratio of common stockholders' equity, adjusted for any liquidation premium on any *preferred* or *preference stock* the firm may have outstanding, to the number of common shares outstanding on that date:

$$\text{Book value per common share} = \frac{\text{Common stockholders' equity}}{\text{Number of common shares outstanding}} \qquad (23.1)$$

Recall from Chapter 2 that the market value per share can differ—and differ very significantly—from the book value per share. In fact, one rough measure of the value a firm has created is its ratio of book to market value per share.

Du Pont's Book Value Per Common Share

EXAMPLE

Book value per common share is the value each share would have if the firm's assets were sold and its liabilities were paid off at the amounts shown on the balance sheet, including preferred stock paid off at its involuntary liquidation value. Of course, book values generally bear no direct relation to the true liquidation values of a firm's assets, because book value is based on historical cost and accounting measures of depreciation. Du Pont's book value per common share at year-end 1994 was $18.48 (= 12,585/681).

Du Pont's preferred stock does not carry any *liquidation premium*. But to illustrate how a liquidation premium affects the calculation of book value per common share, suppose that the liquidation premium is 5%. Thus the liquidation value of the preferred stock would be $249 million (= 1.05 × 237 million), $12 million greater than its face amount. Reducing common stockholders' equity by this amount leaves $12,573 million available to common stockholders, or

$$\text{Book value per common share adjusted for preferred stock liquidation premium} = \frac{12,573}{681} = \$18.46$$

■

Targeted Common Stock

Several firms have issued one or more classes of common stock with dividends tied to the performance of a particular subsidiary. Such shares are called *targeted common stock*. General Motors Corporation was the first firm to issue them. It issued GM class E common stock in October 1984 when it acquired Electronic Data Systems (EDS) from Texas entrepreneur H. Ross Perot.

Targeted common stock enables investors to invest in the businesses of a corporation in whatever proportions they want. For example, one investor might want to invest in USX's steel business (U.S. Steel) but not in its oil and gas business (Marathon Group). Another investor might have the opposite preferences. The first investor can buy shares of USX-U.S. Steel. The second can buy shares of USX-Marathon. Other investors might buy shares of both stocks but in differing proportions. So long as there are no stocks that are perfect substitutes for USX-U.S. Steel and USX-Marathon, creating these series of targeted common stocks gives investors new investment opportunities. Targeted common stock can add value by making the capital market more nearly *complete*.

Targeted common stock can be used for incentive compensation purposes for subsidiary employees. For example, when GM bought EDS, one reason why the class E stock was created was that Perot believed EDS's incentive compensation would be more effective if it was tied to changes in EDS's value rather than to GM's overall value.

23.5 PUBLIC OFFERING OF COMMON STOCK

Common stock is almost always offered on a negotiated basis. Common stock offered to the public must be registered with the SEC.

Costs of the Offering

General cash offers have three cost components: (1) the gross underwriting spread, (2) the market impact of the announcement of the offering and subsequent marketing activity, and (3) out-of-pocket expenses, such as lawyers' and accountants' fees, engraving and printing, and mailing. Out-of-pocket expenses tend to be fixed expenses and are therefore a significant cost factor only in connection with very small offerings.

Market Impact

A firm's share price often declines upon the announcement of a public offering. This may seem puzzling. If the corporation intends to invest the proceeds of the issue in positive-NPV projects, the share price should increase. But evidence indicates that the Signaling Principle is at work. The share price falls because the offering sends a negative signal to investors. In Chapter 15 we illustrated this type of signaling with examples of how the problem of *adverse selection* affects the firm's financing decisions.

If management acts in its shareholders' best interest, it will refrain from issuing shares when it believes the firm's stock is relatively undervalued in the market and will instead sell new shares when it believes the firm's shares are relatively overvalued. Accordingly, the announcement of the new issue may signal overvaluation and lead to a negative market reaction. Taking this line of reasoning a step further, the larger the size of the offering, the more the share price should decrease.

23.6 RIGHTS OFFERINGS

Instead of offering common stock directly to the general public, a firm may offer new stock to its current shareholders on a privileged-subscription basis. This is called a **rights offering**, because the firm distributes to its shareholders *rights* (options) to subscribe for additional shares at a specified price.

From World War II to the 1960s, roughly two-thirds of all common stock issues were rights offerings. But beginning in the late 1960s, virtually all large U.S. firms, which tend to have widely dispersed shareholdings, obtained shareholder approval to eliminate preemptive rights. However, firms outside the United States tend to rely heavily on rights offerings to raise additional equity capital. For example, the London Stock Exchange changed its rules in 1975 to allow general cash offers. Nevertheless, rights offerings continue to be the predominant method of external equity financing in the U.K. In some countries, firms are required by law to sell new share issues through rights offerings.

The Eurotunnel project, begun in 1984 and completed in 1994, involved the construction of twin-bore rail tunnels beneath the English Channel to link the rail systems of France and the United Kingdom. When cost overruns made it necessary to raise additional common equity, Eurotunnel conducted an underwritten rights offering in November 1990 that raised the equivalent of about $1 billion (£532 million, net of expenses).

Further cost overruns necessitated another equity offering. This time Eurotunnel raised £816 million (net of expenses) through an underwritten rights offering in May and June 1994. ■

Eurotunnel's Two Rights Offerings

EXAMPLE

How a Rights Offering Works

In a rights offering, the firm distributes to each shareholder one right for each share the holder owns as of the specified *record date* for the offering. Rights are call options on newly issued shares. The firm will indicate the number of rights required to purchase one new share of stock. For instance, stockholders may be given rights to buy one new share for every three shares already owned. As with other market-traded options, a right has a time until expiration and a strike price. The time until expiration is called the *subscription period*. The strike price for a specified number of rights is called the *subscription price*.

Shareholders can either (1) exercise the rights and subscribe for shares or (2) sell the rights if they are transferable (they usually are). If the shareholders do neither, the rights expire, worthless, at the close of business on the expiration date. If shareholders wish to purchase extra shares, they can purchase additional rights from other shareholders who choose to sell their rights. Or if the firm gives shareholders an *oversubscription privilege* to purchase the shares for which other shareholders fail to subscribe, they can buy them from the issuer to the extent that they are available.

Value of Rights

The Options Principle states that options are valuable. Because a right is a call option, it will always have a positive value prior to its expiration. Recall from Chapter 8 that the value of an option, and therefore of a right, is a function of (1) the strike price, (2) the value of the underlying stock, (3) the time until expiration, (4) the variance of the underlying stock's return, and (5) the riskless return. In addition, the value of a right depends on its dilutive effect, which is caused by its creation of new equity. Loosely speaking, the *dilutive effect* is the difference between the strike price (the new equity) and the market value (existing equity). Recall that when the value of the underlying stock is more than the strike price, a call option is in-the-money. The smaller the strike price relative to the share price, the more valuable the call option.

To encourage subscription, rights are issued in-the-money. That is, the issuer sets the subscription price at less than the market price of its stock on the record date. Because of the short time until expiration, the exercise value—which is based on the difference between the strike price and the share price—is the main thing that determines the value of a right. That is, with a very short life, the option's time premium is negligible.

The initial value of each right just after the offering is announced, and when the stock is trading *rights-on* (that is, the rights are still attached to the stock), is approximately

$$R_C = \frac{P_R - S}{N + 1} \tag{23.2}$$

where R_C is the value of the right, P_R is the market value of a share trading rights-on, S is the strike price, and N is the number of rights to purchase one new share. Where does $N + 1$ come from? The firm will issue one new share for every N shares currently outstanding.[7]

EXAMPLE

The Long Island Lighting Company Rights Offering

Some years ago the Long Island Lighting Company offered 6,402,515 additional shares of its common stock to its current stockholders on the basis of one new share for seven rights (that is, each seven shares already owned) plus a subscription price of $17.15 per new share during the 18-day subscription period. At the time, shares were trading at $18.375.

The initial value of each right issued in connection with this rights offering was

$$R_C = \frac{\$18.375 - \$17.15}{7 + 1} = \$0.1531$$

Equation (23.2) is only an approximation of the value of a right, because it ignores the right's time premium. But it is a very good approximation because the time premium is very small. This is because the time until expiration is very short, the right is significantly in-the-money, and the dilutive effect of a single right is negligible.

After the ex-date, the stock is said to trade *ex-rights* because the purchaser of the shares is not entitled to receive the rights. On the ex-date, then, the share price decreases by the value of the right, which is no longer attached to it. Therefore, the share price ex-rights, P_E, is

$$P_E = P_R - R_C \tag{23.3}$$

In the case of the Long Island Lighting rights,

$$P_E = \$18.375 - \$0.1531 = \$18.2219$$

Immediately after the rights offering, the market value of each right will vary with the price of the firm's common stock:

$$R_C = \frac{P_E - S}{N} \tag{23.4}$$

We divide by N, rather than $N + 1$, because the rights have been separated from the shares.

---

[7] Compare equation (23.2) to Equation (17.2). Note the symmetry. The strike price is set below the share price in a rights offering (Equation 23.2) but above it for transferable put rights (Equation 17.2). The purpose in both cases is to make the option in-the-money. Also, one new share is issued for every N outstanding shares in a rights offering (Equation 23.2); transferable put rights eliminate one out of N shares (Equation 17.2).

Underwritten Rights Offering

Rights offerings are frequently underwritten. The underwriters are paid a stand-by fee for each subscription share, plus a take-up fee on shares the underwriters acquire through exercise of rights and on unsubscribed shares.

Advantages and Disadvantages of a Rights Offering

The fundamental idea underlying a rights offering is to provide shareholders with the option to retain their proportionate ownership in a firm when it sells additional common shares. However, because of the separation of ownership and control, this probably benefits only shareholders with large holdings.

It is often argued that a rights offering is beneficial to shareholders because they can buy shares at a bargain price or because they perceive the rights as a kind of dividend. But a stockholder receives no benefits from the rights other than the option of retaining proportionate ownership. The firm's share price falls on the ex-date, and the decrease in price offsets the value of a right, as in the case of a stock dividend. The shareholder is just as well off after the rights offering as before it, provided that he either sells the rights or exercises them.

The main benefit of a rights offering is that it protects existing shareholders from a potential loss of wealth that can result from a public offering. To induce sales, shares are offered at a price below the current market value. In a public offering, this inducement transfers wealth from existing shareholders to the purchasers of the newly created shares. The rights offering avoids this wealth transfer. It gives the inducement to existing shareholders, so long as they sell or exercise their rights.

A rights offering may also be more beneficial than a public offering to a firm that does not have broad market appeal or a firm that has concentrated stock ownership, because it enables the selling effort to be focused on investors who already own shares and are therefore familiar with the firm. In addition, common stock issued in a rights offering can be purchased on margin, whereas common stock issued in a public offering cannot.

On the other hand, there are two principal disadvantages to a rights offering: It generally takes longer to complete, and it eliminates the possible transaction cost savings of selling large blocks of shares to institutions that do not currently hold the stock.

Dividend Reinvestment Plans

Many firms sponsor dividend reinvestment plans. A **dividend reinvestment plan (DRP)** allows each common stockholder to use her dividends to purchase shares of the firm's common stock. In a *new-issue DRP*, the firm sells newly issued shares to its shareholders. The price is often slightly (up to 5%) below the stock's market price. New-issue DRPs resemble rights offerings; in effect, the firm offers new shares pro rata to existing shareholders. An *open-market DRP* is different. In such a plan, the firm uses the reinvested dividends to repurchase shares on behalf of shareholders. A new-issue DRP is a source of new capital; an open-market DRP is not.

Self-Check Questions

1. Rights offerings of common stock involve what type of option?

2. How does a rights offering work?

3. What determines the value of a right?

4. What is the difference between a share trading rights-on and a share trading ex-rights?

5. What are the advantages and disadvantages of a rights offering as compared to a general cash offer?

23.7 GOING PUBLIC AND GOING PRIVATE

When a firm's common stock is not registered for listing on an exchange or for trading in the over-the-counter market, it is said to be privately held. Privately held firms normally do not have to file regular quarterly financial reports with the SEC. Therefore they are also private in the sense that much of the information concerning them is not public.

When a firm makes an **initial public offering (IPO)**, selling its common stock to the investing public for the first time, it becomes publicly held. It also becomes subject to the regular reporting requirements of the securities laws. On the other hand, when a small group of investors (usually including the firm's managers), buys up all the common stock, the firm is said to *go private* because it becomes privately held.

Going Public

Firms go public through an initial public offering. An IPO is a major event in a firm's life. The decision to go public depends on a number of factors. The key stockholders must conclude that the advantages outweigh the disadvantages.

To make a successful IPO, a firm must (1) find capable underwriters to sponsor and assist it and (2) complete its offering at an acceptable price. Its ability to achieve these goals will depend largely on its profitability and future prospects. A firm that wishes to go public normally tries to do so when it believes the stock market is most receptive.

Table 23-8 shows how the volume of IPOs varied during the 20-year period from 1975 to 1994. The receptivity of investors depends to a great extent on the overall prospect for capital gains, which depends on the tone of the stock market and on how investors expect these capital gains to be taxed. The new-issues boom of 1980 to 1983 coincided with a major stock market rally, when the S&P 500 index increased by nearly 50% between 1979 and 1983. It

TABLE 23-8
IPO (initial public offering) volume, 1975–1994 (dollar amounts in millions).

| YEAR | INITIAL PUBLIC OFFERINGS | | | S&P 500 INDEX | |
	Number	Aggregate Value	Average Size	Beginning of Year	Change During Year
1975	5	$ 176	$35.2	68.6	31.5%
1976	40	337	8.4	90.2	19.2
1977	31	221	7.1	107.5	−11.5
1978	38	225	5.9	95.1	1.1
1979	62	398	6.4	96.1	12.3
1980	149	1,387	9.3	107.9	25.9
1981	347	3,055	8.8	135.8	−9.7
1982	122	1,339	10.9	122.6	14.7
1983	683	12,438	18.2	140.6	17.3
1984	355	3,808	10.7	164.9	1.4
1985	353	8,348	23.6	167.2	26.4
1986	702	18,088	25.8	211.3	14.6
1987	522	17,109	32.8	242.2	2.0
1988	228	5,940	26.1	247.1	12.4
1989	209	6,082	29.1	277.7	27.3
1990	172	4,519	26.3	353.4	−6.6
1991	367	16,411	44.7	330.2	26.3
1992	517	24,138	46.7	417.1	4.5
1993	709	41,721	58.8	435.7	7.1
1994	607	28,341	46.7	466.5	−1.5

Sources: Securities Data Company, Inc., and *S&P 500 1994 Directory,* Standard & Poor's Corporation, New York, pp. 423 and 424.

also began soon after the 1978 reduction in the capital gains tax rate and was enhanced by another reduction in 1981.

PREPARING THE FIRM TO GO PUBLIC   Before going public, firms may have to modify some of their practices and put dealings with insiders on an arm's-length basis. Individuals from outside the firm usually have to be added to the board of directors to monitor the firm's performance on behalf of public investors. The firm will have to change its accounting procedures to conform to generally accepted accounting principles, including regular audits, if they do not conform already.

PRICING THE OFFERING   Underwriters generally try to price an IPO 10% to 15% below the expected trading price. In some cases it is substantially more than 15% "underpriced." Underwriters apparently underprice IPOs to increase their attractiveness and the likelihood that the shares will perform well in the aftermarket. However, research shows that IPOs generally underperform the market for up to three years after the initial price surge following their issuance.

Advantages of Going Public.

Going public offers several advantages.

Raise New Capital.   Going public raises additional capital. Also, shares generally bring a higher price in the public market than in the venture capital or private placement markets.

Achieve Liquidity and Diversification for Current Shareholders.   Existing shareholders usually sell portions of their shares as part of the IPO. This gives them a cash return on their investment and allows them to diversify their investment portfolios.

Create a Negotiable Instrument.   Going public makes the common stock negotiable and creates a visible market value. After going public, the firm usually finds it easier to acquire other firms in exchange for shares of its stock. If all else is equal, marketable securities are worth more because of their greater liquidity.

Increase the Firm's Equity Financing Flexibility.   A publicly traded firm is able to raise additional equity more quickly and more cheaply than it could if it were not public.

Enhance the Firm's Image.   Because of the standards that investment bankers apply before agreeing to take a firm public, going public represents a milestone in a firm's development.

Disadvantages of Going Public

Going public is not without disadvantages, however.

Disclosure Requirements.   A public firm is subject to regulations governing regular reporting to shareholders, proxy solicitation and insider trading, and to other regulations. A public firm must publicly report on a regular basis information regarding its operating results, financial condition, significant business developments, and other sensitive matters such as officers' compensation and transactions between the firm and its management.

Accountability to Public Shareholders and Market Pressure to Perform Short Term.   As a result of information asymmetries, the managers of a publicly held firm might make decisions that look good in the short run but are significantly inferior in the long run. "Managing" quarter-to-quarter earnings can also hamper a firm's operating flexibility.

Pressure to Pay Dividends.   Public shareholders expect the firm to begin paying dividends eventually. This may not be best if the firm is able to reinvest the funds in positive-NPV projects, as we showed in Chapter 5.

Dilution of Ownership Interest.   Existing shareholders lose a portion of their ownership interest to public shareholders. This can be a significant change, and existing shareholders can even lose voting control.

Expense of Going Public.   Going public involves significant expenses—generally from 6% to 13% of the amount of the offering, and even more for very small offerings. Going public can also take a substantial amount of valuable management time.

Higher Estate Valuation.   Negotiability increases a stock's value because of liquidity. Estate tax obligations are consequently greater when a stock is publicly traded. On the other hand, a public market provides a way of selling shares to get cash to pay the tax.

Decision to List the Shares on an Exchange

When a firm goes public, it must decide where its shares will trade. Each of the exchanges and NASDAQ have established minimum listing requirements (net income, shares held by other than insiders, etc.) and reporting requirements. The NYSE's minimum requirements for listing are the most demanding. In order to have its stock listed on an exchange or quoted in the NASDAQ, a firm that meets the listing/quotation criteria files an application, pays a modest fee, and agrees to abide by the disclosure requirements and other rules.

Are there benefits to listing the stock on the NYSE or some other exchange rather than having it quoted on NASDAQ? An exchange appoints a single market maker for each stock it lists. The market maker commits its capital to maintain an orderly market and must adhere to the rules of the exchange. In contrast, there is no central market and no single market maker committed to an over-the-counter (OTC) stock. Many firms feel that prestige is associated with their stock being exchange-listed. Research shows that exchange markets have lower transaction costs. However, they are not necessarily more liquid than the NASDAQ market. And many prestigious firms, including Apple Computer, Intel, and Microsoft, have remained with NASDAQ even though they could qualify for exchange listing.

Going Private

Going private is the reverse of going public. When a small group of investors (usually in conjunction with members of senior management) purchases the entire common equity of a publicly traded firm, the firm becomes privately held. It is no longer subject to the financial reporting requirements of a public firm. If the disadvantages of being publicly owned outweigh the advantages, it is possible to revert to private ownership. Because both going public and going private involve substantial transaction costs, we do not observe firms frequently switching back and forth.

Self-Check Questions
1. What is an IPO?
2. What are the critical steps involved when a firm goes public?
3. What are the advantages and disadvantages of going public?
4. What is "going private"?

23.8 FEATURES OF PREFERRED STOCK AND PREFERENCE STOCK

Preferred stock and **preference stock** are "hybrid" securities. They combine features of common stock and features of debt. They rank senior to common stock, and junior to debt, in claims on the firm's operating income and on the firm's assets in the event of liquidation. The only significant difference between preferred stock and preference stock is that preferred stock is senior.

Dividends must be paid in full on the preferred stock before the firm can pay dividends on its preference stock. Firms normally issue preference stock only when charter limitations prevent them from issuing additional preferred stock. Because of their similarity, we will refer simply to preferred stock.

Preferred stock has the following key features:

1. A *par value* or *stated value*, generally $25, $50, or $100 per share. Issues that are to be sold mainly to institutional investors are usually given a $100 par value. Issues targeted to individual investors are usually given a $25 par value so that a round lot (100 shares) will cost only $2500.

2. A stated *dividend rate or dividend rate formula*. Preferred stock pays dividends quarterly, like common stock, but at a stated rate, like debt. The dividends are not tax-deductible. Also, preferred stock issues usually have a *cumulative dividend feature*. That is, missed dividends are accumulated. The issuer must pay this cumulative amount in full before paying any cash dividends on its common stock.

   Regulated utility firms have been the heaviest issuers of fixed-dividend-rate preferred stock. Preferred stock generally represents between 10% and 15% of an electric utility firm's capitalization. Banking institutions have been the heaviest issuers of floating-rate preferred stock.

3. An *optional redemption provision*. Preferred stock usually has optional redemption provisions similar to those found in debt issues. They give the firm the option to redeem the preferred stock at a stated price per share that is fixed at the time of issue.

4. A *mandatory redemption provision*. Sinking fund preferred stock contains a *sinking fund*. It requires the issuer to redeem the preferred stock, usually at par value, according to a specified schedule. *Perpetual preferred stock* is not required to be redeemed.

Why do firms issue preferred stock? Sinking fund preferred stock is like debt except that dividend payments are not tax-deductible. However, missing a scheduled dividend payment will not force the issuer into default. Preferred stock dividends qualify for a 70% dividends-received deduction when the preferred stockholder is a corporation.

Suppose a firm does not have taxable income.[8] It could sell preferred stock to tax-paying corporate investors instead of issuing debt. This creates a tax asymmetry that can make preferred stock cheaper than debt. Because the issuer is non-tax-paying, issuing preferred stock does not involve any loss of tax shield benefits, but it might result in a lower after-tax required return. Preferred stock yields are usually lower than the yields on comparable debt instruments because of the 70% dividends-received deduction available to corporate investors. This tax-based rationale might explain the tremendous growth in the market for adjustable-rate preferred stock, which is discussed in the appendix at the end of this chapter.

There is a second rationale for preferred stock financing. We noted that regulated utility companies frequently issue preferred stock. They can pass preferred dividends, but not common dividends, through to their customers. This provides an incentive to issue preferred stock. The utility's customers, rather than its shareholders, suffer the tax disadvantage when the regulators let the utility substitute some preferred stock for debt. A high-dividend clientele might find preferred stock more attractive than the utility's common stock, because dividends compose a greater percentage of the preferred stock's return. But the amount of preferred stock that is "just right" remains a mystery.

Self-Check Questions

1. What is preferred stock? What is preference stock? What is the difference between the two?

2. What are the main features of preferred stock?

3. Why do firms issue preferred stock?

---

[8] A combination of carrying forward tax losses from prior years and having substantial deductions for depreciation and other expenses currently could give rise to such a situation.

NORTHWEST'S INITIAL PUBLIC OFFERING

Recall that Northwest had initially hoped to get about $20 per share. But Northwest's investment bankers found they had to reduce the price to $13 to induce purchases. With 108 million shares to be outstanding after the IPO, the price difference would be $756 million [= (20 − 13)108 million]. Table 23-9 shows the dilution from the IPO. Following the IPO, public shareholders would own 18.5% of Northwest. Checchi's and Wilson's ownership would fall to 21.2% from 26.0%, but they would still be able to choose 3 of the 15 directors.

After carefully weighing the pros and cons of an IPO at the lower price, Northwest sold 20,000,000 shares of common stock to the public at $13 per share on March 18, 1994. The offering increased Northwest's outstanding common shares (excluding those not yet issued to the employee trusts) by approximately one-third, an unusually large percentage. The shares were approved for quotation on the NASDAQ market. The NYSE had earlier rejected Northwest's listing application. Northwest had been unprofitable during the preceding 3 years.

The shares were marketed internationally by a syndicate of underwriters. Lehman Brothers was the global coordinator for the offering of 16 million shares in the United States and Canada, 2.5 million in Europe (KLM Royal Dutch Airlines, the owner of roughly 18% of Northwest's shares, had recently formed a strategic alliance with Northwest Airlines), and 1.5 million shares in Asia (Northwest maintains a hub in Tokyo). Nevertheless, press reports characterized investor interest in the offering as lukewarm and noted the reduced price. On the plus side, Moody's announced that it was considering raising Northwest's long-term senior unsecured debt rating to B3 from Caa as a result of the offering.

Figure 23-6 shows the post-IPO performance of Northwest's common stock price for 3 months following the IPO. As noted, the firm went public at $13 per share. The closing price on the offering date was also $13. The Standard & Poor's Airlines Index was 246.65 on that

TABLE 23-9

Dilution in equity ownership of Northwest Airlines Corporation.

	PRIOR TO THE OFFERING		AFTER THE OFFERING	
SHAREHOLDERS	**Number of Shares[a]**	**Percentage Ownership**	**Number of Shares[a]**	**Percentage Ownership**
Alfred A. Checchi	11,400,117	13.0%	11,400,117	10.6%
Gary L. Wilson	11,400,117	13.0	11,400,117	10.6
Employee trusts[b]	29,923,616	34.0	29,923,616	27.7
KLM	16,189,030	18.4	16,189,030	15.0
Investment firms[c]	18,329,721	20.8	18,329,721	17.0
Other officers and directors	690,961	0.8	690,961	0.6
Public shareholders	—	—	20,000,000	18.5
Total	87,933,562	100.0%	107,933,562	100.0%

[a] Includes shares of class B common stock, which is nonvoting but which is convertible share for share into voting class A common stock.
[b] 17,777,026 shares of class A common stock and preferred stock convertible into 12,146,590 shares of class A common stock to be issued to employee trusts as part of the leveraged buyout agreement with the unions.
[c] Three investment firms that helped finance the leveraged buyout.

date. It serves as an indicator of the movement in airline stocks generally.[1] Following North-west's IPO, the share price fell more or less steadily for three weeks to a low of $11.50. Airline stocks also fell, but not as much. Northwest's share price subsequently rose above the IPO price and increased faster than the S&P Airlines Index.

---

[1] Four airlines compose the index (AMR Corp.—41%, Delta Airlines—25%, Southwest Air—27%, and USAir Group—7%).

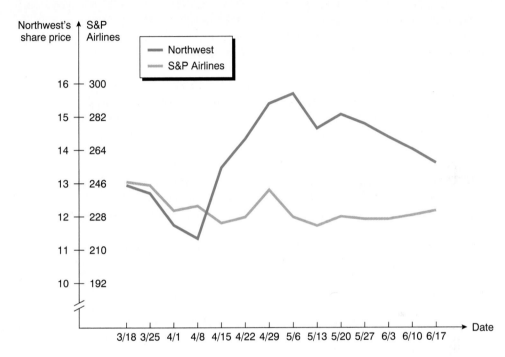

FIGURE 23-6
Northwest's post-IPO share price performance.

SUMMARY

A firm that needs to raise long-term funds externally can sell securities in the public market or in the private market. It can sell them directly to investors or engage a securities firm to assist it. The bulk of the securities issued by U.S. firms are sold in the domestic market in negotiated underwritten offerings.

　　The initial decision involves what type of security to sell. Most important, the firm must decide, in light of its capital structure objectives and its current financial condition, whether to sell debt or equity securities. Economies of scale involved in issuing securities make it impractical for a firm to sell small amounts of debt and equity in its exact capital structure proportions every time it needs funds. Thus the firm will not be able to stick rigidly to its target capital structure.

　　After choosing the security type, the firm must decide on a market. The private market has both advantages and disadvantages relative to the public market. The private market is generally more attractive than the public market for small debt issues or for debt issues backed by complex security arrangements.

There are a number of sources of additional common equity capital: retained earnings, public offerings of new shares, rights offerings of new shares to current shareholders, private placement of new shares, sale of new shares through a dividend reinvestment or employee stock plan, and a contribution of shares in lieu of cash to the firm's pension plan. Public offerings account for most of the new common equity capital that firms raise from external sources.

DECISION SUMMARY

- There are many types of financial securities. For example, securities may be equity, debt, or some combination of these. Securities may also be public or private and domestic or international.
- Most external financing involves debt.
- New issues of securities can be marketed in a variety of ways. For example, they may be underwritten, sold on a best-efforts basis, sold directly to investors, or, in the case of common stock, sold through either a rights offering or a dividend reinvestment plan to current shareholders.
- The stock market usually reacts negatively when a firm announces a new issue of common stock or an issue of debt convertible into common stock. Adverse selection is thought to be the reason for this reaction.
- The stock market usually reacts favorably when a firm announces a private placement of debt, convertible debt, or equity. Private placements reduce information asymmetries, permit better monitoring, and provide a certification of the issuer.
- Issuance costs are proportionately lower for larger issues.
- Bonds have lower explicit issuance costs than common stock for comparable dollar amounts.
- Common stock is the most junior security a firm can issue. Common stock has voting, dividend, and liquidation rights. Issuing additional common stock to new investors dilutes the voting interest of existing shareholders.
- Common stock is most often issued through a general cash offer on a negotiated basis. Rights offerings are rare in the United States but are the typical method of offering additional common stock in many other countries.
- Going public is a major event in a firm's life. It enables a firm to raise capital and creates a negotiable instrument for use in acquisitions and for other purposes. Simultaneously, it obligates a firm to make regular financial disclosures and to deal with a new constituency, its public shareholders. A firm should go public only if it has determined that the advantages of being publicly held outweigh the disadvantages.
- Preferred stock is a hybrid financial instrument. Adjustable-rate preferred stock, which has undergone a number of refinements, gives rise to a tax arbitrage when the issuer is non-tax-paying and the investors are corporations that can use the 70% dividends-received deduction.

EQUATION SUMMARY

(23.1) $\text{Book value per common share} = \dfrac{\text{Common stockholders' equity}}{\text{Number of common shares outstanding}}$

(23.2) $R_C = \dfrac{P_R - S}{N + 1}$

(23.3) $$P_E = P_R - R_C$$

(23.4) $$R_C = \frac{P_E - S}{N}$$

KEY TERMS

public offering...728

general cash offer...729

Eurodollar bond market...729

primary offering...732

secondary offering...732

investment banker...734

underwritten offering...734

syndicated public offering...734

gross underwriting spread...734

direct stock-purchase programs...737

competitive bidding...737

negotiated offering...737

private placement...738

cumulative voting...741

proxy contest...741

rights offering...744

dividend reinvestment
    plan (DRP)...747

initial public offering (IPO)...748

preferred stock...750

preference stock...750

EXERCISES

PROBLEM SET A

A1. What are the principal features of common stock? How are the principal features of common stock and preferred stock different?

A2. How do public and private financing differ? How do the roles of the investment banker differ?

A3. Cite three advantages and the major disadvantage of private financing.

A4. Why does the par value of common stock have little real significance?

A5. What is by far the largest source of new external financing?

A6. What is by far the largest source of new equity financing?

A7. Name the three explicit transaction cost components of the gross underwriting spread in an underwritten public offering.

A8. Explain why the real transaction cost of an issue consists of the market impact as well as the gross spread.

A9. What is a rights offering?

A10. How can a dividend reinvestment plan raise new equity capital?

A11. Explain the difference between a negotiated and a competitive offering.

A12. Why is preferred stock viewed as a "hybrid" security?

A13. Explain why the announcement of a public offering of common stock generally has a negative impact on the firm's share price.

A14. Explain each of the following rights and privileges associated with common stock: (a) dividend rights, (b) liquidation rights, (c) preemptive rights, and (d) voting rights.

PROBLEM SET B

B1. A common stockholder owns 30% of a firm's 1 million outstanding shares. The firm plans to sell 200,000 new shares.

a. By how much is the stockholder's percentage ownership diluted if the firm sells all the shares to new investors?

b. How could the stockholder maintain her 30% ownership interest?

B2. A firm announces a new issue of common stock.

a. How would you expect the stock market to react? Why?

b. Would it make a difference if the firm announced that it would place the shares privately with three of the largest life insurance companies in the United States?

B3. A firm's share price is $30. It has 5 million shares outstanding. When it announces a public offering of 1 million shares of its common stock, its share price falls to $29.

a. Compute the reduction in shareholder wealth that results from the announcement.

b. The firm issues the shares at $29 each. Express the reduction in wealth as a percentage of the gross proceeds of the issue.

c. The gross underwriting spread is 5%. Which factor, the impact of the announcement or flotation expense, had the greater effect on shareholder wealth?

B4. According to Microsoft's 1995 annual report, the firm had $5.333 billion of total stockholders' equity at June 30, 1995. Microsoft had 588 million common shares outstanding. Calculate Microsoft's book value per common share.

B5. Your friend has asked your help in calculating Exxon's book value per common share. She has obtained a copy of Exxon's 1994 annual report from the library. The balance sheet contains the following information as of December 31, 1994:

Total shareholders' equity	$37.415 billion
Preferred stock	554 million
Authorized common shares	2 billion
Issued common shares	1.813 billion
Treasury shares	571 million

There is a 3% preferred stock liquidation premium. Compute Exxon's book value per common share.

B6. Consider a firm about to make a new equity issue. The firm feels it can make either a public offering or a rights offering to all existing shareholders. The firm wants to raise $14.4 million net new equity capital. The current share price is $30, with 3 million shares outstanding. Under Plan I, a public offering would be made as follows: 600,000 new shares would be underwritten at a market price of $26 per share and a net price to the firm of $25 per share. Theoretically, after the issue is completed, the market price per share will be $29.17. Under Plan II, a rights offering (one right per share issued to each current shareholder) would be made with the following features: 1 million new shares would be sold at $15 each, and 3 rights would be necessary to buy each share. Total flotation costs would be $600,000 for Plan II. Theoretically, after the issue is completed, the market price per share will be $26.25. Assuming that the firm's actual goal is to maximize shareholder wealth, which of these plans would be better, and why?

B7. The A. B. Sea Company wants to raise $100 million through a rights offering. It has 70 million shares outstanding, trading at $25 per share. It wishes each right to be worth at least $0.20 initially.

a. Find the subscription price and the subscription ratio.

b. After the offering commences, the shares trade at a price of $23 per share. What is the value of 1 right?

c. In what situations is a rights offering more appropriate than a general public offering?

d. What is the principal drawback to a rights offering?

B8. A firm has a large group of dissident shareholders who control 20% of the firm's stock.

a. Suppose there are 15 board members all up for reelection and that voting is cumulative. How many directors could the dissident shareholders elect?

b. Suppose voting is noncumulative. How many directors could the dissidents elect?

c. Suppose there is cumulative voting but that only 5 directors are up for reelection because the directors' terms are staggered. How long would it take for the dissidents to get in the same position they would be in immediately after the election in part a?

d. Explain why the firm's top management would prefer to have noncumulative voting for directors.

B9. How is stockholders' wealth affected when a firm sells new shares of common stock for a price (a) greater than its book value? (b) less than its book value?

B10. In what sense is preferred stock (a) "expensive" debt? (b) "cheap" equity?

B11. Explain why a firm making a new securities issue, especially one that includes some component of equity, must be concerned with more than simply the explicit transaction costs such as underwriter fees.

B12. (Review from Chapter 5.) A firm is considering issuing preferred stock that bears an 8% dividend rate (payable quarterly). The issue is perpetual. Issuance expenses are 1%.

a. What is the cost of this preferred stock?

b. How does your answer to part a change if the preferred stock matures in one lump sum after 10 years?

c. How does your answer to part b change if the issue has a sinking fund that calls for equal payments in years 9 and 10?

B13. Explain why a preferred stock issue that contains a sinking fund provision is similar to debt. How does the design of this feature affect how debt-like the preferred stock is?

B14. (Review from Chapter 7.) The riskless return is 6%. The expected excess return on the market portfolio is 8%. A stock's beta is 1.35. Calculate the cost of equity capital.

B15. (Review from Chapter 5.) A stock's current market price is $25. The expected annual cash dividend is $1 per share. In addition, investors expect the firm to pay a 4% dividend in common stock. The expected growth rate of the cash dividend is 10% per annum.

a. Calculate the cost of retained earnings.

b. If a new share issue would require 5% flotation costs, what is the cost of the new issue?

B16. (Review from Chapter 7.) A stock's unleveraged beta is 0.8. The firm's debt ratio is $L = 0.4$. The riskless return is 5%, and the expected return on the market portfolio is 15%. What is the firm's cost of equity capital?

B17. (Review from Chapter 5.) A perpetual preferred stock issue can be sold for $25 per share. It would require a quarterly dividend rate of $0.50 per share. The underwriting fees and out-of-pocket expenses amount to 1.75% of the public offering price. What is the cost of preferred stock?

B18. Venture capitalists invest funds that enable firms to start up. They also finance the early stages of development before the firm goes public. They usually ask for preemptive rights, at least at the time of their initial investment. What is their rationale?

B19. In the case of many European firms, a few large institutions or wealthy individuals are the dominant shareholders. Why would you expect such firms to use rights offerings rather than general cash offers to raise additional common equity?

B20. Suppose a firm has 100 million shares outstanding that are worth $20 each. It has 1 million shareholders each of whom owns 100 shares. The firm wants to sell $50 million of common stock.

a. State an argument in favor of a rights offering.

b. State the arguments in favor of a general cash offer.

B21. Suppose General Motors has decided it needs to raise additional equity. Its investment bankers recommend that GM issue preferred stock, because a recent change in tax law has increased the dividends-received deduction. How can GM design the preferred stock issue to be as much like common stock as possible?

PROBLEM SET C

C1. Explain why shelf registration might lead to a more efficient capital market.

C2. In June 1991, Time Warner Inc. announced an innovative rights offering that proved controversial among the firm's shareholders. Time Warner stated that it would distribute transferable rights to purchase approximately 34,450,000 shares. Each Time Warner shareholder would receive 0.6 right for each Time Warner share held. Each full right would entitle the holder to purchase 1 Time Warner share at a subscription price of $105. Any shares that were not subscribed for when the offering terminated would be distributed pro rata among subscribers at no additional cost to them. However, Time Warner would complete the offering only if at least 60% of the rights were exercised (and the shares purchased for cash).

   a. If only 60% of the shares were purchased for cash, and the rest were distributed free, what would be the effective subscription price?

   b. Express the share price ex-rights (P_E) in terms of the share price rights-on (P_R), the fraction of a right distributed for each share (F), and the (exercise) value of 1 right (R).

   c. If the fraction of rights that will be exercised (G) is known with certainty, express the share price ex-rights in terms of the share price rights-on, the subscription price (S), the fraction F, and the fraction G.

   d. Use the expressions in parts b and c to obtain an expression for the value of 1 right.

   e. Some institutional investors said they found the structure of the offering a "brilliant coercive measure." How would you explain this reaction?

C3. A rights offering involves the distribution of call options to a firm's shareholders. A transferable put rights offering, discussed in Chapters 17 and 18, involves the distribution of put options to shareholders. In what sense are these transactions "mirror images" of one another?

Real-World Application: Lucent Technologies' IPO

In 1995, AT&T Corp. announced that it intended to separate into three firms—telecommunications services, telecommunications equipment, and computers. AT&T planned to create a new firm, Lucent Technologies Inc., which would operate AT&T's former telecommunications equipment business. It would design, develop, and manufacture a wide range of communications networks and software, consumer and business telephone systems, and microelectronic components. AT&T planned to take Lucent public early in 1996 and then distribute the remaining shares of Lucent to its own stockholders through a tax-free spin-off later in the year.

AT&T announced in March 1996 that it would offer for sale 112 million Lucent shares, representing about 18% of Lucent's stock. AT&T projected an offering price in the range of $22 to $25 per share. Taking the midpoint of this range, $23.50 per share, the Lucent IPO would raise $2.6 billion. This would make it the largest IPO ever in the United States.

Pricing the IPO would be difficult because Lucent was at the beginning of a potentially stressful period. It had taken a $2.8 billion pretax restructuring charge in 1995, which resulted in a loss of $867 million. The restructuring would cut 23,000 jobs. Also, the spin-off would sever the umbilical cord to its financially stronger parent. Finally, Lucent's business was becoming increasingly competitive. For example, AT&T had recently announced that Lucent was negotiating an equipment contract with Sprint that would require it to provide $1 billion in vendor financing.

Table 23-10 furnishes financial information concerning Lucent, AT&T, and three comparable publicly traded firms. Securities underwriters use such information to price an IPO.

TABLE 23-10

Selected financial information concerning telecommunications firms (millions except per-share amounts).

| FIRM | STOCK LISTED | NUMBER OF SHARES OUTSTANDING | CLOSING PRICE (4/3/96) | MARKET VALUE | | | LATEST 12 MONTHS | | PROJECTED ANNUAL EARNINGS PER SHARE | BOOK VALUE OF EQUITY | INDICATED ANNUAL DIVIDEND RATE[b] |
				Common Equity	Preferred Equity	Long-Term Debt	Earnings Per Share	EBITDA[a]			
Lucent Technologies	NYSE[c]	637	—	—	—	$ 3,965	$1.56[d]	$3457	$1.62	$ 2,329	$3.00[c]
AT&T	NYSE	1596	$64.125	$102,344	—	11,635	2.71[e]	6060	3.71	18,001	1.32
British Telecommunications[f]	NYSE	623	57.00	35,511	—	5,330	5.00	8445	4.97	20,170	3.95
Cable & Wireless[g]	NYSE	733	24.25	17,775	—	1,362	1.30	2319	1.19	6,025	0.70
Northern Telecom	NYSE	256	49.75	12,736	73	1,236	1.93	277	2.43	4,454	0.44

[a] EBITDA = Earnings Before Interest, Taxes, Depreciation, and Amortization.
[b] Calculated by multiplying the latest quarterly dividend rate by 4 or the latest semiannual rate by 2.
[c] Planned.
[d] Before a $1.85 billion after-tax restructuring charge.
[e] Before a $4.18 billion after-tax restructuring charge.
[f] Per-share amounts are expressed in terms of American Depository Receipts (ADRs) (1 ADR = 10 shares).
[g] Per-share amounts are expressed in terms of ADRs (1 ADR = 3 shares).
Sources: Bloomberg, L. P., and *Value Line Investment Survey.*

1. Calculate the price/earnings ratio for each of the comparable firms on the basis of
   a. Latest 12 months earnings per share.
   b. Projected annual earnings per share.

2. Which price/earnings ratio do you think is more meaningful in an efficient market, one based on the latest 12 months earnings per share, or one based on projected annual earnings per share? Explain.

3. Calculate the ratio of (a) the total market value of equity and debt to (b) EBITDA, for each of the comparable firms.

4. Calculate the book value per share and the market-to-book ratio for each of the comparable firms.

5. Calculate the indicated annual dividend yield for each of the comparable firms.

6. Calculate the ratios in questions 1, 3, 4, and 5 for Lucent assuming a share price of $30.

7. Calculate the ratios in questions 1, 3, 4, and 5 for Lucent assuming a share price of $25.

8. Calculate the ratios in questions 1, 3, 4, and 5 for Lucent assuming a share price of $20.

9. Use the information in questions 1 through 8 to estimate a price range within which Lucent's shares should trade.

10. Underwriters generally price an IPO 10% to 15% below the expected trading price. Estimate the price for Lucent's IPO.

11. Lucent's IPO was priced at $27. Compare this price to the price range you estimated in question 10. If the IPO price falls outside your estimated range, can you explain what might account for this?

APPENDIX: EVALUATING THE MERITS OF INNOVATIVE FINANCING ARRANGEMENTS

Investment bankers spend considerable time and effort trying to come up with valuable new securities ideas. As you may know, when an investment banker develops a new security, she generally gives it a cute name (built on an acronym). The list includes LYONs, TIGRs, PRIDES, PERCS, SPINs, DECS, SABRES, SIGNs, and many more.

The rapid pace of securities innovation has produced an almost overwhelming number of new financing instruments. Some of these new instruments include complex and difficult-to-evaluate options structures. Confronted with the choice among existing financing alternatives and yet another innovative security, managers must try to strip away the veneer and determine whether the bankers' claim that the new security is valuable is valid.

In addition to the pursuit of valuable ideas, two important developments account for the revolution in securities innovation. First, the investment banking business has become more competitive. Developing an innovative security provides an opportunity for the developer to solicit business from firms that have been using other investment bankers. It usually also enables the innovator to obtain the mandate to market the new security on a negotiated basis, rather than having to bid for securities.

Second, inflation rates and interest rates have become more volatile, tax changes have become more frequent, and regulatory changes have become more profound as a result of deregulation. Financial innovation is, at least in part, a response to the changing economic and financial environment. For example, increased interest rate volatility led to the development of adjustable-rate preferred stock—and a series of refinements—designed to eliminate the exposure of the securityholder's principal to interest rate changes.

A new security is truly valuable only if it enables an investor to realize a higher after-tax risk-adjusted return, or an issuer a lower after-tax required return, than previously existing securities. Just being different is not enough. There must be real value to the issuing firm's shareholders. A new security could accomplish this by creating a pattern of risk-return combinations that investors could not have achieved previously, thereby making the financial markets more nearly *complete*. A new security could also reduce taxes, reduce transaction costs, or resolve information asymmetries, thereby lessening the impact of market imperfections on valuation.

Sources of Value Added

A new security can enhance shareholder value in any of the following ways.

1. The lower the after-tax required return is, compared to that for conventional securities, the greater the value to the firm. The lower the required return is, the higher the price the firm can get for the security.

   If a firm can repackage a payment stream—create a new type of security—so that it either involves less risk or reallocates risk from one class of investors to another that is less risk-sensitive, then shareholder value will be enhanced because the firm will pay a smaller risk premium. Collateralized mortgage obligations (CMOs) are an example. CMOs include multiple classes of claims against a pool of mortgages. The different classes of securities that make up the CMO package are prioritized with respect to their right to receive principal payments from the underlying mortgage portfolio. For example, class A might get the first priority, giving it a very short average life, and class Z might have the lowest priority, giving it a very long average life (because all prior classes have to be paid off before class Z holders receive anything).

2. The smaller the percentage underwriting commissions and other expenses, the greater the value to the firm. Lower transaction costs increase the *net* proceeds the firm gets. If a firm can structure a new issue so that underwriting commissions are reduced, shareholder value will be enhanced. Extendible notes are an example. Their maturity can be extended by mutual agreement of issuer and investors, effectively rolling over the notes without additional underwriting commissions.

3. The lower the agency costs associated with a particular security, the greater the market value of the firm, if all else is equal. If a firm can structure a new security to reduce agency costs, then shareholder wealth can be enhanced. For example, interest rate reset notes protect bondholders against a deterioration in the issuer's credit standing prior to the reset date. The interest rate is reset automatically if the rating agencies reduce the rating they assign to the notes. Under the Principle of Capital Market Efficiency, without such protection we would expect bondholders to increase their required return to compensate for this risk. As a result of asymmetric information, they might charge

a significant risk premium even if management had no intention of engaging in such things as *asset subsitution*. Interest rate reset notes would be mutually advantageous in that case.

4. The smaller the holders' tax liability associated with the new security, the greater the value to the firm. If a firm can structure a new security to reduce investor taxes without increasing corporate income taxes, shareholder value will be enhanced as a result of this tax arbitrage. For example, a firm that is currently not a taxpayer can create such an arbitrage by issuing adjustable-rate preferred stock in lieu of commercial paper. Industrial firms and banking institutions that have large tax loss carryforwards have accounted for a high percentage of adjustable-rate preferred stock issues. Both adjustable-rate preferred stock and commercial paper are purchased by corporate money managers, but preferred stock dividends are more valuable to a corporation than interest payments, because the corporation is tax-exempt on 70% of the dividends it receives. Consequently, adjustable-rate preferred stock carries a lower pretax yield than similarly rated commercial paper.

5. The greater the corporate tax shield, all else equal, the greater the market value of the firm. If a firm can structure a new security to increase the present value of tax shields available to the issuer or to reduce the issuer's income tax liability without simultaneously increasing the investors' tax liabilities, shareholder value will again be enhanced through tax arbitrage. For example, selling zero-coupon bonds to tax-exempt investors before the Tax Equity and Fiscal Responsibility Act of 1982 (TEFRA) resulted in such an arbitrage, because the issuer could deduct the original issue discount on a straight-line basis—that is, faster than interest on the notes implicitly compounded. TEFRA changed the method of amortization to the scientific interest method, as interest implicitly compounds, and eliminated this arbitrage opportunity.

Other reasons are often given to explain securities innovations. Examples include a desire to achieve a particular accounting treatment or a particular regulatory treatment. The value added by innovations introduced only for their accounting advantages is highly suspect. An efficient capital market can "see through" accounting transformations to determine the true financial benefits, if any, arising out of a new financial instrument.

The Evolution of Adjustable-Rate Preferred Stock

As we have just noted, corporate cash managers have a tax incentive to purchase preferred stock rather than commercial paper or other short-term debt instruments. Nontaxable corporate issuers find preferred stock cheaper than debt, because corporate investors are willing to pass back part of the value of the tax arbitrage by accepting a lower dividend rate.

Purchasing long-term, fixed-dividend-rate preferred stock, however, exposes the purchaser to interest rate risk. A variety of preferred stock instruments have been designed to deal with this problem.

Adjustable-rate preferred stock was designed to reduce interest rate risk by adjusting the dividend rate as interest rates change. The dividend rate adjusts according to a formula that specifies a fixed margin over the maximum of three specified Treasury yields.[9] Despite the dividend adjustment, other risks continue to cause significant deviations in the value of the security. For example, investors might require a higher return because the risk of the firm defaulting had increased.

Convertible adjustable preferred stock (CAPS) was designed to eliminate this deficiency by making the security convertible, on each dividend payment date, into enough shares of common stock (or the equivalent value in cash) to make the security worth its par value. But although CAPS generally traded closer to the respective face amounts than adjustable-rate preferred stock, there have been few such issues. Issuer reluctance may have stemmed from the security's conversion feature, which could force the issuer to issue common stock or raise a large amount of cash on short notice.

---

[9] There is a short-term Treasury yield (usually the 3-month bill yield), an intermediate-term yield (usually the 10-year yield), and a long-term bond yield (generally the 30-year yield).

Auction-rate preferred stock carried the evolutionary process a step further. The dividend rate is reset by Dutch auction every seven weeks, which represents just enough time to meet the 46-day holding period required to qualify for the 70% dividends-received deduction. There are various versions of auction-rate preferred stock that are sold under different acronyms, such as MMP (Money Market Preferred) and AMPS (Auction Market Preferred Stock), coined by the different securities firms that offer the product. Although the names differ, the securities are the same.

In an effort to refine further the adjustable-rate preferred stock, there have been at least two attempts to design a superior security, but only one was successful. *Single-point adjustable-rate stock* (SPARS) has a dividend rate that adjusts automatically every 49 days to a specified percentage of the 60-day high-grade commercial paper rate. The security is designed so as to afford the same degree of liquidity as auction-rate preferred stock, but with lower transaction costs because no auction need be held. The problem with SPARS, however, is that the fixed-dividend-rate formula involves a potential agency cost that auction-rate preferred stock does not. Because the dividend formula is fixed, investors will suffer a loss if the issuer's credit standing falls. Primarily for this reason, there have been only two SPARS issues.

Remarketed preferred stock, by contrast, pays a dividend that is reset at the end of each dividend period to a dividend rate that a specified remarketing agent determines will make the preferred stock worth par. Such issues allow the issuer considerable flexibility in selecting the length of the dividend period (it can be as short as one day). Remarketed preferred also offers greater flexibility in selecting the other terms of the issue. In fact, each share of an issue could have a different maturity, dividend rate, or other terms, provided the issuer and holders so agree. Remarketed preferred has not proved so popular with issuers as auction-rate preferred stock, but that could change because of the greater flexibility that remarketed preferred affords.

Variable cumulative preferred stock was born out of the controversy over whether auction-rate preferred stock or remarketed preferred stock results in more equitable pricing. This variation effectively allows the issuer to decide, at the beginning of each dividend period, which of the two reset methods will determine the dividend rate at the beginning of the next dividend period.

APPENDIX EXERCISES

PROBLEM SET A

A1. When is a new security truly valuable to the issuer's shareholders?

A2. What is the difference between adjustable-rate preferred stock and auction-rate preferred stock?

A3. What are the relative advantages of auction-rate preferred stock and remarketed preferred stock?

A4. What is the principal drawback to convertible adjustable preferred stock?

PROBLEM SET B

B1. What are the principal incentives that encourage financial innovation?

B2. An issue of adjustable-rate preferred stock pays an annual dividend rate equal to 100 basis points plus the greatest of (1) the 3-month Treasury yield, (2) the 10-year Treasury yield, and (3) the 30-year Treasury yield.

a. The 3-month Treasury yield is 8.00% (on a bond-equivalent-yield basis); the 10-year Treasury yield is 8.50%; and the 30-year Treasury yield is 8.70%. What is the annual dividend rate?

b. The issue pays dividends quarterly. The par value is $100 per share. What is the quarterly dividend for the next quarter?

PROBLEM SET C

C1. Suppose General Electric sells a 5-year zero-coupon debt issue. The principal amount is $1000 per bond. The yield to maturity is 12% (annual).

a. Compute the annual interest deductions for tax purposes. [*Hint*: Interest compounds annually.]

b. Compute the annual interest deductions, assuming that General Electric can deduct the original issue discount on a straight-line basis.

c. Why is the straight-line method more valuable to General Electric? Can you quantify the value of the straight-line method? What is the source of this value?

BIBLIOGRAPHY

Affleck-Graves, John, Shantaram P. Hegde, Robert E. Miller, and Frank K. Reilly. "The Effect of the Trading System on the Underpricing of Initial Public Offerings," *Financial Management*, 1993, 22(1):99–108.

Aggarwal, Reena, and Pietra Rivoli. "Fads in the Initial Public Offering Market?" *Financial Management*, 1990, 19(4):45–57.

Alderson, Michael J., and Donald R. Fraser. "Financial Innovations and Excesses Revisited: the Case of Auction Rate Preferred Stock," *Financial Management*, 1993, 22(2):61–77.

Arshadi, Nasser, and Thomas H. Eyssell. "Regulatory Deterrence and Registered Insider Trading: the Case of Tender Offers," *Financial Management*, 1991, 20(2):30–39.

Asquith, P., and D. W. Mullins. "Equity Issues and Offering Dilution," *Journal of Financial Economics*, 1986, 15(1/2):61–89.

Bae, Sung C., and Haim Levy. "The Valuation of Firm Commitment Underwriting Contracts for Seasoned New Equity Issues: Theory And Evidence," *Financial Management*, 1990, 19(2):48–59.

Barry, Christopher B. "New Directions in Research on Venture Capital Finance," *Financial Management*, 1994, 23(3):3–15.

Barry, Christopher B., and Robert H. Jennings. "The Opening Price Performance of Initial Public Offerings of Common Stock," *Financial Management*, 1993, 22(1):54–63.

Barry, Christopher B., Chris J. Muscarella, and Michael R. Vetsuypens. "Underwriter Warrants, Underwriter Compensation, and the Costs of Going Public," *Journal of Financial Economics*, 1991, v29(1):113–136.

Benveniste, Lawrence M., and William J. Wilhelm. "A Comparative Analysis of IPO Proceeds Under Alternative Regulatory Environments," *Journal of Financial Economics*, 1990, 28(1/2):173–208.

Bhagat, Sanjai. "The Effect of Management's Choice Between Negotiated and Competitive Equity Offerings on Shareholder Wealth," *Journal of Financial and Quantitative Analysis*, 1986, 21(2):181–196.

Bhagat, Sanjai, James A. Brickley, and Ronald C. Lease. "The Authorization of Additional Common Stock: An Empirical Investigation," *Financial Management*, 1986, 15(3):45–53.

Bhagat, Sanjai, M. Wayne Marr, and G. Rodney Thompson. "The Rule 415 Experiment: Equity Markets," *Journal of Finance,* 1985, 40(5):1385–1401.

Bowers, Helen M., and Robert E. Miller. "Choice of Investment Banker and Shareholders' Wealth of Firms Involved in Acquisitions," *Financial Management*, 1990, 19(4):34–44.

Brickley, James A., and Kathleen T. Hevert. "Direct Employees Stock Ownership: An Empirical Investigation," *Financial Management*, 1991, 20(2):70–84.

Carey, Mark, Stephen Prowse, John Rea, and Gregory Udell. *The Economics of the Private Placement Market*. Washington, DC: Board of Governors of the Federal Reserve System, December 1993.

Carter, Richard B., and Frederick H. Dark. "The Use of the Over-Allotment Option in Initial Public Offerings of Equity: Risks and Underwriter Prestige," *Financial Management*, 1990, 19(3):55–64.

Carter, Richard, and Steven Manaster. "Initial Public Offerings and Underwriter Reputation," *Journal of Finance*, 1990, 45(4):1045–1067.

Chang, Saeyoung. "Employee Stock Ownership Plans and Shareholder Wealth: An Empirical Investigation," *Financial Management*, 1990, 19(1):48–58.

Dawson, Steven M. "Initial Public Offer Underpricing: The Issuer's View—A Note," *Journal of Finance*, 1987, 42(1):159–162.

Drake, Philip D., and Michael R. Vetsuypens. "IPO Underpricing and Insurance Against Legal Liability," *Financial Management*, 1993, 22(1):64–73.

Eckbo, B. Espen, and Ronald W. Masulis. "Adverse Selection and the Rights Offer Paradox," *Journal of Financial Economics*, 1992, 32(3):293–332.

Ferreira, Eurico J., Michael F. Spivey, and Charles E. Edwards. "Pricing New Issues and Seasoned Preferred Stocks: A Comparison of Valuation Models," *Financial Management*, 1992, 21(2):52–62.

Fields, L. Paige, and Eric L. Mais. "Managerial Voting Rights and Seasoned Public Equity Issues," *Journal of Financial and Quantitative Analysis*, 1994, 29(3):445–457.

Garfinkel, Jon A. "IPO Underpricing, Insider Selling and Subsequent Equity Offerings: Is Underpricing a Signal of Quality?" *Financial Management*, 1993, 22(1):74–83.

Greene, Jason T., and Susan G. Watts. "Price Discovery on the NYSE and the NASDAQ: The Case of Overnight and Daytime News Releases," *Financial Management*, 1996, 25(1):19–42.

Grinblatt, Mark, and Chuan Yang Hwang. "Signalling and the Pricing of New Issues," *Journal of Finance*, 1989, 44(2):393–420.

Gupta, Atul, and Leonard Rosenthal. "Ownership Structure, Leverage, and Firm Value: The Case of Leveraged Recapitalizations," *Financial Management*, 1991, 20(3):69–83.

Handa, Puneet, and A. R. Radhakrishnan. "An Empirical Investigation of Leveraged Recapitalizations with Cash Payout as Takeover Defense," *Financial Management*, 1991, 20(3):58–68.

Hanley, Kathleen Weiss. "The Underpricing of Initial Public Offerings and the Partial Adjustment Phenomenon," *Journal of Financial Economics*, 1993, 34(2):231–250.

Hanley, Kathleen Weiss, A. Arun Kumar, and Paul J. Seguin. "Price Stabilization in the Market For New Issues," *Journal of Financial Economics*, 1993, 34(2):177–198.

Hansen, Robert S., and Paul Torregrosa. "Underwriter Compensation and Corporate Monitoring," *Journal of Finance*, 1992, 47(4):1537–1556.

Jain, Bharat A., and Omesh Kini. "The Post-Issue Operating Performance of IPO Firms," *Journal of Finance*, 1994, 49(5):1699–1726.

James, Christopher, and Peggy Wier. "Borrowing Relationships, Intermediation, and the Cost of Issuing Public Securities," *Journal of Financial Economics*, 1990, 28(1/2):149–172.

Jegadeesh, Narasimhan, Mark Weinstein, and Ivo Welch. "An Empirical Investigation of IPO Returns and Subsequent Equity Offerings," *Journal of Financial Economics*, 1993, 34(2):153–175.

Johnson, James M., and Robert E. Miller. "Investment Banker Prestige and the Underpricing of Initial Public Offerings," *Financial Management*, 1988, 17(2):19–29.

Kadapakkam, Palani-Rajan, and Sarabjeet Seth. "Trading Profits in Dutch Auction Self-Tender Offers," *Journal of Finance*, 1994, 49(1):291–306.

Karpoff, Jonathan M., and Daniel Lee. "Insider Trading Before New Issue Announcements," *Financial Management*, 1991, 20(1):18–26.

Kidwell, David S., M. Wayne Marr, and G. Rodney Thompson. "Eurodollar Bonds, Alternative Financing for U.S. Companies: A Correction," *Financial Management*, 1986, 15(1):78–79.

Levis, Mario. "The Long-Run Performance of Initial Public Offerings: The UK Experience 1980–1988," *Financial Management*, 1993, 22(1):28–41.

Loderer, Claudio F., and David C. Mauer. "Corporate Dividends and Seasoned Equity Issues: An Empirical Investigation," *Journal of Finance*, 1992, 47(1):201–226.

Loderer, Claudio F., Dennis R. Sheehan, and Gregory B. Kadlec. "The Pricing of Equity Offerings," *Journal of Financial Economics*, 1991, 29(1):35–58.

Logue, Dennis E., James K. Seward, and James P. Walsh. "Rearranging Residual Claims: A Case for Targeted Stock," *Financial Management*, 1996, 25(1):43–61.

Masulis, Ronald W., and A. N. Korwar. "Seasoned Equity Offerings: An Empirical Investigation," *Journal of Financial Economics*, 1986, 15(1/2):91–118.

Megginson, William L., Robert C. Nash, and Matthias Van Randenborgh. "The Financial and Operating Performance of Newly Privatized Firms: An International Empirical Analysis," *Journal of Finance*, 1994, 49(2):403–452.

Megginson, William L., and Kathleen A. Weiss. "Venture Capitalist Certification in Initial Public Offerings," *Journal of Finance*, 1991, 46(3):879–904.

Miller, Merton H. "Financial Innovation: The Last Twenty Years and the Next," *Journal of Financial and Quantitative Analysis*, 1986, 21(5):459–471.

Miller, Robert E., and Frank K. Reilly. "An Examination of Mispricing, Returns, and Uncertainty for Initial Public Offerings," *Financial Management*, 1987, 16(2):33–38.

Moore, Norman H., David R. Peterson, and Pamela P. Peterson. "Shelf Registrations and Shareholder Wealth: A Comparison of Shelf and Traditional Equity Offerings," *Journal of Finance*, 1986, 41(2):451–464.

Myers, Stewart C., and Nicholas J. Majluf. "Corporate Financing and Investment Decisions When Firms Have Information That Investors Do Not Have," *Journal of Financial Economics*, 1984, 13(2):187–222.

Persons, John C. "Signaling and Takeover Deterrence with Stock Repurchases: Dutch Auctions versus Fixed Price Tender Offers," *Journal of Finance*, 1994, 49(4):1373–1402.

Pinegar, J. Michael, and Ronald C. Lease. "The Impact of Preferred-For-Common Exchange Offers on Firm Value," *Journal of Finance*, 1986, 41(4):795–814.

Rogowski, Robert J., and Eric H. Sorensen. "Deregulation in Investment Banking: Shelf Registrations, Structure, and Performance," *Financial Management*, 1985, 14(1):5–15.

Schultz, Paul H., and Mir A. Zaman. "Aftermarket Support and Underpricing of Initial Public Offerings," *Journal of Financial Economics*, 1994, 35(2):199–219.

Slovin, Myron B., Marie E. Sushka, and Yvette M. Bendeck. "The Intra-Industry Effects of Going Private Transactions," *Journal of Finance*, 1991, 46(4):1537–1550.

Stein, Jeremy C. "Convertible Bonds as Backdoor Equity Financing," *Journal of Financial Economics*, 1992, 32(1):3–22.

Viswanath, P. V. "Strategic Considerations, the Pecking Order Hypothesis, and Market Reactions to Equity Financing," *Journal of Financial and Quantitative Analysis*, 1993, 28(2):213–234.

LONG-TERM DEBT

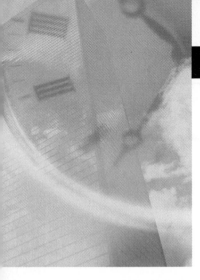

OBJECTIVES

After studying this chapter, you should be able to

1. Describe the four main classes of long-term corporate debt instruments.

2. Briefly explain the maturity, interest rate, sinking fund, call option, and covenants of a long-term debt instrument.

3. Describe the main characteristics of a Eurobond.

4. Explain the debt service parity approach to bond refunding analysis.

5. Calculate the net advantage of refunding a high-coupon debt issue.

No doubt you have borrowed money before. If you have a credit card, you borrow money each time you use it. The card issuer pays the merchant, and you must repay the card issuer. If you always pay the first time you are billed, the loans are *interest-free*. You simply repay the amount you borrowed; no interest is charged. If you do not pay right away, however, you begin to owe interest.

Credit card loans are easy to arrange. (Maybe that's why there is so much credit card debt in the United States![1]) You do not have to sign a new loan agreement each time you use the card. But you did enter into a form of loan agreement when your application was approved. The agreement has a lot of fine print, which spells out the terms of the loans. (Have you ever read it?) For example, it tells you the interest rate and how interest is calculated.

You may have also entered into more formal, longer-term loan arrangements. Have you gotten student loans to pay part of the cost of your education? Have you borrowed to buy a car? It will not be too long before you are taking out a mortgage loan to buy a home. Borrowing money is something individuals normally do. So do firms. In Chapters 15 and 16 we discussed how firms should determine how much to borrow. In this chapter we will look more closely at what forms this borrowing may take.

When a firm decides to issue debt securities, it must decide several things. Should the debt have a fixed or a variable interest rate? When should it mature? Should it include a sinking fund, which will retire it in installments? Should the firm retain a call option so that it can call in the debt and refund it if interest rates drop? These are just a few of the points we will discuss in this chapter.

When a firm has issued debt securities, it usually looks for opportunities to refund the debt at a profit. If interest rates drop, a firm may be able to replace outstanding bonds with lower-cost bonds. This is just what happens when a homeowner refinances her mortgage because rates have moved lower. Well-managed firms actively manage their liabilities. Bond refunding analysis is an important aspect of this activity. We will show you how a firm can evaluate a bond refunding opportunity to decide whether it is in the shareholders' interest to refund.

---

[1] About $400 billion at year-end 1995, according to the Federal Reserve Board.

LONG-TERM DEBT AND THE PRINCIPLES OF FINANCE

◆ *Valuable Ideas*: Look for opportunities to develop new debt securities that reduce issuers' funding costs and raise investors' risk-adjusted after-tax returns.

◆ *Two-Sided Transactions*: Selling new debt securities requires a price and other terms investors find acceptable.

◆ *Signaling*: Announcement of the decision to issue debt and of what type of debt will be issued conveys useful information about the firm.

◆ *Self-Interested Behavior*: Look for profitable opportunities to refund outstanding debt.

◆ *Options*: Recognize the value of a bond's call option. It is valuable because it enables the issuer to redeem the debt and replace it at a lower cost if interest rates drop.

◆ *Incremental Benefits*: Calculate the net advantage of refunding on the basis of its incremental after-tax benefits.

◆ *Risk-Return Trade-Off*: Offering a new debt security that is riskier to investors will require paying a higher rate of interest.

◆ *Time Value of Money*: Use discounted cash flow analysis to compare the costs and benefits of a bond refunding.

GENERAL AVIATION'S FINANCING DECISION

General Aviation Corporation has decided to raise $100 million of long-term funds. The firm has decided that the financing will take the form of a long-term debt issue. Investment bankers have told General Aviation's treasurer that there are three alternatives available. Table 24-1 compares the alternatives.

	U.S. PUBLIC OFFERING	U.S. PRIVATE PLACEMENT	EUROBOND OFFERING
Issue	Debentures	Debentures	Debentures
Amount	$100 million	$100 million	$100 million
Market	U.S. investors in the public securities market	U.S. investors in the private placement market	Foreign investors in the Eurodollar bond market
Maturity	10 years	10 years	10 years
Interest Rate:			
Coupon	9% APR	$9\frac{1}{8}$% APR	$9\frac{1}{8}$% APR
Frequency	Semiannual	Semiannual	Annual
Sinking Fund	None	None	None
Call Provision	None	None	None
Flotation Costs	$1 million	$750,000	$1,250,000

TABLE 24-1
General Aviation's debt financing alternatives.

The third alternative looks unattractive, because the coupon rate and issuance expenses are greater than a domestic public issue would require. The domestic private issue would require a higher coupon rate but would involve lower issuance expenses than the domestic public issue. However, the investment bankers have warned that the private issue might require General Aviation to agree to restrictions that might limit its future operating and financing flexibility.

We will return to this problem after looking at these alternative sources of long-term funds in greater detail.

24.1 TYPES OF LONG-TERM DEBT

There are four main classes of long-term corporate debt instruments: secured debt, unsecured debt, tax-exempt debt, and convertible debt. We will cover the first three here. The fourth class, convertible bonds, is covered in Chapter 26.

Secured Debt

Secured debt is backed by specific assets. This backing reduces both the lenders' risk and the interest rate they require. Mortgage bonds, collateral trust bonds, equipment trust certificates, and conditional sales contracts are the most common types of secured debt.

MORTGAGE BONDS Mortgage bonds are secured by a lien on specific assets of the issuer. The assets are described in detail in the legal document, called a *mortgage*, that grants the lien. If the issuer defaults—fails to make a required payment of principal or interest—or fails to perform some other provision of the loan contract, lenders can seize the assets that secure the mortgage bonds and sell them to pay off the debt obligation. The extra protection that the mortgage provides lowers the risk. In return, that lowers the required return. But the issuer sacrifices flexibility in selling assets. Mortgaged assets can be sold only with the mortgage bondholders' permission or if the borrower provides suitable replacement collateral.

COLLATERAL TRUST BONDS Collateral trust bonds are similar to mortgage bonds except that the lien is against securities, such as common shares of one of the issuer's subsidiaries, rather than against real property such as plant and equipment.

EQUIPMENT TRUST CERTIFICATES AND CONDITIONAL SALES CONTRACTS Equipment trust certificates and conditional sales contracts are frequently issued to finance the purchase of aircraft or railroad "rolling stock". Equipment trust certificates are usually issued to finance a leveraged lease.[2] The trust that issues them owns the asset during the term of the lease. Conditional sales contracts are agreements that manufacturers use to finance customer purchases of their goods. They are long-term receivables. The two financing mechanisms are similar: The borrower obtains title to the assets only after it fully repays the debt.

Unsecured Debt

Unsecured long-term debt consists of notes and debentures. By securities industry convention, **notes** are unsecured debt with an original maturity of ten years or less. **Debentures** are unsecured debt with an original maturity greater than ten years. Notes and debentures are issued on the strength of the issuer's general credit. A financial contract (the bond indenture) specifies

---

[2] Chapter 25 discusses leveraged leases.

their terms. They are not secured by specific property. If the issuer goes bankrupt, noteholders and debentureholders are classified as general creditors.

Debentures may have different levels of seniority. *Subordinated debentures* rank behind more *senior debentures* in payment of interest and principal and in claims on the firm's assets in the event of bankruptcy. This subordinated position exposes lenders to greater risk. Subordinated debentures therefore have a higher required return than senior debt of the same firm.

Tax-Exempt Corporate Debt

Under the Internal Revenue Code, firms can issue tax-exempt bonds for specified purposes. Congress grants tax-exempt bonding authority from time to time to encourage investment in specified types of projects that are in the public interest. The Tax Reform Act of 1986 sharply reduced the list of activities that qualify for tax-exempt financing. Activities that still qualified following that act include solid waste disposal and hazardous waste disposal facilities.

When a project qualifies for tax-exempt debt financing, holders of the tax-exempt bonds do not have to pay federal income tax on the interest payments they receive. Consequently, they are willing to accept a lower interest rate than on taxable debt. This, of course, creates a tax asymmetry. As a general rule, if a firm plans to construct facilities that qualify for tax-exempt financing, it should use such financing to the maximum extent.

Self-Check Questions

1. What are the four main classes of long-term corporate debt instruments?

2. What is the difference between secured debt and unsecured debt?

3. Why is issuing tax-exempt debt advantageous to a firm (when a project qualifies for it)?

24.2 MAIN FEATURES OF LONG-TERM DEBT

Long-term debt issues (initial maturity of one year or greater) are governed by financial contracts. For public debt issues, this contract is called a **bond indenture**. A trustee acts as agent for the bondholders and monitors the issuer's compliance with the provisions of the indenture. For a private issue, the contract is called a **bond agreement** or **note agreement**. These contracts specify the maturity, interest rate, and other terms of the debt issue, and they usually include a number of restrictive covenants.

Long-term debt instruments share several common features, which we described in Chapter 5. We will review them briefly.

1. *Stated maturity*. This is the date by which the borrower must repay the money it borrowed.

2. *Stated principal amount*. This is the amount the borrower must repay.

3. *Stated coupon rate of interest*. The interest rate may be a fixed rate, or it may be a variable rate that is adjusted according to a specified formula.

4. *Mandatory redemption* (or *sinking fund*) *schedule*. Some bonds contain a sinking fund, whereas others are repaid in a single sum at maturity. A sinking fund involves a sequence of principal repayments prior to the maturity date. Bonds are redeemed in cash at their face amount or else through capital market purchases.[3]

---

[3] If the bonds are selling at or above par value, the firm will call individual bonds that have been chosen randomly and pay the owner the par value. If the bonds are selling below par value, the indenture usually permits the firm to repurchase bonds in the open market to satisfy the sinking fund requirement.

5. *Optional redemption provision.* The issuer has the right to call the issue (or some portion of it) for early redemption. A schedule of optional redemption prices is specified at the time of issue. Callable bonds usually provide for a grace period immediately following issuance. Bonds are *noncallable* during this period. Many long-term issues contain a weaker provision. The bonds are only *nonrefundable*. The issuer can call the bonds at the appropriate call premium and redeem them out of excess cash or the proceeds from an equity issue (or in some cases, out of the proceeds of a junior debt issue). During the nonrefundable period, the issuer cannot use the proceeds from a new debt issue that ranks senior to, or on a par with, the outstanding debt to refund it. As we noted in Chapter 9, the optional redemption provision may be useful in reducing a firm's agency costs.

6. *Protective covenants.* **Covenants** impose restrictions on the borrower. They are designed to protect the bondholders.[4] The covenants often spell out financial tests that must be met before the borrower can (1) incur additional indebtedness (*debt limitation*), (2) use cash to pay dividends or make share repurchases (*dividend limitation*), (3) mortgage assets (*limitation on liens* and/or a *negative pledge clause*), (4) borrow through one of its subsidiaries (*limitation on subsidiary borrowing*), (5) sell major assets (*limitation on asset dispositions*), (6) merge with another firm or sell substantially all its assets to another firm (*limitation on merger, consolidation,* or *sale*), or (7) sell assets and lease them back (*limitation on sale-and-leaseback*).

EXAMPLE

Debt Covenants

A debt limitation covenant prohibits issuing additional long-term debt if it would cause the interest coverage ratio (EBIT to total interest) to fall below 3.00 (an *interest coverage test*), or if it would cause the ratio of tangible assets to long-term debt to fall below 1.50 (an *asset coverage test*). A dividend covenant restricts cash dividends or share repurchases to $10,000,000 plus 50% of cumulative earnings (less the cumulative amount already used for this purpose) since the bonds were issued. EBIT is currently $39 million, and interest is $10 million. How much additional 6% debt can the firm incur?

If interest expense rises to $13 million, interest coverage will be 3.00 (= 39/13). The extra $3 million (= 13 − 10) of interest will enable the firm to issue $50 million (= 3/0.06) of debt. ∎

Events of Default

Bond indentures and bond agreements also specify **events of default**. If the borrower fails to pay interest or to repay principal promptly, defaults on another debt issue, or fails to adhere to one of the covenants, the lenders can demand immediate repayment of the debt. Often, however, bondholders will try to negotiate before pursuing default proceedings, because they usually do not want to take ownership of the firm.

✓ Self-Check Questions

1. What are the main features of long-term debt instruments?

2. What is a sinking fund schedule? What is its main purpose?

3. What is an optional redemption schedule? Why is it valuable to a firm?

4. What are covenants? What is their main purpose?

---

[4] Chapter 9 discusses the use of bond covenants in the financial contracting process.

24.3 DESIGNING A LONG-TERM DEBT ISSUE

Firms that wish to borrow offer debt opportunities to potential lenders. Borrowers, therefore, design the terms of long-term debt. Of course, the Principle of Two-Sided Transactions applies. The issuer's choices are constrained by how much compensation investors will require for the package of features selected. In any case, however, a potential borrower first chooses what type of debt to issue. Then it must decide on the key features.

Choice of Debt Maturity

A firm should choose a debt maturity that causes its outflow obligations to be in line with its expected inflows. That is, the debt maturity should bring its *total* debt service stream broadly into line with its projected *total* operating cash flow stream. A debt repayment schedule that bunches repayment obligations within a brief time period involves greater risk of insolvency (that is, insufficient cash to meet required payments on time) than one that spreads these obligations over a longer time period. But the matching does not have to be exact. For example, if a firm is rapidly growing or changing in significant ways (such as improving its profitability), issuing some shorter-maturity debt will enable it to renegotiate these debt contracts in the future after its financial situation has improved.

SIGNIFICANCE OF INCLUDING A SINKING FUND   A sinking fund requires the firm to repay the debt in installments, rather than in a lump sum. It has two important consequences. First, as we noted in Chapter 9, the need to make principal repayments furnishes a monitoring device. Second, a sinking fund reduces the effective life of the debt, thereby reducing the bond's risk in the same way as a shorter maturity. **Average life** is a better measure than maturity of the "average" amount of time the debt will be outstanding. It's defined as

$$\text{Average life} = \frac{\sum_{t=1}^{N} tA_t}{\sum_{t=1}^{N} A_t} \tag{24.1}$$

A_t is the sinking fund payment due t periods from the date of issue. The final sinking fund payment is A_N and occurs at time N. You can think of average life as the weighted average of the time to receipt (t) of the principal payments (with $A_t/\Sigma A_t$ as the weights).

EXAMPLE

Calculating Average Life

A debt issue that matures in 10 years requires equal sinking fund payments at the ends of years 6 through 10. What is the average life?

Average life = 6(0.2) + 7(0.2) + 8(0.2) + 9(0.2) + 10(0.2) = 8 years

On a time-weighted basis, the debt will be repaid in an average of 8 years. ■

Average life uses the sinking fund payments as the weights. Market professionals often make two adjustments to this calculation. They use the total cash flow (interest as well as principal), and they calculate the present value of each payment and use these present values as the weights. The resulting measure is called the **duration** of the bond. It is calculated according to the formula

$$\text{Duration} = \frac{1}{P} \sum_{t=1}^{N} \frac{t\text{CF}_t}{(1+y)^t} \tag{24.2}$$

where P is the price of the bond, CF_t is the total cash flow from the bond at t (that is, interest *and* principal), and y is the bond's yield to maturity expressed as the interest rate per period. For a bond that pays interest semiannually, y is the APR yield divided by 2. The t in the numerator measures the length of time until CF_t will be received. Duration according to Equation (24.2) is the present-value-weighted average number of interest periods until the bond "matures." For a bond that pays interest semiannually, divide the duration calculated from Equation (24.2) by 2 to express it in years.

EXAMPLE

Calculating Duration

A bond pays interest semiannually at a 10% APR. It has a sinking fund that repays $50 million each at the end of years 4 and 5. Total principal is $100 million. The bond's yield to maturity is 9% APR. Calculate the bond's duration.

First calculate the cash flows. There are 10 interest periods. For the first 7 periods, the bond pays interest only. Thus $\text{CF}_1 = \text{CF}_2 = \cdots = \text{CF}_7 = \$5.0$ million $[= 100(0.10/2)]$. The bond pays principal at the end of period 8, so $\text{CF}_8 = \$55.0$ million $(= 50 + 5)$. That leaves $50 million remaining. Therefore, $\text{CF}_9 = \$2.5$ million $[= 50(0.10/2)]$, and $\text{CF}_{10} = \$52.5$ million. The bond's price is

$$P = \sum_{t=1}^{10} \frac{\text{CF}_t}{(1.045)^t} = \$103.63 \text{ million}$$

Now apply Equation (24.2). The bond's duration is

$$\text{Duration} = \frac{1}{103.63} \sum_{t=1}^{10} \frac{t\text{CF}_t}{(1+y)^t}$$

$$= \frac{1}{103.63} \left[\frac{5}{(1.045)^1} + \frac{10}{(1.045)^2} + \frac{15}{(1.045)^3} + \frac{20}{(1.045)^4} + \frac{25}{(1.045)^5} \right]$$

$$+ \frac{1}{103.63} \left[\frac{30}{(1.045)^6} + \frac{35}{(1.045)^7} + \frac{440}{(1.045)^8} + \frac{22.5}{(1.045)^9} + \frac{525}{(1.045)^{10}} \right]$$

$$= 7.48 \text{ periods}$$

With 6-month periods, the duration is 3.74 years $(= 7.48/2)$. Note that the average life of the issue is 4.5 years. Duration provides a better measure of the average timing of the bond's total cash flows. ■

MAXIMUM MATURITY   You may wonder how long a maturity is possible. Within the past few years, firms have issued debt with 40-, 50-, and even 100-year maturities. For example, The Coca-Cola Company sold $150 million of 100-year debentures in July 1993. We are not recommending that you set the longest maturity possible. However, you should recognize that issuing debt with a very long maturity increases the average life of a firm's total debt portfolio. This can be useful when the firm wishes to lengthen the maturity structure of its debt in order to bring it more in line with the time pattern of its operating cash flow stream.

Setting the Coupon Rate

Most issuers of debt select a coupon rate that will make the bonds worth par. However, at times asymmetric taxes or asymmetric information can make it advantageous either to set the coupon rate below the prevailing market rate or to let the interest rate float according to some specified formula.

DEEP-DISCOUNT BONDS   In 1981 and 1982, interest rates were very high by historical standards. Many firms issued *deep-discount bonds*. They carried very low interest rates and were sold at prices well below their principal amounts. For example, Du Pont sold $600 million principal amount of 6% debentures due 2001 at a price of 46.852% ($468.52 per $1000 bond) on November 19, 1981. Recall that in Chapter 5 we discussed *zero-coupon bonds*, which are the deepest-discount bonds possible because they make only a single payment at maturity. Among many others, Beatrice Foods sold $250 million principal amount of zero-coupon notes due February 9, 1992, at a price of 25.50% on February 2, 1982.

Some investors, particularly pension funds, found the deep-discount bonds and zero-coupon bonds attractive. The bonds generally have a call price equal to their par value. Unless the bonds have a call price schedule well below their par value, it is unlikely that a firm would ever exercise its call option. Although a reduced risk of a call benefits the bondholders, it is of course at the expense of the issuer's refunding flexibility.

The discount also reduces the lender's reinvestment risk. In the case of a zero-coupon bond, the investor's "income" each period is effectively reinvested at the issue's yield to maturity, regardless of what interest rates are at the time. This protects the investor's total return from interest rate movements between the dates of issuance and maturity. The absence of reinvestment risk also enables investors such as pension funds to match their investment income against future liabilities more closely than they could with alternative investments. This feature is more valuable the higher is the level of interest rates.

Issuers also found the deep-discount bonds and zero-coupon bonds attractive because of a tax asymmetry. Until May 1982, issuers were permitted to deduct an equal portion of the discount (the difference between par value and the issue price) each period. Thus interest could be deducted at a faster rate than it accrued. This feature is more valuable the higher the bond's yield. It substantially reduced the effective after-tax cost of the debt. Because most purchasers of zero-coupon bonds were tax-exempt, the manner of amortizing the discount did not affect them.

FIXING THE COUPON RATE OR LETTING IT FLOAT   Firms such as banks and finance companies, whose return on assets fluctuates with interest rate movements, often find it best to issue floating-rate long-term debt. Most other firms choose to fix the interest rate on long-term debt issues. They adjust their overall mix of fixed- and floating-rate debt by altering the mix of floating-rate short-term debt and fixed-rate longer-term debt. Before deciding whether to issue floating-rate long-term debt, a firm should at least compare the prospective terms for such an issue against the following alternatives:

1. Issuing a sequence of shorter-term issues, whose successive maturities match the successive interest rate adjustment dates.

2. Issuing fixed-rate debt that matures the day the floating-rate issue does.

In the first case, the sequence of shorter-term issues will involve roughly the same degree of interest rate risk as the longer-term floating-rate issue. The sequence of shorter-term issues will involve greater issuance expenses than the longer-term floating-rate issue. But the issuer can benefit by rolling over shorter-term debt if its credit situation improves, because that will tend to reduce its interest rate. In the second case, the floating-rate issue exposes the issuer to the risk that interest rates will change. Thus it is not surprising that industrial firms generally borrow long term on a fixed-rate basis to fund investments in fixed assets. In contrast, when the issuer's revenues are sensitive to movements in interest rates, borrowing on a floating-rate basis may actually reduce the firm's financial risk by aligning the fluctuations in revenues and interest expense.

Setting the Optional Redemption Provision

The optional redemption provision is a call option that gives the issuer the right to buy back the issue. Setting the optional redemption provision involves answering two questions: Should the issue include a call option? If so, what form should it take? In recent years, however, most corporate debt issues have been noncallable. In a perfect capital market environment, an issuer would not derive any net benefit from including a call provision, because lenders would require a yield premium sufficient to compensate them fully for the risk of a call. However, market imperfections, such as tax asymmetries, agency costs, and transaction costs, might make a call provision advantageous in some situations.

DESIGN OF CALL FEATURES   The call provision included in corporate debt issues has become highly standardized. The first year's call price is normally equal to the public offering price plus the coupon rate. Thereafter, the annual call prices decrease by equal amounts to par, at which price the bonds are callable over the remaining years to maturity. Usually the call provision also imposes limits on the issuer's ability to exercise the option. In the public market, long-term manufacturing firm debt issues are nonrefundable for ten years but can be called and paid for out of excess cash or out of the proceeds of an equity issue. Long-term electric utility debt issues are nonrefundable for five years. Long-term telephone utility debt issues are noncallable (for any reason) for five years.

EXAMPLE		
An Optional Redemption Price Schedule for a Long-Term Bond	Table 24-2 contains an optional redemption price schedule for a long-term bond. The bond has a 25-year maturity. It bears a 10% coupon. Its issue price is 95 (95% of par, or $950 per $1000 principal amount). The initial year's redemption price equals the offering price plus the coupon, 95 + 10 = 105. The bond is callable at par during the last 5 years. The call price steps down annually by equal amounts. There are 20 steps, so each step is 0.25 [= (105 − 100)/20]. ∎	

TABLE 24-2
Optional redemption price schedule.

YEAR	CALL PRICE	YEAR	CALL PRICE	YEAR	CALL PRICE
1	105.00[a]	8	103.25	15	101.50
2	104.75[a]	9	103.00	16	101.25
3	104.50[a]	10	102.75	17	101.00
4	104.25[a]	11	102.50	18	100.75
5	104.00[a]	12	102.25	19	100.50
6	103.75	13	102.00	20	100.25
7	103.50	14	101.75	21–25	100.00

[a] Bond is not refundable out of the proceeds of a debt issue that ranks senior to, or on a par with, this bond.

PUT OPTIONS   Interestingly, within the past few years, some corporate issuers have begun to incorporate put options in their debt issues. The put option gives the lender the right to sell the bond back to the borrower on one or more dates at a specified price, which is usually par. This option gives the lender reassurance against *claim dilution*, such as the loss in value that would result if a firm effected a leveraged buyout and the bonds had to remain outstanding for their original term. The put option limits this impairment in value by permitting holders to force early redemption.

Frequency and Timing of Debt Issues

Economies of scale make larger issues relatively more attractive. Larger issues also help promote a relatively liquid secondary market for the bonds. Consequently, firms issue long-term debt in large discrete amounts, and they plan these issues carefully. Because of capital market efficiency, arbitrage opportunities with respect to interest rate movements will not exist.

When a firm plans to issue debt, it may be possible to obtain a modest reduction in the total cost of the transaction with short-term management. A firm should not issue debt when conditions look volatile or temporarily bad. For example, during periods of tight money or particularly volatile interest rates, the supply of funds for non-investment-grade bonds tends to shrink. Also, a large Treasury financing can temporarily depress the debt market. Therefore, issuers should remain flexible with respect to timing in order to prevent temporary factors from adversely affecting their cost of borrowing.

Self-Check Questions

1. What does the average life of a debt issue measure?

2. What is a deep-discount bond? What is a zero-coupon bond?

3. How do zero-coupon bonds eliminate the investor's reinvestment risk?

4. For what type(s) of firms might issuing floating-rate debt be advantageous?

5. What does the optional redemption price schedule for a long-term bond usually look like?

24.4 RECENT INNOVATIONS IN THE BOND MARKET

In Chapter 23 we discussed the process of securities innovation. We also described some recent innovations and explained the reasons why issuers and investors found them beneficial. (Remember: There are two sides to every transaction). This section describes five recent debt innovations: commodity-linked bonds, collateralized mortgage obligations, floating-rate notes, credit-sensitive notes, and extendible notes.

Commodity-Linked Bonds

Most debt innovations involve some form of risk reallocation as compared to conventional debt instruments. Risk reallocation adds value by transferring risks away from issuers or investors to others better able to bear them. Risk reallocation may also be beneficial if a firm can design a security that better suits the risk-return preferences of a particular class of investors. Investors with a comparative advantage in bearing some types of risks will pay more for innovative securities that enable them to specialize in bearing such risks.

Commodity-linked bonds were developed in response to rising and increasingly volatile prices. The principal repayment, and in some cases the coupon payments, are tied to the price of a particular commodity, such as oil or silver, or to a specified commodity price index. Such bonds are often structured to enable the producer of a commodity to hedge its exposure to a sharp decline in commodity prices and thus in its revenues. Such securities effectively increase a firm's debt capacity by shifting the debt service burden from times when the commodity producer is least able to pay to periods when it is best able to do so.

EXAMPLE	*An Oil-Indexed Debt Issue*	An oil producer could design an "oil-indexed" debt issue with interest payments that rise and fall with the level of oil prices. Investors might be willing to accept significantly lower yields for two reasons. First, the firm's after-interest cash flows would be more stable than in the case of a straight, fixed-rate debt issue. This reduces default risk. Second, some investors may be seeking a "play" on oil prices not otherwise available in the commodity futures or options market. Interest payments rise and fall with the price of oil. In this latter sense, many securities innovations that reallocate risk also add value by "making the market less incomplete." ∎

Collateralized Mortgage Obligations

Collateralized mortgage obligations (CMOs) address a somewhat different kind of "reinvestment risk"—one that investors in mortgage pass-through certificates found troublesome.[5] Most mortgages are prepayable at par at the option of the mortgagor after some brief period. The fact that many mortgages will be paid off if interest rates decline creates a significant prepayment risk for investors. That is, if their principal is returned prematurely, they will have to reinvest at lower rates.

To address this "prepayment" risk, CMOs repackage the mortgage payment stream from a portfolio of mortgages into several series of debt instruments. These are prioritized in terms of their right to receive principal payments. In the simplest form, each series must be repaid in full before any principal payments can be made to the holders of the next series. In this way, a CMO effectively shifts most of the mortgage prepayment risk to the lower-priority class(es) and away from the higher-priority class(es), which benefit from a significant reduction in the uncertainty as to when the debt obligation will be fully repaid.

Floating-Rate Notes

Floating-rate notes are one of the innovative securities developed in response to rising and increasingly volatile interest rates. They adjust interest payments to correspond to changes in market interest rates. Floating-rate notes thus reduce the lender's principal risk by transferring interest rate risk to the borrower. Of course, this transfer exposes the *issuer* to floating interest rate risk. But such a reallocation of interest rate risk can be of mutual benefit to issuers with assets whose values are directly correlated with interest rate changes. For this reason, banks and finance companies are prominent among issuers of these securities.

Credit-Sensitive Notes

A new security can increase shareholder value by reducing agency costs. Recall from Chapter 9 that these costs arise out of the inherent conflicts of interest among professional corporate managers, stockholders, and bondholders. For example, managers in some cases may increase shareholder value at the expense of bondholders by leveraging up the firm. *Credit-sensitive notes* and *floating-rate, rating-sensitive notes* bear a coupon rate that varies inversely with the issuer's credit standing. These securities, however, have a potentially serious flaw: The inter-

---

[5] Mortgage pass-through certificates consist of ownership interests in a portfolio of mortgages. Principal and interest payments are passed through pro rata to certificate holders.

est rate adjustment mechanism will tend to increase the issuer's debt service burden just when it can least afford it—when its credit rating has fallen, presumably as a result of diminished operating cash flow.

A credit-sensitive note bears a 10% coupon rate. The issuer is rated triple-B. The indenture provides that the coupon rate will drop to 9% if the rating improves to single-A and to 8.50% if it rises to double-A or better. It also requires the coupon rate to rise to 11% if the rating drops to double-B and to 13% if it drops to single-B or lower. ■

Credit-Sensitive Notes

EXAMPLE

Extendible Notes

Extendible notes increase stockholder value by reducing the underwriting commissions and other transaction costs associated with raising capital. They give the issuer and investors the option to extend the security's maturity. For example, extendible notes generally provide for such an extension along with a suitable interest rate adjustment every two or three years. They thus represent an alternative to rolling over two- or three-year note issues—an alternative that does not entail additional issuance expenses when the notes are extendible.

Self-Check Questions

1. What is a commodity-linked bond? What type(s) of firms might find it advantageous to issue such bonds?

2. What are collateralized mortgage obligations (CMOs)? How do they reallocate mortgage prepayment risk?

3. Why do banks often issue floating-rate notes?

4. What are credit-sensitive notes?

24.5 INTERNATIONAL DEBT FINANCING

A firm can sell U.S.-dollar-denominated bonds to U.S. investors in the domestic bond market or to foreign investors in the Eurobond market. Alternatively, a firm can sell bonds denominated in a foreign currency. However, issuing bonds denominated in a foreign currency involves a foreign exchange risk. The issuer must either realize foreign currency from its operations or purchase foreign currency to meet its future debt service obligations on the debt. We consider this possibility in Chapter 29.

Dollar-Denominated Borrowing in the Eurobond Market

A **Eurobond** is a bond issued outside the country in whose currency it is denominated. Firms headquartered in the United States issue dollar-denominated Eurobonds to investors in Europe (hence the prefix *Euro*) and in other areas outside the United States. Eurobonds denominated in other currencies are also issued, but U.S. dollar-denominated bonds often represent more than half the total Eurobond market.

The Eurobond market developed during the 1960s when the U.S. government levied an interest equalization tax on the purchase of foreign securities by U.S. investors and imposed restrictions on capital exports by American firms. Large U.S. balance-of-payments deficits continued the outflow of dollar funds. The U.S. also imposed a withholding tax on interest payments by domestic firms to foreign investors, which discouraged foreign investment of these funds in domestic bond issues for many years. Instead, foreign investors avoided this withholding tax by purchasing Eurobonds issued by special-purpose subsidiaries of U.S. firms established in the Netherlands Antilles, which enjoyed a special status as a result of its tax treaty with the United States. The 30% withholding tax was eliminated in 1984, permitting U.S. firms to sell debt directly to foreign investors free of this tax. Nevertheless, the Eurobond market continues to thrive.

Characteristics of Eurobonds

Dollar-denominated Eurobond issues are as varied as domestic bond issues. Most are straight debt issues, but convertible Eurobonds and Eurobonds with warrants are not uncommon. Nevertheless, there are important differences between the domestic bond market and the Eurobond market.

1. Eurobond investors usually own assets denominated in several currencies. The relative attractiveness of dollar-denominated Eurobonds, and hence the relationship between bond yields in the domestic bond market and the dollar-denominated Eurobond market, depends on U.S. dollar exchange rates. When the U.S. dollar is appreciating relative to the other major currencies, Eurobond investors tend to increase their purchasing of dollar-denominated Eurobonds (and of other dollar-denominated assets). This activity can drive Eurobond yields below domestic bond yields and create an attractive borrowing opportunity for U.S. firms, which gives rise to a so-called *Eurobond market window*.

2. Because of investors' exchange rate sensitivity, Eurobond maturities are usually shorter, and issue sizes generally smaller, than in the domestic market.

3. Eurobonds are generally *bearer bonds* that *pay interest annually*. Issuing bonds in bearer form makes it more difficult to refund them prior to maturity, because most buyers can be contacted directly only when they come to the paying agent to claim their interest payments.

4. The Eurobond market is essentially unregulated. It is a truly international market. Hence Eurobond yields are somewhat less susceptible to government influence than domestic bond yields. Nevertheless, arbitrage activity ensures that Eurobond yields normally track domestic bond yields fairly closely.

The Cost of Borrowing in the Eurobond Market

Annual interest payments on Eurobonds make it necessary to compare APYs when comparing domestic and Eurobond borrowing alternatives.

| EXAMPLE | *Comparing Domestic and Eurobond Borrowing Costs* | A firm can issue 10-year public debt in the domestic market at par bearing a 12% coupon. Instead, it could sell a 10-year $12\frac{1}{8}\%$ Eurobond issue. The total issuance expenses are identical for both issues. From Equation (4.7), the APY for the domestic bond is $(1.06)^2 - 1 = 12.36\%$. For the Eurobond issue it is 12.125%. Therefore, the Eurobond issue is slightly cheaper in spite of its higher coupon rate. ■ |

YEAR	DOMESTIC[a]	INTERNATIONAL[a]	TOTAL[a]	PERCENT DOMESTIC	TRADE-WEIGHTED DOLLAR EXCHANGE RATE[b]
1984	$ 81,153	$ 17,986	$ 99,139	81.9%	138.19
1985	84,047	40,889	124,936	67.3	143.01
1986	155,737	42,858	198,595	78.4	112.22
1987	125,185	19,565	144,750	86.5	96.94
1988	117,844	17,958	135,802	86.8	92.72
1989	140,455	18,221	158,676	88.5	98.60
1990	103,523	15,517	119,040	87.0	89.09
1991	197,713	23,141	220,854	89.5	89.84
1992	297,647	26,721	324,368	91.8	86.61
1993	406,146	41,000	447,146	90.8	93.18
1994	343,508	49,914	393,422	87.3	91.32
1995	483,665	66,669	550,334	87.9	84.25
Total	$2,536,623	$380,439	$2,917,062	87.0	

TABLE 24-3
Volume of domestic and international bond financing by U.S. firms, 1984–1995 (dollar amounts in millions).

[a] Includes convertible debt.
[b] Index for which March 1973 = 100.
Sources: Securities Data Company, Inc., and *Federal Reserve Bulletin,* Board of Governors of the Federal Reserve System, Washington, D.C., various issues.

The Eurobond market offers firms an alternative to borrowing domestically. Table 24-3 presents the mix of domestic and international bond financing by U.S. firms from 1984 to 1995. Volume picked up sharply in 1985 and 1993, when the strength of the U.S. dollar and other factors brought about a sharp increase in the foreign demand for dollar-denominated bonds.

Self-Check Questions

1. What is a Eurobond? How did the Eurobond market develop?
2. How do dollar-denominated Eurobonds differ from U.S. domestic bonds?
3. What adjustment do you usually have to make in order to compare the cost of issuing Eurobonds and the cost of issuing domestic bonds?

24.6 BOND REFUNDING

Call options have value. The optional redemption feature of a bond is a call option. It gives the issuer the right to redeem the bond prior to maturity. If interest rates fall sufficiently, the option is in-the-money, and the issuer will call it and replace it with lower-cost debt. Replacing an outstanding bond with a new bond before its scheduled maturity is referred to as a **bond refunding**.

A well-managed firm will look for opportunities to refund its debt at a profit, just as homeowners look for opportunities to refinance their mortgages when interest rates drop. We will show you how a firm can evaluate a bond refunding opportunity to decide whether it is in the shareholders' interest to refund. We will also show you how to quantify the benefit.

The firm can retire outstanding debt in three ways. First, the firm can call the bonds, paying bondholders the cash call (strike) price if the bond indenture includes a call provision. Second, the firm can repurchase the bonds in the open market. Third, the firm can exchange new securities for the bonds, provided that bondholders agree to the exchange. When a firm sells new bonds to raise cash to finance a repurchase or redemption, or when it exchanges new bonds for old bonds, the old bonds are said to be *refunded* with new debt. As with other corporate decisions, a refunding should be undertaken only if it will increase shareholder wealth.

Why Firms Refund Bonds

There are three main reasons why a borrower may find it advantageous to refund a bond issue. The firm may want to (1) take advantage of reduced interest rates to lower the cost of borrowing, (2) eliminate restrictive bond covenants, or (3) lengthen the maturity of the outstanding issue.

The analysis in this chapter is limited to the first reason, which is the most common reason why firms refund. However, the framework developed here also has direct application to the other two motives. For example, suppose a refunding is intended to eliminate restrictive bond covenants, and the firm has determined that the net advantage of the refunding is negative. That negative amount is a cost that must be weighed against the benefit of eliminating the old covenants in order to determine whether the refunding is worthwhile.

The decision to refund involves two basic questions. First, will the refunding be profitable? Second, if it is profitable, would it be more advantageous to wait and refund at some time in the future?

What Gives Rise to Profitable Bond Refunding Opportunities?

Volatile interest rates create profitable bond refunding opportunities. Figure 24-1 illustrates that between 1984 and 1986, and again between 1990 and 1993, interest rates on corporate bonds fell sharply. This gave rise to profitable opportunities to refund outstanding bonds with

FIGURE 24-1

Average yield on AA-rated long-term corporate bonds, 1970–1994.

Sources: Moody's Bond Record, Moody's Investors Service, Inc., New York, various issues.

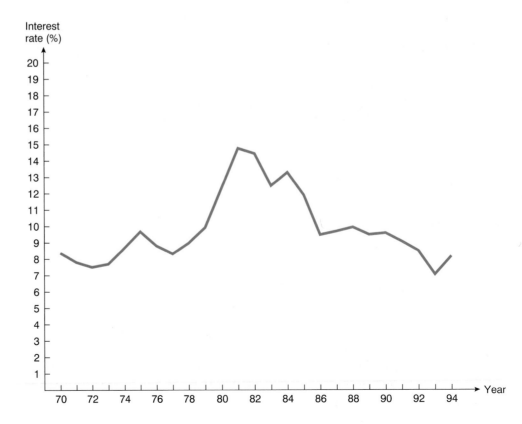

lower-cost bonds. At the same time, many homeowners benefitted by refinancing their mortgages at lower interest rates!

When Refunding Is Profitable: The Debt Service Parity Approach

When a firm refunds debt, there are side effects that often occur. For instance, often its capital structure changes. The effect of this change can complicate the process of accurately determining the net benefit to shareholders of undertaking a refinancing. To avoid confusion, you must be careful to neutralize the side effects when considering a refunding. The refunding decision should be based on a comparison of the after-tax cash flows needed to service the old debt and those needed to service the new debt.

One method of doing this is called the **debt service parity (DSP) approach**. The basic idea is simple. For analytical purposes, construct a hypothetical replacement debt obligation that has the same after-tax payments, period by period, as the outstanding debt obligation. If this stream of after-tax debt service payments will support sufficient new debt to (1) cover the cost of retiring the outstanding issue, (2) pay all transaction costs, and (3) provide a *surplus*, then refinancing will provide a net benefit to the firm's shareholders. The surplus measures the net benefit; it measures how much the call option is in-the-money. *The DSP approach neutralizes side effects by holding fixed the amount of after-tax cash flow from operations required to service debt.*

SIDE ISSUES   Under the DSP approach, whether the new debt issue will *actually* have an identical set of after-tax payments is not important. In order to isolate the refinancing decision and correctly measure the benefits, we measure the net benefit from the refinancing on a debt-service-parity basis by holding the period-by-period after-tax debt service payments fixed. Only after the net benefit (or cost) of the refinancing has been accurately measured on this basis should the firm consider other potential simultaneous changes. Such changes might include borrowing a larger or a smaller amount than the liability that would allow for debt service parity. The choice of the amount to borrow, and the specific terms on which to borrow, however, are separate from the decision to undertake the refinancing. They should be evaluated on their own merits.

OTHER APPLICATIONS   The Principle of Incremental Benefits reveals the advantage of using the DSP approach to analyze a refinancing decision. The incremental cash flows that will result directly from choosing to replace the outstanding liability are made explicit. The DSP approach can also be applied to a variety of other decisions, several of which are illustrated in subsequent chapters.

Self-Check Questions

1. What does it mean to refund a bond issue?

2. What gives rise to profitable bond refunding opportunities?

3. What does the debt service parity approach neutralize? Does this mean that the new issue must be identical to the old one?

True Value: NA

The value of a refunding is its net present value to the firm's shareholders. In order to distinguish the net benefit of a bond refunding from the net present value of a capital investment project, we speak of the **net advantage of refunding** (NA) a bond issue to describe the net present value of the savings derived from the refunding. If the present value of the cash savings from a refunding exceeds the present value of all the costs of refunding, NA is positive and the operation is profitable. We use the debt service parity approach to compute NA. The NA is essentially the net exercise value of the firm's call option.

A Word of Warning

Be careful not to make the mistake of treating a refunding operation as a capital investment. A capital investment involves the purchase of an operating asset whose net cash flows are, in various degrees, uncertain and involve operating risk. Furthermore, a capital investment affects both sides of the firm's balance sheet and is not connected with any specific means of financing. In contrast, a refunding involves replacement of one debt service stream with another that is identical period-by-period on an after-tax basis. The decision affects only the liability side of the firm's balance sheet and is directly connected with a particular means of financing (the refunding issue).

Recall that the opportunity cost of capital is the required return under current capital market conditions. Therefore, although we will be more specific in a moment, loosely speaking, the opportunity cost of capital for a refunding is the after-tax required return on the new debt issue.

Applying the Debt Service Parity Approach to Measure the Net Advantage

Applying the DSP approach is straightforward: Determine the amount of new debt that can be issued today, assuming that the after-tax debt service payments for the new issue are exactly the same, period by period, as those of the old issue. You can think of the after-tax debt service payments on the old debt as a set of promised future cash flows that could be "auctioned off" in the capital market. The amount of new debt the firm can issue today is then the amount it would receive in exchange for that set of promised future cash flows. If the "auction" proceeds are sufficient to cover the cost of repurchasing the old issue, to pay any transaction costs, and to provide a surplus, then the firm should refund the old issue. If there is a deficit, then refunding would decrease shareholder wealth and should not be undertaken.

The DSP principle extends beyond cash flows. Parity implies that all rights and obligations of the old issue must also be maintained in the new. Therefore, the sinking fund schedule and maturity of the hypothetical new issue must be identical to those that remain on the old issue. For example, a debt issue with a remaining life of six years would be evaluated against a hypothetical refunding issue with a six-year life. Note that if the refunding were undertaken, the actual new issue might have a maturity other than six years. The maturity of the actual new issue is a separate decision. The firm should choose the features of the new debt only after it has determined that refunding is advantageous.

Tax Considerations

As with other financial decisions, it is important to reflect the related tax consequences correctly. This involves adjusting the cash flows and the discount rate appropriately. As we have often said, tax code provisions change. Therefore, when undertaking a refunding analysis, it is important to check the tax consequences carefully and ensure that the current tax treatment is accurately reflected in the analysis.

All expenses connected with a refunding are tax-deductible, some during the year of the refunding and the others over the life of the new issue. The basic rule is (1) expenses connected with retiring the old issue may be deducted in the year of the refunding, and (2) expenses connected with the new issue (including any discount or premium) must be amortized over its life.

The expenses that are deductible in the year the refunding occurs include

- The call premium—the difference between the call price and par value.[6]

- The unamortized balance of issuance expenses plus original issue discount (or minus original issue premium) on the old debt.[7]

- Legal fees, printing costs, and fees paid to the trustee for canceling the old bonds.

- Firms often sell the new bonds before retiring the old bonds. In such cases, the difference between the interest cost of, and the investment return on, the surplus funds during the period between the issuance of the new bonds and the retirement of the old bonds is deductible. (If the investment return exceeds the interest cost, of course, the surplus is taxable.)

In general, the current tax law contains a bias in favor of refunding high-coupon debt, because it allows the call premium to be deducted.

Calculating the After-Tax Debt Service Payment Stream   *EXAMPLE*

An outstanding debt issue with a $100 million face amount bears interest at an 8% APR. Interest is payable annually, and principal must be repaid in full at the end of 10 years. The issuer's marginal income tax rate is 40%. The unamortized balance of issuance expenses is $500,000. What is the after-tax debt service payment stream for the debt issue?

For each of years 1 through 9 there will be $4.8 million [$= (1 - 0.4)(0.08)100$] of after-tax interest expense. Annual amortization is $50,000 ($= 500,000/10$). The deduction for expense amortization works just like the deduction for depreciation. It reduces taxable income. The value of a tax deduction equals the amount of the deduction multiplied by the tax rate. The value of annual expense amortization is $20,000 ($= 50,000 \times 0.40$). This is a cash flow benefit. After-tax debt service in years 1 through 9 is $4,780,000 ($= 4,800,000 - 20,000$) per year. For year 10 it will be the same after-tax interest payment *less* amortization *plus* the principal repayment, for a total of $104,780,000 million ($= 4,800,000 - 20,000 + 100,000,000$). Under the DSP approach, the refunding issue would be treated as having a total after-tax debt service obligation of $4.78 million for each of years 1 through 9 and $104.78 million for year 10. ■

Analyzing a High-Coupon Bond Refunding

Now that we have covered the basics, we can show you how to evaluate a high-coupon bond refunding opportunity.

Analyzing a High-Coupon Bond Refunding Opportunity   *EXAMPLE*

Palo Alto Refinancing (PAR) specializes in helping consumers refinance their personal debt. PAR's managers have decided that charity begins at home. The firm has a $100 million bond issue outstanding, which is scheduled to mature in a single lump sum 15 years from today. This issue has a 12% APR coupon rate (6% semiannual). At the current time, the bonds are selling in the capital market for $1035 each. PAR can call them at a strike price of $1050 each. The outstanding bonds cost $1 million to issue 5 years ago. PAR is amortizing this cost on a semiannual straight-line basis [$25,000 ($= 1,000,000/40$) in expense every 6 months] over the

---

[6] Later we will discuss how a firm could purchase noncallable high-coupon bonds through a tender offer. In such cases, the difference between the tender price and par value is tax-deductible.

[7] Original issue discount (premium) occurs when the firm issues debt at a price less than (greater than) its par value. Amortization of issuance expense and original issue discount (premium) parallels the treatment of depreciation on new equipment in a capital budgeting project. That is, the cost is incurred at issuance, but the tax deduction is spread over the life of the bond issue. Just as in the case of depreciation on a piece of machinery that is sold, when the bonds are repurchased, the remaining amount of the cost not yet expensed can be expensed immediately.

20-year total life of the bonds. PAR's marginal tax rate is 34%. Figure 24-2 shows the outstanding debt issue's after-tax debt service stream, its cash flow after taxes (CFATs). Table 24-4 summarizes the results of applying the DSP approach to evaluate the net advantage of refunding the 12% issue.

Current capital market conditions are as follows:

1. PAR can sell 15-year noncallable bullet-maturity debt, with a bond indenture otherwise identical to that of the outstanding bonds, at par value if they carry a 10.4% APR coupon rate (5.2% semiannual).

2. Issuance expenses for the replacement debt that would have to be amortized over the life of the new bonds are $1 million.

3. Expenses that can be deducted for tax purposes immediately, in addition to the call premium, amount to $350,000.

4. PAR can borrow up to $10 million worth of 15-year semiannual installment debt at a semiannual rate of 5.15%, with negligible transaction costs.

Let's say that PAR does nothing with the outstanding bonds. It is obligated to pay the bondholders a tax-deductible $6 million twice a year for the next 15 years and to repay $100 million of principal at the end of 15 years. Also, every 6 months for the next 15 years, PAR can claim, as a tax-deductible expense, part of the original cost of issuing those bonds. The stream of CFATs amounts to $3,951,500 [= (1 − 0.34)6,000,000 − (0.34)25,000] every 6 months plus $100 million 15 years from now. The semiannual after-tax expense is shown on line (c) in Table 24-4.

Suppose PAR issues $100 million worth of new 15-year noncallable debt. It would claim a tax deduction of $33,333 every 6 months (= 1,000,000/30) on the basis of the issuance expenses. The total after-tax payments on that debt would be $3,420,667 [= (1 − 0.34)5,200,000 − (0.34)33,333] twice a year for 15 years, plus a single payment of $100 million 15 years from now. Figure 24-3 shows this set of CFATs as an overlay on the CFATs for the outstanding bonds. The semiannual after-tax expense for the new debt is shown on line (a) in Table 24-4. The clear area in Figure 24-3 represents the difference between the CFATs. It equals $530,833 per year (= 3,951,500 − 3,420,667), which is the "savings" derived from issuing the new and retiring the old issue.

What can the savings CFATs be sold for in the capital market? The savings CFATs are

	AFTER-TAX DEBT SERVICE PER PERIOD	SAVINGS (COST)
TABLE 24-4 Refunding Issues:		
(a) Conventional (5.2% semiannual)	$3,420,667	$100,000,000
(b) Installment (5.15% semiannual)	530,833	9,886,584
Total	3,951,500	109,886,584
(c) Refunded issue (6% semiannual)	3,951,500	100,000,000
Present value savings (PVS)		9,886,584
Transaction Costs:		
(d) After-tax redemption premium		3,300,000
(e) Write-off of unamortized discount		(255,000)
(f) New-issue expenses		1,000,000
(g) Opportunity cost (the time premium of the extinguished option)		1,500,000
(h) Tax-deductible expenses		231,000
Total after-tax transaction costs (Cost)		5,776,000
Net advantage of refunding (NA)		$ 4,110,584

TABLE 24-4
The net advantage of refunding PAR's outstanding 12% bonds.

identical each period, with no final large payment. The debt obtained in exchange for promising the savings CFATs *must be installment debt* in order to maintain debt service parity. Otherwise, the payment pattern would differ from that of the outstanding debt obligation. The amount of installment debt that the savings CFATs can be exchanged for is simply the present value of the savings CFATs. But what is the required return on these cash flows that correctly determines their present value? Because of simultaneous capital structure effects, the required return for these cash flows is the *after-tax cost of new installment debt*. Recall that current capital market conditions allow PAR to issue new installment debt at a before-tax cost of 5.15%. Therefore, the savings can be sold for $9,886,584, which is the present value of $530,833 twice a year for 15 years at 3.40% [= $(1 - 0.34)5.15$]. This amount is shown on line (b) of Table 24-4. Note that the combined after-tax debt service on the two new issues exactly equals the after-tax debt service on the old issue, as the DSP approach requires. ■

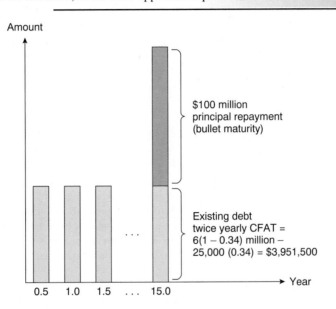

FIGURE 24-2
The schedule of CFATs for PAR's outstanding 12% bonds.

Amount

$100 million principal repayment (bullet maturity)

Existing debt twice yearly CFAT = 6(1 − 0.34) million − 25,000 (0.34) = $3,951,500

0.5   1.0   1.5   . . .   15.0   Year

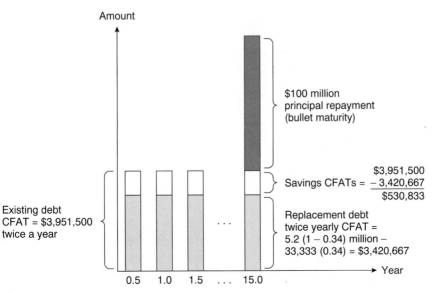

FIGURE 24-3
The schedule of CFATs for the new debt overlaid on the CFATs for the old debt.

Amount

$100 million principal repayment (bullet maturity)

Savings CFATs =
$3,951,500
− 3,420,667
$530,833

Existing debt CFAT = $3,951,500 twice a year

Replacement debt twice yearly CFAT = 5.2 (1 − 0.34) million − 33,333 (0.34) = $3,420,667

0.5   1.0   1.5   . . .   15.0   Year

NET ADVANTAGE   The *net advantage of refunding* then equals the debt proceeds obtained from selling the savings CFATs *minus* the after-tax cost of the transaction. This can be expressed in equation form as

$$NA = PVS - Cost \qquad (24.3)$$

where NA equals the net advantage of refunding, PVS is the present value of the savings, and Cost is the total after-tax transaction costs required to undertake the refunding. Both PVS and Cost should be calculated on a present-value after-tax basis.

TRANSACTION COSTS   There are six types of transaction costs associated with a refunding.

1. *Call premium.* When the call price exceeds par value, there is a call premium. In our example, the call price exceeds the par value by $50 per bond. There are 100,000 bonds ($100 million = $1000 × 100,000) outstanding. PAR will incur an after-tax cost of $3,300,000 [= (1 − 0.34)(50)100,000], which is shown on line (d) in Table 24-4.

2. *Tax credit.* For tax purposes, a firm can deduct any issuance expense that it has not yet claimed on the old bonds. In our example, PAR has already claimed 5 years' worth, or 25%, of the original issuance expense. Therefore, it can claim $750,000 (= 0.75 × 1,000,000) as a tax-deductible expense. This would generate a tax credit of $255,000 (= 0.34 × 750,000),[8] which is shown on line (e) in Table 24-4.

3. *New-issue expenses.* The issuing expenses for the new bonds amount to $1 million in our example. PAR must amortize them over the life of the new bonds. The immediate after-tax expense of $1 million is shown on line (f) in Table 24-4.

4. *Overlapping interest.* When a firm issues the new debt in order to have the net proceeds available before calling the old debt, overlapping interest occurs. This is a net cost. Only an incompetent financial manager would leave the new issue proceeds in a non-interest-bearing investment for the overlapping period. The net cost equals the difference between the interest cost on the old bonds and the interest earned from temporarily investing the proceeds from the new issue. The extra cost is based on the interest rate on the *old* bonds when the savings are computed from the date the new bonds are issued.[9]

5. *The (unexpired) call option's time premium.* Recall from Chapter 8 that it is generally better to sell rather than exercise an American call option. This is also true for the firm's call option. However, to refund, the firm is necessarily exercising its option. PAR's outstanding bonds are selling in the capital market for $1035. But PAR will pay $1050 for each bond when it exercises its option. The difference between the call price of $1050 and the market price of $1035 measures the (unexpired) call option's time premium. This is a real opportunity cost, but it is not a tax-deductible expense. Therefore, PAR will incur a total after-tax cost of $1,500,000 (= 15 × 100,000), which is shown on line (g) in Table 24-4. This transaction cost reflects the fact that the outstanding bonds are callable, whereas the hypothetical new bonds are noncallable. Of course, the new bonds that PAR decides to issue may well be callable, but once again, that is a separate decision.

6. *Immediately tax-deductible expenses,* such as the cost of publishing the redemption notice in newspapers and the fees paid the bond trustee to destroy the old bond certificates. These amount to $350,000 before taxes.

---

[8] This is similar to the writeoff for tax purposes of a machine that is being discarded at a zero salvage value.

[9] Equivalently, the "extra" interest is based on the interest on the new bonds when the savings are computed from the date the old bonds are retired.

The total transaction costs that PAR would incur amount to $5,776,000 (= 3,300,000 − 255,000 + 1,000,000 + 1,500,000 + 231,000). The net advantage of refunding is $4,110,584 (= 9,886,584 − 5,776,000).

Let's review. (1) PAR issues two types of new debt, $100 million of noncallable bonds and $9,886,584 worth of installment debt. (2) $5,776,000 of the installment debt proceeds cover the after-tax transaction costs of the refunding. (3) The future after-tax debt payment schedule is identical to the current payment schedule. (4) Therefore, PAR has a net advantage of $4,110,584 if it undertakes the refunding. ■

Calculating the Net Advantage of PAR's Refunding

EXAMPLE

Accounting Considerations

Generally accepted accounting principles require a bond issuer to account for outstanding bonds on the basis of their historical cost. Any changes in a bond's market price subsequent to issuance are ignored. Consequently, changes in market interest rates can give rise to a significant difference between the book value of a bond and its market price. For example, if current market rates are higher than they were at the time of the bond's issuance, the debt obligation will have a market value lower than its book value. Accounting Principles Board Statement 26 (APB 26) requires a firm to recognize the difference between the old debt's reacquisition price and its net carrying amount in income as a gain or a loss in the period the debt is reacquired. Consequently, reacquiring high-coupon debt generally results in a "loss" for accounting purposes.

You should appreciate that the firm may have to report an accounting loss even though the net advantage of refunding is positive! The reported loss simply reflects the difference between the old bonds' redemption price and their historical cost adjusted for any book amortization.

A firm has a debt issue outstanding that was issued when interest rates were much higher. Consequently, it is selling at a price of $1200 per $1000 face amount. Suppose the firm can redeem it for $1200 per bond. The firm's marginal ordinary income tax rate is 40%.

If the firm redeems the debt, it will record a *loss* for financial reporting purposes (net of taxes) amounting to $120 per bond [= (1 − 0.4)(1200 − 1000)] *regardless of whether the NA of the refunding operation is positive, zero, or negative.* ■

Accounting Impact of a Refunding

EXAMPLE

The provisions of APB 26 are somewhat controversial. Critics claim that APB 26 is misleading and can create opportunities for abuse. This reflects, of course, yet another agency problem wherein financial managers who want to avoid reporting a loss may forgo a profitable opportunity to refund high-coupon debt. One possible remedy would be to amortize the loss over either (1) the life of the new issue or (2) what would have been the remaining life of the refunded issue. This approach would reduce the one-time accounting impact. Of course, the Principle of Capital Market Efficiency holds that market participants will correctly assess the valuation implications of refundings by publicly traded firms. However, as with other corporate decisions, it is important to base the decision to refund on the transaction's impact on shareholder wealth, not on the immediate impact on earnings.

Self-Check Questions

1. What does it mean to say that the net advantage of refunding a bond issue is positive?
2. In applying the debt service parity approach, what are we measuring when we discount the after-tax debt service payment stream for the old issue at the after-tax cost of the new issue?
3. What factors account for the profitability of refunding high-coupon debt?
4. Why does the manner of accounting for calling and refunding high-coupon debt fail to measure properly the net advantage of refunding?

24.7 REFUNDING HIGH-COUPON DEBT IN PRACTICE

Several of the factors noted in the previous section have a fairly small impact on the net advantage of refunding and are often ignored in practice. For example, the cost of the overlapping interest is usually small enough to ignore as long as the proceeds from the new debt are invested for the overlapping period. Also, the difference between the interest rates on the installment debt and on the conventional debt is usually small enough to ignore. Instead, the net advantage of refunding is commonly computed by assuming that all the new debt is conventional debt. Such an approach, of course, does not strictly maintain debt service parity. However, the primary insight that results from the DSP approach remains: We must discount at the *after-tax rate on newly issued debt* in order to reflect the capital structure side effects.

Discounting the Interest Savings

Look again at Table 24-4. By design, the after-tax debt service per period for the installment debt equals the difference between (1) the after-tax debt service per period for the old issue and (2) the after-tax debt service per period for the conventional new issue. This leads to an interesting interpretation of the proceeds from the sale of the installment debt. It represents the present value of the interest savings when (1) an issue of high-coupon debt is replaced by an equivalent principal amount of current-coupon conventional debt and (2) the period-by-period after-tax savings are discounted at the after-tax cost of the new issue. Practitioners usually find this interpretation of the installment debt issue appealing. They calculate the NA by discounting the after-tax debt service savings and subtracting the transaction costs.

In practice, then, the net advantage of refunding high-coupon debt can be expressed in equation form as

$$\text{NA} = \sum_{t=1}^{N} \frac{(1-T)(r-r')D + T[(E-U)/N]}{[1+(1-T)r^*]^t}$$

$$-(1-T)(P-D) - [E + (1-T)F - TU] - (P-B)$$

(24.4)

where
$B =$ market price of the old debt issue (excluding accrued interest)
$D =$ par value of the old debt
$E =$ underwriting commissions and other expenses associated with the new debt issue
$F =$ tax-deductible, out-of-pocket expenses associated with the refunding operation
$N =$ number of periods until the old debt is scheduled to mature
$P =$ call (strike) price of the old debt (excluding accrued interest)
$r =$ coupon rate on the old debt
$r' =$ coupon rate on a conventional new debt issue sold at par

r^* = coupon rate on a new N-period installment debt issue sold at par
T = issuer's marginal ordinary income tax rate
U = unamortized balance of issuance expenses plus original issue discount (or less original issue premium) on the old debt

Equation (24.4) states that the net advantage of refunding high-coupon debt equals the present value of the semiannual savings minus (1) the after-tax call premium, $(1 - T)(P - D)$, (2) the issuance and other expenses net of the write-off of the unamortized discount, $E + (1 - T)F - TU$, and (3) the opportunity cost that is incurred if the call option is exercised prior to its expiration (that is, the unexpired call option's time premium), $P - B$.

EXAMPLE

Using the Alternative Approach to Calculate the NA of PAR's Refunding

Let's apply the alternative approach to Palo Alto's refunding decision. The parameter values are

D = \$100 million	r = 0.06	T = 0.34
E = 1 million	r' = 0.052	U = \$750,000
N = 30	r^* = 0.0515	

The savings per period amount to

$$(1 - T)(r - r')D + T[(E - U)/N] = (1 - 0.34)(0.06 - 0.052)100{,}000{,}000 + 0.34(1{,}000{,}000 - 750{,}000)/30 = 528{,}000 + 2833 = \$530{,}833$$

as indicated in Table 24-4. The proper discount rate is the after-tax cost of the installment debt, 3.4% [=(1 − 0.34)5.15]. The present value of the stream of savings is

$$\sum_{t=1}^{N} \frac{(1 - T)(r - r')D + T[(E - U)/N]}{[1 + (1 - T)r^*]^t} = \sum_{t=1}^{N} \frac{530{,}833}{(1.034)^t} = \$9{,}886{,}584$$

The values of the other parameters required to evaluate Equation (24.4) are B = \$103,500,000, F = \$350,000, and P = \$105,000,000. The net advantage of refunding is

$$\begin{aligned} \text{NA} &= \$9{,}886{,}584 - (1 - 0.34)(105{,}000{,}000 - 100{,}000{,}000) - [1{,}000{,}000 + (1 - 0.34)350{,}000 \\ &\quad - (0.34)750{,}000] - (105{,}000{,}000 - 103{,}500{,}000) \\ &= \$9{,}886{,}584 - 3{,}300{,}000 - 976{,}000 - 1{,}500{,}000 = \$4{,}110{,}584 \end{aligned}$$

The result is the same as that we found by applying the DSP approach directly.

Suppose the coupon rate on the conventional refunding debt issue is used to discount the after-tax debt service savings. Only the sum in Equation (24.4) changes. The discount rate used in this modified calculation is 3.43% [= (1 − 0.34)5.2]. The sum becomes \$9,849,296 (= present value of 530,833 per period for 30 periods at 3.43% per period). Then NA becomes \$4,073,296 (= 9,849,296 − 5,776,000), which is within 1% of the true NA [= (4,110,584 − 4,073,296)/4,110,584 = 0.0091]. ■

A Short Cut

There are two additional points worth noting. First, as we noted in Chapter 5, interest is paid semiannually on domestic U.S. debt issues. To be most precise, we should work with semiannual rather than annual cash flows (except in the case of Eurobond issues, which pay interest annually), as we did in the preceding example. In practice, however, little accuracy is lost by

Refunding the second sinking fund payment would produce 2 years of interest savings. The net advantage of refunding the second $10 million sinking fund payment is

$$NA = \left[\frac{(1 - 0.4)(0.14 - 0.12)}{1.072} + \frac{(1 - 0.4)(0.14 - 0.12)}{(1.072)^2} - (0.60)(0.02) \right](10,000,000)$$

$$= \$96,362$$

The net advantage of refunding the entire issue is just the sum of these two amounts, $88,302. But it is profitable only to refund the second sinking fund amount. The firm's shareholders are better off if the firm calls only the final $10 million of the issue for immediate redemption and waits 1 year to redeem the other $10 million at par through normal operation of the sinking fund. Such a strategy produces a net advantage of $96,362. ■

This example also illustrates the correct procedure for evaluating the net advantage of refunding a high-coupon debt issue that contains a sinking fund. Separate the issue into a serial debt obligation with each series maturing on one of the sinking fund payment dates. If it is profitable for an issuer to call a bond that it would otherwise have redeemed on any particular sinking fund payment date, it must also be profitable for the issuer to call all the bonds that it would otherwise have redeemed on that date. Each series can be analyzed separately to determine whether an immediate call is advantageous.

Tender Offers and Open-Market Purchases

Most long-term bonds contain a "no-call" period. During this period the firm cannot call, or at least is restricted in its ability to call, the debt. Nevertheless, a firm can refund such call-protected high-coupon debt by purchasing bonds in the open market or by tendering for them. Any purchase premium can be deducted for tax purposes in the year of repurchase. Second, the issuer can still deduct the unamortized balance of expenses plus original issue discount in the year of repurchase.

With three adjustments, the method of analysis illustrated in our Palo Alto Refinancing example also applies to refundings accomplished through open-market purchases or a tender offer. First, the issuer must pay the market price or, in the case of a tender offer, some premium over this price, rather than a preset call price. Second, holders are free to accept or reject the issuer's offer. Consequently, both the amount of debt refunded and the effective redemption premium are subject to some degree of uncertainty. These factors can be taken into account by estimating the amount of the issue that can be reacquired at a given price and proceeding with the analysis of refunding this portion of the issue. Third, additional transaction costs are often associated with a repurchase program or a tender offer; an example is fees paid to soliciting dealers when securities firms are engaged to assist with the program.

The open-market purchase method is generally cheaper than a tender offer when the market for the bonds is liquid enough that the repurchase program does not exert much upward pressure on price. Bonds can be repurchased from different holders at a price each is willing to accept. For larger programs, however, firms often prefer the tender offer method because it treats all bondholders equally.

Self-Check Questions

1. True or False? Discounting the change in the after-tax debt service payment stream at the after-tax cost of the new issue is consistent with the debt service parity approach.

2. Why might refunding high-coupon debt involve an opportunity cost?

3. Describe the short-cut technique for evaluating a high-coupon refunding.

4. Why do firms issue callable bonds?

5. How does a sinking fund complicate a bond refunding analysis? What is the best way to handle this problem?

SOLUTION TO GENERAL AVIATION'S FINANCING PROBLEM

You should now be able to help General Aviation's treasurer choose the least costly borrowing alternative. Note that the bonds are noncallable and mature in a lump sum at the end of ten years under each alternative. Also, the covenants for the domestic public issue and the Eurobond issue would be identical, but the domestic private issue covenants would be somewhat more restrictive. You know that the domestic issues pay interest semiannually and that the Eurobond issue pays interest annually. Consequently, care must be taken to express all three costs on a comparable basis. This can be done by comparing their APYs. The role of covenants is more complex, so let's first compute the APYs.

Assuming that General Aviation's marginal income tax rate is 34%, the domestic public debt issue has a semiannual cost of 3.02% on an after-tax basis:

TIME	ITEM	CFBT	CFAT
0	Net proceeds	99,000,000	99,000,000
1–20	Interest payments	−4,500,000	−2,970,000
1–20	Flotation expense[1]	0	17,000
20	Principal repayment	−100,000,000	−100,000,000

$$99,000,000 = \sum_{t=1}^{20} \frac{2,970,000 - 17,000}{(1 + c)^t} + \frac{100,000,000}{(1 + c)^{20}} \quad c = 3.02\%$$

[1] The flotation expense is amortized over the life of the issue on a straight-line basis for tax purposes. This treatment is like using straight-line depreciation for capital equipment: Even though the cash outflow for the flotation cost is incurred now, it is expensed for tax purposes over the life of the issue.

Applying Equation (4.7), the after-tax APY is APY $= (1.0302)^2 - 1 = 6.13\%$. Proceeding in the same manner, we find that the after-tax APY for the domestic private issue is 6.19%. Finally, the after-tax APY for the Eurobond issue is 6.15%.

Therefore, the domestic public issue is the cheapest alternative. Had the private issue been the cheapest alternative, the treasurer would have had to weigh the immediate cost-of-money savings against the cost implicit in the more restrictive covenants.

SUMMARY

There are four main classes of long-term corporate debt: secured debt, unsecured debt, tax-exempt debt, and convertible debt. Debt instruments belonging to these four classes have a stated maturity, a stated principal amount, a stated coupon rate of interest (or interest rate formula, in the case of floating-rate debt), a mandatory redemption schedule, an optional redemption provision, and covenant restrictions designed to protect bondholders.

A firm can increase shareholder wealth by managing its outstanding debt obligations effectively. This process involves exploiting profitable opportunities to call and refund high-coupon debt. The profitability of refunding high-coupon debt is due to two factors. The call option allows the issuer to call the bonds away from holders at a fixed price. Also, the call premium is tax-deductible. A firm should analyze a high-coupon bond refunding opportunity by discounting the change in after-tax debt service payments at the after-tax cost of money for the new issue, and subtracting the after-tax costs and expenses associated with the refunding.

A sinking fund adds a degree of complexity to the refunding analysis. More important, it creates profitable opportunities for the issuer. In a low-interest-rate environment, it may be more profitable for a firm to call less than an entire issue and redeem the balance through the sinking fund.

As with other corporate decisions, a firm should refund bonds only if doing so will increase shareholder wealth. It is very important to analyze a proposed debt refunding on an after-tax basis and to neutralize all financial structure side effects. Some refunding transactions may be advantageous to a firm's shareholders because of tax asymmetries. You must understand the tax consequences and the true economic benefits, as distinct from the purely accounting benefits, of a proposed refunding in order to determine whether it will increase shareholder wealth.

DECISION SUMMARY

- The terms of a debt issue will affect the interest rate that investors require. Provisions such as the covenants contained in an indenture should be carefully examined. Contractual agreements may be able to reduce agency costs, but such provisions are not costless. For example, restrictive covenants may reduce a firm's interest cost, but only at the expense of operating flexibility.

- The exact repayment schedule can affect a firm's cost of financing. Compounding affects the cost because of the time value of money. A sinking fund reduces the maturity of the issue. Therefore, a sinking fund may affect the cost of an issue because of the term structure of interest rates.

- Flotation expenses are normally amortized for tax purposes on a straight-line basis over the life of the issue. This treatment is similar to depreciation on capital equipment.

- A firm should refund outstanding bonds only if doing so will increase shareholder wealth. Discount the change in after-tax debt service payments at the after-tax cost of money for the new issue, and then subtract the after-tax costs and expenses associated with the refunding.

- A firm should call a high-coupon debt issue for optional redemption when its market value (including accrued interest) reaches its effective call price.

- Analyze refunding decisions on a debt-service-parity basis to determine whether the decision is advantageous. Other decisions can then be analyzed in combination with the refunding decision to establish the most profitable combination of decisions.

- When a debt issue contains a sinking fund, treat the debt issue as though it were a serial debt obligation and separately evaluate the profitability of refunding each sinking fund amount.

EQUATION SUMMARY

(24.1) $\text{Average life} = \dfrac{\sum\limits_{t=1}^{N} tA_t}{\sum\limits_{t=1}^{N} A_t}$

(24.2) $\text{Duration} = \dfrac{1}{P} \sum\limits_{t=1}^{N} \dfrac{tCF_t}{(1+y)^t}$

(24.3) $\text{NA} = \text{PVS} - \text{Cost}$

(24.4) $\text{NA} = \sum\limits_{t=1}^{N} \dfrac{(1-T)(r-r')D + T[(E-U)/N]}{[1+(1-T)r^*]^t}$

$\qquad\qquad - (1-T)(P-D) - [E + (1-T)F - TU] - (P-B)$

KEY TERMS

mortgage bonds...768

notes...768

debentures...768

bond indenture...769

bond agreement...769

note agreement...769

covenants...770

events of default...770

average life...771

duration...772

Eurobond...777

bond refunding...779

debt service parity (DSP) approach...781

net advantage of refunding...781

EXERCISES

PROBLEM SET A

A1. What are the two features of debt and equity (one of each) that distinguish them from each other?

A2. Describe the difference between secured and unsecured debt.

A3. What is a Eurobond?

A4. Explain how the presence of a sinking fund affects the effective maturity of a debt issue.

A5. Explain the reasons for including a call option in a corporate bond issue.

A6. Explain the role of debt covenants.

A7. What is a high-coupon bond refunding?

A8. Explain briefly the debt service parity approach to evaluating the net advantage of a proposed bond refunding.

A9. Explain why the manner in which a firm must account for the early retirement of a debt issue is not necessarily indicative of the profitability of bond refunding. How can the accounting treatment give rise to an agency cost?

A10. Explain why a firm should not necessarily refund an outstanding debt issue the instant the net advantage of refunding becomes positive.

A11. What is the opportunity cost of calling bonds for refunding when the market price of the bonds (immediately prior to the call announcement) equals the call price.

A12. Explain why an instantaneously callable high-coupon bond would never trade in a perfect capital market environment at a price (including accrued interest) in excess of the effective call price.

A13. Explain why it may not be most advantageous for a firm to call and refund an entire sinking fund debt issue immediately.

PROBLEM SET B

B1. Show that the semiannual rate for the domestic private issue in General Aviation's financing problem is 3.05%. Show that the APY for the Eurobond issue is 6.15%.

B2. Calculate PAR's net advantage of refunding the 12% debt issue under the assumption that the installment debt requires a 5.2% semiannual coupon rate.

B3. A debt issue bears a 10% coupon and has a sinking fund that makes equal payments at the ends of years 4 and 5. Interest is paid semiannually at the end of each period. If the issuing firm nets a price equal to 95% of the face amount of the debt, what is the pretax APY cost of the debt?

B4. A new debt issue bearing a 12% coupon and maturing in one lump sum at the end of 10 years involves issuance expenses equal to 2% of the gross proceeds.

  a. Assume the issuing firm pays tax at a 50% marginal rate. What is the after-tax cost of debt?

  b. Suppose instead that the firm is not a taxpayer and expects never to be. What is the after-tax cost of debt?

  c. Explain how your answer to part b would change if the firm expected to pay taxes at a 50% rate after 5 years.

B5. A new floating-rate debt issue pays interest annually based on the 1-year Treasury bill rate. Assume zero issuance cost. The issue matures in 5 years. The current 1-year Treasury bill rate is 9%, and the forecasted 1-year rates over the next 4 years are 9.25%, 9.5%, 9.75%, and 10%. The coupon equals the beginning-of-period Treasury rate plus 100 basis points. There is no sinking fund.

  a. Project the debt service payment stream.

  b. Calculate the pretax cost of debt.

  c. Calculate the after-tax cost of debt, assuming a 34% tax rate.

B6. Exxon Corporation has a 34% tax rate, and has decided to issue $100 million of 7-year debt. It has three alternatives. A U.S. public offering would require an 8% coupon with interest payable semiannually and $900,000 of flotation expense. A U.S. private placement would require an $8\frac{3}{8}$% coupon with interest payable semiannually and $500,000 of flotation expense. A Eurobond offering would require an $8\frac{1}{8}$% coupon with interest payable annually and $1,100,000 of flotation expense.

  a. Calculate the cost of borrowing for each alternative.

  b. Which alternative has the lowest cost of borrowing?

  c. What other factors should Exxon consider before it decides how to raise $100 million?

B7. A debt issue contains a dividend limitation. Cumulative dividends cannot exceed the sum of $25 million and 60% of cumulative net income since the debt was issued 3 years ago. The firm earned $50 million net income in each of those years. It paid total dividends of $15 million and $20 million the first 2 years and $25 million so far this year. How large a dividend could the firm pay at the end of the third year without violating the dividend limitation?

B8. A debt issue contains an interest-coverage test that prohibits a firm from issuing additional debt if doing so would reduce its interest coverage below 2.50. Its earnings before interest and taxes are currently $100 million. Its interest expense is currently $25 million. How much additional 10% debt could the firm incur under this test?

B9. Explain why the limitation on sale-and-leaseback provides lenders protection that is similar to the protection that the limitation on liens and the negative pledge clause provide.

B10. An asset-coverage test prohibits a firm from issuing additional long-term debt if doing so would reduce the ratio of tangible assets to long-term debt below 1.50. A firm currently has $1 billion of tangible assets and $400 million of long-term debt. How much additional long-term debt could it issue if it invests the entire proceeds in tangible assets?

B11. A debt issue repays principal in 7 equal installments at the end of years 14 through 20. What is its average life?

B12. A long-term debt issue in the amount of $100 million calls for mandatory redemption payments of $20 million each at the end of years 7, 8, and 9 and for repayment of the remaining balance (called the *balloon*) at the end of year 10. Calculate the issue's average life.

B13. A bond pays interest semiannually at a 7% APR. The bond has a sinking fund that makes equal payments of $20 million at the end of years 6, 7, and 8. The total principal is $60 million. The bond's yield to maturity is 6% APR.

   a. Calculate the bond's price.

   b. Calculate the bond's average life.

   c. Calculate the bond's duration.

   d. Which of the figures calculated in parts b and c is the better measure of the average timing of the bond issue's total cash flow?

B14. A bond pays interest semiannually at a 10% APR. The bond has a sinking fund that makes equal payments at the end of years 8, 9, and 10. The bond's price is 105% of its face amount.

   a. Calculate the bond's yield to maturity.

   b. Calculate the bond's average life.

   c. Calculate the bond's duration.

B15. A firm has outstanding a $50 million debt issue that bears a 15% coupon (7.5% semiannual). It matures in a lump sum at the end of 10 years. The unamortized balance of issuance expenses is $800,000, which the firm is amortizing on a straight-line basis. The call price is $1100 per bond. The bonds are selling in the capital market for $1080 each. A noncallable 10-year bullet-maturity debt issue would require a 12.5% coupon (6.25% semiannual) and $1,000,000 of underwriting and other expenses, and 10-year installment debt would require a 12% coupon (6% semiannual). The firm's marginal income tax rate is 40%.

   a. Calculate the period-by-period after-tax debt service on the 15% debt issue.

   b. Calculate the semiannual after-tax savings that would result if the firm issued $50 million of 12.5% debt.

   c. How much installment debt can the firm issue?

   d. Calculate the net advantage of refunding the 15% debt issue.

B16. Northern Gas Company has outstanding $100 million principal amount of 12% debentures (6%

payable semiannually) that mature in a lump sum at the end of 20 years. The unamortized balance of issuance expenses is $500,000. A par-value $100 million noncallable refunding issue would require a 10% coupon (5% semiannual) and $750,000 of issuance expenses. The 12% issue is callable at a price of $1020 per bond (pretax), and miscellaneous debt retirement costs amount to $3.00 per bond. Northern Gas's marginal income tax rate is 40%.

a. Calculate the net advantage of refunding, assuming the bonds have a market value of $1020 each.

b. How would your answer to part a change if the 12% debentures were selling at a market price of $1017 per bond?

B17. Tara Corporation has $70 million of 12% bonds outstanding that are selling for $1060. It can call the bonds at a price of $1100 each. The bonds have a remaining life of 10 years. Tara is considering refunding the issue with a new $70 million issue of 25-year, 11% bonds. Flotation costs for the new issue would be $500,000. Those of the old issue remaining to be amortized are $350,000. Tara's tax rate is 40%. No overlapping interest payments are expected. What is Tara's net advantage of refunding the outstanding bonds? (Assume that the term structure of interest rates is currently flat.)

B18. The Kaplan Corporation sold $50 million of 25-year, 15% coupon bonds during a period of very high interest rates 10 years ago. Because of changing financial market conditions, the bonds are now selling for $1055. Kaplan can now refund that bond issue with 15-year, 11% coupon bonds, which would sell at par value. The flotation costs for a new bond issue will be $400,000 compared to the $300,000 of unamortized costs for the old bonds. The firm expects a 1-month overlap between the sale of the new bonds and the redemption of the existing bonds. There is a 5% call premium. Kaplan's tax rate is 40%. Kaplan can earn 8% APR on short-term marketable securities. What is Kaplan's net advantage of refunding the outstanding bonds?

B19. The Solamax Corporation issued $20 million worth of 40-year, 10% coupon bonds 14 years ago. Solamax can call the bonds today for $1020 per bond, even though the bonds are selling for $1030 apiece. Management is considering issuing $50 million of new 26-year, 9.2% coupon bonds, with the proceeds being used to expand facilities and to refund their outstanding bonds. Flotation costs for the new bond issue are expected to be $480,000. The old bonds have $185,000 in flotation costs yet to be amortized. An overlap period of 1.5 months is anticipated if the new bonds are issued, Solamax has a tax rate of 35%, and short-term marketable securities are currently yielding 10%. What is the net advantage of refunding to Solamax? (*Hint*: If Solamax can call bonds for redemption at a price less than their current market value, shareholder wealth is enhanced at the expense of bondholder wealth.)

B20. Southern Manufacturing Corporation has $10 million of 14% sinking fund debentures outstanding. The issue amortizes in equal annual amounts at the end of each of the next 5 years. Southern can call the bonds for immediate redemption at a price of 102%. Southern's new issue rate is 12% for 1- and 2-year debt and 13% for 3-, 4-, and 5-year debt. Southern's marginal income tax rate is 34%. Ignoring transaction costs, how much of the issue could Southern economically call for immediate redemption? Which sinking fund amounts should Southern call?

B21. A firm has outstanding a 3-year sinking fund issue that amortizes in 3 equal annual installments of $20 million each, payable at par. The bonds pay interest annually at the rate of 10%. They are callable at 103% of par. The firm's new issue rate is 8% for debt maturing in up to 3 years, and its tax rate is 34%. Ignore issuance expenses.

a. Calculate the net advantage of refunding each sinking fund amount immediately.

b. How much of the 10% issue should the firm call for immediate redemption?

B22. Suppose Ford Motor Credit has $150 million of 10% sinking fund debentures outstanding. The issue amortizes in equal annual amounts at the ends of years 10, 11, and 12. The firm can call the bonds at 103%. Its new issue rate is 8% for 10-year debt, 8.5% for 11-year debt, and 9% for 12-year debt. Its marginal income tax rate is 40%. Which sinking fund amounts should Ford Motor Credit call?

B23. Suppose a firm can profitably refund an entire debt issue. Does that mean it *should* call the *entire* issue immediately? Explain.

PROBLEM SET C

C1. A firm issues a 10-year debt obligation that bears a 12% coupon rate and gives the investor the right to put the bond back to the issuer at the end of the fifth year at 103% of its face amount. The issue has no sinking fund. Interest is paid semiannually. Issuance expenses are 1%. The issuer's tax rate is 34%.

a. Calculate the after-tax cost of debt, assuming the debt remains outstanding until maturity.

b. Calculate the after-tax cost of debt, assuming investors put the bond back to the firm at the end of the fifth year. (Note: Any unamortized issuance expenses and any redemption premium can be deducted for tax purposes in the year of redemption.)

C2. Some years ago, Mountain States Telephone & Telegraph Company tendered at a price of 114.5% for its $250 million principal amount of $11\frac{5}{8}$% debentures due June 8, 2023. At the time of the tender, Mountain States could have issued new 37-year noncallable debt bearing a 9% coupon and requiring $15.00 per bond of issuance expenses. Bondholders tendered $190 million principal amount of the issue. Tax-deductible refunding transaction costs amount to $3.00 per bond. Assume a 34% marginal income tax rate. Interest is payable semiannually, and just prior to the tender the bonds were selling for $1120 each.

a. Mountain States had a tax basis in the $11\frac{5}{8}$% debentures of $965.31 per bond. (The difference between this amount and $1000 represents the unamortized balance of discount and expenses.) Calculate the net advantage of refunding via tender.

b. The $11\frac{5}{8}$% debentures were initially callable 2 years later at a price of 107.50% per debenture. By that date, Mountain States's tax basis in the $11\frac{5}{8}$% debentures would have increased to $967.19 per bond. Calculate the net advantage of waiting 2 years to call the bonds, assuming (1) the same new-issue rate and issuance expenses as of the tender offer date and (2) a flat yield curve on the tender offer date.

c. What procedure could Mountain States have followed in order to determine whether it could expect waiting and calling to be more advantageous than tendering immediately?

C3. A firm is considering refunding $50 million principal amount of its 10% debentures (5% semiannual) that mature in a lump sum in 10 years. The 10% issue has a market price of $777.05 per bond. The unamortized balance of issuance and other expenses is $400,000. The firm's marginal income tax rate is 34%. Debt retirement expenses amount to $150,000. A new issue of 10-year bullet-maturity debt would require a 15% coupon rate (7.5% semiannual) and $380,000 of issuance expenses. Calculate the net advantage of refunding the 10% issue under each of the following three conditions:

a. The gain (the difference between the face amount of the bonds and the price paid to retire them) is nontaxable.

b. The gain is taxable immediately at a 34% rate.

c. The gain is taxable at a 34% rate at the time the 10% issue would have matured.

d. Under what conditions is the refunding profitable?

C4. Gotham Airlines is considering whether to refund its outstanding $100 million principal amount of 6% subordinated debentures, which are scheduled to mature in one lump sum at the end of 6 years. Interest is payable semiannually. The unamortized balance of new-issue expenses is $600,000. Debt retirement expenses amount to $100,000 after taxes. A 6-year refunding issue would require a 12% coupon and $1,200,000 of issuance expenses. Gotham's tax rate is 34%.

a. If the outstanding bonds also yield 12%, what is their market price? Assume the bonds can be repurchased at this price.

b. Suppose the gain is nontaxable. Calculate the net present value of refunding.

c. Suppose the gain is taxable at the end of 6 years at a 34% rate. Calculate the net advantage of re-funding.

d. What is the net advantage of refunding if the gain is currently taxable at a 34% rate?

C5. Martin Aerospace Inc. has $50 million of 20-year non-sinking fund preferred stock outstanding that pays dividends quarterly at the rate of 16% per annum. A new issue of 20-year non-sinking fund preferred stock would require a quarterly dividend rate of 12% per annum and $1 million of issuance expenses. The 16% issue is callable at an aggregate cost of $55 million.

a. Calculate the net advantage of refunding.

b. How would your answer to part a change if both preferred stock issues were perpetual?

C6.

a. Develop a general expression for the net advantage of refunding perpetual preferred stock.

b. Develop, from the net advantage expression in part a, a general expression for the break-even dividend rate for refunding perpetual preferred stock.

C7. A firm can sell a 1-year debt issue bearing a 10% coupon or a 2-year debt issue bearing a 12% coupon. The issuer's tax rate is 34%.

a. Calculate the break-even refunding rate 1 year hence that makes the firm indifferent between the two alternatives.

b. How would you interpret your answer to part a?

c. If the issuer sells the 1-year issue and at the end of 1 year the 1-year new-issue rate is 13%, what is the issuer's actual realized cost of 2-year funds?

d. If the issuer knew with certainty that the 1-year new-issue rate 1 year hence would be 13%, which alternative should it accept?

Real-World Application:
Disney's 100-Year Debt Issue

The Walt Disney Company (Disney) is a diversified, international entertainment firm whose operations include theme parks and resorts, filmed entertainment, and consumer products. The theme parks and resorts segment has generated roughly 40% of its total revenue, filmed entertainment has accounted for roughly 40%, and consumer products has generated the remaining 20%. Disney recently acquired Capital Cities/ABC and with it ABC Television and ABC Radio.

In July 1993, Disney had decided to issue additional long-term debt. Its investment bankers advised that a 100-year debt issue might be possible. Disney was conservatively capitalized. Its long-term debt was rated A1 by

Moody's Investors Service and AA- by Standard & Poor's. Its capitalization on June 30, 1993 was

CAPITALIZATION (Dollar amounts in millions)	BOOK VALUE JUNE 30, 1993
Short-term debt	$503.7
Long-term debt	$1455.5
Stockholders' equity	5169.1
Total capitalization	$6624.6
Total capitalization (including short-term debt)	$7128.3

Its interest coverage for the 12 months ending June 30, 1993 was

INTEREST COVERAGE (Dollar amounts in millions)	12 MONTHS ENDING JUNE 30, 1993
Earnings before interest and taxes	$1640.5
Interest expense	122.4
Interest coverage ratio	13.4x

Interest rates had decreased for the past few years and were near their lowest levels in the past twenty years. This made long-term debt an attractive financing alternative. At the same time, many investors in long-term fixed-rate debt had come to believe that the United States had inflation under control and that long-term interest rates were unlikely to return to the very high levels experienced in the early 1980s. They thought that long-term interest rates might even decline further because the gap between long-term Treasury yields (6.40% for the 30-year bond) and the projected inflation rate (3%) was relatively high by historical standards. Thus, a 100-year maturity, almost unthinkable just a few years before, was now possible according to Disney's investment bankers at Morgan Stanley & Co.

Disney could issue noncallable long-term bonds at the following APRs (with interest payable semiannually):

MATURITY (YEARS)	OFFERING YIELD
3	5.15% APR
5	5.85
7	6.25
10	6.60
20	7.25
30	7.35
100	7.35

If it issued 100-year debt, Disney wanted to preserve some flexibility to retire it before its maturity. Morgan Stanley advised Disney that it could issue $300 million principal amount of 100-year debt that was callable beginning 30 years from the issue date at an interest cost of 7.55% APR. The initial call price would be 103.02%. The call price would step down to par beginning 50 years after the issue date.

1. What did the optional redemption feature cost Disney?
   a. What was the yield premium Disney had to pay?
   b. Calculate the present value of the increase in interest payments Disney would have to make during the first 30 years the bonds are outstanding.

2. Calculate the duration of each of the following bonds bearing the interest rates indicated above:
   a. 5-year bond.
   b. 10-year bond.
   c. 30-year bond.
   d. 100-year (noncallable) bond.

3. Considering your answers in question 2, do you see any pattern between duration and offering yield?

4. Show the pro forma impact on Disney's capitalization and interest coverage from issuing $300 million principal amount of
   a. 30-year bonds.
   b. 100-year noncallable bonds.
   c. 100-year callable bonds.

5. Explain why the optional redemption feature gives Disney the flexibility to transform the callable 100-year bonds into 30-year bonds.

6. Compare the 10-year and 30-year alternatives. If Disney issues 10-year bonds and refunds them with 20-year bonds, what interest rate on the 20-year bonds would make Disney just as well off in July 1993 dollars as if it had issued 30-year bonds in July 1993? (*Hint*: one approach to solving this problem is to find the interest rate on the 20-year bonds that makes the present value of the two 30-year streams of interest payments equal, using the 30-year new issue rate as the discount rate in both cases.)

7. Compare the 30-year and noncallable-100-year alternatives. What interest rate on the 70-year bonds would make Disney just as well off in July 1993 dollars as if it had issued noncallable 100-year bonds in July 1993?

8. Suppose Disney issues callable 100-year bonds. If Disney were to redeem the 100-year bonds at the end of the 30th year and refund them with 70-year bonds, what interest rate on the 70-year bonds

would make Disney just as well off as if it had issued noncallable 100-year bonds instead?

9. Suppose you had a valuation model that could calculate the value to Disney of including the optional redemption feature in the 100-year issue. How large would the value have to be to justify including the optional redemption feature?

10. Should Disney issue callable 100-year bonds, or should it choose one of the other alternatives? Explain.

BIBLIOGRAPHY

Allen, David S., Robert E. Lamy, and G. Rodney Thompson. "Agency Costs and Alternative Call Provisions: An Empirical Investigation," *Financial Management*, 1987, 16(4):37–44.

Allen, David S., Robert E. Lamy, and G. Rodney Thompson. "The Shelf Registration of Debt and Self Selection Bias," *Journal of Finance*, 1990, 45(1):275–288.

Altman, Edward I. "Revisiting the High-Yield Bond Market," *Financial Management*, 1992, 21(2):89–92.

Asquith, Paul, and David W. Mullins, Jr. "Convertible Debt: Corporate Call Policy and Voluntary Conversion," *Journal of Finance*, 1991, 46(4):1273–1290.

Barber, Brad M. "Exchangeable Debt," *Financial Management*, 1993, 22(2):48–60.

Bi, Keqian, and Haim Levy. "Market Reaction to Bond Downgradings Followed by Chapter 11 Filings," *Financial Management*, 1993, 22(3):156–162.

Billingsley, Randall S., Robert E. Lamy, M. Wayne Marr, and G. Rodney Thompson. "Split Ratings and Bond Reoffering Yields," *Financial Management*, 1985, 14(2):59–65.

Bowlin, Oswald D. "The Refunding Decision: Another Special Case in Capital Budgeting," *Journal of Finance*, 1966, 21(1):55–68.

Brick, Ivan E., and Oded Palmon. "The Tax Advantages of Refunding Debt by Calling, Repurchasing, and Putting," *Financial Management*, 1993, 22(4):96–105.

Brick, Ivan E., and S. Abraham Ravid. "Interest Rate Uncertainty and the Optimal Debt Maturity Structure," *Journal of Financial and Quantitative Analysis*, 1991, 26(1):63–82.

Brick, Ivan E., and Buckner A. Wallingford. "The Relative Tax Benefits of Alternative Call Features in Corporate Debt," *Journal of Financial and Quantitative Analysis*, 1985, 20(1):95–105.

Campbell, Cynthia J., Louis H. Ederington, and Prashant

Vankrudre. "Tax Shields, Sample-Selection Bias, and the Information Content of Conversion-Forcing Bond Calls," *Journal of Finance*, 1991, 46(4):1291–1324.

Chance, Don M. "Default Risk and the Duration of Zero Coupon Bonds," *Journal of Finance*, 1990, 45(1):265–274.

Chatfield, Robert E., and R. Charles Moyer. "'Putting' Away Bond Risk: An Empirical Examination of the Value of the Put Option on Bonds," *Financial Management*, 1986, 15(2):26–33.

Christensen, Donald G., and Hugo J. Faria. "A Note on the Shareholder Wealth Effects of High-Yield Bonds," *Financial Management*, 1994, 23(1):10.

Cowan, Arnold R., Nandkumar Nayar, and Ajai K. Singh. "Calls and Out-of-the-Money Convertible Bonds," *Financial Management*, 1993, 22(4):106–116.

Cowan, Arnold R., Nandkumar Nayar, and Ajai K. Singh. "Underwriting Calls of Convertible Securities: A Note," *Journal of Financial Economics*, 1992, 31(2):269–278.

Crabbe, Leland E., and Jean Helwege. "Alternative Tests of Agency Theories of Callable Corporate Bonds," *Financial Management*, 1994, 23(4):3–20.

De, Sankar, and Jayant R. Kale. "Contingent Payments and Debt Contracts," *Financial Management*, 1993, 22(2):106–122.

Diamond, Douglas W. "Seniority and Maturity of Debt Contracts," *Journal of Financial Economics*, 1993, 33(3):341–368.

Emery, Douglas R., J. Ronald Hoffmeister, and Ronald W. Spahr. "The Case for Indexing a Bond's Call Price," *Financial Management*, 1987, 16(3):57–64.

Emery, Douglas R., and Wilbur G. Lewellen. "Refunding Noncallable Debt," *Journal of Financial and Quantitative Analysis*, 1984, 19(1):73–82.

Emery, Douglas R., and Wilbur G. Lewellen. "Shareholder

Gains from Callable-Bond Refundings," *Managerial and Decision Economics*, 1990, 11:57–63.

Fields, L. Page, and Eric L. Mais. "The Valuation Effects of Private Placements of Convertible Debt," *Journal of Finance*, 1991, 46(5):1925–1932.

Finnerty, John D. "Evaluating the Economics of Refunding High-Coupon Sinking-Fund Debt," *Financial Management*, 1983, 12(1):5–10.

Finnerty, John D. *An Illustrated Guide to Bond Refunding Analysis*. Charlottesville, Va.: The Financial Analysts Research Foundation, 1984.

Finnerty, John D. "Indexed Sinking Fund Debentures: Valuation and Analysis," *Financial Management*, 1993, 22(2):76–93.

Finnerty, John D. "Refunding Discounted Debt: A Clarifying Analysis," *Journal of Financial and Quantitative Analysis*, 1986, 21(1):95–106.

Finnerty, John D., Andrew J. Kalotay, and Francis X. Farrell, Jr. *The Financial Manager's Guide to Evaluating Bond Refunding Opportunities*. Cambridge, Mass.: Ballinger Publishing Company, 1988.

Houston, Joel F., and S. Venkataraman. "Optimal Maturity Structure with Multiple Debt Claims," *Journal of Financial and Quantitative Analysis*, 1994, 29(2):179–197.

Hsueh, L. Paul, and David S. Kidwell. "Bond Ratings: Are Two Better Than One?" *Financial Management*, 1988, 17(1):46–53.

Hull, Robert M., and Richard Moellenberndt. "Bank Debt Reduction Announcements and Negative Signaling," *Financial Management*, 1994, 23(2):21–30.

Jalilvand, Abolhassan, and Tae H. Park. "Default Risk, Firm Characteristics, and the Valuation of Variable-Rate Debt Instruments," *Financial Management*, 1994, 23(2):58–68.

Jensen, Marlin R. H., and William N. Pugh. "Valuation Effects of Cancelled Debt Offerings," *Journal of Financial and Quantitative Analysis*, 1991, 26(3):425–432.

Johnson, James M., Robert A. Pari, and Leonard Rosenthal. "The Impact of In-Substance Defeasance on Bondholder and Shareholder Wealth," *Journal of Finance*, 1989, 44(4):1049–1058.

Kalotay, Andrew, and Bruce Tuckman. "Sinking Fund Prepurchases on the Designation Option," *Financial Management*, 1992, 21(4):110–118.

Kaplan, Steven N., and Jeremy C. Stein. "How Risky Is the Debt of Highly Leveraged Transactions?," *Journal of Financial Economics*, 1990, 27(1):215–246.

Kim, In Joon, Krishna Ramaswamy, and Suresh Sundaresan. "Does Default Risk in Coupons Affect the Valuation of Corporate Bonds? A Contingent Claims Model," *Financial Management*, 1993, 22(3):117–131.

Laber, Gene. "Bond Covenants and Forgone Opportunities: The Case of Burlington Northern Railroad Company," *Financial Management*, 1992, 21(2):71–77.

Lewellen, Wilbur G., and Douglas R. Emery. "On the Matter of Parity Among Financial Obligations," *Journal of Finance*, 1981, 36(1):97–111.

Livingston, Miles. "Measuring the Benefit of a Bond Refunding: The Problem of Nonmarketable Call Options," *Financial Management*, 1987, 16(1):38–40.

Long, Michael S., and Stephan E. Sefcik. "Participation Financing: A Comparison of the Characteristics of Convertible Debt and Straight Bonds Issued in Conjunction with Warrants," *Financial Management*, 1990, 19(3):23–34.

Lovata, Linda M., William D. Nichols, and Kirk L. Philipich. "Defeasing Discounted Debt: An Economic Analysis," *Financial Management*, 1987, 16(1):41–45.

Mauer, David C., Amir Barnea, and Chang-Soo Kim. "Valuation of Callable Bonds Under Progressive Personal Taxes and Interest Rate Uncertainty," *Financial Management*, 1991, 20(2):50–59.

Mitchell, Karlyn. "The Call, Sinking Fund, and Term-to-Maturity Features of Corporate Bonds: An Empirical Investigation," *Journal of Financial and Quantitative Analysis*, 1991, 26(2):201–222.

Nayar, Nandkumar, and Michael S. Rozeff. "Ratings, Commercial Paper, and Equity Returns," *Journal of Finance*, 1994, 49(4):1431–1449.

Ogden, Joseph P. "Determinants of the Relative Interest Rate Sensitivities of Corporate Bonds," *Financial Management*, 1987, 16(1):22–30.

Petersen, Mitchell A., and Raghuram G. Rajan. "The Benefits of Lending Relationships: Evidence from Small Business Data," *Journal of Finance*, 1994, 49(1):3–37.

Peterson, Pamela, David Peterson, and James Ang. "The Extinguishment of Debt Through In-Substance Defeasance," *Financial Management*, 1985, 14(1):59–67.

Rajan, Raghuram G. "Insiders and Outsiders: The Choice Between Informed and Arm's-Length Debt," *Journal of Finance*, 1992, 47(4):1367–1400.

Roberts, Gordon S., and Jerry A. Viscione. "The Impact of Seniority and Security Covenants on Bond Yields: A Note," *Journal of Finance*, 1984, 39(5):1597–1602.

Schultz, Paul. "Calls of Warrants: Timing and Market Reaction," *Journal of Finance*, 1993, 48(2):681–696.

Shulman, Joel, Mark Bayless, and Kelly Price. "Marketability and Default Influences on the Yield Premia of Speculative-Grade Debt," *Financial Management*, 1993, 22(3):132–141.

Singh, Ajai K., Arnold R. Cowan, and Nandkumar Nayar. "Underwritten Calls of Convertible Bonds," *Journal of Financial Economics*, 1991, 29(1):173–196.

Thatcher, Janet S. "The Choice of Call Provision Terms: Evidence of the Existence of Agency Costs of Debt," *Journal of Finance*, 1985, 40(2):549–561.

Usmen, Nilufer. "Currency Swaps, Financial Arbitrage, and Default Risk," *Financial Management*, 1994, 23(2):43–57.

Vu, Joseph D. "An Empirical Investigation of Calls of Non-Convertible Bonds," *Journal of Financial Economics*, 1986, 16(2):235–265.

Waheed, Amjad, and Ike Mathur. "The Effects of Announcements of Bank Lending Agreements on the Market Values of U.S. Banks," *Financial Management*, 1993, 22(1):119–127.

Wingler, Tony R., and G. Donald Jud. "Premium Debt Tenders: Analysis and Evidence," *Financial Management*, 1990, 19(4):58–67.

LEASING AND OTHER ASSET-BASED FINANCING

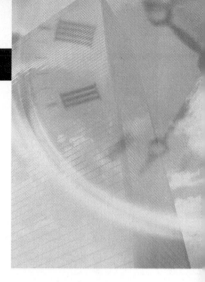

O B J E C T I V E S

After studying this chapter, you should be able to

1. Describe the three types of lease financing, and explain the advantages and disadvantages of lease financing.

2. Explain the concept of the net advantage to leasing.

3. Calculate the net advantage to leasing, the internal rate of return for a lease, and the equivalent loan for a lease.

4. Calculate break-even lease rates for the lessor and the lessee.

5. Describe the distinguishing features of project financing and limited partnership financing, and explain when such financing is advantageous.

You have probably rented a car, a bike, or some other item. Maybe you rented a trailer to take all your belongings to school. Did you consider buying instead? Not if you needed the item for only a few days.

Rentals are typically for short periods, perhaps for only a day. But firms often rent equipment and real estate for much longer periods. Sometimes they even rent entire plants. They rent when renting is cheaper than owning the asset.

We discussed the traditional methods of raising funds in Chapters 23 and 24. Firms retain earnings, or they can sell new issues of bonds, common stock, or preferred stock. They raise those funds on the strength of their general promise to pay and their overall profitability. Investors look to the cash flow from the firm's *entire* asset portfolio to provide the return on their investments.

Asset-based financing is different. The investors involved in **asset-based financing** must look to the cash flow from a specific asset for the return on their investment. In many cases, the lenders involved in asset-based financing lend on a nonrecourse basis. They look *exclusively* to a specific set of assets for the cash flow to service their loans.

The many types of asset-based financing include lease financing, project financing, limited partnership financing, and corporate real estate mortgage financing. Lease financing is the most important. There are a variety of models for analyzing lease financing. The key to proper leasing analysis is making sure that the alternatives are comparable. We will see how to do this by applying the concept of debt service parity (DSP): Each alternative must have the same after-tax payment schedule. Toward the end of the chapter, after we discuss leasing, we will take a quick look at project financing and limited partnership financing.

LEASING AND THE PRINCIPLES OF FINANCE

◆ *Self-Interested Behavior*: Look for profitable opportunities to lease (or rent) an asset rather than borrowing to buy it. Also look for profitable opportunities to arrange project financing or limit partnership financing for an asset you wish to purchase.

◆ *Two-Sided Transactions*: If you can't use the tax benefits of owning an asset, look for a profitable opportunity to lease it.

◆ *Incremental Benefits*: Calculate the net advantage to leasing on the basis of the incremental after-tax benefits that leasing will provide.

◆ *Options*: Recognize that the cancellation option in a lease is valuable to the lessee.

◆ *Capital Market Efficiency*: Use the lease information disclosed in the footnotes to a firm's financial statements to gauge the true financial impact of any leasing or rental agreements that do not appear on the face of the balance sheet.

◆ *Time Value of Money*: Use discounted cash flow analysis to compare the costs and benefits of leasing to those of borrowing and buying.

NORTH AMERICAN COAL'S LEASE-OR-BUY DECISION

Suppose North American Coal Company (NACCO) has a coal mine project under consideration. The project would cost $100 million. Among the equipment that would be required are three electric shovels. Each costs $10 million. NACCO would use each electric shovel for 10 years before selling it. NACCO expects each electric shovel to be worth $500,000 after 10 years. The firm can depreciate each electric shovel on a straight-line basis over 10 years for tax purposes. A finance company has offered to lease each electric shovel to NACCO. The lease would require annual payments of $1.745 million (payable at the end of each year) for 10 years for each shovel. NACCO has a 40% tax rate.

   Should NACCO buy the electric shovels or lease them? NACCO's future tax situation is uncertain. How would the firm's ability to use tax deductions that result from asset ownership affect the buy-or-lease decision? Under the lease alternative, the finance company would own the electric shovels at the end of the lease and would realize their residual value. In view of the residual value that NACCO must forgo, would leasing be a poor alternative?

   We will return to these questions after we learn more about the nature of leasing.

25.1 LEASE FINANCING

Leasing is not new. We know that leasing originated at least 3000 years ago, because records show that the ancient Phoenicians chartered ships. Since that time, chartering, a form of ship leasing, has played a major role in financing maritime activities. Lease financing has also expanded to cover just about any type of capital equipment, and its use has grown very rapidly in recent decades. This is partly because capital equipment has become increasingly complex and costly and quickly grows obsolete. Leasing offers a means of efficiently transferring the risk of obsolescence. More important, firms in capital-intensive industries, such as railroads, airlines, and utilities, have been unable to make full use of the tax deductions that result from asset ownership. Lease financing provides a way effectively to transfer tax deductions from those who cannot use them to those who can.

What Is a Lease?

A **lease** is a rental agreement that extends for one year or longer. Under a lease agreement, the owner of an asset (the **lessor**) grants another party (the **lessee**) the exclusive right to use the asset during the specified term of the lease in return for a specified series of payments. In this way a lease also resembles a secured loan.

Payments are typically made monthly, quarterly, or semiannually. The first lease payment is usually due on the date the lease agreement is signed. Payments are normally level, as are mortgage and car payments. However, this time pattern can be altered—for example, to provide for lower payments during the early years before the asset reaches its full potential to generate cash flow.

Often lease agreements also give the lessee the option to renew the lease or purchase the asset. Sometimes the purchase option specifies a fixed price, but usually the purchase price is the asset's fair market value on the date the lessee exercises the option. If the purchase option is not exercised, the leased asset continues to belong to the lessor.

THE LEASING MARKETPLACE   Leased equipment includes aircraft, ships, railroad cars, communications satellites, mining equipment, computers, and many more items—even entire electric generating plants. Just about any asset can be leased. The principal lessors are equipment manufacturers (such as General Motors Acceptance Corporation), commercial banks, finance companies, and independent leasing companies. Equipment manufacturers arrange leases in order to encourage sales.

TYPES OF LEASES   With a *full-service lease*, the lessor (owner) is responsible for maintaining and insuring the assets and for paying any property taxes due on them. With a *net lease*, the lessee is responsible for these costs.

Leases also differ with respect to their term and the right to cancel during the contract period. **Operating leases** are short-term. They are generally cancelable at the lessee's option before the end of the lease term. **Financial leases** (or capital leases) are long-term. They generally extend over most of the estimated useful economic life of the asset. Usually they cannot be canceled by the lessee before the end of the lease period. Those financial leases that *can* be canceled generally require the lessee to reimburse the lessor for any losses the cancellation causes. The focus of this chapter is on financial leases.

FINANCIAL LEASES   Financial leases represent an important source of long-term financing. Entering into a financial lease is like entering into a loan agreement. The lessee receives an immediate inflow equal to the value of the asset. The lessee realizes this value as though it were cash, because it gets the exclusive use of the asset without having to purchase it. The firm also realizes the same stream of economic benefits (other than tax deductions) that it would if it had purchased the asset.

On the other hand, the lease agreement calls for specified periodic payments, just like a loan agreement. Moreover, if the lessee fails to make timely lease payments, the lessee runs the risk of bankruptcy, just as it would if it missed an interest payment or principal repayment on a loan. Therefore, a lease is very much like a secured loan.

Types of Lease Financing

Most financial leases are direct leases, sale-and-lease-back arrangements, or leveraged leases (Figure 25-1).

DIRECT LEASES   Assets covered by financial leases are generally new. Under a *direct lease*, the lessee identifies the asset it requires. Then it either leases it directly from the manufacturer or arranges for some other lessor to buy it from the manufacturer and lease it to the lessee.

SALE-AND-LEASE-BACK ARRANGEMENTS   A firm may sell an asset it already owns and lease it back from the purchaser. Such arrangements are common in real estate. Under a **sale-and-lease-back** arrangement, the owner of an asset sells it, usually at market value, for cash. The purchaser assumes legal ownership and thereby the right to the tax deductions associated with ownership and to the residual value. The seller gets the exclusive right to use the asset during the basic lease period in return for periodic lease payments.

LEVERAGED LEASES   A lessor who provides lease financing for an expensive piece of equipment, such as an aircraft, may wish to borrow a portion of the funds to make that investment. Under a **leveraged lease**, the lessor borrows a substantial portion of the purchase price of the asset, generally up to 80%. The lessor provides the balance of the purchase price in the

FIGURE 25-1
The types of lease financing.

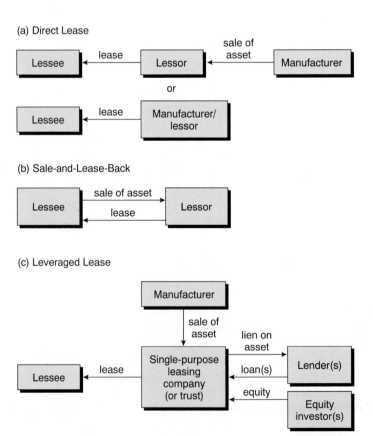

form of equity. To secure the loan, the lessor grants the long-term lender(s) a mortgage on the asset and assigns the lease contract to the lender(s). Thus lenders have a prior claim on the lease payments, as well as what is called a *perfected first lien* on the asset. Under such a lien, if the lessee fails to make timely lease payments, the lenders are entitled to seize the asset.

Advantages of Leasing

Leasing offers a number of real advantages.

- *More efficient use of tax deductions and tax credits of ownership.* The main reason to choose lease financing is the lessor's ability to use the tax deductions and tax credits associated with asset ownership more efficiently than the lessee can.

- *Reduced risk.* Short-term operating leases, in particular, provide a convenient way to use an asset for a relatively short period of time. Cancelable operating leases, such as computer leases, relieve the lessee of the risk of product obsolescence. This risk shifting is efficient. The lessor, such as the equipment manufacturer, is usually in a better position to assume the risk. This motivation for leasing reflects the Options Principle: The cancellation option is valuable.

- *Reduced cost of borrowing.* Lessors of assets that can be sold readily, such as vehicles, generally do not have to perform credit analyses quite as detailed as those conducted by general lenders. They are also more likely to be able to use "standardized" lease documentation. Both factors reduce transaction costs and so can result in a lower cost of borrowing for the lessee. This can especially benefit a smaller firm that may face restricted access to conventional sources of funds.

- *Bankruptcy considerations.* In the case of aircraft and vessels, special provisions of the bankruptcy law give a lessor greater flexibility than a secured lender has to seize the asset in the event of bankruptcy, because the lessor owns the asset. Suppliers of capital to smaller or less creditworthy firms, for which the risk of financial distress is greater, often prefer to advance funds through a lease rather than a loan. Because the lessor retains ownership of the asset, it can seize it if the lessee defaults.

- *Tapping a new source of funds.* Lease financing may permit a lessee to access a new source of funds. For example, finance companies might not customarily purchase the lessee's securities. The new source is beneficial, of course, only if it results in a truly lower cost of borrowing.

    Leasing also offers opportunities to circumvent restrictions.

- *Circumventing restrictive debt covenants or other restrictions.* A firm might be able to borrow funds through lease financing even when conventional debt financing is prohibited by its debt covenants.[1] The leases represent a disguised form of debt financing and so may affect the lessee's agency costs. However, recently drafted indentures and loan agreements usually contain limitations on leasing that foreclose this loophole.

- *Off-balance-sheet financing.* Firms often go to great lengths to design leases that achieve off-balance-sheet treatment. Many firms also try to keep lease payments as low as possible during the early years of the lease term, in order to minimize the impact on reported earnings per share. On the basis of the Principle of Capital Market Efficiency, however, you would expect the leasing information disclosed in the footnotes to the firm's financial statements to enable market participants to gauge the true financial impact of the leasing arrangements. In fact, evidence shows that investors correctly evaluate the financial impact of firms' financial lease obligations. Thus the apparent income statement and balance sheet benefits are of dubious value.

    Of course, as you might also expect, a market imperfection can cause the accounting treatment to affect value. Off-balance-sheet treatment *can* prove beneficial to a regulated firm, such as a bank, in certain situations. Banks are required to maintain a minimum ratio of capi-

---

[1] In a highly publicized leasing arrangement, the U.S. Navy once leased a fleet of oil tankers instead of seeking congressional appropriations to finance the purchase of the vessels.

tal to total assets based on balance sheet figures. Given any particular amount of capital, the minimum required capital-to-assets ratio determines the maximum amount of assets, as reported in the bank's balance sheet. But by leasing assets off-balance-sheet, a bank can increase its assets above the constrained amount. When a bank's assets are already at the permitted maximum, the incremental after-tax cash flow that the bank will realize by employing the leased assets in its business should be included in calculating the benefits of leasing.

Disadvantages of Leasing

There are two main disadvantages to leasing. First, the lessee forfeits the tax deductions associated with asset ownership. Second, the lessee must usually forgo residual value. A prospective lessee should evaluate carefully the cost of losing these benefits. Only then can the firm decide whether leasing is really cheaper than the alternative of borrowing and buying.

Bear in mind the Principle of Two-Sided Transactions. The tax benefits of leasing to the lessor are offset to some extent by certain tax liabilities. The lessor must recognize the full amount of each lease payment as taxable income. As we have pointed out, a lease is like a loan. However, it is a loan in which the entire debt service payment—principal as well as interest—is tax-deductible to the borrower/lessee *and* taxable to the lender/lessor. Leasing is beneficial only when the present value of the benefits of leasing exceeds the present value of the costs of leasing.

Self-Check Questions

1. What is a lease? What is a leveraged lease?

2. How is a financial lease different from an operating lease?

3. What are the main advantages of leasing as compared to conventional debt financing?

4. What are the two main disadvantages to leasing?

25.2 VALUING A FINANCIAL LEASE

Leasing analysis can be complex. A lease financing normally affects a firm's capital structure. Because of its complexity, leasing analysis is one of the more controversial issues in financial management. In the past, there was considerable debate over the correct discount rate. However, this controversy has been essentially resolved. Therefore, we focus our discussion on the generally accepted methods of leasing analysis.

Leasing involves an investment-financing interaction. We discussed capital budgeting in Chapters 10 through 13. The investment–financing interaction can affect the capital investment decision. It is even possible that the net present value of a capital investment project is negative when it is financed on a conventional basis but positive when the asset is leased. Therefore, the firm should not limit its lease-versus-buy analysis to those projects that it can justify on a purchase basis.

Leasing Displaces Borrowing

Lease analysis is similar to bond refunding analysis, which we discussed in Chapter 24. Just as one bond issue displaces another, so lease financing displaces debt. A firm that leases a piece of equipment reduces its borrowing capacity because it must meet its lease payment obligations on time to have uninterrupted use of the leased asset. If the lessee misses a lease pay-

	INITIAL CAPITALIZATION	CONVENTIONAL FINANCING	LEASE FINANCING	TARGET DEBT RATIO RESTORED
Long-term debt:				
Conventional debt	$100	$105	$100	$ 95
Financial lease obligations	—	—	10	10
Total long-term debt	100	105	110	105
Stockholders' equity	100	105	100	105
Net assets	$200	$210	$210	$210
Debt ratio	50%	50%	52.4%	50%

TABLE 25-1

A financial lease displaces conventional debt (dollar amounts in millions).

ment, the lessor can reclaim the asset (which it legally owns) and sue the lessee for the missed lease payment. The consequences of failing to make a lease payment are the same as the consequences of failing to pay interest or repay principal on outstanding debt. The lessor becomes a creditor who can force the lessee into bankruptcy. Consequently, for purposes of financial analysis, a firm's lease payment obligations belong in the same risk category as the firm's interest and principal repayment obligations.

Table 25-1 illustrates why leasing is a form of borrowing. Suppose that NACCO currently has net assets worth $200 million and a debt ratio of 50%. If NACCO financed the $10 million electric shovel on a conventional basis without altering its capital structure, then it would borrow $5 million and raise $5 million of equity funds. That would leave the firm with $105 million of debt and $105 million of equity. Suppose instead that NACCO leased the electric shovel and that the associated lease obligations have a present value of $10 million. NACCO's debt—including this lease obligation—increases to $110 million. No equity funds are required. The lease provides what practitioners like to refer to as "100% financing." However, you can see that leasing has changed the firm's capital structure. NACCO's debt ratio increases from 50% to 52.4% (= 110/210). Thus the two alternatives are not comparable, because they do not leave the firm with identical capital structures.

NACCO can restore its capital structure to 50% debt only if it issues $5 million of equity and reduces its other borrowing by $5 million. In that case, its debt would consist of $95 million of pre-existing debt plus the $10 million new lease obligation. Under both alternatives, NACCO has total debt of $105 million. However, under the leasing alternative, $10 million of that total consists of the new lease obligation. It is in this sense that a financial lease displaces conventional debt *dollar for dollar.*

Only when the alternatives of leasing, or borrowing and buying, are placed on a comparable basis can we make an accurate choice. Such a comparable basis includes the firm's capital structure. The choice of capital structure—and whether the firm will in fact have exactly the same capital structure after implementing either alternative—is a separate decision that should be evaluated on its own merits. The important point is to isolate the decision under consideration. The decision whether to lease or buy should be made separately from the capital structure decision.

Basic Analytic Framework

We have pointed out how the cash flow stream associated with a financial lease is similar in financial effect to the cash flow stream of a secured loan. This suggests an appropriate starting point for analyzing a financial lease: Compare it to the alternative of borrowing to finance the purchase price of the asset and repaying this loan over the lease term.

EXAMPLE	*A Financial Lease is Similar to a Secured Loan*

Consider again the problem posed at the beginning of the chapter. It involves a financial lease. NACCO can either purchase an electric shovel for $10 million or lease it under an agreement that requires payment of $1.745 million at the end of each year for 10 years. Leasing would require NACCO to forgo the tax deductions associated with asset ownership.

Table 25-2 illustrates the direct cash flow consequences to the firm of lease financing an electric shovel. The firm does not have to spend $10 million to purchase the shovel. The effect is equivalent to a cash inflow of $10 million. However, NACCO must make periodic lease payments. These are tax-deductible, so a lease payment of $1,745,000 gives rise to a tax deduction worth $698,000 (= 0.4 × 1,745,000). NACCO must also forgo the depreciation tax deductions and residual value of ownership. Each electric shovel is depreciated to a salvage value of $500,000. Depreciation is straight-line. Each year's deduction is $950,000 [= (10,000,000 − 500,000) ÷ 10]. The value of each year's deduction is $380,000 (= 0.4 × 950,000). Putting all these factors together yields an effective initial net cash inflow of $10.0 million. It is followed by effective net cash outflows of $1.427 million in each of years 1 through 9 and $1.927 million in year 10.

In Table 25-2, we assume that NACCO expects to pay taxes at a 40% marginal rate over the next 10 years. If the firm does not expect to pay income taxes during that period, the value of the depreciation tax deductions forgone is zero. The net cash flow column would change accordingly. ■

TABLE 25-2

Direct cash flow consequences to NACCO of lease financing an electric shovel (dollar amounts in thousands).

YEAR	0	1	2	3	4	5	6	7	8	9	10
Benefits of Leasing:											
Initial outlay (avoided)	+ 10,000										
Costs of Leasing:											
Lease payments[a]		− 1,745	− 1,745	− 1,745	− 1,745	− 1,745	− 1,745	− 1,745	− 1,745	− 1,745	− 1,745
Lease payment tax credit[b]		+ 698	+ 698	+ 698	+ 698	+ 698	+ 698	+ 698	+ 698	+ 698	+ 698
Depreciation tax credits forgone[c]		− 380	− 380	− 380	− 380	− 380	− 380	− 380	− 380	− 380	− 380
Salvage value forgone											− 500
Net cash flow to lessee	− 10,000	− 1,427	− 1,427	− 1,427	− 1,427	− 1,427	− 1,427	− 1,427	− 1,427	− 1,427	− 1,927

[a] Lease payments made annually in arrears.
[b] Assumes the lessee's marginal income tax rate is 40%.
[c] Assumes straight-line depreciation to a $500,000 terminal book value for tax purposes.

APPLYING THE DSP APPROACH   The debt service parity (DSP) approach is useful for this purpose. It applies to leasing analysis much as it does to bond refunding. As we have said, the principal tenet of the DSP approach is that the two alternatives must be evaluated as though the firm's total after-tax obligation (either lease payments or debt service payments) will be exactly the same under either alternative. Maintaining such parity is important. Evaluating the decision whether to lease or to borrow and buy must avoid the complications associated with other possible simultaneous decisions. These complications could bias the calculation of the net advantage to leasing.

When you apply the DSP approach, you ask the question "How much money can I raise today by selling the debt stream promised by the lease?" If this amount is greater than the purchase price of the financed asset, then the lease will not increase shareholder wealth. You could buy the asset more economically using borrowed funds.

First, we must determine the amount of debt the firm can issue *today* if the obligation connected with the *after-tax* period-by-period debt service payments for the borrow-and-buy alternative is exactly the same as that of the lease alternative. Here's how you might view the amount of debt the firm could issue today. Think of the after-tax lease payments as a set of promised future cash flows that could be "auctioned off" in the capital market. The amount of debt the firm can issue today is then the amount it would receive in exchange for that set of promised future cash flows. If the proceeds of the debt are not enough to purchase the equipment, then the leasing alternative has a positive NPV and should be undertaken. Of course, if the debt proceeds are greater than the cost of purchasing the equipment, then leasing would decrease shareholder wealth and should not be undertaken.

THE NET ADVANTAGE TO LEASING   The **net advantage to leasing** equals the purchase price *minus* the present value of the incremental after-tax cash flows—the CFATs—associated with the lease. The net advantage to leasing (NAL) can be expressed in equation form as

$$NAL = P - PV(CFATs) \qquad (25.1)$$

where P is the purchase price and PV(CFATs) is the present value of the CFATs.

What is the appropriate discount rate for determining the present value of the lease payments, any after-tax change in operating or other expenses (due to the lessor becoming responsible for paying them under the terms of the lease), and depreciation tax deductions? They should all be discounted at the lessee's after-tax cost of similarly secured debt (assuming 100% debt financing for the asset). In Chapter 24 we saw that secured debt is debt that provides lenders with a lien on certain assets. This is also the required return for the lease payments, because a firm's lease payments belong to the same risk class as the firm's debt payments. In addition, the lease obligation is secured because the lessor retains ownership of the asset. However, the lessee is effectively borrowing 100% of the purchase price. Thus the financial lease obligation is not *overcollateralized*, as is typically the case with conventional secured debt financing.[2] Accordingly, the secured debt rate used in the financial lease valuation should reflect the absence of overcollateralization. Typically, it is a weighted average of the cost of fully secured debt and the cost of unsecured debt.

The present value of the expected residual value of the asset—the salvage value—is determined by discounting at a higher required return to reflect its greater riskiness. Residual value is more closely related to overall project economic risk than to financing risk. Therefore, the required return for the project is used to determine the present value of the expected residual value.

The relevant incremental cash flows associated with a decision whether to lease or to borrow and buy include (1) cost of the asset (savings), (2) lease payments (cost), (3) incremental differences in operating or other expenses between the leasing and buying alternatives (cost or savings), (4) depreciation tax deductions (forgone benefit), (5) expected net residual value (forgone benefit),[3] and (6) investment tax credit or other tax credits (forgone benefit).

---

[2] An asset's value can decrease, so secured loans are overcollateralized to protect lenders. For example, lenders may require 25% overcollateralization before they will treat a loan as "fully secured" and lend at the lower secured debt rate. In that case, a firm that pledges $100 million of assets can borrow up to $80 million at the secured debt rate. The difference, $20 million, is 25% of $80 million.

[3] The asset's residual value at the end of the lease term is also important for tax reasons. If the asset's residual value is expected to be insignificant, the Internal Revenue Service may take the position that the lease is not a true lease. It would then deny the tax-deductibility of the portion of the lessee's lease payments that effectively represents repayments of principal.

The net advantage to leasing can be rewritten as

$$NAL = P - \sum_{t=1}^{N} \frac{(1-T)(CF_t - \Delta E_t) + TD_t}{[1 + (1-T)r']^t} - \frac{SAL}{(1+r)^N} - ITC = 0 \qquad (25.2)$$

where D_t = the depreciation deduction (for tax purposes, *not* financial reporting purposes) in year t

   ΔE_t = the total incremental difference in operating or other expenses in year t between the leasing and buying alternatives

   ITC = investment tax credit, if available

   CF_t = lease payment in year t

   N = the number of periods in the life of the lease

   NAL = the net advantage to leasing

   P = the purchase price of the asset

   r = the required return for the asset (its after-tax weighted average cost of capital)

   r' = the after-tax cost of debt, assuming 100% debt financing for the asset (typically, this is a weighted average of the fully secured and unsecured debt rates)

   SAL = salvage value of the asset (the expected residual value of the asset at the end of the lease)

   T = the lessee's (asset user's) marginal ordinary income tax rate

Equation (25.2) assumes that the lease payments are made in arrears (that is, at the end of each period), not in advance (at the beginning of each period). Lease agreements often provide for lease payments to be made in advance. In such cases, we must adjust Equation (25.2), as well as the other equations presented in this section, to reflect properly the exact timing of the lease payments. The equation also assumes that the lessor claims any investment tax credit (ITC). Lease agreements sometimes permit the lessee to claim it instead. Before performing a leasing analysis, check the proposed lease terms to determine the timing of the lease payments and who is entitled to claim any available ITC.

Analyzing NACCO's Lease-or-Buy Decision

Let's apply the DSP approach to NACCO's lease-or-buy decision. First, we must specify current capital market conditions. NACCO can borrow 10-year secured installment debt in the amount of 80% of the value of each electric shovel at a pretax interest rate of 11.5% per year. NACCO can borrow unsecured installment debt in the amount of the remaining 20% of the value of each electric shovel at a pretax interest rate of 14.0% per year. Finally, the after-tax required return (weighted average cost of capital) for this project is 15% per year. NACCO's marginal tax rate is 40%.

EXAMPLE

NACCO's Net Advantage to Leasing

NACCO's cost of debt, assuming 100% debt financing with 80% secured and 20% unsecured, is 12.0% [= (0.8)11.5% + (0.2)14.0%] before tax and 7.2% after-tax [= (1 − 0.4)12.0%]. The lease payments are $1,745,000 at the end of each year for 10 years. They are tax-deductible. The amount of the depreciation tax deductions forgone is $950,000 per year [= (10,000,000 − 500,000)/10]. The related tax savings forgone is $380,000 per year (= 0.4 × 950,000). The salvage value is $500,000. There is no ITC. Therefore, applying Equation (25.2) reveals that the net advantage to leasing for NACCO is

$$NAL = 10,000,000 - \sum_{t=1}^{10} \frac{(1 - 0.4)1,745,000 + 380,000}{(1.072)^t} - \frac{500,000}{(1.15)^{10}} - 0$$

$$= 10,000,000 - 9,930,644 - 123,592 = -\$54,236$$

The net advantage to leasing is negative. The firm should borrow and buy rather than leasing the shovel. We will show you later that NACCO's ability fully to use, itself, the tax deductions associated with asset ownership is largely responsible for this negative value. ■

Self-Check Questions
1. How does a lease displace conventional debt?
2. What is the net advantage to leasing?
3. How is the debt service parity approach applied to leasing?
4. Why is the discount rate that is applied to the expected residual value different from the discount rate that is applied to the lease payments?

Other Analytic Approaches

There are two alternative approaches to net-present-value analysis. We should emphasize that the DSP net-present-value approach, which we presented, is the most universally valid analytic method and the one we recommend that you use. The internal-rate-of-return approach is widely used by practitioners. A third approach, called the equivalent-loan approach, is quite similar to the net-present-value approach but yields some interesting insights.

INTERNAL-RATE-OF-RETURN APPROACH   The internal-rate-of-return approach bears the same relation to the net-present-value approach in leasing as it does in capital budgeting analysis, which we discussed in Chapter 11. The internal rate of return, IRR, is the discount rate that makes the net advantage to leasing in Equation (25.2) equal to zero:

$$\text{NAL} = P - \sum_{t=1}^{N} \frac{(1-T)(\text{CF}_t - \Delta E_t) + TD_t}{(1+\text{IRR})^t} - \frac{\text{SAL}}{(1+\text{IRR})^N} - \text{ITC} = 0 \qquad (25.3)$$

where the variables are defined as in Equation (25.2).

The internal rate of return represents the **cost of lease financing**. It is an after-tax cost. If the lessee is taxable, the cost of lease financing includes the interest tax deductions lost on displaced debt. It also includes the tax deductions, tax credits, and residual value forgone as a result of lease financing rather than borrowing and buying the asset. If the cost of lease financing is less than the prospective lessee's after-tax cost of secured debt, the firm should lease finance the asset. Otherwise, it should borrow funds and buy the asset.

Let's apply the IRR approach to NACCO's proposed lease financing. Solving the equation

$$0 = 10{,}000{,}000 - \sum_{t=1}^{10} \frac{1{,}427{,}000}{(1+\text{IRR})^t} - \frac{500{,}000}{(1+\text{IRR})^{10}}$$

for IRR gives IRR $= 0.0758$, or 7.58%. The cost of lease financing is greater than NACCO's 7.20% after-tax cost of comparably (100% financed) secured debt. The firm should therefore borrow funds and buy the asset. ■

The IRR of NACCO's Proposed Lease Financing

EXAMPLE

EQUIVALENT-LOAN APPROACH The equivalent-loan approach has no counterpart in capital budgeting analysis. It involves simply comparing the amount of financing provided by the lease to the amount of financing provided by the **equivalent loan**. The equivalent loan is the maximum amount the lessee could borrow if the lessee dedicates the future incremental cash flow stream (beginning at the end of the first period) to service conventional secured debt. The equivalent loan, by design, involves the same period-by-period after-tax debt service requirements as the lease. This treatment conforms to the DSP principle. In effect, the equivalent loan is the amount for which the after-tax payments could be "auctioned off."

The equivalent loan, EL, can be written

$$EL = \sum_{t=1}^{N} \frac{(1-T)(CF_t - \Delta E_t) + TD_t}{[1+(1-T)r']^t} + \frac{SAL}{(1+r)^N} \qquad (25.4)$$

where the variables are defined as in Equation (25.2). Suppose the purchase price of the asset (*P*) minus the investment tax credit (ITC) exceeds the amount of the equivalent loan. Then the lease effectively provides the greater amount of financing (for the same after-tax debt service stream). The asset should therefore be leased. Otherwise, the asset should be financed on a conventional basis.

EXAMPLE *The Amount of the Equivalent Loan in NACCO's Proposed Lease Financing*	The amount of the equivalent loan is $$EL = \sum_{t=1}^{10} \frac{1,427,000}{(1.072)^t} + \frac{500,000}{(1.15)^{10}} = \$10,054,236$$ which exceeds the \$10 million cost of the asset. Conventional financing is therefore more advantageous than lease financing. ■

Note that the cost of the asset minus the amount of the equivalent loan equals −\$54,236, the net advantage to leasing. Thus the equivalent-loan approach is perfectly equivalent to the net-present-value approach. Nevertheless, we think the equivalent-loan approach is useful in its own right. It makes it easier to interpret the net advantage to leasing. NAL represents the amount by which the magnitude of the funds provided by the lease exceeds (when NAL > 0) or falls short of (NAL < 0) the magnitude of the funds provided by conventional debt financing when debt service parity is preserved.

When Is Lease Financing Advantageous?

As you would expect, leasing would be a zero-sum game between lessor and lessee in a perfect capital market environment. Even with taxes, in an otherwise perfect capital market environment, it will be a zero-sum game if both parties have the same marginal tax rate. In such an environment, the negative of the benefit to the lessee ($-$NAL) will be the cost to the lessor. In the example just given, suppose the lessor has the same marginal tax rate as NACCO. Then the lessor will have a positive NPV of \$54,236 if NACCO undertakes this lease:

$$\text{NPVL} = -P + \sum_{t=1}^{N} \frac{(1 - T')(\text{CF}_t - \Delta E_t) + T'D_t}{[1 + (1 - T')r']^t} + \frac{\text{SAL}}{(1 + r)^N} + \text{ITC} \qquad (25.5)$$

$$\text{NPVL} = -10{,}000{,}000 + \sum_{t=1}^{10} \frac{1{,}427{,}000}{(1.072)^t} + \frac{500{,}000}{(1.15)^{10}} + 0 = \$54{,}236$$

where NPVL is the net present value of the lease to the lessor, T' is the lessor's marginal ordinary income tax rate, and the other variables are defined as in Equation (25.2). Note the symmetry between Equations (25.2) and (25.5). Note also that the discount rates r' and r occur in both equations, because r' measures the riskiness of the lease payments, as determined in the capital market, and r measures the riskiness of the overall project, also as determined in the capital market.

In an imperfect capital market environment, there is a possibility that a tax asymmetry, information asymmetries, or transaction costs may cause leasing to be favorable for both lessor and lessee. For example, if the lessor and the lessee have different marginal income tax rates, the CFATs can have different present values to the two parties.

Suppose NACCO will never be able to use the tax deductions that are potentially available from owning the electric shovels. In that case, its cost of entering into the lease is calculated by discounting the lease payments and the forgone residual asset value. The discount rates for determining the present values of these two costs are the cost of debt, 12%, and the required return for the project, both with $T = 0$. Suppose this required return is 17.5%. Then

$$\text{NAL} = 10{,}000{,}000 - \sum_{t=1}^{10} \frac{1{,}745{,}000}{(1.12)^t} - \frac{500{,}000}{(1.175)^{10}} = \$40{,}685$$

In this case, NACCO should lease the electric shovels. The negative net advantage to leasing calculated earlier was largely caused by NACCO's ability to use the tax deductions associated with asset ownership. ∎

The Net Advantage to Leasing When NACCO Does Not Pay Taxes

EXAMPLE

BREAK-EVEN LEASE PAYMENT   Equations (25.2) and (25.5) can be used to determine a **break-even lease payment** for the lessee and lessor. The lessee's break-even lease payment, L_E, is the lease payment that makes the lessee indifferent between leasing the asset and borrowing the necessary funds on a conventional basis and buying it. NAL = 0 when $\text{CF}_t = L_E$ for all periods t. The lessor's break-even lease payment, L_R, is calculated and interpreted similarly.

Calculating Break-Even Lease Payments

If NACCO never expects to pay income taxes, then L_E = $1,752,200.54 because

$$\text{NAL} = 10,000,000 - \sum_{t=1}^{10} \frac{1,752,200.54}{(1.12)^t} - \frac{500,000}{(1.175)^{10}} = 0$$

What is the lessor's break-even lease rate? Assume T' = 0.4. Then L_R = $1,732,010.75 because

$$\text{NPVL} = -10,000,000 + \sum_{t=1}^{10} \frac{0.6(1,732,010.75) + 380,000}{(1.072)^t} + \frac{500,000}{(1.15)^{10}} = 0$$

So long as $L_R < L_E$, it is possible to find a lease payment (or set of lease payments, one for each period t) CF_t such that $L_R < \text{CF}_t < L_E$ and leasing is mutually advantageous to lessor and lessee. Where CF_t lies in relation to L_R and L_E determines how the net (tax) advantage to leasing is allocated between lessee and lessor. ∎

Therefore, you can see that tax considerations can alter the otherwise zero-sum game. In some cases, tax considerations make lease financing more advantageous than conventional debt financing for both lessee and lessor. In this example, the leasing arrangement effectively allows NACCO to sell tax deductions that would otherwise expire worthless because of NACCO's inability to claim them itself. The value of these tax deductions to the lessor, which is reflected in the lease rate, is sufficient to make lease financing advantageous for both parties. On the other hand, we found previously that if NACCO can claim the tax deductions, then leasing is not advantageous. The value of the tax deductions reflected in the lease rate is lower than the value NACCO would realize by claiming the tax deductions itself.

ASYMMETRIC TAXES AND THE REQUIRED LEASE PAYMENT   It is not true that in *every* case a low taxpayer or nontaxpayer should lease from a relatively high-taxpaying entity. Whether it is advantageous depends on the required lease payment. That payment reflects the value the lessor is effectively willing to pay for the tax deductions transferred under the lease.

The Impact of the Lease Payment the Lessor Charges

Suppose NACCO expects to pay income taxes at a 40% rate. It has been offered a second lease opportunity with payments of $1,792,000 required at the end of each of the next 10 years. All the other information is identical to what was given previously. The net advantage to leasing for NACCO is

$$\text{NAL} = 10,000,000 - \sum_{t=1}^{10} \frac{(1-0.4)1,792,000 + 380,000}{[1 + (1-0.4)0.12]^t} - \frac{500,000}{(1 + 0.15)^{10}}$$

$$= 10,000,000 - 10,126,891 - 123,592 = -\$250,483$$

NACCO's net advantage to leasing is negative under this lease arrangement if NACCO pays taxes at a 40% tax rate.

But consider what happens if NACCO expects never to pay income taxes. Its net advantage to leasing would be

$$\text{NAL} = 10,000,000 - \sum_{t=1}^{10} \frac{1,792,000}{(1.12)^t} - \frac{500,000}{(1.175)^{10}} = -\$224,876$$

In this case, NACCO should not lease even though it expects never to pay income taxes. The reason is quite simple: The payments of $1,792,000 are too large; the required lease payment exceeds NACCO's break-even lease payment. ■

PAYMENT TIMING   The potential tax asymmetry between lessee and lessor is situation-specific. Situations may arise in which there are lease payment amounts at which the lessee would prefer leasing to borrowing and buying when the lessee is fully taxable *but* would prefer borrowing and buying to leasing when the lessee is not a taxpayer.

EXAMPLE

The Impact of Cash Flow Timing on the Attractiveness of Leasing

Suppose NACCO expects to pay income taxes at a 40% rate. It has been offered a lease calling for payments of $1,570,000 *at the beginning* of each of the next 10 years. None of the other conditions has changed, except that tax deductions are realized at the beginning rather than at the end of each period. NACCO's net advantage to leasing is

$$NAL = 10,000,000 - \sum_{t=0}^{9} \frac{(1 - 0.4)1,570,000 + 380,000}{[1 + (1 - 0.4)0.12]^t} - \frac{500,000}{[1 + 0.15]^{10}}$$

$$= 10,000,000 - 9,862,333 - 123,592 = \$14,075$$

Thus the firm's net advantage to leasing is positive. NACCO should lease rather than borrow and buy, even though it pays income tax at a 40% rate.

Suppose NACCO expects never to pay income taxes. Its net advantage to leasing would be

$$NAL = 10,000,000 - \sum_{t=0}^{9} \frac{1,570,000}{(1.12)^t} - \frac{500,000}{(1.175)^{10}} = -\$35,028$$

NACCO should not lease if it expects never to pay income taxes, but it should lease if it expects to pay income taxes at a 40% rate! ■

The critical difference between the last two examples lies in the timing of the lease payments, tax deductions, and tax liabilities. The timing of these items has an effect on the value of the lease to each party. In general, the timing of each of these factors, the nature of the depreciation schedule for the asset, and the existence (or lack) of an investment tax credit affect the ability of the parties to create a lease contract that is mutually beneficial. Note that in all cases, however, the proper neutralization of the capital structure side effects is absolutely necessary to isolate and accurately measure the value of the financial lease.

Leasing and Capital Budgeting

As we saw in the case of capital structure, lease financing can affect the value of an investment project by enabling a lessee to take advantage of any potential tax asymmetry. It is possible for a project that would have a negative NPV if the firm financed it on a conventional basis to have a positive NPV if it is lease financed. If one party can benefit from tax deductions and credits and their timing but the other cannot, leasing can enhance the value of the project.

<table>
<tr><td rowspan="8">**EXAMPLE**</td><td rowspan="8">*Lease Financing Can Affect the Value of an Investment Project*</td><td>The top panel of Table 25-3 illustrates the cash flow streams for an electric power project. The project's owner can lease the power generation equipment. The firm will never be able to claim the tax deductions associated with asset ownership. The firm has determined that debt financing is of no benefit, because it is unable to claim the interest tax deductions. The firm's investments require a 15% return (zero leverage). The NPV of the project, calculated in the manner described in Chapter 11, is −$1,907,113. The project would therefore be unprofitable if it were financed on a conventional basis.</td></tr>
</table>

The top panel of Table 25-3 illustrates the cash flow streams for an electric power project. The project's owner can lease the power generation equipment. The firm will never be able to claim the tax deductions associated with asset ownership. The firm has determined that debt financing is of no benefit, because it is unable to claim the interest tax deductions. The firm's investments require a 15% return (zero leverage). The NPV of the project, calculated in the manner described in Chapter 11, is −$1,907,113. The project would therefore be unprofitable if it were financed on a conventional basis.

Now suppose the project is lease financed instead. The middle panel of Table 25-3 shows the associated cash flows. The lease arrangement calls for lease payments of $10,300,000 at the end of each year. The net advantage to leasing is $2,241,434.

By combining the NPV of the conventionally financed project with the net advantage to leasing (NAL) we get the total NPV of the project if it is lease financed (see the bottom panel of Table 25-3):

$$\text{NPV(leased)} = \text{NPV(conventional)} + \text{NAL} \qquad (25.6)$$

$$= -1,907,113 + 2,241,434 = \$334,321$$

The lease rate is low enough that the net advantage to leasing outweighs the negative net present value of the project when it is financed on a conventional basis. In effect, the lessor is willing to pay enough for the tax deductions to make the project profitable. Thus the project is profitable when lease financed but unprofitable otherwise. ■

TABLE 25-3

Illustration of how lease financing can turn a project profitable.

NPV (CONVENTIONALLY FINANCED)

Time	Item	CFBT	CFAT	PV at 15%
0	Initial outlay	− 50,000,000	− 50,000,000	− 50,000,000
1–7	Δ Rev − Δ Exp.	11,378,903	11,378,903	47,341,013
7	Residual value	2,000,000	2,000,000	751,874
				NPV = − $1,907,113

NET ADVANTAGE TO LEASING

Time	Item	CFBT	CFAT	PV at 12%[a] (15% for residual value)
0	Initial outlay	50,000,000	50,000,000	50,000,000
1–7	Lease payments	− 10,300,000	− 10,300,000	− 47,006,692
7	Residual value	− 2,000,000	− 2,000,000	− 751,874
				NAL = $2,241,434

TOTAL NET PRESENT VALUE

Total net present value = − $1,907,113 + 2,241,434 = $334,321

[a] Assumes a new issue rate of 12.00% for the firm's debt.

Note that the project's residual value can also play an important role in the economics of leasing. Suppose the residual value in the example just given were $10 million. The net present value of the project when financed on a conventional basis would be $1.10 million, and the net advantage to leasing would be $-\$0.77$ million. The sponsor should finance the project in that case on a conventional basis, even though it does not expect to be able to use any of the tax deductions associated with asset ownership.

Self-Check Questions

1. Why does the internal rate of return of a lease's incremental after-tax cash flow stream represent the cost of lease financing?
2. What is the equivalent loan for a lease?
3. Do the net-advantage-to-leasing, internal-rate-of-return, and equivalent-loan approaches to leasing *always* provide the same answer?
4. What is the break-even lease payment?
5. How can lease financing enhance the NPV of a project when the firm that develops it does not pay income taxes?

25.3 TAX AND ACCOUNTING TREATMENT OF FINANCIAL LEASES

There are special tax and accounting provisions that relate to financial leases. It is important for you to understand them—particularly the tax provisions—when you are going to be involved in a leasing transaction.

Tax Treatment of Financial Leases

The Internal Revenue Service (IRS) has established guidelines to distinguish true leases from installment sales agreements and secured loans. If the terms of the leasing arrangement satisfy these guidelines, the lessee can deduct for tax purposes the full amount of each lease payment, and the lessor is entitled to the tax deductions and tax credits of asset ownership. Here are the main guidelines:

- The term of the lease cannot exceed 80% of the useful life of the asset. The term includes all renewal or extension periods other than renewals or extensions that are (1) at the option of the lessee and (2) at the fair market rental prevailing at the time of renewal or extension.

- The lessor must maintain a minimum equity investment in the asset of no less than 10% of the asset's original cost throughout the term of the lease.

- The lessor can grant the lessee a purchase option. However, the exercise price must equal the asset's fair market value at the time the purchase option is exercised. Certain lease transactions do take place with a purchase option that provides for a fixed price equal to the estimated future fair market value, but such a lease does *not* conform to the guidelines and therefore does not qualify for an advance ruling from the IRS.

- The lessee does not pay any portion of the purchase price of the asset. In addition, if the lease is a leveraged lease, the lessee does not lend the lessor funds with which to purchase the leased asset or guarantee loans from others to the lessor for this purpose.

- The lessor must hold title to the property, and it must demonstrate that it expects to earn a pretax profit from the lease transaction—that is, profit apart from any tax deductions and tax credits it will realize.

These and the other requirements the IRS establishes are subject to change from time to time. As we have said repeatedly, it is important to review the applicable tax rules. It is important to verify that a proposed lease arrangement would qualify as a true lease and to confirm that it is advantageous to lease.

Accounting Treatment of Financial Leases

The accounting treatment accorded leases has undergone significant changes in recent decades. At one time, leases represented off-balance-sheet financing. That is, neither the leased asset nor the associated lease obligations were recorded on the face of the lessee's balance sheet. However, generally accepted accounting principles did require a lessee to disclose certain details regarding lease transactions in the footnotes to the lessee's financial statements.

Since 1977 Financial Accounting Standards Board Statement No. 13 (FASB 13) has required lessees to capitalize on their balance sheets all leases entered into on or after that date that have *any one* of the following characteristics:

- The lease transfers ownership of the asset to the lessee before the lease expires.
- The lease agreement grants the lessee the option to purchase the asset at a bargain price.
- The term of the lease equals or exceeds 75% of the estimated useful economic life of the asset.
- The present value of the minimum lease payments, discounted to the beginning of the lease period at the lesser of (1) the lessee's incremental borrowing rate and (2) the interest rate implicit in the lease payment stream (the *lease rate*), equals or exceeds 90% of the asset's value (net of any investment tax credit claimed by the lessor).

Leases that "fail" all four tests are operating leases from an accounting standpoint, and they do not have to be capitalized on the balance sheet.

FASB 13 assumes that if one of the four conditions is met, the lease arrangement is like a purchase of the asset with borrowed funds. Accordingly, FASB 13 requires the lessee to report the present value of the lease payments under capital leases next to long-term debt on the right-hand side of the balance sheet, with a corresponding amount reported as an asset on the left-hand side of the balance sheet. The lessee amortizes the leased asset over the term of the lease. Correspondingly, under the "interest" method, the lessee separates each lease payment into an interest component and a principal repayment component. The amortization amount and the interest component of the lease payment are deducted from income for financial reporting purposes. The principal repayment component reduces the amount of the capitalized lease obligation reported on the lessee's balance sheet.

Self-Check Questions

1. Why does a lessor want to be sure that a lease qualifies as a lease for tax purposes?
2. What are the guidelines a lease must satisfy to qualify as a lease for tax purposes?
3. Are there any advantages to getting a lease off-balance-sheet? Suppose the lessee must provide the details of the lease in the footnotes to its financial statements?

25.4 PROJECT FINANCING

Firms often find it advantageous to finance large capital investment projects that involve discrete assets on a project, or stand-alone, basis. **Project financing** is generally possible when a project possesses the following two characteristics:

1. The project consists of a discrete asset or a discrete set of assets capable of standing alone as an independent economic unit.

2. The economic prospects of the project, combined with commitments from the sponsors or from third parties, ensure that it will generate sufficient revenue net of operating costs to service project debt.

Mines, mineral processing facilities, electric generating facilities, pipelines, dock facilities, paper mills, oil refineries, and chemical plants are examples of assets that firms have financed on a project basis. In each case, the project's assets and the related debt obligations are separated from the sponsoring firms' other assets and liabilities, and the project is analyzed as a separate (though not necessarily independent) unit.

Project Structure

Each project is unique in some respects, and the financing arrangements are designed to suit the project's special characteristics and to resolve potential agency problems.

Project Financing Versus Conventional Financing

EXAMPLE

Suppose NACCO wants to develop the coal mine property discussed previously in order to obtain coal to sell to Electric Generating Company. NACCO could finance the mine on its general credit by selling equity securities or debentures and investing the proceeds in the project. Suppose, however, that in return for being assured of a source of coal, Electric Generating is willing to enter into a long-term coal purchase contract with NACCO. The mine will cost $100 million, which NACCO would like to borrow. The terms of the coal purchase contract can be specified in such a way that the contract will provide support for the loans NACCO will arrange to finance development of the mine and minimize potential agency costs. In the extreme case, the loans may be nonrecourse to NACCO. In that case, lenders will look solely to payments under the coal purchase contract for the payment of interest and the repayment of principal on their loans. The loans are then designed to be self-liquidating from the revenues to be derived from coal sales to Electric, and the project financing has little impact on NACCO's borrowing capacity.

The coal mine is capable of standing alone as an independent economic unit because of the long-term coal purchase contract, which will guarantee a market for its output. Normally, the project sponsor would have to make additional commitments (described in the paragraphs that follow) to lenders as a condition for their agreeing to lend to the project. ∎

Project Financing Arrangements

Financial engineering is crucial in project finance. It is necessary to design contractual arrangements to allocate project risks among the entities involved with the project, allocate the economic rewards among them, convey the credit strength of creditworthy firms to support project debt, and minimize total agency costs. Typical credit support arrangements include the following:

- *Completion undertaking.* Such an undertaking obligates the sponsors or other creditworthy entities either (1) to ensure that the project will pass certain performance tests by some specified date, or (2) to repay the debt. As an example of the former, the coal mine mentioned earlier might be required to produce a certain number of tons of coal per month for a certain specified number of months prior to some specified date. Completion undertakings are designed to control the asset substitution problem. They also prevent the equityholders from abandoning a project without fully compensating lenders if a project becomes unprofitable.

- *Purchase, throughput, or tolling agreements.* These obligate one or more creditworthy entities to purchase the project's output or use its facilities. Purchase agreements that are capable of supporting project financing take the form of take-or-pay contracts or hell-or-high-water contracts. *Take-or-pay contracts* obligate the purchaser to take the project's output or else pay for it if the product is offered for delivery (but normally only if the product is available for delivery). *Hell-or-high-water contracts* obligate the purchaser to pay in all events—that is, whether or not any output is available for delivery. The latter agreement is, of course, stronger and therefore provides greater credit support. *Throughput agreements* are often used in pipeline financing. They require shippers to put some specified minimum amount of a product (for example, oil) through the pipeline each month (or interest period) in order to enable the pipeline to generate sufficient cash to cover its operating expenses and debt service requirements. They can take the form of either *ship-or-pay* (similar to take-or-pay obligations) or hell-or-high-water undertakings. *Tolling agreements* are often used in the financing of processing facilities, such as an aluminum smelter, when the user retains ownership of the item throughout the production process. Such arrangements require users to process a certain specified minimum amount of raw material each month (or interest period).

- *Cash deficiency agreements.* Unless the purchase, throughput, or tolling agreement is of the hell-or-high-water variety, interruptions in availability or deliverability can result in the project realizing insufficient cash to meet its debt service obligations. Sponsors may therefore have to provide supplemental credit support in the form of a *cash deficiency agreement.* Such an agreement obligates the sponsors to invest additional cash as required by the project to meet its debt service obligations.

Advantages of Project Financing

Project financing can provide significant advantages in certain situations.

- *Risk sharing.* A sponsor can enlist one or more joint venture partners to share the equity risk. Such risk sharing is beneficial in the presence of significant costs of financial distress. It should be considered whenever a capital budgeting project is so large, relative to a firm's existing asset portfolio, that pursuing it alone would increase the firm's risk of bankruptcy to an unacceptable level. Under some circumstances, a project sponsor can transfer risks to suppliers, purchasers, and (to a limited degree) lenders through contractual arrangements like those just discussed. Risks can be allocated to parties that are willing to bear them at the lowest cost.

- *Expanded debt capacity.* By financing on a project basis rather than on its general credit, a firm may be able to achieve a higher degree of leverage than would be consistent with its senior debt rating objective if it financed the project entirely on its own. Project-related contractual arrangements transfer portions of the business and financial risk to others. This permits greater leverage.

- *Lower cost of debt.* Suppose the purchasers of the project's output have a higher credit standing than project sponsors. In that case, financing on the purchasers' credit rather than on the sponsors' credit can lead to a lower cost of debt. This benefit is more likely to occur when the output of the project will create a positive NPV for the purchaser that can be realized only if the sponsor undertakes the project. The project sponsor is effectively realizing a portion of the purchaser's positive NPV through the lower cost of borrowing that it achieves.

Disadvantages of Project Financing

Project financing can involve significant transaction costs. The contractual arrangements mentioned earlier are often complex. Consequently, arranging a project financing usually involves significant legal fees. In addition, because of the higher agency costs, lenders generally require a yield premium in return for accepting credit support in the form of contractual undertakings rather than a firm's direct promise to pay.

When To Use Project Financing

A project should be financed on a project basis only if that method of financing maximizes shareholder wealth. This is generally the case when (1) project financing facilitates a higher degree of leverage than conventional financing *and* (2) the tax effects resulting from the higher degree of leverage exceed the sum of the costs associated with the yield premium that lenders require and the higher after-tax transaction costs.

Self-Check Questions
1. When might project financing be a feasible financing alternative?
2. What are the contractual arrangements in a project financing designed to accomplish?
3. What is a completion undertaking?
4. What are the main advantages and disadvantages of project financing?

25.5 LIMITED PARTNERSHIP FINANCING

We said earlier in this chapter that leveraged lease financing represents a cost-effective alternative to debt financing when the lessee is unable to use fully the tax benefits of asset ownership. Limited partnership financing represents another form of tax-oriented financing. But unlike leasing, the sale of limited partnership units represents a form of equity financing.

Limited partnerships have been formed to finance real estate projects, oil and gas exploration, film making, research and development projects, the construction of cable television systems, and various other ventures.

Characteristics of Limited Partnerships

We noted in Chapter 1 that a **limited partnership** is a special form of partnership. Certain partners, called *limited partners*, enjoy limited liability. They are passive investors like the stockholders of a corporation. But a limited partnership, like partnerships generally, does not pay income taxes. Income or loss for tax purposes flows through to the partners. Suppose a firm plans a tax-intensive investment, such as oil and gas drilling, but believes it will not have sufficient taxable income to use fully the tax deductions and tax credits of the venture. It could form a limited partnership in order to direct the tax benefits through to the investors.[4] Particularly in risky projects such as oil exploration, these tax benefits can offer a substantial inducement to individual investors to share the investment risks inherent in such projects.

The limited partnership is operated by a *general partner*. The general partner is responsible for the liabilities of the limited partnership (except for those liabilities specifically assumed or guaranteed by the limited partners). Income, losses, tax credits, and distributions are allocated among the partners in accordance with a sharing formula specified at the time the limited partnership is formed.

Cinema Group Partners was formed some years ago. The general partner contributed 10% of the partnership capital. The limited partners were promised 98% of profits, losses, tax credits, and cash distributions until they recovered their investment. Thereafter, they were promised 80% until they received cash representing, in the aggregate, 200% of their investment. After that, they were promised 70% until they received cash representing in the aggregate 300% of their investment and 60% of any subsequent cash distributions. In addition, the general partner receives a management fee equal to 4% of the limited partnership's net worth. ■

The Cinema Group Partners Limited Partnership

EXAMPLE

---

[4] The tax advantages of a limited partnership (as compared to the corporate form of organization) are greatest for firms with high tax rates and low retention rates (that is, those in "mature" industries). Very rapidly growing firms that need to reinvest all their earnings and have low corporate tax rates are unlikely to find a limited partnership structure beneficial for tax purposes.

Measuring the Cost of Limited Partner Capital

A firm that sets up a limited partnership and serves as general partner effectively experiences the following cash flow benefits and costs:

- Initial cash inflow equal to the net proceeds from the sale of units of limited partnership interest.
- Annual cash inflows equal to the taxes payable on the portion of partnership taxable income that is allocated to the limited partners.
- Initial cash outflow equal to the amount of the investment tax credit, if any, allocated to the limited partners.
- Annual cash outflows equal to (1) the cash distributions to the limited partners plus (2) the tax shields resulting from the portion of partnership losses for tax purposes allocated to the limited partners.
- Terminal cash outflow equal to the residual value of the limited partnership's assets allocated to the limited partners.

EXAMPLE

Calculating the Cost of Limited Partner Capital

Table 25-4 provides the incremental cash flows associated with financing a new cable television system through a limited partnership that the general partner intends to terminate after 10 years. The financing involves the sale of $50 million of units of limited partnership interest that raises $45 million net of issuance expenses. The general partner will invest $5 million for a 10% ownership interest. The limited partnership agreement calls for the limited partners to pay all the issuance expenses and to contribute 90% of partnership capital. The limited partners will also receive 90% of partnership income, losses, tax credits (if any), and cash distributions until they have received aggregate cash distributions equal to their original $50 mil-

---

TABLE 25-4

Calculation of cost of limited partner capital.

END OF YEAR	(1) NET PROCEEDS OF FINANCING[a]	(2) PARTNERSHIP OPERATING CASH FLOW[b]	(3) PARTNERSHIP TAXABLE INCOME[c]	(4) DISTRIBUTION TO LIMITED PARTNERS[d]	(5) TAX ON INCOME (LOSS) FORGONE[e]	(6) RESIDUAL VALUE FORGONE[f]	(7) NET CASH FLOW TO SPONSOR[g]
0	$45.0	—	—	—	—	—	$45.00
1	—	$1.5	−$3.5	$1.35	−$1.26	—	−2.61
2	—	3.0	−2.0	2.70	−0.72	—	−3.42
3	—	3.5	−1.5	3.15	−0.54	—	−3.69
4	—	7.0	2.0	6.30	0.72	—	−5.58
5	—	10.0	5.0	9.00	1.80	—	−7.20
6	—	12.0	7.0	10.80	2.52	—	−8.28
7	—	14.0	9.0	12.60	3.24	—	−9.36
8	—	16.0	11.0	9.82	2.70	—	−7.12
9	—	17.5	12.5	8.75	2.50	—	−6.25
10	—	19.0	14.0	9.50	2.80	$51.30	−58.00

Cost of limited partner capital[h] = <u>12.88%</u>

[a] Calculated as gross proceeds of $50 million less 10% issuance expenses.
[b] As projected by the general partner.
[c] Calculated as operating cash flow less straight-line depreciation amounting to $5 million per year.
[d] Calculated as 90% of operating cash flow until limited partners recover their $50 million investment (during year 8) and as 50% of operating cash flow thereafter.
[e] Taxes payable (credit) by the general partner if the income allocated to the limited partners had instead been included in its income. Limited partners are allocated the same percentage of partnership taxable income as their percentage of partnership operating cash flow. Amount is calculated by multiplying column 3 by the allocation percentage and by the tax rate: for year 3, $-1.5 \times 0.9 \times 0.4 = -0.54$.
[f] Assumes the cable television system is sold for 9 times year 10 operating cash flow, or $171.0 million. Residual value is net of taxes (at a 40% marginal rate) on the half of terminal value that is forgone.
[g] Calculated as the net proceeds of financing plus tax on income (loss) forgone less distribution to limited partners less also residual value forgone.
[h] Calculated as the internal rate of return of the net cash flow stream.

lion investment. After that the limited partners will receive 50% of partnership income, losses, tax credits (if any), and cash distributions. The sponsor's marginal ordinary income tax rate is 40%.

The initial cash flow is the $45 million inflow, representing the net proceeds from the sale of the units of limited partnership interest (column 1). Each annual cash flow thereafter (column 7), except the last year's, is equal to the amount of income taxes saved (tax credits lost) on the portion of partnership income (loss) allocated to the limited partners (column 5) less the cash distributions to limited partners (column 4). Note that in year 8, the limited partners reach $50 million in aggregate cash distributions after the payment of $4.1 million that year. The $4.1 million payment represents 90% of $4.56 million. The remaining $11.44 million of year 8's operating cash flow is divided equally between the general and limited partners, giving the limited partners total cash distributions of $9.82 (= 4.1 + 5.72) million for the year. Table 25-4 assumes that the limited partnership sells the cable television system for nine times the last year's operating cash flow, or $171 million, half of which it must distribute to the limited partners. The general partner forgoes $85.5 million. Because the cable television system has been fully depreciated, there is a $171 million gain on the transaction, half of which is borne by the limited partners. After-tax residual value forgone (column 6) is therefore $51.3 million (= 0.6 × 85.5).

The **cost of limited partner capital** (that is, capital raised from the limited partners, CLPC in the following equation) is just the discount rate that equates the present value of the cash outflows in Table 25-4 to the initial $45 million cash inflow:

$$\text{NP} = \sum_{t=1}^{N} \frac{\text{CFAT}_t}{(1 + \text{CLPC})^t} = \$45.0 \text{ million} \quad \text{CLPC} = 12.88\% \tag{25.7}$$

NP is the net proceeds from the limited partnership financing. CFAT_t is the net after-tax cash flow in year t. CLPC is the cost of limited partner capital, and N is the term of the limited partnership.

Limited partnership financing in this case represents an alternative to all-equity financing.[5] The cost of limited partner capital in Equation (25.7) should therefore be compared to the unleveraged required return for the project (because this limited partnership has no debt). Suppose the capital investment project has a 15% unleveraged required return. Then limited partnership financing is cheaper than conventional all-equity financing. ■

The cost of limited partner capital depends heavily on the limited partners' tax position and on the asset's residual value. The higher the tax rate on the limited partners' income, the greater the value of the tax credits transferred to them. Hence, the lower is likely to be the firm's cost of raising funds through limited partnership financing. In addition, the lower the portion of residual value that needs to be allocated to limited partners, the lower the cost of funds, as was the case with lease financing.

Advantages and Disadvantages of Limited Partnership Financing

Limited partnership financing provides an alternative means of "selling" the tax deductions and tax credits associated with asset ownership. As in the case of lease financing, limited partnership financing can be mutually beneficial to the firm and to the investor when the investor pays income tax at a higher marginal rate than the firm.

---

[5] The limited partnership has no debt. If it did, CLPC would have to be compared to the required return for a conventionally financed and identically leveraged project.

Also as in the case of lease financing, the firm must sacrifice a portion of the asset's residual value. When the forgone residual value is taken into account, limited partnership financing may prove to be more expensive than conventional equity financing.

In contrast to lease financing, limited partnership financing can also be advantageous to profitable firms. A partnership is nontaxable. Organizing a project (or a business) as a limited partnership, rather than having a corporation own it, eliminates a layer of taxation.

Self-Check Questions

1. What is a limited partnership? How do the liabilities of general partners and limited partners differ?

2. How is limited partnership financing similar to lease financing? How is it different?

3. What is the cost of limited partner capital?

4. What are the main advantages and disadvantages of limited partnership financing?

SOLUTION TO NACCO'S LEASE-OR-BUY PROBLEM

NACCO should lease the electric shovels only if leasing will increase the wealth of its shareholders. The net advantage to leasing depends on two critical factors: (1) NACCO's ability to claim the tax benefits of asset ownership on a timely basis and (2) the amount of the residual value NACCO forgoes as a result of leasing. In this case, NACCO estimated the lost residual value at $500,000.

We found in the text that NACCO's net advantage to leasing an electric shovel is negative (−$54,236) if the firm can fully use the tax benefits of asset ownership. But if it can never use these tax benefits, the net advantage to leasing is $40,685. Therefore, NACCO must evaluate its probable future ability to realize the tax benefits of asset ownership before it can reach the lease-or-buy decision.

SUMMARY

A firm can finance a project on the strength of its general promise to pay and overall profitability by promising investors and/or lenders a share of the future cash flow from its entire portfolio of assets. Alternatively, it can finance on an asset-based basis. In that case, the amount providers of capital are paid is tied to the firm's use of a particular asset. Asset-based financing techniques include leasing, various forms of project financing, and limited partnership financing.

Lease financing involves an extended rental agreement. The lessor grants the lessee the exclusive right to use the asset for a specified period. In return, the lessee agrees to make a series of fixed lease payments. The lessor owns the asset. It can claim the tax benefits that accompany asset ownership and the asset's residual value at the end of the lease term. Lease financing can be advantageous to both lessor and lessee when the parties are taxed at different rates. In the case of short-term cancelable operating leases, the lessee benefits from the cancellation option. In addition, lease financing often affords certain advantages over secured lending to providers of capital in the event of bankruptcy. The sale of the tax deductions and tax credits of asset ownership is principally responsible for the widespread use of lease financing.

Lease financing displaces conventional debt. Lease financing should therefore be analyzed as an alternative to borrowing to buy the asset. We recommend using the DSP approach, which neutralizes any capital structure side effects.

Project financing is generally possible when a project involves a discrete asset (or set of assets) capable of standing alone as an independent economic unit. Project loans are designed to be self-liquidating from the project's cash flow. Designing a project financing requires careful financial engineering to allocate the project-related risks among the parties who will bear them at the lowest cost, to apportion the project's economic rewards in a manner commensurate with the allocation of project risks, and to minimize total agency costs. Under certain circumstances, project financing can lead to more efficient risk sharing, expanded debt capacity for the project's sponsor, and a lower overall cost of funds than direct financing by the project's sponsor.

Limited partnership financing provides an alternative means of "selling" the tax benefits of asset ownership. A limited partnership is a special form of partnership in which certain partners, called limited partners, receive a share of partnership profits, losses, tax credits, and cash distributions but enjoy limited liability (just like the shareholders of a corporation). Whereas leasing is a form of debt financing, limited partnership financing is a form of equity financing.

DECISION SUMMARY

- Asset-based financing should be employed only if it increases shareholder wealth.

- Lease financing is equivalent to borrowing to buy the asset. Decision makers must therefore compare leasing to the borrow-and-buy alternative, while neutralizing the capital structure side effects. Use the DSP approach.

- Lease financing can be cheaper than conventional secured debt financing because of a potential tax asymmetry. Lease financing will have a positive net advantage only if the net present value of the net cash flows to the lessee is positive or, equivalently, only if the lease financing provides a greater amount of funds to the lessee than an equivalent loan.

- Lease financing may be beneficial when the lessor is better able to bear the risks of asset obsolescence than the lessee, as may be the case with lessor/manufacturers of high-technology assets such as computers.

- Project financing should be considered whenever a capital budgeting project (1) consists of a discrete asset (or set of assets) *and* (2) has a positive expected net present value *and* (3) is so large relative to the sponsor's existing asset portfolio that pursuing it alone would increase the sponsor's risk of bankruptcy to an unacceptable level.

- Project financing should also be considered whenever there is a readily identifiable set of purchasers for the project's output who would be willing to enter into contractual commitments against which the sponsor could borrow funds for the project on a nonrecourse basis.

- Limited partnership financing can be cheaper than conventional equity financing for a firm that cannot fully use the tax benefits of asset ownership or for a profitable firm that can operate a portion of its business in a separate partnership entity and thereby eliminate corporate taxation of the separate entity's income. Limited partnership financing will have a positive net advantage to a firm only if the cost of limited partner capital is less than the firm's cost of capital for equivalent conventional financing.

EQUATION SUMMARY

(25.1) $\quad \text{NAL} = P - \text{PV(CFATs)}$

(25.2) $\quad \text{NAL} = P - \sum_{t=1}^{N} \dfrac{(1 - T)(CF_t - \Delta E_t) + TD_t}{[1 + (1 - T)r']^t} - \dfrac{\text{SAL}}{(1 + r)^N} - \text{ITC} = 0$

(25.3) $\quad \text{NAL} = P - \sum_{t=1}^{N} \dfrac{(1 - T)(CF_t - \Delta E_t) + TD_t}{(1 + \text{IRR})^t} - \dfrac{\text{SAL}}{(1 + \text{IRR})^N} - \text{ITC} = 0$

(25.4) $\quad \text{EL} = \sum_{t=1}^{N} \dfrac{(1 - T)(CF_t - \Delta E_t) + TD_t}{[1 + (1 - T)r']^t} + \dfrac{\text{SAL}}{(1 + r)^N}$

(25.5) $\quad \text{NPVL} = -P + \sum_{t=1}^{N} \dfrac{(1 - T')(CF_t - \Delta E_t) + T'D_t}{[1 + (1 - T')r']^t} + \dfrac{\text{SAL}}{(1 + r)^N} + \text{ITC}$

(25.6) $\quad \text{NPV(leased)} = \text{NPV(conventional)} + \text{NAL}$

(25.7) $\quad \text{NP} = \sum_{t=1}^{N} \dfrac{\text{CFAT}_t}{(1 + \text{CLPC})^t}$

KEY TERMS

asset-based financing...805

lease...807

lessor...807

lessee...807

operating leases...807

financial leases...807

sale-and-lease-back...808

leveraged lease...808

net advantage to leasing...813

cost of lease financing...815

equivalent loan...816

break-even lease payment...817

project financing...822

limited partnership...825

cost of limited partner capital...827

EXERCISES

PROBLEM SET A

A1. Define the terms *lease, lessor*, and *lessee*. What is the relationship between a lessor and a lessee?

A2. Explain the principal differences among a direct lease, a sale-and-lease-back, and a leveraged lease.

A3. What are the principal advantages and principal disadvantages of lease financing? Which of the purported advantages are really of dubious value?

A4. Explain why a dollar of lease financing displaces a dollar of conventional debt financing.

A5. What are the principal tax benefits associated with asset ownership?

A6. What requirements must a lease satisfy to qualify as a true lease for tax purposes?

A7. Describe how the net advantage to leasing is measured.

A8. What is the appropriate discount rate to use in calculating the present value of the incremental after-tax cash flows associated with a lease financing? Why is the expected residual value of the asset discounted at a higher rate?

A9. Look back at the NACCO example. Suppose the lease rate is $1.7 million payable annually in arrears, and the cost of secured debt is 11%. The required return for the project is 14% assuming NACCO's tax rate is 40% and 17% assuming its tax rate is zero. The depreciation schedule and residual value are unchanged.

a. Calculate the net advantage to leasing if NACCO's tax rate is 40%. Should NACCO lease, or borrow and buy?

b. Calculate the net advantage to leasing if NACCO will never be able to use the tax deductions associated with asset ownership. Should the firm lease, or borrow and buy?

A10.

a. Explain the equivalent-loan approach to the decision whether to lease or to borrow and buy.

b. An asset costs $25 million. If it is leased for a 5-year period, the net cash flow to the lessee is $20 million at the end of year 0, $-$10 million at the end of year 1, and $-$7 million at the end of each of years 2 through 5. The firm's pretax cost of comparably secured debt is 10% and its tax rate is 34%. Calculate the amount of the equivalent loan.

A11. Allied Metals Inc. is considering leasing $1 million worth of manufacturing equipment under a lease that would require annual lease payments in arrears for 5 years. The net cash flow to the lessee over the term of the lease (with zero residual value) is

Year	0	1	2	3	4	5
Net cash flow ($000)	1000	$-$300	$-$275	$-$250	$-$225	$-$200

Allied's cost of comparably secured debt is 12%, and its cost of capital is 16%. Allied pays taxes at a 34% marginal rate.

a. Calculate the net advantage to leasing.

b. Calculate the internal rate of return for the lease.

c. Calculate the amount of the equivalent loan for the proposed Allied lease.

d. Should Allied lease, or borrow and buy?

A12. Define the term *project financing*. Under what circumstances is project financing an appropriate method of financing a capital budgeting project?

A13. What are the principal advantages and disadvantages of project financing?

A14. What do lease financing and limited partnership financing have in common?

A15. Suppose the cable television limited partnership discussed in the text instead enabled the limited partners to receive 90% of partnership income, losses, tax credits, and cash distributions for the life of the limited partnership. Calculate the cost of limited partner capital.

PROBLEM SET B

B1. Leasing enables a firm to acquire the use of an asset just as a cash purchase would, so shouldn't the asset acquisition/lease decision be evaluated by using the lessee's required return for the asset as the discount rate? But lease financing displaces conventional debt financing, so shouldn't the asset acquisition/lease decision be evaluated by using the lessee's cost of secured debt as the discount rate? How would you resolve these apparently contradictory arguments?

B2. A lessor purchases an asset and immediately enters into an agreement to lease the asset to another firm. The lease obligation is a form of secured debt obligation, so shouldn't the lessee's cost of secured debt (as determined in the capital market) be used in the analysis of the net advantage to the lessor of entering into the lease? Alternatively, the lessor must finance its purchase of the asset somehow, so shouldn't the lessor instead use its own cost of capital in evaluating the net advantage to the lessor of entering into the lease?

B3. A firm is considering leasing a computer system that costs $1,000,000 new. The lease requires annual payments of $135,000 in arrears for 10 years. The lessee pays income taxes at a 35% marginal rate. If it purchased the computer system, it could depreciate it to its expected residual value over 10 years. The lessee's cost of similarly secured debt is 10%, and its WACC is 15%.

a. Calculate the net advantage to leasing assuming zero residual value. Should the firm lease the computer system?

b. Calculate the net advantage to leasing assuming $250,000 residual value. Should the firm lease the computer system?

B4. Reconsider the lease in Problem B3. Assume the salvage value is $250,000.

   a. Calculate the IRR of the lease.

   b. How do you interpret the IRR in part a? Should the firm lease the computer system?

   c. Calculate the amount of the equivalent loan. How do you interpret this amount?

B5. Suppose you are considering leasing a personal computer. It would cost $5000 new. You can lease it for 5 years for $100.00 per month payable on the first day of each month. Your mother is willing to lend you the $5000 at 8% APR. The tax code does not permit you to deduct depreciation or personal interest from your (meager) income. Should you lease the PC or borrow from your mother and buy it?

B6. Lake Trolley Company is considering whether to lease or buy a new trolley that costs $25,000. The trolley can be depreciated straight-line over an 8-year period to an estimated residual value of $5000. Lake Trolley's cost of 8-year comparably secured debt is 12%. Its required return for the project is 16% after tax and 20% before tax. National Trolley Leasing Corporation has offered to lease the trolley to Lake Trolley in return for annual payments of $5000 payable at the end of each year.

   a. Specify the incremental cash flow stream associated with the lease assuming Lake Trolley's marginal income tax rate is 40%.

   b. Calculate the net advantage to leasing assuming Lake Trolley's tax rate is 40%. Should Lake Trolley lease, or borrow and buy?

   c. Calculate the net advantage to leasing assuming Lake Trolley's tax rate is zero. Should Lake Trolley lease, or borrow and buy?

   d. How would your answers to parts b and c change if the residual value at the end of 8 years were $500?

B7. Show how to modify Equations (25.2), (25.3), and (25.4) to reflect the timing of lease payments when the lease calls for payments *at the beginning* of each year.

B8. New Horizon Natural Foods is considering whether to lease a delivery truck. A leasing company has offered to lease the truck. It costs $35,000. New Horizon has proposed a 5-year lease that calls for annual payments of $7850 *at the beginning* of each year. New Horizon could depreciate the truck to $5000 at the end of 5 years on a straight-line basis and claim depreciation tax deductions at the beginning of each year. Its marginal tax rate is 34%, its cost of 5-year comparably secured debt is 10%, and its required return for the project is 12% after tax and 16% before tax.

   a. Should New Horizon lease the truck, or borrow and buy?

   b. Suppose instead that New Horizon does not expect to pay income taxes in the foreseeable future. Should New Horizon lease the truck, or borrow and buy?

   c. How do you reconcile your answers to parts a and b?

B9. Neighborhood Savings Bank is considering leasing $100,000 worth of computer equipment. A 4-year lease would require payments in advance of $22,000 per year. The bank does not currently pay income taxes and does not expect to have to pay income taxes in the foreseeable future. If the bank purchased the computer equipment, it would depreciate the equipment on a straight-line basis down to an estimated salvage value of $20,000 at the end of the fourth year. The bank's cost of comparably secured debt is 14%, and its cost of capital is 20%.

   a. Calculate the net advantage to leasing.

   b. Calculate the amount of the equivalent loan.

   c. Calculate the internal rate of return for the lease.

B10. Rashid Singh, the president of Surf-side Beer Distributors of Salina, Kansas, has decided that his firm must acquire a new bottling machine that costs $800,000. The firm's corporate borrowing rate is 12%. The bottling machine can be leased for $110,000 per year for its 10-year life. If the firm leases, it gets no salvage value. If it owns, the expected salvage value is $50,000. Maintenance costs will be the same whether Surf-side leases or buys. The firm uses straight-line depreciation (to the salvage value), and its tax rate is 40%. Can you demonstrate which would be better for Rashid, leasing or buying?

B11. Empire Excavation Corporation plans to acquire a fleet of 10 dump trucks. Each truck costs $75,000. Empire can borrow $750,000 on a comparably secured basis at a pretax cost of 14%. The dump trucks can be depreciated for tax purposes on a straight-line basis to zero over a 5-year useful life. Truck Leasing Corp. has offered to lease the fleet of trucks to Empire under a 5-year lease that calls for lease payments of $190,000 at the end of each year. Empire estimates that forgone after-tax residual value would be $10,000 per truck. Empire's tax rate is 34%. Its cost of capital is 16%.

a. Calculate the stream of net cash flow to Empire under the lease financing.

b. Calculate the net advantage to leasing.

c. Calculate the amount of the equivalent loan.

d. Should Empire lease, or borrow and buy? Justify your answer.

B12. A 3-year lease entails the following stream of net cash flow (in millions of dollars) to the lessee: $10.5, −$3.0, −$5.0, −$5.0. The lessee's pretax cost of comparably secured debt is 13%. The lessee does not pay taxes, and it does not expect to become a taxpayer in the near future. The item will have zero residual value at the end of the lease term.

a. Calculate the net advantage to leasing. Is leasing advantageous?

b. Calculate the amount of the equivalent loan.

c. Calculate the IRR of the lease.

d. Do the three approaches yield consistent results? Explain why you would normally expect them to yield consistent results.

B13. A lease calls for payments of $1 million at the end of each of the next 5 years and for payments of $2 million at the end of each of the following 5 years. The asset to be leased costs $10 million. It can be depreciated in the following manner to a residual value of $500,000 at the end of the lease term:

Year	1	2	3	4	5	6	7	8	9	10
Depreciation ($ thousands)	2000	1750	1500	1250	1000	400	400	400	400	400

The lessee's marginal income tax rate is currently 40%. Its cost of 10-year comparably secured debt is 12.5%. Its required return for the project is 15% after tax and 17.5% before tax.

a. Calculate the net advantage to leasing.

b. How would your answer to part a change if the lessee did not expect to pay any income taxes for the next 3 years but to pay income taxes each year thereafter at a 40% rate? (*Hint*: Any tax losses in years 1–3 can be carried forward and realized in year 4.)

B14. Amalgamated Leasing Corp. would like to submit a leasing proposal to the Sandoval Hardware Manufacturing Company. Sandoval has asked to lease $5 million worth of equipment under a 6-year lease. Amalgamated can depreciate the equipment for tax purposes on a straight-line basis over the 6-year term to an estimated residual value of $250,000. The leasing firm's income tax rate is 40%. Amalgamated has estimated Sandoval's 6-year cost of funds to be 10% for fully secured debt (25% overcollateralized) and 12% for unsecured debt. It has also estimated the required after-tax return for an investment in the assets to be 15%.

a. Calculate Amalgamated's break-even lease rate.

b. Assume Sandoval pays income taxes at a 30% rate. Calculate Sandoval's net advantage to leasing at Amalgamated's break-even lease rate.

c. Calculate Sandoval's break-even lease rate.

d. Is it possible for Amalgamated and Sandoval to find a mutually beneficial lease rate?

B15. A copper mining firm would like to finance the construction of a copper mine on a nonrecourse project basis. It will set up a separate corporation to finance, build, own, and operate the mine. It will also agree to purchase all the mine's output on terms that will be spelled out in a copper purchase agreement. The separate corporation will pledge the copper purchase agreement as security for a bank loan.

   a. Describe the agency costs involved in this arrangement.

   b. Why would the bank charge a higher interest rate on this loan than it would on an otherwise identical loan directly to the mining firm?

B16. Suppose the copper mining firm in Question B15 has outstanding debt that is rated single-B. Suppose also that it can arrange to sell the entire output of the new copper mine to a triple-A-rated Japanese trading company under a hell-or-high-water contract. Explain how this contract could reduce the mining firm's cost of capital for the new mine project.

B17. A limited partnership would involve the following net cash flows to the firm sponsoring it:

Year	0	1	2	3	4	5	6	7
Net cash flow ($ millions)	125.0	−10.5	−12.0	−14.5	−16.5	−18.5	−22.5	−112.5

   a. Calculate the cost of limited partner capital.

   b. Suppose the firm's unleveraged cost of equity is 15% and the limited partnership has no debt. Should the firm employ limited partnership financing?

B18. Suppose a limited partnership has debt.

   a. How would you interpret the cost of limited partner capital?

   b. How would you compare the cost of limited partner capital in that case to the cost of conventional financing?

B19. The Light Rock Cafe plans to raise capital to finance a new restaurant through the sale of limited partnership interests. The firm, as general partner, plans to raise $5.25 million. Of this amount, $5 million will be invested in the restaurant, and the balance will be used to pay issuance expenses. The assets can be depreciated to zero over 8 years on a straight-line basis. The partnership will be terminated at the end of 8 years. Upon termination, the general partner will buy out the limited partners at a price equal to 7 times the last year's operating cash flow. The projected operating cash flow stream for the partnership is

Year	1	2	3	4	5	6	7	8
Net cash flow ($ thousands)	250	1000	1500	2000	2250	2500	2750	3000

   The limited partners will be entitled to receive 75% of each year's partnership income, losses, tax credits (if any), and cash distributions. They will also be entitled to receive 75% of the residual value. The Light Rock Cafe will not invest cash but will contribute its name and "know-how" (that is, its experience) to the project in return for a 25% ownership interest. Assume the general partner's marginal ordinary income tax rate is 40%. Calculate the cost of limited partner capital.

B20. Suppose you can either purchase a new Honda Civic for $20,000 cash or lease it from Honda for $2000 down and $360 per month for 48 months. At the end of the lease, you will be able to purchase the car for $6000, which is your estimate of its residual value. Your cost of borrowing the funds to buy the car is 12% APR.

   a. You cannot depreciate the car for tax purposes. Nor can you deduct the lease payments or interest expense. Should you lease the car, or borrow to buy it?

   b. Honda can depreciate the car straight-line to $6000 over 4 years. Honda's required return on the lease is 12% pretax APR. Honda's marginal income tax rate is 40%. Is leasing advantageous to Honda?

   c. Explain why leasing a car can be mutually advantageous to the manufacturer and the customer.

B21. Explain how the contractual arrangements in a project financing can be designed so as to cover the following contingencies: (a) completion risk (b) technological risk (c) economic risk.

PROBLEM SET C

C1. The break-even tax rate is the income tax rate for the lessee that would make the lessee indifferent between leasing an asset on the one hand and borrowing and buying it on the other.

  a. Calculate the break-even tax rate for Lake Trolley Company in Problem B6 under the assumption that the residual value is $500.

  b. Suppose the statutory income tax rate is 40% and is expected to remain 40% for the foreseeable future. How would you give the break-even tax rate a practical interpretation?

C2. The lessor can claim the tax deductions associated with asset ownership and realize the leased asset's residual value. In return, the lessor must pay tax on the rental income.

  a. Explain why a financial lease represents a secured loan in which the lender's entire debt service stream is taxable as ordinary income to the lessor/lender.

  b. In view of this tax cost, what tax condition must hold in order for a financial lease transaction to generate positive-net-present-value tax benefits for lessor and lessee combined?

  c. Suppose the lease payments in Table 25-2 must be made in advance, not arrears. (Assume that the timing of the lease payment tax deductions/obligations changes accordingly but the timing of the depreciation tax deductions does not change). Show that the net advantage to leasing for NACCO must decrease as a result. Explain why this reduction occurs.

  d. Show that if NACCO is nontaxable, the net advantage to leasing is negative and greater in absolute value than the net advantage of the lease to the lessor.

  e. Either find a lease rate that will give the financial lease a positive net advantage for both lessor and lessee or show that no such lease rate exists.

  f. Explain what your answer to part e implies about the tax costs and tax benefits of the financial lease when lease payments are made in advance.

C3. Derive Equation (25.4) from the debt service parity principle.

C4. C is the cost of equipment, L the amount of each annual lease payment, T_R the lessor's marginal income tax rate, T_E the lessee's marginal income tax rate, and D the lessee's marginal cost of secured debt. Consider a 2-year lease with lease payments in advance. Tax depreciation is calculated on a straight-line basis (tax deductions realized at year-end). There is zero residual value.

  a. Show that the net present value of the lease to the lessor, NPV_R, can be expressed as

$$NPV_R = -C + \left[\frac{(1 - T_R)L[1 + (1 - T_R)D] + T_R C/2}{(1 - T_R)D}\right]\left[1 - \left[\frac{1}{1 + (1 - T_R)D}\right]^2\right]$$

  b. Show that the net present value of the lease to the lessee, NPV_E, can be expressed as

$$NPV_E = C - \left[\frac{(1 - T_E)L[1 + (1 - T_E)D] + T_E C/2}{(1 - T_E)D}\right]\left[1 - \left[\frac{1}{1 + (1 - T_E)D}\right]^2\right]$$

  c. If $T_E = T_R$, is leasing a zero-sum game? Might there be other reasons to lease?

  d. If $T_E = 0 < T_R$, is it possible to find a lease payment L for which $NPV_R > 0$ and $NPV_E > 0$ hold simultaneously?

  e. Suppose instead that lease payments are made in arrears each year. Recalculate NPV_R and NPV_E. Can you find an annual lease payment amount L for which $NPV_R > 0$ and $NPV_E > 0$ hold simultaneously when $T_R = 0.4$ and $T_E = 0$?

C5. A bank wishes to enter into an operating lease for certain equipment it needs because the lease obligation would not appear on the face of the bank's balance sheet. The bank must maintain a capital-to-assets ratio of 8%. This ratio calculation ignores leases that qualify as operating leases under generally accepted accounting principles.

a. If the bank's ratio of capital to assets is currently exactly 8%, explain why $1 of capitalized lease obligations would displace $1 of earning assets (that is, loans or securities).

b. Explain how the net advantage to leasing through an operating lease should be calculated in order to reflect the avoidance of the capital constraint. How would you modify Equation (25.2)?

c. Suppose Binghamton Thrift can lease $736,000 worth of office equipment under an operating lease. The lease requires monthly rental payments in arrears of $13,600 for each of 30 months, followed by monthly rental payments in arrears of $16,600 each for an additional 30 months. The residual value of the equipment at the end of the lease term is expected to be 10% of its original cost. Binghamton Thrift's estimated cost of comparably secured debt is 13% per year, semiannually compounded. The bank is not, and does not expect to become in the foreseeable future, a taxpayer. The bank earns a "spread" of 2% (marginal interest income minus interest payments) on each dollar of deposits that are loaned out to customers. Calculate the net advantage to leasing assuming the bank's capital-to-assets ratio currently equals the required minimum.

d. How would your answer to part c change if the bank's capital-to-assets ratio exceeds the required minimum by a wide margin?

Real-World Application:
Continental Airlines's Lease-Versus-Buy Decision

Continental Airlines (Continental) is the fifth largest airline in the United States. Continental transports passengers, cargo, and mail. It serves 175 airports worldwide, including 58 foreign destinations, and is one of the leading airlines providing service to Mexico and Central America.

The airline industry in the United States is very competitive. It was deregulated in the 1980s. The resulting competitive pressures coupled with an inefficient cost structure have forced Continental into bankruptcy twice since 1983. It emerged from bankruptcy most recently in April 1993.

As of year-end 1995, Continental operated a fleet of 309 aircraft. It owned 47 of these and leased the other 262. At year-end 1995, Continental had the following capitalization:

CAPITALIZATION
(Dollar amounts in millions)

	BOOK VALUE DEC. 31, 1995
Short-term debt	$ 221
Long-term notes and debentures	$ 1352
Capitalized leases	306
Total long-term debt	1658
Preferred stock	283
Stockholders' equity	305
Total capitalization	$ 2246
Total capitalization (including short-term debt)	$ 2467

Continental would like to expand its fleet by adding two Boeing 757s. Each would cost $125 million. Continental has the opportunity to lease the two aircraft. The lease would have a term of 15 years and would require quarterly payments of $4 million in arrears for each aircraft. Leasing is attractive to Continental because it had a total of $2.5 billion of net operating loss carryforwards on December 31, 1995. A loss can be carried forward for only up to 15 years. These loss carryforwards will expire at various times from 1996 through 2009.

Continental's cost of fully secured 15-year debt is 10%. Its cost of unsecured 15-year debt is 12%, and its WACC is 15%. Continental is uncertain about the residual value of a Boeing 757 at the end of the 15-year lease term, but it has estimated the following possible values and probabilities:

Residual value ($ millions)	10	15	20	25	30	35	40	45	50
Probability (%)	5	10	10	15	20	15	10	10	5

1. Calculate Continental's cost of comparably secured debt, assuming that to be fully secured, the face amount of the debt cannot exceed 80% of the value of the collateral securing it.

2. What is the expected residual value of each Boeing 757? What is its expected present value?

3. Specify the lease CFATs assuming

   a. Continental can use all the tax benefits of ownership. (Assume a 40% tax rate and straight-line depreciation to the expected residual value.)

b. Continental cannot use any of these tax benefits.

4. Calculate the net advantage to leasing assuming the expected residual value and

a. Continental can use all the tax benefits of ownership.

b. Continental cannot use any of these tax benefits.

5. Calculate the internal rate of return (IRR) for the lease under the assumptions in question 4.

6. Calculate the net advantage to leasing assuming that Continental cannot use the tax benefits of ownership and that the residual value is

a. $50 million.

b. $10 million.

7. What is the break-even residual value assuming

a. Continental can use all the tax benefits of ownership.

b. Continental cannot use any of these tax benefits.

8. Based on Continental's expected residual value for a Boeing 757, what is Continental's break-even lease rate assuming

a. Continental can use all the tax benefits of ownership.

b. Continental cannot use any of these tax benefits.

9. Suppose Continental believes it will not be in a tax-paying position for a decade or longer. Should it lease, or borrow and buy? Explain.

10. Suppose Continental would have the option to terminate the lease at any time without penalty. Should it lease, or borrow and buy? Explain.

BIBLIOGRAPHY

Bayless, Mark E., and J. David Diltz. "An Empirical Study of the Debt Displacement Effects of Leasing," *Financial Management*, 1986, 15(4):53–60.

Brick, Ivan E., William Fung, and Marti Subrahmanyam. "Leasing and Financial Intermediation: Comparative Tax Advantages," *Financial Management*, 1987, 16(1):55–59.

Cason, Roger L. "Leasing, Asset Lives and Uncertainty: A Practitioner's Comments," *Financial Management*, 1987, 16(2):13–16.

Collins, J. Markham, and Roger P. Bey. "The Master Limited Partnership: An Alternative to the Corporation," *Financial Management*, 1986, 15(4):5–14.

Dyl, Edward A., and Stanley A. Martin, Jr. "Setting Terms for Leveraged Leasing," *Financial Management*, 1977, 6(4):20–27.

Elgers, Pieter T., and John J. Clark. *The Lease/Buy Decision*. New York: The Free Press, 1980.

Fabozzi, Frank J., and Uzi Yaari. "Valuation of Safe Harbor Tax Benefit Transfer Leases," *Journal of Finance*, 1983, 38(2):595–606.

Finnerty, John D. *Project Financing: Asset-Based Financial Engineering*. New York: Wiley, 1996.

Hochman, Shalom, and Ramon Rabinovitch. "Financial Leasing Under Inflation," *Financial Management*, 1984, 13(1):17–26.

Hodges, Stewart D. "The Valuation of Variable Rate Leases," *Financial Management*, 1985, 14(1):68–74.

Krishnan, V. Sivarama, and R. Charles Moyer. "Bankruptcy Costs and the Financial Leasing Decision," *Financial Management*, 1994, 23(2):31–42.

Lease, Ronald C., John J. McConnell, and James S. Schallheim. "Realized Returns and the Default and Prepayment Experience of Financial Leasing Contracts," *Financial Management*, 1990, 19(2):11–20.

Lewis, Craig M., and James S. Schallheim. "Are Debt and Leases Substitutes?," *Journal of Financial and Quantitative Analysis*, 1992, 27(4):497–512.

Mukherjee, Tarun K. "A Survey of Corporate Leasing Analysis," *Financial Management*, 1991, 20(3):96–107.

Schall, Lawrence D. "Analytic Issues in Lease vs. Purchase Decisions," *Financial Management*, 1987, 16(2):17–20.

Schallheim, James S. *Lease or Buy?* Boston, Mass.: Harvard Business School Press, 1994.

Schallheim, James S., Ramon E. Johnson, Ronald C. Lease, and John J. McConnell. "The Determinants of Yields on Financial Leasing Contracts," *Journal of Financial Economics*, 1987, 19(1):45–68.

Slovin, Myron B., Marie E. Sushka, and John A. Polonchek. "Corporate Sale-and-Leasebacks and Shareholder Wealth," *Journal of Finance*, 1990, 45(1):289–300.

Smith, Clifford W., Jr., and Lee M. Wakeman. "Determinants of Corporate Leasing Policy," *Journal of Finance*, 1985, 40(3):896–908.

DERIVATIVES AND HEDGING

Modern financial engineering emerged in the 1970s in response to a very real problem. In comparison to conditions that prevailed in the staid 1950s and 1960s, financial markets had become more volatile, exposing firms to greater risks. Because these risks could affect firm value, managers sought to avoid them. Initially many firms tried to build better forecasting models. If they could predict an adverse price change, they thought, then they could take steps to avoid its impact. Not surprisingly, these forecasting efforts were generally unsuccessful. By nature, the capital markets operate with a significant random component in interest rate and financial price movements that make precise forecasting impossible.

Putting into practice the Principle of Valuable Ideas, financial engineers developed a variety of derivative instruments that firms can use to manage financial risk. A **derivative** is a financial instrument whose value depends on the price of some other asset. An option is an example of a derivative. As you know, the value of a stock option depends on the price of the underlying shares.

There are four basic types of derivatives. We call them the *basic building blocks* because they are used to build more complex derivatives. Once you understand how the basic building blocks work, you will be able to analyze more complex securities. For example, a convertible bond is a *hybrid security* composed of a "plain vanilla" security (a conventional bond) and a derivative (a call option on the issuer's common stock). Once you identify the option and analyze it, you learn a lot about how the price of the hybrid security will behave.

Organized options markets and financial futures markets were two of the most significant financial developments of the 1970s. The development of the swaps markets was one of the most significant events of the 1980s. These new financial instruments increased the ability of investors to alter their return distributions. As a result, it became possible to reallocate financial risk within the capital markets to enable participants to invest in return distributions that better suit their preferences.

In this chapter, we will describe the basic types of derivatives and show how firms use them to manage the financial risks they face.

DERIVATIVES AND HEDGING AND THE PRINCIPLES OF FINANCE

◆ *Valuable Ideas*: Look for opportunities to develop derivatives that enable firms to cope better with the financial risks they face.

◆ *Options*: Recognize the value of options contained in derivative instruments.

◆ *Two-Sided Transactions*: You can use derivatives to transfer financial risks to others. Derivatives do not eliminate financial risk; they only transfer it.

◆ *Risk-Return Trade-Off*: To transfer risk to another party, you must offer a return that fully compensates for the amount of risk transferred.

◆ *Capital Market Efficiency*: You cannot forecast movements in interest rates, commodity prices, and foreign exchange rates precisely because these financial prices have a significant random component in an efficient market. Use the financial markets' consensus forecasts.

◆ *Comparative Advantage*: Transferring risks to other parties can be valuable if they are willing to bear these risks more cheaply.

INDIANTOWN'S INTEREST RATE RISK PROBLEM

Bechtel Enterprises, GE Capital, and Pacific Gas & Electric formed a limited partnership, called Indiantown Cogeneration, L.P., to construct and operate a coal-fired cogeneration plant three miles northwest of Indiantown, Florida. The plant would produce electricity and steam. It would sell the electricity to the local power company and the steam to a citrus juice processor. The expected total cost was $770 million. The partnership planned to borrow up to $535 million.

The partnership arranged a bank loan. Borrowings would carry a floating interest rate. Construction was scheduled to start in October 1992 and to finish by year-end 1995. The partners planned to replace the construction loan with permanent fixed-rate debt as the plant neared completion, perhaps around year-end 1994. Thus for a two-year period, the partnership would face the risk that interest rates might rise and increase the cost of the project.

The partners wanted to eliminate this risk exposure. They knew that long-term fixed-rate financing could not be arranged until the project was just about finished. They talked to their bankers about ways to hedge this risk.

As you read this chapter, think about which of the derivatives might help Indiantown solve its problem. At the end of the chapter, we will tell you what Indiantown decided to do.

26.1 OPTIONS

The first basic building block we will examine is the option. Recall from Chapter 8 that an **option** conveys a right without an obligation. According to the Options Principle, that is why options are valuable. With a *call option* on a stock, you have the right to buy a specified amount of stock (usually 100 shares in the case of a standardized market-traded stock option) at a specified price within some stated time period. A *put option* provides the right to sell. The specified price is the *strike price*. These instruments are traded in the options markets.

Options Markets

Options are traded on organized exchanges and in the over-the-counter (OTC) market. The Chicago Board Options Exchange (CBOE) began operations in 1973. It initially traded only call options on about two dozen stocks. Trading volume grew rapidly, and so did the number of option contracts available. By January 1996 the CBOE listed puts and calls on 767 common stocks. Today it is the largest options exchange in the world in aggregate dollar value of contracts traded. Among U.S. securities exchanges, only the New York Stock Exchange (NYSE) is bigger. Stock options are also traded on four other exchanges: the American Stock Exchange, Philadelphia Stock Exchange, NYSE, and Pacific Stock Exchange. There is also an OTC market. It deals primarily in nonstandardized options.

Figure 26-1 shows a typical price quotation for options listed on an exchange. It comes from the *Wall Street Journal* of October 11, 1995, and shows the previous day's trading in put and call options on Exxon common stock. Newspapers usually provide quotations only for actively traded options. Exxon's stock closed at $73¾. The options have a strike price of $65, $70, or $75. They expire in October 1995, November 1995, or January 1996. The Vol. (volume) column gives the number of contracts to buy or sell 100 shares traded that day. The column headed Last gives the last trading price. For example, the November 70 call last traded at $4.50 per underlying share, or $450 per contract. A total of 101 contracts to buy 10,100 shares traded that day.

On each options exchange, the members meet during trading hours on the floor of the exchange to buy and sell options. Floor brokers execute buy orders and sell orders for their customers. Each exchange employs clerks who observe the trading and transmit the latest trading information to other options exchanges and news services around the world.

The five options exchanges jointly own the Options Clearing Corporation (OCC) and clear all their option trades through the OCC. Figure 26-2 shows how the OCC interposes itself between every option buyer and seller. The option buyer and seller agree on the price and strike a deal. At this point, the OCC steps in. It places itself between the two traders, effec-

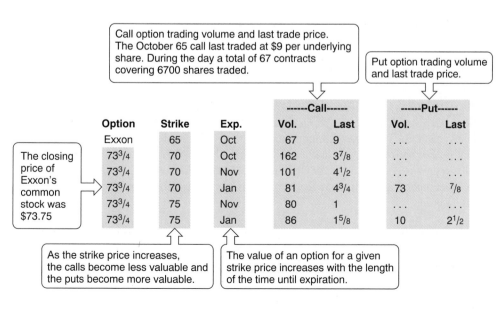

FIGURE 26-1

A typical price quotation for listed options.
Source: Wall Street Journal, October 11, 1995, p. C16.

Call option trading volume and last trade price. The October 65 call last traded at $9 per underlying share. During the day a total of 67 contracts covering 6700 shares traded.

Put option trading volume and last trade price.

Option	Strike	Exp.	------Call------		------Put------	
			Vol.	Last	Vol.	Last
Exxon	65	Oct	67	9	. . .	. . .
73³/4	70	Oct	162	3⁷/8	. . .	. . .
73³/4	70	Nov	101	4¹/2	. . .	. . .
73³/4	70	Jan	81	4³/4	73	⁷/8
73³/4	75	Nov	80	1	. . .	. . .
73³/4	75	Jan	86	1⁵/8	10	2¹/2

The closing price of Exxon's common stock was $73.75

As the strike price increases, the calls become less valuable and the puts become more valuable.

The value of an option for a given strike price increases with the length of the time until expiration.

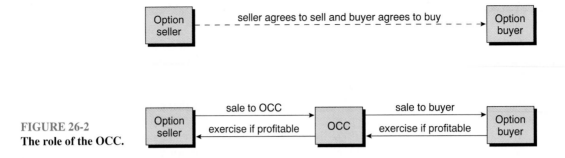

FIGURE 26-2
The role of the OCC.

tively becoming both the buyer of the option from the writer and the writer of the option to the buyer. The OCC substitutes its promise to deliver for the option seller's promise to deliver. When an option holder exercises, the OCC arranges with a member firm whose clients have written that particular option to make good on the option obligation. The OCC stands behind this obligation. The OCC effectively makes all call option contracts written on a particular security that have the same strike price and the same expiration date perfect substitutes for one another, and the same is true for put option contracts. This lowers transaction costs because it saves the cost of having to conduct a separate credit investigation for each seller.

In recent years, the number of traded options has greatly increased. There are options on common stocks, of course. There are also traded options on foreign currencies, on debt instruments such as U.S. Treasury securities, on stock market indexes such as the Standard & Poor's 500 Index (S&P 500), and on futures contracts.

Over-the-Counter Options

The options that are traded on exchanges are standardized with respect to such features as strike price, expiration date, exercise style (for example, American or European), and settlement arrangements. This enhances their liquidity. But there is a drawback. If an investor or a firm wants a nonstandard option, it cannot obtain such an option on an exchange. The investor can try to obtain what she wants in the OTC market. Like the OTC market for stocks, the OTC market for options consists of securities dealers who craft customized options to meet investor demand. A potential option buyer calls an OTC dealer to negotiate an option contract's exercise price, expiration date, underlying stock, and so on and a mutually acceptable price for the option.

To compete with the OTC market, the CBOE recently introduced FLEX options. These allow some flexibility in designing options on the S&P 500, S&P 100, and Russell 2000 indexes. The OTC market still offers greater flexibility in option design.[1]

Options and Corporate Finance

Options have a wide range of uses in corporate finance. As you learned in Chapter 23, firms in many countries sell new common stock to their shareholders through rights offerings. Rights are call options. As you learned in Chapters 17 and 18, firms can repurchase shares by distributing transferable put rights. These rights are put options. As you learned in Chapter 24, firms often include an option to redeem bonds early in a new debt issue. The option to redeem is a call option.

---

[1] For example, the time to expiration for a FLEX option cannot exceed 5 years, and FLEX options are not available for individual stocks. Such options can be purchased in the OTC market.

Firms also issue options to raise cash. They issue call options in the form of warrants, and they issue convertible bonds. A convertible bond is a straight bond with call options attached. We discuss warrants and convertible bonds next.

Self-Check Questions

1. What are the four basic types of derivatives?
2. Explain the basic difference between a call option and a put option.
3. Describe the role of the Options Clearing Corporation (OCC) in the operation of the options exchanges. What is the main benefit of the OCC?
4. How does the OTC options market work? How is it different from the options exchanges?

26.2 WARRANTS

A **warrant** is a long-term call option that is issued by a firm. It entitles the holder to buy shares of the firm's common stock at a stated price for cash. Firms, particularly smaller ones, often find it more attractive to issue convertible bonds, or bonds with warrants, than to issue straight debt. In addition, smaller firms often include warrants as a "sweetener" to a new issue of common stock or a privately placed debt issue.

Recall that standardized call options traded in the options market are written by investors against outstanding shares of a firm's stock. By contrast, warrants are issued by the firm, often as part of a package that includes the issuer's common stock, preferred stock, or bonds. Warrants are like rights because the underlying security is newly issued equity. But warrants usually do not expire for several years, and some firms, such as Allegheny Corporation, have even issued perpetual warrants.

Main Features of Warrants

The provisions of a warrant are essentially the same as those of a conventional call option. A warrant specifies the underlying common stock, the number of shares, a strike price, an expiration date, and the option type (American or European). Sometimes a warrant contains an early redemption feature, which enables the issuer to trigger its exercise prior to the expiration date.

EXAMPLE — *An Issue of Warrants*

A large and actively traded issue of warrants was sold by American Express Company in two *tranches* (parts). American Express distributed 932,000 common share purchase warrants to its common stockholders and then sold an additional 900,000 such warrants to the public at a price of $12.625 per warrant. Each American Express warrant entitled the holder to purchase, at any time within five years of the issue date, one share of American Express common stock at a strike price of $55 per share. The strike price was 17.0% over the previous closing price of American Express common stock. The terms of the warrant permitted American Express to accelerate the expiration date if the price of American Express's common stock traded at or above a price of $95 per share for a period of 10 consecutive trading days.

The American Express warrants were also redeemable at the firm's option beginning two years from the issue date at a price of $40 per warrant. This redemption feature, like the redemption feature on a convertible bond, permits the issuer to force exercise of the call option.

Some warrants provide for a "step-up" or increase in the strike price. Warrants like those issued by American Express provide for adjustment of the strike price if the issuer pays a common stock dividend, splits its common stock, distributes some of its assets (other than cash dividends), or issues stockholders rights to purchase shares at a discount from the prevailing market price, and in some other circumstances.[2] However, as is generally the case, American Express warrant holders are not entitled to vote or to receive dividends, and the strike price is not adjusted for cash dividend payments to common stockholders. ■

Financing with Warrants

Firms can sell warrants separately, as American Express did, or in combination with other securities. When a firm issues warrants at their fair market price, the cash it receives is fair compensation for the potential equity interest given up because of the efficiency of the capital markets. Nevertheless, issuing warrants may add value by reducing agency costs.[3]

Self-Check Questions

1. What is a warrant? How is it like a call option?
2. Describe the main features of warrants. What is the purpose of including a redemption feature in the terms of a warrant issue?
3. Why do firms issue warrants?

26.3 CONVERTIBLE SECURITIES

The conversion features of convertible bonds and convertible preferred stock are very similar. In our discussion we will concentrate on convertible bonds, but our comments will also apply to most convertible preferred stock.

Main Features of Convertible Debt

A **convertible bond** is a bond that is convertible, at the option of the bondholder, into shares of the issuer's common stock. Convertible debt has the same coupon rate, maturity, and optional redemption features that typify a straight bond. It also has the following conversion features:

1. Each bond is convertible at any time prior to maturity into common stock at a stated *conversion price*. This (strike) price usually exceeds the issuer's share price at the time of issue. In other words, the conversion option is normally issued out-of-the-money. The conversion premium is generally between 10% and 20%. Dividing the face amount of the convertible bond by the conversion price gives the *conversion ratio*. It is the number of shares of common stock into which each bond can be converted. The conversion terms are normally fixed for the life of the issue, although some convertible securities provide for one or more step-ups in the conversion price over time.

2. The conversion price is usually adjusted for stock splits, stock dividends, or rights offerings with a discounted offering price. It is also adjusted when the firm distributes assets (other than cash dividends) or indebtedness to its shareholders.

---

[2] As is customary, the strike price is actually adjusted only if the dilutive factors would require an adjustment of at least 5%. In addition, the $40 redemption price and the $95 acceleration price of the American Express warrants would be adjusted along with the strike price.

[3] See Chapter 9 for a discussion of optimal financial contracts.

3. Bondholders who convert do not receive accrued interest. Therefore, bondholders rarely convert voluntarily just before an interest payment date.

4. If the bonds are called, the conversion option will expire just before (usually between three and ten days before) the redemption date.

Convertible Preferred Stock

The main buyers of convertible securities are either entirely tax-exempt investors or those who cannot benefit directly from the corporate 70% dividends-received deduction. Consequently, under most market conditions, issuers of convertible securities have been able to obtain essentially the same terms (chiefly annual interest or dividend rate and conversion premium) whether they issued the convertible security as debt or as preferred stock.

Convertible preferred stock is similar to convertible debt; it is preferred stock that is convertible at the holder's option into shares of the issuer's common stock. Issuers who are in a taxpaying position and expect to remain so for a number of years find it cheaper to issue convertible debt than convertible preferred stock. Interest payments are tax-deductible, whereas dividend payments are not. The tax deductions reduce the cost of capital. Interest deductions are much less valuable to issuers who do not expect to be in a tax-paying position for a number of years. Of course, they are worthless if the issuer will *never* be able to claim them for tax purposes. Thus, in either case, non-tax-paying firms that wish to issue convertible securities issue convertible preferred stock.

Convertible preferred stock is usually perpetual, whereas convertible debt has a stated maturity and usually has a sinking fund. The rating agencies view perpetual convertible preferred stock as "true" equity for credit rating purposes.

CONVERTIBLE EXCHANGEABLE PREFERRED STOCK   A firm that is only temporarily not in an income-tax-paying position can issue *convertible exchangeable preferred stock*. Such securities are convertible preferred stock that is exchangeable at the option of the firm into convertible *debt* of the firm. The firm would exercise this option as soon as it became taxpaying. The annual interest rate on the convertible debt equals the annual dividend yield on the convertible preferred stock issue, and the issues have equivalent conversion terms. A non-tax-paying firm can reap the advantages of issuing convertible preferred stock while preserving the flexibility to reissue it in the form of debt should the firm become a taxpayer before the issue is converted.

PERCS   Preferred equity redemption cumulative stock (PERCS) is a form of convertible preferred stock whose conversion feature differs from that of traditional convertible preferred stock. Conversion of PERCS into common stock is mandatory, not voluntary. The option is European, not American. It is initially at-the-money because PERCS are convertible share for share. However, there is a cap on the option's payoff. The issuer can call the PERCS for redemption prior to maturity, and the holder must surrender the PERCS for the cash redemption price. If the price of the common exceeds the redemption price, the issuer gets the excess.

The issuing firm holds the option, and conversion is ultimately mandatory. Therefore, referring to PERCS as a convertible security is actually somewhat of a misnomer. The contract is in fact more like a futures contract for common stock from a PERCS holder's viewpoint. The PERCS holder has essentially purchased the common stock to be delivered at a future (but not absolutely certain) date.

PERCS pay a higher dividend rate than the underlying common. Investors have to decide whether the incremental dividend stream adequately compensates for the cap on the payoff.[4]

---

[4] Some investors objected to the cap. Practicing the Principle of Valuable Ideas, securities dealers created Dividend-Enhanced Convertible Stock (DECS). Conversion of DECS is mandatory, but the conversion feature is initially out-of-the-money, and the payoff is not capped.

Exchangeable Debentures

Firms have also issued bonds that are exchangeable for the common stock of another firm. The debentures are in effect "convertible" into the common stock of the other firm. But in all other respects, exchangeable debentures are like conventional convertible bonds. Exchangeable debentures may be attractive to a firm that owns a block of another firm's common stock when it would like to raise cash and intends eventually to sell the block. The firm may want to defer the sale, because it believes the shares will increase in value or because it wants to defer the capital gains tax liability.

Forced Conversions

Convertible bonds are normally callable subject to a schedule of fixed redemption (strike) prices that decline over the life of the issue. This call provision allows the issuer to force holders to convert the debt into common stock whenever the conversion value exceeds the call price. Most convertible bond indentures require the issuer to notify bondholders of the call prior to the redemption date, generally 30 days in advance. Securityholders can convert at any time during this notice period.

HOW FORCED CONVERSION WORKS   As we have noted, the market value of a convertible bond always exceeds its conversion value unless the conversion option is about to expire. The difference between the market and conversion values reflects the conversion option's time premium. If the underlying common stock is non-dividend-paying, convertible bondholders never voluntarily convert, no matter how high the conversion value becomes. They can always realize greater value by selling the bond. Even when the underlying common stock is paying cash dividends, convertible bondholders do not voluntarily convert if the dividends they would receive after conversion are less than the interest they receive now.

Suppose the market value of the underlying common stock exceeds the call price. Calling the convertible issue motivates holders to convert, because converting is more profitable than tendering the bonds for cash redemption. A firm should follow the forced conversion strategy that maximizes shareholder wealth. If the firm calls convertible bonds when their conversion value is less than the effective call price, the bonds will not be converted, and wealth will be transferred from shareholders to bondholders. If the firm calls convertible bonds when the conversion value exceeds the call price, bondholders will simply convert. The forced conversion strategy that maximizes shareholder wealth is the one that minimizes bondholder value: In a perfect capital market, a firm should call convertible bonds when their conversion value reaches the *effective call price* (optional redemption price plus accrued interest).[5]

Judged by the standards of the perfect capital market, most firms appear to wait "too long" to call their convertible bonds. They usually wait until the conversion value exceeds the call price by a seemingly wide margin—at least 20% is the practitioner's rule. Why do they behave this way? As we well know by now, actual markets are not perfect. In addition, if the market price of the issuer's common stock falls—and remains—below the conversion price during the 30-day notice period, the redemption value will exceed the conversion value, and bondholders will surrender their bonds for cash rather than convert. In that case, the firm may have to raise enough cash to cover the cash redemption value on short notice. That could involve significant transaction costs. This explains why firms normally wait to call their convertible bonds until the conversion value exceeds the effective call price by a comfortable margin.

Because of put-call parity discussed in Chapter 8, a convertible bond can be modeled either as (1) a straight bond together with a nondetachable call option on the underlying com-

---

[5] This decision rule assumes that the bond's conversion value exceeds its bond value at the time of the call. Suppose interest rates decline following the bond's issuance and the underlying share price also falls, causing the conversion option to have little value. The convertible bond will behave like a nonconvertible bond. The decision whether to redeem the convertible bond is then based on the same criteria as the decision whether to call a nonconvertible bond.

mon stock or as (2) the underlying common stock together with a nondetachable put option on the stock. According to the second interpretation, if the common stock price does not rise above the conversion price, the convertible bondholders can *put* the stock back to the issuer for the bond's redemption value at maturity. When the bond's conversion value exceeds the bond's redemption value, the put option is out-of-the-money. When a firm forces conversion, it expropriates the remaining time premium of a deep-out-of-the-money put option. Therefore, management must weigh the value it can expropriate if the forced conversion succeeds against the cost it will incur if the forced conversion attempt fails. We believe this is why firms *appear* to wait too long to force conversion.

There is also an agency cost involved with trying to force conversion. A failed attempt is very embarrassing for the firm's executives and could even lead to one or more people being fired. This, of course, tends to bias the executives toward waiting for an even larger margin!

A Forced Conversion

EXAMPLE

Time Incorporated called its Series C $4.50 cumulative convertible preferred stock for redemption at a price of $54.9375, including accrued dividends. The issue was convertible into 1.5152 shares of Time common stock at a conversion price of $33 per share. The market price of the common stock was $46⅜, representing a 40.5% premium over the conversion price. Time was paying dividends on its common stock at the rate of $1.00 per share per annum. A holder who converted at that time would suffer a decrease in annual dividend income amounting to $2.98 [= 4.50 − (1.5152)1.00] per preferred share. Consequently, few holders had converted voluntarily.

The market value of the common stock provided a *redemption cushion* over the redemption price amounting to

$$\text{Redemption cushion} = \frac{\left(\begin{array}{c}\text{Conversion}\\ \text{ratio}\end{array}\right)\left(\begin{array}{c}\text{Market price of}\\ \text{common stock}\end{array}\right) - \begin{array}{c}\text{Redemption}\\ \text{price}\end{array}}{\text{Redemption price}} \quad (26.1)$$

$$= \frac{1.5152(46.375) - 54.9375}{54.9375}$$

$$= 27.9\%$$

This cushion gave holders a strong incentive to convert when Time called the issue. With the assistance of investment bankers, the entire issue was converted. ■

TIMING THE FORCED CONVERSION   Investment bankers generally recommend that a firm not call a convertible issue unless the redemption cushion is at least 20%. The greater the cushion, the lower the risk of cash redemption. To eliminate this possibility altogether, the firm can engage the services of an investment banker (as Time did) to underwrite the redemption. The banker agrees to purchase any shares of common stock that would have been issued if bonds (or preferred stock) that were tendered for redemption had instead been converted. Most redemptions of convertible securities are underwritten.

Self-Check Questions

1. What is a convertible bond? What is convertible preferred stock? What are the main differences between them?

2. What are the main features of convertible debt?

3. What is convertible exchangeable preferred stock? Why do firms issue it?

4. Explain how forced conversion works. Why is a 20% redemption cushion recommended?

26.4 OPTION PRICING MODELS

Now let's take a look at how to value options. To keep matters simple, we will value only stock options. We will value calls first and then puts.

Why DCF Analysis Isn't Practical

The value of any asset is the present value of its expected future cash flows. So to value an option, why not just compute its present value? The problem is that an option's required return is very unstable. This is because an option's risk depends on the market value of its underlying asset.

An option has a unique required return for every possible market value an underlying asset can have. Since an asset's market value is virtually constantly changing in an efficient capital market, the required return to an option on such an asset is also constantly changing. Because of this, it is not practical to use discounted cash flow analysis to value options.

Recall from Chapter 8 that owning an option gives you a claim to the asset's "good" outcomes, and yet the option costs less than the asset. How can this be? This seems like a really good deal. The part that is easily forgotten is that you "pay" for this seemingly beneficial situation with higher risk: Owning an option is riskier than owning the underlying asset. As with a lottery ticket, if you invest only a small amount of money, it may not seem that risky.

WHY WE USE THE RISKLESS RETURN   If you're like us, you are probably thinking: If an option is riskier than its underlying asset, how can we use the *riskless* return to value it? In fact, this is precisely why this key to option valuation eluded scholars for many years. We will not prove this result, but we will provide some intuition into it.

When an asset owner sells a call option on the asset, he gives up a claim to the "good" outcomes, but gets the option's value, which he can invest over the remaining life of the option. It might seem like the expected future value of this investment depends on how the money is invested. However, this is not the case.

Recall from Chapter 10 that value can remain constant even if expected return changes, so long as there is also an offsetting change in risk. For example, suppose our asset owner gets $100 for the one-year call option. He can invest the $100 in either the 6% riskless return or a 10% risky return. The riskless investment has an expected future cash flow of $106, and a present value of $100 (= 106/1.06). The risky investment has an expected future cash flow of $110, and a present value of $100 (= 110/1.10).

The present value is the same either way, even though the *realized* return can turn out to be different for the risky investment (that's the nature of risk). Any difference in value would be quickly eliminated in an efficient capital market. We can think of the riskless return as a convenient way to measure the time value of money and the entire risk-return trade-off. Therefore, when we value an option, we use the riskless return to account for differences in the time value of money because of its convenience and simplicity.

Despite the convenience, it is important to remember that, although we use the riskless return to value an option, owning an option is not riskless. It is quite the opposite! ***Owning an option alone is riskier than owning the underlying asset alone.***

A Simple Option Pricing Model

Consider an asset with only two possible outcomes at time $t = 1$, $60 and $160. These outcomes have *risk-adjusted probabilities* of 0.6 and 0.4, respectively. That is, the actual probabilities that the asset may take on the values $60 and $160 are adjusted in the valuation model. We know that investors are risk-averse. Because of the Principle of Risk-Return Trade-Off, the price of the asset at $t = 0$ is less than the expected outcome. By adjusting the actual probabilities downward, we obtain equality between price and the risk-adjusted expected value, which is useful for modeling purposes.[6] The risk-adjusted expected future cash flow is then $100 [= 0.6(60) + 0.4(160)]$. If the riskless return (r_f) is 5%, the present value of the expected future cash flows is $95.24 (= 100/1.05)$.

What is a call option on this asset worth if it has a strike price of $150? If the outcome is $60, then the call option is worthless. If the outcome is $160, then the option is worth $10 at $t = 1$ (exercise value = asset value minus strike price = $160 - 150$). Therefore, the risk-adjusted expected future cash flow is $4 [= 0.6(0) + 0.4(10)]$. The present value of the option is $3.81 (= 4/1.05)$.

Now consider a similar option on a slightly more complex asset. This second asset has a two-period life. Figure 26-3 presents the outcomes and associated risk-adjusted probabilities. At $t = 2$, the asset will be worth $60, $160, or $260. At $t = 1$, there are two possible values. One possibility is a value at time $t = 1$ of $95.24 (as we just calculated, based on the probabilities of the $60 and $160 outcomes). The second possibility at $t = 1$ is based on the likelihood that the asset will be worth $160 or $260 at $t = 2$. It has a value of $190.48 \{= [0.6(160) + 0.4(260)]/1.05\}$.

We just computed $3.81 as the value of a call option on this asset at time $t = 1$ if the asset is worth $95.24 at that time. Similarly, the value of the call option is $47.62 [= 0.6(160 - 150)/1.05 + 0.4(260 - 150)/1.05]$ if the value of the asset is $190.48 at $t = 1$. Therefore, the value of the call option at $t = 0$ must be $20.32 \{= [0.6(3.81) + 0.4(47.62)]/1.05\}$.

We could also "skip over" the option's possible values at $t = 1$. To do so, we need the risk-adjusted probabilities of the three final outcomes. With independent outcomes, the risk-adjusted probability of a terminal outcome of $60 can be computed by multiplying the

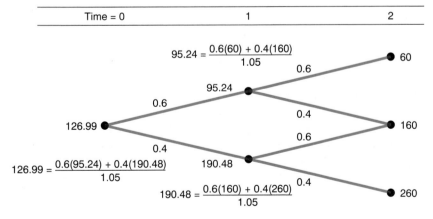

FIGURE 26-3
Possible outcomes in the two-period case.

---

[6] We use risk-adjusted probabilities to calculate a "sure" expected value that is equivalent to the actual risky expected value. We use them to reduce complexity (believe it or not!).

risk-adjusted probabilities along the "path" leading to that outcome: $(0.6)(0.6) = 0.36$. Likewise, the risk-adjusted probability of the $260 outcome is $(0.4)(0.4) = 0.16$. The $160 outcome can result from two paths. Its risk-adjusted probability is the sum of the risk-adjusted probabilities of these paths: $(0.6)(0.4) + (0.4)(0.6) = 0.48$. Then the value of the call option, CALL, is the present value of the expected payoff:

$$\text{CALL} = \frac{1}{(1.05)^2} [0.36(0) + 0.48(160 - 150) + 0.16(260 - 150)] = \$20.32$$

The Black-Scholes Option Pricing Model

The preceding example can be extended beyond two periods. If the number of possible outcomes for the value of the asset increases, an option's value can be computed directly, if tediously, from the possible paths for the expected value of the asset. We can extend this notion and build what is called a *two-state option pricing model* (two-state OPM).

Think of the movement in the asset's value during short time periods as either slightly up or slightly down. Suppose the risk-adjusted probability of an increase or decrease in value is constant over all periods. Then the risk-adjusted probabilities of the terminal outcomes can be computed by using the binomial probability distribution. This is why the two-state OPM is often referred to as the *binomial option pricing model* (binomial OPM).

We can make the time periods and possible price movements as small as we like. They can even be so small that time is virtually continuous. Recall how we examined the effect of more frequent compounding to understand continuous compounding in Chapter 4. We can do something similar here. We can make the time periods and possible movements smaller and smaller to see what happens *in the limit* as the size of each time period approaches zero.

Under a particular set of assumptions, as more time periods are used and the size of each time period approaches zero, the two-state OPM just described converges to the option pricing model derived by Fischer Black and Myron Scholes. Their model is significant because they were the first to prove that time-value-of-money adjustments *must* be made using the riskless return. The Black-Scholes OPM is

$$\text{CALL} = P_0 N(d_1) - SN(d_2)e^{-\Delta tk} \tag{26.2}$$

where

$$d_1 = \frac{\ln(P_0/S) + \Delta tk}{\sigma \Delta t^{1/2}} + \frac{\sigma \Delta t^{1/2}}{2} \tag{26.3}$$

$$d_2 = d_1 - \sigma \Delta t^{1/2} \tag{26.4}$$

and

$N(d) =$ the cumulative distribution function (cdf) for a standardized (mean $= 0$, $\sigma = 1$) normal random variable. This is the probability that an outcome is less than or equal to d. $N(d)$ is given in the table in Appendix B to this book for values of d from $d = -3.09$ to $d = 3.09$, in increments of 0.01.

$\sigma =$ the standard deviation of the (continuously compounded) return on the underlying asset

$\Delta t =$ the time (in years) until the option expires

$k =$ the riskless APR with continuous compounding

$S =$ the strike price of the option

$P_0 =$ the current value of the underlying asset

$\ln =$ the natural (base e) logarithm function

CRITICAL ASSUMPTIONS   This OPM makes the following assumptions:

1. The option and its underlying asset are traded in a continuously operating perfect market environment, including no restrictions on short positions and zero transaction costs.
2. The return distribution from owning the underlying asset is the normal probability distribution, with known and constant σ over the life of the option contract.
3. The value of k, the riskless return, is known and constant over the life of the option contract.
4. The option contract is European (that is, the option is exercisable only just before its expiration).
5. There are no cash flows associated with the asset over the life of the option contract, including no dividends when the asset in question is a stock.

Using the Black-Scholes OPM is very practical for two reasons. First, except for σ, the parameter inputs needed are specified in the option contract or are readily observable in currently operating markets. Second, the model usually provides a very good approximation of the true value of an option, even though not all of the assumptions may be satisfied. In any case, it is almost always a good starting point for analysis. And this is true even though violations of the model's assumptions can dramatically complicate option valuation.

USING THE BLACK-SCHOLES OPM   As you might expect by now, violations of the perfect market assumption do not harm the model's usefulness. However, it may surprise you to find out that the distinction between an American and a European type of option is not important unless there are cash flows associated with the underlying asset before the option expires. Recall that you can exercise an American option any time during its life. Also, you are generally better off selling, rather than exercising, one prior to its expiration. Thus, with a few adjustments, the Black-Scholes OPM can often be used to value American as well as European options.

Applying the Black-Scholes OPM

EXAMPLE

Suppose a non-dividend-paying stock is selling for $28 per share. The standard deviation of the return from owning a share of this stock is estimated from the returns on the stock during a recent, representative historical period and is found to be 0.30. The APR for the riskless return with continuous compounding is 6%. The option has a strike price of $30, and there are 9 months until expiration. What is a call option on this stock worth?

First list the parameter values: $P_0 = 28$, $\sigma = 0.30$, $k = 0.06$, $S = 30$, and $\Delta t = 0.75$. Then, $\sigma \Delta t^{1/2} = 0.259808$. From Equation (26.3), d_1 is

$$d_1 = \frac{\ln(P_0/S)}{\sigma \Delta t^{1/2}} + \frac{\Delta t k}{\sigma \Delta t^{1/2}} + \frac{\sigma \Delta t^{1/2}}{2} = \frac{\ln(26/30)}{0.259808} + \frac{0.75(0.06)}{0.259808} + \frac{0.259808}{2}$$

$$d_1 = -0.265553 + 0.173205 + 0.129904 = 0.037556 \approx 0.04$$

Equation (26.4) yields

$$d_2 = d_1 - \sigma \Delta t^{1/2} = 0.037556 - 0.259808 = -0.222252 \approx -0.22$$

From Appendix B, we have

$$N(d_1) = N(0.04) = 0.5160$$

$$N(d_2) = N(-0.22) = 0.4129$$

Finally, from Equation (26.2),

$$\text{CALL} = P_0 N(d_1) - SN(d_2)e^{-\Delta t k} = 28(0.5160) - 30(0.4129)e^{-0.045} = \$2.61$$

An option like this one should sell in the market for a price of about $2½ to $2¾. Note that the value of the option equals its time premium because it is out-of-the money. ∎

What Happens When the Share Price Falls?

Suppose the non-dividend-paying stock in the previous example was instead selling for $26 per share. With everything else the same, we would have $P_0 = 26$, $\sigma = 0.30$, $k = 0.06$, $S = 30$, and $\Delta t = 0.75$. As before, $\sigma\Delta t^{1/2} = 0.259808$. From Equation (26.3), d_1 is

$$d_1 = \frac{\ln(P_0/S)}{\sigma\Delta t^{1/2}} + \frac{\Delta tk}{\sigma\Delta t^{1/2}} + \frac{\sigma\Delta t^{1/2}}{2} = \frac{\ln(26/30)}{0.259808} + \frac{0.75(0.06)}{0.259808} + \frac{0.259808}{2}$$

$$d_1 = -0.550795 + 0.173205 + 0.129904 = -0.247686 \approx -0.25$$

Equation (26.4) yields

$$d_2 = d_1 - \sigma\Delta t^{1/2} = -0.247686 - 0.259808 = -0.507494 \approx -0.51$$

From Appendix B, we have

$$N(d_1) = N(-0.25) = 0.4013$$
$$N(d_2) = N(-0.51) = 0.3050$$

Finally, from Equation (26.2),

$$\text{CALL} = P_0N(d_1) - SN(d_2)e^{-\Delta tk} = 26(0.4013) - 30(0.3050)e^{-0.045} = \$1.69$$

Although the option is $2 further out-of-the-money, its value decreases by less than $2. ∎

Put-Call Parity

We introduced the concept of put-call parity in Chapter 8. At this point, we will be more explicit about how the time value of money is accounted for in the difference between the value of a put option and the value of a call option.

PUT-CALL PARITY RELATIONSHIP   Recall that the outcome distribution shown in Figure 8-5 can be claimed by either ownership of (a long position in) a call option ($S = \$110,000$) or ownership of both the asset and a put option ($S = \$110,000$). The only difference in value between these two positions is the amount of money that will be invested. In the case of the call option, the investor invests the current value of the call option (CALL) by purchasing the option and must pay $110,000 when the call is exercised. Thus in one case, the investor commits the value of the call option (CALL) now and the present value of the strike price (S_0) that will be paid in the future. In the other case, the investor commits the current value of the put option now (PUT) and the current value of the underlying asset now (P_0). Then, if the outcome is above the strike price, the investor ends up owning the asset in either case. If the outcome is below the strike price, the investor ends up with the strike price in cash but does not own the asset in either case. Therefore, the two positions are equivalent, and we have the following relationship:

$$-P_0 - \text{PUT} = -\text{CALL} - S_0 \tag{26.5}$$

Recall that the present value of the strike price does not change with the risk of the investment. Thus we can use the riskless return to compute the present value of S. With a riskless APR of k and continuous compounding, $S_0 = Se^{-\Delta tk}$, where Δt is the time until expiration. Substitute this expression into Equation (26.5). Rearranging, we can express the value of either option in terms of the other (and the present value of the strike price and the current value of the asset):

$$\text{CALL} = \text{PUT} + P_0 - Se^{-\Delta tk} \tag{26.6}$$

$$\text{PUT} = \text{CALL} + Se^{-\Delta tk} - P_0 \tag{26.7}$$

AN APPLICATION OF PUT-CALL PARITY   Just as we saw in Chapter 8 that common stock can be modeled as a form of option, insights into the value and nature of other securities can be obtained by modeling them in different, but equivalent, terms. We noted previously that a convertible bond can be modeled either as a straight bond plus a call option on shares of the firm's common stock or as the underlying stock plus a put option on the stock. Now you can see that this equivalence is because of put-call parity. As in the case of approximating common stock as a European call option, it is generally a good approximation, even though a convertible bond is *exactly* equivalent to shares of stock plus a put option only under specific conditions.

One insight to be gained from the stock-plus-put-option view of convertible debt concerns how corporations view the issuance of convertible debt. Often, a financial manager refers to convertible debt as *deferred equity*. This term implies that the convertible bondholders are viewed as already being equityholders in the firm. Of course, because of the put option, these particular equityholders have the value of their equity somewhat protected, because (except in the case of bankruptcy) they can sell their equity back to the firm. This view provides further insight into the general lack of concern by practicing financial managers over the issue of calling outstanding convertible debt to force its conversion into equity—it is already viewed as equity.

Valuing Put Options

We can value a put option simply by substituting Equation (26.2) into Equation (26.7).

What is the value of a 9-month put option, with $S = \$30$, on a non-dividend-paying stock that is selling for \$28 per share if $\sigma = 0.30$ and $k = 6\%$? We computed the value of a call option under the same conditions in our first example. It was \$2.61. Therefore, from Equation (26.7),

$$\text{PUT} = \text{CALL} + Se^{-\Delta tk} - P_0 = 2.61 + (30)e^{-0.045} - 28 = \$3.29$$

Note that the option's time premium equals \$1.29, which is its market value minus its exercise value.

Next let's extend our second example. The value of the put option if the stock has a current value of \$26 is

$$\text{PUT} = \text{CALL} + Se^{-\Delta tk} - P_0 = 1.69 + (30)e^{-0.045} - 26 = \$4.37$$

The put option is \$2 further in-the-money. But the option's value does not increase by \$2. Most of the option's value is its exercise value (\$4). Its time premium is only \$0.37. ■

Valuing a Put Option

EXAMPLE

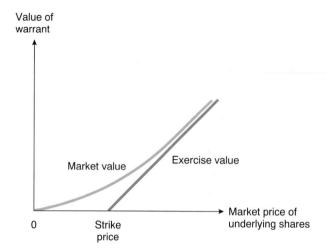

FIGURE 26-4
Relationship between the value of a warrant and the price of the underlying shares.

Valuing Warrants

Figure 26-4 illustrates the relationship between the value of a warrant and the price of the underlying shares. It is, of course, just like the relationship we observed for other call options in Chapter 8.

Warrants are long-term call options. We can value them like any other call option. But there is one important adjustment. Issuing warrants is dilutive because new shares are created. We must take this dilution into account. To do so, divide the call option value by a dilution factor:

$$W = \frac{C}{1 + P} \tag{26.8}$$

where W is the value of the warrant, C is the value of a call option to purchase one common share, and P is the proportionate increase in the number of common shares that would result from exercising the warrants. We use Equation (26.8) to value warrants before they are issued. How about after the issue? In an efficient market, their dilutive impact is already fully reflected in the issuer's common stock price, so $W = C$ after issuance.

Valuing Convertible Bonds

A convertible bond can be modeled as a straight bond plus a nondetachable warrant. From the Options Principle, you know that the value of a warrant can never be negative. Therefore, in a perfect capital market environment, the value of a convertible bond can never fall below its value as a straight bond. Similarly, the value of a convertible bond can also never fall below its conversion value. Figure 26-5 illustrates the relationship among the bond value, conversion value, and actual market value of a convertible bond.

The market value of a convertible bond equals the sum of the bond value and the actual value of the conversion option. Note in Figure 26-5 that the market value of the convertible bond always exceeds both the bond value and the conversion value. When the underlying share price rises above the conversion price, the conversion value exceeds the bond value. In that share price range, the actual market value of the convertible bond equals the bond value plus the exercise value of the conversion option plus the conversion option's time premium. When the underlying share price is very low, the convertible bond's market value approximates the bond value. When the share price is very high, the convertible bond's market value approximates the conversion value.

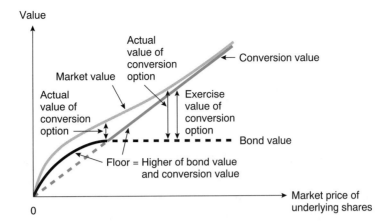

FIGURE 26-5
Bond value, conversion value, and actual market value of a convertible bond.

We can value a convertible bond by valuing the bond and warrant components separately. The value of a convertible bond exactly equals the sum of the two component values in a perfect capital market.

Self-Check Questions

1. What is the main distinguishing feature of the binomial OPM?
2. How does an increase in the strike price affect the value of a call option, according to the Black-Scholes OPM?
3. How does an increase in the underlying share price affect the value of a call option, according to the Black-Scholes OPM?
4. List the five critical assumptions underlying the Black-Scholes OPM.
5. Explain and illustrate with a diagram the meaning of put-call parity.
6. Explain why a convertible bond can be viewed either as (1) a bond with a call option or as (2) common stock with a put option.
7. How can an option pricing model be used to value warrants? How can it be used to value convertible debt or preferred stock?

26.5 INTEREST RATE SWAPS

Often, a firm wishes to replace fixed-rate debt with floating-rate debt, or vice versa. Such a substitution involves transaction costs. The firm can avoid these by entering into an interest rate swap. The swap enables the firm to recharacterize an existing debt obligation rather than having to pay the cost of replacing it in its entirety.

A **swap** contract obligates two parties to exchange specified cash flows at specified intervals. In an **interest rate swap**, the cash flows are determined by two different interest rates. In a **currency swap**, the cash flows are determined by two different exchange rates. We will discuss currency swaps in Chapter 29.

Swaps were introduced in 1981, and their use has grown rapidly. Table 26-1 shows the growth in the interest rate swap market since 1987. The number of contracts grew seven-fold, and the total notional principal amount involved in these transactions grew nine-fold. The market is still growing.

TABLE 26-1

Interest rate swaps outstanding, 1987–1993.

	1987	1988	1989	1990	1991	1992	1993
Number of contracts	34,127	49,560	75,223	102,349	127,690	151,545	236,126
Notional principal amount in billions of U.S. dollars	$682	$1010	$1539	$2311	$3065	$3850	$6178

Source: Smithson (1995), p. 53. Reprinted by permission.

How an Interest Rate Swap Works

The two parties to an interest rate swap exchange interest payment obligations. One might be at a specified fixed rate, say 8%, and the other at a floating rate, say 6-month LIBOR (London Interbank Offer Rate, at which banks in the London money market lend each other funds). Or they might be different floating rates. Coupon payments *but not the principal* are swapped. The payments are based on a *notional principal amount*. The payments are conditional. If one party defaults, the other is released from its obligation.

Figure 26-6 illustrates an interest rate swap. In its simplest form, called a *fixed-rate-floating-rate swap*, one interest rate is fixed and the other is floating. One party pays out a series of cash flows determined by the fixed interest rate R_1. It receives a series of cash flows determined by the floating interest rate R_2. The cash flows for the other party are the mirror image of those shown in Figure 26-6.

A swap has lower default risk than a loan. Two features account for this. No principal changes hands, and the payments are netted. Each party calculates what it owes the other. The party owing the greater amount writes a check to the other for the difference.

EXAMPLE

An Interest Rate Swap

Let's say that McDonald's Corporation enters into the following fixed-rate–floating-rate swap. It agrees to pay 6-month LIBOR and to receive 8%, based on $100 million notional. Net payments will be made semiannually. The amount of the first payment is determined on the swap date. LIBOR is 6%. Six months later McDonald's receives a check for $1,000,000 [= 100,000,000(0.08 − 0.06)/2]. By then LIBOR has risen to 7%. Six months later McDonald's receives a check for $500,000 [= 100,000,000(0.08 − 0.07)/2]. LIBOR has risen further to 9%. At the end of the third period, McDonald's writes a check for $500,000 [= 100,000,000(0.09 − 0.08)/2]. ∎

FIGURE 26-6

An interest rate swap.

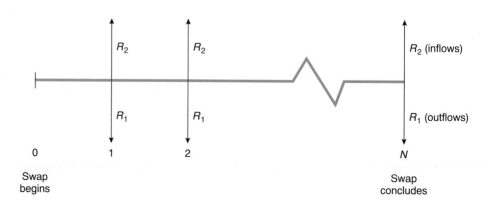

Interest rate swaps are used to change fixed-rate loans into floating-rate loans, and vice versa, or to change the index on a floating-rate loan.

How Interest Rate Swaps are Used

Suppose McDonald's issued $100 million of 10-year fixed-rate bonds 3 years ago. The interest rate is 7.50%. The issue has 7 years remaining. McDonald's now enters into a 7-year fixed-rate–floating-rate swap like the one in the previous example. Every 6 months McDonald's pays interest at a 7.50% rate on the bonds. It receives interest at an 8% rate and pays 6-month LIBOR in the swap. Its net interest cost is

Pay bondholders	7.50%
Receive from swap counterparty	8.00%
Pay swap counterparty	6-month LIBOR
Net interest cost	6-month LIBOR − 0.50%

In effect, McDonald's has converted its fixed-rate bonds to floating-rate bonds paying 6-month LIBOR minus 0.50%. ■

The Changing Market for Swaps

Swaps are not traded on exchanges. In the early days of the swap market, financial institutions arranged swaps by finding two counterparties who wanted to swap. The intermediary took no risk; it simply acted as agent. Swaps have evolved into a standardized product, and the intermediary's role has changed. It became important for intermediaries to put the transactions on their books. This exposed the intermediaries to default risk. The Principle of Comparative Advantage came into play. Commercial banks, with their greater capitalizations and comparative advantages in handling high-volume, standardized transactions and in extending credit, replaced investment banks as the main intermediaries.

Table 26-2 shows the 10 largest swap dealers in 1993. Nine were commercial banks. Three of these (Compagnie Financière de Paribas, Crèdit Lyonnais, and Banque Indosuez) were French.

Value Added by Interest Rate Swaps

In the 1980s, many market participants and academic researchers argued that comparative advantage was responsible for the rapid growth of the interest rate swap market.

TABLE 26-2
Ten largest swap dealers, 1993.[a]

RANK	FIRM	NOTIONAL PRINCIPAL AMOUNT OUTSTANDING ($ MILLIONS)
1	J.P. Morgan	453,080
2	Compagnie Financière de Paribas	431,728
3	Chemical Banking	411,782
4	Bankers Trust New York	315,879
5	Merrill Lynch	308,000
6	Crèdit Lyonnais	302,885
7	Citicorp	254,596
8	Chase Manhattan	237,773
9	BankAmerica	214,817
10	Banque Indosuez	184,924

[a] Interest rate swaps and currency swaps.
Source: Smithson, Smith, and Wilford (1995), p. 248.

THE COMPARATIVE ADVANTAGE ARGUMENT   The argument went like this. Suppose a BBB-rated firm can borrow on a floating-rate basis at LIBOR plus 0.50% and on a fixed-rate basis at 12%. An AAA-rated bank can borrow at LIBOR or at 10.50%. The BBB-rated firm must pay a rate premium of 1.50% in the fixed-rate market but of only 0.50% in the floating-rate market. The BBB-rated firm has a comparative advantage in the floating-rate market. The AAA-rated bank has a comparative advantage in the fixed-rate market. Suppose the bank borrows fixed-rate, the firm borrows floating-rate, and they swap. The firm agrees to pay the bank 11%, and the bank agrees to pay LIBOR. Figure 26-7 illustrates the swap and the net interest cost to each party.

The firm pays a net interest cost of 11.50%. It saves 0.50%. The bank pays LIBOR − 0.50% and also saves 0.50%. Sound too good to be true? It is! The argument is appealing. Unfortunately, it ignores arbitrage. With no barriers to capital flows, arbitrage would eventually eliminate any comparative advantage. Over time, the swap market would shrink, not grow!

A simple comparison of interest rates can be misleading. A swap is mutually beneficial only if it is superior *for each party* to a straight borrowing that is *identical in design and risk*. In a competitive market, there is no reason why the difference in floating rates for two firms should be the same as the difference in fixed rates. Consequently, there is also no reason why the fixed-rate–floating-rate differential should be the same for every firm. This differential depends on the probability distribution of the firm's cash flows. If the distributions for two firms differ, so will their fixed-rate–floating-rate differentials.

A BETTER EXPLANATION   We think there is a better explanation for the growth of the interest rate swap market. Information asymmetries and transaction costs can explain much of the growth. Suppose a firm has information, which is not available to the market, that leads it to believe that its credit quality will improve. It is generally cheaper and easier to refund short-term debt than long-term debt. Issuing short-term floating-rate debt and swapping into fixed-rate will enable the firm to exploit the information asymmetry. In our example, suppose the BBB-rated firm's credit improves so that it can borrow at LIBOR + 0.25%. It replaces its bank loan facility with a new one, leaving the swap in place. Its cost of funds drops to 11.25% [= LIBOR + 0.25% + 11.00% − LIBOR].

We will explain later in the chapter how firms can use interest rate swaps to manage their interest rate risk exposure. Firms can enter into a swap with any number of large financial in-

FIGURE 26-7
The comparative advantage argument.

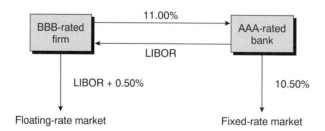

Firm's Net Interest Cost		Bank's Net Interest Cost	
Pay floating rate	LIBOR + 0.50%	Pay fixed rate	10.50%
Swap:		Swap:	
Pay	11	Receive	11
Receive	LIBOR	Pay	LIBOR
Net interest cost	11.50%	Net interest cost	LIBOR − 0.50%

stitutions. The success of swaps should therefore come as no surprise. Recall that the creation of a market for a security increases its liquidity, thus increasing its value by lowering transaction costs. The markets for swaps and other interest rate derivatives have grown with the increase in hedging by firms.

Self-Check Questions

1. What is an interest rate swap? How does one work?
2. Why do firms enter into interest rate swaps?
3. How do interest rate swaps add value? Is comparative advantage responsible for the growth in the interest rate swap market?
4. How are interest rate swaps useful in hedging interest rate risk?
5. Explain why an interest rate swap involves less default risk than simply exchanging two debt obligations.

26.6 FORWARDS AND FUTURES

You probably think derivatives are new. Some are, but others are not. Futures contracts on commodities have been traded on organized exchanges since the 1860s. Forward contracts are even older. The Chicago Board of Trade (CBOT) opened in 1842. It initially traded forwards. It introduced commodity futures in 1865. Financial futures are newer. The International Monetary Market of the Chicago Mercantile Exchange (CME) introduced foreign currency futures in 1972 and interest rate futures in 1975.

Forward Contracts

A **forward contract** obligates the holder to buy a specified amount of a particular asset at a stated price on a particular date in the future. All these terms are fixed at the time the forward contract is entered into. The specified future price is the *exercise price*. Most forward contracts are for commodities or currencies. (We will discuss foreign exchange forwards in Chapter 29.)

At contract origination, the net present value of a forward contract is zero because the exercise price is set equal to the expected future price. Neither buyer nor seller will realize a profit unless the actual market price of the asset differs from the exercise price at maturity. If the actual price exceeds the exercise price, the contractholder profits. If the actual price is lower than the exercise price, the holder suffers a loss. Under the Principle of Two-Sided Transactions, the holder's gain (loss) is the contract seller's loss (gain).

National Refining Corporation enters into a forward contract to purchase 10,000 barrels of oil at $17 per barrel in 90 days from Lone Star Oil & Gas. The purchase obligation is $170,000 ($= 17 \times 10,000$). Suppose the price of oil is $20 when the contract matures. National Refining realizes a profit of $3 per barrel, or $30,000. ■

A Forward Contract

EXAMPLE

A forward contract has two-sided default risk. Lone Star might fail to deliver the oil, and National Refining might fail to pay for it.[7] This credit risk is important in determining who is

---

[7] The CBOT developed futures contracts after many forward contracts defaulted.

able to transact in the forward market. Access is usually limited to large corporations, governments, and other creditworthy parties.

Two other features of forward contracts are noteworthy. First, there are no intermediate cash flows. Value is conveyed only at maturity. Second, most forward contracts require *physical delivery* of the asset in exchange for the cash purchase price. However, some can be *cash-settled*, which requires the party with the loss to pay that sum to the other party.

Futures Contracts

The basic form of a futures contract is identical to that of a forward contract. A **futures contract** obligates the holder to buy a specified quantity of a particular asset at a specified exercise price at a specified date in the future. A futures contract differs from a forward contract with respect to realizing gains or losses. With a forward contract, gains or losses are realized only on the settlement date. With a futures contract, they are realized daily. Also, futures contracts are traded on organized exchanges, whereas forwards are traded over the counter. Futures contracts are actively traded on more than 60 exchanges in more than two dozen countries. There are futures contracts for agricultural commodities, precious metals, industrial commodities, currencies, stock market indexes, and interest-bearing securities. These securities include Treasury bills, Treasury notes, Treasury bonds, and Eurodollar deposits.

Some futures contracts (notably agricultural futures) require physical delivery. Others (notably stock index futures and Eurodollar futures) are cash-settled. In practice, few futures contracts are held to maturity and exercised. Most are closed out by doing a reverse trade on the futures exchange.

MARKET FOR FUTURES   Futures are traded on exchanges through open outcry. Trading takes place in a trading ring on the exchange floor. Exchange members who want to trade enter the ring and announce their intention to trade. When a buyer and seller agree on terms, the updated price is posted on a board near the trading ring.

Unlike the stock exchanges and the options markets, there are no central market makers on the futures exchanges. As a result, futures prices can exhibit considerable volatility. To limit this volatility, the futures exchanges have established price limits. Futures prices cannot change by more than the indicated limit on any particular day.

LOW DEFAULT RISK   A futures contract has less default risk than a forward contract. Three features of futures markets are responsible. (1) Futures contracts are *marked to market* and *settled* at the end of every business day. When a futures contract loses value during the day, the holder pays the seller at the end of the day a sum equal to the day's loss. (2) There are *margin requirements*. Each buyer and seller must post a performance bond, which is adjusted daily. (3) There is a *clearinghouse*. Each party to a futures transaction really enters into a transaction with the clearinghouse. If either party defaults on a payment, the clearinghouse will make the payment. It first applies any funds in the defaulting party's margin account. If that is not enough, then the clearinghouse covers the difference.

GREATER LIQUIDITY   Futures contracts are more liquid than forward contracts for two reasons. Futures are standardized contracts, and they are traded on organized exchanges.

How an Interest Rate Futures Contract Works

We will use the Treasury bond futures contract to illustrate how an interest rate futures contract works. The underlying instrument is a hypothetical bond with a $100,000 par value, a 20-year maturity, and an 8% coupon. The contract price is quoted with respect to this bond. However, the contract seller can choose from among several actual Treasury bonds that are acceptable to deliver. Settlement is made by physical delivery.

Suppose you buy one contract, which specifies delivery in 6 months at a price of 96 (that is, 96% of the face amount, or $96,000 in total). You are said to be *long* the contract, and the seller is said to be *short* the contract. Each day your position and the seller's position will be marked to market as the value of the futures contract changes. As interest rates go up, the value of the futures contract (the value of the 8% bond) goes down. As interest rates go down, the value of the futures contract goes up. Under the Principle of Two-Sided Transactions, as the value of your long position goes down, the value of the seller's short position goes up by the same amount. As the value of your long position goes up, the value of the seller's short position goes down by the same amount.

A Futures Contract

EXAMPLE

At the end of 6 months you will take delivery of Treasury bonds in exchange for the $96,000 agreed-on price. Your gain (or loss) will depend on whether you can sell the bonds for more (or less) than the $96,000 you paid for them. If you do not want to take delivery, you can close out your position by selling one Treasury bond contract. The clearinghouse will net your long and short positions. If the 8% bond increased in value while you owned the futures contract, you will have a profit; in the opposite case, you will have a loss. ∎

Growth of the Futures Market

Figure 26-8 illustrates the growth of the Treasury bond and Eurodollar CD futures markets between 1981 and 1992. The number of Treasury bond contracts traded grew five-fold to 70 million per year. The number of Eurodollar CD contracts traded grew many times faster to 59 million per year. Each Eurodollar CD contract is for $1 million. Thus the underlying principal amount is actually greater in the Eurodollar futures market than in the Treasury bond futures market.

As we observed in the swaps market, the interest rate futures markets have expanded because of the increase in hedging activity.

FIGURE 26-8

Yearly volume of financial futures contracts, 1981–1992.

Source: Smithson, Smith, and Wilford (1995), p. 211.

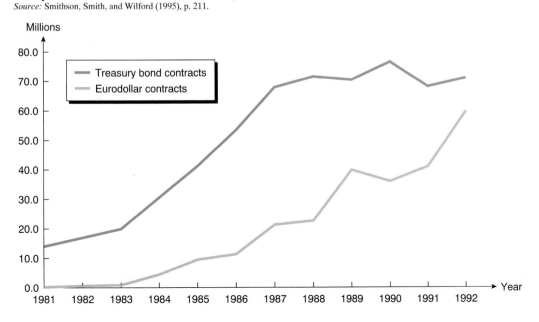

26.7 HEDGING

We have mentioned several times that derivatives are used in hedging and that an increase in hedging helps to explain the growth in the options, swaps, and futures markets. Now we will see how firms use the instruments we have described to hedge.

How a Hedge Works

A firm engages in hedging in order to reduce its sensitivity to changes in the price of a commodity, a foreign exchange rate, or an interest rate. Figure 26-9 illustrates the rationale for

FIGURE 26-9
The rationale for hedging.

(a) An increase in interest rates leads to a decrease in the value of the firm.

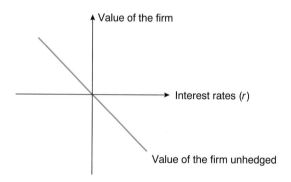

(b) The hedge neutralizes the effect of the rise in interest rates.

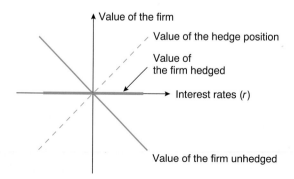

hedging. Suppose an increase in interest rates would decrease the value of the firm. In panel (a), the firm's value decreases as interest rates increase. This may be a result of interest rates increasing on floating-rate debt that the firm has outstanding. It might reflect a rise in long-term interest rates just as the firm is about to issue new bonds. You could also think of *r* as the price of jet fuel to an airline, or the cost of pounds sterling to a U.S. importer of British goods.

If the firm can take a position in a derivative whose value will increase as interest rates increase, it can neutralize the impact of the interest rate increase. In panel (b), the value of the hedge position follows the dashed line. The hedge position is carefully selected so that changes in its value offset changes in the value of the asset being hedged. Panel (b) illustrates a *perfect hedge*. The value changes offset each other precisely, so the value of the firm is unaffected. Perfect hedges are difficult to construct. Nevertheless, proper hedging should substantially reduce the firm's exposure to price risks.

Hedging with Options

Options provide an opportunity to hedge against a bad outcome while preserving the opportunity to benefit from a good outcome. Imagine that General Holding Company has purchased 1 million shares of Family Entertainment's common stock. General Holding would like to sell the stock. However, it is near year-end. Deferring the sale would defer tax on the gain General Holding has realized. But General Holding is concerned that the shares might decline in value before year-end.

General Holding can purchase put options. Family Entertainment's current share price is $28. If General Holding buys put options on 1 million shares at $28 per share, it will be fully hedged against risk of loss. Table 26-3 illustrates the possible outcomes. Suppose Family Entertainment's share price falls to $20. General Holding's 1 million shares lose $8 each. But the put is worth $8 per share. The gain just offsets the loss. On the other hand, if Family Entertainment's share price rises, General Holding has a gain. It has hedged against the risk of a loss without affecting its opportunity to benefit from a rise in Family Entertainment's share price. ■

Using Options to Hedge

EXAMPLE

TABLE 26-3
Possible outcomes for General Holding's option hedge.

SHARE PRICE AT TIME OF SALE	GAIN OR (LOSS) ON SHARES		GAIN OR (LOSS) ON HEDGE		NET GAIN OR (LOSS)
	Per Share	Total	Per Share	Total	
$20	$(8)	$(8,000,000)	$8	$8,000,000	—
25	(3)	(3,000,000)	3	3,000,000	—
30	2	2,000,000	—	—	$2,000,000
35	7	7,000,000	—	—	7,000,000

Hedging with Interest Rate Swaps

A floating-rate borrower can hedge against a change in interest rates by entering into a swap to pay fixed and receive floating. The BBB-rated firm in the comparative advantage example entered into such a swap. The swap converted its interest cost from LIBOR + 0.50% floating to 11.50% fixed.

CAPS AND FLOORS   There are three other interest rate derivative instruments we should mention. *Interest rate caps* pay the holder if the specified interest rate (for example, 3-month

LIBOR) rises above a specified rate. A floating-rate borrower who buys a 7% cap will never have to pay more than 7%. Any period in which 3-month LIBOR exceeds 7%, the seller of the cap contract pays the difference between the actual rate and 7% multiplied by the notional amount and the fraction of the year (in this case 0.25). The cap contract is like a call option on 3-month LIBOR with a strike price of 7%. It hedges the contract holder against a rise in rates.

An *interest rate floor* places a lower limit on the interest rate. For example, an investor in floating-rate notes that pay 3-month LIBOR + 1.00% who purchases a 4.00% floor contract can never receive less than 5.00% interest any period. The floor contract is like a put option on 3-month LIBOR with a strike price of 4.00%. It hedges against a drop in rates.

COLLARS   Finally, an *interest rate collar* is just a package consisting of a cap and a floor. For example, a 4%/7% collar consists of a 4% floor and a 7% cap. It hedges against rates falling outside a particular range.

Hedging with Forwards and Futures

Because forwards and futures are basically identical in structure, we will present a futures example. The critical factor in futures hedging is determining the hedge ratio. The *hedge ratio* is defined by

$$\text{Hedge ratio} = \frac{\text{Volatility of bond to be hedged}}{\text{Volatility of hedging instrument}} \tag{26.9}$$

EXAMPLE

Hedging with Futures

New Age Foods plans to issue $50 million of bonds. It needs 1 month to prepare the documentation. It is concerned that interest rates might rise by a full percentage point before it can sell the issue. It could sell Treasury bond futures to hedge this risk.

If it were prepared to issue debt immediately, it could sell 10% notes that mature in a lump sum at the end of 30 years. If its new-issue rate increases to 11%, the 10% issue will fall in value to

$$PV = \sum_{t=1}^{60} \frac{5}{(1.055)^t} + \frac{100}{(1.055)^{60}} = 91.2751$$

per $100 par value. The change in value is 8.7249 (= 100 − 91.2751).

New Age estimates that the yield on an 8% 20-year Treasury bond would also increase by 1%, from 9% currently to 10%. At a 9% yield, the 8% Treasury bond is worth

$$PV = \sum_{t=1}^{40} \frac{4}{(1.045)^t} + \frac{100}{(1.045)^{40}} = 90.7992$$

per $100 par value. At a 10% yield, it is worth

$$PV = \sum_{t=1}^{40} \frac{4}{(1.05)^t} + \frac{100}{(1.05)^{40}} = 82.8409$$

per $100 par value. The change in value is 7.9583 (= 90.7992 − 82.8409)

From Equation (26.9), the hedge ratio is

$$\text{Hedge ratio} = \frac{8.7249}{7.9583} = 1.0963$$

New Age needs to sell short 1.0963 8% Treasury bonds for each bond to be hedged. New Age needs to sell short

$$\text{Number of contracts} = \text{Hedge ratio}\left(\frac{\text{Principal amount to be hedged}}{\text{Par value of hedging instrument}}\right) \qquad (26.10)$$

Each futures contract covers $100,000 principal amount of bonds, so

$$\text{Number of contracts} = 1.0963\left(\frac{50,000,000}{100,000}\right)$$

$$= 548 \text{ Treasury bond contracts}$$

To verify, suppose interest rates rise by 1%. The missed issuance opportunity will cost New Age

$$50,000,000(0.087249) = \$4,362,450$$

But it will earn a profit on the futures contracts equal to

$$548(100,000)0.079583 = \$4,361,148$$

This profit offsets 99.97% of the opportunity cost. ■

Consider two other hedging situations. Suppose Delta Airlines is concerned about a possible rise in the cost of jet fuel. It could hedge by buying oil futures. Suppose Nike is about to receive payment in French francs for a large shipment of running shoes just like the ones you wear. It could sell French franc futures to hedge against the risk of a decline in the value of the franc.

Self-Check Questions

1. Explain a firm's rationale for hedging.

2. How does a hedge work?

3. A firm might win a contract to sell goods to a British firm in exchange for pounds sterling. How could it go about hedging its sterling/dollar foreign exchange risk?

4. A firm is considering borrowing on a floating-rate basis. How could it hedge its interest rate risk?

5. What are interest rate caps and floors? How are they like options?

6. How could a firm use interest rate futures to hedge an upcoming issue of long-term debt?

INDIANTOWN'S DECISION TO HEDGE

Indiantown entered into six interest rate swap agreements in October 1992. The six were *accreting swaps*. The notional principal amounts would increase according to a specified schedule. This schedule reflected how Indiantown's bank borrowings would increase during the construction period.

The total notional amount would increase from \$16,578,600 in November 1992 to \$535 million in 1995. It would remain at the final amount through December 2010. Indiantown planned to refund the bank debt by the end of 1994, if possible. The 2010 expiration provided plenty of flexibility. Indiantown could delay the refinancing if it felt interest rates were too high in 1994. Indiantown also had the flexibility to terminate the swaps if it paid off the bank debt.

Swap payments were based on the spread between 8.30% and 3-month LIBOR. LIBOR was one of the three indices Indiantown could choose on its bank loan. Indiantown would have to pay its banks a margin over LIBOR between 1.25% and 1.75%. Thus the swaps locked in a fixed rate between 9.55% and 10.05%.

In November 1994, Indiantown sold \$505 million of first mortgage bonds. The bonds were issued in 10 series. The bonds had fixed interest rates between 7.38% and 9.77%. Indiantown used part of the proceeds to pay off the bank loans. Because interest rates had fallen since 1992, it realized a profit of more than \$7 million when it terminated the swaps. All in all, a pretty good outcome for Indiantown!

SUMMARY

The financial markets have become more volatile in recent years. Firms have responded by seeking ways to hedge their risk exposure. Financial engineers have responded by developing new hedging instruments. These do not eliminate risk. Rather, they transfer it to other parties who are willing to bear it at lower cost.

There are four basic derivatives: options, swaps, forwards, and futures. They can be used to build more complex securities. Understanding them is important. Once you do, you will be able to analyze complex securities more easily.

An option conveys a right without an obligation. A call option gives the right to buy, a put option the right to sell. Firms can issue call options, known as warrants, to raise equity. They can package them with debt to create convertible bonds or exchangeable bonds. Valuing options can be difficult. Various option valuation models have been developed. The binomial OPM and the Black-Scholes OPM are two that are widely used.

Financing with convertible debt represents a form of what practitioners call deferred equity financing. The issue is debt until it is converted. A convertible bond derives its value from two sources: its value as a straight bond and the value of the underlying common stock into which it can be converted. Put-call parity allows the security to be modeled as a bond plus a call option or as stock plus a put option.

Firms, particularly smaller ones, often find it advantageous to issue convertible bonds or bonds with warrants. These securities generally have lower agency costs than straight debt. If the firm pursues riskier projects (asset substitution), the option feature lets securityholders share in the payoff from really good outcomes.

Interest rate swaps entered the marketplace in 1981. Their use has grown rapidly. The two parties to a swap exchange interest but not principal. Payments are based on a notional principal amount. Swaps can be used to transform fixed-rate debt into floating-rate debt, and vice versa. Interest rate swaps are useful in hedging interest rate risk. The swaps market has grown in response to the increase in hedging by firms.

Forwards and futures are contracts that obligate the holder to buy a specified amount of a particular asset at a stated price on a particular date in the future. Futures are standardized, forwards are not. Futures are exchange-traded. Forwards are traded over the counter. Forwards allow greater flexibility in design, whereas futures are more liquid and have less default risk. Both are useful for hedging commodity price risk, foreign exchange risk, and interest rate risk.

We will return to the subject of options, swaps, forwards, and futures in Chapter 29 and describe how a firm can use these instruments to hedge foreign exchange risk.

DECISION SUMMARY

- A firm can use options, swaps, forwards, or futures to hedge specific risks. It should hedge when doing so will increase shareholder wealth.
- Smaller, riskier firms may find it advantageous to issue convertible debt rather than straight debt.
- A firm that sells convertible or exchangeable securities should check to make sure that it is receiving full value for the options.
- The Black-Scholes OPM can be used to value options on stocks. It is useful for valuing warrants and the option component of convertible bonds. Remember to adjust for the dilution factor when valuing warrants that have not yet been issued.
- A firm that is not tax-paying, and does not expect to be in the foreseeable future, should issue convertible preferred stock rather than convertible debt. If it expects to become tax-paying soon, it should consider issuing convertible exchangeable preferred stock. It can exchange convertible debt for the convertible preferred when it begins paying income taxes.
- In a perfect capital market, a convertible debt issue should be called for redemption, in order to force its conversion into common stock, when its conversion value reaches its effective call price (the optional redemption price plus accrued interest). With costly transactions, including the chance of a "failed conversion," firms usually call only when the conversion value exceeds the effective call price by at least 20%.
- A firm that wants to transform some fixed-rate debt into floating-rate debt should compare the cost of refunding the fixed-rate debt and the cost of entering into a fixed-rate–floating-rate swap. It should select the lower-cost alternative.
- A firm can use derivatives to reduce its exposure to commodity price, foreign exchange, or interest rate risk. It should decide how much risk it wants to transfer. It should make sure that any transaction it considers will work properly. If it considers more than one alternative, it should select the one with the lowest cost.

EQUATION SUMMARY

(26.1) $$\text{Redemption cushion} = \frac{\left(\begin{array}{c}\text{Conversion}\\\text{ratio}\end{array}\right)\left(\begin{array}{c}\text{Market price of}\\\text{common stock}\end{array}\right) - \begin{array}{c}\text{Redemption}\\\text{price}\end{array}}{\text{Redemption price}}$$

(26.2) $$\text{CALL} = P_0 N(d_1) - SN(d_2)e^{-\Delta tk}$$

where

(26.3) $$d_1 = \frac{\ln(P_0/S) + \Delta tk}{\sigma \Delta t^{1/2}} + \frac{\sigma \Delta t^{1/2}}{2}$$

$$(26.4) \qquad d_2 = d_1 - \sigma \Delta t^{1/2}$$

$$(26.5) \qquad -P_0 - \text{PUT} = -\text{CALL} - S_0$$

$$(26.6) \qquad \text{CALL} = \text{PUT} + P_0 - Se^{-\Delta tk}$$

$$(26.7) \qquad \text{PUT} = \text{CALL} + Se^{-\Delta tk} - P_0$$

$$(26.8) \qquad W = \frac{C}{1 + P}$$

$$(26.9) \qquad \text{Hedge ratio} = \frac{\text{Volatility of bond to be hedged}}{\text{Volatility of hedging instrument}}$$

$$(26.10) \qquad \text{Number of contracts} = \text{Hedge ratio} \left(\frac{\text{Principal amount to be hedged}}{\text{Par value of hedging instrument}} \right)$$

KEY TERMS

derivative...839

option...840

warrant...843

convertible bond...844

convertible preferred stock...845

swap...855

interest rate swap...855

currency swap...855

forward contract...859

futures contract...860

EXERCISES

PROBLEM SET A

A1. Explain why a convertible bond can be viewed as a package consisting of a straight bond and warrants.

A2. Redo the Black-Scholes OPM example assuming $P_0 = 28$ and $\sigma = 0.40$. Why has the value of the call option increased?

A3. Redo Problem A2 assuming $\Delta t = 2.00$. Why has the value of the call option increased?

A4. What is a derivative?

A5. What is a convertible security?

A6. What is an interest rate swap?

A7. What is a warrant?

A8. Warrants are often referred to as "sweeteners" to a bond issue, as though the firm can "throw them into the deal" at no cost. Explain why it is, or is not, costless for the firm to include warrants with a bond issue.

A9. Explain why futures contracts are similar to forward contracts. How are they different?

A10. What is the basic rationale for hedging?

A11. Explain how each of the following instruments is used to hedge interest rate risk: (a) interest rate swap (b) option to buy a bond (c) interest rate future.

PROBLEM SET B

B1. What is the value of a call option with a strike price of $180 on the two-state asset shown in Figure 26-3?

B2. Suppose that the risk-adjusted probabilities for increasing and decreasing prices in Figure 26-3 were reversed. That is, an increase has a 40% chance and a decrease a 60% chance of occurring. What is the value of a call option with a strike price of $140 on such a two-state asset?

B3. What is the value of a put option with a strike price of $185 on the two-state asset shown in Figure 26-3?

B4. Suppose a stock is selling for $48.50 per share, the standard deviation of the return from owning a share of this stock is 24% per year, and the riskless return with continuous compounding is 5% APR. According to the Black-Scholes OPM:

a. What is a call option on this stock worth if the option has a strike price of $50 and 8 months until expiration?

b. What is a put option on this stock worth if the option has a strike price of $50 and 8 months until expiration?

c. What is a call option on this stock worth if the option has a strike price of $50 and 4 months until expiration?

d. What is a put option on this stock worth if the option has a strike price of $50 and 4 months until expiration?

B5. According to the Black-Scholes OPM, what is the value of a 6-month put option with a strike price of $40 on stock selling for $37.75 if the standard deviation of the return to the stock is 28% per year and the riskless return with continuous compounding is 7% APR?

B6. Suppose the standard deviation of a stock's return is 25% per year and the riskless return with continuous compounding is 6% APR. According to the Black-Scholes OPM:

a. What is a 6-month call option on this stock worth if the strike price is $30 and the stock is currently selling for $28? What are the time and exercise values of this option?

b. What is a 6-month call option on this stock worth if the strike price is $30 and the stock is currently selling for $32? What are the time and exercise values of this option?

c. What is a 6-month call option on this stock worth if the strike price is $30 and the stock is currently selling for $34? What are the time and exercise values of this option?

B7. Consider a 9-month call option with a strike price of $25 on a stock that currently sells for $25. According to the Black-Scholes OPM, if the riskless return with continuous compounding is 6% APR:

a. What is the value of this option if σ is 35%?

b. What is the value of this option if σ is 30%?

c. What is the value of this option if σ is 25%?

B8. According to the Black-Scholes OPM, what is the value of a call option with a strike price of $110 and 3 months until expiration on an asset that has a current market value of $90 and a σ of 30% per year if k is 10%?

B9. Consider a 6-month call option with a strike price of $20 on a stock that currently sells for $21. According to the Black-Scholes OPM, if σ is 30%:

a. What is the value of this option if k is 4%?

b. What is the value of this option if k is 7%?

c. What is the value of this option if k is 10%?

B10. What is the current value of a European call option with an exercise price of $20 and an expiration date 9 months from now if the stock is non-dividend-paying and is now selling for $24.38, the variance of the return on the stock is 0.48, and the riskless return is 6%? What is the current exercise value of this call option? What is the current time premium?

B11. Suppose an asset with a two-period life similar to the one shown in Figure 26-3 has three possible terminal values: $150, $200, and $250. Probabilities for the valuation paths are 0.55 for an increase and 0.45 for a decrease.

a. What is the value of a call option on this asset if the option has a strike price of 210 and the riskless return is 10% per period?

b. What is the value of a put option on this asset if the option has a strike price of 210 and the riskless return is 10% per period?

c. Show that direct computation and put-call parity give identical answers to part b. That is, if you used one method to get the answer to part b, now use the other to show its equivalence. (*Hint:* Be sure to note that the riskless return used in the Black-Scholes OPM is an APR but that the riskless return given is an APY.)

B12. Tokai Bank can borrow at a fixed rate of 9% or at LIBOR. A manufacturing firm can borrow at a fixed rate of 12% or at LIBOR + 1%.

a. Is there a mutually advantageous opportunity to engage in an interest rate swap? Explain.

b. Suppose the bank offers to pay the manufacturing firm LIBOR in return for payments at $11\frac{1}{2}\%$. How should the manufacturing firm respond?

c. The manufacturing firm proposes to pay $10\frac{1}{2}\%$ in return for LIBOR. Is such a swap advantageous for the bank?

d. What fraction of the net cost benefit does each party realize under the swap terms in part c?

B13. Triple-A-rated Exxon Corporation can borrow at a fixed rate of 8.5% or at LIBOR + 0.10%. Single-B-rated Cajun Drilling Company can borrow fixed-rate at 12% or floating-rate at LIBOR + 2%.

a. Is there a mutually advantageous opportunity to engage in an interest rate swap? Explain.

b. Suppose Exxon proposes that Cajun pay 11% in return for LIBOR. Should Cajun accept the offer?

c. Suppose Exxon proposes that Cajun pay 9.5% in return for LIBOR. Should Cajun accept the offer?

B14. Petrie Stores holds 200,000 shares of Toys 'R' Us common stock. It plans to sell the shares but would like to delay the sale for 3 months for tax reasons. Toys 'R' Us is trading at $40. The standard deviation of the return on the stock is 28% per year. The riskless return with continuous compounding is 6% APR. The stock is not expected to pay dividends for the next 3 months.

a. How could Petrie Stores hedge the risk of a decline in the Toys 'R' Us share price?

b. How much would an at-the-money put option on 200,000 shares cost?

c. How much would the put option cost with a strike price of $35?

d. Compare the advantages and disadvantages of the two option alternatives.

B15. Dayton, Duvalier, and Dice (Three D) plans to acquire Neptune Candy Company through a leveraged buyout. It will borrow $1 billion of the purchase price from its banks. The interest rate is 3-month LIBOR + 1%. Three D would like to protect against its interest cost rising above 10%.

a. How can Three D hedge this risk?

b. Suppose Three D buys a 9% interest rate cap contract. LIBOR varies over the next eight quarters as shown in the following table.

Quarter	1	2	3	4	5	6	7	8
3-month LIBOR (%)	7.50	6.75	8.50	10.25	11.50	12.25	9.75	7.50

How much interest does Three D pay each quarter?

c. How much does the party who sold the cap contract have to pay Three D each quarter?

B16. An interest rate collar provides for an 8% floor and 10% cap. The notional amount is $100 million. The periodic interest rates are shown in the table in Problem B15. Calculate the amount of the payment the seller of the collar contract will make or receive each quarter.

B17. Kmart plans to issue $100 million of bonds. It needs one month to prepare the documentation. It is concerned that interest rates might rise before it can sell the issue. Its current new issue rate is 9% for 30-year bonds.

  a. How could Kmart use futures contracts to hedge this risk?

  b. The yield on 8% 20-year Treasury bonds is 7.50%. Kmart's treasurer estimates that the yield on these bonds will rise to 8.50% if Kmart's borrowing cost rises to 10%. Calculate the hedge ratio.

  c. Calculate the number of Treasury bond futures contracts Kmart should sell to hedge its risk.

  d. Calculate Kmart's missed issuance opportunity cost and their profit on the futures contracts if interest rates rise by 1%.

  e. Recalculate the hedge ratio, number of contracts, missed issuance opportunity cost, and profit on the futures contracts if the yield on 20-year Treasury bonds rises by 0.5% when Kmart's borrowing cost rises by 1%.

PROBLEM SET C

C1. What standard deviation of the return to a stock is implied for the Black-Scholes OPM for the following situation? A 5-month call option with a strike price of $35 sells for $2.03, k is 6%, and the stock is currently selling for $32.75.

C2. Use put-call parity to show that the combination of buying an asset, buying a put with a strike price of S, and selling a call with a strike price of S is equivalent to simply buying a riskless bond that has a maturity value of S.

C3. A convertible bond can be modeled as a call option plus a straight bond. A warrant is a call option. In a perfect capital market environment, the combined market value of a warrant and a straight bond is identical to the market value of a comparable convertible bond. Explain why you might expect the market value of the warrant-bond combination to be somewhat higher than that of the comparable convertible bond. *Hint:* This can be done by using the Options Principle.

C4. Show that the values of a European put and an American put are different when there is no chance that the option will be out-of-the-money during the remaining time until maturity.

C5. Why does the time premium of an option increase (decrease) as the value of the underlying asset moves toward (away from) the strike price?

C6. Explain why it is possible to view an interest rate swap as a portfolio of forward contracts.

C7. Explain why a futures contract can be viewed as a sequence of forward contracts. Each day the old forward contract is settled and a new one is written.

Real-World Application:
Bally's PRIDES

Bally Entertainment Corporation (Bally) is one of the leading operators of casinos and casino hotels. It has casinos in Atlantic City, New Jersey; Las Vegas, Nevada; New Orleans, Louisiana; and Robinsville, Mississippi.

In September 1995, Bally was considering issuing a new derivative instrument called PRIDES, which Merrill Lynch & Co. had developed. (To help protect its invention, Merrill Lynch also registered the PRIDES ser-vice mark.) Figure 26-10 provides a summary of terms for the proposed issue.

Bally's treasury department analyzed this rather unusual form of convertible preferred stock. In particular, they wanted to understand how the conversion feature worked. At the time, Bally's common stock was trading at $11⅛ and was not dividend paying. The treasury staff gathered the following additional information and began their analysis of PRIDES:

Riskless return	5.50%
Volatility of the return on Bally's common stock (standard deviation)	0.40
Bally's new issue rate for 3-year preferred stock	10.75%

1. The PRIDES contain a mandatory conversion feature.
   a. Explain how it works.
   b. Suppose Bally's common stock price is $20 on October 3, 1999. Would you expect a mandatory conversion to occur? Explain.
   c. Suppose Bally's common stock price is $8 on October 3, 1999. Would you expect a mandatory conversion to occur? Explain.

2. Compare an investment in PRIDES to an investment in Bally's common stock. Explain why the investment in PRIDES involves trading off some of the potential for capital gain in exchange for cash dividends.

3. Specify the cash dividend stream assuming the PRIDES remain outstanding for 4 years and calculate its present value.

4. On a sheet of graph paper, show how the value the holder of a share of PRIDES will realize on October 3, 1999 will depend on the price of Bally's common stock on that date. (*Hint:* Look back at Figure 26-4.)

5. Within which common stock price range on your graph in question 4 will the PRIDES holder get
   a. The value of a share of Bally's common stock.
   b. $11.125 per PRIDES share regardless of Bally's share price.

   c. $11.125 plus 82% of the appreciation in Bally's share price above $13.567.

6. Within which price range for the underlying common stock will a PRIDES holder voluntarily convert it into Bally common stock?

7. Use your answers to questions 4, 5, and 6 to explain how to interpret the voluntary conversion feature as a call option. What is the strike price?

8. Explain why the PRIDES holder effectively owns 0.82 of a call option on Bally common stock with a strike price of $13.567 per underlying share. Who has the other 0.18 of the call option?

9. Explain how a share of PRIDES can be interpreted as a combination of a share of Bally's common stock *plus* a stream of cash dividends paying $0.2225 per quarter for 4 years *minus* the difference between two 4-year call options, one with a strike price of $11.125 and the other with a strike price of $13.567, and *minus also* 0.18 of a 4-year call option with a strike price of $13.567.

10. Value each of the components in question 9 as of October 3, 1995, the date the PRIDES were issued.

11. a. Do you think the PRIDES were overpriced or underpriced? Explain your reasons.
    b. What factor(s) might account for any overpricing or underpricing you found?

FIGURE 26-10
Summary of terms for Bally's PRIDES.

Securities:	Preferred Redeemable Increased Dividend Equity Securities (PRIDES), a form of convertible preferred stock.
Issue Date:	October 3, 1995
Number of Shares:	13,500,000
Price per Share:	$11.125
Dividends:	Dividends are payable quarterly in arrears at the rate of $0.2225 per share. Dividends are cumulative.
Conversion:	
Mandatory:	On October 3, 1999, each share of PRIDES not previously redeemed or converted will be mandatorily converted into one share of Bally's common stock plus the right to receive in cash all accrued but unpaid dividends.
Optional:	Unless previously redeemed (or mandatorily converted), each share of PRIDES is convertible at any time at the option of the holder into 0.82 share of Bally's common stock.
Optional Redemption:	Bally may not redeem shares of PRIDES prior to October 3, 1998. At any time after October 3, 1998 and prior to the mandatory conversion date, each share of PRIDES is redeemable at Bally's option. Upon any such redemption, each holder will receive for each share of PRIDES the *number* of Bally common shares equal to (1) the call price plus all accrued and unpaid dividends divided by (2) the current market price of Bally's common stock. However, this *number* can never be less than 0.82. The call price varies according to the following schedule:

Period	Call Price	Period	Call Price
10/3/98–1/2/99	$11.348	7/3/99–9/2/99	$11.181
1/3/99–4/2/99	11.292	9/3/99–10/3/99	11.125
4/3/99–7/2/99	11.237		

PRIDES holders may convert PRIDES that are called for redemption on or before the redemption date.

Source: Bally Entertainment Corporation, *Prospectus for 13,500,000 Shares of 8% PRIDES Convertible Preferred Stock* (September 28, 1995).

BIBLIOGRAPHY

Arak, Marcelle, Arturo Estrella, Laurie Goodman, and Andrew Silver. "Interest Rate Swaps: An Alternative Explanation," *Financial Management*, 1988, 17(2):12–18.

Bell, David E., and William S. Krasker. "Estimating Hedge Ratios," *Financial Management*, 1986, 15(2):34–39.

Black, Fischer. "Fact and Fantasy in the Use of Options and Corporate Liabilities," *Financial Analysts Journal,* 1975, 31(July-August):36–41, 61–72.

Black, Fischer, and Myron Scholes. "The Pricing of Options and Corporate Liabilities," *Journal of Political Economy*, 1973, 81(May/June):637–654.

Brown, Keith C., and Donald J. Smith. "Default Risk and Innovations in the Design of Interest Rate Swaps," *Financial Management*, 1993, 22(2):94–105.

Chang, Jack S. K., and Soushan Wu. "On Hedging Jump Risks in the Foreign Exchange and Stock Markets," *Financial Management*, 1994, 23(1):15.

Emery, Douglas R., and John D. Finnerty, "Using a PERCS-for-Common Exchange Offer to Reduce the Costs of a Dividend Cut," *Journal of Applied Corporate Finance*, 1995, 7(4):77–89.

Grant, Dwight. "Rolling the Hedge Forward: An Extension," *Financial Management*, 1984, 13(4):26–28.

Howe, John S., and Peihwang Wei. "The Valuation Effects of Warrant Extensions," *Journal of Finance*, 1993, 48(1): 305–314.

Hunter, William C., and Stephen G. Timme. "A Stochastic Dominance Approach to Evaluating Foreign Exchange Hedging Strategies," *Financial Management*, 1992, 21(3):104–112.

Koppenhaver, G. D. "Bank Funding Risks, Risk Aversion, and the Choice of Futures Hedging Instrument," *Journal of Finance*, 1985, 40(1):241–255.

Kumar, Raman, Atulya Sarin, and Kuldeep Shastri. "The Behavior of Option Price Around Large Block Transactions in the Underlying Security," *Journal of Finance*, 1992, 47(3): 879–890.

Lauterbach, Beni, and Paul Schultz. "Pricing Warrants: An Empirical Study of the Black-Scholes Model and Its Alternatives," *Journal of Finance*, 1990, 45(4):1181–1209.

Maldonado, Rita, and Anthony Saunders. "Foreign Exchange Futures and the Law of One Price," *Financial Management*, 1983, 12(1):19–23.

McCabe, George M., and Charles T. Franckle. "The Effectiveness of Rolling the Hedge Forward in the Treasury Bill Futures Market," *Financial Management*, 1983, 12(2):21–29.

Merton, Robert C. "Theory of Rational Option Pricing," *Bell Journal of Economics and Management Science*, 1973, 4(Spring):141–183.

Nance, Deana R., Clifford W. Smith, Jr., and Charles W. Smithson. "On the Determinants of Corporate Hedging," *Journal of Finance*, 1993, 48(1):267–284.

Rendleman, Richard J., Jr., and Brit J. Bartter. "Two-State Option Pricing," *Journal of Finance*, 1979, 34(5):1093–1110.

Smithson, Charles W. *Managing Financial Risk: 1995 Yearbook.* New York: CIBC Wood Gundy, 1995.

Smithson, Charles W., Clifford W. Smith, Jr., and D. Sykes Wilford. *Managing Financial Risk: A Guide to Derivative Products, Financial Engineering, and Value Maximization.* Burr Ridge, Ill: Irwin, 1995.

Sprenkle, Case. "Warrant Prices as Indications of Expectations," *Yale Economic Essays*, 1961, 1:179–232.

Titman, Sheridan. "Interest Rate Swaps and Corporate Financing Choices," *Journal of Finance*, 1992, 47(4):1503–1516.

Part VII

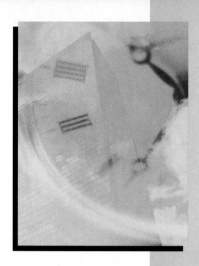

Part VII draws together concepts and techniques we have developed thus far throughout the book. We will discuss three special topics: bankruptcy, mergers and acquisitions, and multinational corporate finance. Each topic involves important issues related to the principles of finance, valuation, capital budgeting, capital structure, financial planning, and long-term financing.

Bankruptcy is part of a firm's natural life cycle. As we have said many times, firms operate in competitive markets. In the face of intense competition, some firms succeed and others fail. Before actually failing, poor performers exhibit signs of *financial distress*. Financial distress occurs when the firm is in danger of not being able to pay its debts as they come due. Often a *financial restructuring*, either privately or in a formal bankruptcy, is required to resolve this condition. If the distress cannot be resolved, then the firm must be *liquidated*.

Growth through acquisition is also an important part of virtually every major firm's development. One firm's acquisition of another is a capital budgeting decision. The basic techniques of *DCF analysis* apply. One firm should acquire another only if doing so creates value—that is, only if it is a positive-NPV investment for the acquiring firm's shareholders. But an acquisition is more complex than a typical capital budgeting project. It involves special legal, tax, and accounting issues. We will show you how to apply DCF analysis, as well as some other useful techniques that allow for these complexities, to determine whether a proposed acquisition is a positive-NPV investment. We will also draw on the techniques we developed in Part IV to illustrate the handling of situations where there is an investment-financing interaction.

Our final chapter concerns multinational corporate finance. Firms with significant foreign operations must consider the special opportunities and risks—particularly the foreign exchange risk—that go along with multinational operations. We will show you how to apply the techniques developed in Parts III and VI to evaluate international investment and financing opportunities. We will also explain how firms use foreign exchange derivatives, which are similar to the other derivatives we discussed in Part VI, to hedge their foreign exchange risk.

BANKRUPTCY, REORGANIZATION, AND LIQUIDATION

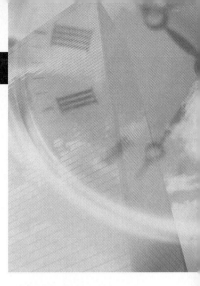

When a firm borrows money, it enters into a contract to pay interest and repay principal in a timely manner. When the firm does not generate enough cash to pay its debt, lenders take steps to make the borrower meet its obligations. If the firm finds it cannot correct the situation, then it tries to renegotiate the terms of the loan. And if that proves impossible, the firm may have no choice but to file for bankruptcy.

The term *bankruptcy* has its origin in medieval Italy. When a merchant did not pay his debts, the lenders would destroy his trading bench. The word *bankruptcy* comes from the Italian term for "broken bench," *banca rotta*.

This chapter describes the bankruptcy process in the United States and, in the last section, abroad. Bankruptcy law offers two ways to resolve financial distress: reorganization and liquidation. **Reorganization** creates a plan to restructure the debtor's business and restore its financial health. **Liquidation** is a more extreme solution. Under liquidation, the debtor stops operating the business, its assets are sold, and the proceeds are used to pay creditors.

We will discuss both forms of bankruptcy, but we will emphasize reorganization, because U.S. bankruptcy law favors reorganization. However, the bankruptcy laws of most other countries favor liquidation, as we will see toward the end of the chapter.

O B J E C T I V E S

After studying this chapter, you should be able to

1. Explain the main causes of corporate financial distress.

2. Describe the difference between reorganization and liquidation under the bankruptcy code.

3. Calculate the *Z*-score for a firm, using the information contained in its financial statements.

4. Describe the difference between reorganization outside bankruptcy and reorganization in bankruptcy.

5. Explain how a "prepackaged bankruptcy" differs from a more traditional reorganization.

BANKRUPTCY AND THE PRINCIPLES OF FINANCE

◆ *Self-Interested Behavior*: When involved in a reorganization, look for opportunities to increase the value of what you recover. The other parties will do the same!

◆ *Two-Sided Transactions*: Increasing your recovery comes at the expense of what some other party to the reorganization will recover.

◆ *Valuable Ideas*: Look for opportunities to redesign securities or other features of a plan of reorganization to enhance value.

◆ *Options*: Use the option to default only when it is beneficial to do so.

◆ *Risk-Return Trade-Off*: Obtaining debtholder consents to modify the terms of a bond indenture requires compensation for the added risk they face.

◆ *Capital Market Efficiency*: Value a security on the basis of the price at which it would trade in an active market.

◆ *Time Value of Money*: Use discounted cash flow analysis to determine whether reorganization is preferable to liquidation and to compare alternative plans of reorganization.

TRANS WORLD AIRLINES'S FINANCIAL DISTRESS

Trans World Airlines (TWA) emerged from bankruptcy in November 1993. Despite its reorganization, TWA was unable to regain its financial footing or take advantage of the mild recovery in the airline industry. During 1994, TWA lost $1 million a day. Too much debt and intense competition from stronger rivals eventually pushed TWA into another financial crisis.

In May 1995, TWA announced that it was considering a prepackaged bankruptcy. Under the proposed reorganization plan, TWA's creditors would forgive $500 million of debt. In return, their equity ownership percentage would increase to about 70% from 55%. As a result, interest expense would decrease by $50 million per year.

TWA's creditors appeared to support the plan, although a formal vote would not occur until the end of June. A prepackaged plan might enable TWA to reorganize its finances in as little as two months. Even so, TWA's managers were concerned about the risks of a Chapter 22 bankruptcy. (The second bankruptcy filing, like the first, would occur under Chapter 11 of the U.S. bankruptcy code, but bankruptcy specialists refer to the *second* filing as a "Chapter 22" bankruptcy.) Bankruptcy carries with it a stigma. Would travel agents and passengers avoid booking trips on a financially shaky airline? However, reorganizing outside bankruptcy could prove difficult, because some of the creditors might refuse to go along.

As you read this chapter, think about TWA's dilemma. At the end of the chapter, we will tell you what TWA decided to do.

27.1 CORPORATE FINANCIAL DISTRESS AND ITS CONSEQUENCES

Recent experience has taught us an important lesson: Even very large firms can fail. Recent experience has also highlighted the risk in leveraged buyouts. In a *leveraged buyout* investors acquire a firm largely by using borrowed money.[1] Leveraged buyouts, which became popular in the 1980s, offered equity investors the opportunity to earn exceptionally high returns. But under the Principle of Risk-Return Trade-Off, leveraged buyouts also had an exceptionally high risk of financial distress. This became evident in the 1990s, when many of these firms began to fail because of their crushing debt loads.

Corporate Financial Distress in the 1990s

The number of business failures accelerated in 1990–1992 (Figure 27-1). Business failures rose by 21% in 1990, by 45% in 1991, and by 10% in 1992. The aggregate liabilities of firms entering bankruptcy increased by 33% in 1990 to $56 billion and by 73% in 1991 to $96.8 billion. Both the number and the aggregate liabilities of firms entering bankruptcy have fallen since 1992, although the number of firms entering remains high. As the number and size of bankruptcies grew, bankruptcy came to be regarded as a more acceptable strategy for dealing with financial distress.

Not only has the number of bankruptcies increased sharply, but unprecedented numbers of very large firms have failed. Table 27-1 lists the 25 largest U.S. bankruptcies involving non-bank firms through the end of December 1994. All but one (Penn Central) occurred since 1982, and 17 took place since the beginning of 1990. Several of these bankruptcies, including those of Federated Department Stores, R.H. Macy, Allied Stores, and Southland, followed on the heels of a leveraged buyout.

This experience was not limited to the United States. Olympia & York (the fourth-largest bankruptcy in Table 27-1) is headquartered in Toronto, and Maxwell Communication (sixth largest) is based in London. Both had extensive operations in the United States and filed for bankruptcy court protection there.

Four Aspects of Financial Distress

A firm is in **financial distress** when it is having significant trouble paying its debts as they come due. A variety of terms are used to describe a financially distressed firm. Four of the more widely used terms are *bankrupt, in default, failed,* and *insolvent.* They have different shades of meaning.

A firm is *bankrupt* when it has filed a petition for relief from its creditors under the bankruptcy code, or when it has consented to a filing by its creditors. The filing signifies either that the firm has not paid debts that have come due or that it will become unable to pay them within the foreseeable future.

A firm is *in default* when it violates one of the terms of a loan agreement or bond indenture. It is useful to distinguish between technical defaults and payment defaults. A technical default occurs when the debtor violates a loan covenant. Technical defaults rarely lead to bankruptcy. They are usually cured through negotiation with creditors. A payment default occurs when the firm misses a scheduled interest payment or principal repayment. If there is a grace period, the default actually occurs after it has expired (usually 30 days for interest payments for publicly traded bonds). A payment default is generally more serious than a technical default. However, even when a firm is in default, it is not necessarily bankrupt. It can continue to operate while it tries to negotiate an out-of-court restructuring with its creditors.

---

[1] Chapter 28 discusses leveraged buyouts in greater detail.

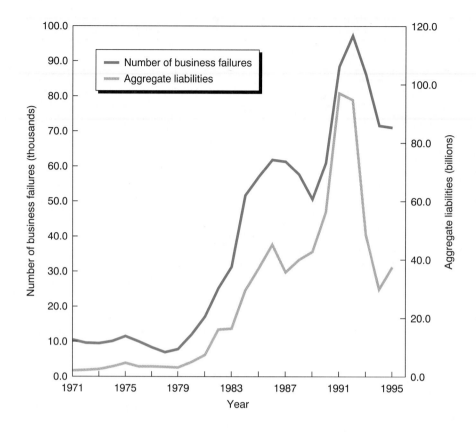

FIGURE 27-1
Number of business failures and aggregate liabilities of firms entering bankruptcy, 1971–1995.
Source: *Business Failure Record* (New York: Dun & Bradstreet, 1996).

A firm is said to have *failed* if it meets one of the criteria that Dun & Bradstreet, a leading provider of data about distressed firms, has adopted in classifying unsuccessful firms as business failures. According to Dun & Bradstreet, business failures include

> …businesses that cease operation following assignment or bankruptcy; those that cease with loss to creditors after such actions as execution, foreclosure, or attachment; those that voluntarily withdraw leaving unpaid obligations, or have been involved in court actions such as receivership, reorganization, or arrangement; and those that voluntarily compromise with creditors.[2]

A firm is *insolvent* when it is unable to pay its debts. It is useful to distinguish between technical insolvency and bankruptcy insolvency. Technical insolvency occurs because of a lack of cash. Bankruptcy insolvency occurs when the firm's total liabilities exceed the fair market value of its total assets. The firm's true net worth is negative, which means that the value of its assets is insufficient to pay its debts. Technical insolvency may be a temporary condition. Bankruptcy insolvency usually indicates a more serious distressed condition.

Causes of Financial Distress

Financial distress results from a deterioration in a firm's business. There can be many causes. Poor management, unwise expansion, intense competition, too much debt, massive litigation, and unfavorable contracts are just a few of the possible causes.

Managerial incompetence is the leading cause of corporate financial distress. Table 27-2 reports the results of two Dun & Bradstreet surveys. In the 1980 survey, lack of management experience, unbalanced experience, or outright management incompetence caused

---

[2] *Business Failure Record* (New York: Dun & Bradstreet, 1992).

RANK	COMPANY	BANKRUPTCY DATE	ASSETS ($ MILLIONS)
1	Texaco, Inc.	04/12/87	35,892
2	Federated Dept. Stores	01/15/90	7,913
3	Continental Airlines Hldgs.	12/03/90	7,656
4	Olympia & York Devel. Ltd.	05/14/92	7,023
5	Penn Central	06/21/70	6,851
6	Maxwell Communication Corp.	12/16/91	6,352
7	LTV Corp.	07/17/86	6,307
8	Columbia Gas System, Inc.	07/31/91	6,196
9	Macy (R.H.) & Co., Inc.	01/27/92	4,812
10	Eastern Air Lines, Inc.	03/09/89	4,037
11	Allied Stores Corp.	01/15/90	3,502
12	Walter Industries, Inc.	12/27/89	3,462
13	Southland Corp.	10/24/90	3,439
14	Trans World Airlines, Inc.	01/31/92	3,277
15	Public Service Co. of New Hampshire	01/28/88	2,639
16	Pan Am Corp.	01/08/91	2,441
17	Farley, Inc.	09/24/91	2,408
18	Manville Corp.	08/26/82	2,298
19	JWP, Inc.	12/21/93	2,281
20	E-II Holdings, Inc.	07/15/92	2,141
21	Ames Department Stores	04/25/90	2,130
22	Carter Hawley Hale Stores	02/11/91	2,045
23	Circle K Corp., The	05/15/90	2,045
24	Continental Info. Systems	01/13/89	1,926
25	NVR L.P.	04/06/92	1,901

TABLE 27-1

Twenty-five largest U.S. bankruptcies of nonbank firms.[a]

[a] Excluding firms whose primary businesses are banking, insurance, brokerage, or similar financial products.
Source: The 1995 Bankruptcy Yearbook and Almanac (Boston, Mass.: New Generation Research, 1995), p. 62.

1980			1992/1993		
Cause	Percent of Failures	Cumulative Percentage	Cause	Percent of Failures	Cumulative Percentage
Lack of or unbalanced management experience	50%	50%	Economic Factors		
			Industry weakness	21%	21%
			Insufficient profits	11	32
Management incompetence	44	94	Inadequate sales	2	34
			Not competitive	1	35
Neglect	1	95	Other	1	36
Fraud	4	99	Experience Causes	1	37
			Finance Causes		
Other	1	100	Burdensome debt	4	41
			Heavy operating costs	40	81
			Insufficient capital	3	84
			Neglect	4	88
			Disaster	6	94
			Strategy	1	95
			Fraud	4	99
			Other	1	100

TABLE 27-2

Causes of business failure.

Source: Business Failure Record (New York: Dun & Bradstreet, 1980 and 1992/1993).

TABLE 27-3
Age of failed businesses.

| Age (years) | PROPORTION OF TOTAL FAILURES | | | | | |
| | 1980 | | 1990 | | 1993 | |
	Percent	Cumulative	Percent	Cumulative	Percent	Cumulative
1 or less	0.9%	0.9%	9.0%	9.0%	7.1%	7.1%
2	9.6	10.5	11.2	20.2	8.5	15.6
3	15.3	25.8	11.2	31.4	8.8	24.4
4	15.4	41.2	10.0	41.4	7.9	32.3
5	12.4	53.6	8.4	49.8	7.4	39.7
6	8.9	62.5	7.2	57.0	6.5	46.2
7	6.3	68.8	5.3	62.3	5.9	52.1
8	5.2	74.0	4.5	66.8	5.5	57.6
9	4.3	78.3	3.8	70.6	5.0	62.6
10	3.4	81.7	3.5	74.1	4.3	66.9
over 10	18.3	100.0	25.9	100.0	33.1	100.0
Number of failures	11,742		60,747		86,133	

Source: Business Failure Record (New York: Dun & Bradstreet, 1980, 1990, and 1993/1994).

94% of business failures. The 1992/1993 survey used a different set of categories. Nevertheless, managerial incompetence is probably responsible for most of the failures charged to "industry weakness," "insufficient profits," or "finance causes," which total 79%.

EXTERNAL FACTORS   Factors external to the firm can also play a role. For example, intense competition within the U.S. airline industry has made it difficult for any airline, regardless of management quality, to make money. The reduced availability of bank credit from 1990 to 1992 also complicated the picture. Nevertheless, how quickly and effectively management responds to changing conditions in the product and financial markets determines to a great extent which firms survive and which do not.

AGE OF THE FIRM   Younger firms are more likely to fail than older firms. Younger firms have less experience. They also tend to be smaller and less well capitalized than older firms in the same industry. Table 27-3 shows the breakdown of business failures according to the age of the firm at the time of the bankruptcy filing. Approximately half of the businesses that failed in 1980 and 1990 were of firms no more than five years old. That percentage was 40% in 1993. The likelihood of failure increases in years two and three and falls after that.

Self-Check Questions

1. What is the main difference between reorganization and liquidation under the bankruptcy code?

2. What happened to the number and aggregate size of business failures in the period 1990–1992?

3. What is financial distress? What aspects of financial distress are involved when a firm is bankrupt? in default? failed? insolvent?

4. What are the main causes of financial distress? To what extent are factors internal to the firm responsible? What about factors external to it?

5. How does the likelihood of financial distress vary with the age of the firm? For which years is the likelihood of failure greatest?

27.2 AN HISTORICAL PERSPECTIVE

Until modern times, the legal system generally favored creditors and treated a financially distressed debtor quite harshly. The first official laws covering bankruptcy were adopted in England in 1542 under Henry VIII. The law treated a bankrupt individual as a criminal. Punishments ranged from imprisonment in debtors' prison to the death penalty!

Origins of U.S. Bankruptcy Law

In the United States, three federal bankruptcy laws were adopted during the nineteenth century. Each was enacted in response to some sort of financial panic and was repealed after the panic ended. These laws were designed to help creditors recover as much of their loans as possible.

Current U.S. bankruptcy law favors reorganizing the financially distressed debtor. The Bankruptcy Act of 1898 was the first U.S. bankruptcy law to give firms in distress the option of being protected from their creditors. The firm could be placed in what is called an *equity receivership* and reorganized under court supervision. Otherwise it had to be liquidated. The equity receivership structure proved to be costly and ineffective. There was no provision for an independent, objective review of the plan of reorganization, as there is today. In keeping with the Principle of Self-Interested Behavior, a debtor and a friendly creditor would often initiate an equity receivership and push through a plan that favored that creditor over the others. Debtors could even offer cash payoffs to powerful dissenters to secure their consent to the proposed plan!

Evolution of Current U.S. Bankruptcy Law

The Great Depression produced a large number of bankruptcies and led to the Chandler Act of 1938. This law substantially improved the procedures for reorganizing distressed firms. It required the court to hold hearings on a proposed plan, and it provided greater protection for creditors.

The bankruptcy rules were overhauled again with passage of the Bankruptcy Reform Act of 1978. The new law replaced the old Chapters X and XI with a new Chapter 11. It established a bankruptcy court system and substantially improved bankruptcy procedures. It made it easier, quicker, and less costly for public firms to seek relief from their creditors while they try to reorganize. Under Chapter 11, the debtor usually continues to operate its business with existing management, except when the bankruptcy court determines that a disinterested trustee should be appointed. This may be for cause[3] or because it would be in the best interests of the creditors or shareholders.

Recent Developments

In 1991 Congress enacted a new provision of the Bankruptcy Code, entitled Chapter 10. This new section allows small and medium-sized businesses to reorganize under a "fast-track Chapter 11" procedure intended to reduce the delay and expense of a Chapter 11 reorganization.

Three years later, Congress enacted the Bankruptcy Reform Act of 1994. This law contains provisions designed to expedite the bankruptcy process. However, U.S. bankruptcy law continues to draw criticism. Bankruptcy is a slow and expensive process. The 1994 act created a National Bankruptcy Commission to investigate further changes in bankruptcy law.

---

[3] Cause includes fraud, dishonesty, incompetence, and gross mismanagement.

27.3 EARLY DETECTION OF FINANCIAL DISTRESS

As a firm's financial condition worsens, it begins to show signs of financial distress. Losses begin to occur. Interest coverage worsens. The firm's operations start to absorb more cash than they generate. Net working capital may turn negative. The debt level tends to rise relative to cash flow. The debt-to-equity ratio also tends to increase. This deterioration reveals itself in a worsening of the firm's key financial ratios. Thus changes in a firm's financial ratios can be used to predict the onset of financial distress.

Multiple Discriminant Analysis

Almost without exception, early studies that used financial ratios to predict corporate bankruptcy tried to pick a single financial ratio that worked best. But it seems unlikely that any single financial ratio will work best for all industries and in all situations.

Multiple discriminant analysis (MDA) is a more appropriate technique for predicting corporate bankruptcy, because it uses more than one variable. MDA places a firm into one of two or more groups based upon the firm's individual characteristics. In bankruptcy prediction, MDA tries to distinguish between two groups, bankrupt and nonbankrupt firms.

MDA is applied in the following manner. A set of financial ratios are calculated for groups of bankrupt and nonbankrupt firms. MDA then determines the *discriminant function* that best distinguishes between the groups. The discriminant function is of the form $Z = V_1X_1 + V_2X_2 + \cdots + V_nX_n$. The discriminant function transforms the individual financial ratios into a single discriminant score, or Z-score. The Z-score is then used to classify the firm as "bankrupt" or "nonbankrupt." In this equation, V_1, V_2, and so on are discriminant coefficients, or weights, and X_1, X_2, and so on are the financial ratios. The MDA technique determines the set of discriminant coefficients, V_i, that maximizes the percentage of firms that are correctly classified.

Figure 27-2 shows a two-variable analysis. Measures of profitability and liquidity are plotted for a sample of nonbankrupt (•) and bankrupt (○) firms. MDA selects the weights in such a way as to position the line where it distinguishes best between bankrupt and nonbankrupt firms. The discriminant function is used to calculate a Z-score for a firm in order to assign it to one of the two groups. This procedure effectively compares the financial profile of an individual firm to the financial profiles of the groups of bankrupt and nonbankrupt firms.[4]

Altman's Z-Score Model

Edward Altman developed a Z-score model based on five financial ratios. Altman's Z-score model[5] is

$$Z = 0.012X_1 + 0.014X_2 + 0.033X_3 + 0.006X_4 + 0.999X_5 \tag{27.1}$$

---

[4] The Z-score model can also be used to predict the likelihood that a reorganized debtor will fail if it is capitalized in a particular manner. It is thus a potentially useful tool in assessing the feasibility of a proposed plan of reorganization.

[5] Values for the variables X_1 through X_4 should be entered as percentage values. For example, if a firm has a ratio of net working capital to total assets (X_1) of 10%, then X_1 should be entered as 10.0%, not 0.10. Variable X_5 (sales to total assets) should be entered as a ratio. For example, a sales-to-total-assets ratio of 200% should be entered as 2.0.

Operating margin (*M*)

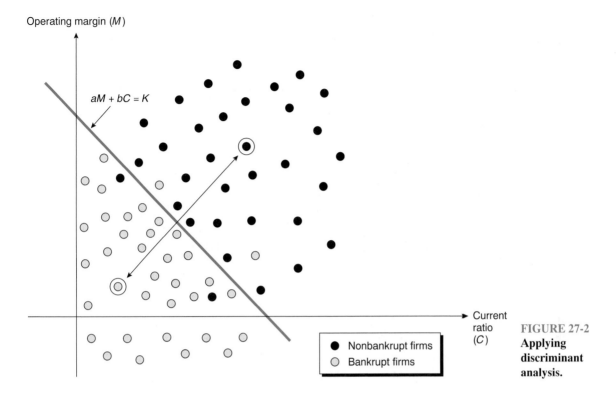

FIGURE 27-2
Applying discriminant analysis.

where X_1 = net working capital/total assets
X_2 = retained earnings/total assets
X_3 = (earnings before interest and taxes)/total assets
X_4 = market value of equity/book value of total liabilities
X_5 = sales/total assets
Z = Z-score.

The greater a firm's Z-score, the lower its risk of going bankrupt.

Applying the Z-score Model

Suppose that Plexus, a manufacturer of luxury cars, has the following financial ratios:

$$X_1 = 15\% \qquad X_2 = 30\% \qquad X_3 = 17\% \qquad X_4 = 225\% \qquad X_5 = 1.5$$

Substituting into the Z-score model (Equation 27.1) gives

$$Z = 0.012(15) + 0.014(30) + 0.033(17) + 0.006(225) + 0.999(1.5) = 4.01$$

In order to interpret this Z-score, we need to examine the Z-scores of Altman's samples of bankrupt and nonbankrupt firms. He found that $Z = 2.675$ discriminated best between bankrupt and nonbankrupt firms (in the sense that it minimized the number of misclassifications). However, he also found that there was a zone of uncertainty between $Z = 1.81$ and $Z = 2.99$ within which errors in classification would occur for firms within 1 year prior to bankruptcy. Thus the range of Z values can be divided into three intervals:

SCORE	PREDICTION
$Z > 2.99$	Firm will not fail within 1 year.
$1.81 \leq Z \leq 2.99$	Gray area within which it is difficult to discriminate effectively.
$Z < 1.81$	Firm will fail within 1 year.

The Z-score model predicts that Plexus will not fail within the next year. ■

Classification Accuracy of the Z-Score Model

Studies have found that Equation (27.1) is not as accurate when it is used to predict bankruptcy in more recent time periods. The mix of variables and the coefficient values tend to change over time. We offer two practical suggestions. Anyone who uses a Z-score model should re-estimate the discriminant function regularly to ensure that it is up to date. Second, a Z-score model is likely to be most reliable when it is applied to firms within a particular industry. For example, a bankruptcy prediction model could be estimated for the oil and gas industry.

Self-Check Questions

1. What is MDA?
2. What does a firm's Z-score measure? How reliable is it?
3. According to Altman's original model, what would a Z-score of 1.50 indicate? a Z-score of 4.50? a Z-score of 2.50?
4. Why is it important to re-estimate the discriminant function regularly?

27.4 REORGANIZATION OUTSIDE BANKRUPTCY

Bankruptcy is time-consuming and expensive. For these reasons, financially distressed firms usually try to reorganize outside bankruptcy before filing for bankruptcy. A firm can restructure its liabilities outside bankruptcy in one of three ways. It can (1) exchange new securities for existing securities, (2) solicit securityholders' consent to modify the terms of existing securities, or (3) repurchase existing securities for cash.

Each technique requires the firm to persuade its securityholders to alter the terms of their investment in the firm. The more complex the debtor's structure is, the less likely out-of-court restructurings are to work. When there are several layers of debt—as in Revco, Public Service of New Hampshire, and LTV Corp., to name just a few—there are several competing constituencies jockeying for position. As we discussed in Chapter 9, financial distress intensifies agent incentives, and some stakeholders may form claimant coalitions. However, recall that even such coalitions are not always stable. And in any case, an out-of-court settlement must satisfy all of the competing stakeholders. This becomes more difficult to achieve when the debtor's capital structure is very complex.

Exchange Offers

Firms that need to restructure usually do not have enough cash to repurchase their outstanding debt securities. They therefore often make an exchange offer. An **exchange offer** trades new securities of the firm for some of its outstanding securities. These new securities might consist of common stock, preferred stock, or new debt securities with a lower interest rate or a longer amortization schedule. These transactions *deleverage* the firm by reducing its debt ratio (L). The idea is to reduce the debt burden to one that the firm will be able to bear.

Many firms conducted exchange offers in the 1990s to deal with a ticking time bomb in their capital structures. Two examples are interest-rate-reset notes[6] and pay-in-kind debentures.[7] If the interest rate reset feature or requirement to pay debt service in cash will substantially increase the firm's debt service requirements, then it may be necessary to eliminate a substantial part of the debt to avert a financial crisis.

<table>
<tr><td>

RJR Nabisco's 1989 leveraged buyout created an issue of convertible debentures and an issue of exchangeable debentures. Each issue had both a pay-in-kind feature and an interest-rate-reset feature. By mid-1990, RJR Nabisco had $20 billion of debt outstanding, including nearly $6.0 billion of pay-in-kind interest-rate-reset securities. In July 1990, the interest rate on the convertible debentures reset to $17\frac{3}{8}\%$, and the interest rate on the exchangeable debentures reset to 17%.

RJR Nabisco immediately took steps to reduce its debt. It offered to exchange $333 of cash and $667 stated value of convertible preferred stock for each convertible debenture and for each exchangeable debenture. It also repurchased other debt for cash. The deleveraging program retired $6.9 billion of debt. These steps eventually helped RJR Nabisco regain an investment-grade rating. ■

</td><td>

RJR Nabisco's Exchange Offer

EXAMPLE

</td></tr>
</table>

Amending the Terms of Outstanding Securities

A firm may try to amend its indenture if it can no longer satisfy some of the terms. For example, because of losses, a firm might no longer satisfy a covenant to maintain a specified minimum net worth. The firm could solicit the written consent of the holders of the debt securities to relax, or perhaps eliminate, the restrictive covenant. Under the Principle of Risk-Return Trade-Off, the firm would have to pay debtholders for their consents. The firm might pay cash or increase the interest rate on the debt.

Repurchasing Securities for Cash

Repurchases for cash by a financially troubled firm are unusual. Such a firm usually does not have enough cash on hand and would probably have trouble arranging credit. Yet some voluntary debt reductions have taken the form of cash repurchases of outstanding debt. For example, we mentioned RJR Nabisco's 1990 recapitalization program. In addition to the exchange offers, RJR Nabisco bought back $1.724 billion principal amount of debentures for $1.504 billion cash. RJR paid a slight premium over their market value. The premium offered debtholders an incentive to sell their debentures.

Creating Incentives to Participate

A financially distressed firm can create incentives—either positive or negative—to encourage bondholders to agree to an out-of-court restructuring. As a positive incentive, the firm can offer to exchange, for the outstanding securities, new securities with a higher interest rate, shorter maturity, more senior ranking (the new securities possibly being secured), or stronger covenants. It can also offer a cash incentive.

---

[6] Interest-rate-reset notes provide for a resetting of the interest rate on a specified date, usually 2 or 3 years after issuance. The interest rate must be reset to an interest rate that will make the securities worth 101% of their principal amount. If the reset issue is large relative to the firm's capitalization, the interest rate reset could itself cause the firm's financial condition to deteriorate. It could even be enough to push the firm "over the edge."

[7] Pay-in-kind debentures pay interest in the form of additional notes for some specified period. Interest payment obligations are thus deferred (to a period when the issuer expects to be better able to service its debt). But if the improvement in operating cash flow does not occur, the initial cash-pay date can threaten serious financial distress.

As a negative incentive (coercion), a firm might structure the exchange offer such that nonexchanging holders will find their securities contractually or structurally subordinated to the new securities if the exchange offer succeeds. Or the firm might combine a consent solicitation with an exchange offer: Bondholders will receive the new securities only if enough of them agreed to modify the covenants of the old bonds. The modification reduces the covenant protection for bondholders who refuse to exchange. A firm might also threaten to file for bankruptcy if the exchange offer fails.

THE HOLDOUT PROBLEM   *Holdouts* are holders of outstanding securities who refuse to exchange their securities for new ones. In keeping with the Principle of Self-Interested Behavior, they hope to get a better deal. Holdouts can usually benefit, because the firm's ability to pay the holdouts in full improves if the exchange offer succeeds. Holdouts benefit at the expense of exchanging bondholders. The right to hold out is yet another hidden option.

Firms employ a variety of techniques to discourage holdouts. They use the positive and negative incentives we just discussed. Many have also used a prepackaged bankruptcy. This strategy is discussed later in the chapter. It is often effective in dealing with the holdout problem, because *all* holders of the outstanding securities are bound by the terms of the plan once the bankruptcy court confirms it.

Self-Check Questions

1. How can a firm restructure its liabilities outside of bankruptcy?

2. How can a firm use an exchange offer to restructure its liabilities? Why did RJR Nabisco feel it necessary to do this in 1990?

3. Why does amending restrictive covenants involve making a payment to the debtholders?

4. What are holdouts, and why are they a problem when a firm is trying to restructure its liabilities? How can a firm discourage holdouts?

27.5 REORGANIZATION IN BANKRUPTCY

As we have said, the U.S. Bankruptcy Code offers two means of dealing with corporate financial distress: reorganization and liquidation. In a reorganization (under Chapter 11 of the bankruptcy code), a plan is developed to reorganize the debtor's business and restore its financial health. In a liquidation (under Chapter 7 of the bankruptcy code), the assets of the firm are sold, usually piecemeal, and the cash proceeds are paid to the firm's creditors according to strict rules of priority. For businesses of any significant size, reorganization is more common than liquidation.

Chapter 11 offers a debtor the opportunity to freeze its debts while it attempts to negotiate a reorganization plan with creditors. Reorganization is an administrative procedure. It allows a distressed, but otherwise economically viable, firm to survive as a going concern. The objective of this process is to preserve the going-concern value of the debtor.

Guiding Principle of Chapter 11

The guiding principle of Chapter 11 reorganizations is that a debtor should be given the opportunity to negotiate with its creditors and achieve a consensual plan of reorganization *provided that the going-concern value of the reorganized debtor exceeds its liquidation value.* Even though a firm may not be able to meet its current financial obligations, it may still be able to operate profitably after its debts are restructured. Chapter 11 gives the debtor the opportunity to determine whether restructuring is feasible and in the best interest of its creditors.

Consider a steel manufacturer with just a single steel mill. The scrap value of the mill is well below its book value. The firm owes $100 million, the economy is in a recession, and the firm cannot cover its interest payment obligations. The scrap value of the mill plus the value of the land it occupies would provide a total liquidation value of $30 million. The firm expects that once the economy recovers from the recession, it will be able to earn a competitive return on its steel-making assets. The present value of the expected cash flows is $60 million. The steel manufacturer cannot service $100 million of debt, and the amount of its liabilities exceeds the value of its assets. But liquidation would be wasteful. The going-concern value is more than the liquidation value, so a higher value can be realized through reorganization.■

Reorganization Value Versus Liquidation Value

EXAMPLE

PROTECTION FROM CREDITORS   The reorganization process could be thwarted if creditors were permitted to seize their security or obtain default judgments and have the sheriff auction off the bankrupt firm's assets to pay these default judgments. The debtor's efforts to reorganize would then quickly deteriorate into a free-for-all liquidation as the creditors ripped apart the firm. This unsavory prospect provides the rationale for bankruptcy court protection from creditors.

FILING FOR BANKRUPTCY   In many Chapter 11 cases, the bankruptcy courts have allowed a firm to file for bankruptcy even though the firm was still solvent at the time. Some firms have argued successfully that they faced potential liabilities that could make them insolvent. Examples include Manville Corporation (product liability), Continental Airlines (burdensome labor contracts), A. H. Robins (product liability), and Texaco (adverse legal judgment). In each case, the firm was able to meet its regular cash commitments as they were coming due.[8] A firm does not have to be insolvent to file for bankruptcy. Nevertheless, the vast majority of firms that file for bankruptcy are insolvent.

INVOLUNTARY FILINGS   Most bankruptcy petitions are filed by the debtor. These are called *voluntary filings*. However, the bankruptcy code permits creditors to file an *involuntary petition* against a delinquent debtor.

Debtor in Possession

Table 27-4 describes the Chapter 11 process. The firm commences this process by filing a *petition for relief*. The firm then becomes a **debtor in possession**. It is in possession of the same assets and business it had before the bankruptcy filing. It can continue to operate its business with the same officers and the same board of directors it had before.

The debtor in possession must open a new set of books and open a new bank account. Its prefiling unsecured debts are frozen. It continues to operate its business but must now comply with the rules and regulations of the bankruptcy process. It must obtain bankruptcy court approval for critical decisions, such as sales of assets and new financing.

THE ROLE OF DIRECTORS IN BANKRUPTCY   Under normal circumstances, a firm's board of directors is charged with ensuring that the firm operates in the best interests of shareholders. (This is referred to as their *fiduciary duty*.) But when a firm files for bankruptcy, the board's role changes. In bankruptcy, a director's fiduciary duty shifts to that of a trustee. The

---

[8] However, Texaco claimed that it was unable to post a $10 billion bond required following an adverse court decision in connection with litigation instituted against Texaco by Pennzoil.

TABLE 27-4
**How Chapter 11
works in a successful
reorganization.**

HOW CHAPTER 11 WORKS

Firm Files for Chapter 11 Protection

A firm files for Chapter 11 protection from its creditors either when it is no longer able to pay its debts as they come due or when it anticipates future liabilities that it will not be able to meet. It has usually attempted an out-of-court restructuring but failed to achieve one.

The Chapter 11 Bankruptcy Process

The bankruptcy judge issues an automatic stay.

The firm becomes a *debtor in possession*. The firm operates its business as before the bankruptcy filing except that the bankruptcy court must approve all significant decisions. All debts are frozen. Creditors are precluded from seizing the debtor's property or trying to enforce collection. Lawsuits are suspended.

Different creditor classes form committees.

Generally, the largest seven creditors within each class of creditors are appointed to the committee. Equityholders may also form a single committee or one committee for preferred stockholders and one for common stockholders, if the firm has preferred stock outstanding. The creditors' committee(s) can ask the bankruptcy court to appoint an examiner to investigate possible fraud or mismanagement. They can also petition the bankruptcy court to appoint a trustee to run the firm.

The committees and the debtor negotiate a plan of reorganization.

For the first 120 days after filing for bankruptcy, the firm has the exclusive right to propose a plan of reorganization. Thereafter, unless the bankruptcy court extends the period of exclusivity, any interested party can submit a plan.

Creditors approve the proposed plan of reorganization.

Generally, each class of creditors must approve the plan.[a] A majority of the creditors holding at least two-thirds of the bonds in the class who vote must approve the plan in order for the class to accept it.

The bankruptcy court confirms the plan of reorganization.

The reorganization plan must satisfy the requirements of the bankruptcy code before the bankruptcy court can confirm it.

Reorganized Firm Emerges from Bankruptcy

The reorganized debtor must execute the plan of reorganization. The debtor emerges from Chapter 11 when it has satisfied the conditions in the plan.

[a] The *cramdown* exception is described in the text.

board of directors becomes responsible for conserving the assets of the estate to pay the firm's creditors. The interests of the firm's existing shareholders are secondary, at best. This shift of responsibility often proves difficult for directors. One study found that more than half the directors of bankrupt firms resigned between the bankruptcy filing and plan confirmation.

Automatic Stay

The bankruptcy code imposes an **automatic stay** of any further efforts by creditors to collect their debts or by secured creditors to seize the collateral securing their loans. This is one of the fundamental protections provided debtors by the bankruptcy code. The automatic stay gives the debtor some breathing room. It is broad and very effective. It stops all collection efforts, all foreclosure actions, and all harassment against the debtor. It is "automatic" because it takes effect as soon as the bankruptcy petition is filed. It enables the debtor to hold onto its assets while it strives to put together a plan of reorganization. The automatic stay also relieves the financial pressures that drove the debtor into bankruptcy. In effect, the automatic stay enables a debtor to operate independently of the liability side of its balance sheet.

Debtor-in-Possession Financing

A bankrupt firm often needs additional working capital. To obtain it, the firm arranges **debtor-in-possession financing**. The debtor might seek additional financing from the same entities that financed it prior to the bankruptcy filing. If they refuse, there are lenders that specialize in debtor-in-possession financing. Such debt is treated as a *priority claim*, which gives it a very high priority in the order of claims against the debtor's assets.

Self-Check Questions

1. What is Chapter 11 of the bankruptcy code, and what is its guiding principle?

2. What is a debtor in possession? What is it required to do in bankruptcy?

3. What does an automatic stay accomplish?

Plan of Reorganization

The main objective of the Chapter 11 process is to come up with a **plan of reorganization**. The plan of reorganization is crucial to the firm's survival as a going concern. It contains a business plan for the firm, establishes a new capital structure, shows how the old debts will be paid off, and provides for the distribution of cash, new securities, and other consideration among the firm's creditors and shareholders. The plan must satisfy requirements specified in the bankruptcy code in order for a bankruptcy court to confirm it.

A debtor in possession has the exclusive right to file a plan of reorganization for 120 days following the bankruptcy filing. The debtor has the exclusive right to solicit acceptance of the plan by creditors and equity securityholders within 180 days following the bankruptcy filing. These periods can be extended by the bankruptcy court.

PRIORITY   The liabilities, called *claims*, and equity interests are classified, in order of decreasing priority, as follows:

1. *Administrative expenses* (such as legal, accounting, and trustee fees).

2. *Priority claims*, which consist of
   (a) Unsecured claims arising in the ordinary course of the debtor's business after the bankruptcy filing, which include supplier claims for goods delivered and debtor-in-possession financing.
   (b) Unsecured claims for wages, salaries, sales commissions, and employee benefits earned by an individual within 90 days before the bankruptcy filing, but only to the extent of $2000 per individual.
   (c) Unsecured claims for contributions to employee benefit plans, but only to the extent of $2000 per individual.
   (d) Small unsecured trade claims.
   (e) Unsecured claims by individuals for deposits made before the bankruptcy filing in connection with the future delivery of goods or provision of services by the debtor, but only to the extent of $900 per individual.
   (f) Unsecured claims by governmental entities for income and other taxes.

3. *Secured debt.* The secured creditors are usually organized into separate classes based on (1) the assets securing their claims and (2) the nature of their security interest (for example, first or second mortgage). To the extent that the funds received from, or value attributable to, the collateral is less than the allowed claim, the balance of the claim is treated as an unsecured claim.

4. *Unsecured senior debt.* Sometimes separate classes of unsecured creditors are designated for administrative convenience. Examples include institutional debtholders, public debenture holders, and trade debt.

5. *Subordinated debt.* Such debt is expressly subordinated by its terms to some classes of senior debt. These claimants may be organized into multiple classes, depending on the subordination provisions.

6. *Preferred stock.*

7. *Common stock.*

ABSOLUTE PRIORITY   The **absolute priority doctrine** holds that the assets of the debtor should be distributed among creditors and shareholders according to the hierarchy just listed. A more senior claim must be paid in full before a junior claim is permitted to receive *any* distribution. However, for reasons we will explain later, senior creditors often find it expedient, in practice, to allow a reorganization plan to deviate from absolute priority.

REQUIREMENTS FOR CONFIRMATION   A plan of reorganization must satisfy five basic conditions in order to be eligible for confirmation by the bankruptcy court. Table 27-5 summarizes these requirements.

A plan of reorganization must be **feasible**. The reorganized debtor cannot be insolvent. It must have a positive net worth. Moreover, the plan of reorganization must include a plan of operations, including specifying provisions for the sale of unneeded assets or unwanted businesses, that makes it unlikely that the debtor will return to bankruptcy in the foreseeable future.

Second, the plan cannot *discriminate unfairly* among creditors. Two creditors holding equivalent claims must receive equivalent distributions. In particular, if cash is distributed to a particular class of creditors, all claims that belong to that class should receive a proportionate cash distribution. If two classes of claims have the same priority, then they should receive equivalent distributions, including equivalent distributions of cash.

Third, at least one class of creditors must accept the plan. In a *consensual plan*, all classes of creditors and all classes of shareholders vote to accept the plan. The bankruptcy code provides for a *cramdown procedure*, which enables the bankruptcy court to confirm a plan over the objections of some classes of creditors.

Fourth, the plan of reorganization must satisfy the **fair-and-equitable test**. This test requires that (1) a class of claims votes to accept the plan, or else (2) the class's claims are paid

TABLE 27-5

Summary of the requirements for confirming a plan of reorganization.

SUMMARY OF THE REQUIREMENTS FOR CONFIRMING A PLAN OF REORGANIZATION
1. The plan must be feasible. • The reorganized debtor must have positive net worth. • It is unlikely that the reorganized debtor will wind up back in bankruptcy in the foreseeable future. 2. The plan cannot discriminate unfairly among creditors of equal classes. 3. At least one class of creditors must accept the plan. • Need at least two-thirds approval in amount of allowed claims that vote *and* • Need more than one-half approval in number of allowed claims that vote. 4. The plan must satisfy the fair-and-equitable test. • If an *impaired* class votes against the plan and would receive less than the full amount of its claims under the plan, all junior classes must get nothing under the plan.[a] • If an *unimpaired* class votes against the plan, it is treated as having approved the plan. 5. The plan must satisfy the best-interests-of-creditors test. • If the holder of a claim or interest votes against the plan, the claim holder must receive at least as much under the plan as the holder would receive if the debtor were liquidated.

[a] A class is impaired when it will receive cash and securities that are worth less than the amount of its claims.

in full, or else (3) if the class rejects the plan and is not paid in full, then no class of claims or interests ranking junior to that class can receive anything.[9]

There is nothing to prevent a class from accepting a plan that provides less compensation than it would get if the absolute priority doctrine were applied. However, the next junior class will have to receive fair and equitable treatment (unless it is also willing to accept less) before a succeeding junior class can receive anything. You are probably wondering why a class of creditors might be willing to accept less than full payment and let a junior class receive something. Interest does not accrue on unsecured debt after the debtor files a bankruptcy petition. Suppose a junior class is challenging the reorganization plan. Paying them enough to convince them not to hold up the bankruptcy process can benefit the senior class(es) because of the Time-Value-of-Money Principle. Such a payment is for the hidden option to "make trouble," and is part of the agency costs involved. (See the Seven-Up—Dr. Pepper example and footnote 13 in Chapter 9.)

The fair-and-equitable test is aptly named. Suppose a class of claims would not be repaid in full under a proposed plan. If the claim holders reject the plan, then it seems only fair that if the bankruptcy court is nevertheless going to confirm the plan over their objections, no junior class should receive anything.

Fifth, the plan must satisfy the **best-interests-of-creditors test**. If the holder of a claim or interest votes against the proposed plan, then the holder must receive at least as much as she would have if the debtor were liquidated.

Like the fair-and-equitable test, the best-interests test has a sound basis. If creditors would receive a greater distribution if the debtor were liquidated, then liquidation is in their best interest. On the other hand, suppose the debtor has going-concern value or net operating loss carryforwards that would be lost in liquidation, and as a result the value of the reorganized debtor exceeds its liquidation value. Then reorganization is in the creditors' best interest.

ACCEPTANCE OF A PLAN   A class of claims accepts a proposed plan of reorganization if it is approved by (1) more than one-half of the number of creditors who vote *and* (2) creditors holding at least two-thirds of the amount of claims belonging to that class that vote. A class of equityholders accepts a plan if at least two-thirds of the number of outstanding shares that are voted are cast in favor of the plan. Creditors and shareholders who do not vote are ignored when these tests are applied.

CRAMDOWN   The cramdown procedure permits the bankruptcy court to confirm a proposed plan over the objections of one or more classes of creditors. The plan must pass the following test. If a class rejects the plan, then (1) the plan must provide the holders with property the value of which is at least equal to the allowed amount of their claims or else (2) no junior class receives anything.[10]

Cramdown

EXAMPLE

Olympic Computer Company is preparing a plan of reorganization. Table 27-6 shows Olympic Computer's latest balance sheet. The firm has 1000 shares of preferred stock with a par value of $100 per share and a liquidation value of $110 per share. It has 1000 shares of common stock with no par value. It also has $3 million of bank debt (secured by accounts receivable), $2 million of mortgage debt (secured by machinery, equipment, and real estate), and $3 million of subordinated debt (expressly subordinated to the bank debt).

Suppose that an appraisal of Olympic Computer's assets reveals a liquidation value of

---

[9] The third alternative applies in a cramdown, which we will discuss later in the chapter.

[10] A cramdown plan satisfies the absolute priority doctrine.

TABLE 27-6
Balance sheet of Olympic Computer Company before reorganization.

OLYMPIC COMPUTER COMPANY
Balance Sheet before Reorganization
($ millions)

Assets		Liabilities and Stockholders' Equity	
Cash	$1.0	Accounts payable	$4.0
Accounts receivable[a]	3.0	Bank debt	3.0
Inventory	2.0	Subordinated debt[c]	3.0
Fixed assets[b]	1.0	Mortgage bonds	2.0
Real estate[b]	1.0	Preferred stock	0.1
		Common stock	(4.1)
		Total liabilities and	
Total assets	$8.0	stockholders' equity	$8.0

[a] Pledged to secure the bank debt.
[b] Pledged to secure the mortgage bonds.
[c] Subordinated to the bank debt.

$1 million for the machinery, equipment, and real estate; $2 million for the receivables; and $1 million for the inventory. The mortgageholder would be paid $1 million, leaving a $1 million deficiency. The banks would be paid $2 million, also leaving a $1 million deficiency. Suppose that administrative claims and tax claims total $1 million. Table 27-7 shows how the available assets would compare to the unsecured claims in a Chapter 7 liquidation.

There is $1 million of cash but $9 million of unsecured claims. Unsecured claimants would be entitled to a cash distribution equal to $\frac{1}{9}$ of their claims. Because of the subordination provision, the bank debt is entitled to the share that would otherwise be paid to the subordinated debt. Therefore, the banks would be entitled to $\frac{4}{9}$ of the cash distribution, and the subordinated debtholders would get nothing. That is, the banks are entitled to a $\frac{1}{9}$ share because of the $1 million deficiency remaining after the receivables are liquidated, plus the sub-

TABLE 27-7
Distributions to Olympic Computer creditors in liquidation.

DISTRIBUTIONS TO OLYMPIC COMPUTER CREDITORS IN LIQUIDATION
($ millions)

Available Cash		Unsecured Claims	
Cash on balance sheet	$1.0	Accounts payable	$4.0
Liquidation of assets	4.0	Banks' deficiency	1.0
Administrative & tax claims	(1.0)	Subordinated debt	3.0
Secured interests	(3.0)	Mortgagee's deficiency	1.0
Total cash available	$1.0	Total unsecured claims	$9.0

CASH DISTRIBUTIONS

	Secured Claim	Unsecured Claim	Total Distribution
Trade creditors	—	$0.444	$0.444
Banks	$2.0	0.444	2.444
Subordinated debtholders	—	—	—
Mortgage bondholders	1.0	0.112	1.112
Total	$3.0	$1.0	$4.0

DISTRIBUTIONS TO OLYMPIC COMPUTER CREDITORS UNDER REORGANIZATION ($ millions)			
Available Consideration		**Unsecured Claims**	
Going-concern value	$6.0	Accounts payable	$4.0
Cash on balance sheet	1.0	Banks' deficiency	1.0
Administrative & tax claims	(1.0)	Subordinated debt	3.0
Secured interests	(3.0)	Mortgagee's deficiency	1.0
Total available consideration	$3.0	Total unsecured claims	$9.0

TABLE 27-8
Distributions to Olympic Computer creditors in a cramdown.

DISTRIBUTIONS			
	Secured Claim	**Unsecured Claim**	**Total Distribution**
Trade creditors	—	$1.333	$1.333
Banks	$2.0	1.0	3.0
Subordinated debtholders	—	0.333	0.333
Mortgage bondholders	1.0	0.334	1.334
Preferred stockholders	—	—	—
Common stockholders	—	—	—
Total	$3.0	$3.0	$6.0

ordinated debtholders' $\frac{3}{9}$ share. They get $0.444 (= 0.111 + 0.333). To satisfy the best-interests-of-creditors test, the plan would have to provide for distributions to creditors no less than the amounts shown in Table 27-7.

Suppose a careful analysis of Olympic Computer reveals that it has a value of $6 million on a going-concern basis. Suppose also that the $1 million of cash is not needed to run the business. Then Olympic Computer's *reorganization value*—its value as a going concern plus the value of any excess assets—is $7 million.

Table 27-8 illustrates the distributions that would occur in a cramdown. Subtracting $1 million of administrative and tax claims and $3 million for the secured claims from the $7 million of reorganization value leaves $3 million available for distribution to the unsecured claims. These claims total $9 million. Unsecured claims can thus realize 33 cents on the dollar. Note that because Olympic Computer is insolvent, the preferred stockholders and common stockholders will not receive anything in a cramdown.

Trade creditors receive $1.333 million. Because of the subordination provision, subordinated debtholders must pay over to the banks the lesser of (1) their entire share or (2) enough to repay the banks in full. That is, a class of creditors cannot receive an amount that exceeds their claims. The subordination provision makes an additional $1.333 million available for the banks. However, $1 million brings their total distribution to $3 million, the amount of their original claims. The $0.333 million excess remains with the subordinated debtholders. The mortgage bondholders receive $\frac{3}{9}$ of their $1 million deficiency, or $0.334 million.

The reorganization plan for Olympic Computer does not discriminate unfairly, and it satisfies both the best-interests-of-creditors test and the fair-and-equitable test. Trade creditors, subordinated debtholders, and mortgage bondholders would have to accept the plan, and the new capital structure of Olympic Computer would have to be crafted so that the plan is feasible in order for the bankruptcy court to confirm it. ■

Advantages and Disadvantages of Bankruptcy

A reorganization under Chapter 11 has advantages and disadvantages compared to an out-of-court restructuring. A financially distressed firm must weigh these advantages and disadvantages in order to decide what to do.

ADVANTAGES OF BANKRUPTCY

1. Filing the bankruptcy petition automatically stays all creditor collection efforts.

2. The bankruptcy process provides the debtor with a single forum—bankruptcy court—for conducting negotiations and resolving disputes.

3. The bankruptcy court can authorize debtor-in-possession financing for working capital purposes.

4. The bankruptcy court can authorize the debtor in possession to reject unfavorable leases and other contracts.

5. All claims (including contingent claims) can be dealt with at one time and a plan developed for discharging them.

6. Interest stops accruing on unsecured claims.

7. Claims resulting from the rejection of leases or contracts are capped.

8. If a proposed plan has been accepted by at least two-thirds in dollar amount of claims, and by more than one-half in number of claims, actually voting in each class of creditors, the bankruptcy court can confirm it over the objection of dissenting creditors.

9. Even if a class of creditors rejects the plan, the court can still confirm it under the cramdown rules.

10. Once the plan is confirmed, all of the debtor's creditors and stockholders are bound by its terms.

11. Restructuring through bankruptcy may enable the debtor to avoid having to pay taxes on the income that results when debt is retired at less than its face amount.

DISADVANTAGES OF BANKRUPTCY

1. The debtor's business is disrupted for some period of time, in part because the debtor cannot pay pre-petition creditors. Some of its former vendors, suppliers, and customers may decline to do business with a bankrupt firm.

2. A debtor in possession must meet stringent reporting requirements.

3. The bankruptcy court must approve all transactions outside the ordinary course of business.

4. A bankruptcy filing may trigger the filing of claims that would not have been asserted in an out-of-court restructuring (for example, a claim concerning a potential environmental cleanup liability).

5. The need for official committees to represent creditors and stockholders, as well as legal and financial advisors for these committees (paid for by the debtor), can make bankruptcy much more expensive than an out-of-court restructuring.

6. The debtor's management might lose control of the firm through either the appointment of a trustee or the adoption of a creditors' reorganization plan.

On balance, a private out-of-court restructuring can save significant direct and indirect costs. It does so mainly by avoiding the delays inherent in a bankruptcy restructuring. The private alternative is more likely to work when the debtor's liabilities are concentrated in the hands of a fairly small number of banks or other large, sophisticated financial institutions.

Self-Check Questions

1. What is the main purpose of the plan of reorganization? For how long does the debtor have the exclusive right to file one with a bankruptcy court?
2. What is the absolute priority doctrine? Is it ever violated in a reorganization? in a liquidation?
3. List the five main requirements a plan of reorganization must satisfy before a bankruptcy court can confirm it.
4. What does it mean to say that a plan of reorganization is feasible?
5. Explain the fair-and-equitable test and the best-interests-of-creditors test.
6. When does a class of claims accept a proposed plan of reorganization?
7. What are the main advantages and disadvantages of bankruptcy?

27.6 PREPACKAGED PLANS OF REORGANIZATION

A prepackaged bankruptcy attempts to combine the advantages—and avoid the disadvantages—of the bankruptcy process and out-of-court restructurings. In a **prepackaged bankruptcy**, the debtor and creditors negotiate a plan of reorganization and then file it along with the bankruptcy petition. The requirements for confirming a prepackaged plan are the same as in a traditional reorganization.

The prepackaged bankruptcy process has four main advantages compared to alternative methods of reorganization. (1) It can alleviate the holdout problem discussed earlier. Exchange offers usually require 90% or 95% of the debtholders to accept the exchange offer. The bankruptcy code sets lower acceptance levels. (2) The confirmed plan is binding on all debtholders, whether they vote to accept the plan or not. (3) Filing for bankruptcy often permits the debtor to realize tax advantages that are not available in an out-of-court restructuring. (4) Filing for bankruptcy allows the debtor to reject burdensome leases and other contracts.

EXAMPLE

Crystal Oil Company's Prepackaged Bankruptcy

The first significant prepackaged bankruptcy was that of Crystal Oil Company. Crystal Oil, an independent oil and gas producer headquartered in Louisiana, filed for bankruptcy on October 1, 1986. It emerged from bankruptcy less than 3 months later with its capital structure completely reorganized. Total indebtedness was reduced from $277 million to $129 million. Debtholders received common stock, convertible notes, convertible preferred stock, and warrants to purchase common stock in exchange for the old debt.

Crystal Oil's reorganization plan had been presented to creditors 3 months prior to the bankruptcy filing. All seven classes of public debtholders accepted the plan. However, Crystal Oil's two most senior creditors, Bankers Trust and Halliburton Company, did not initially accept the plan. Both had liens on Crystal Oil's oil and gas properties. Bankers Trust eventually accepted a revised plan. Halliburton never did. The Bankruptcy Court approved the plan over Halliburton's objection. ◼

The prepackaged process works best when there is only one class of creditors that will be disadvantaged by the plan and when the debtor can obtain the approval of that class before the bankruptcy filing. If a debtor has a large number of separate classes of creditors, the negotiations may be very time-consuming. The debtor may have to file for bankruptcy before it is able to get all the acceptances it needs. Also, trade creditors (who may lack financial sophistication) often resist prepackaging attempts. If the debtor can pay them in full, the prepackaged strategy stands a greater chance of succeeding. Generally, prepackaged bankruptcies work best for holding companies with at most a few classes of debt and few trade creditors.

Self-Check Questions
1. What is a prepackaged bankruptcy? How does it work?
2. What are the four main advantages of a prepackaged bankruptcy?
3. When does the prepackaged process work best?

27.7 LIQUIDATION IN BANKRUPTCY

When the prospects for reorganizing a debtor are so poor that it would be unreasonable to invest further time and financial resources in the effort, the only alternative is liquidation. The firm or its creditors file a petition under Chapter 7 (bankruptcy with intent to liquidate the firm). In some cases, the parties to a Chapter 11 filing cannot agree on a plan of reorganization and decide to convert to a Chapter 7. Pan Am Corporation and Eastern Airlines are examples.

Liquidation is preferable to reorganization when selling the debtor's assets in liquidation would produce value that exceeds the debtor's reorganization value. Usually, the key variables are time and risk. For instance, the financial advisors of the debtor may believe that the realizable economic value of the debtor will eventually exceed the liquidation value. But suppose the value to be realized and the time it would take are highly uncertain. In that case, the expected present value of the debtor's assets as a going concern might be less than their currently realizable liquidation value. Then liquidation is in the best interests of creditors.

Liquidation Value

Liquidation value does not necessarily mean the amount of cash the debtor's estate would realize through a forced sale of the debtor's assets. Rather, it refers to the amount that could be realized though an orderly sale. Liquidation value is usually lower than reorganization value. For example, inventories of items that are protected by manufacturer warranties, such as electronic goods, are heavily discounted in liquidation. This discount is part of the substantial indirect costs of financial distress, which we discussed in Chapter 15, resulting from the consumer-firm principal-agent relationship.

Liquidation value must generally be estimated asset class by asset class. The aggregate liquidation value of all of the debtor's assets, less the costs of the liquidation process, is then compared to the reorganization value. Reorganization value can be estimated by applying the valuation techniques we will describe in Chapter 28.

Table 27-7 illustrates the distributions to creditors in a Chapter 7 bankruptcy. The absolute priority doctrine must be followed in a liquidation. Recall that under this doctrine, claims with a higher priority must be paid in full before junior claims can receive anything. If the going-concern value of Olympic Computer was, say, only $4 million, then liquidation would be in the best interests of creditors.

Liquidation Process

Liquidation can take the form of either an assignment or a formal court-supervised liquidation. *Assignment* is a private method of disposition. Assets are assigned to a trustee, usually selected by the creditors, who liquidates them, usually by auction. Proceeds from the sale are then distributed to the creditors. The firm ceases to exist.[11] Rarely are the funds realized sufficient to pay off all creditors' claims in full. Equity investors generally see their investments in the debtor wiped out. Assignment is usually faster and less costly than the more rigid court-supervised liquidation procedure.

Self-Check Questions

1. When is it better to liquidate a debtor than to attempt a reorganization?

2. What do we mean by the term *liquidation value* of a debtor's assets?

3. Must the absolute priority doctrine be followed in a liquidation?

27.8 AN INTERNATIONAL PERSPECTIVE

Bankruptcy laws vary greatly from country to country.[12] As we have seen, U.S. bankruptcy law emphasizes reorganizing a distressed firm. In contrast, most other nations place more emphasis on recovering creditors' funds and favor liquidation over reorganization. We think this is changing. For example, recent bankruptcy legislation in Canada has struck a better balance between the rights of creditors and those of debtors by providing a new, more effective mechanism for reorganization. In Australia, efforts are underway to develop a reorganization process similar to that of the United States. The failure of large multinational firms that can file for bankruptcy protection in more than one country, as Maxwell Communication and Olympia & York Development did, will increase the pressure for international bankruptcy reform.

An International Comparison of Bankruptcy Filings

Figure 27-3 compares the actual numbers of business bankruptcies in 1994 and the numbers of business bankruptcies per capita in 14 industrial nations. France had more business bankruptcies than the United States. Relative to the size of the countries, Switzerland and the Scandinavian countries had the greatest numbers of business bankruptcies.

In the rest of this section, we will discuss the bankruptcy laws of Canada and Mexico to illustrate different national approaches to resolving financial distress.

Bankruptcy in Canada

In Canada there are three possible strategies for reorganizing a distressed firm: (1) informal restructuring, (2) restructuring under the Companies' Creditors Arrangement Act (CCAA), and (3) reorganization under the Bankruptcy and Insolvency Act (BIA, enacted in 1992). Informal out-of-court restructurings in Canada are similar to those in the United States.

---

[11] Thus the creditors never assume ownership of the firm, as they usually do following a reorganization.

[12] A good source of information on the bankruptcy laws of different countries is *Multinational Commercial Insolvency*, published by the American Bar Association.

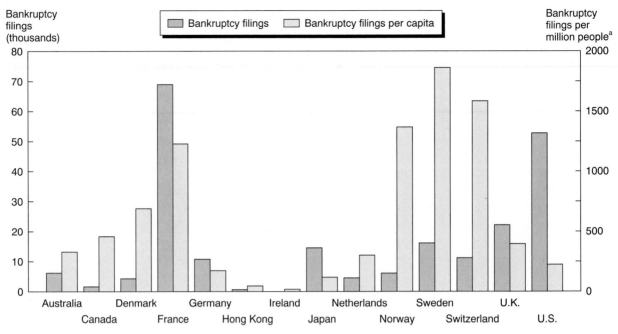

FIGURE 27-3

Business bankruptcies in 14 countries.
[a]Number of business bankruptcy filings per million people.
Source: *The 1995 Bankruptcy Yearbook and Almanac* (Boston, Mass.: New Generation Research, 1995), p. 416.

REORGANIZATION UNDER THE CCAA   The CCAA has been described as one of the most unusual reorganization laws in the world. Adopted during the Great Depression, it was designed for reorganizing large, insolvent public firms with complicated debt structures. But bankruptcy professionals in Canada were dissatisfied with the old, pre-BIA bankruptcy law. They decided to apply the CCAA to small and medium-sized as well as large bankruptcies.

The CCAA has evolved into a rough equivalent of Chapter 11 in the United States. For example, the CCAA provides for a stay against both secured and unsecured creditors. However, there are important differences. The CCAA lacks rules for classifying creditors. It also lacks the detailed procedures of Chapter 11. There is no cramdown or other means of dealing with dissenting creditors. A proposed plan of reorganization must be approved by three-quarters in value, and a majority in number, of the members of each class. If it is rejected by any class, the stay is lifted and creditors are free to move against the debtor to collect on their loans.

EXAMPLE

Olympia & York's Bankruptcy

In May 1992, Olympia & York (O&Y) filed for protection under the CCAA for 29 affiliated firms (mostly subsidiaries), 5 of which also filed for protection under Chapter 11 in the United States. Months of difficult negotiations followed. O&Y presented a restructuring plan in November 1992. A significantly amended plan was approved by creditors and the courts in the spring of 1993. ■

REORGANIZATION UNDER THE BIA   An insolvent firm can file for protection from creditors under the BIA. Creditor actions are stayed, and the debtor must offer a *proposal* to its unsecured creditors. It may also submit the proposal to the secured creditors, but that is not required. The unsecured creditors can be treated as a single class. If each class of unsecured creditors votes to accept the proposal, and the court also approves it, it becomes binding on all unsecured creditors (and on any class of secured creditors that voted to accept it). Class acceptance requires the approval by at least two-thirds in value, and more than one-half in number, of the members of the class who voted (as in Chapter 11). The proposal is not binding on a class of secured creditors that either did not vote or voted to reject. They are free to move against the debtor to seize collateral or collect on their loans. If the unsecured creditors reject the proposal, then the debtor is automatically placed in liquidation.

The BIA shifted the focus of the bankruptcy process in Canada toward reorganization. It was intended to replace the CCAA. But the CCAA affords considerable flexibility in handling reorganizations, which many bankruptcy professionals in Canada find advantageous. Because of the CCAA's popularity, the Canadian government has not repealed it.

Bankruptcy in Mexico

Mexican bankruptcy law also provides for both reorganization and liquidation. Under the first alternative, the debtor requests the bankruptcy court to order a *suspension of payments*. That order halts debt payments and gives the debtor time to try to negotiate a *preventive agreement* with its creditors. At least two-thirds in amount, and more than one-half in number, of the holders of unsecured claims who vote must approve the agreement. If the creditors reject the agreement, then the firm must be liquidated.

A suspension of payments is similar to a U.S. Chapter 11 in that creditors are stayed from enforcing their claims, and the debtor continues to operate its business under court supervision while it negotiates with creditors. But a suspension of payments is really a moratorium on interest and principal payments to creditors. The debtor can propose to reschedule debt repayments for up to three years or to discharge debts at a discount of up to 40% of the face amount of the debt. Under a suspension, however, the agreement is to reschedule or repay existing debt obligations rather than undertake a Chapter 11-style plan to reorganize the debtor's business operations and capital structure.

Self-Check Questions

1. In what critical respect does U.S. bankruptcy law differ from the bankruptcy laws of most other countries?
2. How is reorganization under the Companies' Creditors Arrangement Act of Canada similar to a U.S. Chapter 11 reorganization? How is it different?
3. How is a suspension of payments under Mexican bankruptcy law similar to the automatic stay under U.S. Chapter 11? How is it different?

RESOLUTION OF TRANS WORLD AIRLINES'S FINANCIAL DISTRESS

TWA's managers had already negotiated for several months with representatives of the holders of TWA's 10% notes and 8% notes. By May 1995, the noteholders had concluded that a prepackaged bankruptcy would be preferable to a reorganization outside bankruptcy. Meanwhile, TWA's managers practiced damage control. They assured travel agents that a prepackaged bankruptcy could be accomplished quickly, perhaps in just two months, and that it would not disrupt TWA's operations or inconvenience passengers.

TWA's noteholders approved the prepackaged plan in late June, and TWA filed its petition for bankruptcy within days. The U.S. Bankruptcy Court in St. Louis confirmed TWA's plan just over a month later, and TWA emerged from bankruptcy by the end of August, on schedule.

SUMMARY

A firm seeks protection from its creditors under Chapter 11 when it is no longer able to pay its debts as they come due or when it anticipates future liabilities that it will not be able to meet. The guiding principle of Chapter 11 is that a debtor should be given the opportunity to negotiate with its creditors and achieve a consensual plan of reorganization, provided that the value of the reorganized debtor exceeds its liquidation value.

The bankruptcy process is time-consuming and expensive. Financially distressed firms therefore usually attempt to reorganize outside bankruptcy before resorting to a bankruptcy filing. A firm can seek to restructure its liabilities outside bankruptcy by offering to exchange new securities for the outstanding securities, by seeking securityholders' consent to modify the terms of existing securities, or by repurchasing existing securities for cash. The third alternative is usually available only to firms that can see the possible onset of financial distress far enough in advance that they are able to sell new securities (or borrow from their banks) to raise the cash necessary to make the repurchases. Alternatively, the firm might attempt a prepackaged bankruptcy. This means negotiating a plan of reorganization and using the bankruptcy filing as a means of forcing holdouts to go along with the plan.

Prepackaged bankruptcy represents a "hybrid" form of bankruptcy. It can resolve financial distress relatively quickly and inexpensively. It is effective in dealing with holdouts. It can also result in tax advantages that an out-of-court restructuring cannot. This is because the tax code presumes a firm filing for bankruptcy is insolvent. However, prepackaged bankruptcy is not likely to be feasible when there are many classes of debtholders with sharply divergent interests or when there are complex legal issues that must be resolved through litigation.

An out-of-court restructuring has potential advantages relative to a traditional Chapter 11 reorganization. It is generally less disruptive to the debtor's business, and it is generally less time-consuming than the bankruptcy process. Bankruptcy also has potential advantages relative to an out-of-court restructuring. Filing the bankruptcy petition automatically stays all creditor collection efforts. Bankruptcy provides a single forum for resolving all disputes. The bankruptcy court can authorize debtor-in-possession financing to relieve a liquidity crisis and can authorize the debtor to reject unfavorable leases and other contracts. The percentage of securityholders that must approve a bankruptcy plan of reorganization is usually lower than the percentage required to approve an out-of-court restructuring.

DECISION SUMMARY

- A financially distressed but viable firm should file for protection from its creditors under Chapter 11 when it is unable to pay its debts as they come due (or when such failure is imminent) *and* it cannot reach agreement with its creditors on restructuring its debts out of court.

- An out-of-court restructuring is normally less expensive and less time-consuming than a Chapter 11 reorganization.

- When a distressed firm's liquidation value exceeds its reorganization value, it should file for liquidation under Chapter 7.

- A debtor undergoing reorganization under Chapter 11 has the exclusive right to propose a plan of reorganization for 120 days from the date it filed the bankruptcy petition. It must ensure that the plan it proposes complies with the requirements for plan confirmation contained in the bankruptcy code.

- Financial distress does not occur without warning. Creditors can use multiple discriminant analysis to predict a firm's financial distress.

- A prepackaged bankruptcy has several advantages over an out-of-court restructuring. It is an effective way to deal with the holdout problem. It normally works best when the debtor has a very simple capital structure, such as that of a holding company with no trade creditors and a small number of outstanding debt issues.

- Absolute priority is not always observed in bankruptcy. In many cases, making a small distribution to a dissenting class is advantageous to senior creditors. "Buying their support" is purchasing their hidden option and is likely to speed up the reorganization process and reduce expenses.

- It is not necessary to secure the approval of every class of creditors in Chapter 11. The bankruptcy code contains a cramdown provision to deal with any dissenting class(es). Cramdown should be used when it is cheaper than increasing the distributions to the dissenting class(es).

EQUATION SUMMARY

(27.1) $$Z = 0.012X_1 + 0.014X_2 + 0.033X_3 + 0.006X_4 + 0.999X_5$$

KEY TERMS

reorganization...877	automatic stay...890	fair-and-equitable test...892
liquidation...877	debtor-in-possession financing...891	best-interests-of-creditors test...893
financial distress...879	plan of reorganization...891	prepackaged bankruptcy...897
exchange offer...886	absolute priority doctrine...892	
debtor in possession...889	feasible...892	

EXERCISES

PROBLEM SET A

A1. Define "corporate financial distress."

A2. What are some useful indicators of impending corporate financial distress?

A3. What is the purpose of the bankruptcy code? When should a firm file for bankruptcy?

A4. How do a Chapter 7 liquidation and a Chapter 11 reorganization differ?

A5. What is the main cause of corporate financial distress? What role do factors outside the firm play?

A6. How does the age of the firm affect the probability of bankruptcy?

A7. What is the basic premise of Chapter 11?

A8. Explain the meaning of the following terms: (a) debtor in possession, (b) automatic stay, (c) plan of reorganization, (d) consensual plan of reorganization, (e) cramdown, and (f) prepackaged bankruptcy.

A9. What is the purpose of the cramdown provision of the bankruptcy code?

A10. Under what circumstances is a prepackaged bankruptcy attempt most likely to succeed?

A11.

   a. Under what circumstances will reorganization be preferred over liquidation?

   b. Under what circumstances will liquidation be preferred over reorganization?

A12. Must absolute priority be adhered to when a debtor is liquidated? Explain.

A13. Why can we generally not rely on just one variable to predict the likelihood of bankruptcy?

A14. Describe the sorts of positive and negative incentives that a financially distressed firm can employ to encourage securityholders to participate in an exchange offer.

A15. What is a holdout? How can holdouts frustrate the financial reorganization process?

A16. What are the main advantages and disadvantages of an out-of-court restructuring compared to bankruptcy?

A17. What are the five basic conditions that a plan of reorganization must satisfy in order to be confirmed by the bankruptcy court?

A18.

   a. Describe the best-interests-of-creditors test.

   b. Describe the fair-and-equitable test.

PROBLEM SET B

B1. Explain what the absolute priority doctrine is. What are the arguments for and against enforcing absolute priority in reorganization?

B2. How has the addition of Chapter 10 to the bankruptcy code potentially reduced the costs of bankruptcy?

B3. What role does valuation play in the bankruptcy process?

B4. What are the main advantages of a prepackaged bankruptcy? How might these advantages be exaggerated?

B5. Suppose a firm's financial statements indicate the following financial ratio values:

$$X_1 = 5\% \qquad X_2 = 10\% \qquad X_3 = -5\% \qquad X_4 = 50\% \qquad X_5 = 1.05$$

   a. Calculate the Z-score.

   b. Is the firm likely to go bankrupt within 1 year?

B6. Suppose a firm's financial statements indicate the following financial ratio values:

$$X_1 = 5\% \qquad X_2 = 20\% \qquad X_3 = 2\% \qquad X_4 = 110\% \qquad X_5 = 1.25$$

   a. Calculate the Z-score.

   b. Is the firm likely to go bankrupt within 1 year?

B7. Why does the accuracy of a Z-score model depend on the time period used in estimating the discriminant coefficients?

B8. A reorganization plan provides that creditors will receive new debt. It will pay a 10% coupon annually and will mature in a lump sum at the end of 10 years. The debtor's financial advisors estimate that the required return for new debt is 16%. What is the new debt worth as a percentage of its face amount?

B9. In what sense is a prepackaged bankruptcy a form of private restructuring?

B10. Explain how the following classes of claims and interests would be ordered for bankruptcy purposes.

  a. Accounts payable

  b. Legal fees incurred during the bankruptcy process

  c. First mortgage bonds

  d. Common stock

  e. Unsecured bank debt

  f. Second mortgage bonds

  g. Bank debt secured by inventories and receivables

  h. Preferred stock

  i. Subordinated debentures (subordinated to all bank debt)

  j. Tax claims

B11. Divided Airlines Corporation has $100 million of subordinated debentures outstanding, which are expressly subordinated to the firm's bank debt. Outstanding bank debt totals $500 million. It also has $200 million of accounts payable. Divided Airlines goes bankrupt. The fair market value of its assets is estimated to be $600 million. The firm proposes in its plan of reorganization to pay the banks $400 million, the trade creditors $150 million, and the subordinated debenture holders $50 million.

  a. Against whom does the proposed plan discriminate unfairly?

  b. Suppose the bank creditors vote to reject the proposed plan. Can it meet the fair-and-equitable test?

B12. Assume the same facts as in Problem B11. A revised plan of reorganization proposes to pay the banks $500 million, the trade creditors $100 million, and the subordinated debenture holders nothing.

  a. Against whom does the revised plan discriminate unfairly?

  b. Suppose the trade creditors vote to reject the plan. Can if be crammed down?

B13. Assume the same facts as in Problem B11 except that Divided Airlines is worth $700 million. The banks propose a plan of reorganization in which they would be paid $500 million, the trade creditors would be paid $175 million, and the subordinated debenture holders would be paid $25 million. Against whom does the plan discriminate unfairly?

B14. In the cramdown example presented in the chapter, suppose that Olympic Computer's subordinated debt is subordinated not only to the bank debt but also to the accounts payable and the mortgage bonds. How would the distributions in a cramdown change?

B15. A firm had assets worth $700 million. It borrowed $100 million, which was secured by a mortgage on its newest factory. The firm also borrowed $200 million on an unsecured basis. The firm subsequently went bankrupt, and its assets are now worth just $150 million. Its newest factory can be sold only for $50 million. Who gets what?

PROBLEM SET C

  C1. Should the increase in the number of bankruptcy filings since the Bankruptcy Reform Act of 1978 was enacted be a cause for concern?

  C2. How is the growing importance of financial intermediaries likely to affect the reorganization process?

  C3. Local Business Machines Corporation is a distressed manufacturer of personal computers. Its

TABLE P-1
Balance sheet of Local Business Machines Corporation.

LOCAL BUSINESS MACHINES CORPORATION
Balance Sheet Before Reorganization
($ millions)

Assets		Liabilities and Shareholders' Equity	
Current Assets:		Current Liabilities:	
Cash	$ 10	Bank debt due within one year[a]	$ 50
Accounts receivable	20	Account payable	30
Inventory	20	Total current liabilities	80
Total current assets	50		
		Long-term debt:	
Plant and equipment	100	10% senior debentures	20
Less accumulated depreciation	(60)	9% mortgage bonds due 2006[b]	20
	40	14% subordinated debentures due 1997[c]	30
Other assets	10	Total long-term debt	70
		Accumulated shareholders' deficit	(50)
Total assets	$100	Total liabilities and shareholders' equity	$100

[a] Secured by accounts receivable and inventory.
[b] Secured by all plant and equipment.
[c] Subordinated to senior debentures and bank debt.

TABLE P-2
Income statement for Local Business Machines Corporation.

LOCAL BUSINESS MACHINES CORPORATION

Income Statement for the Latest 12 Months
($ millions)

Gross sales	$100
Cost of goods sold	(90)
Gross profit	10
Depreciation	(5)
Income before interest expense	5
Interest expense	(12)
Loss	$ (7)

balance sheet is shown in Table P-1, and its income statement for the latest 12-month period is shown in Table P-2. Income statements for the previous 5 years show a steady stream of significant losses. Lately, Local Business Machines has been selling assets to meet interest payments.

a. Is the fair market value of Local Business Machine's assets likely to differ from their book value? Explain.

b. Assume that the fair market value of the accounts receivable and that of inventory are $16 million each, that of plant and equipment is $25 million, and that of the other assets is $2 million. How would value be distributed in a cramdown situation?

c. What issues would each of the classes of claims holders be likely to raise as they negotiate a plan of reorganization?

C4. Dissipated Technologies Corporation has a capital structure consisting of (1) $5 million principal amount of secured debt due in 10 years, (2) $2.5 million of unsecured debentures due in 1 year, and (3) common stock. Dissipated Technologies defaults on an interest payment to the unsecured debenture holders. They elect, through their trustee, to accelerate the debt. (How can they do this?) The debenture holders bring suit and obtain a judgment. Dissipated Technologies, not having any cash, cannot pay. Under a cross-default provision in the secured creditor's indenture, the secured debt's maturity is accelerated. The secured creditor demands payment. Dissipated Technologies, still without cash, refuses. The debenture holders begin attachment proceedings on Dissipated Technologies' unpledged property. The secured creditor begins a proceeding to arrange for a sheriff's sale of the property (about one-half of the property of Dissipated Technologies) on which it has a lien. The proceeds of such a sale would be used to satisfy the secured creditor's claim.

a. Dissipated Technologies files a bankruptcy petition. The debenture holders' and secured creditor's proceedings stop. Why? Does any section of the bankruptcy code require this?

  Dissipated Technologies proposes the following reorganization plan: (1) The secured creditor will have its maturity reinstated and interest payments will be paid when due under the old indenture. Its lien on Dissipated Technologies' property will continue. One interest payment was missed during the reorganization proceedings. The secured creditor will be paid the missed interest payment with an added premium for the delay. (2) The unsecured creditors will receive 6 annual installments of $600,000 each. (3) The common stockholders will remain as such. Dissipated Technologies is valued at $6 million.

b. The secured creditor objects to the plan. The unsecured creditors and shareholders accept the plan. Can the bankruptcy court confirm the plan over the secured creditor's objection?

c. Suppose instead that 1 debenture holder (out of the 100 debenture holders in all) who holds 25% of the principal amount of the outstanding debentures objects, but the secured creditor accepts the plan. Can the bankruptcy court confirm the plan over the debenture holder's objection?

d. Suppose instead that *all* the debenture holders object, whereas the secured creditor again accepts the plan. Can the plan be confirmed?

e. What did the balance sheet of Dissipated Technologies look like? What would it look like if the plan were confirmed?

Real-World Application:
Crystal Oil's Prepackaged Bankruptcy

Crystal Oil Company (Crystal Oil) was engaged mainly in crude oil and natural gas exploration and production. Beginning in 1984, a worldwide decline in the demand for crude oil and natural gas led to a decline in oil and gas prices. This decline in prices threatened Crystal Oil's ability to meet its debt service obligations. In 1984 and 1985, the firm took many steps to meet its obligations and reduce its debt. It sold many properties and its refinery assets, greatly reduced drilling for oil and gas, and cut back its investments in producing properties.

  As its financial condition worsened, Crystal Oil also restructured some of its debt by (1) extending the maturity of a large trade payable to Halliburton Company from April 1985 to April 1987; (2) exchanging approximately $125 million face amount of new 15% notes and 7,418,000 shares of its common stock for approximately $234 million face amount of old debentures, which reduced its annual interest cost by $12.7 million; and (3) exercising its option to pay interest on the new 15% notes in common stock rather than cash.

  Crystal Oil lost $10.9 million in 1983, $21.4 million in 1984, $67.8 million in 1985, and an additional $213.7 million in the first 6 months of 1986. As a result of these losses, its balance sheet on June 30, 1986 had a large negative stockholders' equity.

BALANCE SHEET, JUNE 30, 1986 **(Dollar amounts in thousands)**			
Current assets	$21,721	Total liabilities	$370,961
Long-term assets	104,332	Stockholders' equity	(244,908)
Total assets	$126,053	Total capitalization	$126,053

By the beginning of 1986, Crystal Oil was no longer in compliance with some of its debt covenants, although it had thus far met all its required payments. However, in April 1986, it defaulted on a scheduled interest payment. In May, it suspended all payments on its secured trade debt to Halliburton. Over the next 2 months, it defaulted on scheduled interest payments for four other debt issues. By that time, Crystal Oil had concluded that it could not continue as a going concern unless it substantially reduced its outstanding debt.

Crystal Oil put together a plan of reorganization. The plan would reduce the outstanding face amount of debt from $277.4 million to $129.0 million (with a fair market value of $75.8 million). The holders of the old debt that would be eliminated would receive a combination of new notes, new preferred stock, new common stock, and new warrants. On July 10, 1986, Crystal Oil presented its plan to Bankers Trust, Halliburton, and all its unsecured creditors. It asked these creditors to vote on the plan. If it could get enough favorable votes, it would file the prepackaged plan along with a voluntary petition for reorganization under Chapter 11, and simultaneously seek the plan's immediate confirmation. Under the plan, the capitalization of the reorganized Crystal Oil would be (dollar amounts in thousands)

New bank note (issued to Bankers Trust)	$43,651
New Halliburton note (issued to Halliburton)	10,278
New convertible secured notes	21,114
Other liabilities	747
Total liabilities	75,790
Preferred stockholders' equity	1,170
Common stockholders' equity	53,268
Total capitalization	$130,228

Table 27-9 shows the distributions to creditors and stockholders under the proposed plan and, alternatively, what they could expect to get if Crystal Oil were liquidated. Table 27-10 provides a statement of projected cash flows for Crystal Oil.

1. What caused Crystal Oil's financial distress?

2. In mid-1986, Crystal Oil was
   a. bankrupt.
   b. in default.
   c. failed.
   d. insolvent.

3. How does a prepackaged bankruptcy work? What are its advantages relative to the traditional Chapter 11 bankruptcy process?

4. What requirements must Crystal Oil's plan of reorganization satisfy for the bankruptcy court to be able to confirm it?

5. Refer to Table 27-9. Explain why the proposed plan satisfies the best-interests-of-creditors test.

6. Does the proposed plan satisfy the feasibility test? Explain.

7. The class of creditors comprising the 15% Note claims had 234 claimants and $134,542,000 of claims. What must happen for the class of claims to vote in favor of Crystal Oil's plan?

8. Refer to Table 27-9. The holders of the 15% Notes would receive only $43,628,000 for their claims of $134,542,000. How do you explain the distribution of $2,461,000 to common stockholders?

9. If the classes of debenture holders (there are actu-

TABLE 27-9

Distributions to Crystal Oil's creditors and shareholders in liquidation and under the proposed plan of reorganization (dollar amounts in thousands).

CLASS OF CLAIMS OR INTERESTS	LIQUIDATION	REORGANIZATION						
		New Bank Note	New Halliburton Note	New Convertible Notes	Other Liabilities	New Preferred Stock	New Common Stock and Warrants	Total
Bankers Trust	$43,864	$43,651	—	—	—	—	$ 213	$ 43,864
Halliburton	10,515	—	$10,278	—	—	—	237	10,515
15% Notes[1]	14,919	—	—	$21,114	—	$20,784	1730	43,628
Other liabilities[2]	22	—	—	—	$747	—	—	747
Debentures[3]	—	—	—	—	—	27,761	1252	29,013
Common stock	—	—	—	—	—	—	2461	2,461
								$130,228

[1] Ranks junior to the Bankers Trust and Halliburton debt.
[2] Ranks junior to the secured portion of the 15% Notes and to the Bankers Trust and Halliburton debt.
[3] Ranks junior to all other liabilities.
Source: Crystal Oil Company, *Disclosure Statement* (July 9, 1986), pp. 26, 71–72.

TABLE 27-10
Statement of projected cash flows for Crystal Oil (dollar amounts in thousands).

	1986	1987	1988	1989	1990	1991	1992	1993	1994	1995	1996
Cash at beginning of year	$ 9,231	$ 3,153	$ 4,000	$ 3,362	$ 4,000	$10,795	$24,708	$34,720	$52,470	$57,939	$60,167
Cash flow from operations before debt expense	24,683	18,696	25,752	24,903	26,464	23,469	20,928	19,307	17,396	13,276	6,007
Planned capital expenditures	(6,957)	(1,736)	(13,733)	(6,287)	(10,412)	(9,451)	(10,827)	(1,483)	(1,868)	(1,003)	(675)
Cash available for debt service	26,957	20,113	16,019	21,978	20,052	24,813	34,809	52,544	67,998	70,212	65,499
Debt service	(23,804)	(16,113)	(12,657)	(17,978)	(9,257)	(105)	(89)	(74)	(10,059)	(10,045)	(55,122)
Cash at end of year	$ 3,153	$ 4,000	$ 3,362	$ 4,000	$10,795	$24,708	$34,720	$52,470	$57,939	$60,167	$10,377

Source: Crystal Oil Company, *Disclosure Statement* (July 9, 1986), pp. 60–61.

ally two such classes) vote to reject the plan, could it still pass the fair-and-equitable test? Could it pass this test if just one of the debenture holder classes votes to reject?

10. The discussion in the Crystal Oil Company's prepackaged bankruptcy example in the chapter noted that Halliburton never accepted Crystal Oil's plan but that the bankruptcy court approved it anyway. How could that happen?

BIBLIOGRAPHY

Alderson, Michael J., and Brian L. Betker. "Liquidation Costs and Capital Structure," *Journal of Financial Economics*, 1995, 39(1):45–70.

Aziz, Abdul, and Gerald H. Lawson. "Cash Flow Reporting and Financial Distress Models: Testing of Hypotheses," *Financial Management*, 1989, 18(1):55–63.

Barrow, Janice M., and Paul M. Horvitz. "Response of Distressed Firms to Incentives: Thrift Institution Performance Under the FSLIC Management Consignment Program," *Financial Management*, 1993, 22(3):176–184.

Beranek, William, and Steven L. Jones. "The Emerging Market for Trade Claims of Bankrupt Firms," *Financial Management*, 1994, 23(2):76–81.

Betker, Brian L. "An Empirical Examination of Prepackaged Bankruptcy," *Financial Management*, 1995, 24(1):3–18.

Bhagat, Sanjai, James A. Brickley, and Jeffrey L. Coles. "The Costs of Inefficient Bargaining and Financial Distress: Evi-

dence from Corproate Lawsuits," *Journal of Financial Economics*, 1994, 35(2):21–247.

Bi, Keqian, and Haim Levy. "Market Reaction to Bond Downgradings Followed by Chapter 11 Filings," *Financial Management*, 1993, 22(3):156–162.

Brown, David T., Christopher M. James, and Robert M. Mooradian. "The Information Content of Distressed Restructurings Involving Public and Private Debt Claims," *Journal of Financial Economics*, 1993, 33(1):93–118.

Chatterjee, Sris, Upinder S. Dhillon, and Gabriel G. Ramirez. "Coercive Tender and Exchange Offers in Distressed High-Yield Debt Restructurings: An Empirical Analysis," *Journal of Financial Economics*, 1995, 38(3):333–360.

Chatterjee, Sris, Upinder S. Dhillon, and Gabriel G. Ramirez. "Resolution of Financial Distress: Debt Restructurings via Chapter 11, Prepackaged Bankruptcies, and Workouts," *Financial Management*, 1996, 25(1):5–18.

Coats, Pamela K., and L. Franklin Fant. "Recognizing Financial

Distress Patterns Using a Neural Network Tool," *Financial Management*, 1993, 22(3):142–155.

DeAngelo, Harry, and Linda DeAngelo. "Dividend Policy and Financial Distress: An Empirical Investigation of Troubled NYSE Firms," *Journal of Finance*, 1990, 45(5):1415–1432.

DeGennaro, Ramon P., Larry H. P. Lang, and James B. Thomson. "Troubled Savings and Loan Institutions: Turnaround Strategies Under Insolvency," *Financial Management*, 1993, 22(3):163–175.

Eberhart, Allan C., William T. Moore, and Rodney L. Roenfeldt. "Security Pricing and Deviations from the Absolute Priority Rule in Bankruptcy Proceedings," *Journal of Finance*, 1990, 45(5):1457–1470.

Eberhart, Allan C., and Lemma W. Senbet. "Absolute Priority Rule Violations and Risk Incentives for Financially Distressed Firms," *Financial Management*, 1993, 22(3):101–116.

Gertner, Robert, and David Scharstein. "A Theory of Workouts and the Effects of Reorganization Law," *Journal of Finance*, 1991, 46(4):1189–1222.

Gilson, Stuart C. "Bankruptcy, Boards, Banks, and Blockholders: Evidence on Changes in Corporate Ownership and Control when Firms Default," *Journal of Financial Economics*, 1990, 27(2):355–388.

Gilson, Stuart C., Kose John, and Larry H. P. Lang. "Troubled Debt Restructurings: An Empirical Study of Private Reorganization of Firms in Default," *Journal of Financial Economics*, 1990, 27(2):315–354.

Gilson, Stuart C., and Michael R. Vetsuypens. "CEO Commission in Financially Distressed Firms: An Empirical Analysis," *Journal of Finance*, 1993, 48(2):425–458.

Gombola, Michael J., Mark E. Haskins, J. Edward Ketz, and David D. Williams. "Cash Flow in Bankruptcy Prediction," *Financial Management*, 1987, 16(4):55–65.

Gosnell, Thomas, Arthur J. Keown, and John M. Pinkerton. "Bankruptcy and Insider Trading: Differences between Exchange-Listed and OTC Firms," *Journal of Finance*, 1992, 47(1):349–362.

Hotchkiss, Edith Shwalb. "Postbankruptcy Performance and Management Turnover," *Journal of Finance*, 1995, 50(1):3–21.

Jog, Vijay M., Igor Kotlyar, and Donald G. Tate. "Stakeholder Losses in Corporate Restructuring: Evidence from Four Cases in the North American Steel Industry," *Financial Management*, 1993, 22(3):185–201.

John, Kose. "Managing Financial Distress and Valuing Distressed Securities: A Survey and a Research Agenda," *Financial Management*, 1993, 22(3):60–78.

John, Kose, Larry H. P. Lang, and Jeffry Netter. "The Voluntary Restructuring of Large Firms in Response to Performance Decline," *Journal of Finance*, 1992, 47(3):891–918.

John, Teresa A. "Accounting Measures of Corporate Liquidity, Leverage, and Costs of Financial Distress," *Financial Management*, 1993, 22(3):91–100.

Kaen, Fred R., and Hassan Tehranian. "Information Effects in Financial Distress: The Case of Seabrook Station," *Journal of Financial Economics*, 1990, 26(1):143–171.

Kaplan, Steven N. "Campeau's Acquisition of Federated: Post-Bankruptcy Results," *Journal of Financial Economics*, 1994, 35(1):123–136.

Krishnan, V. Sivarama, and R. Charles Moyer. "Bankruptcy Costs and the Financial Leasing Decision," *Financial Management*, 1994, 23(2):31–42.

Loderer, Claudio P., and Dennis P. Sheehan. "Corporate Bankruptcy and Managers' Self-Serving Behavior," *Journal of Finance*, 1989, 44(4):1059–1076.

Mooradian, Robert M., "The Effect of Bankruptcy Protection on Investment: Chapter 11 as a Screening Device," *Journal of Finance*, 1994, 49(4):1403–1430.

Multinational Commercial Insolvency. Chicago, Ill.: American Bar Association, 1993.

The 1995 Bankruptcy Yearbook and Almanac. Boston, Mass.: New Generation Research, 1995.

Opler, Tim C. "Controlling Financial Distress Costs in Leveraged Buyouts with Financial Innovations," *Financial Management*, 1993, 22(3):79–90.

Opler, Tim C., and Sheridan Titman. "Financial Distress and Corporate Performance," *Journal of Finance*, 1994, 49(3):1015–1040.

Scholes, Myron S., and Mark A. Wolfson. "Employee Stock Ownership Plans and Corporate Restructuring: Myths and Realities," *Financial Management*, 1990, 19(1):12–28.

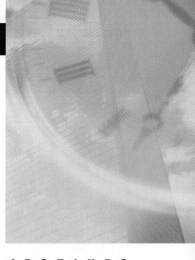

CHAPTER 28

MERGERS AND ACQUISITIONS

F ew financial events attract headlines quite the way a protracted battle for control of a large firm does. Not long ago, the front page of the *Wall Street Journal* carried an article headlined "Bidding War: Offers for RJR Pit KKR and Shearson in a Battle for Turf," which announced the bid of Kohlberg Kravis Roberts & Company (KKR) for control of RJR Nabisco. Five days earlier, a management-led group had announced its intention to develop a proposal, in conjunction with Shearson Lehman Hutton, to acquire RJR Nabisco in a leveraged buyout valued at $75 per common share. A **leveraged buyout** is an acquisition that is financed principally, sometimes more than 90%, by borrowing on a secured basis. The KKR bid amounted to $90 per share. The battle for control unfolded over the ensuing 6-week period. It involved three bidding groups, no fewer than 10 of the leading investment banks, and a veritable army of lawyers, information agents, accountants, and commercial banks. KKR finally prevailed when it offered to pay $109 per common share, 45% more than the management-led group's original proposal and a staggering aggregate bid of $25 billion.

In a corporate acquisition, one firm (the *acquiror*) gains control of another firm (the *acquiree*). A corporate acquisition is a form of capital investment. As with any capital investment, a firm should proceed only if the investment will increase shareholder wealth. The investment is often substantial in relation to the acquiror's size before the acquisition. Table 28-1 lists the 10 largest merger and acquisition transactions that had taken place in the United States through year-end 1994. Because of its size, an acquisition can have a greater impact on shareholder wealth than other forms of capital investment. The analytical tools and basic decision rules of capital budgeting still apply. However, particular care must be taken in applying these tools because of the enormous size and complexity of the investment. This chapter explores the possible benefits and costs of a corporate acquisition and reviews the special legal, tax, and accounting issues involved.

Agency problems are important in corporate acquisitions. How will the target respond? Under the Principle of Self-Interested Behavior, we would

TABLE 28-1
The ten largest merger and acquisition transactions in the United States through year-end 1994 (dollar amounts in billions).

ACQUIRING FIRM	ACQUIRED FIRM	APPROXIMATE PRICE PAID[a]	YEAR ANNOUNCED
Kohlberg Kravis Roberts & Co.	RJR Nabisco, Inc.	$24.6	1988
Beecham Group Plc–U.K.	Smithkline Beckman Corp.	16.1	1989
Chevron Corp.	Gulf Corp.	13.2	1984
Philip Morris Companies, Inc.	Kraft, Inc.	13.1	1988
American Telephone & Telegraph Co.	McCaw Cellular Communications Co.	12.6	1993
Bristol-Myers Co.	Squibb Corp.	12.0	1989
Time, Inc.	Warner Communications, Inc.	11.7	1989
Texaco, Inc.	Getty Oil Co.	10.1	1984
National Amusements, Inc.	Paramount Communications, Inc.	10.0	1993
American Home Products Corp.	American Cyanamid Co. Inc.–99.6%	9.2	1994

[a] Based on the number of shares of common stock acquired.
Source: Merrill Lynch Business Advisory Services, *Mergerstat Review* 1994, p. 47.

expect that managers would not sit by passively when facing a possible acquisition of "their" firm. And in fact, corporate managers go to great lengths to erect barriers to forestall unwanted suitors from acquiring their firms (and perhaps eliminating their jobs in the process). We will describe these measures and their potential impact on shareholder wealth. We will also explain how to tailor the techniques of capital budgeting to corporate acquisitions and will describe other valuation techniques—especially comparative analysis—that are widely used in practice.

MERGERS AND ACQUISITIONS AND THE PRINCIPLES OF FINANCE

◆ *Self-Interested Behavior*: Look for opportunities to make profitable acquisitions. Acquire another firm only if doing so increases shareholder wealth.

◆ *Two-Sided Transactions*: Acquiring another firm usually requires paying a premium over the prevailing market price large enough to get the acquiree's shareholders to sell their shares.

◆ *Comparative Advantage*: Recognize that a merger of firms that have different comparative advantages might have a positive NPV.

◆ *Behavioral Principle*: Look to comparable acquisitions for guidance regarding a reasonable price to pay for an acquisition.

◆ *Valuable Ideas*: Look for opportunities to redesign securities or the structure of an acquisition transaction to enhance value.

◆ *Incremental Benefits*: Calculate the net advantage of an acquisition on the basis of the incremental after-tax cash flows the acquisition will provide.

◆ *Risk-Return Trade-Off*: Merging two firms through an exchange of shares benefits the bondholders of both, because their expected return increases while their risk decreases.

◆ *Diversification*: Diversifying through a conglomerate merger will benefit shareholders only if they could not achieve such diversification on their own.

◆ *Capital Market Efficiency*: The method of accounting for an acquisition does not affect the benefits shareholders derive from it.

◆ *Time Value of Money*: Use discounted-cash-flow analysis to measure the net advantage of an acquisition.

EMPIRE STATE'S ACQUISITION OPPORTUNITY

Empire State Pharmaceutical is a proprietary drug manufacturer with annual sales of $1.2 billion. Empire State is considering acquiring another publicly traded proprietary drug manufacturer, Garden State Drugs. Garden State has annual sales of $600 million. The acquisition would increase Empire State's sales by 50%. It would also lead to significant economies in marketing, and it would expand Empire State's product line more quickly than Empire State could do by developing similar drugs on its own. The net benefit of the potential acquisition depends, of course, on how much Empire State would have to pay to acquire Garden State.

Empire State's board of directors has asked the firm's chief financial officer to (1) determine a reasonable price to offer Garden State's shareholders, (2) estimate the impact on Empire State's shareholders of making the acquisition at the recommended price, (3) determine the maximum price Empire State could afford to pay, and (4) recommend the financial package that Empire State should offer Garden State's shareholders. In this chapter, we will help Empire State's chief financial officer respond to the board's request.

28.1 WHAT'S SPECIAL ABOUT A MERGER?

A **merger** involves a combination of two firms, the acquiror and the acquiree. The acquiror absorbs all the assets and liabilities of the acquiree and assumes the acquiree's business. The acquiree loses its independent existence, often becoming a subsidiary of the acquiror.

In a **consolidation**, two or more firms combine to form an entirely new entity. The distinction between acquiror and acquiree becomes blurred, because shares of each of the consolidated firms are exchanged for shares of the new firm. Both of the consolidating firms lose their independent existence, often becoming subsidiaries of the new firm or, in combination, becoming the new firm.

When two firms of roughly equal size combine, they often choose to consolidate. When they are of unequal size, one firm acquires the other through merger. Usually the larger firm acquires the smaller, although this is not always the case. The distinction between a merger and a consolidation is important in a legal sense, but the same analytical techniques apply to both. Accordingly, we will assume that one party to a corporate combination can be identified, or at least treated for analytical purposes, as the acquiror, and we will use the terms *corporate acquisition* and *merger* interchangeably to refer to corporate combinations in general.

A merger involves the acquisition of an entire firm. Buying a firm, with its own portfolio of assets and its own liabilities, is more complicated than buying a new machine or building a new plant. In addition, complex tax issues must often be resolved. For these reasons, estimating the incremental cash flows is inherently more difficult than the measurement problems encountered in capital investment projects of the types discussed in Chapters 11 through 13.

Also, how a firm finances an acquisition takes on added importance. The economics of the investment and how the firm finances it tend to interact, because the acquisition can alter the acquiror's financial structure. Thus estimating the required return is also inherently more difficult in the case of corporate acquisitions than in other forms of capital investment. Yet accuracy is often crucial because of the amount of corporate funds that the acquiror must commit to the transaction.

There is an additional reason why mergers represent a special form of capital investment. Firms usually have to make very quick decisions on the basis of incomplete information. In unfriendly situations, the acquiror may have only publicly available information on which to base a decision. In such cases, discounted-cash-flow analysis is difficult to apply. Consequently, the other valuation techniques that are used in practice to gauge the reasonableness of an acquisition price take on increased importance in such situations.

Self-Check Questions

1. What is a merger? What is a consolidation? How do they differ?
2. Explain why a corporate acquisition can be viewed as a special type of capital investment project. In what respects is it more complicated than a typical capital investment project?

28.2 WHY FIRMS MERGE

There are a number of possible motives a firm may have for seeking to merge with a particular firm. Each should be judged against the objective of maximizing shareholder wealth.

When Do Mergers Create Value?

The shareholders of an acquiring firm can benefit from a merger only if the two firms are worth more in combination than separately. To provide a framework for discussion, suppose that acquiror and acquiree are worth V_A and V_B in total market value (that is, the total market value of their assets), respectively. They would be worth V_{AB} in total market value in combination. The acquiror must normally offer the acquiree's shareholders some premium, P_B, above V_B to induce them to sell their shares. The acquiror also incurs various costs and expenses, E. The **net advantage to merging**, NAM, to the acquiror's shareholders equals the difference between (1) the total market value of the firm post-merger net of the cost of completing the acquisition and (2) the total market value of the firms before the merger:

$$\text{NAM} = V_{AB} - (V_B + P_B) - E - V_A = [V_{AB} - (V_A + V_B)] - P_B - E \qquad (28.1)$$

If the net advantage to merging is positive, the merger would increase the wealth of the acquiror's shareholders. The term in brackets in Equation (28.1) represents what is commonly referred to as the *synergistic effect* of a merger. The whole is worth more than the sum of the parts when this expression is positive. Under the Principle of Two-Sided Transactions, the premium P_B represents both a gain to the acquiree's shareholders and a cost to the acquiror's shareholders. Even if the synergistic effect is positive, the acquiror's shareholders will benefit only if the premium P_B and the costs and expenses E do not consume the benefits arising out of the synergy. One of the more interesting issues in the area of mergers and acquisitions is the size of P_B in relation to $V_{AB} - (V_A + V_B)$. If P_B is sufficiently large, NAM might even be negative. In that case, the acquiror will have "overpaid" for the acquisition.

Firm A, with a total market value of $50 million, is planning to acquire Firm B, which has a total market value of $15 million. Firm A estimates that the merged firm will be worth $75 million as a result of operating and other efficiencies. Firm A's investment bankers have advised that Firm A will have to pay a $6 million premium in price to acquire Firm B. Merger-related costs and expenses will amount to $1 million. Applying Equation (28.1), we find that the net advantage to merging is

Calculating the Net Advantage to Merging

EXAMPLE

$$\text{NAM} = [75 - (50 + 15)] - 6 - 1 = \$3 \text{ million}$$

Synergy creates $10 million of value (= $75 − [15 + 50]). Of this amount, $6 million is paid to Firm B's shareholders, and $1 million covers transaction-related expenses. Firm A's shareholders wind up with a net increase in their wealth of $3 million. Thus the merger would benefit both firms' shareholders. ■

Evidence suggests that mergers do tend to produce synergy and that the stockholders of acquired firms tend to benefit handsomely. Stockholders generally receive takeover premiums averaging between 30% and 50% for their shares. In contrast, the shareholders of acquiring firms tend to realize only very modest gains. This sharing of benefits is probably due to capital market efficiency, reflecting the impact (actual or potential) of competing acquirors.

Valid Motives for Merging

A merger can be economically beneficial only if the sum of the parts exceeds the whole. There are at least four situations in which this can happen.

ACHIEVE OPERATING EFFICIENCIES AND ECONOMIES OF SCALE   Two firms may decide to merge in order to achieve *operating efficiencies* or to take advantage of *economies of scale.* The merged firms can eliminate duplicate facilities, operations, or departments.[1] Consider two airlines with overlapping routes. By merging their operations, they can better coordinate scheduling and eliminate excess capacity.

Achieving operating efficiencies is more likely to result from a horizontal or vertical merger than from a conglomerate merger. A **horizontal merger** combines two firms in the same line of business. A **vertical merger** involves integrating forward toward the consumer, or backward toward the source of supply, in a particular line of business. A **conglomerate merger** joins firms in unrelated businesses. The merger of two airlines is a horizontal merger. When a firm purchases one of its parts suppliers, that is a vertical merger. Most mergers in the United States since World War II have been of the conglomerate type.

One means of achieving operating efficiencies involves combining two firms that have complementary resources. For example, a small computer firm might have a skilled product engineering staff and one or more unique products but might lack management expertise and a strong sales staff. A second computer firm, perhaps older and larger, might have strong management and an established sales network but lack state-of-the-art products. A merger could be mutually beneficial, because each firm has something the other needs. Such a case is an ap-

---

[1] Something to consider if you are thinking of pursuing a career in corporate financial management: The financial staff of the acquiree is usually one of the first redundancies to be eliminated!

plication of the Principle of Comparative Advantage. But a merger will be beneficial to both only if it enables each firm to obtain what it needs more cheaply than it could have if it had remained on its own.

Two firms in the same line of business might also merge in order to achieve economies of scale in production, distribution, or some other phase of their operation. Economies of scale occur when the average unit cost of goods sold decreases as output expands. For example, a higher volume of production might permit a firm to build larger, more efficient plants than the smaller ones it must build now. Achieving economies of scale in production is a key motive underlying most horizontal mergers.

Operating efficiencies and economies of scale are the main sources of any synergy. A conglomerate merger has the least potential for generating them. In any case, one must be careful in assessing potential operating efficiencies and potential economies of scale. They may never be realized. For example, merging an insurance broker and a securities broker to achieve economies of distribution may fail to yield the anticipated benefits if the brokers cannot (or simply will not) sell each other's products.

| EXAMPLE | *Potential Economies Are Not Always Realized* | After Sears, Roebuck & Co. acquired Dean Witter Reynolds Inc., it placed Dean Witter stockbrokers in more than 300 of its approximately 850 retail stores nationwide. Dean Witter brokers complained about the "socks and stocks" marketing strategy, saying it was difficult to drum up business from people shopping for clothing, vacuum cleaners, and lawn mowers. Within a few years, Sears had reduced the number of Dean Witter outlets by more than two-thirds. ■ |

REALIZE TAX BENEFITS   Suppose a firm has tax loss carryforwards it cannot take full advantage of. Merging with a profitable firm that pays income taxes might prove mutually beneficial. Under some circumstances, the firm with a loss can use its tax loss carryforwards to shelter some—or perhaps all—of the profitable firm's income from taxation. For example, when the Penn Central Corporation emerged from bankruptcy, in effect it was able to use its substantial tax loss carryforwards by acquiring tax-paying firms.[2]

Here is another possible tax benefit. Consider a firm in a mature industry that is generating a large amount of free cash flow. If the firm distributes the cash to its shareholders, they will have to pay tax (unless shares are repurchased at a price that is less than the shareholders' tax basis in the shares). But they will not have to pay tax if the firm instead invests the cash in the shares of other firms. Whether the acquiror's shareholders truly gain depends on whether the acquisition has a positive net present value.

---

[2] Under current tax law, the merger must have a valid business purpose, apart from taxes, in order for the Internal Revenue Service to permit the profitable firm to utilize the other firm's tax net operating loss carryforwards (NOLs). In general, it is easier to survive the scrutiny of the IRS when the acquiror is the one with the NOLs. The Tax Reform Act of 1986 tightened restrictions on one firm's ability to utilize another firm's NOLs to shelter part of its operating income from taxation following an acquisition. If the ultimate ownership of a firm with NOLs changes by more than 50% over a 3-year period, then the amount of the acquiree's NOLs and unused tax credits that the acquiror can utilize in any one year is limited to an amount calculated by multiplying the net worth of the acquiree immediately prior to the acquisition times the long-term tax-exempt bond yield (published by the U.S. Treasury). As a result of more recent changes in tax law, it is no longer possible for an acquiring firm with NOLs to use its NOLs to shelter gain on the sale of the acquiree's assets (for example, assets in a subsidiary with a very low tax basis) following the corporate acquisition, which was one of the strategies Penn Central adopted.

FREE UP SURPLUS CASH Mergers may be motivated by the acquiror's desire to use the acquiree's cash.[3] Firms with substantial cash and a shortage of capital investment opportunities may therefore look like sitting ducks for acquisition unless they can invest the cash or distribute it to their shareholders.

GROW MORE QUICKLY OR MORE CHEAPLY A firm may find that it can grow more quickly or more cheaply by acquiring other firms than through internal development. It is generally quicker to obtain new products, new facilities, or a national distribution network by acquiring a firm that has already developed them. A firm may be able to acquire assets, such as oil and gas reserves, more cheaply by purchasing another firm than by developing—or in this case exploring for—its own. Acquiring a local firm may be the most cost-effective means of establishing a secure market position in a foreign market. The desire to secure a position in the U.S. market probably is largely responsible for the sharp increase in the number of foreign acquisitions of U.S. firms in recent years.

Questionable Motives for Merging

Firms also cite other motives for mergers. Three of the more questionable motives involve diversification, reducing the cost of debt, and enhancing earnings per share.

DIVERSIFICATION Diversification is generally one of the main motives behind a conglomerate merger. At first glance, this motive seems reasonable because of the Principle of Diversification. But diversification will benefit the acquiror's shareholders only if they could not achieve such diversification more cheaply on their own. The following example shows why diversification might not increase shareholder wealth.

Two firms plan to merge through an exchange of shares. The firms are in unrelated businesses, so there is no synergistic effect. Firm A has 1 million shares worth $40 each, and Firm B has 3 million shares worth $20 each. Each firm is debt-free. Firm B will issue 2 new shares of its stock (worth $20 each, for a total of $40) for each share of Firm A (worth $40). (There is no merger premium in this case.) Table 28-2 shows the impact of the merger. The total market value of each firm is the weighted average of its value in the three possible states of the economy. For example, the value of Firm A is

A Conglomerate Merger Might Not Increase Shareholder Wealth

$$\text{Value of Firm A} = 0.4(50) + 0.5(36) + 0.1(20) = \$40 \text{ million}$$

The value of Firm B is calculated the same way. Combining Firms A and B combines their respective values. The value of the combined firm is $100 million (= 40 + 60). Because there are 5 million shares, each share is worth $20 (= 100/5).

Suppose a shareholder owned 1000 shares of Firm A and 500 shares of Firm B prior to the merger. Her shares were worth

$$\$50,000 = (40)(1000) + (20)(500)$$

Following the merger, she owns 2500 shares of Firm B (the original 500 shares plus 2000 more received in exchange for her 1000 shares of Firm A), which are worth the same $50,000 (= 20 × 2500).

---

[3] It has been argued that mergers and threats of merger have unlocked stockpiles of surplus cash in the broadcasting, food, forest products, motion picture, oil, and tobacco industries.

TABLE 28-2
Diversification through merging may not increase shareholder wealth (dollar amounts in millions).

| | NUMBER OF SHARES | TOTAL VALUE IN STATE | | | TOTAL MARKET VALUE | SHARE PRICE |
		Boom	Stable Growth	Recession		
Probability		0.4	0.5	0.1		
Firm A	1 million[b]	$ 50	$36	$20	$ 40	$40
Firm B	3 million	75	54	30	60	20
Combined[a]	5 million[b]	125	90	50	100	20

[a] Firm A and Firm B combine through an exchange of shares. Firm B issues 2 million new shares in exchange for Firm A's 1 million outstanding shares.
[b] Firm A's 1 million shares are eliminated in exchange for 2 million shares of Firm B.

Shareholder wealth has not changed.[4] ■

The homemade diversification argument for mergers is like the personal leverage argument discussed in Chapter 15 and the homemade dividends argument discussed in Chapter 17. They rest on the assumption that there are no market imperfections. Relaxing these assumptions, corporate diversification may create value. For example, as already noted, diversifying at the firm level may be more tax-efficient than paying out the excess cash to shareholders.

FINANCIAL SYNERGY   A larger (merged) firm can take advantage of economies of scale in issuing securities, which we documented in Chapter 23. If the merged firm makes larger issues than the two firms would separately, the merger may result in lower transaction costs. However, lower issuance expenses are not likely to contribute much to the value of a merger.

A merger can benefit bondholders. The problem here is the reverse of what we called (in Chapter 9) the problem of claim dilution with respect to capital structure. Recall that stockholders can expropriate wealth from bondholders by diluting the bondholders' claim on the assets. This same phenomenon can work in reverse, against the stockholders. Diversification via merger can reduce the probability of bankruptcy. The expected return to each class of debtholders increases, and their risk decreases. It follows from the Principle of Risk-Return Trade-Off that the debtholders of each firm are unambiguously better off. But if the merger does not alter the two firms' combined returns, the stockholders must be worse off. The bondholders gain at the expense of stockholders, because each firm effectively guarantees the debt of the other.

EXAMPLE

A Conglomerate Merger Can Benefit Bondholders at the Expense of Stockholders

Table 28-3 illustrates how a conglomerate merger can benefit bondholders at the expense of shareholders. The conditions are the same as in Table 28-2 except that Firm A now has $30 million principal amount of debt. Firm A's bondholders will be paid in full in the boom and stable growth states. But there is only $20 million available in the recession state. The bondholders get it all, though they still come up short by $10 million, and the shareholders get nothing. Therefore, the debt is worth only $29 million [= 0.4(30) + 0.5(30) + 0.1(20)].

If Firm A and Firm B merge, the combined cash flows of the two firms are available to

---

[4] Note that the merger might actually make her *worse off* if there are no close substitutes for each firm, because the merger in that case would reduce her investment opportunities. Before the merger, she owned the shares of the two firms in the ratio 4 : 1 by market value ($40,000 of Firm A and $10,000 of Firm B). They combine in the ratio 2 : 3 ($40 million of Firm A and $60 million of Firm B). After the merger, she effectively owns them in this new ratio. See Problem C2.

	BOOM	STABLE GROWTH	RECESSION	TOTAL MARKET VALUE
Probability	0.4	0.5	0.1	
Firm A				
Debt	$ 30	$30	$20	$ 29
Equity	20	6	—	11
Total	$ 50	$36	$20	$ 40
Firm B				
Debt	$ —	$—	$—	$—
Equity	75	54	30	60
Total	$ 75	$54	$30	$ 60
Combined				
Debt	$ 30	$30	$30	$ 30[a]
Equity	95	60	20	70[b]
Total	$125	$90	$50	$100

TABLE 28-3

Financial synergy can benefit bondholders at the expense of stockholders (dollar amounts in millions).

[a] Bondholder wealth increases by $1 (= 30 − 29) because bondholders are paid in full in each state as a result of the merger.
[b] Shareholder wealth decreases by $1 (= 60 + 11 − 70) because of the coinsurance effect.

service the debt. In the recession state, the bondholders will be paid in full as a result of the merger. In effect, Firm B guarantees Firm A's obligation to repay its bonds. This guarantee is referred to as the *coinsurance effect* of a merger. If both firms had debt, each would effectively guarantee the debt of the other.

The stock of the combined firm is worth $70 million. The sum of the values of the stock in each firm is $71 million (= 60 + 11). The shareholders of the two firms have collectively lost $1 million (= 71 − 70). What happened to this value? The $1 million of value was transferred to the bondholders. Their debt became more valuable because they will be paid in full regardless of the state of the economy. The merger transferred value from the stockholders to the bondholders through the coinsurance effect. ■

ENHANCED EARNINGS PER SHARE   A firm can increase its earnings per share by exchanging its shares for those of another firm whose shares have a lower price-earnings ratio. (We'll return to this point later in the chapter.) Such share-for-share exchanges increase earnings per share *even if no real gain results from the merger*.

Self-Check Questions

1. What is the net advantage to merging? How is it calculated?
2. List four valid motives that firms may have for merging. Explain each one.
3. What is the difference between a horizontal merger and a vertical merger? How are they different from a conglomerate merger?
4. Two unrelated firms plan to merge. Their joint announcement says that the shareholders of both will benefit from diversification. Do you agree? Why or why not?
5. Firm A with high leverage acquires Firm B with a debt-free capital structure. The firms exchange shares on the basis of their respective fair market values. Why might the shareholders of Firm B object to this merger?

28.3 TECHNICAL ISSUES

When one firm acquires another, three sets of technical issues arise: the legal form of the transaction, its tax status, and its accounting treatment. These three sets of issues are interrelated. Figure 28-1 summarizes the alternatives.

Form of Transaction

There are three basic ways of effecting a corporate acquisition:

1. Merger or consolidation
2. Purchase of stock
3. Purchase of assets

Merger or Consolidation.   In a merger, the acquiror absorbs the acquiree. The acquiror automatically obtains all the assets and assumes all the liabilities of the acquiree, which loses its corporate existence. But suppose the acquiror wishes the acquiree to survive as a separate entity. Then the acquiror can merge the acquiree with a special-purpose subsidiary. The acquiree becomes a wholly owned subsidiary of the acquiror.

A merger or consolidation must comply with each corporation's charter. Many corporate charters require a simple majority of the firm's shareholders to approve a merger or consolidation. Some require a two-thirds majority.

A merger or consolidation offers the most flexible means of structuring a tax-free acquisition. It is also generally easier and less costly to complete than either of the other two forms of acquisition.

Acquisition of Stock.   An acquiror can purchase the acquiree's stock. It still obtains the acquiree's assets and liabilities, but no shareholders' meetings are involved. A prospective acquiror can also bypass management and make a *tender offer* directly to the firm's shareholders. It is only an *offer* to purchase; any shareholders who do not like the price offered can refuse to sell their shares. But if the price is high enough, the shareholders will sell their shares. This can create problems for the acquiror, however. If the acquiror purchases fewer than 80% of the acquiree's voting securities, then it will not be able to consolidate the acquiree for tax purposes. Also, if any of the acquiree's shares remain outstanding, then there is a minority interest in the subsidiary, which gives rise to potential agency problems.[5]

Acquisition of Assets.   An acquiror can purchase only the selling firm's assets. The liabilities of the seller, other than those specifically assumed by the buyer, remain the responsibility of the seller. There is thus substantially less likelihood that hidden liabilities will be discovered after the transaction to the detriment of the buyer. There is also no problem with

FIGURE 28-1
Legal, tax, and accounting issues involved in mergers.

LEGAL FORM	TAX STATUS	ACCOUNTING TREATMENT
Merger or consolidation	Tax-free	Pooling of interests
Purchase of stock	Taxable	Purchase accounting
Purchase of assets		

[5] Consequently, an acquiror that purchases shares from less than all of the acquiree's shareholders—for instance, through a tender offer—generally follows this purchase with a formal merger in order to eliminate the minority interest. Under Delaware state law, for example, the acquiror can execute a *statutory merger*, effectively forcing out minority stockholders, without a shareholders' meeting if it owns at least 90% of the voting securities of the acquiree.

minority shareholders. In addition, the buyer's shareholders usually do not have to approve the transaction, and most corporate charters require only 50% approval by the seller's shareholders. The three main drawbacks to this structure are that (1) it is more difficult to achieve a tax-free transaction, (2) transferring the title of ownership to individual assets is costly and time-consuming, and (3) distributing the cash proceeds to shareholders usually triggers an income tax liability to the shareholders in addition to any tax the firm may owe.

Antitrust Considerations

A merger transaction must comply with federal antitrust law, state anti-takeover statutes, the corporate charter of each firm, and federal and state securities laws. There are three main federal antitrust statutes. The Clayton Act has become the chief weapon the government uses to contest mergers that it feels may lessen competition. Section 7 forbids a firm to purchase the assets or the stock of another firm if the purchase might substantially lessen competition, or tend to create a monopoly, in any line of commerce or in any section of the country. For example, the government challenged the merger of Texaco and Getty Oil Company, at the time the third and twelfth largest oil companies in the United States, because of the two firms' overlapping gasoline marketing operations in the northeastern Unites States.

The actual percentage of potential mergers contested on antitrust grounds is small. Those involving very large firms, and horizontal acquisitions, appear to be the most likely to be challenged. Many of those that are questioned can survive the challenge by having the acquiror agree to sell assets in the affected market(s) to restore competition, as Texaco agreed to do.

Other Legal Considerations

Several other legal issues must be addressed in merger situations. For example, there are special rules relating to tender offers. Also, the acquiror should examine the indenture covenants for the acquiree's outstanding debt to determine whether any of its debt issues will have to be repaid at par upon a change in control.

Tax Considerations

The tax issues that arise in connection with mergers are very complex. All we can do is summarize some of the key aspects. The Internal Revenue Service assumes that an acquisition is taxable unless stringent conditions are met. In a **tax-free acquisition**, the selling shareholders are treated as having *exchanged* their old shares for substantially similar new shares. The acquiror's tax basis in each asset whose ownership is transferred in the transaction is the same as the acquiree's. Each selling shareholder who receives only stock does not have to pay any tax on the gain realized as a result of the acquisition until the shares are sold.

In a **taxable acquisition**, the selling shareholders are treated as having *sold* their shares. The acquiror can, if it wants, increase the tax basis in the assets it acquires to the fair market value of the consideration it pays to acquire them (including the fair market value of the acquiree's liabilities assumed by the acquiror). Unless the sale is an installment sale (that is, for debt of the acquiror), each shareholder who sells shares must recognize gain or loss for tax purposes immediately.[6]

From the seller's perspective, the main benefit of a tax-free transaction is deferral of tax on any gain realized on the sale of the business. The seller who receives stock in the acquiror also has a continuing equity interest in the enterprise and can share in any post-merger benefits. From the buyer's perspective, the main benefit derives from the acquiror's ability to take

---

[6] An acquisition can qualify as an *installment sale* only if the acquiree's common stock was not publicly traded *and* the installment debt issued to pay the purchase price is not publicly traded.

BUSINESS-PURPOSE TEST

The transaction must have a sound business purpose. It cannot be solely for tax reasons.

CONTINUITY-OF-BUSINESS TEST

The acquiror must continue to operate the acquiree's business.

MODE-OF-ACQUISITION AND MEDIUM-OF-PAYMENT TESTS
Merger or Consolidation

- Must qualify as a merger or consolidation under applicable state law.
- Acquiree's shareholders must receive at least 50% of the aggregate purchase price in stock of the acquiror (either common or preferred, either voting or nonvoting).

Stock-for-Stock Acquisition

- Acquiror can exchange only its voting stock or the voting stock of its parent.
- Acquiror must gain control of at least 80% of the aggregate voting interest in the acquiree and 80% of the total number of outstanding shares of each class of nonvoting stock.

Stock-for-Assets Acquisition

- Acquiror must obtain *substantially all* of the acquiree's assets in exchange for voting stock of the acquiror or voting stock of its parent.[a]
- Immediately after the stock-for-assets exchange, this voting stock must be distributed to the acquiree's shareholders in liquidation of the acquiree.

[a] If the acquiree is merged into a subsidiary of the acquiror (a so-called *subsidiary merger*), then the Code requires that (1) the medium-of-payment test be met using only stock of the parent firm and (2) the subsidiary acquire substantially all the assets of the acquiree. Under present IRS guidelines, *substantially all* means at least 90% of the fair market value of net assets and at least 70% of the fair market value of gross assets. If a subsidiary of the acquiror is merged into the acquiree (a *reverse subsidiary merger*), the Code requires that (1) at least 80% of the purchase price be paid in voting stock and (2) after the transaction the acquiror hold substantially all of its (pre-merger) assets and substantially all of the acquiree's (pre-merger) assets.

FIGURE 28-2
Requirements for tax-free treatment.

---

advantage of the existing tax attributes of the acquiree, such as net operating loss carryforwards.[7]

REQUIREMENTS FOR TAX-FREE TREATMENT   The Internal Revenue Code imposes a variety of conditions that must be met for a transaction to be tax-free. If these conditions are not met, the transaction is taxable. Figure 28-2 summarizes the requirements for tax-free treatment.

TO BE OR NOT TO BE TAX-FREE   A tax-free transaction benefits a shareholder who has a gain, because it permits deferral of tax on the gain. A taxable transaction benefits a shareholder who has a loss and has sufficient taxable income to offset it, because it creates a tax deduction. A taxable transaction also gives the acquiror greater flexibility in financing the acquisition. And it benefits the acquiror when the acquiree has substantial depreciable or depletable properties, such as oil and gas reserves, that, when written up to market value, will generate depreciation and depletion deductions whose present value exceeds the immediate tax recapture liability triggered by the write-up. Under the Principle of Two-Sided Transac-

---

[7] The Tax Reform Act of 1986 imposed restrictions on the buyer's ability to utilize these tax attributes.

tions, the interests of the acquiror and those of the selling shareholders often conflict. The "high" market value of the assets that can make writing up their tax basis advantageous is likely to be reflected in a "high" share price for the acquiree, which creates the capital gain.

As a general rule, structuring an acquisition as a taxable transaction in order to be able to write up the tax basis of the acquiree's assets is not a tax-effective strategy under current U.S. tax law.[8] The seller must pay tax on the difference between the purchase price received and its tax basis in the assets. In an efficient market, this tax liability will be reflected in the purchase price the buyer pays. Because this difference is then depreciated over several years, the net present value of the asset write-up must be negative.

Accounting Considerations

Acquisitions often involve difficult accounting issues. One of the more important issues, in practice, is whether to structure the acquisition as a pooling of interests or as a purchase. In an efficient capital market, the choice of accounting technique should not affect market value, because it does not affect cash flows. Nevertheless, professional managers often take great pains to structure transactions so as to achieve a particular accounting treatment.

POOLING OF INTERESTS   In a **pooling of interests**, the assets, liabilities, and operating results of the firms involved in the merger are added together without any adjustment to their recorded values. The financial statements of the firms are combined as though the firms had always been commonly owned. That is, no adjustments are made to the recorded values of the firms' assets or liabilities to reflect the merger. The acquiror's financial statements for all disclosed fiscal years (usually 5) preceding the merger must be restated to reflect the pooling (if the impact would be material).

Firm B acquires Firm A. Suppose it gives Firm A's shareholders $60 million of its common stock. Table 28-4 shows the accounting impact. The balance sheets of the two firms are added line by line. The *book values* of equity are combined. The $60 million market value of equity that Firm B pays Firm A's shareholders does *not* enter into this calculation. The combined book equity is $115 million. The new firm is owned jointly by the former shareholders of both firms. The old shareholders of Firm A now own shares of Firm B. ■

EXAMPLE
Pooling-of-Interests Accounting

TABLE 28-4
Accounting for an acquisition: pooling of interests method (dollar amounts in millions).

	FIRM A	FIRM B	COMBINED
Assets			
Working capital	$20	$ 35	$ 55
Fixed assets	30	65	95
Total	$50	$100	$150
Liabilities and Equity			
Debt	$10	$ 25	$ 35
Equity	40	75	115
Total	$50	$100	$150

---

[8] There is one exception. Suppose (1) the seller has tax net operating loss carryforwards (NOLs) that are sufficient to cover the tax liability and (2) the seller or the acquiror could not otherwise use these NOLs (or their realization would be delayed for some years). Then it is possible for the net present value of the write-up to be positive.

PURCHASE METHOD   Under the **purchase method**, one of the firms is identified as the acquiror. It is treated as having purchased the assets of the other firm. The purchase price, after adding the fair market value of the liabilities the acquiror assumes, is allocated to the acquired assets. Any excess of the purchase price over the fair market value of the net assets acquired is recorded as *goodwill*, which the acquiror must amortize over a period not exceeding 40 years. This represents a noncash charge against the acquiror's net income. If instead of an excess there is a deficiency, the deficiency is assigned as a reduction in the carrying value of long-term assets. The reported net income of the acquiror includes the net income of the acquiree only from the date of the acquisition.

EXAMPLE

Purchase Accounting

Firm B acquires Firm A. It issues $60 million of new common stock to investors for cash. It uses the cash to pay for the shares of Firm A. Table 28-5 shows the accounting impact. Firm A's fixed assets have a fair market value of $42 million. Its debt has a book value of $10 million but is worth only $7 million. Firm A's assets are written up by $12 million. Its debt is written down by $3 million. The acquisition eliminates Firm A's equity because Firm A's shares are purchased and retired.

   Table 28-5 also shows the calculation of goodwill. The fair market value of Firm A's assets exceeds that of its liabilities by $55 million. But Firm B paid $60 million. The $5 million excess represents goodwill. You might think of goodwill as a firm's "franchise" value: the reputational capital it has built up for itself and its products through years of successful operation. ■

TABLE 28-5
Accounting for an acquisition: purchase method (dollar amounts in millions).

	FIRM A	FIRM B	ADJUSTMENTS	COMBINED
Assets				
Working capital	$20	$ 35		$ 55
Fixed assets	30	65	$+12^a$	107
Goodwill	—	—	$+5^b$	5
Total	$50	$100		$167
Liabilities and Equity				
Debt	$10	$ 25	-3^c	$ 32
Equity	40	75	-40^d	
			$+60^e$	135
Total	$50	$100		$167

[a] To record the write-up of Firm A's assets to fair market value.
[b] Calculation of goodwill:

Purchase price paid for Firm A's equity		$60
Fair market value of Firm A's assets	$62	
Fair market value of Firm A's liabilities	7	
Fair market value of Firm A's net assets		55
Goodwill		$ 5

[c] To revalue Firm A's debt to fair market value.
[d] The acquisition eliminates Firm A's equity.
[e] To record the equity Firm B issues to raise the cash to pay for Firm A.

   Acquisitions that qualify for pooling-of-interests accounting usually also qualify as tax-free, and taxable acquisitions are usually accounted for as purchases. However, neither statement is always true.

Self-Check Questions

1. What are the three basic ways of effecting a corporate acquisition? What are the distinguishing features of each approach?

2. What are the main differences between a tax-free acquisition and a taxable acquisition? Why would a seller with a low tax basis in her stock prefer a tax-free acquisition, other things being equal?

3. What are the main differences between the pooling-of-interests and the purchase methods of accounting for an acquisition? Does the choice of accounting method affect shareholder wealth?

4. Why do antitrust concerns sometimes arise in connection with mergers? Which type of merger is most likely to raise them?

28.4 COMPARATIVE ANALYSIS OF MERGERS

There are two main ways to value corporate acquisitions: by comparative analysis and by discounted-cash-flow analysis. In a comparative analysis, we infer the value from the prices that were paid for firms in comparable transactions. Comparative analysis is the more widely used technique.

The two approaches differ in one fundamental respect. Comparative analysis is used to determine a "reasonable" price to pay. The discounted-cash-flow approach is used to calculate the impact of an acquisition on shareholder wealth, given a particular acquisition cost. It can also be used to estimate the maximum price an acquiror could pay without reducing the wealth of its shareholders. These two approaches are therefore complementary. When used properly together, they yield more useful information than either approach could separately.

The Merger Premium

Two issues make the analysis of acquisitions difficult. First, the acquiror usually must pay a premium over the price at which the acquiree's shares are trading in the market (or would trade if the target firm were publicly held). The premium reflects the value of obtaining control of the acquiree. Comparative analysis can be used to determine a "reasonable" premium. Second, in many cases the acquiree is large enough, compared to the acquiror, that there are significant debt capacity side effects associated with the merger. The adjusted-present-value approach discussed in Chapter 16 is ideally suited to handling such situations.

The required premium tends to vary from one industry to another, depending on the industry's prospects. It also varies from one firm to another within an industry, depending on that firm's financial and business characteristics and relative prospects. And the required premium may depend on the state of the stock market.

Premiums Paid in Acquisitions

Table 28-6 shows the distribution of premiums paid in acquisitions for the period 1975–1994. The annual average premium has varied between a low of 35% in 1991 and a high of 50% in 1979 and again in 1980. The annual median premium has varied between a low of 28% in 1985 and a high of 48% in 1979. A recent study found that acquisition premiums during the 1974–1985 period were approximately double those of the 1963–1973 period, which was a pe-

TABLE 28-6
Premiums paid in acquisitions of publicly-traded firms, 1975–1994.

| YEAR | NUMBER OF ACQUISITIONS | PERCENT PREMIUM PAID OVER MARKET PRICE | | | | | | AVERAGE | MEDIAN | DOW JONES INDUSTRIAL AVERAGE DURING YEAR | |
| | | 0.1–40.0 | | 40.0–80.0 | | OVER 80.0 | | | | | |
		Amount	%	Amount	%	Amount	%			High	Low
1975	129	74	57	38	30	17	13	41	30	881.81	632.04
1976	168	101	60	45	27	22	13	40	31	1014.79	858.71
1977	218	120	55	70	32	28	13	41	36	999.75	800.85
1978	240	116	48	90	38	34	14	46	42	907.74	742.12
1979	229	95	41	91	40	43	19	50	48	897.61	796.67
1980	169	75	44	61	36	33	20	50	45	1000.17	795.13
1981	166	80	48	54	33	32	19	48	42	1024.05	824.01
1982	176	80	45	66	37	30	18	47	44	1070.55	776.92
1983	168	101	60	53	32	14	8	38	34	1287.20	1027.04
1984	199	118	59	68	34	13	7	38	34	1286.64	1086.57
1985	331	231	70	71	21	29	9	37	28	1553.10	1184.96
1986	333	222	67	82	24	29	9	38	30	1955.60	1502.30
1987	237	155	65	66	28	16	7	38	31	2722.42	1738.74
1988	410	255	62	113	28	42	10	42	31	2183.50	1879.14
1989	303	187	62	88	29	28	9	41	29	2791.41	2144.64
1990	175	105	60	48	27	22	13	42	32	2999.75	2365.10
1991	137	92	67	35	26	10	7	35	29	3168.83	2470.30
1992	142	84	59	40	28	18	13	41	35	3413.21	3136.58
1993	173	110	64	48	28	15	9	39	33	3794.33	3241.95
1994	260	155	60	80	31	25	10	42	35	3978.36	3593.35
Total	4363	2556	58	1307	30	500	12				

Sources: W.T. Grimm & Co., *Mergerstat Review 1988*, pp. 94–95, and Merrill Lynch Business Advisory Services, *Mergerstat Review 1994*, pp. 90–91.

riod of generally rising share prices. That study also found that the acquisition premium behaves countercyclically, varying inversely with the Standard & Poor's 500 Index.[9]

EXAMPLE

Analysis of Premiums Paid

An acquisition target currently has 10,000,000 shares outstanding. They are trading at $27. This gives the target a current market value of $270 million. The acquiror's financial staff analyzes 10 recent acquisitions of firms in the same industry. It finds that the merger premiums fall between 50% and 66%. It also considers whether there has been any merger speculation or other factors that might have inflated the target's share price. It concludes there were none.

The premiums paid suggest that a reasonable acquisition value is between $405 million (= 270 × 1.5) and $448 million (= 270 × 1.66). A reasonable offering price would fall between $40.50 (= 405/10) and $44.80 (= 448/10) per share. Discounted-cash-flow analysis (discussed later) and tactical considerations will determine what price the acquiror should initially offer.[10] ■

---

[9] Nathan and O'Keefe (1989). The reasons for this behavior are not entirely clear. One possibility is that takeovers occur when the target firm is undervalued. Undervaluation may be more severe during recessions (when share prices are depressed).

[10] Discounted-cash-flow analysis will indicate the maximum price the acquiror can afford to pay. The acquiror must then determine an appropriate bidding strategy. Do not offer the maximum initially; give yourself room to raise the bid later.

Comparative Analysis

Investment bankers look at comparable acquisitions to determine a reasonable price for the acquiror to offer for the target firm's shares. They use a table like Table 28-7. Using such a table reflects the Behavioral Principle: Look to comparable acquisitions for guidance regarding a reasonable price to pay for an acquisition. The table provides the following pricing benchmarks for a carefully selected group of acquisitions of publicly traded firms.

$$\frac{\text{Multiple of}}{\text{earnings paid}} = \frac{\text{Purchase price per share}}{\substack{\text{Target's fully diluted earnings per share} \\ \text{before extraordinary items}}} \tag{28.2}$$

$$\frac{\text{Multiple of}}{\text{cash flow paid}} = \frac{\text{Purchase price per share}}{\substack{\text{Target's fully diluted cash flow per share} \\ \text{before extraordinary items}}} \tag{28.3}$$

$$\frac{\text{Multiple of}}{\text{EBIT paid}} = \frac{\substack{\text{Aggregate purchase} \\ \text{price of equity}} + \substack{\text{Market value of} \\ \text{debt assumed}}}{\substack{\text{Target's earnings before interest and taxes (EBIT)} \\ \text{before extraordinary items}}} \tag{28.4}$$

$$\frac{\text{Multiple of}}{\text{EBITDA paid}} = \frac{\substack{\text{Aggregate purchase} \\ \text{price of equity}} + \substack{\text{Market value of} \\ \text{debt assumed}}}{\substack{\text{Target's earnings before interest, taxes, depreciation,} \\ \text{and amortization (EBITDA) before extraordinary items}}} \tag{28.5}$$

$$\frac{\text{Multiple of}}{\text{book value paid}} = \frac{\text{Purchase price per share}}{\text{Target's book value per common share}} \tag{28.6}$$

$$\text{Premium paid} = \frac{\substack{\text{Purchase price} \\ \text{per share}} - \substack{\text{Target's share} \\ \text{price pre-merger}}}{\text{Target's share price pre-merger}} \tag{28.7}$$

The following ratio is often useful for firms that have substantial manufacturing facilities.

$$\frac{\substack{\text{Multiple of} \\ \text{replacement} \\ \text{cost paid}}}{} = \frac{\substack{\text{Aggregate purchase} \\ \text{price of equity}} + \substack{\text{Market value of} \\ \text{debt assumed}}}{\text{Replacement cost of target's assets}} \tag{28.8}$$

The following ratio is useful for natural resource firms whose assets often enjoy relatively liquid secondary markets (such as oil and gas reserves, timber and timberland, and so on).

$$\frac{\substack{\text{Price paid} \\ \text{per unit of} \\ \text{resource}}}{} = \frac{\substack{\text{Aggregate purchase} \\ \text{price of equity}} + \substack{\text{Market value of} \\ \text{debt assumed}}}{\text{Number of units of resource target owns}} \tag{28.9}$$

In Equations (28.2) and (28.3), if the firm is in a highly cyclical industry, then earnings per share and cash flow per share for each firm should be averaged over a period that corresponds to the length of one cycle. Also, if projected earnings are available for each firm as of its acquisition date, it is useful to calculate the multiple of earnings paid on both a historical basis and a projected basis. The multiple of EBIT (Equation 28.4) and the multiple of EBITDA (Equation 28.5) are usually more meaningful than the multiple of earnings (Equation 28.2) or cash flow (Equation 28.3) when the acquirees in the group of comparable transactions have significantly different capital structures. Differences in interest expense will affect earnings and cash flow but not EBIT and EBITDA. In Equation (28.7), the target's share price pre-merger is usually measured 30 days before the initial announcement of the acquisition in order to prevent pre-announcement effects from biasing the analysis.

TABLE 28-7

Illustration of comparative analysis.

DATE ANNOUNCED	ACQUIROR/ ACQUIREE[a]	INFORMATION ON ACQUIREE FOR LATEST 12 MONTHS PRIOR TO ACQUISITION							PURCHASE PRICE PAID FOR EQUITY		PURCHASE PRICE AS MULTIPLE OF					PREMIUM PAID OVER MARKET PRICE ONE MONTH BEFORE ANNOUNCEMENT
		Net Revenue (5-year growth)	Net Income (5-year growth)	Cash Flow (5-year growth)	EBIT (5-year growth)	EBITDA (5-year growth)	Book Value	MARKET VALUE OF DEBT	Aggregate	Per Share	Earnings[b]	Cash Flow[b]	EBIT[c]	EBITDA[c]	Book Value[b]	
	—	—	—	—	—	—	—	—	—	—	—	—	—	—	—	—
	Empire/ Garden State (P)	$600 (12.3%)	$30 (11.2%)	$42 (12.0%)	$53 (11.9%)	$58 (12.1%)	$196	$93	—	—	—	—	—	—	—	—
12/10/95	Atlantic/ Crescent (P)	630 (10.9)	27 (11.0)	40 (10.3)	45 (10.4)	51 (10.2)	177	105	$410	$33.75	15.2x	10.3x	11.4x	10.1x	2.3x	60%
11/5/95	Essex/ Trenton	435 (9.8)	20 (10.0)	30 (10.1)	35 (10.2)	39 (9.9)	142	90	270	39.50	13.5	9.0	10.3	9.2	1.9	45
9/7/95	Sussex/ Brooklyn	465 (7.5)	23 (8.0)	35 (8.7)	39 (9.1)	43 (8.9)	130	87	220	24.50	9.6	6.3	7.9	7.1	1.7	37
8/3/95	Madison/ Washington (P)	833 (12.9)	42 (12.6)	60 (13.2)	80 (12.9)	86 (13.3)	281	175	730	55.25	17.4	12.2	11.3	10.5	2.6	66
4/30/95	Jersey/ Philadelphia (P)	610 (11.7)	29 (12.4)	45 (12.7)	52 (12.5)	60 (12.6)	197	100	450	27.63	15.5	10.0	10.6	9.2	2.3	55
2/1/95	Morris/ Neptune (P)	720 (10.1)	32 (9.9)	42 (10.2)	58 (10.4)	64 (10.0)	210	90	441	38.25	13.8	10.5	9.2	8.3	2.1	53
11/30/94	Salem/ Seaside (P)	415 (13.6)	17 (12.6)	22 (11.1)	30 (11.3)	34 (10.7)	121	75	302	43.50	17.8	13.7	12.6	11.1	2.5	62
10/19/94	Worthington/ Homestead (P)	440 (11.4)	22 (11.7)	35 (11.0)	40 (11.1)	48 (10.5)	161	125	320	31.25	14.5	9.1	11.1	9.3	2.0	50
8/4/94	Ludlow/ Quackenbush	515 (11.1)	24 (8.3)	37 (8.3)	41 (8.7)	45 (8.4)	160	85	300	29.88	12.5	8.1	9.4	8.6	1.9	47
7/16/94	Warren/ Bergen	550 (10.8)	25 (8.7)	37 (9.0)	42 (9.1)	45 (8.8)	130	110	285	44.00	11.4	7.7	9.4	8.8	2.2	43
For all the Comparables:																
High		13.6%	12.6%	13.2%	12.9%	13.3%					17.8x	13.7x	12.6x	11.1x	2.6x	60%
Low		7.5	8.0	8.3	8.7	8.4					9.6	6.3	7.9	7.1	1.7	37
Average		11.0	10.5	10.5	10.6	10.3					14.1	9.7	10.3	9.2	2.2	51
For the Proprietary Pharmaceutical Manufacturers:																
High		13.6%	12.6%	13.2%	12.9%	13.3%					17.8x	13.7x	12.6x	11.1x	2.6x	66%
Low		10.1	9.9	10.2	10.4	10.0					13.8	9.1	9.2	8.3	2.0	50
Average		11.8	11.7	11.4	11.4	11.2					15.7	11.0	11.0	9.8	2.3	58

[a] (P) denotes proprietary pharmaceutical manufacturers.
[b] Based on the purchase price paid for equity.
[c] Based on the combined market value of debt and purchase price paid for equity.

In Equation (28.8), the replacement cost of the acquiree's assets can often be estimated from industry benchmarks (for example, proved developed crude oil reserves located in Texas have an average "finding cost" of so many dollars per barrel). In Equation (28.9), the number of units of resource the target owns is measured in physical units. Different resources can be combined by adopting some standard of equivalence. For example, an oil and gas firm's hydrocarbon reserves can be expressed on a "net equivalent barrel" basis by calculating the number of barrels of oil that would have the same market value as the firm's gas reserves. Then the price paid per unit of resource would be expressed in terms of dollars per net equivalent barrel.

Equations (28.2), (28.3), (28.6), and (28.7) are used to value the target firm's equity. Equations (28.4), (28.5), (28.8), and (28.9), because they all have the market value of debt assumed in the numerator, are used to value the target firm's net assets (that is, debt and equity). You must subtract the market value of the target's debt to get the value of its equity.

Comparative Analysis **EXAMPLE**

Table 28-7 illustrates comparative analysis of Empire State's possible acquisition of Garden State, the two firms we saw in an earlier example. Garden State currently has 10,000,000 shares outstanding, which are trading at a price of $27. This gives Garden State a current market value of $270 million (= 10 × 27). Empire State's financial staff believes that there has been no merger speculation or other factors that might have inflated Garden State's share price. (If there had been, Empire State's financial staff would have to reduce the premium to be offered Garden State's shareholders.)

The comparative analysis table contains data for 10 carefully selected recent acquisitions of pharmaceutical firms that are similar to Garden State in size and in business and financial characteristics. Six are also proprietary drug manufacturers like Garden State.

Comparing the multiples and premiums paid for all 10 firms to those paid for proprietary drug manufacturers reveals that the proprietary manufacturers have commanded higher multiples and premiums. Empire State's financial staff therefore decides to base its calculations on the data concerning the acquisitions of proprietary drug firms.

In terms of its growth (and other characteristics), Garden State compares very favorably with the six proprietary drug manufacturers. "Reasonable" acquisition multiples and a "reasonable" acquisition price would fall within the ranges shown in Table 28-8. The intersection of the six value ranges is $414 to $448 million. This analysis suggests a price per share in the range of $41.40 (= 414/10) to $44.80 (= 448/10) per Garden State share. Any price per share within this range would represent a reasonable price, in the sense that it would not be out of line with the prices that acquirors have paid in comparable situations. This is in keeping with the Behavioral Principle. ■

TABLE 28-8
Estimated ranges of value for Garden State Drugs.

MULTIPLE	RANGE OF MULTIPLES	VALUE FOR GARDEN STATE ($ MILLIONS)	IMPLIED AGGREGATE PURCHASE PRICE ($ MILLIONS)
Earnings	13.8–17.8x	30	414–534
Cash flow	9.1–13.7	42	382–575
EBIT	9.2–12.6	53	395–575[a]
EBITDA	8.3–11.1	58	388–551[a]
Book value	2.0–2.6	196	392–510
Premium paid	50%–66%	270	405–448

[a] After subtracting the market value of Garden State's debt ($93 million).

Comparative analysis does not always work this smoothly. In many cases, it is difficult to identify a well-defined group of comparables. For example, the candidates may all be in different businesses. In such cases, careful judgment must be applied to determine an appropriate value range—for example, by eliminating less closely comparable firms from the table (as we did in the illustration).

Liquidation Approach

The potential liquidation value (or breakup value) of a firm's common equity should also be considered in a merger evaluation. A holding company that operates a number of essentially autonomous firms, or a firm that owns a number of dissimilar assets, investments, and other firms, can be valued by estimating the market value of each class of assets and subtracting the cost of repaying all its liabilities:

$$\text{Liquidation value} = \text{Asset value} - \text{Repayment} - \text{Taxes} - \text{Expenses} \qquad (28.10)$$

where Liquidation value is the liquidation value of the target firm's common equity, Asset value is the liquidation value of all its assets, Repayment is the cost of repaying all its debt and preferred stock obligations, Taxes are the tax obligations incurred in connection with the liquidation, and Expenses are the costs and expenses associated with the acquisition and liquidation.

The liquidation values estimated when applying Equation (28.10) should be based on the values that can be realized within a "reasonable" time frame, say one year, rather than in a "fire sale." Equations (28.2) through (28.6)—and in the case of subsidiaries that hold substantial natural resources, Equation (28.9)—can be used to value subsidiaries that are salable within this reasonable time frame. Equation (28.7) can be used to value any subsidiaries that are publicly traded. The cost of repaying debt and redeeming preferred (and preference) stock will be specified in the documents governing those fixed-income obligations. Finally, the sale of assets usually triggers a corporate tax liability, and disposing of assets generally involves significant expenses.

Self-Check Questions

1. Explain how to use comparative analysis to estimate a reasonable price to pay for an acquisition. What is the rationale underlying this approach?

2. What is a merger premium, and how is it calculated? Why is it wise to calculate the merger premium using the share price 30 days before the initial announcement of the acquisition?

3. What is the multiple of earnings paid? What is the multiple of cash flow paid? What is the multiple of EBITDA paid? Why is the multiple of EBITDA paid more useful than the other two when the comparables have widely differing capital structures?

4. Suppose a holding company has three operating subsidiaries. There is no other firm just like the holding company, but each of its subsidiaries has a number of competitors each involved in only a single business. How would you use the liquidation approach to value this firm?

28.5 DISCOUNTED-CASH-FLOW ANALYSIS: WEIGHTED-AVERAGE-COST-OF-CAPITAL APPROACH

We have pointed out that an acquisition is a special type of capital budgeting problem. A firm acquires another firm, not just an asset. Even though acquisitions are more complex, discounted-cash-flow analysis is still useful. We must be careful not to overlook any of the complexities that might affect shareholder value. But when applied correctly, discounted-cash-flow analysis is helpful to an acquiror in deciding whether an acquisition would benefit its shareholders if it can buy the target for the price it is considering paying. Discounted-cash-

TABLE 28-9

Discounted-cash-flow analysis of the acquisition of Garden State Drugs: weighted-average-cost-of-capital approach.

	0	1	2	3	4	5	6	7	8	9	10
						YEAR					
Purchase of equity[a]	$ 480.0	—	—	—	—	—	—	—	—	—	—
Cost of debt assumed	92.6	—	—	—	—	—	—	—	—	—	—
Transaction costs	5.0	—	—	—	—	—	—	—	—	—	—
Acquiree's excess cash	(35.0)	—	—	—	—	—	—	—	—	—	—
Net acquisition cost	$ 542.6										
Incremental Free Cash Flow:											
Revenue	—	$672	$753	$843	$944	$1057	$1184	$1326	$1486	$1664	$1864
Cost of goods sold[b]	—	336	376	421	472	529	592	663	743	832	932
SG&A	—	251	276	304	334	367	404	444	489	538	591
Depreciation (tax)	—	13	15	15	18	19	22	25	28	30	35
Pretax operating profit	—	72	86	103	120	142	166	194	226	264	306
Income taxes[c]	—	36	43	52	60	71	83	97	113	132	153
Net operating profit	—	36	43	51	60	71	83	97	113	132	153
Depreciation (tax)	—	13	15	15	18	19	22	25	28	30	35
Net operating cash flow	—	49	58	66	78	90	105	122	141	162	188
Net investment in working capital[d]	—	$(15)	$(18)	$(20)	$(25)	$(28)	$(32)	$(36)	$(40)	$(43)	$(50)
Investment in fixed assets	—	(22)	(25)	(30)	(35)	(40)	(45)	(50)	(50)	(50)	(50)
Operating economies net of taxes[e]	—	10	11	12	13	15	15	15	15	15	15
Incremental free cash flow	—	22	26	28	31	37	43	51	66	84	103
Terminal Value of Net Assets:											
Nondisposition basis[f]	—	—	—	—	—	—	—	—	—	—	2472
Disposition basis[g]	—	—	—	—	—	—	—	—	—	—	1842
Incremental Net Cash Flow:											
Nondisposition basis	$(542.6)	$ 22	$ 26	$ 28	$ 31	$ 37	$ 43	$ 51	$ 66	$ 84	$2575
Disposition basis	$(542.6)	$ 22	$ 26	$ 28	$ 31	$ 37	$ 43	$ 51	$ 66	$ 84	$1945

$$\text{Required return} = \text{WACC} = r - T^*Lr_d\left[\frac{1 + r}{1 + r_d}\right] = 0.1659 - 0.25(\tfrac{1}{3})(0.12)\left[\frac{1.1659}{1.12}\right] = 15.55\%$$

IRR (Nondisposition basis) = 20.40%
IRR (Disposition basis) = 17.59%
NPV (Nondisposition basis) = $236.5 million
NPV (Disposition basis) = $ 88.0 million

[a] Estimated as 16 times prior year's earnings (a purchase price of $48.00 per share).
[b] Excluding depreciation.
[c] Assumes a 50% marginal income tax rate.
[d] Increase in inventories and receivables net of increase in payables.
[e] Estimated after-tax savings resulting from eliminating redundant overhead and redundant production facilities and marketing some of Garden State's products through Empire State's distribution network.
[f] Calculated as 16 times terminal year's earnings ($142.7 million) plus the amount of debt outstanding at the investment horizon ($188.3 million). This calculation assumes that Empire State does not sell the shares of Garden State; it continues to hold them (nondisposition case).
[g] Calculated as 16 times terminal year's earnings ($142.7 million) plus the amount of debt outstanding at the investment horizon ($188.3 million) and net of capital gains tax at a 34% rate (with a tax basis of $450 million) and net also of transaction costs ($10 million). This calculation assumes that Empire State sells the shares of Garden State at the end of the 10th year and pays any resulting tax liability if there is a gain (or receives a tax benefit if there is a loss on disposition).

flow analysis is also useful in determining the maximum price the acquiror can afford to pay. We illustrate both uses of the technique in this section.

Table 28-9 illustrates how you could use discounted-cash-flow analysis to evaluate Empire State's possible acquisition of Garden State. We assume that Empire State has already decided that it would not be advantageous to step up the tax basis of Garden State's assets. Empire State elected to use a 10-year time horizon for its analysis. Projected amounts are rounded to the nearest million.

Acquisition Cost

Empire State plans to purchase all of Garden State's outstanding stock for cash through a tender offer at a price of $48 per share (16 times earnings, which approximates the midpoint of the range determined in the preceding section). Garden State currently has $100 million of debt outstanding, which bears interest at a 10% rate, payable annually in arrears. The debt matures in one lump sum at the end of 10 years and is callable at par. Empire State will be able to assume this debt.

Assumption of Acquiree's Debt

Assuming the obligation for servicing this debt reduces the amount of new debt that Empire State can issue to finance (part of) the cost of the acquisition. Cash that Empire State uses to service the debt it assumes is not available to service new debt. In other words, assuming the 10% debt involves an opportunity cost.

We can measure this cost by applying the debt service parity (DSP) approach introduced in Chapter 24. Under the DSP approach, the opportunity cost of assuming Garden State's outstanding debt equals the maximum amount of new debt that Empire State could issue, subject to the constraint that the after-tax period-by-period debt service payments of the hypothetical new issue are the same as those of Garden State's debt that Empire State would assume. If Empire State is permitted to assume the debt, and if the opportunity cost of assuming the debt is less than the cost of retiring it immediately, Empire State should assume the debt rather than retire it. This opportunity cost is part of the cost of the acquisition. It must be subtracted from the amount of new debt Empire State could otherwise issue to finance the acquisition. If instead the opportunity cost of assuming Garden State's debt is greater than the cost of retiring it immediately, the debt should be retired. The cost of retiring it must then be included in the cost of the acquisition.

Empire State's pretax cost of a new debt issue (before issuance expenses) is 12%. Its marginal ordinary income tax rate is 50%. Assuming the 10% debt would require after-tax interest payments of $5 million per year. Newly issued debt would have an after-tax interest cost of 6% per annum. The opportunity cost of assuming Garden State's outstanding debt equals the present value of the after-tax debt service with Empire's after-tax cost of debt serving as the discount rate:

$$PV(\text{assumed debt}) = \sum_{t=1}^{10} \frac{5}{(1.06)^t} + \frac{100}{(1.06)^{10}} = \$92.6 \text{ million}$$

Because the cost of assuming the 10% debt is less than the $100 million cost of retiring it, Empire State is better off assuming the debt. The net advantage is $7.4 million (= 100.0 − 92.6). The DSP approach would also be used to value any debt instruments (or preferred stock instruments) that an acquiror issues to the acquiree's shareholders in payment for some portion of the acquisition price.

Acquiree's Excess Cash

The gross cost of Empire State's acquisition is $572.6 million (= 480.0 + 92.6). However, after analyzing Garden State's financial statements, Empire State believes that Garden State has approximately $35 million of excess cash and marketable securities that it will be able to apply toward the purchase price.[11] Empire State has estimated that investment bankers' fees and other expenses net of taxes will total $5 million.

---

[11] This represents a potential pitfall, however. Firms like to pay as much of the acquisition cost as they can with the acquiree's cash. But what appears as excess cash may in fact be tied up as compensating balances, or it may be overseas and repatriating it could trigger a significant tax liability.

Net Acquisition Cost

Empire State's net acquisition cost of acquiring Garden State's net assets is

Cost of purchasing target's common shares	$480.0
+ Transaction costs and expenses	5.0
− Liquidation value of target's excess assets	(35.0)
Net investment in target's equity	450.0
+ Present value of debt acquiror assumes	92.6
Net acquisition cost (NAC)	$542.6

(28.11)

If the target's debt became payable immediately as a result of the acquisition, the present value of the debt the acquiror assumes would be the face amount, $100 million. In that case, the net acquisition cost would be $550 million. Whenever you evaluate the possible acquisition of a firm that has debt outstanding, check whether the acquisition will trigger immediate repayment. If it will, but if assuming the debt would be cheaper than retiring it, you will probably want to find an alternative legal structure that will avoid acceleration.

Financing

Empire State's financial staff has studied the capital structure policies of large pharmaceutical firms in the manner described in Chapters 15 and 16. On the basis of that analysis, Empire State believes that it could finance the acquisition on a long-term basis with a debt-to-total-value ratio of 1/3 without any adverse impact on its senior debt rating or on how it might choose to finance other projects. The amount of new long-term debt that Empire State can issue is the amount it can have outstanding after the acquisition less the amount of debt displaced by the debt it assumes in the acquisition.

$$\text{Added debt} = \text{NAC}(L) - \text{PV(debt displaced)}$$ (28.12)
$$= 542.6(1/3) - 92.6 = \$88.3 \text{ million}$$

where L is the acquiror's target debt-to-total-value ratio.

Operating Assumptions

Empire State believes that Garden State's revenue will grow at the rate of 12% per annum, the historical growth rate. Empire State also believes that the cost of goods sold will grow at the same rate, whereas selling, general, and administrative expense (SG&A) will grow at 10% per annum. Annual depreciation expense for tax purposes is estimated from Garden State's published financial reports and from Empire State's estimate of Garden State's required capital expenditure program. The forecasted operating economies represent Empire State's estimate of the benefits it will realize by eliminating redundant production facilities and marketing some of Empire State's products through Garden State's distribution network.

There are some important potential pitfalls. It is easy to be too optimistic about the acquiree's growth prospects. It is also easy to be overly optimistic about the synergistic benefits from the merger. The more dissimilar the acquiree's and the acquiror's businesses, the more difficult it will be to find true synergies. It is also easy to underestimate the amount of investment that will be required. The older the acquiree's plant and equipment, the higher the required post-merger capital expenditures.

Terminal Value

An acquiree's terminal value is its estimated value at the end of the time period used in the acquisition analysis. We estimate terminal value by comparing the results of owning the acquiree with the results of selling it. For our example, the first case (nondisposition) assumes that Empire State continues to own Garden State for an indefinite period beyond the investment horizon. The second case (disposition) assumes that Empire State sells all the common stock of Garden State at the investment horizon. If Empire State were to sell Garden State after the investment horizon, the present value of any resulting tax liabilities would have to be taken into account. The value of Garden State in that case would lie between the two values estimated in the following paragraphs.

In the first case, Garden State's terminal value is estimated by applying the acquisition multiple, 16, to Garden State's pro forma earnings in year 10 estimated as though Garden State were on a stand-alone basis. In year 10, Garden State would have $100 million principal amount of 10% debt plus $88.3 million of 12% debt, giving rise to $10.3 million of after-tax interest expense. Subtracting this from Garden State's estimated year-10 net operating profit of $153 million leaves $142.7 million of earnings. Multiplying by 16.0 gives a terminal value of $2283.2 million for Garden State's equity. Adding the terminal value of Garden State's debt, $188.3 million, gives the terminal value of Garden State's net assets.

$$\text{TV(NA)} = \text{TV(equity)} + \text{TV(debt)} - T - E \tag{28.13}$$
$$= 2283.2 + 188.3 - 0 - 0 = \$2471.5 \text{ million}$$

where TV(NA) is the terminal value of net assets, TV(equity) is the terminal value of shareholders' equity, TV(debt) is the terminal value of long-term debt (and capitalized lease and preferred stock) obligations, T represents any taxes incurred in realizing the terminal value, and E represents any other expenses incurred in realizing the terminal value.

In the second case, tax liabilities and transaction costs must be taken into account. Empire State estimates that if it sold Garden State, it would incur $10 million of transaction costs. Its net proceeds are $2273.2 million ($= 2283.2 - 10$). Its tax basis equals what it pays to purchase Garden State's shares (that is, the net investment in target's equity), $450 million. Empire State would realize a long-term capital gain equal to the difference between the net proceeds from the sale of the equity and the net investment in the target's equity, $1823.2 million ($= 2273.2 - 450$).[12] Empire State's financial staff estimates a future capital gains tax rate of 34%. Empire State would incur capital gains tax of $620.0 million ($= 0.34 \times 1823.2$). Substituting into Equation (28.13), this leaves

$$\text{TV(NA)} = 2283.2 + 188.3 - 620.0 - 10 = \$1841.5 \text{ million}$$

The calculation of terminal value is often critical. By assuming a high enough future multiple, an acquiror can justify any purchase price. But it seems more prudent to assume that the future acquisition multiple will be no greater than the current acquisition multiple, as we did in the illustration.

Acquisition Analysis

With the incremental net cash flow stream calculated, we can now apply discounted-cash-flow analysis. The required return for the acquisition, WACC, is estimated by applying the procedure described in Chapter 16 to estimate the unleveraged required return r. We use Equation (16.9) to calculate WACC, which is the weighted average cost of capital for the acquisition.

$$\text{WACC} = r - T^*Lr_d\left(\frac{1+r}{1+r_d}\right) \tag{16.9}$$

Empire State's financial staff analyzed pharmaceutical firms comparable to Garden State. It estimated an unleveraged required return $r = 0.1659$. It also estimated a net-benefit-

---

[12] Its original tax basis in the shares of Garden State equals the purchase price for the shares ($480 million) plus transaction costs ($5 million) minus the portion of the purchase price paid for with the acquiree's cash ($35 million). The net amount is $450 million. The net sales proceeds realized upon the sale of the shares equals the sale price ($2283 million) net of transaction costs ($10 million).

to-leverage factor $T^* = 0.25$. It had previously determined the debt ratio $L = 1/3$ and the cost of debt $r_d = 0.12$. Substituting these values into Equation (16.9) gives

$$\text{WACC} = 0.1659 - 0.25(1/3)(0.12)\left(\frac{1.1659}{1.12}\right) = 0.1555, \text{ or } 15.55\%$$

Note that as in capital budgeting, the debt ratio is the acquiror's long-run target proportion of debt financing.

The incremental net cash flow stream is discounted at the required return WACC = 0.1555 to obtain the net present value of the acquisition, NPV (acquisition).

$$\text{NPV(acquisition)} = -\text{NAC} + \sum_{t=1}^{N} \frac{\text{CFAT}_t}{(1 + \text{WACC})^t} \qquad (28.14)$$

where CFAT_t is the (unleveraged) incremental net cash flow during period t, and N is the investment horizon. CFAT_N includes the terminal value of the acquisition (at the investment horizon) estimated from Equation (28.13).

Applying Equation (28.14) to Empire State's proposed acquisition of Garden State indicates NPV(acquisition) = \$236.5 million on a nondisposition basis and NPV(acquisition) = \$88.0 million on a disposition basis. The weighted-average-cost-of-capital approach indicates that the acquisition of Garden State at a price representing 16 times earnings would be profitable. ■

Calculating the NPV of a Potential Acquisition

EXAMPLE

Calculating terminal value on both bases reveals the sensitivity of the acquisition decision to this value and, in this case, to the multiple applied to the terminal year's earnings. Note that the present value of the incremental net cash flow stream, exclusive of terminal value, is −\$346.1 million. The terminal value must be at least \$1468.6 million (= 346.1×1.1555^{10}) for the NPV to be positive. The NPV of a proposed acquisition is usually very sensitive to the estimated terminal value. Therefore, it is important to consider carefully the assumptions made in arriving at the estimate. It is also wise to calculate the break-even terminal value, which makes NPV(acquisition) equal to zero.

Maximum Price the Acquiror Can Afford to Pay

There is one additional use for discounted-cash-flow analysis. We can calculate the maximum price the acquiror could afford to pay for the target. Given the incremental net cash flow stream and discount rate, the maximum price is the one that makes NPV(acquisition) equal to zero. Valuing Garden State on a disposition basis, Empire State could afford to pay approximately \$568.0 million (the original \$480 million price plus the \$88.0 million net present value), or \$56.80 (= 568/10) per share. At that price, Garden State's shareholders would experience a 110% gain (\$56.80 versus \$27), whereas Empire State's shareholders would only expect to break even at best.[13] But this calculation assumes that Garden State can be sold for

---

[13] Empire State could actually afford to pay an even higher price before NPV becomes zero. A higher price increases Empire State's tax basis in Garden State's shares and reduces the future capital gains tax liability. For a purchase price of \$568.0 million, the tax liability would be \$590.0 million [= 0.34(2273.2 − 538.0)]; it would be \$620.0 million if the price paid for the stock were \$480 million.

16 times earnings at the end of 10 years. A prospective acquiror might not want to make that sort of bet by offering to pay $56.80 per share.

28.6 DISCOUNTED-CASH-FLOW ANALYSIS: ADJUSTED-PRESENT-VALUE APPROACH

The adjusted-present-value approach (Chapter 16) represents an alternative to the weighted-average-cost-of-capital approach to calculating the NPV of an acquisition. Recall that the weighted-average-cost-of-capital approach assumes that the firm's capital structure contains fixed proportions of debt and equity for the life of the investment. It is appropriate to use the APV approach to evaluate leveraged buyouts or other potential acquisitions that assume an acquisition-specific debt financing package with a debt ratio that will change over time in some intended manner.

As noted, Empire State's financial staff has determined that a 1/3 ratio of debt to total value is appropriate. This suggests that $88.3 million of the $450 million of cash Empire State needs to finance the acquisition can be raised through the issuance of new debt without altering Empire State's debt capacity.

Measuring the Net APV of a Potential Acquisition

Modifying Equation (16.5) to incorporate the net acquisition cost (NAC) leads to the following expression for the net adjusted present value (net APV) of an acquisition.

$$\text{Net APV(acquisition)} = -\text{NAC} + \sum_{t=1}^{N} \frac{\text{CFAT}_t}{(1 + r)^t} + \sum_{t=1}^{N} \frac{T^* \text{INT}_t}{(1 + r_d)^t} \tag{28.15}$$

$-$NAC plus the first sum represents the NPV of the acquisition on an all-equity basis. The second sum represents the NPV of the interest tax shields on acquisition-related debt. We will illustrate the APV approach by using the disposition case in Table 28-9.

Empire State's financial staff calculated the unleveraged required return $r = 0.1659$. The NPV of the acquisition on an all-equity basis is

$$\text{NPV(all-equity)} = -\text{NAC} + \sum_{t=1}^{N} \frac{\text{CFAT}_t}{(1 + r)^t} \qquad (28.16)$$

$$= -542.6 + \sum_{t=1}^{10} \frac{\text{CFAT}_t}{(1.1659)^t} = \$41.1 \text{ million}$$

Calculating the Net APV of a Potential Aquisition

EXAMPLE

Next, we must calculate the present value of the interest tax shields. The debt pays interest annually. Empire State's financial staff has been informed by the firm's investment bankers that Empire State can issue 10-year debt for the acquisition without a sinking fund. Issuing \$88.3 million principal amount of 10-year debt bearing a 12% coupon would require interest payments of \$10.60 million ($= 88.3 \times 0.12$) per annum. In addition, Empire State assumes the Garden State debt, which requires interest payments of \$10 million per annum. Total interest expense is \$20.60 million ($= 10.60 + 10$) per year for 10 years. The net-benefit-to-leverage factor is $T^* = 0.25$. The second sum in Equation (28.15) is

$$\text{PV(tax shields)} = \sum_{t=1}^{N} \frac{T^* \, \text{INT}_t}{(1 + r_d)^t} \qquad (28.17)$$

$$= \sum_{t=1}^{10} \frac{0.25(20.60)}{(1.12)^t} = \$29.1 \text{ million}$$

Adding NPV(all-equity) in Equation (28.16) and PV(tax shields) in Equation (28.17), we get

$$\text{Net APV(acquisition)} = 41.1 \text{ million} + 29.1 \text{ million} = \$70.2 \text{ million} \ \blacksquare$$

Comparing the APV and WACC Approaches

The net APV is less than the \$88.0 million NPV(disposition) calculated in Table 28-9 using the WACC approach. What accounts for the difference between the two figures? The required return, the WACC, used in the NPV calculation assumes that Empire State rebalances its capital structure periodically to maintain $L = 1/3$. The APV calculation we performed was for a specific debt structure: \$100 million of 10-year debt bearing a 10% coupon and \$88.3 million of 10-year debt bearing a 12% coupon, both maturing in a lump sum. But if Garden State's operating income increases in the manner shown in Table 28-9, Empire State's debt ratio will gradually decrease. The NPV calculation explicitly takes into account the additional future debt capacity created by the acquisition. The true net APV(acquisition) when this debt capacity side effect is taken into account must equal the NPV. We can modify Equation (28.15) by adding the NPV of these side effects. With this adjustment, net APV(acquisition) will indicate the true net present value. The two are equal when NPV(side effects) = \$17.8 million.

$$\text{Net APV(acquisition)} = \text{NPV(all-equity)} + \text{PV(tax shields)} + \text{NPV(side effects)} \qquad (28.18)$$
$$= 41.1 + 29.1 + 17.8 = \$88.0 \text{ million}$$

Note that if Empire State had decided, say for tax reasons, to finance the acquisition of Garden State on an all-common-stock basis, then there would still have been a positive impact on Empire State's debt capacity that should not be ignored. Repeating the calculation in Equation (28.17) for the debt of Garden State that Empire assumes, we find that PV(tax shields) = $14.1 million. (Use 10.0 in place of 20.60 in Equation 28.17.) The APV and WACC approaches would lead to an $88.0 million net present value when NPV(side effects) = $32.8 million, because then

$$\text{Net APV(acquisition)} = \$41.1 + 14.1 + 32.8 = \$88.0 \text{ million}$$

Which Approach to Use

You can use either the weighted-average-cost-of-capital approach or the adjusted-present-value approach to calculate the NPV of an acquisition. Applied correctly, the two approaches will provide the same NPV. In particular, it is important to hold the acquiror's debt ratio L constant, which requires taking an acquisition's debt capacity side effects into account. Such a procedure is consistent with debt service parity.

We have found the leverage rebalancing formula (Equation 16.9) for the (weighted average) required return to an investment easier to apply than the APV approach. This is because the formula involves adjusting the discount rate to reflect debt capacity side effects rather than estimating these effects period by period, which the APV method requires. As we noted in Chapter 16, the leverage rebalancing formula assumes periodic capital structure rebalancing, which is generally consistent with corporate practice. It thus provides a reasonably accurate adjustment for debt capacity side effects that can result from an acquisition.

Self-Check Questions

1. When is it appropriate to use the APV approach to evaluate a proposed acquisition?
2. What discount rate is used to calculate NPV(all-equity)?
3. What discount rate is used to calculate the present value of the interest tax shields? What is the rationale for using this discount rate?
4. Do the APV approach and the WACC approach produce the same estimate of the net present value of an acquisition? Which method, then, should you use?

28.7 THE MEDIUM OF PAYMENT

Acquirors usually pay for acquisitions in cash, stock, or some combination of the two. Achieving tax-free treatment requires that the acquiror pay at least 50% of the purchase price in its stock, although in many cases the acquiror has the flexibility to issue preferred stock instead of common stock.

Choice of Medium of Payment

Figure 28-3 breaks down merger transactions during the period 1975–1994 according to the medium of payment. Overall, 42% of the acquisitions were cash only, 31% were stock only, 1% were debt only, and the other 26% were paid for in a combination of stock, cash, and debt. The proportion of cash-only transactions fell sharply between 1988 and 1992. The proportion involving a combination of stock, cash, and debt generally increased through the 20-year period. Combinations of stock and debt arise in two-tiered tender offers, wherein shareholders

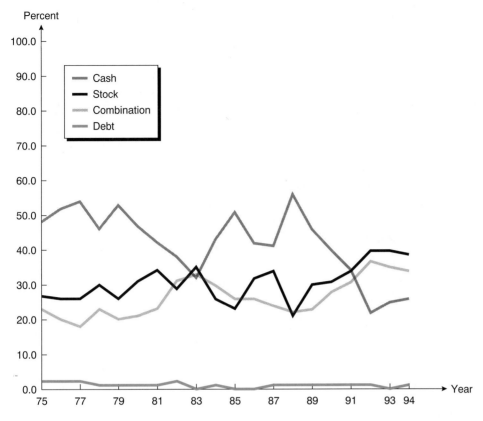

FIGURE 28-3
Trend in medium of payment, 1975–1994.
Source: Merrill Lynch Business Advisory Services, *Mergerstat Review 1994,* p. 55.

of the target usually get debentures in the second tier of the transaction. Combinations of cash and debt are common in acquisitions of privately held firms wherein the sellers often take a note from the buyers as part of the purchase price.

Common Stock and Net Acquisition Cost

Common stock tends to become a more popular medium of payment among acquirors during periods of rising stock prices. Acquirors are reluctant to pay in stock when they feel their shares are depressed in price. However, the shareholders of publicly traded acquirees, particularly the *risk arbitrageurs* who generally replace a significant portion of the public shareholders by buying their shares as soon as an acquisition is announced, prefer cash as the medium of payment. When an acquisition occurs, they want to take their profits and move on. Receiving cash saves them the trouble and cost of having to sell securities in the open market.

Acquirors often decide to pay in common stock when they think their share price is attractive. That is, they think it is "cheaper" to pay in common stock than in cash. But whether it really is cheaper depends on (1) how the transaction is structured and (2) what happens to the share price after the transaction is announced.

Suppose Empire State wished to buy Garden State in an exchange of common stock. If managers of the two firms agreed on a fixed price of $480 million payable in Empire State common stock, the net acquisition cost would remain $542.6 million regardless of what happened to Empire State's share price. But in stock-for-stock acquisitions it is customary to negotiate an *exchange ratio*—that is, so many shares of Empire State for each share of Garden State. If the acquiror's share price then increases, so does the net acquisition cost. Of course, if the acquiror's share price falls, the net acquisition cost falls also.

<table>
<tr><td>

EXAMPLE

</td><td>

Impact on the Net Acquisition Cost in a Stock-for-Stock Acquisition

</td><td>

Assume that Empire State has 50 million shares outstanding that are trading at a price of $32 each. Garden State has 10 million shares outstanding. Suppose Empire State offers to pay $48 for each Garden State share. It would have to exchange 1.5 (= 48/32) of its shares for each Garden State share. Empire State would have to issue 15 million (= 1.5 × 10 million) new shares. As a result, Garden State's former shareholders would own 23% [= 15/(15 + 50)] of Empire State after the acquisition. Suppose the exchange ratio is fixed. Suppose also that stock market investors believe the market value of Empire State's equity should be $2168 million after the acquisition. This value is the sum of Empire State's current market value ($1600 million) plus the value of the shares issued in exchange for Garden State's shares ($480 million) plus the NPV in the disposition case ($88.0 million). In that case, Empire State's share price would rise to $33.35 per share (= 2168/65), and its cost of purchasing Garden State's shares would increase to $500.2 million (= 33.35 × 1.5 × 10). The fixed exchange ratio effectively appropriates 23% of the NPV for Garden State's former shareholders.[14]

Let's assume instead that investors believe the market value of Empire State's equity after the merger should be $1950 million. Then Empire State's share price would fall to $30 (= 1950/65), and its cost of purchasing Garden State's shares would fall to $450 million (= 30 × 1.5 × 10). Its net acquisition cost would fall from the $542.6 million in Table 28-9 to $512.6 million. In this way, Garden State's former shareholders would share the burden of the decline in value of Empire State's shares.[15] Thus an acquiror's shareholders are better off in a stock-for-stock transaction than in a cash-for-stock transaction if the acquiror overpays. ■

</td></tr>
</table>

Dilution in Earnings Per Share

There is one other factor to consider when common stock is the medium of payment. A publicly traded acquiror is usually concerned about the impact an acquisition will have on its future reported earnings per share. As we noted earlier, an acquisition can increase earnings per share under pooling-of-interests accounting when the acquiror's price-earnings multiple exceeds the target's. However, when the acquiree's price-earnings multiple exceeds the acquiror's, the accounting impact is just the opposite.

Table 28-10 illustrates the dilutive case. In the absence of any operating economies or other synergistic benefits, the market value of the combined entity is just the sum of the market values of the acquiror and the acquiree. Because the acquiror has the lower price-earnings multiple, its earnings per share are diluted from $5.00 to $4.29 per share. However, its price-earnings multiple increases from $10.0x$ to $11.7x$.

You should appreciate that as long as transactions take place in an efficient capital market, dilution in earnings per share will have only an accounting impact. Dilution is not an indicator of a proposed acquisition's impact on shareholder wealth. It should not affect which medium of payment the acquiror chooses.

---

[14] Note that 23% of $88.0 million is $20.2 million. Adding this amount to the original purchase price for Garden State's shares ($480 million) gives $500.2 million.

[15] Realizing this possibility, acquirees often try to negotiate a *flexible exchange ratio* designed to assure them a fixed dollar price for their shares. For example, suppose Empire State's share price falls to $30 upon announcement of the acquisition, but the exchange ratio adjusts to 1.60 Empire State shares per Garden State share. Garden State's shareholders would still realize $48 (= 1.60 × 30) per share.

	ACQUIROR	ACQUIREE	COMBINED
Total earnings	$50,000,000	$10,000,000	$60,000,000
Number of shares	10,000,000	5,000,000	14,000,000[a]
Earnings per share	$ 5.00	$ 2.00	$ 4.29
Share price	$50.00	$40.00	$50.00
Price-earnings ratio	10.0x	20.0x	11.7x

TABLE 28-10
Illustration of the dilutive impact of an acquisition on reported earnings per share.

[a] Acquiror exchanges 0.8 common share for each of the acquiree's common shares, issuing a total of 4 million new shares.

Self-Check Questions

1. Over the past 20 years, what has been the most frequent medium of payment in corporate acquisitions? Have there been any changes recently in the relative frequencies of the various methods of payment?

2. Why do risk arbitrageurs prefer to receive cash rather than securities?

3. Explain why paying for an acquisition by issuing common stock raises the cost of a positive-NPV acquisition and reduces the cost of a negative-NPV acquisition.

4. Explain why the acquiror's shareholders are better off in a stock-for-stock transaction than in a cash-for-stock transaction if the acquiror overpays.

28.8 MERGER TACTICS

Many merger and acquisition transactions take place on a "friendly" basis. The two parties agree to merge. Then they negotiate the legal form of the transaction, price, method of payment, and other terms. But many transactions are unfriendly. Management of the target may resist the potential acquiror's overtures. If they refuse to negotiate, the potential acquiror can take its offer directly to the target's shareholders along either of two avenues: a tender offer or a proxy contest. Managers and boards of directors have shown remarkable creativity in designing takeover defenses to thwart such threats to their security. You've probably heard the term *shark repellents,* which is used to describe them in the media.

Tender Offers

Few events in business pack as much drama—or engender as much bitterness—as a hostile tender offer by one firm for the shares of another. A **tender offer** is an offer to purchase shares of stock at a stated price from shareholders who are willing to *tender* shares at that price. In a hostile tender offer, the management of the target firm takes steps, often including litigation, to contest the offer. *Hostile raids* became an established acquisition strategy more than 20 years ago when one of the leading securities firms assisted International Nickel of Canada in a successful hostile tender offer for ESB.

Tender offers are frequently employed when incumbent management refuses to negotiate with the prospective acquiror. An example is the battle for control over RJR Nabisco, which is discussed in the next section. In other cases, management may be indifferent to a proposed acquisition. A tender offer lets the shareholders decide for themselves whether they like the acquiror's offer. The tender price usually represents a substantial premium over the target's prevailing share price, and tender offers are almost always made exclusively in cash.

ADVANTAGES OF TENDER OFFERS   There are a number of potential advantages to cash tender offers as compared to alternative acquisition methods. First, a cash tender offer represents the quickest means of obtaining control of another firm. There are no terms to be negotiated and no securities to be registered. The buyer decides on a tender price and on other terms of the offer and files the tender offer documents with the Securities and Exchange Commission. Tender offers also have a shorter minimum waiting period for government antitrust review. However, tender offers are regulated under the Williams Act amendments to the Securities Exchange Act of 1934, and SEC rules do not permit an all-out blitzkrieg. The Williams Act requires disclosure (within 10 days of reaching the threshold) of all acquisitions of 5% or more of any class of a firm's equity securities, as well as disclosure of tender offers or exchange offers to acquire a class of equity securities of a publicly traded firm.

A second advantage is that a tender offer provides greater flexibility than other acquisition strategies. A firm can tender for just enough shares to give it effective control. In the case of a publicly traded firm whose shares are widely held, this may require tendering for only 20% to 40% of the outstanding shares. The acquiror can set conditions of the offer so that, for example, it does not have to buy any shares unless the required minimum number is tendered. Once the acquiror has purchased these shares, resistance on the part of the acquiree's management normally lessens. The acquiror can then effect a merger structured as a tax-free reorganization to achieve 100% ownership.

Third, a cash tender offer represents the simplest way for a foreign firm to buy a U.S. firm. U.S. investors would generally be reluctant to swap shares of a U.S. firm for securities of a foreign firm for legal and other reasons. A cash tender offer gets around this problem.

Fourth, open-market purchases of the target firm's stock followed by a cash tender offer give the potential acquiror an opportunity for profit. The cash tender price effectively puts a floor under the target's share price and alerts the financial community that the target firm is "in play." If a higher bidder emerges, the original bidder can take some consolation from the profits it realizes on the shares it owns.

CONTESTED TENDER OFFERS   Tender offers are often contested by the target's management, which may mount an aggressive public relations campaign, file lawsuits, bid for the other firm's shares, and take other steps.

Unexpected tender offers are a source of concern to management. The 20-day minimum period that the tender offer must remain open seems painfully short to a firm that gets caught by surprise. In addition, current tender offer regulations require the target firm to disclose its response within 10 business days of the commencement of the offer.

Proxy Contests

Tender offers are expensive because the bidder must purchase enough shares to secure control. Alternatively, one or more individuals who oppose incumbent management can initiate a **proxy contest**. A *proxy* conveys the right to vote the shares of the person who grants the proxy. The dissidents solicit shareholders' proxies to vote their shares in favor of their slate of directors at the next annual meeting of stockholders. However, a proxy fight is expensive and time-consuming, and few succeed.

In December 1995, Brooke Group took the first step in its proxy battle with RJR Nabisco's management. Brooke Group, controlled by investor Bennett LeBow and investor Carl Icahn, had tried unsuccessfully to convince the board of directors of RJR Nabisco to spin off the Nabisco food division in order to separate it from the firm's tobacco business. Nabisco's board expressed a willingness to consider the spinoff but said that it would need time to figure out how best to separate the two businesses.

Brooke Group's Proxy Battle with RJR Nabisco Management

EXAMPLE

Brooke Group then solicited RJR Nabisco's shareholders on the issue. More than 50% of the firm's shareholders voted in favor of a resolution supporting an immediate spinoff and another resolution giving shareholders the right to call a special shareholders' meeting. However, these resolutions were not binding on the board, which still refused to agree to an immediate spinoff. Thus in February 1996, Brooke Group announced that it would propose its own slate of dissident directors with a stated goal of spinning off the food business.

They launched a proxy contest in April 1996 but lost, leaving RJR Nabisco management in place to pursue its own strategy. ▪

Shareholders seem to prefer cash in hand—especially when it represents a large premium over the prevailing share price—to the mere promise that the firm's financial prospects will improve in the future under new management. This observation is consistent with the Principle of Risk-Return Trade-Off. It is not surprising, then, that the vast majority of contests for control take the form of cash tender offers rather than proxy fights.

Defensive Tactics

Corporate managers often react negatively to unsolicited takeover bids. One would hope that their motive in doing so is to achieve the highest possible value for the firm's shares rather than merely exhibiting the Principle of Self-Interested Behavior to protect their jobs. The courts have generally held that the directors of a firm have a responsibility to obtain maximum value for shareholders. Corporate managers have devised a host of defensive tactics. Table 28-11 lists some of the more popular ones. These tactics include anticipatory steps that management and the board take to reduce the risk of getting blind-sided. But they can also entrench management. The poison pill has become controversial. In at least two cases, the Delaware Chancery Court ordered the board of directors to redeem poison pills in order to let shareholders choose between a restructuring plan supported by the board and an outside bidder's cash tender offer. The responsive tactics are more extreme and many involve the sale of assets or securities.

IMPLICATIONS FOR SHAREHOLDER WEALTH   The use of defensive tactics raises serious questions about how they affect shareholder wealth. If they entrench inefficient management, shareholder wealth must suffer. Studies have concluded that corporate charter amendments that authorize a staggered election of directors or supermajority voting do not adversely affect stock prices but that targeted share repurchases (greenmail) cause shareholders who do not receive favored treatment to suffer a loss of wealth.

THE AGENCY PROBLEM IN THE BID RESPONSE   The managers' role in determining the firm's response to an unsolicited takeover bid reflects a potentially serious agency problem. Many firms have established golden parachutes in order to reduce this agency problem. A *golden parachute* provides generous payments to managers who lose their jobs as a result of a takeover. In some cases these payments have been substantial. For example, the RJR Nabisco leveraged buyout discussed in the next section resulted in payments to employees totaling $166 million. Golden parachutes are designed to align the objectives of shareholders

TABLE 28-11	DEFENSIVE TACTIC	DESCRIPTION
Frequently employed takeover defensive tactics.	**Anticipatory Tactics**	
	Dual class recapitalization	Firm distributes a second class of common stock that possesses superior voting rights (for example, 10 votes per share). New shares cannot be sold. Shareholders who wish to sell must exchange new shares for regular shares with only 1 vote per share. Over time, management's voting power increases as other shareholders sell their shares.
	Employee stock ownership plan (ESOP)	Firm sells a large block of common stock (or voting preferred stock) to a company-sponsored ESOP and repurchases an equivalent number of common shares in the open market. Firm votes the ESOP's shares until they are distributed to employees, which typically takes place over several years.
	Poison pill	Firm issues rights to its shareholders (typically, one nondetachable right per common share) that entitle the shareholders to purchase at one-half the market price (1) shares of the firm's common stock if a potential acquiror buys more than a specified percentage of the firm's shares (flip-in poison pill) or (2) shares of the acquiror's common stock following an acquisition of the firm (flip-over poison pill). The acquiree's board of directors can redeem the rights for a nominal sum (typically, $0.05 per right) if it approves of the acquisition.
	Staggered election of directors	Firm's board of directors is divided into three equal classes. Only one class stands for reelection each year. A hostile raider cannot obtain control through a single proxy context.
	Supermajority voting/fair-price provision	Firm's charter is amended to require a supermajority (for example, 80%) of the firm's common shares to be voted in favor of a merger that has not been approved by the firm's board of directors. (If it is board-approved, a simple majority usually applies.) A fair-price provision allows the board of directors to waive the supermajority voting provision if the acquiror agrees to pay all shareholders the same price. The fair-price provision is designed to prevent a two-tier bid, in which shareholders who sell their shares in the initial tender often receive one price and the remaining shareholders who are ''merged out'' in the second stage receive a lower price.
	Responsive Tactics	
	Asset purchases or sales	Firm purchases assets that the bidder does not want or that would block the bidder by creating an antitrust problem. Firm sells the ''crown jewel'' assets that the bidder wants.
	Leveraged recapitalization	Firm borrows a large sum of money and distributes the loan proceeds along with any other excess cash to its shareholders as a dividend. A recapitalization is designed to make it more difficult for a takeover raider to make the acquisition with borrowed funds.
	Litigation	Firm files suit against the bidder alleging violation of state takeover statute(s), antitrust laws, securities laws, or other laws or regulations.
	Pac-Man defense (or counter tender offer)	Firm makes a counterbid for the common stock of the potential acquiror.
	Share repurchases or sales	Firm uses excess cash or borrows cash with which to finance a large share repurchase program. Alternatively, the firm might instead repurchase shares only from the takeover raider, any premium over fair market value representing ''greenmail.'' As a third alternative, the firm can sell shares to a ''friendly'' third party.
	Standstill agreement	Prospective acquiror agrees during the term of the agreement (1) not to increase its shareholdings above a specified percentage and, in many cases, (2) to vote its shares with management.

and managers. However, if they are too generous, then under the Principle of Self-Interested Behavior, they could give management an incentive to sell the firm on terms that may not be the most advantageous ones for shareholders.

Self-Check Questions

1. What is a tender offer? How are tender offers used in battles for corporate control?
2. What are the main advantages of a tender offer as compared to alternative acquisition methods?
3. What is a proxy contest, and how does one work?
4. What are some of the defensive tactics that firms use in their efforts to ward off unwanted suitors?
5. What is a golden parachute? What agency problem is it designed to avoid? How might it create an agency problem of its own?

28.9 LEVERAGED BUYOUTS

Recall that a leveraged buyout (LBO) is an acquisition that is financed principally by borrowing. The debt is secured by a lien on the firm's assets. Lenders look to the operating cash flow from these assets to service this debt. LBOs are often used to take a firm private. Chapter 23 discusses the benefits of going private.

The RJR Nabisco Leveraged Buyout

Kohlberg Kravis Roberts & Co. (KKR) acquired RJR Nabisco, Inc. in 1988 in a leveraged buyout costing $26 billion (including over $1 billion of transaction costs). Its common equity investment was a mere $1.5 billion, just 6% of the cost of the acquisition.

EXAMPLE — The RJR Nabisco Leveraged Buyout

On October 20, 1988, RJR Nabisco announced that a management group, which included its president and chief executive and the chief executive of its tobacco subsidiary, had advised the board of directors that they "intend to seek to develop with a financial partner a proposal to acquire the firm in a leveraged buyout." The management group contemplated paying about $75 per share in cash, for an aggregate value of $17.6 billion.

Four days later KKR announced that it was offering to acquire the firm for $90 per share in cash and securities (plus $108 for each outstanding share of preferred stock). Henry Kravis (the second K in KKR) explained that KKR had to participate in the RJR Nabisco buyout in order to protect its franchise as the leading LBO firm. Several rounds of bidding ensued. KKR finally prevailed when it raised its bid to $109 per share ($81 of it in cash).

Bear in mind the Principle of Self-Interested Behavior, and remember that management had indicated initially its intention to bid $75 per share. RJR Nabisco's board voted unanimously to accept the KKR offer. ■

Agency Problems That Arise in LBOs

The RJR Nabisco LBO illustrates two significant agency problems. First, the management-led group announced that it was contemplating bidding $75 per share—far below the $109 acquisition price. The relatively low initial bid undoubtedly reflects the Principle of Two-Sided Transactions: The better the deal for the managers, the worse the deal would be for the shareholders. If shareholders had sold their shares to the management-led group, that group would have reaped a windfall of $34 per share, or more than $7.5 billion in the aggregate. Fortunately, the board of directors immediately formed a special outside committee and took steps to enable the firm's shareholders to realize "full value" for their shares.

Second, the LBO caused RJR Nabisco's bonds to fall in price by approximately 20% to 30%. The fall in bond value reflected a transfer of wealth to the shareholders from the bondholders. This illustrates the problem of claim dilution with respect to capital structure, a concept we discussed in Chapter 9. Soon after the LBO announcement, Moody's Investors Service downgraded the bonds from A-1 to Ba-2. Worse, the transaction sent shock waves through the corporate bond market as bond investors became concerned that other corporate bonds might be subject to similar *event risk*. Investors began to demand new protective bond covenants, called *super poison puts*, that would force issuers to redeem bonds at par in the event that a change in control occurred. Event risk is, of course, another form of agency cost. The demand for super poison puts represents the bondholders' attempt to reduce this cost.

Financing a Leveraged Buyout

The ideal LBO candidate has relatively low operating risk. This permits the firm to take on an unusually high degree of financial risk. In addition, an issue of subordinated debt provides comfort to senior lenders, much like true equity. The actual financing structure for a leveraged buyout will depend crucially on the perceived riskiness of the firm's business, its cash flow characteristics, and the quality of its assets. These factors determine how much debt the firm's operations can support. Investment bankers (or leveraged buyout firms) try to determine the maximum amount of debt the firm's operations can support. The comparative approach, together with the discounted-cash-flow approach, will suggest a reasonable purchase price. This price, together with the firm's borrowing capacity, will indicate the maximum degree of leverage for the buyout.

EXAMPLE

Financing for the RJR Nabisco Leveraged Buyout

KKR tendered for up to 165.5 million shares of RJR Nabisco's common stock (74% of the outstanding shares) at a price of $109 per share and for the 1.25 million outstanding preferred shares at $108 per share. Common stockholders tendered 98.7% of the outstanding common shares, and KKR purchased 75.2% of these shares at a cost of $18 billion. The transaction was so large that it caused a small blip in the U.S. money supply. The balance of the common stock was eliminated in exchange for a combination of preferred stock and convertible debt through a merger.

Table 28-12 shows how KKR financed the $25.96 billion net cost of the leveraged buyout. The financing occurred in two stages. Senior bank borrowings provided 49% of the funds. Subordinated lenders provided 19% of the funds by privately purchasing two series of increasing-rate notes, whose respective interest rates increase by specified amounts at quarterly intervals. KKR and the other equity investors provided 8% of the funds and invested them in $500 million of pay-in-kind extendible debt securities and $1.5 billion of common stock. The pay-in-kind extendible debt securities were subordinated to the increasing-rate notes. They were *pay-in-kind* because RJR Nabisco could pay interest on them in the form of additional notes rather than cash. The second stage of the financing consisted of $6.326 billion of convertible and exchangeable securities, which provided the remaining 24% of the funds.

INVESTMENT		SOURCES OF FINANCING	
Purchase of common stock	$24,589	Senior bank debt	$12,634 (49%[c])
Purchase of preferred stock	135	Subordinated debt	5,000 (19%)
Fees and expenses	1,100	Junior subordinated notes[a]	500 (2%)
Interest to date of merger	570	Convertible debentures[b]	2,259 (9%)
Payments to employees	166	Exchangeable preferred stock[b]	4,067 (15%)
Other	70	Common stock	1,500 (6%)
Excess cash	(670)		
Total investment	$25,960	Total funds invested	$25,960

TABLE 28-12
Sources of permanent financing for the acquisition of RJR Nabisco (dollar amounts in millions).

[a] Pay-in-kind extendible debt securities purchased by certain equity investors.
[b] Issued in exchange for common stock in the second step of the transaction.
[c] Percentage of funds obtained from this source.
Source: RJR Holdings Capital Corp., *Prospectus* (May 12, 1989).

Self-Check Questions

1. What is a leveraged buyout? What distinguishes it from other acquisitions?

2. Describe two agency problems that can arise in a leveraged buyout.

3. What is event risk? How do bond investors deal with it?

SOLUTION TO EMPIRE STATE'S ACQUISITION OPPORTUNITY

At the beginning of the chapter we posed four problems with respect to Empire State's proposed acquisition of Garden State: (1) determining a reasonable price to pay, (2) estimating the impact of the acquisition on Empire State's shareholders, (3) determining the maximum price Empire State could afford to pay, and (4) recommending a financial package to offer Garden State's shareholders. During our discussion of comparative analysis, we estimated a reasonable acquisition price range of between $414 million and $448 million. This was based on a review of recent comparable acquisitions of proprietary pharmaceutical manufacturers.

During our discussion of discounted-cash-flow analysis, we estimated that even if Empire State offered to pay $48 per share—a price slightly above the estimated reasonable range—the acquisition would have a net present value of $236.5 million on a nondisposition basis and a net present value of $88.0 million on a disposition basis.

On the basis of these estimated NPVs and the disposition scenario, it appears that Empire State could afford to pay up to $8.80 per share (= $88.0 million/10 million shares) more than the $48 price contemplated, for a total of up to $56.80 per share. Actually, Empire State would still have a positive NPV at that price, because the preceding calculation did not take into account the effect of the higher tax basis Empire State would have in Garden State's stock.

Empire State has decided there is no benefit to stepping up the tax basis of Garden State's operating assets. Thus it may pursue a tax-free transaction. At least 50% of the consideration it offers Garden State's shareholders would have to consist of equity securities. Depending on the form of tax-free transaction, Empire State might be limited to using common stock to pay 100% of the purchase price.

If Empire State does decide to initiate a tender offer, it should offer Garden State's shareholders cash in order to maximize the likelihood of a successful tender offer. It would issue securities to raise the needed cash. The mix of securities should be consistent with its long-term capital structure objective.

SUMMARY

A merger represents a special form of capital investment. One firm acquires the entire portfolio of assets, and usually the liabilities as well, of another firm. Such a transaction has special legal, tax, and accounting consequences. A merger is larger, more complex, and thus more difficult to analyze than the purchase of a building or a single machine.

Firms have a variety of motives for merging, but a merger can benefit both the acquiror's shareholders and the acquiree's shareholders only if (1) the two firms are worth more together than they are apart and (2) the increase in value is large enough to offset the transaction costs involved. Merging benefits the acquiror's shareholders only if they can realize some of this net gain.

A proposed merger must comply with federal antitrust and securities laws and with each firm's charter. An acquiror can merge or consolidate with the acquiree, purchase the acquiree's stock, or purchase only (some portion of) the acquiree's assets. An acquiror can structure an acquisition so that it is either taxable or tax-free. The tax treatment of the acquisition can have significant cash flow consequences for the acquiror.

There are two basic approaches to valuing corporate acquisitions: comparative analysis and discounted-cash-flow analysis. The former is more widely used in practice, but the two can be used effectively together. Comparative analysis is used to gauge a reasonable acquisition price. This is done by analyzing the price-earnings multiples, cash flow multiples, EBIT and EBITDA multiples, book value multiples, and premiums paid in comparable acquisitions. This analysis suggests reasonable multiples at which to value the target. Discounted-cash-flow analysis, when supplemented by an analysis of comparable merger transactions, will indicate what net acquisition price is reasonable to pay and can indicate whether a proposed transaction at that price is likely to benefit the acquiror's shareholders.

DECISION SUMMARY

- When one firm acquires another firm, it makes a capital investment. The tools of capital budgeting can be used to evaluate proposed acquisitions. But the size and complexity of acquisition transactions make it more difficult to apply these analytical tools to acquisitions than to an investment in a plant or a piece of equipment.

- The acquiror must select its target. A firm must have a valid motive for acquiring another firm. The benefits of the acquisition for the acquiror's shareholders should be assessed realistically. Pure conglomerate mergers whose only benefit is diversification are beneficial only if the acquiror's shareholders cannot achieve such diversification as cheaply on their own, which is seldom the case.

- The acquiror must assess the antitrust and other regulatory consequences of the proposed acquisition in order to determine its feasibility and advisability.

- The acquiror must choose what legal form the acquisition should take: merger or consolidation, purchase of stock, or purchase of assets.

- The acquiror must evaluate its tax position, the target's tax position, and the tax position of the target's shareholders and decide whether it prefers a tax-free transaction or a taxable transaction.

- Generally, the acquiror is also concerned about the accounting impact of an acquisition, even though the available evidence indicates that the choice of accounting method does not affect valuation. It can choose between pooling-of-interests and purchase accounting treatments. Acquirors also often place a constraint on how much dilution in earnings per share they are willing to accept.

- The acquiror must decide how it wishes to pay for the acquisition: with cash, common stock, other securities, or some combination. Its choice is restricted by the legal form of transaction, tax status, and accounting treatment it chooses. Common stock has a potential advantage in that the target's shareholders bear part of the risk that the acquiror has overpaid.

- The acquiror can use comparative analysis to determine a range of reasonable acquisition prices.

- The acquiror can use discounted-cash-flow analysis to evaluate the net present value of the acquisition. Discounted-cash-flow analysis can (and should!) also be used to determine the maximum price the acquiror can afford to pay (which is likely to depend on the legal form and tax status of the acquisition).

- You can use either the weighted-average-cost-of-capital approach or the adjusted-present-value approach to calculate the NPV of any acquisition. Applied correctly, the two approaches provide the same NPV.

- The adjusted-present-value approach is appropriate to use when you evaluate a leveraged buyout or some other potential acquisition that assumes an acquisition-specific debt financing package with a debt ratio that will change over time in some intended manner.

- Considering all its prior decisions and the probable response(s) of the target, the acquiror must decide how to proceed with the transaction, such as with a cash tender offer or a friendly proposal to merge. The defensive barriers the target has already erected affect this decision. Prior to proceeding with the transaction, the acquiror must comply with all applicable legal and regulatory requirements.

- As the transaction proceeds—or as the battle for control unfolds—the acquiror may have to alter some of its earlier decisions if it finds that its objectives conflict with those of the target. But throughout this process, the acquiror must not lose sight of the fact that its ultimate objective is to maximize the wealth of its stockholders.

EQUATION SUMMARY

General

(28.1) $$NAM = V_{AB} - (V_B + P_B) - E - V_A = [V_{AB} - (V_A + V_B)] - P_B - E$$

(28.10) $$\text{Liquidation value} = \text{Asset value} - \text{Repayment} - \text{Taxes} - \text{Expenses}$$

Comparative Analysis

(28.2) $$\frac{\text{Multiple of}}{\text{earnings paid}} = \frac{\text{Purchase price per share}}{\text{Target's fully diluted earnings per share before extraordinary items}}$$

(28.3) $$\frac{\text{Multiple of}}{\text{cash flow paid}} = \frac{\text{Purchase price per share}}{\text{Target's fully diluted cash flow per share before extraordinary items}}$$

(28.4) $$\frac{\text{Multiple of}}{\text{EBIT paid}} = \frac{\text{Aggregate purchase price of equity} + \text{Market value of debt assumed}}{\text{Target's earnings before interest and taxes (EBIT) before extraordinary items}}$$

(28.5) $$\frac{\text{Multiple of}}{\text{EBITDA paid}} = \frac{\text{Aggregate purchase price of equity} + \text{Market value of debt assumed}}{\text{Target's earnings before interest, taxes, depreciation, and amortization (EBITDA) before extraordinary items}}$$

$$(28.6) \quad \frac{\text{Multiple of}}{\text{book value paid}} = \frac{\text{Purchase price per share}}{\text{Target's book value per common share}}$$

$$(28.7) \quad \text{Premium paid} = \frac{\begin{array}{cc}\text{Purchase price} & \text{Target's share} \\ \text{per share} & - \text{price pre-merger}\end{array}}{\text{Target's share price pre-merger}}$$

$$(28.8) \quad \frac{\text{Multiple of}}{\text{replacement}} = \frac{\begin{array}{cc}\text{Aggregate purchase} & \text{Market value of} \\ \text{price of equity} & + \text{debt assumed}\end{array}}{\text{Replacement cost of target's assets}}$$

$$(28.9) \quad \frac{\text{Price paid}}{\text{per unit of}} = \frac{\begin{array}{cc}\text{Aggregate purchase} & \text{Market value of} \\ \text{price of equity} & + \text{debt assumed}\end{array}}{\text{Number of units of resource target owns}}$$

Discounted-Cash-Flow Analysis

$$(28.11) \quad \begin{array}{l}\text{Cost of purchasing target's common shares} \\ + \text{ Transaction costs and expenses} \\ \underline{- \text{ Liquidation value of target's excess assets}} \\ \text{Net investment in target's equity} \\ \underline{+ \text{ Present value of debt acquiror assumes}} \\ \text{Net acquisition cost (NAC)}\end{array}$$

$$(28.12) \quad \text{Added debt} = \text{NAC}(L) - \text{PV(debt displaced)}$$

Weighted-Average-Cost-of-Capital Approach

$$(28.13) \quad \text{TV(NA)} = \text{TV(equity)} + \text{TV(debt)} - T - E$$

$$(28.14) \quad \text{NPV(acquisition)} = -\text{NAC} + \sum_{t=1}^{N} \frac{\text{CFAT}_t}{(1 + \text{WACC})^t}$$

$$(16.9) \quad \text{WACC} = r - T^*Lr_d\left(\frac{1 + r}{1 + r_d}\right)$$

Adjusted-Present-Value Approach

$$(28.15) \quad \text{Net APV(acquisition)} = -\text{NAC} + \sum_{t=1}^{N} \frac{\text{CFAT}_t}{(1 + r)^t} + \sum_{t=1}^{N} \frac{T^* \text{INT}_t}{(1 + r_d)^t}$$

$$(28.16) \quad \text{NPV(all-equity)} = -\text{NAC} + \sum_{t=1}^{N} \frac{\text{CFAT}_t}{(1 + r)^t}$$

$$(28.17) \quad \text{PV(tax shields)} = \sum_{t=1}^{N} \frac{T^* \text{INT}_t}{(1 + r_d)^t}$$

$$(28.18) \quad \text{Net APV(acquisition)} = \text{NPV(all-equity)} + \text{PV(tax shields)} + \text{NPV (side effects)}$$

KEY TERMS

EXERCISES

PROBLEM SET A

A1. Define the following terms: (a) merger; (b) consolidation, (c) horizontal merger, (d) vertical merger, and (e) conglomerate merger.

A2. Explain the valid motives that two firms may have for merging.

A3. The Diversification Principle states that diversification is beneficial. Diversification is one of the main justifications managers give when undertaking conglomerate mergers. Explain why the justification is usually invalid notwithstanding the Diversification Principle.

A4. How can a merger create financial synergy? How can it create business synergy? What is the difference between these two types of synergy?

A5. Ace Homebuilding and Brace Homebuilding will merge. Ace has a total market value of $50 million, and Brace has a total market value of $75 million. Their merger will lead to operating efficiencies and will produce a present value savings of $10 million.

a. What is the total market value of the merged firms?

b. If the merger would entail expenses amounting to $5 million, is there a net advantage to merging?

c. If Ace buys Brace's outstanding shares, paying Brace's common stockholders a $3 million premium, will the acquisition be advantageous to Ace's shareholders? How is the net advantage to merging divided between the two firms' shareholders?

A6. Two firms plan to merge. Prior to the merger, the acquiror has earnings per share of $5 and a price-earnings ratio of 20. The acquiree has earnings per share of $2 and a price-earnings ratio of 10. The acquiror has 10 million shares of stock, and the acquiree has 5 million shares.

a. How many shares must the acquiror exchange for each of the acquiree's shares if the shares are exchanged at their respective market values (i.e., no premium)?

b. Calculate the acquiror's earnings per share after the merger.

c. Calculate the acquiror's price-earnings ratio after the merger.

d. What conclusion can be drawn from parts b and c?

A7. How is the net advantage to merging usually divided between shareholders of acquirors and shareholders of acquirees?

A8. Describe the three basic ways of effecting a corporate acquisition, and explain the distinguishing features of each.

A9. Describe the main differences between a tax-free acquisition and a taxable acquisition. Which of these does a seller generally prefer and which does a buyer generally prefer?

A10. What are the basic requirements a firm must meet to achieve tax-free treatment of a corporate acquisition?

A11. Describe the main differences between the pooling-of-interests method and the purchase method of accounting for acquisitions. Should the choice of accounting technique affect market value in an efficient market?

A12. Define the term *tender offer,* and explain how a firm can acquire another firm through a tender offer. What are the main advantages of a tender offer relative to the other acquisition methods?

A13. Define the term *proxy contest,* and explain how an investor group can gain control of a firm through a proxy contest. What are the main disadvantages of a proxy contest relative to a cash tender offer?

A14. Describe the main defensive tactics that firms have used in an effort to fight off unwanted suitors. How would you expect the use of such tactics to affect shareholder wealth? Describe the agency problem that arises in connection with defensive tactics to thwart unwanted bids.

A15. What distinguishes a leveraged buyout from other types of acquisitions?

PROBLEM SET B

B1. Firm A intends to acquire Firm B. The acquisition will cost Firm A $100 million. Firm A plans to install new management, "fix" the company, and sell it at the end of 5 years. The projected incremental free cash flow stream that Firm A expects to realize from the acquisition, which reflects the anticipated operating improvements, is

Year	1	2	3	4	5
Cash flow ($ millions)	10	20	30	40	50

In addition, the projected after-tax sales proceeds amount to $200 million.

a. Calculate the NPV of the acquisition, assuming a 20% cost of capital.

b. Calculate the internal rate of return for the acquisition.

c. Calculate the payback period for the acquisition.

d. Should Firm A proceed with the acquisition?

B2. Two firms merge in a stock-for-stock transaction. What happens to stockholder wealth and bondholder wealth as a result of the merger? Must this *always* be the case in a stock-for-stock transaction?

B3. Two firms in unrelated businesses plan to merge. There are three possible states of the economy. The following table shows the returns to the shareholders of each firm and the debtholders of Firm B in each state of the economy. Firm B has $50 million principal amount of debt, and Firm A has no debt.

	Boom	Stable Growth	Recession
Probability	0.3	0.5	0.2
Firm A	$200 million	$100 million	$25 million
Firm B			
Debt	50	50	25
Equity	100	50	—

a. What is each firm worth?

b. A merger would not produce any operating efficiencies or economies of scale. What is the merged firm worth? What is the debt of the merged firm worth? What is the equity of the merged firm worth?

c. Should the firms merge?

B4. Suppose the two firms in Problem B3 are in the same industry and a merger will produce $30 million of synergistic benefits (in all three states of the economy) but require $2 million of expenses.

a. How will a merger affect the bondholders?

b. How will a merger affect the shareholders of each firm?

c. Should the firms merge?

B5. Explain why some shareholders of the acquiree might incur an income tax obligation even though the acquisition qualifies under the Internal Revenue Code as a tax-free acquisition. Must every shareholder of the acquiree necessarily incur an income tax obligation in connection with a taxable acquisition?

B6. The purchase price in an acquisition is $275 million. Consultants estimate that the fair market value of the assets acquired is $180 million. Investment bankers estimate that the fair market value of the liabilities assumed in the acquisition is $30 million. Calculate the amount of goodwill.

B7. National Permanent Credit Corporation just acquired Specific Capital Corporation. National paid $50 per Specific share. Specific's latest 12 months' fully diluted earnings per share before extraordinary items was $5 and fully diluted cash flow per share before extraordinary items was $6.25, the most recent book value per share was $20, and the closing share price 30 days prior to the merger announcement was $35. Calculate the following ratios:

a. Multiple of earnings paid

b. Multiple of cash flow paid

c. Multiple of book value paid

d. Premium paid

B8. International Oil Company has oil and gas reserves consisting of 25 million barrels of oil and 60 billion cubic feet of natural gas. Judging by the prices at which oil and gas reserves have recently sold, 1 barrel of oil is equivalent to 6000 cubic feet of natural gas.

a. Calculate the number of barrels of oil equivalent in International's reserves.

b. Regal Oil Corporation is contemplating a bid for International based on the value of International's assets. Petroleum reserves have recently sold for $8.50 per barrel of oil equivalent, and Regal estimates that International's other assets are worth $52.5 million. Calculate the estimated value of International's assets.

B9. Razorback Computer Corporation is preparing to make a bid for the common shares of Windy City Software. Razorback would acquire the shares for cash but would not write up Windy City's assets. Windy City has 5 million shares outstanding, which are trading at a price of $30 per share and a price-earnings multiple of 10. Windy City has $50 million principal amount of 8% debt, which pays interest annually in arrears and matures in a lump sum at the end of 6 years. Razorback's marginal income tax rate is 40%. Razorback estimates that it will have to pay a 50% premium to acquire Windy City and will also have to pay $3 million of after-tax transaction costs. Windy City has no excess cash. Razorback's target debt-to-equity ratio is 1/3, its pretax cost of new debt is 10%, its cost of capital for the acquisition is 16.5%, and the incremental free cash flow stream for the next 6 years is

Year	1	2	3	4	5	6
Cash flow ($ millions)	25	30	35	40	45	50

a. Calculate the NPV and IRR of the acquisition on a nondisposition basis, assuming the estimated year-6 net operating profit is $75 million.

b. Calculate the NPV and IRR of the acquisition on a disposition basis, assuming a 6-year investment horizon.

c. Should Razorback make the acquisition if it has to pay $45 per share?

d. What is the maximum price Razorback can afford to pay on a disposition basis with a 6-year investment horizon?

B10. Razorback Computer Corporation in Problem B9 has a leveraged beta of 1.25. The riskless return is 10%, and the risk premium on the market portfolio is 8%.

a. Calculate the unleveraged cost of equity capital for Razorback.

b. Calculate the net APV of the acquisition on a nondisposition basis, assuming the debt issued to finance the acquisition matures in a lump sum at the end of 6 years.

c. Calculate the net APV of the acquisition on a disposition basis, assuming the debt issued to finance the acquisition matures in a lump sum at the end of 6 years.

B11. Eastern Shore Chemicals plans to acquire Ocean State Chemicals for $50 million. The two firms' balance sheets follow. The fair market value of Ocean State's working capital is $12 million, of its fixed assets is $32 million, and of its debt is $4 million.

	Ocean State	Eastern Shore
Assets ($ millions)		
Working capital	$ 10	$ 25
Fixed assets	25	125
Total	$ 35	$150
Liabilities and Equity ($ millions)		
Debt	$ 5	$ 50
Equity	30	100
Total	$ 35	$150

a. Suppose Eastern Shore exchanges shares of its common stock for the outstanding shares of Ocean State's common stock. How would the balance sheet of the combined firm look? Which method of accounting did you apply?

b. Suppose Eastern Shore issues new common stock for cash and uses the cash to purchase Ocean State's shares. How would the balance sheet of the combined firm look? Which method of accounting did you apply?

B12. Firm A has 1,000,000 shares outstanding that are trading at $25 each. Firm B has 2,000,000 shares outstanding that are trading at $50 each. Firm A earns $2.50 per share, and Firm B earns $4.00 per share.

a. Calculate each firm's price-earnings ratio.

b. Suppose Firm B acquires Firm A in a stock-for-stock swap based on current market values. What happens to Firm B's earnings per share? Does that mean that Firm B's shareholders are better off as a result of the merger? Explain.

B13. Louisiana Fried Chicken (LFC) is hoping to acquire Arkansas Fried Chicken (AFC). LFC has gathered the following information regarding recent acquisitions of comparable restaurant chains (dollar amounts in millions):

Acquisition	Market Value of Debt	Price Paid for Equity	Earnings	EBIT	EBITDA
1	$225	$450	$ 30	$ 80	$110
2	150	600	50	100	125
3	175	350	25	85	85
4	25	375	35	50	65
5	110	330	30	55	70
6	50	450	45	60	85

a. Calculate the multiples of earnings, EBIT, and EBITDA paid for each firm.

b. AFC has no debt. Which of the three multiples in part a is most useful for determining a reasonable price to pay for AFC?

c. AFC's earnings are $50 million, its EBIT is $75 million, and its EBITDA is $100 million. What is a reasonable range of values? Why do the three ratios appear to give inconsistent value ranges?

B14. With regard to Empire State's acquisition of Garden State, suppose Garden State's new-issue rate is 13%.

a. What is the market value of the $100 million of outstanding bonds?

b. Would the acquisition help or hurt Garden State's bondholders?

c. What is the cause of this transfer of wealth?

B15. Big Sky Airlines would like to acquire Far West Commuter Air and integrate Far West's route structure into its system. Big Sky would acquire Far West's shares for cash but not write up Far

West's assets. Far West has 2 million shares outstanding. Its share price is $24, its earnings per share are $4, and it has no debt and no excess cash. Big Sky's debt-to-equity ratio is 2 to 1. Its pretax cost of debt is 14% (annual interest), its cost of equity is 20%, and its marginal income tax rate is 40%. If Big Sky acquires Far West, it projects a year-8 net operating profit of $45 million and incremental free cash flows of

Year	1	2	3	4	5	6	7	8
Cash flow ($ millions)	6	10	12	14	18	22	25	30

a. Calculate the NPV and IRR of the acquisition on a nondisposition basis, assuming Big Sky pays a 1/3 premium for Far West's shares and $500,000 of after-tax acquisition expenses.

b. Calculate the NPV and IRR of the acquisition on a disposition basis under the same assumptions as in part a and assuming an 8-year investment horizon.

c. Should Big Sky make the acquisition if it has to pay a 1/3 premium for Far West's shares?

B16. Big Sky's unleveraged cost of equity capital is 16%. Calculate the adjusted present value of Big Sky's acquisition of Far West under the assumptions stated in Problem B15 and assuming the debt issued to finance the acquisition matures in a lump sum at the end of 8 years.

B17. Ajax Air Products and Central Combustion have agreed to an exchange of common stock under which Ajax would acquire Central. Ajax's common stock is trading at $40 per share, and Central's common stock is trading at $20 per share. Each firm has 10 million shares outstanding.

a. Calculate the exchange ratio assuming Ajax does not pay a premium.

b. Calculate the exchange ratio assuming Ajax pays a 25% premium to acquire Central.

c. If the exchange ratio determined in part b is fixed and the announcement of the merger causes Ajax's share price to fall 10%, by how much would you expect Central's share price to change?

B18. American Car Rental has agreed to acquire Big Apple Car Rental. American's financial staff has gathered the following data regarding acquisitions involving firms in the automobile industry.

Acquiree	Business	Price/ Earnings	Price/ Cash Flow	(Debt & Equity)/ EBITDA	Price/ Book Value
Central	rental	10x	5.8x	8.2x	1.5x
Eastern	manufacturing	7	4.3	6.5	1.2
Western	manufacturing	6	4.0	6.3	1.1
South Central	rental	11	6.7	8.9	1.6
Southwestern	rental	12	7.8	7.9	1.4
Panhandle	manufacturing	8	4.9	6.9	1.3

Price is the price paid in the acquisition. Big Apple's latest 12 months' earnings are $25 million, its latest 12 months' cash flow is $40 million, its latest 12 months' EBITDA is $30 million, and its current aggregate book value is $175 million. Calculate a reasonable range of acquisition values for Big Apple.

B19. Excelsior Paper Products Company is considering acquiring the Spring Lake Greeting Card Company. Excelsior would have to pay $100 million for Spring Lake, 90% of which it would borrow at a 10% annual interest rate. The $100 million purchase price represents a multiple of 8 times this year's incremental free cash flow. Excelsior's marginal income tax rate is 40%. Its long-term debt ratio is 50%. Spring Lake's incremental free cash flow is expected to grow at the rate of 10% per annum into the foreseeable future. All available free cash flow will be used first to pay interest, next to repay principal (until the acquisition loan is fully repaid), and then to pay dividends. The unleveraged cost of equity capital for similar acquisitions is 14%. The riskless return is 6%, and the excess return on the market portfolio is 8%. Calculate the net present value of the acquisition, assuming a 6-year investment horizon.

PROBLEM SET C

C1. A firm owns two plants that it purchased 10 years ago for $5,000,000. The two plants have been depreciated to zero but have a current fair market value of $6,000,000. An acquiror has offered $8,000,000 to buy the corporation. Following the acquisition, it could depreciate the plants straight-line over 5 years. The acquiror's income tax rate is 40%, and its 5-year new-issue debt rate is 12%. The selling corporation has two shareholders whose tax basis in their shares is their original $5,000,000 investment to purchase the two plants. Their capital gains tax rate is 28%, and they invest most of their funds in municipal bonds yielding 7%. They had originally planned to sell their business and retire in 2 years, but the $8 million offer seems "too good" to refuse.

  a. Calculate the net present value of the tax shields that would result from writing up the tax basis of the plants. Would the acquiror prefer a taxable transaction?

  b. Calculate the incremental cost of a taxable transaction. Would the sellers prefer a tax-free transaction?

  c. Calculate the net advantage of a taxable transaction. Would the acquiror and the sellers benefit mutually from a tax-free transaction?

C2. Arnold Electronics and Beard Oil and Gas plan to combine through merger. Neither firm has any debt. The merger will involve a share-for-share exchange, and there will be no transaction costs. Arnold has total market value $V_A = \$100$ million, and Beard has total market value $V_B = \$200$ million. No synergistic effects will result from the merger.

  a. What is the maximum value the combined firms could have following the merger?

  b. Suppose that if there were no merger, Arnold's shares and Beard's shares would be expected to provide annual returns of 20% and 25%, respectively. Further suppose that there exist two other firms, one of whose shares are a perfect substitute for Arnold's and the other of whose shares are a perfect substitute for Beard's. What must be the expected return on the shares of the merged firm in a perfect market environment?

  c. Show that if the shares of the merged firm were trading at a price that would provide an expected annual return of 23%, then market agents could earn a pure arbitrage profit. Explain how this could be accomplished, and quantify the profit.

  d. Suppose instead that neither the Arnold shares nor the Beard shares has a close substitute. Show that the value of the combined firms following the merger must be less than $300 million.

C3. Two firms are identical, including their capital structures. Each faces two possible states of nature, which are equally likely: F (favorable) or U (unfavorable). The returns to the stockholders of each firm and the returns to debtholders are identical in each state, but the likelihood that state F will occur for Firm A and the likelihood that it will occur for Firm B are uncorrelated. For each firm, debtholders have a prior claim to the first $140 of income. The returns (in $ millions) in each state are

	RETURN IN STATE		EXPECTED	STANDARD
RETURN TO	F	U	RETURN	DEVIATION
Firm	200	100	150	50
Debtholders	140	100	120	20
Stockholders	60	0	30	30

  a. Specify the set of possible outcomes for the merged firm, for the former debtholders of each firm, and for the former stockholders of each firm following a merger through an exchange of shares.

  b. Show that each class of debtholders is better off as a result of the merger.

  c. Show that each class of stockholders is worse off as a result of the merger.

  d. What conclusions can be drawn from parts b and c?

C4. Radnor Publishing would like to acquire Excelsior Publishing from The Miami Media Group. Radnor estimates that the net acquisition cost, before any depreciation recapture, would be $125 million. Radnor estimates that Excelsior's incremental free cash flow is currently $15 million and will grow at 15% per annum into the foreseeable future before allowing for any asset write-up. Radnor believes it could sell Excelsior at the end of 10 years at a multiple of $125/15 = 8\frac{1}{3}$ times incremental free cash flow. The Miami Media Group acquired Excelsior 1 year ago for $100 million, which represents its current tax basis in Excelsior's stock. Excelsior's tax basis in its assets is $25 million, because Excelsior's assets consist primarily of goodwill. Radnor's marginal income tax rate is 40%, and its cost of capital for the acquisition is 16%.

a. Calculate Radnor's NPV of acquiring Excelsior's common stock for $125 million cash, assuming that Radnor can write up Excelsior's assets to $50 million and pay only $10 million in depreciation recapture taxes.

b. Calculate Radnor's NPV of acquiring Excelsior's common stock for $125 million common stock. [*Hint:* The transaction is tax-free.]

c. Would Miami Media prefer a taxable transaction or a tax-free transaction? Calculate the difference in taxes payable.

d. How would you recommend that Miami Media and Radnor structure the acquisition: taxable or tax-free?

C5. At the time the Delaware Chancery Court ruled in favor of Time Inc. and let it proceed with its purchase of Warner Communications, Time's shares were trading at around $144 per share. Paramount Communications had bid $200 per share for Time's common stock. Time's board of directors refused to let the shareholders vote on the proposed Warner Communications transaction and argued that their long-term strategy had greater value for the Time shareholders. After the court decision, Paramount withdrew its bid.

a. What do Time's actions reveal about the existence of agency costs?

b. How could you reconcile the board's argument that its long-term strategy has a present value in excess of $200 per share with the fact that the stock was trading at just $144 per share?

C6. The section on merger tactics discussed Brooke Group's proxy battle with the management of RJR Nabisco. Check the *Wall Street Journal* index and find some articles describing this proxy battle and its outcome.

a. How close did the dissidents come to winning?

b. How did RJR Nabisco's other shareholders make out?

Real-World Application:
The Lockheed-Martin Marietta 'Merger of Equals'

Between 1985 and 1995, the Federal defense budget for research and development, test and evaluation, and procurement had shrunk by almost two-thirds in real terms (dollars of constant purchasing power). This reduction placed pressure on aerospace/defense firms to consolidate in order to maintain production economies and remain competitive. Lockheed Corporation (Lockheed) and Martin Marietta Corporation (Martin Marietta) had been active participants in the industry's consolidation.

In light of the anticipated further decreases in military spending and accelerating consolidation in the aerospace/defense industry, in March 1994, Lockheed and Martin Marietta began exploring the possibility of combining. During the next several months, the two firms each considered other possible acquisitions and joint ventures. In August 1994, the boards of directors of the two firms approved a 'merger of equals'. Both boards believed that a Lockheed-Martin Marietta combination would create a leading aerospace firm that would have the critical mass and economies of scale necessary to compete effectively in the current global business environment. The merger would enhance the combined firms' position in commercial markets, give rise to an estimated $200 million per year of pretax operating cost savings, and create a broader product platform on which to grow the combined business. A 'merger of equals' would also result in lower leverage than a cash acquisition in which one firm borrowed funds to buy the other.

The merger of Lockheed and Martin Marietta would involve the formation of a new corporation, Lockheed Martin Corporation (Lockheed Martin), which would have two special-purpose subsidiaries. One would be merged with and into Lockheed, and the other would be merged with and into Martin Marietta. As a result, Lockheed and Martin Marietta would become wholly owned subsidiaries of Lockheed Martin. Each of Lockheed's 66,179,422 outstanding common shares would be exchanged for 1.63 Lockheed Martin shares. Martin Marietta's 100,680,090 outstanding common shares would be exchanged for Lockheed Martin shares on a share-for-share basis. In addition, General Electric Company, which held 20 million shares of Martin Marietta convertible preferred stock, would receive 20 million shares of Lockheed Martin convertible preferred stock. Both were convertible into 28,941,466 shares of the issuing firm's common stock.

The merger transaction was structured so as to qualify under the Internal Revenue Code as a tax-free exchange of shares. The two firms also expected it to qualify as a pooling of interests for accounting purposes.

Lockheed's financial advisor noted that the ratios of Lockheed's average closing stock price to Martin Marietta's average closing stock price for various historical periods ending just prior to the announcement of the merger were

LAST 5 YEARS	LAST 3 YEARS	LAST 2 YEARS	LAST 12 MONTHS	LAST 6 MONTHS	LAST 3 MONTHS	LAST 30 DAYS	LATEST CLOSING PRICE
1.609	1.597	1.567	1.484	1.438	1.444	1.380	1.309

Lockheed Martin intended to pay cash dividends of $0.35 per share per quarter. Lockheed had paid $0.57 per share per quarter, and Martin Marietta had paid $0.24 per share per quarter.

Table 28-13 provides summary income statements and balance sheets for Lockheed and Martin Marietta for the latest 12 months preceding the merger.

1. What form will the merger take?
2. What is the rationale for the merger? Do you think it makes sense?
3. Describe the merger's
   a. Tax treatment.
   b. Accounting treatment.
4. Prepare each of the following:
   a. Pro forma income statement.
   b. Pro forma balance sheet.
5. Calculate the impact on earnings per share for Lockheed shareholders and for Martin Marietta shareholders.

	LOCKHEED	MARTIN MARIETTA	ADJUSTMENTS
Net sales	$13,025	$10,276	$(116)[a]
Cost of sales	(12,144)	(9,329)	116[a]
Earnings from operations	881	947	
Other income and expenses, net	(6)	203	
Interest expense	(160)	(120)	
Pretax income	715	1,030	
Income taxes	(272)	(415)	
Net income	$ 443	$ 615	
Weighted average shares (millions)	63.5	125.9[b]	
Assets:			
Current assets	$ 4,116	$ 3,325	
Long-term assets	4,909	5,668	
Total assets	$ 9,025	$ 8,993	
Liabilities and Stockholders' Equity:			
Current liabilities	$ 2,723	$ 2,156	
Long-term debt	1,906	1,347	
Other long-term liabilities	1,707	2,220	
Preferred stock	—	1,000	
Common stockholders' equity	2,689	2,270	
Total liabilities and stockholders' equity	$ 9,025	$ 8,993	

TABLE 28-13
Summary financial information for Lockheed and Martin Marietta for the 12 months preceding the merger (dollar amounts in millions).

[a] Intercompany sales.
[b] Fully diluted.
Source: Lockheed Corporation and Martin Marietta Corporation, *Joint Proxy Statement* (February 10, 1995).

6. Calculate the percentages of Lockheed Martin that the former stockholders of Lockheed and Martin Marietta will each own assuming
   a. Martin Marietta convertible preferred stock is not converted.
   b. Martin Marietta convertible preferred stock is fully converted.

7. Immediately prior to the announcement of the proposed terms of the merger (but several months after the two firms' intention to merge had been announced), Lockheed's closing share price was $74⅛, and Martin Marietta's closing share price was $45¾.
   a. What is the total equity value of Lockheed Martin before allowing for the effect of the operating cost savings? (*Hint:* Treat the convertible

preferred stock as though it had been converted.)
   b. How would the operating cost savings affect the value of the firm? (Assume a 40% income tax rate.)

8. How would the merger affect Lockheed's and Martin Marietta's bondholders?

9. How would the merger affect the dividend income of Lockheed's and Martin Marietta's shareholders?

10. Are the proposed exchange ratios fair to
    a. Lockheed's shareholders.
    b. Martin Marietta's shareholders.

11. Lockheed and Martin Marietta described their combining as a merger of equals. Do you think this is an accurate description of the transaction? Explain.

Newbould, Gerald D., Robert E. Chatfield, and Ronald F. Anderson. "Leveraged Buyouts and Tax Incentives," *Financial Management*, 1992, 21(1):50–57.

Niden, Cathy M. "An Empirical Examination of White Knight Corporate Takeovers: Synergy and Overbidding," *Financial Management*, 1993, 22(4):28–45.

Opler, Tim C. "Controlling Financial Distress Costs in Leveraged Buyouts with Financial Innovations," *Financial Management*, 1993, 22(3):79–90.

Opler, Tim C. "Operating Performance in Leveraged Buyouts: Evidence from 1985–1989," *Financial Management*, 1992, 21(1):27–34.

Opler, Tim, and Sheridan Titman. "The Determinants of Leveraged Buyout Activity: Free Cash Flow Versus Financial Distress Costs," *Journal of Finance*, 1993, 48(5):1985–1999.

Palepu, Krishna G. "Predicting Takeover Targets: A Methodological and Empirical Analysis," *Journal of Accounting and Economics*, 1986, 8(March):3–36.

Servaes, Henri. "Tobin's *Q* and the Gains from Takeovers," *Journal of Finance*, 1991, 46(1):409–420.

Shrieves, Ronald E., and Mary M. Pashley. "Evidence on the Association Between Mergers and Capital Structure," *Financial Management*, 1984, 13(3):39–48.

Slovin, Myron B., Marie E. Sushka, and Carl D. Hudson. "Deregulation, Contestability, and Airline Acquisitions," *Journal of Financial Economics*, 1991, 30(2): 231–252.

Smith, Brian F., and Ben Amoako-Adu. "Minority Buyouts and Ownership Characteristics: Evidence from the Toronto Stock Exchange," *Financial Management*, 1992, 21(2):41–51.

Song, Moon H., and Ralph A. Walkling. "The Impact of Managerial Ownership on Acquisition Attempts and Target Shareholder Wealth," *Journal of Financial and Quantitative Analysis*, 1993, 28(4):439–457.

Stulz, Rene M., Ralph A. Walkling, and Moon H. Song. "The Distribution of Target Ownership and the Division of Gains in Successful Takeovers," *Journal of Finance*, 1990, 45(3):817–834.

Sullivan, Michael J., Marlin R. H. Jensen, and Carl D. Hudson. "The Role of Medium of Exchange in Merger Offers: Examination of Terminated Merger Proposals," *Financial Management*, 1994, 23(3):51–62.

Thomas, Hugh. "Seller Selection of M&A Advisors," *Financial Management*, 1993, 22(4):17–18.

Vijh, Anand M. "The Spinoff and Merger Ex-Date Effects," *Journal of Finance*, 1994, 49(2):581–609.

Wansley, James W., William R. Lane, and Ho C. Yang. "Abnormal Returns to Acquired Firms by Type of Acquisition and Method of Payment," *Financial Management*, 1983, 12(3):16–22.

Weaver, Samuel C., Robert S. Harris, Daniel W. Bielinski, and Kenneth F. MacKenzie. "Panel Discussion: Merger and Acquisition Valuation," *Financial Management*, 1991, 20(2):85–96.

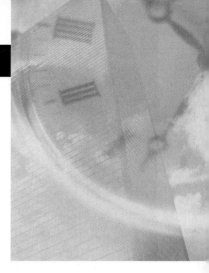

MULTINATIONAL CORPORATE FINANCE

Today's successful firms have a global perspective and operate in many countries. They raise capital, hire employees, and sell their products throughout the world in whichever countries offer the most attractive opportunities. They develop new products specifically for foreign markets and seek new markets for existing products outside their country of incorporation. This is equally true for U.S. and foreign firms. Indeed, the distinction between U.S. firms and foreign firms has become blurred as the leading firms have evolved into truly **multinational corporations**.

Exxon Corporation produces oil and gas in the North Sea, off Norway and the United Kingdom, and in Australia, Indonesia, and Malaysia. Microsoft Corporation has a European manufacturing operation in Ireland. The Walt Disney Company has a huge theme park located near Paris. The Goodyear Tire & Rubber Company produces tires and inner tubes in Brazil and Chile. The Coca-Cola Company sells its familiar soft drink virtually everywhere. Two-thirds of its sales and three-quarters of its operating profits come from outside the United States.

Foreign-based multinationals have significant U.S. operations. Australia's News Corporation owns the Fox Broadcasting Network, Twentieth Century Fox film studio, HarperCollins Publishers, TV Guide, and several TV stations. Germany's Thyssen AG produces automotive products in Indiana and several other states. Japan's Toyota Motor Corporation manufactures automobiles in California and Kentucky. Switzerland's Hoffmann-La Roche Inc. manufactures pharmaceutical products in New Jersey. Korea's Samsung Electronics Co. Ltd. produces semiconductors in California.

Thus far in the book we have made little distinction between domestic and foreign situations for the sake of simplicity. In this chapter our discussion will revolve explicitly around multinational corporations, firms that operate in more than one country.

The principles of finance are equally valid in international and domestic finance. They can be applied no matter where the firm has its base or where it

OBJECTIVES

After studying this chapter, you should be able to

1. Describe the five basic types of foreign exchange transactions: spot transactions, forward transactions, currency futures, currency swaps, and currency options.

2. Describe each of the four key parity relationships: interest rate parity, purchasing power parity, expectations theory of forward exchange rates, and the international Fisher effect.

3. Explain how a firm can use forward market transactions, foreign currency money market transactions, and foreign currency option transactions to hedge its currency risk exposure.

4. Evaluate the net present value of a foreign capital budgeting project.

5. Calculate the cost of borrowing in terms of the domestic currency when issuing debt denominated in a foreign currency.

6. Explain the pitfall in borrowing in whichever currency affords the lowest interest rate.

operates. For the most part, the international dimension merely complicates application of the principles. The fundamental goal of an international firm also remains unchanged: Maximize shareholder wealth. Firms seek out positive-NPV projects in foreign as well as domestic markets, and the analytical tools developed in earlier chapters can also be applied in an international context when we take into account certain complications.

The main complication concerns foreign currencies. A firm headquartered in the United States keeps its accounts in U.S. dollars. When it pursues a project in a foreign market, it will invest in assets in the foreign country and thus incur costs and realize revenues in the local currency. Some currencies, such as the British pound, German mark, Japanese yen, and Swiss franc, are freely convertible into U.S. dollars. But the nonsynchronous timing of revenues and expenses and the fluctuation in exchange rates lead to foreign exchange risks that the firm will want to manage. Some other currencies are not freely convertible into U.S. dollars, which exposes the U.S. firm to even greater foreign exchange risk.

We will help you understand how the foreign exchange markets operate and the methods they afford for handling foreign exchange risk. We will also show you how to take foreign exchange risk into account when evaluating proposed capital budgeting projects and analyzing foreign-currency-denominated financing alternatives.

In addition, we will explain the relationship among foreign exchange rates, interest rates in different countries (and different currencies), and national inflation rates. We will then describe how market imperfections that impede the free flow of capital across national boundaries can give rise to positive-NPV financing opportunities in foreign capital markets.

Our basic objective throughout this chapter is to broaden your perspective and give you a global financial orientation. We hope to convince you that maintaining an international perspective can yield important benefits in the form of finding positive-NPV projects or identifying positive-NPV financing alternatives not available in the domestic market.

MULTINATIONAL CORPORATE FINANCE AND THE PRINCIPLES OF FINANCE

◆ *Self-Interested Behavior*: Seek out investments that offer the greatest expected risk-adjusted real return.

◆ *Two-Sided Transactions*: You can use derivatives to transfer foreign exchange risk to others. Derivatives do not eliminate risk; they only transfer it.

◆ *Valuable Ideas*: Look for opportunities to develop derivatives or design arrangements that enable firms to cope better with the risks they face in their foreign operations. Also, look for opportunities to develop new positive-NPV financing mechanisms.

- *Comparative Advantage*: Transferring foreign exchange risk to other parties can be valuable if they are willing to bear these risks more cheaply.

- *Options*: Recognize the value of hidden options in a situation, such as the foreign exchange options in some derivative instruments.

- *Incremental Benefits*: Calculate the net advantage of a foreign project on the basis of the incremental after-tax cash flows the project will provide.

- *Risk-Return Trade-Off*: To transfer risk to another party, you must offer a return that fully compensates for the amount of risk transferred.

- *Diversification*: Diversifying internationally is valuable when the returns from a foreign investment are not perfectly correlated with the returns on any subset of the U.S. market portfolio.

- *Capital Market Efficiency*: You cannot forecast foreign exchange rate movements precisely, because these movements have a significant random component in an efficient market. Use the foreign exchange market's consensus forecast.

- *Time Value of Money*: Use discounted cash flow analysis to measure the net present value of a foreign investment project.

MOBIL OIL'S FINANCING ALTERNATIVES

Mobil Oil Corporation wants to borrow $100 million, or the foreign currency equivalent to $100 million, to help pay the cost of a new refinery the firm is constructing. Investment bankers have advised the firm's treasurer that Mobil Oil could raise funds in the domestic market by issuing at par 5-year bonds bearing a 9% interest rate (interest payable annually in arrears) and that Mobil Oil could instead sell Swiss-franc-denominated bonds in Switzerland where the firm maintains its international headquarters. The Swiss franc issue would require a 4% interest rate (interest payable annually in arrears) to be worth par.

The 4% interest rate looks very attractive to Mobil Oil's treasurer. However, she wonders why the Swiss franc borrowing rate should be so much lower than the U.S. dollar borrowing rate. The answer lies in the relationship among exchange rates, interest rates, and inflation rates. After we explain these relationships and develop a procedure for taking foreign exchange rates into account in calculating the cost of debt, we will help Mobil Oil's treasurer decide which alternative to choose.

29.1 SOME USEFUL TERMS

Each time you study a new subject, you encounter new terms. International finance has many special terms, some quite colorful. Some are so important that we have a separate section or subsection for them. These include currency futures, currency swaps, exchange rates, foreign currency options, foreign exchange market, and forward exchange rates. Here are some others.

American Depository Receipts

An *American depository receipt*, or ADR, is a receipt that represents ownership of shares of a foreign corporation's common stock. The foreign shares are held in trust, usually by a U.S. bank. ADRs are issued in the United States, and they are publicly traded. Their price is expressed in U.S. dollars. An agent bank converts each dividend into U.S. dollars before paying it to U.S. shareholders. Some ADRs are *firm-sponsored*; others are *unsponsored*.

We discussed registration requirements and ongoing information requirements in Chapter 23. Foreign firms like ADRs because these requirements are less demanding for ADRs than for shares issued directly to U.S. investors.

Unsponsored ADRs can be created by a securities firm without the foreign firm's help. They have weaker information requirements than firm-sponsored ADRs. There are about 700 separate issues of ADRs.

Eurobonds

A *Eurobond* is a bond issued outside the country in whose currency it is denominated. The prefix *Euro* means "outside of." For example, Eurodollar bonds are denominated in U.S. dollars and are issued, held, and traded outside the United States. Eurobonds exist in U.S. dollars, Canadian dollars, German marks, French francs, Japanese yen, British pounds, and many other currencies. Eurobonds have become a major source of capital. The Euromarket is a large, unregulated, supranational market; it is basically free of the restrictions that apply to domestic offerings.

Eurocurrency

The term *Eurocurrency* refers to funds deposited in a bank outside the country in whose currency it is denominated. For example, *Eurodollars*, which are the leading Eurocurrency, consist of U.S. dollar deposits in banks outside the United States. Eurocurrencies represent all the major world currencies.

European Currency Units

A *European currency unit*, or ECU, is an index of ten European currencies. It was developed in 1979. Members of the European Economic Community intended it to serve as the single currency of account for the European Monetary System. Many Eurobonds have been issued in ECUs. However, the ECU has not yet replaced the ten currencies that compose it.

Foreign Bonds

A *foreign bond* is issued by a foreign firm or government in the country in whose currency it is denominated. For example, *Yankee bonds* are denominated in U.S. dollars and issued in the United States by foreign firms or governments. They are different from Eurobonds. A U.S. firm sells Eurobonds outside the United States; a foreign firm sells Yankee bonds in the United States. Other examples of foreign bonds are Bulldog bonds (issued in Britain), Matador bonds (Spain), Rembrandt bonds (Netherlands), and Samurai bonds (Japan).

Foreign bond offerings face tougher restrictions and disclosure standards than bonds sold by domestic issuers. As a result, the Eurobond market has grown more rapidly than the markets for foreign bonds.

London Interbank Offer Rate

The *London Interbank Offer Rate*, or LIBOR, is the interest rate at which large international banks lend each other funds in the London money market. Most loans consist of Eurodollars, and most are overnight. The overnight rate is referred to as *overnight LIBOR*. But banks also lend each other Eurodollars for longer periods, such as for a week at *7-day LIBOR*, for a month at *1-month LIBOR*, and so on. There are similar interest rates for other Eurocurrencies, such as sterling LIBOR, Paris Interbank Offer Rate (PIBOR) for French francs, and so on.

Dollar LIBOR is important in the commercial loan market. Many short-term loans bear interest at a rate tied to LIBOR. For example, the interest rate on a loan might be stated as 3-month LIBOR plus 1%. The interest rate adjusts quarterly. If 3-month LIBOR increases to 6% APR from 5%, the interest rate increases to 7% from 6%. Similarly, floating-rate dollar-denominated Eurobonds usually have an interest rate that is tied to LIBOR.

Self-Check Questions

1. What is an American depository receipt? What is the difference between firm-sponsored and unsponsored ADRs? Why do many foreign firms prefer ADRs over issuing their shares in the United States?

2. What are Eurobonds, and where are they traded?

3. What is a European currency unit? Are bonds issued denominated in ECUs?

4. What is the London Interbank Offer Rate (LIBOR)? Explain why LIBOR is really a set of interest rates. Why is LIBOR useful as a benchmark for pricing floating-rate loans?

29.2 THE FOREIGN EXCHANGE MARKET

A large American department store chain has signed an agreement to import fine English china. The contract calls for the American firm to pay the British exporting firm in British pounds. To do so, the American firm must purchase British pounds in the foreign exchange market. The **foreign exchange market** is the market within which one country's currency is traded for another country's currency. In our example, the American firm would exchange U.S. dollars for British pounds in the foreign exchange market and pay the exporter's invoice. Alternatively, if the contract had specified payment in U.S. dollars, the exporter would have received dollars and then sold the dollars for British pounds in the foreign exchange market.

The foreign exchange market is the world's largest financial market. It is a worldwide market, but London, New York, and Tokyo are the major centers of activity. It is also an over-the-counter market. The larger commercial and investment banks and the central banks are the principal market participants, and corporations generally buy and sell currencies through a commercial bank. The many other participants include importers, who need foreign currency to pay for the goods they import; money managers who buy and sell foreign stocks and bonds; and multinational firms that invest in facilities and sell goods in foreign markets. Most of the trading takes place in six currencies: U.S. dollar ($), German mark (or simply mark; DM), French franc (FF), Swiss franc (SF), Japanese yen (¥), and British pound (£).

Exchange Rates

An **exchange rate** is the price of one country's currency expressed in terms of another country's currency. For example, a rate of $1.70 per £1 (written simply $1.70/£) means that 1 British pound costs $1.70 (£1 = $1.70). To put it another way, 1 U.S. dollar costs 0.5882 British pound, because 1/1.70 = 0.5882 ($1 = £0.5882).

An exchange rate is used to convert an amount expressed in one currency into another.

Using an Exchange Rate to Convert From One Currency to Another

Your sorority can buy a used two-decker London bus for £15,000. (You will use it to drive everyone to home football games and other important events.) How many dollars will you need to buy it?

The exchange rate is $1.70 per £1. Purchasing the bus will cost you £15,000 × 1.70 per £1 = $25,500. ■

The U.S. dollar–British pound exchange rate can be expressed equivalently in terms of either dollars per pound or pounds per dollar. The exchange rates could also be expressed indirectly in terms of a third currency—say, the Swiss franc: SF1.50/$ and SF2.55/£. Figure 29-1 illustrates these currency relationships. Given any two, it is easy to find the third.

The direct and indirect methods of expressing an exchange rate are equivalent. In our example, the dollar–pound exchange rate implicit in the exchange rates SF1.50/$ and SF2.55/£ is £0.5882/$ (or, equivalently, $1.70/£) because

$$\frac{SF1.50}{\$} \div \frac{SF2.55}{£} = \frac{£0.5882}{\$}$$

If the equivalence did not hold, there would be a riskless arbitrage opportunity.

A Riskless Currency Arbitrage Opportunity

Suppose British pounds were trading at a price of SF2.60/£ in Switzerland and at a price of $1.70/£ in New York while Swiss francs were trading for SF1.50/$ in New York. In that case, the pound would be overvalued in Switzerland relative to the other two currencies. A foreign exchange trader who purchased $100 worth of pounds in New York would obtain £58.82 (= 100 × 0.5882). Selling the pounds in Switzerland would yield SF152.93 (= 58.82 × 2.60). The Swiss francs could be sold in New York for $101.96 (= 152.93 × 0.6667), yielding a riskless arbitrage profit of $1.96 per $100 invested. ■

In practice in foreign exchange trading, all exchange rates are expressed in terms of the U.S. dollar. For example, SF1 = $0.66, DM1 = $0.60, £1 = $1.70, and so on. Traders find it convenient to quote exchange rates indirectly in terms of a single currency, the U.S. dollar.

Types of Foreign Exchange Transactions

There are five types of foreign exchange transactions: spot transactions, forward transactions, currency futures, currency swaps, and currency options. Let's take a look at each.

FIGURE 29-1
The relationship among the values of three currencies.

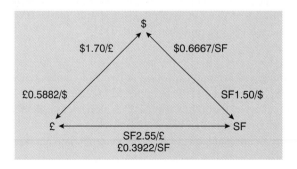

SPOT TRANSACTIONS   *Spot trades* involve the purchase and sale of a currency for "immediate" delivery, which actually occurs two business days after the trade takes place. Figure 29-2 illustrates what a typical table of foreign exchange rates published in a financial newspaper looks like. Suppose the exchange rates shown in the table applied on February 15, 1996. The table furnishes the *spot foreign exchange rates* quoted by Bankers Trust Co. for trading amounts of $1 million or greater as of 3 P.M. the preceding two trading days. For example, the British pound is quoted in the table at £1 = $1.6865 for February 15 and at £1 = $1.6950 for February 14, indicating a slight decrease in the value of the pound (relative to the dollar) between February 14 and February 15.

The table also reports currency *cross rates* for actively traded currencies. These rates show the value of any currency in terms of any other currency. For example, considering the Canadian dollar (C$)–US dollar ($) exchange rate, C$1.2035 = $1 (in the upper left-hand corner) is equivalent to $0.83091 = C$1 (in the lower right-hand corner).

FORWARD TRANSACTIONS   *Forward trades* involve the purchase and sale of a currency for future delivery on the basis of exchange rates that are agreed to today. Figure 29-2 shows *forward exchange rates* in addition to spot exchange rates for British pounds, Canadian dollars, French francs, Japanese yen, Swiss francs, and German marks. In each case the rates are shown for 30-, 90-, and 180-day forward contracts. Forward contracts typically have a term between 1 and 52 weeks. For example, a firm could purchase pounds for immediate delivery at an exchange rate of £1 = $1.6865 on Thursday, February 15, 1996. On that same day, a firm could also contract for 30-day delivery at an exchange rate of £1 = $1.6779, called the forward exchange rate, and for 180-day delivery at a forward rate of £1 = $1.6341. A firm entering into a 30-day forward contract on February 15 to purchase British pounds agrees to exchange $1.6779 per pound on February 19 (two *business* days later) when the contract settles.

Note that the forward rates for pounds are lower than the spot rate. In the next section we will see why. If a firm purchased pounds for 30-day delivery, it would get more pounds for its dollar than it would in a spot purchase (£0.5960/$ versus £0.5929/$). The pound is therefore said to trade at a *forward discount* relative to the dollar, because forward pounds are "cheaper" than spot pounds. For a one-month contract, this forward discount can be expressed on an APR basis as

$$\text{Forward discount} = 12\left(\frac{\text{30-Day Forward rate} - \text{Spot rate}}{\text{Spot rate}}\right) = 12\left(\frac{0.5960 - 0.5929}{0.5929}\right) = 6.27\% \quad (29.1)$$

FIGURE 29-2
Foreign exchange rate tables.

				KEY CURRENCY CROSS RATES Late New York Trading Feb. 15, 1996					
	Dollar	**Pound**	**SFranc**	**Guilder**	**Yen**	**Lira**	**D-Mark**	**FFranc**	**CdnDlr**
Canada	1.2035	2.0283	.79834	.63027	.00831	.00096	.71024	.20896	—
France	5.7595	9.706	3.8206	3.0162	.03976	.00458	3.3989	—	4.7856
Germany	1.6945	2.8557	1.1240	.88741	.01170	.00135	—	.29421	1.4080
Italy	1258.7	2121.3	834.96	659.18	8.689	—	742.81	218.54	1045.9
Japan	144.86	244.13	96.093	75.863	—	.11509	85.488	25.151	120.37
Netherlands	1.9095	3.2181	1.2667	—	.01318	.00152	1.1269	.33154	1.5866
Switzerland	1.5075	2.5406	—	.78947	.01041	.00120	.88964	.26174	1.2526
U.K.	.59337	—	.39361	.31074	.00410	.00047	.35017	.10302	.49303
U.S.	—	1.6853	.66335	.52370	.00690	.00079	.59014	.17363	.83091

Continued on next page

FIGURE 29-2
(continued)

EXCHANGE RATES
Thursday, February 15, 1996

The New York foreign exchange selling rates below apply to trading among banks in amounts of $1 million and more as quoted at 3 p.m. Eastern time by Bankers Trust Co. Retail transactions provide fewer units of foreign currency per dollar.

Country	U.S. $ equiv. Thurs.	U.S. $ equiv. Wed.	Currency per U.S. $ Thurs.	Currency per U.S. $ Wed.	Country	U.S. $ equiv. Thurs.	U.S. $ equiv. Wed.	Currency per U.S. $ Thurs.	Currency per U.S. $ Wed.
Argentina					Forward	.17252	.17437	5.7965	5.7350
(Peso)	1.0004	1.0004	.9996	.9996	180-Day				
Australia					Forward	.17132	.17313	5.8370	5.7760
(Dollar)	.7503	.7450	1.3328	1.3423	Germany				
Austria					(Mark)	.5908	.5970	1.6925	1.6750
(Schilling)	.08397	.08478	11.91	11.80	30-Day				
Bahrain					Forward	.5909	.5970	1.6924	1.6750
(Dinar)	2.6522	2.6522	.3771	.3771	90-Day				
Belgium					Forward	.5904	.5966	1.6937	1.6763
(Franc)	.02828	.02856	35.36	35.01	180-Day				
Brazil					Forward	.5892	.5953	1.6971	1.6797
(Real)	.04129	.04264	24.22	23.45	Greece				
Britain					(Drachma)	.006266	.006333	159.60	157.90
(Pound)	1.6865	1.6950	.5929	.5900	Hong Kong				
30-Day					(Dollar)	.12802	.12806	7.8110	7.8090
Forward	1.6779	1.6865	.5960	.5929	India (Rupee)	.05907	.05907	16.93	16.93
90-Day					Indonesia				
Forward	1.6595	1.6683	.6026	.5994	(Rupiah)	.0005568	.0005568	1796.01	1796.01
180-Day					Ireland (Punt)	1.5785	1.5830	.6335	.6317
Forward	1.6341	1.6427	.6120	.6088	Israel (Shekel)	.5378	.5378	1.8594	1.8594
Canada					Italy (Lira)	.0007955	.0008034	1257.01	1244.76
(Dollar)	.8299	.8288	1.2050	1.2065	Japan (Yen)	.006911	.006930	144.70	144.30
30-Day					30-Day				
Forward	.8269	.8261	1.2093	1.2105	Forward	.006919	.006938	144.53	144.13
90-Day					90-Day				
Forward	.8207	.8201	1.2185	1.2193	Forward	.006929	.006948	144.33	143.93
180-Day					180-Day				
Forward	.8125	.8123	1.2307	1.2310	Forward	.006943	.006965	144.04	143.57
Chile					Jordon				
(Peso)	.003448	.003448	290.03	290.03	(Dinar)	1.5328	1.5328	.6524	.6524
China					Kuwait				
(Renminbi)	.211757	.211757	4.7224	4.7224	(Dinar)	3.4596	3.4596	.2891	.2891
Colombia					Lebanon				
(Peso)	.002208	.002208	453.00	453.00	(Pound)	.001825	.001825	548.00	548.00
Denmark					Malaysia				
(Krone)	.1532	.1547	6.5295	6.4625	(Ringgit)	.3704	.3698	2.6995	2.7045
Ecuador					Malta (Lira)	3.0534	3.0534	.3275	.3275
(Sucre)					Mexico (Peso)				
Floating					Floating				
rate	.001445	.001445	692.00	692.00	rate	.0003670	.0003670	2725.02	2725.02
Finland					Netherland				
(Markka)	.25310	.25336	3.9510	3.9470	(Guilder)	.5244	.5299	1.9070	1.8870
France					New Zealand				
(Franc)	.17375	.17558	5.7555	5.6955	(Dollar)	.5850	.5825	1.7094	1.7167
30-Day					Norway				
Forward	.17342	.17525	5.7664	5.7060	(Krone)	.1544	.1548	6.4775	6.4605
90-Day									

Continued on next page

FIGURE 29-2
(continued)

Country	U.S. $ equiv.		Currency per U.S. $		Country	U.S. $ equiv.		Currency per U.S. $	
	Thurs.	*Wed.*	*Thurs.*	*Wed.*		*Thurs.*	*Wed.*	*Thurs.*	*Wed.*
Pakistan (Rupee)	.0471	.0471	21.25	21.25	30-Day Forward	.6642	.6688	1.5055	1.4952
Peru (new Sol)	.4237	.4237	2.3600	2.3600	90-Day Forward	.6624	.6673	1.5097	1.4986
Philippines (Peso)	.04533	.04533	22.06	22.06	180-Day Forward	.6607	.6649	1.5135	1.5040
Portugal (Escudo)	.006769	.006769	147.73	147.73	Taiwan (Dollar)	.038387	.038461	26.05	26.00
Saudi Arabia (Riyal)	.26681	.26681	3.7480	3.7480	Thailand (Baht)	.03911	.03911	25.57	25.57
Singapore (Dollar)	.5365	.5366	1.8640	1.8635	Turkey (Lira)	.0004264	.0004264	2345.05	2345.05
South Africa (Rand)	.3927	.3931	2.5465	2.5439	United Arab (Dirham)	.2723	.2723	3.6725	3.6725
South Korea (Won)	.0014584	.0014584	685.70	685.70	Uruguay (New Peso)				
Spain (Peseta)	.009153	.009234	109.25	108.30	Financial	.001247	.001247	801.75	801.75
Sweden (Krona)	.1637	.1632	6.1100	6.1275	Venezuela (Bolivar)				
Switzerland (Franc)	.6647	.6693	1.5045	1.4940	Brady rate	.02137	.02137	46.80	46.80
					SDR	1.32768	1.32790	.75319	.75307
					ECU	1.21633	1.21899		

Special Drawing Rights (SDR) are based on exchange rates for the U.S., German, British, French and Japanese currencies. Source: International Monetary Fund.
European Currency Unit (ECU) is based on a basket of community currencies. Source: European Community Commission.

Note that the Japanese yen is trading at a *forward premium* relative to the dollar, because forward yen are more expensive than spot yen.

Forward contracts can be customized to suit a corporation's particular requirements as to amount, currency, settlement date, and other matters. Voiding a forward contract is difficult and is subject to negotiation with the other party to the contract.

CURRENCY FUTURES   Currency futures markets also exist. A **currency future** is really a standardized forward contract that is exchange-traded. Because of this standardization, currency futures generally are less costly and enjoy more liquid markets than (non-exchange-traded) forward contracts. With a futures contract, a firm can close out its position at any time simply by selling the contract (or repurchasing the contract if it has sold short). The choice between a forward contract and a futures contract thus involves a trade-off between the customization the forward contract provides and the low transaction costs and liquidity of a futures contract.

CURRENCY SWAPS   In the third type of foreign exchange transaction, the **currency swap**, two parties swap currencies and agree to exchange a series of specified payment obligations denominated in one currency for payment obligations denominated in another. When payments are due, one party generally pays the other the difference in value caused by changes in the exchange rate. Currency swaps can be arranged directly between two firms seeking to borrow in each other's home currency. More commonly, firms swap currency with commercial banks, which are in a better position to effect such transactions.

EXAMPLE

A Currency Swap

Beecham Group plc, a British firm, would like to make an investment in the United States. Pfizer, Inc. is an American firm that would like to make an investment in the United Kingdom. They can both borrow in their respective national currencies and enter into a currency swap. Suppose a 10-year British pound loan to Beecham requires a 12% APR, whereas a 10-year U.S. dollar loan to Pfizer requires a 9% APR. Pfizer and Beecham agree to exchange interest and principal payment obligations.

Suppose each firm needs the equivalent of $100 million. Each firm borrows this sum in its home currency, and the two firms enter into a currency swap. Pfizer's debt service stream (assuming the debt matures in a lump sum and pays annual interest) under a currency swap arrangement with Beecham is given in Table 29-1.

In this example, Pfizer borrows $100 million and exchanges the $100 million with Beecham for £62.5 million. In each of the subsequent 10 years, Pfizer agrees to pay Beecham £7.5 million (= 0.12 × 62.5), and Beecham agrees to pay Pfizer $9 million (= 0.09 × 100). Pfizer then makes an interest payment of $9 million on its loan. At the time of the last interest payment, Pfizer agrees to pay Beecham £62.5 million, and Beecham agrees to pay Pfizer $100 million. Pfizer then pays $100 million to repay its loan. The payment obligations of Beecham and Pfizer are netted: On the basis of prevailing exchange rates, one party will have to write the other party a check for the net amount owed when each payment is due.

The currency swap effectively converts Pfizer's $100 million 9% dollar loan into a £62.5 million 12% sterling loan. ■

TABLE 29-1

Pfizer's debt service stream (currency amounts in millions).

	YEAR 0		YEARS 1–10		YEAR 10	
	$	£	$	£	$	£
Borrow $	+100					
Swap $ for £	−100	+62.5				
Interest on $ loan			−9			
Swap payments			+9	−7.5	+100	−62.5
Repay $ loan					−100	
Net cash flow	0	+62.5	0	−7.5	0	−62.5

Why does a currency swap offer a cost advantage over simply borrowing the needed foreign currency directly in the foreign capital market? Briefly, the answer is market imperfections. Tax asymmetries and national regulations that restrict international capital flows have segmented the world capital markets and restricted the free flow of capital across national boundaries. This segmentation can result in differences in relative borrowing costs that give a comparative advantage to two firms to engage in a currency swap. Recently, firms have been swapping currency with commercial banks, which can process the transactions and benefit from asymmetries more efficiently than other firms.

CURRENCY OPTIONS   A forward contract or a futures contract obligates the parties to make the foreign currency exchange specified in the contract. A **currency option** conveys the right to buy (in the case of a call option) or to sell (for a put option) a specified amount of a particular foreign currency at a stated price within a specified time period. Commercial banks sell customized currency options, and standardized currency options are traded on option exchanges. In addition, a number of options on currency futures contracts are traded on the Chicago Mercantile Exchange, which is the main foreign currency futures exchange in the United States. As discussed later in the chapter, firms use these options to hedge certain types of foreign currency risks.

Self-Check Questions

1. What is the foreign exchange market?
2. What is an exchange rate? If the dollar–pound exchange rate is $1.75/£, what is it when expressed in pounds per dollar?
3. What is a spot exchange rate? What is a forward exchange rate?
4. What is a currency future? How is it different from a currency forward?
5. What is a currency swap? How can a firm use a currency swap to convert a dollar loan into, say, a French franc loan?

29.3 INTERNATIONAL FINANCIAL PARITY RELATIONSHIPS

If the international capital markets were perfect, each financial asset would provide the same risk-adjusted expected return in every market in which it is traded. A financial asset traded in two different markets would have the same price in both. Otherwise, there would be opportunities for arbitragers to earn riskless profits. Economists refer to this principle as the **Law of One Price**. We also mentioned the Law of One Price in explaining the Principle of Capital Market Efficiency in Chapter 3.

We noted in our discussion of domestic capital markets that transaction costs and other market imperfections cause departures from the perfect market model. Nevertheless, we have often assumed a perfect capital market environment as a starting point in this book. By examining the implications of that assumption and then exploring the effect of market imperfections, we have gained some useful insights into corporate financial management. So too with international corporate finance.

Let's begin, then, by assuming that the international capital markets and foreign exchange markets are perfect. Arbitrage activity enforces the Law of One Price throughout these markets. We can characterize the resulting equilibrium relationships among exchange rates, interest rates, and inflation rates. Figure 29-3 summarizes four key parity relationships: interest rate parity, purchasing power parity, expectations theory of forward exchange rates, and the international Fischer effect. These relationships give rise to the combined market equilibrium conditions, also shown in Figure 29-3.

We will take a closer look at the four parity relationships using British pounds (£) and U.S. dollars ($). Figure 29-3 expresses the parity relationships in the more general form, comparing foreign (F) and domestic (D) conditions.

Interest Rate Parity

Interest rate parity states a relationship between the interest rates and the currency exchange rates for two countries. The following example illustrates this important relationship by showing the arbitrage opportunity available when these rates are in disequilibrium.

Interest Rate Parity (29.2)[a]

$$\frac{1 + r_F(t)}{1 + r_D(t)} = \frac{s_{DIF}}{f_{DIF}(t)}$$

Purchasing Power Parity (29.3)

$$\frac{E[1 + i_F(t)]}{E[1 + i_D(t)]} = \frac{s_{DIF}}{E[s_{DIF}(t)]}$$

Expectations Theory of Forward Exchange Rates (29.4)

$$E[s_{DIF}(t)] = f_{DIF}(t)$$

International Fisher Effect (29.5)

$$\frac{1 + r_F(t)}{1 + r_D(t)} = \frac{E[1 + i_F(t)]}{E[1 + i_D(t)]}$$

Combined Market Equilibrium Conditions

$$\frac{1 + r_F(t)}{1 + r_D(t)} = \frac{E[1 + i_F(t)]}{E[1 + i_D(t)]} = \frac{s_{DIF}}{E[s_{DIF}(t)]} = \frac{s_{DIF}}{f_{DIF}(t)}$$

Definitions of Variables

$r_F(t)$ = t-period foreign currency interest rate
$r_D(t)$ = t-period domestic currency interest rate
s_{DIF} = spot exchange rate between the domestic and foreign currencies
$f_{DIF}(t)$ = t-period forward exchange rate between the domestic and foreign currencies
$i_F(t)$ = average annual inflation rate over next t periods in the foreign economy
$i_D(t)$ = average annual inflation rate over next t periods in the domestic economy
$s_{DIF}(t)$ = spot exchange rate between the domestic and foreign currencies t periods in the future

[a] Formulas used in the examples are expressed in pounds (£) and dollars ($). Here they are shown more generally in foreign (F) and domestic (D) currencies.

FIGURE 29-3
Key parity relationships in international financial market equilibrium.

EXAMPLE

Interest Rate Parity

Suppose you have the following two investment alternatives. You can buy a 1-year U.S. dollar-denominated note that pays 10% interest at maturity or a 1-year British pound-denominated note that pays 12% interest at maturity. Which would you select?

You cannot answer this question until you take into account how many pounds you get for your dollars today and how many dollars you would get for your pounds 1 year from today. The forward exchange market provides the needed information.

Suppose the dollar-pound spot rate is $1.70/£ and the 1-year forward rate is $1.60/£. The pound is trading at a forward discount. This example will demonstrate why. If you invest $1000 in the U.S. dollar-denominated note, you will receive $1100 at maturity. If you instead convert the $1000 into British pounds at the spot rate, you will receive £588.24 (= 1000/1.70). If you purchase the British pound-denominated note, then you will receive £658.83 (= 588.24 × 1.12) at maturity. By selling the pounds forward, you would ensure that the £658.83 would purchase $1054.13 (= 658.83 × 1.60). The dollar-denominated note is the more profitable investment.

Moreover, you can earn a riskless arbitrage profit by borrowing British pounds, selling them in the spot market for U.S. dollars, investing the dollars at 10%, and selling the dollars you will receive at maturity forward against the pound.

If you borrowed £588.24 and bought $1000 (= 588.24 × 1.70), the investment of those dollars would yield $1100, which would produce £687.50 (= 1100/1.60) under the forward contract. After paying £70.59 (= 588.24 × 0.12) of interest and repaying the sterling borrowing, you have a £28.67 (= £687.50 − 588.24 − 70.59) arbitrage profit. Arbitrage will continue until the interest rate differential is equivalent to the differential between the spot and forward rates. The interest rate differential between U.S. dollars and British pounds for investments of identical risk maturing at time t can be expressed as

$$\frac{1 + r_£(t)}{1 + r_\$(t)}$$

where $r_£(t)$ and $r_\$(t)$ are the t-period pound and dollar interest rates, respectively. The differential between the spot exchange rate ($s_{\$/£}$) and the forward exchange rate for t periods forward, $f_{\$/£}(t)$, can be expressed as

$$\frac{s_{\$/£}}{f_{\$/£}(t)}$$

Equating these two expressions reflects the fact that **interest rate parity** must hold for every period t in equilibrium:

$$\frac{1 + r_£(t)}{1 + r_\$(t)} = \frac{s_{\$/£}}{f_{\$/£}(t)} \tag{29.2}$$

In this example, interest rate parity will hold if arbitrage activity raises the 1-year forward rate to $1.67/£, for then

$$\frac{1 + r_£(1)}{1 + r_\$(1)} = \frac{1.12}{1.10} = 1.02 = \frac{\$1.70/£}{\$1.67/£} = \frac{s_{\$/£}}{f_{\$/£}(1)}$$

When Equation (29.2) holds, interest rate parity ensures that the forward discount exactly offsets the higher interest rate on British pound investments of comparable duration and risk. If U.S. dollar-denominated investments provided a higher interest rate, then the British pound would trade at a forward premium. In that case, the larger number of dollars to be received upon future sale of pounds would fully compensate for the lower British interest rate.

Interest rate parity, expressed by Equation (29.2), requires the difference between the forward and spot exchange rates to offset the difference between the interest rates in the two countries. *The higher interest rate is fully offset by the forward discount.* Evidence indicates that interest rate parity normally holds, at least to a close approximation, in the Eurocurrency markets. It probably does not hold nearly so closely for domestic money markets. A variety of government-imposed restrictions and national differences in taxation inhibit investing in foreign currencies in many countries. These restrictions interfere with the arbitrage activity needed to maintain interest rate parity.

Purchasing Power Parity

Suppose a loaf of bread costs $1 in the United States. What should it cost in South Korea? According to the Law of One Price, $1 should also buy a loaf of bread in South Korea and in every other market. This will happen only if the foreign exchange rate between two currencies adjusts by the difference in the rates of inflation in the countries that issued the two currencies. If the rate of inflation is 3% in the United States and 5% in South Korea, then the Korean won would have to fall by (1.05/1.03) − 1, or about 2% per annum, for the (equivalent) dollar price of a loaf of bread to remain the same in both countries. This equilibrium condition is referred to as **purchasing power parity**.[1]

Purchasing power parity is formally stated in terms of expected inflation rates. It requires that the expected difference in inflation rates equal the difference between the spot exchange rate now and the spot exchange rate expected in the future. More specifically, the difference in inflation rates over a time period is expressed as

$$\frac{E[1 + i_£(t)]}{E[1 + i_\$(t)]}$$

where E is the expected value of the quantity in brackets and $i_£(t)$ and $i_\$(t)$ are the British and U.S. inflation rates, respectively. This ratio must equal the difference between the spot exchange rate ($s_{\$/£}$) and the spot exchange rate expected t periods in the future ($E[s_{\$/£}(t)]$), which can be expressed as

$$\frac{s_{\$/£}}{E[s_{\$/£}(t)]}$$

Equating these two expressions reflects the fact that purchasing power parity must hold for every period t in equilibrium:

$$\frac{E[1 + i_£(t)]}{E[1 + i_\$(t)]} = \frac{s_{\$/£}}{E[s_{\$/£}(t)]} \tag{29.3}$$

EXAMPLE

Purchasing Power Parity

Let's continue the previous example. Suppose the expected inflation rate is 8% in the United States and 10% in Great Britain. Purchasing power parity will hold if the current spot rate is $1.70 = £1 and the expected spot rate 1 year forward is $1.67 = £1, for then

$$\frac{E[1 + i_£(1)]}{E[1 + i_\$(1)]} = \frac{1.10}{1.08} = 1.02 = \frac{\$1.70/£}{\$1.67/£} = \frac{s_{\$/£}}{E[s_{\$/£}(1)]}$$

When Equation (29.3) holds, purchasing power parity ensures that the expected change in the spot exchange rate offsets the difference between the expected inflation rates in the two countries. *The higher inflation rate is fully offset by the expected rate of depreciation of that country's currency.* Empirical evidence supports the existence of purchasing power parity, as we have defined it in terms of expectations.[2]

Expectations Theory of Forward Exchange Rates

There are two other conditions that will hold in a well-behaved market. One links forward and spot exchange rates. The other explains how real interest rates between two countries are related.

---

[1] Purchasing power parity differs from the Law of One Price referred to earlier in that the Law of One Price refers to individual goods, whereas purchasing power parity refers to the general price level for all goods—for example, as measured by the consumer price index.

[2] Strictly speaking, the Law of One Price, from which purchasing power parity is derived, requires that the *actual* inflation rate differential *always* be equal to the *actual* change in the foreign exchange rate. Equation (29.3) requires only the equality of *expected* inflation differentials and the *expected* change in the spot rate.

Suppose foreign exchange market participants could perfectly hedge their foreign currency risks or that they did not care about risk—that is, suppose they were risk neutral. Then the forward rate would depend solely on what market participants expected the future spot rate to be. For example, suppose the expected spot rate for British pounds were £1 = $1.50. What would be the forward rate? It would have to be £1 = $1.50. If it were higher than this rate, everyone would want to sell pounds, but no one would be willing to sell dollars forward. If it were lower than this rate, everyone would want to sell dollars, but no one would be willing to sell pounds forward. Therefore, the **expectations theory of forward exchange rates** maintains that the expected spot exchange rate t periods in the future equals the t-period forward rate:

$$E[s_{\$/£}(t)] = f_{\$/£}(t) \qquad (29.4)$$

This condition does not require the actual future spot rate to equal the historical forward rate. Foreign exchange market participants are not assumed to be perfect forecasters. All that is required is that, on average, the forward rate equals the future spot rate. Evidence shows that it does. However, the evidence also indicates that when the forward rate predicts a sharp change (either up or down) in the spot rate, the forecasted change tends to overstate the actual change. This finding is at variance with the expectations theory; the forward rate is not *always* an unbiased predictor of the future spot rate. Thus it appears that firms that hedge their foreign currency risk by buying or selling foreign currencies forward usually do not have to bear any added cost for this insurance. However, it also appears that during unsettled periods, when concerns about foreign currency risk are heightened, firms are willing to sacrifice some expected return in order to transfer the foreign exchange risk to someone else. Such behavior reflects the Principle of Risk-Return Trade-Off.

International Fisher Effect

In Chapter 12 we showed that the required return in nominal terms (r_n) results from simply compounding the required real return (r_r) and the *expected* inflation rate (i):

$$r_n = r_r + i + ir_r \qquad (12.3)$$

We noted that the cross-product, ir_r, is relatively small and is sometimes ignored in practice, so that

$$r_n = r_r + i + ir_r \approx r_r + i$$

Many years ago, Irving Fisher argued that the nominal rate of interest observed in the financial markets fully reflects investors' collective expectation regarding the rate of inflation. It does so in order to compensate them for inflation's effects on the real value of their investments. This phenomenon is now called the *Fisher effect*. If follows from the Principle of Self-Interested Behavior: Investors seek out investments that offer the greatest expected risk-adjusted real return. Arbitrage ensures that in a perfect capital market, two debt instruments denominated in different currencies but of equivalent risk will offer the same expected real return. If in addition the Fisher effect holds, then the difference in nominal interest rates must equal the difference in expected inflation rates:

$$\frac{1 + r_£(t)}{1 + r_\$(t)} = \frac{E[1 + i_£(t)]}{E[1 + i_\$(t)]} \qquad (29.5)$$

We refer to Equation (29.5) as the **international Fisher effect** because it follows from the (domestic) Fisher effect.

Equation (29.5) follows from Equations (29.2), (29.3), and (29.4). Interest rate parity, coupled with purchasing power parity and the expectations theory of forward exchange rates, implies the international Fisher effect. More generally, the four parity relationships are mutually consistent. If any three of them hold, then so must the fourth.

We can rewrite Equation (29.5) as

$$\frac{1 + r_{\pounds}}{1 + E[i_{\pounds}]} = \frac{1 + r_{\$}}{1 + E[i_{\$}]} = 1 + r_r$$

The international Fisher effect says that the real rate of interest is the same in every country.

EXAMPLE

International Fisher Effect

Let's continue the investments example. We know that $r_{\pounds}(1) = 0.12$, $r_{\$}(1) = 0.10$, $i_{\pounds}(1) = 0.10$, and $i_{\$}(1) = 0.08$. We can verify that Equation (29.5) holds:

$$\frac{1.12}{1.10} \approx 1.02 \approx \frac{1.10}{1.08}$$

There isn't much empirical evidence concerning the international Fisher effect. We can observe that, as a general rule, the countries with the highest inflation rates also tend to have the highest interest rates. Thus we are at least able to say that real interest rates vary less than nominal interest rates. But strict equality usually does not hold. Probably because of various national impediments to the free international flow of capital, the national capital markets are segmented to some degree. As a result, arbitrage activity is prevented from achieving a single real rate of interest that applies in all market segments.

Self-Check Questions

1. List the four key parity relationships. Is it always true that if any three of them hold, then so must the fourth?
2. Explain what interest rate parity means. Does it usually hold in the Eurocurrency markets?
3. Explain what purchasing power parity means. Does it usually hold in the markets for actively traded currencies? In what sense does it usually hold?
4. Explain the expectations theory of forward exchange rates. Does it usually hold in the markets for actively traded currencies?
5. Explain the international Fisher effect.

29.4 HEDGING AGAINST FOREIGN CURRENCY RISKS

We introduced you to the basics of hedging in Chapter 26. When some of the cash flows a firm expects to receive, or anticipates having to pay, are denominated in a foreign currency, the firm faces foreign currency risk. **Foreign exchange risk** (or foreign currency risk) is the risk that the receipt or payment, when translated into the domestic currency, will change as a result of a change in the exchange rate. For example, suppose that Pratt & Whitney has a contract to sell aircraft engines to British Airways. The contract calls for delivery in one year against payment in British pounds. The value of the contract is £100 million. Suppose the spot dollar–pound exchange rate expected one year hence is £1 = $1.60. Then the aircraft engine contract has an expected value of $160 million. But suppose the dollar–pound exchange rate is £1 = $1.50 when British Airways makes payment. In that case, British Airways will still pay £100 million, but Pratt & Whitney will receive only $150 million when it converts the pounds into dollars.

Exchange Rate Volatility

The exchange rates between the major currencies are not fixed by government policy. Rather, they can float up or down in response to supply and demand. The central bank of each major country does intervene in the foreign exchange market from time to time. It buys or sells its currency in order to smooth exchange rate fluctuations. It tries to keep its exchange rate at a level it deems appropriate. For example, it may wish to reduce its exchange rate in order to boost exports. However, intervention can affect the situation only temporarily when exchange rates are floating because they are determined by supply and demand. Attempts to impose a different exchange rate are soon swamped by market forces.

Figure 29-4 shows how the values of the Australian dollar, British pound, German mark, and Japanese yen moved in relation to the U.S. dollar between 1980 and 1995. All four currencies exhibit considerable volatility.

FIGURE 29-4

Exchange rate fluctuations for four currencies relative to the U.S. dollar, 1980–1995.
[a] $/A$ = U.S. dollars per Australian dollar, $/DM = U.S. dollars per German mark, and $/£ = U.S. dollars per pound.
[b] ¥/$ = yen per U.S. dollar.
Source: Federal Reserve Bulletin.

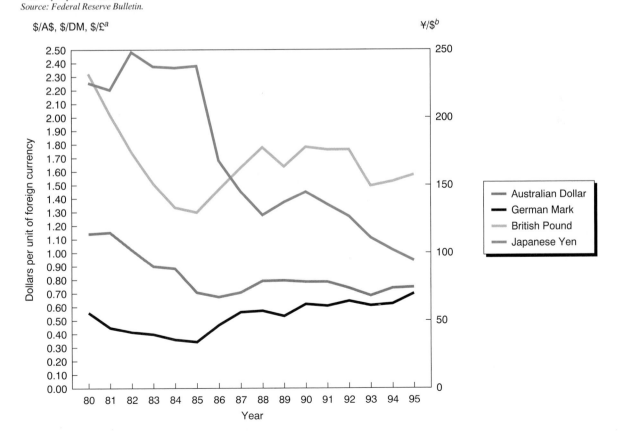

Hedging Techniques

Pratt & Whitney can eliminate its foreign currency risk exposure by hedging. **Hedging** a particular foreign currency risk exposure involves establishing an offsetting position in the same foreign currency. Designed correctly, the hedging position will generate a gain or loss that will offset the loss or gain, respectively, on the original foreign currency exposure.

In the preceding example, Pratt & Whitney's hedging strategy would involve entering into a foreign currency transaction that would generate an offsetting gain in case the pound's value depreciated relative to the expected future spot rate before receipt of payment (a $10 million gain if the pound were to depreciate to $1.50/£). There are three basic foreign currency hedging techniques: (1) forward market transactions, (2) foreign currency money market transactions, and (3) currency option transactions.

Before describing the three hedging techniques, we should mention one other strategy for Pratt & Whitney that you may have thought of. Pratt & Whitney could negotiate payment in U.S. dollars.[3] But the Principle of Two-Sided Transactions should indicate why invoicing in dollars does not eliminate foreign currency risk. It eliminates *Pratt & Whitney's* foreign currency risk exposure but transfers it to British Airways, which must now pay in dollars. The Principle of Risk-Return Trade-Off implies that the risk transfer will require compensation to British Airways in the form of a reduced transaction price. The three hedging techniques also involve risk shifting, but risk shifting to third parties not involved in the commercial transaction. As always, only market imperfections can make the transaction something other than a zero-sum game.

Forward Market Transactions

Continuing with our Pratt & Whitney illustration, let's see how forward market transactions can be used to hedge foreign currency risk.

| EXAMPLE | *Hedging Pratt & Whitney's Foreign Currency Risk in the Forward Market* | Pratt & Whitney could hedge its foreign currency risk exposure by selling a £100 million forward contract for delivery in 1 year. That strategy converts the 100 million receivable into a known dollar amount. Suppose the 1-year forward rate is £1 = $1.60. Then the forward sale will net Pratt & Whitney $160 million 1 year hence. Table 29-2 shows the consequences to Pratt & Whitney of hedging in this manner in three different future exchange rate scenarios. |

Suppose the British pound depreciates to £1 = $1.50. Pratt & Whitney receives £100 million from British Airways, which is worth $150 million. But Pratt & Whitney delivers the £100 million under the forward contract for $160 million. There is a $10 million profit (160 − 150) on the forward contract that restores the value of the contract to the originally expected $160 million value. Suppose instead that the British pound appreciates to £1 = $1.70. The £100 million Pratt & Whitney receives is worth $170 million. But it must deliver pounds at an exchange rate of £1 = $1.60 to settle the forward contract. The $10 million loss on the forward contract leads to a net (of gain or loss on hedging) realized value of $160 million on the engine contract. Indeed, regardless of what happens to the spot rate 1 year hence, Pratt & Whitney will realize $160 million because of the forward contract. Losses are avoided—but so are gains—under a forward contract hedge. ■

---

[3] Equivalently, the engine contract could contain a price adjustment clause that would adjust the pound price for changes in the dollar–pound exchange rate.

SPOT EXCHANGE RATE, 1 YEAR HENCE	VALUE OF ORIGINAL CONTRACT (MILLIONS)	GAIN (LOSS) ON FORWARD CONTRACT (MILLIONS)	NET REALIZED DOLLAR VALUE (MILLIONS)
£1 = $1.50	£100 = $150	$10	$160
£1 = $1.60	£100 = $160	—	160
£1 = $1.70	£100 = $170	(10)	160

TABLE 29-2
Possible outcomes of Pratt & Whitney's forward market hedge.

THE COST OF A FORWARD CONTRACT   What is the cost of a forward contract? Managers often calculate the cost of a forward contract by annualizing the forward discount or premium, but that procedure is wrong. It is based on the difference between the current spot rate and the forward rate, as shown in Equation (29.1). The true cost of a forward contract is its opportunity cost. It depends on the proceeds the firm would realize if it did not hedge. That cost depends on the difference between the forward rate and the *expected* future spot rate:

$$c \approx \left(\frac{365}{n}\right)\left(\frac{E[s_{D/F}(n)] - f_{D/F}(n)}{s_{D/F}}\right) \tag{29.6}$$

where n is the length of the forward contract measured in days, $E[s_{D/F}(n)]$ is the expected spot rate n days hence, $f_{D/F}(n)$ is the forward rate specified in an n-day forward contract, and $s_{D/F}$ is the current spot rate.

Calculating the Cost of a Forward Contract **EXAMPLE**

Suppose the current spot rate is £1 = $1.70. The cost to Pratt & Whitney of a 1-year ($n = 365$) forward contract is

$$c = \left(\frac{365}{365}\right)\left(\frac{\$1.60 - 1.60}{1.70}\right) = 0$$

Under the expectations theory of forward exchange rates, the forward rate equals the expected future spot rate. Consequently, the cost of a forward contract is zero in an efficient market. The foreign exchange market seems reasonably efficient. Thus although the cost of insuring against foreign exchange risk may not be exactly zero in practice, such insurance is nevertheless quite cheap.

Foreign Currency Money Market Transactions

Pratt & Whitney could instead hedge its foreign currency risk exposure by borrowing in British pounds for one year against its future receivable, exchanging at the current spot exchange rate into dollars, and investing the dollar proceeds in a one-year financial instrument.

EXAMPLE

Hedging Pratt & Whitney's Foreign Currency Risk in the Money Market

Suppose that the current spot exchange rate is £1 = $1.70 and that 1-year interest rates are 10% in dollars and 16.875% in British pounds. Pratt & Whitney could borrow £85,561,497 (= 100/1.16875) for 1 year, convert it into $145,454,545 (= 85,561,497 × 1.70) in the spot market, and invest the dollar proceeds at 10% interest for 1 year to realize $160 million (= 1.10 × 145,454,545). Pratt & Whitney could then use the £100 million it receives from British Airways to pay interest and repay principal on its British pound loan.

Table 29-3 shows the consequences to Pratt & Whitney of hedging in this manner. The gain or loss on the money market hedge fully offsets the loss or gain, respectively, on the value of the original contract. Pratt & Whitney's net realized dollar value is the same regardless of the future dollar–pound spot exchange rate. ■

TABLE 29-3

Possible outcomes of Pratt & Whitney's foreign currency money market hedge.

SPOT EXCHANGE RATE, 1 YEAR HENCE	VALUE OF ORIGINAL CONTRACT (MILLIONS)	GAIN (LOSS) ON MONEY MARKET HEDGE (MILLIONS)	NET REALIZED DOLLAR VALUE (MILLIONS)
£1 = $1.50	£100 = $150	$10	$160
£1 = $1.60	£100 = $160	—	160
£1 = $1.70	£100 = $170	(10)	160

The fact that the net realized dollar value is the same under the two different hedging methods is not a coincidence. Under interest rate parity, any difference between selling a foreign currency forward (as in the forward market hedge) and selling it spot (as in the foreign currency money market hedge) will be fully offset by the difference between the interest rates in the two currencies. The foreign currency money market hedge might be thought of as a "homemade" forward contract. Which form of hedging is more effective in practice depends, to a large extent, on whether government restrictions favor one method over the other.

Currency Option Transactions

The hedging techniques discussed so far are useful for hedging foreign currency risk exposures that are certain as to amount and timing. But life is not always quite so simple. Suppose that Pratt & Whitney and Mitsubishi are competing for the order and that British Airways will not make a decision for several weeks (while it studies the bids). If Pratt & Whitney sells pounds forward but does not win the contract, it will lose money if the British pound appreciates. Pratt & Whitney can avoid this outcome and still hedge its foreign currency risk by purchasing a British pound put option, which will let it sell £100 million at a stated exchange rate in one year. The most Pratt & Whitney can lose in that case is the cost of the option.

Currency options represent a useful hedging tool when the quantity of foreign currency to be received or paid is uncertain. The following rules indicate how to choose between forward contracts (or foreign currency money market hedging) and currency options.

• When the quantity of foreign currency to be received (to be paid) is known, sell (buy) the currency forward.

• When the quantity is unknown, buy a put option (call option) on the foreign currency sufficient to cover the maximum amount of foreign currency that might be received (paid).

29.5 INTERNATIONAL CAPITAL INVESTMENT DECISIONS

Suppose General Electric Company is considering building a plant in Germany to manufacture electric motors for the Central European market. The plant is expected to cost DM50 million. As you know by now, General Electric should choose the alternative with the largest positive NPV from mutually exclusive alternatives. The same rule applies to international capital investment projects.

But a foreign project involves several complications. The incremental after-tax cash flows are denominated in foreign currencies. These foreign currencies may not be freely convertible into U.S. dollars. Foreign investment projects may also entail a risk of expropriation by the host country's government. In addition, foreign taxes must be considered, the cost of capital for a foreign project may differ from that for a domestic project, and there may be a cost advantage to raising funds in the foreign country or in the international capital market.

There are two alternative methods of applying the NPV criterion to foreign projects. The first is to calculate the incremental cash flows in the local currency, convert nondollar incremental cash flows into dollars at appropriate projected foreign exchange rates, and discount at the dollar-denominated required return. The second method is to do the entire NPV calculation in the local currency and then convert the foreign-currency-denominated NPV into dollars at the current exchange rate. The two procedures, applied correctly, will produce the same NPV.

Estimating the Incremental Cash Flows

So long as General Electric can hedge its foreign currency risk exposure, it should refrain from basing its investment decision on its internal foreign exchange forecasts. General Electric would be wise to apply the Principle of Capital Market Efficiency. It should base its decision on the foreign exchange market's consensus forecast, which can be obtained by applying the key parity relationships in Figure 29-3. If it wishes to speculate on foreign currency movements, it should do so by trading in the foreign currency market, not by building an electric motor plant.

General Electric's project staff has projected the following incremental after-tax cash flows in German marks:

Year	1	2	3	4	5
Cash flow (DM millions)	15	17	20	20	17

The current dollar–mark exchange rate is DM1 = $0.60. This implies a $30 million (= 0.60 × 50) project cost. General Electric can project future exchange rates by applying interest rate parity, purchasing power parity, and the expectations theory of forward exchange rates.

The Incremental After-Tax Cash Flows for General Electric's German Project

EXAMPLE

Suppose the 1-year riskless return is 8% in the United States (the equivalent annual 1-year Treasury note rate) and 6% in Germany and that the expected inflation rate in the United States is 5% per annum for each of the next 5 years. Under interest rate parity, (Equation 29.2) and the expectations theory (Equation 29.4), the expected spot rate 1 year hence satisfies

$$\frac{1.06}{1.08} = \frac{\$0.60}{E[s_{\$/DM}(1)]}$$

$$E[s_{\$/DM}(1)] = \$0.6113$$

Under purchasing power parity (Equation 29.3),

$$\frac{E[1 + i_{DM}(1)]}{1.05} = \frac{0.60}{0.6113}$$

$$E[1 + i_{DM}(1)] = 1.03059$$

The expected inflation rate in Germany for the next year is 3.059%. Suppose the real interest rate is expected to remain constant over the next 5 years in each country. Then the projected German inflation rate is 3.059% per annum for each of the next 5 years. General Electric should check to make sure that its cash flow forecast is consistent with a 3.059% German inflation rate.

Under purchasing power parity (Equation 29.3), the expected spot rate t years hence ($1 \leq t \leq 5$) satisfies

$$E[s_{\$/DM}(t)] = \$0.60(1.05/1.03059)^t$$

Now this equation can be applied to convert the projected German mark cash flows into U.S. dollars:

	YEAR				
	1	2	3	4	5
Cash flow (DM millions)	15	17	20	20	17
Exchange rate ($/DM)	0.6113	0.6228	0.6345	0.6465	0.6586
Cash flow ($ millions)	9.17	10.59	12.69	12.93	11.20

LACK OF CONVERTIBILITY   Unlike Germany, many foreign countries place restrictions on a firm's ability to convert local currency into dollars or other "hard" currencies. This is often the case in Third World countries that have very limited hard currency reserves. If the free cash flow is not freely convertible into U.S. dollars—that is, if the U.S. parent is not free to convert the foreign currency into U.S. dollars and transfer the dollars outside the foreign country—then the annual cash flows may overstate the true benefits that the project sponsor can expect to realize. Recall from Chapter 11 that the NPV calculation implicitly assumes that interim cash flows can be reinvested at the project's cost of capital. When the local currency is not freely convertible into U.S. dollars, the incremental cash flow stream should reflect the actual expected U.S. dollar cash remittances (including interest on reinvested balances that can be remitted in U.S. dollars) at the time the project sponsor expects to realize these U.S. dollar flows.

EXPROPRIATION AND OTHER POLITICAL RISKS   Investing in a foreign country entails political risk. An incoming foreign government might not honor a previous government's agreement to permit convertibility, or the foreign government might impose discriminatory taxes or, worst of all, expropriate the firm's property for its own use (euphemistically called *nationalization*).

Political risks should be incorporated in discounted-cash-flow analysis by adjusting the incremental cash flows, rather than by adjusting the discount rate.

Suppose that the expected cash flows for a project are

Year	1	2	3	4
Cash flow ($ millions)	20	30	30	40

Let's say the project sponsor fears there is a 50% probability that the project will be expropriated at the end of 2 years when a new government may come to power. The expected cash flow stream to be discounted is

Year	1	2	3	4
Cash flow ($ millions)	20	30	15	20

Adjusting for Political Risk

EXAMPLE

Calculating the probability of expropriation is highly subjective. But that does not mean the risk should be ignored. If expropriation risk is significant, it is important to gauge the sensitivity of NPV to the probability of expropriation. Break-even analysis—determining the probability of expropriation during any particular year that would reduce the NPV to zero—is often used.

FOREIGN TAXES   The method of cash remittance can affect the amount of taxes. In addition to local income taxes, countries generally levy withholding taxes on dividend and interest payments, often at different rates. Management fees and royalty payments are not generally subject to withholding taxes and are generally tax-deductible in the foreign country. Dividends, interest, management fees, and royalty payments are subject to U.S. taxation if the payments are remitted to the United States. It may be possible, however, to remit payments from a high-tax jurisdiction to a low-tax jurisdiction and thereby reduce worldwide corporate taxes. Multinational firms spend considerable sums on worldwide tax planning and on structuring payments so as to minimize overall taxes. The incremental U.S. and foreign taxes the project sponsor will have to pay because of the project should be taken into account when calculating the incremental after-tax cash flow stream.

Estimating the Cost of Capital for a Foreign Project

Should the required return on a foreign project be greater than the required return on an otherwise identical domestic project? Yes, many financial executives believe, because of the additional economic and political risk associated with foreign projects. However, this view is not necessarily correct. See Section 7.7 for a discussion of this issue.

APPROXIMATE BETA CALCULATION   We cannot give you a precise procedure for calculating the project beta, and hence the cost of capital, for a foreign project. The relevant portfolio for purposes of calculating beta depends on the sponsoring firm's shareholders' degree of international diversification. In view of the limited international diversification of most

U.S. firms' shareholders, we recommend using the U.S. market portfolio (with the Standard & Poor's 500 Index serving as a useful proxy) in the project beta calculation. Here are the steps to take:

1. Find a set of comparable publicly traded firms located in the same country and in the same industry as the project under consideration.

2. Calculate the historical total returns adjusted for exchange rate changes: the sum of (a) end-of-period share value converted to U.S. dollars minus beginning-of-period share value converted to U.S. dollars and (b) dividends paid converted to U.S. dollars, all divided by (c) beginning-of-period share value converted to U.S. dollars.

3. Calculate beta using linear regression in the same manner as for a domestic project.

If no comparable publicly traded foreign firms can be identified, use the beta calculated for domestic projects of the same type. This will normally lead to a conservative (somewhat higher) estimate of the foreign project's required return, because international corporate diversification tends to involve lower systematic risk, and therefore a lower beta and a lower required return, than an otherwise identical domestic project.

EXAMPLE

Calculating the NPV for General Electric's German Investment

Let's return to the problem facing General Electric. General Electric's marginal income tax rate for the project is 23.8%. The pretax cost of debt for the project is 10% based on a project debt ratio (L) of 25%, so $r_d = 0.10$. The debt ratio is consistent with General Electric's capital structure objective. General Electric calculates a (leveraged) project beta of 1.10. The riskless return is 8%, and the expected return on the market portfolio is 16.6%. The (leveraged) required return on equity for the project is

$$r_e = 8 + 1.10(8.6) = 17.46\%$$

The required return for the dollar-denominated incremental cash flow stream is then the weighted average cost of capital:

$$\text{WACC} = 0.25(0.762)(0.1) + 0.75(0.1746) = 15.00\%$$

The project NPV is

$$\text{NPV} = -30.0 + \frac{9.17}{1.15} + \frac{10.59}{(1.15)^2} + \frac{12.69}{(1.15)^3} + \frac{12.93}{(1.15)^4} + \frac{11.20}{(1.15)^5}$$

$$= \$7.29 \text{ million}$$

Let's verify that calculating the project NPV in German marks does not alter the dollar NPV. First we calculate the approximate German mark required return. This rate must satisfy the relationship[4]

$$\frac{1 + r_{\text{DM}}(1)}{1 + r_{\$}(1)} = \frac{1 + r_{\text{DM}}^*}{1 + r_{\$}^*} \tag{29.7}$$

where $r_{\text{DM}}(1)$ and $r_{\$}(1)$ are the 1-year riskless returns, and r_{DM}^* and $r_{\$}^*$ are the required returns in DM and $, respectively. Applying Equation (29.7) gives

$$\frac{1.06}{1.08} = \frac{1 + r_{\text{DM}}^*}{1.15} \quad \text{or} \quad r_{\text{DM}}^* = 12.87\%$$

---

[4] We give you the opportunity in Problem C8 to verify that Equation (29.7) must hold.

The NPV of the project in German marks is

$$NPV = -DM50.0 + \frac{15.00}{1.1287} + \frac{17.00}{(1.1287)^2} + \frac{20.00}{(1.1287)^3} + \frac{20.00}{(1.1287)^4} + \frac{17.00}{(1.1287)^5}$$

$$= DM12.15 \text{ million}$$

Converting this amount to U.S. dollars gives

$$DM12.15 \text{ million}(\$0.60/DM) = \$7.29 \text{ million}$$

Self-Check Questions

1. Describe the two alternative methods of applying the NPV criterion to foreign capital budgeting projects. Will they both lead to the same answer?

2. Why is it usually unwise to use an internally generated set of foreign exchange forecasts when estimating the incremental cash flows for a foreign project?

3. How should you allow in the NPV analysis for lack of free convertibility?

4. How should you allow in the NPV analysis for expropriation risk?

5. Explain why, in estimating the cost of capital for a foreign project, it is usually not a good idea simply to calculate the cost of capital for a domestic project and "tack on" a risk premium.

29.6 FINANCING FOREIGN INVESTMENTS

A firm that wants to borrow funds to finance a foreign capital budgeting project can (1) borrow U.S. dollars in the United States and export the funds to the foreign country, (2) borrow U.S. dollars in the Euromarket, (3) borrow in the foreign country, or (4) borrow in whichever currency and in whichever market affords the lowest interest cost. The fourth strategy is particularly tempting, but is also very risky, as many *former* corporate treasurers will attest!

Financing in the Euromarket

In addition to the separate domestic capital markets, there is a large supranational Euromarket. As we have said, the prefix *Euro* means "outside of." The *Eurodollar bond market* was discussed in Chapter 24 and redefined for you at the beginning of this chapter. It consists of bonds denominated in U.S. dollars that are issued, held, and traded outside the United States. Similarly, there are Euromarkets for bonds denominated in British pounds, French francs, Japanese yen, and several other major currencies.

The Euromarket offers a viable alternative to the domestic capital market for a firm that wants to raise short-term or long-term funds. From time to time, U.S. firms have found it advantageous to sell entire bond issues in the Eurobond market, rather than domestically, and to borrow in different currencies. In 1989 the World Bank introduced *global bonds*, which are designed to qualify for immediate trading in any domestic capital market and in the Euromarket and hence to reach the broadest group of investors.[5] In all these cases, the issuer enters the Euromarket hoping to exploit an opportunity to raise funds at a lower cost than domestically.

---

[5] International Bank for Reconstruction and Development, 8⅜% U.S. Dollar Bonds of 1989, due October 1, 1999, *Prospectus* (September 19, 1989).

Choice of Currency

General Electric could borrow $30 million and purchase DM50 million, or it could borrow DM50 million. Borrowing dollars to fund a German mark investment entails foreign exchange risk. If General Electric borrows dollars and the mark depreciates relative to the dollar, the firm's German electric motor plant will be worth fewer dollars. Also, in that case, General Electric will have to dedicate a larger proportion of its mark-denominated project cash flow to service its U.S. dollar-denominated debt. The opposite would occur if the mark appreciated relative to the dollar. General Electric can hedge against this foreign exchange risk either by borrowing in dollars and selling marks forward or by borrowing in marks. The latter strategy will result in a German mark liability that at least partially offsets the German mark asset. We said "at least partially" because General Electric would still face foreign exchange exposure on any equity (DM assets minus DM liabilities) that it has invested in the plant.

Not all foreign investments involve foreign exchange risk. Suppose a foreign project's revenues are denominated in U.S. dollars, as is the case with international oil and gas projects because petroleum products are typically invoiced in U.S. dollars. More generally, the Law of One Price implies that the price of a foreign good, denominated in the local currency, will adjust to offset exchange rate changes. In our example, the price in marks of General Electric's motors would adjust under the Law of One Price to preserve the dollar price. The Law of One Price does not hold exactly, although it is probably not too bad an approximation in the case of goods that enjoy an active international trade. To the extent that the Law of One Price does hold for a particular project, the project sponsor is best off borrowing in its currency of account. General Electric should borrow a mixture of U.S. dollars and marks, with the dollar proportion directly related to the extent to which General Electric expects to be able to preserve the price of its electric motors in dollars in the face of changes in the dollar–mark exchange rate.

ROLE OF INTEREST RATE PARITY   Interest rate parity implies that when credit risk is held constant, any difference in nominal pretax yield between two different currencies is exactly offset by the expected change in the spot exchange rate during the term of the loan. If one currency affords a relatively low interest rate, it is because market participants expect the country to have a relatively low inflation rate and its currency to appreciate in value. Nominal interest cost savings will be offset exactly by expected exchange rate changes. The currency of borrowing does not matter.

BORROWING IN A FOREIGN CURRENCY   In practice, there are international capital market frictions that may make it advantageous to borrow in one currency rather than another. Tax asymmetries, government-imposed capital and credit controls, and other market frictions can create opportunities to reduce a borrower's after-tax cost of debt (expressed in terms of the borrower's currency of account) by choosing one currency rather than another in which to borrow.

EXAMPLE

Calculating General Electric's Cost of Borrowing in a Foreign Currency

Suppose that General Electric can borrow 5-year funds in U.S. dollars for its new plant at an interest rate of 10% APR or 5-year funds in German marks at an interest rate of 8% APR. The mark-denominated loan calls for sinking fund payments of DM10 at the end of years 2 and 3 and DM15 at the end of years 4 and 5. First we verify that the pretax dollar cost of debt (before transaction costs) is 10%. Table 29-4 presents General Electric's debt service in U.S. dollars. The cost of debt is the return c that solves the equation

$$0 = -30.0 + \frac{2.4452}{1 + c} + \frac{8.7192}{(1 + c)^2} + \frac{8.3754}{(1 + c)^3} + \frac{11.2491}{(1 + c)^4} + \frac{10.6693}{(1 + c)^5}$$

so that $c = 10.0\%$.

General Electric's marginal ordinary income tax rate is 50% on both its U.S. income and its German income. Its after-tax cost of debt on the U.S. dollar loan (before transaction costs) is $0.10(1 - 0.5) = 5.00\%$.

Suppose instead that General Electric borrows and repays the German marks through its German subsidiary. Its after-tax cost of debt, expressed in terms of dollars, is given in Table 29-5. In this case, the cost of debt is the return c that solves the equation

$$0 = -30.0 + \frac{1.2226}{1 + c} + \frac{7.4736}{(1 + c)^2} + \frac{7.3602}{(1 + c)^3} + \frac{10.4733}{(1 + c)^4} + \frac{10.2742}{(1 + c)^5}$$

so that $c = 5.96\%$.

The after-tax cost of the loan in German marks exceeds the after-tax cost of the U.S. dollar loan. Note that the mark is appreciating relative to the dollar, but only the actual interest expense, not the cost to General Electric of repaying the more expensive marks, is tax deductible.

	YEAR				
	1	2	3	4	5
Principal amount (DM millions)	50	50	40	30	15
Interest at 8% (DM millions)	4	4	3.2	2.4	1.2
Principal payment (DM millions)	—	10	10	15	15
Total debt service (DM millions)	4	14	13.2	17.4	16.2
Exchange rate ($/DM)	0.6113	0.6228	0.6345	0.6465	0.6586
Debt service ($ millions)	2.4452	8.7192	8.3754	11.2491	10.6693

TABLE 29-4
General Electric's debt service in U.S. dollars.

	YEAR				
	1	2	3	4	5
Debt service (DM millions):					
Principal payment	—	10	10	15	15
Interest payment	4	4	3.2	2.4	1.2
Tax saving (at 50%)	(2)	(2)	(1.6)	(1.2)	(0.6)
Total	2	12	11.6	16.2	15.6
Exchange rate	0.6113	0.6228	0.6345	0.6465	0.6586
Debt service ($ millions)	1.2226	7.4736	7.3602	10.4733	10.2742

TABLE 29-5
After-tax debt service for General Electric's German mark loan.

Borrowing in the weaker currency usually minimizes the expected after-tax cost of debt. That is, interest rate parity applies to pretax yields, not after-tax yields. Also, it is normally cheaper to borrow in high-tax-rate countries. However, neither statement is *always* true. We recommend that when evaluating alternative currency borrowing options, you calculate the after-tax cost of each before deciding which to select.

Investment-Financing Interactions

The net present value of a foreign investment project generally depends to some extent on the manner in which it is financed. This is true because the manner of financing affects the project sponsor's ability to repatriate funds and can have important tax consequences because of the complex interplay of domestic and foreign taxes. We cannot discuss these tax factors here, but we do wish to emphasize their importance to project NPV. Because of these factors, international projects often have significant financing side effects.

When financing side effects are significant, we recommend using the adjusted-present-value approach:

1. Calculate the base case NPV assuming (a) all-equity financing from the U.S. parent and (b) that all incremental free cash flow is repatriated to the U.S. parent in the form of dividends.

2. Determine how much debt the project is capable of supporting without compromising the firm's target capital structure. Then calculate the present-value tax shields that would result (a) if funds were borrowed in the United States, (b) if funds were borrowed in the foreign country, and (c) if funds were borrowed in the Euromarket. Select the most advantageous alternative.

3. Calculate the present-value benefit of any support provided by the host country in the form of loan guarantees, subsidized loans, loans obtained from the World Bank or other organizations to finance infrastructure improvements, and so on.

4. Calculate the present-value benefit (chiefly in the form of reduced taxes) of alternative forms of remitting funds, or of remitting funds to low-tax jurisdictions rather than to the United States.

5. Calculate the present-value benefit of any other side effects.

6. Add all these present-value amounts to obtain project NPV.

We cannot give you a complete checklist. But we can remind you to bear in mind the Principle of Incremental Benefits when you evaluate a foreign investment project. Carefully think through the incremental costs and benefits of the project, and try to devise ways to enhance each incremental benefit and reduce each incremental cost.

Self-Check Questions

1. What is the Eurodollar bond market? Are there Euromarkets for bonds denominated in other currencies? Name a few.

2. Under strict interest rate parity and ignoring taxes, would there be any advantage to borrowing in one currency rather than another? Why might there be an advantage in practice?

3. What is the best approach to follow when comparing borrowing alternatives in different currencies?

4. Taking tax factors into account, is it usually better to borrow in a weaker currency or in a stronger currency? in a high-tax-rate country or in a low-tax-rate country?

SOLUTION TO MOBIL OIL'S FINANCING PROBLEM

Mobil Oil must avoid the temptation to borrow in Swiss francs simply because the interest rate is so much lower than the dollar interest rate. Because of interest rate parity and purchasing power parity, the interest rate differential reflects the expectation that the rate of inflation in the United States will exceed the rate of inflation in Switzerland by 5% per year over the next 5 years. Consequently, the Swiss franc is expected to appreciate by 5% per year relative to the U.S. dollar. However, all of Mobil Oil's revenues are in U.S. dollars because oil shipments are invoiced in U.S. dollars (which is the standard industry practice).

Thus borrowing in Swiss francs does not provide a hedging benefit. Unless there are special tax advantages or transaction cost savings that might result from borrowing in Switzerland, Mobil Oil should borrow in U.S. dollars.

SUMMARY

A multinational firm's objective is the same as that of a purely domestic firm: to maximize shareholder wealth. But an international financial manager needs additional analytical tools to cope with complications in the form of cash flows denominated in foreign currencies, foreign political risk, foreign government regulations and capital constraints, and foreign tax systems. Managers need these tools to take advantage of opportunities that are available in the foreign exchange market and in foreign capital markets to reduce foreign exchange risk. Information can be obtained from those markets that enables a financial manager to ensure that financial decisions are not biased, perhaps unknowingly, by foreign exchange rate factors.

A critical first step toward developing these tools involves understanding the four key parity relationships in international financial market equilibrium: interest rate parity, purchasing power parity, the expectations theory of forward exchange rates, and the international Fisher effect. Interest rate parity requires the difference between the forward and spot exchange rates to offset the difference between the interest rates in the two countries. Purchasing power parity states that the difference between the expected inflation rates in two countries equals the expected change in the spot exchange rate. The expectations theory states that the forward exchange rate equals the expected future spot exchange rate. The international Fisher effect holds that real rates of interest must be the same in all the world's capital markets.

The four key parity relationships do not hold exactly because of government regulations, particularly capital controls, asymmetric taxes, and other market imperfections. But they are a useful approximation to reality and represent a good starting point for analysis.

The foreign exchange market offers a low-cost means of hedging foreign exchange risk. International financial managers would be wise to utilize this relatively cheap insurance and not to speculate on exchange rate movements. We explained how to use forward and futures contracts, currency swaps, foreign currency money market transactions, and currency options to reduce or eliminate exposure to foreign exchange risk.

International projects often involve an interaction between investment and financing. In such cases, the adjusted-present-value approach is useful in evaluating the project.

DECISION SUMMARY

- The four key parity relationships provide a useful framework for gauging future foreign exchange rate movements.
- The incremental cash flow stream and the discount rate should be calculated with respect to the same currency; which currency does not matter, so long as the key parity relationships all hold.
- The incremental free cash flow stream should be adjusted for any political risks and/or tax differences. Adjust cash flows, not the discount rate, for any political risk.
- Base the cash flow calculation on the timing of the repatriation of funds from the foreign country, and plan how to accomplish the intended timing.
- The discount rate should reflect appropriately the opportunity cost of funds to the sponsoring firm's shareholders. As a result of the somewhat limited degree of international portfolio diversification of

U.S. investors, the cost of capital for a foreign project may actually be less than the cost of capital for a comparable domestic project.

- Use the key parity relationships to project future exchange rates when calculating the incremental cash flow stream. In particular, ensure that the inflation rate implicit in the forecasted cash flow stream is consistent with purchasing power parity.

- In applying the CAPM, calculate beta on the basis of a set of comparable publicly traded firms in the host country that are in the same industry as the project. Also, unless there is reason to believe that the sponsoring firm's shareholders are well diversified internationally, a domestic proxy, such as the Standard & Poor's 500 Index, should be used as the market portfolio. Using the domestic beta is likely to overstate the true beta and understate the project's present value.

- Foreign currency risk should be hedged, whenever it is advantageous to the firm's shareholders, either by entering into forward or futures transactions, by engaging in foreign currency option transactions, by arranging currency swaps, or by borrowing in the host country's capital market.

- A foreign project can be financed in the sponsoring firm's domestic capital market, in the Euromarket, in the host country's capital market, or in some other country's capital market. A firm should evaluate each feasible borrowing alternative, particularly borrowing in the Euromarket. The cost of funds for each alternative should be calculated after-tax on a consistent basis. It should be expressed in terms of the same currency, the same frequency of compounding, and so on. The firm should select the lowest-cost alternative, taking into consideration any particular benefit from tax savings and from hedging foreign exchange, political, or other risks.

- An international financial manager should maintain a global financing perspective but should *not* simply borrow in whichever currency affords the lowest stated interest rate.

EQUATION SUMMARY

(29.1) $\text{Forward discount} = 12\left(\dfrac{\text{30-Day Forward rate} - \text{Spot rate}}{\text{Spot rate}}\right)$

(29.2) $\dfrac{1 + r_£(t)}{1 + r_\$(t)} = \dfrac{s_{\$/£}}{f_{\$/£}(t)}$

(29.3) $\dfrac{E[1 + i_£(t)]}{E[1 + i_\$(t)]} = \dfrac{s_{\$/£}}{E[s_{\$/£}(t)]}$

(29.4) $E[s_{\$/£}(t)] = f_{\$/£}(t)$

(29.5) $\dfrac{1 + r_£(t)}{1 + r_\$(t)} = \dfrac{E[1 + i_£(t)]}{E[1 + i_\$(t)]}$

(29.6) $c = \left(\dfrac{365}{n}\right)\left(\dfrac{E[s_{D/F}(n)] - f_{D/F}(n)}{s_{D/F}}\right)$

(29.7) $\dfrac{1 + r_{DM}(1)}{1 + r_\$(1)} = \dfrac{1 + r_{DM}^*}{1 + r_\$^*}$

KEY TERMS

EXERCISES

PROBLEM SET A

A1. Explain the important differences between a forward contract for a particular foreign currency and a futures contract for the same currency. What are the relative advantages of each?

A2. Use the foreign currency cross rates in Figure 29-2 to:

a. Find the price of a Canadian dollar in Swiss francs.

b. Find the price of a Swiss franc in Canadian dollars.

c. Show that the currency cross rates in parts a and b are equivalent.

A3. Use the foreign exchange rates for Thursday in Figure 29-2 to answer the following questions.

a. Is the German mark trading at a forward discount or at a forward premium to the U.S. dollar? Calculate the 30-day, 90-day, and 180-day forward premium or discount.

b. Is the Japanese yen trading at a forward discount or at a forward premium to the U.S. dollar? Calculate the 30-day, 90-day, and 180-day forward premium or discount.

A4. Explain each of the following parity relationships: (a) interest rate parity, (b) purchasing power parity, (c) expectations theory of forward exchange rates, and (d) equality of expected real returns.

A5. The Swiss franc–Japanese yen exchange rate is SF1 = ¥96.18. The Swiss franc–German mark exchange rate is SF1 = DM1.125. What is the Japanese yen–German mark exchange rate?

A6. The dollar–pound exchange rate is £1 = $2.00. The expected rates of inflation in the United States and Great Britain are 4% and 8% APR, respectively. Calculate the forward exchange rate required under purchasing power parity.

A7. What happens if the conditions required for the expectations theory of forward exchange rates to hold are satisfied in the market for US dollars and British pounds but:

a. The forward rate (expressed as $ per £) is greater than the expected future spot rate (expressed as $ per £).

b. The forward rate (expressed as $ per £) is less than the expected future spot rate (expressed as $ per £).

A8. Explain which of the following represents the stronger requirement: (a) the forward rate always equals the expected future spot rate, or (b) the forward rate always equals the future spot rate.

A9. Suppose the interest rates in the United States and Switzerland are 8% and 4% APR, respectively, and the projected inflation rates are 5% and 1% APR, respectively. Verify that Equation (29.5) holds. What is the real rate of interest?

A10. Explain why the difference between the current spot exchange rate and the forward exchange rate is not an accurate measure of the cost of a forward contract.

A11. In what sense can a foreign currency money market hedge be thought of as a "homemade" forward contract? Discuss the significance of this relationship for practical foreign currency risk management.

A12. Using the Pratt & Whitney example, show that if the future spot rate is £1 = $1.25, both the forward contract hedge and the foreign currency money market hedge will produce a net realized dollar value of $160 million. Show that the same result occurs in each case if the future spot rate is £1 = $2.00.

A13. Calculate the U.S. dollar and German mark internal rates of return for General Electric's electric motor plant, and apply the IRR criterion. Which criterion is superior, IRR or NPV?

A14. Explain why a corporate treasurer would be unwise to follow a policy of always borrowing in whichever currency affords the lowest stated interest rate.

PROBLEM SET B

B1. A firm faces two borrowing alternatives. It can issue 6-year debt domestically that bears a 10% APR coupon and that matures in a lump sum at the end of 6 years. Issuance expenses are 1% of the principal amount. Alternatively it can issue a 10¼% Eurobond that matures in a lump sum at the end of 6 years. Issuance expenses are 1.25% of the principal amount. The issuer's tax rate is 50%.

    a. Calculate the after-tax cost of the domestic issue.

    b. Calculate the after-tax cost of the Eurobond issue, and express this cost on an equivalent semi-annually compounded basis.

    c. Which issue is cheaper? Explain.

B2. Look back at General Electric's cost of borrowing in German marks. Suppose General Electric Company's marginal ordinary income tax rate is 34%. Ignore issuance expenses.

    a. Calculate the after-tax cost of the U.S. dollar-denominated issue.

    b. Calculate the after-tax cost of the German-mark-denominated issue expressed in U.S. dollars.

B3. The 3-month riskless interest rate in U.S. dollars is 8% APR. The 3-month riskless interest rate in Swiss francs is 3%. The dollar–franc exchange rate is SF1 = $0.66.

    a. Calculate the 3-month forward rate required under interest rate parity.

    b. Suppose the 3-month forward rate is SF1 = $0.68. Describe how a riskless arbitrage profit could be earned.

    c. Quantify the profit in both dollars and Swiss francs.

B4. The spot rate for U.S. dollars and German marks is $1 = DM1.50. The 1-year forward rate is $1 = DM1.40.

    a. Under interest rate parity, what is the 1-year U.S. dollar interest rate if the 1-year German mark interest rate is 5%?

    b. Under interest rate parity, what is the 1-year German mark interest rate if the 1-year U.S. dollar interest rate is 10%?

    c. What mathematical relationship must hold between the U.S. dollar and German mark 1-year interest rates if interest rate parity prevails?

B5. Gold is selling for $450 an ounce in New York and £300 an ounce in London.

    a. Suppose it were costless to transport gold between New York and London. What would the dollar–pound exchange rate have to be for the Law of One Price to hold?

    b. Suppose the dollar–pound exchange rate is £1 = $1.70. Describe how arbitrageurs could realize a riskless arbitrage profit.

    c. Quantify the profit in both dollars and British pounds.

B6. Show that if interest rate parity, purchasing power parity, and the expectations theory of forward exchange rates all hold, then so does the international Fisher effect. What happens when any one of the first three parity relationships fails to hold?

B7. The Swiss franc–German mark spot exchange rate is SF1 = DM1.20. The 1-year forward rate is SF1 = DM1.30.

    a. What is your best estimate of the spot rate expected 1 year from now?

    b. If the expected spot rate were SF1 = DM1.40, would anyone want to sell Swiss francs forward? to sell German marks forward?

    c. If the expected spot rate were SF1 = DM1, would anyone want to sell Swiss francs forward? to sell German marks forward?

B8. Suppose the Japanese yen–German mark spot exchange rate is ¥1 = DM0.012 and the expected spot rate 1 year hence is ¥1 = DM0.015. What is the relationship between the expected inflation rates in Japan and Germany for the coming year?

B9. Suppose the expected average annual inflation rates in Canada and Great Britain over the next 5 years are 7% and 10%, respectively, and the first three parity relationships in Figure 29-3 hold. What is the relationship between the 5-year interest rates in Canada and Great Britain?

B10. TransAtlantic Airlines (TAA) expects to receive DM5 million from a German tour operator in 30 days. Because TAA's expenses are in U.S. dollars, the firm wishes to hedge its foreign currency risk. The current spot exchange rate is DM1 = $0.60, and the 30-day forward exchange rate is DM1 = $0.58.

    a. How many U.S. dollars should TAA expect to receive if it does not hedge?

    b. Suppose the spot exchange rate at the time the tour operator pays is DM1 = $0.56. How much would hedging have saved TAA?

    c. If the 30-day interest rates are 10% APR in the United States and Germany, which method of hedging would you recommend?

    d. If the 30-day interest rates in the United States and Germany are 10% and 14% APR, respectively, which method of hedging would you recommend?

B11. In Problem B10, suppose the 30-day interest rate in the United States is 12% APR. What would the 30-day interest rate have to be in Germany in order for TAA to be indifferent between entering into a 30-day forward contract and effecting a 30-day foreign currency money market hedge?

B12. Consider again General Electric's proposed electric motor plant. What are the expected real rates of interest in Germany and in the United States? Why must these rates of interest be equal when interest rate parity, purchasing power parity, and the expectations theory of forward exchange rates hold?

B13. With General Electric's proposed electric motor plant, suppose that the projected riskless interest rates (APR) in the United States and Germany are as follows:

MATURITY (YEARS)	1	2	3	4	5
United States	8%	9%	9%	10%	10%
Germany	6%	7%	8%	9%	10%

    a. Calculate the spot exchange rates expected 1, 2, 3, 4, and 5 years hence.

    b. Calculate the projected incremental cash flow stream in dollars on the basis of the projected spot exchange rates in part a.

    c. Calculate the NPV of the project based on the cash flow stream in part b.

B14. Northern Chemical Company is considering building a petrochemical plant in Scotland. The plant would cost $100 million. The projected incremental cash flow stream is

Year	1	2	3	4	5	6	7
Cash flow (£ millions)	30	40	40	50	50	50	50

The current spot exchange rate is £1 = $1.50. The 1-year riskless rate is 8% in the United States and 12% in the United Kingdom. The expected inflation rate in the United States is 5% per year for the next 7 years.

    a. What is the expected inflation rate in the United Kingdom for the next 7 years?

    b. Calculate the expected spot exchange rates for each of the next 7 years.

    c. Calculate the projected incremental cash flow stream in dollars.

    d. If the dollar required return is 14%, what is the NPV in dollars?

    e. Calculate the British pound required return.

    f. Calculate the NPV in British pounds.

    g. Are the project NPVs in parts d and f equal? Explain.

B15. Verify that if General Electric can deduct for tax purposes the appreciation in the cost of marks that must be repaid, its after-tax cost of the mark-denominated loan, expressed in U.S. dollars, closely approximates the after-tax cost of the U.S. dollar-denominated loan, 5.00%.

PROBLEM SET C

C1. The 2-year interest rate is 10% per year compounded semiannually. The 1-year interest rate is 8% per year compounded semiannually. If there is no opportunity for riskless arbitrage, what is the 1-year forward interest rate?

C2.

a. If the interest rates $r_£(t)$ and $r_\$(t)$ are continuously compounded interest rates, re-express Equation (29.2).

b. If the inflation rates $i_£(t)$ and $i_\$(t)$ are continuously compounded inflation rates, re-express Equation (29.3).

c. Derive Equation (29.5) from Equation (29.4) and the modified Equations (29.2) and (29.3).

d. Given $r_£(1) = 0.12$, $r_\$(1) = 0.10$, $i_£(1) = 0.10$, and $i_\$(1) = 0.08$, show that Equation (29.5) holds as a strict equality.

e. What is the real rate of interest? Show that the international Fisher effect implies that a single real rate of interest exists in the two markets.

C3. Show that if any one of the four parity relationships in Figure 29-3 fails to hold, at least one other must also fail to hold.

C4. Use the key parity relationships in Figure 29-3 to demonstrate the perfect equivalence of a forward contract and a foreign currency money market hedge.

C5. Generalize the Pratt & Whitney example to demonstrate that:

a. The net realized dollar value will be $160 million regardless of the future spot exchange rate when the British pounds are sold forward.

b. The net realized dollar value will be $160 million regardless of the future spot exchange rate when the British pounds are sold spot and the dollar proceeds invested at an interest rate that satisfies interest rate parity.

C6. Let ^FR_t be the total return on a foreign security when the share price and dividend payments are measured in the local currency. Let $^\$R_t$ be the total return when the components are measured in U.S. dollars. Let $^FR_{mt}$ and $^\$R_{mt}$ be the total return on the U.S. market portfolio when the components are measured in the local currency and in U.S. dollars, respectively. By applying the key parity relationships in Figure 29-3, show that in equilibrium:

$$\frac{1 + {}^\$R_t}{1 + {}^FR_t} = \frac{E[1 + i_\$(t)]}{E[1 + i_F(t)]} = \frac{1 + {}^\$R_{mt}}{1 + {}^FR_{mt}}$$

C7. Use the relationship between stock returns and expected inflation rates established in Problem C6 to show that the following procedures for calculating the beta for a foreign project are equivalent:

a. Convert ^FR_t to $^\$R_t$ and regress $^\$R_t$ on $^\$R_{mt}$.

b. Convert $^\$R_{mt}$ to $^FR_{mt}$ and regress ^FR_t on $^FR_{mt}$.

C8. Use the results obtained in Problems C6 and C7, together with the key parity relationships in Figure 29-3, to demonstrate that

$$\frac{1 + r_F(t)}{1 + r_\$(t)} = \frac{1 + r_F^*}{1 + r_\$^*}$$

where r_F^* is the project's cost of capital when the incremental cash flows are expressed in the foreign country's currency and $r_\$^*$ is the project's cost of capital when the incremental cash flows are converted to dollars.

C9. *The Economist* (April 15, 1995) reported the following prices for a Big Mac hamburger in different countries, along with these exchange rates:

COUNTRY	PRICE OF A BIG MAC	EXCHANGE RATE
Australia	A$2.45	A$1.35/US$
Britain	£1.74	£0.62/US$
Canada	C$2.77	C$1.39/US$
France	FFr18.5	FFr4.80/US$
Germany	DM4.80	DM1.38/US$
Japan	¥391	¥84/US$
United States	$2.32	—

a. Calculate the exchange rates implied by the Law of One Price.

b. Are the prices consistent with the Law of One Price?

c. How would you interpret your answers to parts a and b? Are exchange rates out of equilibrium? Is the Law of One Price invalid? Or is there some other explanation?

Real-World Application:
Emerson Electric's Financing Alternatives[1]

Emerson Electric Company (Emerson) manufactures a broad range of electrical and electronic equipment. It has roughly 200 subsidiaries that operate in more than two dozen countries. In the mid-1980s, Emerson began to place increased emphasis on its international operations. As its total sales grew past $5 billion, the proportion made up of international sales increased to more than 20% of the total. As part of its international strategy, Emerson shifted from exporting domestically produced items to manufacturing goods offshore, and it nearly doubled the number of foreign plants.

In the spring of 1987, Emerson wanted to raise $65 million (or the equivalent in a foreign currency) to finance its overseas expansion. Its debt was rated triple-A, and thus it would be able to borrow funds in virtually any market it chose. Emerson's investment bankers presented several financing alternatives. These alternatives included three possible two-year debt issues, each with a bullet maturity:

- A domestic U.S. dollar issue bearing a coupon rate of 8.65% APR (with interest payable semiannually in arrears).

- A Swiss-franc-denominated Eurobond issue bearing a coupon rate of 4.60% APR (with interest payable annually in arrears).

- A domestic issue denominated in New Zealand dollars bearing a coupon rate of 18.55% APR (with interest payable semiannually in arrears). (Certain U.S. institutions wanted to invest in New Zealand dollar securities but could only buy securities from a U.S. issuer.)

Emerson had subsidiaries operating in both Switzerland and New Zealand, and it therefore realized free cash flow in Swiss francs and New Zealand dollars. Nevertheless, it intended to hedge fully its currency risk exposure if it issued non-U.S. dollar debt. Its investment banker informed Emerson that it would be able to purchase Swiss francs and New Zealand dollars in the futures market at the following prices:

Months forward	6	12	18	24
Swiss francs/U.S. dollar	1.510	1.470	1.440	1.410
New Zealand dollars/U.S. dollar	1.905	1.992	2.079	2.166

The spot foreign exchange rates at the time were 1.530 Swiss francs per U.S. dollar and 1.762 New Zealand dollars per U.S. dollar.

[1] This real-world application is based on Robert F. Bruner, *Case Studies in Finance,* 2nd ed. (Burr Ridge, Ill.: Irwin, 1994), chapter 35.

1. How would you explain
   a. The pattern of decreasing forward exchange rates for Swiss francs.
   b. The pattern of increasing forward exchange rates for New Zealand dollars.
2. Explain why the Swiss franc issue may not be the least expensive, and why the New Zealand dollar issue may not be the most expensive, in spite of their interest rates.
3. What principal amount of foreign-currency-denominated bonds would Emerson have to issue to raise $65 million, assuming it issues bonds denominated in
   a. Swiss francs.
   b. New Zealand dollars.
4. Specify the debt-service stream (principal and interest) for each alternative and express it in equivalent amounts of U.S. dollars. What have you assumed in performing this calculation?
5. Calculate the cost of borrowing for each alternative. What calculation must you perform to make the three alternatives truly comparable?
6. Which of the three borrowing alternatives has the lowest cost?
7. Suppose the three debt issues would require the following flotation costs, which are tax-deductible in the United States on a straight-line basis over the life of each issue: 1% for the Swiss franc issue, 0.75% for the New Zealand dollar issue, and 0.50% for the U.S. dollar issue. Assume a 40% income tax rate for Emerson. Which of the three alternatives has the lowest after-tax cost?
8. How would you expect the restriction on investors' ability to purchase New Zealand dollar securities to have affected the interest cost of the New Zealand dollar debt issue?

BIBLIOGRAPHY

Aggarwal, Reena, Ricardo Leal, and Leonardo Hernandez. "The Aftermarket Performance of Initial Public Offerings in Latin America," *Financial Management*, 1993, 22(1):42–53.

Alexander, Gordon, Cheol S. Eun, and S. Janakiramanan. "Asset Pricing and Dual Listing on Foreign Capital Markets: A Note," *Journal of Finance*, 1987, 42(1):151–158.

Anvari, M. "Efficient Scheduling of Cross-Border Cash Transfers," *Financial Management*, 1986, 15(2):40–49.

Baldwin, Carliss Y. "Competing for Capital in a Global Environment," *Midland Corporate Finance Journal*, 1987, 5(Spring):43–64.

Cebenoyan, A. Sinan, George J. Papaioannou, and Nickolaos G. Travlos. "Foreign Takeover Activity in the U.S. and Wealth Effects for Target Firm Shareholders," *Financial Management*, 1992, 21(3):58–68.

Chang, Jack S. K., and Soushan Wu. "On Hedging Jump Risks in the Foreign Exchange and Stock Markets," *Financial Management*, 1994, 23(1):15.

Chen, Haiyang, Michael Y. Hu, and Joseph C. P. Shieh. "The Wealth Effect of International Joint Ventures: The Case of U.S. Investment in China," *Financial Management*, 1991, 20(4):31–41.

Collins, J. Markham, and William S. Sekely. "The Relationship of Headquarters Country and Industry Classification to Financial Structure," *Financial Management*, 1983, 12(3):45–51.

Constand, Richard L., Lewis P. Freitas, and Michael J. Sullivan. "Factors Affecting Price Earnings Ratios and Market Values of Japanese Firms," *Financial Management*, 1991, 20(4):68–79.

Cooper, Ian A., and Evi Kaplanis. "Cost to Crossborder Investment and International Equity Market Equilibrium." ed. J. Edwards, Julian Franks, C. Mayer, and Stephen Schaefer. In *Recent Developments in Corporate Finance*, Cambridge, England: Cambridge University Press, 1986.

Cornell, Bradford. "Spot Rates, Forward Rates and Exchange Market Efficiency," *Journal of Financial Economics*, 1977, 5(1):55–65.

Cornell, Bradford, and Alan C. Shapiro. "Managing Foreign Exchange Risks," *Midland Corporate Finance Journal*, 1983, 1(Fall): 16–31.

Crutchley, Claire, Enyang Guo, and Robert S. Hansen. "Stockholder Benefits from Japanese–U.S. Joint Ventures," *Financial Management*, 1991, 20(4):22–30.

Doukas, John, and Nickolaos G. Travlos. "The Effect of Corporate Multinationalism on Shareholders' Wealth: Evidence from International Acquisitions," *Journal of Finance*, 1988, 43(5):1161–1175.

Dufey, Gunter, and S.L. Srinivasulu. "The Case for Corporate Management of Foreign Exchange Risk," *Financial Management*, 1983, 12(4):54–62.

Eun, Cheol S., and Bruce G. Resnick. "Exchange Rate Uncertainty, Forward Contracts, and International Portfolio Selection," *Journal of Finance*, 1988, 43(1):197–215.

Fatemi, Ali M. "Shareholder Benefits from Corporate International Diversification," *Journal of Finance*, 1984, 39(5): 1325–1344.

Fisher, Irving. *The Theory of Interest.* New York: Augustus M. Kelley, 1965.

Frankel, Jeffrey A. "The Japanese Cost of Finance: A Survey," *Financial Management*, 1991, 20(1):95–127.

Gultekin, Mustafa N., N. Bulent Gultekin, and Alessandro Penati. "Capital Controls and International Capital Market Segmentation: The Evidence from the Japanese and American Stock Markets," *Journal of Finance*, 1989, 44(4):849–870.

Hodder, James E. "Evaluation of Manufacturing Investments: A Comparison of U.S. and Japanese Practices," *Financial Management*, 1986, 15(1):17–24.

Howe, John S., and Kathryn Kelm. "The Stock Price Impacts of Overseas Listings," *Financial Management*, 1987, 16(3):51–56.

Hunter, William C., and Stephen G. Timme. "A Stochastic Dominance Approach to Evaluating Foreign Exchange Hedging Strategies," *Financial Management*, 1992, 21(3):104–112.

John, Kose, Lemma W. Senbet, and Anant K. Sundaram. "Cross-Border Liability of Multinational Enterprises, Border Taxes, and Capital Structure," *Financial Management*, 1991, 20(4):54–67.

Kaplan, Steven N., and Bernadette A. Minton. "Appointments of Outsiders to Japanese Boards: Determinants and Implications for Managers," *Journal of Financial Economics*, 1994, 36(2):225–258.

Kaufold, Howard, and Michael Smirlock. "Managing Corporate Exchange and Interest Rate Exposure," *Financial Management*, 1986, 15(3):64–72.

Levis, Mario. "The Long-Run Performance of Initial Public Offerings: The UK Experience 1980–1988," *Financial Management*, 1993, 22(1):28–41.

Manzon, Gil B., Jr., David J. Sharp, and Nickolaos G. Travlos. "An Empirical Study of the Consequences of U.S. Tax Rules for International Acquisitions by U.S. Firms," *Journal of Finance*, 1994, 49(5):1893–1904.

Marr, M. Wayne, John L. Trimble, and Raj Varma. "On the Integration of International Capital Markets: Evidence from Euroequity Offerings," *Financial Management*, 1991, 20(4):11–21.

Medewitz, Jeanette N., and Keith A. Olson. "An Investigation Into the Market Valuation Process of Closed-End Country Funds," *Financial Management*, 1994, 23(1):13–14.

Megginson, William L., Robert C. Nash, and Matthias Van Randenborgh. "The Financial and Operating Performance of Newly Privatized Firms: An International Empirical Analysis," *Journal of Finance*, 1994, 49(2):403–452.

Merton, Robert C. "Presidential Address: A Simple Model of Capital Market Equilibrium with Incomplete Information," *Journal of Finance*, 1987, 42(3):483–510.

Pettway, Richard H., Neil W. Sicherman, and D. Katherine Spiess. "Japanese Foreign Direct Investment: Wealth Effects from Purchases and Sales of U.S. Assets," *Financial Management*, 1993, 22(4):82–95.

Prowse, Stephen D. "The Structure of Corporate Ownership in Japan," *Journal of Finance*, 1992, 47(3):1121–1140.

Rhee, S. Ghon, and Rosita P. Chang. "Intra-Day Arbitrage Opportunities in Foreign Exchange and Eurocurrency Markets," *Journal of Finance*, 1992, 47(1):363–380.

Rogalski, Richard J., and James K. Seward. "Corporate Issues of Foreign Currency Exchange Warrants: A Case Study of Financial Innovation and Risk Management," *Journal of Financial Economics*, 1991, 30(2):347–366.

Shapiro, Alan C. *International Corporate Finance,* 2nd ed. Cambridge, Mass.: Ballinger, 1988.

Shapiro, Alan C. *Multinational Financial Management*, 3rd ed. Boston: Allyn and Bacon, 1989.

Smith, Clifford W., Jr., Charles W. Smithson, and L. Macdonald Wakeman. "The Evolving Market for Swaps," *Midland Corporate Finance Journal*, 1986, 3(Winter):20–32.

Thomadakis, Stavros, and Nilufer Usmen. "Foreign Project Financing in Segmented Capital Markets: Equity versus Debt," *Financial Management*, 1991, 20(4):42–53.

Usmen, Nilufer. "Currency Swaps, Financial Arbitrage, and Default Risk," *Financial Management*, 1994, 23(2): 43–57.

Using a Business Calculator

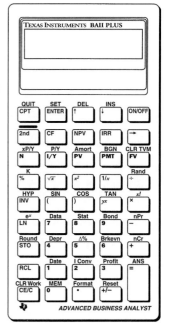

A business calculator is an absolute must in today's corporate environment whether you are doing finance, accounting, marketing, production, strategy, or human resource management. You can easily learn to make the time-value-of-money calculations we illustrate here. However, with just a little more effort, you can also learn to do so much more with your calculator, such as calculating averages, standard deviations, depreciation, linear regression coefficients, and breakeven amounts. The list is almost endless.

There are many different business calculators on the market today. The one you choose depends on your own personal preferences. We have chosen the Texas Instruments BAII PLUS to illustrate the use of a business calculator.

Key strokes are illustrated by boxes. An unshaded box indicates the function shown on the face of the key. For example, the four-key-stroke sequence 3 + 2 = adds the numbers 3 and 2 using the red keys with + and = on them. A shaded box preceded by a 2nd indicates the function shown in grey above the key. For example, 4 2nd x! computes 4 factorial (4 times 3 times 2 times 1) using the secondary function shown above the times key, which is the red key with × on it.

Assumed Payments per Period *(very important)*

Your calculator can assume any number of payments per period. For simplicity, our calculations here, and throughout the book, *always* assume the mode is set to 1.00. For example, if there are 12 monthly payments per year over 5 years, we make the conversion and use N = 60.

To set your calculator for use with our calculations:

2nd P/Y 1 ENTER CE/C CE/C

This setting continues indefinitely (even though the calculator is turned off and on), until it is changed.

Decimal Place Display

Your calculator always *calculates* with 9-digit accuracy. However, the numbers it displays depend on the number of decimal places to which you have it set. Our calculations generally display 2, 3, or 4 decimal places.

To set the number of decimal places displayed to three:

2nd Format 3 ENTER [the display will show: DEC = ☐ 3.000] CE/C CE/C

This setting also continues indefinitely (even though the calculator is turned off and on), until it is changed.

End-of-Period Annuity Cash Flows

Your calculator can assume that annuity cash flows occur either at the end of the period or at the beginning of the period. For simplicity, our calculations *always* assume the mode is set to end-of-period annuity cash flows. If a small BGN appears above the number display, the mode is set to beginning-of-period annuity cash flows. Otherwise, the mode is already set to end-of-period annuity cash flows.

To set the mode to end-of-period annuity cash flows:

[2nd] [BGN] [the display should show BGN; if it shows END, hit [CE/C]] [2nd] [SET] [CE/C] [CE/C]

This setting also continues indefinitely (even though the calculator is turned off and on), until it is changed.

EXAMPLES

Present Value of a Single Future Cash Flow

The present value of $5000 to be received in 4 years at 12% APY is $3177.59:

[4] [N] [1] [2] [I/Y] [0] [PMT] [5] [0] [0] [0] [FV] [CPT] [PV] = −3,177.59

Future Value of a Current Amount

The future value of $2000 to be received in 7 years at 9% APY is $3656.08:

[7] [N] [9] [I/Y] [2] [0] [0] [0] [PV] [0] [PMT] [CPT] [FV] = −3,656.08

Present Value of an Annuity

The present value of $200 per month for 5 years (60 months) at 9% APR (0.75% per month) is $9634.67:

[6] [0] [N] [.] [7] [5] [I/Y] [2] [0] [0] [PMT] [0] [FV] [CPT] [PV] = −9,634.67

Future Value of an Annuity

The future value of $50 per week for 3 years (156 weeks) at 6% APR (0.5% per week) is $11,772.37:

[1] [5] [6] [N] [.] [5] [I/Y] [0] [PV] [5] [0] [PMT] [CPT] [FV] = −11,772.37

Annuity Cash Flows for a Present Value

The monthly payments for a $100,000 20-year (240 months) mortgage at 8.16% APR (0.68% per month) are $846.43:

[2] [4] [0] [N] [.] [6] [8] [I/Y] [1] [0] [0] [0] [0] [0] [PV] [0] [FV] [CPT] [PMT] = −846.43

Annuity Cash Flows for a Future Value

Suppose you are going to save some money from the paycheck you get every 2 weeks, and you will earn 4.42% APR (0.17% per 2-week period) on your savings. To save up $10,000 over 2.5 years (65 pay periods), you will need to put aside $145.63 from each paycheck:

[6] [5] [N] [.] [1] [7] [I/Y] [0] [PV] [1] [0] [0] [0] [0] [FV] [CPT] [PMT] = −145.63

Interest Rate for a Present Value

A $15,000 10-year (120-month) loan requiring monthly payments of $206.96 has an APR of 11.04%:

[1] [2] [0] [N] [1] [5] [0] [0] [0] [PV] [2] [0] [6] [.] [9] [6] [+/−] [PMT] [0] [FV] [CPT] [I/Y] = 0.92 [×] [1] [2] [=] 11.04

Interest Rate for a Future Value

To save $1,000,000 by investing $155.50 per month for 35 years (420 months), your investments must earn an APR of 12.00%:

[4] [2] [0] [N] [0] [PV] [1] [5] [5] [6] [5] [0] [+/−] [PMT] [1] [0] [0] [0] [0] [0] [0] [0] [FV] [CPT] [I/Y] = 1.00 [×] [1] [2] [=] 12.00

Present Value of Annuity Cash Flows and a Future Value

The present value of a 10%-coupon ($50 semiannually) corporate bond that pays $1000 at maturity in 8 years (16 semiannual periods) and has a yield to maturity of 12% (6% semiannually) is $898.94:

[1] [6] [N] [6] [I/Y] [5] [0] [PMT] [1] [0] [0] [0] [FV] [CPT] [PV] = −898.94

Interest Rate for Annuity Cash Flows and a Future Value

The yield to maturity of a 6%-coupon ($30 semiannually) corporate bond that pays $1000 at maturity in 5.5 years (11 semiannual periods) and currently sells for $833.87 is 10%:

[1] [1] [N] [8] [3] [3] [.] [8] [7] [+/−] [PV] [3] [0] [PMT] [1] [0] [0] [0] [FV] [CPT] [I/Y] = 5.00 [×] [2] [=] 10.00

NPV and IRR for Uneven Cash Flows

CF0	CF1	CF2	CF3	CF4	CF5
−110,000	45,000	45,000	45,000	10,000	60,000

The NPV at a cost of capital of 12% and the IRR for the above cash flows from a capital budgeting project are $38,483.20 and 25.73%, respectively:

[CE/C] [CE/C] [CF] [2nd] [CLR Work] [1] [1] [0] [0] [0] [0] [+/−] [ENTER] [↓] [4] [5] [0] [0]

[0] [ENTER] [↓] [3] [3 is the number of times the cash flow repeats] [ENTER] [↓] [1] [0] [0]

[0] [0] [ENTER] [↓] [ENTER] [↓] [6] [0] [0] [0] [0] [ENTER] [↓] [ENTER] [2nd] [QUIT] [all the cash flows have been entered]

[NPV] [1] [2] [12 is the cost of capital (required return)] [ENTER] [↓] [CPT] = 38,483.20

[IRR] [CPT] = 25.73

at a 20% cost of capital, the NPV is $13,726.85:

[NPV] [2] [0] [ENTER] [↓] [CPT] = 13,726.85

Appendix B

Cumulative Distribution Function for the Standard Normal Random Variable

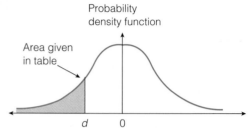

For example, N[−1.15] = .1251 and N[1.57] = .9418

d	0.00	0.01	0.02	0.03	0.04	0.05	0.06	0.07	0.08	0.09
−3.0	.0013	.0013	.0013	.0012	.0012	.0011	.0011	.0011	.0010	.0010
−2.9	.0019	.0018	.0018	.0017	.0016	.0016	.0015	.0015	.0014	.0014
−2.8	.0026	.0025	.0024	.0023	.0023	.0022	.0021	.0021	.0020	.0019
−2.7	.0035	.0034	.0033	.0032	.0031	.0030	.0029	.0028	.0027	.0026
−2.6	.0047	.0045	.0044	.0043	.0041	.0040	.0039	.0038	.0037	.0036
−2.5	.0062	.0060	.0059	.0057	.0055	.0054	.0052	.0051	.0049	.0048
−2.4	.0082	.0080	.0078	.0075	.0073	.0071	.0069	.0068	.0066	.0064
−2.3	.0107	.0104	.0102	.0099	.0096	.0094	.0091	.0089	.0087	.0084
−2.2	.0139	.0136	.0132	.0129	.0125	.0122	.0119	.0116	.0113	.0110
−2.1	.0179	.0174	.0170	.0166	.0162	.0158	.0154	.0150	.0146	.0143
−2.0	.0227	.0222	.0217	.0212	.0207	.0202	.0197	.0192	.0188	.0183
−1.9	.0287	.0281	.0274	.0268	.0262	.0256	.0250	.0244	.0239	.0233
−1.8	.0359	.0351	.0344	.0336	.0329	.0322	.0314	.0307	.0301	.0294
−1.7	.0446	.0436	.0427	.0418	.0409	.0401	.0392	.0384	.0375	.0367
−1.6	.0548	.0537	.0526	.0516	.0505	.0495	.0485	.0475	.0465	.0455
−1.5	.0668	.0655	.0643	.0630	.0618	.0606	.0594	.0582	.0571	.0559
−1.4	.0808	.0793	.0778	.0764	.0749	.0735	.0721	.0708	.0694	.0681
−1.3	.0968	.0951	.0934	.0918	.0901	.0885	.0869	.0853	.0838	.0823
−1.2	.1151	.1131	.1112	.1093	.1075	.1056	.1038	.1020	.1003	.0985
−1.1	.1357	.1335	.1314	.1292	.1271	.1251	.1230	.1210	.1190	.1170
−1.0	.1587	.1563	.1539	.1515	.1492	.1469	.1446	.1423	.1401	.1379
−0.9	.1841	.1814	.1788	.1762	.1736	.1711	.1685	.1660	.1635	.1611
−0.8	.2119	.2090	.2061	.2033	.2005	.1977	.1949	.1922	.1894	.1867
−0.7	.2420	.2389	.2358	.2327	.2296	.2266	.2236	.2206	.2177	.2148
−0.6	.2743	.2709	.2676	.2643	.2611	.2578	.2546	.2514	.2483	.2451
−0.5	.3085	.3050	.3015	.2981	.2946	.2912	.2877	.2843	.2810	.2776
−0.4	.3446	.3409	.3372	.3336	.3300	.3264	.3228	.3192	.3156	.3121
−0.3	.3821	.3783	.3745	.3707	.3669	.3632	.3594	.3557	.3520	.3483
−0.2	.4207	.4168	.4129	.4090	.4052	.4013	.3974	.3936	.3897	.3859
−0.1	.4602	.4562	.4522	.4483	.4443	.4404	.4364	.4325	.4286	.4247
−0.0	.5000	.4960	.4920	.4880	.4840	.4801	.4761	.4721	.4681	.4641

d	0.00	0.01	0.02	0.03	0.04	0.05	0.06	0.07	0.08	0.09
0.0	.5000	.5040	.5080	.5120	.5160	.5199	.5239	.5279	.5319	.5359
0.1	.5398	.5438	.5478	.5517	.5557	.5596	.5636	.5675	.5714	.5753
0.2	.5793	.5832	.5871	.5910	.5948	.5987	.6026	.6064	.6103	.6141
0.3	.6179	.6217	.6255	.6293	.6331	.6368	.6406	.6443	.6480	.6517
0.4	.6554	.6591	.6628	.6664	.6700	.6736	.6772	.6808	.6844	.6879
0.5	.6915	.6950	.6985	.7019	.7054	.7088	.7123	.7157	.7190	.7224
0.6	.7257	.7291	.7324	.7357	.7389	.7422	.7454	.7486	.7517	.7549
0.7	.7580	.7611	.7642	.7673	.7704	.7734	.7764	.7794	.7823	.7852
0.8	.7881	.7910	.7939	.7967	.7995	.8023	.8051	.8078	.8106	.8133
0.9	.8159	.8186	.8212	.8238	.8264	.8289	.8315	.8340	.8365	.8389
1.0	.8413	.8439	.8461	.8485	.8508	.8531	.8554	.8577	.8599	.8621
1.1	.8643	.8665	.8686	.8708	.8729	.8749	.8770	.8790	.8810	.8830
1.2	.8849	.8869	.8888	.8907	.8925	.8944	.8962	.8980	.8997	.9015
1.3	.9032	.9049	.9066	.9082	.9099	.9115	.9131	.9147	.9162	.9177
1.4	.9192	.9207	.9222	.9236	.9251	.9265	.9279	.9292	.9306	.9319
1.5	.9332	.9345	.9357	.9370	.9382	.9394	.9406	.9418	.9429	.9441
1.6	.9452	.9463	.9474	.9484	.9495	.9505	.9515	.9525	.9535	.9545
1.7	.9554	.9564	.9573	.9582	.9591	.9599	.9608	.9616	.9625	.9633
1.8	.9641	.9649	.9656	.9664	.9671	.9678	.9686	.9693	.9699	.9706
1.9	.9713	.9719	.9726	.9732	.9738	.9744	.9750	.9756	.9761	.9767
2.0	.9773	.9778	.9783	.9788	.9793	.9798	.9803	.9808	.9812	.9817
2.1	.9821	.9826	.9830	.9834	.9838	.9842	.9846	.9850	.9854	.9857
2.2	.9861	.9864	.9868	.9871	.9875	.9878	.9881	.9884	.9887	.9890
2.3	.9893	.9896	.9898	.9901	.9904	.9906	.9909	.9911	.9913	.9916
2.4	.9918	.9920	.9922	.9925	.9927	.9929	.9931	.9932	.9934	.9936
2.5	.9938	.9940	.9941	.9943	.9945	.9946	.9948	.9949	.9951	.9952
2.6	.9953	.9955	.9956	.9957	.9959	.9960	.9961	.9962	.9963	.9964
2.7	.9965	.9966	.9967	.9968	.9969	.9970	.9971	.9972	.9973	.9974
2.8	.9974	.9975	.9976	.9977	.9977	.9978	.9979	.9979	.9980	.9981
2.9	.9981	.9982	.9982	.9983	.9984	.9984	.9985	.9985	.9986	.9986
3.0	.9987	.9987	.9987	.9988	.9988	.9989	.9989	.9989	.9990	.9990

Appendix C

Answers to Selected Problems

CHAPTER 2

B3. $150 million

B5. $47,388 million; $7964 million; $5520 million

B7. a. $400   b. $1.5x$

B9. a. 28%; 16.17%   b. 31%; 24.85%   c. 31%; 27.31%

B11. a. $5092.50   b. $2065.50; $2065.50; $4125.00   c. none
     d. +$2800.00

C1. $750,000

CHAPTER 3

B1. According to the Principle of Self-Interested Behavior, each party to a financial transaction will choose the course of action that is most financially advantageous to that party, given the information they possess. A particular piece of information may result in a particular action when the decision maker acts in his own self-interest. In that case, observing the decision maker's action may allow us to deduce the information that is known to the decision maker.

B3. *Limited liability* is a legal concept stating that the financial liability of an asset owner is limited in some manner. For example, a stockholder in a publicly traded firm such as IBM or General Motors cannot be held responsible for a liability of the corporation. If a borrower's financial liability is limited to a particular amount, that limit gives the borrower the option to default and not fully repay the loan.

B5. According to the Signaling Principle, an action we observe is the optimal action of a self-interested player, given a particular information set. If a second player expects to face the same (or nearly the same) information set but does not know exactly what is in the information set and it is costly (or impossible) to determine the information with accuracy, the second player can infer that the action taken by the first player will also be in the second player's best interest. As a result, we have the Behavioral Principle—when all else fails, look at what others are doing for guidance.

B7. You would want to guard against the free-rider problem in any situation where you expend resources to determine a best course of action and others can receive the same benefits by simply imitating your actions. For example, if you have researched and developed a new, cost-saving way to manufacture automobile tires, you would want to apply for a patent so that other firms in the tire industry cannot costlessly imitate your new production process.

B9. $3259.84

B11. The Principle of Two-Sided Transactions is important to financial decision making because when we analyze any transaction, we must remember that someone else is analyzing that same transaction from the opposite point of view. This is much like any game of strategy, such as chess.

CHAPTER 4

B1. $6035.23

B3. a. 0.665%   b. 8%   c. 8.3%

B5. 16.183%

B7. $2444.34

B9. $3517.88

B11. $12,940.88

B13. $10,775.51

B15. In 5.5 years

B17. 9.2%

B19. $5531.66

B21. a. $569.47   b, No

B23. $430.38

B25. $16,790.88

C1. a. $4628.21   b. $3441.79

C3. a. $61,857.65   b. $32.65

C5. a. $47,912.83   b. $49,881.47

C7. $290.28

C9. $1093.60

C11. $739.33

C13. $566.58

CHAPTER 5

B1. 8.107%

B3. Oct. 9, 2012

B5. 5.98%

B7. 3.33%

B9. a. 9.692%; 9.927%   b. 9.942%; 10.189%

B15. $5.13

B17. 9.2%

B19. 20%

C1. -$0.11

C3. 9.868%

CHAPTER 6

B3.   46.4%

B7.   a. 10.5%; 4.8%   b. 317.25; 202.76   c. 235.6   d. 0.93

B9.   56.25% invested in portfolio 1

B11. a. 2.49%; 0.58%   b. 2.01; 54.46   c. 5.84   d. 0.56

B15. a. 8%   b. 16%

B21. By the portfolio separation theorem, every investor will choose to own a portion of every asset in the portfolio M and will never choose to hold an asset that is not in the portfolio M. Because there is never an owner for an asset that is not in M, M must contain every asset that has an owner—that is, every asset available in the market.

CHAPTER 7

B2.   13.68%

B5.   3.92

B7.   Both statements are correct. Beta measures the risk of the asset when it is held in a well-diversified portfolio. Sigma measures the risk when the asset is held alone.

B9.   14.14%

B11. 25.92%

B13. 12%

B16. 1.03

B19. 15.79%

B21. a. 15.2%   b. 11.7%

CHAPTER 8

B6.   Stockholders can sell (put) the firm's assets to the debtholders at the strike price of $0.

B9.   An American option is never worth less. An American option has all the rights of a European option plus the right to exercise anytime before expiration.

B11. $742,924.53

B14. $9142.99

CHAPTER 9

B1.   Monitoring is not always the best choice because minimizing agency costs involves a trade-off of the three types of agency costs. For example, the costs of monitoring may exceed the costs due to occasional agent misbehavior.

B4.   Human capital consists of the unique capabilities and expertise that belong to an individual. A person's human capital is largely invested in a particular firm or industry, and these skills are not likely to be perfectly transferable to another job. As a result, human capital is rarely well-diversified; instead, it is concentrated in one area or profession.

B8.   Without bond covenants, shareholders may have the ability as well as the incentive to expropriate debtholder wealth through asset substitution, underinvestment, or claim dilution. Because rational debtholders expect the shareholders to act in their own self-interest, they will require a higher interest rate on bonds without covenants than they would otherwise accept on identical bonds with covenants.

B11. An optimal contract is one that balances the three types of agency costs so that the total cost is minimized. High contracting costs or high monitoring costs should result in lower costs of misbehavior, and low contracting and monitoring costs may result in higher costs of misbehavior, so there is a trade-off of costs involved. The optimal contract achieves the trade-off that minimizes the total cost.

B14. Because a high-risk project increases the variability of returns on the firm's assets, it increases the value of a call option on those assets. The shareholders gain more in positive outcomes and don't lose any more in negative outcomes with the high-risk project. Thus, even if the project has a negative NPV, the loss in total firm value comes entirely at the expense of the firm's debtholders while the shareholders' claim is increased in value.

CHAPTER 10

B1.   B and C

B3.   13.73%

B5.   a. 10%   b. Balance due: $210.00, 220.50, 231.53, 243.11, 255.27, 268.03, 281.43, 295.50

B8.   15.2%

B10. 30%

C4.   1.10

C6.   6.17%

CHAPTER 11

B2. $13,254.32

B3. $681.91

B5.   −$48.75

B7.   a. $87.75, accept   b. −31.12%, reject

B11. 4.5 years

B13. −$9494

B15. $4,159,983

C2. $3,207,797

C3. $43,579.37

CHAPTER 12

B1. $24,008

B3.   Choose A, EAC = $31,691

B5.   Japanese truck, EAC = $165,417

B7.   a. 1.5   b. $15,427.58   c. $4418.44

B9.   a. $155,260   b. $155,260

B10. NPV becomes $145,061

B13. −$670,201

B15. a. No   b. $4,104,087

B17. Do not test market.

C3.   Yes, NPV = $18,972.63

C7.   Yes, EAC = $1970.20

CHAPTER 13

B1.   Undertake B, NPV = $1,126,284

B4.   Choose A, EAC = $658.14

B6.   NPV = $878,500

B8.   NPV = $1,493,500

B11. $33,333

B13. $34,396

B15. a. Buy A, EAC = $8509.03   b. Buy B, EAC = $8293.87

C5.   NPV = $1,158,000

CHAPTER 14

B3.   False. Competition drives arbitrageurs' NPVs to zero, where the expected return is fair for the risk taken on.

B5.   The homogeneity of assets contributes to the efficiency of the capital markets by reducing the evaluation of financial securities to considerations involving risk and return. Investors trading to increase the return on their investments (for a given level of risk) will identify the same opportunities that an arbitrageur would, thus increasing the competition for those opportunities and increasing the efficiency of the market.

B7.   Inductive reasoning requires inferring the cause from the result. When multiple causes lead to the same result, it is extremely difficult to apply the Signaling Principle and determine the *actual* cause.

B9.   According to the law of value conservation, value is neither created nor destroyed when assets (cash flows) are combined, separated, or exchanged.

B12. The blessing would be that you would never have to worry about whether you were paying a fair price because all prices would be fair. The curse would be that absolutely no positive-NPV investments would ever exist.

B14. 26.25%; 29.83%

C1.   6.94237%

C2. $57,326.57

CHAPTER 15

B1.   18.17%

B4.   Not necessarily. The opportunity costs of the restrictive covenants can outweigh the benefits.

B5.   a. $40,625   b. $7109

B7.   a. $5000   b. $3500   c. $3920; 35.7%   d. $3150   e. $3318   f. $5000

CHAPTER 16

B2.   Research shows that a firm's debt rating is highly correlated with its size. Therefore, size is an important consideration when a firm chooses comparable firms to compare itself to.

B6.   The firm would maintain less leverage than a cross section of single-A-rated firms if it were not able to fully utilize its interest tax shields or if debt management considerations, such as issuance expenses, caused it to issue less debt.

B7.   a. 2.5x b. 2.0x c. 2.16x

B8. $243,486

B11. a. 16.1%   b. 12.67%   c. 14.16%   d. 1.36   e. Since the market model provides a better estimate, use r_e = 19.2%.

B13. 13.0%

B14. a. $613,702   b. 28%   c. 23.81%   d. 29%

CHAPTER 17

B3.   a. 80%   b. 1600

B5. $2.15

B8.   With the firm's capital budget and capital structure fixed, dividend policy involves a risk and time-value trade-off between present and future dividends. In a perfect capital market, however, the present value of the entire dividend stream, and therefore the stock price, is unaffected by this trade-off.

B11. Since the projects are expected to earn their required return, the reinvestment alternative has a zero NPV. Therefore, the alternatives are equally beneficial.

B13. a. Yes, 25 cents is larger than half of 42 cents.   b. On average, stock prices increase in reaction to such changes. We believe this is due to the information conveyed by the dividend change because no change would be expected in a perfect capital market.

B15. The firm might pay a dividend in spite of a need for expansion capital and the flotation costs associated with a new issue because of the information content of dividends. If the dividend payment was expected based on the firm's past dividend policy, investors are likely to interpret the missed dividend as a negative signal of future earnings prospects rather than as a positive signal of the existence of a positive-NPV investment opportunity. As a result, the share price would drop in response to the missed dividend, and this price decrease might more than offset the flotation cost savings associated with avoiding the new issue.

B17. The current capital gains rate is higher than 10%, so such a change would increase the tax bias in favor of retained earnings. Therefore, the average payout ratio of NYSE-traded firms might be expected to drop. However, such a drop would probably not be significant because of the tax-timing option and the large proportion of investment that is either tax exempt or tax deferred.

CHAPTER 18

B1. a. 18%   b. Nothing. Dividend policy is irrelevant in a perfect capital market.

B5. a. 33.86%   b. $1.70, 1.90, 2.10, 2.35, 2.60

B6. a. 27.3%   b. Firms in a cyclical business.

B7. a. 12.55%   b. $8.33   c. $7.97; the time value of money causes the difference. You can earn money on the reinvested quarterly dividends.   d. Pattern 3

B11. a. $95 million; $98.75 million   b. $95 million; 99.46 million   c. A lower capital gains tax rate favors share repurchases.

B13. a. $29.44   b. They suffered an aggregate $5 million loss.

B16 Yes. If shares are sold between the ex-dividend date and the payment date.

B19. The Dutch auction procedure only allows shareholders to select the share repurchase price within the firm-specified range. If the firm would have been willing to pay the range maximum for all the shares in any case, it may benefit by getting to pay less for at least some of them.

CHAPTER 19

B1. 60.8 days; 36.5 days; 30.4 days; 66.9 days

B4. a. $208,967; $626,901   b. Purchase $417,934 at the upper limit, and sell $208,967 at the lower limit c. $278,623

B5. a. 18.43%; 20.13%   b. 38.83%; 45.70%   c. 24.83%; 27.86%

B7. $100, 300, 500, 300, 0

B9. a. 15.00%   b. 17.65%   c. 16.67%   d. 20.00%

B11. 11.11%

B13. 23.70%

B15. 11.98%

B17. $10,500

C1. Take alternative 1, APY = 12.68%

CHAPTER 20

B2. $42,298.50

B3. $137.87

B6. 33 days

B8. a. $1,262,598 b. $1,132,846 c. The current policy.

B10. a. $26,300 b. 17.66 c. $8966; $9476; the higher

B12. a. 16 b. 26

B13. 30; 10

CHAPTER 21

B1. a. $15,500 per month   b. $2,405,706

B3. a. $$12,762.82 per year   b. $17,121 surplus

B7. $81,663 per year for Lacey; $115,595 per year for Logan

B9. a. $66,034   b. $1,490,634

B11. $973,020 at the end of the 10 years

B13. a. $600   b. $170   c. No. The debtholders are protecting themselves.

CHAPTER 22

B1. Cumulative borrowing balances will be (in $1000s) 0, 60, 110, 80, 0, 0

B3. a. $2,200,000 b. 5.77% c. $220,000 d. 9.56%

B4. Cumulative loan balances will be $50, 150, 225, 225, 100, 0

B7. $110,000

B8. a. 5.96%   b. 10.92%

CHAPTER 23

B1. a. 5%   b. Buy 60,000 of the new shares

B3. a. $5 million   b. 17%   c. Announcement

B5. $30.11

B8. a. 6   b. Cannot be certain of electing any   c. 3 elections d. It makes it more difficult for a dissident group to exert control

B12. a. 8.329%   b. 8.399%   c. 8.405%

B14. 16.8%

B16. 18.3%

B17. 8.39%

CHAPTER 24

B2. $4,070,817

B3. 11.78%

B5. b. 10.45%   c. 6.91%

B7. $55 million

B8. $150 million

B10. $800 million

B12. 8.8 years

B14. a. 9.8%   b. 9 years   c. 8.39 years

B17. −$4,277,235

B19. $1,177,285

B22. Refund entire issue

C1. a. 8.20%   b. 8.61%

C3. a. $475,193   b. −$3,314,957   c. −$966,948   d. Only if the gain is nontaxable

C5. a. $9,100,382   b. $10,666,667

CHAPTER 25

B3. a. $117,571; yes   b. $118,678; yes

B5. Lease, NAL = $102.85

B8. a. Lease, NAL = $260.31   b. Borrow and buy, NAL = −$114.01

B10. Leasing, NAL = $120,592

B12. a. $0.46 million; yes   b. $10.04 million   c. 10.58%

B13. a. $1,130,211   b. $4,393,938

B17. a. 9.86%   b. Yes

B19. 22.31%

CHAPTER 26

B1. $11.61

B2. $47.89

B3. $51.70

B5. $3.34

B7. a. $3.50   b. $3.12   c. $2.74

B9. a. $2.48   b. $2.66   c. $2.84

B10. $6.75; 4.38; 2.37

B11. a. $10   b. $14.13

B13. a. Yes   b. No   c. Yes

B15. a. Buy an interest rate cap or sell (short) futures on short-term debt.   b. $18.75 million, 16.88, 21.25, 22.50, 22.50, 22.50, 22.50, 18.75   c. $0.00 million, 0.00, 0.00, 3.13, 6.25, 8.13, 1.88, 0.00

C1. 32%

CHAPTER 27

B2. Chapter 10 was intended to allow small and medium-sized businesses to reorganize under a "fast-track Chapter 11" procedure, which was designed to reduce the delay and cost of Chapter 11.

B5. a. 1.43   b. Yes

B6. a. 2.36   b. No

B8. 71%

B11. a. The banks   b. No

B13. No one

CHAPTER 28

B1. a. $59.3 million   b. 34.45%   c. 4 years   d. Yes

B3. a. Firm A, $115 million; Firm B, 100   b. $215 million; 50; 165   c. No

B6. $125 million

B8. a. 35 million   b. $350 million

B10. a. 17.50%   b. $157.84 million   c. $165.41 million

B14. a. $83.72 million   b. Helps them, value increases to $88.70 million   c. Risk reduction, Empire would then be guaranteeing the bonds

B16. $98.94

B19. $49.08 million

CHAPTER 29

B1. a. 5.19% APY   b. 5.27% APY   c. Domestic

B2. a. 6.60%   b. 7.26%

B4. a. 12.5%   b. 2.67%   c. Equation (29.2)

B5. a. $1.50 per pound   b. Buy gold in NY, sell it in London   c. $60, or 35.29 pounds, per ounce of gold

B7. a. SF1 = DM1.30   b. Yes; no   c. No; yes

B8. Higher in Germany by 25%

B9. Higher in Great Britain by 3%

B10. a. $2.9 million   b. $100,000   c. Foreign currency money market transaction   d. Forward contract

B13. a. 0.6113$/DM, 0.6226, 0.6168, 0.6223, 0.6000   b. $9.1695 million, 10.5842, 12.336, 12.446, 10.200   c. $6,275,018

C1. 12.38%

Glossary

Abandonment option   The option of terminating an investment earlier than originally planned.

Absolute priority doctrine   The idea that any distribution of a debtor's assets should be according to claim priority.

Accelerated depreciation   A depreciation method that permits a firm to claim greater depreciation expense than it could under the *straight-line depreciation* method during the early years (and lesser in later years) of an asset's life.

Accounts receivable   Money owed a firm by its customers.

Acid test ratio   The difference between current assets and inventories divided by current liabilities.

Acquiree   A firm that is being acquired.

Acquiror   A firm or individual who is acquiring something; for example, a firm that is acquiring another firm.

Acquisition   See *Corporate acquisition*.

Acquisition of assets   A *merger* or *consolidation* in which an acquiror purchases the selling firm's assets.

Acquisition of stock   A *merger* or *consolidation* in which an acquiror purchases the acquiree's stock.

Adjusted present value (APV)   A method that determines total value by adding the "basic" present value of unleveraged cash flows to the present value of net benefits to leverage.

Adverse selection   A situation in which market participation is a negative signal.

Affirmative covenant   A *bond covenant* that specifies certain actions the firm must take. Also called a *positive covenant*.

Agency cost view (of capital structure)   The argument that the various agency costs create a complex environment in which total agency costs are at a minimum with some, but less than 100%, debt financing.

Agency costs   The incremental costs of having an agent make decisions for a principal.

Agency problem   A potential conflict of interest in a principal-agent relationship.

Agency theory   The analysis of principal-agent relationships, wherein one person, an *agent*, acts on behalf of another person, a **principal**.

Agent   The decision maker in a principal-agent relationship.

Aging schedule   A table of accounts receiv-able broken down into age categories (such as 0–30 days, 30–60 days, and 60–90 days), which is used to see whether customer payments are keeping close to schedule.

American option   An option that can be exercised at any time during its life.

AMEX   The American Stock Exchange.

Amortize   To spread out over a future time period, such as repayment of a loan by installment payments or tax deductions for depreciation expense.

Annual percentage rate (APR)   The periodic rate times the number of periods in a year. For example, 2% per quarter is an 8% APR.

Annual percentage yield (APY)   The effective (true) annual rate of return. The APY is the rate you actually earn or pay in one year, taking into account the effect of compounding. For example, as shown in Table 4-3, 1% per month is a 12.68% APY.

Annual report   A report issued annually by a firm. It includes, at a minimum, an income statement, a balance sheet, a statement of cash flows, and accompanying notes.

Annuity   A series of identical cash flows each period for *n* periods.

Annuity due   An *annuity* with *n* payments, wherein the first payment is made at time $t = 0$ and the last payment is made at time $t = n - 1$.

Antidilutive effect   Result of a transaction that increases earnings per common share (e.g., by decreasing the number of common shares outstanding).

APB   The Accounting Principles Board.

APR   See *Annual percentage rate*.

APT   See *Arbitrage pricing theory*.

APV   See *Adjusted present value*.

APY   See *Annual percentage yield*.

Arbitrage   The act of buying and selling an asset simultaneously, where the sale price is larger than the purchase price, so that the difference provides a riskless profit.

Arbitrage pricing theory (APT)   A theory of asset pricing in which the risk premium is based on a specified set of risk factors in addition to (or other than) the correlation with the expected excess return on the market portfolio.

arbitragers   Persons who search for and exploit arbitrage opportunities. Also spelled *arbitrageurs*.

Asset activity ratios   Ratios that measure how effectively the firm is managing its assets.

Asset-based financing   Methods of financing in which lenders and equity investors look principally to the cash flow from a particular asset or set of assets for a return on, and the return of, their investment.

Asset-coverage test   A *bond indenture* restriction that permits additional borrowing only if the ratio of assets (typically net tangible assets) to debt (typically long-term debt) does not fall below a specified minimum.

Asset pricing model   A model for determining the *required return* on an asset.

Asset substitution   A firm's investing in assets that are riskier than those that the debtholders expected.

Asset substitution problem   Arises when the stockholders substitute riskier assets for the firm's existing assets and expropriate value from the debtholders.

Assets   A firm's productive resources.

Asymmetry   A lack of equivalence between two things, such as the unequal tax treatment of interest expense and dividend payments.

Asymmetric information   Information that is known to some people but not to others.

Asymmetric taxes   A situation wherein participants in a transaction have different net tax rates.

At-the-money   Said of an option when the value of the underlying asset equals the *strike price*.

Auction markets   Markets in which the prevailing price is determined through the free interaction of prospective buyers and sellers, as on the floor of a stock exchange.

Auction rate preferred stock   Floating-rate *preferred stock*, the dividend rate on which is adjusted every seven weeks through a *Dutch auction*.

Authorized shares   Number of shares authorized for issuance by a firm's *corporate charter*.

Automated Clearing House (ACH)   A collection of 32 regional electronic interbank networks used to process transactions electronically with a guaranteed one-day *bank collection float*.

Automatic stay   The restricting of liability holders from collection efforts of collateral seizure, which is automatically imposed when a firm files for bankruptcy under Chapter 11.

Average age of accounts receivable   The

G1

weighted average age of all the firm's outstanding invoices.

Average life   The effective maturity of a debt issue, taking into account the effect of sinking fund payments.

Average rate of return (ARR)   The ratio of the average cash inflow to the average amount invested.

Average tax rate   Taxes as a fraction of income; total taxes divided by total taxable income.

Back-to-back loan   A form of loan barter arrangement whereby two firms lend each other funds denominated in different currencies for an agreed-upon period.

Balance sheet   A statement of a firm's financial position at one point in time, including its assets and the claims on those assets by creditors (liabilities) and owners (stockholders' equity).

Balance sheet identity   Total Assets = Liabilities + Stockholders' Equity.

Balloon payment   A debt payment that is larger than the loan's other payments. It is typically the final payment that repays the outstanding balance of the loan.

Bank collection float   The time that elapses between when a check is deposited into a bank account and when the funds are available to the depositor (during which period the bank is collecting payment from the payer's bank).

Bankers' acceptances   *Drafts* that are accepted by a commercial bank. They are often used by importers and exporters to help facilitate international trade.

Bankruptcy   A formal legal process under which a firm experiencing financial difficulty is protected from its creditors while it works out a plan to settle its debt obligations under the supervision of the bankruptcy court.

Bankruptcy cost view (of capital structure)   The argument that expected indirect and direct bankruptcy costs offset the other benefits from leverage so that the optimal amount of leverage is less than 100% debt financing.

Bankruptcy risk   The risk that a firm will be unable to meet its debt obligations. Also called default risk and *insolvency risk.*

Bankruptcy view (of capital structure)   The argument that expected bankruptcy costs preclude firms from being financed entirely with debt.

Basic business strategies   Key strategies a firm intends to pursue in carrying out its business plan.

Basis point   1/100 of 1%; 1% equals 100 basis points.

Bearer bonds   Bonds that are not registered on the books of the issuer. Such bonds are held in physical form by the owner, and the owner obtains interest payments by physically detaching coupons from the bond certificate and delivering them to the paying agent.

Benefit-cost ratio   The present value of the future cash flows divided by the initial investment. Also called the *profitability index.*

Best-efforts sale   A method of securities distribution in which the securities firm undertakes only to use its best efforts to sell the securities on behalf of the issuer, as contrasted with a *purchase and sale.*

Best-interests-of-creditors test   The requirement that a claim holder voting against a *plan of reorganization* must receive at least as much as she would have if the debtor were liquidated.

Beta   A linear measure of how much an individual asset contributes to the standard deviation of the market portfolio; calculated as the covariance between the return on the asset and the return on the market portfolio, divided by the variance of the return on the market portfolio.

Bid-ask spread   The spread, or difference, between the bid price (at which a market agent is willing to buy) and the ask price (at which a market agent is willing to sell).

Binomial option pricing model   An option pricing model in which the underlying asset can take on only two possible (discrete) values in the next time period for each value that it can take on in the preceding time period. Also called the *two-state option pricing model.*

Black-Scholes option pricing model   Formula developed by Fischer Black and Myron Scholes to value a *European option* on a non-dividend-paying stock.

Block trade   Commonly, a trade involving a large amount of stock. The NYSE defines a block trade as consisting of the lesser of (1) 10,000 or more shares or (2) shares (regardless of the number) with a market value of $200,000 or more, that are sold in a single transaction.

Block voting   A group of shareholders banding together to vote their shares in a single block.

Book value   The net amount (net book value) for something shown in accounting statements.

Bond   A long-term obligation for borrowed money; that is, a long-term *debt security.*

Bond agreement   A contract for *privately placed* debt.

Bond covenant   A contractual provision in a bond indenture. A positive covenant requires certain actions. A negative covenant limits certain actions.

Bond equivalent yield   True interest cost expressed on the basis of a 360-day year.

Bond indenture   The explicit legal contract for a bond.

Bond points   A conventional unit of measure for bond prices set at $10 and equivalent to 1% of the $1000 face value of the bond. A price of 50 bond points means that the bond sold for $500 (50 times $10), or 50% of its face value.

Bond value   With respect to a *convertible bond,* the value the security would have if it were not convertible; the value of the security apart from the value of the conversion option.

Book value per common share   The amount of owners' equity on a firm's balance sheet divided by the number of the firm's outstanding shares.

Break-even concept   The notion of equating costs and revenues. At times this is misleading, because computations typically disregard the time value of money.

Break-even lease payment   The lease payment at which a party to a prospective lease is indifferent between entering and not entering into the lease arrangement.

Break-even point   An accounting term defined as the point at which the total contribution margin equals the total fixed costs of producing a product or service.

Break-even tax rate   The tax rate at which a party to a prospective transaction is indifferent between entering and not entering into the transaction.

Broker   Someone who assists in securities trading but never actually owns the securities.

Budget   A detailed schedule of a financial activity, such as an advertising budget, a sales budget, or a capital budget.

Bullet maturity   Refers to debt that requires repayment of the entire principal at maturity.

Business risk   The inherent or fundamental risk of a business, without regard to financial risk. Also called *operating risk.*

Buy   To purchase an asset. Also called taking a long position.

Buy orders   Orders for securities purchases.

Call an option   To exercise a call option.

Call option   The right to *buy* something at a given price during the life of the option.

Call premium   Premium in price above the par value of a bond (or share of preferred stock) that must be paid holders to redeem the bond (or share of preferred stock) before its scheduled maturity date.

Call price   The price for which a bond can be repaid before maturity under a call provision.

Call provision   A provision that gives the firm the right to repay the bonds before the maturity date.

Callable   A financial security such as a bond with a call option attached to it (i.e., the issuer has the right to call the security).

Capital   Money invested in a firm.

Capital asset pricing model (CAPM)   A model for determining the *required return* on an asset, taking into account the risk of the asset. A model for specifying the risk-return trade-off in the capital markets.

Capital budget   A firm's set of planned capital expenditures.

Capital budgeting   The process of choosing the firm's long-term capital investments.

Capital expenditure   Investment in additional *assets*.

Capital gain   The difference between what an asset is sold for and its book value, typically referring to an asset that has been owned for a sufficiently long time, such as a year or more.

Capital gains yield   The price change portion of a stock's return.

Capital lease   A lease obligation that has to be capitalized on the face of the balance sheet.

Capital market   A market in which securities are bought and sold.

Capital market efficiency   Reflects the relative amount of wealth wasted in making transactions. An efficient capital market allows the transfer of assets with little wealth loss.

Capital market imperfections view (of capital structure)   The view that issuing debt is generally valuable but that the firm's optimal choice of capital structure is a dynamic process that involves the other views of capital structure (net corporate/personal tax, agency cost, bankruptcy cost, and pecking order), which result from considerations of asymmetric taxes, asymmetric information, and transaction costs.

Capital market line (CML)   The line of investment possibilities extending outward from the *riskless rate*, r_f, and passing through the expected return on the *market portfolio*.

Capital rationing   Placing one or more limits on (rationing) the amount of new investment undertaken by a firm, either by using a higher cost of capital or by setting a maximum on parts of, and/or the entirety of, the capital budget.

Capital structure   The makeup of the liabilities and stockholders' equity side of the balance sheet, especially the ratio of debt to equity and the mixture of short and long maturities.

Capitalize   (1) To record on the books of a firm at cost for allocation as an expense over the life of the asset or liability (see *Depreciate*). (2) To summarize as the present value of a series of future obligations, as in capitalizing a lease.

Capitalized   A cost that is allocated to two or more time periods.

Capitalized lease obligation   See *Capital lease*.

Capitalization rate   A stock's *required return*.

Capitalization ratio   The ratio of the amount of *capital* raised from a particular source (for example, long-term debt) to the total capitalization of the firm.

Capitalization table   A table showing the capitalization of a firm, which typically includes the amount of *capital* obtained from each source (e.g., long-term debt and common equity) and the respective *capitalization ratios*.

CAPM   See *Capital asset pricing model*.

Cash budget   A forecasted summary of a firm's expected cash inflows and cash outflows as well as its expected cash and loan balances.

Cash concentration services   See *Concentration services*.

Cash conversion cycle   The length of time between a firm's purchase inventory and the receipt of cash from its accounts receivable.

Cash deficiency agreement   An agreement to invest cash in a project to the extent required to cover any cash deficiency the project may experience.

Cash discount   An incentive offered to purchasers of a firm's product for payment within a specified time period, such as 10 days.

Cash equivalent   A short-term security that is sufficiently liquid that it may be considered the financial equivalent of cash.

Cash flow   See *Cash flow from operations*.

Cash-flow break-even point   The point below which the firm will need either to obtain additional financing or to liquidate some of its assets to meet its fixed costs (for example, salaries and administrative costs, interest and principal payments, and planned cash dividends).

Cash flow coverage ratio   The number of times that financial obligations (for interest, principal payments, preferred stock dividends, and rental payments) are covered by earnings before interest, taxes, rental payments, and depreciation.

Cash flow from operations   A firm's net cash inflow resulting directly from its regular operations (disregarding extraordinary items such as the sale of fixed assets or transaction costs associated with issuing securities), calculated as the sum of net income plus non-cash expenses that were deducted in calculating net income.

Cash flow per common share   Cash flow from operations minus preferred stock dividends, divided by the number of common shares outstanding.

Cash ratio   The proportion of a firm's assets held as cash.

CBOE   Chicago Board Options Exchange. A securities exchange created in the early 1970s for the public trading of standardized option contracts.

Certainty equivalent   An amount that would be accepted in lieu of a chance at a possibly higher, but uncertain, amount.

Certificate of deposit (CD)   An obligation of a bank, with a maturity of six months to five years, that evidences a deposit.

CFAT   Cash flow after tax.

Claim dilution   A reduction in the likelihood that one or more of the firm's claimants will be fully repaid, including time-value-of-money considerations.

Claimant   A party to an explicit or implicit contract. Sometimes also called a *stakeholder* in the *set-of-contracts model*.

Clear a position   To eliminate a long or short position, leaving no ownership or obligation.

Clientele effect   The grouping of investors who have a preference that the firm follow a particular financing policy, such as the amount of leverage it uses.

Closing price   The price of a financial security in the last trade before the market closed.

Collateral   Assets that can be repossessed if the borrower defaults.

Collateral trust bond   A bond that is secured by other securities.

Collection float   The negative float that is created between the time when you deposit a check in your account and the time when funds are made available.

Collection fractions   The percentage of a given month's sales collected during the month of sale and each month following the sale.

Collective wisdom   The combination (net result) of all of the individual opinions about a stock's value.

Commercial paper   A promissory note sold by a large, creditworthy corporation in large denominations with maturities of 1 day to 270 days.

Commission broker   A broker on the floor

of an exchange who acts as an agent for a particular brokerage house and who buys and sells stocks for the brokerage house on a commission basis.

Commitment fee A fee paid to a commercial bank in return for its legal commitment to lend funds that have not yet been advanced.

Common-base-year analysis The representing of accounting information over multiple years as percentages of amounts in an initial year.

Common-size analysis The representing of balance sheet items as percentages of assets and of income statement items as percentages of sales.

Common stock A proportional equity ownership interest — that is, a proportionate residual ownership interest in a corporation. Common stock is the most junior security a corporation can issue.

Common stock equivalents Securities, including certain types of convertible securities, stock options, and warrants, that are considered the substantial equivalent of common stock.

Common stock ratios Ratios that are designed to measure the relative claims of stockholders to earnings (earnings per share and payout ratio), cash flow (cash flow per share), and equity (book value per share) of a firm.

Comparative credit analysis A method of analysis in which a firm is compared to others that have a desired target debt rating in order to infer an appropriate financial ratio target.

Compensating balance An excess balance that is left at a bank to provide indirect compensation for loans extended or other bank services.

Competitive bidding A securities offering process in which securities firms submit competing bids to the issuer for the securities the issuer wishes to sell.

Competitive offering An offering of securities through *competitive bidding*.

Complete capital market A market in which there is a distinct marketable security for each and every possible outcome.

Completion risk The risk that a project will not be brought into operation successfully.

Completion undertaking An undertaking either (1) to complete a project such that it meets certain specified performance criteria on or before a certain specified date or (2) to repay project debt if the completion test cannot be met.

Compound interest Interest paid on previously earned interest as well as on the principal.

Compounding The process of accumulating the time value of money forward in time. For example, interest earned during one period earns additional interest during each subsequent time period.

Compounding frequency The number of compounding periods in a year. For example, quarterly compounding has a compounding frequency of 4.

Compounding period The length of the time period (for example, a quarter in the case of quarterly compounding) that elapses before interest compounds.

Comprehensive due diligence investigation The investigation of a firm's business in conjunction with a securities offering to determine whether the firm's business and financial situation and its prospects are adequately disclosed in the *prospectus* for the offering.

Concentration account A single centralized account into which funds collected at regional locations (lockboxes) are transferred.

Concentration services Movement of cash from different lockbox locations into a single *concentration account* from which disbursements and investments are made.

Conditional sales contracts Similar to *equipment trust certificates* except that the lender is either the equipment manufacturer or a bank or finance company to whom the manufacturer has sold the conditional sales contract.

Conglomerate A firm engaged in two or more unrelated businesses.

Conglomerate merger A merger involving two or more firms that are in unrelated businesses.

Consol A type of bond that has an infinite life but is not issued in the U.S. capital markets.

Consolidation The combining of two or more firms to form an entirely new entity.

Consumer credit Credit granted by a firm to consumers for the purchase of goods or services. Also called *retail credit*.

Contingent claim A claim that can be made only if one or more specified outcomes occur—that is, a claim that is contingent on the value of some other asset or on a particular occurrence.

Continuous compounding The process of accumulating the time value of money forward in time on a continuous, or instantaneous, basis. Interest is earned continuously, and at each instant, the interest that accrues immediately begins earning interest on itself.

Continuous random variable A random value that can take on *any* fractional value within specified ranges, as contrasted with a *discrete* value.

Contribution margin The difference between variable revenue and variable cost.

Control 50% of the outstanding votes plus one.

Controlled disbursement A service that provides for a single presentation of checks each day (typically in the early part of the day).

Controller The corporate manager responsible for the firm's accounting activities.

Conventional project A project with a negative initial cash flow (an outflow), which is expected to be followed by one or more future positive cash flows (cash inflows).

Conversion premium The percentage by which the *conversion price* in a *convertible security* exceeds the prevailing common stock price at the time the convertible security is issued.

Conversion price The contractually specified price per share at which a convertible security can be converted into (exchanged for) shares of common stock.

Conversion ratio The number of common shares into which a *convertible security* may be converted; the ratio of the face amount of the convertible security to the *conversion price*.

Conversion value The market value of the number of shares into which a *convertible security* can be converted; that is, the value of the security as common stock.

Convertible bond A bond that, at the option of its owner, can be exchanged for a contractually specified number of shares of the firm's common stock.

Convertible exchangeable preferred stock *Convertible preferred stock* that may be exchanged, at the issuer's option, into *convertible bonds* that have the same conversion features as the convertible preferred stock.

Convertible preferred stock *Preferred stock* that can, at the option of its owner, be converted into (exchanged for) a contractually specified number of shares of the firm's common stock. See also *Convertible security*.

Convertible security A security (bond or preferred stock) that, at the option of its owner, can be converted into (exchanged for) a contractually specified number of shares of the firm's common stock.

Corporate acquisition The acquisition of one firm by another; a merger.

Corporate bond A financial security issued, typically with a *par value* of $1000, by a firm that contractually agrees to make future payments to the bond's owner.

Corporate charter A legal document creating a corporation.

Corporate finance One of the three areas

of the discipline of finance. It deals with the operation of the firm (both the *investment decision* and the *financing decision*) from that firm's point of view.

Corporate financial management The application of financial principles within a corporation to create and maintain value through decision making and proper resource management.

Corporate financial planning Financial planning conducted by a firm that encompasses preparation of both the *long-term financial plan* and the *short-term financial plan*.

Corporate processing float The time that elapses between receipt of payment from a customer and the depositing of the customer's check in the firm's bank account; the time required to process customer payments.

Corporate tax view (of capital structure) The argument that double (corporate and individual) taxation of equity returns makes debt a cheaper financing method.

Corporation A legal "person" that is separate and distinct from its owners. A corporation is allowed to own assets, incur liabilities, and sell securities, among other things.

Correlation coefficient The covariance between two random variables divided by the product of the standard deviations of those random variables.

Cost-benefit ratio The net present value of an investment divided by the investment's initial cost. Also called the *profitability index*.

Cost of capital The required return for a capital budgeting project.

Cost of lease financing A lease's *internal rate of return*.

Cost of limited partner capital The discount rate that equates the after-tax inflows with outflows for capital raised from limited partners.

Counter trade The exchange of goods for other goods rather than cash; barter.

Coupon equivalent yield True interest cost expressed on the basis of a 365-day year.

Coupon payments A bond's interest payments.

Coupon rate A bond's annual percentage rate.

Coupon rate of interest (for a bond) The sum of interest payments to be made within one year divided by the *par value* of the bond. Often called simply coupon or coupon rate.

Covariance The mathematical expectation of the product of two random variables' deviations from their mean.

Covenants Provisions in a *bond indenture*

(or *preferred stock agreement*) that require the bond (or preferred stock) issuer to take certain specified actions (*affirmative covenants*) or to refrain from taking certain specified actions (*negative covenants*).

Cover To *clear a position* that was *short*.

Coverage ratios Ratios that show the amount of funds available to "cover" a particular financial obligation compared to the size of that obligation.

Covered call optionwriter A person who sells (writes) a call option on an asset that she owns.

Cramdown The ability of the bankruptcy court to confirm a *plan of reorganization* over the objections of some classes of creditors.

Credible signal A signal that provides accurate information; a signal that can distinguish among "senders."

Credit period The length of time for which the customer is granted credit.

Credit scoring A statistical technique wherein several financial characteristics are combined to form a single score to represent a customer's creditworthiness.

Cross-default A provision under which default on one debt obligation triggers default on another debt obligation.

Cross rates The *exchange rate* between two currencies expressed as the ratio of two foreign exchange rates that are both expressed in terms of a third currency.

Cross-sectional approach A statistical methodology applied to a set of firms at a particular point in time.

Crossover rate The return at which two alternative projects have the same net present value.

Crown jewel A particularly profitable or otherwise particularly valuable corporate unit (or asset) of a firm.

Cumulative dividend feature A requirement that any missed preferred or preference stock dividends be paid in full before any common dividend payment is made.

Cumulative voting A system of voting for directors of a corporation in which a shareholder's total number of votes is equal to her number of shares held times the number of candidates; the shareholder's votes can be cast for candidates in any proportion. In other words, all votes could be cast for a single candidate.

Currency future A *financial future* contract for the delivery of a specified foreign currency.

Currency option An *option* to buy or sell foreign currency.

Currency swap An agreement to swap a series of specified payment obligations de-

nominated in one currency for a series of specified payment obligations denominated in a different currency.

Current assets Assets that are expected to become cash within one year.

Current liabilities Liabilities that mature, or are expected to be paid off, within one year.

Current ratio A liquidity ratio that measures the number of times a firm's current assets cover its current liabilities.

Current yield The annual coupon payment divided by the closing price.

Customary payout ratios A range of *payout ratios* that is typical based on an analysis of comparable firms.

Date of record Date on which the owners of securities are established for the purpose of determining who is entitled to receive scheduled securities payments, such as dividends on common stock.

Days' sales in inventory ratio The average number of days' worth of sales that is held in inventory.

Days' sales outstanding (DSO) The approximate number of days required to collect a firm's accounts receivable. Also called *average collection period*.

Dealer Someone who assists securities trading by buying and selling out of his own inventory of securities.

Debenture Long-term bonds (typically of longer than 10-year maturity) not secured by specific assets.

Debt A legal obligation to make contractually agreed-upon future payments.

Debt capacity Optimal amount of debt in the firm's capital structure.

Debt/equity ratio Total debt divided by total common stockholders's equity; the amount of debt per dollar of equity.

Debt limitation A *bond covenant* that restricts in some way the firm's ability to incur additional indebtedness.

Debt ratio Total debt divided by total assets; the fraction of the assets of the firm that are financed by debt.

Debt service The payment obligations connected with a debt contract.

Debt-service coverage ratio Earnings before interest and income taxes plus one-third rental charges, divided by interest expense plus one-third rental charges plus the quantity principal repayments divided by one minus the tax rate. See Equation (16.3).

Debt service parity (DSP) approach An analysis wherein the alternatives under consideration will provide the firm with the exact same schedule of after-tax debt payments (including both interest and principal).

Debtor in possession   A firm that is continuing to operate its business under Chapter 11 bankruptcy protection.

Debtor-in-possession financing   New debt obtained by a firm during the Chapter 11 bankruptcy process.

Decision tree   A diagram that illustrates the interdependence of decisions in situations that require a sequence of decisions, such as the progression of decisions from formulation of an idea for a new product through several stages either to cancellation of the product development project or to market introduction of the product.

Deductive reasoning   The use of a general fact to provide accurate information about a specific situation.

Deep-discount bond   A bond that is issued at a price significantly below its par value.

Defeasance   Rendering null and void.

Deferred equity   A common term for convertible bonds because of their equity component and the expectation that the bond will ultimately be converted into shares of common stock.

Defined benefit pension plan   A pension plan wherein the covered employee's pension benefit is determined by a formula that takes into account the employee's years of service to the firm and the employee's final salary.

Defined contribution pension plan   A pension plan wherein the employer makes an agreed-upon, regular contribution to the employee's own retirement savings account.

Demand master notes   Short-term securities that are repayable immediately upon the holder's demand.

Dependent   (capital budgeting project) Acceptance of the project is contingent on acceptance of another project.

Depository transfer check (DTC)   A check on the firm's account at a regional location that is deposited into the *concentration account* to initiate automatically the transfer of funds into that account from another bank account.

Depreciate   To allocate the purchase cost of an asset over its life.

Depreciation   A noncash expense claimed for tax or accounting purposes in connection with a capital asset.

Derivatives   Securities that derive their value from another asset.

Detachable warrant   A warrant that can be sold separately from the bond with which it was issued.

Dilution   Reduction in earnings per common share resulting from a financial transaction.

Dilutive effect   Result of a transaction that decreases earnings per common share.

Direct-estimate method   A method of cash budgeting based on detailed estimates of cash receipts and cash disbursements category by category.

Direct lease   A lease arrangement under which the manufacturer of an asset leases it (directly) to some entity.

Direct stock-purchase programs   The purchase by investors of securities directly from the issuer.

Disbursement float   The positive float that is created between the time when a check is written and the time when it is finally cleared out of the checking account.

Discount   The percent a customer can deduct from the net amount of the bill if payment is made before the end of the *discount period*.

Discount bond   A bond that is selling for less than its par value.

Discount period   The period during which a customer can deduct the *discount* from the net amount of the bill when making payment.

Discount rate   A generic term for a rate of return that measures the time value of money.

Discounted basis   Selling something on a discounted basis is selling it below what its value will be at maturity, so that the difference makes up all or part of the interest.

Discounted-cash-flow (DCF) analysis   The process of valuing capital budgeting projects by discounting their future expected cash flows.

Discounted-cash-flow (DCF) framework   The valuing of an asset by discounting its expected future cash flows at some discount rate.

Discounted payback   The length of time it takes for an investment's *discounted* future cash flows to equal the investment's initial cost.

Discounting   The process of adjusting for the time value of money backward in time.

Discrete compounding   *Compounding* the time value of money (e.g., interest) for discrete time intervals (time periods).

Discrete random variable   A random variable that can take on only a certain specified set of discrete possible values—for example, the positive integers 1, 2, 3, … .

Discretionary cash flow   Cash flow that is available after the funding of all positive-NPV capital investment projects; it is available for paying cash dividends, repurchasing common stock, retiring debt, and so on.

Discriminant analysis   A statistical procedure that links the probability of default to a specified set of financial ratios.

Diversifiable risk   Risk that can be eliminated by diversification.

Dividend   Periodic payment made to stockholders (of either *preferred stock* or *common stock*).

Dividend clawback   With respect to a *project financing*, an arrangement under which the sponsors of a project agree to contribute as equity any prior *dividends* received from the project to the extent necessary to cover any cash deficiencies.

Dividend clientele   A group of shareholders who prefer that the firm follow a particular dividend policy. For example, such a preference is often based on comparable tax situations.

Dividend limitation   A *bond covenant* that restricts in some way the firm's ability to pay cash dividends.

Dividend policy   An established guide for the firm to determine the amount of money it will pay out as dividends.

Dividend rate   Dividends paid per common share per annum.

Dividend reinvestment plan   A firm-sponsored program that enables common stockholders to pool their dividends (and, in many cases, supplementary cash) for reinvestment in shares of the firm's common stock.

Dividend rights   A shareholder's right to receive per-share dividends identical to those other shareholders receive.

Dividend yield   The dividend income portion of a stock's return; more specifically, the dividend per share divided by the share price.

Diversification   Spreading investments across several alternatives instead of concentrating them in a single or a few investments.

Double-declining-balance method   A method of computing depreciation expense.

Draft   An unconditional written order for payment.

DSAT   Debt service after tax.

DSP   Debt service parity.

Duration   The time until the "average" dollar of present value is received from an asset.

Dutch auction   An auction process in which the market-clearing price is determined by accepting the highest bid, then the next highest bid, and so on, until a price is found for which all the securities offered for sale will be purchased. All securities transactions then take place at the market-clearing price.

Dutch auction tender offer   A "reverse" tender process, wherein shareholders can offer to sell shares at prices with a specified range.

EAA   See *Equivalent annual annuity.*

EAB   See *Equivalent annual benefit.*

EAC   See *Equivalent annual cost.*

Earning power   Earnings before interest and taxes (EBIT) divided by total assets.

Earnings Earnings available for common stock; net income minus preferred stock dividends.

Earnings per share (EPS) A firm's annualized earnings divided by the share price.

Earnings before interest and taxes (EBIT) Operating profit plus nonoperating profit, such as investment income, calculated before the deduction of interest and income taxes.

Earnings yield The earnings per share divided by the market price per share; equals the reciprocal of the price/earnings ratio.

Economic defeasance See *In-substance defeasance.*

Economic dependence Exists when the costs and/or revenues of one project depend on those of another.

Economic order quantity (EOQ) The order quantity that minimizes total inventory costs.

Economic risk In project financing, the risk that the project's output will not be salable at a price that will cover the project's operating and maintenance costs and its debt service requirements.

Economies of scale The decrease in the marginal cost of production as a plant's scale of operations increases.

Effective annual rate (r_a) An annual measure of the time value of money that fully reflects the effects of *compounding.*

Effective call price The *strike price* in an *optional redemption provision* plus the accrued interest to the redemption date.

Effective rate A measure of the time value of money that fully reflects the effects of *compounding.*

Effective spread The *gross underwriting spread* adjusted for the impact of the announcement of the common stock offering on the firm's share price.

Efficiency Reflects the amount of wasted energy.

Efficient capital market A market in which new information is very quickly (within at most a few hours) reflected accurately in share prices.

Efficient frontier The combinations of securities portfolios that maximize expected return for any given level of risk or, equivalently, minimize risk for any given level of expected return.

Electronic data interchange (EDI) The exchange of information electronically, directly from one firm's computer to another's, in a structured format.

Electronic depository transfers The transfer of funds between bank accounts through the *Automated Clearing House* (ACH) system.

Employee stock plan A firm-sponsored program that enables employees to purchase shares of the firm's common stock on a preferential basis.

Endogenous variable A value determined within the context of a model. Also called simply a variable.

Enhancement An innovation that has a positive impact on one or more of a firm's existing products.

EOQ See *Economic order quantity.*

EPS See *Earnings per share.*

Equipment trust certificates Certificates issued by a trust that was formed to purchase an asset and lease it to a lessee. When the last of the certificates has been repaid, title of ownership of the asset reverts to the lessee.

Equity An ownership interest in a firm.

Equity contribution agreement An agreement to contribute equity to a project under certain specified conditions.

Equityholders Those holding some shares of the firm's equity. Also called *stockholders* and *shareholders.*

Equity multiplier Total assets divided by total common stockholders' equity; the amount of total assets per dollar of equity.

Equivalent annual annuity (EAA) The equivalent amount per year for some number of years that has a present value equal to a given amount.

Equivalent annual benefit The *equivalent annual annuity* for the net present value of an investment project.

Equivalent annual cost (EAC) The equivalent cost per year of owning an asset over its entire life.

Equivalent loan Given the after-tax payment stream associated with a lease, the maximum amount of conventional debt that the same period-by-period after-tax debt service stream is capable of supporting.

Erosion An innovation that has a negative impact on one or more of a firm's existing products.

Ethics Standards of conduct or moral judgment.

Eurobond A bond that is sold outside the country in whose currency the bond is denominated.

Eurodollar U.S. dollar-denominated deposit account in a bank outside the United States.

Eurodollar bond market The market for U.S. dollar-denominated bonds outside the United States.

European option An option that can be exercised only at its expiration.

Events of default Contractually specified events that allow lenders to demand immediate repayment of a debt

EVPI See *Expected value of perfect information.*

Excess return on the market portfolio The difference between the return on the market portfolio and the riskless rate (i.e., r_m minus r_f).

Exchange offer An offer by the firm to give one security, such as a bond or preferred stock, in exchange for another security, such as shares of common stock.

Exchange rate The price of one country's currency expressed in terms of another country's currency.

Ex-date See *Ex-dividend date.*

Ex-dividend Without the holder having the right to receive the declared but as yet unpaid dividend.

Ex-dividend date The date beginning on which a dividend is not paid to a new owner of a share of the stock.

Exercise To make the exchange specified in the option contract.

Exercise price The price for which the asset will be exchanged in an option contract if the option is exercised. Also called *strike price.*

Exercise value The amount of advantage over a current market transaction provided by an in-the-money option.

Exogenous variable A variable whose value is determined outside the model in which it is used. Also called a *parameter.*

Expectations hypothesis A theory of the *term structure of interest rates* that holds that each *forward rate* equals the expected future interest rate for the relevant period.

Expectations theory of forward exchange rates A theory of foreign exchange rates that holds that the expected future spot foreign exchange rate t periods in the future equals the current t-period forward exchange rate.

Expected future cash flows Projected future cash flows associated with an asset or decision.

Expected future return The return that is expected to be earned on an asset in the future. Also called simply the *expected return.*

Expected return The return one would expect to earn on an asset if it were purchased.

Expected value The mathematical expectation. See Equation (6.4).

Expected value of perfect information (EVPI) The expected value if the future uncertain outcomes could be known minus the expected value with no additional information.

Expensed An expenditure that is entirely recognized at the time it is incurred.

Expiration   The time when the option contract ceases to exist (expires).

Expiration date   The date on which a financial security will cease to exist. Also called *maturity date.*

Expire   To cease to exist. Also called *mature.*

Ex-rights   In connection with a *rights offering*, shares of stock that are trading without the *rights* attached.

Ex-rights date   The date on which a share of common stock begins trading *ex-rights.*

Extendible notes   Notes the maturity of which can be extended by mutual agreement of the issuer and investors.

Extraordinary positive value   A positive net present value.

Extra or special dividends   A dividend that is paid in addition to a firm's "regular" quarterly dividend, either at the same time as one of the quarterly dividends or at some other time.

Factor analysis   A statistical procedure that seeks to explain a certain phenomenon (e.g., the actual return on common stock) in terms of the behavior of a specified set of predictive factors.

Fair price   A price that does not favor either the buyers' or the sellers' side of the transaction—that is, a zero-NPV investment.

Fair-and-equitable test   A set of requirements for a *plan of reorganization* to be approved by the bankruptcy court.

FASB   The Financial Accounting Standards Board.

Feasible   A *plan of reorganization* that can be successful.

Feasible target payout ratios   *Payout ratios* that are consistent with the availability of excess funds to make cash dividend payments.

Fed   The Federal Reserve System.

Fed funds wire transfer   Electronic transfer of *federal funds* through the Federal Reserve's wire transfer system to achieve same-day availability.

Federal agency securities   Debt securities issued by a federal agency and backed to varying degrees by the federal government.

Federal funds   Uncommitted reserves that a bank has available to sell to other banks.

Finance   A discipline concerned with determining value and making decisions. The finance function allocates resources, which includes acquiring, investing, and managing the resources.

Financial asset   A contract that provides for the exchange of money at various points in time.

Financial control   The day-to-day management of the firm's costs and expenses in order

to control them in relation to the budgeted amounts.

Financial distress   When a firm is having significant trouble paying its debts as they come due.

Financial future   A contract entered into now that provides for the delivery of a specified asset in exchange for the selling price at some specified time in the future.

Financial intermediary   A firm that purchases financial securities and pays for them by issuing claims against itself (its own financial securities).

Financial lease   See *Capital lease.*

Financial leverage   The degree to which a firm's assets are financed by debt as opposed to equity.

Financial leverage clientele   A group of investors who have a preference for investing in firms that adhere to a particular financial leverage policy.

Financial markets   Markets where financial securities are bought and sold.

Financial markets and intermediaries   One of the three areas of the discipline of finance. It deals with the firm's *financing decision* from a third party's point of view.

Financial objectives   Objectives of a financial nature that the firm will strive to accomplish during the period covered by its *financial plan.*

Financial plan   A financial blueprint for the financial future of the firm.

Financial planning   The process of evaluating the investing and financing options available to the firm. It includes attempting to make optimal decisions, projecting the consequences of these decisions for the firm in the form of a financial plan, and then comparing future performance against that plan.

Financial press   That portion of the media that is devoted to reporting financial news.

Financial ratio   The result of dividing one financial statement item by another. Ratios help analysts interpret financial statements by focusing on specific relationships.

Financial risk   Risk that is created by financial leverage, which is the financial makeup, or *capital structure,* of the firm.

Financial security   A standardized financial asset such as common stock, preferred stock, bond, convertible bond, or financial future.

Financing decisions   Decisions concerning the liabilities and stockholders' equity (right) side of the firm's balance sheet, such as the decision to issue bonds.

Fisher's separation theorem   The firm's choice of investments is separate from its owners' attitudes toward investments. See also *Portfolio separation theorem.*

Five C's of Credit   Five characteristics that are used to form a judgment about a customer's creditworthiness. The five C's of credit are character, capacity, capital, collateral, and conditions.

Fixed asset turnover ratio   The ratio of sales to fixed assets.

Fixed-charge coverage ratio   Generally, the number of times that interest charges and rental payments are covered by earnings before interest, taxes, and rental payments. More specifically, earnings before interest and income taxes plus one-third rental charges, divided by interest expense plus one-third rental charges. See Equation (16.2).

Fixed-price basis   An offering of securities at a fixed price.

Fixed-price tender offer   A one-time offer to purchase a stated number of shares at a stated fixed price above the current market price.

Flight to quality   The tendency for bond investors to sell lower-grade corporate bonds and purchase Treasury bonds during periods of heightened uncertainty.

Float   The difference between the firm's available or collected balance at its bank and the firm's book or ledger balance.

Floor brokers   Independent brokers who are not affiliated with a particular brokerage house and who execute buy and sell orders for commission brokers.

Floor traders   Independent stock exchange members who buy and sell stocks only for their own account.

Flotation cost   The cost of selling a new issue of securities.

Force majeure risk   (project financing) The risk that there will be an interruption of operations for a prolonged period after the project has been completed as a result of fire, flood, storm, or some other factor beyond the control of the project's sponsors.

Foreign currency option   An option that conveys the right to buy (in the case of a call option) or sell (put option) a specified amount of a specified foreign currency at a specified price within a specified time period.

Foreign currency risk   The risk that the value of one currency expressed in terms of another currency—the foreign exchange rate—may fluctuate over time.

Foreign exchange market   The market within which one country's currency is traded for another country's currency.

Foreign exchange risk   See *Foreign currency risk.*

Formula basis   A method of selling a new issue of common stock in which the Securities and Exchange Commission declares the registration statement effective on the basis of a price formula rather than a specific price.

Forward contract A contract to exchange an asset for cash at a specific future date.

Forward discount The difference between the spot price and the forward price when the spot price exceeds the forward price.

Forward exchange rate The foreign exchange rate for a forward trade.

Forward premium The difference between the forward price and the spot price when the forward price exceeds the spot price.

Forward rate An interest rate that is expected to prevail during a future time period—for example, the 1-year borrowing rate expected to prevail two periods in the future.

Forward trade The purchase or sale of a foreign currency, commodity, or other item for future delivery for a price that is agreed to today.

Fourth market Over-the-counter market in which transactions in financial securities are made directly between institutions.

Free cash flow *Cash flow from operations* contributed by a particular capital investment project minus net incremental capital expenditures for the project.

Free rider A follower who avoids the cost and expense of finding the best course of action and by simply mimicking the behavior of a leader who made these investments.

Friction costs The costs connected with a transaction.

Frictions The "stickiness" in making transactions; the total "hassle," including the time, effort, money, and associated tax effects of gathering information and making a transaction such as buying stock or borrowing money.

Full-service lease A lease in which the lessor agrees to pay all costs of maintaining the leased item in good working condition, the cost of insurance, and any property taxes.

Fully diluted earnings per share Earnings per share calculated under the assumption that all convertible securities have been converted into common equity and all stock options have been exercised.

Future See *Financial future.*

Future A standardized forward contract that is traded on a futures market.

Future investment opportunities The options to identify additional, more valuable investment opportunities in the future that result from a current opportunity or operation.

Future value The amount of cash at a specified date in the future that is equivalent in value to a specified sum today.

Future-value annuity factor Equation (4.1) without CF.

Future-value factor Equation (3.2) without PV.

Future-value formula Equation (3.2).

General cash offer A *public offering* made to investors at large.

General partner A partner who has unlimited liability for the obligations of the partnership.

General partnership A partnership in which all the partners are *general partners.*

Generally accepted accounting principles (GAAP) A technical accounting term that encompasses the conventions, rules, and procedures necessary to define accepted accounting practice at a particular time.

Global bonds *Bonds* that are designed so as to qualify for immediate trading in any domestic capital market and in the Euromarket.

Goodwill Excess of the purchase price over the fair market value of the net assets acquired under *purchase accounting.*

Greenmail A firm's paying a takeover raider a premium to repurchase shares from the raider.

Gross profit margin Gross profit divided by sales, which is the amount of each sales dollar left over after paying the cost of goods sold.

Gross spread The fraction of the (gross) proceeds of an underwritten securities offering that is paid as compensation to the underwriters of the offering.

Gross underwriting spread See *Gross spread.*

"Hard" capital rationing Capital rationing that under no circumstances can be violated.

Hedge A transaction that reduces the risk of an investment.

Hedging Reducing the risk of an investment through the use of financial security transactions.

Hell-or-high-water contract A contract that obligates a purchaser of a project's output to make cash payments to the project in all events, even if no product is offered for sale (no matter what the circumstances, "come hell or high water").

High-coupon bond refunding *Refunding* of a high-coupon bond with a new, lower-coupon bond.

High-yield bond See *Junk bond.*

Homemade dividend Sale of some shares of stock to get cash that would be similar to getting a cash dividend.

Homogeneity The degree to which items are similar.

Homogeneous Exhibiting high degree of *homogeneity.*

Horizontal merger A merger involving two or more firms in the same industry that are both at the same stage in the production cycle—that is, two or more competitors.

Hubris An arrogance due to excessive pride and an insolence toward others.

Human capital The unique capabilities and expertise of individuals.

Hurdle rate The required return in *capital budgeting.*

Imputation tax system A tax system that reduces the impact of the two-tier tax system of double taxing of income going to shareholders by eliminating or reducing the tax on dividend income with a tax credit.

In-substance defeasance The deposit of cash and risk-free securities into an irrevocable trust sufficient to enable the issuer to remove a debt obligation from its balance sheet.

In-the-money Said of an option that currently would provide an advantage, if exercised.

Income bond A bond contract under which a firm may be allowed to forgo one or more interest payments if the firm has insufficient income.

Income statement A financial statement that reports the income, expenses, and profit (or loss) for a specific interval of time, usually a year or a quarter of a year.

Incremental cash flow Net increase in the firm's cash flow attributable to a particular capital investment project after allowing for any negative impact the project may have on existing product sales or corporate expenses; the difference between *free cash flow* with the project and free cash flow without it.

Incremental costs and benefits Costs and benefits that would occur if a particular course of action were taken compared to those that would occur if that course of action were not taken.

Independent project A project that can be chosen without requiring or precluding any other investment.

Inductive reasoning The attempt to use information about a specific situation to draw a general conclusion.

Inflation uncertainty The fact that future inflation rates are not known. It is a possible contributing factor to the makeup of the *term structure of interest rates.*

Information asymmetry A situation involving *asymmetric information*—that is, information that is known to some, but not all, participants.

Information services Organizations that furnish investment and other types of information, such as information that helps a firm monitor its cash position.

Informational efficiency The speed and accuracy with which prices reflect new information.

Initial public offering (IPO) A first-time public issuing of stock in a corporation.

Insiders Managers, controlling stockholders, and any other persons who possess privileged, nonpublic information regarding a firm.

Insolvency risk The risk that a firm will be unable to discharge its debt. Also called *bankruptcy risk*.

Insolvent When a firm is unable to pay its debts.

Installment sale The sale of an asset in exchange for a specified series of payments (the installments).

Intangible assets Real assets that do not have a physical presence, such as patents, copyrights, trademarks, and technical expertise.

Interest The cost of borrowed money.

Interest coverage ratio Earnings before interest and income taxes divided by interest expense. See Equation (16.1).

Interest coverage test A debt limitation that prohibits the issuance of additional long-term debt if the issuer's interest coverage would, as a result of the issue, fall below some specified minimum.

Interest payments Contractual debt payments based on the *coupon rate of interest* and the *principal amount* (typically calculated by multiplying these two amounts and dividing by the number of interest periods per year).

Interest rate parity A theory of relative exchange rates that states that the difference in interest rates in two currencies for a stated period should just offset the difference between the spot foreign exchange rate and the forward exchange rate corresponding to that period.

Interest rate risk The risk of a change in the value of a bond because of a change in the interest rate.

Interest rate swap An agreement to swap interest payment obligations.

Interest tax shield The reduction in income taxes that results from the tax-deductibility of interest.

Intermediate-term Typically indicates 1 to 10 years.

Intermediate-term funds Typically, funds that are lent for an initial term of between 1 and 10 years.

Internal growth rate The maximum growth rate that the firm can obtain if it relies only on spontaneous short-term liabilities and retained earnings to finance growth.

Internal rate of return (IRR) The expected return of a capital budgeting project.

International Fisher effect A theory that holds that the difference between the interest rates in two currencies should just offset the difference between the expected inflation rates in the two countries that issued the currencies.

Inventory turnover ratio An asset turnover ratio that shows how many times inventory turns over in a year.

Investment banker A *financial intermediary* that specializes in marketing new securities issues and assisting with *mergers*.

Investment decisions Decisions concerning the asset (left) side of the firm's balance sheet, such as the decision to offer a new product.

Investment-grade ratings A long-term debt rating in one of the four highest rating categories.

Investment project market line (IPML) The line of required returns for investment projects as a function of beta (nondiversifiable risk).

Investment tax credit A provision of the tax code that permits a firm that makes qualifying capital expenditures to credit a specified percentage of those expenditures against its income tax liability for the period in which the qualifying expenditures are made. The Tax Reform Act of 1986 eliminated the investment tax credit, but the credit has been eliminated and restored several times during the postwar period.

Investments As a discipline, the study of financial securities, such as stocks and bonds, from the investor's viewpoint. This area deals with the firm's financing decision, but from the other side of the transaction.

Investor relations The process by which the corporation communicates with its investors.

Invoice The written statement from a supplier about goods that were shipped, along with the amount due and the payment dates.

Invoice billing Billing system in which the invoices that are sent off at the time of customer orders are all separate bills to be paid.

Invoice date Usually the date when goods are shipped. Payment dates are set relative to the invoice date.

Involuntary liquidation preference A premium that must be paid to preferred or preference stockholders if the issuer of the stock is forced into involuntary liquidation.

IPML See *Investment Project Market Line*.

Issued shares Shares that are currently owned by investors (*outstanding shares*) or have been at one time owned by investors (*treasury shares*).

IRR See *Internal Rate of Return*.

Junk bond A bond with a *speculative-grade rating*.

Just-in-time (JIT) inventory systems Systems that schedule materials to arrive exactly as they are needed in the production process.

Law of large numbers The mean of a random sample approaches the mean (expected value) of the population as the sample grows large.

Law of One Price If two different prices exist for an asset, *arbitragers* will execute transactions until the price differential no longer exists.

Lease A long-term rental agreement; a form of secured long-term debt.

Lease rate The payment per period stated in a lease contract.

Legal defeasance The deposit of cash and permitted securities, as specified in the bond indenture, into an irrevocable trust sufficient to enable the issuer to discharge fully its obligations under the bond indenture.

Legal investments Investments that a regulated entity is permitted to make under the rules and regulations that govern its investing.

Lessee An entity that leases an asset from another entity.

Lessor An entity that leases an asset to another entity.

Letter of credit A form of guarantee of payment issued by a bank; used to guarantee the payment of interest and repayment of principal on bond issues.

Leverage The use of debt financing.

Leveraged beta The *beta* of a *leveraged required return*; that is, the beta as adjusted for the degree of leverage in the firm's *capital structure*.

Leveraged buyout The purchase of a firm that is financed with a very high proportion of debt.

Leverage clientele A group of shareholders who, because of their personal leverage, seek to invest in corporations that maintain a compatible degree of corporate leverage.

Leveraged lease A lease arrangement under which the lessor borrows a large proportion of the funds needed to purchase the asset and grants the lenders a lien on the asset and a pledge of the lease payments to secure the borrowing.

Leverage ratios Generally, measures of the relative contribution of stockholders and creditors, and of the firm's ability to pay financing charges. More specifically, the ratio of the value of the firm's debt to the total value of the firm.

Leverage rebalancing Making transactions to adjust (rebalance) a firm's leverage ratio back to its target.

Leveraged required return The *required return* on an investment when the investment is financed partially by debt.

Liability A debt claim against the firm's assets.

LIBOR The London interbank offer rate; the rate of interest that major international banks in London charge each other for borrowing.

Lien A security interest in one or more assets that is granted to lenders in connection with a secured debt financing.

Limitation on asset dispositions A *bond covenant* that restricts in some way a firm's ability to sell major assets.

Limitation on liens A *bond covenant* that restricts in some way a firm's ability to grant liens on its assets.

Limitation on merger, consolidation, or sale A *bond covenant* that restricts in some way a firm's ability to merge or consolidate with another firm.

Limitation on sale-and-leaseback A *bond covenant* that restricts in some way a firm's ability to enter into sale-and-leaseback transactions.

Limitation on subsidiary borrowing A *bond covenant* that restricts in some way a firm's ability to borrow at the subsidiary level.

Limited liability Limitation of possible loss to what has already been invested.

Limited partner A partner who has limited legal liability for the obligations of the partnership.

Limited partnership A partnership that includes one or more partners who have *limited liability*.

Line of credit An *informal* arrangement between a bank and a customer establishing a maximum loan balance that the bank will permit the borrower to maintain.

Linear regression A statistical technique for fitting a straight line to a set of data points.

Liquidation When a firm's business is terminated, all its assets are sold and the proceeds are used to pay its creditors, and any leftover proceeds are distributed to its shareholders.

Liquidation rights The rights of a firm's securityholders in the event the firm liquidates.

Liquidity The extent to which something can be sold quickly and easily without loss of value.

Liquidity preference The argument that greater *liquidity* is valuable, all else equal. A possible contributing factor to the make up of the *term structure of interest rates*.

Liquidity ratios Ratios that measure a firm's ability to meet its short-term financial obligations on time.

Loan amortization schedule The schedule for repaying the interest and principal on a loan.

Lockbox A collection and processing service provided to firms by banks, which collect payments from a dedicated postal box that the firm directs its customers to send payment to. The banks make several collections per day, process the payments immediately, and deposit the funds into the firm's bank account.

Log-linear least-squares method A statistical technique for fitting a curve to a set of data points. One of the variables is transformed by taking its logarithm, and then a straight line is fitted to the transformed set of data points.

Lognormal probability distribution A standardized probability distribution wherein the logarithm of the *random variable* follows the *standard normal probability distribution*.

Long position Ownership of a financial security.

Long-term In accounting information, one year or more.

Long-term debt Debt with more than one year remaining to maturity.

Long-term debt ratio The ratio of long-term debt to total capitalization.

Long-term financial plan Financial plan covering two or more years of future operations.

Low-coupon bond refunding *Refunding* of a low-coupon bond with a new, higher-coupon bond.

Mail float The time that elapses while an invoice or payment of an invoice is in the mail.

Majority voting A system of voting for directors of a corporation in which each shareholder has one vote for each director and a simple majority can elect each director.

Management fee The portion of the *gross underwriting spread* that compensates the securities firms that manage a public offering for their management efforts.

Management's discussion A report from management to the stockholders that accompanies the firm's financial statements in the annual report. This report explains the period's financial results and enables management to discuss other ideas that may not be apparent in the financial statements in the annual report.

Managerial decisions Decisions concerning the operation of the firm, such as the choice of firm size, firm growth, and employee compensation.

Managers Decision-making employees.

Mandatory redemption schedule Schedule according to which *sinking fund* payments must be made.

Margin of safety With respect to working capital management, the difference between (1) the amount of long-term financing and (2) the sum of fixed assets and the permanent component of current assets.

Margin requirements In a securities transaction, regulations that specify the minimum portion of the purchase price that must be paid in cash.

Marginal Incremental.

Marginal tax rate The tax rate applied to the last, or marginal, dollar of income.

Market maker A person who facilitates liquidity by transacting in the asset. Called a *specialist* in a stock market.

Market overhang The theory that in certain situations, institutions wish to sell their shares but postpone share sales because large sell orders under current market conditions would drive down the share price and that the consequent threat of securities sales will tend to retard the rate of share price appreciation. Support for the theory is largely anecdotal.

Market portfolio A value-weighted portfolio of every asset in a market.

Market return The return on the market portfolio.

Market segmentation The theory that the *term structure of interest rates* is determined by the relative demand for and supply of bonds within different maturity ranges. See also *Segmented market*.

Market-to-book ratio The ratio of the market price per share to the book value per share.

Market value The price for which something could be bought or sold in a reasonable length of time, where "reasonable length of time" is defined in terms of the item's liquidity.

Market value ratios Ratios that relate the market price of the firm's common stock to selected financial statement items.

Master limited partnership (MLP) A publicly traded limited partnership.

Materials requirement planning (MRP) systems Computer-based systems that plan backward from the production schedule to make purchases and manage inventory levels.

Mature   To cease to exist; to *expire*.

Maturity   The end of a bond's life.

Maturity date   The date a bond's life ends; the date by which it must be fully repaid.

Max function   A mathematical function that selects the item of greatest value from a list.

Mean   The *expected value* of a *random variable*.

Mean of the sample   The arithmetic average; that is, the sum of the observations divided by the number of observations.

Medium-term notes   Unsecured notes, similar to *commercial paper*, that are registered with the SEC and whose maturities range from 9 months to 30 years.

Merger   A combination of two firms in which the *acquiror* absorbs all the assets and liabilities of the *acquiree* and assumes the acquiree's business.

Mimic   An imitation that sends a false signal.

Min function   A mathematical function that selects the item of least value from a list.

Minority interest   An outside ownership interest in a subsidiary that is consolidated (with the parent) for financial reporting purposes.

MLP   See *Master limited partnership*.

Modeling   The process of creating a depiction of reality, such as a graph, picture, or mathematical representation.

Money market   Market for short-term financial instruments.

Money market preferred stock   See *Auction rate preferred stock*.

Money market security   A short-term, low-risk obligation without collateral.

Monitor   To seek information about an agent's behavior; a device that provides such information.

Monte Carlo simulation   An analytical technique for solving a problem by performing a large number of trial runs (called simulations) and inferring a solution from the collective results of the trial runs. Also called simply *simulation*.

Moral hazard   A situation wherein an agent can take unseen actions for personal benefit when such actions are costly to the principal.

Mortgage   A legal document granting a lien on one or more specific assets.

Mortgage bond   A bond that is secured by a lien on one or more specific assets.

Multinational corporation   A firm that operates in more than one country.

Mutual funds   Funds that pool money contributed by individuals or other entities and invest the money in portfolios of securities.

Mutually exclusive   Two projects that cannot both be undertaken; that is, choosing one precludes choosing the other.

NASDAQ   The National Association of Securities Dealers Automated Quotations system.

Natural logarithm   Logarithm to the base e (approximately 2.7183).

Negative covenant (of a bond)   A *bond covenant* that limits or prohibits altogether certain actions unless the bondholders agree.

Negative pledge clause   A *bond covenant* that requires the borrower to grant lenders a lien equivalent to any liens that may be granted in the future to any other currently unsecured lenders.

Negotiated markets   Markets in which each transaction is separately negotiated between buyer and seller (i.e., an investor and a *dealer*).

Negotiated offering   An offering of securities for which the terms, including underwriters' compensation, have been negotiated between the issuer and the underwriters.

Net adjusted present value   The *adjusted present value* minus the initial cost of an investment.

Net advantage of refunding   The net present value of the savings from a *refunding*.

Net advantage to leasing   The net present value of entering into a lease financing arrangement rather than borrowing the necessary funds and buying the asset.

Net advantage to merging   The difference in total post- and pre-merger market value minus the cost of the merger.

Net assets   The difference between total assets on the one hand and current liabilities and noncapitalized long-term liabilities on the other.

Net-benefit-to-leverage factor   A linear approximation of a factor, T^*, that enables us to operationalize the total impact of leverage on firm value in the capital market imperfections view of capital structure.

Net book value   The current book value of an asset or liability; that is, its original book value net of any accounting adjustments such as depreciation.

Net lease   A lease arrangement under which the lessee is responsible for all property taxes, maintenance expenses, insurance, and other costs associated with keeping the asset in good working condition.

Net period   The period of time between the end of the *discount period* and the date payment is due.

Net present value (NPV)   The present value of the expected future cash flows minus the cost.

Net present value of future investments (NPVFI)   The present value of the total sum of NPVs expected to result from all of the firm's future investments.

Net profit margin   Net income divided by sales; the amount of each sales dollar left over after all expenses have been paid.

Net salvage value   The after-tax net cash flow for terminating the project.

Net working capital   Literally, current assets minus current liabilities. Often referred to simply as *working capital*. See also "A Simple Example of Working Capital" in Chapter 11.

Net worth   Common stockholders' equity (consisting of common stock, surplus, and retained earnings).

Nexus (of contracts)   A set or collection of something.

Nominal   In name only. Differences in compounding cause the nominal rate to differ from the effective rate. Inflation causes the purchasing power of money to differ from one time to another.

Nominal annual rate   An effective rate per period multiplied by the number of periods in a year.

Noncash charge   A cost, such as depreciation, depletion, and amortization, that does not involve any cash outflow.

Nondiversifiability of human capital   The difficulty of diversifying one's *human capital* (the unique capabilities and expertise of individuals) and employment effort.

Nondiversifiable risk   Risk that cannot be eliminated by diversification.

Nonrecourse   Without recourse, as in a nonrecourse lease.

Nonredeemable   Not permitted, under the terms of the indenture, to be redeemed.

Nonrefundable   Not permitted, under the terms of the indenture, to be refunded.

Normal probability distribution   A probability distribution for a *continuous random variable* that is symmetric around the mean, completely specified once the *mean* and *variance* (or *standard deviation*) are known, and bell-shaped when graphed.

Normal random variable   A random variable that has a *normal probability distribution*.

Note   A debt obligation with an initial maturity between one and ten years.

Note agreement   A contract for *privately placed* debt.

Notes to the financial statements   A detailed set of notes immediately following the financial statements that explain and expand on the information in the financial statements.

NPV See *Net present value.*

NPV profile A graph of NPV as a function of the discount rate.

NPVFI See *Net present value of future investments.*

NYSE The New York Stock Exchange.

Odd lot A number of securities not equal to a *round lot*; in the case of common stock, fewer than 100 shares.

Odd-lot dealer A broker who combines *odd lots* of securities from multiple *buy orders* or *sell orders* into *round lots* and executes transactions in those round lots.

Off-balance-sheet financing Financing not required to be reported on the firm's balance sheet.

Offering memorandum A document prepared to outline the terms of securities to be offered in a *private placement.*

Open account A credit account where the customer makes purchases and the signed invoices are evidence of indebtedness.

Open-market purchase The purchase of securities in one or more transactions arranged in the open market.

Open-market purchase program A systematic program of repurchasing shares of stock in market transactions at current market prices, in competition with other prospective investors.

Operating lease A lease obligation that does not have to be capitalized on the face of the balance sheet.

Operating leverage The relative mix of fixed and variable costs to provide a product or service.

Operating profit margin The ratio of operating income to net sales.

Operating risk The inherent or fundamental risk of a firm, without regard to *financial risk.* The risk that is created by *operating leverage.* Also called *business risk.*

OPM See *Option pricing model.*

Opportunity cost The difference between the value of a course of action and the value of the next best alternative.

Opportunity cost of capital The price per unit of financial capital that users of funds must pay suppliers of funds in the capital market.

Optimal contract The contract that balances the three types of agency costs (contracting, monitoring, and misbehavior) against one another to minimize the total cost.

Option A right to do something without an obligation to do it.

Option pricing model (OPM) A model for valuing options.

Optional redemption provision Provision of a bond indenture that governs the issuer's ability to call the bonds for redemption prior to their scheduled maturity date.

Optionholder The person in the long-position side of an option transaction; the owner.

Optionwriter The person in the short-position side of an option transaction; the person with the obligation; the seller of the option.

Organized exchange A securities marketplace wherein purchasers and sellers regularly gather to trade securities according to the formal rules adopted by the exchange.

Original maturity The length of a bond's life when it is issued.

OTC See *Over-the-counter market.*

Out-of-the-money Said of an option that currently would provide a disadvantage, if exercised.

Outstanding shares Shares that are currently owned by investors.

Oversubscription privilege In connection with a rights offering, the opportunity to subscribe for additional shares that other shareholders have not subscribed to.

Over-the-counter market (OTC) Any alternative to an *organized exchange.* Often used loosely to refer to NASDAQ, a securities market that is less structured than the NYSE, AMEX, CBOE, and other exchanges.

Pac-Man strategy Takeover defense strategy in which the prospective acquiree retaliates against the acquiror's tender offer by launching its own tender offer for the other firm.

Par value The amount of money to be repaid for a bond at the end of its life. The par value is also called the *face value.*

Parameter A representation that characterizes a part of a model (e.g., a growth rate), the value of which is determined outside of the model. Sometimes called an *exogenous variable.*

Partnership Shared ownership among two or more individuals, some of whom may, but do not necessarily, have limited liability. See *General partnership, Limited partnership,* and *Master limited partnership.*

Payable through drafts A method of making payment that is used to maintain control over payments made on behalf of the firm by personnel in noncentral locations. The payer's bank delivers the payable through draft to the payer, which must approve it and return it to the bank before payment can be made.

Payback The length of time it takes to recover the initial cost of an project, without regard to the time value of money.

Payment date The date on which each *shareholder of record* will be sent a check for the declared dividend.

Payout ratio Generally, the proportion of earnings paid out to common stockholders as cash dividends. More specifically, the firm's cash dividend divided by the firm's earnings in the same period.

P/E ratio The current stock price divided by the most recent annualized earnings per share.

Pecking-order view (of capital structure) The argument that external financing transaction costs, especially those associated with the problem of adverse selection, create a dynamic environment in which firms have a preference, or pecking, order of preferred sources of financing, when all else is equal. Internally generated funds are the most preferred, new debt is next, debt-equity combinations is next, and new external equity is the least preferred source.

Perfect capital market A market in which there are never any arbitrage opportunities.

Perfect competition An idealized market environment in which every market participant is too small to affect the market price by acting on its own.

Perfect market view (of capital structure) Analysis of a decision (capital structure), in a perfect capital market environment, that shows the irrelevance of capital structure in a perfect capital market.

Perfect market view (of dividend policy) Analysis of a decision (dividend policy), in a perfect capital market environment, that shows the irrelevance of dividend policy in a perfect capital market.

Perfected first lien A first lien that is duly recorded with the cognizant governmental body so that the lender will be able to act on it should the borrower default.

Perpetuity An infinite annuity. A series of identical cash flows each period forever.

Perquisites Personal benefits, including direct benefits, such as the use of a firm car or expense account for personal business, and indirect benefits, such as an up-to-date office decor.

Personal tax view (of capital structure) The argument that the difference in personal tax rates between income from debt and income from equity eliminates the disadvantage from the double taxation (corporate and personal) of income from equity.

Plan of reorganization A plan for reorganizing a firm during the Chapter 11 bankruptcy process.

Planned capital expenditure program

Capital expenditure program as outlined in the corporate *financial plan*.

Planned financing program   Program of short-term and long-term financing as outlined in the corporate *financial plan*.

Planning horizon   The length of time a model projects into the future.

Poison pill   Anti-takeover device that gives a prospective acquiree's shareholders the right to buy shares of the firm or shares of anyone who acquires the firm at a deep discount to their fair market value. Named after the cyanide pill that secret agents are instructed to swallow if capture is imminent.

Pooling of interests   A method of accounting for a merger in which the merging entities' financial results are combined as though the two entities had always been a single entity.

Portfolio   (1) The collection of securities that an investor owns. (2) The collection of real and financial assets that a firm owns.

Portfolio separation theorem   An investor's choice of a risky investment portfolio is separate from her attitudes toward risk. See also *Fisher's separation theorem*.

Position   Having a claim on (owning) (long), or obligation concerning (owing) (short), an asset or option; that is, having bought or sold an asset or option.

Positive covenant   (of a bond) A *bond covenant* that specifies certain actions the firm must take. Also called an *affirmative covenant*.

Post-audit   A set of procedures for evaluating a capital budgeting decision after the fact.

Postponement option   The option of postponing a project without eliminating the possibility of undertaking it.

Preauthorized checks (PACs)   Checks that are authorized by the payer in advance and are written either by the payee or by the payee's bank and then deposited in the payee's bank account.

Preauthorized electronic debits (PADs)   Debits to its bank account authorized in advance by the payer. The payer's bank sends payment to the payee's bank through the *Automated Clearing House* (ACH) system.

Precautionary demand (for money)   The need to meet unexpected or extraordinary contingencies with a buffer stock of cash.

Precautionary motive   A desire to hold cash in order to be able to deal effectively with unexpected events that require a cash outlay.

Preemptive right   The existing shareholders' right to subscribe for a new common share issue or for a new issue of securities that are convertible into common shares be-

fore any shares can be offered to other investors.

Preference stock   A security that ranks junior to *preferred stock* but senior to *common stock* in the right to receive payments from the firm; essentially junior preferred stock.

Preferred stock   A hybrid security that combines certain features of debt and certain features of common stock, ranking between the two in the right to receive payment from the firm.

Preferred stock agreement   A contract for *preferred stock*.

Preliminary prospectus   A preliminary version of the *prospectus*.

Premium bond   A bond that is selling for more than its par value.

Prepackaged bankruptcy   A *bankruptcy* in which a debtor and its creditors pre-negotiate a *plan or reorganization* and then file it along with the bankruptcy petition.

Present value   The amount of cash today that is equivalent in value to a payment, or to a stream of payments, to be received in the future.

Present-value annuity factor   Equation (4.2) without CF.

Present-value factor   Equation (3.3) without FV.

Present-value formula   Equation (3.3).

Price-earnings ratio, or P/E   A stock's market price per share divided by the firm's annual earnings per share.

Primary market   A market consisting of newly created securities.

Primary offering   A firm selling some of its own newly issued shares to investors.

Prime rate   The benchmark interest rate that banks charge large, creditworthy firms.

Principal   (1) The total amount of money being borrowed. (2) The party affected by agent decisions in a principal-agent relationship.

Principal-agent relationship   A situation that can be modeled as one person, an *agent*, who acts on behalf of another person, a *principal*.

Principal amount   The face amount of debt; also, the amount borrowed. Often called simply *principal*.

Private placement   The sale of securities directly to investors (often institutions) without a *public offering*.

Pro forma capital structure analysis   A method of analyzing the impact of alternative capital structure choices on a firm's credit statistics and reported financial results, especially to determine whether the firm will be able to use projected tax shield benefits fully.

Pro forma financial statements   Financial

statements as adjusted to reflect a projected or planned transaction.

Pro forma statement   A financial statement showing the forecast (or projected) operating results or impact of a particular transaction, as in pro forma income statements in the *long-term financial plan* or the pro forma *balance sheet* for a share repurchase.

Probability   The relative likelihood of a particular outcome among all possible outcomes.

Probability density function   The probability function for a *continuous random variable*.

Probability function   A function that assigns a *probability* to each and every possible outcome.

Production payment financing   A method of nonrecourse asset-based financing in which a specified percentage of revenue realized from the sale of the project's output is used to pay debt service.

Profitability index (PI)   The present value of the future cash flows divided by the initial investment. Also called the *benefit-cost ratio*.

Profitability ratios   Ratios that focus on the profitability of the firm. *Profit margins* measure performance in relation to sales, and *rate of return ratios* measure performance relative to some measure of the size of the investment.

Progress review   A periodic review of a capital investment project to evaluate its continued economic viability.

Progressive tax system   A tax system wherein the average tax rate increases for some increases in income but never decreases with an increase in income.

Project financing   A form of asset-based financing in which a firm finances a discrete set of assets (project) on a stand-alone basis.

Prospectus   A legal disclosure document that must be distributed both to purchasers and to persons whose purchase interest is solicited in connection with a public offering of securities.

Proxy contest   A battle for the control of a firm in which the dissident group seeks, from the firm's other shareholders, the right to vote those shareholders' shares in favor of the dissident group's slate of directors.

Proxy fight   See *Proxy contest*.

Public offering   The sale of registered securities by the issuer (or underwriters acting on behalf of the issuer) in the public market.

Publicly traded assets   Assets that can be traded in a public market, such as the *stock market*.

Purchase   To *buy*, or take a *long position*.

Purchase accounting Method of accounting for a *merger* in which the *acquiror* is treated as having purchased the assets and assumed the liabilities of the *acquiree*, which are all written up or down to their respective fair market values, the difference between the purchase price and the net assets acquired being attributed to *goodwill*.

Purchase agreement As used in connection with project financing, an agreement to purchase a specific amount of project output per period.

Purchase and sale A method of securities distribution in which the securities firm purchases the securities from the issuer for its own account at a stated price and then resells them, as contrasted with a *best-efforts* sale.

Purchase method A *merger* or *consolidation* in which one of the firms is identified as the acquiror.

Purchasing power parity A theory of relative exchange rates that states that the expected difference in inflation rates for two countries over some period must equal the differential between the spot exchange rate currently prevailing and the spot exchange rate expected at the end of the period.

Pure-discount bond A bond that will make only one payment of principal and interest. Also called a *zero-coupon bond* or a *single-payment bond*.

Put an option To *exercise* a put option.

Put-call parity The relationship between the value of a put option and the value of a call option.

Put option The right to *sell* something at a given price during the life of the option.

Put price The price at which the asset will be sold if a put option is exercised. Also called the *strike price* and the *exercise price*.

Pyramid scheme An illegal, fraudulent scheme in which a con artist convinces victims to invest by promising an extraordinary return but simply uses newly invested funds to pay off any investors who insist on terminating their investment.

Quick (acid test) ratio A liquidity ratio that measures the number of times a firm can cover its current liabilities using its current assets (but not including its inventories, which are less liquid).

Random variable A function that assigns a real number to each and every possible outcome of a random experiment.

Randomized strategy A strategy of introducing into the decision-making process a random element that is designed to reduce the information content of the decision-maker's observed choices.

Range The difference between the highest and the lowest possible values.

Rate of interest The rate, as a proportion of the principal, at which *interest* is computed.

Rate of return ratios Ratios that are designed to measure the profitability of the firm in relation to various measures of the funds invested in the firm.

Raw material supply agreement As used in connection with project financing, an agreement to furnish a specified amount per period of a specified raw material.

Real assets Identifiable assets, such as buildings, equipment, patents, and trademarks, as distinguished from a financial obligation.

Real capital Wealth that can be represented in financial terms, such as savings account balances, *financial securities*, and real estate.

Real rate of interest The rate of interest excluding the effect of inflation; that is, the rate that is earned in terms of constant-purchasing-power dollars.

Realized return The return that is actually gotten over a given time period.

Rebalancing (a debt level) The process of making transactions that change the firm's capital structure back to its target.

Receivables balance fractions The percentage of a month's sales that remain uncollected (and part of accounts receivable) at the end of the month of sale and at the end of succeeding months.

Receivables turnover ratio The number of times receivables turn over in a year, measured as the total annual credit sales divided by the current accounts receivable balance.

Record date A date established to determine who will actually get the dividend check for a share of stock, in case the share is sold between when the dividend is declared and when it is paid.

Red herring A *preliminary prospectus*.

Redeemable Eligible for redemption under the terms of the indenture.

Redemption cushion The percentage by which the *conversion value* of a convertible security exceeds the redemption price (*strike price*).

Refundable Eligible for refunding under the terms of the indenture.

Refunding Issuing new debt and using the net proceeds to retire previously outstanding debt.

Registration statement A legal document that is filed with the Securities and Exchange Commission to register securities for public offering.

Regression toward the mean The tendency for subsequent observations of a *random variable* to be closer to its mean.

Reinvestment rate assumption The return that the cash flows from a capital budgeting project are expected (assumed) to earn from being reinvested.

Remaining maturity The length of time remaining until a bond's maturity.

Remote disbursement Technique that involves writing checks drawn on banks in remote locations so as to increase disbursement float.

Reoffering yield In a *purchase and sale*, the yield to maturity at which the *underwriter* offers to sell the bonds to investors.

Reorganization Creating a plan to restructure a debtor's business and restore its financial health.

Replacement cycle The frequency with which an asset is replaced by an equivalent asset.

Repo An agreement in which one party sells a security to another party and agrees to repurchase it on a specified date for a specified price.

Repurchase agreements See *Repo*.

Required return The minimum *expected return* you would require to be willing to purchase the asset (that is, to make the investment).

Residual assets Assets that remain after sufficient assets are dedicated to meet all senior securityholders' claims in full.

Residual claim The claim on what is left after all prior claims have been settled; the "last" claim.

Residual method A method of allocating the purchase price for the acquisition of another firm (a merger) among the acquired assets.

Residual risk All the (remaining) risk that is not borne by senior providers of capital. The common stockholders of a firm bear the residual risk of the firm.

Retail credit Credit granted by a firm to consumers for the purchase of goods or services. Also called *consumer credit*.

Retained earnings Accounting earnings that are retained by the firm for reinvestment in its operations; earnings that are not paid out as dividends.

Retire To extinguish a security, as in paying off a debt. Also expressed as *clearing a position*.

Return on assets (ROA) Net income divided by total assets.

Return on average assets The ratio of the sum of operating income and other income to average total tangible assets.

Return on average common equity The ratio of earnings available for common stock before extraordinary items to average common stockholders' equity.

Return on average invested capital The ratio of the sum of operating income and other income net of income taxes to average net tangible assets.

Return on equity (ROE) Net income available to common stockholders divided by common stockholders' equity.

Return on investment (ROI) A measure of investment return, the definition for which varies from firm to firm.

Reverse stock split A recombination of outstanding shares of common stock that reduces the number of shares outstanding proportionately. See also *stock split*.

Reverse subsidiary merger A merger involving a subsidiary of the *acquiror* and an *acquiree* in which the acquiree is the surviving entity (and becomes a subsidiary of the acquiror).

Revolving credit An agreement that represents a legal commitment to lend up to a specified maximum amount any time during a specified period.

Revolving credit agreement A *legal* commitment wherein a bank promises to lend a customer up to a specified maximum amount during a specified period.

Right A short-lived (typically less than 90 days) call option for purchasing additional stock in a firm, issued by the firm to all its shareholders on a pro rata basis.

Rights offerings The process of issuing *rights*.

Rights-on Shares trading with the rights attached.

Risk Typically defined as the standard deviation of the return on total investment.

Risk-adjusted probability A probability used to determine a "sure" expected value (sometimes called a *certainty equivalent*) that would be equivalent to the actual risky expected value.

Risk-averse Choosing lower risk when alternative returns are equal, or choosing higher returns when alternative risks are equal.

Risk classes Groups of projects that have approximately the same amount of risk.

Risk management The process of identifying and evaluating risks and selecting and managing techniques to adapt to risk exposures.

Risk-neutral Insensitive to risk.

Risk-prone Willing to pay money to transfer risk from others.

Riskless arbitrage The simultaneous purchase and sale of the same asset to yield a profit. See also *arbitrage*.

Riskless rate The rate earned on a riskless investment. Denoted r_f, it is typically modeled as the rate earned on 90-day U.S. Treasury bills.

Risky debt Debt that has some possibility of not being fully repaid on time.

Round lot A standardized number of financial securities, 100 shares in the case of most common stocks. (For some high-priced stocks, a round lot consists of 10 shares.)

Rule 415 Rule enacted in 1982 that permits firms to file *shelf registration* statements.

Safety stock Inventory buffer stock that a firm holds to hedge uncertainties in delivery times, usage, or sales.

Sale-and-leaseback An agreement to sell an asset and lease it back from the purchaser.

Salvage value The before-tax difference between the sale price of the assets and the clean-up and removal expenses.

Seasoned offering A public issuing of shares by a corporation that already has shares that are trading in the capital markets.

SEC See *Securities and Exchange Commission*.

Secondary market A market where securities that are already outstanding are traded.

Secondary offering Shareholders (usually insiders or large institutions) selling previously issued shares they own to investors at large in an offering that has been registered with the *SEC*.

Secured debt Debt that identifies specific assets that can be taken over by the debtholder in case of default.

Securities and Exchange Commission (SEC) Federal government agency established in 1933 to regulate the public securities markets.

Security A claim on future cash flows.

Security analysts Financial professionals who study individual firms and industries in order to make earnings forecasts, prepare research reports, and make buy/sell/hold recommendations for individual stocks.

Security market line (SML) The linear relationship between required return and beta.

Segmented market A market in which participants provide or demand products with only certain attributes—for example, debt of a particular maturity, firms with a particular capital structure, or firms with a particular dividend policy. See also *Clientele effect*.

Sell To sell, or *take a short position*.

Sell order A directive to *sell* one or more financial securities.

Selling concession The portion of the *gross underwriting spread* that compensates the se-

curities firms for their efforts to sell the securities.

Semi-strong form of capital market efficiency Prices reflect all *publicly available* information about an asset's value.

Senior Having a prior claim, as in senior debt, which has, relative to *subordinated* debt, a prior claim to the cash flow and the assets of the firm in the event of liquidation.

Sensitivity analysis Varying key parameters of a process to determine the sensitivity of outcomes to that variation.

Separation theorem The choice of investments is separate from investor attitudes. See also *Fisher's separation theorem* and *Portfolio separation theorem*.

Set-of-contracts model A model that describes the firm as a collection of implicit and explicit contracts among the *stakeholders*.

Share repurchase A firm's purchase of its own shares of stock.

Shareholders Those holding some shares of the firm's equity. Also called *stockholders* and *equityholders*.

Shareholder of record The owner as determined by the *record date*.

Shareholder wealth maximization Maximizing the value of the firm to its owners. For a publicly traded firm, the value of the firm to its owners is the market value of the shares owned.

Shark repellents Defensive measures taken by a prospective takeover target to try to ward off potential suitors.

Shelf basis The process of issuing securities that have previously been registered by filing a *shelf registration* statement.

Shelf registration The process of registering a two-year inventory of securities by filing a single registration statement.

Shirking An agent's putting forth less than "full effort."

Short The obligation side of the transaction. With respect to options, the party that must deliver (call option) or take (put option) the asset in the event the option is exercised; the party that has the obligation (to buy or sell) without the right to do so.

Short position The mirror image of owning an asset (a *long position*). A position of obligation, for example, to return borrowed securities, to deliver on a futures contract, or to sell (call) or buy (put) when the option-holder exercises his option.

Short selling Borrowing an asset, such as a bond or stock, and selling it to a third party.

Short-term Typically, less than a year.

Short-term debt Debt with one year or less remaining to maturity.

Short-term financial plan A financial plan that covers the coming fiscal year.

Short-term funds See *Short-term debt.*

Short-term investment services Services that assist firms in making short-term investments.

Signaling The process of conveying information through a firm's actions.

Signaling view (of dividend policy) The argument that dividend changes are important signals to investors about changes in management's expectation about future earnings.

Simple compound growth method A method of calculating the growth rate by relating the terminal value to the initial value and assuming a constant percentage annual rate of growth between these two values.

Simple interest Interest that is received on the initial principal amount only, rather than compounded.

Simulation The use of a mathematical model to imitate a situation many times in order to estimate the likelihood of various possible outcomes.

Single-payment bond A bond that will make only one payment of principal and interest.

Sinking fund A bond provision specifying principal repayments prior to the maturity date.

SML See *Security market line.*

"Soft" capital rationing Capital rationing that under certain circumstances can be violated or even viewed as made up of targets rather than absolute constraints.

Sole proprietorship A firm wherein a single individual owns all the firm's assets directly and is responsible for all its liabilities.

Span To cover all contingencies within a specified range.

Specialist A person charged by a stock exchange with the responsibility of maintaining an orderly, continuous market in a stock (that is, a market wherein its price changes smoothly); a *market maker* in a stock market.

Speculative demand (for money) The need for cash to take advantage of investment opportunities that may arise.

Speculative-grade rating A long-term debt rating other than an *investment-grade rating.*

Speculative motive A desire to hold cash for the purpose of being in a position to exploit any attractive investment opportunity requiring a cash expenditure that might arise.

Speculator One who engages in a speculative activity by taking a position (for example, in a security) in the hope of earning an extraordinary return.

Split-rate tax system A tax system that taxes retained earnings at a higher rate than earnings that are distributed as dividends.

Spot foreign exchange rate Foreign exchange rate for a spot trade.

Spot market A market to trade today an asset that is also traded on a futures market.

Spot rate The rate that applies in transactions executed for "immediate" delivery.

Spot trade The purchase or sale of a foreign currency, commodity, or other item for "immediate" delivery.

Stakeholder Anyone with a legitimate claim of any sort on the firm, such as stockholders, bondholders, creditors, employees, customers, the community, and the government.

Standard deviation The square root of the *variance.*

Standard normal probability distribution A *normal probability distribution* in which the *mean* is zero and the *variance* is 1.

Standby agreement Agreement under which a securities firm agrees to stand ready to buy any unsold shares at a predetermined price following a rights offering or to buy any shares resulting from bonds that were not converted during a forced conversion, also at a predetermined price.

Standby fee A fee paid to an underwriter in connection with an underwritten rights offering or an underwritten forced conversion to compensate the underwriter for standing ready (standing by) to take up rights or acquire convertible bonds, exercise the options, and sell the shares obtained upon exercise.

Stated Specified, as in stated rate of interest.

Statement billing Billing method in which the sales for a period such as a month (for which a customer also receives invoices) are collected into a single statement, and the customer must pay all of the invoices represented on the statement.

Statement of cash flows Financial statement that shows cash receipts and payments over a period of time.

Statement-of-cash-flows method A method of cash budgeting that is organized along the lines of the *statement of cash flows.*

Step up To increase, as in step up the tax basis of an asset.

Stock A share of stock is equity in a corporation.

Stock dividends A bookkeeping reapportioning of the claim size of a share of stock so that there are more shares and each share has a proportionately smaller ownership interest. For example, if a firm declares a 5% stock dividend, a shareholder will receive 5 new

shares for every 100 shares owned. Money from the retained earnings account is transferred to the "Paid-in Capital" and "Capital Contributed in Excess of Par Value" accounts.

Stock market The collective stock exchanges, most notably the New York, American, NASDAQ, London, and Tokyo markets.

Stock repurchase A firm's repurchase of outstanding shares of its own *common stock.*

Stock split A bookkeeping reapportioning of the claim size of a share of stock so that there are more shares and each share has a proportionately smaller ownership interest. For example, if a firm declares a 2-for-1 stock split, then each shareholder owns twice as many shares, but each new share has half the claim size of each old share. The stock's par value per share is adjusted to reflect the change, but no money is transferred among balance sheet accounts.

Stockholders Those holding some shares of the firm's equity. Also called *shareholders* and *equityholders.*

Stockholders' equity Residual ownership claims against the firm's assets.

Stopping curve A curve showing the refunding rates for different points in time at which the expected value of refunding immediately equals the expected value of waiting to refund.

Stopping curve refunding rate A refunding rate that falls on the *stopping curve.*

Straight-line An amount divided into equal per-period amounts over some number of periods, as in *straight-line depreciation.*

Straight-line depreciation Depreciation calculated under the *straight-line* method— that is, into equal annual amounts.

Strategic Related to the long-range strategy of the firm.

Stratified random sampling A sampling procedure in which the population is divided into strata, each with a different set of characteristics, and the sample is drawn randomly from each stratum; the procedure is designed to increase the likelihood of achieving a "representative" sample.

Strike price The price specified in the option contract for buying or selling the underlying asset. That is, the asset is exchanged for the strike price.

Strong form of capital market efficiency Prices reflect *all* information that exists about an asset's value.

Subjective probabilities Probabilities that are determined subjectively (for example, on the basis of judgment rather than using statistical sampling.

Subordinated Of lesser priority with respect to payment obligations, as in subordinated debentures.

Subscribe To purchase financial securities, as in subscribing for additional shares through a *rights offering* or subscribing for shares of newly issued securities.

Subscription period The time until the option to *subscribe* expires.

Subscription price The price at which an investor can *subscribe*.

Subsidiary merger A merger involving a subsidiary of the *acquiror* and an *acquiree* in which the subsidiary of the acquiror is the surviving entity.

Sufficient statistic A statistic that contains all of the information pertaining to the value of a parameter that is in a sample.

Sum-of-the-years'-digits A method of computing depreciation expense.

Sunk cost A cost that has already been incurred and cannot be altered by subsequent decisions. Previously incurred sunk costs can be ignored when making most decisions.

Sustainable growth rate The rate at which the firm can grow without increasing its financial leverage. Sustainable growth is financed with spontaneous short-term funds, retained earnings, and additional long-term debt that maintains its financial leverage.

Sweep account A non-interest-bearing transaction bank account out of which all funds remaining at the end of each business day are automatically "swept" and deposited into an interest-bearing account or invested in some other manner that the account holder has previously specified.

Syndicate A group of securities firms formed to share the underwriting risk in connection with an *underwritten offering* of securities.

Syndicated public offering A *public offering* that is *underwritten* by a *syndicate*.

Synergistic effect A violation of value-additivity whereby the value of the combination is greater than the sum of the individual values.

Systematic risk Risk that cannot be diversified away by combining securities into portfolios.

Take a position To *buy* or *sell*; that is, to have some amount that is owned or owed on an asset or option.

Take-or-pay contract A contract that obligates the purchaser to take any product that is offered to it (and pay the cash purchase price) or pay a specified amount if it refuses to take the product.

Take-up fee A fee paid to an underwriter in connection with an underwritten rights offering or an underwritten forced conversion as compensation for each share of *common stock* the underwriter obtains and must resell upon exercise of rights or conversion of bonds.

Tangible assets Real assets that have a physical presence, such as buildings, equipment, and raw materials.

Tax clawback agreement An agreement to contribute as equity to a project the value of all previously realized project-related tax benefits (not already clawed back) to the extent required to cover any cash deficiency of the project.

Tax differential view (of dividend policy) The view that shareholders prefer capital gains over dividends, and hence low payout ratios, because capital gains are effectively taxed at a lower rate than dividends.

Tax-free acquisition A *merger* or *consolidation* in which (1) the acquiror's tax basis in each asset whose ownership is transferred in the transaction is generally the same as the acquiree's and (2) each seller who receives only stock does not have to pay any tax on the gain he realizes until the shares are sold.

Tax shield The reduction in income taxes that results from taking an allowable deduction from taxable income.

Tax-timing option The option to sell an asset and claim a loss for tax purposes or not to sell the asset and defer a capital gain tax.

Taxable acquisition A *merger* or *consolidation* that is not a *tax-free acquisition*. The selling shareholders are treated as having sold their shares.

Taxable transaction Any transaction that is not tax-free to the parties involved, such as a *taxable acquisition*.

Tender offer A general offer to purchase securities that is made publicly and directly to all holders of the desired securities.

Tender offer premium The premium offered above the current market price in a tender offer.

Term loan A bank loan, typically with a floating interest rate, for a specified amount that matures in between one and ten years and requires a specified repayment schedule.

Term structure of interest rates A graph showing the relationship between interest rates and maturity.

Terminal value The value of a bond at maturity, typically its par value, or the value of an asset (or an entire firm) on some specified future valuation date.

Thinly traded Infrequently traded.

Third market Exchange-listed securities trading in the over-the-counter market.

Throughput agreement An agreement to put a specified amount of product per period through a particular facility—for example, an agreement to ship a specified amount of crude oil per period through a particular pipeline.

Time premium of an option The value of an option beyond its current exercise value representing the optionholder's control until expiration, the risk of the underlying asset, and the riskless return.

Time until expiration The time remaining until a financial security expires. Also called the *time to maturity*.

Time to maturity The time remaining until a financial security expires. Also called the *time until expiration*.

Time value of an option The difference between the market value of an option and its exercise value.

Time value of money The idea that a dollar today is worth more than a dollar in the future, because the dollar received today can earn interest up until the time the future dollar is received.

Times-interest-earned ratio The ratio of EBIT to interest expense, also called the interest coverage ratio.

Tolling agreement An agreement to put a specified amount of raw material per period through a particular processing facility—for example, an agreement to process a specified amount of alumina into aluminum at a particular aluminum plant.

Total asset turnover ratio The ratio of sales to total assets.

Trade credit Credit granted by a firm to another firm for the purchase of goods or services.

Traders Persons engaged in short-term speculation.

Trading Buying and selling securities.

Trading posts The posts on the floor of a stock exchange where the specialists stand and securities are traded.

Traditional view (of dividend policy) An argument that "within reason," investors prefer a larger to a smaller dividend, because the dividend is sure but the future return is uncertain.

Tranches Two or more quantities of the same loan or security. For example, a firm may issue new bonds in two tranches six months apart.

Transaction costs The time, effort, and money necessary to make a transaction, including such things as commission fees and the cost of physically moving the asset from seller to buyer.

Transaction loan A loan extended by a bank for a specific purpose. In contrast, lines of credit and revolving credit agreements involve loans that can be used for various purposes.

Transactions motive A desire to hold cash for the purpose of conducting cash-based transactions.

Transactions demand (for money) The need to accommodate a firm's expected cash transactions.

Transferable put right An option issued by the firm to its shareholders to sell the firm one share of its common stock at a fixed price (the strike price) within a stated period (the time to maturity). The put right is "transferable" because it can be traded in the capital markets.

Treasurer The corporate officer responsible for designing and implementing many of the firm's financing and investing activities.

Treasury bill A short-term security issued by the U.S. government usually with a maturity of 91 days, 182 days, or 52 weeks.

Treasury shares Shares that have been repurchased from investors by the firm.

True interest cost For a security such as commercial paper that is sold on a discount basis, the coupon rate required to provide an identical return assuming a coupon-bearing instrument of like maturity that pays interest in arrears.

True lease A contract that qualifies as a valid lease agreement under the Internal Revenue Code.

Turnkey construction contract A type of construction contract under which the construction firm is obligated to complete a project according to prespecified criteria for a price that is fixed at the time the contract is signed.

Two-state option pricing model An option pricing model in which the underlying asset can take on only two possible (discrete) values in the next time period for each value it can take on in the preceding time period. Also called the *binomial option pricing model*.

Two-tier tax system A method of taxation in which the income going to shareholders is taxed twice, as shown in Figure 15–6.

Underinvestment problem The mirror image of the *asset substitution problem*, wherein stockholders refuse to invest in low-risk assets to avoid shifting wealth from themselves to the debtholders.

Underlying asset The asset that an option gives the optionholder the right to buy or to sell.

Underwrite To guarantee, as to guarantee the issuer of securities a specified price by entering into a *purchase and sale* agreement.

Underwriter A party that guarantees the proceeds to the firm from a security sale, thereby in effect taking ownership of the securities.

Underwriting Acting as the *underwriter* in a *purchase and sale*.

Underwriting fee The portion of the *gross underwriting spread* that compensates the securities firms that underwrite a public offering for their *underwriting* risk.

Underwritten offering A *purchase and sale*.

Unleveraged beta The *beta* of an *unleveraged required return*; that is, the beta when the firm has a debt-free capital structure.

Unleveraged required return The *required return* on an investment when the investment is financed entirely by equity.

Unlimited liability Full liability for the debt and other obligations of a legal entity. The general partners of a partnership have unlimited liability.

Unsecured debt Debt that does not identify specific assets that can be taken over by the debtholder in case of default.

Unsystematic risk Risk that cannot be eliminated by diversification. Also called *nondiversifiable risk*.

Up-tick A term used to describe a transaction that took place at a higher price than the preceding transaction (involving the same security).

Value additivity Prevails when the value of the whole (a group of assets) exactly equals the sum of the values of the parts (the individual assets).

Value-additivity principle The principle that the value of two or more assets that are combined in a single entity is equal to the sum of the values of the separate assets.

Variable A value determined within the context of a model. Also called *endogenous variable*.

Variable cost A cost that is directly proportional to output.

Variance The mathematical expectation of the squared deviations from the mean. See Equation (6.5).

Vertical merger A merger in which one firm acquires another that is in the same industry but at another stage in the production cycle—for example, the acquiree serves as a supplier to the acquiror or purchases the acquiror's goods or services.

Voting rights The right to vote on matters that are put to a vote of securityholders—for example, the right to vote for directors.

WACC See *Weighted average cost of capital*.

Warrant A long-term call option issued by a firm on its own stock.

Weak form of capital market efficiency Prices reflect information about an asset's value that is *contained in past asset market prices*.

Weighted average cost of capital (WACC) The weighted average of financing costs for a financing package that would allow a project to be undertaken.

White knight A firm that steps in at a potential acquiree's behest and acquires the firm in a friendly merger in order to save the firm from a hostile raider.

Withholding taxes Taxes that must by law be collected by the paying corporation before payment is made to securityholders.

Without recourse Without the lender having any right to seek payment or seize assets in the event of nonpayment from anyone other than the party (such as a special-purpose entity) specified in the debt contract.

Working capital Current assets minus current liabilities.

Working capital management The management of current assets and current liabilities.

Working capital ratio Net working capital expressed as a proportion of sales.

Write (an option) To create and sell an option. Also called *taking a short position* in an option.

Yield curve The relationship between the yields to maturity of coupon-paying bonds selling at *par value* and the maturities of those bonds.

Yield to call (YTC) The annual percentage rate of a bond, assuming it will be paid off at the first possible time.

Yield to maturity (YTM) The annual percentage rate that equates a bond's market price to the present value of its promised future cash flows.

Zero-balance account A bank account that is managed so as to have just enough cash to cover checks that will be presented for payment during the day, which results in the balance returning to zero at the end of each business day.

Zero-coupon bond A bond that will make only one payment of principal and interest. Also called a *pure-discount bond* and a *single-payment bond*.

Zero-one integer programming An analytical method that can be used to determine the solution to a capital rationing problem.

Zero-sum game A type of game wherein one player can gain only at the expense of another player.

Author Index

Subject Index

IMPORTANT IMPLICIT PRINCIPAL-AGENT RELATIONSHIPS CONNECTED WITH A FIRM

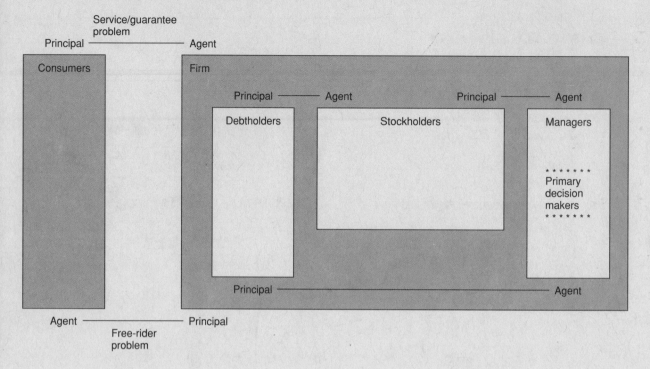

TIME-VALUE-OF-MONEY NOTATION

t A time period. For example, $t = 3$ is time period 3.

CF_t The net cash flow at time t. For example, CF_3 is the net cash flow at the end of time period 3.

CF   The net cash flow each period for an annuity.

r The discount rate per period. For example, $r = 0.02$ is 2% per time period.

m The number of compounding periods per year.

APR   The annual percentage rate (nominal annual rate). The APR equals r times m.

APY   The annual percentage yield (effective annual rate). The APY is the amount you would actually earn if you invested for exactly one year and if the investment paid interest at r per period for m periods.

n A number of time periods. For example, n might be 36 months.

FV_t A future value at time t. For example, FV_5 is a future value at the end of time period 5.

FVA_n The future value of an n-period annuity (at $t = n$).

PV   A present-value amount.

PVA_n The present value of an n-period annuity (at $t = n$).

NPV   The net present value.